UNDERSTANDING AND APPLYING MEDICAL ANTHROPOLOGY

Second Edition

Peter J. Brown
Emory University

Ron Barrett
Macalester College

Boston Burr Ridge, IL Dubuque, IA New York San Francisco St. Louis
Bangkok Bogotá Caracas Kuala Lumpur Lisbon London Madrid Mexico City
Milan Montreal New Delhi Santiago Seoul Singapore Sydney Taipei Toronto

The McGraw·Hill Companies

Published by McGraw-Hill, an imprint of The McGraw-Hill Companies, Inc., 1221 Avenue of the Americas, New York, NY 10020.

This book is printed on recycled paper.

1 2 3 4 5 6 7 8 9 0 QPD/QPD 0 9

ISBN: 978-0-07-340538-4
MHID: 0-07-340538-8

Editor in Chief: *Michael Ryan*
Publisher: *Frank Mortimer*
Sponsoring Editor: *Gina Boedeker*
Marketing Manager: *Pam Cooper*
Developmental Editor: *Phil Butcher*
Managing Editor: *Nicole Bridge*
Project Manager: *Meghan Durko*
Manuscript Editor: *Thomas L. Briggs*
Design Manager and Cover Designer: *Margarite Reynolds*
Production Supervisor: *Louis Swaim*
Composition: *10/12 Palatino by Hurix*
Printing: *45# New Era Matte Plus Recycled, Quebecor World, Dubuque*

Credits: The credits section for this book begins on page 455 and is considered an extension of the copyright page.

Library of Congress Cataloging-in-Publication Data

Understanding and applying medical anthropology/[edited by] Peter J. Brown and
Ronald L. Barrett. —2nd ed.
p. cm.
ISBN-13: 978-0-07-340538-4
ISBN-10: 0-07-340538-8
1. Medical anthropology—Methodology. 2. Medical anthropology—Philosophy.
I. Brown, Peter J. II. Barrett, Ronald L.
GN296.U54 2010
306.4'61—dc22 2009009176

www.mhhe.com

Peter J. Brown is a professor in the Department of Anthropology, Emory College of Arts and Sciences, and also a professor in the Hubert Department of Global Health, Rollins School of Public Health. He serves as the director of Emory's Center for Health, Culture and Society. He has co-edited *The Anthropology of Infectious Diseases; Emerging Illnesses and Society: Negotiating the Public Health Agenda; Applying Anthropology* (9th ed.); and *Applying Cultural Anthropology* (8th ed.). His research primarily deals with sociocultural aspects of malaria and its control, and he serves on a malaria-related Scientific Advisory Committee for the World Health Organization. He has an additional research interest in cultural issues in obesity and its related chronic diseases. Recipient of several teaching awards, he is a director of a new program, Global Health, Culture and Society, at Emory College. He is associate editor of the journal *Medical Anthropology*.

Ron Barrett is a medical anthropologist and assistant professor at Macalester College. His research interests concern the social dynamics of infectious diseases, religious healing, and decision making at the end of life in both India and the United States. His study of religious healing and the stigma of leprosy is the subject of a book: *Aghor Medicine: Pollution, Death, and Healing in Northern India* (University of California Press). Barrett is also a registered nurse with clinical experience in hospice, neuro-intensive care, and brain injury rehabilitation.

For Betsy Nico, LiLi, Patrick, and Thomas —PJB
For Kate, Tara, and Maya —RB

To the Instructor

Teaching medical anthropology is both exciting and challenging. Undergraduates are able to relate to sickness and healing because they have had some experience with these central issues and because many are thinking of careers in the health care industry. Learning about the multiple causes of disease and the cultural variation in healing practices makes students examine their own lives and culture with a fresh perspective; one of the real satisfactions of being a teacher comes from watching students get excited by such an intellectual journey. It is also satisfying when students become increasingly aware of the health problems of others. At the same time, teaching medical anthropology is challenging due to its amorphous yet undeniably growing body of knowledge. How does a professor organize such a course?

We have divided this book into two main parts. Part I illustrates the variety of theoretical and analytical approaches used by medical anthropologists. Part II provides examples of those approaches as they are relevant to a variety of health issues and problems; hence, the title of the reader—*Understanding and Applying Medical Anthropology*. From looking at the first part of the book, it should be apparent that we hold a very broad view of the scope of medical anthropology and that we are committed to the traditional four-field approach of general anthropology. We believe that the application of anthropological knowledge—the job of making our research useful—is part of the responsibility of all anthropologists. Aspects of nearly all anthropological work are relevant to understanding and solving human problems. That is why we use the term *applying* medical anthropology rather than the narrower and more specific *applied* anthropology (in both this and other edited readers). The latter refers to anthropological work done for a client on a problem identified by the client. We think students want to read about anthropological research and analysis on relevant topics, and the second part of the collection provides some good examples of this. At times we have included two or more selections on a similar topic in order to enhance in-class discussions. The organization of this book, we believe, will suit a heterogeneous approach to a medical anthropology course.

As far as we can tell, there is no agreement about how a basic course in medical anthropology should be taught. Almost thirty years ago, the first special publication of the new Society for Medical Anthropology concerned teaching medical anthropology; the volume included nine different model courses (Todd and Ruffini 1979). The diversity of those courses—ranging from ethnomedicine, to biomedical anthropology, to family structure and health—was impressive. Theoretical diversity has been a continuing hallmark of medical anthropology, and it is reflected in most of the edited textbooks of the field. On the other hand, the relatively few regular textbooks in the field have had, by necessity, a more narrow theoretical focus, like the ecological approach (McElroy and Townsend 1996) or cultural aspects of healing and medicine (Foster and Anderson 1978; Helman 1994). Recently, some new books have provided a synthesis of medical anthropology, even as the discipline has expanded and the theoretical basis of research has become more sophisticated (Anderson 1996; Hahn 1995; Janzen 2001; Singer and Baer 2007: Wiley and Allen 2008; Winkelman 2008).

This second edition is long overdue. The first edition was very well received, and there have been many requests for a new edition. We revised this reader in medical anthropology because there is a need for a book of original research articles to accompany the texts, ethnographies, and case studies that we use in such courses. As we have collected course syllabi from other medical anthropologists over the years, we have been struck by the diversity and richness of the teaching resources available. For the first edition, we thought it would be easy to assemble such a reader, but it turned out to be quite a difficult task. This is partially because of the expanding breadth of the field and partially because there are so many fascinating articles available. Our first list included more than 220 articles, and when we asked colleagues to help, they simply suggested more titles. The list got much longer for the second edition. We eventually pared the list to the current number through a long and painful process. We were at times forced to cut entire articles that we really admired and to edit out portions of articles due to space constraints.

In the end, we selected the readings with five criteria in mind:

- Readability
- A mix of classic articles and more recent contributions
- A range in theoretical orientation
- A range of theoretical difficulty or sophistication
- Ethnographic variation

We expect the reading level to be appropriate for upper-division undergraduates who have already taken a basic anthropology course. Many selections are from the standard professional journals in the field, including *Medical Anthropology Quarterly, Medical Anthropology, Social Science and Medicine, Human Organization, Anthropology and Medicine,* and *Culture, Medicine and Psychiatry*. Interestingly, there has been no new textbook reader in medical anthropology since the launching of many of these journals. The growth of medical anthropology has been astounding; both the quantity and quality of ethnographic, biocultural, and critical medical anthropological research is impressive.

To add to the pedagogical value of this collection, we have included section and reading introductions. In section introductions, we emphasize the "conceptual tools" that are put to work in each kind of medical anthropology. It is important for students to be reminded of the central concepts before they start reading the details of a particular case. In selection introductions, we describe the context for the problem at hand by raising related issues and by listing some questions for discussion. Most introductions and conceptual tools sections include bibliographic suggestions for further reading, which are listed at the back of the book. These references might be useful for undergraduates who are writing term papers or for graduate students who are developing a stronger grasp of the field. There are, of course, a great many other resources in medical anthropology, many of which are available through the Society for Medical Anthropology (SMA). Those who are interested may want to consult the SMA's web page: http://www.medanthro.net.

We are painfully aware that, due to space constraints, there are many important topics in medical anthropology that are not represented here, including ethnopharmacology, health policy, childbirth, gerontology, and clinical cases. We hope that instructors using this book will feel free to contact us with their opinions about selections that work (or do not work) and with suggestions for future editions.

New to the Second Edition

One of the main challenges in revising this reader after a ten-year hiatus has been to bring it up to date without completely changing a text that has been warmly received. The combination of newer articles and "classics" was designed for maximum pedagogical benefit. We believe that the seventeen new selections will be great vehicles for teaching and encouraging class discussion. We have even added some more "classics"—like "The Doctor's White Coat"—because we have found that many students in medical anthropology courses have not taken an anthropology course before, and these older articles can assist in the teaching of basic concepts.

We have reorganized the section and subsection headings to fit current themes in medical anthropology, based on our readings of the literature over the past decade. New sections emphasize the anthropological analysis of biotechnologies, the phenomenological experience of illness, and work within the context of biomedicine. One section that has been deleted is the one spotlighting critical medical anthropology (CMA). We believe that this was an awkward label, borrowed from postmodern critical theory, that combined political economic approaches (e.g., Singer) and epistemological inquiries into the cultural assumptions of biomedicine (e.g., Scheper-Hughes and Lock). At this historical juncture, we think that these ideas have become mainstream medical anthropology. The critiques have been incorporated, we believe, into applied medical anthropology as well. Therefore, we explain the ideas of CMA in the *conceptual tools* and the *context sections* rather than in a separate section.

An important new feature is the *context sections* found at the bottom of the introduction to each selection. These are intended for more advanced students interested in knowing where the articles fit within the intellectual history of medical anthropology. These short entries often describe the author's larger research agenda and discuss why this particular article was written. This background information can help students appreciate the reading more fully. These sections also include the full source citation, something that was unfortunately hidden in the first edition.

Over the years, we have heard that the *conceptual tools* section introductions are much appreciated by students. Therefore, we have updated and expanded these bullet points where appropriate. For some teachers, these sections play the role of a minitextbook (or an expanded glossary).

Finally, we have made an effort to shorten many articles, and we greatly appreciate the authors who have allowed us to do this. It permits us to include more selections and increases the chance that students will actually read the assignments.

Acknowledgments

Many people have aided us in developing this second edition, and they deserve our most sincere thanks. First and foremost, Erin Finley and Kate Cummings were a terrific help in organizing the text, reading potential selections, giving advice and encouragement, and cutting, pasting, and proofing. Thanks.

Several colleagues at Emory have been quite helpful, especially George Armelagos, Craig Hadley, Chikako Osawa-de Silva, Kate Barrett, Lynn Sibley, Leandris Liburd, and Carol Worthman. Colleagues at other institutions have also offered very useful advice, including Merrill Singer, Jill Flueriet, Mark Nichter, Christ Kuzawa, and Alan Goodman. We appreciate the advice of the reviewers of the first edition of the book. They include Pamela Erickson, University of Connecticut; Dean Wheeler, Glendale College; Peter Benson, Washington University; Daniel Benyshek, University of Nevada, Las Vegas; and Daniel Minderhout, Bloomsburg University.

PJB wants to thank graduate students with whom he has cotaught medical anthropology and global health over the past several years, including Dredge Kang, Svea Closser, Michelle Parsons, Erin Finley, and Alexa Dietrich. PJB is particularly grateful for all that he has learned from the undergraduate and graduate students who have been in his medical anthropology classes over the past thirty years.

To the Student

We think it is exciting that you have decided to take a course in medical anthropology. What initially sparked your interest? The prospect of studying other medical systems, like shamanism? The thought of discovering what made disease rates increase in ancient societies? Your concern about the serious health problems both in the United States and throughout the world? All these topics—exotic and mundane—are related to medical anthropology. Or maybe your interest is related to your career ambitions or current work in the health care field. Whatever the case, you will find the study of medical anthropology to be intriguing and intellectually rewarding. You will also find the study of medical anthropology to be relevant to your life—if only because disease, illness, healing, and death are universal in the human experience. All cultures have medical systems. Whether you participate in that medical system as a patient or a healer, there is real value in understanding the big picture of how and why that system works. Medical anthropology is an exciting field both for intellectual understanding and for social action. As the title of this book suggests, you first need to understand medical anthropology and then use it to make a difference in the world.

As you skim through this book, notice the extremely wide variety of topics that are included within medical anthropology. That is because anthropology itself takes a broad, holistic approach to the study of human biology and cultures. In the United States, anthropology traditionally includes four fields; biological or physical anthropology, archaeology, cultural anthropology, and anthropological linguistics. Medical anthropology is *not* one of the four fields; rather, it involves the use of anthropological concepts and methods from all four fields in the study of health, disease, and healing. One of the hallmarks of medical anthropology, therefore, is the theoretical and practical diversity within the field; this is one reason we refer to "medical anthropologies" in the first selection.

Your instructor may not cover all of these approaches during your particular course. Most medical anthropologists, like most anthropologists in general, concentrate on the cultural end of the field. Many courses in medical anthropology do not deal with evolutionary or biological questions. Your course instructor will likely pick and choose selections according to his or her orientation to the field. That is as it should be, but we hope that you will also see this book as a resource for independently exploring other approaches.

We have selected the readings here with you, the student, in mind. Primarily, we picked selections that were readable and that contained interesting case studies. Some were picked because they are controversial in order to help spark class discussions. But we also wanted the selections to reflect diversity—in terms of both sophistication and the areas of the world represented. Some readings are "classics" in the field written by famous anthropologists. Although they may be older, they usually make for wonderful reading. Most of the articles are from professional scholarly publications (e.g., *Medical Anthropology Quarterly, Medical Anthropology, Social Science and Medicine, Culture, Medicine and Psychiatry,* and *Anthropology and Medicine*), and they will, on occasion, require concentrated reading on your part. When reading primary sources, you may want to skim the article first in order to familiarize yourself with the overall structure of the argument. Prereading for the main ideas is not a substitute for the real reading, but it can better prepare you to understand the article.

In the introductions to the sections and to the readings themselves, we have provided an orientation to the general context and framework of the material. Section introductions provide a thumbnail description of important "conceptual tools." It will be useful for you to put these concepts and vocabulary into your own personal intellectual toolbox. Each selection introduction includes thought questions to ponder. The aim is to help you place a particular selection into the larger scheme of things; so the introductions are designed to get you to think about the broader (and sometimes unanswerable) questions involved. At the end of each introduction, you will find a "context box" that will tell you something about the author and why the article was written.

Because medical anthropology is such a diverse field, we have divided this book into two main parts. Part I is designed to introduce you to the multiple approaches used by medical anthropologists in their research and other work. As you can see, we have identified four major approaches in biosocial-oriented medical anthropology and six distinct approaches in culturally oriented medical anthropology. These different approaches are described in the first reading by Brown, Barrett, Padilla, and Finley.

The second part of the book is about applying medical anthropology. In Part II, we have identified seven different problem areas—from doctor–patient communication to global health programs—and selections that illustrate how anthropological analysis can be *relevant* to understanding and solving those real problems. There is an important field called "applied anthropology" in which" people, including medical anthropologists, do research, program implementation, and program evaluation for particular clients who hire them to work on particular problems. The writings of those applied anthropologists are often reports for their clients. The selections in Part II do not all fit neatly within the domain of applied anthropology. Although many discuss the particular solution to a problem—such as the AIDS epidemic or social stigma related to disease—the main purpose of other selections is to get readers to "rethink" the problem in a new way. That is what is meant by "applying" medical anthropology (Podolefsky, Brown, and Lacy 2009).

If you are interested in learning more about medical anthropology, you may want to consult the "handbook" of the field by Carolyn Sargent and Thomas Johnson (1996), which includes nineteen review articles about different aspects of medical anthropology. It also has a terrific bibliography. If you are thinking about graduate study, you may want to consult the directory *Graduate Programs in Medical Anthropology,* produced by the Society for Medical Anthropology (a unit of the American Anthropological Association [AAA]), or the *Guide to Departments,* published annually by the AAA. For further information, contact the AAA on the Internet: <http: //www.aaanet.org>. The major academic journals in the field, including *Medical Anthropology Quarterly, Medical Anthropology, Social Science and Medicine, Culture, Medicine and Psychiatry,* and *Medicine and Anthropology,* are also useful places to look for information.

We hope you enjoy the selections here and that you learn a lot from your study of medical anthropology. More important, we hope that what you learn in this course will be useful to you in the future because you were encouraged to think about disease, healing, and medicine in new ways.

Contents

Part I

UNDERSTANDING MEDICAL ANTHROPOLOGY Biosocial and Cultural Approaches

This book is divided into two parts: the first deals with understanding medical anthropology, and the second is devoted to applying medical anthropology. Understanding must come before utilization. But what does it mean to understand something (or somebody)? Of course, understanding requires knowledge, but that is not enough. Four things come to mind. First, understanding means being able to take another point of view or at least imagine another point of view. It follows, then, that understanding also means you have mastered the basic vocabulary and conceptual framework used by another so that you can articulate or communicate that point of view. Third, understanding means that you have a grasp of the range of interests and abilities of the "other." Finally, understanding requires that you have a basic knowledge of the history and future goals of another.

The selections in this first part of the book will acquaint you with the fundamental goals, concepts, and theoretical approaches used by medical anthropologists. You will come to understand what medical anthropology is all about. As you will learn in the first selection, there is no single field that can be called "medical anthropology." There is so much diversity of theoretical approaches that it is more accurate to think of multiple medical anthropologies. This diversity can be considered in two fundamental areas—biosocial approaches and cultural approaches. In general, anthropologists are very tolerant and encouraging of a multidisciplinary approach to understanding humans. In the simplest sense, medical anthropology refers to an anthropological way of exploring issues of health, disease, healing, and sickness. But what is anthropology?

Anthropology is the holistic and comparative study of people or, more properly, humankind. Obviously, many other disciplines study people: psychology, sociology, medicine, political science, biology, history, and so on. However, to understand ourselves in a complete way, we must join these separate and somewhat narrow views into a single framework. Anthropology attempts to integrate these disparate views by beginning with our biological and evolutionary roots, by exploring the development of culture through prehistoric and historical time, by examining the unique human ability for language, and, finally, by examining the diversity of present-day cultures throughout the world.

The effort to integrate these different views has resulted in the four fields that characterize U.S. anthropology: cultural anthropology, biological (or physical) anthropology, archaeology, and anthropological linguistics. These different fields have three basic things in common. First, their approaches are all comparative, although these comparisons may be across cultures, time periods, or species. Second, all four fields emphasize the importance of the concept of culture. Third, they share an interest in understanding humans holistically, within a broader context. However, the four fields differ greatly in the kind of data or information they use and the methods they employ, with some fields borrowing from the biological sciences, some the humanities, and some the social sciences.

Medical anthropology provides a unique way of understanding the human experience. This is because all human beings—irrespective of culture, class, or historical epoch—experience sickness and death. Simultaneously, all cultures—irrespective of technological complexity—have medical systems that help people cope with the inevitability of sickness, just as all cultures have religious systems that deal with the inevitability of death. Medical anthropology tries to understand the causes of health and illness in societies. Our own health is influenced by the environment, our genetic inheritance, and, most important, our socioeconomic circumstances; all of these factors interact in complex ways.

In the first half of this book, we have divided medical anthropology into two basic approaches: biosocial and cultural. Although this distinction is a bit artificial, we think it is useful. In our view, the term *biosocial* (or *biocultural*) refers to an anthropological view of the ways in which people adapt to their environment and change that environment that makes health conditions better or worse. On the other hand, cultural approaches in medical anthropology emphasize the role of ideas, beliefs, and values in creating systems of illness classification and medical programs for curing illness. In other words, biocultural approaches focus on health, and cultural approaches focus on aspects of medicine or ethnomedicine.

In general, biosocial approaches try to combine the concepts and questions that are common in biological (physical) anthropology, archaeology, and ecology. Cultural approaches are more influenced by ethnography, linguistics, psychology, sociology, and philosophy. All these approaches reflect slightly different theoretical orientations and consequently use slightly different methods for research and analysis.

Why should you learn about the diversity of the theoretical perspectives in medical anthropology? Certainly, it is an important part of the process of understanding a field of study. Knowing about diverse theoretical orientations can help you understand why certain questions about health and illness have been asked in particular ways.

Anthropological research projects usually begin with three elements that, when combined, allow researchers to do their work. First, there is a problem or question that the anthropologist wants to explore. Second, there is an ethnographic site, a particular society, or a historical period that will provide the information and the context for answering the question. Third, the researcher has a theoretical approach that is used to ask questions in a certain way, to pay attention to particular things, or to determine what research methods to use. When a researcher proposes a project, all three factors come into play; in a sense, the researcher focuses on the topic by sharpening each of these dimensions, like triangulating a target. In this regard, the theoretical orientation is of primary importance. To a significant extent, the theoretical orientation determines what questions get asked and how they get answered.

 1

Medical Anthropology: An Introduction to the Fields

Peter J. Brown
Ronald L. Barrett
Mark B. Padilla
Erin P. Finley

Chances are, you just started taking this course in medical anthropology, and you are not sure what exactly it is going to be about. Chances are also that one of your friends—or your roommate or even your parents—will ask, "Sounds interesting, but what is medical anthropology?" The purpose of this selection is to help you be prepared to answer that question. As you will see, it is not an easy one to answer. We have this problem, for example, at cocktail parties. Part of the issue is that many people—even well-educated ones—do not really know what anthropology is. Therefore, when some people ask the question, they have a preconception that anthropology means only archaeology. In this situation, your challenge is to gently dissuade them of this idea by saying something like this: "While some medical anthropologists do study the health of prehistoric populations, most medical anthropologists use a cultural *orientation to study health and medicine in contemporary populations, especially multiethnic ones like our own." But in actuality, if you answered the question with a long, run-on sentence like that, the person asking the question might start backing away from you! Therefore, to keep the conversation interesting, it is always best to have a few examples of medical anthropological research at hand. This selection should be helpful in that regard.*

Medical anthropology studies human health problems and healing systems in their broad social and cultural contexts. Medical anthropologists engage in both basic research on issues of health and healing systems and applied research aimed at improving therapeutic care in clinical settings or improving public health programs in community settings. Drawing from biological and social sciences, as well as clinical sciences, medical anthropologists engage in academic and applied research, contributing to the understanding and improvement of human health and health services worldwide.

Medical anthropology is inherently interdisciplinary in focus. It is not characterized by a single theoretical paradigm. For example, medical anthropology is not limited to the study of exotic, non-Western medical systems, even though the ethnographic description of religion and healing systems is as old as anthropology itself. The field also has other areas of research using tools of critical cultural inquiry, like the cultural analysis of underlying assumptions of biomedicine or the globalization of biomedical technologies, which are products of more recent intellectual trends.

As you read this selection, consider these questions:

- **What do anthropologists mean by "culture," and how is it related to health and healing?**
- **Why is the distinction between disease and illness important in medical anthropology? Why might this difference not be very important to physicians and other health care providers?**
- **Which of the different approaches in medical anthropology do you think will be of most interest to you? Why?**

Context: This article is original to this reader and has been substantially updated for the current edition. Peter Brown is a professor of anthropology and global health at Emory; Ron Barrett is an assistant professor of nursing and anthropology at Emory; Mark Padilla is an assistant professor of health behavior and health education at the University of Michigan; Erin Finley is completing her PhD in medical anthropology at Emory. This article was originally written at a time (1998) when medical anthropology had expanded a great deal from its modest origins. Few people had attempted to describe the whole field and how it relates to both four-field anthropology and as applied anthropology. In the past decade, medical anthropology has grown exponentially, developing into a rich and varied field. It is a measure of the field's diversity and ongoing evolution that not all medical anthropologists will agree with the structure of the discipline as presented here.

Source: P. J. Brown, R. Barrett, M. Padilla, and E. Finley (2009). "Medical Anthropology: An Introduction to the Fields." In P. J. Brown and R. Barrett (eds.), Understanding and Applying Medical Anthropology. New York: McGraw-Hill.

WHAT IS MEDICAL ANTHROPOLOGY?

The Society for Medical Anthropology defines medical anthropology as follows:

> This field is broadly taken to include all inquiries into health, disease, illness, and sickness in human individuals and populations that are undertaken from the holistic and cross-cultural perspective distinctive of anthropology as a discipline—that is, with an awareness of species' biological, cultural, linguistic, and historical uniformity and variation. It encompasses studies of ethnomedicine, epidemiology, maternal and child health, population, nutrition, human development in relation to health and disease, health-care providers and services, public health, health policy, and the language and speech of health and health care. (SMA 2008)

This definition can be daunting to someone coming to anthropology for the first time, but its essential point is this: Medical anthropology encompasses all anthropological studies of health and healing. Medical anthropology takes the tools of anthropology and applies them to human illness, suffering, disease, and well-being.

Therefore, in order to give a proper rendering of medical anthropology, we must first introduce its parent discipline and some of the key concepts within it. Introductory anthropology courses usually begin with some variation of the short and classic definition "Anthropology is the study of humankind." Although a bit vague, this definition underscores that anthropology is a holistic and interdisciplinary enterprise that uses many different approaches to important human issues. In the broadest sense, these approaches are usually categorized into four major fields: cultural anthropology, physical or biological anthropology, archaeology, and linguistics.

These days, however, introductory courses are often the first and last places where anyone gives much thought to the relationships between the four fields of anthropology. In recent decades, anthropology has gone the way of many academic disciplines. Its fields and subfields have become increasingly specialized, each with its own lexicons and theoretical orientations. As a result of these increasingly specialized differences, the academic discussions between the fields of anthropology have diminished considerably, especially between many areas of biological and cultural anthropology. Such trends are unfortunate because the compartmentalization of anthropology often undermines the discipline's greatest strengths: its holistic approach and interdisciplinary nature.

Despite their specialized perspectives, cultural and biological anthropologists share a great deal of common ground. For example, one useful definition of culture describes it as learned patterns of thought and behavior shared by a social group. (Anthropologists have many different definitions of culture, and the lack of complete agreement about this term should be taken as evidence of the concept's centrality.) Cultural patterns might be considered to have three basic and interconnected domains: (1) infrastructure—the domain of material and economic culture; (2) structure—the domain of social organization, power, and interpersonal relations; and (3) the belief system or superstructure—the domain of symbols, cognitive models, and ideology. For example, in the traditional culture of a North Indian village, all three levels of the cultural system are important—in agriculture and the economy of the village, in the social organization of the caste system, and in the religious beliefs and rituals of Hinduism. All three domains are closely related, and all three satisfy human needs. Many anthropologists argue that all three domains of culture are influenced by the biological aspects of the human experience as a group-living organism within an ecological setting. Likewise, the individual human organism is an open system, highly permeable to cultural influences, many of which can have a profound impact on growth and development. Human biology and culture are intimately related, and it is important to have a holistic perspective on these interrelationships when studying human issues pertaining to health and sickness.

Given the history of anthropology itself, medical anthropology is a relatively new area of specialization. Medical anthropology is not really a *subfield* (like biological anthropology, archaeology, cultural anthropology, or anthropological linguistics), partly because those subfields generally have a central theoretical paradigm. Medical anthropologists use a wide variety of theoretical perspectives, and they often do not agree on which ones are best. Therefore, medical anthropology is essentially the application of anthropological theories and methods to questions of health, illness, medicine, and healing. As such, it is more correct to refer to a variety of *medical anthropologies.*

Medical anthropologists engage in basic research on issues of health and healing systems, as well as applied research aimed at the improvement of therapeutic care in clinical settings or public health programs in community settings. The purpose of basic research is to expand knowledge; the purpose of applied research is to help solve specific human problems. There is a great deal that we do not know about the causes of sickness and the processes of healing—and anthropologists can contribute to the growth of human knowledge in these important areas. On the other hand, the health problems facing people in all parts of the world are overwhelming and complex, and anthropologists can contribute to the design and implementation of programs to alleviate those problems.

In regard to the four traditional fields of American anthropology, the most common type of anthropologist is a cultural anthropologist. Similarly, it is most common to find that practicing medical anthropologists were trained in cultural anthropology. On the other hand, as you will see by the readings in this book, biological anthropologists, archaeologists, and even anthropological linguists can be interested in, and contribute to, studies in medical anthropology. Medical anthropology includes a range of anthropological subfields, theories, and methods applied to issues of human health, sickness, and healing.

BASIC CONCEPTS

As with the concept of culture, the notion of health is difficult to define. According to the charter of the World Health Organization, health refers not merely to the absence of disease but to a state of physical, social, and psychological well-being (Dubos 1959). What constitutes well-being in one society, however, may be quite different in another. The ideal of a lean-figured body—a sign of health in the West—may indicate sickness and malnutrition in sub-Saharan Africa (Brown 1991). In the fishing villages that line Lake Victoria, the parasitic disease schistosomiasis is so prevalent that the bloody urine of young males is considered a healthy sign of approaching manhood (Desowitz 1981). In the United States, the "elegant pallor" and "hectic flush" of *consumption* (tuberculosis) was often mimicked at the turn of the twentieth century because of its association with famous writers and artists (Sontag 1978). Any conceptualization of health must therefore depend on an understanding of how so-called normal states of well-being are constructed within particular social, cultural, and environmental contexts.

Sickness is an inclusive term that includes all unwanted variations in the physical, social, and psychological dimensions of health. Hahn defines sickness as "unwanted conditions of self, or substantial threats of unwanted conditions of self" (Hahn 1995:22). These conditions may include "states of any part of a person—body, mind, experience, or relationships" (ibid.). More specifically, the criteria that people use when they assign sickness to a given state of health are based upon complex interactions between human biology and culture.

Sickness can be further divided into two basic categories: *illness* and *disease.* Disease refers to the outward, clinical manifestations of altered physical function or infection. It is a clinical phenomenon, defined by the pathophysiology of certain tissues within the human organism. Illness, on the other hand, encompasses the human experience and perceptions of alterations in health, as informed by its broader social and cultural dimensions. The distinction between illness and disease is a useful one because it helps to explain the phenomenon of patients who seek medical attention in the absence of clinically identifiable symptoms (illness without disease) and those exhibiting pathophysiology who do not seek medical help (disease without illness).

This distinction also explains differences in the quality of communication and therapeutic exchange between patients and healers. For example, a physician using a disease model may see the patient's symptoms as the expression of clinical pathology, a mechanical alteration in bodily processes that can be "fixed" by a prescribed biomedical treatment. From the patient's perspective, however, an illness experience may include social as well as physiological processes. His or her problem may just as easily be caused by an evil spirit, a germ, or both. The physician's diagnosis may not make sense in terms of the patient's theory of illness, and his or her "cure" may not take into consideration the patient's family dynamics, the potential for social stigma in the community, or lack of adequate resources to make follow-up visits or afford long and expensive therapies.

Healing systems often cross-cut categories of religion, medicine, and social organization. Therapeutic modalities can range from cardiac bypass surgery, to amulets worn for protection against the evil eye, to conflict resolution between kin groups. Shamans, priests, university-trained physicians, and members of one's own family may assume a healing role at any given time in a person's life. In recent decades, medical anthropologists have distinguished between biomedical systems of healing based upon Western scientific notions of medicine and ethnomedical systems of healing based upon all other notions of healing. As we shall see, this distinction may be more of a convenience than a reality.

BASIC APPROACHES TO MEDICAL ANTHROPOLOGY

While the scope of anthropological inquiry into issues of human health, sickness, and healing is very diverse, and the subfields engaged in these inquiries often overlap, one can nevertheless identify six basic approaches to medical anthropology: (1) biological, (2) ecological, (3) critical, (4) ethnomedical, (5) experiential, and (6) applied. The first two of these approaches emphasize the interaction of humans and their environment in a way that we consider biosocial, that is, with a focus on the interaction between biological/health questions and socioeconomic and demographic factors. The last four of these approaches in medical anthropology emphasize the concept of culture (the patterns of thought and behavior characteristic of a group).

We believe that all six of these approaches in medical anthropology share four essential premises: first, that illness and healing are basic human experiences that are best understood holistically in the complex and varied interactions between human biology and culture; second, that disease is an aspect of human environments influenced by culturally specific behaviors and sociopolitical circumstances; third, that the human body and symptoms are interpreted through cultural filters of beliefs and epistemological assumptions; and fourth, that the cultural aspects of healing systems have important pragmatic consequences for the acceptability, efficacy, and improvement of health care in human societies.

Biological Approaches

Much of the research in biological anthropology concerns important issues of human health and illness, and therefore often intersects with the domains of medical anthropology. Many of the contributions of biological anthropologists help to explain the relationships between evolutionary processes, human genetic variation, and the different ways that humans are sometimes susceptible, and other times resistant, to disease and other environmental stressors. The evolution of disease in ancient human populations helps us to better understand current health trends. For example, the recent global trend of emerging and reemerging infectious diseases, such as tuberculosis and AIDS, is influenced by forces of natural and cultural selection that have been present throughout modern human evolution. During the time of the Paleolithic, early human populations lived in small bands as nomadic hunters and gatherers. The low population densities during this period would not have supported the acute infectious diseases found today (Hart 1983); instead, chronic parasitic and arthropod-born diseases were more prevalent (Klicks 1983; Lambrecht 1964). In recent years, the development of evolutionary medicine has emphasized this long prehistoric period—the "environment of evolutionary adaptiveness."

The shift toward sedentary living patterns and subsistence based upon plant and animal domestication, sometimes called the Neolithic Revolution, had a profound effect on human health. Skeletal evidence from populations undergoing this transition indicate an overall deterioration in health consistent with the known relationship between infectious disease and malnutrition (Pelletier et al. 1993). These emerging infections have been attributed to increasing population density, social stratification, decreased nutritional variety, problems of clean water and sanitation, and close contact with domesticated animals (Cockburn 1971; Fenner 1970). These changes had a disproportionate impact on women, young children, the elderly, and the emerging underclass, who were most susceptible to infections in socially stratified societies (Cohen and Armelagos 1984).

A more recent threat to human health has come from chronic degenerative conditions. These so-called diseases of civilization, such as heart disease, diabetes, and cancer, are the leading causes of adult mortality throughout the world today. Many of these diseases share common etiological factors related to human adaptation over the last 100,000 years. For example, obesity and high consumption of refined carbohydrates and fats are related to increased incidences of heart disease and diabetes. Human susceptibility to excess amounts of these substances can be explained by the evolution of human metabolism over millions of years of seasonal food shortages and diets low in fat (Konner and Eaton 1985).

A related theory of "thrifty genes" has been proposed to explain relatively shorter-term evolutionary changes that account for genetic variation in the susceptibility to chronic diseases between different contemporary populations (Neel 1982). For example, certain Native American and other recently acculturated populations have significantly higher prevalences of adult-onset diabetes and hypertension in comparison to populations that have been subsisting on high-calorie and fatty diets for many generations.

The thrifty gene hypothesis proposes that the differences in susceptibility to chronic diseases in these populations are related to differences in the degree of genetic adaptiveness to changes in diet and activity lifestyles that have occurred in recent human history (McGarvey 1995). In other words, during times of "feast or famine" in the past, genes affecting insulin physiology were selected for that allowed people to adapt to irregular food supply; some populations may have been forced through an evolutionary "bottleneck" of natural selection resulting in higher gene frequencies of this particular adaptation. In the context of modern diets, however, these genes add to the burden of chronic disease. Other biological/medical/anthropological approaches, in recent years, have focused on the "fetal origins of chronic disease." This means that, rather than genetic determination, fetal development is programmed to meet the demands of the mother's environment.

As in the case of infectious disease, variation in human susceptibility to chronic diseases cannot be accounted for by genes alone. Environmental and sociocultural factors play a major role as well. Here, human physiological measurements have demonstrated the impact of sociocultural conditions upon human health. For example, a recent anthropological study of African Americans suggests that the psychological stress related to racial discrimination may contribute to higher prevalences of hypertension in these populations (Dressler 1996).

Some biological contributions to medical anthropology actually critique the misapplication of biological concepts. During the late nineteenth century, measurements of cranial size were taken of Jewish and Southern European immigrants to the United States and compared with those of Anglo-American residents. The differences in cranial size between these populations were used to support a theory of racial hierarchy based upon hereditary differences in brain size. By careful comparisons between first- and second-generation groups from these immigrant populations, Franz Boas was able to demonstrate that these differences were attributable to environmental influences on body size (Boas 1940). Subsequent analyses have discredited previous studies relating measurements of intelligence to those of cranial capacity (Gould 1981), and categories of human races have been shown to have little validity in the study of human variation.

Biological anthropologists can also provide important information regarding the ethnopharmacological aspects of traditional medical systems. Etkin defines ethnopharmacology as "the study of indigenous medicines that connects the ethnography of health and healing to the physical composition of medicines and their physiologic actions" (Etkin 1996:151). Eschewing biological reductionism, she asserts that ethnopharmacologists consider not only the physiological properties of plant substances but also issues related to their selection, preparation, and intended uses within particular social settings and broader biocultural frameworks.

More recently, biological anthropology has begun to play a central role in the relatively new field of "evolutionary medicine". It takes a view on human health that considers how survival pressures over the course of evolution may have shaped facets of human biology. Health researchers who incorporate an appreciation of the ongoing effects of natural selection on the physiology of people and other organisms may be equipped to develop more sophisticated approaches in their efforts to treat or prevent disease (Nesse and Williams 1999). For example, encouraging the use of condoms not only reduces the number of sex partners who are likely to acquire a sexually transmitted disease from an infected individual, it may also—over time—help to reduce the virulence of the disease. This reliance on biological anthropology's appreciation for the interconnectedness between genes and environment has led to a number of new developments in the field of evolutionary medicine, and holds promise for many more.

Ecological Approaches

Ecology refers to the relationships between organisms and their total environment. Within medical anthropology, the ecological perspective has three major premises. First, the interdependent interactions of plants, animals, and natural resources comprise an "ecosystem" with characteristics that transcend its component parts. Second, the common goal of the species within an ecosystem is homeostasis, a balance between environmental degradation and the survival of living populations. In this homeostatic system, infectious disease agents (pathogens) and their human hosts are understood to exist in a dynamic adaptive tension with one another that strives toward a relatively stable balance between pathogens and human responses. Third, modern human adaptations include cultural and technological innovations that can dramatically alter the homeostatic relationship between host and disease, occasionally creating severe ecological imbalances. In some cases, these imbalances may benefit humans in the short term, decreasing the prevalence of a particular disease in a population and improving human health. In other cases, homeostatic imbalances favor disease agents, providing an opportunity for diseases to reach epidemic proportions and dramatically increase human morbidity and mortality.

Thus, an ecological approach to medical anthropology emphasizes that the total environment of the human species includes the products of large-scale human activity, as well as "natural" phenomena, and that health is affected by all aspects of human ecology. The term *medical ecology* has been used to describe this approach as the intersection of culture, disease ecology, and medicine in the study of medical issues (McElroy 1996). This approach can be further distinguished by two levels of analysis. At the micro level, *cultural ecology* examines how cultural beliefs and practices shape human behavior, such as sexuality and residence patterns, which in turn alter the ecological relationship between host and pathogen. At a broader level, *political ecology* examines the historical interactions of human groups and the effects of political conflict, migration, and global resource inequality on disease ecology (Brown 1996). Many ecological approaches to medical anthropology include some aspects of both cultural and political ecology. Malaria and schistosomiasis provide two useful examples.

Malaria is a disease caused by a microscopic *Plasmodium* parasite that is transmitted to human hosts through contact with mosquitoes of the genus *Anopheles.* These mosquitoes breed and multiply in stagnant pools of water in warm climatic regions of the world. Malaria has a long and sordid history in many societies, and it continues to be a major cause of human morbidity and mortality today (Brown 1997a). At a cultural ecological level, adaptations to malaria include the highland Vietnamese building practices, in which stilted houses allowed people to live above the 10-foot mosquito flight ceiling (May 1958). Although malaria has since been eradicated in the southern Italian island of Sardinia, Brown (see, selection 9) discovered that, while perhaps unintended, many of its continued cultural practices function to reduce contact with malaria-carrying mosquitoes. These included settlement and land use patterns, in which nucleated villages are located in highland areas and flocks of sheep are taken to the lowlands in the winter, thus minimizing contact with the mosquitoes during peak malaria seasons.

At a political ecological level, however, we find that these adaptive cultural practices were probably motivated by historical threats of military raids and expropriation of land by foreigners. Furthermore, wealthy Sardinians had less contact with the mosquitoes because they did not have to leave the safety of the village to work in the fields as did the laborers, nor did they have to stay in the village during peak malaria season when they could afford to take summer vacations abroad. Thus, the example of malaria demonstrates that multiple ecological variables—biological, cultural, political, and economic—interact to influence the prevalence of particular diseases in a given environmental context. In recent years—marked by the advent of global warming—more areas of the world have become vulnerable to malaria; this is a political ecological phenomenon.

Finally, schistosomiasis, a parasitic disease spread by snails, provides one of the most dramatic examples of the relationship between political ecology and disease. As Heyneman (1974) has described, economic development programs throughout the world have often focused on the building of dams in order to prevent seasonal flooding, improve irrigation, and provide hydroelectric power. Enormous dams, such as the Aswan High Dam on the Nile River, have dramatically altered the ecology of surrounding areas by preventing seasonal flooding and creating one of the largest man-made bodies of water in the world. A by-product of such changes, however, is that they create homeostatic imbalances between human populations and certain water-borne parasitic infections, such as schistosomiasis. The small snails that carry schistosomiasis thrive in the numerous irrigation canals emanating from the dams, increasing human exposure to the parasites. The result has been continual increases in the prevalence of debilitating schistosomiasis, an infection that primarily affects children, in numerous developing countries.

The story of schistosomiasis demonstrates that political-economic forces, such as dam development programs, can dramatically shape the relationship between host and disease in human populations. This, in turn, emphasizes the need for medical ecology to widen its definition of "environment" beyond the purely "natural" to include the political-economic consequences of collective human activity. In this globalizing world characterized by out-of-control carbon emissions and global warming that will have serious health impacts, there is no doubt that political-economic policies directly influence local disease ecologies.

Ethnomedical Approaches

All societies have medical systems that provide a theory of disease etiology, methods for the diagnosis of illness, and prescriptions and practices for curative or palliative treatment. The initial development of medical anthropology derived from anthropological interest in the healing beliefs and practices of different cultures. These interests stemmed from a growing recognition of the complex relationship between issues of health and sickness, culture-specific beliefs and healing practices, and the opportunities and constraints afforded by larger social forces (Wellin 1978).

Promoting the need for ethnomedical science, Fabrega defines ethnomedical inquiry as "the study of how members of different cultures think about disease and organize themselves toward medical treatment and the social organization of treatment itself" (Fabrega 1975:969). As a domain of inquiry, ethnomedical research is as broad as the discipline of anthropology. Generally speaking, medical anthropologists studying ethnomedical systems have focused upon six major areas of research: (1) ethnographic descriptions of healing practices, (2) explanatory models of health and sickness, (3) linguistic taxonomies of illness categories, (4) health-seeking behaviors, (5) the efficacy of ethnomedical systems, and (6) the comparison of and interaction between ethnomedical systems in a rapidly globalizing world.

At the beginning of this century, anthropological studies of medical systems were confined to ethnographic descriptions of "exotic" practices within non-Western societies. Many of the observations about sickness and therapeutic rituals were analyzed as a window on underlying cosmological beliefs and cultural values within comparative studies of myth and religion. However, some aspects of these works have been criticized for a tendency to sensationalize the differences of "primitive" people in comparison to their readership in Western industrialized societies (Rubel and Hass 1996).

In later decades, cultural notions of disease etiology around the world were described, classified, and mapped in order to trace the evolution of culture. The classification of ethnomedical beliefs and practices continued into the 1960s with projects emphasizing cross-cultural comparisons, such as the Human Relations Area Files (HRAF—a cross-indexed survey of hundreds of world cultures). One of the major questions that arose from these comparisons was the relationship between Western and non-Western medical systems. The term *ethnomedicine* was first defined as "beliefs and practices related to disease which are the products of indigenous cultural development and are not explicitly derived from the conceptual framework of modern medicine" (Rubel and Hass 1996). In order to describe another medical system, anthropologists must learn about the way different illnesses are named and categorized; to do this they must work with local healers to describe illness taxonomies.

In the simplest sense, all ethnomedical systems have three interrelated parts: (l) a theory of the etiology (causation) of sickness, (2) a method of diagnosis based on the etiological theory, and (3) the prescription of appropriate therapies based upon the diagnosis.

While this initial definition of ethnomedicine is convenient for many applications, it also forces an arbitrary distinction between supposedly "indigenous," "traditional," and "nonscientific" medical systems and supposedly "Western," "modern," and "scientific" medical systems. In India, for example, many Ayurvedic practitioners receive university training, practice in commercial institutions, and supplement their therapies with antibiotics, x-rays, and other tools of "biomedicine" (Nichter 1996). Likewise, many Indian physicians trained in "English medicine" use indigenous categories to explain health issues to their patients. Furthermore, in her comparison of biomedical systems in Europe and North America, Payer (1988) found considerable variability in the health beliefs and practices that constitute "biomedicine." Because of these issues of *medical pluralism,* it may be more useful to consider ethnomedicine as the study of any form of medicine as a cultural system. In other words, biomedicine can be considered as just another ethnomedical system.

In contemporary society, clinicians frequently find themselves treating patients from a different ethnomedical tradition. In the context of such medical pluralism, clinicians can elicit the person's *explanatory model* of his or her sickness rather than memorizing the details of a specific ethnomedical belief system (Brown 1997b). An explanatory model (EM) is a personal interpretation of the etiology, treatment, and outcome of sickness by which a person gives meaning to his or her condition. Although EMs are personal, they are also learned cultural models, so that an EM shared by a group might be considered a folk model of disease. These models constitute health belief systems that, from a cross-cultural perspective, generally fall into two categories: (1) *personalistic belief systems* that explain sickness as the result of supernatural forces directed at a patient, by either a sorcerer or an angry spirit; and (2) *naturalistic belief systems* that explain sickness in terms of natural forces, such as the germ theory of contagion in Western biomedicine or the imbalance of humours in many forms of Chinese, Indian, and Mediterranean systems (see selection 12). There is often disparity between the explanatory models of patients and healers, which may lead to problems of communication and nonadherence to prescribed therapies (Brown 1997b). A great deal of research in medical anthropology over the past decade has focused on cross-cultural encounters between patients and healers with different explanatory models of illness—particularly within biomedical settings—in an attempt to understand how these interactions are navigated by both clinicians and patients, and with what consequences for health outcomes and health care delivery.

Health-seeking behaviors refer to when people seek medical assistance and whom they turn to initially for help. Information on such behaviors is important for public health programs aimed at disease prevention and treatment. While stated health beliefs may influence treatment decisions, explanatory models alone are not good predictors of people's observed patterns of health seeking. This is because, as anthropologists have long noted, there is often a significant difference between cultural "ideals"—what people say they do—and "real" behavior of observable action. For example, a study of Nepalese patients found that people often sought multiple medical resources for a single illness despite verbal claims to the contrary (Durkin-Longley 1984). Many different factors may weigh upon decisions concerning when and where to seek treatment, such as the influence of family members (Janzen 1978), social networks, and geographic access to health resources (Kunitz 1983). In many cases, economic resources can severely limit treatment options, as in the case of Uganda, where the annual per capita health expenditures are less than the cost of a single HIV test.

An emerging area of interest among medical anthropologists concerns the efficacy of ethnomedical systems to meet the health needs of patients in particular cultural settings. Yet it is no accident that the criteria of medical efficacy are precisely as problematic as those of health. One solution may be to base the effectiveness of a particular treatment on the patient's own criteria. However, Csordas and Kleinman (1990) note that patients often claim satisfaction with their therapies while still retaining symptoms. These same authors suggest a broader set of criteria involving structural, clinical, discursive, persuasive, and social indices for the evaluation of ethnomedical therapies.

Experiential Approaches

In 1988, renowned anthropologist and psychiatrist Arthur Kleinman published a book titled *The Illness Narratives,* in which he advocated paying close attention to how people make sense of their illness experiences through narrative. In other words, he pointed out that the stories people tell about their illnesses can provide great insight into how they cope with the dilemmas that disease and suffering create in their lives. Since that time, what can broadly be called an *experiential approach* in medical anthropology has become increasingly resonant throughout the fields. Anthropologists using this approach frequently put illness-related suffering—whether due to pain, disability, or the awareness of one's own mortality—at the center of their analysis. They focus on three aspects of illness, in particular: (1) narrative—the stories that people tell about their illness; (2) experience—the way that people feel, perceive, and live with illness; and (3) meaning—the ways that people make sense of their illness, often linking their experience to larger moral questions. For example, in selection 19, Linda Hunt considers narratives from two individuals with cancer in southern Mexico; although these two have different cancers and face different life situations, both explain their illness in relation to the disappointments and obligations they have borne in their social lives.

In fact, experiential approaches often reference the links between sickness and problems in the social world. Illness narratives in particular may demonstrate how a symptom is experienced as troubling because of its impact on relationships with others, as when pain or fatigue interferes with a mother's ability to care for her children. Narratives may also provide a venue for negotiating the meaning of an illness, particularly in the social space between family members, patients, healers, and so forth. Kohn (2000) writes of how care providers treating children with facial disfigurements in Northern California create "therapeutic emplotments"—essentially, complex narratives—that are intended to help the children feel more comfortable with their appearance. In trying to transform the children's narratives of themselves and their appearance, the care providers are in fact trying to shift the children's experience of their disfigurement from one of embarrassment and shame to one of acceptance and confidence. Narrative, then, is not just a story of what has happened, or is happening, or might happen. It can also represent an active attempt to negotiate both individual selfhood and social relations amidst sickness and suffering.

The experiential approach has been applied most often in the exploration of illness experiences that are highly subjective, such as chronic pain and mental illness. These experiences, internal as they are, may be difficult to share or explain through the usual channels of communication. Mental disorders like schizophrenia have received significant attention as medical anthropologists attempt to understand the phenomenon of psychosis from within, interacting closely with and listening to the voices of those who might otherwise be ignored because of their difficulties in behaving and expressing themselves in normative ways (Jenkins 2004). In addition to helping social scientists rethink the cultural boundaries between what is considered "normal" verses "pathological," these studies have the potential to explore the connection between body and mind—often considered in Western societies to be separate and distinct entities—in a more holistic way.

The experience of illness is something that evolves in the space between body and mind and between individuals and those in their social environment; it may change over time as the disease progresses or resolves. In understanding how illness is experienced, medical anthropologists gain insight into how people endure and make meaning in some of the most vulnerable moments of their lives, and can better appreciate how these processes play out in people's explanatory models, care-seeking behaviors, and coping strategies.

Critical Approaches

In the last part of the twentieth century, medical anthropology witnessed a significant break from its disciplinary past. During this period, there were intense intellectual debates surrounding the approaches—sometimes called "critical theories"—which include postmodernism, Marxism, and deconstructionism. In general, these approaches require people to critically examine their own intellectual assumptions about how the world works; the basic idea is that reality is "socially constructed" and that some versions of "reality" conceal complex political relationships. These debates have influenced cultural anthropology in general and medical anthropology specifically. An important outcome has been the development of *critical medical anthropology* (CMA), a perspective that coalesced in the 1980s and 1990s (Singer 1989). Though CMA subsumes much theoretical diversity, it expresses at least two broad critiques.

The first critique is that many medical anthropologists have incorrectly attributed regional disparities in health to local sociocultural differences without examining the influence of global political-economic inequality on the distribution of disease. The intellectual tendency of medical anthropologists in the past has been to view illness only within local cultural systems and to neglect the larger political and economic context within which these cultures are found. Critical medical anthropologists, on the other hand, describe how large-scale political, economic, and cognitive structures constrain individuals' decisions, shape their social behavior, and affect their risk for disease (see selection 10 by Farmer). For example, in an analysis of the political-economic dimensions of disease in Tanzania, Meredeth Turshen has described how a history of colonialism drastically affected the country's nutritional base, altered its kinship structure, and imposed constraints on its health care system. This analysis is specifically designed to question the hidden assumptions of an ahistoric, scientific, epidemiological, "natural history" approach to understanding disease and international health problems. As such, she questions the epistemology (the way of creating knowledge) of standard studies, and she emphasizes an alternative she calls the "unnatural history of disease" (Turshen 1984). This study exemplifies the CMA approach in two ways: (1) the questioning of epistemological assumptions in standard analyses and recognition that those assumptions highlight some causes and obfuscate others; and (2) the emphasis on how historical political factors shape contemporary decision making, as well as the distribution of present-day health problems (Turshen 1984). This approach is also called the "political economy of health" (Morsy 1996).

Critical medical anthropologists make similar arguments concerning health disparities *within* industrialized Western societies. Due to their interest in macrolevel forces (e.g., world capitalism), critical medical anthropologists are generally skeptical of public health policies that propose microlevel solutions. Thus, CMA not only challenges the "socioculturalism" of traditional medical anthropology but also criticizes the narrow focus of international health agencies whose policies and interventions rarely address the large-scale factors influencing disease (Morsy 1996). Recently, Merrill Singer (see selection 36) has provided examples of ways that CMA can be merged with applied anthropology.

The second important critique offered by CMA emerges from an epistemological debate on the nature of biomedicine. Some critical medical anthropologists, influenced by the work of postmodern thinkers such as Michel Foucault (1990), challenged the medical anthropological presumption that Western biomedicine is an empirical, law-governed science that is unbiased by its own cultural premises. They point to the assumptions and generalizations underlying the theory and practice of Western medicine, which have been historically exempt from cultural analysis in medical anthropology. Scheper-Hughes and Lock, for example, critically question and analyze ("deconstruct") the mind–body distinction—a fundamental premise of biomedicine of the separation of "mind from body, spirit from matter, and real from unreal"—as a way to gain insight into how health care is planned and delivered in Western societies (1987:6). They suggest that the dominance of science and medicine has made the separation of mind and body so pervasive that people currently lack a precise vocabulary to express the complex interactions between mind, body, and society (Lock and Scheper-Hughes 1996; Scheper-Hughes and Lock 1987). Even within the new integrated paradigm of health in medicine, the "bio-psycho-social" approach, there is an assumed predominance of biology and a neglect of the fact that the most important phenomena are the *interactions* of mind, body, and society (Hahn and Kleinman 1983). In the 1980s and 1990s, critical medical anthropologists therefore proposed a new paradigm that viewed sickness not just as an isolated event but as a product of complex interactions involving nature, society, and culture.

Since the end of the 1990s, CMA—rather than remaining a distinct subsection of the fields—has been incorporated into medical anthropology more broadly. Rather than being a separate, renegade intellectual approach, CMA has become "mainstream" medical anthropology. From our perspective, CMA has also resulted in three developments with particular importance for contemporary medical anthropology.

The first development from CMA has been an energetic engagement with issues related to social justice and disparities in health across populations. Paul Farmer, a physician and anthropologist who is also the director of the nonprofit organization Partners in Health, has been highly influential in this area. He has become a widely recognized figure, highlighting the impact of global political ecologies on the emergence of infectious diseases like HIV/AIDS and multi-drug resistant tuberculosis (MDR-TB). In providing a critical perspective on global inequalities in health, Farmer and other authors writing in the same vein have placed a direct challenge to epidemiological research that too often explains health disparities in terms of race or other presumed biological difference, thus leaving out the crucial role of socioeconomic, political, and cultural determinants in shaping the differential distribution of health and illness across and within societies.

The second development resulting from CMA has been the bridging of experiential and critical approaches into a theoretical framework known as *critical phenomenology,* which examines how macrolevel processes of power and political economy are experienced at the microlevel by the individuals and communities they affect. Anthropologist Joao Biehl (2005), for example, has traced the paths by which ongoing socioeconomic changes in Brazil, accompanied by an increasing medicalization of illness and infirmity in that country, have resulted in families leaving their mentally and physically disabled members to live in ragged communities on the margins of society. Following this social progression to its outcome at the level of individual experience, he describes how mentally ill individuals in Brazil perceive and make sense of this "social abandonment." By situating the illness experience within its broader social context, critical phenomenology links processes occurring at the national or global level with their consequences at the level of individual lives.

The third development stemming from CMA has been so influential over the last decade that it deserves attention as its own approach, as described below.

Anthropology in and of Biomedicine

This relatively new approach reflects an increased focus on studying biomedicine as an ethnomedical system of knowledge and practice as deserving of critical scholarship as any other. This focus includes an emphasis on biotechnologies such as medical testing, the use of pharmaceuticals, and scientifically derived treatments. In viewing how such new technologies are taken up (or rejected) within existing biomedical systems, it is possible to observe how they come to be associated with different social circumstances across different cultural settings. Reproductive technologies such as in vitro fertilization, for example, may come to epitomize one set of concerns among women in the United States (selection 23) and a very different set among men in Egypt and Lebanon (selection 22).

In addition, explorations within biomedicine provide an opportunity to study the epistemology of scientific and medical knowledge. Studying the processes by which these forms of knowledge acquire their status *as* "knowledge"—rather than as "beliefs," the word Western societies often use to describe the knowledge of other cultures—forces us to test the distinctions between knowledge and belief and to find them highly questionable (Good 1994). Medical anthropologist Allan Young (1995), for example, has shown how post-traumatic stress disorder (PTSD) became accepted in the late 1970s as a distinct mental illness. It was not a process of psychiatrists suddenly "discovering" a new disorder. Instead, PTSD came to be included in the *Diagnostic and Statistical Manual for Mental Disorders* (DSM), psychiatry's official list of accepted diagnoses, when a group of psychiatrists came together and—urged by a vocal lobby of Vietnam veterans and their advocates—agreed that PTSD should be recognized despite a lack of medical and epidemiological research available to describe it. Likewise, studying the processes of knowledge creation in other areas of biomedicine has provided important insight into how "the gold standard of care" becomes the gold standard and how "evidence-supported treatments" acquire the evidence supporting their use.

Applied Approaches

As its name implies, applied anthropology emphasizes the direct application of anthropological theory and method to particular social problems. Within medical anthropology, applied approaches can be categorized into two general domains: (1) applied anthropology in clinical (e.g., hospital) settings, and (2) applied anthropology in public health programs. *Clinically applied anthropology* focuses on health care within biomedical settings and analyzes the effects of cultural and socioeconomic factors on doctor–patient interaction, adherence to treatment, and the experience of healing. A growing body of literature within clinically applied anthropology demonstrates how knowledge of explanatory models can be used to improve cultural sensitivity in physician–patient communications (Kleinman et al. 1978).

Explanatory models may be of particular importance in understanding the relationship between ethnicity and disease (Brown 1997b; Chrisman and Johnson 1996). For example, Heurtin-Roberts and Reisin (1990) have shown that the explanatory models of "high blood" and "high-pertension" among African American women can cause clinical communication difficulties in the treatment of high blood pressure, as well as affecting patient adherence to treatment. Because the explanatory model of "high-pertension" refers to an episodic illness that cannot be treated (except to avoid stressful situations), patients who believe that their illness is "high-pertension" see no point in taking daily medication prescribed by a biomedical doctor; they are "non-compliant." Similar obstacles to clinical treatment have been described in studies of the explanatory models of other ethnic groups, such as the hot-cold theory of disease among Hispanics (see selection 28). Such studies suggest that greater attention to patients' explanatory models of illness—and the specific ways in which they conflict with or conform to biomedical models—can facilitate mutual understanding between physicians and their patients, and ultimately improve health outcomes (Csordas and Kleinman 1996; Helman 1994).

Medical anthropologists working within health care settings have often been called to assist in solving problems created by the cultural differences between patients and health care providers. Some of these problems involve difficulties in communication across both language and cultural barriers. Such problems have been described in the well-known book by Anne Fadiman *The Spirit Catches You and You Fall Down* (1998), which deals with the conflicts between the family of a Hmong child and her American doctors. Sometimes the context of health care in a multiethnic society is referred to as "cross-cultural medicine." For a significant period of its history, medical anthropology dealt with the health beliefs and practices of ethnic minorities. Margaret Clark's *Health in the Mexican-American Community* (1959) is a good example of this work. Her analysis emphasizes, for example, that it is insufficient simply to translate medical instructions when the patient population has limited literacy and biomedical language (in any language) is unfamiliar to them. Another well-known volume of this work, edited by Alan Harwood, is *Ethnicity and Medical Care* (1981). The training of health care providers in basic knowledge about cultural differences among patients and skills in cross-cultural communication is called "cultural competence." Many medical anthropologists are critical of this approach and such training programs.

The second major branch of applied medical anthropology deals with public health—policy-making, program development, and intervention. Medical anthropologists are often called upon to consult with international and domestic health agencies in an effort to formulate health programs that are more culturally sensitive, applicable to local needs, and effective in obtaining community support. Anthropological perspectives are relevant at all levels of the public health process, from the interpretation of disease trends to the design, implementation, and evaluation of programs. Anthropologists have been influential in the recent philosophical changes that are reflected in the shift from "international health" to "global health." The latter approach underscores the fact that health improvements in the developing world require mutual cultural understanding and cooperation, and that in our globalized and interconnected world, there are no epidemiological borders.

One of the areas in which anthropologists have contributed their insights to public health is in their collaboration with epidemiologists (Trostle 1997). Through ethnography, anthropologists have assisted epidemiologists in identifying some of the specific behaviors that increase risk for disease and the cultural norms or beliefs that promote them (Nations 1986). One of the classic examples of this is the prominent role of anthropologists in unraveling the social etiology of *kuru*, an infectious disease found among the South Fore of New Guinea and probably transmitted through funerary practices (Lindenbaum 1979). Thus, while some medical anthropologists have been somewhat disdainful of the methods and assumptions of epidemiology itself, applied anthropologists have increasingly found ways to bridge what they view as the complementary strengths of epidemiology and medical anthropology (Inhorn 1995). Other applied anthropologists have focused on creating more effective public health programs by appealing to local cultural values and personnel. For example, in the area of HIV/AIDS, several anthropologists have advocated the use of traditional healers as educators and trusted health advisors in local communities (Green 1994; Schoepf 1992). The use of traditional healers as collaborators in the introduction of health technologies and information avoids many of the problems of distrust, translation, applicability, and sustainability that often plague public health programs.

Finally, some medical anthropologists have examined the cultural dimensions of the public health bureaucracy itself. Like scholars who frame studies of biomedicine as a cultural system, applied anthropologists are increasingly turning their attention to the cultural beliefs, norms, and implicit premises upon which public health funding and administration are based (Justice 1986). Some medical anthropologists have begun to study nongovernmental organizations (NGOs) working in global health. Frequently, such research seeks to expose the cultural and bureaucratic assumptions within public health that create obstacles to the implementation of locally relevant, effective, and culturally sensitive programs.

CONCLUSION

Medical anthropology, like its parent discipline, is a holistic and interdisciplinary enterprise. We began this article quoting the definition of the field offered by the Society for Medical Anthropology. That definition includes so many topics covering such a diverse set of questions that some readers may think that it was written by a committee. In the simplest sense, medical anthropology refers to studies of health and healing from biosocial and cross-culturally comparative perspectives. In this regard, *healing* refers to all medical systems, including modern biomedicine and its sophisticated technologies, as cultural products. Because there is such a remarkable diversity of theories and methods used in medical anthropology, it seems more appropriate to talk about it as a number of related fields; that is why we used the plural form in the title. In this article, we have outlined seven major approaches that medical anthropologists use to better understand issues of human health, healing, and sickness: biological ecological, ethnomedical, critical, experiential, applied, and anthropology *in* and *of* biomedicine. When we explore the specific examples, however, it becomes clear the seven categories are, in fact, overlapping. The first part of this book—the part devoted to *understanding* medical anthropology—contrasts biosocial approaches and cultural approaches; this seems to be a fundamental distinction. Yet even this simple distinction seems artificial because the culturally oriented analyses focus on biological/medical processes, and the biological approaches almost always emphasize the role of human (cultural) behavior. Within all of this theoretical and methodological diversity, however, there are essential commonalities in an anthropological study of health, illness, and healing. These commonalities all stem from an anthropological view of the world.

REFERENCES

Biehl, Joao. 2005. *Vita: Life in a Zone of Social Abandonment.* Berkeley: University of California Press.

Boas, Franz. 1940. *Race, Language, Culture.* New York: Macmillan.

Brown, Peter J. 1981. Cultural Adaptation to Endemic Malaria in Sardinia. *Medical Anthropology* 5(4): 311–339.

———. 1991. Culture and the Evolution of Obesity. *Human Nature* 2:31–57.

Brown, Peter J., Daniel Smith, and Marcia Inhorn. 1996. Disease, Ecology, and Human Behavior. In *Medical Anthropology: Contemporary Theory and Method.* C. F. Sargent and T. F. Johnson, eds. Pp. 183–219. Westport, CT: Praeger.

Brown, Peter J. 1997. Culture and the Global Resurgence of Malaria. In *The Anthropology of Infectious Disease: International Health Perspectives.* Marcia Inhorn and Peter J. Brown, eds. Pp. 119–141. Newark, NJ: Gordon and Breach.

Brown, Peter J., Jessica Gregg, and Bruce Ballard. 1997b. Culture, Ethnicity, and the Practice of Medicine. In *Human Behavior for Medical Students.* A. Stoudemire, ed. New York: Lippincott.

Chrisman, Noel J., and Thomas M. Johnson. 1996. Clinically Applied Anthropology. In *Medical Anthropology: Contemporary Theory and Method.* C. F. Sargent and T. M. Johnson, eds. Pp. 88–109. Westport, CT: Praeger, 1996.

Clark, Margaret. 1959. *Health in the Mexican American Community: A Community Study.* Berkeley: University of California Press.

Csordas, Thomas, and Arthur Kleinman. 1996. The Therapeutic Process. In *Medical Anthropology: Theory and Method.* C. F. Sargent and T. M. Johnson, eds. Pp. 3–20. Westport, CT: Praeger.

Desowitz, R. S. 1981. *New Guinea Tapeworms and Jewish Grandmothers: Tales of Parasites and People.* New York: Norton.

Dubos, Rene. 1959. *The Mirage of Health.* New York: Harper and Row.

Durkin-Longley, Maureen. 1984. Multiple Therapeutic Use in Urban Nepal. *Social Science and Medicine* 19:867–872.

Dressier, W. H., J. R. Bindon, and M. J. Gilliland. 1996. Sociocultural and Behavioral Influences on Health Status among the Mississippi Choctaw. *Medical Anthropology* 17:165–180.

Etkin, Nina. 1996. Ethnopharmacology: The Conjunction of Medical Ethnography and the Biology of Therapeutic Action. In *Medical Anthropology: Contemporary Theory and Method.* C. F. Sargent and T. M. Johnson, eds. Westport, CT: Praeger.

Farmer, Paul. 1996. Social Inequalities and Emerging Infectious Diseases. *Emerging Infectious Diseases* 2(4):259–269.

Fabrega, Horacio. 1975. The Need for an Ethnomedical Science. *Science* 189:969–975.

Fadiman, Anne. 1998. *The Spirit Catches You and You Fall Down.* New York: Farrar, Straus and Giroux.

Foucault, Michel. 1990. *The History of Sexuality Volume I: An Introduction.* New York: Vintage.

Good, Byron. 1994. *Medicine, Rationality, and Experience: An Anthropological Perspective.* Cambridge: Cambridge University Press.

Green, Edward C. 1994. *AIDS and STDs in Aftica: Bridging the Gap between Traditional Healing and Modern Medicine.* Boulder, CO: Westview Press.

Gould, Jay Stephen. 1981. *The Mismeasure of Man.* New York: Norton.

Hahn, Robert A. 1995. *Sickness and Healing: An Anthropological Perspective.* New Haven, CT: Yale University Press.

Hahn, Robert A., and Arthur Kleinman. 1983. Belief as Pathogen, Belief as Medicine: "Voodoo Death" and the "Placebo Phenomenon" in Anthropological Perspective. *Medical Anthropology Quarterly* 14(3):16–19.

Harwood, A. 1971. The Hot-Cold Theory of Disease: Implications for the Treatment of Puerto Rican Patients. *Journal of the American Medical Association* 216:1153–1158.

———. 1981. *Ethnicity and Medical Care.* Cambridge: Harvard University Press.

Helman, Cecil G. 1994. *Culture, Health, and Illness: An Introduction for Health Professionals,* 3rd ed. Oxford: Butterworth-Heinemann.

Heurtin-Roberts, S., and E. Reisin. 1990. Health Beliefs and Compliance with Prescribed Medication for Hypertension among Black Women. *Morbidity and Mortality Weekly Report* 39(40):701–703.

Heyneman, Donald. 1974. Dams and Disease. *Human Nature* 2:50–57.

Inhorn, Marcia C. 1995. Medical Anthropology and Epidemiology: Divergences or Convergences? *Social Science and Medicine* 40(3):285–290.

Janzen, John. 1978. *The Quest for Therapy: Medical Pluralism in Lower Zaire.* Berkeley: University of California Press.

Jenkins, Janis, and Robert J. Barrett. 2004. *Schizophrenia, Culture, and Subjectivity: The Edge of Experience.* Cambridge: Cambridge University Press.

Justice, Judith. 1986. *Policies, Plans, and People: Foreign Aid and Health Development.* Berkeley: University of California Press.

Kleinman, Arthur M., Leon Eisenberg, and Byron J. Good. 1978. Culture, Illness and Care: Clinical Lessons from Anthropologic and Cross-cultural Research. *Annals of Internal Medicine* 88:251–258.

Kohn, Abigail. 2000. "Imperfect Angels": Narrative "Emplotment" in the Medical Management of Children with Craniofacial Abnormalities. *Medical Anthropology Quarterly* 14(2):202–223.

Kunitz, Stephen. 1983. *Disease Change and the Role of Medicine: The Navajo Experience.* Berkeley: University of California Press.

Lindenbaum, Shirley. 1979. *Kuru Sorcery: Disease and Danger in the New Guinea Highlands.* Mountain View, CA: Mayfield.

Lock, Margaret, and Nancy Scheper-Hughes. 1996. A Critical-Interpretive Approach in Medical Anthropology: Rituals and Routines of Discipline and Dissent. In *Medical Anthropology: Contemporary Theory and Method.* C. F. Sargent and T. M. Johnson, eds. Pp. 41–70. Westport, CT: Praeger.

Martorell, Reynaldo. 1989. Body Size, Adaptation and Function. *Human Organization* 48:15–20.

May, J. M. 1958. *The Ecology of Human Disease.* New York: MD Publications.

McElroy, Ann, and Patricia K. Townsend. 1996. *Medical Anthropology in Ecological Perspective.* Boulder, CO: Westview Press.

Morsy, Soheir A. 1996. Political Economy in Medical Anthropology. In *Medical Anthropology: Contemporary Theory and Method.* C. F. Sargent and T. F. Johnson, eds. Pp. 21–40. Westport, CT: Praeger.

Nations, Marilyn K. 1986. Epidemiological Research on Infectious Disease: Quantitative Rigor or *Rigor Mortis?* Insights from Ethnomedicine. In *Anthropology and Epidemiology: Interdisciplinary Approaches to the Study of Health and Disease.* C. R. Janes, R. Stall, and S. M. Gifford, eds. Dordrecht: D. Reidel.

Nichter, Mark, and Mimi Nichter. 1996. *Anthropology and International Health: Asian Case Studies.* Newark, NJ: Gordon and Breach.

Payer, Lynn. 1988. *Medicine and Culture.* New York: Penguin.

Rubel, Arthur J. 1964. The Epidemiology of a Folk Illness: *Susto* in Hispanic America. *Ethnology* 3:268–283.

Rubel, Arthur J., and Michael R. Hass. 1996. Ethnomedicine. In *Medical Anthropology: Contemporary Theory and Method.* C. F. Sargent and T. F. Johnson, eds. Pp. 113–130. Westport, CT: Praeger.

Scheper-Hughes, Nancy, and Margaret M. Lock. 1987. The Mindful Body: A Prolegomenon to Future Work in Medical Anthropology. *Medical Anthropology Quarterly* 1(1):6–41.

Schoepf, Brooke Grundfest. 1992. AIDS, Sex and Condoms: African Healers and the Reinvention of Tradition in Zaire. *Medical Anthropology* 14:225–242.

Seckler, D. 1982. "Small but Healthy": A Basic Hypothesis in the Theory, Measurement, and Policy of Malnutrition. In *Newer Concepts in Nutrition and Their Implications for Policy.* P. V. Sukhatme, ed. Pp. 127–137. Pune, India: Maharashtra Association for the Cultivation of Science Research Institute.

Singer, Merrill. 1989. The Coming of Age of Critical Medical Anthropology. *Social Science and Medicine* 28(11): 1193–1203.

Society for Medical Anthropology. 2008. http://www.medanthro.net.maq/index.html, October 6.

Sontag, Susan. 1978. *Illness as Metaphor.* New York: Farrar, Straus and Giroux.

Trostle, J., and J. Sommerfeld. 1996. Medical Anthropology and Epidemiology. *Annual Review of Anthropology* 25:253–274.

Turshen, Meredith. 1982. *The Political Ecology of Disease in Tanzania.* New Brunswick, NJ: Rutgers University Press.

Wellin, Edward. 1978. Theoretical Orientations in Medical Anthropology: Change and Continuity over the Past Half-Century. In *Health and the Human Condition.* M. Logan and E. Hunt, eds. Pp. 23–39. North Scituate, MA: Duxbury.

Young, Allan. 1997. *The Harmony of Illusions: Inventing Post-Traumatic Stress Disorder*. Princeton, NJ: Princeton University Press.

Evolution, Health, and Medicine

CONCEPTUAL TOOLS 

■ ***Evolution is the central theoretical concept in all the biological sciences, including anthropology.*** Many people misunderstand evolution, thinking that it is just a theory or that it has to do with perfectibility and progress. In fact, evolution is a powerful, awesome idea. Evolutionary theory is able to explain literally millions of biological observations of the natural world. The fact that scientists argue about specific cases or that there are parts of the evolutionary record that we know little about should not detract from our appreciation of this important concept.

■ ***Evolution means three things: Things change over time, change occurs because of natural forces, and these changes occur in predictable directions.*** Evolutionary change includes the possibility that, over generations, a species can change into another species. The primary driving force determining the direction, character, and speed of that change is *natural selection.* Natural selection means that because some inherited traits affect the ability of individuals to survive and reproduce, traits that enhance reproductive fitness will, over generations of individuals living and dying in a particular ecological context, tend to increase. On the other hand, genetic traits that make it more likely that individuals or their offspring will die early will tend to decrease. Evolutionary change, therefore, depends on the interaction of organisms and their environment. That interaction results in differential rates of morbidity (sickness), mortality, and fertility for individuals with different traits. Geographic isolation of a population undergoing selection is necessary for a species to change into another species.

■ ***There are other forces in evolution besides natural selection.*** These include mutation, gene flow or migration, and genetic drift.

■ ***Humans are special because of our dual system of inheritance.*** Humans are unique in that we have a dual system of inheritance—through both genes and culture—and in that we largely depend on culture for survival. Genetic evolution works through Darwinian principles. That means that, first, there is variation in a population based on inherited characteristics. When that genetic variation affects different individuals' ability to survive and reproduce, those successful individuals will pass the genes down to the next generation with greater frequency. Darwinian evolution means that individuals with other, less-adapted characteristics will die at greater frequencies, or their offspring will die more often, or they will have fewer offspring. These are the same rules of life that apply to all living things.

■ ***On the other hand, cultural evolution is a more flexible and potentially faster process.*** Cultural systems change as people evaluate the influence of their behavior in interaction with the environment. Simply put, people tend to do things that improve their conditions and avoid things that harm them or make them sick. Cultural evolution is partly related to the processes of problem solving and evaluation and partly related to issues of social power structures that influence behavior. Cultural learning can be based on borrowing ideas from nonkin, so that it doesn't take generations to occur. In many ways, cultural evolution has outstripped biological evolution for humans.

■ ***Understanding the evolutionary strategies of pathogens can be very useful for health care providers and people working in preventive medicine.*** Evolution shapes the reproductive strategies used by pathogens to pass their genes on to the next generation. Symptoms like coughing or diarrhea can be the pathogen's mechanism for infecting another host. On the other hand, pathogens like intestinal worms may not cause drastic symptoms in their hosts and therefore live in a commensal relationship with the host. When health care workers and patients understand how incomplete antibiotic treatment can result in "unnatural selection" for resistant strains of bacteria, there is more likelihood of patients' adherence to correct medical therapies. New antibiotic-resistant strains of disease are a major threat to human health.

 2

Stone Agers in the Fast Lane: Chronic Degenerative Diseases in Evolutionary Perspective

S. Boyd Eaton
Marjorie Shostak
Melvin Konner

This selection was written for a medical journal by anthropologist-physicians interested in using an evolutionary approach to explain what our diet and exercise patterns should be if we want to prevent chronic degenerative diseases like cardiovascular disease, hypertension, and some cancers. The primary argument here is an important one: There is a "discordance," or biological estrangement, between our genes and contemporary patterns of diet and activity. The result of this discordance is that, in rich countries like the United States, there has been a marked increase in a variety of chronic diseases. These diseases, sometimes called diseases of civilization, are largely preventable. The prescription is a familiar one—a low-fat, high-fiber diet and an increase in exercise—but the reasoning behind it is evolutionary, rather than authoritative moralism. The authors wrote a popular book on this subject (Eaton, Shostak, and Konner 1988), and some cartoonists even poked fun at their work, calling it the "cave man diet." But medical anthropologists would argue that there are a lot of lessons modern people could learn from so-called cave men.

Two of the authors (Shostak and Konner) did anthropological fieldwork among the !Kung San hunter-gatherers who live in the Kalahari Desert in southern Africa. Hunter-gatherers today cannot be thought of as some type of living fossil; these peoples are affected by significant historical and political-economic pressures (Solway and Lee 1990). On the other hand, their lives more closely resemble those of our remote ancestors (as this selection says, in the "environment of evolutionary adaptedness"). Most anthropologists strongly believe that so-called modern people have a lot to learn from so-called primitive people. Those practical lessons include not only diet and exercise but things like breast-feeding patterns, child-rearing rules, and the organization of schools.

When you read this selection, think about your own health or that of your friends and family. Do you smoke cigarettes or drink alcohol? Do you eat a diet high in saturated fat? Do you get enough exercise? Why is that?

As you read this selection, consider these questions:

- **How can you tell that this selection was written for physicians reading a medical journal? What kind of assumption may be embedded here regarding the nature and causation of health?**
- **If there is a "discordance" in the evolution of our genes and culture, why haven't our genes caught up?**
- **Can you devise an evolutionary explanation for why we like to eat things (say, ice cream or alcohol) that are bad for us?**

Context: This article was written toward the early days of the field of evolutionary medicine (a.k.a. Darwinian medicine). Eaton's primary interests were in the prevention of chronic disease, while Konner and Shostak had done field research on the !Kung San people of the Kalahari Desert. After an article in the prestigious New England Journal of Medicine on this topic in 1985, these three authors wrote a popular book titled The Paleolithic Prescription: A Program of Diet & Exercise and a Design for Living (1989). Boyd Eaton is a physician, radiologist, and researcher in the evolutionary medicine of chronic diseases at Emory University. Melvin Konner is a biological anthropologist and physician at Emory University; he is a prolific author, best known for his volume The Tangled Wing: Biological Constraints on the Human Spirit. The late Marjorie Shostak made remarkable contributions to ethnographic writing with her book Nisa: The Life and Words of a !Kung Woman.

Source: S. Boyd Eaton, Marjorie Shostak, and Melvin Konner (1988). *"Stone Agers in the Fast Lane: Chronic Degenerative Diseases in Evolutionary Context."* American Journal of Medicine. 84:739–749.

From a genetic standpoint, humans living today are Stone Age hunter-gatherers displaced through time to a world that differs from that for which our genetic constitution was selected. Unlike evolutionary maladaption, our current discordance has little effect on reproductive success; rather it acts as a potent promoter of chronic illnesses: atherosclerosis, essential hypertension, many cancers, diabetes mellitus, and obesity among others. These diseases are the results of interaction between genetically controlled biochemical processes and a myriad of biocultural influences—lifestyle factors—that include nutrition, exercise, and exposure to noxious substances. Although our genes have hardly changed, our culture has been transformed almost beyond recognition during the past 10,000 years, especially since the Industrial Revolution. There is increasing evidence that the resulting mismatch fosters "diseases of civilization" that together cause 75 percent of all deaths in Western nations, but that are rare among persons whose lifeways reflect those of our preagricultural ancestors.

In today's Western nations, life expectancy is over 70 years—double what it was in preindustrial times. Infant death rates are lower than ever before and nearly 80 percent of all newborn infants will survive to age 65 or beyond. Such vital statistics certify that the health of current populations, at least in the affluent nations, is superior to that of any prior group of humans. Accordingly, it seems counterintuitive to suggest that, in certain important respects, the collective human genome is poorly designed for modern life. Nevertheless, there is both epidemiologic and pathophysiologic evidence that suggests this may be so.

In industrialized nations, each person's health status is heavily influenced by the interaction between his or her genetically controlled biochemistry and a collection of biobehavioral influences that can be considered lifestyle factors. These include nutrition, exercise, and exposure to harmful substances such as alcohol and tobacco. This report presents evidence that the genetic makeup of humanity has changed little during the past 10,000 years, but that during the same period, our culture has been transformed to the point that there is now a mismatch between our ancient, genetically controlled biology and certain important aspects of our daily lives. This discordance is not genetic maladaptation in the terms of classic evolutionary science—it does not affect differential fertility. Rather, it promotes chronic degenerative diseases that have their main clinical expression in the postreproductive period, but that together account for nearly 75 percent of the deaths occurring in affluent Western nations.

THE HUMAN GENOME

The gene pool from which current humans derive their individual genotypes was formed during an evolutionary experience lasting over a billion years. The almost inconceivably protracted pace of genetic evolution is indicated by paleontologic findings that reveal that an average species of late Cenozoic mammals persisted for more than a million years,[1] by biomolecular evidence indicating that humans and chimpanzees now differ genetically by just 1.6 percent even though the hominid-pongid divergence occurred seven million years ago,[2] and by dentochronologic data showing that current Europeans are genetically more like their Cro-Magnon ancestors than they are like 20th-century Africans or Asians.[3] Accordingly, it appears that the gene pool has changed little since anatomically modern humans, *Homo sapiens sapiens*, became widespread about 35,000 years ago and that, from a genetic standpoint, current humans are still late Paleolithic preagricultural hunter-gatherers.

THE IMPACT OF CULTURAL CHANGES

It has been proposed that chronic degenerative disorders, sometimes referred to as the "diseases of civilization," are promoted by discordance between our genetic makeup (which was selected over geologic eras, ultimately to fit the life circumstances of Paleolithic humans) and selected features of our current bioenvironmental milieu. The rapid cultural changes that have occurred during the past 10,000 years have far outpaced any possible genetic adaptation, especially since much of this cultural change has occurred only subsequent to the Industrial Revolution of 200 years ago.

The increasing industrialized affluence of the past two centuries has affected human health both beneficially and adversely. Improved housing, sanitation, and medical care have ameliorated the impact of infection and trauma, the chief causes of mortality from the Paleolithic era until 1900, with the result that average life expectancy is now approximately double what it was for preagricultural humans. The importance of these positive influences can hardly be overstated; their effects have not only increased longevity, but also enhanced the quality of our lives in countless ways. But, on the other hand, the past century has accelerated the biologic estrangement that has increasingly differentiated humans from other mammals over the entire two-million-year period since *Homo habilis* first appeared. Despite the increasing importance of culture and technology during this time, the basic lifestyle elements of *Homo sapiens sapiens* were still within the broad continuum of general mammalian experience until recently. However, in today's Western nations, we have so little need for exercise, consume foods so different from those available to other mammals, and expose ourselves to such harmful agents as alcohol and tobacco that we have crossed an epidemiologic boundary and entered a watershed in which disorders such as obesity, diabetes, hypertension, and certain cancers have become common in contrast to their rarity among remaining preagricultural and other traditional humans.

METHODS

Pertinent data on fitness, diet, and disease prevalence in non-industrial societies were reviewed, tabulated, and contrasted with comparable data from industrialized nations. The literature cited is based on studies of varied traditional groups: pastoralists, rudimentary horticulturalists, and simple agriculturalists, as well as technologically primitive hunter-gatherers. We would have preferred to present data derived solely from studies of pure hunter-gatherers, since they are most analogous to Paleolithic humans. Unfortunately, only a few such investigations have been performed, so that inclusion of selected non-foraging populations constitutes a necessary first approximation. However, there is a continuum of human experience with regard to lifestyle factors that now affect disease prevalence, and on this continuum, traditional peoples occupy positions much closer to those of our preagricultural ancestors than to those of affluent Westerners. In each case, the groups analyzed resemble late Paleolithic humans far more than ourselves with respect to factors (such as exercise requirements and dietary levels of fat, sodium, and fiber) considered likely to influence the prevalence of the disease entity under consideration.

THE LATE PALEOLITHIC LIFESTYLE

The Late Paleolithic era, from 35,000 to 20,000 B.P., may be considered the last time period during which the collective human gene pool interacted with bioenvironmental circumstances typical of those for which it had been originally selected. It is because of this that the diet, exercise patterns, and social adaptations of that time have continuing relevance for us today.

Nutrition

The diets of Paleolithic humans must have varied greatly with latitude and season just as do those of recently studied hunter-gatherers; undoubtedly, there were periods of relative plenty and others of shortage; certainly there was no one universal subsistence pattern. However, the dietary requirements of all Stone Age men and women had to be met by uncultivated vegetables and wild game exclusively; from this starting point, a number of logically defensible nutritional generalizations can be extrapolated. (1) The amount of protein, especially animal protein, was very great. The mean, median, and modal protein intake for 58 hunter-gatherer groups studied in [the 20th] century was 34 percent[4] and protein intake in the Late Paleolithic era may have been higher still.[5,6] The current American diet derives 12 percent of its energy from protein (Table I). (2) Because game animals are extremely lean, paleolithic humans ate much less fat than do 20th-century Americans and Europeans, although more than is consumed in most Third-World countries. (3) Stone Age hunter-gatherers generally ate more polyunsaturated than saturated fat. (4) Their cholesterol intake would ordinarily have equaled or exceeded that now common in industrialized nations. (5) The amount of carbohydrate they obtained would have varied inversely with the proportion of meat in their diet, but (6) in almost all cases they would have obtained much more dietary fiber than do most Americans. (7) The availability of simple sugars, especially honey, would have

TABLE I Late Paleolithic, Contemporary American, and Currently Recommended Dietary Composition

	Late Paleolithic Diet	*Contemporary American Diet*	*Current Recommendations*
Total dietary energy (percent)			
Protein	33	12	12
Carbohydrate	46	46	58
Fat	21	42	30
Alcohol	~0	7–10*	–
P:S ratio	1.41	0.44	1.00
Cholesterol (mg)	520	300–500	300
Fiber (g)	100–150	19.7	30–60
Sodium (mg)	690	2,300–6,900	1,100–3,300
Calcium (mg)	1,500–2,000	740	800–1,600
Ascorbic acid (mg)	440	87.7	60

Updated from Eaton and Konner, note 4. Data base now includes 43 species of wild game and 153 types of wild plant food.

*Inclusion of calories from alcohol would require concomitant reduction in calories from other nutrients—mainly carbohydrate and fat.

P.S.–polyunsaturated to-saturated fat.

varied seasonally. For a two- to four-month period, their intake could have equaled that of current humans, but for the remainder of the year it would have been minimal. (8) The amounts of ascorbic acid, folate, vitamin B_{12}, and iron available[7, 8] to our remote ancestors equaled, and likely exceeded, those consumed by today's Europeans and North Americans; probably this reflects a general abundance of micronutrients (with the possible exception of iodine in inland locations). (9) In striking contrast to the pattern in today's industrialized nations,[9] Paleolithic humans obtained far more potassium than sodium from their food (as do all other mammals). On the average, their total daily sodium intake was less than a gram—barely a quarter of the current American average. (10) Because they had no domesticated animals, they had no dairy foods; despite this, their calcium intake, in most cases, would have far exceeded that generally consumed in the 20th century.

Physical Exercise

The hunter-gatherer way of life generates high levels of physical fitness. Paleontologic investigations and anthropologic observations of recent foragers[10] document that among such people, strength and stamina are characteristic of both sexes at all ages.

Skeletal remains can be used for estimation of strength and muscularity. The prominence of muscular insertion sites, the area of articular surfaces, and the cortical thickness and cross-sectional shape of long bone shafts all reflect the forces exerted by the muscles acting on them. Analyses of these features consistently show that preagricultural humans were more robust than their descendants, including the average inhabitants of today's Western nations. This pattern holds whether the population being studied underwent the shift to agriculture 10,000[11] or only 1,000[12] years ago, so it clearly represents the results of habitual activity rather than genetic evolution. The fact that hunter-gatherers were demonstrably stronger and more muscular than succeeding agriculturalists (who worked much longer hours) suggests that the intensity of intermittent peak demand on the musculoskeletal system is more important than the mere number of hours worked for the development of muscularity.

The endurance activities associated with both hunting and gathering involve considerable heat production. The long-standing importance of such behaviors for humankind is apparently reflected in the unusual mechanisms for heat dissipation with which evolution has endowed us: we are among the very few animal species that can release heat by sweating; also, our hairless, exposed skin allows heat to escape readily, especially during rapid movement, like running, when airflow over the skin is increased. These physiologic adaptations suggest the importance of endurance activities in our evolutionary past,[13] and evaluation of recent preliterate populations confirms that their daily activities develop superior aerobic fitness (Tables II and III). Whereas actual measurements of maximal oxygen uptake capacity have been made almost exclusively on men, anthropologic observations suggest commensurate aerobic fitness for women in traditional cultures as well.[15]

Alcoholic Beverages

Honey and many wild fruits can undergo natural fermentation, so the possibility that some preagricultural persons had alcoholic beverages cannot be excluded. However, widespread regular use of

TABLE II Aerobic Fitness

Subsistence Pattern	*Population*	*Average Age*	*Maximal Oxygen Uptake (ml/kg/minute)*	*Fitness Category**
Hunter-gatherers	Canadian Igloolik Eskimos	29.3	56.4	Superior
	Kalahari San (Bushmen)	Young men	47.1	Excellent
Rudimentary horticulturists	Venezuelan Warao Indians	Young men	51.2	Excellent
	New Guinea highland Lufas	25	67.0	Superior
Simple agriculturists	Mexican Tarahumara Indians	29.8	63.0	Superior
Pastoralists	Finnish Kautokeino Lapps	25–35	53.0	Superior
	Tanzanian Masai	32–43	59.1	Superior
Industrialized Westerners	Canadian Caucasians	20–29	40.8	Fair
	Canadian Caucasians	30–39	38.1	Fair
	Canadian Caucasians	40–49	34.9	Fair

*From note 14.

TABLE III Fitness Classification for American Males*

	Maximal Oxygen Uptake (ml/kg/minute)					
Age	*Very Poor*	*Poor*	*Fair*	*Good*	*Excellent*	*Superior*
20–29	<33.0	33.0–36.4	36.5–42.4	42.5–46.4	46.5–52.4	>52.5
30–39	<31.5	31.5–35.4	36.5–40.9	41.0–44.9	45.0–49.4	>49.5
40–49	<30.2	30.2–33.5	33.6–38.9	39.0–43.7	43.8–48.0	>48.1

*Data modified from note 14.

alcohol must have been a very late phenomenon: of 95 preliterate societies studied in this century,[16] fully 46, including the San (Bushmen), Eskimos, and Australian Aborigines, were unable to manufacture such beverages. It is estimated that 7 to 10 percent of the average adult American's daily energy intake is provided by alcohol; such levels are far in excess of what Late Paleolithic humans could have conceivably obtained.

In general, native alcoholic beverages are prepared periodically and drunk immediately.[17] Their availability is subject to seasonal fluctuation, and as products of natural fermentation, their potency is far less than that of distilled liquors. Their consumption is almost invariably subject to strong societal conventions that limit the frequency and place of consumption, degree of permissible intoxication, and types of behavior that will be tolerated. In small-scale preliterate societies, drinking tends to be ritualized and culturally integrated.[18] Solitary, addictive, pathologic drinking behavior does not occur to any significant extent; such behavior appears to be a concomitant of complex, modern, industrialized societies.[17]

Tobacco Abuse

Recent hunter-gatherers such as the San (Bushmen), Aché, and Hadza had no tobacco prior to contact with more technologically advanced cultures, but the Australian Aborigines chew wild tobacco, so seasonal use by Paleolithic humans in geographically limited areas cannot be excluded. However, widespread tobacco usage began only after the appearance of agriculture in the Americas, perhaps 5,000 years ago. With European contact, the practice spread rapidly throughout the world. Pipes and cigars were the only methods employed for smoking until the mid-19th century, when cigarettes first appeared. Cigarettes had three crucial effects: they dramatically increased per capita consumption among men; after World War I, they made smoking socially acceptable for women; and they made inhalation of smoke the rule rather than the exception. Although the hazards of chewing tobacco, snuff, pipes, and cigars are not insignificant, the major impact of tobacco abuse is a post-cigarette phenomenon of this century.

HOW ALTERED LIFESTYLE FACTORS AFFECT DISEASE PREVALENCE

In many, if not most, respects, the health of humans in today's affluent countries must surpass that of typical Stone Agers. Infant mortality, the rate of endemic infectious disease (especially parasitism), and the prevalence of post-traumatic disability were all far higher 25,000 years ago than they are at present. Still, pathophysiologic and epidemiologic research conducted over the past 25 years supports the concept that certain discrepancies between our current lifestyle and that typical of preagricultural humans are important risk factors for the chronic degenerative diseases that account for most mortality in today's Western nations. These "diseases of civilization" are not new: Aretaeus described diabetes 2,000 years ago, atherosclerosis has been found in Egyptian mummies, paleolithic "Venus" statuettes show that Cro-Magnons could be obese, and the remains of 500-year-old Eskimo burials reveal that cancer afflicted hunter-gatherers isolated from contact with more technologically advanced cultures.[19] However, the lifestyle common in 20th-century affluent Western industrialized nations has greatly increased the prevalence of these and other conditions. Before 1940, diabetes was rare in American Indians,[20] but now the Pimas have one of the world's highest rates;[21] hypertension was unknown in East Africans before 1930, but now it is common,[22] and in 1912, primary malignant neoplasms of the lungs were considered "among the rarest forms of disease."[23] It is not only because persons in industrialized countries live longer that these illnesses have assumed new importance. Young persons in the Western world commonly harbor developing asymptomatic atherosclerosis,[24] whereas youths in technologically primitive cultures do not;[25,26] the age-related rise in blood pressure so typical of affluent society is not seen in unacculturated groups,[27] and older members of preliterate cultures remain lean[28–30] in contrast to the increasing proportion of body fat that is almost universal among affluent Westerners.[31]

Obesity

Obesity is many disorders: its "causes"—genetic, neurochemical, and psychologic—interact in a complex fashion to influence body energy regulation. Superimposed upon this underlying etiologic matrix, however, are salient contrasts between the Late Paleolithic era and the 20th century that increase the likelihood of excessive weight gain (Table IV). (1) Most of our food is calorically concentrated in comparison with the wild game and uncultivated fruits and vegetables that constituted the Paleolithic diet.[4] In general, the energy-satiety ratio of our food is unnaturally high: in eating a given volume, enough to create a feeling of fullness, Paleolithic humans were likely to consume fewer calories than we do today.[32] (2) Before the Neolithic Revolution, thirsty humans drank water; most beverages consumed today provide a significant caloric load while they quench our thirst. (3) The low levels of energy expenditure common in today's affluent nations may be more important than excessive energy intake for development and maintenance of obesity.[33] Total food energy intake actually has an *inverse* correlation with adiposity, but obese persons have proportionately even lower levels of energy expenditure—a low "energy throughput" state. Increased levels[33] of physical exercise raise energy expenditure proportionately more than caloric intake[34] and may lower the body weight "set point."

Diabetes Mellitus

Mortality statistics for New York City between 1866 and 1923 show a distinct fall in the overall death rate, but a steady, impressive rise in death rates from diabetes. For the over-45 age group, there was a 10-fold increase in the diabetic death rate during this period.[35] This pattern anticipated the more recent experience of Yemenite Jews moving to Israel,[36] Alaskan Eskimos;[37] Australian Aborigines,[38] American Indians,[39] and Pacific Islanders of Micronesian, Melanesian, and Polynesian stock.[40] In these groups, diabetic prevalence, if not the actual mortality rate, has risen rapidly and it has been observed that obesity and maturity-onset diabetes are among the first disorders to appear when unacculturated persons undergo economic development. At present, the overall prevalence of non-insulin-dependent diabetes among adults in industrialized countries ranges from 3 to 10 percent,[41] but among recently studied, unacculturated native

TABLE IV Triceps Skinfold Measurements in Males[*]

Subsistence Pattern	*Population*	*Age*	*Thickness (mm)*
Hunter-gatherers	Australian Aborigines	25–29	4.7
	Kalahari San (Bushmen)	Young men	4.6
	Canadian Igloolik Eskimos	20–29	4.4
	Congo Pigmies	20–29	5.5
	Tanzanian Hadza	25–34	4.9
Rudimentary horticulturists	New Guinea Tukisenta	16–37	5.0
	Venezuelan Warao Indians	Young men	5.9
	New Guinea Biak	25	5.3
	Solomon Islanders	19–70	5.4
	New Guinea Lufa	21–35	5.1
	Surinam Trio Indians	21 and over	6.0
Simple agriculturists	Peruvian Quechua Indians	35	4.0
	Japanese Ainu	Young men	5.3
	Tarahumara Indians	21 and over	6.3
	Rural Ethiopian peasants	20–30	5.3
Mean			5.2
Industrialized Westerners	Canadian Caucasians	20–29	11.2
	American Caucasians	18–24	9.0
Mean			10.1

TABLE V Diabetes Prevalence*

Subsistence Pattern	*Population*	*Prevalence (percent)*
Hunter-gatherers	Alaskan Athabaskan Indians	1.3
	Greenland Eskimos	1.2
	Alaskan Eskimos	1.9
Rudimentary horticulturists	Papua, New Guinea Melanesians	0.9
	Loyalty Island Melanesians	2.0
	Rural Malaysians	1.8
Simple agriculturists	Rural villagers, India	1.2
	"New" Yemenite immigrants, Israel	0.1
	Rural Melanesians, New Caledonia	1.5
	Polynesians on Pukapuka	1.0
	Rural Figians	0.6
Pastoralists	Nomadic Broayas, North Africa	0.0
Mean		1.1
Industrialized Westerners	Australia, Canada, Japan, United States	Range 3.0–10.0**

*See footnote to Table IV.

*Data are from note 41.

populations that have managed to continue a traditional lifestyle, rates for this disorder range from nil to 2.0 percent (Table V).

Like obesity, diabetes mellitus is a family of related disorders, each of which reflects the interplay of genetic and environmental influences. But again, in comparison with Paleolithic experience, the lifestyle of affluent, industrialized countries potentiates underlying causal factors to promote maturity-onset diabetes by several mechanisms. (1) A 1980 World Health Organization expert committee on diabetes concluded that the most powerful risk factor for type II diabetes is obesity.[42] The obese persons common in Western nations have reduced numbers of cellular insulin receptors. They manifest a relative tissue resistance to insulin,[43] and therefore their blood insulin levels tend to be higher than those of lean persons. (2) Conversely, high-level physical fitness, characteristic of aboriginal persons, is associated with an increased number of insulin receptors and better insulin binding;[44] these effects enhance the body's sensitivity to insulin.[45] Serum insulin levels are typically low in hunter-gatherers[46] and trained athletes;[44] cellular insulin sensitivity can be improved by physical conditioning that increases cardiorespiratory fitness.[47] This effect is independent from,[47] but may be augmented by, an associated effect on body weight and composition.[43] (3) Diets containing ample amounts of non-nutrient fiber and complex carbohydrate have been shown to lower both fasting and post-prandial blood glucose levels.[48] Diets with high intakes of fiber and complex carbohydrates are the rule among technologically primitive societies, but are the exception in Western nations. The recommendation by the American Diabetes Association underscores the merit of these Paleolithic dietary practices.

Hypertension

Across the globe, there are many cultures whose members do not have essential hypertension nor experience the age-related rise in average blood pressure that characterizes populations living in industrialized Western nations. These persons are not genetically immune from hypertension since, when they adopt a Western style of life, either by migration or acculturation, they develop, first, a tendency for their blood pressure to rise with age and, second, an increasing incidence of clinical hypertension.[27, 49] These normotensive cultures exist in varied climatic circumstances—in the arctic, the rain forest, the desert, and the savanna—but they share a number of essential similarities, each of which is the reciprocal of a postulated causal factor for hypertension. These include diets low in sodium and high in potassium.[50] In addition, the pastoralists and those groups still subsisting as hunter-gatherers have diets that provide a high level of calcium.[51] These persons are slender,[52] aerobically fit,[53] and, at least in their unacculturated state, have limited or no access to alcoholic beverages.[54]

More than 90 percent of the hypertension that occurs in the United States and similar nations is idiopathic or "essential" in nature. Many theories about the origin of this hypertension have been advanced and it may represent a family of conditions that share a final common pathway resulting in blood pressure elevation. Although its "causes" remain obscure, its occurrence in most cases probably reflects the interaction between individual genetic predisposition and pertinent modifiable lifestyle characteristics. Accordingly, a promising approach to its prevention is suggested by the practices of traditional persons who are spared this disorder; the common features they share reflect components of our ancestral lifestyle.

Atherosclerosis

Clinical and postmortem investigations of arctic Eskimos,[55–57] Kenyan Kikuyu,[58] Solomon Islanders,[59] Navajo Indians,[60] Masai pastoralists,[61] Australian Aborigines,[62] Kalahari San (Bushmen),[30] New Guinea highland natives,[63] Congo Pygmies,[64] and persons from other preliterate societies reveal that, in the recent past, they experienced little or no coronary heart disease. This is presumably because risk factors for development of atherosclerosis were so uncommon in such cultures. Like our Paleolithic ancestors, they traditionally lacked tobacco, rarely had hypertension, and led lives characterized by considerable physical exertion. In addition, their serum cholesterol levels were low (Table VI). The experience of hunter-gatherers is of special interest in this regard: their diets are low in total fat and have more polyunsaturated than saturated fatty acids (a high polyunsaturated-to-saturated fat ratio), but contain an amount of cholesterol similar to that in the current American diet. The low serum cholesterol levels found among them suggest that a low total fat intake together with a high polyunsaturated-to-saturated fat ratio can compensate for relatively high total cholesterol intake.[65] This supposition is supported by the experience of South African egg farm workers. Their diets include a mean habitual cholesterol intake of 1,240 mg per day, but fat (polyunsaturated-to-saturated fat ratio = 0.78) provides only 20 percent of total energy and their serum cholesterol

TABLE VI Serum Cholesterol Values*

Subsistence Pattern	*Population*	*Gender*	*Cholesterol Value (mg/dl)*
Hunter-gatherers	Tanzanian Hadza	M	114
		F	105
	Kalahari San (Bushmen)	M	130
		F	109
	Congo Pygmies	M	101
		F	111
	Australian Aborigines	M	146
		F	132
	Canadian Eskimos		141
Rudimentary horticulturists	Palau Micronesians	M	160
		F	170
	New Guinea Chimbu		130
	New Guinea Wabag		144
	Brazilian Xavante Indians	M	107
		F	121
	Brazalian Kren-Akorore Indians		100
	Solomon Islands Aita	M	135
		F	142
	Solomon Islands Kwaio	M	114
		F	125
	New Guinea Bomai	M	130
		F	140
	New Guinea Yongamuggi	M	139
		F	140
Simple agriculturists	Mexican Tarahumara Indians	M	136
		F	139
	Rural Samoans	M	167
		F	180
	Guatemalan Mayan Indians	M	132
		F	143
Pastoralists	Kenyan Samburu	M	166
	Kenyan Masai	F	135

levels average 181.4 mg/dl (with high-density lipoprotein cholesterol = 61.8 mg/dl).[66]

The adverse changes that occur in atherosclerotic risk factors when persons from societies with little such disease become westernized recapitulate the pattern observed for the other diseases of civilization. The experiences of Japanese,[67] Chinese,[68] and Samoans[69] migrating to the United States, of Yemenite Jews to Israel,[70] and of Greenland Eskimos to Denmark[71] parallel those of Kalahari Bushmen,[72] Solomon Islanders,[59] Ethiopian peasants,[73] Canadian Eskimos,[74] Australian Aborigines,[38] and Masai Pastoralists[75] who have become increasingly westernized in their own countries.

Abnormalities of coagulability may contribute to both the development and the acute clinical manifestations of atherosclerosis.[76] Platelet function has received considerable attention in this respect.[77] Fibrinolytic activity is enhanced by physical exercise,[78] but decreased by smoking cigarettes,[79] obesity,[80] and hyperlipoproteinemia,[81] so it is not surprising that preliterate peoples have more such activity than do average Westerners.[82,83] Platelet aggregation is influenced by hypercholesterolemia,[84] by physical exercise,[85] and by blood levels of long-chain polyunsaturated omega-3 class fatty acids.[86] The latter, in turn, are related to dietary intake of fats containing these constituents; fish oils have especially high concentrations of such fatty adds. Meat from domesticated animals is deficient in this regard[87] but the wild game consumed by our ancestors contained a moderate amount,[4,87] possibly enough to induce blood levels comparable to those of the Japanese[88] or Dutch,[89] although almost certainly not those of the Eskimos.[71]

Coronary atherosclerosis was apparently uncommon in the United States before about 1930,[90,91] but its importance thereafter rapidly increased to a peak in the 1960s, then began a gradual decline. Whereas many factors ranging from changes in the diagnostic classification codes to improvements in treatment are involved in these trends, both the "epidemic" and the decline have been linked to alterations in lifestyle—initially away from and subsequently back toward the pattern that prevailed among preagricultural humans.[92]

Cancer

The perception of cancer as a disease primarily related to the environment has been progressively strengthened over the past decade.[93] International studies reveal large differences in cancer incidence rates between countries; for example, age-standardized analyses reveal that Canadian women have seven times more breast cancer than do non-Jewish women in Israel.[94] Genetic variation cannot account for these major differences, since groups migrating from an area with a characteristic pattern of cancer incidence rates acquire different rates typical of their new geographic location within a few generations. Age-standardization data show that Japanese men in Hawaii have 11 times more prostatic cancer than do Japanese men in Japan and that black Americans have 10 times more colon cancer than do black Nigerians.[94] Also, there have been large changes in incidence rates for many types of cancer within genetically stable populations: in Ireland, lung cancer mortality increased 177 percent between 1950 and 1975.[94] In Canada, acculturation of western and central Arctic Eskimos has led to an increase in overall cancer morbidity together with marked change in the relative frequency of specific tumor types. Between 1950 and 1980, the number of proven salivary gland cancers decreased by two thirds, whereas lung cancers increased 550 percent.[95] Furthermore, tumor incidence in laboratory animals can be readily altered by manipulating external factors ranging from radiation exposure to dietary composition.

On the basis of these observations, epidemiologists have argued that it should be theoretically possible to reduce site-specific incidence for each type of cancer to the lowest rate found in any population.[96] By summing the lowest national or regional rates observed for each cancer site, basal or "naturally occurring" minimal incidence rates can be developed. When these minimal rates are compared with the rates observed in countries where each type of tumor is common, it appears that from 70 to 90 percent of cancers are the result of environmental influences and hence potentially preventable.[94,96]

The factors considered most likely to affect the development of cancer are tobacco abuse[93,97] and nutritional influences.[98] Extensive tobacco usage (and the regular consumption of alcoholic beverages) postdate the Agricultural Revolution, whereas current cancer-preventive nutritional recommendations[99,100]—to avoid obesity, reduce total fat intake, consume a wide variety of fruits and vegetables (including considerable dietary fiber, vitamin C, and vitamin A or beta carotene), and to drink alcohol only in moderation if at all—are a fairly accurate, if incomplete, summary of Paleolithic nutritional practices.

CONCLUSION

The diseases considered, as well as others ranging from dental caries to diverticulosis, share important features. In each case, the condition is uncommon, rare, or almost unknown in cultures whose pertinent essential features mimic those of our Late Paleolithic ancestors. However, in each instance, the prevalence of disease increases dramatically when the previously unaffected society adopts a Western lifestyle, whether by migration or acculturation. Furthermore, extensive pathophysiologic research has identified bioenvironmental factors that are likely etiologic agents for each condition. Such factors (e.g., caloric concentration, tobacco abuse, sedentary living, diets high in fat and salt, and so on) are pervasive in affluent industrialized society, but not in traditional cultures where the lifestyle is, in important ways, similar to that of preagricultural humans—similar to that for which the current human genome was selected. These considerations are consistent with the hypothesis that discordance between our genes and the affluent 20th-century lifestyle (defined to include diet, exercise, and exposure to harmful substances) accentuates underlying causal factors and thereby promotes the chronic "diseases of civilization."

Of course, cancer, atherosclerosis, non-insulin-dependent diabetes mellitus, and other afflictions of affluence are all disorders whose clinical manifestations become increasingly common with advancing age; might not the prevalence of these conditions in 20th-century Western nations result simply from the unprecedented life expectancy that characterizes these countries? The population's greater age must certainly be a contributing factor, but the failure of young persons in traditional cultures to exhibit the early stages of these chronic diseases[58,101] contrasts with the experience of youths in Western nations,[24] indicating that age is not the primary determinant. Furthermore, those persons in traditional societies who do reach age 60 and beyond remain lean[28,30] and normotensive,[27] while clinical[57] and postmortem[58] examinations reveal little or no significant coronary atherosclerosis. Findings like these suggest that chronic degenerative diseases need not be the inevitable consequence of advancing years.

Evolution has endowed Homo sapiens with the ability to adapt and thrive under an extraordinary range of conditions, and this adaptability allows us to benefit enormously from the manifold advantages of today's civilization. In 20th-century industrialized nations, parameters such as infant mortality, childhood growth rates, and average life expectancy all indicate a state of public health far exceeding that which was obtained in the Stone Age or at any time thereafter until the current century. Indeed, more than half the persons who have ever lived beyond age 65 are alive today. Nevertheless, we can still profit from the experience of our remote ancestors. We still carry their inheritance—genes selected for their way of life, not ours. Despite the achievements of science and technology, we remain collectively fearful of diseases that available evidence suggests were uncommon, rare, or unknown in the Late Paleolithic era. In order to regain relative freedom from these illnesses, we need to take a step backward in time. For each disorder, we may anticipate increasingly sophisticated and effective treatments, but the crucial corrective measure will almost certainly be prevention. This will entail reintroduction of essential elements from the lifestyle of our Paleolithic ancestors.

REFERENCES

1. Stanley SM: Chronospecies' longevities, the origin of genera, and the punctuational model of evolution. Paleobiology 1978; 4: 26–40.
2. Sibley CG, Ahlquist JE: The phylogeny of the hominoid primates, as indicated by DNA-DNA hybridization. J Mol Evol 1984; 20: 2–15.
3. Turner CG: The dental search for native American origins. In: Kirk R, Szathmary E. eds. Out of Asia: peopling the Americas and the Pacific. Canberra, Australia: Journal of Pacific History, 1985; 31–78.
4. Eaton SB, Konner MJ: Paleolithic nutrition. A consideration of its nature and current implications. N Engl J Med 1985; 312: 283–289.
5. Ember CR: Myths about hunter-gatherers. Ethnology 1978; 17: 439–148.
6. Foley R: A reconsideration of the role of predation on large mammals in tropical hunter-gatherer adaptation. Man 1982; 17: 393–402.
7. Metz J, Hart D, Harpending HC: Iron, folate and vitamin B_{12} nutrition in a hunter-gatherer people: a study of the !Kung Bushman. Am J Clin Nutr 1971; 24: 229–242.
8. Ellestad-Sayed J, Hildes JA, Schaefer O, Lobban MC: Twenty-four hour urinary excretion of vitamins, minerals and nitrogen by Eskimos. Am J Clin Nutr 1975; 28: 1402–1407.
9. Holbrook JT, Patterson KY, Bodner JE, et al: Sodium and potassium intake and balance in adults consuming self-selected diets. Am J Clin Nutr 1984; 40: 786–793.
10. Clastres P: The Guayaki. In: Bicchieri MG. ed. Hunters and gatherers today. New York: Holt, Rinehart and Winston, 1972; 138–174.
11. Smith P, Bloom RA, Berkowitz J: Diachronic trends in humeral cortical thickness of Near Eastern populations. J Hum Evol 1984; 13: 603–611.
12. Larsen CS: Functional implications of post cranial size reduction on the prehistoric Georgia coast, U.S.A. J Hum Evol 1981; 10: 489–502.
13. Carrier DR: The energetic paradox of human running and hominid evolution. Curr Anthropol 1984; 25: 483–495.
14. Cooper KH: The aerobics way. New York: Bantam Books, 1977; 257–266.

15. Macpherson RK: Physiological adaptation, fitness, and nutrition in peoples of the Australian and New Guinea regions. In: Baker PT, Weiner JS, eds. The biology of human adaptability. Oxford: Clarendon Press, 1966; 431–468.
16. Bacon MK, Barry H, Child IL, Snyder CR: A cross-cultural study of drinking. V. Detailed definitions and data. Q J Studies Alcohol 1965; suppl 3: 78–111.
17. Horton D: The functions of alcohol in primitive societies: a cross cultural study. Q J Studies Alcohol 1943; 4: 199–320.
18. Bacon MK, Barry H, Child IL: A cross-cultural study of drinking. II. Relations to other features of culture. Q J Studies Alcohol 1965; suppl 3: 29–48.
19. Hart Hansen JP, Meldgaard J, Nordquist J: The mummies of Qilakitsoq. Natl Geograph 1985; 162: 190–207.
20. West KM: Diabetes in American Indians and other native populations in the new world. Diabetes 1974; 23: 841–855.
21. Bennett PH, LeCompte PM, Miller M, Rushforth NB: Epidemiological studies of diabetes in the Pima Indians. Recent Prog Horm Res 1976; 32: 333–376.
22. Trowell HC: From normotension to hypertension in Kenyans and Ugandans 1928–1978. East Afr Med J 1980; 57: 167–173.
23. Adler I: Primary malignant growths of the lungs and bronchi. New York: Longmans, Green. 1912; 3.
24. Velican D, Velican C: Atherosclerotic involvement of the coronary arteries of adolescents and young adults. Atherosclerosis 1980; 36: 449–460.
25. Schaeffer O: Medical observations and problems in the Canadian arctic. Can Med Assoc J 1959; 81: 386–391.
26. Kennelly BM, Truswell AS, Schrive V: A clinical and electrocardiographic study of !Kung Bushmen. S Afr Med J 1972; 46: 1093–1097.
27. Page LB: Epidemiologic evidence on the etiology of human hypertension and its possible prevention. Am Heart J 1976; 91: 527–534.
28. Glanville EV, Geerdink RA: Skinfold thickness, body measurements and age changes in Trio and Wajana Indians of Surinam, Am J Phys Anthropol 1970, 32: 455–462.
29. Sinnett PF, Keig G, Craig W: Nutrition and age-related changes in body build in adults: studies in a New Guinea highland community. Hum Biol Oceania 1973; 2: 50–62.
30. Truswell AS, Hansen DL: Medical research among the !Kung. In: Lee RB, DeVore I, eds. Kalahari hunter-gatherers. Cambridge, Massachusetts: Harvard University Press 1976; 166–195.
31. Durnin JVGA, Womersley J: Body fat assessed from total body density and its estimation from skinfold thickness: measurements on 481 men and women aged from 16 to 72 years. Br J Nutr 1974; 32: 77–97.
32. Duncan KH, Bacon JA, Weinsier RL: The effects of high and low energy density diets on satiety, energy intake, and eating time of obese and nonobese subjects. Am J Clin Nutr 1983; 37: 763–767.
33. Stern JS: Is obesity a disease of inactivity? In: Stunkard AJ, Stellar E, eds. Eating and its disorders. New York: Raven Press, 1984; 131–139.
34. Woo R, Garrow JS, Pi-Sunyer FX: Effect of exercise on spontaneous calorie intake in obesity. Am J Clin Nutr 1982; 36: 470–477.
35. Emerson H, Larimore LD: Diabetes mellitus. A contribution to its epidemiology based chiefly on mortality statistics. Arch Intern Med 1924; 34: 585–630.
36. Cohen AM, Chen B, Eisenberg S, Fidel J, Furst A: Diabetes, blood lipids, lipoproteins and change of environment. Restudy of the 'new immigrant Yemenites' in Israel. Metabolism 1979; 28: 716–728.
37. Mouratoff GJ, Scott EM: Diabetes mellitus in Eskimos after a decade. JAMA 1973; 226: 1345–1346.
38. O'Dea K, Spargo RM, Nestle PJ: Impact of Westernization on carbohydrate and lipid metabolism in Australian Aborigines. Diabetologia 1982; 22: 148–153.
39. West K: North American Indians. In: Trowell HC, Burkitt DP, eds. Western diseases: their emergence and prevention. Cambridge, Massachusetts: Harvard University Press, 1981; 129–137.
40. Taylor R, Zimmet P: Migrant studies in diabetes epidemiology. In: Mann JI, Pyorala K, Teuscher A. eds. Diabetes in epidemiological perspective. London: Churchill Livingstone, 1983; 58–77.
41. Hamman RF: Diabetes in affluent societies. In: Mann JI, Pyorala K, Teuscher A, eds. Diabetes in epidemiological perspective. London: Churchill Livingstone, 1983; 7–42.
42. Zimmet P: Type 2 (non-insulin-dependent) diabetes—an epidemiological overview. Diabetologia 1982; 22: 399–411.
43. Yki-Jarvinen H, Koivisto VA: Effects of body composition on insulin sensitivity. Diabetes 1983; 32: 965–969.
44. Koivisto VA, Somon V, Conrad P, Hendler R, Nadel E, Felig P: Insulin binding to monocytes in trained athletes. Changes in the resting state and after exercise. J Clin Invest 1979; 64: 1011–1015.
45. Rosenthal M, Haskell WL, Solomon R, Widstrom A, Reaven GM: Demonstration of a relationship between level of physical training and insulin-stimulated glucose utilization in normal humans. Diabetes 1983; 32: 408–411.
46. Merimee J, Rimoin DL, Cavalli-Sforza LL: Metabolic studies in the African Pygmy. J Clin Invest 1972; 51: 395–401.
47. Jennings G, Nelson L, Nestel P, et al: The effects of changes in physical activity on major cardiovascular risk factors, hemodynamics, sympathetic function, and glucose utilization in man: a controlled study of four levels of activity. Circulation 1986; 73: 30–40.
48. Villaume C, Beck B, Gariot P, Desalme A, Debry G: Long term evolution of the effect of bran ingestion on meal-induced glucose and insulin responses in healthy man. Am J Clin Nutr 1984; 40: 1023–1026.
49. Blackburn H, Prineas R: Diet and hypertension: anthropology, epidemiology, and public health implications. Prog Biochem Pharmacol 1983; 19: 31–79.

50. Meneely GR, Battarbee HD: High sodium low potassium environment and hypertension. Am J Cardiol 1976; 38: 768–785.
51. McCarron DA, Morris CD, Cole C: Dietary calcium in human hypertension. Science 1982; 217: 267–269.
52. Tobian L: Hypertension and obesity. N Engl J Med 1978; 298: 46–48.
53. Nelson L, Jennings GL, Esler MD, Korner PI: Effect of changing levels of physical activity on blood-pressure and haemodynamics in essential hypertension. Lancet 1986; 11: 473–476.
54. Klatsky AL, Friedman G, Armstrong MA: The relationships between alcoholic beverage use and other traits to blood pressure: a new Kaiser Permanente study. Circulation 1986; 73: 628–636.
55. Gottman AW: A report of one hundred three autopsies on Alaskan natives. Arch Pathol 1960; 70: 117–124.
56. Arthaud JB: Cause of death in 339 Alaskan natives as determined by autopsy. Arch Pathol 1970; 90: 433–138.
57. Kronmann N, Green A: Epidemiological studies in the Upernavik district, Greenland. Incidence of some chronic diseases 1950–1974. Acta Med Scand 1980; 208: 401–406.
58. Vint FW: Post-mortem findings in the natives of Kenya. E Afr Med J 1937; 13: 332–340.
59. Page LB, Danion A, Moellering RD: Antecedents of cardiovascular disease in six Solomon Islands societies. Circulation 1974; 49: 1132–1146.
60. Fulmer HS, Roberts RW: Coronary heart disease among the Navajo Indians. Ann Intern Med 1963; 59: 740–764.
61. Ho K-J, Biss K, Mikkelson B, Lewis LA, Taylor CB: The Masai of East Africa: some unique biological characteristics. Arch Pathol 1971; 91: 387–410.
62. Woods JD: The electrocardiogram of the Australian Aboriginal. Med J Aust 1966; 1: 438–441.
63. Sinnett PF, Whyte HM: Epidemiological studies in a total highland population, Tukisenta, New Guinea. Cardiovascular disease and relevant clinical, electrocardiographic, radiological and biochemical findings. J Chronic Dis 1973; 26: 265–290.
64. Mann GV, Roels OA, Price DL, Merrill JM: Cardiovascular disease in African Pygmies: a survey of the health status, serum lipids and diet of Pygmies in Congo. J Chronic Dis 1962; 15: 341–371.
65. Schonfeld G, Patsch W, Rudel LL, Nelson C, Epstein M, Olson RE: Effects of dietary cholesterol and fatty acids on plasma lipoproteins. J Clin Invest 1982; 69: 1072–1080.
66. Vorster HH, Silvis N, Venter CS, et al: Serum cholesterol, lipoproteins, and plasma coagulation factors in South African blacks on a high-egg but low-fat intake. Am J Clin Nutr 1987; 46: 52–57.
67. Kato H, Tillotson J, Nichaman M, Rhoads GG, Hamilton HB: Epidemiologic studies of coronary heart disease and stroke in Japanese men living in Japan, Hawaii, and California. Serum lipids and diet. Am J Epidemiol 1973; 97: 372–385.
68. Gerber LM, Madhavan S: !Epidemiology of coronary heart disease in migrant Chinese populations. Med Anthropol 1980; 4: 307–320.
69. Hornick CA, Hanna JM: Indicators of coronary risk in a migrating Samoan population. Med Anthropol 1982; 6: 71–79.
70. Brunner D, Meshulan N, Altman S, Bearman JE, Loebl K, Wendkos ME: Physiologic and anthropometric parameters related to coronary risk factors in Yemenite Jews living different time spans in Israel. J Chronic Dis 1971; 24: 383–392.
71. Dyerberg J, Bang HO, Hjorne N: Fatty acid composition of the plasma lipids in Greenland Eskimos. Am J Clin Nutr 1975; 28: 958–966.
72. Wilmsen EN: Studies in diet, nutrition, and fertility among a group of Kalahari Bushmen in Botswana. Social Science Information 1982; 21: 95–125.
73. Ostwald R, Gerbre-Medhin M: Westernization of diet and serum lipids in Ethiopians. Am J Clin Nutr 1978; 31: 1028–1040.
74. Schaefer O, Timmermans JFW, Eaton RDP, Matthews AR: General and nutritional health in two Eskimo populations at different stages of acculturation. Can J Public Health 1980; 71: 397–405.
75. Day J, Carruthers M, Bailey A, Robinson D: Anthropometric, physiological, and biochemical differences between urban and rural Masai. Atherosclerosis 1976; 23: 357–361.
76. Kannel WB, Wolf PA, Castelli WP, D'Agostino RB: Fibrinogen and risk of cardiovascular disease. The Framingham study. JAMA 1987; 258: 1183–1186.
77. Rao AK, Mintz PD, Lavine SJ, et al: Coagulant activities of platelets in coronary artery disease. Circulation 1984; 69: 15–21.
78. Khanna PK, Seth HN, Balasubramanian V, Hoon RS: Effects of submaximal exercise on fibrinolytic activity in is chaemic heart disease. Br Heart J 1975; 37: 1273–1276.
79. Fuster V, Cheseboro JH, Frye RL, Elveback LR: Platelet survival and the development of coronary artery disease in the young adult: effects of cigarette smoking, strong family history and medical therapy. Circulation 1981; 633: 546–551.
80. Shaw DA, MacNaughton D: Relationship between blood fibrinolytic activity and body fatness. Lancet 1963; 1: 352–354.
81. Lowe GDO, McArdle BM, Stromberg P, Lorimer AR, Forbes CD, Prentice CRM: Increased blood viscosity and fibrinolytic inhibitor in type II hyperlipoproteinaemia. Lancet 1982; I: 472–475.
82. Goldrick RB, Whyte HM: A study of blood clotting and serum lipids in natives of New Guinea and Australians. Aust Ann Med 1959; 8: 238–244.
83. Gillman T, Naidoo SS, Hathorn M: Fat, fibrinolysis and atherosclerosis in Africans. Lancet 1957; II: 696–697.
84. Stuart MJ, Gerrard JM, White JG: Effect of cholesterol on production of thromboxane B_2 by platelets in vitro. N Engl J Med 1980; 302: 6–10.
85. Rauramaa R, Salonen JT, Seppanen K, et al: Inhibition of platelet aggregability by moderate-intensity physical exercise: a randomized trial in overweight men. Circulation 1986; 74: 939–944.
86. Glomset JA: Fish, fatty acids, and human health. N Engl J Med 1985; 312: 1253–1254.

87. Crawford MA, Gale MM, Woodford MH: Linoleic acid and linolenic acid elongation products in muscle tissue of Syncerus caffer and other ruminant species. Biochem J 1969; 115: 25–27.
88. Hirai A, Hamazaki T, Terano T, et al: Eicosapentaeroic acid and platelet function in Japanese. Lancet 1980; II: 1132–1133.
89. Kromhaut D, Bosschieter EB, DeLezenne Coulander C: The inverse relation between fish consumption and 20-year mortality from coronary heart disease. N Engl J Med 1985; 312: 1205–1269.
90. White PD: The historical background of angina pectoris. Mod Concepts Cardiovasc Dis 1974; 43: 109–112.
91. Perry TM: The new and old diseases: a study of mortality trends in the United States, 1900–1969. Am J Clin Pathol 1975; 63: 453–474.
92. Walker WJ: Changing U.S. lifestyle and declining vascular mortality—a retrospective. N Engl J Med 1983; 308: 649–651.
93. Cairns J: The treatment of diseases and the war against cancer. Sci Am 1985; 253: 51–59.
94. Doll R, Peto R: The causes of cancer: quantitative estimates of avoidable risks of cancer in the United States today. JNCI 1981; 66: 1191–1308.
95. Hildes JA, Schaefer O: The changing picture of neoplastic disease in the western and central Canadian Arctic (1950–1980). Can Med Assoc J 1984; 130: 25–32.
96. Wynder EL, Gori GB: Contribution of the environment to cancer incidence: an epidemiologic exercise. JNCI 1977; 58: 825–832.
97. Public Health Service: The health consequences of smoking—cancer: a report of the Surgeon General (DHHS publication no. [PHS] 82-50179). Washington: Government Printing Office, 1982.
98. Byers T, Graham S: The epidemiology of diet and cancer. Adv Cancer Res 1984; 41: 1–69.
99. National Research Council: Diet, nutrition, and cancer. Washington: National Academy Press, 1982.
100. American Cancer Society: Nutrition and cancer: cause and prevention. CA—A cancer journal for clinicians 1984; 34: 21–128.
101. Oliver WJ, Cohen EL, Neel JV: Blood pressure, sodium intake and sodium related hormones in the Yanamamo Indians, a "no-salt" culture. Circulation 1975; 52: 146–151.

 3

How Is Darwinian Medicine Useful?

Randolph Nesse

Biologically oriented medical anthropologists look at problems of human health through the lens of evolution. Human biology has been shaped by millions of years of evolutionary pressures—especially the pressures created by our coexistence with microbes that can sicken and even kill us. The use of evolutionary theory to understand the epidemiology and etiology of human diseases is called Darwinian (or evolutionary) medicine.

One of the shortcomings of clinical biomedicine is that it only tells us how *individual people get sick. It does not tell us* why *humans are more susceptible to certain kinds of diseases than others. Darwinian medicine addresses this latter question by applying basic principles of adaptation and natural selection to particular physical conditions. In this brief selection, Randolph Nesse, one of the early proponents of Darwinian medicine, outlines some evolutionary reasons for a list of common human health problems such as obesity, anxiety disorders, and basic symptoms ranging from pain to vomiting. The discussion of obesity has particular relevance to the Eaton, Shostak, and Konner article (reading selection 2).*

People often find the evolutionary medicine argument persuasive and straightforward. However, there have been criticisms by both biological and cultural anthropologists. Some biologically oriented medical anthropologists find that evolutionary medicine runs the risk of finding an adaptation for almost any symptom. However, it is often the case that natural selection occurs via a series of imperfect compromises that have nothing to do with a particular adaptation. For example, some proponents of Darwinian medicine, such as Paul Ewald, argue that fever is an adaptive defense against certain infections that occurred at an earlier stage of mammalian evolution. But an alternative explanation is that fever is a physiological by-product of an inflammatory response that was adapted for a different set of health problems. Note, however, that both hypotheses are based on evolutionary reasoning.

Some cultural anthropologists are wary of evolutionary explanations for human emotions and other psychological states. While no one challenges the basic scenario for a flight-or-fight response, the notion that the human can be simplified to a set of evolutionary response mechanisms seems to discount the influence of culture on the way people think and feel. This is essentially a nature-versus-nurture debate. However, an emerging set of studies attempts to strike some middle ground between the two extremes of biological and cultural determinism. Many medical anthropologists emphasize the interaction of biology and culture in demonstrating that natural selection is one of several processes that determine our health.

As you read this selection, consider these questions:

- **Why do people tend to think that evolution is a process that only happened in the past?**
- **How could some of the ideas of "Darwinian medicine" be tested scientifically?**
- **How might an evolutionary approach to health and disease help us understand why certain microbes become resistant to antibiotics?**
- **What are the practical benefits of evolutionary medicine? In what ways could it help improve public health efforts or the practice of clinical biomedicine?**

Context: Randolph Nesse is a psychiatrist and professor of medicine at the University of Michigan. He became interested in evolutionary medicine while trying to understand why human beings are susceptible to certain kinds of mental and emotional problems. He then teamed up with George Williams, an emeritus professor of marine biology and evolutionary theorist at the State University of New York in Stony Brook, to write a seminal article titled "The Dawn of Darwinian Medicine" in 1991. Since then, there have been several edited volumes on the topic by Wenda Trevathan, James McKenna, and Paul Ewald. This article was written for an audience of physicians to explain why this new evolutionary approach to understanding the causes and treatment of illnesses can shed new light relevant to the practice of medicine.

Source: R. Nesse (2001). "How Is Darwinian Medicine Useful?" Western Journal of Medicine 174: 358–360.

INTRODUCTION

Evolution by natural selection has been biology's organizing principle for more than a century, but only in the last few decades has it been applied to the social sciences and medicine. Its application to medicine, known as evolutionary or Darwinian medicine, uses an evolutionary perspective to understand why the body is not better designed and why, therefore, diseases exist at all.[1-3] This article outlines some basic principles of Darwinian medicine, summarizes the usefulness of evolutionary principles for medicine, and provides some examples from key literature sources.

For example, traditional clinical medicine looks at the problem of obesity in terms of individual differences that explain why one person becomes obese and another does not. These factors may be due to genes, early environment, or current lifestyle. Now that one half of Americans are overweight, however, it is time to answer the evolutionary question: why are our bodies designed so that most of us eat too much and exercise too little?

EVOLUTIONARY EXPLANATIONS FOR OBESITY

An initial answer is simple. In the environment in which we evolved, natural selection shaped appetite regulation mechanisms to ensure that we survived periods of famine. In those ancient times, eating required walking for hours each day to get food, a caloric cost that made it impossible for most people to accumulate much surplus as fat.[4] Exposure to intermittent periods of food shortage sets off a system that prepares for a coming famine by increasing appetite and basal weight above the starting point. Dieting activates the same system, so weight can rebound to above what it was when the diet began. When young people try to lose weight by using willpower to drastically limit their food intake, their regulation mechanisms react with a response that is adaptive: they often gorge themselves. These episodes of uncontrolled eating can make the dieter even more fearful of becoming obese, so still further efforts of will arouse the mechanism more strongly, setting in cycle the positive feedback spiral we see in anorexia and bulimia.

As for our food preferences, one would think we would be designed to eat what is good for us. The system would work fine if we lived on the African savanna. In the natural environment, fat, salt, and sugar are in such short supply that when they are encountered, the useful response is to consume them. Fat provides twice as many calories per gram as carbohydrates. Sugar is often associated with ripe fruits, and seeking it out was usually beneficial. Now that we can choose our foods, we prefer what was in short supply on the African savanna.

We also choose our levels of exercise to minimize caloric expenditure—a wise strategy in the Paleolithic era when wasting calories could bring death. This tendency to be sedentary, in combination with our preferences for large amounts of high-calorie, high fat food, has resulted in an epidemic of atherosclerotic disease. Natural selection will eventually fix such design problems, but it will take hundreds or thousands of generations to do so.

EVOLUTION AND ANXIETY DISORDERS

Anxiety disorders offer another example of Darwinian medicine in action.[5] We know anxiety can be useful, but why do so many people experience so much of it, so often, when it seems worse than useless?

In ancient times, anxiety was necessary for humans to flee from a predator. This "fight and flight" mechanism is built into our nervous systems. It is triggered at the wrong time in people with panic disorder. If a panther were approaching, however, it would be valuable. Agoraphobia, the fear of open spaces and the tendency to stay close to home or to flee at the least hint of danger, is considered a phobia in modern societies, but is the optimal response if predator attacks have been frequent.[5]

SYMPTOMS AS EVOLUTIONARY DEFENSES

An evolutionary approach can fundamentally change how we think about the body and disease.[6] Instead of seeing disease as a defect in a previously perfect machine, Darwinian medicine allows us to see the body as a product of natural selection, full of trade-offs and vulnerabilities that all too often lead to disease. Physicians are not mechanics repairing broken parts; they are guides who understand the trade-offs that give rise to disease and come up with strategies that will oppose the effects of other organisms, compensate for what the body cannot repair, and relieve suffering when possible.

For example, pain, nausea, cough, fever, vomiting, diarrhea, fatigue, and anxiety are common medical problems. Much of medical practice focuses on relieving suffering by prescribing medications that block these responses. A different view is that these responses are not problems themselves but represent the body's attempt to remedy a problem. If defenses are so useful, and natural selection is potent, then prescribing medicines may be unsafe. If fever, cough, and diarrhea are useful defenses, blocking them might make people sicker, Treating Shigella-induced diarrhea, for example, substantially increases complications.[7] The excessive suppression of cough can cause death. Extreme circumstances require a balanced approach, however; for example, blocking fever can prevent febrile seizures, and stopping vomiting can prevent dehydration.

Why has natural selection shaped the body so these defenses are expressed so readily and intensely? The answer is the same as the explanation for why we tolerate smoke detectors that sound a false alarm every time the toast burns. You could design a detector that went off only when there was extensive smoke, but the disadvantage would be the absence of the alarm in response to some fires. Defenses such as pain and fever are inexpensive compared with the dangers they avert, so natural selection has shaped regulation mechanisms that express them whenever they might be useful. As a result, it is usually possible to block them safely.[8] As for that most hackneyed bit of medical advice, "take aspirin and drink plenty of fluids," perhaps studies will soon be conducted to determine if this speeds or slows recovery from everyday infections.

CLINICAL APPLICATIONS OF DARWINIAN MEDICINE

Understanding Common Illnesses

Most medical research asks why one person gets a disease and another does not. Darwinian medicine suggests asking an additional and different line of questioning: why are we all vulnerable to certain diseases?[6,9] Why are we all likely to get hemorrhoids, impacted wisdom teeth, and pneumonia? Why will so many of us experience myocardial infarction, cancer, or rheumatoid arthritis?

Most people think that the answer is simply that natural selection cannot make the body any better than it has. After all, it is a random process with no direction or coordination. In fact, the body is not better designed for specific evolutionary reasons.

One important reason is that natural selection does not shape organisms for health or longevity but for maximizing reproduction, even at the expense of a shortened life span. When there is a conflict—for instance, when a gene improves bone healing in youth but also causes arterial calcification—that gene will be selected for even though it leads to fatal outcomes in later life. Where there is a conflict between reproductive success and health, reproduction always wins out.[10]

Answering Questions about Etiology

Another way in which evolutionary biology is useful in medicine is to answer classic questions about the etiology of disease. For instance, evolutionary medicine can provide specific approaches to the problem of antibiotic resistance. The story of pathogen virulence provides the best example. It seems that it would not be in their interests for pathogens to kill the host that supports them. Given sufficient time, virulent pathogens should gradually evolve into a benign mutualism with their hosts. The steady decrease in the virulence of syphilis over the past 5 centuries has often been interpreted in this way, probably correctly. Pathogens that cause severe and often fatal disease, such as cholera, are thought to be still in the process of adapting to their host.

This notion is incorrect, however. In work summarized by Ewald, it became clear that natural selection shapes whatever level of virulence maximizes the replication of bacteria and viruses.[11,12] Often, as with rhinovirus, the pathogen spreads more rapidly if the host is up and around. Other pathogens, however, such as Plasmodium species, are spread by vectors. Mosquitoes are more effective vectors when the host is prostrate. Genetic variants that replicate more quickly are selected for and increase in prevalence.

This fact has immediate practical implications for infection control. The hands of medical staff are a vector, so it is not surprising that nosocomial *Escherichia coli* strains tend to become increasingly virulent with the duration of circulation in a medical setting. Furthermore, these organisms are exposed to antibiotics, so they are likely to become resistant to treatment. A neonatal nursery is well designed for breeding "superbugs." The difficulty of exterminating these bugs may warrant cutting off their evolutionary pathway occasionally by moving nurseries at intervals to a completely different sterile room with fresh supplies and no transfer of infants from the previous nursery. The prospect of interrupting the further evolution of nosocomial pathogens might justify the considerable expense.

Identifying Improvements for Public Health

Where water supplies are contaminated by sewage, selection acts to increase virulence. Public sanitation changes the selection forces, giving the advantage to less virulent organisms. Where new sources of clean well water have been provided, especially in India, virulent pathogens such as *Shigella dysenteriae* and classic *Vibrio cholerae* have been replaced by less virulent *Shigella flexneri* and the El Tor subtype of *V. cholerae*.[13]

CONCLUSION

Everyone uses metaphors to understand the world. The dominant metaphor for the body has been a machine. Disease has been viewed as a defect arising in an otherwise perfect device. An evolutionary view offers a richer and more nuanced view of the body as a product of natural selection: extraordinary in many ways, but also flawed in many ways, for good evolutionary reasons. Furthermore, it reveals that the body has no master plan and there is no such thing as "the" human genome. Humans have genes that make phenotypes that effectively make new copies of themselves. We care less about the fate of our genes, however, and more about the health and welfare of individuals.

Darwinian medicine will most powerfully advance our goal of helping individuals by inspiring research that yields solid new findings to guide health care practice. Even at this early stage, however, Darwinian medicine can help clinicians answer old questions, pose new questions, and provide a more natural view of disease.

REFERENCES

1. Williams GW, Nesse RM. The dawn of Darwinian medicine. Q Rev Biol 1991;66:1–22.
2. Nesse RM, Williams GC. Why We Get Sick: The New Science of Darwinian Medicine. New York, NY: Vintage; 1994.
3. Stearns S, ed. Evolution in Health and Disease. Oxford: Oxford University Press; 1998.
4. Eaton SB, Konner M. Paleolithic nutrition: a consideration of its nature and current implications. N Eng J Med 1985;312:283–289.
5. Marks IM, Nesse RM. Fear and fitness; an evolutionary analysis of anxiety disorders. Ethol Sociobiol 1994;15:247–261.
6. Nesse RM, Williams GC. Research designs that address evolutionary questions about medical disorders. In: Steams SC, ed. Evolution in Health and Disease. New York, NY: Oxford University Press; 1999:16–26.
7. DuPont HL, Hornick RB. Adverse effect of lomotil therapy in shigellosis. JAMA 1973;226:1525–1528.
8. Nesse R. The smoke detector principle: natural selection and the regulation of defenses. In: Damasio AR, Harrington A, Kagan J, McEwen B, Moss H. Shaikh R, eds. Unity of Knowledge: The Convergence of Natural and Human Science. New York, NY: New York Academy of Sciences; in press.
9. Trevathan WR, McKenna JJ, Smith EO, eds. Evolutionary Medicine. New York, NY: Oxford University Press; 1999.
10. Williams GC. Pleiotropy, natural selection, and the evolution of senescence, Evolution 1957;11:398–411.
11. Ewald P. Evolution of Infectious Disease. New York, NY: Oxford University Press; 1994.
12. Ewald PW. The evolution of virulence: a unifying link between ecology and parasitology. J Parasitol 1995;81:659–669.
13. Ewald PW. Evolutionary biology and the treatment of signs and symptoms of infectious disease. J Theor Biol 1980;86:169–176.

Human Biological Variation

 CONCEPTUAL TOOLS 

■ ***Human biological variation can be genetic or phenotype.*** Anthropologists study human similarities and differences; the variation from individual to individual and from one human group to another can be both biological and cultural (Lasker 1969). Some biological variation among contemporary humans is related to health—either phenotypic variation is the result of different health and nutritional experiences or genotypic variation affects patterns of morbidity and mortality. Differences in stature (height), for example, may reflect the adequacy of childhood diet whereas genetic differences are involved with predispositions to a wide variety of diseases (Frisancho 1993).

Genetic variation among populations can be measured in the frequency of particular gene forms (alleles). Gene frequency differences usually reflect historical forces of natural selection or migration. Comparative studies of anthropological genetics can help in reconstructing prehistoric patterns of population movement—for example, the movement of Siberian people to the New World. Difference in gene frequencies among populations can also reflect historical exposure to particular factors in natural selection—including diseases and food shortages.

Phenotype refers to expressed biological features resulting from the interaction of genes and environment. People living for a long period at high elevations, for example, can physiologically adapt to the shortage of oxygen by developing greater hemoglobin density as well as greater lung capacity. Babies born in higher altitudes tend to be smaller than babies born at sea level. Probably the most important mechanism for phenotypic variation involves nutrition. Biological anthropologists studying human growth and development have shown that poor growth—stunting and wasting—is a sensitive measure of lack of adequate food in childhood. Other kinds of malnutrition, such as deficiencies in the micronutrients iodine or vitamin A, may have permanent effects on mental capacity. Therefore, observed biological variations among groups often reflect environmental rather than genetic difference.

■ ***Race is not a useful biological concept. Ethnicity is a construct of cultural identity.*** Race is not a viable biological concept because it cannot be adequately defined either genetically or phenotypically. Most genetic variation can be found within so-called racial groups, whereas the differences among groups are extremely small and have little physiological significance. All humans today are part of the same species. The rule of racial hypodescent found in North America (a "mixed race" child is categorized as African American) strongly supports that race is a concept of folk biology rather than a useful scientific category.

Ethnicity is an important social construction, and ethnic groups are sometimes thought to be recognizably different by phenotype. Nearly all of the difference, however, is in culture—dress, language, religion, and so forth. Ethnicity is related to subcultural differences in a pluralistic society, and there is often an additional overlap with social class.

■ ***The study of human biology is comparative.*** Human biology is different from biomedicine in its aims and scope. The explanation of human biological variation is important to biologically oriented medical anthropologists; such variation requires careful documentation and analysis using principles of adaptation and evolution. In biomedicine, such variation is largely considered "noise" that sometimes complicates the identification of a single etiology (cause) of an illness and the prescription of a therapy. In human biology, the history of particular populations is relevant to understanding their characteristic genetic and physiological traits. By doing cross-cultural comparisons, for example, anthropologists find that Western girls are early maturers with regard to menarche, and this physiological trend has both health repercussions and reproductive implications. It is important not to assume that a particular group (say, white Americans) is the "normal" standard for growth patterns, reactions to drugs, and so forth. Comparative medical research, such as that by the National Institutes of Health on women's health, is central to understanding human biological variation.

 4

The Tall and Short of It

Barry Bogin

Some biologically oriented medical anthropologists focus on issues of child growth and development—that is, measuring and explaining patterns of growth through the life cycle. Measurement of the variations in the human body—in stature, weight, fat, and so forth—is called anthropometry. *In clinical pediatrics, a standard tool for evaluating a baby's health is the use of a growth chart for judging whether the child is growing as expected. Failure to grow is an indicator to the doctor that something is wrong.*

Most of the time, poor growth is a consequence of inadequate nutrition. However, most people believe that differences in stature are primarily determined by our genes. Of course there is genetic variation that has some effect on stature (e.g., the height differences between men and women, which average about 10 percent in all populations). But final height is influenced by disease experience as well as nutritional status. When children live in poverty, both their adult stature and their health are affected.

In this selection, the nutritional anthropologist Barry Bogin describes the idea of human plasticity. *The way that someone looks (phenotype) reflects the interaction between the individual's genotype and his or her environment. It is important to remember that the environment, in this case, is culturally constructed. This is an issue identified by the father of American anthropology, Franz Boas, who compared immigrant populations and their children raised in the United States during the 1920s. He documented a rapid increase in anthropometric measurements, including stature and brain size, for the U.S.-raised offspring. This was a case where the genetic composition of the immigrants and their children was identical, but their bodies were different. Boas used these data to refute the notion of fixed biological characteristics in so-called races—a fundamental assumption of the scientific racism of that time.*

As you read this selection, consider these questions:

- **Why are the Dutch the tallest nation in the world? Might public health policies begun after the Dutch famines during the Second World War have had an effect?**
- **What does plasticity mean?**
- **If child nutrition affects growth and stature, do you think it might also affect brain development? What might this mean in terms of the consequences of growing up in poverty?**
- **Are pygmies short only because of nutrition?**

Context: Barry Bogin teaches in the Centre for Human Development and Aging at the University of Loughborough in the United Kingdom. He previously taught at Wayne State University and the University of Michigan at Dearborn. His original research concerned growth and development among Mayan people in Guatemala and the United States. A prolific author, his most recent book is The Growth of Humanity (2001). Some of his work has focused on the "nutrition transition" (historical shifts in nutrition patterns and their health consequences) and the growing problem of obesity in the developing world. Note: Some readers might not recognize that the first line of this article is a reference to the advice given to Dustin Hoffman's character at the beginning of the classic movie The Graduate (1967).

Source: Barry Bogin (1998). "The Tall and Short of It." Discover Magazine, February, pp. 40–44.

As a biological anthropologist, I have just one word of advice for you: plasticity. *Plasticity* refers to the ability of many organisms, including humans, to alter themselves—their behavior or even their biology—in response to changes in the environment. We tend to think that our bodies get locked into their final form by our genes, but in fact we alter our bodies as the conditions surrounding us shift, particularly as we grow during childhood. Plasticity is as much a product of evolution's fine-tuning as any particular gene, and it makes just as much evolutionary good sense. Rather than being able to adapt to a single environment, we can, thanks to plasticity, change our bodies to cope with a wide range of environments. Combined with the genes we inherit from our parents, plasticity accounts for what we are and what we can become.

Anthropologists began to think about human plasticity around the turn of the century, but the concept was first clearly defined in 1969 by Gabriel Lasker, a biological anthropologist at Wayne State University in Detroit. At that time scientists tended to consider only those adaptations that were built into the genetic makeup of a person and passed on automatically to the next generation. A classic example of this is the ability of adults in some human societies to drink milk. As children, we all produce an enzyme called lactase, which we need to break down the sugar lactose in our mother's milk. In many of us, however, the lactase gene slows down dramatically as we approach adolescence—probably as the result of another gene that regulates its activity. When that regulating gene turns down the production of lactase, we can no longer digest milk.

Lactose intolerance—which causes intestinal gas and diarrhea—affects between 70 and 90 percent of African Americans, Native Americans, Asians, and people who come from around the Mediterranean. But others, such as people of central and western European descent and the Fulani of West Africa, typically have no problem drinking milk as adults. That's because they are descended from societies with long histories of raising goats and cattle. Among these people there was a clear benefit to being able to drink milk, so natural selection gradually changed the regulation of their lactase gene, keeping it functioning throughout life.

That kind of adaptation takes many centuries to become established, but Lasker pointed out that there are two other kinds of adaptation in humans that need far less time to kick in. If people have to face a cold winter with little or no heat, for example, their metabolic rates rise over the course of a few weeks and they produce more body heat. When summer returns, the rates sink again.

Lasker's other mode of adaptation concerned the irreversible, lifelong modification of people as they develop—that is, their plasticity. Because we humans take so many years to grow to adulthood, and because we live in so many different environments, from forests to cities and from deserts to the Arctic, we are among the world's most variable species in our physical form and behavior. Indeed, we are one of the most plastic of all species.

One of the most obvious manifestations of human malleability is our great range of height, and it is a subject I've made a special study of for the last 25 years. Consider these statistics: in 1850 Americans were the tallest people in the world, with American men averaging 5′6″. Almost 150 years later, American men now average 5′8″, but we have fallen in the standings and are now only the third tallest people in the world. In first place are the Dutch. Back in 1850 they averaged only 5′4″—the shortest men in Europe—but today they are a towering 5′10″. (In these two groups, and just about everywhere else, women average about five inches less than men at all times.)

So what happened? Did all the short Dutch sail over to the United States? Did the Dutch back in Europe get an infusion of "tall genes"? Neither. In both America and the Netherlands life got better, but more so for the Dutch, and height increased as a result. We know this is true thanks in part to studies on how height is determined. It's the product of plasticity in our childhood and in our mothers' childhood as well. If a girl is undernourished and suffers poor health, the growth of her body, including her reproductive system, is usually reduced. With a shortage of raw materials, she can't build more cells to construct a bigger body; at the same time, she has to invest what materials she can get into repairing already existing cells and tissues from the damage caused by disease. Her shorter stature as an adult is the result of a compromise her body makes while growing up.

Such a woman can pass on her short stature to her child, but genes have nothing to do with it for either of them. If she becomes pregnant, her small reproductive system probably won't be able to supply a normal level of nutrients and oxygen to her fetus. This harsh environment reprograms the fetus to grow more slowly than it would if the woman was healthier, so she is more likely to give birth to a smaller baby. Low-birth-weight babies (weighing less than 5.5 pounds) tend to continue their prenatal program of slow growth through childhood. By the time they are teenagers, they are usually significantly shorter than people of normal birth weight. Some particularly striking evidence of this reprogramming comes from studies on monozygotic twins, which develop from a single fertilized egg cell and are therefore identical genetically. But in certain cases, monozygotic twins end up being nourished by unequal portions of the placenta. The twin with the smaller fraction of the placenta is often born with low birth weight, while the other one is normal. Follow-up studies show that this difference between the twins can last throughout their lives.

As such research suggests, we can use the average height of any group of people as a barometer of the health of their society. After the turn of the century both the United States and the Netherlands began to protect the health of their citizens by purifying drinking water, installing sewer systems, regulating the safety of food, and, most important, providing better health care and diets to children. The children responded to their changed environment by growing taller. But the differences in Dutch and American societies determined their differing heights today. The Dutch decided to provide public health benefits to all the public, including the poor. In the United States, meanwhile, improved health is enjoyed most by those who can afford it. The poor often lack adequate housing, sanitation, and health care. The difference in our two societies can be seen at birth: in 1990 only 4 percent of Dutch babies were born at low birth weight, compared with 7 percent in the United States. For white Americans the rate was 5.7 percent, and for black Americans the rate was a whopping 13.3 percent. The disparity between rich and poor in the United States carries through to adulthood: poor Americans are shorter than the better-off by about one inch. Thus, despite great affluence in the United States, our average height has fallen to third place.

People are often surprised when I tell them the Dutch are the tallest people in the world. Aren't they shrimps compared with the famously tall Tutsi (or "Watusi," as you probably first encountered them) of Central Africa? Actually, the supposed great height of the Tutsi is one of the most durable myths from the age of European exploration. Careful investigation reveals that today's Tutsi men average 5'7" and that they have maintained that average for more than 100 years. That means that back in the 1800s, when puny European men first met the Tutsi, the Europeans suffered strained necks from looking up all the time. The two-to-three-inch difference in average height back then could easily have turned into fantastic stories of African giants by European adventurers and writers.

The Tutsi could be as tall or taller than the Dutch if equally good health care and diets were available in Rwanda and Burundi, where the Tutsi live. But poverty rules the lives of most African people, punctuated by warfare, which makes the conditions for growth during childhood even worse. And indeed, it turns out that the Tutsi and other Africans who migrate to Western Europe or North America at young ages end up taller than Africans remaining in Africa.

At the other end of the height spectrum, Pygmies tell a similar story. The shortest people in the world today are the Mbuti, the Efe, and other Pygmy peoples of Central Africa. Their average stature is about 4'9" for adult men and 4'6" for women. Part of the reason Pygmies are short is indeed genetic: some evidently lack the genes for producing the growth-promoting hormones that course through other people's bodies, while others are genetically incapable of using these hormones to trigger the cascade of reactions that lead to growth. But another important reason for their small size is environmental. Pygmies living as hunter-gatherers in the forests of Central African countries appear to be undernourished, which further limits their growth. Pygmies who live on farms and ranches outside the forest are better fed than their hunter-gatherer relatives and are taller as well. Both genes and nutrition thus account for the size of Pygmies.

Peoples in other parts of the world have also been labeled pygmies, such as some groups in Southeast Asia and the Maya of Guatemala. Well-meaning explorers and scientists have often claimed that they are genetically short, but here we encounter another myth of height. A group of extremely short people in New Guinea, for example, turned out to eat a diet deficient in iodine and other essential nutrients. When they were supplied with cheap mineral and vitamin supplements, their supposedly genetic short stature vanished in their children, who grew to a more normal height.

Another way for these so-called pygmies to stop being pygmies is to immigrate to the United States. In my own research, I study the growth of two groups of Mayan children. One group lives in their homeland of Guatemala, and the other is a group of refugees living in the United States. The Maya in Guatemala live in the village of San Pedro, which has no safe source of drinking water. Most of the water is contaminated with fertilizers and pesticides used on nearby agricultural fields. Until recently, when a deep well was dug, the townspeople depended on an unreliable supply of water from rain-swollen streams. Most homes still lack running water and have only pit toilets. The parents of the Mayan children work mostly at clothing factories and are paid only a few dollars a day.

I began working with the schoolchildren in this village in 1979, and my research shows that most of them eat only 80 percent of the food they need. Other research shows that almost 30 percent of the girls and 20 percent of the boys are deficient in iodine, that most of the children suffer from intestinal parasites, and that many have persistent ear and eye infections. As a consequence, their health is poor and their height reflects it: they average about three inches shorter than better-fed Guatemalan children.

The Mayan refugees I work with in the United States live in Los Angeles and in the rural agricultural community of Indiantown in central Florida. Although the adults work mostly in minimum-wage jobs, the children in these communities are generally better off than their counterparts in Guatemala. Most Maya arrived in the 1980s as refugees escaping a civil war as well as a political system that threatened them and their children. In the United States they found security and started new lives, and before long their children began growing faster and bigger. My data show that the average increase in height among the first generation of these immigrants was 2.2 inches, which means that these so-called pygmies have undergone one of the largest single-generation increases in height ever recorded. When people such as my own grandparents migrated from the poverty of rural life in Eastern Europe to the cities of the United States just after World War I, the increase in height of the next generation was only about one inch.

One reason for the rapid increase in stature is that in the United States the Maya have access to treated drinking water and to a reliable supply of food. Especially critical are school breakfast and lunch programs for children from low-income families, as well as public assistance programs such as the federal Women, Infants, and Children (WIC) program and food stamps. That these programs improve health and growth is no secret. What is surprising is how fast they work. Mayan mothers in the United States tell me that even their babies are bigger and healthier than the babies they raised in Guatemala, and hospital statistics bear them out. These women must be enjoying a level of health so improved from that of their lives in Guatemala that their babies are growing faster in the womb. Of course, plasticity means that such changes are dependent on external conditions, and unfortunately the rising height—and health—of the Maya is in danger from political forces that are attempting to cut funding for food stamps and the WIC program. If that funding is cut, the negative impact on the lives of poor Americans, including the Mayan refugees, will be as dramatic as were the former positive effects.

Height is only the most obvious example of plasticity's power; there are others to be found everywhere you look. The Andes-dwelling Quechua people of Peru are well adapted to their high-altitude homes. Their large, barrel-shaped chests house big lungs that inspire huge amounts of air with each breath, and they manage to survive on the lower pressure of oxygen they breathe with an unusually high level of red blood cells. Yet these secrets of mountain living are not hereditary. Instead the bodies of young Quechua adapt as they grow in their particular environment, just as those of European children do when they live at high altitudes.

Plasticity may also have a hand in determining our risks for developing a number of diseases. For example, scientists have long been searching for a cause for Parkinson's disease. Because Parkinson's tends to run in families, it is natural to think there is a genetic cause. But while a genetic mutation linked to some types of Parkinson's disease was reported in mid-1997, the gene accounts for only a fraction of people with the disease. Many more people with Parkinson's do not have the gene, and not all people with the mutated gene develop the disease.

Ralph Garruto, a medical researcher and biological anthropologist at the National Institutes of Health, is investigating the role of the environment and human plasticity not only in Parkinson's but in Lou Gehrig's disease as well. Garruto and his team traveled to the islands of Guam and New Guinea, where rates of both diseases are 50 to 100 times higher than in the United States. Among the native Chamorro people of Guam these diseases kill one person out of every five over the age of 25. The scientists found that both diseases are linked to a shortage of calcium in the diet. This shortage sets off a cascade of events that result in the digestive system's absorbing too much of the aluminum present in the diet. The aluminum wreaks havoc on various parts of the body, including the brain, where it destroys neurons and eventually causes paralysis and death.

The most amazing discovery made by Garruto's team is that up to 70 percent of the people they studied in Guam had some brain damage, but only 20 percent progressed all the way to Parkinson's or Lou Gehrig's disease. Genes and plasticity seem to be working hand in hand to produce these lower-than-expected rates of disease. There is a certain amount of genetic variation in the ability that all people have in coping with calcium shortages—some can function better than others. But thanks to plasticity, it's also possible for people's bodies to gradually develop ways to protect themselves against aluminum poisoning. Some people develop biochemical barriers to the aluminum they eat, while others develop ways to prevent the aluminum from reaching the brain.

An appreciation of plasticity may temper some of our fears about these diseases and even offer some hope. For if Parkinson's and Lou Gehrig's diseases can be prevented among the Chamorro by plasticity, then maybe medical researchers can figure out a way to produce the same sort of plastic changes in you and me. Maybe Lou Gehrig's disease and Parkinson's disease—as well as many others, including some cancers—aren't our genetic doom but a product of our development, just like variations in human height. And maybe their danger will in time prove as illusory as the notion that the Tutsi are giants, or the Maya pygmies—or Americans still the tallest of the tall.

 5

Why Genes Don't Count (for Racial Differences in Health)

Alan Goodman

Medical anthropologists are interested in human biological variation because, at its essence, anthropology is the study of human similarities and differences. Biological differences described using the term "race" are more than just problematic—they are wrong. This is because race is not a useful or relevant biological concept. Contemporary knowledge of population genetics demonstrates that there is no such thing as clearly defined "racial" groups. In other words, "race" is a scientific myth. Racism *and* racialization, *however, are social and cultural realities. As this selection by a noted biological anthropologist shows, "race" is a cultural invention about human biological variation. The American Anthropological Association's "Statement on Race" (1998) provides an excellent summary of these fundamental facts.*

In the United States, we consistently collect epidemiological data for racial and ethnic groups, and the data consistently demonstrate significant differences among these groups in all measures of morbidity and mortality. The question is, how do we understand and deal with these health disparities? Do health inequalities between "racial" groups reflect biological differences among the groups?

In the previous selection, Barry Bogin demonstrated how differences in height between groups must be understood in terms of plasticity and the interaction of environment and genes. Genetic differences exist, but they are only a small part of the overall story. This selection shows that since there is more genetic variation within *groups* than *between groups, it is inappropriate to ascribe health inequalities to genes. This is a hard thing for some people to swallow because the cultural ideas of race, biology, skin color, and genes seem so obvious. They may seem obvious, but they are illogical and based on faulty assumptions.*

Modern geneticists and molecular biologists have made enormous discoveries about genes that cause (or play a role in causing) certain diseases. There has been a great deal of scientific effort devoted to mapping the human genome (or, more precisely, the genome of one person). There has also been a great and expensive search for the particular genes "for" certain diseases. In light of the complex causal web of most chronic diseases—type 2 diabetes is the central example in this selection—thinking that there is a single genetic cause for a disease clearly is too simplistic, especially when we are asking questions about health differences between social groups. Finally, there is an unmistakable pessimism in the overemphasis on genetic predispositions to health problems; it is fatalistic, or it implies that the only solution is changing our genetic structure or function. On a more positive note, it is important to recognize that diseases are preventable by changing our behaviors and changing our culture.

As you read this selection, consider these questions:

- **Why is race not a useful way to think about human biological variation?**
- **Is race real?**
- **If the author is right about genes, why are there inequalities in health measures between different "racial" and ethnic groups? What about economic classes?**
- **What might be the effects of racism on risk of disease or access to health care?**
- **How is our understanding of biological variations—like resistance to malaria, an adult's ability to digest milk, or the risk of developing diabetes—not aided by the concept of race?**

Context: Alan Goodman, recent president of the American Anthropological Association (AAA), teaches at Hampshire College. He has been a leader in expanding the AAA's mission to educate the American public about "race." A biological anthropologist with a specialization in the teeth of ancient populations, Goodman has worked to promote a productive dialogue between biologically oriented and culturally oriented medical anthropologists. Historically, these dialogues occurred at a time when there was great divisiveness between biological and cultural anthropologists. These efforts at reintegration are reflected in two of his co-edited books: Genetic Nature/Culture: Anthropology and Science beyond the Two-Culture Divide (2003) and Building a New Biocultural Synthesis:

Political-Economic Perspectives on Human Biology (1999). He has a personal interest in understanding human variation in regard to stature.

Source: Goodman A. (2000). "Why Genes Don't Count (for Racial Differences in Health)." American Journal of Public Health. 90(11):1699–1702.

In 1973, I took a course titled "Introduction to Physical Anthropology" with Professor George Armelagos. In the course, he taught that "race" was once a core worldview in anthropology and that it had spread to other sciences and practices such as medicine and public health. Natural historians in the 18th and 19th centuries thought in terms of idealized and unchanging types of objects, including human beings. The big question of the time concerned the degree and significance of racial differences. The church's monogenetic position held that the "races" were created together as a species with clear subspecies. Men of science such as Philadelphia physician George Morton and Cambridge natural historian Louis Agassiz supported a polygenetic position, asserting that the races were separately created species.

Professor Armelagos explained that human biological variation is continuous, complex, and ever changing. As a static and typological concept, race is inherently unable to explain the complex and changing structure of human biological variation. As in the decennial census, individuals will always fail to fit neatly into racial boxes. Moreover, the placement of an individual in a given box says little about his or her biology: the racial mean is meaningless. To begin to comprehend the human biological variation, one needed an evolutionary theory that focused on gradual change and populations rather than on race. Professor Armelagos went on to say that although race is still real, it is not biologically based; rather, it is social with biological consequences.

Students' responses ranged from disbelief to transformation. After having long assumed the biological basis of race, many in the room could not accept his claims. Others misunderstood his message, thinking he was denying the reality of biological variation itself. Still others were transformed forever by this new idea.

I recollect that it made almost instant sense to me that human races are social constructions. Although I saw Professor Armelagos as a White man, his birth certificate stated that he was Greek. I had grown up in a working-class family in a town composed mostly of second-generation immigrants from Italy and Ireland, and as a boy I was aware of being perceived as Jewish and different from my Irish and Italian friends in some fundamental way. Yet when I began attending a more diverse university, something striking happened: I became "White." I was no longer perceived as very distinct from other students of European descent. It was then that I learned about the fluidity of race and how social and political-economic processes were constantly changing color lines.

Professor Armelagos hinted at a powerful lesson: that scientific ideas can endure and be made to seem real if they have social and political-economic utility. An evolutionary framework that explained human variation had been established for more than a century, ever since the publication of Darwin's *Origin of Species*.[1] In the 1940s, Montagu used the "new evolutionary synthesis" to explain clearly why race was a biological myth.[2,3] Yet the idea of race as biology persists today in science and society.[4]

I was aware of the power of race as a worldview in 1973. But what I understood less was the idea's ability to persist after it had been proven unscientific. If I had been asked in the 1970s whether race would survive as a way to think about human biological variation in 2000, I would have answered emphatically, "No!" I was naive to the durability of an economically useful idea.

Acceptance of the notion of race-as-biology declined in anthropology throughout the late 1970s and early 1980s.[5,6] Yet, during the past decade, racialized notions of biology have made a comeback.[4,7] This is especially true in human genetics, a field that, paradoxically, once drove the last nail into the coffin of race-as-biology.

In this commentary, I explain why race should not be used as a proxy for genetic or biological variation. I then explain and illustrate the 2 unfounded assumptions that are needed for an acceptance that racial differences in disease are due to genetic differences among races.

THE MYTH OF RACE AS BIOLOGY

The first of 6 reasons why race is an inadequate and even harmful way to think about human biological differences is based on the history and theoretical underpinnings of the idea of race. The next 3 have to do with the structure of human biological variation. The last 2 pertain to the use of race in practice.

1. *The concept of race is based on the idea of fixed, ideal and unchanging types.* Race was first a European folk concept from an era in which the world was seen as fixed and unchanging.[8,9] Such an idea, however, is completely incompatible with evolutionary theory. In response, some who still adhere to the concept of race might say that as it is now used in science, it is dynamic, flexible, and even evolutionary.[10,11] But the new race is the old race, typological and ideal. Like a chameleon changing its color to better hide in a chromatically different environment, race changes superficially to fit into a new intellectual environment.

2. *Human variation is continuous.* Allele frequencies tend to vary gradually. Therefore, there is no clear place to designate where one race begins and another ends. Skin color, for example, slowly changes from place to place. Templeton has shown that most human variation is explained by geographic distance[12]: individuals tend to be most similar to those who live nearby and least similar to those who live farthest away.

3. *Human variation is nonconcordant.* Traits tend to vary independently of other traits. Race classifications vary, therefore, by the traits used in the classification. A classification based on sickle cell trait might include equatorial Africans, Greeks, and Turks, while another based on lactase enzyme deficiency might include eastern and southern Africans along with southern Europeans, Japanese, and Native Americans. There is no possibility for consistency. Because skin color correlates with only a few other phenotypic traits such as hair and eye color, it is true that "race is only skin deep."

4. *Within-group genetic variation is much greater than variation among "races."* Starting with Lewontin,[13] studies have statistically apportioned variation in different genetic systems to different levels, among "races" and within "races" and smaller populations such as the Hopi, the Ainu, and the Irish.[14] Lewontin collected data on blood group polymorphisms in different groups and races.[13] He found that blood group variation among races statistically explained about 6% of the total variation.[13] The implication of Lewontin's results is that if one is to adopt a racial paradigm, one must acknowledge that race will statistically explain only a small proportion of variations. These variations are better explained by geographic distance.[12]

5. *There is no way to consistently classify by race.* Race is impossible to define in a stable and universal way because race-as-biology varies with place and time, and the socially determined color line is even more dynamic. A problem with race classification is that there is no agreed-upon "race scale" as there are hat and shoe size scales. Ideas about race are fluid and based on different phenotypic cues; the salient cues change over time, place, and circumstance. One study of infants who died in their first year showed that 37% of infants classified as Native American on their birth certificates were classified as some other race on their death certificates.[15] If race "changes" so quickly in less than a year, one can only imagine the degree of misclassification that could occur over decades and across regions.

6. *There is no clarity as to what race is and what it is not.* Other key methods of classification involve inconsistencies as well. For example, definitions of socioeconomic class vary widely. Although always imperfect, they begin to provide a glimpse of the underlying processes by which social and economic positions affect lived experiences and health. Race differs critically from other classification methods in the breadth of potential interpretations of the underlying processes. Some individuals view racial differences in disease as owing to genes, while others see race differences as the consequence of the lived experience of "racing"—the taxonomic practice of assigning individuals to races—and of racism. Obviously, this confusion has serious implications for theory and practice: One cannot practice predictive science on the basis of a changing and undefinable cause.

Probably none of these reasons is by itself sufficient to throw race onto the scrap heap of surpassed scientific ideas. But considered together, they clearly suggest that race-as-biology is obsolete. Just as we have moved beyond thinking that the sun revolves around the moon and that a fully-formed, tiny human lives in sperm, so too it is time to move beyond believing that race is a valid method for classifying human biological differences.

THE DOUBLE ERROR INHERENT IN GENETIC EXPLANATIONS OF RACIAL DIFFERENCES

Two errors—2 leaps of illogic—are necessary for acceptance of the idea that racial differences in disease are due to genetic differences among races. The first leap is a form of geneticization, the belief that most biology and behavior are located "in the genes."

Genes, of course, are often a part of the complex web of disease causality, but they are almost always a minor, unstable, and insufficient cause. The presence of Gm allotype, for example, might correlate to increased rates of diabetes in Native Americans,[16] but the causal link is unknown. In other cases, the gene is not expressed without some environmental context, and it may interact with environments and other genes in nonadditive and unpredictable ways.

The second necessary leap of illogic is a form of scientific racialism, the belief that races are real and useful constructs. Importantly, this leap propels one from explaining disease variation as caused by genetic variation to explaining that racial differences in disease are caused by genetic variation among races. To accept this logic, one needs to also accept that genetic variation occurs along racial divides: that is, most variation occurs among races. However, we know from Lewontin's work that this assumption is false for simple genetic systems.[13] For a disease of complex etiology, genetics is an illogical explanation for racial differences.

WHY RACE-AS-GENES FAILS IN PRACTICE

Scientifically, race-as-biology has been and is still used both as a means of identification and classification and as a means of explanation. As the former, it is often applied in the forensic sciences. As the latter, it requires the former and, depending on what is to be explained, may be used in many fields, including biological anthropology, exercise physiology, psychology, and public health.

Identification of humans from skeletal remains provides a clear example of the poor performance of a racial model of human variation.[4] The most widely referenced method for identifying race from the skeleton is Giles and Elliot's discriminant function for determining race from cranial remains.[17] In the original study of crania of individuals of known "race" and sex, Giles and Elliot were able to correctly classify about 85% of individuals as members of 1 of 3 races—Native American, White, or Black. This rate of correct racial classification is often cited in texts and popular articles.[18,19] However, in 4 retests of the method's ability to correctly classify Native Americans, the rate dropped to an average of approximately 33%.[4] In other words, the retest performance was about what one would expect by random assignment. Failure to extend the method to other times and places illustrates the nature of temporally and geographically changing color lines and biologies.

The attribution of racial differences in disease to genetic differences illustrates both geneticization and scientific racialism. For example, the rise in diabetes among some Native Americans is often thought to be caused by a genetic variation that separates Native Americans from European Americans.[17,20,21] Type II diabetes, along with obesity, gallstones, and heart disease, is part of what has been called "New World Syndrome."[21] The designation of a panracial syndrome may fix in one's mind the idea of homogeneity within race and the notion that the syndrome is innate.

Contemporary variation in diabetes rates among Native North American groups is tremendous, however, and the rise in diabetes rates is a relatively recent phenomenon.[22] Other groups experiencing shifts from complex carbohydrates to colas, from fast-moving foods to fast foods, and from exercise to underemployment have experienced very similar increases in diabetes rates. Rather than accept that diabetes is "in our blood," as articulated by the Pima,[23] it might be more productive to locate diabetes in changeable lifestyles.

FROM STUDIES OF RACE-AS-GENETICS TO STUDIES OF RACIALISM AND RACISM

As the 19th century turned into the 20th century, anthropology was united in viewing race as a powerful explanation for biology, culture, and behavior. As the 20th century turns to the 21st, anthropologists have begun to reach a consensus on the limits and significance of race. As is illustrated in the recently ratified American Anthropological Association statement on race, the new consensus maintains that

- Human biological variation should not be reduced to race. It is too complex and does not fit this outdated idea.
- Race is real. Rather than being based on biology, it is a social and political process that provides insights into how we read deeper meaning into phenotypes.
- Racialization and racism come about because, in a racialized culture, we read meaning into skin color and other phenotypic variants. Rather than biology affecting behavior, ideology and behavior affect individuals "under the skin."

The 20th century was a highly racialized century. All signs suggest that the 21st may be, too. A central confusion about race—one that is reflected in census debates and the use of census data—is that we use the concept differently. Although the Office of Management and Budget Directive 15 makes no claim that race is a scientific term or is biological in meaning, this disclaimer is hidden in the small type of an official document.

Until there are no racial distinctions in aspects of life such as access to employment and health care, a society that purports to be just, such as our own, needs to track racial differences and the political-economic consequences of a racial system. Professor Armelagos and others like him, extending back to Montagu, Franz Boas, W.E.B. Du Bois, and Frederick Douglass, paved the way toward rejecting race-as-biology.

NOTES

1. Darwin C. *On the Origin of Species by Means of Natural Selection or the Preservation of Favored Races in the Struggle for Life.* London, England: John Murray; 1859.
2. Montagu MFA. The concept of race in the human species in light of genetics. *J Hered.* 1941; 32: 243–247.
3. Montagu MFA. *Man's Most Dangerous Myth: The Fallacy of Race.* New York, NY: Columbia University Press; 1942.
4. Goodman AH. Bred in the bone? *The Sciences.* March/April 1997:20–25.
5. Lieberman L, Stevenson BW, Reynolds LT. Race and anthropology: core concept without consensus. *Anthropol Educ Q.* 1989;20(2):67–73.
6. Barkan E. *The Retreat of Scientific Racism.* New York, NY: Cambridge University Press; 1992.
7. Goodman AH, Armelagos GJ. Race, racism and the new physical anthropology. In: Reynolds LT, Lieberman L, eds. *Race and Other Misadventures: Essays in Honor of Ashley Montagu in His Ninetieth Year.* Dix Hills, NY: General Hall Inc; 1996:174–186.
8. Smedley A. *Race in North America: Origin and Evolution of a World View.* 2nd ed. Boulder, Colo: Westview Press; 1999.
9. Stepan N. *The Idea of Race in Science: Great Britain 1800–1960.* London, England: Macmillan Press; 1982.
10. Gill GW. A forensic anthropologist's view of the race concept. In: Abstracts of the 46th Annual Meeting of the American Academy of Forensic Sciences. 1996.
11. Brues AM. The objective view of race. In: Gordon CC, ed. *Race Ethnicity, and Applied Bioanthropology.* Richmond, Va: American Anthropological Association; 1993:74–78. NAPA bulletin 13.
12. Templeton A. Human races: a genetic and evolutionary perspective. *Am Anthropologist.* 1998;100: 632–650.
13. Lewontin RC. The apportionment of human diversity. *Evol Biol.* 1972;6:381–398.
14. Nei M, Roychoudhury AK. Genetic relationship and evolution of human races. In: Hecht M, Wallace B, Prance G, eds. *Evolutionary Biology.* Vol 14. New York, NY: Plenum Press; 1982:1–59.
15. Hahn R, Mulinare J. Teutsch S. Inconsistencies in coding race and ethnicity between birth and death in US infants. *JAMA.* 1992;267:259–263.
16. Knowler WC, Williams RC, Pettitt DJ, Steinberg AG. Gm and type 2 diabetes mellitus: an association in American Indians with genetic admixture. *Am J Hum Genet.* 1988;43:520–526.
17. Giles E, Elliot O. Race identification from cranial measurements. *J Forensic Sci.* 1962;7:247–257.
18. St. Hoyme LE, Iscan MY. Determination of sex and race: accuracy and assumptions. In: Iscan MY, Kennedy KAR, eds. *Reconstruction of Life from the Skeleton.* New York, NY: Alan R Liss; 1989:53–93.
19. Sauer N. Forensic anthropology and the concept of race: if races don't exist, why are forensic anthropologists so good at identifying them? *Soc Sci Med.* 1992;34:107–111.
20. Weiss K. Transitional diabetes and gallstones in Amerindian peoples: genes or environment? In: Swedlund AC, Armelagos GJ, eds. *Disease in Populations in Transition.* Hadley, Mass: Bergen & Garvey; 1992: 105–123.
21. Weiss K, Ferrell R. Hanis CL. A new world syndrome of metabolic diseases with a genetic and evolutionary basis. *Yearbook Phys Anthropol.* 1984;27:153–178.
22. Young TK. *The Health of Native Americans.* New York, NY: Oxford University Press; 1994.
23. Kozak D. Surrendering to diabetes: an embodied response to perceptions of diabetes and death in the Gila Indian community. *Omega J Death Dying.* 1996;35: 347–359.

 6

Skin Deep

Nina Jablonski
George Chaplin

Skin color is an incredibly salient aspect of human biological variation worldwide. Variations in skin color—determined by the size of melanin globules in the epidermis—are hard not to notice. But as the last reading made clear, skin color and the entire concept of "race" are worthless for understanding human biological *variation. In the United States, however, "race" is an extremely important* social *concept linked to a legacy of slavery and racial discrimination. In the past, race was also (erroneously) used as a scientific explanation for a variety of differences between social groups. For example, it was once believed that higher rates of tuberculosis in African Americans were due to some unidentified inherited biological weakness—instead of conditions of poverty that increased transmission and of chronic undernutrition that exacerbated the expression of the disease. Similarly, psychiatrists even described a so-called mental illness in slaves called "drapetomania," a condition that caused slaves to want to run away from plantations! The social inequalities of "race" and ethnicity continue to cause great differences in health outcomes not only in the United States but also in many countries throughout the world.*

Obviously, there is a spectrum of skin colors among human beings, and this spectrum is, in large measure, caused by genetic variations. Human genetic variations occur in a wide range of attributes, from height, to bone density, to blood characteristics such as sickle-cell trait. Such differences require explanation using the most important biological theory: evolution through natural selection. Natural selection occurs because of differential rates of fertility and mortality, including differences in the experiences of health and disease. Diseases are important agents of natural selection. In environments characterized by certain diseases—as where malaria is endemic, for example—people who have inherited particular genetic traits—like the sickle-cell trait—have a better chance of survival and reproduction. In this case, the problem of mortality caused by malaria is worse than the mortality caused by sickle-cell disease.

When anthropologists examine the distribution of skin color throughout the world, the oddity that needs explanation is the light pigmentation of "white" skin, for reasons that Nina Jablonski and George Chaplin explain in this selection describing the relationship between skin color and ultraviolet radiation from the sun. Ultraviolet radiation is necessary for the body to synthesize vitamin D, which in turn is necessary for calcium production for bones and the immune system. Too much ultraviolet radiation can result in low levels of the essential B vitamin called folate. Too little absorption of ultraviolet radiation, something that is more likely to happen in cold, cloudy climates, results in a deficiency of vitamin D. Other diseases resulting from improper absorption include rickets, neural-tube defects, low sperm counts, and skin cancer. In demonstrating these relationships between skin color and radiation, Jablonski and Chaplin reveal how such biological characteristics are the result of interactions between humans and their environment, although it is important to remember that humans, to a large degree, create their environments. Thus, biologically oriented medical anthropologists examine human diversity in the context of both biological and cultural evolution.

As you read this selection, consider these questions:

- **Why did theories of scientific racism persist for such a long time? How did science eventually correct itself?**
- **What is the relationship between exposure to ultraviolet radiation and the spectrum of skin color in the world?**
- **Why might skin cancer be less important in natural selection for skin color than neural-tube defects and low spermatogenesis caused by different levels of folate?**
- **Why is the distribution of skin color in the Americas not as closely correlated with ultraviolet radiation as in the Old World?**
- **Why is "race" not a useful concept in understanding human variation in skin color?**

Context: Nina Jablonski is professor and head of the Department of Anthropology at Penn State University. She is a biological anthropologist with a special interest in primate evolution; she has done fieldwork in Kenya, Nepal, and China. Her research on Old World prehistoric primates has focused on the history of adaptations to environmental change. This led her to research on the evolution of human skin and skin coloration, using physiological, paleontological, epidemiological, and environmental data. George Chaplin is a geographer and a senior research associate in anthropology at Penn State University. He is particularly interested in geographical information systems. His research includes work on human ecology and evolution, spatial epidemiology, and biodiversity. This article was written for a general audience. After anthropologists stopped using race as a biological concept, the question of the evolution of skin color was relatively neglected. Although the relationship of skin color, UVR, and rickets had been described in anthropology texts for some time, the research in this article adds important new evidence about the role of folate and other factors.

Source: N. Jablonski and G. Chapin (2002). "Skin Deep." Scientific American 287(4):74–81.

Among primates, only humans have a mostly naked skin that comes in different colors. Geographers and anthropologists have long recognized that the distribution of skin colors among indigenous populations is not random: darker peoples tend to be found nearer the equator, lighter ones closer to the poles. For years, the prevailing theory has been that darker skins evolved to protect against skin cancer. But a series of discoveries has led us to construct a new framework for understanding the evolutionary basis of variations in human skin color. Recent epidemiological and physiological evidence suggests to us that the worldwide pattern of human skin color is the product of natural selection acting to regulate the effects of the sun's ultraviolet (LTV) radiation on key nutrients crucial to reproductive success.

FROM HIRSUTE TO HAIRLESS

The evolution of skin pigmentation is linked with that of hairlessness, and to comprehend both these stories, we need to page back in human history. Human beings have been evolving as an independent lineage of apes since at least seven million years ago, when our immediate ancestors diverged from those of our closest relatives, chimpanzees. Because chimpanzees have changed less over time than humans have, they can provide an idea of what human anatomy and physiology must have been like. Chimpanzees' skin is light in color and is covered by hair over most of their bodies. Young animals have pink faces, hands, and feet and become freckled or dark in these areas only as they are exposed to sun with age. The earliest humans almost certainly had a light skin covered with hair. Presumably hair loss occurred first, then skin color changed. But that leads to the question, When did we lose our hair?

The skeletons of ancient humans—such as the well-known skeleton of Lucy, which dates to about 3.2 million years ago—give us a good idea of the build and the way of life of our ancestors. The daily activities of Lucy and other hominids that lived before about three million years ago appear to have been similar to those of primates living on the open savannas of Africa today. They probably spent much of their day foraging for food over three to four miles before retiring to the safety of trees to sleep.

By 1.6 million years ago, however, we see evidence that this pattern had begun to change dramatically. The famous skeleton of Turkana Boy—which belonged to the species *Homo ergaster*—is that of a long-legged, striding biped that probably walked long distances. These more active early humans faced the problem of staying cool and protecting their brains from overheating. Peter Wheeler of John Moores University in Liverpool, England, has shown that this was accomplished through an increase in the number of sweat glands on the surface of the body and a reduction in the covering of body hair. Once rid of most of their hair, early members of the genus *Homo* then encountered the challenge of protecting their skin from the damaging effects of sunlight, especially UV rays.

BUILT-IN SUNSCREEN

In chimpanzees, the skin on the hairless parts of the body contains cells called melanocytes that are capable of synthesizing the dark-brown pigment melanin in response to exposure to LTV radiation. When humans became mostly hairless, the ability of the skin to produce melanin assumed new importance. Melanin is nature's sunscreen: it is a large organic molecule that serves the dual purpose of physically and chemically filtering the harmful effects of UV radiation; it absorbs LTV rays, causing them to lose energy, and it neutralizes harmful chemicals called free radicals that form in the skin after damage by UV radiation.

Anthropologists and biologists have generally reasoned that high concentrations of melanin arose in the skin of peoples in tropical areas because it protected them against skin cancer. James E. Cleaver of the University of California at San Francisco, for instance, has shown that people with the disease xeroderma pigmentosum, in which melanocytes are destroyed by exposure to the sun, suffer from significantly higher than normal rates of squamous and basal cell carcinomas, which are usually easily treated. Malignant melanomas are more frequently fatal, but they are rare (representing 4 percent of skin cancer diagnoses) and tend to strike only light-skinned people. But all skin cancers typically arise later in life, in most cases after the first reproductive years, so they could not have exerted enough evolutionary pressure for skin protection alone to account for darker skin colors. Accordingly, we began to ask what role melanin might play in human evolution.

THE FOLATE CONNECTION

In 1991 one of us (Jablonski) ran across what turned out to be a critical paper published in 1978 by Richard F. Branda and John W. Eaton, now at the University of Vermont and the University of Louisville, respectively. These investigators showed that light-skinned people who had been exposed to simulated strong sunlight had abnormally low levels of the essential B vitamin folate in their blood. The scientists also observed that subjecting human blood serum to the same conditions resulted in a 50-percent loss of folate content within one hour.

The significance of these findings to reproduction—and hence evolution—became clear when we learned of research being conducted on a major class of birth defects by our colleagues at the University of Western Australia. There Fiona J. Stanley and Carol Bower had established by the late 1980s that folate deficiency in pregnant women is related to an increased risk of neural tube defects such as spina bifida, in which the arches of the spinal vertebrae fail to close around the spinal cord. Many research groups throughout the world have since confirmed this correlation, and efforts to supplement foods with folate and to educate women about the importance of the nutrient have become widespread.

We discovered soon afterward that folate is important not only in preventing neural tube defects but also in a host of other processes. Because folate is essential for the synthesis of DNA in dividing cells, anything that involves rapid cell proliferation, such as spermatogenesis (the production of sperm cells), requires folate. Male rats and mice with chemically induced folate deficiency have impaired spermatogenesis and are infertile. Although no comparable studies of humans have been conducted, Wai Yee Wong and his colleagues at the University Medical Center of Nijmegen in the Netherlands have recently reported that folic acid treatment can boost the sperm counts of men with fertility problems.

Such observations led us to hypothesize that dark skin evolved to protect the body's folate stores from destruction. Our idea was supported by a report published in 1996 by Argentine pediatrician Pablo Lapunzina, who found that three young and otherwise healthy women whom he had attended gave birth to infants with neural tube defects after using sun beds to tan themselves in the early weeks of pregnancy. Our evidence about the breakdown of folate by UV radiation thus supplements what is already known about the harmful (skin-cancer-causing) effects of UV radiation on DNA.

HUMAN SKIN ON THE MOVE

The earliest members of *Homo sapiens*, or modern humans, evolved in Africa between 120,000 and 100,000 years ago and had darkly pigmented skin adapted to the conditions of UV radiation and heat that existed near the equator. As modern humans began to venture out of the tropics, however, they encountered environments in which they received significantly less UV radiation during the year. Under these conditions their high concentrations of natural sunscreen probably proved detrimental. Dark skin contains so much melanin that very little UV radiation, and specifically very little of the shorter-wavelength UVB radiation, can penetrate the skin. Although most of the effects of UVB are harmful, the rays perform one indispensable function: initiating the formation of vitamin D in the skin. Dark-skinned people living in the tropics generally receive sufficient UV radiation during the year for UVB to penetrate the skin and allow them to make vitamin D. Outside the tropics this is not the case. The solution, across evolutionary time, has been for migrants to northern latitudes to lose skin pigmentation.

The connection between the evolution of lightly pigmented skin and vitamin D synthesis was elaborated by W. Farnsworth Loomis of Brandeis University in 1967. He established the importance of vitamin D to reproductive success because of its role in enabling calcium absorption by the intestines, which in turn makes possible the normal development of the skeleton and the maintenance of a healthy immune system. Research led by Michael Holick of the Boston

University School of Medicine has, over the past 20 years, further cemented the significance of vitamin D in development and immunity. His team also showed that not all sunlight contains enough UVB to stimulate vitamin D production. In Boston, for instance, which is located at about 42 degrees north latitude, human skin cells begin to produce vitamin D only after mid-March. In the wintertime there isn't enough UVB to do the job. We realized that this was another piece of evidence essential to the skin color story.

During the course of our research in the early 1990s, we searched in vain to find sources of data on actual UV radiation levels at the earth's surface. We were rewarded in 1996, when we contacted Elizabeth Weatherhead of the Cooperative Institute for Research in Environmental Sciences at the University of Colorado at Boulder. She shared with us a database of measurements of UV radiation at the earth's surface taken by NASA's Total Ozone Mapping Spectrophotometer satellite between 1978 and 1993. We were then able to model the distribution of UV radiation on the earth and relate the satellite data to the amount of UVB necessary to produce vitamin D.

We found that the earth's surface could be divided into three vitamin D zones: one comprising the tropics, one the subtropics and temperate regions, and the last the circumpolar regions north and south of about 45 degrees latitude. In the first, the dosage of UVB throughout the year is high enough that humans have ample opportunity to synthesize vitamin D all year. In the second, at least one month during the year has insufficient UVB radiation, and in the third area not enough UVB arrives on average during the entire year to prompt vitamin D synthesis. This distribution could explain why indigenous peoples in the tropics generally have dark skin, whereas people in the subtropics and temperate regions are lighter-skinned but have the ability to tan, and those who live in regions near the poles tend to be very light skinned and burn easily.

One of the most interesting aspects of this investigation was the examination of groups that did not precisely fit the predicted skin-color pattern. An example is the Inuit people of Alaska and northern Canada. The Inuit exhibit skin color that is somewhat darker than would be predicted given the LTV levels at their latitude. This is probably caused by two factors. The first is that they are relatively recent inhabitants of these climes, having migrated to North America only roughly 5,000 years ago. The second is that the traditional diet of the Inuit is extremely high in foods containing vitamin D, especially fish and marine mammals. This vitamin D–rich diet offsets the problem that they would otherwise have with vitamin D synthesis in their skin at northern latitudes and permits them to remain more darkly pigmented.

Our analysis of the potential to synthesize vitamin D allowed us to understand another trait related to human skin color: women in all populations are generally lighter-skinned than men. (Our data show that women tend to be between 3 and 4 percent lighter than men.) Scientists have often speculated on the reasons, and most have argued that the phenomenon stems from sexual selection—the preference of men for women of lighter color. We contend that although this is probably part of the story, it is not the original reason for the sexual difference. Females have significantly greater needs for calcium throughout their reproductive lives, especially during pregnancy and lactation, and must be able to make the most of the calcium contained in food. We propose, therefore, that women tend to be lighter-skinned than men to allow slightly more UVB rays to penetrate their skin and thereby increase their ability to produce vitamin D. In areas of the world that receive a large amount of UV radiation, women are indeed at the knife's edge of natural selection, needing to maximize the photoprotective function of their skin on the one hand and the ability to synthesize vitamin D on the other.

WHERE CULTURE AND BIOLOGY MEET

As modern humans moved throughout the Old World about 100,000 years ago, their skin adapted to the environmental conditions that prevailed in different regions. The skin color of the indigenous people of Africa has had the longest time to adapt because anatomically modern humans first evolved there. The skin-color changes that modern humans underwent as they moved from one continent to another—first Asia, then Austro-Melanesia, then Europe and, finally, the Americas—can be reconstructed to some extent. It is important to remember, however, that those humans had clothing and shelter to help protect them from the elements. In some places, they also had the ability to harvest foods that were extraordinarily rich in vitamin D, as in the case of the Inuit. These two factors had profound effects on the tempo and degree of skin-color evolution in human populations.

Africa is an environmentally heterogeneous continent. A number of the earliest movements of contemporary humans outside equatorial Africa were into southern Africa. The descendants of some of these early colonizers, the Khoisan (previously known as Hottentots), are still found in southern Africa and have significantly lighter skin than indigenous equatorial Africans do—a clear adaptation to the lower levels of LTV radiation that prevail at the southern extremity of the continent.

Interestingly, however, human skin color in southern Africa is not uniform. Populations of Bantu-language speakers who live in southern Africa today are far darker than the Khoisan. We know from the history of this region that Bantu speakers migrated into this region recently—probably within the past 1,000 years—from parts of West Africa near the equator. The skin-color difference between the Khoisan and Bantu speakers such as the Zulu indicates that the length of time that a group has inhabited a particular region is important in understanding why they have the color they do.

Cultural behaviors have probably also strongly influenced the evolution of skin color in recent human history. This effect can be seen in the indigenous peoples who live on the eastern and western banks of the Red Sea. The tribes on the western side, which speak so-called Nilo-Hamitic languages, are thought to have inhabited this region for as long as 6,000 years. These individuals are distinguished by very darkly pigmented skin and long, thin bodies with long limbs, which are excellent biological adaptations for dissipating heat and intense LV radiation. In contrast, modern agricultural and pastoral groups on the eastern bank of the Red Sea, on the Arabian Peninsula, have lived there for only about 2,000 years. These earliest Arab people, of European origin, have adapted to very similar environmental conditions by almost exclusively cultural means—wearing heavy protective clothing and devising portable shade in the form of tents. (Without such clothing, one would have expected their skin to have begun to darken.) Generally speaking, the more recently a group has migrated into an area, the more extensive its cultural, as opposed to biological, adaptations to the area will be.

PERILS OF RECENT MIGRATIONS

Despite great improvements in overall human health in the past century, some diseases have appeared or reemerged in populations that had previously been little affected by them. One of these is skin cancer, especially basal and squamous cell carcinomas, among light-skinned peoples. Another is rickets, brought about by severe vitamin D deficiency, in dark-skinned peoples. Why are we seeing these conditions?

As people move from an area with one pattern of UV radiation to another region, biological and cultural adaptations have not been able to keep pace. The light-skinned people of northern European origin who bask in the sun of Florida or northern Australia increasingly pay the price in the form of premature aging of the skin and skin cancers, not to mention the unknown cost in human life of folate depletion. Conversely, a number of dark-skinned people of southern Asian and African origin now living in the northern U.K., northern Europe or the northeastern U.S. suffer from a lack of UV radiation and vitamin D, an insidious problem that manifests itself in high rates of rickets and other diseases related to vitamin D deficiency.

The ability of skin color to adapt over long periods to the various environments to which humans have moved reflects the importance of skin color to our survival. But its unstable nature also makes it one of the least useful characteristics in determining the evolutionary relations between human groups. Early Western scientists used skin color improperly to delineate human races, but the beauty of science is that it can and does correct itself. Our current knowledge of the evolution of human skin indicates that variations in skin color, like most of our physical attributes, can be explained by adaptation to the environment through natural selection. We look ahead to the day when the vestiges of old scientific mistakes will be erased and replaced by a better understanding of human origins and diversity. Our variation in skin color should be celebrated as one of the most visible manifestations of our evolution as a species.

Bioarchaeology and the History of Health

■ ***The importance of the Neolithic Revolution and other epidemiological transitions must be stressed.*** The Neolithic Revolution refers to the domestication of plants and animals, a process that began about 10,000 years ago. The invention and spread of agriculture and pastoralism was a process that probably took several thousand years to complete, but there is no doubt that the social and cultural implications of this economic transformation were revolutionary. Agriculture meant that there was a fundamentally different relationship between humans and their environment than was the case with hunter-gatherers. Agriculture both allowed and required local populations to grow: It *allowed* population growth because it provided a more predictable source of carbohydrate foods and because people settled in permanent villages; it *required* growth because more people were necessary to labor in the fields and to process food (Cohen and Armelagos 1984). A denser population and permanent ties to the land resulted in concentrated power in the hands of fewer people and the creation of systems of social stratification (Armelagos and Dewey 1970).

■ ***Paleopathologists have documented the negative effect of the Neolithic Revolution on health status.*** One excellent source of epidemiological, paleopathological, and ethnographic information on this topic is Mark Cohen's *Health and the Rise of Civilization* (1989). Another edited volume, *Paleopathology at the Origins of Agriculture* (Cohen and Armelagos 1984), provides seventeen specific case studies of health at this important historical juncture and demonstrates the controversy surrounding this issue; twelve cases show definite negative health effects, whereas five cases do not.

■ ***Historians of health have documented how the spread of epidemic diseases, and the mortality caused by them, influenced larger historical processes.*** One classic example is the spread of the Spanish empire into the New World, particularly in Cortez's conquest of Mexico. William H. McNeill (1976) has shown how Cortez's party (inadvertently) introduced infectious diseases to the Amerindian population and how these diseases caused massive mortality because the local populations lacked childhood immunities to European diseases. Massive die-offs caused economic collapse, famine, and social unrest. European conquest was greatly aided by this native die-off and cultural collapse. In this regard, McNeill has described world history as the "confluence of disease pools," in which populations with a larger number of childhood endemic diseases historically win out over more isolated populations. Recently, Stephen Kunitz (1994) has disputed the universality of such a historical law by demonstrating that the health consequences of initial interactions between aboriginal populations and European colonizers shows much more variation. Finally, epidemics have historically brought social and ethnic tensions to the forefront of social interaction.

■ ***The modern decline in mortality and increase in population growth is primarily the result of socioeconomic changes (affecting hygiene, nutrition, and so forth) and not because of therapeutic inventions of biomedicine.*** Health historians using demographic data have documented a decline in mortality in Europe primarily during the 19th century. The reasons for this improved health are not completely known, but Thomas McKeown (1979) provides convincing evidence that these health improvements historically preceded the development of scientific therapies in modern medicine (see selection 8). He credits public health interventions affecting hygiene, nutrition, and birth spacing as the primary reasons for these improvements. Demographic historians have made significant progress in understanding the role of breast-feeding and birth-spacing patterns on total fertility that also play an important role in population change—most strikingly in the demographic transition from large completed families to small completed families (and the zero population growth that characterized some of the richest countries of the world) (Caldwell 1982).

 7

Health and Disease in Prehistoric Populations in Transition

George J. Armelagos

It is hard for people to know if things are getting better or worse. On the one hand, there is the myth of progress, which claims that technological innovation makes our lives less grueling, healthier, more productive, and happier. On the other hand, there is the myth of the good old days, with people bemoaning crumbling morality, increased misery throughout the world, and backlashes from progress, such as antibiotic-resistant diseases. Perhaps it's a question of personal optimism and pessimism—our individual perception. But aren't there historical facts about this? Isn't it the case that, given the choice to live in the prehistoric past, everyone would choose the comforts of today?

This selection is about the health of populations who undergo rapid historical change, particularly with the domestication of plants and animals during the Neolithic Revolution. The author reviews paleopathological research methods to examine skeletal remains uncovered in archaeological excavations. A variety of infectious diseases leave definitive traces on the bones; some conditions, such as porotic hyperostosis, reflect nutritional anemias in childhood; other markers, such as Harris lines and enamel hypoplasia, resemble the rings in tree trunks that reflect the availability of adequate nutrition in the past.

A large area of concern in bioarchaeology is the cause of population growth. In this selection, George Armelagos considers the effects of sedentary village life on fertility and child mortality.

As you read this selection, consider these questions:

- **In what ways can the domestication of plants and animals be considered the worst mistake or the most important event in human history?**
- **Why is it important for bioarchaeologists and paleopathologists to study disease history and biochemistry as well as anatomy?**
- **Why do you think that family size and fertility would increase when humans changed from hunter-gatherers to farmers?**

Context: George Armelagos and Alan Swedlund are biological anthropologists who have written a great deal about health in prehistoric and historical populations. Armelagos is a paleopathologist who has contributed to the medical anthropological studies of race, emerging infectious disease, and the origins of syphilis. In 2008, he was awarded the prestigious Franz Boas Award for Exemplary Service to Anthropology. Swedlund's work focuses primarily on issues of demography. When this article was written in 1990, controversy was brewing over whether the advent of agriculture always brought about a decrease in health and an increase in population.

Source: G. J. Armelagos (1990). "Health and Disease in Populations in Transition." In Alan Swedlund and George Armelagos (eds.), Diseases in Populations in Transition. Westport, CT: Bergin & Garvey.

The study of disease in prehistory offers a unique opportunity for the anthropologist. Paleopathologists have contributed significantly to our knowledge about the history and geography of numerous pathological conditions. While there is still a vigorous debate concerning the chronology and geographic distribution of diseases such as syphilis, tuberculosis, and rheumatoid arthritis, we know a great deal about their occurrence in many regions. However, paleopathology can potentially provide a broader understanding of the relationship between disease and human populations. For example, the interaction between human populations and the disease process provides information about biocultural adaptation. The cultural system can dramatically influence the disease process, and disease can significantly alter the cultural adaptation.

Populations in transition often experience change in ecological relationships that alter their disease patterns. The paleopathology of prehistoric populations provides a means for examining these changes from an evolutionary perspective. While early human populations subsisted primarily as gatherer-hunters, there was a dramatic shift to primary food production about 10,000 years ago. I will discuss the impact of this shift and subsequent changes on the disease profile of populations undergoing these major transitions.

During the last four million years human disease ecology has changed significantly as a function of changes in the environment, evolution of the species, and cultural adaptation. These processes created different environments for the pathogens and altered their interaction with human populations. There is a substantial literature that describes the evolutionary impact of disease on human populations. These studies (Armelagos 1967; Armelagos and Dewey 1970; Armelagos and McArdle 1975; Cockburn 1971; Boyden 1970; Fenner 1970; Polgar 1964) agree that there has been dramatic change in the pattern of disease and the human response, especially within the last 10,000 years. When gathering and hunting were the sole means of human subsistence (a period lasting from 4,000,000 years ago to the beginning of the Neolithic), population size was small, and density was quite low.

Human population size and density presumably remained quite low throughout the Paleolithic. It is assumed that fertility and mortality rates in these small gathering-hunting populations were balanced and that population growth was low and stable. Controversy continues as to the demographic factors which created this stability. Some demographers argue that gatherer-hunters were at their maximum natural fertility and this was balanced by high mortality. Other demographers argue that gatherer-hunters maintained a stable population with controlled moderate fertility balanced by moderate mortality.

A critical key to resolving this controversy is to understand the demographic changes that occurred during the Neolithic period. The Neolithic not only heralded a major shift in subsistence, it also resulted in a dramatic increase in population size and density. The reasons for this increase are complex. There are those who have argued that the Neolithic economy generated food surpluses which provided the key to population growth. The abundance of food would have led to a better nourished and healthier population with a reduced rate of mortality. Since populations were at their natural maximum fertility, there would have been a rapid increase in population.

While this scenario is appealing in its simplicity, the empirical evidence paints a different picture. The biological consequence of the shift from gathering and hunting to agriculture presents a much bleaker picture of health and disease. Instead of experiencing improved health, there is evidence of an increase in infectious and nutritional disease.

DISEASE IN GATHERER-HUNTERS

A consideration of the disease ecology of contemporary gatherer-hunters provides insights into the types of disease that would have affected our gatherer-hunter ancestors. Polgar (1964) suggests that gatherer-hunters would have two types of disease to contend with in their adaptation to their environment. One class of disease would be those organisms that had adapted to prehominid ancestors and persisted with them as they evolved into hominids. Head and body lice (*Pediculus humanus*), pinworms, yaws, and possibly malaria would be included in this group. Cockburn (1967b) adds to this list most of the internal protozoa found in modern humans and such bacteria as salmonella, typhi and staphylococci.

Livingstone (1958) dismisses the potential of malaria in early hominids because of the small population size and an adaptation to the savannah, which would not have been within the range of the mosquitos that carry the malaria plasmodium. The second class of diseases is the zoonotics, which have nonhuman animals as their primary host and only incidentally infect humans. Humans can be infected by zoonoses through insect bites, by preparing and eating contaminated flesh, and from wounds inflicted by animals. Sleeping sickness, tetanus, scrub typhus, relapsing fever, trichinosis, tularemia, leptospirosis, and schistosomiasis are among the zoonotic diseases which could have afflicted earlier gatherers and hunters.

The range of the earliest hominids was probably restricted to the tropical savannah. This would have limited the pathogens that were potential disease agents. During the course of human evolution there was eventually an expansion of habitat into the temperate and eventually the tundra zones. As Lambrecht (1964, 1985) points out, the hominids would have avoided large areas of the African landscape because of tsetse flies and thus avoided the trypanosomes they carried.

The evolution of the human species and its expansion into new ecological niches would have led to a change in the pattern of trypanosome infection. While this list of diseases that plagued our gathering-hunting ancestors is informative, those diseases that would have been absent are also of interest. The contagious community diseases such as influenza, measles, mumps, and smallpox would have been missing. Burnet (1962) states that there would have been few viruses infecting these early hominids. On the other hand, Cockburn (1967b), in a well-reasoned argument, suggests that the viral diseases found in non-human primates would have been easily transmitted to humans.

DISEASE IN AGRICULTURAL POPULATIONS IN TRANSITION

Given the limited list of diseases found in gatherer-hunters, it should not have been surprising that a shift to primary food production (agriculture) would increase the number and the impact of disease in sedentary populations. Sedentism would undoubtedly increase parasitic disease spread by contact with human waste. In gathering-hunting groups, the frequent movement of the base camp and frequent forays away from base camp by men and women would decrease their contact with human wastes. In sedentary populations the proximity of habitation area and their waste deposit sites to the water supply would be a source of contamination. While sedentism could and did occur prior to the Neolithic period in those areas with abundant resources (acorns in California and marine resources in the Northwest Coast), the shift to agriculture would necessitate sedentary living.

The herding of animals would also increase the frequency of contact with zoonotic diseases. The domestication of animals in the Neolithic would have provided a steady supply of disease vectors. The zoonotic infections would likely increase because of domesticated animals, such as goats, sheep, cattle, pigs, and fowl. Products of domesticated animals such as milk, hair, and skin, as well as the dust raised by the animals, could transmit anthrax, Q fever, brucellosis, and tuberculosis (Polgar 1964). Breaking the sod during cultivation exposes workers to insect bites and diseases such as scrub typhus (Audy 1961). Livingstone (1958) showed that slash-and-burn agriculture in west Africa exposed populations to *Anopheles gambiae*, a mosquito which is the vector for *Plasmodium falciparum*, which causes malaria.

The development of urban centers is a recent event in human history. In the Near East, cities as large as 50,000 people were established by 3000 B.C. In the New World, urban settlements of half a million were in existence by 500 B.C. Settlements of this size increase the already difficult problem of removing human wastes and delivering uncontaminated water to the people. Cholera, which is transmitted by contaminated water, was a potential problem. Diseases such as typhus (carried by lice) and the plague bacillus (transmitted by fleas or by the respiratory route) could be spread from person to person. Viral diseases such as measles, mumps, chicken pox, and smallpox could be spread in a similar fashion. We had, for the first time, populations which were large enough to maintain disease in an endemic form. Cockburn (1967b) estimates that populations of one million would be necessary to maintain measles as an endemic disease.

There were also social changes and social upheavals, which resulted in a different mode of disease transmission; for example, the crowding of urban centers, changes in sexual practices, such as prostitution, and an increase in sexual promiscuity may have been factors in the venereal transmission of the treponema, the pathogen which causes syphilis (Hudson 1965). The period of urban development can also be characterized by the exploration and expansion into new areas which would result in the introduction of novel diseases to populations that had little resistance to them (McNeill 1976).

The evolutionary picture of infectious disease suggests that agriculturalists faced considerable difficulties. However, there exists a possible paradox that deserves further consideration. Zoonotic diseases in gatherer-hunters would likely have the greatest impact on the segment of the society that contains the producers (those between age 20 and 40). This segment, in its daily rounds, is more likely to come into contact with the animals that are the vector of disease. As Lambrecht (1985: 642) points out, exposure to fly bites is unavoidable in tsetse fly country. The degree of exposure to fly bites is influenced by the choice of habitat and the behavior of the potential host. He writes, "In many areas, Rhodesian sleeping sickness is significantly higher in men than women. This is related to men's activity such as hunting and honey collecting which brings them in close contact with *morsitans* savanna flies, major vector of *T. b. rhodesiense.*" The infection is called "honey collector's disease" by the native groups.

The occurrence of endemic diseases in larger urban agriculturalist areas would most likely kill the very young infants, young children, and the very old adults. In this situation, the predictability of mortality allows them to reduce birth spacing to meet the increase in mortality. Sedentary societies can wean infants earlier, allowing the women to become pregnant again. The social costs of disruption from this pattern of endemic disease mortality may not be as great as the impact of zoonotic diseases on the gatherer-hunters. Even the energetic costs of endemic diseases that are fatal would not be as great. Infants require relatively little energetic investment when compared to older children and young adults. Those who do survive (because of acquired immunity) will be protected from these pathogens. The protected producers segment would be able to reproduce and continue to extract the resources essential for survival.

The process of industrialization, which began a little over 200 years ago, would lead to an even greater environmental and social transformation. City dwellers would have to contend with industrial wastes and polluted water and air. Slums that rise in industrial cities become the focal point for poverty and the spread of disease. Epidemics of smallpox, typhus, typhoid, diphtheria, measles, and yellow fever in urban settings are well documented (Polgar 1964). Tuberculosis and respiratory diseases such as pneumonia and bronchitis are even more serious problems with harsh working situations and crowded living conditions.

In the modern era, there are organized public health and medical practices to control infectious diseases in many western societies. Yet, in many of the developing nations, infectious diseases still extract a great toll on human life. Even with public health and medical advances, nations such as the United States experience new outbreaks of infectious disease which they find very threatening. The current AIDS epidemic generates great fear among the public.

The above discussion has focused our concerns on the ecology of disease in these populations in transition. The issue of the biological response of the host and pathogen remains. It has been assumed that the pathogen–host interaction would result in a decrease in the virulence of the pathogen and an increase in the resistance of the host. The short generation time of the pathogens makes it possible for them to evolve mechanisms which decrease their pathogenicity. This evolutionary strategy would be effective if the virulence of the pathogen threatened the extinction of the host. A dead host is of little value in maintaining the reproductive potential of the pathogen.

The potential response of the human host is still an open question. It is often assumed that human populations have developed genetic resistance to disease. For example, generalized host factors and highly specific genetically determined resistance factors (r) would have evolved (Motulsky 1963). The development of resistance factors (r) is assumed but difficult to demonstrate. Since the interaction of the endemic pathogen and the human host is quite recent in evolutionary terms, there is a question of the potential for a human genetic response to have evolved. The 5,000 years since the development of large urban centers may not have been an adequate time for evolution to occur. However, according to Lederberg (1963), it is possible that the human host–pathogen contact may have preceded the Neolithic period. He suggests that during the Paleolithic period, animals may have acted as a reservoir for diseases. If there had been intense and continuing contact between the human population and the animals, then a potential for humans to develop a genetic response to diseases would have existed.

NUTRITIONAL DEFICIENCY AND THE ORIGIN OF AGRICULTURE

The evidence suggesting that nutritional problems plagued Neolithic groups is more surprising. It would seem that agriculturalists could control their food supply by generating surpluses. Even though there is the potential of periodic famines and blight, the surpluses should be theoretically able to buffer the society through these critical periods.

The nutritional difficulties of agriculturalists may be more problematical. Periodic famines have been and remain a problem. Hollingsworth (1973) has documented thousands of famines that occurred during the historical period. Presently, vast areas of Africa are experiencing famines that are extracting a toll on the populations. It is estimated that a million people will die during a single year.

Even without the occurrence of famine or blight nutritional deficiencies can result from the intensification of agricultural production. The intensification of agriculture through irrigation often leads to a reliance on cereal grains. Diets which rely on cereal grains can be deficient in essential nutrients. Maize, for example, is deficient in the essential amino acid lysine. Other cereal grains contain phytates which combine with important minerals decreasing their bioavailablility.

The development of social classes within Neolithic societies also has nutritional implications. Since class, by definition, reflects differences in the access to resources, there is the probability that there will be individuals within the society who are not receiving adequate nutrition.

THE EVIDENCE FROM SKELETAL REMAINS: DEAD MEN (AND WOMEN) DO TELL TALES

The response of the human skeleton to normal and abnormal growth is deceptively simple. Bone is limited to a process by which osteons (the building unit of bone) can be deposited or they can be resorbed—or they can combine these processes in response to a stimulus.

An individual who weighs 160 pounds will have a skeleton comprised of 206 bones the sum weighing about thirty pounds. These thirty pounds of bones, which are composed of about twenty-two pounds of calcium, two pounds of water, seven pounds of organic matter, and a few ounces of major, minor, and trace minerals, are responsible for supporting our muscle structure, protecting vital organs such as the brain and the eyes, producing red blood cells, and maintaining chemical balance in the body.

Many diseases leave their mark on bone, and these marks can be used to diagnose disease occurrence. Tuberculosis, syphilis, and leprosy have skeletal "signatures" which aid in their diagnosis. In severe cases of tuberculosis, for example, there is often a collapse of the vertebral body and frequently resorptive lesions in other parts of the skeleton which are diagnostic.

Many pathogens leave only generalized changes in the skeleton. For example, we often find a periosteal reaction that reflects a pathogenic change to a number of organisms. These nonspecific lesions (periosteal reactions) are confined to the outer layer of bone and show a roughened appearance caused by the inflammatory process. The periosteal reaction occurs when the fibrous outer layer is stretched and subperiosteal hemorrhages occur. Micro-organisms such as staphylococcus and streptococcus and other pathogens can cause these changes. Unfortunately, there are many pathogens (viruses) that leave no evidence on bone. These viruses can cause an illness and even death without any skeletal response.

Nutritional deficiencies can also leave specific lesions which are easily diagnosed from bone. Deficiencies of vitamin D (rickets) result in a constellation of characteristics that are very distinct. Similarly, vitamin C deficiency (scurvy) leaves unique changes but these are more difficult to diagnose in prehistoric remains.

A major breakthrough in analyzing nutritional disease resulted from a movement away from using single indicators of stress to an approach that considers multiple indicators which are systematically analyzed to provide an understanding of nutritional disease stress. For example, there are a number of lesions such as porotic hyperostosis, defects in enamel development, and premature bone loss that, when coupled with evidence of growth retardation, can provide clues to a pattern of nutritional deficiency.

Porotic hyperostosis, which potentially occurs on the cranium and the roof of the eye orbits, can be used to diagnose iron deficiency anemia. The lesion, as the name implies, has a very porous, coral-like appearance, which develops when diploe (the trabecular portion of the cranial bone that separates the inner and outer surfaces) expands. Then the outer layer of bone becomes thinner and may eventually disappear, exposing the trabecular bone (diploe) which is quite porous. The expansion of the diploe can be caused by any anemia that stimulates red blood cell production. While there are a number of anemias (sickle cell anemia, thalassemia, iron deficiency) that can cause these changes, the relatively minor manifestation of the lesion on the cranial surface and roof of the orbits and its high frequency in children between ages one and three and in young adult females would suggest iron deficiency anemia as the most likely cause.

In conjunction with the analysis of porotic hyperostosis, other stress indicators such as a decrease in long bone growth may provide information about the individual's physiological state. Since we are by necessity using cross-sectional data, comparisons with longitudinal growth studies are very difficult. Growth patterns are determined by averaging long bone lengths of individuals whose developmental age is determined by tooth eruption patterns. These lengths are then compared to standards that exist for living populations. There are few growth standards from peasant agriculturalists, and it is often necessary to use growth standards developed from well-nourished children from the United States. Even with these difficulties, we can often see indications of growth retardation. However, internal comparison of populations experiencing shifts in subsistence may be the most useful method for understanding the impact of these changes on growth.

Recently, histological techniques have provided additional tools for analyzing the impact of nutritional deficiencies on bone growth and maintenance. Microscopic analysis of cross-sections of femora reveal that some children have very thin cortical bone. By examining the percentage of cortical bone for each individual and comparing it with an age-matched sample, we can determine those individuals experiencing nutritional difficulties. It is even possible to ascertain if the bone loss is the result of a lack of osteonal deposition or an increase in bone resorption.

Finally, two additional methods can be used to determine disruption of normal growth and development. Harris lines (lines of increased radiopaque density) found by radiographic analysis have been used as an indicator of growth arresting and recovery. Recent research suggests that Harris lines are more likely to be evidence of recovery and therefore can be used to assess the ability of the individual to respond to stress.

The Harris lines can also be used to assess the age at which an individual experienced growth disruption and subsequent recovery. Since growth occurs at both ends of a long bone, the Harris lines will maintain their relative position to the midshaft. If a researcher knows the relative growth rates of the proximal and distal portion of the long bone, then the age at which a line developed can be estimated.

The analysis of defects in dental enamel is another measure of growth disruption. Dental enamel hypoplasia is a deficiency in enamel thickness that results from a disruption in the formation of the matrix. Enamel defects can result from systemic disruption, hereditary conditions, or localized trauma. Since systemic disruption is likely to affect more than one tooth, we use the occurrence on multiple teeth as the criteria for assessing a systemic cause. Unlike bone, once enamel matures it cannot be remodeled. Enamel is secreted in a regular ringlike pattern, and the crown development provides a permanent chronological record of any physiological disruption. An understanding of rates of enamel formation allows one to define the time in development at which the metabolic disruption occurred.

There are two ways in which the chronological distribution can be used. First, we can examine the chronological pattern of hypoplasia in adults to see the age at which they were exposed to physiological disruption. Second, we can evaluate the impact of this disruption on other aspects of their morbidity and mortality. Do adults who were stressed as children suffer from other insults, and do they live as long as those who were not stressed?

Trauma is another insult that provides information on the adaptation of the group. The location of the callus formation which results from the healing of the fracture provides clues to their cause. For example, fractures of the bones of the forearm (the radius and ulna) at the midshaft usually result from raising the arm to parry or ward off a blow. These fractures, called "parry fractures," are a good index of strife in a population. When individuals extend an arm to break a fall, however, they frequently fracture the bones of the forearm at the wrist. These fractures, "Colles and Potts" fractures, are indices of klutziness.

DICKSON MOUNDS: A PREHISTORIC POPULATION IN TRANSITION

The change in subsistence from 900 to 1250 A.D. at the Dickson Mounds, Illinois, was profound. In the period from 900 A.D. to 1175 A.D., there was a shift from a Late Woodland adaptation, which can be characterized as a general gathering-hunting strategy, to one which emphasized agriculture. The latter phase of this development (Mississippian Acculturated Late Woodland) was a period in which maize agriculture became established at Dickson Mounds.

From 1175 to 1250 A.D. there was an intensification of agriculture in what has been called the Middle Mississippian period. When these earlier groups from Dickson Mounds are compared to the Middle Mississippian people, there is evidence of a remarkable deterioration of health. In this short period there was a fourfold increase in iron deficiency anemia (porotic hyperostosis) and a threefold increase in infectious disease (periosteal reaction) (see Table 1). The frequency of individuals with both iron deficiency and infectious lesions increases from 6 percent in the Late Woodland period to 40 percent in the Middle Mississippian period. Furthermore, individuals with both conditions display a synergistic disease interaction (Lallo et al. 1977; Lallo et al. 1978), that is, they experience more severe manifestation of each condition.

The relationship of infection and anemia in children can be ascertained by examining the age of onset and distribution of the lesions by age. The infectious lesion in children under ten years of age peaks during the first year while the anemia shows its highest frequency during the second and third year. This pattern

TABLE 1 Frequency of Infectious Lesions (Periostitis and Osteomyelitis) and Porotic Hyperostosis

		Postcranial Infectious Lesions		Porotic Hyperostosis		Porotic Hyperstosis and Infectious Lesions	
Dickson Population	*N*	*N*	*%*	*N*	*%*	*N*	*%*
Late Woodland	44	9	20.5	6	13.6	3	6.5
Mississippian Acculturated Late Woodland	93	45	48.4	29	31.2	20	21.5
Middle Mississippian	101	74	73.3	52	51.5	41	40.6
Total	238	128	53.8	87	36.5	64	26.9

Source: Huss-Ashmore, Goodman, and Armelagos (1982).

suggests that individuals who do survive the infectious pathogen may have problems in maintaining adequate iron reserves. The exposure to the pathogens that are the consumers of iron and iron deficiencies due to nutritional intake are the most likely explanation of this pattern. The biological cost of infection and anemia can be determined from an analysis of a life expectancy constructed for individuals who died before their tenth year (Figure 1). It is apparent that individuals with infections show a dramatic decrease in life expectancy. Those children in the group with periosteal lesions at birth can be expected to live less than a year. Even those suffering from iron deficiency display a decrease in life expectancy of up to six months at each age group.

The impact of the shift to agriculture at Dickson Mounds can be seen in other aspects of growth and development. There is evidence of delayed growth in the long bone length and circumference of Mississippian children from their fifth through fifteenth year (Goodman et al. 1984).

The frequency and the chronology of hypoplastic defects in the dental enamel of the Dickson Mounds population supports the argument that the shift to agriculture had deleterious effects on the health of the group. There is an increase in hypoplasia from 0.90 defects per individual (Late Woodland) to 1.61 per individual in the Middle Mississippian period. The proportion of individuals with one or more hypoplasias increases from 45 percent to 80 percent during the same period (Goodman et al. 1984). Since the chronological development of the enamel is well understood, it is possible to determine the age at which the hypoplasias occurred during the life of the individual. The hypoplastic lines in adults provide "metabolic memory" of events which occurred during their childhood.

The chronology of enamel hypoplasia shows that the Dickson Mounds population experienced peak stress between the ages of two and four, which corresponds to the period of weaning. The pattern of porotic hyperostosis in this population occurs at about the same phase of development. The comparison of the chronology between the earlier groups and the intensive agriculturalists at Dickson Mounds (Figure 2) shows an earlier age of onset of hypoplasia, suggesting an earlier age of weaning.

Enamel hypoplasia is considered a relatively benign pathology. However, Goodman and Armelagos (1988) have calculated the mean age at death for those with and without hypoplasias and find significant differences. Individuals with no lesions have a mean age at death five years greater than individuals with one hypoplasia and nine years greater than individuals with two or more hypoplastic episodes (Figure 3).

Two hypotheses have been proposed to explain the difference in mean age at death. The first suggests that those with hypoplasia represent a group of individuals who were challenged by the insult early in their lifetime and continued to be subjected to insults during the rest of their lives. This increased "wear-and tear" throughout their lives leads to an earlier death. Another hypothesis suggests that major insults occur at a critical period of immunological development. Individuals experiencing severe stress during the development of their immunological system may irreparably damage their ability to fight

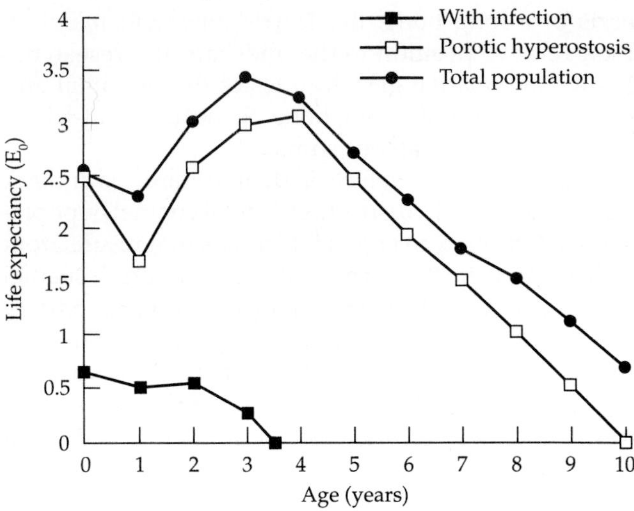

FIGURE 1 Life Expectancy for the Dickson Mounds Population for Those Dying Within the First Ten Years.
(Source: Huss-Ashmore, Goodman, and Armelagos [1982].)

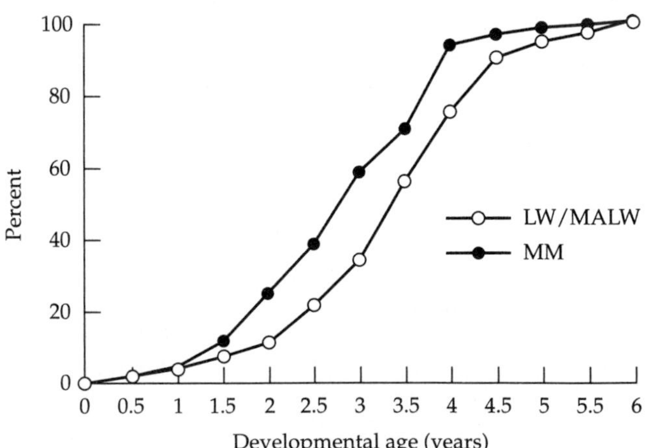

Key: LW = Late Woodland
MALW = Mississippian Acculturated Late Woodland
MM = Middle Mississippian

FIGURE 2 The Cumulative Frequency of Enamal Hypoplasias in Two Dickson Mounds Populations.
(Source: Goodman, and Armelagos, and Rose [1984].)

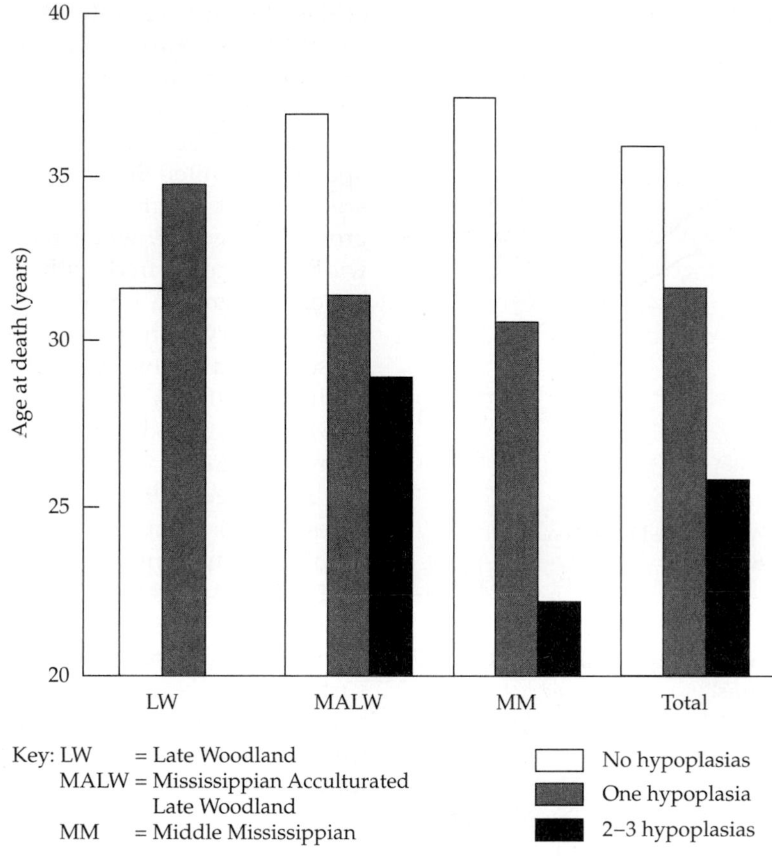

FIGURE 3 Mean Ages at Death of Dickson Mounds Adolescent/Adults by Number of Hypoplasias-Stress Periods Between 3.5–7.0 Years Development Age. *(Source: Goodman and Armelagos [1988].)*

infection throughout their lifetime. The "damaged goods" hypothesis suggests that significant thymolymphatic growth, which is essential for developing effective immunological competence, occurs prenatally, in infancy and early childhood.

Clark (1985) and co-workers (Clark et al. 1986) use the growth of the vertebral column to offer support to the "damaged goods" hypothesis. The size of the vertebral neural canal (VNC) is a good measure of childhood growth. The VNC is completed in childhood and is not subjected to catch-up growth. Since the VNC is growing during the phase of the neurological (of which it is a part) and the thymolymphatic development, it may reflect disruptions that occur during this period which affect immunological development. Multivariate, bivariate, and nonparemetric analyses show that small VNC are associated with greater vertebral wedging (a measure of morbidity) and decreased mean age at death (Clark et al. 1986).

The impact of multiple stressors affected the mortality pattern of the Dickson Mounds population. Change in the mortality profile is the final measure of the biological cost of the shift to agriculture at Dickson Mounds. A comparison of life expectancy (Figure 4) shows a decrease in life expectancy at all ages for the intensive agriculturalists.

In summary, the population at Dickson Mounds suffered biologically from the shift to intensive agriculture. The success of the cultural system occurred at the expense of individuals and the population. The ability to reduce birth spacing allowed the population not only to meet the increase in mortality but also to meet the increased labor needs for intensifying agriculture. But there was an increase in nutritional and infectious disease load that affected all segments of the population but especially women, infants, and children.

SUDANESE NUBIA: AGRICULTURAL INTENSIFICATION AND DISEASE

The archaeological record for the Wadi Halfa area of Sudanese Nubia is remarkably complete. There are

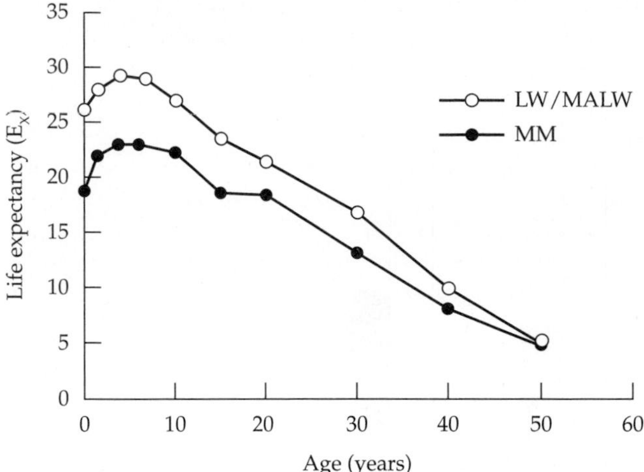

Key: LW = Late Woodland
MALW = Mississippian Acculturated Late Woodland
MM = Middle Mississippian

FIGURE 4 Comparison of Life Expectancies for Two Dickson Mounds Populations. *(Source: Goodman et al. [1984]. Reprinted by permission.)*

biological remains which date back to the Mesolithic period. Although the critical material from the earliest agriculturalists is not available, there are two series of populations which reflect a less intensive (A-Group and G-Group) and a more intensive agricultural adaptation (Meroitic, X-Group, and Christians). These samples provide a wealth of data for understanding the impact of change in subsistence.

Populations from the Meriotic (350 A.D.), X-Group (350–550 A.D.) and Christian (550–1300 A.D.) periods show a pattern of pathology similar to that at the Dickson Mounds. There is, for example, similarity in the distribution of porotic hyperostosis (iron deficiency anemia) in which the children between two and six years of age and young adult females are affected. A significant difference did exist in frequency of infectious disease in the Nubian population. The frequency of periosteal reaction was much lower. This surprising finding can be explained by the consumption of a broad spectrum antibiotic. The Nubians ingested tetracycline (Basset et al. 1981) produced by mold-like bacteria (*Streptomycetes*) which contaminated the grain. The contaminated grain may have been brewed into beer that provided them with therapeutic doses of the antibiotic, a serendipitous factor in controlling infectious diseases which affect bones.

Growth retardation in the Nubians is extremely difficult to demonstrate from the cross-sectional data (Armelagos et al. 1972). Since we are not able to follow the growth of individuals during the various phases of their lifetime, we rely on averaging the long bone lengths for the various developmental ages and infer growth pattern from these data. Long bone length and widths fail to show any definitive evidence of growth retardation. The comparison with standards developed from United States data shows that the Nubians are smaller but are experiencing similar patterns of growth. However, when the long bone lengths and widths are compared with the thickness of cortical bone, problems in growth become evident. The cortices are very thin and are equivalent to the thicknesses found in two-year-old children. Microscopic analysis confirms this observation. Huss-Ashmore (1981) finds that the premature osteoporosis results from an increase in intercortical resorption. Martin and Armelagos (1979) show that young adult women (ages 19–25) from this same population also have problems maintaining cortical bone. There is a significant increase in rates of endosteal resorption (when compared to males of the same age). While these women are able to form osteons on their periosteal surface, there is no indication that these osteons are being mineralized. Instead, the resorption of osteons from the endosteal surface is the source for calcium for the lactating women.

THE TEST: PREHISTORIC POPULATIONS IN TRANSITION

These two case studies do not prove that a shift to agriculture will always result in a deterioration of health. There is other evidence that provides information to further test this hypothesis. In *Paleopathology at the Origins of Agriculture* (Cohen and Armelagos 1984a), there are seventeen case studies (in addition to the Nubian and Dickson Mounds examples) that examine the impact of subsistence change on the health of both New World and Old World populations. In general, the shift to a sedentary habitation pattern (with or without agriculture) may have triggered the most significant changes in disease profile. As expected, the sedentary populations show a dramatic shift in infectious diseases. The increased contact between individuals and close contact with human wastes which contaminate the environment are undoubtedly the major causes of this change in disease pattern.

Twelve of the case studies published in *Paleopathology at the Origins of Agriculture* (Cohen and Armelagos 1984a), for which observations on the pattern of infectious disease were available, show an increase in infections in the agricultural groups when compared with the gatherer-hunters. This increase is due to the increase in sedentism, the increase in population size, and the synergism between malnutrition and infection (Cohen and Armelagos 1984b). One study records a decrease in infections from the gathering-hunting to the early farming period, with an increase as agriculture became intensified (Norr 1984).

The same sample demonstrates that the intensification of agriculture consistently led to poorer nutrition as evidenced by the occurrence of porotic hyperostosis (an indicator of iron deficiency anemia). In sixteen groups where data are available, twelve show an increase with the intensification of agriculture.

CONCLUSIONS

1. The small population size of Paleolithic gatherer-hunters made contagious or infectious disease a relatively minor problem for these earlier groups.

2. The impact of zoonotic diseases may have presented more of a problem to gatherer-hunters because of the greater impact of disease on the producer segment of the population. In small populations an increase in mortality among the producers would be potentially more socially and economically disruptive.

3. The transition to sedentism among gatherer-hunters with a stable and abundant food supply and among early agriculturalists potentially represents a new ecological setting. Population and pathogens are placed in new relationships that can result in an increase in parasitic and infectious diseases.

4. Beyond the problems associated with sedentism, the transition to agriculture increases the potential problems with infectious diseases. The increase in population size and density will increase the possibility of infectious disease transmission.

5. Although primary food production can generate surpluses, there is a potential for nutritional deficiencies from blight, drought, and the reliance on single crops which may be deficient in essential nutrients.

6. Agricultural populations which experienced an increase in nutritional and infectious disease were able to increase their population size. The predictability of mortality in these sedentary populations (deaths of the very young and very old) and a producer segment of the population with acquired immunity to disease may have been able to respond to the increase in mortality. The population size can be maintained or increased by decreasing the birth spacing. Furthermore, the acquired immunity of those who survive these childhood diseases may act to protect the producer segment of the population and thus make infectious disease socially less disruptive.

7. The rise of population in urban centers was relatively late in human history. In the Old World, preindustrial urban centers developed only 5,000 years ago and 2,400 years ago in the New World. This suggests that human populations have been exposed to endemic diseases for a relatively short time in evolutionary terms. For this reason, specific genetic adaptation to specific pathogens is unlikely. The development of a generalized physiological response is more likely than the evolution of a specific genetic response.

8. Lederberg (1963) argues that a genetic response may have occurred earlier than the post-Neolithic period. He claims that a specific genetic response may have evolved in situations in which humans and animals develop an intense and long-term interaction. In that situation the animals could act as reservoirs for pathogens and repeatedly infect humans.

9. In the last 10,000 years, Homo sapiens has experienced a number of periods of rapid transition that have had a dramatic impact on health and disease patterns. The shift to a Neolithic economy that relied on primary food production, the development of urban centers, the Industrial Revolution, and the development of rapid long distance travel changed the pattern of disease in human populations. The interaction of pathogens and people has been influential in shaping our biology and culture.

REFERENCES

Armelagos, G. J. 1967. Man's changing environment. In *Infectious Diseases: Their Evolution and Eradication.* T. A. Cockburn, ed. Springfield, Ill.: Charles C. Thomas.

Armelagos, G. J., and J. Dewey. 1970. Evolutionary response to human infectious disease. *Bioscience* 20(5):271–75.

Armelagos, G. J., and A. McArdle. 1975. Population, disease, and evolution. In *Population Studies in Archaeology and Biological Anthropology: A Symposium.* A. C. Swedlund, ed. *Memoir of the Society of American Archaeology,* No. 30.

Armelagos, G. J., J. H. Mielke, K. H. Owen, D. P. Van Gerven, J. R. Dewey, and P. E. Mahler. 1972. Bone growth and development in prehistoric populations from Sudanese Nubia. *Journal of Human Evolution* 1:89–119.

Audy, J. R. 1961. The ecology of scrub typhus. In *Studies in Disease Ecology.* J. M. May, ed. New York: Hafner.

Basset, E., Margaret Keith, George J. Armelagos, Debra L. Martin, and A. Villanueva. 1981. Tetracycline-labeled human bone from prehistoric Sudanese Nubia (A.D. 350). *Science* 209:1532–34.

Boyden, S. V. 1970. *The Impact of Civilization on the Biology of Man.* Toronto: University of Toronto Press.

Burner, F. M. 1962. *Natural History of Infectious Disease.* Cambridge: Cambridge University Press.

Clark, G. A. 1985. Hetrochrony, allometry and canalization in the human vertebral column: Examples from prehistoric American populations. Ph.D diss., University of Massachusetts, Amherst.

Clark, G. A., N. R. Hall, G. J. Armelagos, G. A. Borkan, M. M. Panjabi, and G. T Wetzel. 1986. Poor growth prior to early childhood: Decreased health and life-span in the adult. *American Journal of Physical Anthropology* 70:145–60.

Cockburn, T. A. 1971. Infectious disease in ancient populations. *Current Anthropology* 12(1):45–62.

———. 1967a. Infections of the order primates. In *Infectious Diseases: Their Evolution and Eradication.* T. A. Cockburn, ed. Springfield, Ill: Charles C. Thomas.

———. 1967b. The evolution of human infectious diseases. In *Infectious Diseases: Their Evolution and Eradication.* T. A. Cockburn, ed. Springfield, Ill.: Charles C. Thomas.

Cohen, M. N., and G. J. Armelagos, eds. 1984a. *Paleopathology at the Origins of Agriculture.* Orlando: Academic Press.

———. 1984b. Paleopathology at the origins of agriculture: Editors' summation. In *Paleopathology at the Origins of Agriculture.* M. N. Cohen and G. J. Armelagos, eds. Orlando: Academic Press.

Fenner, F. 1970. The effects of changing social organization on the infectious diseases of man. In *The Impact of Civilization on the Biology of Man.* S. V. Boyden, ed. Canberra: Australia National University Press.

Goodman, A. H., and G. J. Armelagos. 1988. Childhood stress, cultural buffering, and decreased longevity in a prehistoric population. *American Anthropologist* 90:936–44.

Goodman, A. H., G. J. Armelagos, and J. C. Rose. 1984. The chronological distribution of enamel hypoplasia from prehistoric Dickson Mounds. *American Journal of Physical Anthropology* 65:259–266.

Goodman, A. H., J. Lallo, G. J. Armelagos, and J. Rose. 1984. Health changes at Dickson Mounds, Illinois (A.D. 950–1300). In *Paleopathology at the Origins of Agriculture.* M. N. Cohen and G. J. Armelagos, eds. Orlando: Academic Press.

Goodman, A. H., D. L. Martin, and G. J. Armelagos. 1984. Indications of stress from bone and teeth. In *Paleopathology at the Origins of Agriculture.* M. N. Cohen and G. J. Armelagos, eds. Orlando: Academic Press.

Haldane, J. B. S. 1949. Disease and evolution. Supplement to *La Ricerca Scientifica* 19:68–76.

Hollingsworth, T. H. 1973. Population crises in the past. In *Resources and Population.* B. Cox and J. Peel, eds. New York: Academic Press.

Hudson, E. H. 1965. Treponematosis and man's social evolution. *American Anthropologist* 67:885–901.

Huss-Ashmore, R. 1981. Bone growth and remodeling as a measure of nutritional stress. In *Biocultural Adaptation: Comprehensive Approaches to Skeletal Analysis.* University of Massachusetts, Department of Anthropology, Research Reports No. 20, pp. 84–95.

Huss-Ashmore, R., A. H. Goodman, and G. J. Armelagos. 1982. *Advances in Archaeological Method and Theory,* vol. 5. Orlando: Academic Press.

Lallo, J., G. J. Armelagos, and R. P. Mensforth. 1977. The role of diet, disease and physiology in the origin of porotic hyperostosis. *Human Biology* 40:471–83.

Lallo, J., G. J. Armelagos, and J. C. Rose. 1978. Paleoepidemiology of infectious disease in the Dickson Mounds population. *Medical College of Virginia Quarterly* 14:17–23.

Lambrecht, F. L. 1985. Trypanosomes and hominid evolution. *Bioscience* 35(10):640–46.

———. 1964. Aspects of evolution and ecology of tsetse flies and trypanosomiasis in prehistoric African environments. *Journal of African History* 5:1–24.

Lederberg, J. 1963. Comments on A. Motulsky's "Genetic systems in disease susceptibility in mammals." In *Genetic Selection in Man.* W. J. Schull, ed. Ann Arbor: University of Michigan Press (comments are interspersed with the Motulsky text).

Livingstone, F. B. 1958. Anthropological implications of sickle-cell gene distribution in West Africa. *American Anthropologist* 60:533–62.

McNeill, W. H. 1976. *Plagues and People.* Garden City: Anchor/Doubleday.

Martin, D. L., and G. J. Armelagos. 1979. Morphometrics of compact bone: An example from Sudanese Nubia. *American Journal of Physical Anthropology* 51:571–78.

Motulsky, A. G. 1963. Genetic systems involved in disease susceptibility in mammals. In *Genetic Selection in Man.* W. J. Schull, ed. Ann Arbor: University of Michigan Press.

Norr, L. 1984. Prehistoric subsistence and health status of the Coastal peoples from the Panamanian Isthmus of Lower Central America. In *Paleopathology at the Origins of Agriculture.* M. N. Cohen and G. J. Armelagos, eds. Orlando: Academic Press.

Polgar, S. 1964. Evolution and the ills of mankind. In *Horizons of Anthropology.* S. Tax, ed. Chicago: Aldine.

 8

Determinants of Health

Thomas McKeown

The question of what determines health is very important. If we, as a society, can agree about what causes health, then we should be able to agree on where our financial resources should be placed in order to get the best results from our investment. If there is a single most important lesson to be obtained from studying the history of health, it must be this one.

It turns out, of course, that defining "health" is not as simple as it might first appear. The World Health Organization says that health is not merely the absence of disease but an overall state of physical, mental, and social well-being. You may think such a definition seems utopian. Most scientists and scholars would agree, however, that levels of disease in a population (morbidity) *and the frequency of death at particular ages in a population* (mortality) *represent essential, if gross, measures of health. In other words, improved health is reflected in the decline of mortality.*

We can ask this historical question more specifically: What is the role of medicine in the improvement of health? If by "medicine" we mean biomedical clinical care including modern inventions like x-rays, antibiotics, and immunizations, then it is possible to compare mortality rates before and after significant medical interventions were introduced. This is exactly the topic of Thomas McKeown's famous book. The Role of Medicine: Dream, Mirage, or Nemesis? *(1979), as well as this selection. McKeown demonstrates that the biggest advancements in health occurred* after *specific medical interventions became available. He suggests (but he doesn't have the data to prove this) that more significant factors regarding health improvement involved sanitation, better food, and birth spacing. This argument has been controversial, largely because there is a widespread presumption in our society that improved health in developed countries is due to advances in medical knowledge and the technological and scientific breakthroughs in biomedical science. McKeown disputes this premise.*

Medical anthropologist Stephen Kunitz has done a similar, focused study of historical changes in health status on the Navajo reservation and the impact of improved medical care because of Indian Health Service facilities (1983). His findings suggest that the determinants of health are more complicated than McKeown suggests and that access to medical facilities (in this case, a free health care system) has a measurable although rather small effect. Other influences of the dominant white society—for example, drinking and automobile accidents—are also important factors.

In the end, the study of health history does not hinge on an either/or decision. Solutions to health problems are going to be found not in technology but in the more equitable distribution of adequate food, sanitation, housing, health information, and *medical care services.*

As you read this selection, consider these questions:

- **In the United States today, we spend about 15 percent of our gross national product on health care. What do you think McKeown would say about this expenditure?**
- **Do many people actually believe the presumption that McKeown is arguing against—that modern health improvements are caused by modern medicine? What do your friends think are the determinants of health?**
- **What implications does McKeown's discussion have for combating infectious diseases in the Third World, where they are still a very significant cause of morbidity and mortality?**

Context: Thomas McKeown (1918–1988) was a medical historian at the University of Birmingham. Despite his earlier training in biochemistry and medicine, he became famous for the thesis that the major mortality declines in industrial societies were due to improved living standards rather than biomedical technology. Scholars continue to debate his demographic methodology and the question of whether he focused too much on economic change and nutrition at the expense of other factors such as sanitation, vaccination, or the provision of basic clinical medicine. This controversial thesis also has political and policy ramifications. Nevertheless, the McKeown thesis stands as a major contribution to social medicine and public health.

Source: T. McKeown (1978). "Determinants of Health." Human Nature Magazine. New York: Harcourt Brace.

Modern medicine is not nearly as effective as most people believe. It has not been effective because medical science and service are misdirected and society's investment in health is misused. At the base of this misdirection is a false assumption about human health. Physicians, biochemists, and the general public assume that the body is a machine that can be protected from disease primarily by physical and chemical intervention. This approach, rooted in 17th century science, has led to widespread indifference to the influence of the primary determinants of human health—environment and personal behavior—and emphasizes the role of medical treatment, which is actually less important than either of the others. It has also resulted in the neglect of sick people whose ailments are not within the scope of the sort of therapy that interests the medical professions.

An appraisal of influences on health in the past suggests that the contribution of modern medicine to the increase of life expectancy has been much smaller than most people believe. Health improved, not because of steps taken when we are ill, but because we become ill less often. We remain well, less because of specific measures such as vaccination and immunization than because we enjoy a higher standard of nutrition, we live in a healthier environment, and we have fewer children.

For some 300 years an engineering approach has been dominant in biology and medicine and has provided the basis for the treatment of the sick. A mechanistic concept of nature developed in the 17th century led to the idea that a living organism, like a machine, might be taken apart and reassembled if its structure and function were sufficiently understood. Applied to medicine, this concept meant that understanding the body's response to disease would allow physicians to intervene in the course of disease. The consequences of the engineering approach to medicine are more conspicuous today than they were in the 17th century largely because the resources of the physical and chemical sciences are so much greater. Medical education begins with the study of the structure and function of the body, continues with examination of disease processes, and ends with clinical instruction on selected sick people. Medical service is dominated by the image of the hospital for the acutely ill, where technological resources are concentrated. Medical research also reflects the mechanistic approach, concerning itself with problems such as the chemical basis of inheritance and the immunological response to transplanted tissues.

No one disputes the predominance of the engineering approach in medicine, but we must now ask whether it is seriously deficient as a conceptualization of the problems of human health. To answer this question, we must examine the determinants of human health. We must first discover why health improved in the past and then go on to ascertain the important influences on health today, in the light of the change in health problems that has resulted from the decline of infectious diseases.

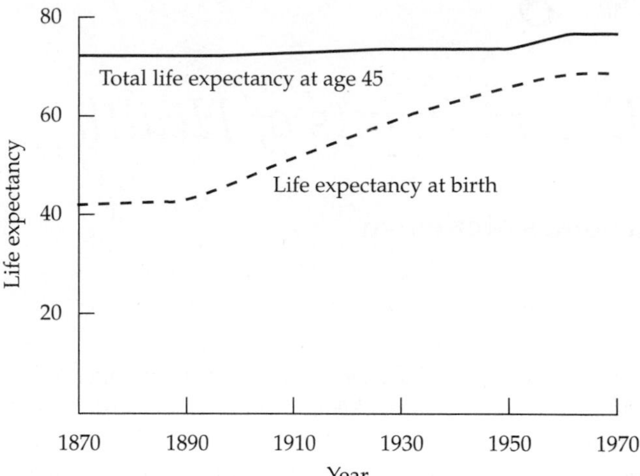

Life Expectancy

It is no exaggeration to say that health, especially the health of infants and young children, has been transformed since the 18th century. For the first time in history, a mother knows it is likely that all her children will live to maturity. Before the 19th century, only about three out of every 10 newborn infants lived beyond the age of 25. Of the seven who died, two or three never reached their first birthday, and five or six died before they were six. Today, in developed countries fewer than one in 20 children die before they reach adulthood.

The increased life expectancy, most evident for young children, is due predominantly to a reduction of deaths from infectious diseases. Records from England and Wales (the earliest national statistics available) show that this reduction was the reason for the improvement in health before 1900 and it remains the main influence to the present day.

But when we try to account for the decline of infections, significant differences of opinion appear. The conventional view attributes the change to an increased understanding of the nature of infectious disease and to the application of that knowledge through better hygiene, immunization, and treatment. This interpretation places particular emphasis on immunization against diseases like smallpox and polio, and on the use of drugs for the treatment of other diseases, such as tuberculosis, meningitis, and pneumonia. These measures, in fact, contributed relatively little to the total reduction of mortality; the

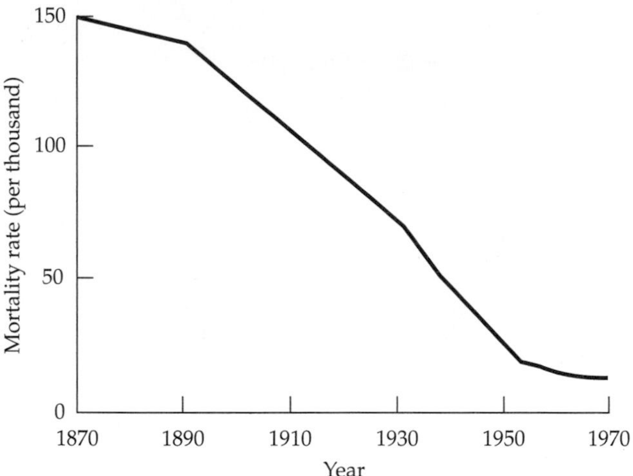

Infant Mortality Rate

main explanation for the dramatic fall in the number of deaths lies not in medical intervention, but elsewhere.

Deaths from the common infections were declining long before effective medical intervention was possible. By 1900, the total death rate had dropped substantially, and over 90 percent of the reduction was due to a decrease of deaths from infectious diseases. The relative importance of the major influences can be illustrated by reference to tuberculosis. Although respiratory tuberculosis was the single largest cause of death in the mid-19th century, mortality from the disease declined continuously after 1838, when it was first registered in England and Wales as a cause of death.

Robert Koch identified the tubercle bacillus in 1882, but none of the treatments used in the 19th or early 20th centuries significantly influenced the course of the disease. The many drugs that were tried were worthless; so, too, was the practice of surgically collapsing an infected lung, a treatment introduced about 1920. Streptomycin, developed in 1947, was the first effective treatment, but by this time mortality from the disease had fallen to a small fraction of its level during 1848 to 1854. Streptomycin lowered the death rate from tuberculosis in England and Wales by about 50 percent, but its contribution to the decrease in the death rate since the early 19th century was only about 3 percent.

Deaths from bronchitis, pneumonia, and influenza also began to decline before medical science provided an effective treatment for these illnesses. Although the death rate in England and Wales increased in the second half of the 19th century, it has fallen continuously since the beginning of the 20th. There is still no effective immunization against bronchitis or pneumonia, and influenza vaccines have had no effect on deaths. The first successful treatment for these respiratory diseases was a sulfa drug introduced in 1938, but mortality attributed to the lung infections was declining from the beginning of the 20th century. There is no reason to doubt that the decline would have continued without effective therapeutic measures, if at a slower rate.

In the United States, the story was similar; Thomas Magill noted that "the rapid decline of pneumonia death rates began in New York State before the turn of the century and many years before the 'miracle drugs' were known." Obviously, drug therapy was not responsible for the total decrease in deaths that occurred since 1938, and it could have had no influence on the substantial reduction that occurred before then.

The histories of most other common infections, such as whooping cough, measles, and scarlet fever, are similar. In each of these diseases, mortality had fallen to a low level before effective immunization or therapy became available.

In some infections, medical intervention *was* valuable before sulfa drugs and antibiotics became available. Immunization protected people against smallpox and tetanus; antitoxin treatment limited deaths from diphtheria; appendicitis, peritonitis, and ear infections responded to surgery; Salvarsan was a long-sought "magic bullet" against syphilis; intravenous therapy saved people with severe diarrheas; and improved obstetric care prevented childbed fever.

But even if such medical measures had been responsible for the whole decline of mortality from these particular conditions after 1900 (and clearly they were not), they would account for only a small part of the decrease in deaths attributed to all infectious diseases before 1935. From that time, powerful drugs came into use and they were supplemented by improved vaccines. But mortality would have continued to fall even without the presence of these agents; and over the whole period since cause of death was first recorded, immunization and treatment have contributed much less than other influences.

The substantial fall in mortality was due in part to reduced contact with microorganisms. In developed countries an individual no longer encounters the cholera bacillus, he is rarely exposed to the typhoid organism, and his contact with the tubercle bacillus is infrequent. The death rate from these infections fell continuously from the second half of the 19th century when basic hygienic measures were introduced: purification of water; efficient sewage disposal; and improved food hygiene, particularly the pasteurization of milk, the item in the diet most likely to spread disease.

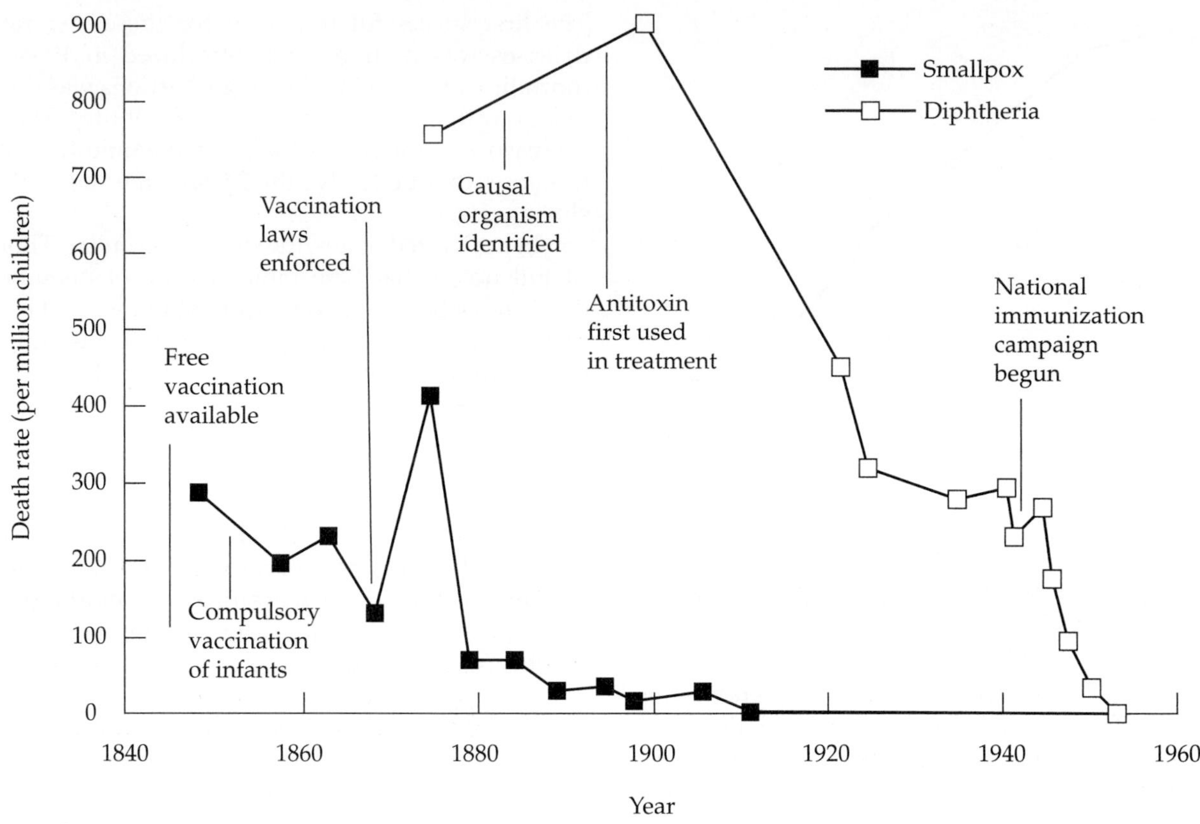

Child Death Rates Reduced by Medicine

Pasteurization was probably the main reason for the decrease in deaths from gastroenteritis and for the decline in infant mortality from about 1900. In the 20th century, these essential hygienic measures were supported by improved conditions in the home, the work place, and the general environment. Over the entire period for which records exist, better hygiene accounts for approximately a fifth of the total reduction of mortality.

But the decline of mortality caused by infections began long before the introduction of sanitary measures. It had already begun in England and Wales by 1838, and statistics from Scandinavia suggest that the death rate had been decreasing there since the first half of the 18th century.

A review of English experience makes it unlikely that reduced exposure to microorganisms contributed significantly to the falling death rate in this earlier period. In England and Wales that was the time of industrialization, characterized by rapid population growth and shifts of people from farms into towns, where living and working conditions were uncontrolled. The crowding and poor hygiene that resulted provided ideal conditions for the multiplication and spread of microorganisms, and the situation improved little before sanitary measures were introduced in the last third of the century.

Another possible explanation for the fall in mortality is that the character of infectious diseases changed because the virulence of microorganisms decreased. This change has been suggested in diseases as different as typhus, tuberculosis, and measles. There is no infection of which it can be said confidently that the relationship between host and parasite has not varied over a specified period. But for the decline of all infections, this explanation is obviously inadequate because it implies that the modern improvement in health was due essentially to a fortuitous change in the nature of the infections, independent of medical and other identifiable influences.

A further explanation for the falling death rate is that an improvement in nutrition led to an increase in resistance to infectious diseases. This is, I believe, the most credible reason for the decline of the infections, at least until the late 19th century, and also explains why deaths from airborne diseases like scarlet fever and measles have decreased even when exposure to the organisms that cause them remains almost unchanged. The evidence demonstrating the impact of improved nutrition is indirect, but it is still impressive.

Lack of food, and the resulting malnutrition were largely responsible for the predominance of the infectious diseases, from the time when men first aggregated in large population groups about 10,000 years

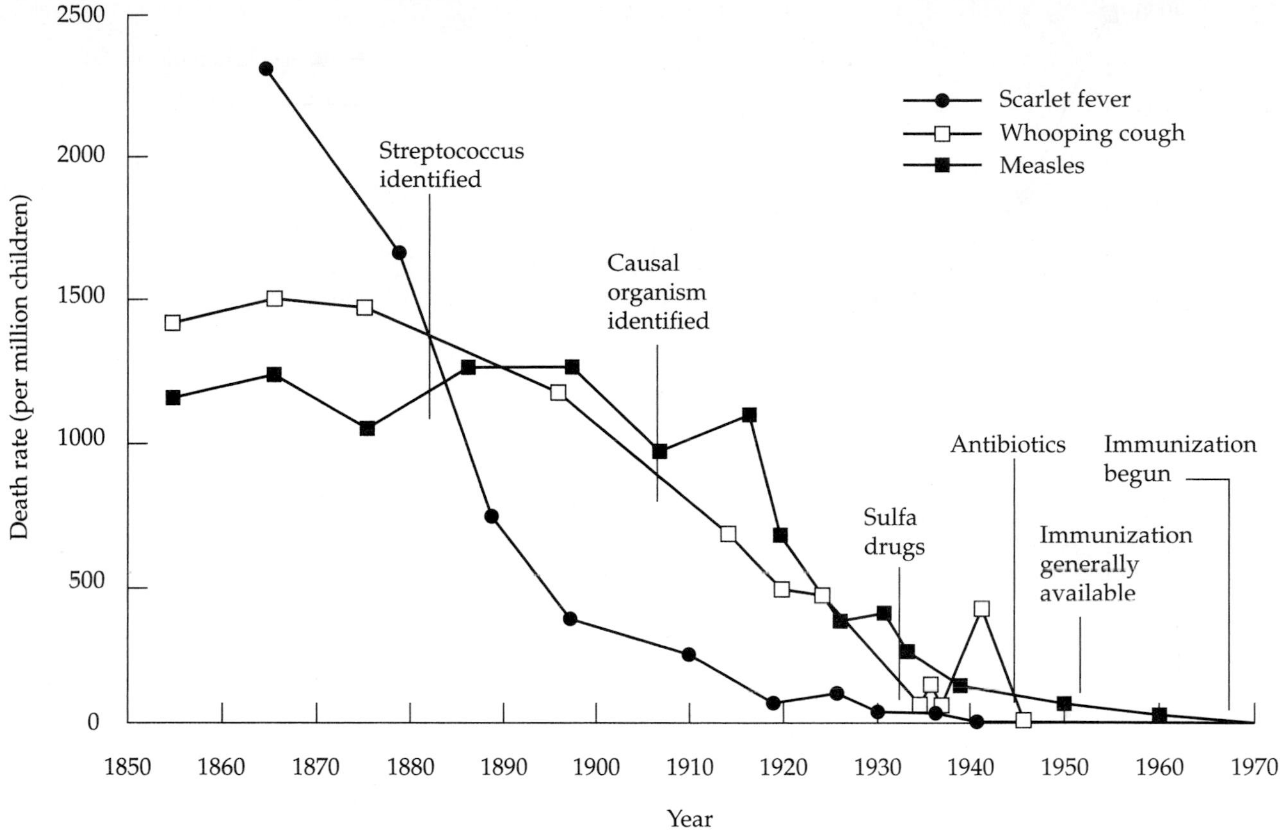

Other Childhood Diseases

ago. In these conditions an improvement in nutrition was necessary for a substantial and prolonged decline in mortality.

Experience in developing countries today leaves no doubt that nutritional state is a critical factor in a person's response to infectious disease, particularly in young children. Malnourished people contract infections more often than those who are well fed and they suffer more when they become infected. According to a recent World Health Organization report on nutrition in developing countries, the best vaccine against common infectious diseases is an adequate diet.

In the 18th and 19th centuries, food production increased greatly throughout the Western world. The number of people in England and Wales tripled between 1700 and 1850 and they were fed on home-grown food.

In summary: The death rate from infectious diseases fell because an increase in food supplies led to better nutrition. From the second half of the 19th century this advance was strongly supported by improved hygiene and safer food and water, which reduced exposure to infection. With the exception of smallpox vaccination, which played a small part in the total decline of mortality, medical procedures such as immunization and therapy had little impact on human health until the 20th century.

One other influence needs to be considered: a change in reproductive behavior, which caused the birth rate to decline. The significance of this change can hardly be exaggerated, for without it the other advances would soon have been overtaken by the increasing population. We can attribute the modern improvement in health to food, hygiene, and medical intervention—in that order of time and importance—but we must recognize that it is to a modification of behavior that we owe the permanence of this improvement.

But it does not follow that these influences have the same relative importance today as in the past. In technologically advanced countries, the decline of infectious diseases was followed by a vast change in health problems, and even in developing countries advances in medical science and technology may have modified the effects of nutrition, sanitation, and contraception. In order to predict the factors likely to affect our health in the future, we need to examine the nature of the problems in health that exist today.

Because today's problems are mainly with non-communicable diseases, physicians have shifted their

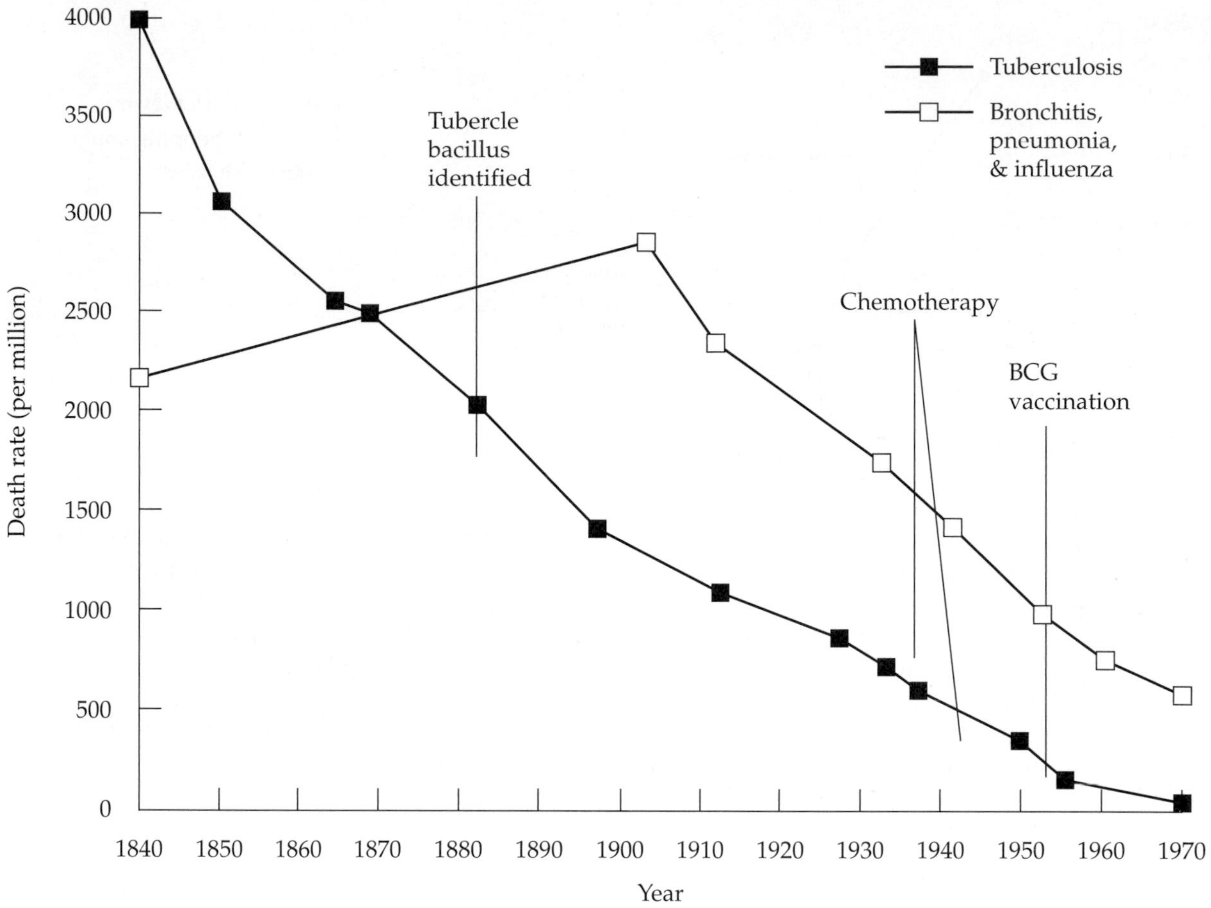

Pulmonary Diseases

approach. In the case of infections, interest centers on the organisms that cause them and on the conditions under which they spread. In noninfective conditions, the engineering approach established in the 17th century remains predominant and attention is focused on how a disease develops rather than on why it begins. Perhaps the most important question now confronting medicine is whether the commonest health problems—heart disease, cancer, rheumatoid arthritis, cerebrovascular disease—are essentially different from health problems of the past or whether, like infections, they can be prevented by modifying the conditions that lead to them.

To answer this question, we must distinguish between genetic and chromosomal diseases determined at the moment of fertilization and all other diseases, which are attributable in greater or lesser degree to the influence of the environment. Most diseases, including the common noninfectious ones, appear to fall into the second category. Whether these diseases can be prevented is likely to be determined by the practicability of controlling the environmental influences that lead to them.

The change in the character of health problems that followed the decline of infections in developed countries has not invalidated the conclusion that most diseases, both physical and mental, are associated with influences that might be controlled. Among such influences, those which the individual determines by his own behavior (smoking, eating, exercise, and the like) are now more important for his health than those that depend mainly on society's actions (provision of essential food and protection from hazards). And both behavioral and environmental influences are more significant than medical care.

The role of individual medical care in preventing sickness and premature death is secondary to that of other influences; yet society's investment in health care is based on the premise that it is the major determinant. It is assumed that we are ill and are made well, but it is nearer the truth to say that we are well and are made ill. Few people think of themselves as having the major responsibility for their own health, and the enormous resources that advanced countries assign to the health field are used mainly to treat disease or, to a lesser extent, to prevent it by personal measures such as immunization.

The revised concept of human health cannot provide immediate solutions for the many complex problems facing society: limiting population growth and providing adequate food in developing countries, changing personal behavior and striking a new balance between technology and care in developed nations. Instead, the enlarged understanding of health and disease should be regarded as a conceptual base with implications for services, education, and research that will take years to develop.

The most immediate requirement in the health services is to give sufficient attention to behavioral influences that are now the main determinants of health. The public believes that health depends primarily on intervention by the doctor and that the essential requirement for health is the early discovery of disease. This concept should be replaced by recognition that disease often cannot be treated effectively, and that health is determined predominantly by the way of life individuals choose to follow. Among the important influences on health are the use of tobacco, the misuse of alcohol and drugs, excessive or unbalanced diets, and lack of exercise. With research, the list of significant behavioral influences will undoubtedly increase, particularly in relation to the prevention of mental illness.

Although the influences of personal behavior are the main determinants of health in developed countries, public action can still accomplish a great deal in the environmental field. Internationally, malnutrition probably remains the most important cause of ill health, and even in affluent societies sections of the population are inadequately, as distinct from unwisely, fed. The malnourished vary in proportion and composition from one country to another, but in the developed world they are mainly the younger children of large families and elderly people who live alone. In light of the importance of food for good health, governments might use supplements and subsidies to put essential foods within the reach of everyone, and provide inducements for people to select beneficial in place of harmful foods. Of course these aims cannot exclude other considerations such as international agreements and the solvency of farmers who have been encouraged to produce meat and dairy products rather than grains. Nevertheless, in future evaluations of agricultural and related economic policies, health implications deserve a primary place.

Perhaps the most sensitive area for consideration is the funding of the health services. Although the contribution of medical intervention to prevention of sickness and premature death can be expected to remain small in relation to behavioral and environmental influences, surgery and drugs are widely regarded as the basis of health and the essence of medical care, and society invests the money it sets aside for health mainly in treatment for acute diseases and particularly in hospitals for the acutely ill. Does it follow from our appraisal that resources should be transferred from acute care to chronic care and to preventive measures?

Restricting the discussion to personal medical care, I believe that neglected areas, such as mental illness, mental retardation, and geriatric care, need greatly increased attention. But to suggest that this can be achieved merely by direct transfer of resources is an oversimplification. The designation "acute care" comprises a wide range of activities that differ profoundly in their effectiveness and efficiency. Some, like surgery for accidents and the treatment of acute emergencies, are among the most important services that medicine can offer and any reduction of their support would be disastrous. Others, however, like coronary care units and iron treatment of some anemias are not shown to be effective, while still others—most tonsillectomies and routine check-ups—are quite useless and should be abandoned. A critical appraisal of medical services for acute illnesses would result in more efficient use of available resources and would free some of them for preventive measures.

What health services need in general is an adjustment in the distribution of interest and resources between prevention of disease, care of the sick who require investigation and treatment, and care of the sick who do not need active intervention. Such an adjustment must pay considerable attention to the major determinants of health: to food and the environment, which will be mainly in the hands of specialists, and to personal behavior, which should be the concern of every practicing doctor.

REFERENCES

Burnet, Macfarlane. *Genes, Dreams and Realities.* Basic Books, 1971.

Cochrane, A. L. *Effectiveness and Efficiency.* Nuffield Provincial Hospitals Trust, 1972.

Dubos, Rene. *Mirage of Health.* Harper & Row, Publishers, 1971.

McKeown, Thomas. *The Modern Rise of Population.* Academic Press, 1977.

McKeown, Thomas. *The Role of Medicine: "Dream, Mirage or Nemesis?* Nuffield Provincial Hospitals Trust, 1976.

Thomas, Lewis. *The Lives of a Cell: Notes of a Biology Watcher.* Viking Press, 1974.

Cultural and Political Ecologies of Disease

CONCEPTUAL TOOLS

■ ***What is disease?*** From an ecological perspective, disease does not exist as a thing in and of itself. *Disease* is a process that is triggered by the interaction between a host and an environmental insult, often a pathogenic organism or germ. Disease is one possible outcome of the relationship between the host and the potential pathogen. Since the advent of bacteriology and germ theory, it has been recognized that infection is a necessary but not sufficient condition for disease to occur. For tuberculosis, for example, this principle has been recognized since the work of the turn-of-the-century bacteriologist Robert Koch. Normal, healthy individuals typically harbor many different colonies of viruses and bacteria that are not pathogenic (i.e., disease-producing), primarily because these agents are held in check by the human immune system. Indeed, individuals are constantly being challenged by microorganisms in their environment (Burnet and White 1978). Disease only occurs when the host's immunological system is unable to keep pace with the reproduction of the pathogen—a process that is affected by age and that can be accelerated through malnutrition, co-infection, or immunosuppression.

■ ***What is ecology?*** *Ecology* is the study of the relationship between a species and its total environment. Most often considered a subfield of biology, ecology deals with the interactions of organisms and their environments with the population, community, and ecosystem levels of organization (Moran 1990). Integral to most ecological studies is the idea that the complex set of interactions among organisms in an ecological niche (territory) makes up a system. This ecosystem includes not only natural resources (e.g., water, minerals) but also plants, animals, and humans. Two of the assumptions of this model are that the ecosystem is maintained through mutually dependent interactions among members of the system and that the common goal of the various species in the system is homeostasis. The primary benefit of homeostatic balance is the prevention of environmental degradation and thus mutual survival. In this view, human activities, such as agriculture, create imbalances in natural ecosystems.

Humans are capable not only of ecological change but also of ecological destruction. There is no doubt that humans have often been responsible for radical changes in their environment and that such ecological changes have had negative effects on health (e.g., the impact of the construction of dams on the prevalence of schistosomiasis).

■ ***What are adaptation and maladaptation?*** Adaptation is an important concept in biology and in ecologically oriented medical anthropology. *Adaptation* refers to a general process through which either genes or cultural traits are shaped (i.e., selected for) to fit a particular environment. The term comes from the Latin *ad aptus*, meaning "toward a fit," and it refers to the relative direction of change in the evolutionary process. It is important to remember, however, that the mechanisms of biological adaptation and cultural adaptation are quite different (Durham 1991; Wiley 1992). *Maladaptation* refers to a trait or process that results in decreased chances of survival and reproduction. Contrary to what a naïve interpretation of the theories of ecology and evolution might suggest, there are an amazing number of examples of maladaptive behaviors in the anthropological record (Edgerton 1992). Some maladaptations exist because of unequal power relationships between groups. Other maladaptations persist because of the inertia of culture and the fact that the linkage of cause and effect might be obscured by time or complexity. Poor states of health may be, in a general sense, a reflection of maladaptation, but more often they reflect political-economic inequities or other pressures limiting people's choices.

■ ***What is the political ecology of disease?*** *Political ecology* is a relatively new term referring to a theoretical orientation emphasizing political-economic factors—such as the history of colonialism—and macrosociological factors—such as social stratification, ethnic conflicts, and migration—within a general ecological framework. Political ecology contrasts with the more traditional anthropological approach of cultural ecology (associated with theorists like Julian Steward and Roy Rappaport) and with the medical anthropological orientation attempting to link biological and cultural anthropology (associated with the work of Alexander Alland [1970]). The primary difference is in the recognition and emphasis of higher levels of analysis than a singular culture—for example, the nation-state, colonial powers, or multinational corporations. In other words, it combines political economy with ecology. Within medical anthropology, Meredith Turshen was one of the first to use this term in *Political Ecology of Disease in Tanzania,* as she emphasized the German colonial policies regarding labor reserves, plantation agriculture, and colonial medicine that together shaped the social epidemiological distribution of disease (Trostle and Sommerfeld 1996). More recently, Hans Baer, arguing that "political ecology" is a useful label related to "green politics," has provided an excellent review of current work and ongoing challenges (1996).

▪ ***The "natural history" of disease refers to the study of disease transmissions and disease processes within an ecological setting.*** The term itself refers to the approach used by scientists Macfarlane Burnet and David White in their textbook *The Natural History of Infectious Disease* (1978), which examines diseases and disease rates "in the wild," as naturalists would. The problem is that many naturalists, in describing the interaction of species in an ecosystem, neglect to recognize that the larger ecological context has been shaped by political forces; in other words, they tend to see external conditions as natural when in fact they are the result of cultural activities or political policies.

The approach to understanding disease that "naturalizes" the context is limited. The term *unnatural history* encapsulates this political-ecological critique of the limitations of a traditional ecological or epidemiological analysis. Scholars who use this term argue that it is dangerous to assume that the underlying ecological context is a given or natural. They argue that by focusing on the microbiological or individual behavioral levels of analysis, people are not only ignoring but also reinforcing the larger political-economic systems of inequality. Scholars who defend traditional ecology and epidemiology respond that they recognize the limitations of their approach and the importance of the larger political context but that the traditional scientific approaches can yield tangible applications to combat disease.

▪ ***Colonialism and so-called tropical diseases are found most often in the poorer countries of the "developing" world and are encountered by citizens of rich, developed countries through international travel.*** The main problem with the term *tropical diseases* is that it implies that the prevalence of diseases is somehow rooted in the climate and geography of a region. In fact, many so-called tropical diseases like malaria used to be common in the American Midwest and southern England. In modern world history, most of the industrialized countries that became colonial powers were located in temperate climates, and most of the colonies were located in warmer tropical environments. The two kinds of countries had, and continue to have, substantially different epidemiological profiles. But these differences are not the result of temperature and humidity. Rather, there is clear evidence that the primary factor involved in the transmission of so-called tropical diseases is simply poverty. Thomas McKeown (1988) suggests that scientists rename these diseases "diseases of poverty." A history of colonialism and, more important, postcolonial patterns of economic inequity play a central role in the creation of poverty and therefore the continuation of "tropical" disease.

▪ ***Global warming is an excellent example of ecological change with serious health implications.*** Global warming is a serious and scary fact, and there is indisputable evidence that it is caused by human activity. The primary causes of global warming are human activities that increase greenhouse gas emissions (in carbon dioxide and methane), which trap the sun's heat in the atmosphere. By driving cars, using electricity from coal-fired power plants, and heating our homes with oil or natural gas, we release carbon dioxide and other heat-trapping gases into the atmosphere. Deforestation is another significant source of greenhouse gases, because fewer trees means less carbon dioxide conversion to oxygen. As temperatures rise, disease-carrying mosquitoes and rodents spread, infecting people with diseases like malaria, dengue fever, and cholera. Extreme weather events also result in the loss of human life, not to mention property. These health effects will affect the impoverished world more than the developed world.

 9

Cultural Adaptations to Endemic Malaria in Sardinia

Peter J. Brown

The sickle-cell trait in West Africa is the textbook example of a genetic trait that has increased in frequency because it confers selective advantage to individuals in the context of a particular disease. The sickle-cell trait, in its heterozygous form, protects people who have the gene from P. falciparum *malaria, which is fatal. Sickle cell is a very expensive adaptation, however, because in its homozygous form it causes a painful and deadly condition called sickle-cell anemia. For people of African descent in the United States, for example, sickle cell can be a serious worry—a "birth defect" that serves no obvious purpose. For people living in West Africa today, where up to one-quarter of the population can carry the gene, the sickle-cell trait is less of a problem than malaria. Therefore, the protection against malaria made possible by this "'birth defect" is very valuable indeed, as malaria is a serious and growing problem throughout the world today. Estimates are that of the 30 million people who get malaria each year, 3 million of them—most often small children in Africa and Asia—will die from the disease (Oaks et al. 1991).*

Malaria is a very old disease, but there is little mystery surrounding it. Scientists have known the basic cycle of transmission (through anopheles mosquitoes) for a hundred years, and medical doctors have had effective medicines for prevention and treatment for fifty years. Right after World War II, a new residual insecticide (DDT) was used to kill malarial mosquitoes and stop the disease; this strategy was effective in Europe and the United States. Given that we have the scientific knowledge and technology, why does malaria continue to be such a problem? There are some new problems of insecticide resistance in the mosquitoes and chemical resistance in the malaria parasite, but the largest obstacles continue to be money and political will (Brown 1997).

This selection is a case study analyzing cultural *adaptations to malaria on the island of Sardinia, Italy. In doing this work, I wanted to understand the role of traditional Sardinian economy, social organization, and folk medical beliefs in protecting certain groups from malaria. To do this, I first needed to understand the particular disease ecology (in this case, temperate climate malaria is different from malaria in Africa) and to describe the social epidemiological distribution of the disease. Then I could examine the microsociological behaviors that helped explain the distribution of the disease. Note that this analysis of cultural traits as having an adaptive function in the context of malaria does* not *imply that malaria is the reason for the origins of the cultural traits.*

Malaria no longer exists in Sardinia, thanks, in small part, to a U.S.-funded malaria eradication project. People used their cultural technology to change their ecology and stop the transmission of malaria. That is a good example of an ecologically adaptive change. At the same time, the sudden conquest of malaria might be seen as a natural experiment for understanding the relationship between improved health, economic development, and population change (Brown 1986).

As you read this selection, consider these questions:

- **How is it that people can culturally adapt to a disease without being aware that they are doing so?**
- **If malaria is such a problem in the world today, why don't cultural systems adapt to solve the problem? Has cultural evolution stopped working?**
- **What is ecological about this case study?**
- **If malaria did not cause these cultural traits to exist, might the disease have played a role in maintaining the cultural traits?**

Context: This article was influenced by the field of "cultural ecology" that was developed at Columbia and Michigan universities in the 1970s. Peter Brown, a professor at Emory and co-editor of this volume, was interested in the social effects of a sudden improvement in population health, like the one experienced in 1951 in Sardinia when malaria was eradicated using DDT. Societies adapt to diseases culturally as well as genetically (as in the case of sickle cell). This article shows how the social-epidemiological distribution of malaria was related to the local economy and customs. Malaria continues to be a huge global health problem today, especially in Africa.

Source: P. J. Brown (1981). "Cultural Adaptations to Endemic Malaria in Sardinia." Medical Anthropology 5(3):311–339.

The analysis of how human populations adapt to specific disease entities in their environment is an important goal of medical anthropology (Alland 1966). It may be argued that humans are unique because they rely on culture as the primary mechanism for adaptation and hence survival. Diseases act as agents of natural selection and therefore affect human evolution, both biological and cultural (Alland 1970). As such, the study of the interaction between disease and the persistence of particular cultural patterns is an important area for study in medical anthropology. This paper examines some basic features of traditional Sardinian culture and economy for possible adaptive features and functions in the context of endemic malaria. These cultural adaptations to malaria are found at three levels of traditional Sardinian culture: economic production, social organization, and folk medical beliefs.

The importance of malaria as a force in human evolution has been well documented by Livingstone (1958, 1964, 1971) and others (Motulsky 1960; Wiesenfeld 1967). Often called the "queen of diseases," malaria has historically been the largest single cause of human mortality (Bruce-Chwatt 1979). Anthropologists have made major contributions to the understanding of the interaction between agricultural change, increased malaria prevalence, and the processes of genetic selection for abnormal hemoglobins. The study of cultural adaptations to malaria in Sardinia is of particular interest because the island has been a classic case study in population genetics (Mourant et al. 1978), and there is extensive data linking the geographical distribution of malaria with thalassemia and G-6-PD deficiency (Bernini et al. 1960; Siniscalco et al. 1966; Brown 1981). Nevertheless, there is very little understanding of how traditional behavior and beliefs may have affected malaria prevalence, or conversely, how the ecological variable of malaria may have influenced the persistence of cultural traits.

Some of the cultural elements discussed here in the Sardinian context are relatively common in the ethnographic literature of southern European societies. The analysis of these elements in relation to malaria, however, can provide a new, ecologically oriented interpretation of such features. Cultural adaptations to malaria in Sardinia either limited exposure to anopheles mosquitoes, or prescribed behaviors which decreased the probability of malaria relapses. From the native viewpoint, these traditions reflected rational choices based upon an ethnomedical theory in which malaria was caused by "bad air." Nevertheless, such traditions did function to interrupt the transmission of malaria through anopheles mosquitoes; they had positive preventive functions despite being founded on an erroneous supposition.

This paper will first discuss the concept of cultural adaptation and its importance in medical anthropology. It will then describe the ecology and epidemiology of malaria in Sardinia, including the geographic and socioecological distribution of the disease. This background information is necessary for understanding the mechanisms of cultural adaptation to malaria. The core of the paper involves an analysis of cultural traits, characteristic of lowland zones, which had adaptive functions in the context of malaria. The findings of this paper are the result of field and archival research on the socioeconomic effects of malaria and its eradication, conducted in a lowland district of north-western Sardinia during 1976 and 1977.

THE CONCEPT OF CULTURAL ADAPTATION

The concept of adaptation refers to the fundamental process of evolution in which particular traits are selected in a given environment because they increase an organism's chances for survival and reproduction. While primarily used in evolutionary biology, the concept of adaptation has been central to anthropological discussions of cultural evolution and cultural ecology (Alland 1966, 1970; Alland and McCay 1973; Netting 1964; Rappaport 1979). Adaptation implies that the environment sets certain "problems" which organisms need to "solve," and that natural selection is the mechanism by which such solutions are found. In this regard, it is obvious that diseases are primary environmental "problems" and agents of natural selection; anthropologists therefore expect that diseases shape both biological and cultural evolution (Alland 1970). The concept of adaptation does not imply that the resulting biological or cultural traits are the *only* solution to a specific environmental problem, nor does it imply that they are the optimal solutions. Rather, adaptation means that the biological or cultural traits are tolerable or have minimally sufficient positive consequences to improve an organism's chances for survival in a particular environment. Some of the confusion which surrounds the use of the concept of adaptation (Alland and McCay 1973; Lewontin 1978) stems from the fact that the single term is sometimes used to describe the basic evolutionary process (i.e. adaptation used as a verb), while in other contexts the term is used as an identification of traits which have "adaptive value" in a particular environment (i.e. adaptation used as a noun).

In this paper, the concept of cultural adaptations refers to certain culture traits or social institutions which function to increase the chances of survival for a society in a particular ecological context. This sweeping definition implies that many culture traits are adaptations, but one cannot assume that all culture traits have adaptive value. To avoid this type of tautology, this paper is concerned with a single important environmental "problem," endemic malaria. In the analysis of cultural adaptations, the question of ultimate causation for the traits described here is irrelevant (Alland 1966:41). I do not argue that endemic malaria caused Sardinian culture to develop in a certain way, but rather that particular traits functioned to limit malaria prevalence and malaria mortality. The practice of such traits therefore increased the fitness, or probability of survival, for the Sardinian population. As such, the analysis of cultural adaptations is not concerned with the origin of cultural features, but with the explanation of the persistence of such traits over time. None of the traits described here exclusively functioned to limit malaria, since they also satisfied more directly functional needs.

Cultural adaptations differ from biological ones, not only due to diverse mechanisms of transmission, but also because human cultural behavior can be volitional and maintained by choice. Cultural adaptations need not be the result of conscious processes; indeed, many of the adaptations discussed in this paper occurred without subjective awareness. However, some cultural adaptations are the result of cultural theories and willful behavior. As described by Alland and McCay, cultural adaptation is both a functional and volitional concept, since "humans, because they think, can be stimulated to think about environmental problems" (1973:172). Cultural theories designed to solve environmental "problems" can in fact retard adaptation if they block other solutions; Alland (1970) has made this argument in reference to ethnomedical curative practices. In the case of cultural adaptations to malaria in the Sardinian context, many practices function adaptively despite being based on a faulty epidemiological model.

THE ECOLOGIC AND ETHNOGRAPHIC SETTING

Sardinia, an autonomous region of the Italian Republic, is located near the center of the western Mediterranean basin. The island is roughly rectangular in shape, with an approximate length of 270 kilometers and a width of 100 kilometers [figure 1]. Though only slightly smaller than Sicily in territory, the Sardinian population historically totaled fewer than one-third of the neighboring island. The single most important historical cause of this low population density has been endemic malaria (Brown 1979). Certain elements of Sardinian geography may also have contributed to this low population density.

For over two thousand years, Sardinia was the most malaria-ridden territory of the western Mediterranean. The disease was hyperendemic and comprised the major cause of mortality on the island. The annual incidence and case-mortality rates for Sardinia rivaled those of many tropical zones. Italian scholars have long noted the importance of endemic malaria as a limiting factor in the economic history of Sardinia and the rest of the Italian *Mezzogiorno* (Celli 1933; Carta-Raspi 1971; Boscolo et al. 1962; Braudel 1972). In fact, in the first half of this [20th] century, a large body of public health literature argued that malaria was the underlying cause of economic underdevelopment in many areas of the world, including Sardinia (re: Tornu 1907; Jones 1908; Conti 1910; Dettori 1911; Brambilla 1912; Fermi 1925; Brotzu 1934; Hackett 1937).

Due to the high prevalence of malaria on the island, Sardinia was selected as the site of a pioneering malaria eradication project conducted by the Rockefeller International Health Foundation between 1947 and 1951. This project, labeled ERLAAS (*Ente Regionale per la Lotta Anti Anofelica in Sardegna*), marked the first use of DDT attempting species eradication of an indigenous anopheline vector (Logan 1953). Because of the ERLAAS campaign, there are detailed data available concerning the epidemiology of malaria in Sardinia and the entomology of the malaria vector. *Anopheles labranchiae.*

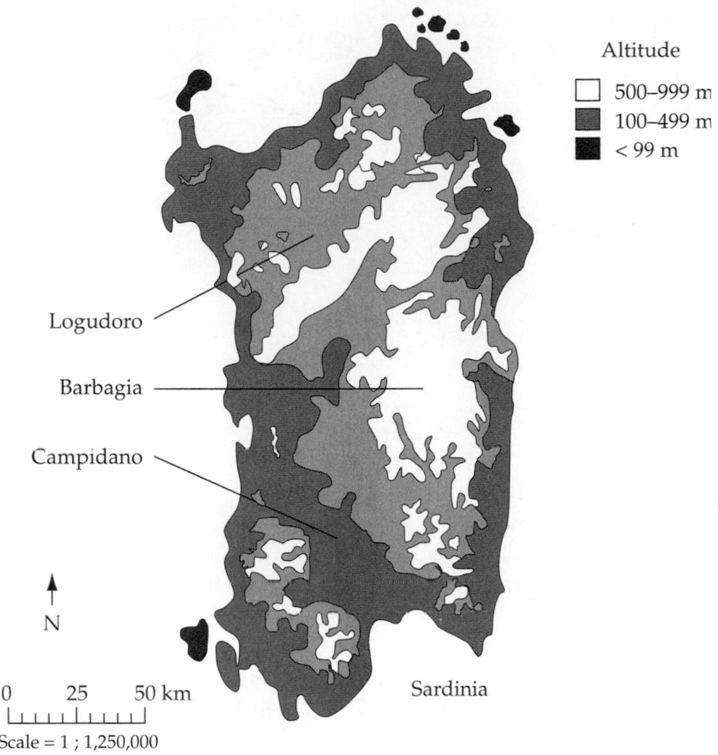

FIGURE 1 Map of Altitude and Major Geographical Zones of Sardinia

THE EPIDEMIOLOGY OF MALARIA IN SARDINIA

The discovery of cultural adaptations to any disease requires information on disease ecology, the social and geographic distribution of the disease, and ethnographic details concerning the organization of daily life. The central question in such a study is whether culturally prescribed behavior patterns affect the mechanisms of disease transmission. In relation to malaria, one must ask whether certain behaviors functioned to reduce the probability of being bitten by an infected anopheles mosquito. Endemic malaria in Sardinia was characterized by two epidemiological factors which are of critical importance: first, the seasonal cycle of malaria prevalence; and secondly, the sylvatic, or nonanthrophilic, nature of the principal vector, *A. labranchiae*. These ecological variables directly affected the pattern of malaria transmission in Sardinia, and the analysis of cultural adaptations must take them into account.

Different anopheline populations show remarkable variability in breeding habits and feeding preferences; this variability has compounded the difficulties of malaria control programs worldwide (Harrison 1978:228). Obviously, precise entomological information is crucial for a successful malaria eradication effort. The lack of such data was probably a critical factor in the failure of the ERLAAS project, since differences in the behavior of the Sardinian population of *A. labranchiae* from their mainland con-specifics were not anticipated by program malariologists (Aitken 1953:303).

The single most important behavioral difference was the *sylvatic* nature of the Sardinian population of *A. labranchiae*. This meant that the mosquitoes did not regularly rest or hibernate in human habitations, nor were they totally dependent on humans as a source of blood feasts. An important discovery of the ERLAAS campaign was that the spraying of interior house walls with a residual insecticide, which is a successful strategy against domestic anopheline vectors, was totally ineffective against a sylvatic species. The sylvatic nature of *A. labranchiae* is evidence that it is a well-adapted indigenous species, which possibly predated human occupation of the island (Trapido 1953:369).

In addition to the sylvatic nature, several other features of the behavior of the Sardinian *A. labranchiae* are important to recognize. First, the vector preferred fresh water to brackish water for breeding. Second, the mosquitoes were found in all ecological zones of the island, including highland regions, but predominated in low elevation zones with fresh water suitable for breeding. In this regard, the highest concentrations of

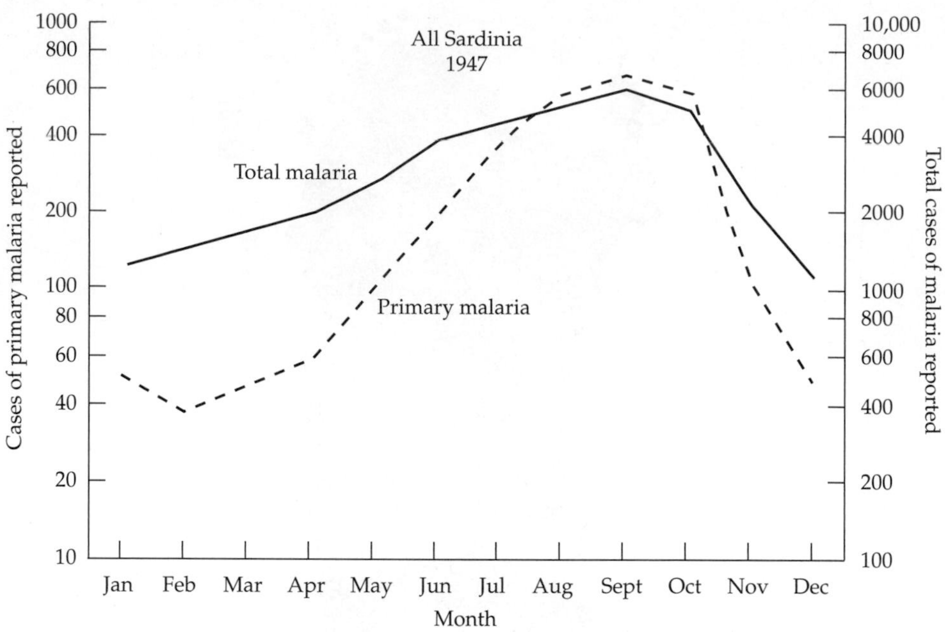

FIGURE 2 The Seasonal Epidemiological Cycle of Malaria in Sardinia *(Based on data for 1947 reported in Logan [1953])*

A. labranchiae were found in areas immediately surrounding human settlements. Finally, like most anophelines, the Sardinian vector is an active feeder primarily in the hours around dawn and dusk (Aitken 1953:329). Because of the marked variation in breeding and feeding habits of different anopheline species, it should be remembered that the cultural adaptations to malaria described here may not always be applicable to ecological zones where *A. labranchiae* is not the primary malaria vector.

The epidemiology of malaria in temperate climates like Sardinia is very different from that of tropical zones because of a characteristic seasonal, or epidemic, cycle (Hackett 1937; Logan 1953:181). The seasonal cycle of malaria in Sardinia is graphically depicted in figure 2; this cycle is often labeled *estivo-autumnal.* The fact of a "malarial season" in Sardinia is of critical importance for understanding cultural adaptations. The incidence of primary malaria transmission reaches an epidemic peak during the months of August, September, and October. The epidemic peak is contrasted with a hiatus of primary infections during the winter and early spring. It is important to recognize, however, that malaria relapses can occur at any time during the year, and for this reason the incidence of total malaria cases remains at constantly high endemic levels. The epidemic cycle of malaria is causally related to the ecological parameter of temperature which affects both larval development of the *A. labranchiae* and the extrinsic reproductive cycle of the malaria protozoa, *Plasmodium* (Aitken 1953:313). Because of this seasonal cycle, adults cannot gain immunity to malaria as they do in tropical zones, since acquired immunity is possible only from constant exposure to the disease.

The epidemiology of malaria in Sardinia is rather complex because both *Plasmodium vivax* and *P. falciparum* coexisted, and neither strain was predominant. In this regard, multiple infections were not uncommon (Hackett 1937:167). In general, *P. vivax* had a consistently high annual incidence which accounted for the stable, endemic nature of malaria on the island; this can be seen in the curve for "total malaria" in figure 2. *P. vivax* mainly affected children, and was characterized by high morbidity but low mortality rates. On the other hand, *P. falciparum,* the more deadly strain, had an unstable annual incidence (also shown in figure 2). *P. falciparum* had a more seasonal nature and accounts for the annual epidemic during late summer and early fall; the size of this annual epidemic primarily depended upon variable ecological conditions, such as the amount of summer precipitation (Aitken 1953:312).

THE GEOGRAPHIC AND SOCIAL DISTRIBUTION OF MALARIA

There are difficulties in reconstructing the geographic and social distribution of malaria in Sardinia because of the variability of the annual incidence of the disease

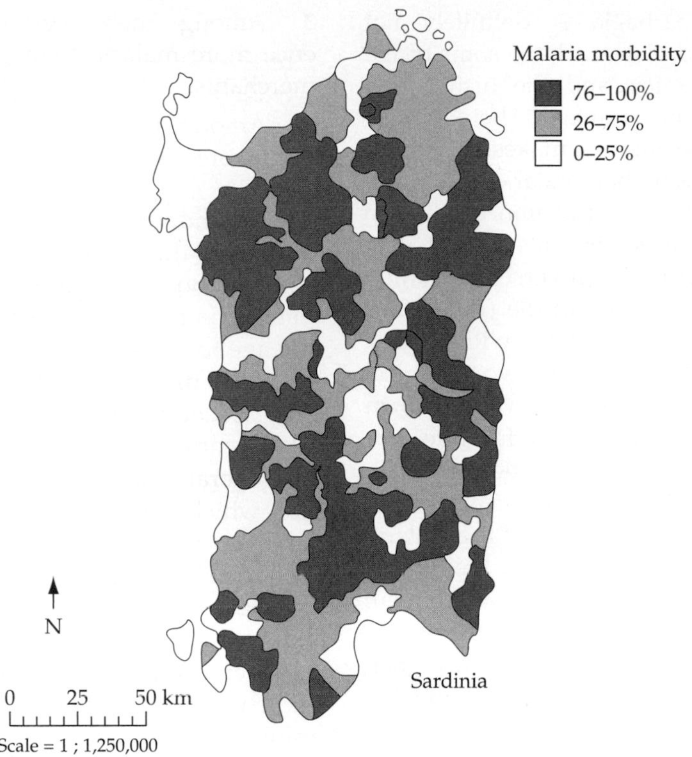

FIGURE 3 The Geographic Distribution of Malaria Morbidity *(Based on the malaria survey by Fermi [1934, 1938])*

and certain weaknesses inherent in the historical health statistics. Nevertheless, in comparison with most parts of the world, the specificity of the historical epidemiological data for Sardinia is unique. This is primarily because of the work of the malariologist Claudio Fermi, who conducted an island-wide village survey for malaria prevalence between 1933 and 1937 (Fermi 1937, 1939). The magnitude of Fermi's survey is impressive—the final publication totals more than 2,000 pages and includes analyses of forty one variables, for each of the island's 337 settlements. Fermi's database incorporates a number of measures in malaria morbidity, including physicians' records, quinine consumption, and site visits; although unsophisticated by modern standards, the Fermi survey is an impressive and important database. Before this survey, the traditional interpretation of the geographic distribution of malaria on the island was that certain subregions, like the Campidano plain in the southern sector of the island, and all coastal zones were characterized by the most malaria. Conversely, the central highlands of the Barbagia were generally thought to be malaria-free. However, by mapping the malaria morbidity prevalence data from Fermi's survey, one must recognize a more complex geographical distribution. The geographic distribution of malaria on the island is shown in figure 3 (. . .); this distribution can be compared with the pattern of elevation depicted in figure 1. It must be understood that although underpopulated coastal zones may have developed strong historical reputations for malaria, the data show that no ecological zone, including the mountainous highlands, was totally impervious to the disease.

The geographic distribution of malaria in Sardinia can be predicted by two primary ecological variables: elevation and settlement size. Fermi's malaria survey data reveal a relatively weak, but statistically significant, inverse correlation between malaria morbidity and settlement size ($r = -0.203$, $p \leq .001$). This inverse correlation means that urban centers, with populations greater than 10,000, had relatively low malaria rates; conversely, the smallest agricultural communities, with populations less than 1,500, generally had the highest malaria rates. Malaria was a *rural* disease. The rationale for this ecological distribution is obvious when one remembers the sylvatic nature of the Sardinian malaria vector. In general, the ecological settings of cities are inhospitable to anopheles mosquitoes, and consequently the probability of malaria transmission in cities is low. Urban inhabitants may have low risks of exposure to infected anophelines during most of the year; however, this situation is sometimes reversed during the peak of the seasonal epidemic cycle.

The map of malaria morbidity in figure 3 (. . .) is relatively complex, and yields no striking geographical pattern. The highland Barbagia is definitely not malaria-free; the Logudoro plateaus have some of the island's highest malaria rates; and the distribution within the Campidano plain is mixed. The complexity of this geographic distribution makes one question the simple assumption that malaria morbidity rates can be considered a direct function of altitude (cf. Brown 1981). Nevertheless, Fermi's survey data indicate a statistically significant inverse correlation between malaria prevalence and altitude ($r = -0.223$, $p \leq .001$). Altitude is inversely correlated with malaria prevalence because of its relationship to two ecological parameters—temperature and standing water (Brown 1979:113). These parameters directly affect the size and life span of the Anopheline population; as such, altitude has only an *indirect* relation to malaria transmission. Temperature affects the length of the malaria epidemic season since the Plasmodium lifecycle is interrupted at low temperatures. For this reason, there is a longer season of possible malaria transmission in lowland zones where average temperatures are higher. Because of a history of deforestation beginning with the Carthaginian epoch, many highland zones have been severely eroded and lowland areas are characterized by poor drainage and inland swamps (*stagni*). Because they provided good breeding conditions for *A. labranchiae,* lower elevation zones had higher densities of the malaria vector. As such, elevation provides a gross measure of local ecological conditions and can be used as an adequate predictor of malaria prevalence.

The sociological distribution of malaria in Sardinia is difficult to reconstruct, particularly for the small rural villages characteristic of the island. In these rural areas, there was never an adequate system for accurate recording of malaria cases. However, three available data sources permit a general understanding of social epidemiological patterns. These sources include: ERLAAS data from a sample of fifty-two Sardinian communities (Logan 1953); historical records of rural physicians in malarious communities (for example, Martinelli 1883); and interviews with older residents of ex-malarious communities (Brown 1979). Despite the lack of standardized prevalence data, these sources allow one to make generalizations of malaria morbidity prevalence based upon age, sex, and occupation categories. Similar social epidemiological distributions of malaria based upon prevalence survey data have been reported for other parts of the world (Hackett 1937; Russell 1955). Four generalizations concerning the social distribution of malaria in Sardinia can be supported:

1. Children experience more malaria than adults.
2. Among adults, men experience more malaria than women.
3. Among men, agro-pastoral workers experience more malaria than professionals, artisans, and merchants.
4. Among agro-pastoral workers, peasants experience more malaria than shepherds.

If standardized social epidemiological data were available, these basic generalizations would probably be found island-wide, despite local variations in malaria prevalence. The first generalization, relating age to malaria morbidity, is characteristic of any endemic disease. Higher rates for children probably reflect more *P. vivax* to which adults have possibly acquired a mild immunity (Hackett 1937:167). In general, the portion of the Sardinian population which experienced the highest rates of malaria infection were rural-dwelling, male agriculturalists. Conversely, the portion of the population with lowest malaria prevalence were urban-dwelling, upper-class adult females. It is important to understand how culturally prescribed behavior patterns for these groups may help account for this social epidemiological pattern.

CULTURAL ADAPTATIONS TO MALARIA

Having described the basic ecological and epidemiological context, the present analysis will examine cultural adaptations to malaria in reference to three levels of a single cultural system: human ecology; social organization; and ethnomedicine. On the level of human ecology, the cultural adaptations to malaria included characteristic settlement patterns, and the traditional land utilization of inverse transhumance. Although the ultimate causation of these traits can be traced to other factors, the settlement and land usage patterns had important adaptive value because they reduced exposure to the malaria vector. On the level of social organization, the analysis will focus on two aspects: first, cultural rules limiting the geographical mobility for particular social groups; and secondly, class-related behaviors which limited malaria exposure for the landed elite. This second adaptation is illustrated in the ethnographic example of the social organization of one of the grape harvests in Bosa, a town on the western coast of the island. Finally, cultural adaptations on the ideological level of ethnomedicine are considered. Traditional Sardinian folk-medical theories of fever causation and preventive medicine are examined in relation to the concept of *buon aria* (good air). This ethnomedical theory reinforced all three levels of cultural adaptations, and it is hypothesized that behaviors prescribed by this belief system reduced the probability of malaria relapses.

The cultural adaptations discussed here were predominant in *traditional* Sardinia, which for present purposes can be considered as before 1947. Contemporary Sardinian society is undergoing rapid change (Weingrod and Morin 1971), but it is important to note that most of the fundamental aspects of these cultural adaptations have persisted into the post-eradication epoch. However, not all of the cultural traits described here, particularly those of traditional ethnomedicine, are important or elaborated features of modern Sardinian culture. For this reason, the methodology used in this research combined historical analysis with traditional ethnographic techniques.

NUCLEATED SETTLEMENT PATTERN AND INVERSE TRANSHUMANCE

Both the formation and distribution of settlements in Sardinia have been influenced by the ecological restrictions of malaria. The settlement pattern found in all ecological zones of the island is characterized by extreme nucleation and a clear preference for "high ground" locations, specifically hilltops, precipices, and foothills (Pinna and Corda 1956; Alivia 1954; Anfossi 1915). This settlement pattern is not unique to Sardinia, and can be found in many non-malarious parts of Europe. However, the pattern has been particularly characteristic for the Italian *Mezzogiorno,* where it has affected both the political economy and history (Schneider and Schneider 1976). To a visitor on the island, this settlement pattern appears picturesque but irrational, since it requires rigorous daily commutes to agricultural fields. The adaptive value of the nucleated settlement pattern is linked to the sylvatic behavior of *A. labranchiae.* The man-made environment of nucleated settlements decreases anopheles densities and therefore the probability of anopheles-human contact. It therefore lowers the prevalence of malaria. Anthropological discussions of this Mediterranean settlement pattern (Blok 1969) have been correct in not viewing the ecological threat of malaria as a primary, causal variable. More direct factors, such as the historical threat of pirate raids, military conquests, and the expropriation of land by foreigners, were probably more important than malaria in driving people from coastal plains to hilltop settlement sites. It was malaria, however, which made the resettlement of abandoned lands extremely difficult, if not impossible, because it threatened the health of individuals in isolated farmsteads. The constant threat of malaria transmitted by a sylvatic vector gave an advantage to relatively large, densely populated communities. It also made the formation of new settlements a risky venture at best. The historical disappearance of 300 hamlets in the Campidano plain during the fifteenth century (Loddo-Canepa 1932) may be taken as evidence of the insuitability of a dispersed settlement pattern in a malarious environment. The disastrous failure of agricultural development schemes to repopulate low-lying plains in Sardinia (Tyndale 1849 III:28), as well as malarious areas of mainland Italy (Celli 1933), further document this point. Although it cannot be claimed to have originally caused the nucleated hilltop settlement pattern, malaria may help to explain its persistence long after historical periods of political insecurity.

In the native ideology, the most important quality for a settlement site is buon aria, which means that a hilltop village is subjected to healthful, cleansing breezes. The location of nucleated settlements in sites with buon aria, yet also within walking distance to agricultural flatlands, is an important modal pattern. The settlement pattern reflects an essential compromise between health and economic productivity since it allows the agricultural exploitation of malarial flatlands without the habitation of them. This appears to be an example of cultural adaptations following a minimax strategy, as suggested by Alland (1970:184). It is possible to view the nucleated hilltop settlement pattern as minimizing the malaria-related costs associated with agriculture in low elevation zones of the island.

The practice of inverse transhumance in the traditional pastoral economy in Sardinia is a clear example of the unconscious, adaptive value of settlement pattern in land utilization. The concept of transhumance refers to the seasonal movement of flocks to higher and lower elevation zones corresponding to the seasonal availability of pasture and water. As used by human geographers, the distinction between normal and inverse transhumance centers on the location of permanent settlements, since pasture utilization is nearly identical (LeLannou 1941:171). In normal transhumance, settlements are located at lower elevations and flocks are taken up to mountain pastures for the summer. In inverse transhumance, permanent settlements are located in the mountains and flocks travel down to the lowlands for winter. Figure 4 (. . .) diagrams the pattern of inverse transhumance which has been prevalent in Sardinia, particularly for the central highlands (LeLannou 1941; Berger 1981). However, this inverse pattern is problematic because it creates hardships for the pastoral population, since shepherds spend the greater part of the year (approximately from November to June) in winter pastures, far from their hometown and family. Inverse transhumance has

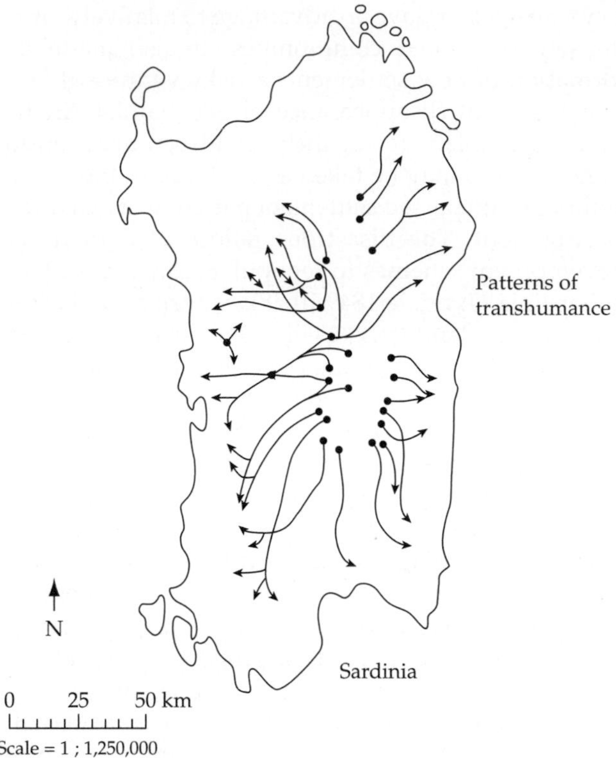

FIGURE 4 Flock Movements in the Traditional Pattern of Inverse Transhumance *(After LeLannou [1941])*

disadvantages, not only because isolation in winter pastures compounds the difficulty in protecting sheep from theft, but also because the winter is the most important economic season in pastoral production. Lambing, milking, cheese making, and shearing must all be accomplished in isolated winter pastures, and this is associated with significant problems of labor recruitment.

The adaptive value of the inverse transhumance pattern rests on the coinciding seasonality of flock movements and the annual malaria cycle. In short, this land use pattern allows for the exploitation of fertile but malarial lowland pastures during the "safe" season of November to May, while it also permits shepherds to escape those high risk zones during the peak of the malarial cycle. This may be an efficient solution to the problem of malaria seasonality in the plains, but it is also an economic necessity for the maintenance of relatively large settlements in mountainous districts. Women and children, as year-round inhabitants of mountainous communities, enjoyed greatly reduced chances of contracting malaria. As shepherds transferred flocks from burnt-out lowland pastures to more lush mountain zones, they unconsciously reduced their exposure to malaria. In contrast to the pastoral pattern, the labor demands of agricultural production are greatest during the late summer harvest which corresponds directly with the peak of the seasonal malaria epidemic. Since fertile agricultural districts were also characterized by the greatest densities of anopheles, the increased incidence of malaria during the late summer often resulted in labor shortages for the harvest. The land use pattern of inverse transhumance resulted in greater risk of exposure for peasants than shepherds, and this differential risk has been borne out in social epidemiological data.

ADAPTIVE ASPECTS OF SOCIAL ORGANIZATION

Analysis of traditional Sardinian social organization may enhance the understanding of the observed social distribution of malaria. Since culture determines the daily behavior patterns for different social groups, it also influences the risk of exposure to anopheles and hence malaria rates. Lower malaria prevalence for adult women and upper class individuals may be understood in this manner. It is also important to recognize that patterns of social organization vary between ecological zones of the island, particularly the agricultural lowlands and the pastoral highlands. This significant intracultural variation may be related to the differential influence of malaria as a factor shaping cultural behavior. In this regard, the adaptive aspects of social organization analyzed here are characteristic of the culture of lowland Sardinia, and not the pastoral highlands.

Traditional cultural rules restricted the geographical mobility of women, and these rules were given particular emphasis in the case of pregnant women. In general, women were expected not to leave the confines of the *paese*, or nucleated settlement, during most of their lives. Limited geographical mobility for women is a cultural ideal which corresponds to a pattern of sexual segregation wherein men operate in the public sphere and women control the domestic sphere. The woman's world centers on her house and the immediate neighborhood setting. Except in limited circumstances, women are *not* expected to do agricultural labor, since, from an emic viewpoint, such work would reduce the social prestige of a family. Because of these rules of social organization, women were generally able to stay within the confines of the nucleated settlement, and therefore had limited exposure to the malaria vector. As such, the lower malaria prevalence rates for women are predicated on the adaptive value of the settlement pattern.

Restrictions on mobility were even more rigorously applied during pregnancy and the immediate postpartum period. During this time, the ideal behavior was for women to remain within the house itself. The adaptive value of such a restriction becomes important and obvious when one remembers that a malaria attack during pregnancy carries a high risk of spontaneous abortion. From the Sardinian viewpoint, pregnancy (*gravidanza*) is perceived as a seriously dangerous state, and this certainly was the case with the constant threat of malaria. A famous Sardinian novel begins with the statement, "The pregnancy went well, she did not contract malaria . . ." (Dessí 1951:3). It is clear that the threat of malaria-induced spontaneous abortions may have increased the adaptive value of cultural restrictions on the geographical mobility of females. Evidence of this includes the historical fact that with the eradication of malaria, there has been a significant increase in Sardinian fecundity rates (Brown 1979:351).

The traditional behavior of Sardinian upper classes, particularly large land holders, can be seen to have similar adaptive value. The social organization of production in the agricultural lowlands meant that, like women, the traditional elites did not regularly commute to the fields, and therefore had low exposure to the malaria vector. Members of the upper classes usually remained within the safe confines of the nucleated settlement. This principle was often extended when upper class families took up permanent residence in malaria-free urban areas and appointed intermediaries to handle agricultural affairs on the village level. This social organization of production has been described for many southern European societies (Davis 1970; Schneider and Schneider 1976). This strategy, which was predominant for most small villages in the Campidano, allowed absentee landlords to escape the threat of endemic rural diseases. Obviously, the better health of the upper class was not simply the result of limited contact with the malaria vector, but also due to better living conditions and medical care. By virtue of their access to capital, however, the upper classes were able to escape from the epidemic peak of the malaria cycle during the summer. The "summer vacation" is a European aristocratic tradition which historically may have had important health implications.

An example of a behavioral adaptation by elites who lived in a highly malarial community is illustrated by the traditional social organization of the grape harvest (*vendemmia*) in the community of Bosa, in western Sardinia. This specific ethnographic example cannot be generalized for all Sardinia because, unlike most settlements, this town had a markedly high concentration of land ownership and a small number of aristocratic families. It is, however, a possible example of intracultural variation partly shaped by the ecological threat of malaria. The aristocratic tradition of Bosa is symbolically represented by a particular precious wine, *La Malvasia,* which was produced solely by these few families. Near the La Malvasia vineyards, the elites built houses (*case coloniche*) on sites which they considered to have the healthful characteristic of buon aria. Every year the upper class of Bosa transferred their residence from town to country for a period from August 15 to approximately the middle of October; ostensibly, this transfer was necessary for the supervision of the vendemmia. Yet this is inadequate as a final explanation for the residence change.

It is important to recognize the seasonal coincidence between the grape harvest and the annual epidemic cycle of malaria. This traditional residence movement allowed the elite to be absent from the nucleated settlement during the height of the malaria epidemic (see figure 2). Based upon fieldwork interviews, it seems clear that many upper class members were aware of the antimalaria function of this movement to their summer houses. Within the traditional ethnomedical model, low rates of malaria in the upper-class children of Bosa were considered to be due to their increased exposure to buon aria; however, there is also an epidemiological rationale for the observed lower rates of malaria for individuals absent from the nucleated settlement during the late summer. It has been argued above that remaining within the nucleated settlement during most of the year is adaptive against endemic, or stable, malaria because of decreased risk of exposure to the anopheles vector. But the adaptive value of remaining within the nucleated settlement is insignificant during the peak of the epidemic cycle despite the relative paucity of mosquitoes, because there is a greater chance that any *A. labranchiae* within the settlement has been infected by the malaria protozoa. While the overall vector populations may have been larger in the countryside, the greatest concentration of infected anopheles were located on the fringes of the nucleated settlement (Aitken 1953). Only during this epidemic peak period was the probable exposure to an *infected* anopheles lower in the countryside than in the village.

While the social organization of the vendemmia allowed the upper class families to escape the summer epidemic of malaria, this was not true of the laboring classes who actually did the work of the harvest. In the traditional pattern, workers commuted to the Malvasia vineyards around dawn and dusk. Since the paths to the vineyards passed by a large fresh water swamp, these workers were subjected to the prime feeding periods of *A. labranchiae.* This behavioral adaptation by the elite of Bosa seems to reflect a conscious decision to escape from the malaria epidemic of the town to the buon aria of hillside vineyards. Such behavioral adaptations may have been "right for the wrong reason," but in the study of cultural adaptations, it is the ultimate function of a particular trait which is most significant (Netting 1974:46).

ETHNOMEDICINE AND MALARIA RELAPSE RATES

On the level of cultural ideology, one can raise the hypothesis that traditional Sardinian folk theories of fever causation had adaptive value by reducing malaria relapse rates. In this regard, two folk theories are discussed here, *Intemperie* and *Colpo d'Aria.* These elements of the traditional ethnomedical system are concerned with rules of general health, and have particular attention to the etiology of fevers. These theories are associated with a variety of behavioral prescriptions and admonitions which comprise the nucleus of traditional folk preventive medicine. These prescriptions stress the necessity of moderation in daily life and the danger of sudden mixtures of hot and cold elements which may cause physiological shock and bring on fevers. In Sardinia, these folk theories predated the miasmic theory of malaria causation (Brown 1979:244). Today, the concept of Colpo d'Aria is used regularly in lowland communities, but particular details concerning Intemperie can be found only in archival sources. Although the importance of both theories may have dwindled in recent years, the behavioral prescriptions for health maintenance based upon them have persisted in contemporary Sardinian society. The adaptive value of these folk theories involves the prevention of spontaneous malaria relapses rather than primary transmission. In a population with endemic, temperate-climate malaria, relapses regularly account for more attacks than primary transmission. The present goal is to examine how culturally prescribed behaviors may be related to the mechanisms of malaria relapses.

Before the twentieth century and the discovery of the relationship between malaria, anopheles, and plasmodium protozoa, there was no standardization of the name "Malaria," nor was there a consistent method of diagnosis or treatment of the disease (Russell 1955; Harrison 1978). Endemic intermittent fevers had a variety of names because they were thought to be geographically specific; for example, in nineteenth century Sardinia, malaria was called *Intemperie Sarda.* Archival sources emphasize the irregular spacing of fevers and chills as unequivocal evidence of the unique character of the Sardinian fevers (Aquenza-Mossa 1702; Leo 1801; Tendas 1881; Sachero 1833). This symptomological irregularity, however, was actually the result of the coexistence and multiple infections of vivax and falciparum strains of malaria.

The emic term Intemperie referred to both this specific illness of malaria and its etiology. The ethnomedical theory of Intemperie is analogous to the hot-cold theory of illness prevalent in many parts of the world, but they are clearly not identical. With Intemperie, illness is thought to be caused by a sudden and dangerous shift from hot to cold, or from dry to wet. An important distinction is that the external environment, not internal equilibrium, is implicated as a causal element. There is a meteorological analogy throughout this literature, and the earliest source (Aquenza-Mossa 1702) argues that climatic conditions which cause sudden storms also cause human fevers. Nineteenth century Sardinian physicians (Sachero 1833; Tendas 1881) adapted the folk theory to the then-scientific theory of *miasma* by arguing that *intemperosi* climatic conditions created miasmic reactions in lowland areas which in turn caused malaria. But the underlying concept is that for individual health, like weather, abrupt changes in temperature cause violent reactions.

It is probable that the ethnomedical theory of Intemperie relates seasonal climatic changes with the seasonal epidemic cycle of malaria. The concept of Intemperie finds a correlate in contemporary Sardinia with a pervasive idea that the *cambiamento delle stagione* (change of seasons) is a dangerous period for personal health. In Sardinia's climate, the "change of seasons" refers to two periods—the increasing temperature of the spring and decreasing temperature of the fall. In this regard, it is significant that in temperate climate malaria, relapse rates sharply increase during the spring; these seasonally-related relapses function as an infection pool which is a prerequisite for the late summer epidemic (Hackett 1937:165).

The health danger of a change in temperature is also a central theme to the ethnomedical concept of *Colpo d'Aria,* which means "blast of air." An individual exposed to a Colpo d'Aria is prone to a variety of minor illnesses, such as the common cold or flare-ups of chronic pains. In everyday life, the concept of Colpo d'Aria is reflected in precautions and concern about drafts. The Sardinians' belief is that an individual with a warm physiological equilibrium is at a great health risk when "shocked" by a sudden blast of cold. A sudden change in an individual's internal temperature equilibrium results in an unhealthy physiological shock and possibly illness; the principle holds true for a drafty room in winter, or drinking a cold beer in summer. As such, a fever represents the body's efforts for renewed equilibrium after being exposed to cold. The chills and fevers characteristic of malaria, therefore, are thought to be analogous to a pendulum, swinging back and forth between hot and cold.

The adaptive value of the folk theories of both Intemperie and Colpo d'Aria depends upon how they shape daily behavior. Both theories aim at a similar strategy of preventive medicine: the avoidance of conditions where a sudden mixing of hot and cold would upset the temperature equilibrium. Both archival sources and contemporary informants produce similar lists of behavioral restrictions which, it is argued, will, if followed, reduce the risk of temperature imbalance and illness. Such a list of Sardinian folk-medical recommendations based on both ethnomedical theories would include: avoiding drafts and dampness; avoiding overexertion; keeping one's stomach full; drinking spirits regularly, but not to excess; wearing hats and layers of clothing; avoiding cold beverages when hot; not sleeping outside without shelter; closing shutters at dusk; never getting overly hot or cold; special care when bathing; and general moderation in all things. Such suggestions should not appear exotic, since they are very similar to "common sense" guidelines for good health in our own culture. It is generally accepted that such recommendations concerning diet, rest, and clothing are important for personal health maintenance and guarding against the common cold.

. . .

When one thinks of malaria causation only in terms of the mosquito vector and primary transmissions, then the folk theories of Intemperie and Colpo d'Aria appear to be nothing but quaint, yet interesting customs. However, by remembering the unique ability of malaria to relapse long after the initial infection, and that certain behaviors can provoke such relapses, then the traditional folk theories of fever causation may have had significant adaptive value.

CONCLUSIONS

This paper has examined particular traits of traditional Sardinian culture in relation to the epidemiology of malaria. It has been suggested that cultural adaptations to the disease can be found at three levels of behavior: human ecology, social organization, and ideology. Cultural traits based on the folk concept of buon aria (good air) have been seen to have adaptive value because they tend to reduce exposure to the malaria vector. Behaviors associated with traditional ethnomedical theories possibly lowered the probability of spontaneous malaria relapses. On the level of human ecology, the nucleated hilltop settlement pattern and the pastoral land use system of inverse transhumance have the function of allowing the exploitation of malaria lowlands without habitation of them. On the level of social organization, it has been argued that lower malaria prevalences for women are the result of cultural rules restricting their mobility outside of the nucleated settlement. Such rules are most important for pregnant women, since reduced exposure to the malaria vector would decrease the risk of spontaneous abortions. Although there was considerable intracultural variation for all Sardinia, the elite classes of Bosa were able to escape the annual summer epidemic of malaria by transferring their residences during the grape harvest. Finally, on the level of ideology, the folk medical theories of Intemperie and Colpo d'Aria provide a functional explanation of the seasonality of malaria. More importantly, culturally prescribed behaviors associated with those theories may have reduced the probability of malaria relapses.

The analysis of cultural adaptations to specific diseases stems directly from cultural evolution theory and can lead to a more thorough understanding of the interaction of biological and cultural evolution. Since diseases directly affect survival rates, they function as selective agents for biological characteristics and, more importantly, cultural traits. The analysis of how cultural behaviors reduce disease prevalence provides examples of cultural systems evolving to meet the demands of specific environmental conditions. In the case of malaria in Sardinia, this search for cultural adaptations has emphasized the intersection between the behavior to the malaria vector, *Anopheles labranchiae,* and the daily activities of particular social groups. Endemic malaria did not cause these cultural traits to first appear, but the fact that they functioned to protect the population from malaria may help explain their persistance over time. The cultural elements discussed here in the Sardinian context are relatively common in the ethnographic literature of southern European societies. This paper, hopefully, provides a new, ecologically-oriented interpretation of those cultural features.

REFERENCES

Aitken, T. 1953. The Anopheline Fauna of Sardinia. *In* The Sardinian Project. J. Logan, ed. Baltimore: Johns Hopkins Press.

Alivia, G. 1954. Poplazione ed Economia: il Problema della Sardegna, Milano: Iglesias.

Alland, A. 1966. Medical Anthropology and the Study of Biological and Cultural Adaptation. American Anthropologist 68:40–50.

———. 1969. Ecology and Adaptation to Parasitic Diseases. *In* Environment and Cultural Behavior. A. Vayda, ed. New York: Natural History Press.

———. 1970. Adaptation in Cultural Evolution: Art Approach to Medical Anthropology. New York: Columbia University Press.

Alland, A. and B. McCay. 1973. The Concept of Adaptation in Biological and Cultural Evolution. *In* Handbook of Social and Cultural Anthropology. J. Honigmann, ed. Chicago: Rand McNally.

Anfossi, G. 1915. Ricerche sulla Distribuzione della Popolazione in Sardegna. Sassari: Galizzi.

Aquenza et Mossa, P. 1702. Tractus de Febre Intemperie. Typographia Emmanuelis Ruiz de Murgia. Barcelona.

Belgind, G. 1942. Textbook of Clinical Parasitology. New York: Holmes and Meier.

Berger, A. 1981. The Effects of Capitalism on the Social Structure of Pastoral Villages in Highland Sardinia. Michigan: Discussions in Anthropology.

Bernini, L., V. Carcassi, B. Latte, A. G. Motulsky, M. Siniscalco, G. Montalenti. 1960. Indagini Genetiche Sulla Predispozione al Favismo—III. Distribuzione della Frequenze Geniche per il Locus Gd. *In* Sardegna: Interazione con la Malaria e la Talassemia al Livello Popolazionistico. Accademia Nazionale dei Lincei (Roma) 29:115–25.

Blok, A. 1969. South Italian Agro-Towns. Comparative Studies in Society and History 11:121–35.

Boscolo, A., L. Bulferetti, L. Delpiano. 1962. Profilo Storico Economico della Sardegna dal Riformismo Sette-Centesco al Piano di Rinasata. Padova: CEDAM.

Brambilla, G. 1912. La Malaria Sotto L'Aspetto Economico-Sociale. Milano: Gorlini.

Braudel, F. 1972. The Mediterranean and the Mediterranean World in the Age of Phillip II. New York: Harper and Row.

Brotzu, G. 1934 La Malaria nella Storia della Sardegna. Mediterranea 8:3–10.

Brown, P. J. 1979. Cultural Adaptations to Endemic Malaria and the Socioeconomic Effects of Malaria Eradication in Sardinia. Ph.D. Dissertation. S.U.N.Y. Stony Brook.

———. 1981. New Considerations on the Distribution of Malaria, Thalassemia, and Glucose 6-Phosphate Dehydrogenase in Sardinia. Human Biology (in press).

Bruce-Chwatt, L. J. 1979. Man against Malaria: Conquest or Defeat. Transactions of the Royal Society of Tropical Medicine and Hygiene 73:605–17.

Carta-Raspi, R. 1971. Storia della Sardegna. Milano: Mursia.

Celli, A. 1933. The History of Malaria in the Roman Campagna. London: John Bale and Sons.

Coggeshall, L. T. 1963. Malaria. *In* Cecil-Loeb Textbook of Medicine. P. B. Beeson and W. McDermott, eds. St. Louis: C. V. Mosby.

Conti, A. 1910. La Malaria con Rilevi Fatti in Sardegna. Sassari: Gallizzi.

Davis, J. 1970. Land and Family in a South Italian Town. London: Athlone.

Dessí, G. 1951. Forests of Norbio. New York: Harcourt.

Dettori, G. 1911. La Malaria in Sardegna. Cagliari: Giva-Falconi.

Fermi, C. 1925. La Malaria e la Decadenze della Civilia. Grottaferrla: San Nilo.

———. 1937. Regioni Malariche, Decadenze, Risanamento e Spesa. "Sardegna" Vol. 1—Sassari Province. Rome: Tipografia dello Stato.

———. 1939. Regioni Malariche, Decadenza, Risanamento e Spesa. "Sardegna" Vol. 2—Nuoro Province, Vol. 3—Caligari Province. Rome: Tipografia dello Stato.

Hackett, L. W. 1937. Malaria in Europe: An Ecological Study. Cambridge: Oxford University Press.

Hackett, L. W. and A. Missiroli. 1935. The Varieties of *Anopheles Maculipennis* and Their Relation to the Distribution of Malaria in Europe. Rivista di Malariologia 14:45–109.

Harrison, G. 1978. Mosquitoes, Malaria, and Man: A History of the Hostilities Since 1880. New York: E. P. Dutton.

Jones, W., R. Ross, R. Ellet. 1908. Malaria: A Neglected Factor in the History of Greece and Rome. Naples: Dethen and Rocholl.

Katz, S. H. and J. Schall. 1979. Fava Bean Consumption and Biocultural Evolution. Medical Anthropology 3:459–76.

LeLannou, M. 1941. Patres et Paysans de la Sardaigne. Tours: Arrault.

Leo, P. A. 1801. Di Alcuni Antichi Pregiudizi sulla Cosi-detta Sarda Intemperie, e sulla Malattia Conosciuta con Questo Nome: Lezione Fisico-Medica. Cagliari: Reale Stamperia.

Lewontin, R. C. 1978. Adaptation. Scientific American 239:212–30.

Livingstone, F. B. 1958. Anthropological Implications of Sickle Cell Gene Distribution in West Africa. American Anthropologist 60:533–62.

———. 1964. The Distribution of the Abnormal Hemoglobin Genes and Their Significance for Human Evolution. Evolution 18:685–99.

———. 1971. Malaria and Human Polymorphisms. Annual Review of Genetics 5:33–64.

Loddo-Canepa, M. 1932. Lo Spopolamento della Sardegna durante le Dominazione Aragonese e Spagnuola. Roma: Comitato Italiano per lo Studio dei Problema della Popolazione.

Logan, J. A. 1953. The Sardinian Project. Baltimore: Johns Hopkins Press.

Martinelli, G. 1883. Relazione del Medico Chirugico Giuseppe Martinelli nelle sue Qualita de Medico Condotto e Necroscopico Medico della Sanità Maritima de Commune di Bosa dall'Anno 1852 al 1881. Sassari: Tipografia Chiarella.

Motulsky, A. 1960. Metabolic Polymorphisms and the Role to Infectious Diseases in Human Evolution. Human Biology 32:28–62.

Mourant, A. E., A. C. Kopéc, and K. Domiewska-Sobczak. 1978. Blood Groups and Diseases. Oxford: Oxford University Press.

Netting, R. MC. 1974. Agrarian Ecology. Annual Review of Anthropology 3:21–56.

Pinna, M. and L. Corda. 1957. La Distribuzione della Popolazione e i Centri Abitati della Sardegna. Pisa: Libreria Goliardica.

Rappaport, R. A. 1979. Ecology, Meaning and Religion Richmond, California: North Atlantic.

Russell, P. F. 1955, Man's Mastery of Malaria. London: Oxford University Press.

Sachero, C. G. 1833. Dell Intemperie di Sardegna e delle Febbri Periodiche Perniciose. Torino: Tipografia Fodratti.

Schneider, J. and P. Schneider. 1976. Culture and Political Economy in Western Sicily. New York: Academic Press.

Silverman, S. 1968. Agricultural Organization, Social Structure, and Values in Italy: Amoral Familism Reconsidered. American Anthropologist 70:1–20.

Siniscalco, M. L., L. Bernini, G. Filippi, B. Latte, P Merra Khan, and S. Piomelli. 1966. Population Genetics of Haemoglobin Variants, Thalassemia and Glucoses-6-Phosphate Dehydrogenase Deficiency, with Particular Reference to the Malaria Hypothesis. Bulletin of the World Health Organization 34:379–93.

Tendas, D. A. 1881. La Sardegna e le Sue Febbri Telluriche—Riflessioni Fiolosofico, Scientifico, Critiche. Cagliari: Tipografia di Alagna.

Tornu, A. 1907. Lo Stato Attuale del Problema Malarico e i Suoi Rapporti con Agricolura. Iglesias: Canelles.

Trapido, H. 1953. Biological Considerations in the ERLAAS Project. *In* The Sardinian Project. J. Logan, ed. Baltimore: Johns Hopkins Press.

Tyndale, J. W. 1849. The Island of Sardinia. London: Richard Bently.

Weingrod, A. and E. Morin. 1971. Post Peasants: The Character of Contemporary Sardinian Society. Comparative Studies in Society and History 13:301–24.

Wiesenfeld, S. L. 1967. Sickle-cell Trait in Human Biological and Cultural Evolution. Science 157:1134–38.

 10

Social Inequalities and Emerging Infectious Diseases

Paul Farmer

Emerging diseases are thought of as "new" diseases that are a threat to the health of people in the United States. The movie Outbreak *and the best-seller* The Hot Zone*—both scary stories about strange hemorrhaghic fevers like Ebola—represent popularizations of the topic of emerging infectious disease. But emerging disease also refers to old diseases, such as malaria or tuberculosis, that may have evolved chemotherapy-resistant strains. The evolution of antibiotic resistance, as we saw in the selections on Darwinian medicine, is certainly the result of humans changing the environment in which pathogens reproduce. But how do we define the environment? The epidemiological study of emerging infectious diseases generally recognizes the importance of human factors in disease transmission. Things like ecological disruption from the building of roads, overuse of agricultural pesticides, or rapid spread of infections by air travel are often pointed out. These are thought to reflect environmental influences.*

Anthropologists believe that it is also important to recognize what is not *pointed out or discussed when it comes to these new public health threats. One issue that seems left out of discussions of disease ecology is a simple and obvious one: the role of poverty and social inequalities. The goal of this selection, published for an audience of researchers in emerging infectious diseases, is to ask some difficult questions about what is not currently being investigated. This "critical" approach fits into the area of political ecology. As the author says, the questions are less about pig–duck agriculture (the Asian ecological setting that is thought to play a key role in the continuation of annual influenza epidemics) and more about the influence of World Bank policies on the spread of infectious disease. The political dimensions of his argument for diseases such as Ebola, TB, and AIDS, or the idea of the unnatural history of disease, are clear in this selection. The political-ecological approach is still young, but the author prescribes some key areas for more research.*

Political ecology challenges some of the standard presuppositions that are used in defining health problems. In many ways, this selection announces a research agenda rather than demonstrating ecological research results. The challenge to political-ecological medical anthropology will be to demonstrate the causal chain at different levels of reality—the microbe, the individual, the society, the nation, and the World Bank.

As you read this selection, consider these questions:

- **If the political-ecological argument is true, what are the implications for the distribution of resources to deal with emerging infectious diseases?**
- **Why do many people (including physicians and epidemiologists) feel uncomfortable when an ecological analysis is expanded to the world of politics? Are political dimensions so complicated and thorny that they make solutions seem less imaginable?**
- **How accurate is the metaphor of semipermeable national borders that allow diseases to pass freely but bureaucratically restrict the flow of cures?**

Context: Paul Farmer is a medical anthropologist and medical doctor who specializes in the treatment of infectious diseases. When he was a medical student, Farmer founded a clinic for the treatment of AIDS and TB in a very poor rural area of Haiti. His first book, AIDS and Accusation, described how large-scale historical, political, and economic events place many of his patients at high risk for such diseases. Farmer's clinic has since grown into a large international organization, Partners in Health, which provides health care and advocacy for poor communities throughout the world. A readable biography of Farmer, by Tracy Kidder, is Mountains Beyond Mountains (2003). This particular article was written at a time when public attention was just turning to so-called emerging infectious diseases because they represented threats to the United States. The major contribution of this article, published in a journal for public health epidemiologists, was to refocus this attention on the long-standing socioeconomic inequalities that make people more vulnerable to these diseases in the first place.

Source: P. Farmer (1996). "Social Inequalities and Emerging Infectious Diseases." Emerging Infectious Diseases 2(4):259–269.

The past decade has been one of the most eventful in the long history of infectious diseases. There are multiple indexes of these events and of the rate at which our knowledge base has grown. The sheer number of relevant publications indicates explosive growth; moreover, new means of monitoring antimicrobial resistance patterns are being used along with the rapid sharing of information (as well as speculation and misinformation) through means that did not exist even 10 years ago. Then there are the microbes themselves. One of the explosions in question—perhaps the most remarked upon—is that of "emerging infectious diseases." Among the diseases considered "emerging," some are regarded as genuinely new; AIDS and Brazilian purpuric fever are examples. Others have newly identified etiologic agents or have again burst dramatically onto the scene. For example, the syndromes caused by Hantaan virus have been known in Asia for centuries but now seem to be spreading beyond Asia because of ecologic and economic transformations that increase contact between humans and rodents.

Neuroborreliosis was studied long before the monikers Lyme disease and *Borrelia burgdorferi* were coined, and before suburban reforestation and golf courses complicated the equation by creating an environment agreeable to both ticks and affluent humans. Hemorrhagic fevers, including Ebola, were described long ago, and their etiologic agents were in many cases identified in previous decades. Still other diseases grouped under the "emerging" rubric are ancient and well-known foes that have somehow changed, in pathogenicity or distribution. Multidrug–resistant tuberculosis (TB) and invasive or necrotizing Group A streptococcal infection are cases in point.

Like all new categories, "emerging infectious diseases" has benefits and limitations. The former are well known: a sense of urgency, notoriously difficult to arouse in large bureaucracies, has been marshaled, funds have been channeled, conferences convened, articles written, and a journal dedicated to the study of these diseases has been founded. The research and action agendas elaborated in response to the perceived emergence of new infections have been, by and large, sound. But the concept, like some of the diseases associated with it, is complex. Its complexity has, in some instances, hampered the learning process. A richly textured understanding of emerging infections will be grounded in critical and reflexive study of how learning occurs. Units of analysis and key terms will be scrutinized and defined more than once. This process will include regular rethinking not only of methods and study design, but also of the validity of causal inference and reflection on the limits of human knowledge. This study of the process, loosely known as epistemology, often happens in retrospect, but many of the chief contributors to the growing research in emerging infectious diseases have examined the epistemologic issues surrounding their work and are familiar with the multifactorial nature of disease emergence: "Responsible factors include ecological changes, such as those due to agricultural or economic development or to anomalies in the climate; human demographic changes and behavior; travel and commerce; technology and industry; microbial adaptation and change; and breakdown of public health measures."[1] A recent Institute of Medicine report on emerging infections does not even categorize microbial threats by type of agent, but rather according to factors held to be related to their emergence.[2]

In studying emerging infectious diseases, many thus make a distinction between a host of phenomena directly related to human actions—from improved laboratory techniques and scientific discovery to economic "development," global warming, and failures of public health—and another set of phenomena much less common and related to changes in the microbes themselves. Close examination of microbial mutations often shows that, again, human actions have played a large role in enhancing pathogenicity or increasing resistance to antimicrobial agents. In one long list of emerging viral infections, for example, only the emergence of Rift Valley fever is attributed to a possible change in virulence or pathogenicity, and this only after other, social factors for which there is better evidence.[1] No need, then, to call for a heightened awareness of the sociogenesis, or "anthropogenesis," of emerging infections. Some bench scientists in the field are more likely to refer to social factors and less likely to make immodest claims of causality about them than are behavioral scientists who study disease. Yet a critical epistemology of emerging infectious diseases is still in its early stages of development; a key task of such a critical approach would be to take existing conceptual frameworks, including that of disease emergence, and ask, What is obscured in this way of conceptualizing disease? What is brought into relief? A first step in understanding the "epistemological dimension" of disease emergence, notes Eckardt, involves developing "a certain sensitivity to the terms we are used to."[3]

A heightened sensitivity to other common rubrics and terms shows that certain aspects of disease emergence are brought into relief while others are obscured. When we think of "tropical diseases," malaria comes quickly to mind. But not too long ago, malaria was an important problem in areas far from the tropics. Although there is imperfect overlap between malaria as currently defined and the malaria of the mid-19th century, some U.S. medical historians agree with contemporary assessments: malaria "was the most important disease in the country at the time." In the Ohio River Valley, according to Daniel Drake's 1850 study, thousands died in seasonal epidemics. During the second decade of the 20th century, when the population of 12 southern states was approximately 25 million, an estimated million cases of malaria occurred each year. Malaria's decline in this country was "due only in small part to measures aimed directly against it, but more to agricultural development and other factors some of which are still not clear."[4] These factors include poverty and social inequalities, which led, increasingly, to differential morbidity with the development of improved housing, land drainage, mosquito repellents, nets, and electric fans—all well beyond the reach of those most at risk for malaria. In fact, many "tropical" diseases predominantly affect the poor; the groups at risk for these diseases are often bounded more by socioeconomic status than by latitude.

Similarly, the concept of "health transitions" is influential in what some have termed "the new public health" and in the international financial institutions that so often direct development efforts.[5] The model of health transitions suggests that nation-states, as they develop, go through predictable epidemiologic transformations. Death due to infectious causes is supplanted by death due to malignancies and to complications of coronary artery disease, which occur at a more advanced age, reflecting progress. Although it describes broad patterns now found throughout the world, the concept of national health transitions also masks other realities, including intranational illness and death differentials that are more tightly linked to local inequalities than to nationality. For example, how do the variables of class and race fit into such paradigms? In Harlem, where the age-specific death rate in several groups is higher than in Bangladesh, leading causes of death are infectious diseases and violence.[6]

Units of analysis are similarly up for grabs. When David Satcher, director of the Centers for Disease Control and Prevention (CDC), writing of emerging infectious diseases, reminds us that "the health of the individual is best ensured by maintaining or improving the health of the entire community,"[7] we should applaud his clearsightedness but go on to ask, What constitutes "the entire community"? In the 1994 outbreak of cryptosporidiosis in Milwaukee, for example, the answer might be "part of a city."[8] In other instances, community means a village or the passengers on an airplane. But the most common unit of analysis in public health, the nation-state, is not all that relevant to organisms such as dengue virus, *Vibrio cholerae* O139, human immunodeficiency virus (HIV), penicillinase-producing *Neisseria gonorrhoeae,* and hepatitis B virus. Such organisms have often ignored political boundaries, even though their presence may cause a certain degree of turbulence at national borders. The dynamics of emerging infections will not be captured in national analyses any more than the diseases are contained by national boundaries, which are themselves emerging entities—most of the world's nations are, after all, 20th-century creations.

Here I have discussed the limitations of three important ways of viewing the health of populations—tropical medicine, "the" epidemiologic transition, and nation health profiles—because models and even assumptions about infectious diseases need to be dynamic, systemic, and critical. That is, models with explanatory power must be able to track rapidly changing clinical, even molecular, phenomena and link them to the large-scale (sometimes transnational) social forces that manifestly shape the contours of disease emergence. I refer, here, to questions less on the order of how pig–duck agriculture might be related to the antigenic shifts central to influenza pandemics, and more on the order of the following: Are World Bank policies related to the spread of HIV, as has recently been claimed?[9] What is the relationship between international shipping practices and the spread of cholera from Asia to South America and elsewhere in the Western Hemisphere?[10,11] How is genocide in Rwanda related to cholera in Zaire?[12]

The study of anything said to be emerging tends to be dynamic. But the very notion of emergence in heterogeneous populations poses questions of analysis that are rarely tackled, even in modern epidemiology, which, as McMichael has recently noted," assigns a primary importance to studying interindividual variations in risk. By concentrating on these specific and presumed free-range individual behaviors, we thereby pay less attention to the underlying social-historical influences on behavioral choices, patterns, and population health."[13] A critical (and self-critical) approach would ask how existing frameworks might limit our ability to discern trends that can be linked to the emergence of diseases. Not all social-production-of-disease theories are equally alive to the importance of how relative social and economic positioning—inequality—affects risk for infection. In its report on emerging infections, the Institute of Medicine lists neither poverty nor inequality as "causes of emergence."[2]

A critical approach pushes the limits of existing academic politesse to ask harder and rarely raised questions: What are the mechanisms by which changes in agriculture have led to outbreaks of Argentine and Bolivian hemorrhagic fever, and how might these mechanisms be related to international trade agreements, such as the General Agreement on Tariffs and Trade and the North American Free Trade Agreement? How might institutional racism be related to urban crime and the outbreaks of multidrug-resistant TB in New York prisons? Does the privatization of health services buttress social inequalities, increasing risk for certain infections—and death—among the poor of sub-Saharan Africa and Latin America? How do the colonial histories of Belgium and Germany and the neocolonial histories of France and the United States tie in to genocide and a subsequent epidemic of cholera among Rwandan refugees? Similar questions may be productively posed in regard to many diseases now held to be emerging.

EMERGING HOW AND TO WHAT EXTENT? THE CASE OF EBOLA

Hemorrhagic fevers have been known in Africa since well before the continent was dubbed "the white man's grave," an expression that, when deployed in reference to a region with high rates of premature death, speaks volumes about the differential valuation of human lives. Ebola itself was isolated fully two decades ago.[14] Its appearance in human hosts has at times been insidious but more often takes the form of explosive eruptions. In accounting for recent outbreaks, it is unnecessary to postulate a change in filovirus virulence through mutation. The Institute of Medicine lists a single "factor facilitating emergence" for filoviruses: "virus-infected monkeys shipped from developing countries via air."[2]

Other factors are easily identified. Like that of many infectious diseases, the distribution of Ebola outbreaks is tied to regional trade networks and other evolving social systems. And, like those of most infectious diseases, Ebola explosions affect, researchers aside, certain groups (people living in poverty, health care workers who serve the poor) but not others in close physical proximity. Take, for example, the 1976 outbreak in Zaire, which affected 318 persons. Although respiratory spread was speculated, it has not been conclusively demonstrated as a cause of human cases. Most expert observers thought that the cases could be traced to failure to follow contact precautions, as well as to improper sterilization of syringes and other paraphernalia, measures that in fact, once taken, terminated the outbreak.[15] On closer scrutiny, such an explanation suggests that Ebola does not emerge randomly: in Mobutu's Zaire, one's likelihood of coming into contact with unsterile syringes is inversely proportional to one's social status. Local elites and sectors of the expatriate community with access to high-quality biomedical services (viz., the European and American communities and not the Rwandan refugees) are unlikely to contract such a disease.

The changes involved in the disease's visibility are equally embedded in social context. The emergence of Ebola has also been a question of our consciousness. Modern communications, including print and broadcast media, have been crucial in the construction of Ebola—a minor player, statistically speaking, in Zaire's long list of fatal infections—as an emerging infectious disease.[16] Through Cable News Network (CNN) and other television stations, Kikwit became, however briefly, a household word in parts of Europe and North America. Journalists and novelists wrote best-selling books about small but horrific plagues, which in turn became profitable cinema. Thus, symbolically and proverbially, Ebola spread like wildfire—as a danger potentially without limit. It emerged.

EMERGING FROM WHERE? THE CASE OF TB

TB is said to be another emerging disease, in which case, emerging is synonymous with reemerging. Its recrudescence is often attributed to the advent of HIV—the Institute of Medicine lists "an increase in immunosuppressed populations" as the sole factor facilitating the resurgence of TB[2]—and the emergence of drug resistance. A recent book on TB, subtitled "How the battle against tuberculosis was won—and lost," argues that "Throughout the developed world, with the successful application of triple therapy and the enthusiastic promotion of prevention, the death rate from tuberculosis came tumbling down."[17] But was this claim ever documented? Granted, the discovery of effective anti-TB therapies has saved the lives of hundreds of thousands of TB patients, many in industrialized countries. But TB—once the leading cause of death among young adults in the industrialized world—was already declining there well before the 1943 discovery of streptomycin. In the rest of the world, and in pockets of the United States, TB remains undaunted by ostensibly effective drugs, which are used too late, inappropriately, or not at all: "It is sufficiently shameful," notes one of the world's leading authorities on TB, "that 30 years after recognition of the capacity of triple-therapy . . . to elicit 95%+ cure rates, tuberculosis prevalence rates for *many* nations remain unchanged."[18] Some estimate that more than 1.7 billion persons are infected with quiescent, but viable, *Mycobacterium tuberculosis* and, dramatic shifts in local epidemiology aside, a global analysis does not suggest major decreases in the importance of TB as a cause of death. TB has retreated in certain populations, maintained a steady state in others, and surged forth in still others, remaining, at this writing, the world's leading infectious cause of adult deaths.[19]

At mid-century, TB was still acknowledged as the "great white plague." What explains the invisibility of this killer by the 1970s and 1980s? Again, one must turn to the study of disease awareness, that is, of consciousness and publicity, and their relation to power and wealth. "The neglect of tuberculosis as a major public health priority over the past two decades is simply extraordinary," wrote Murray in 1991. "Perhaps the most important contributor to this state of ignorance was the greatly reduced clinical and epidemiologic importance of tuberculosis in the wealthy nations."[20] Thus TB has not really emerged so much as emerged from the ranks of the poor.[21,22] An implication, clearly, is that one place for diseases to hide is among poor people, especially when the poor are socially and medically segregated from those whose deaths might be considered more important.

When complex forces move more poor people into the United States, an increase in TB incidence is inevitable. In a recent study of the disease among foreign-born persons in the United States, immigration is essentially credited with the increased incidence of TB-related disease.[23] The authors note that in some of the immigrants' countries of origin the annual rate of infection is up to 200 times that registered in the United States; moreover, many persons with TB in the United States live in homeless shelters, correctional facilities, and camps for migrant workers. But there is no discussion of poverty or inequality, even though these are, along with war, leading reasons for both the high rates of TB and for immigration to the United States. "The major determinants of risk in the foreign born population," conclude the authors, "were the region of the world from which the person emigrated and the number of years in the United States."

GOING WHERE? THE CASE OF HIV

To understand the complexity of the issues—medical, social, and communicational—that surround the emergence of a disease into public view, consider AIDS. In the early 1980s, the public was informed by health officials that AIDS had probably emerged from Haiti. In December 1982, for example, a physician affiliated with the National Cancer Institute was widely quoted in the popular press stating that "We suspect that this may be an epidemic Haitian virus that was brought back to the homosexual population in the United States."[24] This proved incorrect, but not before damage to Haitian tourism had been done. Result: more poverty, a yet steeper slope of inequality and vulnerability to disease, including AIDS. The label "AIDS vector" was also damaging to the million or so Haitians living elsewhere in the Americas and certainly hampered public health efforts among them.[25]

HIV disease has since become the most extensively studied infection in human history. But some questions are much better studied than are others. And error is worth studying, too. Careful investigation of the mechanisms by which immodest claims are propagated (as regards Haiti and AIDS, these mechanisms included "exoticization" of Haiti, racism, the existence of influential folk models about Haitians and Africans, and the conflation of poverty and cultural difference) is an important yet neglected part of a critical epistemology of emerging infectious diseases. Also underinvestigated are considerations of the pandemic's dynamic. HIV may not have come from Haiti, but it was going to Haiti. Critical reexamination of the Caribbean AIDS pandemic showed that the distribution of HIV does not follow national borders, but rather the contours of a transnational socioeconomic order. Furthermore, much of the spread of HIV in the 1970s and 1980s moved along international "fault lines," tracking along steep gradients of inequality, which are also paths of migrant labor and sexual commerce.[26]

In an important overview of the pandemic's first decade, Mann and co-workers observe that its course "within and through global society is not being affected—in any serious manner—by the actions taken at the national or international level."[27] HIV has emerged but is going where? Why? And how fast? The Institute of Medicine lists several factors facilitating the emergence of HIV: "urbanization; changes in lifestyles/mores; increased intravenous drug abuse; international travel; medical technology."[2] Much more could be said. HIV has spread across the globe, often wildly, but rarely randomly. Like TB, HIV infection is entrenching itself in the ranks of the poor or otherwise disempowered. Take, as an example, the rapid increase in AIDS incidence among women. In a 1992 report, the United Nations observed that "for most women, the major risk factor for HIV infection is being married. Each day a further three thousand women become infected, and five hundred infected women die."[28] It is not marriage per se, however, that places young women at risk. Throughout the world, most women with HIV infection, married or not, are living in poverty. The means by which confluent social forces, such as gender inequality and poverty, come to be embodied as risk for infection with this emerging pathogen have been neglected in biomedical, epidemiologic, and even social science studies on AIDS. As recently as October 1994—15 years into an ever-emerging pandemic—a *Lancet* editorial could comment, "We are not aware of other investigators who have considered the influence of socioeconomic status on mortality in HIV-infected individuals."[29] Thus, in AIDS, the general rule that the effects of certain types of social forces on health are unlikely to be studied applies in spite of widespread impressions to the contrary.

AIDS has always been a strikingly patterned pandemic. Regardless of the message of public health slogans—"AIDS is for Everyone"—some are at high risk for HIV infection, while others, clearly, are at lower risk. Furthermore, although AIDS eventually causes death in almost all HIV-infected patients, the course of HIV disease varies. Disparities in the course of the disease have sparked the search for hundreds of cofactors, from *Mycoplasma* and ulcerating genital lesions to voodoo rites and psychological predisposition. However, not a single association has been compellingly shown to explain disparities in distribution or outcome of HIV disease. The only well-demonstrated cofactors are social inequalities, which have structured not only the contours of the AIDS pandemic, but also the course of the disease once a patient is infected.[30–31] The advent of more effective antiviral agents promises to heighten those disparities even further: a three-drug regimen that includes a protease inhibitor will cost $12,000 to $16,000 a year.[34]

QUESTIONS FOR A CRITICAL EPISTEMOLOGY OF EMERGING INFECTIOUS DISEASES

Ebola, TB, and HIV infection are in no way unique in demanding contextualization through social science approaches. These approaches include the grounding of case histories and local epidemics in the larger biosocial systems in which they take shape and demand exploration of social inequalities. Why, for example, were there 10,000 cases of diphtheria in Russia from 1990 to 1993? It is easy enough to argue that the excess cases were due to a failure to vaccinate.[35] But only in linking this distal (and, in sum, technical) cause to the much more complex socioeconomic transformations altering the region's illness and death patterns will compelling explanations emerge.[36,37]

Standard epidemiology, narrowly focused on individual risk and short on critical theory, will not reveal these deep socioeconomic transformations, nor will it connect them to disease emergence. "Modern epidemiology," observes one of its leading contributors, is "oriented to explaining and quantifying the bobbing of corks on the surface waters, while largely disregarding the stronger undercurrents that determine where, on average, the cluster of corks ends up along the shoreline of risk."[13] Neither will standard journalistic approaches add much: "Amidst a flood of information," notes the chief journalistic chronicler of disease emergence, "analysis and context are evaporating . . . Outbreaks of flesh eating bacteria may command headlines, but local failures to fully vaccinate preschool children garner little attention unless there is an epidemic."[38]

Research questions identified by various blue-ribbon panels are important for the understanding and eventual control of emerging infectious diseases.[39,40] Yet both the diseases and popular and scientific commentary on them pose a series of corollary questions, which, in turn, demand research that is the exclusive province of neither social scientists nor bench scientists, clinicians, or epidemiologists. Indeed, genuinely transdisciplinary collaboration will be necessary to tackle the problems posed by emerging infectious diseases. As prolegomena, four areas of corollary research are easily identified. In each is heard the recurrent leitmotiv of inequality.

Social Inequalities

Study of the reticulated links between social inequalities and emerging disease would not construe the poor simply as "sentinel chickens," but instead would ask, What are the precise mechanisms by which these diseases come to have their effects in some bodies but not in others? What propagative effects might social inequalities per se contribute?[41] Such queries were once major research questions for epidemiol and social medicine but have fallen out of favor, leaving a vacuum in which immodest claims of causality are easily staked. "To date," note Krieger and co-workers in a recent, magisterial review, "only a small fraction of epidemiological research in the United States has investigated the effects of racism on health."[42] They join others in noting a similar dearth of attention to the effects of sexism and class differences; studies that examine the conjoint influence of these social forces are virtually nonexistent.[43,44]

And yet social inequalities have sculpted not only the distribution of emerging diseases, but also the course of disease in those affected by them, a fact that is often downplayed: "Although there are many similarities between our vulnerability to infectious diseases and that of our ancestors, there is one distinct difference: we have the benefit of extensive scientific knowledge."[7] True enough, but who are "we"? Those most at risk for emerging infectious diseases generally do not, in fact, have the benefit of cutting-edge scientific knowledge. We live in a world where infections pass easily across borders—social and geographic—while resources, including cumulative scientific knowledge, are blocked at customs.

Transnational Forces

"Travel is a potent force in disease emergence and spread," as Wilson has reminded us, and the "current volume, speed, and reach of travel are unprecedented."[45] Although the smallpox and measles epidemics following the European colonization of the Americas were early, deadly reminders of the need for systemic understandings of microbial traffic, there has been, in recent decades, a certain reification of the notion of the "catchment area." A useful means of delimiting a sphere of action—a district, a county, a country—is erroneously elevated to the status of explanatory principle whenever the geographic unit of analysis is other than that defined by the disease itself. Almost all diseases held to be emerging—from the increasing number of drug-resistant diseases to the great pandemics of HIV infection and cholera—stand as modern rebukes to the parochialism of this and other public health constructs.[46] And yet a critical sociology of liminality of both the advancing, transnational edges of pandemics and also the impress of human-made administrative and political boundaries on disease emergence has yet to be attempted.

The study of borders qua borders means, increasingly, the study of social inequalities. Many political borders serve as semipermeable membranes, often quite open to diseases and yet closed to the free movement of cures. Thus may inequalities of access are created or buttressed at borders, even when pathogens cannot be so contained. Research questions might include, for example, What effects might the interface between two very different types of health care systems have on the rate of advance of an emerging disease? What turbulence is introduced when the border in question is between a rich and a poor nation? Writing of health issues at the U.S.-Mexican border, Warner notes that "It is unlikely that any other binational border has such variety in health status, entitlements, and utilization."[47] Among the infectious diseases registered at this border are multidrug-resistant TB, rabies, dengue, and sexually transmitted diseases including HIV infection (said to be due, in part, to "cross-border use of 'red-light' districts").

Methods and theories relevant to the study of borders and emerging infections would come from disciplines ranging from the social sciences to molecular biology: mapping the emergence of diseases is now more feasible with the use of restriction fragment length polymorphism and other new technologies.[48] Again, such investigations will pose difficult questions in a world where plasmids can move, but compassion is often grounded.

The Dynamics of Change

Can we elaborate lists of the differentially weighted factors that promote or retard the emergence or reemergence of infectious diseases? It has been argued that such analyses will perforce be historically deep and geographically broad, and they will at the same time be processual, incorporating concepts of change. Above all, they will seek to incorporate complexity rather than to merely dissect it. As Levins has recently noted, "effective analysis of emerging diseases must recognize the study of complexity as perhaps the central general scientific problem of our time."[49] Can integrated mathematical modeling be linked to new ways of configuring systems, avoiding outmoded units of analyses, such as the nation-state, in favor of the more fluid biosocial networks through which most pathogens clearly move? Can our embrace of complexity also include social complexity and the unequal positioning of groups within larger populations? Such perspectives could be directed towards mapping the progress of diseases from cholera to AIDS, and would permit us to take up more unorthodox research subjects—for example, the effects of World Bank projects and policies on diseases from onchocerciasis to plague.

Critical Epistemology

Many have already asked, What qualifies as an emerging infectious disease? More critical questions might include, Why do some persons constitute "risk groups," while others are "individuals at risk"? These are not merely nosologic questions; they are canonical ones. Why are some approaches and subjects considered appropriate for publication in influential journals, while others are dismissed out of hand? A critical epistemology would explore the boundaries of polite and impolite discussion in science. A trove of complex, affect-laden issues—attribution of blame to perceived vectors of infection, identification of scapegoats and victims, the role of stigma—are rarely discussed in academic medicine, although they are manifestly part and parcel of many epidemics.

Finally, why are some epidemics visible to those who fund research and services, while others are invisible? In its recent statements on TB and emerging infections, for example, the World Health

Organization uses the threat of contagion to motivate wealthy nations to invest in disease surveillance and control out of self-interest—an age-old public health approach acknowledged in the Institute of Medicine's report on emerging infections: "Diseases that appear not to threaten the United States directly rarely elicit the political support necessary to maintain control efforts."[2] If related to a study under consideration, questions of power and control over funds must be discussed. That they are not is more a marker of analytic failures than of editorial standards.

Ten years ago, the sociologist of science Bruno Latour reviewed hundreds of articles appearing in several Pasteur-era French scientific reviews to constitute what he called an "anthropology of the sciences" (he objected to the term epistemology). Latour cast his net widely. "There is no essential difference between the human and social sciences and the exact or natural sciences," he wrote, "because there is no more science than there is society. I have spoken of the Pasteurians as they spoke of their microbes."[50] (Here, perhaps, is another reason to engage in a "proactive" effort to explore themes usually relegated to the margins of scientific inquiry: those of us who describe the comings and goings of microbes—feints, parries, emergences, retreats—may one day be subjected to the scrutiny of future students of the subject.)

Microbes remain the world's leading causes of death.[51] In "The conquest of infectious diseases: who are we kidding?" the authors argue that "clinicians, microbiologists, and public health professionals must work together to prevent infectious diseases and to detect emerging diseases quickly."[52] But past experience with epidemics suggests that other voices and perspectives could productively complicate the discussion. In every major retrospective study of infectious disease outbreaks, the historical regard has shown us that what was not examined during an epidemic is often as important as what was[53,54] and that social inequalities were important in the contours of past disease emergence. The facts have taught us that our approach must be dynamic, systemic, and critical. In addition to historians, then, anthropologists and sociologists accountable to history and political economy have much to add, as do the critical epidemiologists mentioned above.[55–58]

My intention, here, is ecumenical and complementary. A critical framework would not aspire to supplant the methods of the many disciplines, from virology to molecular epidemiology, which now concern themselves with emerging diseases. "The key task for medicine," argued the pioneers Eisenberg and Kleinman some 15 years ago, "is not to diminish the role of the biomedical sciences in the theory and practice of medicine but to supplement them with an equal application of the social sciences in order to provide both a more comprehensive understanding of disease and better care of the patient. The problem is not 'too much science,' but too narrow a view of the sciences relevant to medicine."[59]

A critical anthropology of emerging infections is young, but it is not embryonic. At any rate, much remains to be done and the tasks themselves are less clear perhaps than their inherent difficulties. The philosopher Michel Serres once observed that the border between the natural and the human sciences was not to be traced by clean, sharp lines. Instead, this border recalled the Northwest Passage: long and perilously complicated, its currents and inlets often leading nowhere, dotted with innumerable islands and occasional floes.[60] Serres' metaphor reminds us that a sea change is occurring in the study of infectious disease even as it grows, responding, often, to new challenges—and sometimes to old challenges newly perceived.

REFERENCES

1. Morse S. Factors in the emergence of infectious diseases. Emerging Infectious Diseases 1995;1:7–15.
2. Lederberg J, Shope RE, Oaks SC. Emerging infections: microbial threats to health in the United States. Washington, D.C.: National Academy Press, 1992.
3. Eckardt I. Challenging complexity: conceptual issues in an approach to new disease. Ann New York Acad Sci 1994;740:408–17.
4. Levine N. Editor's preface to selections from Drake D. Malaria in the interior valley of North America. Urbana: University of Illinois Press, 1964 (1850).
5. Frenk J, Chacon F. Bases conceptuales de la nueva salud international. Salud Pública Méx 1991;33:307–13.
6. McCord C, Freeman H. Excess mortality in Harlem. N Engl J Med 1990;322:173–7.
7. Satcher D. Emerging infections: getting ahead of the curve. Emerging Infectious Diseases 1995;1:1–6.
8. MacKenzie W, Hoxie N, Proctor M, Gradus MS, Blair KA, Peterson DE, et al. A massive outbreak in Milwaukee of Cryptosporidium infection transmitted through the water supply. N Engl J Med 1994;331:l61–7.
9. Lurie P, Hintzen P, Lowe RA. Socioeconomic obstacles to HIV prevention and treatment in developing countries: the roles of the International Monetary Fund and the World Bank. AIDS 1995;9:539–46.
10. World Health Organization. Cholera in the Americas. Weekly Epidemiol Rec. 1992;67:33–9.
11. McCarthy S, McPhearson R, Guarino A. Toxigenic Vibrio cholera O1 and cargo ships entering the Gulf of Mexico. Lancet 1992;339:624.
12. Goma Epidemiology Group. Public health impact of Rwandan refugee crisis: what happened in Goma, Zaire, in July, 1994? Lancet 1995;345:339–44.

13. McMichael A. The health of persons, populations and planets: epidemiology comes full circle. Epidemiology 1995;6:633–6.
14. Johnson KM, Webb PA, Lange JV, Murphy FA. Isolation and partial characterization of a new virus causing acute hemorrhagic fever in Zaire. Lancet 1977;1:569–71.
15. World Health Organization. Ebola haemorrhagic fever in Zaire, 1976. Report of an international commission. Bull WHO 1978;56:271–93.
16. Garrett L. The coming plague. New York: Farrar, Straus and Giroux, 1995.
17. Ryan F. The forgotten plague: how the battle against tuberculosis was won and lost. Boston: Little, Brown, 1993.
18. Iseman M. Tailoring a time-bomb. Am Rev Respir Dis 1985;132:735–6.
19. Bloom B, Murray C. Tuberculosis: commentary on a resurgent killer. Science 1992;257:1055–63.
20. Murray C. Social, economic and operational research on tuberculosis: recent studies and some priority questions. Bull Int Union Tuberc Lung Dis 1991;66:149–56.
21. Farmer P, Robin S, Ramilus St-L, Kim J. Tuberculosis and "compliance": lessons from rural Haiti. Seminars in Respiratory Infections 1991;6:373–9.
22. Spence D, Hotchkiss J, Williams C, Davies P. Tuberculosis and poverty. British Medical Journal 1993;307:759–61.
23. McKenna MT, McCray E, Onorato I. The epidemiology of tuberculosis among foreign-born persons in the United States, 1986 to 1993. N Engl J Med 1995; 332: 1071–6.
24. Chabner B. Cited in the Miami News, December 2, 1982;8A.
25. Farmer P. AIDS and accusation: Haiti and the Geography of blame. University of California Press, Berkeley, 1992.
26. Farmer P. The exotic and the mundane: human immunodeficiency virus in the Caribbean. Human Nature 1990;l:415–45.
27. Mann J, Tarantola D, Netter T. AIDS in the world. Cambridge, MA: Harvard University Press, 1992.
28. United Nations Development Program. Young women: silence, susceptibility and the HIV epidemic. New York, UNDP, 1992.
29. Sampson J, Neaton J. On being poor with HIV. Lancet 1994;344:1100–1.
30. Chaisson RE, Keruly JC, Moore RD. Race, sex, drug use, and progression of human immunodeficiency virus disease. N Engl J Med 1995;333:75l–6.
31. Farmer P, Connors M, and Simmons J, eds. Women, poverty, and AIDS: sex, drugs, and structural violence. Monroe, ME: Common Courage Press, 1996.
32. Fife E, Mode C. AIDS incidence and income. JAIDS 1992;5:1105–10.
33. Wallace R, Fullilove M, Fullilove R, Gould P, Wallace D. Will AIDS be contained within U.S. minority populations? Soc Sci Med 1994;39:1051–62.
34. Waldholz M. Precious pills: new AIDS treatment raises tough question of who will get it. Wall Street Journal, July 3, 1996, p. 1.
35. Centers for Disease Control and Prevention. Diphtheria outbreak—Russian Federation, 1990–1993. MMWR 1993;42:840–1847.
36. Field M. The health crisis in the former Soviet Union: a report from the "post-war" zone. Soc Sci Med 1995;1469–78.
37. Patz J, Epstein P, Burke T, Balbus J. Global climate change and emerging infectious diseases. JAMA 1996; 275:217–33.
38. Garrett L. Public health and the mass media. Current Issues in Public Health 1995;l:147–50.
39. Centers for Disease Control and Prevention. Addressing emerging infectious disease threats: a prevention strategy for the United States. Atlanta, USA. Department of Health and Human Services, 1994.
40. Roizman B, ed. Infectious diseases in an age of change: the impact of human ecology and behavior on disease transmission. Washington, D.C.: National Academy Press, 1995.
41. Farmer P. On suffering and structural violence: a view from below. Daedalus 1996;125:261–83.
42. Krieger N, Rowley D, Herman A, Avery B, Phillips M. Racism, sexism, and social class: implications for studies of health, disease, and well-being. Am J Prev Med 1993; (Supplement)9:82–122.
43. Navarro V. Race or class versus race and class: mortality differentials in the United States. Lancet 1990;336:1238–40.
44. Marmot M. Social differentials in health within and between populations. Daedalus 1994;123:197–216.
45. Wilson M. Travel and the emergence of infectious diseases. Emerging Infectious Diseases 1995;1:39–46.
46. Haggett P. Geographical aspects of the emergence of infectious diseases. Geogr Ann 1994;76:91–104.
47. Warner DC. Health issues at the US-Mexican border. JAMA1991;265:242–7.
48. Small P, Moss A. Molecular epidemiology and the new tuberculosis. Infect Agents Dis 1993;2:132–8.
49. Levins R. Preparing for uncertainty. Ecosystem Health 1995;1:47–57.
50. Latour B. The pasteurization of France. Sheridan A, Law J, trans. Cambridge, MA: Harvard University Press, 1988.
51. Global Health Situation and Projections. Geneva: World Health Organization, 1992.
52. Berkelman RL, Hughes JM. The conquest of infectious diseases: who are we kidding? Ann Int Med 1993;119: 426–8.
53. Epstein PR. Pestilence and poverty—historical transitions and the great pandemics. Am J Prev Med 1992;8:263–8.
54. Packard R. White plague, black labor: tuberculosis and the political economy of health and disease in South Africa. Berkeley: University of California Press.
55. Aïach P, Carr-Hill R, Curtis S, Illsley R. Les inégalités sociales de santé en France et en Grande-Bretagne. Paris: INSERM, 1987.
56. Fassin D. Exclusion, underclass, marginalidad. Revue Française de Sociologie 1996;37:37–75.
57. Inhorn M, Brown P, eds. The anthropology of infectious diseases. New York: Gordon and Breach, 1996.
58. Krieger N, Zierler S. What explains the public's health? A call for epidemiologic theory. Epidemiology 1996;7: 107–9.
59. Eisenberg L, Kleinman A. The relevance of social science to medicine. Dordrecht: Reidel, 1981.
60. Serres M. Le passage du nord-ouest. Paris: Editions de Minuit, 1980.

 11

Why Is It Easier to Get Drugs Than Drug Treatment in the United States?

Merrill Singer

Medical anthropologists have made many contributions to our understanding of addictions to illegal drugs. Drug problems differentially affect the poor and members of ethnic minorities. The behavior of drug addicts is illegal, yet their opportunities for drug treatment are limited. In fact, society seems conflicted about the question of whether drug addiction is a medical or law enforcement problem. The "War on Drugs," which includes tough criminal-sentencing mandates, has resulted in a remarkable increase in U.S. prison populations.

Much of the medical anthropological research on drug issues has focused on the sociocultural context of addiction—what the lives of addicts are like and how they survive. Research by anthropologists like Philippe Bourgois (2003) and Claire Sterk (1999) has shed light on these people, who are often invisible to mainstream society. Because addicts are at high risk for contracting HIV if they use dirty needles, and because needle exchange programs are effective public health measures for preventing spread of this disease, drug abuse is a very important issue.

The ecology of drug addiction is not simply a matter of drugs being available and people making "bad decisions." The ecology of drug addiction is political. *This selection illustrates a medical anthropological approach that emphasizes the political ecology of a health problem. Rather than simply analyzing health problems at the level of individual decisions, anthropologists must study the larger context of politics, economics, and social power. In other words, the ecology of drug addiction is shaped by political and moral decisions that create the environment of drug addiction. There are many parallels to the author's sophisticated analysis of a legal drug—alcohol—abuse in selection 36. This selection illustrates this political-economic and political-ecological approach in medical anthropology.*

As you read this selection, consider these questions:

- **What is the answer to the author's question in the title? Do profits make a difference?**
- **Why does the author use a historical approach that emphasizes the cultural factors shaping drug policy?**
- **From a medical anthropological viewpoint, why do some people become drug addicts?**
- **How might political policies like the War on Drugs affect the environment of drug abuse?**
- **How is drug abuse in the United States related to the global political economy?**

Context: Merrill Singer, a professor at the University of Connecticut, worked for a large portion of his career as director of research at the Hispanic Health Council in Hartford, Connecticut. Along with his frequent co-author, Hans Baer, he has been an important leader in "critical medical anthropology," an approach that particularly emphasizes a political-economic and political-activist approach to diverse health problems. Much of Singer's research has been funded by the National Institute of Drug Abuse, part of the National Institutes of Health. He is a prolific author; this selection was originally published in a recent edited volume on the negative health effects of health policy.

Source: M. Singer (2004). "Why Is It Easier to Get Drugs Than Drug Treatment in the United States?" In Unhealthy Health Policy: A Critical Anthropological Examination, pp. 287–302. Walnut Creek, CA: Altamira Press.

On the front page of its Sunday edition on June 8, 2002, the *New York Times* ran an article titled "Latin American Poppy Fields Undermine U.S. Drug Battle." This article encapsulates one half of the purpose of this [reading], namely documentation of the failure of the War on Drugs to stop the flow of drugs to U.S. cities, towns, and rural areas. As the article notes, amid this long-fought war, drugs are readily available and new users are joining the ranks of illicit drug consumers (Forero and Weiner 2002). If we add to this picture the rapid spread of so-called club drugs, and their movement toward becoming a new wave of street drugs, as well as the domestic production and widespread use of substances like methamphetamine, and under the counter sales of pharmaceutical narcotics and tranquilizers on the street, it is evident that the War on Drugs can claim few real victories: it is still easy to get drugs anywhere in the United States, from down the street from the White House to the least populated county in the country and from inner-city streets to Wall Street suites. Getting into effective drug treatment, on the other hand, remains a major challenge for the many drug users who would like to overcome their drug dependency. In short, a burning question for health policy in the United States is "Why is it easier to get drugs than drug treatment?"

The unhealthy state of policies and strategies enacted in response to illicit drug use is captured in the following anecdote. In response to the AIDS epidemic, I helped develop a study of the role of syringes in HIV infection among drug users (see . . . Singer et al. 2000). The study design called for the collection of syringes acquired on the street by drug users for laboratory testing for the presence of human DNA (to determine if syringes sold on the street are being recycled and are a possible source of infection). Additionally, ethnographers were to visit abandoned buildings or other frequently used illicit drug-injection sites to collect discarded syringes to be tested for HIV and hepatitis C antibodies (indicating that the syringe has been used by an infected individual and that reuse by another individual could transmit infection). While many of the procedures used in this project reflect strategies implemented elsewhere in AIDS prevention research, in Springfield, Massachusetts, one of the three northeastern U.S. cities in which the project was to be implemented—and despite the full support from the local public health department, AIDS prevention programs, and community-based organizations—the local police flatly told the research team that if they were caught in possession of syringes in transit to the laboratory, they would be arrested for violation of state paraphernalia laws. No attempts to explain the public health procedures employed in the project or its HIV risk-reduction goals convinced police officials that arresting AIDS researchers would only retard AIDS prevention and not further the cause of the War on Drugs. At several meetings, the police unswervingly affirmed their commitment to arresting drug users or anyone else that violated a strict reading of existing paraphernalia laws.

This vignette reflects in microcosm the enormous difficulties our society has had in responding effectively and reasonably to the AIDS epidemic in light of prevailing attitudes, laws, and criminal justice practices directed at drug users. As a result of the War on Drugs, every 20 seconds someone in the United States is arrested for a drug violation and, at the rate of one per week, a new prison is completed to house the unprecedented throng of inmates that are now locked up in the world's largest and most populous penal system (Egan 1999). Perhaps the logic of this approach might be defended if it actually achieved its intended goal of stopping the production, distribution, and use of dangerous substances. However, as noted above, there is abundant evidence that the War on Drugs has been an unmitigated failure in achieving its publicly expressed purposes. The War on Drugs continues unabated, presidential administration after administration, one bloated "drug-fighting" annual budget after the other, seemingly headed toward a modern reenactment of the 100 Years' War.

It seems reasonable to ask why this apparently futile war continues. The conclusion reached by a growing number of people concerned with this public health and social issue is that even while the War on Drugs can claim little in terms of achieving its primary goals, it has, in fact, produced enormously useful secondary gains. This [reading] argues that the War on Drugs, seen *not* as a war on drug use per se but as a social war on *those who can be classified as drug users (or pushers),* functions as a well-financed societal control mechanism that redundantly reinforces and reproduces the most overtly inegalitarian features of the structure of American society.

ANATOMY OF THE WAR ON DRUGS

The 1960s left an indelible mark on American drug use patterns. Prior to this time, the United States had experienced various waves of drug use, all of which were shaped in their character and composition by distinctive historic forces and prevailing social relationships, but the 1960s marked a significant shift in prevailing patterns. This shift—which can be seen as the ever-widening expansion of illicit drug use from the social margins (e.g., ethnic minorities and other devalued social groups like jazz musicians or beat generation writers) to the mainstream core—provided the initial public motivation for the War on Drugs. This war was publicly declared in 1969 by Richard Nixon early in his presidential term as part of his campaign to restore "law and order" to American society. As Musto (1987:254) notes, "No President has equaled Nixon's antagonism to drug abuse, and he took an active role in organizing the federal and state governments to fight the onslaught of substance abuse." In fiscal year 1969, the antidrug budget was $86 million (Drug Abuse Council 1980). Nixon resolutely declared that illicit drugs were now "public enemy number one" (cited in Chambers and Inciardi 1974:221). The war was on!

Without doubt, drug use had expanded greatly just prior to (and during) the Nixon administration. Survey data from 1971 suggest that as many as 24 million Americans admitted that they had broken with convention and tried marijuana, a drug that had been nationally condemned as a "killer weed" in previous decades. Most notably, among young adults (18–21 years), 40 percent reported having used marijuana. Moreover, so-called hard drug use also was growing. It is estimated that the number of heroin users jumped from a relative handful during World War II to 50,000 by 1960 and to 500,000 a decade later (Domestic Council Drug Abuse Task Force 1975; National Commission on Marijuana and Drug Abuse 1972). By 1972, a Gallup Poll found that drug abuse was seen as the major cause of urban decay (cited in Inciardi 1986), although others would see drug abuse and urban decay as common consequences of social policies and economic practices such as the exportation of industrial production and the federal financing of suburban flight (Baer, Singer, and Susser 2003). With the expressed purpose of turning the tide against the ever-widening circle of drug use, Nixon quickly established the Special Action Office for Drug Abuse Prevention, the Office of Drug Abuse Law Enforcement, and the Office of National Narcotics Intelligence. At all appearances, the Nixon administration seemed quite serious about fighting a full-scale war to extinguish illicit drug use. A closer look at the oft-cited Nixon opposition to drug abuse, however, suggests a somewhat different understanding of his widely heralded War on Drugs. [Nixon had multiple motivations for launching a war on drugs, using new drug enforcement institutions for his own political agenda being among them. In fact, motivation for opposition to drug use has historically been complicated by varying political influences. . . .]

U.S. opposition to drug use did not begin until the late nineteenth century. Importantly, congressional debate on the first narcotics laws *did not focus on the negative health effects* of drugs like opium and cocaine, nor even on the rising rate of addiction in the U.S. population, but rather was driven in no small measure by concern with America's rising position in international trade. Specifically, Congress's first action against drugs developed in direct response to the fact that the British were gaining an economic bonanza from their forced opium sales (from their Indian colony) to China, profits that enabled England to achieve a competitive edge against U.S. businesses globally.

At this time, public drug use was widespread in the United States as well. Drugs like heroin and cocaine were readily available. A study done in 1888 of the contents of prescriptions purchased from pharmacies in Boston, for example, found that of the 10,200 prescriptions filled that year, 15 percent contained opiates, and that opiate-based proprietary drugs had the highest sales (Eaton 1888). The end result was that during the 1800s, opium use was treated as a "normal" behavior that was both legal and integrated into everyday experience.

Indeed, the only behavior that was labeled as a "drug problem" per se was the smoking of opium in opium dens often located in the Chinese sections of U.S. cities, although not only used by Chinese clients. From this moment on, U.S. societal reactions to drug use and attitudes about particular racial/ethnic groups have been closely intertwined. In the case of Chinese opium smoking, a major underlying factor in social condemnation was the depression that began in the 1860s and the resulting redefinition of the Chinese as surplus labor in the American West. As with opium, attitudes about cocaine also were colored by societal racism. Throughout the American South, a publicly expressed fear developed that if blacks had access to cocaine, they "might become oblivious of their prescribed bounds and attack white society" (Musto 1987:6). These examples reveal an important aspect of U.S. experience with illicit drugs that is often hidden behind moral, legal, and even public health initiatives like the War on Drugs. . . . In the early 1940s, . . . rates of drug addiction in the United States took a sudden drop. The decline, caused by [WW II's] disruption of drug trafficking systems, was short-lived. Soldiers who had used drugs overseas began to bring their addictions and knowledge of drug use home with them. And it was in the ghettos and barrios along the East and West coasts that drug injection found a new home after the war, especially among young men whose hopes for equality, raised by a war against totalitarianism, were smashed by racism and the postwar economic downturn.

In addition to the press of social conditions, the postwar U.S. inner-city drug epidemic was the end result of several events, including: (1) the 1949 retreat of defeated Kuomintang Nationalist Chinese forces into eastern Burma and their takeover of opium production in the Golden Triangle poppy-growing region of Southeast Asia, (2) the emergence of Hong Kong and Marseilles as heroin-refining centers, and (3) the reestablishment of Mafia-controlled international drug trafficking networks (Inciardi 1986; Schultheis 1983; Singer et al. 1990). The individual responsible for the latter was none other than Lucky Luciano. Arrested in 1936 on drug charges, from his jail cell he sent messages to Sicily directing the Mafia to support the U.S. Army during World War II. It is widely believed that in return for helping the Allies during the invasion of Sicily, and for opposing communism in Italy after the war, the Mafia was made various promises by the U.S. government, including the return of weapons confiscated by Mussolini's Fascists (McCoy 1991). In addition, Luciano was able to build an unparalleled international narcotics syndicate soon after his arrival in Italy in 1946 (McCoy, Read, and Adams 1986:114). As Musto (1987:236) notes, a key factor in Lucky Luciano's "success" as a drug kingpin was "police collusion with drug suppliers in communities like Harlem."

In short, Nixon's War on Drugs, although launched with great fanfare and, in fact, accompanied by a significant expansion in the availability of drug treatment, followed a long tradition of contradictory motivations and actions that undercut the expressed goal of fighting illicit drug use. The same types of patterns also characterize America's continually renewed War on Drugs *since* the Nixon presidency. For example, after the fall of the Shah of Iran, the CIA developed a growing presence in Afghanistan—which had become one of the world's largest opium-producing areas—including developing supportive relationships with opium-growing Baluchi and Pashtun peoples. When the Soviet Union invaded Afghanistan in 1979, the CIA, on the authority of President Jimmy Carter, began supplying arms and logistic support to the northern tribes. As a result of "high-powered CIA largess" (Levins 1986:125) and a record poppy crop in the region, there appeared a new "monster source of opium production [that] . . . promise[d] to send a veritable hurricane of heroin swirling once again through the streets of Europe and America: Afghanistan" (Levins 1986:125).

That wave struck in the early 1980s. In response, Presidents Reagan and Bush resuscitated a somewhat indolent drug war (again without any real success), and Bill Clinton joined the battle by appointing a general, Barry McCaffrey, to lead America's charge. In the introduction to his 1996 National Drug Control Strategy, President Clinton (1996:3) claimed: "In the last few years our Nation has made significant progress against drug use and related crime. We have dealt serious blows to the international criminal networks that import drugs into America."

A street-level view of the drug scene, however, does not support these rosy pronouncements (Singer 1999). Drops in the levels of some kinds of drug use appear to be unrelated to supply issues and are offset by rises in other kinds of drug use (Community Epidemiological Work Group 1998). Cocaine use, for example, may be down, but use of heroin, methamphetamine, and designer drugs is up significantly. Indeed, data from the U.S. Substance Abuse and Mental Health Services Administration indicate that since 1988 there has been a significant drop in the mean age of first-time heroin users, from 27.4 years in 1988 to 17.6 years in 1997 (Dee 1999). Recent studies have shown that teenagers report that marijuana is readily available in high school and can be easily acquired within a short period of time. In fact, there has been little change in the level of adolescent access to marijuana in 25 years, with approximately 90 percent currently reporting that it is "very easy" or "fairly easy" to obtain (Johnson, Bachman, and O'Malley 1997).

Now in its fourth decade, the War on Drugs, in short, continues to fail at achieving its primary goal of significantly stemming the flow of illicit drugs into the United States (Guttman 1996). Indeed, as Bertram and Sharpe (1996:C-I), coauthors of the book *Drug War Politics: The Price of Denial,* argued, "Drug law-enforcement budgets increased from $1 billion to $9 billion annually during the past 15 years, but heroin and cocaine are cheaper and more available than ever." Notably, since 1996, the drug law enforcement price tag has jumped another $3 billion annually without any significant record of success.

Consequently, during the War on Drugs, the National Institute on Drug Abuse has reported a steady increase in the drug abuse cost to society. Indeed, in the thick of the recent War on Drugs years, from 1985 to 1992, there was a 50 percent increase in the estimated cost to society of illicit drug use in terms of the combined impact of drug-related crime, health care expenditures, and lost wages. In light of this reassessment of somewhat hidden features of the War on Drugs, a rationale appears for why the program has continued, year after year, decade after decade, at great cost and with little overt success. This rationale consists of the following secondary gains of the "war."

GLOBAL DESIGNS

At the international level, the War on Drugs serves to further U.S. geopolitical and geo-economic interests (as some in power would define them) when overt actions toward serving those ends are illegal or embarrassing, or would prove unpopular with the American people. Repeatedly, as has been noted, behind the public face of the drug war has been a backstage effort to collude with (and hence foster) drug producers/distributors and the use of the drug war as a Trojan Horse for the achievement of other political economic aims. At the same time, while political enemies like Castro of Cuba or the Sandinistas of Nicaragua have been repeatedly publicly accused by U.S. government spokespersons of having deep involvement in drug trafficking (often without much evidence)—and this accusation has been used to demonstrate to the American people the immoral character of hated regimes—the clear involvement of U.S. clients and intelligence personnel in the drug trade has been hidden from public view. Exploiting the drug problem in the service of international political power in this way reflects the phenomenon that Chomsky (1988:169) has referred to as "the reality that must be effaced."

THE BENEFITS OF BLAME

Secondly, by scapegoating drug users as the nefarious cause of contemporary urban suffering and decay—a practice that is even more common among government spokespersons than accusations made against foreign heads of state—attention is diverted from the role of class inequality as a source of social misery. Since the full implementation of federal laws banning the sale of some substances, and ever more so since the formal declaration of the War on Drugs, there has been an effort to paint the drug addict as the very essence of deviance and badness in U.S. society. Addicts are not simply socially devalued, they are portrayed as the reason why our streets and homes are unsafe, our inner cities are eyesores that must be avoided by suburbanites at all costs, and our ability to experience a traditional American feeling of community has been shattered. Lost in this interpretation is any assessment of the role of corporate policy—including rampant mergers, buyouts, restructuring, downsizing, hiring and training policies, shrinking public giving patterns, and factory closings—in reshaping American social life. The inner-city areas commonly identified in the popular imagination with drug use are the very areas that have been abandoned in corporate shifts, producing rampant unemployment, deteriorating services, failing schools, and the resulting short-term coping strategies for surviving social misery that come to be seen as the causes and not the consequences of pressing urban problems (Bourgois 1995; Singer 1994; Waterston 1993).

RACISM AND THE DEMONIZATION OF (SOME) DRUGs

Thirdly, by widely promoting the image of the drug user of color as a modern social bogey man, the War on Drugs effectively reinforces divisive racist stereotypes that contribute to a well-contained labor force with negligible working-class consciousness. Consistently, the demonized image of the drug user and drug dealer presented to society through all arms of the mass media is that of the African American male nationally and the Latino male internationally. At the neighborhood level, these threatening images are used to justify nightly police assaults in full battle gear on minority neighborhoods, a campaign that has telling social consequences. As Chambliss (1994:679) points out, "The war on drugs in the United States has produced another war as well: it is a war between the police and minority youth from the 'ghetto underclass,'" as reflected in rap song lyrics.

Indeed, whatever its failures, one of the things that the War on Drugs has done quite well is to arrest a lot of people and put them in prison. A profile of those incarcerated on drug-related charges, however, suggests that enforcement of drug policy is a better reflection of the "politics of race" than it is of a meaningful effort to stop the sale and use of illicit drugs. While studies show that 15 percent of the nation's cocaine users are African American, they account for approximately 40 percent of those charged with powder cocaine violations and 90 percent of those convicted on crack cocaine charges (Davidson 1999). Overall, African Americans, who comprise 12 percent of the U.S. population, make up 55 percent of those convicted for illicit drug possession. One in 15 African American males currently is incarcerated, primarily as a result of drug laws. Moreover, in 1995, approximately 30 percent of African American males between the ages of 20 and 29 years were under some form of criminal justice supervision, up from 23 percent in 1990.

The significantly higher proportion of African Americans charged with crack cocaine offenses has been found to be "the single most important difference accounting for the overall longer sentences imposed on blacks, relative to other groups" according to a 1993 Justice Department report (quoted in Muwakkil 1996:21). Ironically, while still clinging to patriotic slogans about the unparalleled freedoms of American society, compared to other industrialized countries on a per capita basis the United States is the most incarcerating nation in the world. Lost in the "lock 'em up" drug war mentality is any systematic assessment of why socially marginalized working-class youth turn to drugs and the drug trade, including any examination of the direct contributions of structurally imposed inequality of access to socially valued statuses, avenues of social success, and coveted material wealth. As Bourgois (1995:320) notes, the drug trade is "the biggest equal opportunity employer" for inner-city youth. By hiding this painful reality behind demonized images of drug users of color, the War on Drugs blocks a full public consideration of reality.

THE WAGES OF SIN

Fourth, by sustaining the existence of an exploitable pariah subcaste of low-cost, drug-dependent workers, and by allowing a revolving system for warehousing segments of this labor pool behind publicly funded prison walls, the War on Drugs slashes production costs and bolsters corporate profits. While street drug users often lack steady full-time employment, they do acquire shorter-term blue-collar jobs of various sorts in the formal economy. Sociologists of work have long recognized that an effective means of lowering salaries across the board in the working class is the existence of a sector of semi-employed workers at the bottom of the labor market. This desperate pool of workers who are resigned to accept socially marginal, low-status jobs at minimal wages functions to competitively pull down the wage levels of other strata of labor. As Waterston (1993:241) notes, "As a special category, addicts are politically weak and disconnected from organized labor, thereby becoming a source of cheap, easily expendable labor. Moreover, the costs of daily reproduction are absorbed by addict-workers themselves."

Moreover, the dramatic increase in the number of imprisoned Americans has created a large pool of potentially available superexploited workers, some of whom earn as little as 17 cents an hour. As Chien, Connors, and Fox (2000:319) point out, "[Prison] employers can freely dismiss and recall workers, need not deal with unions, and do not have to pay for benefits or even work facilities, as these costs are borne by taxpayers." The prison industry, they note, which has a number of subsectors, including the building and running of prisons and the leasing of prison labor, is but one arena in which the private sector directly profits from the War on Drugs.

Unfortunately, as the director of the National Institute on Drug Abuse has argued, there remains "a widespread misperception that drug abuse treatment is not effective. . . . [However] there are now extensive data showing that addiction is eminently treatable if the treatment is well delivered and tailored to the needs of the particular patient" (Leshner 1999:1314). Rates of success in drug treatment are comparable to those for other chronic diseases such as diabetes, hypertension, and asthma. Ironically, studies of the social benefits of drug treatment support the very kinds of changes that those who demonize drug users would most support. First, criminal activity among individuals in and after drug treatment is two-thirds of that of comparable out-of-treatment drug users (Gerstein et al. 1994). Rajkumar and French (1996), for example, calculated that the costs of crime averaged $47,971 per drug user per year prior to drug treatment, compared to $28,657 in the year following drug treatment. Second, French and Zarkin (1992) have found that even a 10 percent increase in the amount of time spent in a residential drug treatment program increases the subsequent legal earning of a drug user by 2.4 percent and decreases illegal earnings by 4.1 percent. Similar findings exist for methadone treatment (French and Zarkin 1992). Third, cost savings in terms of AIDS infection, tuberculosis, and other diseases that are much more common among drug users who are out of treatment compared to those in treatment significantly adds to the demonstrated cost and health benefits of drug treatment (French, Mauskopf, Teague, and Roland 1996). Injection drug users who are not in treatment have been found to be six times more likely to be infected with HIV than those who enroll and stay in drug treatment (Metzger et al. 1993). Further, there is a consistent finding indicating an association between duration of drug treatment and protection from HIV infection (Metzger, Navaline, and Woody 1998).

Currently, of the $18 billion in the federal drug budget, only one-third is directed toward prevention and treatment efforts. However, only 10 percent of the approximately $6 billion of federal money targeted to reduce the demand for drugs is earmarked for the treatment of the estimated 4 million hardcore drug users in the United States (Stocker 1998). Importantly, as a widely cited 1994 RAND study found, from a cost-benefits standpoint, drug treatment is seven times more cost effective than domestic law enforcement and incarceration, ten times more effective than interdiction programs designed to stop drugs at the U.S. border, and 23 times more effective than efforts to attack the sources of illicit drug production abroad (cited in Massing 1999). In other words, the least funded aspect of the federal drug strategy—treatment—produces the greatest benefit in terms of lowering the use of illicit drugs.

While there are shortcomings to a fully medicalized model of drug treatment (Waterston 1993)—one that does not recognize and respond to the social origins of drug abuse—and sound concerns about the growing "commodification of treatment" (Murphy and Rosenbaum 1999), nonetheless a radical shift toward an emphasis on treatment would go a long way toward creating a healthy drug abuse policy orientation. Of special note, in her ethnographic study of cocaine-using women in Atlanta, the women Sterk (1999:209-210) interviewed emphasized the need for community-based programs that addressed all aspects of their lives. They proposed a harm-reduction approach, which included low-threshold programs that do not penalize drug users who have not quit totally or who re-lapse, that provide psychological services to help them cope with their past experiences as well as practical services such as basic education, life-skills training, job preparation, and employment opportunities. They yearned for large social changes as well, especially for an end to poverty and an increase in welfare benefits for the poor.

As this finding suggests, while U.S. policy makers haven't figured out how to effectively address our national drug crisis, drug users—those who bear the painful burden of their own addictions—often have a very clear sense of a healthy drug policy. Perhaps it is time that we listen.

REFERENCES

Agar, M., and H. Schacht Reisinger. (2002). "A Tale of Two Policies: The French Connection, Methadone, and Heroin Epidemics." *Culture, Medicine and Psychiatry* 26 no. 3: '371–96.

Baer, H., M. Singer, and I. Susser. (2003). *Medical Anthropology and the World System,* 2nd ed.Westport, CT: Praeger.

Bertram, E., and K. Sharpe. (1996, September 26). "Drug Abuse: Is the Cure Worse than the Crime—Candidates Lack Answers to Questions." *Hartford Courant,* C-I, C-4.

Bourgois, P. (1995). *In Search of Respect: Selling Crack in El Barrio.* Cambridge: Cambridge University Press.

Browning, F., and B. Garrett. (1986). "The CIA and the New Opium War." In *Culture and Politics of Drugs,* edited by Peter Park and Wasyl Matveychuk, 118–24. Dubuque, Iowa: Kendall/Hunt.

Castillo, F. (1987). *Los Jinetes de la Cocaina.* Bogota: Editorial Documentos Periodisticos.

Chambers, C, and J. Inciardi. (1974). "Forecasts for the Future: Where We Are and Where We Are Going." In *Drugs and Criminal Justice System,* edited by J. Inciardi and C. Chambers, 218–34. Beverly Hills, CA: Sage.

Chambliss, W. (1994). "Why the U.S. Government Is Not Contributing to the Resolution of the Nation's Drug Problem." *International Journal of Health Services* 24, no. 4: 675–90.

Chien, A., M. Connors, and K. Fox. (2000). "The Drug War in Perspective." In *Dying for Growth,* edited by J. Y. Kim, J. Millen, A. Irwin, and J. Gershman, 293–327. Monroe, ME: Common Courage Press.

Chomsky, N. (1988). *The Culture of Terrorism.* Boston: South End Press.

Clinton, W. (1996). "Transmittal Letter from the President." In *The National Drug Control Strategy,* 3. Washington, DC: White House.

Coffin, P. (1999). *Safer Injection Rooms.* New York: Lindesmith Center.

Community Epidemiological Work Group. (1998). *Epidemiologic Trends in Drug Abuse, vol. 1: Highlights and Executive Summary.* Rockville, MD: National Institute on Drug Abuse.

Davidson, J. (1999). "The Drug War's Color Line: Black Leader's Shift Stances on Sentencing." The Nation 269, no. 8: 42–43.

Dee, J. (1999, November 15). "New Face of Heroin: First-Time Users Getting Younger." *Hartford Courant,* Al, A6.

Domestic Council Drug Abuse Task Force. (1975). *White Paper on Drug Abuse.* Washington, DC: U.S. Government Printing Office.

Drug Abuse Council. (1980). *The Facts about "Drug Abuse."* New York: Free Press.

Eaton, V. (1888). "How the Opium Habit Is Acquired." *Popular Science* 33: 665–66.

Egan, T. (1999). "The War on Drugs Retreats, Still Taking Prisons." *New York Times,* February 28, I.

Epstein, E. (1977). *Agency of Fear.* New York: G. P. Putnam's.

Forero, J., and T. Weiner. (2002, June 8). "Latin American Poppy Fields Undermine U.S. Drug Battle." *New York Times,* Sunday, I.

French, M., and G. Zarkin. (1992). "Effects of Drug Abuse Treatment on Legal and Illegal Earnings." *Contemporary Policy Issues* 10: 98–110.

French, M., J. Mauskopf, J. Teague, and E. Roland. (1996). "Estimating the Dollar Value of Health Outcomes from Drug Abuse Interventions." *Medical Care* 34: 890–910.

Fresia, J. (1988). *Toward an American Revolution: Exposing the Constitution and Other Illusions.* Boston: South End Press.

Gerstein, D., R. Johnson, H. Harwood, D. Fountain, N. Suter, and K. Mallory. (1994). *Evaluating Recovery Services: The California Drug and Alcohol Treatment Assessment (CALDATA).* Contract No. 92-00110. Sacramento: State of California, Health and Welfare Agency, Department of Alcohol and Drug Programs.

Goode, E. (1984). *Drugs in American Society.* New York: Alfred A. Knopf.

Guttman, W. E. (1996, January). "The War No One Wants to Win." *Z Magazine,* 1–5.

Helmer, J. (1983). "Blacks and Cocaine." In *Drugs and Society,* edited by M. Kelleher, B. Mac-Murray, and T. Shapiro, 14–29. Dubuque, Iowa: Kendall/Hunt.

Inciardi, J. (1986). *The War on Drugs: Heroin, Cocaine, Crime, and Public Policy.* Mountain View, CA: Mayfield.

Johnson, L., J. Bachman, and P. O'Malley. (1997). *National Survey Results on Drug Use from the Monitoring the Future Study.* Rockville, MD: National Institute on Drug Abuse.

Kleber, H. (1996). "Outpatient Detoxification from Opiates." *Primary Psychiatry* 1: 42–52.

Kruger, H. (1976). *The Great Heroin Coup.* Boston: South End Press.

Leshner, A. (1999). "Science-Based Views of Drug Addiction and Its Treatment." *Journal of the American Medical Association* 282, no. 14: 1314–16.

Levins, H. (1986). "The Shifting Source of Opium." In *Culture and Politics of Drugs,* edited by P. Park and W. Matveychuk, 124–25. Dubuque, Iowa: Kendall/Hunt.

Massing, M. (1999, September 20). "It Is Time for Realism." *The Nation,* 11–15.

McCoy, A. (1991). *The Politics of Heroin.* Brooklyn: Lawrence Hill.

McCoy, A., C. Read, and L. Adams. (1986). "The Mafia Connection." In *Culture and Politics of Drugs,* edited by P. Park and W. Matveychuk, 110–18. Dubuque, Iowa: Kendall/Hunt.

Metzger, D., H. Navaline, and G. Woody. (1998). "Drug Abuse Treatment as AIDS Prevention." *Public Health Reports* 113, supp. 1: 97–106.

Metzger, D., G. Woody, A. McLellan, C. O'Brien, P. Druly, and H. Navaline. (1993). "Human Immunodeficiency Virus Seroconversion Among in- and out-of-Treatment Intravenous Drug Users: An 18-Month Prospective Follow-Up." *Journal of Acquired Immune Deficiency Syndromes* 6: 1049–1056.

Murphy, S., and M. Rosenbaum. (1999). *Pregnant Women on Drugs.* New Brunswick, NJ: Rutgers University Press.

Musto, D. (1987). *The American Disease: Origins of Narcotic Control.* New York: Oxford University Press.

Muwakkil, S. (1996, March 18). "Politics by Other Means." *In These Times,* 20–21.

National Commission on Marijuana and Drug Abuse. (1972). *Marijuana: A Signal of Misunderstanding.* Washington, DC: U.S. Government Printing Office.

Rajkumar, A., and M. French. (1996). *Drug Abuse, Crime, Costs and the Economic Benefits of Treatment.* Unpublished manuscript, University of Maryland.

Schultheis, R. (1983). "Chinese Junk." In *Drugs and Society,* edited by M. Kelleher, B. Mac Murray, and T. Shapiro, 234–41. Dubuque, Iowa: Kendall/Hunt.

Singer, M. (1994). "AIDS and the Health Crisis of the U.S. Urban Poor: The Perspective of Critical Medical Anthropology." *Social Science and Medicine* 39, no. 7: 931–48.

———. (1999). "The Ethnography of Street Drug Use Before AIDS: A Historic Review." In *Cultural, Observational, and Epidemiological Approaches in the Prevention of Drug Abuse and HIV/AIDS,* edited by P. Marshall, M. Singer, and M. Clatts, 228–64. Bethesda, MD: National Institute on Drug Abuse.

Singer, M., C. Flores, L. Davison, G. Burke, Z. Castillo, K. Scanlon, and M. Rivera. (1990). "SIDA: The Sociocultural and Socioeconomic Context of AIDS Among Latinos." *Medical Anthropology Quarterly* 4: 72–114.

Singer, M., T. Stopka, C. Siano, K. Springer, G. Barton, K. Khoshnood, et al. (2000). "The Social Geography of AIDS and Hepatitis Risk: Qualitative Approaches for Assessing Local Differences in Sterile Syringe Access among Injection Drug Users." *American Journal of Public Health* 90, no. 7: 1049–1056.

Singer, M., Z. He, and H. Salaheen. (2004). "Cross-border Trafficking in Women for Commercial Sex Work and the Spread of HIV." Presented at the Society for Applied Anthropology, Dallas, Texas.

Sterk, C. (1999). "Fast Lives: Women Who Use Crack Cocaine" Philadelphia: Temple University Press.

Stocker, S. (1998). "Drug Addiction Treatment Conference Emphasizes Combining Therapies," *NIDA Notes* 13, no. 3: I, 13.

U.S. Congress, House Select Committee on Narcotics Abuse and Control. (1977). *Southeast Asian Narcotics.* Hearings, 95th Congress, 1st Session. Washington, DC: U.S. Government Printing Office.

Waterston, A. (1993). "Street Addicts in the Political Economy." Philadelphia: Temple University Press.

Ethnomedicine and Healers

CONCEPTUAL TOOLS

■ ***Healers have special knowledge, and anthropologists may use the ethnographic strategy of becoming apprentices to study them.*** Individual healers—their practices and performances—can be studied apart from a general ethnomedical system. The study of ethnomedicine may emphasize an idealized theory linking etiological categories, diagnostic techniques, and therapies. But many ethnomedical systems are not codified; there are no textbook ways to cure. The actual practice of an ethnomedical system can be highly idiosyncratic to a particular healer. As we will see in the story of Quesalid told by Lévi-Strauss, a shaman's knowledge is not generally shared with others. A shaman will have personal relationships with particular spirit helpers. The healer's medical knowledge is a product of his or her personal experience and biography, and the healers' theories and techniques may combine components from radically different belief systems. For example, in David Jones's ethnography *Sanapia: A Comanche Medicine Woman* (1972), that medical system combined traditional Comanche beliefs and herbal knowledge with fundamentalist Christian beliefs, as well as the peyote practices of the Native American church. These diverse elements are combined in Sanapia's unique "medicine way" that seems logically consistent to her.

■ ***One research methodology used by medical anthropologists is the intensive study of a single healer in his or her medical context.*** When anthropologists study a cultural system, they often depend on a small number of key informants who are intensively interviewed and followed over a period of time. The relationship between informants and anthropologists is like the relationship between teachers and students. But because the healer-informants' knowledge is very powerful—and takes years of devoted study to master—informants sometimes reveal the knowledge very gradually. In this regard, anthropologists become apprentices. This methodology has been used often. Some cases, like the work of Carlos Casteneda (1973), who wrote about a probably fictitious Yaqui Indian shaman called Don Juan, are famous but not anthropologically reliable. Other anthropologists have studied Tibetan Buddhist priests (DesJarlais 1992), Malayan midwives, and South American rain forest shaman (Harner 1968), as well as biomedical internists (Hahn and Gaines 1985) and surgeons (Katz 1990). These are cases of participant observation (although the anthropologist in the operating room is really observing rather than participating!).

One anthropologist, Michael Harner, has become famous among New Age healers because he travels the country teaching the basic techniques of shamanism described in his book *The Way of the Shaman* (1990). There is a remarkable demand for this type of knowledge, possibly indicating people's distrust of and discontent with biomedicine. Nevertheless, very few anthropologists condone the work of Harner, who has become a shaman and teaches others how to be spiritual healers.

■ ***All acts of healing, however mundane, have an important element of ritual and drama.*** To what extent are taking one's temperature with a thermometer and reading blood pressure with a cuff and stethoscope ritual acts? From the point of view of the patient, ritual may be the most important attribute. Because they have special knowledge, healers symbolically differentiate themselves with particular technologies, clothes, and vocabularies. The practice of an ethnomedical system must involve the correct use of these symbols in order to achieve the beliefs discussed previously. Therefore, a healing ritual can be described from a dramatic and theatrical point of view. Mystery is an important element in performing healing rituals throughout the world.

■ ***The use of meaningful symbols is essential in the healer's role.*** All healers use symbolic paraphernalia and words as necessary parts of their practice. These symbols communicate the meaning of the illness, and their manipulation communicates the process of healing. Symbols also signify the authoritative knowledge of the healer.

- ***Trance, song, and consultation are often important in the healer's craft.*** Consultation can be with supernatural beings as well as humans. Trance allows a healer to directly enter other realms of reality where the actual causes of illness may reside.

- ***Biomedicine is an ethnomedicine of Western culture.*** In a cultural sense, a medical system is an organized set of ideas referring to a particular healing tradition (e.g., Chinese, Ayurvedic, homeopathic, or biomedical). Medical anthropologists use the term *biomedicine* to refer to the tradition of scientific, biologically oriented methods of diagnosis and cure.

Biomedicine is a relatively recent tradition that is technologically sophisticated and often extremely successful in curing. Historically known as allopathic medicine, the knowledge and technology of biomedicine has grown extremely quickly, and with it, the prestige and professionalization of biomedical practitioners. The scientific medical system is international, cosmopolitan, dominant, and hegemonic. It is not, however, culture-free. The cultural and epistemological assumptions of biomedicine have been studied by medical anthropologists (Rhodes 1996); researchers have also studied the significant and fascinating national and regional differences in the practice of biomedicine, especially between European countries and the United States (e.g., differences in the interpretation of schizophrenia or low blood pressure and rates and styles of surgery) (Payer 1988).

When viewed as a cultural system, biomedicine becomes one ethnomedicine among many others. All ethnomedicines are rooted in cultural presuppositions and values, associated with rules of conduct, and embedded in a larger context (Hahn 1995). There is little doubt that *belief* in the healer and the power of the medicine by a patient and family plays a fundamental role in the process of healing. All medical systems manipulate symbols to invoke and enhance belief; in this regard, all medical systems involve symbolic healing processes (sometimes labeled the "placebo effect").

 12

Disease Etiologies in Non-Western Medical Systems

George M. Foster

If every culture in the world has a medical system, or, more properly, an ethnomedical system, then how is it possible to talk about this great variation? How is it possible to compare medical systems that are based on completely different ideas of what causes illness—from spirits to germs? The first thing that social scientists do when faced with such a problem is to survey the range of variation and then construct a system of categorization, also called a typology. This is a comparative method in which like is grouped with like. The next step is to define these groups with descriptive labels using what the famous sociologist Max Weber called "ideal types."

In this classic article, George Foster surveys the range of variation in medical systems and focuses on an essential aspect of such systems: the etiology or theory of disease causation. This is a good place to start, because medical systems must have three basic components: a theory of etiology, a system of diagnosis, and techniques of appropriate therapy. Theories of causation are actually cognitive blueprints, something that medical anthropologists often refer to as explanatory models.

The distinction between naturalistic and personalistic ethnomedical systems is quite useful. Naturalistic systems tend to have etiological explanations that are restricted to the disease symptomatology and a single level of causality. In contrast, personalistic explanations extend to the domains of social relations—with living people, ancestors, and other spiritual entities. Naturalistic cures tend to be oriented to-ward the physical body; personalistic cures must not only deal with immediate causes for an illness (like witchcraft) but also the underlying social rifts that have provoked the witchcraft.

One of the most interesting aspects of this distinction is that personalistic and naturalistic systems have completely different attitudes about the sharing of medical knowledge. In a personalistic system, a shaman gains prestige as a healer in part because he jealously guards his personal ethnomedical knowledge. In a naturalistic system, a healer gains prestige by producing and giving away medical knowledge—by teaching it to others. The more open information system has adaptive advantages because therapies can be openly compared and evaluated. Naturalistic systems are associated with the great traditions of complex civilizations; medical knowledge becomes codified and taught as a profession.

Notice that the author doesn't clearly come out and say that scientific biomedicine is a naturalistic ethnomedical system. But a careful reading will reveal that biomedicine has more of the attributes of the naturalistic ideal type. Also notice that these ideal types do not really work as a clean and neat categorization scheme. There are two reasons for this: First, many ethnomedical systems have attributes of both naturalistic and personalistic etiologies (the Navajo medical system is an example of one that doesn't fit the typology); second, many societies have multiple medical systems operating simultaneously, or medical pluralism.

As you read this selection, consider these questions:

- **Why is it that the author believes that personalistic systems are evolutionarily older than naturalistic ethnomedical systems?**
- **Are personalistic ethnomedical systems kinder to the victim of the disease because they do not blame a person for getting sick? Or is a person really responsible for keeping peaceable social relations to prevent spiritual attacks?**
- **What is the logical connection between etiologic theories and therapeutic practices?**

Context: This article was written by one of the founders of medical anthropology, George Foster. He taught at the University of California at Berkeley and was co-author of the first textbook in the field, also published in 1976. Foster did extensive fieldwork in peasant societies in Tzintzuntzan, Mexico, over a forty-year period. He was also a frequent consultant to the World Health Organization. His last book was on the origins and variations of the hot-cold theory of disease. This article, generally considered a classic, was published in the flagship journal of the American Anthropological Association; it suggested that there were two basic types of non-Western medical systems. After this period, medical anthropologists began exploring Western biomedicine rather than focusing solely on technologically simple societies.

Source: Foster G. (1976)."Disease Etiologies in Non-Western Medical Systems." American Anthropologist 78(4):773–782.

Impressive in ethnographic accounts of non-Western medicine is the tendency of authors to generalize from the particulars of the system(s) within which they have worked. Subconsciously, at least, anthropologists filter the data of all exotic systems through the lens of belief and practice of the people they know best. Whether it be causality, diagnosis, the nature and role of the curer, or the perception of illness within the wider supernatural and social universe, general statements seem strongly influenced by the writers' personal experiences. Glick, for example, in one of the most interesting of recent general essays, notes that in many cultures, religion and medical practices are almost inseparable, and he adds that "We must think about how and where 'medicine' fits into 'religion'. . . . In an ethnography of a religious system, where does the description of the medical system belong; and how does it relate to the remainder?" (Glick 1967:33).

Yet in many medical systems, as, for example, those characterizing mestizo villagers and urbanites in Latin America, medicine would have the most minimal role in an ethnography of religious beliefs and practices. Illness and curing are dealt with largely in nonreligious terms. In Tzintzuntzan, for example, in many hours of recording ideas about origins and cures of illness, not once has religion been mentioned—even though most villagers, if asked, would certainly agree that illness ultimately comes from God.

The ethnologist analyzing medical beliefs and practices in an African community can scarcely avoid dealing with witchcraft, oracles, magic, divining, and propitiation, all of which are categories of only modest concern to the student of Indian Ayurvedic medicine. In short, there has been all too little dialogue between anthropologists who have studied dramatically different non-Western medical systems. So striking is the parochialism at times that one is tempted to agree with the medical sociologist Freidson who notes the existence of a "very large body of sociological and anthropological information" about popular knowledge of and attitudes toward health and disease, but finds most of it to be "grossly descriptive." "Aside from cultural designations like Mexican, Subanun, and Mashona," he writes, "there is no method by which the material is ordered save for focusing on knowledge about *particular* illnesses. Such studies are essentially catalogues, often without a classified index" (Freidson 1970:10).

Yet if we can successfully classify kinship, political and economic systems, and witchcraft and sorcery beliefs, and find the significant behavioral correlates associated with each, then certainly we can do the same with medical systems. We are, after all, dealing with limited possibilities in each of these cases. In this paper I am concerned with the cross-cultural patterning that underlies non-Western medical systems, and with identifying and explicating the primary independent variable—disease etiology—around which orbit such dependent variables as types of curers, the nature of diagnosis, the roles of religion and magic, and the like. This is, then, an essay on comparative ethnomedicine, a term Hughes aptly defines as "those beliefs and practices relating to disease which are the products of indigenous cultural development and are not explicitly derived from the conceptual framework of modern medicine" (Hughes 1968:99).

THE PROBLEMS OF TERMINOLOGY

Throughout most of anthropology's brief history ethnologists have labeled the institutions of the peoples they have studied as "primitive," "peasant," or "folk," depending on the basic societal type concerned. Until relatively recently we investigated primitive religion, primitive economics, primitive art—and, of course, primitive medicine. The seminal writings of the ethnologist-physician Ackerknecht during the 1940s display no uncertainty as to what interested him: it was "primitive medicine," a pair of words that appeared in the title of nearly every article he published (Ackerknecht 1971). Caudill, too, in the first survey of the new field of medical anthropology spoke unashamedly of "primitive medicine" (Caudill 1953).

When, following World War II, studies of peasant communities became fashionable, these peoples were described as possessing a "folk culture." Not surprisingly their medical beliefs and practices were labeled "folk medicine," a frequent source of confusion since the popular medicine of technologically complex societies also often was, and is, so described.

In recent years, however, this traditional terminology has come to embarrass us. In a rapidly changing world, where yesterday's nonliterate villagers may be today's cabinet ministers in newly independent countries, the word "primitive"—initially a polite euphemism for "savage"—is increasingly outmoded. Ackerknecht himself recognizes this change, for in the 1971 collection of his classic essays most titles have been edited to eliminate the word "primitive." "Peasant" and "folk" are less sensitive words, but they too are being replaced by "rural," "agrarian," or something of the kind. The extent to which we have been troubled by terminology is illustrated by the circumlocutions and quotation marks found in the major review articles of recent years: "popular health culture," "indigenous or folk medical roles," "non-scientific health practices," "native conceptual traditions about illness," "culture specific illness," "the vocabulary of Western scientific medicine," "indigenous medical systems," and the like (e.g., Polgar 1962; Scotch 1963; Fabrega 1972; Lieban 1973).

ETIOLOGY: THE INDEPENDENT VARIABLE

Yet the greatest shortcoming of our traditional medical terminology—at least within the profession itself—is not that it may denigrate non-Western people, but rather that, by focusing on societal types it has blinded us to the basic characteristics of the medical systems themselves. There is more than a grain of truth in Freidson's comments, for many accounts *are* "grossly descriptive," with lists of illnesses and treatments taking precedence over interpretation and synthesis. So where do we start to rectify the situation? Glick (1967:36), I believe, gives us the critical lead when he writes that "the most important fact about an illness in most medical systems is not the underlying pathological process but *the underlying cause.* This is such a central consideration that most diagnoses prove to be statements about causation, and most treatments, responses directed against particular causal agents" (emphasis added).

A casual survey of the ethnomedical literature tends to confirm Glick's statement. In account after account we find that the kinds of curers, the mode of diagnosis, curing techniques, preventive acts, and the relationship of all these variables to the wider society of which they are a part, derive from beliefs about illness causality. It is not going too far to say that, if we are given a clear description of what a people believe to be the causes of illness, we can in broad outline fill in the other elements in that medical system. It therefore logically follows that the first task of the anthropologist concerned with medical systems is to find the simplest taxonomy for causality beliefs. Two basic principles, which I call *personalistic and naturalistic,* seem to me to account for most (but not all) of the etiologies that characterize non-Western medical systems. While the terms refer specifically to causality concepts, I believe they can conveniently be used to speak of entire systems, i.e., not only causes, but all of the associated behavior that follows from these views.

A personalistic medical system is one in which disease is explained as due to the *active, purposeful intervention* of an *agent,* who may be human (a witch or sorcerer), nonhuman (a ghost, an ancestor, an evil spirit), or supernatural (a deity or other very powerful being). The sick person literally is a victim, the object of aggression or punishment directed specifically against him, for reasons that concern him alone. Personalistic causality allows little room for accident or chance; in fact, for some peoples the statement is made by anthropologists who have studied them that *all* illness and death are believed to stem from the acts of the agent.

Personalistic etiologies are illustrated by beliefs found among the Mano of Liberia, recorded by the physician Harley, who practiced medicine among them for 15 years. "Death is unnatural," he writes, "resulting from the intrusion of an outside force," usually directed by some magical means (Harley 1941:7). Similarly, among the Abron of the Ivory Coast, "People sicken and die because some power, good or evil, has acted against them. . . . Abron disease theory contains a host of agents which may be responsible for a specific condition. . . . These agents cut across the natural and supernatural world. Ordinary people, equipped with the proper technical skills, sorcerers, various supernatural entities, such as ghosts, bush devils, and witches, or the supreme god *Nyame,* acting alone or through lesser gods, all cause disease" (Alland 1964:714–715).

In contrast to personalistic systems, naturalistic systems explain illness in impersonal, systemic terms. Disease is thought to stem, not from the machinations of an angry being, but rather from such *natural forces or conditions* as cold, heat, winds, dampness, and, above all, by an upset in the balance of the basic body elements. In naturalistic systems, health conforms to an *equilibrium* model: when the humors, the yin and yang, or the Ayurvedic *dosha* are in the balance appropriate to the age and condition of the individual, in his natural and social environment, health results. Causality concepts explain or account for the upsets in this balance that trigger illness.

Contemporary naturalistic systems resemble each other in an important historical sense: the bulk of their explanations and practices represent simplified and popularized legacies from the "great tradition" medicine of ancient classical civilizations, particularly those of Greece and Rome, India, and China. Although equilibrium is expressed in many ways in classical accounts, contemporary descriptions most frequently deal with the "hot-cold dichotomy" which explains illness as due to excessive heat or cold entering the body. Treatment, logically, attempts to restore the proper balance through "hot" and "cold" foods and herbs, and other treatments such as poultices that are thought to withdraw excess heat or cold from the body.

In suggesting that most non-Western etiologies can be described as personalistic or naturalistic I am, of course, painting with a broad brush. Every anthropologist will immediately think of examples from his research that appear not to conform to this classification. Most troublesome, at least at first glance, are those illnesses believed caused by emotional disturbances such as fright, jealousy, envy, shame, anger, or grief. Fright, or *susto,* widespread in Latin America, can be caused by a ghost, a spirit, or an encounter with the devil; if the agent *intended* harm to the victim, the etiology is certainly personalistic. But often accounts of such encounters suggest chance or accident rather than purposive action. And, when an individual slips beside a stream, and fears he is about to fall into the water and drown, the etiology is certainly naturalistic.

The Latin American *muina,* an indisposition resulting from anger, may reflect a disagreeable interpersonal episode, but it is unlikely that the event was staged by an evil doer to bring illness to a victim. In Mexico and Central America the knee child's envy and resentment of its new sibling-to-be, still in the mother's womb, gives rise to *chipil,* the symptoms of which are apathy, whining, and a desire to cling to the mother's skirt. The foetus can be said, in a narrow sense, to be the cause of the illness, but it is certainly not an active agent, nor is it blamed for the result. Since in a majority of emotionally explained illnesses it is hard to identify purposive action on the part of an agent intent upon causing sickness, I am inclined to view emotional etiologies as more nearly conforming to the naturalistic than to the personalistic principle. Obviously, a dual taxonomy for phenomena as complex as worldwide beliefs about causes of illness leaves many loose ends. But it must be remembered that a taxonomy is not an end in itself, something to be polished and admired; its value lies rather in the understanding of relationships between apparently diverse phenomena that it makes possible. I hope that the following pages will illustrate how the personalistic-naturalistic classification, for all its loose ends, throws into sharp perspective correlations in health institutions and health behavior that tend to be overlooked in descriptive accounts.

Before proceeding, a word of caution is necessary: *the two etiologies are rarely if ever mutually exclusive* as far as their presence or absence in a particular society is concerned. Peoples who invoke personalistic causes to explain most illness usually recognize some natural, or chance, causes. And peoples for whom naturalistic causes predominate almost invariably explain some illness as due to witchcraft or the evil eye. But in spite of obvious overlapping, the literature suggests that many, if not most, peoples are committed to one or the other of these explanatory principles to account for a majority of illness. When, for example, we read that in the Venezuelan peasant village of El Morro 89% of a sample of reported illnesses are "natural" in origin, whereas only 11% are attributed to magical or supernatural causes (Suárez 1974), it seems reasonable to say that the indigenous causation system of this group is naturalistic and not personalistic. And, in contrast, when we read of the Melanesian Dobuans that all illness and disease are attributed to envy, and that "Death is caused by witchcraft, sorcery, poisoning, suicide, or actual assault" (Fortune 1932:135, 150), it is clear that personalistic causality predominates.

Although in the present context I am not concerned with problems of evolution, I believe the personalistic etiology is the more ancient of the two. At the dawn of human history it seems highly likely that *all* illness, as well as other forms of misfortune, was explained in personalistic terms. I see man's ability to depersonalize causality, in all spheres of thought, including illness, as a major step forward in the evolution of culture.

ETIOLOGIES: COMPREHENSIVE AND RESTRICTED

We now turn to the principal dependent variables in medical institutions and health behavior that correlate with personalistic and naturalistic etiologies. The first thing we note is that personalistic medical etiologies are parts of more comprehensive, or general, explanatory systems, while naturalistic etiologies are largely restricted to illness. In other words, in personalistic systems *illness is but a special case in the explanation of all misfortune.* Some societies, to quote Horton (1967), have adopted a "personal idiom" as the basis of their attempt to understand the world, to account for almost everything that happens in the world, only incidentally including illness. In such societies the same deities, ghosts, witches, and sorcerers that send illness may blight crops, cause financial reverses, sour husband–wife relationships, and produce all manner of other misfortune. To illustrate, Price-Williams states "The general feature of illness among the Tiv is that it is interpreted in a framework of witchcraft and malevolent forces" (1962:123). "In common with a great many other people, Tiv do not regard 'illness' or 'disease' as a completely separate category distinct from misfortunes to compound and farm, from relationships between kin, and from complicated matters relating to the control of land" (1962:125).

Similarly, the Kaguru of Taznazia "believe most misfortunes, however small, are due to witchcraft. Most illness, death, miscarriages, sterility, difficult childbirths, poor crops, sickly livestock and poultry, loss of articles, bad luck in hunting, and sometimes even lack of rain are caused by witches" (Beidelman 1963:63–64).

In contrast, naturalistic etiologies are restricted to disease as such. Although a "systemic idiom" may prevail to account for much of what happens in the world, a humoral or a yin-yang imbalance which explains an illness is not invoked to explain crop failure, disputes over land, or kin quarreling. In fact, the striking thing is that while in naturalistic systems disease etiologies are disease specific, other areas of misfortune, such as personal quarrels, are, not surprisingly, explained in personalistic terms. In Tzintzuntzan, for example, misunderstandings between friends may be due to natural-born trouble makers, who delight in spreading rumors and falsehoods. Financial reverses, too, may be accounted for by bad luck, or dishonesty and deceit on the part of false friends. But these explanations are quite divorced from illness etiology, which has its own framework, exclusive to it.

DISEASE, RELIGION, AND MAGIC

When Glick (1967:32) writes that "it is common knowledge that in many cultures, ideas and practices relating to illness are for the most part inseparable from the domain of religious beliefs and practices," he is speaking only of those systems with personalistic etiologies. Jansen (1973:34) makes this clear in writing of the Bomvana (Xhosa) that "religion, medicine and magic are closely interwoven, . . . being parts of a complex whole which finds its religious destination in the well-being of the tribe. . . . The Bomvana himself does not distinguish between his religion, magic and medicine." When curers are described as "priests" and "priestesses," as is often the case in Africa (e.g., Warren 1974–75:27), we are clearly in the domain of religion.

In contrast, in naturalistic systems religion and magic play only the most limited roles *insofar as we are dealing with etiology,* and to the extent that religious rituals are found, they are significantly different in form and concept from religious rituals in personalistic systems. For example, in those Latin American societies whose etiological systems are largely naturalistic, victims of illness sometimes place votive offerings on or near "miraculous" images of Christ, the Virgin Mary, or powerful saints, or light votive candles for these supernatural beings, asking for help. These are certainly religious acts. But it is important to note that in personalistic systems the beings supplicated, and to whom propitiatory offerings are made, are themselves held responsible for the illness. It is to appease their anger or ill will that such offerings are made. In contrast, in Catholic countries the beings to whom prayers are raised and offerings made *are not* viewed as causes of the illness. They are seen as merciful advocates who, if moved, can intervene to help a human sufferer. It should be noted, too, that most of these acts conform to a general pattern in which aid of supernaturals is sought for any kind of misfortune, such as financial reverses or the release of a son from jail, as well as illness or accident.

Thus, there is a significant contrast in structure and style between the two systems. In societies where personalistic etiologies predominate, all causality is general and comprehensive, and not specific to illness; but paradoxically, when ritual supplications and sacrifices are made, usually they are narrowly limited in scope, specific to a particular illness, or to prevent feared illness. In contrast, in societies where naturalistic etiologies predominate, illness causality is specific to illness alone, and does not apply to other kinds of misfortune. But, insofar as religion is a part of curing, it is comprehensive or general, conforming to the same patterns that characterize a pious person in the face of any misfortune.

LEVELS OF CAUSALITY

Personalistic and naturalistic etiologies further differ importantly in that, for the former, it is necessary to postulate at least two levels of causality: the deity, ghost, witch, or other being on whom ultimate responsibility for illness rests, and the instrument or technique used by this being, such as intrusion of a disease object, theft of the soul, possession, or witchcraft. In the literature on ethnomedicine the first level—the being—is often referred to as the *efficient* cause, while the second level—the instrument or technique—is referred to as the *instrumental,* or *immediate* cause. A few anthropologists recognize three levels of causation. Goody (1962:209–210), for example, describes both efficient and immediate causes, to which he adds a final cause, an ancestor or earth shrine that withdraws its protection from a person so that he falls victim to a sorcerer. In Honduras (Peck 1968:78) recognizes essentially the same three levels: an instrumental cause ("i.e., what has been done to the patient, or what is used"), an efficient cause ("i.e., who or what has done it to the patient"), and a final, or ultimate, cause ("i.e., an attempt to answer the question, 'why did *this* happen to *me* at *this time*?'").

Naturalistic etiologies differ significantly in that levels of causation are much less apparent; in most cases they tend to be collapsed. Although it can be argued that a person who willfully or through carelessness engages in activities known to upset his bodily equilibrium is the efficient cause of his illness, in practice this line of argument has little analytical value.

It was failure to recognize levels of causality that limited the value of Clements' pioneering study of disease etiology (1932), a defect first pointed out by Hallowell (1935). This distinction, as we are about to see, is critical to an understanding of basic differences in curing strategies found in the two systems.

SHAMANS AND OTHER CURERS

The kinds of curers found in a particular society, and the curing acts in which they engage, stem logically from the etiologies that are recognized. Personalistic systems, with multiple levels of causation, logically require curers with supernatural and/or magical skills, for the primary concern of the patient and his family is not the immediate cause of illness, but rather "Who?" and "Why?" Among the Bomvana (Xhosa) Jansen (1973:39) puts it this way: "They are less interested to know: *How* did it happen? rather than: *Who* is responsible?" Similarly, in Mali we read that "In general the Bambara want to know *why* they are ill and not how they got ill" (Imperato 1974–75:44). And in the Indian village studied by Dube the Brahmin or a local seer is essential to find out what ancestor spirit is angry, and why (Dube 1955:128).

The shaman, with his supernatural powers, and direct contact with the spirit world, and the "witch doctor" (to use an outmoded term from the African literature), with his magical powers, both of whom are primarily concerned with finding out who, and why, are the logical responses in personalistic, multiple causality, etiological systems. After the who and why have been determined, treatment for the immediate cause may be administered by the same person, or the task may be turned over to a lesser curer, perhaps an herbalist. Thus, among the Nyima of the Kordofan mountains in the Sudan, the shaman goes into a trance and discovers the cause and cure of the disease. But he himself performs no therapeutic acts; this is the field of other healing experts, to whom the patient will be referred (Nadel 1946:26).

Naturalistic etiological systems, with single levels of causation, logically require a very different type of curer, a "doctor" in the full sense of the word, a specialist in symptomatic treatment who knows the appropriate herbs, food restrictions, and other forms of treatment such as cupping, massage, poultices, enemas, and the like. The curandero or the Ayurvedic specialist is not primarily concerned with the who or why, for he and the patient both usually are in complete agreement as to what has happened.

DIAGNOSIS

Personalistic and naturalistic etiological systems divide along still another axis, the nature of diagnosis. In personalistic systems, as we have just seen, the shaman or witch doctor diagnoses by means of trance, or other divinatory techniques. Diagnosis—to find out who and why—is the primary skill that the patient seeks from his curer. Treatment of the instrumental cause, while important, is of secondary concern.

In contrast, in naturalistic systems diagnosis is of very minor importance, as far as the curer is concerned. Diagnosis usually is made, not by the curer, but by the patient or members of his family. When the patient ceases treatment with home remedies and turns to a professional, he believes he knows what afflicts him. His primary concern is treatment to cure him. And how is diagnosis done by the layman? The answer is simple, pointed out many years ago by Erasmus (1952:414), specifically for Ecuador. When an individual whose disease etiology is largely naturalistic feels unwell, he thinks back to an earlier experience, in the night, the day before, or even a month or a year earlier, to an event that transpired, or a situation in which he found himself, that is known to cause illness. Did the patient awaken in the morning with swollen tonsils? He remembers that on going to bed the night before he carelessly stepped on the cold tile floor of his bedroom in his bare feet. This, he knows, causes cold to enter his feet and compress the normal heat of his body into the upper chest and head. He suffers from "risen heat." *He* tells the doctor what is wrong, and merely asks for an appropriate remedy.

Does a woman suffer an attack of painful rheumatism? She remembers that she had been ironing, thereby heating her hands and arms, and that without thinking she had washed them in cold water. The cold, to her vulnerable superheated arms and hands, caused her discomfort. She needs no diviner or shaman to tell her what is wrong. The striking thing about a naturalistic system is that, in theory at least, the patient can, upon reflection, identify *every* cause of illness that may afflict him. So powerful is this pattern today in Tzintzuntzan that when people consult medical doctors, their standard opening statement is "Doctor, please give me something for————," whatever their diagnosis may be. Doctors, traditional or modern, are viewed as curers, not diagnosticians.

To summarize, we may say that in personalistic systems the primary role of the shaman or witch doctor is *diagnostic,* while in naturalistic systems it is *therapeutic.*

PREVENTIVE MEASURES

Preventive medicine, insofar as it refers to individual health-oriented behavior, can be thought of as a series of "dos" and "don'ts," or "shoulds" and "shouldn'ts." In contemporary America we "should" get an annual physical examination, our eyes and teeth checked regularly, and make sure out immunizations are up to date when we travel abroad. We "should not" smoke cigarettes, consume alcohol to excess, breathe polluted air, or engage in a series of other activities known or believed to be inimical to health. Our personal preventive measures are, perhaps, about equally divided between the "dos" and "don'ts."

In all other societies similar "shoulds" and "shouldn'ts" can be identified. Although my grounds are highly impressionistic, I rather have the feeling that naturalistic etiologies correlate predominantly with "don'ts," while personalistic etiologies correlate with "dos." In naturalistic systems a personal health strategy seems to consist of avoiding those situations or not engaging in behavior known to produce illness. In Tzintzuntzan, and many other Latin American communities, the prudent person doesn't stand on a cold floor in bare feet, doesn't wash hands after whitewashing a wall, doesn't go out into the night air immediately after using the eyes, and a host of other things. In theory, at least, a hypercautious individual should be able to avoid almost all illness *by not doing certain things.*

In contrast, in personalistic systems the basic personal health strategy seems to emphasize the "dos," and especially the need to make sure that one's social networks, with fellow human beings, with ancestors, and with deities, are maintained in good working order. Although this means avoiding those acts known to arouse resentment—"don'ts"—it particularly means careful attention being paid to the propitiatory rituals that are a god's due, to positive demonstrations to ancestors that they have not been forgotten, and to friendly acts to neighbors and fellow villagers that remind them that their good will is valued. In short, recognizing major overlapping, the primary strategies to maintain health in the two systems are significantly different. Both require thought. But in one—the personalistic—time and money are essential ingredients in the maintenance of health. In the other—the naturalistic—knowledge of how the system works, and the will to live according to its dictates, is the essential thing; this costs very little, in either time or money.

THE LOCUS OF RESPONSIBILITY

With respect to personal responsibility for falling ill, do the two etiological systems differ? To some extent I think they do. In Tzintzuntzan, as pointed out, the exercise of absolute care in avoiding disease producing situations should, in theory, keep one healthy. Hence, illness is *prima facie* evidence that the patient has been guilty of lack of care. Although illness is as frightening as in any other society, and family members do their best to help a sick member, there is often an ambivalent feeling that includes anger at the patient for having fallen ill. I have seen worried grown daughters losing a night's sleep as they sought medical care for a mother they feared was suffering a heart attack. When the mother confessed that she had not taken her daily pill to keep her blood pressure down (and after she was back to normal, the crisis past), the daughters became highly indignant and angry at her for causing them to lose sleep.

In personalistic systems people also know the kinds of behavior—sins of commission and omission—that may lead to retaliation by a deity, spirit, or witch. To the extent they can lead blameless lives they should avoid sickness. But personalistic causality is far more complex than naturalistic causality, since there are no absolute rules to avoid arousing the envy of others, for doing just the right amount of ritual to satisfy an ancestor, for knowing how far one can shade a taboo without actually breaching it. Consequently, in such systems one has less control over the conditions that lead to illness than in the other, where the rules are clearly stated. Spiro (1967:4) makes this contrast clear among the Burmese. Since suffering (including illness) is the "karmic" consequence of one's demerits accumulated in earlier incarnations, the responsibility for suffering rests on the shoulders of the sufferer himself. But, says Spiro, to accept this responsibility is emotionally unsatisfying. On the other hand, if one subscribes to a supernatural-magical explanatory system, in which all suffering comes from ghosts, demons, witches, and *nats*, in at least some cases the sufferer is entirely blameless. He simply happens to be the victim of a witch who, from malice, chooses him as victim. "In other cases he is only inadvertently responsible—he has unwittingly offended or neglected a nat who, annoyed by his behavior, punishes him." Spiro sees this reasoning as underlying the juxtaposition of Buddhism and supenaturalism—of personalistic and naturalistic etiologies—in Burma.

SUMMARY

By way of summary the two systems of disease etiology and their correlates may be tabularized as follows:

System:	Personalistic	Naturalistic
Causation:	Active agent	Equilibrium loss
Illness:	Special case of misfortune	Unrelated to other misfortune
Religion, Magic:	Intimately tied to illness	Largely unrelated to illness
Causality:	Multiple levels	Single level
Prevention:	Positive action	Avoidance
Responsibility:	Beyond patient control	Resides with patient

REFERENCES

Ackerknecht, Erwin H. 1971. Medicine and Ethnology: Selected Essays. Baltimore: Johns Hopkins Press.

Alland, Alexander, Jr. 1964. Native Therapists and Western Medical Practitioners among the Abron of the Ivory Coast. Transactions of the New York Academy of Sciences. Vol. 26. Pp. 714–725.

Beidelman, T. O. 1963. Witchcraft in Ukaguru, In Witchcraft and Sorcery in East Africa. J. Middleton and E. H. Winter, eds. Pp. 57–98. London: Routledge and Kegan Paul.

Caudill, William. 1953. Applied Anthropology in Medicine. In Anthropology Today. A. L. Kroeber, ed. Pp. 771–806. Chicago: University of Chicago Press.

Clements, Forrest E. 1932. Primitive Concepts of Disease. University of California Publications in American Archaeology and Ethnology, Vol. 32, Part 2. Pp. 185–252.

Dube, S. C. 1955. Indian Village. London: Routledge and Kegan Paul.

Erasmus, Charles J. 1952. Changing Folk Beliefs and the Relativity of Empirical Knowledge. Southwestern Journal of Anthropology 8:411–428.

Fabrega, Horacio, Jr. 1972. Medical Anthropology. In Biennial Review of Anthropology: 1971. Bernard J. Siegel, ed. Pp. 167–229. Stanford: Stanford University Press.

Fortune, Reo F. 1932. Sorcerers of Dobu: The Social Anthropology of the Dobu Islanders of the Western Pacific. London: George Routledge.

Freidson, Eliot. 1970. Professional Dominance: The Social Structure of Medical Care. New York: Atherton.

Glick, Leonard B. 1967. Medicine as an Ethnographic Category: The Gimi of the New Guinea Highlands. Ethnology 6:31–56.

Goody, Jack. 1962. Death, Property and the Ancestors: A Study of the Mortuary Customs of the Lodagas of West Africa. Stanford: Stanford University Press.

Hallowell, A. Irving. 1935. Primitive Concepts of Disease. American Anthropologist 37:365-368.

Harley, George Way. 1941. Native African Medicine: With Special Reference to Its Practice in the Mano Tribe of Liberia. Cambridge: Harvard University Press.

Horton, Robin. 1967. African Traditional Thought and Western Science. Africa 37:50–71,155–187.

Hughes, Charles C. 1968. Ethnomedicine. In International Encyclopedia of the Social Sciences, Vol. 10. Pp. 87–93. New York: Free Press/Macmillan.

Imperato, Pascual James. 1974–75. Traditional Medical Practitioners among the Bambara of Mali and Their Role in the Modern Health-Care-Delivery System. In Traditional Healers: Use and Non-Use in Health Care Delivery. I. E. Harrison and D. W. Dunlop, eds. Rural Africana 26:41–53.

Jansen, G. 1973. The Doctor–Patient Relationship in an African Tribal Society. Assen, The Netherlands: Van Goreum.

Lieban, Richard W. 1973. Medical Anthropology. In Handbook of Social and Cultural Anthropology. John J. Honigmann, ed. Pp. 1031–1072. Chicago: Rand McNally.

Nadel, S. F. 1946. A Study of Shamanism in the Nuba Mountains. Journal of the Royal Anthropological Institute 76:25–37.

Peck, John G. 1968. Doctor Medicine and Bush Medicine in Kaukira, Honduras. In Essays on Medical Anthropology. Thomas Weaver, ed. Pp. 78–87. Southern Anthropological Society Proceedings, Vol. 1.

Polgar, Steven. 1962. Health and Human Behavior: Areas of Interest Common to the Social and Medical Sciences. Current Anthropology 3:159–205.

Price-Williams, D. R. 1962. A Case Study of Ideas Concerning Disease Among the Tiv. Africa 32:123–131.

Scotch, Norman A. 1963. Medical Anthropology. In Biennial Review of Anthropology. Bernard J. Siegel, ed. Pp. 30–68. Stanford: Stanford University Press.

Spiro, Melford E. 1967. Burmese Supernaturalism: A Study in the Explanation and Reduction of Suffering. Englewood Cliffs: Prentice-Hall.

Suárez, María Matilde. 1974. Etiology, Hunger, and Folk Diseases in the Venezuelan Andes. Journal of Anthropological Research 30:41–54.

Warren, Dennis M. 1974–75. Bono Traditional Healers. In Traditional Healers: Use and Non-Use in Health Care Delivery. I. E. Harrison and D. W. Dunlop, eds. Rural Africana 26:25–39.

13

Transcendental Medication

Melvin Konner

The author of this selection is a biological anthropologist, a skeptical scientist, and a physician (Konner 1982, 1987; see also selection 2). Here Melvin Konner tells the story of becoming an apprentice healer when he and his wife, Marjorie Shostak, were doing anthropological fieldwork among the !Kung San hunter-gatherers of the Kalahari Desert of Botswana. The !Kung do not take any drugs in order to induce the altered state of consciousness—the trance—necessary for healing. Rather, they use a technique that might be considered a form of both sensory deprivation and overload, by a long and repetitive dance and song called the N/um Tchai, *or medicine dance. This is the most common and important ritual of the San peoples, and it has been studied in depth (Katz 1982; Shostak 1981). In this ritual, the* n/um*—medicine or sweat—that is stored in the stomachs of the "owners of medicine" is heated through dance and song until it causes the dancer to fall into a trance. In this state the healer can "lay on hands," transferring his protective sweat and energy to the assembled group or pull out the sicknesses from people. The* N/um Tchai *ritual is well depicted in an ethnographic* film *of the same name.*

!Kung call the trance state kwi, *or "half death." This interesting term reminds us of the ideas of Edward Tylor, one of the founders of the discipline of anthropology, who in his early book* Primitive Religion *(1889) argued that the most fundamental religious belief, called* animism, *referred to a belief in souls. Tylor thought that the belief in souls meant a recognition that living things have a visible, corporeal element as well as an invisible, spiritual, life-giving element. He thought that the idea of souls was reinforced by and helped explain the everyday experiences of death, dreams, and trances—times when the body and soul become separated; the idea of animism also agrees with the relatively common experience of spirit possession in other cultures. Because a trance is temporary, it might be considered "half death," but it is clearly recognized as a dangerous and somewhat painful state. Among the !Kung, both men and women can become "owners of medicine," but women, because of the danger involved, usually curtail their healing careers when they first get pregnant.*

In this selection, there is little doubt that trance involves an altered state of consciousness and that this ritual is quite dramatic. N/um Tchai *ceremonies often continue all night. Like the band societies themselves, there is no clear leader and little job specialization. Some men, however, simply have a greater gift for going into trance, and they are afforded some prestige for this.*

By trying his hand at the trance dance, Melvin Konner followed the long ethnographic tradition of participant observation. Although his research among the !Kung focused on patterns of infant rearing and the biology of breast-feeding, his research interests were much broader than that. The questions at the end of this selection about biology of belief and healing are currently being addressed in a new field called psychoneuroimmunology (Desowitz 1987).

As you read this selection, consider these questions:

- **Why do you think that the touching of the patient by the healer seems so important in this healing ritual? Is the fact that n/um also means "sweat" relevant here? In what other cultures is the "laying on of hands" important?**
- **How was Konner's "experienced-based learning" of being an apprentice essential for his particular view of this ritual?**
- **If the !Kung really believe that the trance is "half death," why would anyone be willing to take this risk to become a healer?**
- **Do you think that any ritual can have therapeutic power as long as it is culturally relevant?**

Context: Melvin Konner is a biological and medical anthropologist with doctorates in both anthropology and medicine. He is widely read and published, with books ranging from human nature to child development and the state of the U.S. health care system. This selection describes his role as a participant observer of traditional healing practices while he and his wife, Margorie Shostak, were conducting ethnographic research among the !Kung San hunter-gatherers of the Kalahari Desert in Botswana. Konner's work on child development among the !Kung was part of a much larger set of studies known as the Harvard Kalahari Project. During this same time, Marjorie Shostak conducted interviews for her famous book Nisa; Life of a !Kung Woman. Konner is a professor of Anthropology at Emory University.

Source: M. Konner (1985). "Transcendental Medication." The Sciences, May/June.

Dusk is closing. The horizon of the Kalahari Desert makes a distant, perfect circle, broken only by scrub bush and an occasional acacia. The human sounds of the evening meal are heard throughout the village camp, a rough ring of small grass shelters with a fire and a family in front of each. For some reason, on this night, there is an unusually high level of excitement among the people of the !Kung San band. Perhaps there is meat in the camp, or perhaps it is just the round moon rising. Perhaps someone has been ill. Or maybe no one has; what is about to happen will benefit the healthy almost as much as the sick.

The women have talked among themselves and decided to try. They may have been prodded by the men, or they may have tested the men's interest with questions—or they may have just decided, simply and unilaterally. They begin to clap in complex rhythms and to sing in a strange yodeling style that bridges octaves gracefully, creating a mesmerizing array of sounds. Gradually, they collect into a circle around a fire. Emotionally and musically they echo one another's enthusiasm. Someone stokes the fire as the dusk turns to dark.

Two of the men sitting cross-legged in front of a hut poke each other and stir. "These women are really singing," says one. "But we men are worthless." They chuckle and then become more serious, although the joking will begin again as the night wears on. They strap dance rattles onto their lower legs and get the feel of the sound that bounces back when their feet slap the ground. "Look," one of the women says, smiling. "These things might become men tonight." The dancing begins as other men join in, tracing a circle around the singing women. The men's feet slam to the ground repetitively and solidly. That sound becomes orchestrated with the clapping and singing of the women, and the network of echoing enthusiasm widens.

A newborn baby wakes and cries, and is adjusted in the sling at her mother's side. A toddler stumbles over to his mother, leans against her, and stares, wide-eyed, at the dancers. A pretty young woman whispers something into the ear of the woman next to her, both of them glance at one of the men dancing and burst out laughing. The fire is stoked again, and it burns more brightly.

Suddenly a man falls to the ground. Because he is in late middle age, the naïve observer wants to rush to his aid, but for the same reason his !Kung companions are unconcerned. (They have been expecting someone to fall, and the older and wiser among them, because of their experience, are most susceptible.) He lies there for a time, moaning softly and trembling. Other men drift over to him and kneel. They rub him gently, then vigorously, as one of them lifts the fallen man onto his lap. Finally, the man comes to a semblance of his senses and gets to his feet. Now he is in another state entirely, still trembling and moaning but walking, fully charged with energy. He bends over one of the women in the circle and places his hands on her shoulders. The trembling intensifies, taking on the rhythm of his breathing. With each breath, the amplitude of his voice and the tremor of his arms increase until the crescendo ends with a piercing shriek: "Kowhee-deedee!" He seems to relax momentarily, then moves on and repeats the ritual with each woman in the circle.

Meanwhile, the circle of singers has swelled, more men have joined the dancing, and other villagers, mostly children and adolescents, have formed a spectators' circle outside the inner two. One of the onlookers is a pregnant woman with a fever. The man in the healing trance goes to her for the laying on of hands, exerting himself at exceptional length and with exceptional vigor. At one point he pauses and stares out into the blackness, shouting almost hysterically, "You all! You all get out of here! You all get out of here!" Then he stares for a time into the void beyond the circle of spectators, before returning to the task of healing.

How does the healing trance come about? Does it truly impart the power to heal? And if so, how?

If Lorna Marshall, Richard Lee, and Richard Katz—the three great students of this ritual—could be at your elbow while you watched the !Kung dance, they might provide the following information. The trance and its power to heal are due in large part to the energy of the community. If the women sing and clap well, the men will dance well; if the sound of the dance rattles is good and someone begins to fall into a trance, the clapping and singing will rise to a new plane of excitement; if that plane is high enough and the men are sufficiently trusting of the women and of one another, several may enter deep and prolonged trances, and their healing power may last until after dawn.

The power itself, called *n/um,* is said to reside in the flanks of the abdomen, the pit of the stomach, or the base of the spine, and to boil up in a very painful way during the trance. The power to heal is not exactly the same as susceptibility to trances, but both are said to grow steadily during early adulthood and then diminish after middle or late middle age. A young man may have all the courage and energy he needs but, lacking experience and control, may be quite useless as a healer; an elder may have all the experience required, but his energy will not be what it was. (The parallel to the life cycle of male sexuality is striking, and perhaps significant.) As many as half of all men in the tribe can attain the healing power, which is an act of great courage, since the !Kung San believe that in a deep enough trance the soul may leave the body forever. The trance itself is at once exotically self-involved and heroically selfless. The individual is elevated in a way that is almost unique in this egalitarian culture, and yet his identity is dissolved; the ritual is of, by, and for the whole community.

If the dancer is experienced, his soul can travel great distances, to the world of the spirits and gods, and communicate with them about the illnesses and problems of the people. This marginal condition, between life and death, can be controlled only by the healer's own skill and by the vigorous ministrations of other healers. Their taking him in their arms, embracing him, and rubbing him with their sweat are considered lifesaving. In the process, the healing power can be transferred from an older, "big" healer to a novice; the novice places himself and his life in the hands of the older man, who must convey the power while protecting the novice from the grave dangers—both spiritual and real—that lie in wait.

In 1970, when I lived with the !Kung San in northwestern Botswana, along the fringe of the Kalahari Desert, I became an apprentice healer myself. The music created by the combined instruments of voice, clapping, and dance rattles struck me as being what used to be called psychedelic. Its eerie beauty seemed to bore into my skull, loosening the moorings of my mind. The dancing delivered a shock wave to the base of the head each time my heels hit the ground. This happened perhaps a hundred times a minute and lasted between two and ten hours. The effects on the brain and its blood vessels, and on the muscles of the head and neck, were direct and physical. Hyperventilation probably played a role, and perhaps smoke inhalation did as well. The sustained exertion may have depleted the blood of sugar, inducing light-headedness. And staring into the flames, while dancing those monotonous steps around and around the circle, seemed to have an effect all its own. ("Look not too long into the fire," warns Ishmael, the narrator of *Moby Dick,* for it may unhinge the mind.)

But more than any of these factors, what made it possible for me to enter into the trance (to the limited extent that I did) was trust. On the one night that was followed by a morning full of compliments, especially from the women, on how well I had done, I had it in the extreme—that "oceanic" feeling of oneness with the world, which Freud viewed as echoing our complete, blissful infant dependency. Whom did I trust? Everyone—the women; the other dancers, apprentices, and healers; the whole community—but especially my teacher, a man in his late forties (I was then twenty-six). He was not one of the most powerful healers, but he was strong enough to teach a novice like me. God had strengthened his healing power (and given him his own dancing song) in a dream, during the course of a long illness. He was a well-respected leader in the community, and most important, he was my friend.

Over the two years during which we worked closely together, my regard and affection for him matured into love. He was sensitive, wise, loyal, witty, bright, vigorous, generous—in a word, the perfect father. During that night I committed myself entirely into his hands, much as a suggestible person might do with a hypnotist. And as I drifted into a mental world not quite like any other I have experienced (although it shared some features with states induced by alcohol or marijuana), my mind focused on him and on my feeling for him. I felt sure that he would take care of me. He left me to my own devices for hours, and then at last, when I most needed some human contact, he took my arms and draped me over his shoulders. I suppose we looked rather comical—a six-foot-tall white man slumped over a five-foot-high African hunter-gatherer—but to me it seemed one of the most important events of my long and eventful stay in Africa.

All folk healing systems—and modern scientific medicine, too—are based on the relationship between the healer and the victim of illness. The behavioral and psychological features of this relationship—such elements as authority, trust, shared beliefs, teaching, nurturance, and kindness—significantly, and sometimes dramatically, affect the course of illness, promoting healing and preventing recurrence. Counseling and psychotherapy speed recovery from surgery and heart attack and mitigate the suffering of patients receiving radiotherapy for cancer. Even a room with a view reduces the amount of pain medication requested by patients recovering from surgery.

Call it placebo if you like, but the human touch has a real and measurable effect. Some aspects of it appear to act directly, through neuroendocrine mechanisms, which, though poorly understood, clearly serve as intermediaries between mind and body. Meditation, for example, decreases heart rate and blood pressure and thus helps relieve hypertension, and psychological stress has been shown in laboratory animals to decrease the number of "natural killer cells," which seek and destroy tumors and may provide resistance to cancer. On a more mundane level, the human touch can improve the patient's compliance with medical advice—an area in which modern physicians have not exactly excelled.

In my case, the deep and all-encompassing sense of trust did not last the whole night through. I drifted into a delusion that something terrible was happening to my wife, who was back resting in our grass hut, a mile or so away. This idea arose from an almost completely irrational fear of the Kalahari and all the creatures in it, animal and human. I darted from the circle, jumped into a Jeep truck, and began to drive. The trance was broken by the sound of the Jeep lodging itself on a tree stump.

What was happening in my mind and brain? No one can really say. We can guess that the neocortex, which is centrally involved in logical thought, was dulled, and probably have a piece of the truth; but it is possible as well that selected parts of my brain were heightened in their functioning. Because of the trance's superficial resemblance to a seizure and, more important, because of the powerful shifts in emotion, we can presume the involvement of the limbic system, the structure, between the brain stem and the neocortex, that mediates the emotions and has been implicated in epilepsy. Finally, we can be pretty sure that the trance involves some alteration of the brain stem's reticular activating system, which is the regulator of consciousness, ushering us from sleep to waking, from concentration to reverie. But this is all what mathematicians call "hand waving"—lines of argument so vague and sweeping as to satisfy no one.

So, it is too soon to conclude that !Kung healing "works" (according to scientific standards), and too soon to give an adequate explanation of the trance itself. I suspect, though, that in the end we will have convincing evidence. In the meantime, we can give the !Kung credit for discovering a deeply insightful system of psychology, based on knowledge and methods comparable in interest to anything in the West—and with at least equal symbolic richness. Consider the case of a young mother who had a serious bout with malaria in the wake of her middle-aged father's death. The healer in charge of her care entered a deep trance, during which his soul left his body. Traveling the road to the spirit world, it caught up with her father, who held the daughter's soul in his arms. After much discussion, the father was convinced that his daughter's need to remain on earth outweighed his own need for her and even his own considerable grief, so he returned her soul to the world of the living. A few days later, her fever and chills were gone.

Could the healer's report of his encounter with the father have influenced the course of the daughter's parasitic illness? Your guess is as good as mine. But mine is that the !Kung may have something to teach Western physicians about the psychological, and even spiritual, dimensions of illness.

14

The Doctor's White Coat: The Image of the Physician in Modern America

Dan W. Blumhagen

This selection offers a historical analysis of an important symbol in biomedicine, one that every patient and health care provider runs into on a daily basis. As with most aspects of culture, the use of the doctor's white coat is expected, and it usually goes unremarked and unanalyzed. A medical anthropological view of biomedical culture and behavior, however, requires us to examine this symbol for what it may reveal about the ethnomedical system of which it is part. This analysis demonstrates that cultural symbols have a cultural history and tells us how, as the white coat became commonly used in clinical settings, it came to be imbued with some important meanings. The author, a physician who was studying anthropology at the time, argues that the white coat is a symbol of science, purity, modernity, authoritative knowledge, and even supernatural power. Symbolic analysis is an important and standard method in medical anthropology; the cultural meanings of items used in the modern hospital—from white coats and badges to sophisticated scanning machines—exist in addition to *their obvious technological purposes. The values reflected in these symbols may also be uniquely American, particularly the value placed on the latest and most sophisticated technology. Finally, not all doctors are distinguished by the white coat—for example, surgeons (who have been studied intensively by medical anthropologists) often wear "scrubs" in the hospital and white coats only when in their offices. In some ways, the image of the doctor described in this selection may be a bit dated; changing public perceptions of doctors have eroded some of the original meanings. Nevertheless, physicians still wear white coats, while patients often get stuck in those gowns that gape open in the back.*

As you read this selection, consider these questions:

- **According to the author, what is the *attitude* of the physician that is communicated by the symbol of the white coat?**
- **How might the white coat enhance the beliefs of both the patient and the doctor about the possibility of successful healing?**
- **Given contemporary knowledge that germs are invisible to the naked eye, why might doctors and their patients think that the white coat is "clean" or "pure"?**
- **Sometimes the members of the society described by an anthropologist disagree with her symbolic analysis. Do you think that might be the case with the white coat? Why?**
- **Since the AIDS epidemic, the use of masks and gloves has become standard procedure in clinical settings. Do you think this might affect the rapport between healer and patient?**
- **According to the author, the white coat originated in the context of the scientific laboratory. Do you think that the typical doctor practicing in a clinic is really a scientist?**

Context: Dan W. Blumhagen is a medical doctor and anthropologist who worked for much of his career at the United States Agency for International Development. He wrote this classic article in 1979, when he was a graduate student in anthropology and a clinical research fellow in a hospital. His anthropological eye was caught by the obvious symbolism of the doctor's white coat. This article explores the cultural history of this clear and important symbol, and the ideological mechanisms by which the symbol enhances the image and authority of a biomedical practitioner.

Blumhagen wrote this at a time when physician-anthropologists were just beginning to have an impact on the field and when medical anthropological inquiries were beginning to examine the culture of biomedicine itself. This article was published in a prominent medical journal.

Source: D. W. Blumhagen (1979). "The Doctor's White Coat: The Image of the Physician in Modern America." *Annals of Internal Medicine* 91:111–116.

All societies have healers who care for the sick (1). The healer's interaction with a patient is often surrounded by a symbolic system that expresses the implicit cultural concepts of what "healing" means (2). As changes occur in the social meanings attributed to healing, the symbols used to express those concepts also change. This paper will use the symbol-analysis approach, widely used in cultural anthropology, to examine the historical origins and the function of the symbol systems that surround American physicians and their patients. An understanding of how these were adopted first by the profession and then by the greater society will elucidate what it means to be a healer in American culture. This knowledge can be usefully applied to problematic patient consultations, as well as to understanding some of the conflicts that have arisen between the medical profession and society at large.

THE NATURE OF SYMBOL ANALYSIS

Most physicians are aware of the importance of symbol analysis in individual psychotherapy (3). What is less widely appreciated is the application of a similar approach to understanding entire cultures. Anthropologists have found that symbols are often used as a way to express and reaffirm the fundamental belief systems that a society holds (4). This is often done in ritualized events. Perhaps cultural symbols can be most usefully viewed as a form of communication, analogous to words in a natural language (5). Like wards, they can be used in social settings to define the shared interpretation of "what's really going on here," to direct each actor's behavior, and to express the dominance relationships that exist between the various individuals who are interacting. Since most symbol analyses have dealt with small-scale preliterate societies, there is no well-defined formula for doing such a study in a complex, literate society such as modern America. My approach here will be to look at doctor–patient interactions to determine what symbols may be used, then to examine historical data documenting how these came into use and the original meanings they bore. Finally, the use of these symbols in the medical setting will be compared with similar symbols used in other American rituals to develop the full spectrum of meaning that they communicate.

SYMBOLS OF THE PHYSICIAN

What, then, are the symbols surrounding physicians, and what do they mean? Table 1 shows how physicians are depicted in advertisements for medical journals and in newspaper comic strips. These sources were chosen because they represent stereotypes of the doctor as presented to the profession and to the public. They represent "all physicians in general" and do not merely reflect the idiosyncracies of a particular physician.

TABLE I Depiction of Physicians in Medical and Lay Media

	Medical Journals*	Newspaper Comics†
Number	45	11
White coats	29	7
Stethoscopes	13	5
Head mirror	6	5
Black bag	0	5
No special identifiers	14‡	0

* Advertisements showing individuals clearly identified as physicians that appeared in *JAMA*. 1978:239(1–5); *N Engl J Med*. 1978:298 (1-4); *Am Fam Physician* 1977–8:16(6) to 17(2); and *J Fam Pract*. 1977–8:5(6) to 6(2). Each illustration was counted once, regardless of how many times it appeared.

† Syndicated comic strips that ran in the *Seattle Times* and *Seattle Post-Intelligencer* in January 1978. Each individual identified as a physician or medicine man was counted once, regardless of how frequently he appeared in a single strip.

‡ Two advertisements that show "clinical experts" making decisions about drug use or continuing medical education, that is, decisions that would affect the physician's behavior rather than the patient's, account for 13 or these.

Table 1 shows that although there are some differences in the way physicians are depicted in medical and popular media, there appear to be four principal objects used to depict the doctor: the white coat, stethoscope, head mirror, and black bag. In this survey, there was only one physician depicted in a patient-care setting who did not have at least one of these items. The most frequent component of the image seems to be the white coat. Of 43 doctors pictured in patient-care settings (Table 1), 36 were wearing white. In the symbolism of white coats, the social concept of "what it means to be a physician" is summarized, intensified, and extended. Its importance as *the* symbol of physicians is seen in that when the advertising media—a reflection of the current social stereotypes—wish to depict a person with the authority of a physician, he is usually shown wearing a white coat. Although professionals are reluctant to articulate the meanings they attribute to white coats, on occasion, under stress, such interpretations may be given.

> The relationship between a physician and his patient is serious and purposeful, not social, casual or random. In this relation the patient unburdens himself or herself of a set of concerns regarding health matters and transfers them to the accepting physician. For a very long time it

> has been customary for individuals in society to dress rather formally when conducting serious business, and less formally when they are at leisure. The physician's dress should convey to even his most anxious patient a sense of seriousness of purpose that helps to provide reassurance and confidence that his or her complaints will be dealt with competently. True, the white coat is only a symbol of this attitude, but it also has the additional practical virtue of being identifiable, easily laundered, and more easily changed than street clothes if accidentally soiled. Casual or slovenly dress is likely to convey, rightly or wrongly, casual or inattentive professional handling of their problem. Such a patient may respond in an inhibited manner, fail to volunteer information, refuse to carry out a recommended diagnostic or management program, fail to keep appointments, and be uncomfortable enough to seek help elsewhere. The rapport, so anxiously sought for with your patient, may be irretrievably lost (6).

To fully understand how the white coat has achieved this position, we must look at the historical origins of white coats as the symbol of physicians. I have been able to identify three major origins for the white coat as it has been used until fairly recently: the operating room, the scientific, specifically microbiological, laboratory, and the hospital. Each adds a layer of meaning.

THE WHITE COAT IN THE OPERATING ROOM

Operating-room garb appears to have originated with the concept of aseptic surgery, which began in this country about 1889 (7). Photographs from that year in the Massachusetts General Hospital Archives show the surgeons and nurses (but not the anaesthesiologist or observers in the balcony) wearing short-sleeved white coats over their street clothes. Masks and gloves had not yet come into use. The purpose of the coats in this setting appears to be twofold: to protect the patient from being contaminated by the physician, and to protect the physician from contamination by the patient during the procedure being performed. We will find that the white coat repeatedly serves to protect both the patient and the physician.

Another implication that surgery has for the public image of the physician is its incredible power to send a person into a deathlike state, open the previously inviolable body cavities, correct whatever was "wrong," and resurrect the patient, healed.

> I have said that the modern surgeon has become a popular hero. . . . One has only to glance through the month's illustrated magazines, or to turn a few pages of the latest novel to find him in the act of revealing his demonical subtlety or demonstrating his incredible skill. The tall spare frame is capable on emergency of strength and endurance that would make Sandow stand aghast (8).

White coats had not yet become symbolic of this heroism, but the newly developing film industry ground out a remarkable number of amplifications of this theme (9). One such film, "Society Doctor," is described as being "played in spotless white . . . and with an appropriate sense of glamor and nobility. . . . [The hero] persuades his best friend to operate on him, directing the work himself with the aid of mirrors" (10). In these quotations we see that the social image of the physician had become one of immense power and authority. These attributes were associated with the white clothing he wore.

Even though the operating room provided one of the earliest examples of doctors wearing white, and provides some of the basic cultural meaning, it does not appear to be the main source. Stahel's otherwise valuable article (11) confuses this point. With the goal of better aseptic technique, the white coats of 1889 rapidly became full-length gowns, and were referred to as such (12). Aseptic surgery required that these gowns only be used in the operating room to avoid the risk of cross contamination. The back opening, a necessity for sterile technique, also made it impractical for other patient-care settings (11). Additionally, the term "gown" in our culture usually refers to women's clothing, and thus is not suitable as a symbol for those who were "active, scientific men, virile, ambitious . . . upon whose shoulders the actual work of the institution will fall" (12, p. 265).

Photographs of surgeries at Massachusetts General Hospital in 1908 clearly show the divergence of white coats from operating-room gowns. There are three types of dress in the audience: the scrub suits of the surgeons who are clustered on one side; the street clothes of the vast majority in the middle; and the white coat of a single individual who looks as if he had just walked out of his laboratory to observe the procedure. The step that took the garb of the scientific laboratory into a clinical setting appears to be the main source of our current white coats. The term "lab coat," the primary term used for the white coat, refers to this origin.

THE WHITE COAT IN THE LABORATORY

The representation of the physician as a scientist has a long history that culminated during the first decades of this century. In the middle of the 19th century, science had nearly destroyed the reputability of medicine by demonstrating that its cures were worthless, but it was unable to substitute more effective remedies. Medicine became simply one of a wide variety of healing cults and quackery (13). Despite this inauspicious start, both the profession and public turned to science as the means by which healing would come. After all, the laboratories, whose inventions had transformed night into day, could transmit messages instantaneously, and had revolutionized transportation, were certainly the most important hope for the conquest of disease. Physicians were urged to present themselves as scientists. Cathell, whose book *The Physician Himself* went through many editions between 1882 and 1922, advised: "Show aesthetic cultivation in your office arrangement, and make it look fresh, neat, clean *and scientific*" (14) (emphasis added). Above all, one must avoid "forcing on everybody the conclusion that you are, after all, but an ordinary person" (14, p. 56). By 1922, Cathell had become more emphatic in describing "*the office, the sanctuary—of an earnest working scientific medical man . . .*" (emphasis in original) as the place where one will make 'judicious and intelligent use of your scientific instruments of precision . . . to assist you in curing nervous and terrified people by increasing their confidence in your armamentarium and in your professional ability" (15). The authority of science is seen as validating the practice of medicine.

Demonstrations of the efficacy of modern science, such as the construction of the Panama Canal (1915), led to its public acceptance as the foundation of modern healing. An intense feeling of hope about the future of scientific medicine was expressed in cartoons. . . . Other healing cults, particularly homeopathy and eclecticism, which had threatened the existence of scientific medicine only a few years earlier, withered away. Their schools closed or converted to biomedicine.

The medical profession rapidly consolidated its position as a part of the scientific enterprise. Within a decade of the publication of the *Flexner Report* in 1910, medical education was restructured around laboratory science. The *content* of medicine changed. Textbooks were rewritten: Of all the books popular enough to go through multiple editions before the "progressive era," almost none were still being printed when it ended. (This was ascertained by a review of the books in the open stacks of the Countway Library. The most notable exceptions, of course, are *Gray's Anatomy* and Osler's *Textbook of Medicine* (1892), both of which are still being printed in revised editions. There were no technical or theoretical advances that would outdate the former, and the latter was written by one of the men who led medical education during this change.) Towards the end of this radical transformation of the profession of medicine, and as a reflection of it, physicians became stereotyped as scientists wearing white coats. The message of power and protection emerged: While wearing a white coat the physician is able to handle safely the deadly scourges that plague mankind and is able to render them innocuous: One result of this perception of power was that physician-scientists were granted tremendous authority. No mere individual desires or beliefs were allowed to stand in the way of the public's health as determined by medical laboratories (16).

THE WHITE COAT IN THE HOSPITAL

The shift in locus of sick care from the home to the hospital was the third historical trend. The basis for this lay in the development of aseptic surgery and modern diagnostic and therapeutic techniques, which necessitated the use of personnel and resources that could not readily be taken to the patient's home. With the impact of the change in medical care, the image of the hospital changed from that of being a place where social outcasts died to being the only place where the sick could be healed. The image changed from death to life. This was reflected in the change of the clothing of the healing staff. The black habits of the religious nursing orders, for example, became the white uniforms of the modern nursing profession (17). Hornsby, then director of Michael Reese Hospital in Chicago, tells us in *The Modern Hospital* (12, pp. 543–5) that all people connected with the healing process (including patients and visitors) were to be dressed in white whereas the *nonmedical* employees were to be given colored uniforms. White became associated with the *institutions* of healing, and it was within their halls that the use of white coats as the symbol of medicine was most pronounced. Physicians in private practice have never completely adopted their use.

This transition is most clearly indicated in the photographs of house staff that often accompany a hospital's annual report. These pictures show that during the period 1905–15 apprentice physicians exchanged their street clothes for white coats and pants. Hornsby indicates that this was not merely for the convenience of the hospital laundry; indeed, "Intern's white uniforms are difficult to launder, and should be done by hand" (12, p. 601). In other words, there were compelling reasons for dressing interns in white that outweighed the economic disadvantages.

THE MEANING OF WHITENESS

Given the historical backdrop of the meaning of the white coat, what is added by the cultural conception of the meaning of whiteness? Originally, laboratory coats were tan and appear to have changed to white as they became associated with medicine. Why was not another, perhaps more functional, color adopted? Why were both the profession and the public so profoundly disturbed when Nobel Laureate Alexis Carrel wore *black* gowns in his laboratories and operating rooms at the fledgling Rockefeller Institute of Medicine (18)?

The significance of white as a symbol of life has already been mentioned. Since there are few celebrations of life in our society, this meaning is derived from its opposite color, black, which is clearly the color of death and mourning. The association with purity has also received comment. But this purity contains two strands of meaning: First is the concept of innocence. No shadow of malice, of intentional harm, can mar the white coat—the patient is safe in the hands of this powerful figure. Second is the purity of unaroused sexuality, particularly as this meaning is evoked in another ritual that uses the white bridal gown.

Closely allied to the concept of purity is the concept of superhuman power. The saying "cleanliness is next to godliness" originated long before the germ theory of disease! Whiteness as an attribute of superhuman power, at once irresistibly attractive and infinitely dangerous, is clearly expressed in Melville's *Moby Dick* (19) and, as has been shown, was explicitly applied to physicians. In religious symbolism, Christ and the saints who have exercised their power over death and all other human frailties are robed in white (Bible, Revelations 7:9–17). But these are not merely powerful, they are supremely good.

A final meaning comes from the term candor, itself derived from the Latin *candidus* (white). This impartial truth-telling is often portrayed in statues of "justice," who is usually depicted wearing white.

If symbols affect behavior, the use of the white coat should affect how patients and physicians act. There appear to be two behavioral changes that have been mediated by the white coat: the physician's access to his patient's body, and the shift in the locus of the sick role from the home to an institution.

BODY AND SEXUAL TABOOS IN AMERICAN CULTURE

In many societies, the most powerful symbol systems are found in situations where strong social values appear to be challenged (20). One of the strongest beliefs in our society is the inviolability of a person's physical body (21, 22). There is even a legal term for the violation of a person's rights over his own body: battery. Merely touching another individual without that person's permission is to be at jeopardy of civil and criminal action (23). The extent to which the physical examination is a serious breach of social custom has been clearly stated by Lief and Fox (24).

> The amounts and occasions of bodily contact are carefully regulated in all societies, and very much so in ours. The kind of access to the body of the patient that a physician in our society has is a uniquely privileged one. Even in the course of a so-called routine physical examination, the physician is permitted to handle the patient's body in ways otherwise permitted to special intimates, and in the case of procedures such as rectal and vaginal examination in ways normally not even permitted to a sexual partner.

The physical body is not merely a threat to the person whose body is revealed, it is also considered to be dangerous to the one who is exposed to it. This is the basis of much of the American film rating system. Given these taboos, the perfunctory way that physicians are given permission to do the most intimate examination is remarkable.

> The individual must stand before his doctor man to man, unclothed physically, mentally and morally, revealing to him as he does to no other mortal, not even to his father confessor, the secrets of his inmost soul; submiting his person to the most thorough scrutiny of the physician and to varied tests, physical, clinical, instrumental and what not, and without hesitation committing to his keeping the keys of the family skeleton closet (25).

Physical examinations of apparently healthy people are a relatively recent phenomenon. Referring to the late 19th century, Duffy writes: "Physical diagnosis remained handicapped by the reluctance of patients, particularly females, to bare their skins to the probing, palpation or percussion of the physicians" (26). Rectal and pelvic examinations do not appear to have been frequently used. As late as 1927, Richard Cabot, a prominent medical educator, claimed that "it is not and should not be a part of the routine physical examination to examine the rectum" (27). Buttressed, however, by the successes of medicine in improving public health, a campaign was waged from 1922 to 1929 that promoted periodic physical examinations as a means of improving the *individual's* health (28). These included pelvic and rectal examinations.

For this crusade to be successful, the cultural dangers of the physical contact had to be muted. A mechanism was needed that would reinterpret an ordinarily taboo activity into a socially acceptable, even desirable, one (29). A set of symbols was needed to protect both the doctor and patient in this dangerous setting. The white coat, with its meanings of bilateral protection, purity, goodness, and unaroused sexuality, was ideally suited for this task. In the less-threatening situation where a male physician examined a man, the white coat was all that was needed: the patient was nude (30). When the physician examined a woman, however, a reciprocal symbolic dress was required, leading to the development of the examination gown. In one of the early descriptions of such a garment, the symbolic themes come out. Fisk (30) claims that this gown "gives the examinee a sense of protection and lessens embarrassment." The disparate treatment of men and women could not be maintained, and soon men, too, were offered the protection of examination gowns.

The second behavioral change was a shift in the concept of where it was appropriate to act sick (31). Previously, of course, illness had been a personal drama played in the bedroom, the most secluded, intimate, and protective area of the home. The physician could enter at the invitation of the family and be made privy to the physical and behavioral secrets contained therein without violating any social norms. Only those unfortunate persons who lacked a protective home sought care in an institution. It was only the "fallen women who enter hospitals" (32), that is, only those people without anything worth concealing or without anyone to shield them. Symbols were required that would protect patients from the unwarranted intrusions that could occur in an institution and that would legitimize private behavior in a public place. The physician's white coat and the patient's examination gown met these needs perfectly.

These shared meanings direct patient and physician behavior in the following way: The physician is an active scientist, the patient is passive material; the physician prescribes, the patient complies; the physician is self-concealing, the patient is self-revealing. Clearly, as long as this social definition of the healing encounter exists, the physician will dominate the setting.

DEVELOPMENTS FROM 1930 TO 1960

The above set of symbols appears go have been fully functional by the early 1930s and remained largely intact until recently. There were minor changes, such as the adoption of blue or green garb in operating rooms when high-intensity lighting made the glare from white drapes unbearable, but these pastel shades did not conflict with the underlying value system as black or red, for example, would have.

Other practitioners found that some of the meanings communicated by the white coat were so overpowering that it interfered with their practice. Pediatricians and psychiatrists have discovered that this mark of authority has a tendency to overwhelm their patients, and they therefore tend to wear pastel coats or normal street clothes. As has been noted, many physicians, particularly those in private practice, did not adopt the white coat. Nonetheless, these trends did not affect the public image of what a physician should be. If anything, the beliefs were intensified, as is evidenced by the meteoric rise in the funding of medical research after World War II, which resulted in the National Institutes of Health and much of the rest of the academic medical enterprise (33).

CURRENT TRENDS

During the past decade, however, much of this has changed. Physician-scientists who were once seen as validating medical practice no longer necessarily protect and heal patients, but may endanger them. A good example of this attitude is seen in the widespread laetrile movement, which is perceived as a direct assault on the biomedical establishment. Other social symbols of authority are also being rejected. Hospitals are often accused of prolonging agony rather than renewing life. Body taboos do not seem to be as strong as they once were.

These social changes strike at the heart of the meanings communicated by white coats. No new consensus has developed that will define the nature of healing and give direction for patient behavior. This has had an effect on the use of both white coats and examination gowns.

The quote from Kriss (6) earlier in this paper that expounded the significance of white coats is the result of widespread student challenges of the authority of this symbol. Debate over whether medical students should wear one still continues (34). Voices from some of the countercultural movements recognize the implications of this symbolism and reject it. Some feminists, for example, "advise women to discard the drape by throwing it on the floor when the doctor enters. If he replaces it, throw it on the floor again" (35). This type of symbolic action tends to make physicians uncomfortable, for the rejection of symbols of established roles means that there is little guidance as to how they or their patients should act.

Cousins (36) comments on this redefinition of roles in the healing encounter when he claims that "the most important thing happening in American medicine today is not the discovery of magical new drugs but the new relationship that is emerging between physicians and patients" (36). The old model of the scientist-healer is rejected for a more humanistic relationship. He continues: "Traditionally the doctor is the authoritarian figure . . . the new relationship is more in the nature of a partnership." Note that the "traditional authoritarian figure" is, as has been documented here, a tradition that has only existed since the turn of the century. There were reasons for adopting that role at the time: there may be similar reasons for abandoning it now.

The dynamic relationship that exists between physicians and American culture is only beginning to be explored. As we learn more about the social meaning and function of healing, we will better understand some of the conflicts that we feel between society and the profession. This in turn may enable us to devise better institutional and individual means of meeting these needs. But even before that global understanding is reached, there may be benefits that accrue on a smaller scale. In all patient-physician encounters, careful consideration of the symbolic and other nonverbal communication may be important. In particularly unsettled interactions, painstaking, explicit discussion and negotiation on the exact role that the patient and the physician will take may be required for healing to occur.

REFERENCES

1. Landy D, ed. *Culture, Disease and Healings; Studies in Medical Anthropology.* New York: Macmillan Publishing Co.; 1977:1.
2. Kleinman AM. The symbolic context of Chinese medicine: a comparative approach to the study of traditional medical and psychiatric forms of care in Chinese cultures. *Am J Chin Med.* 1975;3:103–24.
3. Freun S. *The Interpretation of Dreams.* New York: Macmillan Publishing Co.; 1900.
4. Dolgin JL, Klmnitzer DS, Schneider DM. *Symbolic Anthropology: A Reader in the Study of Symbols and Meaning.* New York: Columbia University Press; 1977:3-47.
5. Leach E. *Culture and Communication: The Logic by Which Symbols Are Connected.* Cambridge: Cambridge University Press; 1976:10.
6. Kriss JP. On white coats and other matters. *N Engl J Med.* 1975:292:1024–5.
7. Potter RA, ed. *Surgery in the United States.* The American College of Surgeons and the American Surgical Association: 1976:17.
8. Whitby CJ. *The Doctor and His Work.* London, Swift and Co.: 1912:23.
9. Spears J. The doctor on the screen. *Films in Review.* 19 November 1955:6:436-44.
10. *New York Times Film Review; 1913–1968: Volume 2, 1932–1938.* New York: New York Times: 1970:1143.
11. Stahel HR. Der weisse Mantel in der Medizin. *Zürcher Medizinges-chichtliche Abhandlungen* 1970;78:1–22.
12. Hornsby JA, Schmidt RE. *The Modern Hospital.* Philadelphia: W. B. Saunders: 1913:543.
13. Sharyock RH. *The Development of Modern Medicine.* New York: Alfred A. Knopf, Inc.; 1947:248-72.
14. Cathell DW. *The Physician Himself and What He Should Add to the Strictly Scientific.* Baltimore: Chrishay and Barley; 1882:10.
15. Cathell DW. *Book on the Physician Himself from Graduation to Old Age.* Emerson Hotel, Baltimore: Published by the author; 1922:10.
16. Rosen G. *A History of Public Health.* New York: MD Publications: 1958:464–78.
17. Dietz LD, Lehozky AR. *History and Modern Nursing.* Philadelphia: F.A. Davis; 1967:168–73.
18. Conner GW. *A History of the Rockefeller Institution.* New York: Rockefeller Foundation: 1964:154.
19. Melville H. *Moby Dick or The White Whale.* New York: The Modern Library: 1930:272–83.
20. Berger PL, Luckmann T. *The Social Construction of Reality.* Garden City, New York: Doubleday and Co.; 1966:96.
21. Miner H. Body ritual among the Nacirema. In: Spradley JP, Rynklewich MA, eds. *The Nacirema.* Boston: Little, Brown and Co.; 1975.
22. Glaser BG, Strauss AL. *Awareness of Dying.* Chicago; Aldine Publishing Co.; 1965:162.
23. Black HC. *Black's Law Dictionary.* St. Paul, Minnesota: West Publishing Co.: 1957:193.
24. Lief HI, Fox RC: Training for detached concern in medical students: In: Lief HI, Lief VF, Lief NR, eds. *The Psychological Basis of Medical Practice.* New York: Harper and Row; 1963:32.
25. Finney JMT. *The Physician.* New York: Charles Scribner and Sons; 1923.
26. Duffy J. *The Healers.* New York: McGraw-Hill; 1976:232.
27. Cabot RC. *Physical Diagnosis.* New York: William Wood and Co.; 1927:435.
28. Rosen G. *Preventive Medicine in the United States, 1900–1975.* New York: Science History Press; 1975:59.
29. Emerson JP. Behavior in private places; sustaining definitions of reality in gynecological examinations. In: Drettizerl HP, ed. *Recent Sociology: No. 2 Patterns of Communicative Behavior.* New York Macmillan Publishing Co.; 1970.
30. Fisk EL, Crawford JR. *How to Make the Periodic Physical Examination.* New York: Macmillan Publishing Co.; 1928:41.
31. Freidson E. *Profession of Medicine.* New York: Harper and Row; 1970:220.
32. Trousseau A. *Clinical Medicine Lectures.* Philadelphia: Blinkerston; 1882:43.
33. Bordley J III. Harvey AM. *Two Centuries of American Medicine; 1776–1976.* Philadelphia: W.B. Saunders; 1976:419.
34. McKinnon JA. Life in a short white coat. *New Physician.* November 1977;26:24-30.
35. Dreifus C. ed. *Seizing Our Bodies.* New York: Random House; 1977:266.
36. Cousins N. "A Better Rx for Patients." Los Angeles Times Syndicate; 2 April 1978. Syndicated editorial column.

Belief and Healing

CONCEPTUAL TOOLS

■ ***The distinction between disease and illness has had central importance.*** Disease refers to outward, objective clinical manifestations of abnormality of physical function or infection by a pathogen in an individual or host. The concept of disease is fundamental to biomedicine; the official listing of disease categories, grouped by causal agents, is found in the *International Classification of Diseases,* currently in its ninth edition (the analogous reference for mental disorders is the *Diagnostic and Statistical Manual of Mental Disorders,* 4th ed.). *Disease* refers to observable, organic, and pathological abnormalities in organs and organ systems, whether or not they are culturally recognized. On the other hand, *illness* refers to a person's perceptions and lived experience of being sick or "diseased"—that is, socially disvalued states including (but not limited to) disease. The study of illness involves cognitive and social psychological issues like stigma.

Disease is considered a biological phenomenon, whereas illness includes psychological and social dimensions as well. Within a population, the distribution of disease and illness do not completely overlap: There are people with diagnosable diseases (e.g., hypertension) who do not know or think of themselves as ill; correspondingly, a significant percentage of patients visiting physicians are ill but do not have an identifiable disease. In biomedicine, the illness of a patient with symptoms but no diagnosable disease can be termed as psychosomatic, referring to a psychological etiology. Although this term is infrequently used today, the negative implication of the "psychosomatic" label was that the illness was not real because the patient's "abnormal" mind caused the abnormalities of the body. The patient, therefore, could be blamed as the cause of her or his own symptoms. The traditional biomedical logic subsumed under the concept of psychosomatic illness (and the disease–illness distinction) has been a central target of analysis in critical medical anthropology.

■ ***All cultures have medical systems comprised of both cognitive and behavioral components.*** The cognitive component of a medical system centers on theories of etiology, or causation, of illness. It usually involves a taxonomy of disease categories grouped by causal agent. The study of cultural knowledge about illness and its linkages to differential diagnosis and curative actions is called *ethnomedicine.* The behavioral component of medical systems concerns the social interactions of healers and their patients in a cultural and economic context. Social mechanisms through which healers are trained, division of labor among healers, and organization of the institutions through which medical services are delivered to a population are all important parts of medical systems.

In technologically simple societies like bands and tribes, with shamans as the principal healers, the medical system is integrated into and often indistinguishable from the local religion. In technologically complex societies, the primary medical system is more likely to be secular; complex societies also are often characterized by the simultaneous practice of multiple medical systems or traditions, a situation called *medical pluralism.*

■ ***Healing is a biopsychosocial process.*** Medical anthropology is concerned with both the experience of illness and the experience of healing. Healing is a process that often involves the self-repair of the body. Frequently, biomedical practitioners are able to treat symptoms while the body heals itself. With the advent of biomedical technologies like antibiotics and surgeries, the doctor is able to cure the disease by killing it or removing or repairing tissue. After such interventions, the body needs time, rest, nutrition, and social support in order to complete the healing process. The healing process is linked to the rights and responsibilities associated with the sick role. On the other hand, there are many chronic diseases that simply cannot be cured; they must be *managed,* and the afflicted person must learn to cope with the disease. In these common cases, healing has a different meaning since the sufferer must reshape his or her life. Chronic illnesses often involve a long series of acute episodes and remissions. Coping with illnesses is a psychological process not just for the individual but also for the larger social unit. The social support aspect of healing is central to the entire process. If the social group (including the physician) believes that the patient will get better, then the likelihood of recovery from (or successful adaptation to) the chronic disease is increased.

- ***Belief and healing often involve the cultural constructs of religion.*** Anthropologists argue that religion, defined in its broadest sense, is a universal aspect of all cultures. Religion includes beliefs that help people make sense of the world in times of crisis—like the crises of disease and death. Religion also involves rituals and practices that are associated with the belief system. Some of these practices are aimed at keeping people healthy by reducing risk of divine retribution, while other can be requests for divine healing. In most societies characterized by simple technologies, it is almost impossible to separate religion from medicine.

- ***Belief in healing involves three different social actors.*** As explained in the classic article by Claude Lévi-Strauss, the healing process requires belief and trust at three different levels. First, the healer must believe in her or his own powers to heal, or at least symbolically communicate confidence in that knowledge. Second, the patient must believe in the power of the healer; such a belief is enhanced by the desire to get well and the fact that seeking help is actually an "act of faith." Third, and perhaps most important, the social group must believe in the power of the healer and the possibility that the patient will get well.

- ***Both placebo and nocebo are powerful.*** The importance of belief is seen in studies of the placebo and nocebo effects. In randomized controlled studies, the placebo effect often accounts for up to one-third of the effectiveness of medical interventions. The term *placebo effect* is an oxymoron because a placebo is supposed to have no effect; the effect of placebos is probably related to the beliefs and perceptions of both patients and health care providers. The nocebo effect in groups is related to socially contagious fear.

 15

The Sorcerer and His Magic

Claude Lévi-Strauss

This selection, foundational in medical anthropology, is about the role of belief in both healing and harm—what are today called the placebo and nocebo effects. Written by the famous French anthropologist who pioneered the study of structuralism and the analysis of myth, this selection may be a little difficult, but it is well worth the effort. Claude Lévi-Strauss uses four compelling stories: "voodoo death" among Australian aborigines; a Nambicuara shaman and political leader from the Amazonian rain forest; a teenage boy accused of witchcraft among the Zuni, a Pueblo people of New Mexico; and Quesalid, a Kwakiutl shaman from the Pacific Northwest coastal tribe studied by Franz Boas. Each story illustrates Lévi-Strauss's argument that there are three levels of belief involved in a shamanistic cure. These beliefs in the power of the sorcerer are socially constructed and socially maintained. Belief is enhanced by the manipulation of symbols in a ritual setting.

The interaction of belief and experience is very important. Being cured by a spiritualist healer can be a life-altering experience. The story of Quesalid in this selection by Lévi-Strauss is a powerful and poignant story; it is a story of knowledge, power, a "trick," and ultimately the transformation of an individual's life. Lévi-Strauss comments that Quesalid "did not become a great shaman because he cured his patients; he cured his patients because he had become a great shaman." This delineates precisely the relationship between belief and healing. Belief plays a central role in the "shamanistic complex." It provides the mechanism for the "fabulation" of an unknown reality—the cultural process of controlling something by naming and telling a story about it.

The use of symbols, like the doctor's white coat, plays an important role in reinforcing the patient's beliefs; these symbols can be objects or words, but they have special meaning to participants. Participants do not often see the symbolic dimension to their activities; anthropologists tend to see them, partly because that is a benefit of being an outsider looking in. The bone pointed at the sorcerer's victim, in the voodoo death case described at the beginning of this selection, is a good example of a powerful object-symbol. Quesalid's scrap of bloody feather is another.

The manipulation of symbols, however, is only a means to an end. Its purpose is to bring a cure. That is done, psychosomatic research tells us, by harnessing the power of the mind and the body's own ability to heal itself. The exact mechanisms for this process remain unknown. Lévi-Strauss uses the idea of "abreaction" (a powerful turning point of reliving an event), borrowed from psychoanalytic theory, to explain this mechanism. Although this part of the analysis generally has not been accepted by anthropologists, recent theories about symbolic healing by James Dow (1986), Daniel Moerman (1991), and Robert Hahn (1995) should be of interest to advanced students.

As you read this selection, consider these questions:

- **What are the three levels of belief that Lévi-Strauss thinks form the core of the "shamanistic complex"? Which of these beliefs do you think is the most important?**
- **Why does Quesalid change from a nonbeliever to a believer? How does he get incorporated into the system? Why doesn't he tell the truth at the end of his life?**
- **To what extent do patients expect that their biomedical doctor act like a shaman?**
- **How does the use of symbols facilitate belief?**

Context: Claude Lévi-Strauss is one of France's best-known intellectuals and a major contributor to the field of cultural anthropology. He became an important figure in the mid-1950s because his analyses of cultural products (especially mythologies) used a new approach called *structuralism,* which is both a theory and method influenced by linguistic theory, brain science, and existentialism. The importance of his theoretical contributions is reflected in the fact that much of contemporary cultural anthropological theory is referred to as "post-structuralist." This article appeared in his collection of essays titled *Structural Anthropology,* which was translated into English in 1963. This classic article, emphasizing the role of belief in curing, uses narrative analysis as well as a psychoanalytic approach. Lévi-Strauss turned 100 in 2008.

Source: C. Lévi-Strauss (1963). "The Sorcerer and His Magic." In *Structural Anthropology,* Vol. 1, C. Jacobson (trans.). New York: Basic Books.

Since the pioneering work of Cannon, we understand more clearly the psycho-physiological mechanisms underlying the instances reported from many parts of the world of death by exorcism and the casting of spells.[1] An individual who is aware that he is the object of sorcery is thoroughly convinced that he is doomed according to the most solemn traditions of his group. His friends and relatives share this certainty. From then on the community withdraws. Standing aloof from the accursed, it treats him not only as though he were already dead but as though he were a source of danger to the entire group. On every occasion and by every action, the social body suggests death to the unfortunate victim, who no longer hopes to escape what he considers to be his ineluctable fate. Shortly thereafter, sacred rites are held to dispatch him to the realm of shadows. First brutally torn from all of his family and social ties and excluded from all functions and activities through which he experienced self-awareness, then banished by the same forces from the world of the living, the victim yields to the combined effect of intense terror, the sudden total withdrawal of the multiple reference systems provided by the support of the group, and, finally, to the group's decisive reversal in proclaiming him—once a living man, with rights and obligations—dead and an object of fear, ritual, and taboo. Physical integrity cannot withstand the dissolution of the social personality.[2]

How are these complex phenomena expressed on the physiological level? Cannon showed that fear, like rage, is associated with a particularly intense activity of the sympathetic nervous system. This activity is ordinarily useful, involving organic modifications which enable the individual to adapt himself to a new situation. But if the individual cannot avail himself of any instinctive or acquired response to an extraordinary situation (or to one which he conceives of as such), the activity of the sympathetic nervous system becomes intensified and disorganized; it may, sometimes within a few hours, lead to a decrease in the volume of blood and a concomitant drop in blood pressure, which result in irreparable damage to the circulatory organs. The rejection of food and drink, frequent among patients in the throes of intense anxiety, precipitates this process; dehydration acts as a stimulus to the sympathetic nervous system, and the decrease in blood volume is accentuated by the growing permeability of the capillary vessels. These hypotheses were confirmed by the study of several cases of trauma resulting from bombings, battle shock, and even surgical operations; death results, yet the autopsy reveals no lesions.

There is, therefore, no reason to doubt the efficacy of certain magical practices. But at the same time we see that the efficacy of magic implies a belief in magic. The latter has three complementary aspects: first, the sorcerer's belief in the effectiveness of his techniques; second, the patient's or victim's belief in the sorcerer's power; and, finally, the faith and expectations of the group, which constantly act as a sort of gravitational field within which the relationship between sorcerer and bewitched is located and defined.[3] Obviously, none of the three parties is capable of forming a clear picture of the sympathetic nervous system's activity or of the disturbances which Cannon called homeostatic. When the sorcerer claims to suck out of the patient's body a foreign object whose presence would explain the illness and produces a stone which he had previously hidden in his mouth, how does he justify this procedure in his own eyes? How can an innocent person accused of sorcery prove his innocence if the accusation is unanimous—since the magical situation is a consensual phenomenon? And, finally, how much credulity and how much skepticism are involved in the attitude of the group toward those in whom it recognizes extraordinary powers, to whom it accords corresponding privileges, but from whom it also requires adequate satisfaction? Let us begin by examining this last point.

It was in September, 1938. For several weeks we had been camping with a small band of Nambicuara Indians near the headwaters of the Tapajoz, in those desolate savannas of central Brazil where the natives wander during the greater part of the year, collecting seeds and wild fruits, hunting small mammals, insects, and reptiles, and whatever else might prevent them from dying of starvation. Thirty of them were camped together there, quite by chance. They were grouped in families under frail lean-tos of branches, which give scant protection from the scorching sun, nocturnal chill, rain, and wind. Like most bands, this one had both a secular chief and a sorcerer; the latter's daily activities—hunting, fishing, and handicrafts—were in no way different from those of the other men of the group. He was a robust man, about forty-five years old, and a *bon vivant*.

One evening, however, he did not return to camp at the usual time. Night fell and fires were lit; the natives were visibly worried. Countless perils lurk in the bush: torrential rivers, the somewhat improbable danger of encountering a large wild beast—jaguar or anteater—or, more readily pictured by the Nambicuara, an apparently harmless animal which is the incarnation of an evil spirit of the waters or forest. And above all, each night for the past week we had seen mysterious campfires, which sometimes approached and sometimes receded from our own. Any unknown band is always potentially hostile. After a two-hour wait, the natives were convinced that their companion had been killed in ambush and, while his two young wives and his son wept noisily in mourning for their dead husband and father, the other natives discussed the tragic consequences foreshadowed by the disappearance of their sorcerer.

Toward ten that evening, the anguished anticipation of imminent disaster, the lamentations in which the other women began to join, and the agitation of the men had created an intolerable atmosphere, and we decided to reconnoiter with several natives who had remained relatively calm. We had not gone two hundred yards when we stumbled upon a motionless figure. It was our man, crouching silently, shivering in the chilly night air, disheveled and without his belt, necklaces, and arm-bands (the Nambicuara wear nothing else). He allowed us to lead him back to the camp site without resistance, but only after long exhortations by his group and pleading by his family was he persuaded to talk. Finally, bit by bit, we extracted the details of his story. A thunderstorm, the first of the season, had burst during the afternoon, and the thunder had carried him off to a site several miles distant, which he named, and then, after stripping him completely, had brought him back to the spot where we found him. Everyone went off to sleep commenting on the event. The next day the thunder victim had recovered his joviality and, what is more, all his ornaments. This last detail did not appear to surprise anyone, and life resumed its normal course.

A few days later, however, another version of these prodigious events began to be circulated by certain natives. We must note that this band was actually composed of individuals of different origins and had been fused into a new social entity as a result of unknown circumstances. One of the groups had been decimated by an epidemic several years before and was no longer sufficiently large to lead an independent life; the other had seceded from its original tribe and found itself in the same straits. When and under what circumstances the two groups met and decided to unite their efforts, we could not discover. The secular leader of the new band came from one group and the sorcerer, or religious leader, from the other. The fusion was obviously recent, for no marriage had yet taken place between the two groups when we met them, although the children of one were usually betrothed to the children of the other; each group had retained its own dialect, and their members could communicate only through two or three bilingual natives.

This is the rumor that was spread. There was good reason to suppose that the unknown bands crossing the savanna belonged to the tribe of the seceded group of which the sorcerer was a member. The sorcerer, impinging on the functions of his colleague the political chief, had doubtless wanted to contact his former tribesmen, perhaps to ask to return to the fold, or to provoke an attack upon his new companions, or perhaps even to reassure them of the friendly intentions of the latter. In any case, the sorcerer had needed a pretext for his absence, and his kidnapping by thunder and its subsequent staging were invented toward this end. It was, of course, the natives of the other group who spread this interpretation, which they secretly believed and which filled them with apprehension. But the official version was never publicly disputed, and until we left, shortly after the incident, it remained ostensibly accepted by all.[4]

Although the skeptics had analyzed the sorcerer's motives with great psychological finesse and political acumen, they would have been greatly astonished had someone suggested (quite plausibly) that the incident was a hoax which cast doubt upon the sorcerer's good faith and competence. He had probably not flown on the wings of thunder to the Rio Ananaz and had only staged an act. But these things might have happened, they had certainly happened in other circumstances, and they belonged to the realm of real experience. Certainly the sorcerer maintains an intimate relationship with the forces of the supernatural. The idea that in a particular case he had used his power to conceal a secular activity belongs to the realm of conjecture and provides an opportunity for critical judgment. The important point is that these two possibilities were not mutually exclusive; no more than are, for us, the alternate interpretations of war as the dying gasp of national independence or as the result of the schemes of munitions manufacturers. The two explanations are logically incompatible, but we admit that one or the other may be true; since they are equally plausible, we easily make the transition from one to the other, depending on the occasion and the moment. Many people have both explanations in the back of their minds.

Whatever their true origin, these divergent interpretations come from individual consciousness not as the result of objective analysis but rather as complementary ideas resulting from hazy and unelaborated attitudes which have an experiential character for each of us. These experiences, however, remain intellectually diffuse and emotionally intolerable unless they incorporate one or another of the patterns present in the group's culture. The assimilation of such patterns is the only means of objectivizing subjective states, of formulating inexpressible feelings, and of integrating inarticulated experiences into a system.

. . .

These mechanisms become clearer in the light of some observations made many years ago among the Zuni of New Mexico by an admirable field-worker, M. C. Stevenson.[5] A twelve-year-old girl was stricken with a nervous seizure directly after an adolescent boy had seized her hands. The youth was accused of sorcery and dragged before the court of the Bow priesthood. For an hour he denied having any knowledge of occult power, but this defense proved futile. Because the crime of sorcery was at that time still punished by death among the Zuni, the accused changed his tactics. He improvised a tale explaining the circumstances by which he had been initiated into sorcery. He said he had received two substances from his teachers, one which drove girls insane and another which cured them. This point constituted an ingenious precaution against later developments. Having been ordered to produce his medicines, he went home under guard and came back with two roots, which he proceeded to use in a complicated ritual. He simulated a trance after taking one of the drugs, and after taking the other he pretended to return to his normal state. Then he administered the remedy to the sick girl and declared her cured. The session was adjourned until the following day, but during the night the alleged sorcerer escaped. He was soon captured, and the girl's family set itself up as a court and continued the trial. Faced with the reluctance of his new judges to accept his first story, the boy then invented a new one. He told them that all his relatives and ancestors had been witches and that he had received marvelous powers from them. He claimed that he could assume the form of a cat, fill his mouth with cactus needles, and kill his victims—infants, three girls, and two boys—by shooting the needles into them. These feats, he claimed, were due to the magical powers of certain plumes which were used to change him and his family into shapes other than human. This last detail was a tactical error, for the judges called upon him to produce the plumes as proof of his new story. He gave various excuses which were rejected one after another, and he was forced to take his judges to his house. He began by declaring that the plumes were secreted in a wall that he could not destroy. He was commanded to go to work. After breaking down a section of the wall and carefully examining the plaster, he tried to excuse himself by declaring that the plumes had been hidden two years before and that he could not remember their exact location. Forced to search again, he tried another wall, and after another hour's work, an old plume appeared in the plaster. He grabbed it eagerly and presented it to his persecutors as the magic device of which he had spoken. He was then made to explain the details of its use. Finally, dragged into the public plaza, he had to repeat his entire story (to which he added a wealth of new detail). He finished it with a pathetic speech in which he lamented the loss of his supernatural power. Thus reassured, his listeners agreed to free him.

This narrative, which we unfortunately had to abridge and strip of all its psychological nuances, is still instructive in many respects. First of all, we see that the boy tried for witchcraft, for which he risks the death penalty, wins his acquittal not by denying but by admitting his alleged crime. Moreover, he furthers his cause by presenting successive versions, each richer in detail (and thus, in theory, more persuasive of guilt) than the preceding one. The debate does not proceed, as do debates among us, by accusations and denials, but rather by allegations and specifications. The judges do not expect the accused to challenge their theory, much less to refute the facts. Rather, they require him to validate a system of which they possess only a fragment; he must reconstruct it as a whole in an appropriate way. As the field-worker noted in relation to a phase of the trial, "The warriors had become so absorbed by their interest in the narrative of the boy that they seemed entirely to have forgotten the cause of his appearance before them."[6] And when the magic plume was finally uncovered, the author remarks with great insight, "There was consternation among the warriors, who exclaimed in one voice: 'What does this mean?' Now they felt assured that the youth had spoken the truth."[7] Consternation, and not triumph at finding a tangible proof of the crime—for the judges had sought to bear witness to the reality of the system which had made the crime possible (by validating its objective basis through an appropriate emotional expression), rather than simply to punish a crime. By his confession, the defendant is transformed into a witness for the prosecution, with the participation (and even the complicity) of his judges. Through the defendant, witchcraft and the ideas associated with it cease to exist as a diffuse complex of poorly formulated sentiments and representations and become embodied in real experience. The defendant, who serves as a witness, gives the group the satisfaction of truth, which is infinitely greater and richer than the satisfaction of justice that would have been achieved by his execution. And finally, by his ingenious defense which makes his hearers progressively aware of the vitality offered by his corroboration of their system (especially since the choice is not between this system and another, but between the magical system and no system at all—that is, chaos), the youth, who at first was a threat to the physical security of his group, became the guardian of its spiritual coherence.

But is his defense merely ingenious? Everything leads us to believe that after groping for a subterfuge, the defendant participates with sincerity and—the word is not too strong—fervor in the drama enacted between him and his judges. He is proclaimed a sorcerer; since sorcerers do exist, he might well be one. And how would he know beforehand the signs which might reveal his calling to him? Perhaps the signs are there, present in this ordeal and in the convulsions of the little girl brought before the court. For the boy, too, the coherence of the system and the role assigned to him in preserving it are values no less essential than the personal security which he risks in the venture. Thus we see him, with a mixture of cunning and good faith, progressively construct the impersonation which is thrust upon him—chiefly by drawing on his knowledge and his memories, improvising somewhat, but above all living his role and seeking, through his manipulations and the ritual he builds from bits and pieces, the experience of a calling which is, at least theoretically, open to all. At the end of the adventure, what remains of his earlier hoaxes? To what extent has the hero become the dupe of his own impersonation? What is more, has he not truly become a sorcerer? We are told that in his final confession, "The longer the boy talked the more absorbed he became in his subject. . . . At times his face became radiant with satisfaction at his power over his listeners."[8] The girl recovers after he performs his curing ritual. The boy's experiences during the extraordinary ordeal become elaborated and structured. Little more is needed than for the innocent boy finally to confess to the possession of supernatural powers that are already recognized by the group.

. . .

We must consider at greater length another especially valuable document, which until now seems to have been valued solely for its linguistic interest. I refer to a fragment of the autobiography of a Kwakiutl Indian from the Vancouver region of Canada, obtained by Franz Boas.[9]

Quesalid (for this was the name he received when he became a sorcerer) did not believe in the power of the sorcerers—or, more accurately, shamans, since this is a better term for their specific type of activity in certain regions of the world. Driven by curiosity about their tricks and by the desire to expose them, he began to associate with the shamans until one of them offered to make him a member of their group. Quesalid did not wait to be asked twice, and his narrative recounts the details of his first lessons, a curious mixture of pantomime, prestidigitation, and empirical knowledge, including the art of simulating fainting and nervous fits, the learning of sacred songs, the technique for inducing vomiting, rather precise notions of auscultation and obstetrics, and the use of "dreamers," that is, spies who listen to private conversations and secretly convey to the shaman bits of information concerning the origins and symptoms of the ills suffered by different people. Above all, he learned the *ars magna* of one of the shamanistic schools of the Northwest Coast: The shaman hides a little tuft of down in a corner of his mouth, and he throws it up, covered with blood, at the proper moment—after having bitten his tongue or made his gums bleed—and solemnly presents it to his patient and the onlookers as the pathological foreign body extracted as a result of his sucking and manipulations.

His worst suspicions confirmed, Quesalid wanted to continue his inquiry. But he was no longer free. His apprenticeship among the shamans began to be noised about, and one day he was summoned by the family of a sick person who had dreamed of Quesalid as his healer. This first treatment (for which he received no payment, any more than he did for those which followed, since he had not completed the required four years of apprenticeship) was an outstanding success. Although Quesalid came to be known from that moment on as a "great shaman," he did not lose his critical faculties. He interpreted his success in psychological terms—it was successful "because he [the sick person] believed strongly in his dream about me."[10] A more complex adventure made him, in his own words, "hesitant and thinking about many things."[11] Here he encountered several varieties of a "false supernatural," and was led to conclude that some forms were less false than others—those, of course, in which he had a personal stake and whose system he was, at the same time, surreptitiously building up in his mind. A summary of the adventure follows.

While visiting the neighboring Koskimo Indians, Quesalid attends a curing ceremony of his illustrious colleagues of the other tribe. To his great astonishment he observes a difference in their technique. Instead of spitting out the illness in the form of a "bloody worm" (the concealed down), the Koskimo shamans merely spit a little saliva into their hands, and they dare to claim that this is "the sickness." What is the value of this method? What is the theory behind it? In order to find out "the strength of the shamans, whether it was real or whether they only pretended to be shamans" like his fellow tribesmen,[12] Quesalid requests and obtains permission to try his method in an instance where the Koskimo method has failed. The sick woman then declares herself cured.

And here our hero vacillates for the first time. Though he had few illusions about his own technique, he has now found one which is more false, more mystifying, and more dishonest than his own. For he at least gives his clients something. He presents them with their sickness in a visible and tangible form, while his foreign colleagues show nothing at all and only claim to have captured the sickness. Moreover, Quesalid's method gets results, while the other is futile. Thus our hero grapples with a problem which perhaps has its parallel in the development of modern science. Two systems which we know to be inadequate present (with respect to each other) a differential validity, from both a logical and an empirical perspective. From which frame of reference shall we judge them? On the level of fact, where they merge, or on their own level, where they take on different values, both theoretically and empirically?

Meanwhile, the Koskimo shamans, "ashamed" and discredited before their tribesmen, are also plunged into doubt. Their colleague has produced, in the form of a material object, the illness which they had always considered as spiritual in nature and had thus never dreamed of rendering visible. They send Quesalid an emissary to invite him to a secret meeting in a cave. Quesalid goes and his foreign colleagues expound their system to him: "Every sickness is a man: boils and swellings, and itch and scabs, and pimples and coughs and consumption and scrofula; and also this, stricture of the bladder and stomach aches. . . . As soon as we get the soul of the sickness which is a man, then dies the sickness which is a man. Its body just disappears in our insides."[13] If this theory is correct, what is there to show? And why, when Quesalid operates, does "the sickness stick to his hand"? But Quesalid takes refuge behind professional rules which forbid him to teach before completing four years of apprenticeship, and refuses to speak. He maintains his silence even when the Koskimo shamans send him their allegedly virgin daughters to try to seduce him and discover his secret.

Thereupon Quesalid returns to his village at Fort Rupert. He learns that the most reputed shaman of a neighboring clan, worried about Quesalid's growing renown, has challenged all his colleagues, inviting them to compete with him in curing several patients. Quesalid comes to the contest and observes the cures of his elder. Like the Koskimo, this shaman does not show the illness. He simply incorporates an invisible object, "what he called the sickness" into his head-ring, made of bark, or into his bird-shaped ritual rattle.[14] These objects can hang suspended in mid-air, owing to the power of the illness which "bites" the house-posts or the shaman's hand. The usual drama unfolds. Quesalid is asked to intervene in cases judged hopeless by his predecessor, and he triumphs with his technique of the bloody worm.

Here we come to the truly pathetic part of the story. The old shaman, ashamed and despairing because of the ill-repute into which he has fallen and by the collapse of his therapeutic technique, sends his daughter to Quesalid to beg him for an interview. The latter finds his colleague sitting under a tree and the old shaman begins thus: "It won't be bad what we say to each other, friend, but only I wish you to try and save my life for me, so that I may not die of shame, for I am a plaything of our people on account of what you did last night. I pray you to have mercy and tell me what stuck on the palm of your hand last night. Was it the true sickness or was it only made up? For I beg you have mercy and tell me about the way you did it so that I can imitate you. Pity me, friend."[15]

Silent at first, Quesalid begins by calling for explanations about the feats of the head-ring and the rattle. His colleague shows him the nail hidden in the head-ring which he can press at right angles into the post," and the way in which he tucks the head of his rattle between his finger joints to make it look as if the bird-were hanging by its beak from his hand. He himself probably does nothing but lie and fake, simulating shamanism for material gain, for he admits to being "covetous for the property of the sick men." He knows that shamans cannot catch souls, "for . . . we all own a soul"; so he resorts to using tallow and pretends that "it is a soul . . . that white thing . . . sitting on my hand." The daughter then adds her entreaties to those of her father: "Do have mercy that he may live." But Quesalid remains silent. That very night, following this tragic conversation, the shaman disappears with his entire family, heartsick and feared by the community, who think that he may be tempted to take revenge. Needless fears: He returned a year later, but both he and his daughter had gone mad. Three years later, he died.

And Quesalid, rich in secrets, pursued his career, exposing the impostors and full of contempt for the profession. "Only one shaman was seen by me, who sucked at a sick man and I never found out whether he was a real shaman or only made up. Only for this reason I believe that he is a shaman; he does not allow those who are made well to pay him. I truly never once saw him laugh."[16] Thus his original attitude has changed considerably. The radical negativism of the free thinker has given way to more moderate feelings. Real shamans do exist. And what about him? At the end of the narrative we cannot tell, but it is evident that he carries on his craft conscientiously, takes pride in his achievements, and warmly defends the technique of the bloody down against all rival schools. He seems to have completely lost sight of the fallaciousness of the technique which he had so disparaged at the beginning.

. . .

We see that the psychology of the sorcerer is not simple. In order to analyze it, we shall first examine the case of the old shaman who begs his young rival to tell him the truth—whether the illness glued in the palm of his hand like a sticky red worm is real or made up—and who goes mad when he receives no answer. Before the tragedy, he was fully convinced of two things—first, that pathological conditions have a cause which may be discovered and second, that a system of interpretation in which personal inventiveness is important structures the phases of the illness, from the diagnosis to the cure. This fabulation of a reality unknown in itself—a tabulation consisting of procedures and representations—is founded on a threefold experience: first, that of the shaman himself, who, if his calling is a true one (and even if it is not, simply by virtue of his practicing it), undergoes specific states of a psychosomatic nature; second, that of the sick person, who may or may not experience an improvement of his condition; and, finally, that of the public, who also participate in the cure, experiencing an enthusiasm and an intellectual and emotional satisfaction which produce collective support, which in turn inaugurates a new cycle.

These three elements of what we might call the "shamanistic complex" cannot be separated. But they are clustered around two poles, one formed by the intimate experience of the shaman and the other by group consensus. There is no reason to doubt that sorcerers, or at least the more sincere among them, believe in their calling and that this belief is founded on the experiencing of specific states. The hardships and privations which they undergo would often be sufficient in themselves to provoke these states, even if we refuse to admit them as proof of a serious and fervent calling. But there is also linguistic evidence which, because it is indirect, is more convincing. In the Wintu dialect of California, there are five verbal classes which correspond to knowledge by sight, by bodily experience, by inference, by reasoning, and by hearsay. All five make up the category of knowledge as opposed to conjecture, which is differently expressed. Curiously enough, relationships with the supernatural world are expressed by means of the modes of knowledge—by bodily impression (that is, the most intuitive kind of experience), by inference, and by reasoning. Thus the native who becomes a shaman after a spiritual crisis conceives of his state grammatically, as a consequence to be inferred from the fact—formulated as real experience—that he has received divine guidance. From the latter he concludes deductively that he must have been on a journey to the beyond, at the end of which he found himself—again, an immediate experience—once more among his people.[17]

The experiences of the sick person represent the least important aspect of the system, except for the fact that a patient successfully treated by a shaman is in an especially good position to become a shaman in his own right, as we see today in the case of psychoanalysis. In any event, we must remember that the shaman does not completely lack empirical knowledge and experimental techniques, which may in part explain his success. Furthermore, disorders of the type currently termed psychosomatic, which constitute a large part of the illnesses prevalent in societies with a low degree of security, probably often yield to psychotherapy. At any rate, it seems probable that medicine men, like their civilized colleagues, cure at least some of the cases they treat and that without this relative success magical practices could not have been so widely diffused in time and space. But this point is not fundamental; it is subordinate to the other two. Quesalid did not become a great shaman because he cured his patients; he cured his patients because he had become a great shaman. Thus we have reached the other—that is, the collective—pole of our system.

The true reason for the defeat of Quesalid's rivals must then be sought in the attitude of the group rather than in the pattern of the rivals' successes and failures. The rivals themselves emphasize this when they confess their shame at having become the laughingstock of the group; this is a social sentiment *par excellence.* Failure is secondary, and we see in all their statements that they consider it a function of another phenomenon, which is the disappearance of the *social consensus,* re-created at their expense around another practitioner and another system of curing. Consequently, the fundamental problem revolves around the relationship between the individual and the group, or, more accurately, the relationship between a specific category of individuals and specific expectations of the group.

In treating his patient the shaman also offers his audience a performance. What is this performance? Risking a rash generalization on the basis of a few observations, we shall say that it always involves the shaman's enactment of the "call," or the initial crisis which brought him the revelation of his condition. But we must not be deceived by the word *performance.* The shaman does not limit himself to reproducing or miming certain events. He actually relives them in all their vividness, originality, and violence. And since he returns to his normal state at the end of the seance, we may say, borrowing a key term from psychoanalysis, that he *abreacts.* In psychoanalysis, abreaction refers to the decisive moment in the treatment when the patient intensively relives the initial situation from which his disturbance stems, before he ultimately overcomes it. In this sense, the shaman is a professional abreactor.

We have set forth elsewhere the theoretical hypotheses that might be formulated in order for us to accept the idea that the type of abreaction specific to each shaman—or, at any rate, to each shamanistic school—might symbolically induce an abreaction of his own disturbance in each patient. In any case, if the essential relationship is that between the shaman and the group, we must also state the question from another point of view—that of the relationship between normal and pathological thinking. From any nonscientific perspective (and here we can exclude no society), pathological and normal thought processes are complementary rather than opposed. In a universe which it strives to understand but whose dynamics it cannot fully control, normal thought continually seeks the meaning of things which refuse to reveal their significance. So-called pathological thought, on the other hand, overflows with emotional interpretations and overtones, in order to supplement an otherwise deficient reality. For normal thinking there exists something which cannot be empirically verified and is, therefore, "claimable." For pathological thinking there exists experiences without object, or something "available." We might borrow from linguistics and say that so-called normal thought always suffers from a deficit of meaning, whereas so-called pathological thought (in at least some of its manifestations) disposes of a plethora of meaning. Through collective participation in shamanistic curing, a balance is established between these two complementary situations. Normal thought cannot fathom the problem of illness, and so the group calls upon the neurotic to furnish a wealth of emotion heretofore lacking a focus.

An equilibrium is reached between what might be called supply and demand on the psychic level—but only on two conditions. First, a structure must be elaborated and continually modified through the interaction of group tradition and individual invention. This structure is a system of oppositions and correlations, integrating all the elements of a total situation, in which sorcerer, patient, and audience, as well as representations and procedures, all play their parts. Furthermore, the public must participate in the abreaction, to a certain extent at least, along with the patient and the sorcerer. It is this vital experience of a universe of symbolic effusions which the patient, because he is ill, and the sorcerer, because he is neurotic—in other words, both having types of experience which cannot otherwise be integrated—allow the public to glimpse as "fireworks" from a safe distance. In the absence of any experimental control, which is indeed unnecessary, it is this experience alone, and its relative richness in each case, which makes possible a choice between several systems and elicits adherence to a particular school or practitioner.[18]

In contrast with scientific explanation, the problem here is not to attribute confused and disorganized states, emotions, or representations to an objective cause, but rather to articulate them into a whole or system. The system is valid precisely to the extent that it allows the coalescence or precipitation of these diffuse states, whose discontinuity also makes them painful. To the conscious mind, this last phenomenon constitutes an original experience which cannot be grasped from without. Because of their complementary disorders, the sorcerer-patient dyad incarnates for the group, in vivid and concrete fashion, an antagonism that is inherent in all thought but that normally remains vague and imprecise. The patient is all passivity and self-alienation, just as inexpressibility is the disease of the mind. The sorcerer is activity and self-projection, just as affectivity is the source of symbolism. The cure interrelates these opposite poles, facilitating the transition from one to the other, and demonstrates, within a total experience, the coherence of the psychic universe, itself a projection of the social universe.

Thus it is necessary to extend the notion of abreaction by examining the meanings it acquires in psychotherapies other than psychoanalysis, although the latter deserves the credit for rediscovering and insisting upon its fundamental validity. It may be objected that in psychoanalysis there is only one abreaction, the patient's, rather than three. We are not so sure of this. It is true that in the shamanistic cure the sorcerer speaks and abreacts *for* the silent patient, while in psychoanalysis it is the patient who talks and abreacts *against* the listening therapist. But the therapist's abreaction, while not concomitant with the patient's, is nonetheless required, since he must be analyzed before he himself can become an analyst. It is more difficult to define the role ascribed to the group by each technique. Magic readapts the group to predefined problems through the patient, while psychoanalysis readapts the patient to the group by means of the solutions reached. But the distressing trend which, for several years, has tended to transform the psychoanalytic system from a body of scientific hypotheses that are experimentally verifiable in certain specific and limited cases into a kind of diffuse mythology interpenetrating the consciousness of the group, could rapidly bring about a parallelism. (This group consciousness is an objective phenomenon, which the psychologist expresses through a subjective tendency to extend to normal thought a system of interpretations conceived for pathological thought and to apply to facts of collective psychology a method adapted solely to the study of individual psychology.) When this happens—and perhaps it already has in certain countries—the value of the system will no longer be based upon real cures from which certain individuals can benefit, but on the sense of security that the group receives from the myth underlying the cure and from the popular system upon which the group's universe is reconstructed.

Even at the present time, the comparison between psychoanalysis and older and more widespread psychological therapies can encourage the former to reexamine its principles and methods. By continuously expanding the recruitment of its patients, who begin as clearly characterized abnormal individuals and gradually become representative of the group, psychoanalysis transforms its treatments into conversions. For only a patient can emerge cured; an unstable or maladjusted individual can only be persuaded. A considerable danger thus arises: The treatment (unbeknown to the therapist, naturally), far from leading to the resolution of a specific disturbance within its own context, is reduced to the reorganization of the patient's universe in terms of psychoanalytic interpretations. This means that we would finally arrive at precisely that situation which furnishes the point of departure as well as the theoretical validity of the magico-social system that we have analyzed.

If this analysis is correct, we must see magical behavior as the response to a situation which is revealed to the mind through emotional manifestations, but whose essence is intellectual. For only the history of the symbolic function can allow us to understand the intellectual condition of man, in which the universe is never charged with sufficient meaning and in which the mind always has more meanings available than there are objects to which to relate them. Torn between these two systems of reference—the signifying and the signified—man asks magical thinking to provide him with a new system of reference, within which the thus-far contradictory elements can be integrated. But we know that this system is built at the expense of the progress of knowledge, which would have required us to retain only one of the two previous systems and to refine it to the point where it absorbed the other. This point is still far off. We must not permit the individual, whether normal or neurotic, to repeat this collective misadventure. The study of the mentally sick individual has shown us that all persons are more or less oriented toward contradictory systems and suffer from the resulting conflict; but the fact that a certain form of integration is possible and effective practically is not enough to make it true, or to make us certain that the adaptation thus achieved does not constitute an absolute regression in relation to the previous conflict situation.

The reabsorption of a deviant specific synthesis, through its integration with the normal syntheses, into a general but arbitrary synthesis (aside from critical cases where action is required) would represent a loss on all fronts. A body of elementary hypotheses can have a certain instrumental value for the practitioner without necessarily being recognized, in theoretical analysis, as the final image of reality and without necessarily linking the patient and the therapist in a kind of mystical communion which does not have the same meaning for both parties and which only ends by reducing the treatment to a fabulation.

In the final analysis we could only expect this fabulation to be a language, whose function is to provide a socially authorized translation of phenomena whose deeper nature would become once again equally impenetrable to the group, the patient, and the healer.

NOTES

1. W. B. Cannon, "'Voodoo' Death," *American Anthropologist*, n.s., XLIV (1942).
2. An Australian aborigine was brought to the Darwin hospital in April 1956, apparently dying of this type of sorcery. He was placed in an oxygen tent and fed intravenously. He gradually recovered, convinced that the white man's magic was the stronger. See Arthur Morley in the *London Sunday Times*, April 22, 1956, p. 11.
3. In this study, whose aim is more psychological than sociological, we feel justified in neglecting the finer distinctions between the several modes of magical operations and different types of sorcerers when these are not absolutely necessary.
4. C. Lévi-Strauss, *Tristes Tropiques* (Paris: 1955), Chapter XXIX.
5. M. C. Stevenson, *The Zuni Indians*, 23rd Annual Report of the Bureau of American Ethnology (Washington, D.C.: Smithsonian Institution, 1905).
6. *Ibid.*, p. 401.
7. *Ibid.*, p. 404.
8. *Ibid.*, p. 406.
9. Franz Boas, *The Religion of the Kwakiutl*, Columbia University Contributions to Anthropology, Vol. X (New York: 1930), Part II, pp. 1–41.
10. *Ibid.*, p. 13.
11. *Ibid.*, p. 19.
12. *Ibid.*, p. 17.
13. *Ibid.*, pp. 20–21.
14. *Ibid.*, p. 27.
15. *Idid.*, p. 3l.
16. *Ibid.*, pp. 40–41.
17. D. D. Lee, "Some Indian Texts Dealing with the Supernatural," *The Review of Religion* (May, 1941).
18. This oversimplified equation of sorcerer and neurotic was justly criticized by Michel Leiris. I subsequently refined this concept in my "Introduction à l'oeuvre de Marcel Mauss," in M. Mauss, *Sociologie et Anthropologie* (Paris: 1950), pp. xviii–xxiii.

 16

Doctors and Patients: The Role of Clinicians in the Placebo Effect

Daniel Moerman

The placebo phenomenon is a fascinating aspect of the healing process and poses an interesting challenge to medical research. The author of this selection argues that the term "placebo effect" is an oxymoron. This is because placebo *means "having no effect" despite the fact that giving a patient a chemically inert medicine (the placebo) clearly can have a substantial positive outcome; in other words, how can "no effect" have an effect? However it is defined, the placebo effect is very powerful.*

For medical anthropologists, the importance of the beliefs of both patients and healers is central to any ethnomedical system, including biomedicine. These beliefs are mutually reinforced during a therapeutic interaction. The role of belief (as described in the work of Claude Lévi-Strauss in selection 15) involves the healer's belief in his or her own power, the patient's belief in the healer, and society's belief in the overall process. Dan Moerman raises the question of which level of belief is the most important. Most of the time, medical researchers assume that certain patients are more prone to the "power of suggestion" and therefore should be excluded from research. This selection, however, presents evidence that beliefs of the health care providers *in the power of the medicine they are administering are much more important. These beliefs are often rooted in the cultural ideology of science and technology.*

For some people, it is difficult to understand why a particular medicine (pharmaceutical) loses its effectiveness when it goes off patent and becomes an over-the-counter product. Similarly, it may seem surprising that recipients of "sham surgeries" get better. Research on the placebo effect is difficult to do today because of ethical concerns of the medical community. Nevertheless, both doctors and patients are part of a cultural context that shapes the healing process. The most effective healers probably make the best use of the placebo effect in combination with their biomedical treatments.

As you read this selection, ask yourself these questions:

- **How might health care providers unconsciously communicate their beliefs to patients?**
- **In the history of medical research, why might doctors have been unaware of their role in the placebo effect?**
- **Do you think it is wrong for a doctor to prescribe a placebo drug to a patient? Why? Given the studies described by Moerman, would a placebo be effective if the doctor did not believe that it could be effective?**
- **How might the placebo effect be related to the work of nonbiomedical practitioners, including healers in traditional ethnomedicines and complementary and alternative medicine (CAM)?**

Context Daniel Moerman teaches anthropology at the University of Michigan in Dearborn. His first health-related research was conducted with a rural black population in coastal South Carolina. St. Helena Islanders told him of their complex theory of health involving a system of pressures and flavors of the blood, which, if things went badly, could cause various illnesses that they treated with a series of plants (called "weeds") gathered from fields or planted in their gardens. Since then, he has done research primarily in two areas—medicinal plants of North America (primarily of Native Americans) and the impact of health knowledge and beliefs on the healing process. His book Native American Ethnobotany received the Annual Literature Award of the Council on Botanical and Horticultural Libraries in 2000. Moerman's book on the placebo effect (which he calls the *meaning effect*) is a very readable introduction to this area of research.

Source: D. Moerman (2002). *Meaning, Medicine and the "Placebo Effect."* Cambridge: Cambridge University Press, pp. 32–46.

The standard explanation for why people respond to placebos is a psychological one: people are suggestible, or they are neurotic, or something like that. But consider an interesting experiment described by Richard Gracely, one of the leading pain researchers in the United Slates. It shows clearly that clinicians—doctors, dentists, nurses, and so on—play a very important role in this response.

WHAT THE DOCTOR KNOWS MAKES A DIFFERENCE

Sixty people who were having their wisdom teeth removed participated in an experiment designed by Dr Gracely. They were told they would receive either placebo (which might reduce the pain of having the tooth removed, or might do nothing), naloxone (which might increase their pain, or do nothing), fentanyl (which might reduce their pain, or do nothing), or no treatment at all. Subjects were all recruited from the same patient stream, with consistent selection criteria by the same staff. The tricky part of the experiment is this: What Gracely was actually studying was not so much patients as *clinicians.* In the first phase of the study, the clinicians (the dentists and nurses)—but not the patients—were told fentanyl was not yet a possibility because of administrative problems with the study protocol, yielding the PN group. In the second phase, a week later, clinicians were told that the problems had been resolved, and now patients might indeed receive fentanyl, yielding the PNF group. Figure 1 shows the effects of placebo treatment in the two groups. "Pain after placebo administration in group PNF was significantly less than pain after placebo in group PN at 60 minutes (1[23df] = 3.56, $P < .01$). The two placebo groups differed only in the clinician's knowledge of the range of possible double-blind treatments."[1] Note that Dr. Gracely attributed this difference not to the varying personalities of the dentists involved, but to their knowledge. And somehow, without even realizing it, these clinicians conveyed to their patients (who were receiving inert medication) that they *might* receive a powerful painkiller (PNF group) or they might *not* (PN group). And this was sufficient to make a substantial and statistically significant difference in the experience of their patients, to soothe the pain of the extraction of wisdom teeth; remember that the patients represented in the figure, are only those who received placebo injections. These two patient groups are similar to the two placebo groups in a study on brand name aspirin, in which individuals who took aspirin labeled with the brand name of a popular aspirin-based drug had greater headache pain relief than those who took aspirin labeled "analgesic tablet," and those who took placebo labeled with the same brand name had greater pain relief than those who took the unbranded placebo[2] except [in Gracely's study], the "reputation" of the inert treatment came not from a brand name, but from physician knowledge and enthusiasm.

PATIENT PSYCHOLOGY AND THE SEARCH FOR "PLACEBO RESPONDERS"

The traditional approach to this issue has been quite different, and has focused on the psychological characteristics of patients. The standard experimental design was to divide a group of patients or experimental subjects into two groups, a group which responded to a placebo of some sort and a group which didn't. These groups were then compared on a variety of personality measures. These studies have yielded a variety of results indicating, for example, that placebo responders were more neurotic and extroverted than nonreactors in one study[3] more "acquiescent" in another,[4] "outgoing, verbally and socially skilled, and generally well, adjusted" as opposed to "belligerent, aggressive and antagonistic to authority" in another,[5] tending to exhibit "higher anxiety and lower ego strength and self-sufficiency" in another,[6] and so on. So, placebo reactors are neurotic yet well-adjusted, outgoing and socially skilled yet acquiescent to authority, extroverted yet with low ego strength. No one has ever been able to find a reliable way to predict who is going to respond to inert treatment and who is not.[7,8]

It is also important to note that the same people respond differently at different times to medication, active or inert; the response is very inconsistent. In a classic study in the 1950s, researchers—working with Veterans' Hospital inpatients with sleep disturbances—studied the possible uses of an antihistamine (methapyrilene hydrochloride) as a hypnotic to induce sleep. They tell us that "No patient was accepted for the study who . . . was a known placebo reactor." They aren't clear on just how they knew this, but they tried. They then gave varying drugs—active or inert—to their subjects, to see their influence on sleep. "Although all known placebo reactors were excluded from the study, it was found that over 30% of the patients scored the placebo as excellent in inducing and maintaining sleep."[9]

Similarly, many contemporary studies, especially of chronic conditions, begin with some sort of "placebo washout" or '"run-in" stage: in these cases,

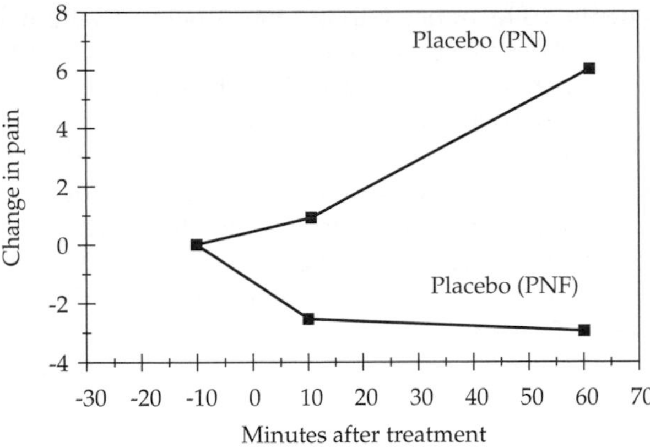

FIGURE 1 Effects of Physician Knowledge on Patient Response to Inert Medication *(Source: Gracely et al. 1985)*

patients are given inert medication for several weeks before the study actually begins.[10–12] Researchers are rarely very clear about why they are doing this, but there seem to be two reasons: one more overt, one more covert. The overt reason is to "clear the patient of any previous medication," while the more covert is to eliminate what Straus and his colleagues in the 1950s called "known placebo responders."[9] This technique is common in studies of hypertension. In such studies, patients with blood pressure over a certain level are entered into the trial, then given inert medication for three to five weeks; individuals whose blood pressure falls below the low-level cutoff point for entry into the study are then usually dropped from the trial. Such studies have a bias against individuals responsive to meaningful treatment. These "washout/run-in" rates can be substantial. In one study from Hong Kong, 16 of 52 patients (31%) originally recruited were excluded because their blood pressure dropped below entry requirements for the study after four weeks of placebo treatment.[13] In a study in the United States, 125 of 507 recruited patients (25%) were dropped during the four-to-six week placebo lead-in phase, "most often because their diastolic blood pressure fell below 92 mmHg."[14] In the Chinese trial, even after eliminating a third of the patients for responding to placebos, the mean diastolic blood pressure (mDBP) of the control group patients dropped from 104 to 97, while the mDBP of the drug group (taking nebivolol) dropped from 99 to 83. In the American study, even after eliminating a quarter of the patients, the mDBP of the control group dropped from 98 to 95 while the drug treatment group (taking captopril) mDBP dropped from 100 to 92. One cannot eliminate "placebo responders" from a trial.

This has also been shown in a large study of drug trials for the treatment of depression: "Meta-analyses" of 101 studies reveal that a placebo run-in does not (1) lower the placebo response rate, (2) increase the drug-placebo difference, or (3) affect the drug response rate after the patients are randomized to drug and placebo treatment.[15]

So, you can't identify in advance those people who might respond to inert medication. And if you try to do so using, for example, a placebo run-in, it won't make any difference in the outcome (except that you will have a smaller sample size). The general conclusion is that the characteristics and qualities of individual patients make no significant impact on the character and quality of meaning effects. What then does make a difference?

DOCTOR EFFECTS AND THE SEARCH FOR "PLACEBOGENESIS"

It seems quite clear that the most important single factor shaping the meaningful quality of medicine springs from doctors. Consider the following text, the testimony of a 76-year-old veteran of the Second World War, who was one of ten men in a study of knee surgery.[16] Although he didn't know it for certain until somewhat later, he had been one of five in the study to have sham surgery on his knee to treat his arthritis; he was mildly anesthetized and given three stab wounds in the knee to mimic the visible results of arthroscopic surgery. And it worked quite nicely. Here, the patient describes the outcome of his surgery, and his surgeon, Dr. Brace Moseley:

> I was very impressed with, him, especially when I heard he was the team doctor with the [Houston] Rockets. . . . So, sure, I went ahead and signed up for this new thing he was doing. . . . The surgery was two years ago and the knee never has bothered me since. It's just like my other knee now. I give a whole lot of credit to Dr. Moseley. Whenever I see him on TV during a basketball game, I call the wife in and say, "Hey, there's the doctor that fixed my knee."[17]

Surely this man's knee was healed by Dr Moseley, not by three stab wounds, but in some more complex and much more interesting way. I have met and spoken with Bruce Moseley, and I agree with the arthroscopy patient. He is a very impressive man. He's tall, strong, and athletic looking. He has a firm, friendly, and persuasive manner. I'm not certain how I "know" something like this, but he sure looks like a good surgeon to me even though I've never seen him on TV, and I'm not much of a basketball fan.

That is the general finding of most of the research looking into these matters. In 1938, W. R. Houston told the American College of Physicians, meeting in St. Louis, about "The Doctor Himself as a Therapeutic Agent." He urged the adoption of a higher scientific medicine, one which would allow the "doctor himself, as therapeutic agent, [to] be refined and polished to make of himself a more potent agent," adding that this would "lead to the physician's occupying a position of even greater dignity in the social order than the high place he now holds."[18]

Arthur K. Shapiro, one of the most eminent students of the placebo effect, described a variation on this theme which he called "the indirect interest of the physician in the patient."[19] He derived this perspective from a complex case of his where a depressed woman, whenever treated with any medication, immediately developed a long and intolerable list of physical complaints requiring her doctor to stop her treatment. Shapiro prescribed for her "an elaborate dosage schedule of twelve placebo tablets daily." She reacted, as in the past, with multiple physical complaints. He then told her that she had been taking inert placebos "to convince her that the symptoms were caused by psychological factors and not by the medication." Subsequently, he treated her with imipramine (Tofranil), and she got much better without the kinds of complaints she had previously experienced. He then considers what factors might have accounted for her improvement.

> This patient's remarkable response was probably more related to my interest in the treatment than to any other factor. It is obvious that I am intellectually and emotionally interested in the placebo phenomenon and therefore in this patient's negative placebo response. The management was an attempt to explore and innovate a treatment procedure. There was an element of danger in my not knowing how the patient would respond; she did consider suicide for a short period following the confrontation. In other words, my interest in the phenomenon was experienced by the patient as an interest in her.

Several years later the patient told Shapiro that she had understood that he "'was really trying to help her' . . . whereas physicians previously 'were too busy,' uninterested, and 'would only give her boxes of pills'; and that she was then 'able to have faith in the clinic and doctors' which enabled her to take medication and finally improve." Shapiro's perspective—that the patients understanding (knowledge) of the physician's interest in her, genuine or not (she interpreted his interest in his experiment as interest in her)—seems to me to be as productive as it is (surprisingly) honest.

John Whitehorn did ingenious research in the 1950s with psychiatrists working with schizophrenic patients.[20] He noticed that some doctors (whom he called "A") had substantially better results with their patients than others ("B") did; three-quarters of A doctors' patients improved while only a quarter of B doctors' did. He examined the doctors, and found that there were persistent differences in the ways they responded to questions on the Strong Vocational Interest Test. He noted "definite differences in the interest patterns [in 4 vocations] of the A and B physicians. These 4 vocations are lawyer and C.P.A. (A's high B's low); printer and mathematics physical science teacher (A's low B's high)." In a much closer examination of these test scores, Whitehorn came to some interesting conclusions about this difference. The A's, he wrote, "resembling lawyers, [may] have a problem-solving . . . approach [while] B doctors, with attitudes resembling printers—black or white, right or wrong—are likely to view the patient as a wayward mind needing correction."[20†]

There is also experimental evidence which bears on this issue and can be interpreted in the same way. A pioneering and elegant study by Uhlenhuth,[21] for example, showed that the mild tranquilizer meprobamate (Elavil) was more effective than placebo in treating anxious outpatients only in one of three clinics, and then only when physicians adopted a very positive "therapeutic" attitude through which they "maintained a solicitous, confident and enthusiastic attitude, [toward the patient, and] . . . communicated a pervasive assurance that the medication was effective for his particular complaint," etc. In the same clinic, when physicians adopted an "experimental" attitude—"detached, uncertain and observing, . . . [and] communicated to the patient that the medication was as yet of uncertain value for the patients condition"—there was no difference in outcome between drug and placebo groups, and both groups did worse than the patients with the enthusiastic physician.

This finding was confirmed by an even more complex study,[22] which compared four variables—the status of the communicator (dentist vs. technician), the attitude of the dentist, the attitude of the dental technician, and the message of drug effects—on the effectiveness of a placebo.

The subjects in the study were dental patients who were given a pill (an inert capsule) before they received a mandibular block injection of local anesthetic (the shot you get in the jaw before dental work). Then they were asked to rate the pain of the injection. The amount of pain varied depending on just what they were told, and who told them. The most important factor was the message of the drug effect. Patients were given either an "Oversell message" ("This is a recently developed

† Then again , I have a brother who's a printers. Believe me, not all printers are "black and white, right or wrong" kind of guys.

pill that I've found to be very effective in reducing tension, anxiety, and sensitivity to pain. It cannot harm you in any way. The pill becomes effective almost immediately") or an "Undersell message" ("This is a recently developed pill that reduces tension, anxiety and sensitivity to pain in some people. Other people receive no benefit from it. I personally have not found it be very effective. It cannot harm you in any way. The pill becomes effective almost immediately if it's going to have an effect"). Patients who received the Oversell message "exhibited the least pain from the injection, and significant post-placebo reductions in both . . . anxiety and fear of injection." The message was much more significant than the "attitude" of the dentist or technician—a warm versus a neutral attitude to the patient. In this case, the patient's knowledge (even though based on "false" information) trumped the "chair side manner" of the professionals.

In a more recent study of general practice consultation. Thomas showed the effect of a "positive" diagnosis compared with a more neutral approach on the part of the physician.[23] A series of 200 patients with symptoms but no abnormal physical signs (characteristic of roughly half of office visits to the general practitioner) were randomly assigned to a "positive" consultation with or without a prescription (of a generally neutral drug—3 mg tablets of thiamine hydrochloride), or a "negative" or "neutral" consultation with or without the same prescription. In the positive consultations, "the patient was given a firm diagnosis and told confidently that he would be better in a few days." In the negative consultations, the doctor said "I cannot be certain of what is the matter with you." In a survey of patients two weeks later, 64% of positive consultation patients said they were all better, while only 39% of those who had negative consultations thought they were better (P <.001; this could occur as a chance result less than one time in a thousand experiments). Receiving a treatment in this study made no difference; physician attitude to the patient's illness overrode any consideration of the pills patients might have received.

Herbert Benson and David McCallie reviewed the medical literature on the history of the medical treatment of angina pectoris.[24] They found that in the recent past, in the 1940s and 1950s just before the age of the double blind trial, there were a number of drugs which had been in widespread use for treating angina and which had been intensively studied. They also noted that a number of these drugs, after being in widespread use, were subjected to placebo controlled trials. In those trials, the drugs were no more effective than the placebos! They note a consistent pattern: "The initial 70 to 90 percent effectiveness in the enthusiasts reports decreases to 30 to 40 percent 'base-line' placebo effectiveness in the [later] skeptics' reports."[24] Thus, for this grave condition, skeptics can heal 30% to 40% of their patients with inert medication, while enthusiasts can heal 70% to 90%. There is little reason to think that, in the studies Benson reviewed, the later doctors attracted to them more skeptical patients. The difference here is that enthusiastic doctors could heal twice as many people as skeptical ones could with the same drugs.

So far we have seen that the doctors' attention (or "indirect interest," their interest in the patient as a "case"), their aptitudes (as lawyers or printers), and their attitudes and enthusiasms all make a difference; all can influence patients and can enhance (or retard) their healing processes. But how are these factors conveyed to patients? What sorts of communication have effects?

DOCTOR–PATIENT COMMUNICATION

Moira Stewart recently reviewed a large number of studies which, in a way bear on this problem.[25] She wanted to know if the quality of physician–patient communication made a significant difference in patient health outcomes. She found, generally, that they did. But she focused more on the form of communication than on its content: She compared several studies involving patient choice: "In one (Morris and Royle 1988),[26] the fact that a woman [with breast cancer] was able to choose the kind of breast surgery to have was not found to be related to emotional health outcomes. In another (Fallowfield et al. 1990),[27] going to a surgeon who permitted (but did not force) the choice was found to be related to positive outcomes. I would suggest, therefore, that it was not simply the decision-making power of the patient that was effective but, rather, the provision of a caring, respectful and empowering context in which a woman was enabled to make an important decision with both support and comfort."[25] It is also possible to put another interpretation on this. In the study cited, women were assigned to physicians of three sorts: those who preferred mastectomy; those who preferred lumpectomy; or those who offered their patients a choice of treatment. The women who saw the third type of physician had less post-operative depression than women treated by either of the other two types. It could be that the physicians who gave women a choice had to explain the benefits and costs of both procedures, rather than only explaining one. Hence the woman with choice had more real information, she knew more, and the physician shared with her the knowledge; that is, both were in agreement on the better way to proceed. Stewart also notes that "agreement between physician and patient was found to be a key variable that influenced outcomes."[28, 29]

Table 1, redrawn from Stewart's article, can be similarly interpreted. In each case, one can infer that the patient actually gained some information from the physician, and probably came to understand something of the level of the physician's commitment to it (compared to, some sort of relevant control); in each case, there was some evidence of symptom mitigation. In the first row of the table, for example, one study has shown that, when patients were encouraged to ask questions, anxiety was reduced; in three additional studies, such encouragement, led to an improvement in role and physical limitation. Knowledge can mitigate the effects of illness.

CONCLUSIONS

What we find here is, first, that the psychological makeup or the personality of the patient has little to do with the outcome of a medical procedure, and, in particular, that one cannot predict who will respond to inert medication by referring to patient character. By contrast, there is ample evidence to indicate that the nature, character, personality, behavior, and style of doctors can influence a good deal of human response not only to inert but also to active medication. It is as if the physician's demeanor activates medication, inert or otherwise. I think it is probably the case that the most important aspect of that demeanor is its "certainty." This might appear as enthusiasm, but need not, at least not in the sense of the "enthusiastic cheerleader." A common quality of clinicians the world around, regardless of how they understand their practice, is a quiet assurance, a certainty, that things will turn out well. Hence, successful clinicians will have a deep and abiding commitment to the character and nature of their techniques.

An ethnographic anecdote: in the late 1990s, I attended a conference with a number of people interested in the placebo effect. A meeting was held to consider forming some sort of association addressing this area of interest. As is common at such meetings, everyone was asked to introduce him- or herself. Near the back of the room, seated next to one another, were two Korean-American gentlemen, both of them acupuncturists. I had observed them earlier in animated and friendly conversation. However, after the first had introduced himself, and while the second was doing so, they first realized something about the acupuncture technique of the second. Unlike himself, who used a "deep needling" technique, the second used a "shallow needling" technique. Unable to contain himself, the first loudly interrupted the second's self-introduction, saying "But that means your whole technique is based on the placebo effect!" The second shouted back to the effect that, no, it was the first practitioner's technique that was "all placebo." Although they did not come to blows, a budding friendship foundered on the shoals of the placebo effect. More important, the incident shows how deep and fundamental was the commitment of each to his own technique. Of course, a biomedically trained internist or surgeon (more polite than our acupuncturists) might have muttered to himself that the techniques of both were "only" the placebo effect. The sheer intensity of this interchange can show us something important about how any sort of healing might work, and how important the healer's commitment to the method is to its success.

In a similar way, but from another direction, it is a commonplace in the non-Western world that many people who become healers of some sort or other are those who have been cured of some serious illness by the medical system they subsequently join. Edgerton's famous account of Abedi, a "traditional African psychiatrist," is a good example.[40] Abedi turned to a specialization in mental illnesses after suffering a series of hallucinations which occurred at the beginning of his medical apprenticeship with his father. He was terrorized when he heard voices of people he couldn't see; it was weeks later before he was cured of this bout of illness which was diagnosed as being due to witchcraft. He had a long subsequent career curing the most violently psychotic individuals.

For a more recent case, see the marvelous account of "Sister Grace," a Navajo Catholic nun who blended charismatic Christianity, elements of both the Native American Church (NAC) and classical Navajo tradition, and conventional Western medicine in her healing ministry, which began after her immersion in these traditions led to her emergence from a profound depression. She has become a very well known and respected healer on the Navajo reservation. Sister

TABLE 1 Elements of effective discussion of the medical management plan

Element	Patient Outcomes Affected
Patient is encouraged to ask more questions.	Anxiety,[30] role limitation and physical limitation[31-33]
Patient is successful at obtaining information	Functional status[36,32] and physiological status[32,33]
Patient is provided with information programs and packages	Pain,[34] function,[35] mood and anxiety[36]
Physician gives clear information programs and packages	Psychologic distress,[37] symptom resolution,[38] blood pressure[39]
Physician and patient agree about the nature of the problem and need for follow-up	Problem[28] and symptom[29] resolution
Physician is willing to share decision making	Patient anxiety[27]

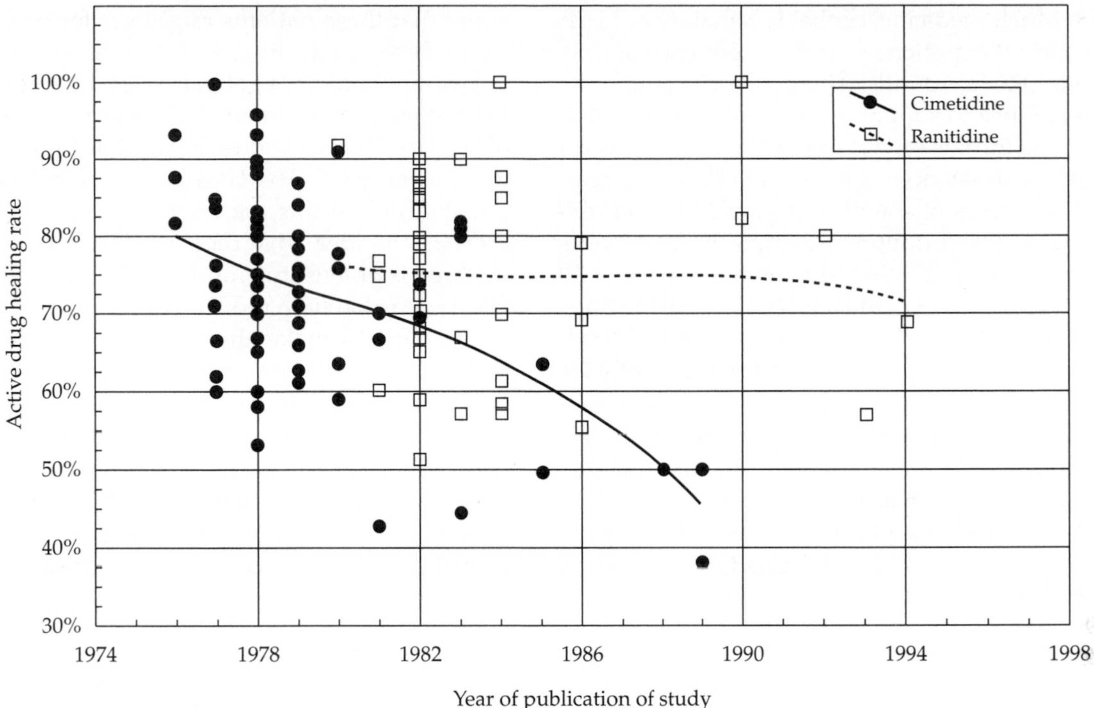

FIGURE 2 The healing rate of the first effective treatment for gastric ulcer disease (Cimetidine) declined significantly after the introduction of a new, "better" drug (Ranitidine). This suggests changes in physician's enthusiasm for new drugs.

Grace's father, healed from an accident with help from the Native American Church, himself became an accomplished "roadman" of the NAC.[41]

The personal experience of these people is, in itself, undeniable evidence, powerful proof for them of the power and usefulness of their healing art. This is uncommon in biomedicine—the great majority of oncologists have not had cancer; most cardiologists do not have heart disease; few geriatric specialists seem much older than forty. The only persistent exception in (or, perhaps, at the margins of) conventional medicine is for psychiatrists who specialize in psychoanalysis; it is still generally the case that psychoanalysts have undergone psychoanalysis during their training (and usually continue it during their practice). The changes which this experience brings to their lives—like those that transform the man or woman who becomes a shaman—can be powerful and convincing evidence of its effectiveness.[††]

But for more ordinary physicians, who have not experienced the treatments they prescribe for their patients, other devices must serve to create this assurance. In Western medicine, the primary device for achieving this end is the extraordinary romance medicine has with science. Medical students are steeped in science. Doctors routinely argue that their work "is scientific." By this, they mean that it is somehow based on real scientific analysis or experiment: that is, that it's "true." Modern medical education is steeped in science—from the MCATs to the fixation on "data"; "show me the data" is the first thing any doctor will ever ask. When I explained to my family doctor once that a recurring minor but annoying skin problem seemed to abate when I took a course of antibiotics for some other condition, she laughed and said, "Well, you're ahead of the data on that one!" And, of course, much of medicine is based on real scientific research and practice. But much

[††] If there is a common thread among many autobiographical accounts of physicians who have experienced serious illness, it is their shock and dismay at how hard, how humiliating, how exhausting, and how painful it can be to be a patient; Robert Hahn has written a thoughtful and interesting review, titled "Between Two Words." Of the ways doctors report on their experience with serious illness.[42] Here, for example, is some testimony from a nephrologist who, diagnosed with metastatic lung cancer, had to have chemotherapy among other things:

> I have spent a tremendous percentage of my time telling my patients that they needed to show up for dialysis, needed to stay for the full treatment. I have heard every type of excuse for cutting times and treatments. Some patients have cussed me out. One said "Get out of my face," Another said, "You have no idea what it is like to go through this. "I have sometimes become unpopular among patients because I would not accept the selfish remark, "It's my life." My response, "But what about your wife, your little children and grandchildren, your friends. It is selfish to rob them of your beauty just because you are too impatient to sit to a chair for four hours. Maybe it is fate, but my chemotherapy time is the exact time as my average patient's dialysis—four hours." I go to a state hospital, and sometimes have to wait two and a half hours to be put on. I have pesky pump as my companion, and can either watch boring soap operas, read or sleep. I can complain, laugh, or cry. There is only one thing and one thing only I cannot let myself do—cut my time short With a great deal of humbleness and humility to my patients, I can now very safely proclaim. "It is a lot easier to be the doctor than the patient.[43] For another view of this situation, watch William Hurt in The Doctor. Where a surgeon learns what medicine is really like after he contracts cancer. This film is often shown to medical students.

of it is not. Much medicine, probably a majority of it, is based on clinical experience, on the experience of doctors in their clinical rounds. There is, for example, no scientific evidence to support giving antibiotics to children with sore throats except under the most stringent and special circumstances; a review of studies of treatment of 10,484 cases of sore throat showed that antibiotics shortened the duration of symptoms by 8 hours over the course of an illness lasting about a week or 10 days.[44] Yet, regardless of evidence, it is done all the time. There are many other similar examples.[45] But it doesn't really matter given the issue we are addressing. What is important is that doctors—healers of any sort or type—are convinced that their techniques are powerful and effective, and that there is undeniable evidence of this effectiveness. In some places, such proof comes from gods or spirits, in some places from personal experience, and in other places from the assertions of science. Insofar as these convictions are somehow conveyed to patients and, in the process, convince them of their doctor's power, then they are likely (within the bounds of our physical mortality) to be effective.

In August 1920, my wife's great-grandfather, her mother's father's father, wrote some memoirs of his life. Born in 1840, he had trained in Strasbourg, France to be a physician. After about twenty years of practice, he began to doubt his abilities: "My feeling of being impotent against the fatal progress of most diseases drove me little by little to be disgusted with the practice of medicine. It is obvious that a doctor, to exercise his profession properly and not become a charlatan, must be convinced that his prescriptions can only have a favorable effect on the course of the disease." Losing this conviction, Dr Schmidt left medicine and became a tax collector.

The ways in which doctors convince themselves of the effectiveness of their techniques changes through time. For example, I cited above Dr. Houston's account of "The Doctor Himself as a Therapeutic Agent."[18] This paper (the record of a distinguished address to the American College of Physicians in 1938) contained not a single reference, no charts, no data at all. The paper by Dr. Stewart with which I brought the discussion to a close, published in 1995, compared the results of 21 randomized controlled trials which examined the effects of various interventions in 3,753 different patients. Both papers seem quite convincing; but the styles of evidence and presentation, and the sense of what it means to be "scientific," have changed.

It is also important to note that doctors don't really have to work very hard at this much of the time. Look again at Figure 1, and recall that the difference in pain relief these patients experienced after receiving inert medication can be attributed to the fact that, in the PNF group, the doctors, but not the patients, knew that these patients might get fentanyl (which is certainly very effective) and that those patients in the PN group would not get it. It's not that they got it—all the patients represented in the figure got an injection of sterile saline solution—it was that the doctors knew they *might* get it. The cues being given to patients in a situation like this are extremely subtle, indeed, no one has any idea what they are. But doctors *know* that fentanyl is potent stuff, and just the possibility of your getting it is likely to reduce your pain.

Finally, to make the case that it is doctors, not patients, who are the primary active ingredient here, one can demonstrate the proposition that old treatments became less effective as new treatments come along. Figure 2 shows the results of 117 studies of treatment of gastric ulcers with two different drugs.[46] The points show the percentage of people in each study who were healed by the drug (based on an endoscopic examination). The studies are plotted in terms of their dates of publication. The points represented by solid circles are studies of one of the first really effective treatments for ulcer disease, cimetidine (trade-name Tagamet), a drug which inhibits the production of acid in the gut. The earliest studies were done in 1975, and they continued for about ten years. But in 1981, the first studies were done of a new, "better" drug which also blocked acid called ranitidine (trade-name Zantac). Before ranitidine came along in 1981, cimetidine healed 72% of the patients treated with it in trials. After ranitidine came along, the effectiveness of cimetidine dropped so that only 64% of patients treated with it were cured: ranitidine cured 75% of patients treated with it in trials. It is, of course, research physicians (those doing these studies), not patients, who are fully aware of (and excited by) newly emerging drugs. As they convey their enthusiasm for their new drugs, they may simultaneously disparage the "older" ones, even though they may not be aware they are doing it.

In summary, what patients know (not what kinds of people they are), and what things mean, is what accounts for the effectiveness of much of medical treatment. And, of course, the single most important source of knowledge and meaning for patients is their doctors. Doctors know lots of things. Many of the things that they know they are unaware of knowing (as is true for most of us in this life). But it is the depth of their convictions which conveys to patients the power of their treatments.

REFERENCES

1. Gracely RH, Dubner R, Deeter WR, Wolskee PJ. Clinicians' expectations influence placebo analgesia. *Lancet* 1985 Jan 5; 1(8419):43.

2. Braithewaite, A, Cooper, P. Analgesic effects of branding in treatment of headaches. *BMJ* (Clinical Research Ed.), 282, no. 6276: 1576–1981.
3. Gartner MA Jr. Selected personality differences between placebo reactors and nonreactors, *Journal of the American Osteopath Association* 60:377-8, 1961.
4. Fisher S, Fisher RL. Placebo response and acquiescence. *Psychopharmacologia* 4, 298–301, 1963.
5. Muller BP. Personality of placebo reactors and nonreactors. *Diseases of the Nervous System* 26:58-61, 1965.
6. Walike BC, Meyer B. Relation between placebo reactivity and selected personality factors. *Nursing Research*, 15, 119–23, 1966.
7. Liberman RP. The elusive placebo reactor. Neuro-Psycho-Pharmacology: Proceedings of the Fifth International Congress of the Collegium Internationale Neuro-Psycho-Pharmacologicum. Chief Editor H. Brill 557–66. Amsterdam: Excerpta Medica Foundation, 1967.
8. Fisher S. The placebo reactor: thesis, antithesis, synthesis, and hypothesis. *Diseases of the Nervous System* 28:510–5, 1967.
9. Straus B, Eisenberg J, Gennis J. Hypnotic effects of an antihistamine–methapyrilene hydrochloride. *Ann Intern Med* 42:574–582, 1955.
10. Knipschild P, Leffers P, Feinstein AR. The qualification period. *J Clin Epidemiol* 44(6):461–4, 1991.
11. Lang JM, No free Lunch. *J Clin Epidemiol* 1992 May;45(5):563–5.
12. Knipschild P, Leffers P, Feinstein AR. Value for money. *J Clin Epidemiol* 45:564–65, 1992.
13. Schoenberger JA, Wilson D J. Once-daily treatment of essential hypertension with captopril. *J Clin Hypertens* 1986; Dec; 2(4):379–87. (quote is from p.381).
14. Trivedi MH, Rush J. Does a placebo run-in or a placebo treatment cell affect the efficacy of antidepressant medications? *Neuropsychopharmacology* 1994. Aug; 11(1): 33–43.
15. Mosely JB Jr, Wray NP, Kuykendell D, Willis K, Landon G. Arthroscopic treatment of osteoarthritis of the knee: a perspective, randomized, placebo-controlled trial. Results of a pilot study, *Am J Sports Med* 1996, Jan–Feb; 24(1):28–34.
16. Talbot M. The placebo prescription. *New York Times Magazine*. January 9, 2000 34–9, 44, 58–60.
17. Houston, WR. The doctor himself as a therapeutic agent. *Ann Intern Med*, 11, no.8:1416-25, 1938.
18. Shapiro AK. Etiological factors in placebo effect. *JAMA* 187, no 10:712–15, 1964.
19. Whitehorn, JC Betz, BJ. Further studies of the doctor as a crucial variable in the outcome of treatment with schizophrenic patients. *Am J Psychiat* 117, no. 3:215–233, 1960.
20. Uhlenhuth EH, Rickels K, Fisher S, Park LC, Lipman RS, Mock JE. Drug, doctor's verbal attitude and clinic setting in the symptomatic response to pharmacotherapy. *Psychopharmacologia* 1966; 9:392-418.
21. Gryll SI., Katahn M. Situational factors contributing to the placebo effect, *Psychopharmacology* (Berl), 1978 May 31; 57(3): 253–61.
22. Thomas KB. General practice consultations: is there any point in being positive? *Br Med J* (Clin Res Ed). 1987 May 9; 294:1200–2.
23. Benson H, McCallie DP Jr. Angina pectoris and the placebo effect. *N Engl J Med* 1979 June 21; 300(25):1424–9 (quote is from 1424).
24. Stewart MA. Effective physician-patient communication and health outcomes: a review. *CMAJ* 1995 May; 152(9):1423-33.
25. Morris J, Royle GT. Offering patients a choice of surgery for early breast cancer: a reduction in anxiety and depression in patients and their husbands. *Soc Sci Med* 1988;26(6):583-5.
26. Fallowfield LJ. Hall A, Maguire GP, Baum M. Psychological outcomes of different treatment policies in women with early breast cancer outside a clinical trial. *BMJ* 1990 Sep 22; 301(6752): 575–80.
27. Starfield B, Wray C, Hess K, Gross R, Birk PS, D'Lugoff BC. The influence of patient-practitioner agreement on outcome of care. *Am J Public Health*. 1981 Feb; 71(2): 127–34.
28. Bass MJ, Buck C, Turner L, Dickie G, Pratt G, Robinson HC. The physician's actions and the outcome of illness in family practice. *J Fam Pract* 1986 Jul;23(1):43–7.
29. Thompson SC, Nanni C, Schwankovsky L. Patient-oriented interventions to improve communication in a medical office visit. *Health Psychol*, 1990; 9(4):390–404.
30. Greenfield S, Kaplan S, Ware JE Jr. Expanding patient involvement in care. Effects on patient outcomes. *Ann Intern Med* 1985 Apr;102(4):520–8.
31. Kaplan SH, Greenfield S, Ware JE Jr. Assessing the effects of physician-patient interactions on the outcomes of chronic disease. *Med Care* 1989 Mar;27(3 Suppl):S110–27. *Erratum in Med Care* 1989 Jul;27(7):679.
32. Greenfield S, Kaplan SH, Ware JE Jr, Yano EM, Frank HJ. Patients' participation in medical care: effects on blood sugar control and quality of life in diabetes. *J Gen Intern Med*. Sep–Oct;3(5):448–57.
33. Egbert LD. Reduction of postoperative pain by encouragement and instruction of patients. *N Engl J Med*. 1964; 270:825–7.
34. Roter DL, Hall JA. Health education theory: an application to the process of patient–provider communication. *Health Edu Res* 1991 Jun;6(2):185-93.
35. Heszen-Klemens I, Lapinska E. Doctor-patient interaction, patients' health behavior and effects of treatment. *Soc Sci Med* 1984;19(1):9–18.
36. Edgerton, RB. A traditional African psychiatrist. *Southwestern Journal of Anthropology* 27:259–78, 1971.
37. Begay DH, Maryboy NC. The whole universe is my cathedral: a contemporary Navajo spiritual synthesis. *Med Anthropol* Q 2000 Dec;14(4):498–520.
38. Hahn RA. Sickness and Healing. An Anthropological Perspective. New Haven: Yale University Press, 1995.
39. Fadem SZ. A Doctor Gets Sick. Nephron Information Center. Http://www.Nephron.com/life.html, 2000.
40 Moerman, DE. Medical romanticism and the sources of medical practice. *Complementary Therapies in Medicine*. 6:198-202, 1998.
41. Del Mar CB, Glasziou PP, Spinks AB. Antibiotics for sore throat *Cochrane Database Sys*. Rev. The Cochrane Library, Issue 1, 2000.
42. Moerman DE. Cultural variations in the placebo effect: ulcers, anxiety, and blood pressure. *Med Anthropol Q* 2000 Mar;14(1):51-72.

 17

The Nocebo Phenomenon: Concept, Evidence, and Implications for Public Health

Robert A. Hahn

This selection is about the flip side of the placebo effect. The nocebo phenomenon *refers to the process by which negative expectations result in negative effects. In one hospital-based study reported here, 80 percent of patients who were given a glass of sugar water and told that it would make them vomit actually did vomit. Is "power of suggestion" this powerful? Certainly, this is a central theme in the selection by Lévi-Strauss, but surprisingly, this topic has not been systematically evaluated in biomedicine. In general, the placebo and nocebo phenomena seem to be viewed by biomedical scientists as a type of "noise" that contaminates the "real" interactions of cause and effect. It would be worthwhile to change this conception—to see the placebo effect instead as something to be understood and as power to be harnessed in order to improve medical care.*

This selection was written by an anthropologist for biomedical scientists in the field of preventive medicine. Robert Hahn suggests that the nocebo phenomenon should be considered in health education programs. He suggests that the creation of medical categories of disease may be a double-edged sword: "Categories of an ethnomedicine may not only describe conditions of sickness, but may also foster those conditions by establishing expectations that they may occur." A similar point is made by Lynn Payer in The Disease Mongers *(1994), in which she argues that the explosion of medical testing for risk factors like cholesterol may actually do patients more harm than good, although they generate enormous revenue for biomedical corporations.*

The value of looking at the nocebo phenomenon is not merely that we will remember the possible harm of engendering negative expectations. It is also important to think about the power of belief in all types of medical treatments. In what ways do ethnomedical treatments function by providing patients and their families with hope and by distracting everyone while the body heals itself? In this regard, if ethnomedical treatments are to be effective, they must follow the first rule of Hippocrates: "First do no harm." The value of examining the nocebo phenomenon is that it provides an important insight into the placebo effect, something that typically plays a role in the healing process.

This selection was written for a public health–oriented audience, so it offers many specific case studies as evidence. Readers interested in medical anthropological studies of the placebo effect may want to look at the work of Daniel Moerman (1991) and James Dow (1986), or earlier work by Robert Hahn and Arthur Kleinman (1983).

As you read this selection, consider these questions:

- **What is the relationship between nocebos and placebos? Why do you think beliefs or expectations can be so powerful? Or do you?**
- **Is a person more suggestible to the nocebo effect as a member of a group (e.g., children in a cafeteria)? What role does social context play?**
- **Many cultures have a custom of not talking specifically about a disease—for example, not using the term cancer to the patient. What do you think about this custom in relation to the nocebo effect, as well as the principle of informed consent in doctor–patient communication?**

Context: Robert Hahn is a medical anthropologist and epidemiologist at the Centers for Disease Control and Prevention. He has conducted epidemiological fieldwork in numerous countries throughout Latin America and Africa, and edited a volume on the links between anthropology and public health. This article explores the dark side of the placebo phenomenon by introducing the concept of the nocebo, a symbol or action that *increases* pain and suffering in patients. The nocebo phenomenon is particularly relevant for considering the potential for untherapeutic interactions between health providers and their patients.

Source: R. A. Hahn (1997). "The Nocebo Phenomenon: Concept, Evidence, and Implications for Public Health." *Preventative Medicine* 26(5): 607–611.

The nocebo hypothesis proposes that expectations of sickness and the affective states associated with such expectations cause sickness in the expectant. Resultant pathology may be subjective as well as objective conditions. Some nocebo effects may be transient; others may be chronic or fatal. An extreme form of the nocebo phenomenon was described in Cannon's classic paper (1942) as "voodoo death." Because expectations are largely learned from the cultural environment, nocebo effects are likely to vary from place to place.

The nocebo phenomenon, first named by Kennedy (1961) and then elaborated by Kissel and Barrucand (1964), has not been systematically assessed. In this review, I formulate a working definition of the nocebo phenomenon that relates nocebos and placebos; present a range of examples of nocebo phenomena; and draw several implications for public health.

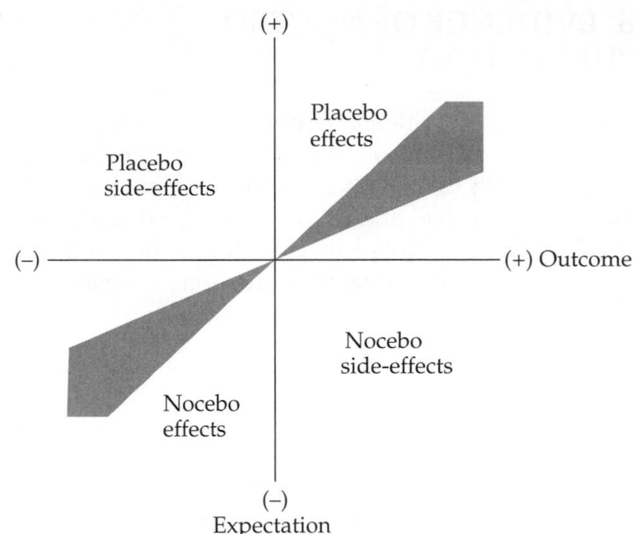

FIGURE 1 The Placebo Thesis: Relations Between Expectation and Outcome (*From R. Hahn,* Sickness and Healing: An Anthropological Perspective, *New Haven, CT: Yale University Press, 1995*)

A. A WORKING DEFINITION OF THE NOCEBO PHENOMENON

The nocebo effect is the causation of sickness (or death) by expectations of sickness (or death) and by associated emotional states. Two forms of the nocebo effect should be recognized: In the *specific* form, the subject expects a particular negative outcome and that outcome consequently occurs; for example, a surgical patient expects to die on the operating table and does die—not from the surgery itself, but from the expectation and associated affect (Weisman and Hackett 1961; Cannon 1942). In the *generic* form, subjects have vague negative expectations—for example, they are diffusely pessimistic—and their expectations are realized in terms of symptoms, sickness, or death—none of which was specifically expected. Again, expectation plays a causal role.

The nocebo phenomenon considered in this review is distinct from placebo side-effects (Figure 1). Placebo side-effects occur when expectations of healing produce sickness, i.e., a positive expectation has a negative outcome. For example, a rash that occurs following administration of a placebo remedy may be a placebo side-effect. Diverse placebo side-effects have been documented; one review reports an incidence of 19% in the subjects of pharmacologic studies (Rosenzweig, Brohier, and Zipfel 1993). In the nocebo phenomenon, however, the subject expects sickness to be the outcome, i.e., the expectation is a negative one. Nocebos may also have side-effects, i.e., when negative expectations produce positive outcomes or outcomes other than those expected.

When Kennedy (1961) and Kissel and Barrucand (1964) first referred to the nocebo phenomenon, they did not distinguish placebo side-effects from the effects of negative expectations. However, reference to voodoo death, for example, as an instance of the placebo phenomenon is etymologically inappropriate. Kennedy and Kissel and Barrucand distinguished placebos from nocebos only in terms of positive and negative *outcomes,* not *also* in terms of expectations. Kennedy's examples are all placebo side-effects, and Kissel and Barrucand did not separate examples of placebo side-effects from an example of nocebo in the sense proposed here: 80% of hospitalized patients given sugar water and told that it was an emetic subsequently vomited. What distinguishes nocebos is that the subject has negative expectations and experiences a negative outcome. Schweiger and Parducci (1981) refer to nocebos as "negative placebos."

Nocebos are causal in the same way that commonly recognized pathogens are, e.g., cigarette smoke of lung cancer, the tubercular bacillus of tuberculosis (Surgeon General 1989; Harris and McClement 1983). That is, nocebos increase the likelihood that the sickness they refer to will occur, and this effect is not the result of confounding, i.e., the empirical association of the hypothesized nocebo with another cause of the condition. None of these exposures is a necessary or a sufficient cause of the given outcome.

B. EVIDENCE OF NOCEBO PHENOMENA

This review of evidence is divided according to the source or manner of acquisition of expectations. It begins with (1) the effects of inner, mental worlds, moves to (2) the effects of nosological categories and self-scrutiny, (3) sociogenic illness, or mass hysteria, and (4) the deliberate induction of sickness or symptoms.

Inner, Mental World

Mood, affect, and some psychiatric conditions are often associated with negative expectations (American Psychiatric Association 1980). For example, hopelessness is a prominent component of diverse forms of depression. Somatoform disorders such as hypochondriasis and conversion disorder may also be associated with expectations of pathology. And some anxiety disorders, too, may be associated with expectations of pathology. Panic disorder, for example, may involve a sense of "impending doom" and a fear of death (American Psychiatric Association 1980).

Although several studies indicate an association of negative expectations and affect associated with psychiatric conditions and pathological outcomes (Black et al. 1985a, 1985b; Newman and Bland 1991; Bruce et al. 1994; Weissman et al. 1990; Reich 1985; Friedman and Booth Kewley 1987; Wells, Stewart, Hays et al. 1989), only the study by Anda and colleagues (1993) uses epidemiologic methods to control for the confounding effects of other risk factors. Anda and colleagues examined the effects of depression on ischemic heart disease (IHD) incidence and mortality in a sample of U.S. adults. They examined persons who were free from heart disease at the outset of the study and excluded subjects whose initial depressed affect might have been the *consequence* of chronic disease. Depression was assessed from the General Well-Being Schedule (Dupuy 1977). Anda and colleagues found that persons with depressive affect were 1.6 times more likely to have nonfatal IHD and 1.5 times more likely to have fatal IHD than persons who did not have depressive affect, independent of other known risk factors for ischemic heart disease. These researchers also examined the effects of hopelessness on heart disease incidence and mortality, and found a dose response—a critical criterion in the inference of causality. Greater hopelessness was associated with greater incidence and mortality.

Considering that an 11.1% prevalence of depressed affect was assessed in the study cohort—a sample of U.S. adults—it can be estimated (as the "population attributable risk") that approximately 26,000 deaths a year (i.e., more than 5% of U.S. IHD mortality and more than 1% of all U.S. deaths) may be attributable to depression, independent of other risk factors. Mortality associated with depressive expectations is an example of the generic form of the nocebo phenomenon. The other examples in this review are of specific nocebo phenomena.

Nosological Categories and Self-Scrutiny

In one specific form, cardiac neurosis or cardiophobia, patients are persistently fearful of heart attacks or other cardiac symptoms, and report chest pain, described by physicians as "non-specific." Although these patients may not manifest recognized cardiac symptoms, there is evidence that belief that one is susceptible to heart attacks is itself a risk factor for coronary death. Eaker examined women, 45 to 64 years of age, in the Framingham study for the 20-year incidence of myocardial infarction and coronary death (Eaker 1992). Women who believed they were more likely than others to suffer a heart attack were 3.7 times as likely to die of coronary conditions as were women who believed they were less likely to die of such symptoms, independent of commonly recognized risk factors for coronary death (e.g., smoking, systolic blood pressure, and the ratio of total to high density lipoprotein cholesterol).

Sociogenic Illness

Sickness or symptoms may also occur when one person observes or learns of the sickness or symptoms in others. Knowledge of sickness in others fosters an expectation that one may also be subject to the same condition. Perhaps the best recognized form of contagion by observation are epidemics referred to as "sociogenic," "psychogenic illness," "mass hysteria," or, in the workplace, "assembly line hysteria" (Colligan and Stockton 1978).

Sirois (1974) reviewed 78 documented outbreaks of "epidemic hysteria" reported between 1872 and 1972. Of these, 44% occurred in schools, 22% in towns, and 10% in factories. Twenty-eight percent involved fewer than 10 persons, 32% involved 10–30 persons, and 19% more than 30 persons; 5% were of unreported magnitude. (Whereas the largest outbreak noted by Sirois involved approximately 200 persons, an outbreak has been described that involved 949 persons [Modan, Tirosh, Weissenberg et al. 1983].) Only females were involved in 74% of the outbreaks, only males in 4% (Sirois 1974). Outbreaks occurred more commonly among persons from lower socioeconomic classes and in periods of uncertainty and social stress. Convulsions were reported in 24% of outbreaks, abnormal movements in 18%, and fainting, globus/cough/laryngismus, and loss of sensation in 11.5% each. Symptomatology changed over the 100 years surveyed, from more globus/cough/laryngismus and abnormal movements to more fainting, nausea, abdominal malaise, and headaches.

Colligan and Murphy (1979) point out that sociogenic outbreaks are commonly associated with a source believed to be related to the symptoms, e.g., a strange odor or gas, new solvent, or an insect bite. However, sometimes reported symptoms do not fit biomedical knowledge of associations between potential toxins or pathogens and pathophysiology. Persons affected often have repetitive jobs, are under unusual stress, and/or have poor relations with superiors. They may be in poorer general health and have been absent more often than persons who are not affected. Colligan and Murphy indicate that sociogenic outbreaks in workplace settings are substantially underreported.

Sirois (1975) estimates that sociogenic outbreaks occur in approximately one out of every 1,000 schools per year in the province of Quebec. A review of recent school outbreaks in diverse countries indicates attack rates (i.e., the proportion of persons exposed who experience the condition) of 6%–48% (Arcidiacono, Brand, Coppenger, and Calder 1990).

The study of Kerckhoff and Back (1968) of the 1962 "June Bug" outbreak in a Montana mill is one of the few to carefully reconstruct social patterns of the spread of a sociogenic condition. In the June Bug event, those affected fainted or complained of pain, nausea, or disorientation. Sixty-two (6.4%) of 965 workers were affected, 59 (95.2%) of them women; all those affected worked in dressmaking departments. Persons affected were 70% more likely than controls to believe that the cause of the outbreak was an insect or other physical object. Persons affected were 62% more likely to have worked overtime at least two or three times a week than those not affected. Persons affected were less likely to go to a supervisor with a complaint or to be members of the union. They were 2.2 times as likely to be sole breadwinners, 5.6 times as likely to be divorced, and 30% more likely to have a child under 6 years of age. The outbreak began among women who were socially isolated, subsequently spread among women connected by links of close social relations, and finally diffused among women less closely connected. The phenomenon analyzed by Kerckhoff and Back might be described as "mass somatization."

The effects of a person's social environment on sickness or illness behavior need not involve direct personal contact. An association has been found between traumatic death or violence in the community environment and subsequent suicide or suicide-like behavior (Phillips 1974, 1977; Phillips and Carstenen 1986). In this instance, the first victim serves as a model with whom others may "identify." For example, when newspaper or television stories about a suicide are released, the rate of suicide may increase in the following week; the greater the circulation of the newspaper, the greater the increase (Phillips 1974). After Marilyn Monroe's suicide in 1962, 197 suicides occurred in the United States during the following week—12% more than the number expected on the basis of past suicide patterns (Phillips 1974). A recent study indicates that teenagers are more susceptible to televised publicity about suicide and that increases in suicides are greater for girls than boys (Phillips and Carstensen 1986).

Motor-vehicle fatalities also follow newspaper stories of suicide. Phillips (1977) calculates that, on average, motor vehicle fatalities increase 9% above the expected rate in the week following front-page reporting of suicides in newspaper stories, and that, reporting in newspapers with greater than average circulation, the increase is 19%.

Sickness/Symptoms Induced

Social psychologists have conducted diverse experiments that demonstrate the effects of negative suggestion on the experience of negative symptoms (Schachter and Singer 1962; Lancman et al. 1994; Jewett, Fein, and Greenberg 1990; Sternbach 1964; Schweiger and Parducci 1981). In one experiment, 47.5% of asthmatics who were exposed to (normally innocuous) nebulized saline solution and told they were inhaling irritants or allergens experienced substantially increased airway resistance and changes in airway resistance and thoracic gas volume (Luparello, Lyons, Bleecker, and McFadden 1968). Controls who did not have asthma were unaffected by exposure to the same stimulus. Twelve asthmatic subjects developed full-blown attacks that were relieved by the same saline solution presented therapeutically. (The researchers also refer to an asthmatic patient in another study whose allergy to roses was induced by plastic as well as natural roses, indicating that the effect of the rose did not result entirely from its botanical properties.)

In a follow-up, double-blind experiment, Luparello, Leist, Lourie, and Sweet (1968) randomized asthmatic patients to four conditions: Two groups were given a bronchodilator, the other two a bronchoconstrictor; half of the group given each substance was told they were being given a bronchodilator, the other half that they were being given a bronchoconstrictor. For each substance administered, expectations induced by misinformation about the substance reduced its physiologic effectiveness by 43% (for the bronchoconstrictor) and 49% (for the bronchodilator).

Another study was designed to evaluate a method for the diagnosis of psychogenic seizures, reported to account for as many as 20% of "refractory epilepsy" (Lancman et al. 1994). Lancman and colleagues compared the effect of suggestion on the induction of seizure behavior in patients with psychogenic seizures and others with known epilepsy. Patients were told that a medicine administered through a skin patch would induce seizures within 30 seconds, and that removal of the patch would end the seizure. Of patients with psychogenic seizures, 77% manifested seizures when the patch was applied, with symptoms such as nonresponsiveness, generalized violent thrashing, and uncoordinated movements; 19% of these patients reported auras, and 44% showed postictal confusion and/or sleepiness. None of the patients with diagnosed epilepsy manifested seizures.

Finally, another study (Jewett, Fein, and Greenberg 1990), designed to evaluate a controversial method of food allergy testing, compared the effect of injecting the food substances—the test to be evaluated—with the effect of injecting saline diluent without the substance in question on symptoms that included itching of the nose, watering or burning eyes, plugged ears, tight or scratchy throat, nausea, dizziness, sleepiness, and depression. (Patients with a history of anaphylactic reactions or documented cardiac irregularity, or other severe reactions to their allergies were excluded.) In this double-blind study, the proportion of patients who experienced symptoms was not statistically different in patients given test (27%) and *nocebo* diluent injections (24%). "Neutralizing" injections, given to eliminate the reactions, were also equally effective whether they contained the food substance or—in this case—the diluent *placebo.* An injection becomes a nocebo (or placebo) not because of its contents, but because of the pessimistic (or optimistic) expectations of its consumer.

C. DISCUSSION

I have reviewed a range of studies indicating that socially given negative expectations and their emotional associations facilitate their own realization. Beliefs can make us sick as well as healthy. The nocebo phenomenon is a little-recognized facet of culture that may be responsible for a substantial variety of pathology throughout the world. However, the extent of the phenomenon is not yet known, and evidence is piecemeal and ambiguous. There is evidence that inner, mental states affect pathological outcomes, independent of other risk factors; that symptoms may spread in communities by being witnessed; and that symptoms may be caused by experimentally induced expectations. Further investigations should explore the ways in which, like the placebo phenomenon, the expectations of the nocebo phenomenon translate diverse cultural beliefs into physiological process.

I conclude with two implications of the nocebo phenomenon for public health.

First, the nocebo phenomenon is a side-effect of human culture. A society's culture tells its members how the world is divided, inter-connected, and known; it specifies what is valued and what is not, what is good, beautiful, right, wrong, and indifferent; it provides rules of conduct whereby the society's members know how to behave and how to judge the behavior of others (Hahn 1995). One element of cultures has been referred to as an "ethnomedicine." A society's ethnomedicine tells societal members what sicknesses there are, how they are acquired, how manifested, how treated. The nocebo phenomenon suggests that the categories of an ethnomedicine may not only describe conditions of sickness, but may also foster those conditions by establishing expectations that they may occur. Thus, a cultural system commonly thought to serve a healing function may also have a contrary outcome, fostering the same pathologies intended to be healed. The assessment of the extent of this noxious facet of ethnomedicines, including our own system of biomedicine, is an important public health challenge.

Second, and more immediately practical, if communication about pathological conditions may serve not only to describe, but, in a sense, also to foster sickness by creating expectations, then we must be cautious in both public health communications and in clinical medicine. We need to know more about how health messages affect their audience. Such knowledge may enhance our ability to minimize the pathological consequences of negative messages. The placebo/nocebo phenomenon suggests that it may be healthier to err on the side of optimism than on the side of pessimism.

REFERENCES

American Psychiatric Association. 1980. *Diagnostic and Statistical Manual of Mental Disorders,* 3rd ed. Washington, D.C: American Psychiatric Association.

Anda, R., D. Williamson, D. Jones, C. Macera, E. Eaker, A. Glassman, and J. Marks. 1993. "Depressed Affect, Hopelessness, and the Risk of Ischemic Heart Disease in a Cohort of U.S. Adults." *Epidemiol* 4(4):285–294.

Arcidiacono, S., J. I. Brand, W. Coppenger, and R. A. Calder. 1990. "Mass Sociogenic Illness in a Day-care Center—Florida." *MMWR* 31(18):301–304.

Black, D. W., G. Warrack, and G. Winokur. 1985a. "Excess Mortality among Psychiatric Patients." *JAMA* 253(1):58–61.

———. 1985b. "The Iowa Record-Linkage Study: II. Excess Mortality among Patients with 'Functional' Disorders." *Arch Gen Psychiatry* 42:82–88.

Bruce, M. L., P. J. Leaf, G. P. M. Rozal et al. 1994. Psychiatric Status and 9 Year Mortality Data in the New Haven Epidemiologic Catchment Area Study." *Am J Psychiatry* 151(5):716–721.

Cannon, W. B. 1942. "Voodoo Death." *American Anthropologist* 44(2):169–181.

Colligan, M. J., and L. R. Murphy. 1979. "Mass Psychogenic Illness in Organizations: An Overview." *Journal of Occupational Psychology* 52:77–90.

Colligan, M. J., and W. Stockton. 1976. "The Mystery of Assembly-line Hysteria." *Psychology Today* 12:93–116.

Conti, S., G. Savron, G. Bartolucci et al. 1989. "Cardiac Neurosis and Psychopathology." *Psychother Psychosom* 52:88–91.

Dupuy, H. J. 1977. "A Concurrent Validational Study of the NCHS General Well-Being Schedule." *Vital Health Statistics*, Series 2, No. 73. DHEW Pub. No. (HRA)78–1347. Washington, D.C.: U.S. Government Printing Office.

Eaker, E., J. Pinsky, and W. P. Castelli. 1992. "Myocardial Infarction and Coronary Death among Women: Psychosocial Predictors from a 20-Year Follow-up of Women in the Framingham Study." *Am J Epidemiology* 135:854–864.

Friedman, H. S., and S. Booth-Kewley. 1987. "The 'Disease-Prone Personality': A Meta-Analytic View of the Construct." *Am Psychol* 42(6):539–555.

Hahn, R. A. 1995. *Sickness and Healing; An Anthropological Perspective.* New Haven, Conn.: Yale University Press.

Harris, H. W., and J. H. McClement. 1983. "Pulmonary Tuberculosis." In Hoeprich, P. D., ed., *Infectious Diseases*, pp. 378–404. New York: Harper and Row.

Jewett, D. L., G. Fein, and M. H. Greenberg. 1990. "A Double-blind Study of Symptom Provocation to Determine Food Sensitivity." *N Engl J Med* 323(7):429–433.

Kennedy, W. P. 1961. "The Nocebo Reaction." *Medical World* 91:203–205.

Kerckhoff, A. C., and K. W. Back. 1968. *The June Bug: A Study of Hysterical Contagion.* New York: Appleton Century-Crofts.

Kissel, P., and D. Barrucand. 1964. *Placebos et Effet Placebo En Medecine.* Paris: Masson.

Lancman, M. E., J. J. Asconape, W. J. Craven, G. Howard, and J. K. Penry. 1994. "Predictive Value of Induction of Psychogenic Seizures by Suggestion." *Annals of Neurology* 35(3):559–361.

Luparello, T. J., N. Leist, C. H. Lourie, and P. Sweet. 1970. "The Interaction of Psychologic Stimuli and Pharmacologic Agents on Airway Reactivity in Asthmatic Subjects." *Psychosomatic Medicine* 32(5):509–513.

Luparello, T., H. A. Lyons, E. R. Bleecker, and E. R. McFadden. 1968. "Influences of Suggestion on Airway Reactivity in Asthmatic Subjects." *Psychosomatic Medicine* 30: 819–825.

Modan, B., M. Tirosh, E. Weissenberg, et al. 1983. "The Arjenyattah Epidemic: A Mass Phenomenon: Spread and Triggering Factors." *Lancet* 24/31:1472–1474.

Newman, S. C., and R. C. Bland. 1991. "Mortality in a Cohort of Patients with Schizophrenia: A Record Linkage Study." *Can J Psychiatry* 36:239–245.

Phillips, D. P. 1974. "The Influence of Suggestion on Suicide: Substantive and Theoretical Implications of the Werther Effect." *American Sociological Review* 39:340–354.

———. 1977. "Motor Vehicle Fatalities Increase Just after Publicized Suicide Stories." *Science* 196:1464–1465.

Phillips, D. P., and L. L. Carstensen. 1986. "Clustering of Teenage Suicides after Television News Stories about Suicide." *N Eng J Med* 315:685-689.

Reich, P. 1985. "Psychological Predisposition to Life-threatening Arrhythmias. "*Ann Rev Med* 36:397–405.

Rosenzweig P., S. Brohier, and A. Zipfel. 1993. "The Placebo Effect in Healthy Volunteers: Influence of Experimental Conditions on the Adverse Events Profile during Phase I Studies " *Clinical Pharmacology and Therapeutics* 54(5):578–583.

Schachter S., and J. E. Singer. 1962. "Cognitive, Social, and Physiological Determinants of Emotional State." *Psychological Review* 69(5):379–399.

Schweiger, A., and A. Parducci. 1981. "Nocebo: The Psychologic Induction of Pain." *Pao J Biol Sci* 16:140–143.

Sirois, F. 1974. "Epidemic Hysteria." *Ada Psychiatrica Scandinavia* 51(252):7–44.

———. 1975. "À Propos de la Fréquence Des Épidémies D'hystérie." *Union Med Canada* 104:121–123.

Sternbach, R. A. 1964. "The Effects of Instructional Sets on Autonomic Responsivity." *Psychophysiology* 1(1):67–72.

Weisman, A. D., and T. P. Hackett. 1961. "Predilection to Death: Death and Dying as a Psychiatric Problem." *Psychosomatic Medicine* 23(3):232–256.

Weissman, M. M., J. S. Markowitz, R. Ouellette, S. Greenwald, and J. P. Kahn. 1990. "Panic Disorder and Cardiovascular/Cerebrovascular Problems: Results from a Community Survey." *Am J Psychiatry* 147:1504–1508.

Wells, K. B., A. Stewart, R. D. Hays et al. 1989. "The Functioning and Well-being of Depressed Patients." *JAMA* 262(7):914–919.

The Meaning and Experience of Illness

■ ***The illness experience may be powerful.*** Practitioners of biomedicine are so unfamiliar with the illness experience that a significant number of physicians have written books about their personal stories of being sick (Hahn 1995). The movie *The Doctor* is an example of this genre, wherein the personal illness experience functions as a revelation and results in a conversion to a new way of practicing medicine. However, medical anthropologists have traditionally taken the patient's point of view in understanding the illness experience, and the ethnographic method emphasizes the native's *emic* analysis (i.e., explaining things from the insider's point of view). More recently, some anthropologists have become autobiographical and reflexive in their ethnographic descriptions. This means that the position of the anthropologist and his or her relationship with the subject of study is included in the ethnography, in part because the author recognizes that it is impossible to be completely objective. A good example of this approach is found in selection 20 by Robert Murphy on the subject of his own paralysis.

■ ***The illness experience may include social and psychological dimensions that cannot be cured with medicine.*** Medical anthropologists use the term *illness experience* to refer to a patient-centered view of sickness, especially the social and psychological aspects (Kleinman 1988). Attention to the overall illness experience—the human aspects of the illness experience—is not a strength of biomedicine. In fact, many see that this major failing of biomedicine is the reason more and more people in the United States use alternative health care systems (Eisenberg et al. 1993). The human suffering of some illnesses may be in the form of discrimination, stigma, damaged self-concept, and social ostracism. Suffering related to the social and psychological dimensions of illness may be worse and last longer than the disease itself; this is especially the case with chronic illnesses. The social meanings of illnesses can also vary from culture to culture.

■ ***Illness—and the suffering associated with it—is a human experience profoundly shaped by culture.*** All humans experience illness and all humans die; this is a biological reality that is interpreted through culture. Culture provides a label for sickness and shapes people's explanatory model of their illness experience. Cultural beliefs, social roles, and economic constraints influence health-seeking behavior. Illness and death create human suffering, which can be experienced on an individual level or a social level.

■ ***Often, the "meaning" of an illness in a particular setting is reflective of larger social, political, economic, or moral concerns.*** Some people cannot afford to become ill, or their illness exacerbates their preexisting social and economic problems. In a context with a very high prevalence of a particular disease—for example, diabetes among Native Americans of the Southwest—experience of the illness might be considered "normal." In other cases, identification with a particular disease may give an individual access to particular resources (as in the case of HIV in particular contexts). In a world of gross economic inequalities, there are significant moral elements reflected in the illness experience of individuals.

■ ***People use narratives to help understand illness and also to forge a way of better managing their own and others' suffering.*** Narratives are stories. People construct stories to explain—for themselves and others—how and why something happened. The suffering involved in the illness experience and death requires such explanations. In addition, there is therapeutic value in the telling and retelling of these stories. Often, the narratives are mutually shaped by the patient and those around her or him. Constructing narratives helps people manage the chaos that can be created by illness. Medical anthropologists often collect these stories as data to describe and analyze the illness experience.

- ***The sick role is an important concept.*** One area of sociological theory involves social statuses and roles—patterns of behavior that are expected by people filling particular positions in a social system. The metaphor "all life is a stage" is intended here—we are actors playing roles. As individuals, we can simultaneously occupy different roles in relation to other people. For example, you may be somebody's son or daughter, somebody's student, somebody's lover, somebody's co-worker, and so on. How you act in a particular context depends in large part on what role you are playing at the time. Appropriate role behavior is learned as part of our culture. Society as a whole can function because people agree on what the roles are and what the expected behavior of a person is in each role. Cognitive psychologists and anthropologists have argued that we know the "play" (or the social scene), including the roles and scripts that they involve, because we share cultural models or schemata (general conceptions about how the world is supposed to function). This idea is closely linked to the social construction of reality that has been previously discussed.

In the inevitable event of sickness, our culture provides us with particular social roles: the sick patient, the healer, the supportive friend or family member. That way, everyone is expected to know what to do. When an individual adopts the sick role, a person's regular social responsibilities are temporarily suspended (e.g., going to work or school). The sick role has its benefits, as we all know. At the same time, new social expectations and responsibilities are enforced (e.g., following the doctor's orders, gradually decreasing dependence on medical care, getting better). If people fail to meet these expectations—for example, if they get up and play instead of staying in bed and acting sick—then others think they are malingering, faking the sick role to reap its benefits. The same thing happens if patients fail to get well, as in the example of chronic fatigue syndrome.

18

Learning to Be a Leper: A Case Study in the Social Construction of Illness

Nancy E. Waxler

This selection returns us to the anthropological enterprise of cross-cultural comparison by examining the social meanings of a particular illness—leprosy—in the contexts of South Asia, North America, and Africa. The biomedical label for leprosy is Hansen's disease *(HD); contrary to myth, this disease, characterized by a progressive degeneration of nerves in the limbs, is not highly infectious. The deformities associated with leprosy are the result of untreated secondary infections, partly because the victim has no sensation of pain in the extremities. With modern biomedical care, HD can be completely arrested. Although it may be possible to cure the disease, the illness and its social stigma are less easily treated.*

An important research strategy in medical anthropology is cross-cultural comparison. Leprosy is a particularly interesting topic for such a comparison because the disease has undergone a striking social transformation. Even though biomedical science has disproved the idea of leprosy as being "unclean," these notions persist. Westerners fear and are disgusted by leprosy; it is, after all, a disease of biblical proportions. But is this social stigma a cultural universal? Is the social reaction related to particular pathological features of the disease? What is it like to be a leper?

When people are diagnosed with a chronic disease, they must learn to adapt to it. The mechanisms for coping, however, are learned in a cultural context. People in the United States with leprosy react differently than people with HD in Ethiopia. In this selection, Nancy Waxler argues that the Mycobacterium *germ that causes leprosy the disease plays only a small part in the large drama that is leprosy the illness. Also note her description of how charitable institutions, established to serve those suffering from leprosy, in the long term may function to perpetuate the problems of stigmatization.*

Notice in this selection that the medical anthropologist is describing the experience of illness from the patient's perspective. This is an example of experience-near *ethnographies that are based on the qualitative research techniques of participant observation and interviewing. The phenomenon of the social construction of a stigmatized illness cannot be studied only by talking to people who have the disease. The social reaction to the disease—the social construction of a moral judgment about the condition—is equally important.*

As you read this selection, consider these questions:

- **How is the social stigma of leprosy different from the stigma of AIDS?**
- **If you were a physician and were able to stop a case of HD so that there were no deformities or long-term effects, what do you think could be done about the experience of the illness of leprosy?**
- **How is it that agencies designed to help people might in fact contribute to their stigmatization?**
- **What does the author mean when she says that people have "careers" with a chronic disease?**

Context: Nancy Waxler was a medical sociology professor in the Department of Psychiatry at Harvard Medical School and later in the School of Social Work at the University of British Columbia. She has done extensive fieldwork on heath care delivery in India, Sri Lanka, and Malaysia, and has co-edited a book on cross-cultural caring. This article is notable for at least two important contributions to the study of health-related stigma. The first is that no disease, even leprosy, is automatically stigmatized—stigma arises from a variety of social, cultural, and historical factors. The second contribution is a better understanding of how health providers may inadvertently stigmatize the patients they are trying to help.

Source: N. E. Waxler (1981). "Learning to Be a Leper: A Case Study in the Social Construction of Illness." In *Social Contexts in Health, Illness, and Patient Care*, E. G. Mishler (ed.). Cambridge: Cambridge University Press.

People who feel ill often first discuss their symptoms with family members or friends and then later go to a physician who questions, evaluates, and perhaps prescribes treatment. In the course of this exploration the "trouble" itself is transformed from vague and disconnected symptoms to a labeled condition, that is, an illness that others in the society understand to have a particular explanation and social meaning. Thus, social negotiations turn symptoms into social facts that may have significant consequences for the sick person.

... [W]e shall look at several aspects of this "social labeling" process.[1] In particular, we shall stress that the definition of a specific disease and associated social expectations often depend as much on the society and culture as on the biological characteristics of the disease itself. People diagnosed as having a particular disease learn "how" to have it by negotiating with friends and relations as well as with people in the treatment system; this process is affected by society's beliefs and expectations for that disease. Finally, society's definition of and expectations for a particular disease are sustained by social and organizational forces that may have little to do with the disease itself as a biological process.

Leprosy is a disease in which the process of social transformation is clear. Leprosy has a known cause, an effective treatment (but no cure), and thus a predictable outcome. From the perspective of the medical model, if the patient is treated quickly and regularly, the bacillus is controlled and the patient will recover; routine and scientifically neutral treatment is all that is required. But Westerners and many Asians—even those who have never seen a leprosy patient—may suspect that scientific treatment of the biological phenomenon misses the point. Often leprosy is feared; lepers are shunned; we say of a deviant community member, "He's like a leper." Doctors in Indian hospitals refuse to see cases; attendants in Ceylonese hospitals refuse to change dressings; wives begin divorce proceedings when husbands are diagnosed as lepers; patients leave their villages to become urban beggars. In some societies, then, routine treatment is neither given nor received. Responses to the disease by patient, family, and doctor are strongly influenced by social expectations and not simply by the biological characteristics of leprosy.

If the social transformation of the disease has such profound effects on those who experience it, then we must ask how a biological phenomenon has taken on such a definition. Is there some inherent quality of the disease—perhaps its communicability, threat to life, its disfiguring effects—that determines social expectations? Or are social definitions of particular diseases specific to certain societies and historical circumstances? Finally, why are certain social definitions perpetuated, for example, the terrible fear of leprosy, in the face of a known cause and effective treatment?

One way to consider these questions is to examine disease and illness cross-culturally. A cross-cultural analysis of leprosy controls for the nature of the disease but varies societal and historical factors, giving us an opportunity to ask whether the stigma of leprosy is universal (thus perhaps associated with biological phenomena) or whether social definitions differ from society to society. . . . [W]e shall document the truth of the second alternative, that there is considerable variation in the social and moral definition of leprosy across cultures, and speculate that this variation may be linked to specific historical events.

We shall also ask how patients respond when caught up in their own society's definition of the disease, and we shall show that the career of the diseased person reflects society's expectations. American lepers, though stigmatized, tend to respond aggressively, "taking on" the disease and the society; Ethiopian and Indian lepers stigmatize themselves and withdraw, complying with society's definition even before others recognize the disease.

Finally, we shall question how and why particular moral definitions of disease continue unchanged. Why are the stigma and fear of leprosy still prevalent in many countries when an effective treatment is readily available? In this regard we shall examine the organizational and social context in which care is offered and shall show that the medical organizations that treat leprosy may have had an important although inadvertent part in perpetuating the stigma of the disease.

Leprosy is an exotic disease, one that most of us have never seen. We examine it here for the same reasons that many anthropologists examine exotic cultures, to reflect on common phenomena. Studies of diseases such as leprosy that have clear and strong moral definitions in some societies provide insights into the moral component of all diseases. We can expect, then, that similar analytic principles might be useful in understand our own society's definitions of tuberculosis, heart disease, schizophrenia, and cancer.

SOME MEDICAL FACTS ABOUT LEPROSY

Leprosy has been known for thousands of years as a chronic and communicable disease affecting the skin, eyes, internal organs, peripheral nerves, and mucous membranes. Not until 1873, however, did Hansen report the discovery of *Mycobacterium leprae*, now thought to be a causal factor in the disease, and only recently has an agent, the nine-banded armadillo, been discovered in which the bacteria can be cultivated experimentally. Pending effective cultivation and experimental tests, the exact relationship between the bacterium and the disease is not clear, although researchers assume that the bacterium plays a part in the disease.

Leprosy is assumed to be only mildly communicable, even though the mode of transmission is not entirely understood. It is usually suggested that long-term skin or respiratory contact of ten or fifteen years' duration is required for transmission. Alternatively, however, a long incubation period is also known. American soldiers, who presumably were infected abroad during World War II, became symptomatic 2.9 years later (for tuberculoid leprosy) and 9.3 years later (for lepromatous leprosy).[2] Further, some immunity factor also is hypothesized.

The common stereotype of the disease, in novels, films, even in fund-raising literature, is of a person whose fingers have fallen off, without a nose, with terrible ulcers on the skin. In fact, the most common symptoms of leprosy, especially in the early stages, are mild and unremarkable. Anesthetic skin (causing secondary problems such as accidental burns), raised patches resembling eczema, skin ulcers that do not heal, for example, are usual; the unremarkability of the symptoms often contribute to late treatment. Only after many years without treatment do leprosy patients experience severe malformation and dysfunction of the kind that might be readily recognized by the layperson.

Currently the most common treatment is sulfone drugs administered over a long period. In Sri Lanka, for example, leprosy patients are expected to continue treatment for a minimum of five years following diagnosis. No one terms these drugs a "cure," and presumably no cure will be known until the causal factors are understood more clearly. These drugs are known to arrest the growth of the bacteria, however, and to cause a drop in the bacteria count in most but not all patients; after three months the disease is usually no longer communicable. For patients whose disease has progressed to the stage of physical malformation, surgery is also used.

The World Health Organization[3] estimates the worldwide prevalence of leprosy to be about 10 million cases or 0.8 per thousand. Ninety-four percent of these cases are in tropical Africa and Asia. Of the total number of estimated cases, only one-third are registered with a health agency and only one-fifth are being treated. Although Westerners usually think of leprosy as a problem "over there," an average of 100 new cases of leprosy was reported each year in the United States during the twenty-year period following World War II; of these, approximately one-half were foreign-born residents.[4] In the Commonwealth of Massachusetts, an average of one case of leprosy per year has been reported since 1970.

If we construct a picture of the "typical" leprosy patient from the medical facts, then, we see a man or woman whose symptoms are mild enough to be unrecognizable to the layperson, who sometime in the past may have lived or worked closely with a leper. During the time the disease was harbored it is relatively unlikely that it was passed along to others. If the disease is diagnosed early and treated regularly with the appropriate drugs, the patient's symptoms will disappear and the disease will be arrested if not cured, leaving no visible signs.

This should be the "medical career" of the typical leprosy patient today. Even in many African and Asian countries, treatment is available and known to ordinary villagers, and thus it is quite possible for a leprosy patient to receive early outpatient treatment, exhibit few visible symptoms, and carry on ordinary social activities. Why is it possible, then, for lepers in Nigeria to follow this career and for Indian lepers, on the other hand, to experience profound changes in their whole life, to lose their occupations, their wives, their children, their very identities? That is, how and why does the moral definition of the disease vary across cultures?

IS LEPROSY UNIVERSALLY STIGMATIZED?

It is easy for Westerners to assume that leprosy is stigmatized in all societies. . . . This assumption has been made without question by a number of authors who have then offered a functional hypothesis about stigma. These authors suggest that because leprosy is universally stigmatized, stigma must function as a sort of social protection device. That is, the moral definition of leprosy was developed to explain and justify society's need to isolate lepers from the majority group that the communicable disease threatened. The assumption, then, is that the disease is indeed inherently life-threatening, that society must protect itself from such a disease by isolating those who are afflicted, and that the moral ideology regarding leprosy is society's justification for its own self-protection.

But does the moral definition of the disease come from the quality of the disease itself or from the social and historical conditions in which the disease exists?

One way of answering this question is to investigate the extent to which the stigma of leprosy differs across societies. If we assume that the basic biological characteristics of leprosy are much the same everywhere in the world and we find that social and moral definitions are not, then we must conclude that these social definitions cannot be explained simply in terms of the biological nature of the disease itself. Reflecting on this hypothesis, we shall look at the social definitions of leprosy in India, Sri Lanka, and Nigeria.

The Indian definition of leprosy can be quickly understood by reference to one set of facts. Of 100 people with leprosy being treated in the city of Lucknow, 53 percent had been born and raised in rural villages; after their leprosy was discovered, all but 18 percent of this group had migrated to the city, away from home and family; 66 percent of these migrants never returned to visit their homes; many became beggars.[5] As Kapoor reports, "The attitude of the society towards these unfortunate people is so cruel and cynical that the victim of the disease feels isolated, despised and virtually excommunicated."[6] Such rejection of people with leprosy is also apparent in Indian leprosy hospitals themselves, where it has been reported that doctors in charge sometimes refuse to touch the patient's body when treatment or diagnosis is required.[7]

These informal norms were formalized in Indian law. Before the 1950s in India, all pauper lepers were segregated regardless of the level of infectiousness. Lepers were excluded from all inheritance in the joint family, were barred from traveling in trains with nonlepers, were not eligible for insurance and were not allowed to serve in the military. In the 1950s the laws were changed to allow normal inheritance of property by leprosy patients but at the same time to provide for judicial separation and divorce when leprosy appeared in a married man or woman. A proposal has also been made for compulsory sterilization of all infectious male patients.[8]

From all reports, then, lepers are often physically and socially rejected in Indian society; some modern laws perpetuate these norms. There is great fear of contagion (an Indian friend advised, "If you talk to a leper, put your handkerchief in front of your nose and mouth"), and repulsion at the sight or even thought of a leper. Those who discover that they have the disease often leave or are pushed out of their homes, to migrate to the cities to the "normal" role of a beggar.

...

But if we look at Sri Lanka (formerly Ceylon), we see a different picture. Here, again, the general population fears leprosy, believes it to be extremely contagious, and to result in hideous deformities; few have seen a leper, however, even in a population where best estimates indicate that the prevalence is 0.37 per thousand.[9] One might expect that the Sri Lankan leper's life experience would be similar to the Indian's, including rejection and mobility. Our interviews of lepers receiving outpatient treatment indicate that this is not so.[10] Instead, we found that leprosy patients, after diagnosis, remain in their own homes and carry on the same occupation that they had before the disease appeared. The schoolteacher continues teaching; the housewife continues cooking and caring for children; only one man, a baker, left his job, he reported, because the physical symptoms prevented him from doing his work.

Families of patients remain intact as well. Those who were married before diagnosis remained married; several more were married after the disease appeared.

...

Thus, there is little of the overt rejection reported in India. Yet life is not entirely unchanged for Sri Lankan lepers. Most patients, in fact, withdraw from society to some extent; they stigmatize themselves. When asked what advice they would give to other patients, our leprosy patients said, "Do not move around the village," "Do not visit others' homes unless it is absolutely necessary." They apply similar advice within their own families (and usually follow this advice), saying, "Use separate eating utensils and sleep separately." And there is general but not unanimous agreement that it is better *not* to tell nonfamily members about the illness; "Others will be afraid," "Others might stop visiting, even stop working with us." Leprosy patients, then, are fully aware of the stigma of the disease; their response is to avoid possible rejection by mild withdrawal and secrecy.

Yet often the secret of leprosy cannot be kept forever. When villagers discover that someone they know has leprosy, their first response is fear and rejection; but that often disappears over the years and relationships return to normal. One patient reported that when the villagers found out about his illness, "They went to the Montessori school my son was attending and asked the teachers to separate him from the others. Then the children began to harass my son. So I wrote a letter to the rural development society telling them they could call any doctor and give me an examination. They didn't do that but the harassment of my son stopped after that. I know the doctors would not say I had leprosy because the treatment is kept secret and they wouldn't tell what it was." For this man stigmatization early in the course of his illness also meant that villagers stopped using his well for bathing. "But now (seven years later) they use the well again and relations are back to normal."

Although the general population in Sri Lanka seems to favor rejection and isolation of lepers, the actual experience of many of these patients is quite different. Families accept the patient, marriages continue, and, over the years, neighbors who might have been afraid at first resume normal relations. Patients themselves sometimes withdraw into their families and avoid unnecessary nonfamily contact. This is not true, naturally, for all those with leprosy, but the general pattern, relative to the Indian one, is of acceptance or at least tolerance.

Nigeria provides an even more benign example.[11] Among the Hausa of Northern Nigeria, leprosy is highly prevalent, as it is in India. In this peasant agricultural, largely Muslim, society, indigenous beliefs about the cause of leprosy include gluttony, swearing falsely by the Koran, [and] washing in the water a leprosy patient has used. Treatments may consist of burning and scraping the skin, purges, and potions. Although leprosy is common, modern methods and theories not understood, and traditional treatments probably ineffective, no one is afraid. "The Hausa, in contrast to the West, exhibit little fear or disgust concerning leprosy. They do not seem to regard it with any special apprehension; it is not necessarily more unusual than any other of the great range of diseases that assail them."[12] Lepers continue to reside with their families, living a normal life until the very advanced stages of the disease. "At this point there seems to be a distinct change in vocation with many of the victims becoming beggars,"[13] but begging itself is an accepted, nonstigmatized role among Muslims.

. . .

Variation in the degree to which leprosy is stigmatized is apparent across Africa, with reports from Ethiopia[14] that resemble the experiences of Indian lepers (divorce, migration, begging), and mild rejection or none at all in Nigeria and Tanzania.[15]

How can we account for differences in the moral definition of leprosy that are apparent in different cultures? Perhaps the incidence of the disease, variations in subtypes, patterns of immunity, or effectiveness of treatment contribute to a society's perceptions. But these may play a minor role in comparison with the culture norms and historical circumstances in which the disease is found. Lepers in India may easily be rejected because a clear and elaborate hierarchical caste structure, justified by the ideology of impurity and sin, is available into which a threatening person may be placed. Caste beliefs and caste practices (not eating with, not touching, not sitting with) serve very well to handle society's fear of the leper. It is easy, then, for normal people in Indian society to equate leprosy with punishment of sins and to treat lepers as outcastes. The cultural background of Sri Lanka is quite similar to that of India, but with two crucial differences. The caste structure is less hierarchical (more than half of the population belongs to the high cultivators' caste), and the majority of the population is Buddhist, not Hindu. The Sinhalese experience with low-caste, and particularly outcaste groups, is relatively small; traditional caste obligations of family to family have generally disappeared, and the concern with who is who and how to behave in the company of other castes is narrowing. Further, Buddhism's stress on tolerance of differences and on compassion for others contrasts with Hindu values. These cultural and structural differences, then, may help explain why the general population in Sri Lanka fears and wants to reject lepers but the family and neighbors of leprosy patients actually accept them with little permanent stigma.

By examining leprosy in India, Sri Lanka, and Africa we have shown that lepers are not universally stigmatized. Thus it is unlikely that the social definition of leprosy arises entirely from biological qualities of the disease itself, that is, from its degree of contagion or visible symptoms. Instead, stigma may be linked to particular historical and cultural conditions, specific to each society.

HOW DOES THE MORAL DEFINITION OF LEPROSY DEVELOP?

How does a disease come to be feared and stigmatized in some cultures, yet remain an unremarkable fact of life in others? This is obviously a complicated question to which there can be no single answer. We might, however, find some answers in historical conditions or in the cultural and social matrix in which the disease is embedded. Many explanations are buried in the past; in India the extreme stigma of leprosy is certainly not new. Nineteenth-century Hawaii, however, provides one well-documented case in which the moral definition of leprosy is related to specific historical, economic, and social circumstances.[16]

In the 1840s in Hawaii, and elsewhere in the West, leprosy had almost disappeared, and when it did occur was considered to be a hereditary household disease. It was of minor importance, not stigmatized, a disease that most people did not encounter. Soon after mid-century, however, Hawaii's economic and social situation began to change, reflecting the worldwide movement of people at the height of colonialism. Europeans moved out to the colonies; Americans traveled for purposes of trade. Chinese began to move the other way, to Hawaii to work on the plantations and to the American West during the gold rush. In 1851 the first group of 180 Chinese immigrants arrived in Hawaii, and by the 1860s the movement of Chinese to Hawaii had become a flood.

The Hawaiians believed that the Chinese had brought leprosy. In the 1850s Hawaiian authorities noted an increase in leprosy, but newspaper reference to leprosy "was purposely omitted . . . for fear of injuring . . . commercial development."[17] By 1862 it could not be ignored and was publicly described as a major outbreak of the disease. This raised several questions in the minds of Hawaiians, and in the minds of health officials around the world. If Hawaii had suddenly experienced a serious increase in leprosy, could one still cling to the idea that leprosy was hereditary? And if it were not hereditary, who carried the disease?

In 1865 Hawaii's official response to the outbreak of leprosy was quarantine of lepers, implying a belief in contagion. This was confirmed in 1874 by Hansen's discovery of the bacillus, *Mycobacterium leprae.* Within one or two decades, at a time of vastly increasing population movements, world opinion shifted from belief in inheritance to belief in contagion.

The Chinese who were believed to have brought leprosy to Hawaii and the western United States were "industrious, painstaking, persevering and frugal—qualities which in Caucasian Protestants undoubtedly would have been considered virtues."[18] Yet they were also viewed by white people, in that age of social Darwinism, as natural cultural inferiors. Further, they provided cheap labor, and their industriousness perhaps threatened poor Westerners who wanted work. Thus, "while there were many demographic–environmental factors at work other than the coincidence of Chinese immigration with the leprosy outbreak in Hawaii that might have triggered the epidemic, the Chinese, nevertheless, almost immediately came to bear the full brunt of responsibility, a stigmatization of them that soon reached monstrous proportions."[19]

. . .

The Chinese were blamed, stigmatized, and excluded. Yet if we look more carefully at Hawaiian Board of Health records, it is not at all clear that the Chinese actually brought leprosy. Writing in 1886, the then superintendent of the Molokai Leprosy Hospital inquired about early cases to discover that leprosy was recognized by missionaries in 1823 and by a physician familiar with the disease in 1840, a decade or more before the great influx of Chinese laborers.[20] Health data support the conclusion that the Chinese were not an important source of leprosy. In the period 1866–85, the Molokai Hospital admitted 3,076 patients, 2,997 of whom were native Hawaiians, 22 Chinese, and the remainder Europeans, Americans, and Africans.[21]. . .

In analyzing this phenomenon a hundred years later, we might conclude that the Chinese became convenient scapegoats for Western society. Whether they actually brought leprosy—and it is not clear that they did—the presence of the disease in Hawaii provided a rationale for rejection that in fact had other basic causes. First was the potential or real economic threat that native Western workers may have felt from Chinese laborers. If Chinese could be believed to have leprosy, that fact made a convenient excuse for excluding economic competitors. Second was the nineteenth-century belief in the inherent inferiority of nonwhite people. If the Chinese could be believed to have a threatening contagious disease, so much the better because that would confirm the Westerner's sense of superiority.

If the Chinese were stigmatized ostensibly because they brought leprosy, then the association could also work the other way; leprosy became stigmatized because it was common among the Chinese. This phenomenon may have occurred in the Western world, and particularly in Hawaii. The result, by the end of the nineteenth century, was the transformation of a relatively unknown disease into a socially and morally threatening phenomenon. In this case the moral definition of the disease came from and was reinforced by the moral and social definition of those believed to carry it.

The association between particular historical events and the appearance of leprosy in Hawaii may explain why leprosy became a stigmatized disease there. In other cultures quite different circumstances may influence the moral definition of the disease. We can look again at Africa for evidence of another definitional process, the introduction of stigma by Western medicine.

In northern Tanzania, . . . there was traditionally little stigma attached to leprosy; patients lived with, ate with, slept with their families. Leprosy was an unremarkable disease. But in 1966 the Geita Leprosy Scheme was inaugurated, focusing not only on case finding and treatment but also on public education. Talks were given to school children in grades 5, 6, and 7 once every two years; key members of the community were also reached, although the general public was not directly educated about the disease. Information on cause, symptoms, mode of transmission, treatment, and social problems was included in each additional effort; thus Western medical notions about leprosy were introduced into the traditional system, largely through the children.

A survey conducted five years later showed how effective this educational effort had been. In response to almost all information questions about the disease, "The majority of the school children expressed the modern view of leprosy as being caused by certain bacteria and by physical contact with a patient, whereas the adult population and the leaders associated leprosy more frequently with such factors as heredity, witchcraft. . . ."[22] Whereas the educational program "stressed that there is no need to isolate the patient provided certain basic rules of hygiene are maintained, and that there is no reason to discontinue marriage to a leprosy patient, "[23] there was a surprising finding. School children, targets of this education, opposed the idea of leprosy patients sharing food and sleeping space with family members, and objected to leprosy patients marrying. "Another illustrative example of attitudes derived from health education is that of the sellers at the Sengerema market who, after a health education session by the Geita Leprosy Scheme some years ago, for the first time in Sengerema's history, urged their colleagues suffering from leprosy not to enter the market again."[24] Thus, together with scientific medicine's facts about causation and treatment, other attitudes had inadvertently been added to the society; the new idea of infection had presumably led Tanzanians to recommend avoidance and even rejection of people with leprosy.

In Tanzania, we see what could be the beginning of a new moral definition of leprosy, introduced without intent by public health educators. A somewhat similar phenomenon seems to have occurred in Nigeria[25] and elsewhere[26] when Western modes of treatment—isolation in leper colonies—were introduced by Christian missionaries. In neither instance is there evidence that the general public's attitude toward leprosy underwent a radical shift toward stigmatization. Yet what we see in this [20th] century in Tanzania and Nigeria may appear, in the next century, in a more institutionalized form.

The cases of Hawaii and Africa provided examples of two different processes through which an ordinary disease may take on a particular social and moral definition. In Hawaii it appears that the status of those believed to carry the disease—the inferior yet economically threatening Chinese coolies—may have been transferred to the disease itself. In Africa a new moral definition may have been inadvertently suggested by scientific medicine's public health educators. Thus, depending on specific historical/economic/cultural/medical "accidents," leprosy, and by implication perhaps all diseases, are transformed into illnesses having culture-specific social and moral definitions.

LEARNING TO BE A LEPER

A society's expectations for lepers, its beliefs about them, have a significant influence on their experiences as sick people. If we examine what a particular patient does when he discovers he has leprosy, we find that his response to leprosy is consistent with society's expectations for lepers. In fact, he learns to be a leper, the kind of leper his family and neighbors, even his doctors, expect him to be.

Ethiopia provides one example of the leprosy patient's confirmation of his society's beliefs about his disease. Leprosy there is feared and stigmatized. "People entering the bus which links the area around the leprosy hospital to the center of town will cover their nose and mouth. When there is an important visitor to the hospital . . . the patients may be confined to their wards."[27]

Those who discover that they have leprosy respond to this social definition in the way we might expect. Often they stigmatize themselves. In a sample of 100 leprosy patients interviewed in the leprosy outpatient clinic in Addis Ababa, Ethiopia, a fairly common patient career was apparent. One-fifth of the patients had been rejected by their families or had voluntarily left their homes. Half of the lepers continued to attend church, "although this does not mean that they actually entered the building. Seventeen refrained from going, mainly out of fear of being rejected."[28] Of those who remained married, one-third stopped having sexual relationships. But many marriages did not continue. One-half of all lepers who were married at the outbreak of the disease were later divorced; of these divorces, one-half were actually initiated by the patient. (This divorce rate is much higher than that of the general population.) Finally, one-fifth had migrated to the city to become beggars.

. . .

The response of Ethiopian lepers to their predicament is consistent with the fatalism of the Ethiopian peasant. Many American lepers, on the other hand, take a role that is almost a caricature of American values: They "fight back."

Leprosy patients treated at the U.S. Public Health Service Hospital at Carville, Louisiana, begin with the assumption that the public fears and stigmatizes lepers. Some report experiences with families or communities that confirm the existence of fear and even rejection. And some leprosy patients accept the public definition of the disease by withdrawing to the haven of the Carville hospital, where they are allowed to live the remainder of their lives. Yet those who make this choice do not willingly accept the beliefs about leprosy that are associated with stigma, beliefs about extreme contagion, deformity, and incurability.

Instead, patients who voluntarily withdraw from society support another segment of the patient population, those whom Gussow and Tracy call "career patients."[29] It is these career patients who take on a peculiarly "American" role, one that is undoubtedly respected by the public. They become professional educators, acting as representatives of all lepers in an attempt to change the public's view of the disease. They give talks at Rotary clubs, organize seminars, speak about leprosy on the radio, conduct tours of the leprosy hospital, publish *The Star.* The content of their educational attempts is a new set of beliefs about leprosy, beliefs that are designed to replace the "old" ideas that justified stigma.

. . .

The assumption behind this new ideology, promoted by the career patients, is that American society's fear of leprosy will wither away as the public learns the "truth" about the disease. No longer will lepers feel wrongly labeled and no longer will they be stigmatized.

In a sense, these career patients are America's version of the Ethiopian beggar. Their response to leprosy is consistent with American values on activism, self-sufficiency, and change; when they see a problem, especially a problem for themselves, they try to solve it. They do not respond like the Ethiopian fatalists. At the same time, however, from the point of view of the public, they are not "normal." They are still lepers, whose role as educators depends on existence of the disease itself. "At the present time this status [as career patient] appears to be the only legitimate one the leprosy patient has available to him for life in open society."[30]

Lepers in the United States learn to be the kind of lepers Americans expect. To confirm the lay American's fears of leprosy, they withdraw, avoid, protect themselves, and protect others. But they do these things reluctantly and temporarily, until their active educational efforts succeed in changing public opinion. In the meantime, those who go openly into the outside world go labeled as "leper," fulfilling our expectations that lepers are indeed "different."

There is a world of difference between the Ethiopian leper begging in front of the train station and the American leper showing a film to the Lions' club. But underlying that difference is a more basic similarity: Lepers learn how to be lepers from the beliefs and expectations their society has for them. In every society the sick person is socialized to take a role the society expects.

HOW IS THE MORAL DEFINITION OF LEPROSY PERPETUATED?

Even though leprosy is sometimes feared and lepers stigmatized, and even though leprosy patients often willingly take on the deviant role that society expects, why do such moral definitions continue far beyond the time when effective treatment is readily available? Wouldn't one expect that as the disease becomes easily treatable the fear and threat would subside?

To examine this question we must return to the situation at the end of the nineteenth century, when although a pandemic of leprosy was feared by European and American observers, it did not occur. The public at the time believed leprosy to be highly contagious, but very few people actually contracted the disease. The panic died down. Leprosy was limited to tropical people, usually the poor, and did not become a threat to colonial settlers. Although an official statement was made in 1909 that leprosy was incurable,[31] by the 1920s a moderately successful treatment had been instituted, and by the 1940s a more effective one. We must ask why fear of leprosy and rejection of lepers continued in many societies when, in reality, most people in those societies had discovered that leprosy was relatively nonthreatening. Here, again, we shall look at social and organizational contexts in which the disease exists rather than at the biological qualities of the disease itself.

In the second half of the nineteenth century, when it was believed that leprosy was not only highly contagious but life-threatening, the churches acted. Father Damien established the leper hospital at Molokai, Hawaii, in 1860 and died there, from leprosy, in 1889. The Mission to Lepers was established in Great Britain in 1874. The Louisiana Home for the Lepers, now the U.S. Public Health Service Hospital at Carville, was founded by the Catholic church in 1894. During this time, of course, numerous missionaries were sent out, to Africa, India, Oceania, to treat lepers. Not until the 1920s did nonreligious organizations enter the field, and they still remain of minor importance compared with the worldwide involvement of missionaries. Even today the nursing staff at the U.S. Public Health Service Hospital at Carville is provided by the Sisters of Charity of St. Vincent de Paul.[32] Also today the American Leprosy Missions and the Leprosy Mission (of Great Britain), foundations that finance treatment centers all over the world, integrate Christian ideology with treatment goals. "The main object of the Mission is to minister in the name of Jesus Christ to the physical, mental and spiritual needs of sufferers from leprosy, to assist in their rehabilitation, and to work toward the eradication of leprosy."[33]

Thus certain groups, church groups in this case, came to "own" the disease. They set up hospitals, trained staff, searched for patients, collected and disseminated information, and spoke and acted "for" the lepers. Because leprosy was in many places greatly feared, those who did this work took on an aura of saintliness. . . .

We have introduced two important facts about leprosy since 1920. First, private church-related organizations became the main providers of treatment to leprosy patients, collecting funds mainly from the industrial West and funneling money to nonindustrial tropical countries. Second, in many (but not all) of these nonindustrial countries, leprosy was strongly stigmatized. One might expect that, once an effective treatment became known and once the missionary organizations began to provide this treatment, the stigmatization of leprosy would decline. Changes in definition of the disease might be slow, might take decades, but with effective and available treatment fear and thus stigma would disappear, even in India and Ethiopia.

Yet they have not disappeared. In fact we suspect that the organizations most committed to treating and curing may have, inadvertently, had a part in perpetuating the stigma of leprosy, through a complex and circular relation between the expectations that some societies have for people with leprosy and the organizational constraints and requirements for the leprosy organizations' own survival.

"Normals" in the community prefer to have deviant people of many sorts removed from view and cared for by others. . . .

Leprosy organizations have taken the responsibility for the care of lepers from "normals" and have in many societies done just what the community wants, removed the leper from view. Inpatient facilities are often completely contained villages providing not only treatment but also employment, education, and recreation. There is often no need for a leprosy patient to leave this "asylum" and, in fact, it is sometimes physically difficult to do so because leprosy hospitals are often found on islands (e.g., in Sri Lanka and the Philippines) or in the remote countryside. In fact, organizations justify the isolation of leprosy patients by reference to the community's stigmatization of lepers. "Some are rejected by their homes and families . . . for some there is, humanly speaking, no hope; their disabilities mean that they will be dependent for the rest of their lives. The Mission cares for such as these also."[34] Removal of lepers from the "normal" community serves to confirm the idea of stigma. People in Sri Lanka may say, "If lepers must be sent to a remote island for treatment then there must be something very terrible about them and their disease." Stigma is thus confirmed.

Leprosy organizations have not only removed threatening people from community view, they have also demanded little change on the part of "normals" by focusing their work largely on treatment and rehabilitation rather than on prevention or on public education to reduce stigma. . . .

Thus, leprosy organizations, by building permanent inpatient hospitals and stressing treatment of stigmatized patients rather than change in the public's view of the disease, have acted "for" the normal community. In many cases leprosy patients, even in the United States, remain permanently under organizational control and do not return to their communities.[35] We expect that so long as these organizations continue to remove leprosy patients, they will be supported by the community. . . .

Leprosy organizations, like many medical foundations, are dependent on public donation of funds. As Scott has suggested, funds may be contributed more generously if such organizations confirm popular beliefs by medical and social science. Spokespersons for these foundations have suggested as much, in discussions of the change from "leprosy" to "Hansen's disease," when they say: "There is a case for retaining the substance of current terminology related to *leprosy* particularly because of its value to fund-raising." They explain that appeals for "overseas" charity, for Asian and African patients, must compete with 77,000 charities at home and "the evocation of a reaction to the word *leprosy* is an essential factor."[36] Thus, leprosy foundations may, to sustain themselves, find it necessary to allude to the idea of threat and to support the community in its willingness to stigmatize.

. . .

Westerners, vaguely threatened by a terrible disease, and certainly somewhat guilty about but very willing to turn the care of such patients over to others, can do only one thing: give donations. As the American Leprosy *Bulletin* suggests, the fact that immunity to standard drugs is occurring more frequently ". . . is nothing short of terrifying, simply because, to date, there is absolutely no other drug which is readily available, as free of negative side effects, as inexpensive and as effective as DDS has been up until now. . . . The quality of care must be raised until a high proportion of cases are found early and treated regularly. Five dollars per year is not enough. Thirty dollars is a more reasonable figure, but in many areas adequate care cannot be given for less than fifty to sixty dollars per patient per year."[37] All one needs to do, then, to be relieved of the burden of dealing with stigmatized people, is to give money, in this case, to keep the disease out of sight in the poor tropical countries.

Much of what is stated in these messages is, according to current scientific knowledge about leprosy, factually wrong. Leprosy is not a terrible or life-threatening disease, nor a real threat to Westerners. Service to lepers, like all service, requires devotion, but the degree of risk is not great. In fact, in a growing number of countries service to lepers is provided by government health service employees in the same way as it is for other diseases. It is apparently true that the immunity of some bacilli has become a problem that must be handled by greater expenditure and / or better planning based on epidemiological knowledge.[38]

Why do foundations dealing with leprosy arouse fears and suggest stigma—particularly in the face of scientific and experiential knowledge that leprosy is not highly contagious and can be treated effectively on an outpatient basis while the patient carries on normal activities? We have suggested that the economic and social commitments of the organizations, justified by an ideology about "important work that remains undone," requires continued financial and other support. To sustain financial support these organizations have learned that they survive only if they confirm society's preference for removal of deviant people from view. Thus, the organizations whose goals are "to assist in their [leprosy patients'] rehabilitation and to work toward the eradication of leprosy" at the same time perpetuate, through their actions (building inpatient hospitals and providing long-term care) and words (public education programs and fund-raising brochures) the community's ideas of stigma. It is not insignificant that the 1978 brochure of the Leprosy Mission is entitled *Set Apart*.

CONCLUSION

We began with a bacillus, mildly communicable, treatable, not life-threatening nor even deforming if treated early. Now we see that the bacillus itself is only a minor actor in the drama of leprosy. Instead, surrounding the disease in many societies is a set of social beliefs and expectations that profoundly affect the patient's experience and the doctor's work.

First we showed that the stigma of leprosy is not universal. In many societies, even where leprosy is common, leprosy is believed to be just another of the debilitating illnesses that many families must tolerate. Patients remain at home and marriages continue. In other societies, lepers are quickly divorced, pushed out of their homes, to end up as beggars. This cross-cultural variation in the stigma of leprosy led us to conclude that the source of a particular response is in the social and cultural matrix in which the disease exists.

In many societies beliefs about leprosy developed and stabilized long before written records were kept. In nineteenth-century Hawaii, however, we saw the economic and social threat of the Chinese immigrants become transformed into the social threat of the disease they were believed to carry. In Africa, we pointed to the very beginning of what could be a new, and stigmatized, notion of leprosy inadvertently introduced by public health educators. Thus, the moral definition of leprosy may arise from particular historical / social / medical circumstances, different in each society.

Second, we showed that the ideology surrounding leprosy provides a map for the leper. Moral definitions tell the leper how to "have" the illness. We contrasted Ethiopian and American experiences, profoundly different, but each exemplifying the effect of society's expectations on the leper's career.

Finally, once the moral definition becomes established, it is often perpetuated for reasons having very little to do with the disease itself. In the case of leprosy, even though effective treatment is available in the tropical countries where the disease is prevalent, and even though the Christian missionary organizations that are often the main providers of treatment certainly do not intend to stigmatize, the stigma of leprosy continues. We have suggested that this moral definition of leprosy is often perpetuated by the very organizations that treat the disease through a complex and circular relationship between the community's preference for removing deviant people and the leprosy organizations' needs for society's support in order to survive. Both the organizations' actions (removing leprosy patients from society) and their ideologies (in the form of public educational materials) sustain the idea that leprosy is horrible and threatening, requires treatment by "special" people, and is an enormous, often hidden, and unending problem. These actions and beliefs, though not based on medical facts, are consistent with the normal community's definitions of the disease and thus receive most sympathy from prospective donors. To continue their work, then, the organizations that "own" leprosy must sustain the stigma of leprosy.

We have examined leprosy because it provides a clear example of the social transformation of disease. In some societies leprosy is transformed into an illness that has serious implications for the social career of the sick person. Similar transformations might occur with other diseases. The effects may be milder and the social transformations less obvious, but if we examine the beliefs, practices, and experiences of patients who suffer from other disease, we should see similar processes.

. . .

The social definition of illness [also] has an obvious effect on doctors. For example, not only must they treat the leprosy bacillus, they must also recognize and deal with the culture's beliefs about the disease. In India and Sri Lanka they must find the hidden patients and convince those in treatment to return for more. In Hawaii and Louisiana doctors must care for and also justify the continued hospitalization of large proportions of leprosy patients with inactive diseases who do not want to go home.[39] The social and cultural context in which the disease exists must be seen as part of the disease process itself.

Our understanding of leprosy can move beyond this "conservative" analysis of the relationship between social factors and disease. It is not simply that doctors are waiting outside the society with neutral values, waiting to step in to treat and to take into account society's peculiar transformations of disease. Instead the medical institution is part of society itself, and thus is implicated in the social and moral definition of disease. We have seen that missionary doctors who went to Africa and India took with them a particular conception of leprosy that required isolation hospitals, and this new treatment method implied that it was right and good that lepers be taken from their homes and isolated from their families. New threats and fears—even the idea of stigma—were thus introduced. These threats and fears, predominant in the West, have been strengthened over the years by medical and missionary organizations whose basic needs are to survive.

NOTES

1. Schur, E. M. *Labeling Deviant Behavior: Its Sociological Implications.* New York: Harper & Row, 1971.
2. Feldman, R. A. "Leprosy surveillance in the USA: 1949–1970," *International Journal of Leprosy*, 1968, 37: 458–60.
3. World Health Organization Expert Committee on Leprosy. *World Health Organization Technical Report Services,* No. 459. Geneva: World Health Organization, 1970.
4. Feldman. "Leprosy surveillance in the USA."
5. Kapoor, J. N. "Lepers in the city of Lucknow," *Indian Journal of Social Work,* 1961, 22:239–46.
6. Ibid., p. 239.
7. Ryrie, G. A. "The psychology of leprosy," *Leprosy Review,* 1951, 22:1,13–24.
8. Kapoor, "Lepers in the city of Lucknow," p. 245.
9. Heffner, L. T "A study of Hansen's disease in Ceylon," *Southern Medical Journal,* 1969, 62:977–5.
10. Waxier, N. E. "The social career of lepers in Sri Lanka." Unpublished study, 1977. The fact that our sample of leprosy patients was obtained from the outpatient leprosy clinic means that we have no information on half of the group estimated to remain untreated. Our conclusions may be biased but in ways that we cannot determine.
11. Shiloh, A. "A case study of disease and culture in action: leprosy among the Hausa of northern Nigeria," *Human Organization,* 1965, 24:140–7.
12. Ibid., p. 143.
13. Ibid.
14. Giel, R. and van Luijk, J. N. "Leprosy in Ethiopian society," *International Journal of Leprosy,* 1970, 33:187–98.
15. Hertroijs, A. R. "A study of some factors affecting the attendance of patients in a leprosy control scheme," *International Journal of Leprosy,* 1974, 42:419–27; van Etten and Anten, "Evaluation of health education."
16. For some of the analysis presented, the author is indebted to Gussow, Z., and Tracy, G., "Stigma and the leprosy phenomenon: the social history of a disease in the nineteenth and twentieth centuries," *Bulletin of the History of Medicine,* 1970, 44:424–49; Gussow, Z., and Tracy, G. "The use of archival materials in the analysis and interpretation of field data: a case study in the institutionalization of the myth of leprosy as 'leper,'" *American Anthropologist,* 1971, 73:695–709.
17. Gussow and Tracy, "Stigma and the leprosy phenomenon," p. 433.
18. Ibid., p, 441.
19. Gussow and Tracy, "The use of archival materials," p. 706.
20. Mouritz, A. "Report of the Superintendent of the Molokai Leprosy Hospital," in *Appendix to the Report on Leprosy of the President of the Board of Health to the Legislative Assembly.* Honolulu, Hawaii, 1886.
21. Ibid.
22. van Etten and Anten, "Evaluation of health education," p. 405.
23. Ibid., p. 417.
24. Ibid., p. 408.
25. Shiloh, "A case study of disease and culture in action."
26. "There was . . . no stigma attached to the disease amongst the Australian Aboriginals until segregation became law and sufferers were taken from their families and isolated. It seems that the Aboriginal people have known and coped with the disease at least since the influx of immigrants from leprosy endemic areas in the middle of the last century—and had no fear of it." Editorial, *The Medical Journal of Australia,* 1977,2(11):345–7.
27. Giel and van Luijk. "Leprosy in Ethiopian society," p. 194.
28. Ibid., p. 190.
29. Gussow, Z., and Tracy, G. "Status, ideology, and adaptation to stigmatized illness; a study of leprosy," *Human Organization,* 1968, 27:316–25, p. 322. These authors assert that in the West the stigma of leprosy is a myth perpetuated by treatment agents. This "myth" is taken quite seriously by the patients themselves, whether it is actually true is not important for our analysis here.
30. Ibid., p. 324.
31. Gussow and Tracy, "The use of archival materials," p. 700.

32. Ibid., p. 703.
33. "Set apart." London: The Leprosy Mission, 1978.
34. "Set apart."
35. Bloombaun, M., and Gugelyk, T. "Voluntary confinement among lepers," *Journal of Health and Social Behavior,* 1970, 12:16–20.
36. Hansen: Research, Notes, 1975, 6(l–2):202.
37. American Leprosy Missions, *Bulletin,* Fall 1978.
38. Some have suggested that drug-resistance requires development of a new treatment strategy that will interrupt transmission in large populations of leprosy patients. One part of this strategy, ironically, may be the need to provide "facilities for the hospitalization of a larger number of patients than at present during the first few months of treatment. This will require building or remodeling of facilities . . ." Lechat, M. "Sulfone resistance and leprosy control," *International Journal of Leprosy,* 1978, 46:64–7.
39. Bloombaum and Gugelyk, "Voluntary confinement among lepers."

 19

Strategic Suffering: Illness Narratives as Social Empowerment among Mexican Cancer Patients

Linda M. Hunt

Medical anthropologists recognize that when people get sick, especially with serious illnesses, they try to understand why *this misfortune has happened to them. They develop a story—a narrative—that helps explain why they got sick and what is going to happen to them. The influential medical anthropologist Arthur Kleinman developed the* explanatory mode *to describe the cognitive processes by which people understand their illness. In his early research, he also demonstrated how patients create narratives about their illness experience (with the help of other people) and that these stories fulfill certain social and psychological functions. Illness narratives include very useful cultural information that can improve the communication and trust between the patient and the physician/healer. As this selection demonstrates, these illness narratives are also particularly valuable for anthropological analysis.*

The sick role *provides a person experiencing an illness with a set of privileges and responsibilities. The person is relieved of certain obligations (like going to school or work) but is also expected to get better. The cultural script of the sick role is modeled after infectious disease. When a person has a chronic disease (like diabetes), a long-lasting and potentially fatal disease (like cancer), or a disability, the situation is different. The illness narratives are different and relationships with other people change.*

In this selection, Linda Hunt describes the illness narratives of a man and a woman with cancer in Mexico. Cancer is a disease that is particularly laden with powerful symbolic meanings; in fact, cancer is regularly used as a metaphor (see Sontag 1978). The experience of reproductive cancers involves questions of gender identity and culturally prescribed social roles. This anthropological analysis also shows how illness narratives can be used as unconscious social strategies.

As you read this selection, ask yourself these questions:

- **The author begins this article by reminding us of the distinction between disease and illness. How is this relevant in the experience of cancer?**
- **How is cancer different from other diseases or illnesses?**
- **In these illness narratives, how might cultural beliefs about appropriate behavior influence the decision to seek medical attention?**
- **Can getting cancer make a person socially empowered? How might a diagnosis of cancer transform someone's life? Can you think of examples?**
- **Why does the author call the experiences of Isabella Martinez and Robert Juarez "strategic suffering"?**

Context: Linda Hunt teaches medical anthropology at Michigan State University. She is a faculty member in the Center for Ethics and Humanities in the Life Sciences, which is part of the medical school. She studied at Harvard University, with Arthur Kleinman, and has done research both in the United States and Mexico. Much of her work concerns Latino patients' experiences with the health care system; she pays particular attention to issues of chronic disease management for conditions like cancer and diabetes. This article appeared in a collection about narrative and the cultural construction of illness and healing.

Source: L. Hunt (2000) "Strategic Suffering: Illness Narratives as Social Empowerment among Mexican Cancer Patients." In Narrative and the Cultural Construction of Illness and Healing, C. Mattingly and C. Garro (eds.), pp. 88–107. Berkeley: University of California Press.

The disruption experienced by people living with chronic illnesses such as cancer is at once that of the "disease" itself (the physical disruptions it produces as an objective, biological entity) and that of the "illness"[1] (the experience of disruption of the expected, the taken-for-granted). Chronic illness thus may present the afflicted with permanent challenges to their identity: it does not permit one to go on living in an undisputed, familiar world (Good 1994; Garro 1994; Good and Good 1982). The core experience of serious chronic illness has often been characterized as an existential loss, a break in the usual rhythm of life (Cassell 1982; Erwin 1984; Kaufman 1988; Williams 1984; Williams and Wood 1986). Bury (1982) describes chronic illness as introducing "biographical disruption," a time in which the normal social structures and roles of reciprocity and support are disrupted. A critical dilemma that people encounter when struggling to face such permanent loss of normal roles is how to reconstruct a sense of continuity of self and role responsibilities, since in many ways performance of roles is what defines one's personhood (Bury 1982; Cassell 1982).

When viewed in these terms, the disruption introduced by chronic illness may appear in purely negative terms: something has been lost, and the loss is something to be coped with and endured. However, examination of people's long-term adaptations to chronic illness reveals that the initial phase of disruption is often followed by a period of reorganization and reconstruction of the self and one's place in the world. Becker (1997) has shown that people confronted by major disruptions to their lives, such as chronic illness, use narratives to restructure their sense of self and social location, telling stories that both articulate and mediate disruption. She argues that narrative thus holds a potent constructive capacity, through which people find the power to resist and restructure ideas of normalcy that do not fit with their experience, as they reconfigure their disrupted identity.

Because chronic illness can produce major disruptions to core components of identity, such as social roles and relationships, narratives concerning such illnesses hold the potential not only of articulating the disruptions experienced but also of reconfiguring one's very social identity. This is so because the narrative portrayal of events is in essence performative, and as such is capable of both expressing and enacting visions of reality. Brodwin (1994), in examining the rhetorical aspect of chronic pain representations, notes that illness can provide an idiom for communication that is capable of at once expressing a lack of sense of control and of generating a sense of mastery. This performative nature of narrative is especially compelling when considered in terms of the permanent disruptions to identity that chronic illness implies. The restructuring of self and social identity that occurs in response to chronic illness requires a long-lasting performance, a kind of pilgrimage into a sustainable construction of a changed self and roles (Frankenberg 1986).

Within the process of narrative reconstruction of the chronically ill self, the individual may enter into a period of self-reflection and reorientation: a moment where conventional structure is realigned with personal endeavor as well as social constraint (Monks and Frankenberg 1988). As patients move from the liminality of illness crisis back into a complex lifeworld, their illness narratives have a potential for affecting strategic changes in terms of the broad context of their lives. Some take this opportunity to redefine the self and social roles in ways that address broader personal and social conflicts and contradictions than those encountered in the illness itself. In naming the heroes and villains, dramatic conflicts and resolutions that compose the illness narrative, the teller may influence the ways the illness and, indeed, the self are conceived and understood.

An important function of illness narratives is to integrate illness into the larger context of life (Jackson 1989; Mattingly 1994, 1998; Mattingly and Garro 1994). Illness narratives are produced intersubjectively. In dialogue with those around them, patients produce stories about the causes and effects of their illness that connect it in direct ways with their evolving life story (Hunt 1994, 1998). Illness representations are thus constituted as a sum of patient presentations and audience interactions (Strauss and Corbin 1984). The narrative reconstruction of the chronically ill self is thus necessarily positioned within power relationships.

Becker (1997), in examining the process of narrative reorganization of the self and social life following disruptive events, found that such reconstructions often serve to create a sense of biographical continuity. However, in cases where the preexisting power relationships were dysfunctional, continuity may not be a desirable end. I wish to propose that in such cases, the telling of illness narratives may be taken up as an opportunity to reorder contentious elements of the social field, creating new meanings and relationships. Illness narratives may thus respond to the disruption of identity introduced by chronic illness by generating a strategically revised identity, creating a new place in the social world that resolves conflicts and difficulties rooted in the broad context of the teller's life. In examining the strategic implications of illness narratives, we open a window onto understanding the rhetorical processes (Brodwin 1994) by which chronic illness and its associated role disruptions are woven into ongoing negotiations over questions of power and powerlessness within patients' lives.

To explore these dynamics, this chapter presents an analysis of the illness narratives of two Mexican patients who have undergone surgical removal of part of their reproductive systems as a treatment for cancer. It will examine how their illness narratives transform the gender liminality resulting from the illness and surgery into revised social identities that address their long-standing difficulties with the ideal gender roles of their culture. An important aspect of these narratives is that while they legitimize nonconformity to prescribed gender roles, they do so without challenging the authority of the larger cultural concept of appropriate behavior for men and women in their society. It will be argued that, in these cases, use of illness narratives is neither manipulative nor revolutionary but instead reflects the practical outcome of people creatively constructing a revised identity when confronted with the permanent disruptions presented by living with chronic illness.

CHANGES IN SOCIAL IDENTITY AND ILLNESS NARRATIVES

In Mexico, as in much of the world, cancer has a powerful metaphoric dimension; it conjures images of an insidious invasion of the victim by a ruthless aggressor that slowly, but inevitably, destroys the person from within (Adonis 1978; American Cancer Society 1980; Antonovsky 1972; Balshem 1991, 1993; Brody 1988; Chavez et al. 1995; Dreifuss-Kattan 1990; Finkler 1991; Garro 1990; M. J. Good et al. 1990, 1992, 1994; Gordon 1990; Hunt 1992, 1993, 1994; Kagawa-Singer 1993; Mathews, Lannin, and Mitchell 1994; Panourgia 1990; Patterson 1987; Saillant 1990; Sontag 1977). Coming to terms with having such an illness necessarily presents a myriad of challenges to the everyday sense of self in the world.

Previous studies of cancer patients' changing identities have primarily considered the cognitive or psychological adjustments that individuals make to cope with their disease (Aaronson 1990; Bolund 1990; Dreifuss-Kattan 1990; Haes 1988; Lowitz and Casciato 1988; Weisman 1979). These studies commonly focus on the intrapsychic dimension of responding to the challenges of cancer. They examine the psychological "coping mechanisms" that patients may draw upon in learning to live with their illness. However, when considered within their larger social and cultural context, such "coping mechanisms," in addition to their psychological functions, are necessarily constrained by and responsive to the pressing problems of negotiating mutual rights and responsibilities between individuals, in terms appropriate to the local moral and cultural world (cf. Kleinman and Kleinman 1991). "Having cancer" requires mobilizing resources for treatment, eliciting assistance for caring for the patient, and renegotiating the privileges and obligations of the patient within familial and other social hierarchies. Shifts in personal identity in having cancer therefore emerge in the context of a larger social framework, subsuming questions of domination and subordination.

The disruptions in social identity introduced by cancer and its treatment not only present a challenge to existing social relations but also, in thrusting patients into a state of indeterminacy and ambiguity, provide an opportunity to negotiate new identities in what Rosaldo has called "the social space within which creativity can flourish" (Rosaldo 1993: 112; see also Gutmann 1996). Chronic patienthood, in its very liminality and marginality, implies a level of role flexibility that may contain a moment of potential empowerment (cf. Frankenberg 1986; Turner 1969; Van Gennep 1960). At these moments, illness narratives have the potential to constructively redefine one's place within the social world (cf. Mattingly 1994, 1998; Mattingly and Garro 1994), simultaneously articulating and configuring the disaster of having cancer in innovative and strategic ways. Individuals, in the process of producing illness narratives, thus move between multiple ways that the sick role could be constructed, achieving altered identities not passively but through selective action (Uzell 1974). The orientations to the illness and its treatment they thereby generate have relevance in the specific terms of their broader sets of interests, needs, and circumstances (cf. Bourdieu 1977; Sahlins 1976).

In analyzing the illness stories that Mexican cancer patients shared with me, I have found that often, in the course of rebuilding a workable image of themselves, the world, and their place in it, patients generate narratives that forge an identity around patienthood in ways that negotiate issues of social empowerment. Such illness narratives may result in a revised version of old roles that constitute a new and enhanced place for the patient within the social world.

THE RESEARCH PROJECT

The case material presented here is drawn from an ethnographic study of hospital-based cancer care in Santo Domingo,[2] a provincial capital in southern Mexico of about five hundred thousand people. The study included extensive interviews with forty-three cancer patients and their families, as well as observations in the oncology clinics of the three major hospitals in town.[3]

Two case examples will be presented in order to explore how illness narratives may be used to reconstruct the altered self in response to the serious existential challenges presented by cancer and its treatment, and how that reconstruction is related to the broader social field. It will be shown that, in generating a revised identity in the face of chronic illness, illness narratives embed ongoing negotiations over contentious elements in patients' social world such as struggles over legitimacy or victimization.

This argument is built on interpreting the stories that patients and their families told me in interviews, but it is extended to contexts beyond the interview situation. In so doing, it is presumed that these stories reflect the intersubjective nature of narrative, having been developed within the more generalized social dialogue of everyday life, wherein the disruptive aspects of chronic illness and its treatment are integrated into ongoing social life. This presumption is based on two sets of observations. First, the narratives themselves cite negotiations and resolutions that have taken place with others in the social lives of the patients. It therefore seems reasonable to assume that similar narrative constructions have been used in interactions with the people to whom they refer. Second, in many cases family members participated in the interview and often jointly produced the illness narrative related to me, indicating that such illness narratives both are publicly generated within the social sphere and represent a habitual rhetorical style.

The variety of conflicts and strategies expressed and configured in the narratives of the group studied were nearly as numerous as the patients. This discussion will therefore be limited to the circumstances of two specific cases. Still, it should be noted that almost all those interviewed had, over the course of many months and often years, constructed the chronic aspect of cancer patienthood in a way that had important implications for resolving contentious aspects of their lifeworld. It will be argued here that this reflects the embeddedness of the process of generating an illness story. In integrating chronic illness and its treatment into everyday life, the pressing issues encountered in everyday social interactions, and the conflicts and goals of those interactions are the material out of which the illness narratives are constructed. The narratives therefore necessarily have salience for addressing the issues most at stake for the person telling the story.

GENDER ROLES AND REPRODUCTIVE CANCERS

The two cases chosen for detailed examination here present an interesting set of contrasts. Both patients suffered from cancer of their reproductive systems, and both had been successfully treated some time earlier by surgical removal of the affected organs. The specific nature of these cancers and their obvious close relationship to disruptions of gender identity have opened parallel opportunities for these patients to reflect on and reformulate their respective gender roles. Preexisting conflicts which each experienced around the ideal roles of dutiful wife and devoted son, respectively, have become the focus of their narrative reconstructions of a larger, culturally normative narrative of appropriate gender roles. They each exhibit a strategic use of their illness stories in which they have found legitimacy for nonconformity to prescribed gender roles through narrative representations in ongoing negotiations over the impact of their illness and treatment.

Sexual Politics and Cervical Cancer

First, let us consider the case of Isabela Martinez, a sixty-eight-year old indigenous woman, the mother of thirteen children. She, like most women in this study, employed a rhetoric consistent with the cultural norm that the greatest achievements women can strive for lie in their devout fulfillment of their role as mother and wife. In Latin American culture, the ideal wife is often characterized as selfless, morally pure, and dedicated to children and husband.[4] This image includes an expectation that she be unfailingly receptive to her husband's sexual advances (Bartra 1987; Foster 1967; Lewis 1963; Rubel 1966; Shedlin and Hollerbach 1981). In her discussion of her illness with me, Isabela made it clear that she did indeed view sexual submission to her husband as a marital duty, but one that had been abused by him. In examining her illness narrative, we can see that she has reconstructed her postsurgical self in ways that both express and reformulate the difficulties she has suffered in this domain.

Isabela and her husband were both from poor campesino families, but they had established a successful business of buying and selling shoes. They lived in considerable comfort in a nice brick house near the center of town in a large indigenous village outside of Santo Domingo. What Isabela at first thought were symptoms related to the miscarriage of her fourteenth child she later discovered were caused by advanced cervical cancer. I spoke with her in her home, three years after she had a hysterectomy as treatment for the cancer. Her prognosis was very good, and she continued to go to the oncology clinic every six months for follow-up visits.

In the course of discussing her illness with me, Isabela made frequent references to the number and frequency of her pregnancies. Her reproductive history was central in her story of the etiology of her illness. The timing and number of her children were things over which she clearly felt she had had no control. Interestingly, she began her illness narrative with reference to her husband's sexual expectations of her. When asked how she had become ill, she said:

> I married when I was seventeen years old, and when I was eighteen I had my first child. And right away, in one year I turned around and had another. And right away again, the next year, and again, another child. . . . That was because when each child was just eight days old my husband wanted to have relations with me. On the eighth day after the birth, my husband would want to have relations with me. Like that, like that, like that. That is how it was. That's why every year, every year, every year, I had a child, that's why there are thirteen.

Isabela went on to describe her current experience of her illness, indicating that she had constructed her illness in a way that had turned the suffering associated with the illness into a resource for dealing with the long-term conflicts she had experienced regarding her wifely role obligations. She told me:

> [Since the hysterectomy] I have had burning pain [*ardores*], burning pains. That's why not anymore, I haven't been able to—I still haven't had relations with him. I don't have any relations with my husband, because I'm afraid. "I don't know if it's going to hurt me," I say . . . "No, no, no, no I can't." Because this pain burned me, and that was because I had relations with my husband. So no, I don't have relations with him. Because I had been ill. So no more, he's touched me only two times. But I don't want to anymore because I imagine that I'm going to feel more pain.

In Isabela's narrative of the etiology and effect of her illness, we see that she has seized the opportunity to reconstruct her identity such that her rejection of her husband's advances is normalized and legitimized. She has turned her suffering into a form of social empowerment. The destructive force of the cancer and the defeminizing nature of the surgery allowed her the flexible moment of liminality wherein it was possible to reformulate her gendered identity. Her illness narrative shows her employing a previously unavailable power to refuse her husband's sexual demands. She has thus managed to preserve her social identity as dutiful wife, while resisting the culturally mandated marital requirement for sexual submission. Her narrative emphasizes and elaborates the suffering she experienced related to her cancer and surgery, such that she is able to effectively resist what she views as exploitative behavior on the part of her husband. She accomplishes this while avoiding any necessity to question or revise the normative moral code of wifely compliance.

Her unusual openness in confiding this rather intimate story allows us some understanding of a phenomenon that was hinted at by four other women in the study. They each mentioned that they had ceased sexual activity following hysterectomies or mastectomies, but only Isabela's narrative offered detailed insight into the sexual politics underlying such behavior. Additionally, the illness narratives of several other women were constructed around a history of physical and emotional abuses suffered at the hands of their husbands or other male relatives. Their illness narratives display and challenge issues of abuse of social power, articulating a previously suppressed voice—a voice made available to them by virtue of the liminality found in being a cancer patient.

In a similar vein, the following case shows how a young man's illness narrative reconstructs a male identity disrupted by cancer and its treatment, in a way that effectively legitimizes nonconformity to culturally defined male role responsibility.

Family Obligation and Testicular Cancer

Latin American male identity, often glossed as "machismo," has been the subject of a great deal of speculation among literary critics and social scientists (see, e.g., Goldwert 1982; Bartra 1987; Paz 1961; Limon 1994). The Latin American male identity is often characterized, in simple terms, as a dominating assertive figure, ruling his wife and family. However, as Gutmann (1996) has argued, gender identity is never simple but instead is profoundly complex. His analysis of male gender identity in Mexico City examines this complexity. He points out that the obligation of taking responsibility for the well-being and support of one's family is also a central aspect of what it means to be a "good man" in Latin America. The dilemma faced by the man in the next case stemmed from conflicts surrounding this caretaking identity. Even prior to becoming ill, he had struggled to be a "good son" but found himself in a nearly impossible situation. In collaboration with his family, he produces an illness narrative that reconstructs a post-illness identity which provides a more tenable social role for himself. As in the case of Isabela, this is accomplished without having to revise the central cultural norm of appropriate male behavior.

Although at twenty-five Roberto Juarez had no children and had never married, he was single-handedly supporting a large family, including his parents, five younger siblings, an alcoholic brother-in-law, and assorted nephews and nieces. The family lived in a small, crowded adobe hut in a farming village twenty miles to the south of Santo Domingo. They owned two small plots of rocky, unproductive land on which they grew corn and beans for the family to eat. In recent years, Roberto's three older brothers had left to start their own families, and his father had become incapacitated with a back injury, leaving Roberto to work the land alone. In addition to the hard labor of tilling, planting, and harvesting, he also worked a few days a week for a bricklayer, working long hours carrying cement and bricks for very low wages.[5] Between the farm and his job, Roberto worked constantly, but still the family was desperately poor. His mother kept a few goats and pigs, and she made tortillas to sell, but that was the extent of the family's resources.

Roberto was in follow-up care for testicular cancer when I met him. A year and half earlier he had been diagnosed with early-stage cancer (seminoma in situ), and one testicle had been surgically removed at that time as treatment. This type of cancer is considered extremely treatable, and Roberto's postsurgical prognosis was excellent.[6]

When I went to their house to talk to Roberto, his whole family sat with us on the ground in front of their hut, and both parents joined him in answering my questions about his illness. They said that when Roberto had first become ill, his testicle had become extremely swollen, he was unable to walk, and his skin had turned dark green, as though he were being poisoned. Frightened, they took him to see a doctor, who told them that he needed an operation. He said it would cost a lot of money, which they didn't have. They took Roberto to another doctor and were told the same thing. The family faced a real dilemma: the cost of the surgery was prohibitive, but Roberto couldn't work to support the family in the condition he was in. Roberto explained: "At first I was thinking of making the sacrifice, and not having the operation. Well, that it might be better if I would die. . . . But then I thought: 'If this is taken away, I'll be better and I will work more and harder.' That's what I thought . . ."

Thus Roberto's narrative is structured in a way that foregrounds his desire to fulfill his obligation as caretaker. However, as the plot unfolds, we see this desire quickly thwarted. He explained that the family finally sold some of their few belongings and one of their plots of land and he had the surgery. He said:

> So we all pitched in and put together the money. It was everything we had. It came to three million pesos.[7] We paid cash. . . . And because of this, for my fault, I've left them poorer than they were before. The doctor told me that with just the operation I would get better, but here it is a year and a half later, and I still can't work hard. . . . Now I don't have the tumor, but I still can't work. It made it harder because now I can't lift heavy things, I can't. I can't work like I worked before . . . I had the surgery, and it came out well. After a year I wanted to work, but I still can't. I'm only half working now, which is all I can do. . . . What I think is that since they cut the testicle from me, I can't anymore. . . . I try to be like everyone else, but . . . I'm not the same as I was when I was born.

His mother interrupted: "That's why now he can't work like before, like he used to work. . . . He always worked hard, he didn't want to give in, but it's beat him. His illness has beat him. . . . He's suffered a lot."

Roberto, as the only able-bodied adult male in his family, was faced with the impossible obligation of single-handedly sustaining a large family with very limited resources. His illness narrative elaborates the emasculating aspect of his cancer treatment, the loss of his testicle, into a loss of his strength and stamina, and thus redefines his role in the household. His mother's reiteration of this construct illustrates how this configuration has become an effective and accepted part of his reconstructed social identity.

It is interesting to consider the joint nature of how Roberto's illness narrative has been constructed. It is not a simple matter of his convincing others to grant him release from role obligations. It is a mutual construction by him and his mother, which has a rather sophisticated strategic payoff. It at once achieves the desired role release, while salvaging Roberto's reputation as a "good son" without requiring a challenge or revision of the authoritative cultural model of male identity.

DISCUSSION

It is perhaps counterintuitive to think of becoming a cancer patient as a means of empowerment, but this was a striking feature of these case examples. Both Isabela and Roberto had been thrust into a liminal state with regard to their gender identity by the nature of their particular types of cancer and the surgical removal of part of their gendered organs. They have thus found themselves in a somewhat ambiguous moment, wherein the applicability of the cultural gender norms is subject to renegotiation. In dialogue with those about them, they produce illness narratives that reconstruct their gendered social roles such that they are exempt from participation in certain prescribed behaviors which prior to their illness had proved untenable for them.

In the process of narratively reconstructing an identity in the face of the disruption posed by their chronic condition, these patients addressed pressing gender role issues that had long plagued them in the course of their everyday lives. The nature of their particular cancers and the disruptive effect of their symbolically emasculating and defeminizing treatments had created a moment of indeterminate gender role identity for each of them. Through their illness narratives they had at once found a voice for their role frustrations and created legitimated new roles for themselves, both expressing and resolving some of the difficult social issues with which they had long been grappling. Through her narrative, Isabela both underscored the burden she felt in the sexual demands of her husband and found the power to resist the situation. Roberto's narrative focused on the loss of his manhood and effectively produced a social accord about the limits of his abilities to fulfill excessive familial obligations.

These cases were not unique. The illness narratives of many patients in this study had similar strategic effects, configuring the illness and its impact on their identities in ways that were socially empowering. For example, there was the illiterate wife who had sustained thirty years of beatings from an abusive husband. Her illness narrative cited his abuse as the cause of her brain cancer, and she thereby publicly challenged her husband and for the first time was able to be recognized as his victim. Another was the aging patriarch whose struggle with his sons to maintain control over the family farm was manifest and negotiated in the competing narratives both he and they told of the father's illness (Hunt 1992).

The clinical literature might construct the phenomenon to which I refer as "secondary gain": the interpersonal advantages that result when one has the symptom of a physical disease, including such things as increased attention from family members, financial gain, and release from work or other social obligations (Barsky and Klerman 1983). This literature is concerned with the impact of these factors on individual patients' motivations to stay ill or become well, and on the tendency toward somatization. This implies that patients may consciously or unconsciously hold ulterior motives that may underlie their failure to get well (see, e.g., Fishbain et al. 1995; Schoen 1993).

The central concern in identifying secondary gain is to determine the validity of subjective reports of pain and disability. It is a judgmental and simplistic model, devised to evaluate the authenticity, in medical terms, of patient complaints. By focusing the present analysis on the embeddedness of illness narratives in broader contexts of personhood and social life, we move toward a fuller understanding of narrative's performative nature. The complex process of reorganization of identity and social relations cannot be credibly reduced to the rudimentary terms of the specific advantages that may accrue to the patient. Characterizing the strategic suffering accomplished by the illness narratives described here as expressions of patients' manipulative or duplicitous motives would fail utterly to comprehend the highly intricate relationship between the expressive and instrumental aspects of the narrative reconstruction of the chronically ill self (Becker 1997; Frankenberg 1986). Instead, the strategic success of these narratives should be seen as an expression of the resilience and adaptability of the human spirit. These patients are neither exploitative nor inauthentic, but rather are involved in a process wherein adversity is incorporated into their ongoing biographies in creative and useful ways. They have effectively reconstructed a place for themselves in the world that is in some ways better for them than the place they occupied prior to the illness's disruptive effects.

Social researchers examining issues of political and economic domination have often argued that the disempowered find and use whatever resources are available to them to gain some ability to deal with oppressive conditions (see, e.g., Ong 1987; Scott 1985). This is in some ways what we have seen in the cases of Isabela and Roberto. As they narratively connect the cause and effects of their illness and treatments to their ongoing lives, they effectively convert the liminality of cancer patienthood into a social resource. In a fascinating process of inversion carried out through narrative, weakness becomes power, and disability becomes a tool.

Should the strategic impact of these illness narratives then be understood in political terms, as a form of resistance to class- and gender-based oppression? Previous researchers working from the feminist and critical anthropology traditions have explained the power relationships expressed in patients' constructions of cancer and other health problems as manifestations of class and gender conflict (see, e.g., Balshem 1993; Martin 1987). In drawing such a conclusion, two important assumptions are necessary: first, that disempowered people perceive their situation as oppressive, and second, that they act out of a motivation to resist that oppressive structure.

Neither of these assumptions is supported by the present analysis. In the two case examples, it is noteworthy that the role reconstructions the narratives produce do not challenge core local cultural concepts of gender roles, but instead are consistent with them. The narratives act to resolve the disjuncture each has encountered between personal experiences and normative expectations about how life should be (Becker 1997), without contesting the cultural constructs of ideal gender roles. Rather than undertake a major revision of standard conventions and mores, these transformations instead draw on normative cultural roles to construct and articulate the new model itself. In these examples we see that cultural ideals give the images and motives that are simultaneously the basis of disruption and of reorganization. Through intersubjective narrative representations of the causes and consequences of their illnesses, these patients produce a revised notion of order that restructures their disrupted identities in ways that transcends victimhood (Ortner 1995; cf. Bruner 1990; MacIntyre 1981). In the process of reconstructing their disrupted identities, they manage to resolve long-standing social conflicts, without needing to take the more radical epistemological step of defining the existing structure as oppressive, and resisting it.

Through their strategic use of illness narratives, these patients responded to the permanent identity loss produced by the chronic illness and its treatment in socially empowering ways. They accomplish this without the need to question the authority of the dominant cultural ideologies about power and obligation. In the very identity loss and liminality that chronic illness introduces, they have found an opportunity for socially empowering reflection and reorientation (Monks and Frankenberg 1988). As these cases have illustrated, illness narratives may be used to restructure one's social roles in strategically advantageous ways, both without losing legitimacy and without having to challenge the dominant model.

By examining the constructive nature of illness narratives, we have seen that patients' narrative performance is capable of enacting (Brodwin 1994) a new, more empowered position for themselves. In the process of defining a changed self, a self with a chronic illness, these patients have effectively enacted social change. In the process of weaving alternative forms of coherence, they simultaneously reflect cultural norms, address contradiction, and realign power relations (cf. Ortner 1995).

CONCLUSION

Illness narratives are generated in an intersubjective dialogue, articulating the illness and its effects with the broader context of life's issues and goals. Through strategically constructed illness narratives, many patients in this study effectively turned suffering into a social asset, and role destruction into an opportunity for personal empowerment. In the long-term frame of the process of adjustment to chronic illness and its treatment, the illness became a central element in the plot of an altered life story with new themes, tensions, and antagonists, a revised system of power, and a transformed protagonist. In the process of forging revised identities in place of those disrupted by the cancer and its treatment, these patients rebuilt workable versions of the world and their place in it.

The examination of the strategic implications of illness narratives does not require making judgments about the manipulative or political intentions of the actors. The purposes and tactics of the patients in this study, while perhaps encompassing some of these motives, are more completely understood as expressive and instrumental narratives that are highly complex, individual and socially located efforts to generate a new, viable place in the social world.

This analysis has allowed us to consider the highly integrated nature of the physical and social disruptions produced by chronic illness and the embeddedness of the process of reorganization people undertake in reconstructing an identity in the context of such an illness. We have seen how illness narratives can result in a reorientation to the self that is shaped not simply as a reconstructive effort to create a sense of continuity in the face of disruption, but also can be a means of affecting change in contentious social roles and relationships. As part of the ongoing interpersonal interactions of patients and those around them, illness narratives may perform important work in ongoing negotiations about mutual rights and responsibilities in the social world. They can become potent micropolitical tools, reforging the disrupted identities of patients. Strategic use of illness narratives can act to legitimize nonconformity to prescribed roles while averting the necessity to call for revision of the moral principles underlying those roles.

. . .

NOTES

1. The word *disease* is used here to refer to physiological dysfunction itself, as understood according to physicians' theories of disorder, and is contrasted with *illness,* which is the experiential aspect of disorder (Kleinman 1988).
2. All proper names are pseudonyms.
3. A full description of the methodology and sample used in this study appears in Hunt 1992.
4. For a critique of this characterization, see Browner and Lewin (1982).
5. About $3.50 U.S. per day.
6. In the United States the five-year survival rate for surgically treated early stage seminoma is 99 percent (Einhorn et al. 1988).
7. About $1,070 U.S.

REFERENCES

Aaronson, Neil. 1990. Quality of life assessment in cancer clinical trials. In *Psychosocial aspects of oncology,* edited by J. Holland and R. Zittoun. Berlin: Springer-Verlag.

Adonis, Catherine. 1978. French cultural attitudes toward cancer. *Cancer Nursing* 1:111–13.

American Cancer Society. 1980. *A study of black America's attitude toward cancer and tests.* New York: American Cancer Society.

Antonovsky, A. 1972. The image of four diseases held by the urban Jewish population of Israel. *Journal of Chronic Diseases* 25:375–84.

Balshem, Martha. 1991. Cancer, control and causality: Talking about cancer in a working-class community. *American Ethnologist* 18:152–72.

———. 1993. *Cancer in the community: Class and medical authority.* Washington, D.C.: Smithsonian Books.

Barsky, A. J., and G. L. Klerman. 1983. Overview: Hypochondriasis, bodily complaints and somatic styles. *American Journal of Psychiatry* 140:273–82.

Bartra, Roger. 1987. *La jaula de la melancolia: Identidad y metamorfosis del Mexicano.* Mexico City: Grijalbo.

Becker, Gay. 1997. *Disrupted lives: How people create meaning in a chaotic world.* Berkeley and Los Angeles: University of California Press.

Bolund, Christina. 1990. Crisis and coping: Learning to live with cancer. In *Psychosocial aspects of oncology,* edited by J. C. Holland and R. Zittoun. Berlin: Springer-Verlag.

Bourdieu, Pierre. 1977. *Outline of a theory of practice.* Cambridge: Cambridge University Press.

Brodwin, Paul. 1994. Symptoms and social performance: The case of Diane Reden. In *Pain as human experience: An anthropological perspective,* edited by M. J. DelVecchio Good, P. Brodwin, B. Good, and A. Kleinman. Berkeley and Los Angeles: University of California Press.

Brody, Howard. 1988. *Stones of sickness.* New Haven, Conn.: Yale University Press.

Browner, Carole, and Ellen Lewin. 1982. Female altruism reconsidered: The Virgin Mary as economic woman. *American Ethnologist* 9:61–75.

Bruner, Jerome. 1990. *Acts of meaning.* Cambridge, Mass.: Harvard University Press.

Bury, Michael. 1982. Chronic illness as a biographical disruption. *Sociology of Health and Illness* 4: 167–82.

Cassell, Eric. 1982. The nature of suffering and the goals of medicine. *New England Journal of Medicine* 306:639–45.

Chavez, Leo, F. Allan Hubbell, Juliet M. McMullin, Rebecca G. Martinez, and Shiraz I. Mishra. 1995. Structure and meaning in models of breast and cervical cancer risk factors: A comparison of perceptions among Latinas, Anglo women, and physicians. *Medical Anthropology Quarterly* 9:40–74.

Dreffuss-Kattan, Esther, 1990. *Cancer stories: Creativity and self-repair.* Hillsdale, N.J.: Atlantic Press.

Einhorn, Lawrence, Barry Lowitz, and Dennis Casciato. 1988. Testicular cancer. In *Manual of clinical oncology,* edited by D. Casciato and B. Lowitz. 2d ed. Boston: Little, Brown.

Erwin, Deborah Oates. 1984. Fighting cancer, dying to win: The American strategy for creating a chronic sick role. Ph.D. diss., Southern Methodist University.

Finkler, Kaja. 1991. *Physicians at work, patients in pain: Biomedical practice and patient response in Mexico.* Boulder, Colo.: Westview Press.

Fishbain, David, H. L. Rosomoff, R. B. Cutler, and R. S. Rosomoff. 1995. Secondary gain concept: A review of the scientific evidence. *Clinical Journal of Pain* 11:6–21.

Foster, George. 1967. *Tzintzuntzan.* Boston: Little, Brown.

Frankenberg, Ronald. 1986. Sickness as cultural performance: Drama, trajectory, and pilgrimage root metaphors and the making of social disease. *International Journal of Health Sciences* 16:603–26.

Garro, Linda. 1990. Culture, pain and cancer. *Journal of Palliative Care 6* (3): 34–44.

———. 1994. Chronic pain and the construction of narratives. In *Pain as human experience: An anthropological perspective,* edited by M. J. DelVecchio Good, P. Brodwin, B. Good, and A. Kleinman. Berkeley and Los Angeles: University of California Press.

Goldwert, Marvin. 1982. *Psychic conflict in Spanish America: Six essays on the psychohistory of the region.* Washington, D.C.: University Press of America.

Good, Byron. 1994. *Medicine, rationality and experience: An anthropological perspective.* Cambridge: Cambridge University Press.

Good, Byron, and Mary-Jo DelVecchio Good. 1982. Toward a meaning-centered analysis of popular illness categories: "Fright illness" and "heart distress" in Iran. In *Cultural conceptions of mental health and therapy,* edited by A. Marsella and G. White. Dordrecht: Reidel.

Good, Mary-Jo DelVecchio, Byron Good, Cynthia Schaffer, and Stuart E. Lind. 1990. American oncology and the discourse on hope. *Culture, Medicine and Psychiatry* 14:59–79.

Good, Mary-Jo DelVecchio, L. Hunt, T. Munakata, and Y. Kobayashi. 1992. A comparative analysis of the culture of biomedicine: Disclosure and consequences for treatment in the practice of oncology. In *Health and health care in developing societies: Sociological perspectives,* edited by P. Conrad and E. Gallagher. Philadelphia: Temple University Press.

Good, Mary-Jo DelVecchio, T. Munakata, Y. Kobayashi, C. Mattingly, and B. J. Good. 1994. Oncology and narrative time. *Social Science and Medicine* 38:855–62.

Gordon, Deborah. 1990. Embodying illness, embodying cancer. *Culture, Medicine and Psychiatry* 14:275–97.

Gutmann, Matthew. 1996. *The meanings of macho: Being a man in Mexico City.* Berkeley and Los Angeles: University of California Press.

Haes, J. C. J. M. de. 1988. Quality of life: Conceptual and theoretical considerations. In *Psychosocial oncology,* edited by M. Watson, S. Greer, and C. Thomas. Oxford: Pergamon Press.

Hunt, Linda M. 1992. Living with cancer in Oaxaca, Mexico: Patient and physician perspectives in cultural context. Ph.D. diss., Harvard University.

———. 1993. The metastasis of witchcraft: The interrelationship between traditional and biomedical concepts of cancer in southern Mexico. *Collegium Antropologicum* 17:249–56.

———. 1994. Practicing oncology in provincial Mexico: A narrative analysis. *Social Science and Medicine* 38:843–53.

———. 1998. Moral reasoning and the meaning of cancer: Causal explanations of oncologists and patients in southern Mexico. *Medical Anthropology Quarterly* 12:298–318.

Jackson, Michael. 1989. *Paths toward a clearing: Radical empiricism and ethnographic inquiry.* Bloomington: Indiana University Press.

Kagawa-Singer, Marjorie. 1993. Redefining health: Living with cancer. *Social Science and Medicine.* 37:295–304.

Kaufman, Sharon. 1988. Toward a phenomenology of boundaries in medicine: Chronic illness experience in the case of stroke. *Medical Anthropology Quarterly* 2:338–54.

Kleinman, Arthur. 1988. *The illness narratives; Suffering, healing and the human condition.* New York: Basic Books.

Kleinman, Arthur, and Joan Kleinman. 1991. Suffering and professional transformation: Toward an ethnography of interpersonal experience. *Culture, Medicine and psychiatry* 15:275–301.

Lewis, Oscar. 1963. *Life in a Mexican village: Tepoztlan revisited.* Urbana: University of Illinois Press.

Limón, José. 1994. *Dancing with the devil: Society and cultural poetics in Mexican-American south Texas.* Madison: University of Wisconsin Press.

Lowitz, Barry, and Dennis Casciato. 1988. Psychosocial aspects of cancer care. In *Manual of clinical oncology,* edited by D. Casciato and B. Lowitz 2nd ed. Boston: Little, Brown.

Maclntyre, Alasdair. 1981. *After virtue: A study in moral theory.* Notre Dame, Ind.: University of Notre Dame Press.

Martin, Emily. 1987. *The woman in the body: A cultural analysis of reproduction.* Boston: Beacon Press.

Mathews, Holly, Donald Lannin, and Toni Mitchell. 1994. Coming to terms with advanced breast cancer: Black women's narratives from eastern North Carolina. *Social Science and Medicine* 38:789–800.

Mattingly, Cheryl, 1994. The concept of therapeutic "emplotment," *Social Science and Medicine* 38:811–22.

———. 1998. *Healing dramas and clinical plots: The narrative structure of experience.* Cambridge: Cambridge University Press.

Mattingly, Cheryl, and Linda Garro. 1994. Narrative representations of illness and healing: Introduction. *Social Science and Medicine* 38:771–74.

Monks, Judith, and Ronald Frankenberg. 1988. Being ill and being me: Self, body and time in multiple sclerosis narratives. In *Disability and culture,* edited by B. Ingstad and S. Reynolds Whyte. Berkeley and Los Angeles: University of California Press.

Ong, Aihwa. 1987. *Spirits of resistance and capitalist, discipline: Factory women in Malaysia.* Albany: State University of New York Press.

Ortner, Sherry. 1995. Resistance and the problem of ethnographic refusal. *Comparative Studies in Society and History* 37:173–93.

Panourgia, E. Neni K. 1990. Death by cancer: Local and unlocal knowledge. Paper presented at the annual meetings of the American Anthropological Association, New Orleans.

Patterson, James T. 1987. *The dread disease: Cancer and modern American culture.* Cambridge, Mass.: Harvard University Press.

Paz, Octavio. 1961. *The labyrinth of solitude: Life and thought in Mexico.* New York: Grove Press.

Rosaldo, Renato. 1993. *Culture and truth: The remaking of social analysis.* Boston: Beacon Press.

Rubel, Arthur. 1966. *Across the tracks: Mexican-Americans in a Texas city.* Austin: University of Texas Press.

Sahlins, Marshall. 1976. *Culture and practical reason.* Chicago: University of Chicago Press.

Saillant, Francine. 1990. Discourse, knowledge and experience of cancer: A life story. *Culture, Medicine and Psychiatry* 14:81–104.

Schoen, Marc. 1993. Resistance to health: When the mind interferes with the desire to become well. *American Clinical Hypnosis* 36:47–54.

Scott, James C. 1985. *Weapons of the weak: Everyday forms of peasant resistance.* New Haven, Conn.: Yale University Press.

Shedlin, Michele, and Paul Hollerbach. 1981. Modern and traditional fertility regulation in a Mexican community: The process of decision-making. *Studies in Family Planning* 12:278–96.

Sontag, Susan. 1977. *Illness as metaphor.* New York: Random House.

Strauss, Anselm, and Juliet Corbin. 1984. *Chronic illness the quality of life.* St. Louis: Mosby.

Turner, Victor. 1969. *The ritual process: Structure and anti-structure.* Ithaca, N.Y.: Cornell University Press.

Uzell, Douglas. 1974. *Susto* revisited: Illness as strategic role. *American Ethnologist* 1:369–78.

Van Gennep, Arnold. 1960. *The rites of passage.* Chicago: University of Chicago Press.

Weisman, A. D. 1979. *Coping wiih cancer.* New York: McGraw-Hill.

Williams, G. 1984. The genesis of chronic illness: Narrative re-construction. *Sociology of Health and Illness* 6:175.

Williams, G., and P. Wood. 1986. Patients and their illnesses. *Lancet,* December 20/27:1435.

 20

The Damaged Self

Robert F. Murphy

This selection is autobiographical, written by an anthropology professor at Columbia University. Robert Murphy has done anthropological fieldwork in the Amazon and other parts of the world (Murphy and Murphy 1985; Murphy and Quoin 1955). His research into the world of the disabled and wheelchair-bound began after a slow-growing cancer began pinching his spinal cord, ultimately leaving his legs paralyzed. This selection is a chapter from his book The Body Silent *(1987), which both tells a poignant personal story and provides keen anthropological observations on the illness experiences of disabled people.*

The focus of this selection is on the self*; the cultural construction of the individual as a social, corporeal, and psychological entity. Murphy uses Freudian theory to explore the notion of self and how the illness experience changes that notion. The relationship between the self and the body is particularly important. In recent years, the anthropology of the body—the study of the symbolic meanings of the body and the embodiment of meaning through lived experience—has become an increasingly important theme. Murphy's experience with a damaged body and an incurable disease resulted in many powerful insights about the world. (A similarly powerful book from this perspective is Reynolds Price's* A Whole New Life *[1994].) Some insights come from the daily struggle to do simple things and the loss of taken-for-granted abilities. Murphy talks about the sex life of paraplegics in this vein. Further insights come from interactions with others who are affected not only by the physical reality of the wheelchair but also by cultural notions of stigma and the social creation of the "other." The necessity of adapting to new life circumstances—and the emotional impact of those adaptions—is a theme we saw in the selection by Gaylene Becker on the lives of deaf people. The disabled must adapt to limitations in mobility and to living daily with pain, but the nonphysical aspects of the illness experience remain very important. In this selection, Robert Murphy frankly discusses the suffering caused by depression and decreased self-esteem, as well as criticizing biomedicine for its inability to deal with the entire self.*

As you read this selection, consider these questions:

- **Why are children often afraid when they see a disabled person? How are definitions of "normal" learned?**
- **Murphy's paralysis developed relatively slowly, whereas most spinal cord injuries occur suddenly as a result of car crashes and other accidents. Would the cause of the injury have any relation to the illness experience? To the way that others treat the disabled?**
- **What does Murphy mean by "unmarked categories" and the creation of the "other"? Is his analogy to the importance of race and the experience of racism relevant here?**
- **Think for a moment about what your life would be like if you were suddenly confined to a wheelchair. How would your life be different? How would your relationship with your body be different? How would people treat you differently?**

Context: Robert Murphy, who taught anthropology at Columbia University, died in 1990. Murphy's original fieldwork, conducted with his spouse Yolanda, dealt with social structure of the Mundurucu, who live in the Amazon rain forest of Brazil. An anthropologist with wide-ranging theoretical interests, Murphy made significant contributions to cultural-ecological, social structural, and symbolic approaches to the field; he was a spirited teacher and author of a well-known textbook. Probably his best-known book, *Women of the Forest (1974)*, was co-written with Yolanda Murphy and was influential in the women's liberation movement of the seventies. In 1974, he began to lose control of his lower extremities and was diagnosed with a slow-growing spinal tumor; two years later he was wheelchair bound. He began research on the anthropology of disability, funded by the National Science Foundation, and produced an important, reflective, and experience-near ethnography of physical disability.

Source: R. Murphy (1987). "The Damaged Self." *In The Body Silent*. New York: Norton.

As Gregor Samsa awoke one morning from uneasy dreams he found himself transformed in his bed into a gigantic insect. He was lying on his hard, as if it were armor-plated, back and when he lifted his head a little he could see his domelike brown belly divided into stiff arched segments. . . . What has happened to me? he thought. It was no dream.

—Franz Kafka, The Metamorphosis

From the time my tumor was first diagnosed through my entry into wheelchair life, I had an increasing apprehension that I had lost much more than the full use of my legs. I had also lost a part of my self. It was not just that people acted differently toward me, which they did, but rather that I felt differently toward myself. I had changed in my own mind, in my self-image, and in the basic conditions of my existence. It left me feeling alone and isolated, despite strong support from family and friends; moreover, it was a change for the worse, a diminution of everything I used to be. This was particularly frightening for somebody who had clawed his way up from poverty to a position of respect. I had become a person of substance, and that substance was oozing away. It threatened everything that Yolanda and I had put together over the years. In middle age, the ground beneath me had convulsed. And I had no idea why and how this had happened.

I cannot remember ever before thinking about physical disability, except as something that happened to other, less fortunate, people. It certainly had no relevance to me. A disabled person could enter my field of vision, but my mind would fail to register him—a kind of selective blindness quite common among people of our culture. During a year that I spent in the Sahel and Sudan zones of Nigeria and Niger, a region of endemic leprosy and missing hands, feet, and noses, the plight of those people was as alien to me as were their language, culture, and circumstances. Because of this gulf, I had no empathy for them and just enough sympathy to drop coins into cups extended from the ends of stumps. A few pennies were all that it took to buy the dubious grace of almsgiving. It was a bargain, a gesture that did not assert my oneness with them, but rather my separation from them.

With the onset of my own impairment, I became almost morbidly sensitive to the social position and treatment of the disabled, and I began to notice nuances of behavior that would have gone over my head in times past. One of my earliest observations was that social relations between the disabled and the able-bodied are tense, awkward, and problematic. This is something that every handicapped person knows, but it surprised me at the time. For example, when I was in the hospital, a young woman visitor entered my room with a look of total consternation on her face. She exclaimed that she had just seen an awful sight, a girl who was missing half of her skull. I knew the girl as a very sweet, but quite retarded, teenaged patient who used to drop in on me a few times a day; we always had the same conversation. I asked my guest why the sight bothered her so much, but she couldn't tell me. She in turn asked why it didn't trouble me. After a moment's thought, I replied that I was one of "them," a notion that she rejected vehemently. But why did my visitor, a poised and intelligent person, react in this way? It aroused my curiosity.

There is something quite significant in this small encounter, for it had elements of what Erving Goffman called "one of the primal scenes of sociology."[1] Borrowing the Freudian metaphor of the primal scene (the child's traumatic witnessing of the mother and father in sexual intercourse), Goffman used the phrase to mean any social confrontation of people in which there is some great flaw, such as when one of the parties has no nose. This robs the encounter of firm cultural guidelines, traumatizing it and leaving the people involved wholly uncertain about what to expect from each other. It has the potential for social calamity.

The intensely problematic character of relations between those with damaged bodies and the more-or-less unmarked cannot be shrugged off simply as a result of the latter's ineptitude, bias, stupidity, and so forth, although they do play a part. Even the best-intentioned able-bodied people have difficulty anticipating the reactions of the disabled, for interpretations are warped by the impairment. To complicate matters, the disabled also enter the social arena with a skewed perspective. Not only are the bodies altered, but their ways of thinking about themselves and about the person and objects of the external world have become profoundly transformed. They have experienced a revolution of consciousness. They have undergone a metamorphosis.

Nobody has ever asked me what it is like to be a paraplegic—and now a quadriplegic—for this would violate all the rules of middle-class etiquette. A few have asked me what caused my condition, and, after hearing the answer, have looked as though they wished they hadn't. After all, tumors can happen to anybody—even to them. Polite manners may protect us from most such intrusions, but it is remarkable that physicians seldom ask either. They like "hard facts" obtainable through modern technology or old-fashioned jabbing with a pin and asking whether you feel it. These tests supposedly provide good, "objective" measures of neurological damage, but, like sociological questionnaires, they reduce experience to neat distinctions of black or white and ignore the broad range of ideation and emotion that always accompanies disability. The full subjective states of the patient are of little concern in the medical model of disability, which holds that the problem arises wholly from some anatomic or physiological disorder and is correctable by standard modes of therapy—drugs, surgery, radiation, or whatever. What goes on inside the patient's head is another department, and if there are signs of serious psychological malaise, he is packed off to the proper specialist.

The medical people have had little curiosity about what I think about my condition, although they do know its sensory symptoms: a constant tingling in my hands, forearms, and feet and a steady, low threshold of pain in my legs. The discomfort is similar to the soreness and burning sensation experienced with torn or severely strained muscles and has much to do with the fact that the musculature of my trunk and legs is always in spasm, despite a generous daily dosage of muscle relaxants. The curious thing about this condition is that a knife could be run through my leg now and I wouldn't feel it. Aside from the tingle and the ache, my legs are otherwise numb and bereft of sensation. For the past four years, I have not tried to move them, for the tumor has long since passed the point at which therapy could maintain function; they don't even twitch anymore.

For a while, I occasionally tried to will the legs to move, but each futile attempt was psychologically devastating, leaving me feeling broken and helpless. I soon stopped trying. The average nondisabled person could be driven to the edge of breakdown if his legs were pinioned and rendered totally immobile for long periods, and an accident victim in a body cast finds his only comfort in the fact that his situation is temporary. I was saved from this, however, because the slow process of paralysis of my limbs was paralleled by a progressive atrophy of the need and impulse for physical activity. I was losing the will to move.

My upper body functions have suffered some impairment ever since the tumor became symptomatic, although the lower body has deteriorated at a much faster rate. In addition to the diminished lung capacity and, consequently, more rapid and shallow breathing, the musculature of the arms and hands has progressively weakened, their range of movement has become steadily more narrow, my fingers have stiffened, and my hands have become increasingly numb and insensitive to touch and temperature. In common with other paralytics, I have to be careful with hot water or hot dishes and pots, for I can burn myself without knowing it. To complicate the hand problems, the fingers of quadriplegics curl inward toward the palms, a process that by the spring of 1986 had made my left hand almost useless.

Beyond these physical symptoms, I have been overtaken by a profound and deepening sense of tiredness—a total, draining weariness that I must resist every waking minute. It starts in the morning when I struggle to awaken, fighting my way out of the comfort and forgetfulness of sleep into self-awareness and renewed disability. Facing the world every day is an ordeal for everybody, and it is no accident that strokes and heart attacks peak at 8 to 9 A.M. It is much worse to confront the day with a serious deficit. The wish to turn my back to the world continues through the daily ablutions, which grow longer and more tedious every year; it now takes me a quarter hour to shave. I am fully able to face life by 10 A.M., but by 4 or 5 P.M., I start to flag. Between these hours, I teach, talk to students, and attend meetings, after which I go home and lie down for a couple of hours. I also conserve strength by spending two, or at most three, days a week at the university. Like most professors, I don't pass the other days in idleness. I read student exams, reports, and doctoral dissertations; I keep up on books and journals in my field; and I do research and writing. But the professorial life allows me to work at home at my own tempo, sometimes while lying in bed. In no other line of work, I tell my graduate students, could such a wreck be 100 percent employed—it has to be an easy job!

But there is another aspect of my fatigue that cannot be eased by rest. This is a sense of tiredness and ennui with practically everything and everybody, a desire to withdraw from the world, to crawl into a hole and pull the lid over my head. The average person will recognize this wish, for everybody at some time or other feels that things have become too much to handle and he or she wishes for surcease, for even temporary remission. How tempting to tell all and sundry—family, work, and society—to go to hell and leave him alone. Who hasn't said this, even if only under his breath? When an ordinary citizen is overcome by these feelings every day and all day, however, his family and friends will urge him to seek professional help, for these are the sure symptoms of depression. In contrast, the deeply impaired harbor these urges chronically, sometimes because they are depressed but more often because they must each day face an inimical world, using the limited resources of a damaged body.

Many give in to the impulse to withdraw, retreating into a little universe sustained by monthly Social Security disability checks, a life circumscribed by the four walls of an apartment and linked to outside society by a television set. Constantina Safilios-Rothschild, a sociologist, has noted that disability may provide a pretext for withdrawal from work for some older workers dissatisfied and weary with their jobs, a kind of "secondary gain" bought at great price.[2] But this is not the source of the isolation; it's just making the best of a bad thing. Many other disabled people go forth to battle the world every day, but even they must wage a constant rear-guard action against the backward pull. This is a powerful centripetal force, for it is commonly exacerbated by an altered sense of selfhood, one that has been savaged by the partial destruction of the body. Disability is not simply a physical affair for us; it is our ontology, a condition of our being in the world.

Of all the psychological syndromes associated with disability, the most pervasive, and the most destructive, is a radical loss of self-esteem. This sense of damage to the self, the acquisition of what Erving Goffman called a "stigma," or a "spoiled identity"[3] grew upon me during my first months in a wheelchair, and it hit me hardest when I returned to the university in the fall of 1977. By then, I could no longer hold on to the myth that I was using a wheelchair during convalescence. I had to face the unpalatable fact that I was wedded permanently to it; it had become an indispensable extension of my body. Strangely, I also felt this as a major blow to my pride.

The damage to my ego showed most painfully in an odd and wholly irrational sense of embarrassment and lowered self-worth when I was with people on my social periphery. Most of my colleagues in the anthropology department were old friends, some even from our undergraduate years, and they generally were warm and supportive. But people from other departments and the administration were another matter. During my first semester back at the university, I attended a few lunch meetings at the Faculty Club, but I began to notice that these were strained occasions. People whom I knew did not look my way. And persons with whom I had a nodding acquaintance did not nod; they, too, were busily looking off in another direction. Others gave my wheelchair a wide berth, as if it were surrounded by a penumbra of contamination. These were not happy encounters.

My social isolation became acute during stand up gatherings, such as receptions and cocktail parties. I discovered that I was now three-and-a-half feet tall, and most social interaction was taking place two feet above me. When speaking to a standing person, I have to crane my neck back and look upward, a position that stretches my larynx and further weakens my diminished vocal strength. Conversation in such settings has become an effort. Moreover, it was commonplace that I would be virtually ignored in a crowd for long periods, broken by short bursts of patronization. There was no escape from these intermittent attentions, for it is very difficult to maneuver a wheelchair through a crowd. My low stature and relative immobility thus made me the defenseless recipient of overtures, rather than their instigator. This is a common plaint of the motor-disabled: They have limited choice in socializing and often must wait for the others to come to them. As a consequence, I now attend only small, sit-down gatherings.

Not having yet read the literature on the sociology of disability, I did not immediately recognize the pattern of avoidance. Perhaps this was for the best, as my initial hurt and puzzlement ultimately led me to research the subject. In the meantime, I stopped going to the Faculty Club and curtailed my contacts with the university-at-large. This is not hard to do at Columbia, as each department lies within a Maginot Line, everybody is very busy, and the general social atmosphere runs from tepid to cool. None of this is surprising, for it is also the dominant ethos of New York City. On the positive side, this same general mood allows one to work in peace. They leave you alone at Columbia, and I wanted more than ever to be left alone.

Withdrawal only compounds the disabled person's subjective feelings of damage and lowered worth, sentiments that become manifest as shame and guilt. I once suggested to a housebound elderly woman that she should use a walker for going outside. "I would never do that," she replied. "I'd be ashamed to be seen." "It's not your fault that you have arthritis," I argued. I added that I used a walker, and I wasn't ashamed—this was untrue, of course, and I knew it. But why should anyone feel shame about his disability? Even more mysterious, why should anyone feel a sense of guilt? In what way could I be responsible for my physical state? It could not be attributed to smoking or drinking, the favorite whipping boys of amateur diagnosticians, and it wasn't the result of an accident, with its possibilities for lifestyle culpability, the accusation that one bought it by living dangerously. No, I didn't do a damned thing to earn my tumor, nor was there any way that I could have prevented it. But such feelings are endemic among the disabled. One young woman, who had been born without lower limbs, told me that she had felt guilt for this since childhood, as had her parents (from whom she probably acquired the guilt). Indeed, a mutuality of guilt is the very life-stuff of the paralytic's family, just as it is, on a smaller scale, central to the cohesion—and turmoil—of all modern families.

Guilt and shame are not in fact as separate as they are often represented to be. In simple form, both are said to involve an assault on the ego: Guilt is the attack of the superego, or conscience, and shame arises from the opprobrium of others. Of the two, I believe that shame is the more potent. The sociologist George Herbert Mead wrote that an individual's concept of his or her self is a reflection, or, more accurately, a refraction, as in a fun-house mirror, of the way he or she is treated by others.[4] And if a person is treated with ridicule, contempt, or aversion, then his own ego is diminished, his dignity and humanity are called into question. Shaming is an especially potent means of social control in small-scale societies, where everybody is known and behavior is highly visible, but it is less effective in complex societies like our own, where we can compartmentalize our lives and exist in relative anonymity. But a wheelchair cannot be hidden; it is brutally visible. And to the extent that the wheelchair's occupant is treated with aversion, even disdain, his sense of worth suffers. Damage to the body, then, causes diminution of the self, which is further magnified by debasement by others.

Shame and guilt are one in that both lower self-esteem and undercut the facade of dignity we present to the world. Moreover, in our culture they tend to stimulate each other. The usual formula is that a wrongful act leads to a guilty conscience; if the guilt becomes publicly known, then shame must be added to the sequence, followed by punishment. There is then a causal chain that goes from wrongful act to guilt to shame to punishment. A fascinating aspect of disability is that it diametrically and completely reverses this progression, while preserving every step. The sequence of the person damaged in body goes from punishment (the impairment) to shame to guilt and, finally, to the crime. This is not a real crime but a self-delusion that lurks in our fears and fantasies, in the haunting, never-articulated question: What did I do to deserve this?

In this topsy-turvy world of reversed causality, the punishment—for this is how crippling is unconsciously apprehended—begets the crime. All of this happens despite the fact that the individual may be in no way to blame for his condition; real responsibility is irrelevant. This transmutation of body impairment into guilt is a neat inversion of the Freudian Oedipal drama. According to the psychoanalytic interpretation of the myth, Oedipus unknowingly kills his father and marries his own mother, for which crime the Fates pursue him to Colonus, where he blinds himself. Blinding is seen as a symbolic form of castration, which is, in turn, the fitting punishment for incest. According to Freud, in male socialization it is the threat of castration by the father—even if only a fantasized threat—that forces the child to relinquish and repress the guilt-ridden wish to possess the mother. It should be noted, however, that in the myth the father did not blind Oedipus; Oedipus did it to himself. What is usually forgotten in discussions of the Greek tragedy is that the father, after hearing from a soothsayer that his son would one day slay him, crippled young Oedipus. In fact, the name Oedipus can be translated as "Swollen Foot" or, loosely, "Gimpy."

That crippling can be just as proper a punishment for incest as blinding finds ethnographic support. In my own fieldwork, I recorded a Mundurucu myth in which a man who committed incest with his surrogate mother was physically deformed by her husband, a god, and later blinded. And among West African Moslems there is a widespread religious cult centered on a female succubus named Dogwa. (In Morocco, this cult figure is called Aisha Kandisha.) Dogwa is both nuturant and sexually seductive to her devotees; she is both mother and lover. In the former role, she can bring wealth to her followers, but in the latter, she jealously takes swift retaliation against infidelity. Appropriately, the punishment is crippling or blinding. It is worth noting that no father figure is involved here. Instead there is the ambivalent mother, the giver and nurturer of life and its potential destroyer. Incest, or even the unconscious wish for it, is a dangerous game, and I would hazard the guess that the unconscious, diffuse sense of guilt that so often bedevils the disabled arises in the first place from the chimerical notion that the crippling is a punishment for this repressed, elusive, and forbidden desire. There may be no such thing as Original Sin, but original guilt lurks in the dark recesses of the minds of all humans. These ashes of our first love are the basic stuff of the indefinable, unarticulated, and haunting sense that the visitation of paralysis is a form of atonement—a Draconian penance.

Paralytic disability constitutes emasculation of a more direct and total nature. For the male, the weakening and atrophy of the body threaten all the cultural values of masculinity: strength, activeness, speed, virility, stamina, and fortitude. Many disabled men, and women, try to compensate for their deficiencies by becoming involved in athletics. Paraplegics play wheelchair basketball, engage in racing, enter marathons, and do weight-lifting and many other active things. Those too old or too impaired for physical displays may instead show their competence by becoming "super-crips." Just as "super-moms" supposedly go off to work every morning, cook Cordon Bleu dinners at night, play with the kids, and then become red-hot lovers after the children are put to bed, the super-crip works harder than other people, travels extensively, goes to everything, and takes part in anything that comes along. This is how he shows the world that he is like everybody else, only better.

Becoming a super-crip, or super-mom, often depends less on the personal qualities of the individual than on very fortunate circumstances. In my own case, I was well established in my profession at the time of my disability, so my activity was just a matter of persistence. The real super-crips are those who do it all after they become impaired, like one woman who, after partial remission from totally paralytic multiple sclerosis, went on to finish college and then obtain a Ph.D. She refused to let the disease rob her of a future. There are many such people, but, like super-moms, they are still a minority. The vast majority, as we will see, are unable to conquer the formidable physical and social obstacles that confront them, and they live in the penumbra of society, condemned to lives as outsiders.

Afflictions of the spinal cord have a further devastating effect upon masculinity, aside from paralysis, for they commonly produce some degree of impotence or sexual malfunction. Depending on the extent of damage to the cord, the numbed genital area sends no signals to the brain, nor do the libidinal centers of the brain get messages through to the genitalia and the physiological processes that produce erections. This can result in total and permanent impotence, sporadic impotence, or difficulty in sustaining an erection until orgasm. There are some paraplegic men, on the other hand, who can maintain an erection but are unable to achieve orgasm, even after steady intercourse of a half hour to an hour. The effects of this on the male psyche are profound. We usually think of "castration anxiety" as an Oedipal thing, but there is a sort of symbolic castration in impotence that creates a kind of existential anxiety among all men. It is no accident that impotence is a major problem in those lands where masculine values are strongest, nor was it fortuitous that the new sexual freedom in America, with its emphasis on female gratification and male performance, has yielded a bumper crop of impotent men. After all, being a man does not mean just having a penis—it means having a sexually useful one. Anything less than that is indeed a kind of castration, although I am using this lurid Freudian term primarily as a metaphor for loss of both sexual and social power.

Most forms of paraplegia and quadriplegia cause male impotence and female inability to orgasm. But paralytic women need not be aroused or experience orgasmic pleasure to engage in genital sex, and many indulge regularly in intercourse and even bear children, although by Caesarean section. Human sexuality, Freud tells us, is polymorphously perverse, meaning that the entire body is erogenous, and the joys of sex varied. Paraplegic women claim to derive psychological gratification from the sex act itself, as well as from the stimulation of other parts of their bodies and the knowledge that they are still able to give pleasure to others. They may derive less physical gratification from sex than before becoming disabled, but they are still active participants. Males have far more circumscribed anatomical limits. Other than having a surgical implant that produces a simulated erection, the man can no longer engage in genital sex. He either becomes celibate or practices oral sex—or any of the many other variations in sexual expression devised by our innovative species. Whatever the alternative, his standing as a man has been compromised far more than has been the woman's status. He has been effectively emasculated.

Even in those cases in which the paraplegic male retains potency, his stance during the sex act changes. Most must lie still on their backs during intercourse, and it is the woman who must do the mounting and thrusting. In modern America, this is an acceptable alternative position, but in some cultures it would be considered a violation of male dominance: Men are on top in society and they should be on top in sex, and that's the end of the matter. And even in the relatively liberated United States of the 1980s, the male usually takes the more active role and the position on top. But the paraplegic male, whether engaging in genital or oral sex, always takes a passive role. Most paralytic men accept this limitation, for they discover that the wells of passion are in the brain, not between the legs, and that pleasure is possible even without orgasm. One man, who had enjoyed an intensely erotic relationship with his wife before an auto accident made him paraplegic and impotent, reported that they simply continued oral sex. The wife derives complete orgasmic satisfaction and the husband achieves deep psychological pleasure, which he describes as a "mental orgasm." The sex lives of most paralyzed men, however, remain symbolic of a more general passivity and dependency that touches every aspect of their existence and is the antithesis of the male values of direction, activity, initiative, and control.

The sexual problems of the disabled are aggravated by a widespread view that they are either malignantly sexual, like libidinous dwarfs, or, more commonly, completely asexual, an attribute frequently ascribed to the elderly as well. These erroneous notions, which I suspect arise from the sexual anxieties of their holders, fail to recognize that a large majority of disabled people have the same urges as the able-bodied, and are just as competent in expressing them. Spinal cord injuries raise special problems, but motor-disabled people with cerebral palsy, the aftereffects of polio, and many other conditions often can lead almost normal sex lives. That asexuality is also attributed sometimes to the blind underlines the utter irrationality of the belief.

Given the prevalence of such ignorance, I was pleased to read in 1985 that educational television was airing a film on sex among the disabled, and I made it a point to watch it. At the beginning of the film, there appeared on the screen a warning that there would be nude scenes, leading me to the happy expectation that a para—or quadriplegic would be shown making love. Not so, for the only nudes were a couple of very healthy-looking young women. And, in deliberate counterpoint, most of the disabled people shown were grossly disfigured. It was a modern-day version of *Beauty and the Beast,* a film that served to perpetuate, not combat, a prejudice. The producers meant well, but they merely illustrated the depth of the problem. This episode reminded me that when one young woman began research among paraplegics, a female friend asked her, "But you wouldn't go to bed with one of them, would you?" These are indeed primal scenes.

One of Sigmund Freud's enduring contributions to our age was his rejection of classical philosophy's disembodiment of the mind. Instead, Freud started with a theory of instincts that located much of human motivation and thought in the needs of the body, especially the sexual drive. This was not a simple single-direction mechanical determinism, however, for Freud's theories held that causality is a two-way street. The human mind also uses its symbolic capacity to reach out and encompass the body, making it just as much a part of the mind as the mind is of the body. The body, particularly the more explicitly erogenous zones, becomes incorporated into human thought, into the very structure of the personality, and the sexual symbolism of pleasure and desire is used by the mind in molding one's orientation to the world. Sex thus invades thought, but is also intensified and transformed by thought. And so it is that the loss of the use of one's legs, or any other vital function, is an infringement also on the integrity of the mind, an assault on character, a vitiation of power.

The unity of mind and body is also an important element in phenomenological philosophy. This school, which arose in the early twentieth century from the writings of Edmund Husserl, sidesteps the old philosophical question of "how do we know the world [or reality, or truth]" and says that the world is whatever we make it out to be; it is created within the stream of conscious experience. And the way we experience and understand reality is in good part shaped by the language categories through which we sort out what we take to be real, and by the cultural symbolism through which we find significance and meaning in the mess of sense impressions continually bombarding us. Reality, then, isn't a hard-and-fast thing, the same for everybody, but a consensual matter, a social construct, that must be reaffirmed and re-created in all our interactions with other people. It would follow from this relativistic view of the human grasp of the world that people of different cultures inhabit somewhat different realities, as do people of the same culture but of radically different circumstances—people, for example, who can't walk.

In his 1962 book *The Phenomenology of Perception,* the French philosopher Maurice Merleau-Ponty states that the starting point for our apprehension and construction of the world is the body.[5] This goes beyond the obvious fact that our sense organs are parts of the body, for he stresses that the landscape of the body is, explicitly or implicitly, the means and the perspective by which we place ourselves in environments and experience their dimensions. As Simone de Beauvoir says, the body is not a thing, an entity separate from the mind and from the rest of the world in which it is situated. The body is also a set of relationships that link the outer world and the mind into a system. Merleau-Ponty illustrates this by reference to the phenomenon of the "phantom limb," the amputee's illusion that he still possesses the missing arm or leg. He writes, "What it is in us which refuses mutilation and disablement is an *I* [Merleau-Ponty's emphasis] committed to a certain physical and interhuman world, who continues to tend towards his world despite handicaps and amputations and who, to this extent, does not recognize them *de jure* [openly and avowedly]."[6] The amputee is missing more than a limb: He is also missing one of his conceptual links to the world, an anchor of his very existence.

Gelya Frank, an anthropologist, has written a life history of a woman born without her four limbs, documenting the laborious process by which she became "embodied" and grew to accept her condition and develop self-love.[7] Frank sees her as a kind of Venus de Milo whose beauty is curiously enhanced, like the statue's, by her lack of limbs. Embodiment is a problem for those born with deficiencies, but at least they can be socialized to their limitations from infancy. On the other hand, most paraplegics and quadriplegics come to their lot through "the slings and arrows of outrageous fortune" and have a different problem—they have to become reembodied to their impairments. And if the loss of function is grave enough, they may even have to become disembodied,

My own sense of disembodiment is somewhat akin to that of Christina, the "disembodied lady" discussed by Oliver Sacks in his book *The Man Who Mistook His Wife for a Hat.*[8] Because of an allergic reaction to an antibiotic drug, Christina lost all sense of her body—a failure of her faculty of proprioception, the delicate, subliminal feedback mechanism that tells the brain about the position, tension, and general feeling of the body and its parts. It is this "sixth sense" that allows for coordination of movement; without it, talking, walking, even standing, are virtually impossible. In similar fashion, I no longer know where my feet are, and without the low-level pain I still feel, I would hardly know I had legs. Indeed, one of the early symptoms of my malady was a tendency to lose my balance when I would take off my pants in the dark, something that happened to me often in my drinking days. Christina's troubles differ from those of the paralytic, however, for her loss has been more complete. Besides, she became disembodied while still capable of movement, and she compensated by using her eyes to coordinate her physical actions. Quadriplegics, too, must watch what they are doing, and I have spilled drinks held in my hand because my wrist had turned and my brain didn't register it. But by the time the paralytic's failure of proprioception is as complete as Christina's, the limb is no longer movable, and the condition is moot.

I have also become rather emotionally detached from my body, often referring to one of my limbs as *the* leg or *the* arm. People who help me on a regular basis have also fallen into this pattern ("I'll hold the arms and you grab the legs"), as if this depersonalization would compensate for what otherwise would be an intolerable violation of my personal space. The paralytic becomes accustomed to being lifted, rolled, pushed, pulled, and twisted, and he survives this treatment by putting emotional distance between himself and his body. Others join in this effort, and I well remember that after I came to from neurosurgery in 1976, there was a sign pinned to my sheet that read, DO NOT LIFT BY ARMS. I weakly suggested to the nurse that they print another sign saying this THIS SIDE UP.

As my condition has deteriorated, I have come increasingly to look upon my body as a faulty life-support system, the only function of which is to sustain my head. It is all a bit like *Donovan's Brain,* an old science-fiction movie in which a quite nefarious brain is kept alive in a jar with mysterious wires and tubes attached to it. Murphy's brain is similarly sitting on a body that has no movement or tactile sense below the arms and shoulders, and that functions mainly to oxygenate the blood, receive nourishment, and eliminate wastes. In none of these capacities does it do a very good job. My solution to this dilemma is radical dissociation from the body, a kind of etherealization of identity. Perhaps one reason for my success in this adaptation is that I never did take much pride in my body. I am of medium height, rather scrawny, and militantly nonathletic. I was never much to look at, but that didn't bother me greatly. From boyhood onward, I cultivated my wits instead. It is a very different matter for an athletically inclined boy or a girl on the threshold of dating and courtship.

Those who have lost use of some parts of their bodies learn to cultivate the others. The blind develop acute sensitivity to sounds, and quadriplegics, who cannot handle heavy telephone directories, have a remarkable knack for remembering phone numbers. But of a more fundamental order, the quadriplegic's body can no longer speak a "silent language" in the expression of emotions or concepts too elusive for ordinary speech, for the delicate feedback loops between thought and movement have been broken. Proximity, gesture, and body-set have been muted, and the body's ability to articulate thought has been stilled. It is perhaps for this reason that writing has become almost an addiction for me, for in it thought and mind become a system, united in conjunction with the movements of my hands and the responses of the machine. Of even more profound impact on existential states, the thinking activity of the brain cannot be dissolved into motion, and the mind can no longer be lost in an internal dialogue with physical movement. This leaves one adrift in a lonely monologue, an inner soliloquy without rest or surcease, and often without subject matter. Consciousness is overtaken and devoured in contemplation, meditation, ratiocination, and reflection without end, relieved only by one's remaining movements, and sleep.

My thoughts and sense of being alive have been driven back into my brain, where I now reside. More than ever before, it is the base from which I reach out and grasp the world. Many paralytics say that they no longer feel attached to their bodies, which is another way of expressing the shattering of Merleau-Ponty's mind–body system. But it also has a few positive aspects. Just as an anthropologist gets a better perspective on his own culture through long and deep study of a radically different one, my extended sojourn in disability has given me, like it or not, a measure of estrangement far beyond the yield of any trip. I now stand somewhat apart from American culture, making me in many ways a stranger. And with this estrangement has come a greater urge to penetrate the veneer of cultural differences and reach an understanding of the underlying unity of all human experience.

My own disembodied thoughts are crude when compared with those of many people. A blind Milton painted sweeping landscapes of the heavens in *Paradise Lost,* and Beethoven crafted the Ninth Symphony despite—or perhaps because of—being deaf. And today one of the world's leading cosmologists, a Cambridge physicist named Stephen Hawking, travels through quarks and black holes in a journey across space and time to the birth of the universe. These are voyages of the mind, for Hawking has an advanced case of amyotrophic lateral sclerosis (familiarly known as Lou Gehrig's disease), which has left him with only slight movement in one hand and an inability to speak above a whisper. There are not many Miltons, Beethovens, and Hawkings, however, and their example may be small comfort to a twenty-year-old quadriplegic who has made the mistake of diving into shallow water. For most disabled people, the loss of synchrony between mind and body has few compensations.

Many years ago, long before I became disabled, I was talking to a black anthropologist, a friend from our days as fellow graduate students, and the subject turned to race. In the course of our conversation, my friend said, "I always think of myself as being black, just as you always think of yourself as white." I protested this, saying that even though I did think of myself as white when talking to a black person, my skin color was not in the forefront of my conscious mind at other times. My friend didn't believe me. But I was neither mistaken nor misleading in my observation, for I grew up in and still lived in a white world. Whiteness was taken for granted; it was standard and part of the usual order of things. I lived in white neighborhoods; I sailed on a white warship (except for the officers' stewards, who were black); I went to white schools (P.S. 114 in Rockaway Beach never had a black student during my eight years there); and I work in a profession that is still ninety-five percent white. Why think of my whiteness when most of my contacts are with white people? The comedian Martin Mull once did a television program entitled "The History of White People in America," a howlingly funny title because its redundancy fractures logic. White is normal; it's what ethnolinguists call an "unmarked category," a word that is dominant within its class and against which other words of that class are contrasted. Why, I would no more have thought of myself as white than I would have thought of myself as walking on two legs.

Before my disability, I was standard White, Anglo-Saxon, Agnostic Male (WASAM?), a member of the dominant part of the society. My roots in tattered-lace-curtain Irish Catholicism made me uneasy in academia, but I never gave much thought to the other components of my identity. My black friend was forced by the reality of white society always to think of himself as black. It was his first line of defense against a hostile environment. His was an embattled identity. And in exactly the same way, from the time I first took to the wheelchair up to the present, the fact that I am physically handicapped has been in the background of my conscious thoughts. Busy though I might be with other matters and problems, it lingers as a shadow in the corner of my mind, waiting, ready to come out at any moment to fill my meditations. It is a Presence. I, too, had acquired an embattled identity, a sense of who and what I was that was no longer dominated by my past social attributes, but rather by my physical defects.

One of the more interesting parallels between the stigma of handicap and other forms of embattlement is a sensitivity to nomenclature. One must refer to Negroes as *blacks* today, a term that would have been insulting forty years ago, when the polite word was *colored.* Likewise, the term *lady* is now considered patronizing, and *girl* seems reserved for the prepubescent. It is not surprising, then, that many people in wheelchairs take offense at the brutally direct word *paralysis,* and I have heard spirited arguments over the relative meanings and virtues of *handicapped* and *disabled.* Words such as *crip* and *gimp* are forbidden to the able-bodied, although they are used by the disabled among themselves; ethnic pejorative words are bandied about in the same way. I have treated *handicapped* and *disabled* as synonyms, for what I find most interesting about the debate over the words is the debate itself. It reveals a stance of defensiveness against belittlement that is seldom relaxed; it bespeaks a constant awareness of one's deficiencies. And in the process, even the vocabulary of disability has become emotionally charged. People have a hard time deciding what to say to the disabled, and their troubles are compounded by the fact that they are uncertain about what words to use.

In all the years since the onset of my illness, I have never consciously asked, "Why me?" I feel that this is a foolish question that assumes some cosmic sense of purpose and direction in the universe that simply does not exist. My outlook is quite fatalistic, an attitude that actually predisposes me to get all the pleasure out of life that I can, while I can. Nonetheless, though I may not brood over my impairment, it is always on my mind in spoken or unspoken form, and I believe this is true of all disabled people. It is a precondition of my plans and projects, a first premise of all my thoughts. Just as my former sense of embodiment remained taken for granted, positive, and unconscious, my sense of disembodiment is problematic, negative, and conscious. My identity has lost its stable moorings and has become contingent on a physical flaw.

This consuming consciousness of handicap even invades one's dreams. When I first became disabled, I was still walking, after a fashion, and I remained perfectly normal in my dreams. But as the years passed and I lost the ability to stand or walk, a curious change occurred. In every dream I start out walking and moving freely, often in perilous places; significantly, I am never in a wheelchair. I am climbing high on the mast of a ship in rough seas—something I did occasionally in an earlier incarnation—or I am on a ladder, painting a house. But in the middle of the dream, I remember that I can't walk, at which point I falter and fall. The dream is a perfect enactment of failure of power, the realization that what most men unconsciously fear had in fact happened to me. In other dreams, I am just walking about aimlessly when suddenly I remember my disability. Sometimes I sit down, but often I just stand puzzled until I awaken, the dream dissolves, the room comes into view, and I return to the reality that my paralysis is not a transient thing—it is an awakening much like that of Gregor Samsa in Kafka's *The Metamorphosis.* But perhaps more significant than the content of my dreams is the fact that since 1978 I have never once dreamed of anything else. Even in sleep, disability keeps its tyrannical hold over the mind.

The totality of the impact of serious physical impairment on conscious thought, as well as its firm implantation in the unconscious mind, gives disability a far stronger purchase on one's sense of who and what he is than do any social roles—even key ones such as age, occupation, and ethnicity. These can be manipulated, neutralized, and suspended, and in this way can become adjusted somewhat to each other. Moreover, each role can be played before a separate audience, allowing us to lead multiple lives. One cannot, however, shelve a disability or hide it from the world. A serious disability inundates all other claims to social standing, relegating to secondary status all the attainments of life, all other social roles, even sexuality. It is not a role; it is an identity, a dominant characteristic to which all social roles must be adjusted. And just as the paralytic cannot clear his mind of his impairment, society will not let him forget it.

Given the magnitude of this assault on the self, it is understandable that another major component of the subjective life of the handicapped is anger,[9] a disposition so diffuse and subtle, so carefully managed, that I became aware of it in myself only through writing this book. The anger of the disabled takes two forms. The first is an existential anger, a pervasive bitterness at one's fate, a hoarse and futile cry of rage against fortune. It is a sentiment fueled by the self-hate generated by unconscious shame and guilt, and it bears more than casual resemblance to the anger of America's black people. And, just as among blacks, it becomes expressed in hostility toward the dominant society, then toward people of one's own kind, and finally it is turned inward into an attack on the self. It is a very destructive emotion. In my own case, I have escaped its worst ravages only because my impairment has been so slow that I have been able to adjust to it mentally, and I am old enough to know that I am just a statistic, not the victim of a divine conspiracy. I suspect, although I lack conclusive data on this, that anger is much greater among those suddenly disabled and the young, for their impairment happens too quickly to permit assimilation, and it clouds an entire lifetime.

The other kind of anger is a situational one, a reaction to frustration or to perceived poor treatment. I have a good supply of this type. A paralytic may struggle to walk and become enraged when he cannot move his leg. Or a quadriplegic may pick up a cup of coffee with stiffened hands and drop it on his lap, precipitating an angry outburst. I had to give up spaghetti because I could no longer twirl it on my fork, and dinner would end for me in a sloppy mess. This would so upset me that I would lose my appetite. Or I may try unsuccessfully for a minute or so to pick up a paper from my desk or turn a page, casual maneuvers for most but a major challenge to me, because my fingers have lost both strength and dexterity. Such frustrations happen to me, and to other paralytics, several times a day. They are minor but cumulative, and they acquire special intensity from the more generalized existential anger often lurking below the surface.

The kind and virulence of the anger of the disabled vary greatly, for each person has a different history, but I have the impression that the depth and type of disability are critical. The extent of disablement obviously influences both existential and situational rage, but anger also seems to be most intense among people with communication disorders—primarily deaf-mutes and people with cerebral palsy and certain kinds of stroke. Most of us have watched the transparent suffering of the speech-impaired as they struggle to convey meaning to their agonized listeners. It is small wonder that the deaf form tightly circumscribed little communities, or that they occasionally explode into overt hostility at those who can hear and speak.

The anger of the disabled arises in the first place from their own lack of physical functions, but, as we will see, it is aggravated by their interaction with the able-bodied world. They daily suffer snub, avoidance, patronization, and occasional outright cruelty, and even when none of these occur, they sometimes imagine the affronts. But whatever the source of the grievance, the disabled have limited ways of showing it. Quadriplegics cannot stalk off in high (or low) dudgeon, nor can they even use body language. To make matters worse, as the price for normal relations, they must comfort others about their condition. They cannot show fear, sorrow, depression, sexuality, or anger, for this disturbs the able-bodied. The unsound of limb are permitted only to laugh. The rest of the emotions, including anger and the expression of hostility, must be bottled up, repressed, and allowed to simmer or be released in the backstage area of the home. This is where I let loose most of the day's frustrations and irritations, much to Yolanda's chagrin. But I never vent to her the full despair and foreboding I sometimes feel, and rarely even express it to myself. As for the rest of the world, I must sustain their faith in their own immunity by looking resolutely cheery. Have a nice day!

In summary, from my own experience and research and the work of others I have found that the four most far-reaching changes in the consciousness of the disabled are: lowered self-esteem; the invasion and occupation of thought by physical deficits; a strong undercurrent of anger; and the acquisition of a new, total, and undesirable identity. I can only liken the situation to a curious kind of "invasion of the body snatchers," in which the alien intruder and the old occupant coexist in mutual hostility in the same body. It is also a metamorphosis in the exact sense. One morning in the hospital, a nurse was washing me when she was called away by another nurse, who needed help in moving a patient. "I'll be right back," she said as she left, which all hospital denizens know is but a fond hope. She left me lying on my back without the call bell or the TV remote, the door was closed, and she was gone for a half hour. Wondering whether she had forgotten me, I tried to roll onto my side to reach the bell. But I was already quadriplegic, and, try as I might, I couldn't make it. I finally gave up and was almost immediately overcome by a claustrophobic panic, feeling trapped and immobile in my own body. I thought then of Kafka's giant bug, as it rocked from side to side, wiggling its useless legs, trying to get off its back—and I understood the story for the first time.

At the beginning of this [article], I spoke of the feeling of aloneness, the desire to shrink from society into the inner recesses of the self, that invades the thoughts of the disabled—a feeling that I attributed in part to the deep physical tiredness that accompanies most debility and the formidable physical obstacles posed by the outside world. But we have added other elements to this urge to withdraw. The individual has also been alienated from his old, carefully nurtured, and closely guarded sense of self by a new, foreign, and unwelcome identity. And he becomes alienated from others by a double-barreled mechanism: Due to his depreciated self-image, he has a tendency to withdraw from his old associations into social isolation. And, as if in covert cooperation with this retreat, society—or at least American society—helps to wall him off.

The physical and emotional sequestering of the disabled is often dramatic. One quadriplegic man, married and the father of two children, told us that he never leaves the house and nobody visits their home, not even the friends of his children. He confessed to feelings of shame about his condition. I was struck by the similarity between that family and the one begotten by my father. Another quadriplegic we met attends college through a program that allows home study. Even though he is capable of leaving his house with help, he never does so, and instructors from the college have to meet him at his home. He is trying to break out of his shell, but he is not quite ready. Many disabled people blame their isolation on a hostile society, and often they are right. But there is also that powerful pull backward into the self. It is an urge that I have felt all my life, a centripetal force that is a universal feature of the emotional makeup of our species. Our lives are built upon a constant struggle between the need to reach out to others and a contrary urge to fall back into ourselves. Among the disabled, the inward pull becomes compelling, often irresistible, outlining in stark relief a human propensity that is often perceived only dimly.

The generality of my inquiry was brought home to me vividly one day while listening to a paper delivered by my colleague Katherine Newman. Newman has been doing important research on four groups of people who have experienced severe economic loss: divorced women, air traffic controllers fired after going out on strike in 1981, laid-off blue collar workers, and long-time-unemployed middle-management people. Newman described a pattern of consistent responses from all four groups. All experienced a deep sense of loss and went through a period of "mourning" quite similar to that reported among the traumatically disabled. Their feelings of depression were aggravated by a process of self-abasement, accentuated in the case of the divorcées by a sense of sexual inadequacy. Common to most members of the four groups was the idea that they somehow were responsible for the loss, that they had failed as providers. They felt culpable, even in cases where they clearly were innocent victims of impersonal economic circumstance. Here, too, the American ideology of success, combined with vestiges of Calvinism, takes the anger that should be aimed at the system and turns it inward upon the self. With their guilt came shame, and Newman's informants frequently surrendered to that sentiment by sharp curtailment of their social contacts. These tendencies often were reinforced by society's penchant for blaming the victim; their self-condemnation was joined by the censure of others. The stricken individual, and his or her family, withdraws into humiliation, and all tend to be avoided just as if a pox had visited them.

The psychological devastation wrought by unemployment has been studied for more than half a century, but Newman's brilliant exposition makes vividly clear the striking parallels between economic and physical disability, the despoilment of identity that is the common fallout of the damaged self. It is a commentary on the importance of economic status in America that downward mobility fosters the same social and psychological results as crippling. And it is worth noting at this point that the social and emotional ravages of physical disability often are magnified by the individual's loss of livelihood. My own case is a rare exception.

Most of Newman's subjects will eventually make their way back to some kind of economic viability, and here they part company with the handicapped, to whom something more devastating has happened. The disabled have become changed in the minds of the rest of society into a kind of quasi-human. In only a few months, I had moved subtly from the center of my society to its perimeter. I had acquired a new identity that was contingent on my defects and that either compromised or radically altered my prior claims to personhood. In my middle age, I had become a changeling, the lot of all disabled people. They are afflicted with a malady of the body that is translated into a cancer within the self and a disease of social relationships. They have experienced a transformation of the essential condition of their being in the world. They have become aliens, even exiles, in their own lands.

REFERENCES

1. Erving Goffman, *Stigma: Notes on the Management of Spoiled Identity* (Englewood Cliffs, N.J.: Prentice-Hall, 1963).
2. Constantina Safilios-Rothschild, *The Sociology, and Social Psychology of Disability and Rehabilitation* (New York: Random House, 1970).
3. Goffman, *Stigma.*
4. George Herbert Mead, *Mind, Self and Society* (Chicago: University of Chicago Press, 1934).
5. Maurice Merleau-Ponty, *The Phenomenology of Perception* (New York: Humanities Press, 1962).
6. Ibid., p. 81.
7. Gelya Frank, "Venus on Wheels: The Life History of a Congenital Amputee," Ph.D. dissertation, Department of Anthropology, University of California, Los Angeles, 1981.
8. Oliver Sacks, *The Man Who Mistook His Wife for a Hat,* pp. 42–52.

Biomedicine, Technology, and the Body

CONCEPTUAL TOOLS

- ***Some of the problematic aspects of new biomedical technologies are focused on the beginning and end of life.*** New technologies can force us to challenge essential views on life itself, such as what constitutes a state of "life" versus "death." Premature infants who recently would have had no chance of survival can now be "saved," although at high cost, both economicaly and in terms of health. Similarly, death can be postponed for a very long time with the use of heart-lung machines, feeding tubes, and intensive health care. New technologies often bring new ethical questions with them. Medical anthropologists have made important contributions to these ethical debates, often by articulating the cultural assumptions, diverse voices, and social power aspects of the arguments.

- ***New reproductive technologies like in vitro fertilization represent interesting case studies of the process of medicalization.*** Medical anthropologists have documented enduring sexism in biomedicine, most often in the field of obstetrics (Hahn 1987). Historically, biomedicine has medicalized and often pathologized normal physiological processes, like pregnancy, childbirth, and breast-feeding. Normal parts of a woman's reproductive life cycle are turned into "diseases." For example, "moodiness" around the time of menstruation becomes "PMS," which in turn becomes a DSM-IV psychiatric condition. The result has often been the imposition of male medical authority over women's bodies and health. In other words, women's lives—and especially their reproductive lives—have increasingly come under medical control. New reproductive technologies have spread throughout the world via globalization.

- ***In North American biomedicine, the human body is often conceptualized as a machine.*** The body-as-machine metaphor is linked to questions of organ transplants and artificial body parts. An assumption of a strict dichotomy between body and mind makes it seem "natural" to fix the body as if it were a machine, substituting parts when necessary. The decisions people make for or against using a new technology often rely on many factors, including the economic costs, their judgment of how effective a new technology may be, and whether use of the technology constitutes an appropriate moral act.

- ***Organ transplantation is an area of cultural contestation.*** In recent years, medical anthropologists have done a great deal of work on cultural issues surrounding organ procurement and transplantation. The technical possibility of transplantation has led to the "commodification" of organs—treating them as a market good of which there is always a shortage. The transplantation process can be a powerful experience for recipients, living donors as well as the families of deceased donors. Anthropologists have also studied, and been politically active in trying to stop, a disturbing international "trade" in human organs.

 21

Accounting for Amniocentesis

Rayna Rapp

The term accounting *in the title of this selection has two meanings. First, an account is an individual's story, like the three stories about amniocentesis at the beginning of the selection. An account represents an individual's creation of meaning out of life experiences. Medical anthropologists, as ethnographers, regularly collect people's stories—about their lives, their illness experiences, their decisions, and so forth. An account is one part of the discourse, or talk, that an ethnographer can directly observe. The second meaning of* accounting *in the title is a kind of analysis—the breaking down of a phenomenon into its essential components. To do an accounting of the complex procedure of amniocentesis, it is necessary to take on the viewpoints of different actors—in this case, the mothers, genetic counselors, and laboratory workers. The single term* accounting *has multiple layers of meaning that cannot be reconciled because they often involve contradictions or binary opposites* (antinomies, *in the author's terms).*

New reproductive technologies—in vitro fertilization (so-called test-tube babies), sonograms (ultrasound pictures), genetic screening through amniocentesis, and other testing procedures—have been both wondrous and troubling biomedical developments with regard to women's health. On the one hand, these technologies might prevent untold suffering due to infertility or prevent the birth of children with terrible medical problems. Also, biomedical technology gives people more control over their reproductive lives. On the other hand, they can be seen as symbols of biomedical dominance (hegemony) over women's lives and as technological intrusions into normal physiological processes. Some people wonder if this is a good thing—for example, consider the use of amniocentesis for preferential abortions of females in some cultures (Miller 1987).

Genetic screening through amniocentesis is closely bound up with the ongoing U.S. cultural debate over abortion, a debate that is poised at the intersection of politics, religion, women's rights, biomedicine, and social class. Faye Ginsburg's book Contested Lives *is an ethnographic case study of the debate in a single U.S. community (1989). In that book, Ginsburg centers her research on women's stories from both sides of the abortion debate; as an ethnographer, she uses women's accounts grounded in the context of their own lives to provide honest and insightful analyses of the plurality of U.S. culture. In this selection, Rayna Rapp uses the same ethnographic attention to women's stories analyzed from multiple viewpoints to demonstrate the cultural complexities of gender and women's health.*

As you read this selection, consider these questions:

- **Why did Rayna Rapp include working in a laboratory setting as part of her field research on amniocentesis? What does the author mean by a "gendered workplace"?**
- **What does Rapp mean by the idea of the anthropologist "situating herself within the context of the research"? Why is this relevant?**
- **Why is amniocentesis stressful for mothers? Why would some women not need the test and others refuse the test?**
- **How is ethnicity a factor in amniocentesis and reproductive decision making?**
- **What does Rapp mean by her sixth point, that "disabilities, like pregnancies, are socially constructed"?**

Context: Rayna Rapp is a professor of anthropology at New York University. She has been an important leader both in feminist anthropology and in the medical anthropological study of biomedical technologies. Her 1999 book, *Testing Women, Testing the Fetus: The Social Impact of Amniocentesis in America*, was the winner of the prestigious Staley Prize in Anthropology and has become a classic in the field. Her research on the emerging technology of amniocentesis, a prenatal diagnostic test used to screen fetuses for chromosomal anomalies, was originally inspired by feminist concerns. Her fieldwork, encompassing multiple viewpoints, emphasized the fact that the practice of amniocentesis is consistent with the stratification of reproduction along social class lines. This research has led her to more recent work on genetics, disabilities, genetic counseling, and new reproductive technologies. This article was first published in a collection that signaled an important turn toward the study of biomedicine in medical anthropology.

Source: R. Rapp (1993). "Accounting for Amniocentesis." In *Knowledge, Power and Practice: the Anthropology of Medicine in Everyday Life,* S. Lindenbaum and M. Lock (eds.), pp. 55–78. Berkeley and Los Angeles: University of California Press.

MULTIPLE BEGINNINGS

Here are three amniocentesis stories, drawn from my New York–based fieldwork, any one of which raises the problem of how to understand the development and routinization of prenatal diagnosis:

On Tuesdays, Alfredo returns to the lab around three o'clock in the afternoon. On this particular Tuesday, there are four fluids in the specimen case he carries, two from Woodhull Hospital in Bushwick, Brooklyn, and two from St. Luke's on Manhattan's Upper West Side. Susan, the head of the lab, assigns one fluid each to Shedeh, Tom, Doris, and Moira. Shedeh will team up with Doris, who is still in training, to make sure all steps of the lab protocol are followed as the samples are logged and numbered, spun down, siphoned, divided, fed, and incubated. The fluids (or soup, as the lab techs call it) will be fed at six days and again at eleven. At fourteen days, there should be enough fetal cells in metaphase ready to read. By that time, the techs will have completed staining, scoping, photographing, and karyotyping cells from the earlier cases on which each was working. Turnaround time at the lab is twenty-one days, and it would be shorter if there were more technicians. The techs cooperate on cutting and scoping under time pressure, completing one another's karyotypes, rushing results, and feeding one another's soup. Seated on swivel chairs at the microscope, or around the cutting table, they talk about baby showers and lunch menus, rock concerts and New York rents as they work. Moira declares that "her" fetus is a wimp: "It's got a wimpy Y and the bikini on the X is pretty gross." Wimpy or not, this fetus is 46XY, which will be reported as a normal diagnosis. I am at the cutting table, struggling to tell number 13 chromosomes from number 14s, listening attentively to lab banter, and wondering what is happening to the woman from whose pregnant belly these "wimpy" fetal cells have been drawn.

Upstairs, Elena is answering telephones, directing patients calling for results to various genetic counselors; Henrietta is the most reassuring, the least likely to tell a twenty-one-week pregnant woman to call back in another week. She'll walk downstairs, trace a sample from the day it was logged to the scope on which it is being read, and try hard to get information she can share on the phone: "The chromosome studies aren't completed yet, but the biochemical results are just fine, and we should have the chromosomes by Friday. Call back, it's okay to call back." But in this case, Mrs. Ramirez speaks only Spanish, and Henrietta doesn't. Iris Mendez, the Sarah Lawrence student on an internship, may do the phone work, or Elena will take matters into her own hands—pestering, then translating for one of the counselors who says she is too busy to take on the case.

Mrs. Ramirez is a Honduran immigrant domestic worker who settled in East Harlem three years ago. Before coming to New York, she had three children, the last in a hospital. Before she registered at St. Luke's prenatal clinic in her fifteenth week of this pregnancy, she had never heard of "the needle test." Now she is having amniocentesis. Why and how has this "choice" to use a new and very expensive reproductive technology been made? What must I learn about migration, medicine, and motherhood to understand how amniocentesis becomes routinized for both the lab techs and women like Mrs. Ramirez?

In February, Tom found something ambiguous on the number 9 chromosomes of the sample he was scoping. Susan told him to check forty cells from all three flasks, rather than twenty from two. But the ambiguity persisted; it wasn't an in vitro artifact, or a random find. He, Susan, and the techs discussed it, and then called Dr. Judith Schwartz, the geneticist in charge of the lab. Judith agreed: there was additional chromosomal material on the top, short arm of the number 9 chromosomes. She called it "9P+": 9 for the pair of chromosomes on which it was located, P to designate the short arm, and plus to indicate additional chromosomal material. First she scanned the literature for an interpretation. Then she phoned the head obstetrician at Woodhull's prenatal clinic in charge of the case and made an appointment for the woman to be called in.

A week's research revealed nothing on "9P+," but twelve clinical reports on "trisomy 9," the closest diagnosis to which Judith could assimilate her case. The move to stabilize a label and an interpretation was not frivolous: the added material (the "plus" on the P arm) had banding patterns that suggested it was a partial replication of the #9, a trisomymanqué. After careful reading, many phone consultations with colleagues, and a meeting with Malve, the genetic counselor who had done the intake interview with the patient at Woodhull, Judith sent Malve off to explain the problem. The patient listened, and decided to keep the pregnancy. Malve was upset by her decision, and thought she hadn't understood what Judith's research revealed: in all twelve cases she could find of trisomy 9, the babies were born with visible and structurally significant physical anomalies and some degree of mental retardation. She asked Judith to counsel the patient directly. Judith did. The patient kept the pregnancy.

The baby was born in early June, and in late July, Judith Schwartz contacted the new mother through her obstetrician, asking if she would be willing to bring her child to the genetics laboratory for a consultation. The mother agreed. On a Wednesday afternoon, the "trisomy 9" came visiting: he was a six-week-old Haitian boy named Étienne St.-Croix. His mother, Veronique, spoke reasonable English and good French. His grandmother, Marie-Lucie, who carried the child, spoke Creole and some French. The two geneticists spoke English, Polish, Hebrew, and Korean between them. I translated in French, ostensibly for the grandmother and mother. Here is what happened:

Judith was gracious with Veronique but after a moment's chit-chat asked to examine the baby. She never spoke directly to the mother again during the examination. Instead, she and Maxine, the other geneticist, both trained in pediatrics, handled the newborn with confidence and interest. Malve took notes as Judith measured and consulted with Maxine. "Note the oblique palpebral fissure and micrognathia," Judith called out. "Yes," answered Veronique in perfect time to the conversation, "he has the nose of my Uncle Hervé and the ears of Aunt Mathilde." As the geneticists pathologized the mother "genealogized," the genetic counselor remained silent, furiously taking notes, and the anthropologist tried to keep score. When the examination was over, the geneticists apologized to the baby for any discomfort they had caused him, and Judith, herself a practicing Jew, asked the mother one direct question. "I notice you haven't circumcised your baby. Are you planning to?" "Yes," Veronique replied, "we'll do it in about another week." "May we have the foreskin?" Judith queried. "With the foreskin, we can keep growing trisomy 9 cells for research, and study the tissue as your baby develops." Veronique gave her a firm and determined "yes," and the consultation was over.

Walking Veronique and Marie-Lucie to the subway to direct them home to Brooklyn, I asked what Veronique had thought about the experience: from the amniocentesis to the diagnosis to the genetic consultation.

> At first, I was very frightened. I am thirty seven, I wanted a baby, it is my husband's second marriage, my mother-in-law is for me, not the first wife, my mother-in-law wanted me to have a baby, too. If it had been Down's, maybe, just maybe I would have had an abortion. Once I had an abortion, but now I am a Seventh Day Adventist, and I don't believe in abortion anymore. Maybe for Down's, just maybe. But when they told me this, who knows? I was so scared, but the more they talked, the less they said. They do not know what this is. And I do not know, either. So now, it's my baby. We'll just have to wait and see what happens. And so will they.

How do geneticists, genetic counselors, pregnant Haitians and anthropologists come to their interpretations of inherently ambiguous situations? How are the intersecting discourses of "genetics," "marriage and family life," and "medical anthropology" constructed, and how do they express contradictory processes?

. . .

Pat was thirty-seven when she accidentally got pregnant, and decided to keep the baby. "It was my best shot at ever having a second child. My first one was already eighteen, she didn't want this, but ever since I divorced her father, I knew I wanted another marriage, another baby. I couldn't get the marriage, but I got the kid." Pat's obstetrician recommended amniocentesis because she was over thirty-five and without much reflection she undertook the test. When the results came back positive, no one was more shocked than she. Her OB wanted to perform an abortion right away, but she stalled for time. The more she thought, the more ambivalent she became.

> I did some research, I visited this group home for adult retardeds in my neighborhood. You know, it was kind of nice. They looked pretty happy, they had jobs, they went bowling. I thought about it. Maybe if I was married, maybe if I had another shot at it. But this was it: take it or leave it. So I took it. I called the Mormons back. Oh, I hadn't been to temple for years. But I knew, in my heart of hearts, they'd convince me not to have an abortion. And they did. One man, he just came and prayed with me, he still comes. Stevie gets a lot of colds, I can't always make it to temple. But when we don't make it, he comes over and prays with us. And the Down's support group, that's helpful too. They told me about schools, and special programs. Stevie's doing really well, he'll learn to read this year, I know he will. And if he doesn't, that's okay, too. This kid has been a blessing, he makes me ask myself, "why are we put here on earth?" There must be a reason, and Stevie's reason was to teach love, to stop haters dead in their tracks. Everyone who meets him loves him. They may start out talking behind his back, but pretty soon, they're rooting for him, 'cause he's such a neat kid. He's taught me a lot about love, and acceptance. So when I see a girl who's pregnant, I always tell her about Stevie, I always say, "don't have that test, you don't need that test to love your baby the way it is." Oh,

> for some of them, maybe abortion is a good thing, I don't know. But for me, Stevie was just what I needed.

How can I account for Pat's "choice" in a way that preserves her agency while noting the power of religion, class, gender ideology, and personal reproductive history in it? How can I describe the shifting powers of sexual mores and medicalization in American culture as they both construct and constrain the range of what she might "choose"?

THE PROBLEM OF THE EXCLUDED MIDDLE

> If anthropology can be said to have one foot in the sciences and one in the humanities, medical anthropology is thus doubly marked. . . . [It] must find a workable bridge linking biology and culture, matter and symbol, body and mind, action and thought. Medical anthropologists are challenged . . . to resolve the central issues in anthropological theory . . . and to contribute to contemporary discussions concerning the status of science as a component of culture.
>
> —LINDENBAUM AND LOCK (1993)

Like all fields of critical inquiry, medical anthropology must simultaneously construct and deconstruct itself. The field seems balanced on a fulcrum, seesawing between biology and history, medicine and meaning systems, epidemiology and emic explanations. This construction tempts us to investigate an amalgam of the body biological and the body politic. When we begin with this orientation, the terrain on which our investigation rests appears stable: we can describe or measure how biology and culture intersect, assuming that each "factor" is distinct, if interactive.

Yet we also know that such bounded representations of biological and social bodies are deeply linked to nature/culture oppositions in the history of Western thought. Deconstructing such antimonies is a prerequisite for providing more powerful accounts of how illness and health operate in the lives of our informants, as well as in the disciplines of medicine and medical anthropology. Antimonies of nature and culture exclude precisely that "middle ground" on which the contest for the meaning and management of illness and health is constructed. It is not a coincidence that such antimonies also position "science" or "medicine" on the high ground of the theoretical seesaw, thus silencing competing interpretations or reducing them to ethnosciences. Binary formulations leave medical anthropologists remarkably free to construct an external role for themselves: we view ourselves as participant-*observers* with license to describe the relation between the parts, rather than observing *participants* in the social phenomena our narratives help to construct.

This triple exclusion—of the middle ground on which contests for meaning occur, of all other interpretations as less-than-scientific, and of medical anthropologists as "outside" their objects of study—became especially clear to me as I began to study the routinization of amniocentesis beginning in 1983. Combing the literature on "patient reactions to prenatal diagnosis," I found four overlapping medical discourses: geneticists spoke of the benefits and burdens their evolving technical knowledge conferred on patients (a discourse that has rapidly intensified as the Human Genome Initiative gets under way); health economists deployed their famous cost/benefit analysis to suggest which diseases and patient populations should be most effectively screened; social workers and sociologists interrogated the psychological stability and decision-making strategies of "couples" faced with "reproductive choices"; and bioethicists commented on the legal, ethical, and social implications of practices in the field of human genetics. Later, a fifth discourse, penned by feminists who are on the whole opposed to the new reproductive technologies as a "male takeover" of motherhood, was added to the literature (Arditti, Duelli-Klein, and Minden 1984; Baruch, d'Amato, and Seager 1988; Corea 1985; Rothman 1986; Spallone & Steinberg 1987; Stanworth 1987). Absent from the published texts were descriptions of the multilayered and contradictory processes by which a new reproductive technology was being produced, a new work force and patient populations created, or a language articulated to describe the impact of these processes on representations of pregnancy, maternity, children, and family life.

Yet if we return to the stories that open this chapter, we can identify many multilayered forces at work. They include (at least) the following seven processes, in narrative order:

First, it is important to analyze "laboratory life." The laboratory labors through which prenatal diagnoses are constructed and carried out by a class-stratified, multiethnic new work force, most of whose members are women. From the Puerto Rican driver to the Iranian, Polish Catholic, Southern African-American, and suburban Jewish lab techs, to the Polish Israeli-American and Korean-American geneticists, this is a work force that resembles the multinational make-up of New York's population. Brain drains, civil wars, labor migrations, upward and downward mobility: these world-scale political economic forces structure the possibilities of who becomes a worker in the scientific labor force. During the two months that I "interned" at the lab, three of the twelve technicians left and were replaced. One Lebanese, one Chinese, and one U.S.-born white Anglo-Saxon were succeeded by an Armenian-Iranian, a Southern African-American, and a New York–born Puerto Rican.

This rapid turnover in the labor force of medical technology is business-as-usual, according to the two geneticists who run the lab. And genetic counseling, too, is a field where job mobility is fast and continuous. During the three years that I have been observing their rounds, five lab counselors have filled two and a half permanent slots, and three to five student interns pass through the lab each year. Work culture is thus based on medical language, and there is little continuity for long-term connections through which counter-discourses might develop.

The world of prenatal diagnosis is distinctly female. Not only are pregnant women the clients for this new reproductive service, but virtually all the workers in this "industry" are female as well. Most lab technicians are women. Geneticists working in this field are disproportionately women, and more than 98 percent of all genetic counselors are female. This new "allied health professional" has been created in the last fifteen years explicitly to serve as "interface" between the DNA revolution and the public who will reap its consequences. Janus-faced experts in a technical and rapidly changing science, genetic counselors balance between science and social work, speaking both epidemiology and empathy to their clients. Trained in aspects of molecular genetics which many physicians do not understand, they are situated in the medical hierarchy like social workers. The cytogenetics, human genetics, molecular genetics, and counseling labors that construct prenatal diagnoses are often described as appropriately "feminine" because they focus on pregnancy, and the nine-to-five working hours do not disrupt family responsibilities. A new field of employment on the frontier of genetics thus emerges with job descriptions, prestige, and pay scales that reproduce familiar gender hierarchies.

Second, we need to consider the recruitment of highly diverse female patient populations. While nationally amniocentesis is becoming something of a ritual for white, middle-class families in which women have delayed childbearing to further education and careers, in New York City the situation is somewhat different. The Prenatal Diagnosis Laboratory of the Health Department was set up in 1978 explicitly to offer amniocentesis to low-income, hence disproportionately non-white, women. The lab is subsidized by both the state and city of New York. It accepts Medicaid and all third-party insurance, and has a sliding-scale fee that begins at zero. The amniotic fluid samples it analyzes reflect this economic outreach to the urban poor: the lab population is approximately one-third Hispanic, one-third African-American, and one-third white; half are private patients, and half are seen at public clinics, according to the racial/ethnic categories provided by both the city and state health departments.

. . .

New York City's Health Department has historically been a leader in providing maternal and child health services, at least since the Progressive Era, providing the most liberal, expansive, and often the earliest nutritional, well-baby, and family planning services (Duffy 1968; Rosenberg 1976, 1987; Rosenkrantz et al., 1978; Rosner 1982). But this cutting edge, then and now, is also a double-edged sword. Services and surveillance, routine care and social control are inextricably linked in extending public health measures to the poor. It is not only "their" well-being, but "our" cost-effectiveness which is continually at issue. There is thus no way to separate eugenic and choice-enhancing aspects of prenatal diagnosis when provided by public health planning and moneys.

Third, science itself can be viewed as constructed by social and cultural processes (e.g., Latour 1987; Traweek 1988; Woolgar 1988). There is an immense lumpiness to science once one steps through the looking-glass into the laboratory. The neutral and distanced discourse of medical journals, the triumphalism of the Tuesday *New York Times* "Science" section, the reassuring "commonsense solutions" of the Phil Donahue show all occasionally claim to evaluate progress in human genetics. But none can contain the ambiguities of the DNA research frontier. There is an anxiety-provoking plethora of "information" disembedded from any cultural context for its interpretation that genetics currently represents. Prenatal diagnosis provides a proliferation of information for consumers without guideposts, for doctors to deploy as stage directions in a play whose acts are as yet unwritten, for technicians in search of metaphors. All participants are constantly negotiating a system of interpretation for both producers and consumers of "scientific knowledge." The laboratory is at once the factory of prenatal diagnoses and an empire of signs. While medical genetic discourse claims universal authority, it continuously confronts the contested nature of much of its findings, and the diversity of interpretations to which even "universal biological facts" lend themselves. The path connecting "scientific information" to "medical policy," "counseling protocols," and "popular culture" is rocky at best.

Fourth, we should note that the relationship between science and religion is unstable in many ways. Not only do different religions hold diverse stances toward reproductive technologies (Office of Technology Assessment 1988) but practitioners within religions may vary widely in their interpretations of official doctrine and personal adherence. Mrs. Ramirez, whose story opened this essay, is a practicing Catholic, but she would consider abortion of a fetus with a serious disability despite church teachings. One of her coreligionists from Ecuador expressed it succinctly:

> Could I abort if the baby was going to have that problem? God would forgive me, surely, yes, I could abort. Latin Catholics, we are raised to fear God, and to believe in His love and mercy. Now, if I were Evangelical, that's another story. It's too much work, being Evangelical. My sisters are both Evangelicals, they go to church all the time. There's no time for abortion for them. (Maria Acosta, 41)

Many Hispanic Catholic women reported multiple early abortions. To them, late abortion was a mortal sin. Finely honed, female-centered theological distinctions and practices are carved out of a monolithic theology. Likewise, "Protestants" display a wide array of beliefs and practices. Some of these differences can be linked to specific churches. Fundamentalists are most likely to preach against the test and Pat Carlson beat a beeline to her Mormon roots when she wanted to be talked out of an abortion following a positive prenatal diagnosis. Mainline groups like Episcopalians, Dutch Reformists, and Methodists are either silent or supportive on the topic of amniocentesis.

. . .

These many stories should alert us to the fact that religions continue to proliferate and make claims on personal, ethnic, and communal identity throughout American cultural life. Far from representing a "culture lag" that science will soon overtake, religious adherence might better be viewed as a continuous aspect of contemporary social life (Harding 1987). Religious identity provides one resource in the complex and often contradictory repertoire of possible identities a pregnant woman brings to her decision to use or reject amniocentesis. There is no definitive "Catholic" or "Jewish" or "Protestant" position on reproductive technology, when viewed from the pregnant woman's point of view. Rather, each pregnancy is assessed in light of the competing claims on maternity the individual acknowledges and to which she responds.

Fifth, both maternalist and medical discourses require careful deconstruction. The debates (between "pharmocrats and feminists," in Gena Corea's felicitous phrase) over whether the new reproductive technologies, including amniocentesis, offer progress or degradation to family life are phrased "as if" motherhood were being revolutionized. The discourse of maternalism—technocratic or resistant romantic, the one aligned with science, the other with nurture—obviously holds ideological weight in the words of a Pat Carlson or a Veronique St.-Croix. But it is not the only or overriding basis on which a decision to use or reject amniocentesis, or pursue its consequences, is made. The dramatic discourses of modern pregnancy as allied with either nature or culture too often echo each other. Each sounds like a unified voice, but the women with whom I have spoken are always polyphonic.

Every pregnancy is embedded in its own specific context: the proximity and judgment of male partners, mothers, sisters, and friends all weigh heavily on an amniocentesis decision. Many women told me they brought their partners to see the sonogram: "Frank just isn't as committed to this pregnancy as he should be," commented white middle-class psychologist Marcia Lang, "but once he sees the baby moving, I know he'll get excited." Juana Martes, a Dominican home care attendant, also thought men should see the sonogram that accompanies the test: "When the little creature moves, they begin to know what women feel, how they suffer for it to be born, and then they respect their wives." Ecuadorian-born Coralina Bollo felt pressured into having the test by her U.S.-born husband; Flora Blanca had to keep her decision to have it secret from her disapproving *companero*. Laura Escobar's Egyptian-born Muslim husband Ibrim reluctantly agreed to the test, stressing that he didn't believe in abortion. He *knew* God would protect his unborn child. Laura turned to me, and in Spanish (which her husband does not speak) said, "When God provides a problem, he also provides a cure."

The fact of decision making involved in amniocentesis reveals the existing gender negotiations within which a specific pregnancy is undertaken. There is a complex choreography of domination, manipulation, negotiation, and, sometimes, resistance in the gender tales women tell about their decisions to use or reject this piece of reproductive technology.

Sixth, disabilities, like pregnancies, are socially constructed. Pat Carlson's decision to continue her pregnancy after a prenatal diagnosis of Down's syndrome is quite a rare event: 90 to 95 percent of women receiving this diagnosis go on to terminate their pregnancies. Likewise, a diagnosis like Tay-Sachs disease carries an abortion rate that is almost 100 percent, although prenatal diagnosis of a similarly recessively transmitted disease, sickle cell anemia, probably leads to abortion only 40 percent of the time.[1] Different rates of abortion seem linked to at least two factors: the knowledge pregnant women and their supporters have about the condition's consequences (which vary, of course, by disease), and the local values (suggested by religious, familial, and ethnic experiences) they hold about it. One genetic counselor encountered two patients, each of whom chose to abort a fetus after learning that its status included XXY sex chromosomes (Klinefelter's syndrome, which affects growth, fertility, and possibly intelligence and learning abilities). One professional couple told her, "If he can't grow up to have a shot at becoming the President, we don't want him." A low-income family said of the same condition, "A baby will have to face so many problems in this world, it isn't fair to add this one to the burdens he'll have."

From a patient's point of view, most diagnoses are inherently ambiguous (Rothman 1986). An extra chromosome spells out the diagnosis of Down's syndrome, but it does not distinguish mildly from severely retarded children, or indicate whether this particular fetus will need open heart surgery. A missing X chromosome indicates a Turner's syndrome female (who will be short-statured and infertile), but cannot speak to the meaning of fertility in the particular family into which she may be born. Homozygous status for the sickle cell gene cannot predict the severity of anemia a particular child will develop. All such diagnoses are interpreted in light of prior reproductive histories and experiences, community values, and aspirations that particular women and their families hold for the pregnancy being examined.

And some constituencies contest the powerful medical definitions of disabilities that predominate in contemporary American society. The disability rights movement points out that socially constructed attitudes of stigma and prejudice, not absolute biological capacities, lie behind the segregation of disabled children and adults.[2] Many disability rights groups focus on legal and policy solutions to their members' problems, often using a civil rights perspective. The discourse of civil rights influenced a series of federal laws in the mid-1970s and the recent "Americans With Disabilities Act," which explicitly deployed models developed in the battles against racial discrimination to mandate access to education, housing, employment, and public facilities for disabled citizens. The movement contains many divided allies and is continuously debating such questions as the relation of mental to physical disabilities and the ethics of prenatal diagnosis for any or all disability. But virtually all members of and advocates for disabled groups insist on the social, rather than the medical, definition of the problems they must confront.

The discursive and material resources available for families of disabled children vary greatly along the fault lines set up by race, class, religious, and ethnic differences in contemporary America. Disability is socially constructed, reflecting not only the hegemonic claims of medicine and counterclaims of families and activists, but cross-cutting differences within the very category of "disability" as well.

Seventh, medical anthropologists must account for their own presence in the problems they study. Why should an anthropologist learn to cut karyotypes in a basement laboratory on First Avenue, follow genetic counselors through their rounds at Harlem hospital, and take the E train to Queens for home visits? Without indulging in a narcissistic exercise, it seems evident that this investigation into the social impact and cultural meaning of prenatal diagnosis is supported by almost twenty years of feminist mobilization in the discipline of anthropology. "People like me" teach women's studies courses, as well as anthropology courses, where the contradictions generated around the concepts of "reproduction" or "motherhood" glide across disciplinary boundaries. They also surface in our personal lives. Members of the same generation who produced the field of "feminist anthropology" often delayed childbearing for the establishment of education and careers, and now we study comparative reproduction. That a cultural anthropologist who has sustained two amniocenteses should query the power of medical discourse and the meaning of cultural differences in this experience seems like an obvious next move.

These seven proliferating processes make it difficult ever to completely frame our "unit" of analysis. Some of the layers described here are clearly local and particular—for example, the funding priorities of New York City's health department or the existence of a permanently and luxuriantly polyglot class of working poor women in the city. Other forces pertain more generally to the political economy of advanced capitalism, where scientific discourse and practices deeply influence contemporary cultural representations of health and illness, pregnancy, disability, and gender. And all layers are, of course, historically contingent.

ENDINGS ARE REALLY BEGINNINGS

In the "middle ground" partially described above, science (in medicine and medical anthropology) cannot provide stable, authoritative discourses against which to measure all other cultural practices. For scientific knowledge, like the other cultural discourses and social practices described above, is also historically contingent. To say that accounts of science (or pregnancy, or ethnic diversity, or anything else) are historically contingent is not to deny their power to intervene in what used to be called "the real world," nor to collapse this discussion into rampant relativism. The temptations of pure relativism can be avoided if the study of power relations, rather than pluralism, lies at the heart of the investigation.

This focus on power is one that was given to me by the people who consented to be interviewed for this study, for they frequently provided insightful comments on the force fields within which their own options and possibilities were inscribed. In the narratives of pregnant women and mothers of disabled children, for example, television looms large. Sonograms provide images of the fetus in utero on a television screen. These images of floating fetuses, beating hearts, and imagined sex organs all have multiple medical, religious, and political interpretations for parents-to-be and the health professionals who orchestrate the viewing (Rapp 1991). Televisions provide multiple viewing points for the cultural problem of prenatal diagnosis. When I asked where women had first learned about amniocentesis, many respondents without formal education answered, "Dallas." In 1986, it took three episodes for the drama of a prenatal diagnosis of Down's syndrome to unfold on the show, with a predictably genderized outcome: "the mother" wanted to keep the pregnancy, "the father" pressured for an abortion, "the resolution" was a miscarriage, rather than a decision. My seven-year-old daughter has accompanied me part of the way on this intellectual journey, learning to identify children and adults with Down's syndrome from her avid addiction to watching "Life Goes On" on Sunday nights. And when I asked Pat Carlson, whose story opens this essay, what would make her son Stevie's life more integrated, I expected an answer about "education" but I got one about television. "Pampers commercials," she replied. "Why Pampers?" I asked. "If they can show all those black and brown kids on TV ads these days, why can't they just show kids like Stevie?" Pat asked. Television is not a neutral presence in the life ways of health care workers, pregnant women, or families with Down's syndrome members. It may well be the most powerful panopticon through which the "information revolution" is constructed, represented, and enforced. The power of television vibrates through any "history of the present" in contemporary American culture.

Power relations are, of course, historically contingent. If, for example, the Chinese invent an earlier fetal sex chromosomal detection technology via maternal-fetal blood centrifuge to mediate the contradiction between their one-child family policy and a patriarchal kinship system, it will surely echo through protocol studies funded in Washington, D.C. down to the basement of the Prenatal Diagnosis Laboratory in New York City. There, visiting Chinese geneticists will undoubtedly enhance international scientific cooperation by teaching it to American colleagues. If the Reagan and Bush appointments to the Supreme Court do, indeed, augur the piecemeal reversal of legal abortion in the United States, prenatal diagnosis might fall victim to our particular, contemporary politicization of the court system. However, a more likely scenario would have to take into account powerful national polls indicating that over 80 percent of Americans support legal abortion when the fetus is defective, a consensus that makes disability rights activists desperate. This hypermedicalization of abortion rights, which posits a "grave fetal defect" as the only basis for a legal abortion, lies at the heart of *Doe v. Bamgaertner,* a legal case generated in Utah explicitly to test *Roe v. Wade.* Geneticists and genetic counselors were brought into the construction of the oppositional brief to describe the arcane range of possible, diagnosable fetal conditions on the one hand, and the subjective meaning of "grave" on the other. The cultural contest over abortion rights thus includes medical experts as liberals; a century ago, physicians served as strategists for campaigns to illegalize the procedure. As this moment in struggles over reproductive rights plays itself out, we can imagine that abortion services could become severely restricted and entirely remedicalized, and prenatal diagnosis would become one obvious and popular route to ending an undesired pregnancy.

Finally, power must remain central to any analysis of the permanent condition of heterogeneity that characterizes the culture of advanced capitalism. The relation of world-structured power domains and local cultures is intimately tied to this question of heterogeneity. If advanced capitalism has enormously homogenizing tendencies that threaten to engulf and flatten cultural particularities, it also sets up uneven conditions for the continuous production of cultural heterogeneity. I want to claim this as a historical as well as contemporary truth. Had I been studying childbirth in New York City at the turn of the century, it would have been Lithuanian holdouts against hospitals, rather than Haitian incomprehension of genetic testing that I would have been querying. There is no way out of this problem. And it has for me a politics that needs underlining. At least two concrete goals flow from this understanding. The first, a familiar theme in medical anthropology, is that health care professionals who often come from the dominant culture can never escape confrontation with multicultural rationalities.

They may, however, be able to learn about cultural differences. Genetic counselors, unlike doctors, are new health professionals in a small and still-developing "woman's" field. Helping them to pluralize would be a service to wo*men,* rather than wo*man,* I imagine. Their commitment to medical discourse and dominant representations of pregnancy and motherhood makes this task a difficult one, but many conscientious counselors are committed to exploring how best to serve underserved, often minority, patient populations (Marfatia, Punales, and Rapp 1990; cf. Rapp 1988).

Second, we need a discussion of what popular scientific literacy might mean, especially but not exclusively for diverse American women, given the gender biases, racial prejudices, class structures, and attitudes toward disability which serve as effective barriers to restructuring the power dynamics of scientific discourse as it shapes American cultural life. While one subtext of the present account is to demedicalize prenatal diagnosis and disability, another, paradoxically, is to suggest that many, perhaps the majority, of women whose lives it affects *still lack access* to the discursive tools and social services on which both scientific literacy and a truly "informed consent" might rest. Historically contingent accounts lead us back to the problem of coping with diversity in a complex society that simultaneously and continuously produces, reproduces, and then denies its own heterogeneous nature. Beyond its theoretical recognition, what are we to do with the abundant inequalities and differences a critical, feminist, medical anthropology must represent amongst American women?

NOTES

1. These statistics were compiled from the Laboratory's "positive diagnosis" files covering the last five years. There is no national monitoring of either amniocentesis or abortion following positive prenatal diagnosis, although the Council of Regional Networks of Genetic Services is currently developing a national data base. The best comparative figures, which approximate those of the Lab, are provided by Hook 1981.
2. For a popular, inspiring, and highly controversial digest of disability rights activism, see *The Disability Rag.* Other resources by and for disabled people and their supporters include *The Exceptional Parent* and the *Siblings Network Newsletter,* and newsletters published by many of the groups organized around specific disabilities (e.g., *National Down's Syndrome Society Newsletter; Neurofibromatosis Newsletter).* Social scientific analyses of the impact of disabilities on family life are provided by Gliedman 1980; Featherstone 1981; Goffman 1963. Personal narratives concerning the lives of families with disabled children appear in Featherstone 1981 and Jablow 1982. Stray-Gundersen 1986 combines perspectives by parents and health professionals.

REFERENCES

Arditti, Rita, Renate Duelli-Klein, and Shelley Minden, eds. 1984. *Test-Tube Woman: What Future for Motherhood?* Boston: Routledge & Kegan Paul.

Baruch, Elaine H., Amadeo F. D'Amado, and Joni Seager, eds. 1988. *Embryos, Ethics and Women's Rights.* New York: Harrington Press.

Corea, Gena. 1984. *The Mother Machine.* New York: Harper & Row.

Duffy, John. 1968. *A History of Public Health in New York City.* New York: Russell Sage Foundation.

Featherstone, Helen. 1981. *A Difference in the Family: Living with a Disabled Child.* New York: Penguin.

Goffman, Erving. 1963. *Stigma: Notes Toward the Management of a Spoiled Identity.* Englewood Cliffs, NJ: Prentice-Hall.

Gliedman, John, and William Roth. 1980. *The Unexpected Minority: Handicapped Children in America.* New York: Harcourt, Brace, Jovanovich.

Harding, Susan. 1987. Convicted by the Holy Spirit. *American Ethnologist* 14:167–181.

Hook, Ernest B. 1981. Rates of Chromosomal Abnormalities at Different Maternal Ages. *Obstetrics and Gynecology* 58: 282–285.

Jablow, Martha. 1982. *Cara: Growing with a Retarded Child.* Philadelphia: Temple University Press.

Latour, Bruno. 1987. *Science in Action.* Cambridge, Mass.: Harvard University Press.

Lindenbaum, Shirley, and Margaret Lock, eds. 1993. Preface. In *Knowledge, Power, and Practice: The Anthropology of Medicine and Everyday Life.* Berkeley, Los Angeles, Oxford: University of California Press.

Marfatia, Lavanya, Diana Punales, and Rayna Rapp. 1990. When an Old Reproductive Technology Becomes a New Reproductive Technology: Amniocentesis and Underserved Populations. *Birth Defects* 26:109–126.

Office of Technology Assessment, Congress of the United States. 1988. *Appendix F: Religious Perspectives in Infertility. Medical and Social Choices.* Washington, D.C.: Government Printing Office.

Rapp, Rayna. 1988. Chromosomes and Communication: The Discourse of Genetic Counseling. *Medical Anthropology Quarterly* 2:143–157.

——— 1991. Constructing Amniocentesis: Medical and Maternal Voices. In *Uncertain Terms: Negotiating Gender in American Culture,* 28–42, Faye Ginsburg and Anna Tsing, eds. Boston: Beacon.

Rosenberg, Charles. 1976. *No Other Gods: On Science in American Social Thought.* Baltimore: Johns Hopkins University Press.

———1987. *The Care of Strangers: The Rise of America's Hospital System.* New York: Basic Books.

Rosenkrantz, Barbara Gutmann, and Elizabeth Lomax. 1978. *Science and Patterns of Child Care.* San Francisco: W. H. Freeman.

Rosner, David. 1982. *A Once Charitable Enterprise: Hospitals and Health Care in Brooklyn and Cambridge.* New York: Cambridge University Press.

Rothman, Barbara Katz. 1986. *The Tentative Pregnancy.* New York: Norton.

Stanworth, Michelle, ed. 1987. *Reproductive Technologies.* Minneapolis: University of Minnesota Press.

Spallone, Patricia, and Deborah Steinberg, eds. 1987. *The Myth of Genetic Engineering and Reproductive Progress.* Elmsford, N.Y.: Pergamon.

Stray-Gundersen, Karen, ed. 1986. *Babies with Down Syndrome.* Kensington, Maryland: Woodbine House.

Traweek, Sharon. 1988. *Beamtimes and Lifetimes.* Cambridge, Mass.: Harvard University Press.

Woolgar, Steven. 1988. *Science: The Very Idea.* London: Tavistock.

 22

Religion and Reproductive Technologies

Marcia C. Inhorn

The new biomedical technologies, especially involving reproduction, have been an important topic of research for medical anthropologists for the past two decades. Reproductive health is often thought of as a highly gendered issue—in other words, a women's question. But infertility is, in fact, a problem of couples. As seen in the previous selections, feminist social theory has greatly influenced contemporary anthropological analysis of biomedical technologies. This is especially the case in reproductive health, childbirth, and infertility. Reproductive technologies and their legality, however, are areas for cultural debates based on religious and ethical beliefs. Certainly, in the United States, the abortion issue is one that continues to be hotly debated by people with different opinions and cultural social beliefs.

In this era of globalization, new reproductive technologies like in vitro fertilization (IVF) have become available for couples who can afford it all over the world. But throughout history, societies have chosen which technologies and ideas they want to adopt. The question is whether newly developed biomedical technologies that raise important issues in biomedical ethics in the United States are likely to be accepted in other societies. Surrogate motherhood, sperm donation, egg donation, and embryo implantation—not to mention the issue of what to do with stem cells—have been areas of cultural contestation in North America. What happens in other societies?

One of the most obvious cultural rifts in the contemporary world is between the "West" and Islamic nations and populations. Most biomedical research and technological development is done in the "West." For Muslims, the moral acceptability of new technologies must be studied and interpreted by scholar/clerics. In this selection, Marcia Inhorn discusses the role of Islam in the interpretation of and ultimate decisions about the acceptability of new reproductive technologies in the Middle East. In the case of IVF, differences between Sunni and Shi'ite branches of Islam are very important in this regard. Sunni religious leaders were quite quick to issue fatwas *allowing IVF. In the long run, however, it has been the most conservative, male Shi'ite religious leaders in Iran who have shown the most "adventurous" attitudes about third-party gamete donation.*

As you read this selection, consider these questions:

- **Why should medical anthropologists be interested in the globalization of new biomedical technologies like IVF?**
- **Why might couples in other societies think that infertility is such a terrible thing?**
- **How are Muslim interpretations of IVF—including the role of the clergy—different from those found in the United States? What is the role of patriarchy in this regard?**
- **How are religious beliefs and medical decision making linked?**
- **What are differences between Sunni and Shi'ite beliefs and practices related to the new reproductive technologies?**

Context: Marcia Inhorn is professor of medical anthropology and international affairs at Yale University, where she is also chair of the Council on Middle East Studies. She is a past president of the Society for Medical Anthropology. She is an influential scholar particularly in the area of gender, health, and new reproductive technologies. Inhorn has conducted multisite research on the social impact of infertility and new reproductive technologies in Egypt, Lebanon, the United Arab Emirates, and Arab America. She is the author of three books on that subject, including *Local Babies, Global Science: Gender, Religion and In Vitro Fertilization in Egypt; Infertility and Patriarchy: The Cultural Politics of Gender and Family Life in Egypt;* and *Quest for Conception: Gender, Infertility and Egyptian Medical Traditions.* In recent years, she has begun to focus on masculinity and male factor infertility. This article was published in a newspaper for professional anthropologists that often highlights the relevance of anthropological research in relation to contemporary society.

Source: M. Inhorn (2005). "Religion and Reproductive Technologies." Anthropology News, February 2005, pp. 17–18.

For infertile couples around the globe, "reproductive health" means achieving a much-desired pregnancy, thereby overcoming the stigmatization and heartbreak of childlessness. At the dawn of the 21st century, achieving pregnancy through resorting to new reproductive technologies has become a global reality. Indeed, since the birth in 1978 of Louise Brown, the world's first test-tube baby, new reproductive technologies to overcome infertility have spread around the globe, reaching countries far from the technology-producing nations of the West. Perhaps nowhere is this globalization process more evident than in the more than 20 nations of the Muslim Middle East, where a private in vitro fertilization (IVF) industry is flourishing. For example, Egypt alone (population > 70 million) hosts 50 IVF clinics, while the tiny country of Lebanon (population > 5 million) boasts more than 15 IVF clinics, one of the highest per capita concentrations in the world.

In the Muslim world, religion has profoundly affected the practice of IVF in ways that are not commonly seen in Euro-America. Thus it is extremely important for anthropologists working in this region to examine the "local moral worlds" of Muslim IVF patients as they attempt to access reproductive technologies according to religious guidelines. In my own research in Egypt and Lebanon, infertile Muslim couples have been extremely concerned about making their testtube babies in the Islamically correct fashion. To that end, many have sought out the "official" Islamic opinion on the practice of IVF in the form of a *fatwa* or a nonbinding but authoritative religious proclamation made by an esteemed religious scholar.

In recent years, many such *fatwas* on a wide variety of reproductive health concerns have been issued in Muslim countries. With regard to IVF specifically, *fatwas* were issued early on in both Egypt and Saudi Arabia, the first two countries to open IVF centers (along with Jordan). In Egypt, the Grand Sheikh of Egypt's famed religious university, Al Azhar, issued the first *fatwa* on medically assisted reproduction on March 23, 1980. This *fatwa*—formulated only two years after the birth of the first IVF baby in England, but a full six years before the opening of Egypt's first IVF center—has proved to be truly authoritative and enduring in all its main points for the Sunni Muslim world. Sunni Islam, it is important to note, is the dominant form of Islam found throughout the Muslim world. Nearly 90% of the world's 1.3 billion Muslims are Sunni Muslims, with the strictest form of Sunni Islam emanating from Saudi Arabia. In Egypt, approximately 90% of citizens are Sunni Muslims.

What is the Sunni position on IVF? As currently practiced in Sunni-majority Muslim countries such as Egypt, in vitro fertilization *is* allowed, as long as it entails the union of ova from the wife with the sperm of her husband and the transfer of the resulting embryo(s) back to the uterus of the same wife. However, the use of a third-party donor is *not* allowed, whether he or she is providing sperm, eggs or embryos. Furthermore, all forms of surrogacy are strictly forbidden.

A global survey of sperm donation among assisted reproductive technology centers in 62 countries provides some indication of the degree of convergence between official Islamic discourse and actual practice. In all of the Muslim countries surveyed—including the Middle Eastern Muslim countries of Egypt, Iran, Kuwait, Jordan, Lebanon, Morocco, Qatar and Turkey, as well as the non–Middle Eastern Muslim countries of Indonesia, Malaysia and Pakistan—sperm donation in IVF and all other forms of gamete donation were strictly prohibited, with these prohibitions mandated by law and/or professional ethical guidelines in all of the countries studied.

Having said this, it is very important to point out how things have changed for Shi'ite Muslims, particularly in Iran and Lebanon, since this global survey was published in 1997. Shi'a is the minority branch of Islam found in Iran and parts of Iraq, Lebanon, Bahrain, Saudi Arabia, Afghanistan, Pakistan and India, and it is much in the news because of the US-led war in Iraq. In the late 1990s, the Supreme Jurisprudent of the Shi'ite branch of Islam, Ayatollah Ali Hussein Khamanei, who is the handpicked successor to Iran's Ayatollah Khomeini, issued a *fatwa* effectively permitting donor technologies to be utilized. With regard to both egg and sperm donation, Ayatollah Khamanei stated that *both* the donor and the infertile parents must abide by the religious codes regarding parenting. However, the donor child can only inherit from the sperm or egg donor, as the infertile parents are considered to be like "adoptive" parents.

For infertile Shi'ite Muslim couples, third-party gamete donation is even more complicated than this *fatwa* would suggest. Because of the Shi'ite practice of *ijtihad*, or individual religious reasoning, some Shi'ite religious authorities continue to denounce sperm and egg donation, prohibiting it for their followers. Others accept egg donation as being like polygyny (which is permitted in Islam), but decry sperm donation for its implications of polyandry (which is not allowed). In Iran itself, Ayatollah Khamanei's position on sperm donation was reversed when the Iranian parliament made sperm donation illegal in 2003. However, embryo donation from one married couple to another *is* allowed in Iran, because embryo donation insures that all parties are married, and it is akin to adoption, which is allowed in Iran, unlike any other Middle

Eastern Muslim country. Egg donation is also allowed in Iran, as long as the husband conducts a temporary *muta* marriage with the egg donor, thereby insuring that all three parties are married. Such *muta* marriages are allowed in Shi'ite Islam and have been encouraged in recent Iranian history, but are not recognized by Sunni religious authorities. In addition, Iran is the only Muslim-majority country in the Middle East to have allowed surrogacy in a very recent turn of events.

As a result of these unprecedented Iranian religious rulings favoring third-party gamete donation and surrogacy, infertile Shi'ite Muslim couples in Iran, as well as in Shi'ite-majority Lebanon, are beginning to receive donor gametes, as well as donating their gametes to other infertile couples. For the Shi'ite religious authorities, IVF physicians and infertile couples who accept the idea of gamete donation, the introduction of donor technologies has been described as a "marriage savior," helping to avoid the "marital and psychological disputes" that may arise if the couple's case is otherwise untreatable.

In Lebanon, Shi'ite *fatwas* allowing egg donation have, in fact, been a great boon to marital relations. There, both fertile and infertile men with reproductively elderly wives (those with poor ova quality) are signing up on waiting lists at IVF clinics to accept the eggs of donor women. Some of these donors are other IVF patients, and some are friends or relatives. And in at least one clinic, some are young women being recruited from the US, who may unwittingly serve as anonymous egg donors for conservative Shi'ite Hizbullah couples! Furthermore, quite interestingly, in multisectarian Lebanon, the recipients of these donor eggs are not necessarily only Shi'ite Muslim couples. Some Sunni Muslim patients from Lebanon and from other Middle Eastern Muslim countries (as well as minority Christian couples), are quietly saving their marriages through the use of donor gametes, thereby secretly "going against" the dictates of Sunni Muslim orthodoxy.

Indeed, new reproductive technologies have brought great joy to thousands of infertile Muslim couples who have borne test-tube babies over the last 20 years since these technologies were first introduced in the Sunni Muslim world. Furthermore, the more recent globalization of these technologies to the Shi'ite Muslim world has fundamentally altered understandings of the ways in which families *can* be made and the ways in which marriages *can* be saved through the uses of donor technologies. Pardoxically, the most conservative, male Shi'ite religious leaders in Iran have been the ones to adopt the most "adventurous" attitudes toward third-party gamete donation. In doing so, they have offered reproductive *fatwas* with real potential to transform infertile gender relations in ways heretofore unanticipated in the Muslim world.

For infertile Shi'ite Muslim couples already benefiting from donor gametes in IVF clinics in Iran and Lebanon, the donor children they bear represent the happy outcome of the "brave new world" of third-party gamete donation as it enters the Muslim world in the 21st century. For those of us in anthropology who study the social and cultural implications of the new reproductive technologies, the striking and rapidly evolving case of the Muslim world reminds us why religion does, indeed, matter in reproductive health, particularly as we enter a religiously troubled new millennium.

23

Rethinking the Biological Clock: Eleventh-Hour Moms, Miracle Moms, and Meanings of Age-Related Infertility

Carrie Friese
Gay Becker
Robert Nachtigall

This article addresses some of the issues and controversies surrounding the notion of a "biological clock." This clock describes a time window of fertility between a woman's late teens and late thirties, after which she is significantly less able to bear children. The biological clock challenges two important milestones of the women's movement: equal opportunity in the workplace and reproductive choice. Since the 1960s and 1970s, women have increasingly moved into the workplace. Like their male counterparts, many of these professional women have delayed having children in order to pursue their careers. Yet unlike males, who remain relatively fertile for most of their lives, older women face the increasing likelihood of age-related infertility and an increasing risk of bearing children with birth defects. Although many women successfully pursue both careers and families, the specter of a "ticking clock" can place an additional burden on those wrestling with these important life decisions.

In contrast to the biological clock, there is a common myth that age-related infertility can be readily overcome with today's assistive reproductive technologies (ARTs). Many of the "eleventh-hour moms" in this study believed that this was the case, only to learn much later that ARTs are mainly effective for women with non-age-related fertility problems and that they have low success rates for helping healthy older women conceive children with their own eggs. In any case, a series of ART treatments can cost more than $100,000, and they are almost never covered by health insurance. Such options, therefore, do not even exist for middle-class and poor people. Indeed, the average household income of these study subjects was over $180,000 a year.

In addition to these issues, this study describes a biomedical category known as "diminished ovarian reserve," which is sometimes referred to as "old eggs" (and sounds like "old age"). In reading about this category, you may wonder whether diminished ovarian reserve should be considered a disease if it is a normal part of the aging process. Yet, at the same time, we might consider it to be an illness insofar as it can cause a great deal of suffering in people's lives. This also brings up the dilemma of medicalization in genetic testing. On the one hand, a medical label can help bring attention and resources to important problems. On the other hand, it can also stigmatize people. Such is the case for many women who have been made to feel inadequate because they—or rather, their eggs—are no longer able to bear biological offspring.

As you read this selection, consider these questions:

- **Why would the eleventh-hour moms feel differently about egg donation than the "miracle moms"?**
- **The authors suggest that most of these women were not sufficiently informed about their reproductive choices. How could so many affluent and well-educated women know so little about age-related infertility and assistive reproductive technologies?**
- **When should an age-related physical change be considered an illness or a disease? If and when should infertility be considered a disease?**
- **In what ways do reproductive technologies change women's notions of the body and of motherhood?**

Context: Carrie Friese is a medical sociologist and postdoctoral fellow at the University of California–Los Angeles Center for Society and Genetics. In addition to reproductive technologies, she has studied the social implications of cloning endangered animals. The late Gay Becker was a much-admired medical anthropologist at the University of California–San Francisco (UCSF) who brought a strong sense of social justice to her research, which ranged from infertility, to aging, to the social stigma of certain health conditions (see selection 38). Robert Nachtigall is a physician at UCSF who specializes in reproductive endocrinology with a research interest in the social and emotional aspects of infertility. This article is based on a subset of data from a large, NIH-funded study on people's decisions regarding whether to publicly disclose that they have used egg or sperm donors to have children.

Source: C. Friese, G. Becker, and R. D. Nachtigall (2006). *"Rethinking the Biological Clock: Eleventh-Hour Moms, Miracle Moms, and Meanings of Age-Related Infertility."* Social Science & Medicine 63:1550–1560.

INTRODUCTION

A wealth of social science literature focusing on unwanted childlessness and advanced reproductive technologies (ART) has emerged over the past 20 years that addresses a wide range of topics. These include the experience of infertility and its treatment (Becker, 1997, 2000; Greil, 1991; Inhorn, 1994; Sandelowski, 1993; Thompson, 2005), its pervasive and problematic nature globally (Inhorn, 1994, 2003; Inhorn & Van Balen, 2003; Kahn, 2000), the complexities ART poses for understandings of kinship (Edwards, Franklin, Hirsch, Price, & Strathern, 1993; Franklin, 1997; Franklin & Ragone, 1998; Strathern, 1992), and the dilemmas arising out of third-party parenting (Becker, Butler, & Nachtigall, 2005; Nachtigall, Becker, Quiroga, & Tschann, 1998; Nachtigall, Tschann, Quiroga, Pitcher, & Becker, 1997; Ragone, 1994; Whiteford, 1989). Yet despite the considerable attention given to these and other "reproductive disruptions" (Van Balen & Inhorn, 2003), limited work has addressed the experience of "older women" who conceive with ART using donor eggs (Becker, 1997, 2000; Thompson, 2005).

For a generation, aging and female reproduction have been lodged within the gendered and gendering debates regarding women's involvement in the workforce and demographic shifts toward delayed parenting which culminate in discourses on the "biological clock." The biological clock is a heterogeneous concept that carries a range of connotations, emerging in the 1970s to capture the interconnections and fissures between social and physiological domains regarding women's bodies and reproduction. Central to the biological clock discourse is the notion that the public domain, organized around paid labor, interferes and competes with a woman's fertile years. By the early 1980s, the biological clock came to be stereotypically identified with a cohort of largely Caucasian, educated, upper-middle class, baby-boom women (McKaughan, 1987). Access to medical technologies and techniques, specifically effective birth control and safe and legal abortions, allowed large numbers of women to voluntarily postpone childbearing. Subsequently, women who chose to have children in their mid-to-late 30s triggered a much-publicized "infertility epidemic" (Aral & Cates, 1983), characterized as women anxiously pursing pregnancy before it was "too late" (McKaughan, 1987). Marsh and Ronner (1996, pp. 245–246) observe that the extent of this infertility epidemic is contested because precise historical infertility statistics are difficult to obtain. Nonetheless, there is a predominant *belief* that infertility is a greater problem now than previously. Some women began to see the biological clock as a kind of deadline as they made decisions about childbearing, a notion through which women have been implicitly blamed for their infertility.

The question underlying the notion of a biological clock has been: "How late can a woman wait to have children?" Menstruation and reproduction have long been interconnected both physiologically and socio-culturally. The cessation of menses has been understood to mark the end of female reproductive capability, thereby separating women's lives into the discrete time frames of menstruating/reproductive and menopausal/non-reproductive years (Formanek, 1990; Utian, 1990). Yet as increasing numbers of women in their late 30s and early 40s attempted to conceive, it became increasingly clear to medical infertility specialists that the later a woman waited to embark on a first pregnancy, the greater the chance that age-related factors would diminish her ability to become pregnant at all, even following the introduction and proliferation of ART (Edwards et al., 1984). This impression has been confirmed by two large data sets, one a widely publicized report from France in the early 1980s (Schwartz & Mayaux, 1982), and more recently a report based on US data that indicated that the chances of a live birth after a cycle of in vitro fertilization (IVF) treatment fall from 1 in 3 for women under age 35, to 1 in 10 for women over 40, to less than 1 in 20 for women over 42 (Centers for Disease Control and Prevention, 2004). This led to the widespread conclusion among infertility specialists that there is an age (arguably older than 43–44) that precludes the likelihood of pregnancy resulting from infertility treatment using a woman's own gametes.

New reproductive technologies have long been associated with the concept of medicalization, the process by which human experiences are redefined as medical problems (Zola, 1972). This medicalization process may be initiated either from within biomedicine or by members of the public who seek legitimacy for a social condition (McLean, 1990) and is epitomized by the growth of medical treatment for infertility, a condition formerly viewed as a social problem but now perceived as a medical condition (Becker & Nachtigall, 1992). Moreover, consumers may, and often do, embrace medicalization (Becker, 2000; Becker & Nachtigall, 1992). Clarke and her colleagues have reframed this concept as "biomedicalization," to encompass its interactive process which engages all the elements of technology development and use, including the roles of biomedicine and consumers (Clarke, Shim, Mamo, Fosket, & Fishman, 2003).

Technological solutions to the biological clock, specifically the use of IVF and its related technologies that employ donor oocytes (eggs) to achieve a pregnancy, have increasingly been at the forefront of medical treatment. Here we see the complexity of the process of biomedicalization at work. Thompson (2005, pp. 90–91) notes that initially a woman's age was not particularly seen as "biological" despite its correlation with a rapid decline in fertility. However, the growing public and legislative demand for clinic accountability with respect to IVF pregnancy rates led infertility specialists to search for criteria that could more accurately predict the likelihood of success of particular ART procedures. Those qualitative and quantitative changes in the ovary that correlate with the probability of a woman becoming pregnant if she undergoes IVF using her own oocytes were referred to as "ovarian reserve" (Scott & Hofmann, 1995). The concept of ovarian reserve is significant because it ruptures the longstanding historical connections between menstruation and female reproductive capacity by specifically focusing on the aging of a woman's eggs. Furthermore, the traditional clinical emphasis on menstrual regularity and ovulatory function as characteristics of continued fertility has given way to an assessment driven by the consideration of a woman's suitability as a candidate for advanced reproductive technologies.

It should be noted that although over 13 different procedures have been described for evaluating a woman's ovarian reserve, the criteria for normal ovarian function is not precise, there is no universal agreement among clinicians about what it might be, and only women embarking on IVF procedures are actually tested for it (Bukulmez & Arici, 2004). Despite these uncertainties, Thompson (2005) notes that the clinical designation of "diminished ovarian reserve" has come to imply that a woman has "old eggs" and is associated in practitioners' and patients' minds with the eclipse of a woman's reproductive potential and with hidden harbingers of menopause. She found that many women experienced these evaluations as an additional insult to their already compromised gender identity and linked the denial of access to treatment using their own (as opposed to donor) eggs to an assault on their biological age.

The medical implications of being identified as having "diminished ovarian reserve" are profound: a woman's treatment options are reduced to conception using the "donated" eggs of another, usually much younger, woman. At the same time, women in their mid- to late 40s and older—an age traditionally thought of as being menopausal and thereby nonreproductive—are told that not only is pregnancy using a donor egg possible, but that their chances of pregnancy are equal to those of women 10–20 years their junior. In this article we examine how women who used a donor egg to conceive their child(ren) ascribed meaning to their own aging as they confronted infertility. As the idea of having "old eggs" took root, women incorporated their thoughts and feelings about cultural categories such as gender, aging, and the biological clock in reconstituting their sense of self after infertility.

METHODS

Respondents were recruited through 12 IVF centers and one sperm bank in four counties in a West Coast state of the USA to participate in a study addressing the disclosure decision, i.e., how parents of children conceived with donor gametes decided whether or not to tell their children of the true genetic origins. Practitioners sent letters to couples who had conceived using donor gametes alerting their former patients to the study, and those interested sent a postcard to the investigators stating their willingness to consider participation in the study. The criteria for entry into the study were the presence of one or more living children who had been conceived with the use of a gamete donor, heterosexual, and in a marital relationship at the time of the child's conception. Data collection is complete.

In most cases initial couple interviews were followed by solo interviews with each partner approximately 3 months later. The purpose of doing both types of interviews was to collect data on how couples jointly perceived the process as well as to allow individuals to discuss differences or conflicts without their partner present. Occasionally solo interviews preceded couple interviews. If one but not both members of a couple agreed to be interviewed, those respondents were also interviewed. One- to two-hour long interviews were semi-structured with many open-ended questions that focused on how the couple decided on whether or not to tell the child about the use of a donor. Related topics included philosophy of family, family relationships, feelings about having used a donor, and approaches taken to telling children and others. Questions about age were not on the interview schedule but age inevitably arose in the course of many couples' discussions about their experiences with infertility, parenthood, and disclosure. This was particularly true among couples who used donor eggs to conceive their child(ren). Although interviewers did not probe about age systematically, interviewers did pursue questions about age when participants raised related concerns. Interviews were tape-recorded and transcribed verbatim.

Data were divided by whether the child(ren) were conceived by using donor eggs or donor sperm. A specific procedure was followed to further develop the data analysis: core categories that repeatedly reappeared in the data were identified and compared with other emergent categories, a process that emerges out of ongoing reading and analysis of transcripts by the entire team. Out of these preliminary core categories generated from meanings in the data, an in-depth process of code development was followed. Codes are highly discrete categories. Each code is a very specific topic that appears in the data. Sections of interview text are analyzed using all codes so that the multiple meanings of a portion of text can be considered. Successive phases of trial coding were conducted until pairs of coders reached a level of agreement of 95 percent or more. The entire data set was then coded using QSR Nud*ist, a data-sorting software program, resulting in over 100 discrete codes, of which age [of parent] was one. The definition of the "age" code was broadly construed: "discussion of age of wife and/or husband, as factor in decisions, attitudes." This article is based on an analysis of this code, which was cross-checked by reading transcripts from which excerpts had been identified to ascertain that excerpts were not misinterpreted by being read out of context. This approach enabled us to scrutinize all the data on age at the same time rather than focusing only on certain cases, as well as to analyze the data within their broader context. Women discussed age far more often than did men, and this article addresses women's narratives only. This allowed for an assessment of how age figured into women's narratives about infertility and parenting as well as how cultural discourses on age informed their experiences. The excerpts in the findings section were taken from this code print-out.

FINDINGS

Findings are based on interviews with 79 couples who used a donor egg to conceive at least one living child. This is a sub-set of a larger sample of 148 heterosexual couples who used a donor gamete to conceive at least one living child. The average age of women at the time of the first interview was 45.8 (range 35–59) with 89% of the women being aged 39 or older at the time of the first interview. The average age of men was 47.5 (range 32–64). The average age of women at birth of first donor egg child was 42.2 (range 32–54) and the average age of men at birth of first donor child was 44.1 (range 30–62). The average age of the first child conceived through donor egg was 3.5. Of the 79 couples, 29 couples (37%) had more than one child conceived by donor eggs. Thirty-three couples (42%) had one or more child(ren) conceived without using donor eggs. Average annual household income for this sub-sample was $185,069.

We found that an important juncture in many women's narration of their infertility experience involved their recollection of being shown graphs or tables that illustrated sharply declining rates of conception after age 38. Although these tables were usually representations of data derived from women attempting pregnancy by using IVF, for many women, they were interpreted as graphic illustrations of the consequences of having "old eggs." Furthermore, we found that when confronted with the apparent age-related decline in their fertility, women in our study voiced two different narratives that described their experience and attitudes. The first narrative was that of "eleventh-hour moms," women who initially tried to become pregnant with treatment that utilized their own eggs but were unsuccessful and turned to donated oocytes as a second-choice option. Here, the socio-biological project of the biological clock was reproduced, but now rooted in the metaphor of "old eggs" rather than menopause. The second narrative was expressed by women who were generally older, some of whom had entered infertility treatment hoping to conceive with their own eggs, but some who knew from the outset that it was not going to be possible. These "miracle moms" rejoiced that their bodies had the ability to become pregnant even into the perimenopause and after, an age they previously thought of as "non-reproductive." Across these differing experiences, women connected the notion of "old eggs" with discourses on gender and the cultural, social, structural/organizational, symbolic and physical aspects of aging.

Eleventh-Hour Moms

Women who voiced the "eleventh-hour mom" narrative expressed the view that their "old eggs" had, in effect, condensed and shortened their years of potential fertility, making them "too old" to conceive a child earlier than they had supposed. Women often believed that they were still fertile if they were menstruating regularly and assumed they could in turn get pregnant up until they were approximately 45 years old. One woman, age 40 at her child's birth, stated, "I honest to God thought if I was still cycling, life was good." For many, it came as a surprise when they realized that these assumptions could be wrong. For example, one woman, 44 at the birth of her child, gave this description of her initial meeting with a reproductive endocrinologist:

> I ended up at what now is the [infertility clinic]. Total novice. I purely was thinking that I needed a better kind of thing [treatment]. And that was a rude awakening because I started to see some real statistics on what my chances were. . . . It never occurred to me that age could be an issue because I was still in my thirties. After all, wasn't that still young? Maybe, but not reproductively it wasn't.

The treatment trajectory that women experienced was shaped by where they saw themselves in the graphic displays of rapidly declining conception. For example, one woman, 40 at the birth of her child, stated: ". . . then we went to the [infertility] clinic. We had to go through their lecture, which talked about old age and the gray—we were in the gray area. We weren't in the black yet." Women who saw themselves as being in the gray area often described a treatment trajectory wherein they first used in vitro fertilization in the hopes that they would be able to become pregnant using their own ova and turned to donor egg only after failures, believing that their eggs were too old. Here, the use of donor egg was often configured as a second-choice option that must be rapidly pursued because of having lost time and having reached the end of fertility.

For many women, learning of age-related infertility was the first time they were being categorized as old, which led some to the self-perception that they were themselves both aged and unhealthy. One woman, 39 at the birth of her child, stated in an interview: "I felt that my infertility—it felt like I was unhealthy, to me. That's how it felt. And that I was older, and I was trying to get pregnant. So I felt old, a little bit." Martin (1987) has shown how the themes of decline and decay work to negatively evaluate menopause. Here, old eggs are similarly construed, which shapes this woman's self-perception. At times, this made women feel self-conscious about their pursuit of pregnancy, which is viewed culturally as a symbol of youth. Another woman, 42 at her child's birth, stated: "It's hard when you're thinking about having a child—that whole sense is one of youthfulness. The person is youthful and useful if they can bear children. And if you can't, then you're old."

Lost Time and Medical Care Women described a condensation, shortening, or curtailment of their reproductive years that was experienced not only as premature aging but as having lost time or being in a state where precious time was constantly slipping away. For some, lost time also implied waste: in time, opportunity, or eggs. Through the notion of waste, one woman blamed herself for her infertility:

> I walked around with all these little, bubbling eggs inside me, and I didn't give it a thought. I didn't show appreciation. I didn't give thanks for it. I didn't think it was something valuable. I just pissed on it, you know. And now, that I want it, it's gone (43 at birth of child).

Another expression of lost time was the notion that time had sped up after women were told they had old eggs. The notion that women's ova age in a manner that lowers the chances of pregnancy despite continuing normal menstruation collapses women's number of fertile years. In turn, time condensation propels a greater sense of urgency in getting pregnant quickly. Procedures like in vitro fertilization require much preparatory time and, for women given an age prognosis, are likely to fail. One woman, who was 37 at the time of her first birth, stated: "By the standard of IVF stuff, every month is a lot for someone trying to get pregnant that way—every week really, especially after forty. You have to be thrown into the fire."

Some women blamed their obstetrician/gynecologist for this lost time and were upset that they did not have proper information to make their reproductive decisions. They were resentful of the medical community for not providing them with information about the ways in which aging eggs have consequences for female infertility. Some women noted that they would have done things differently if they had been provided with this information. For example, one woman recounted how she was given an 8-month supply of clomiphene from her obstetrician/gynecologist to assist her in getting pregnant at the age of 42 after having tried with her husband to become pregnant for over 1 year. After 2 months of taking medication without getting pregnant, she requested a more comprehensive fertility plan and was sent to an infertility clinic. In her first meeting with the reproductive endocrinologist she was told that, due to her age, the only option available for her in achieving pregnancy would be donor egg. She stated: "So when I was 40 I should have been at the fertility clinic, not 42. And so I feel like I lost those two years and I had a lot of resentment [at being in] that position." Another woman went to see her obstetrician/gynecologist at the age of 38 to find out if she needed to make pregnancy an immediate priority or if she had some time to wait. Her physician said she would be fine unless she waited until she was 44. Because she was in the midst of a number of stressful life events, she decided to wait. When she reached the age of 43 and started trying to conceive, she learned her eggs were no longer viable.

Educating Others about Age-Related Infertility Many women were upset that they did not have adequate information in making their reproductive decisions, and some became vocal advocates engaged in educating women about the implications of age and fertility. This was particularly evident among women who gave birth between the ages of 39 and 43, but also among women who delivered before age 39. These women advocated that other women, given the knowledge that they had lacked, have children earlier, were it possible to do so. They believed this would be preferable compared to undergoing the emotional and physical stress associated with invasive infertility treatments. One woman, 35 at the birth of her child, stated:

> I tell people, "don't wait too long." I wouldn't wish this on anybody. . . . I don't love my daughter any less, and I'm not angry that I had to go through this, but I would never wish this on anybody else. I would not want somebody to have to go through this way of conceiving children. But it doesn't mean that, in the end, it didn't turn out okay for me.

Furthermore, some women were concerned that younger women would interpret their successful pregnancies at an older age as a signal that it is possible to get pregnant later in life:

> I think they're creating false hopes for women over forty when other women over forty hear that these women have had children and they ask, "How did you have them?" and they say, "We tried hard and we finally got our child." They're creating false hopes. . . . I'm sad that this myth is prolonged, that you can do everything in life and still have a child at age forty. They're probably going to more extreme measures but they're not telling people (44 at birth of child).

Another respondent, 43 at the birth of her child, noted how easy it would be for her to perpetuate the notion that woman are fertile until they reach menopause, but her sense of social responsibility in educating other women took precedence:

> My desire to make this right . . . is to put my ego to the side, versus get all the accolades of "She's so beautiful, she's got your eyes and your hair". . . I would rather have them know the real story and have them say "Oh my gosh, you're kidding," and then take that information and again be more beneficial. Versus going, "I ran into a 44-year-old woman and she has a baby. Oh, don't worry. It's no problem."

Many women, however, also believed that technological solutions should be available to women and some argued for more and better technologies that could serve as "back-up plans" or "insurance policies" for women who did not have control over the contexts that shaped their reproductive practices. Women defended themselves against those who would blame them for their status as infertile by pointing out that the social practice of delayed parenting is often not a choice and gave reasons for the reproductive decisions they made, including their formerly single status, financial insecurity, or meeting their husband later in life. For these women, delayed parenting was a fact of life and technological solutions were the only means available for contending with their situation. Some women argued for even greater technological intervention in reproduction.

Miracle Moms

A second cluster of attitudes and experiences held by women regarding their use of donor eggs reflects a narrative that we call "miracle moms." A typical example of a "miracle mom" can be seen in one woman's description of her pregnancy as "at the edge of miracles" and her description of her son as "definitely a miracle child." Although miracle moms were generally less prevalent than eleventh-hour moms, through this narrative women described a novel conceptualization of the relationship between infertility, age, and donor egg that may provide insights into changing notions about the body. Miracle moms asserted that there was not just one biological clock, but rather many clocks that differentially shaped the possibilities of the body. Although women who gave birth at age 45 or later often espoused this view, it was sometimes voiced by Women who gave birth between 38 and 44, as well.

Whereas eleventh-hour moms discussed the ways in which new medical concepts about age prematurely curtail the body's potentiality, miracle moms expressed relief and surprise in learning all the reproductive functions that women's bodies are still capable of when a younger egg is used to conceive. One woman, age 50 at the birth of her child, stated: ". . . I'm still breastfeeding. I didn't know you could do that after menopause. They [clinical staff] were very supportive. [They joked] 'Of course your nipples are sore. They've been there for fifty years.'" In contrast to the rueful old eggs dialogue voiced by eleventh-hour moms, miracle moms expressed relief in the realization that the use of a donor egg obviates some of the concerns about maternal age, infertility, and infant health. For example, one woman, 41 at the birth of her child, stated: "I was relieved to think that it was not going to be my advanced, old eggs that weren't doing me much good right now and how much were we going to try to manipulate these things to try to produce a child. . . . It really was such a relief."

The Extension of Fertility Rather than the eleventh-hour mom view of fertility being curtailed by age, miracle moms view fertility as being extended. Many of the women in our study were concerned about the potential health risks to both the woman and the fetus due to their age. They reported learning that age limits a woman's ability to conceive and older eggs increase the risks to the fetus. However, they also learned that age does not limit a woman's ability to sustain a healthy pregnancy. One woman recounted:

> We were trying to find out from somebody who was an Ob/Gyn [obstetrician/gynecologist] what issues might come up for an older mother. Basically medical [issues], but anything that they wanted to tell us, because there's just not that much research out there. And his advice was that there is really no difference. The uterus is still capable of bearing a child to term, even though you're past menopause (54 at birth of child).

Whereas many eleventh-hour moms extrapolated the old eggs diagnosis to define themselves and their bodies in a holistic manner, miracle moms viewed eggs as one exchangeable part of the body that does not define one's total self. This represents a more plastic view of the body, wherein exchanging one bodily part can make the whole body operate anew, creating new kinds of possibilities in pursuing social identities across the life course.

In contrast to the eleventh-hour mom perspective of "lost time," a prominent theme within the miracle mom narrative was the notion that donor eggs allow one to turn back time. Many women discussed their ability to avert the risks associated with older pregnancy by using "young eggs" and making their pregnancy into one that was "like that of a younger woman." One woman, 44 at the birth of her child, stated: "Once I was pregnant with her [donor's] eggs, it's like you're a 24-year-old. I didn't have to worry about amniocentesis. I didn't have to worry about the risk of miscarriage of 43-year-old eggs. It's very interesting. There's a certain relief that comes with having young eggs. . . . It's like the fountain of youth."

The Donor Solution Miracle moms often gave birth at or after the age of 45 and thereby experienced a different clinical trajectory when compared to eleventh-hour moms. Miracle moms were often told right from the start that pregnancy with their own eggs, even using IVF, would be essentially impossible. Women felt that this clinical decision was legitimately supported by the statistical evidence that women have extremely low rates of conception with their own eggs after the age of 43, high rates of miscarriage, and high rates of disability. Some women also entered the infertility clinic when they were menopausal or post-menopausal and thereby "knew" that they could not become pregnant.

As a result, women who gave birth at age 44 or older were presented with fewer options as they pursued pregnancy compared to younger women. Many women noted that their age barred them from adoptive services, which meant that donor egg was the only route through which they could raise a child. Whereas donor egg was frequently viewed as a fall-back option by eleventh-hour moms, donor egg was the only option for miracle moms. One woman stated: "I didn't have a problem [with infertility]. I mean, I never had issues with infertility because I wasn't ever trying to have a baby. When I finally decided to have a baby, I was 48. And we just went right to IVF. I was told that I couldn't try 'cause after 44, they won't let you—they won't even attempt to have a woman use her own eggs. So we went right to the donor solution."

Despite being informed that there were no known physiological reasons for why a woman who is peri-menopausal, menopausal or post-menopausal could not sustain a pregnancy using a donor egg, many miracle moms nonetheless experienced some type of stigmatization as a result of this reproductive decision. Some couples were excluded from treatment altogether on the basis of age. Others experienced age-related negative reactions from physicians and/or therapists as they sought information before pursuing pregnancy. One woman stated: "One of the clinics said that they used a rule of thumb that if the combined age of the parents was over one hundred, they wouldn't do a donor egg procedure. We wouldn't be eligible, which we found kind of ridiculous—more than ridiculous. We found it offensive" (49 at birth of child). Another woman stated:

> Some medical professionals injected their personal opinions in, and would not always give us medical understanding. Some were very careful to just answer our questions. It didn't feel like we were trying to do something immoral or improper. We just wanted information. We're quite capable of making the moral decision (54 at birth of child).

DISCUSSION

The fact that new reproductive technologies have made it possible to extend the child-bearing years beyond the traditional historic biologic barrier of the menopause has far-reaching implications for the restructuring of the entire course of life (Becker, 2000). Women have become actively engaged in and even proponents of the biomedicalization of infertility and aging as the child-bearing stage of life has been lengthened for an additional 20 years. With the possibility for restructuring the life course so dramatically, the question is raised of why women seek out and subject themselves to such intensive and invasive medical treatment at this time of life. Considerable literature interrogates reasons for the pursuit of children. Van Balen and Inhorn (2003, pp. 8–9) summarize these as: (1) social security desires, that children are necessary for their later support of aging parents; (2) social power desires, that children serve as a valuable power resource; (3) social perpetuity desires, the perceived need to continue group structures such as lineage; and (4) political investment, as children are used to promote causes and engage in demographic wars. The desires of women and men who are growing older to parent can easily be identified as reflecting concerns about security in old age and continuity through the generations.

It should be noted, however, that biomedicalization is uneven—that is, it is not a uniform process. That many women felt their physicians, often general obstetrician/gynecologists, had not adequately informed them about the consequences of an age-related decline in fertility raises the question of medical ignorance, incompetence, or negligence. These narratives highlight two phenomena: (1) the "risks" of age-related infertility are not adequately assessed and appreciated by either the general medical profession or the popular culture, and (2) the medical evaluation of age-related fertility in the US is almost solely the provenance of a small number of highly specialized reproductive endocrinologists who provide IVF services to a relatively small percentage of all women experiencing infertility. Furthermore, the medical evaluation of "ovarian reserve" is an evolving clinical process that is subject to interpretation and is rarely employed except as a precursor to IVF treatment. Although the concept of medicalization has traditionally been seen as something "done to" patients, it must be noted that women in both this study and in other studies of reproductive technologies wanted more medicalization to ameliorate the problem, not less (Becker, 2000; Inhorn, 2003).

In our study, eleventh-hour moms discussed their infertility trajectory as a deeply disruptive experience that inhibited their pursuit of a desired future. On the other hand, miracle moms had given up the expectation of motherhood, especially with their own eggs, so they retell their stories of conception, pregnancy and birth through a narrative structure in which initially pessimistic expectations are happily overturned. Both of these narrative structures make the evolving concept of age-related infertility meaningful in a manner that connects with broader discourses on and around the biological clock. Consistent with the notion of a biological clock, eleventh-hour moms positioned infertility in women's behavior, specifically in the act of delaying parenthood, but redefined and temporally advanced the endpoint from menopause to the late 30s, coincident with recent observations concerning the age-related decline in the fertilization potential of oocytes. As such, eleventh-hour moms re-ground the biological clock discourse in a different root metaphor, that of old eggs.

The notion of old eggs represents a fissure in both medical and popular discourses and practices that have been created in and through a menses/menopause model of female reproduction. The sense of surprise women experienced at being told their fertility is challenged by their age and the notion that time has been lost are based on assumptions that follow from the menses/menopause model. Eleventh-hour moms reacted to the shifting biomedical perspective on female reproduction from a menses/menopause model to one that is centered specifically upon the aging of ova.

By recapitulating the biological clock narrative, eleventh-hour moms considered their reproductive choices in a context through which they perceived others to be blaming them for their age-related infertility. To defend themselves against this attack on their reproductive decision-making, women who drew on the eleventh-hour mom narrative structure frequently pointed to the fact that there has been changing knowledge about female fertility that precluded them from conducting themselves differently. In other words, women used the *changing* status of expert knowledge on female reproduction to contend that they themselves are not culpable for their infertility. This narrative reinforces the notion that the etiology of female infertility is embedded in women's behavior and can work to deem women responsible for their status as infertile. Many women who articulated the eleventh-hour mom perspective engaged with the politics of blame as they discussed aging and reproduction. While women articulated varied responses to politicized discourses that blame women for their infertility, the eleventh-hour mom process is nonetheless engaged with these discourses.

Miracle moms also configured themselves in the context of the biological clock but in a very different way. For miracle moms, the surprising component of the notion of old eggs was that there is not a single biological clock but instead a variety of biological clocks. These women did acknowledge that there is a physiological deadline for women to conceive with their own eggs. However, they contended that their eggs are just one part of the reproductive process and that the rest of their body is capable of sustaining a pregnancy. By dispersing reproduction, miracle moms did not extrapolate old eggs to mean that their bodies are past reproductive capacity. Indeed, miracle moms rarely considered themselves infertile per se. This fracturing of reproduction problematizes the notion that female fertility has a discrete end and allows miracle moms to consider their reproductive practices outside of the politics of blame. Whereas eleventh-hour moms engaged in the discourses of blame in various forms, miracle moms often bypassed this discourse completely.

Rather, miracle moms often expressed joy and relief in the kinds of possibilities dispersing reproductive functioning made possible. Clarke (1995) has discussed how the focus in reproductive sciences is on controlling reproductive bodies in "modernity" and on changing reproductive bodies in "postmodernity." Miracle moms could be understood as women's embodiment of postmodern reproduction, wherein an understanding of bodies as malleable allows for the pursuit of desired social identities. Featherstone and Hepworth (1991) have argued that in postmodernity the life course is deinstitutionalized and dedifferentiated, resulting in a blurring of what had previously been considered clearly differentiated life stages. Miracle moms fit within what Hepworth and Featherstone (1982) have called the "new middle age," the baby-boom generation rejoicing in the fragmentation of social expectations associated with aging.

This analysis has shown that two interconnected threads in women's lives were central to the ways in which they made age-related infertility meaningful. The first thread centered broadly upon the woman's life course and her (and her husband's) expectations upon entering the infertility clinic. Specifically, a woman's own understanding of her body as (in)fertile in relation to age shaped her reception of information regarding the declining quantity and quality of eggs. How women understood their bodies as (in)fertile connected with medico-scientific and popular-cultural discourses and practices around the biological clock and menopause. The second thread occurred when women are presented with data that demonstrated a rapid decline in the response to infertility treatment after the age of 38. Because women between 38 and 41 are frequently counseled to try in vitro fertilization with their own eggs first and then, if unsuccessful, "move on" to the use of donor eggs, they construed donor eggs as a second-choice option within the context of this clinical encounter and frequently felt propelled by a sense of urgency to conceive before time runs out. While loss of time is prominent in narratives about infertility generally (Becker, 2000; Martin-Matthews & Matthews, 2001; Sandelowski, Harris, & Holditch-Davis, 1990), by narrativizing this urgency vis-à-vis cultural discourses on the biological clock, some women discussed their experiences of infertility in a context through which they perceived blame.

It appears from this research that women in the 38–41-year-old age group experienced a more complex infertility treatment trajectory than women 42 and older. This age group commonly tried to use in vitro fertilization with their own ova first but when these attempts were deemed failures and women turned to donor eggs, they felt rushed to achieve a pregnancy. This sense of urgency, in turn, reinforced the notion that reproductive capacity is ending. By turning to donor eggs because they believed they had waited too long, eleventh-hour moms considered their reproductive decision-making through a discourse of blame. In retrospect, some women felt they had waited too long and cited a variety of reasons (that were beyond their control) that range from lack of readiness for children to time invested in IVF with their own eggs. Disappointment in shifting from the anticipation of a biogenetic child to a child conceived with a donor egg is undoubtedly part of the adjustment process women in the 38–41 age group undergo.

On the other hand, women who began infertility treatment after 42 were more often advised to use a donor egg immediately. While severing the genetic connection with their potential child was certainly difficult for many women in this age group, these women did not express the same kind of urgency as they recounted their infertility trajectory because using their own eggs was precluded by the policies of medical practices. These women were apparently able to enjoy their reproductive capacity outside the politics of blame.

In conclusion, the extension of the child-bearing years into later phases of the life course is a complex process that has been growing in scale since the introduction of donor eggs, yet the phenomenon has been largely overlooked except by those immediately affected. Historical shifts in the twentieth century in how women's reproduction is viewed, combined with the process of biomedicalization, have led to a new era in how the life course and its potentialities are viewed. Life stages are no longer discrete. They have become much more fluid and indeterminate. In the process, women who use new reproductive technologies are forced to rethink their gender identity in relationship to ideas about what age means for women who reproduce later in life. This research suggests that women's views about age and infertility shift rapidly during the 38–45 age range as part of this process of reconceptualizing age and gender identity. The narratives of these women speak to the profound social changes that engulf them and provide a window into a social life transition that is occurring globally. The resulting social changes are currently being experienced as upheaval, but it is likely they will be seen in the future as commonplace.

REFERENCES

Aral, S. O., & Cates, W. (1983). The increasing concern with infertility—Why now? *Journal of the American Medical Association, 250*(17), 2327.

Becker, G. (1997). *Healing the infertile family.* Berkeley, CA: University of California Press.

Becker, G. (2000). *The elusive embryo: How women and men approach new reproductive technologies.* Berkeley, CA: University of California Press.

Becker, G., Butler, A., & Nachtigall, R. D. (2005). Resemblance talk: A challenge for parents whose children were conceived with donor gametes in the U.S. *Social Science & Medicine, 61,* 1300–1309.

Becker, G., & Nachtigall, R. D. (1992). Eager for medicalization: The social production of infertility as a disease. *Sociology of Health & Illness, 14*(4), 456–471.

Bukulmez, O., & Arici, A. (2004). Assessment of ovarian reserve. *Current Opinion in Obstetrics and Gynecology, 16,* 231-237.

Centers for Disease Control and Prevention (2004). *2002 Assisted reproductive technology success rates: National summary and fertility clinic reports.* US Department of Health and Human Services, December, p. 25.

Clarke, A. E. (1995). Modernity, postmodernity, & reproductive processes, ca. 1890–1990, or "Mommy, where do cyborgs come from anyway?" In C. H. Gray (Ed.), *The cyborg handbook* (pp. 139–155). New York: Routledge.

Clarke, A. E., Shim, J. K., Mamo, L., Fosket, J. R., & Fishman, J. R. (2003). Biomedicalization: Technoscientific transformations of health, illness, and US biomedicine. *American Sociological Review, 68*(2), 161–194.

Edwards, J., Franklin, S., Hirsch, E., Price, F., & Strathern, M. (1993). *Technologies of procreation: Kinship in the age of assisted conception.* London: Routledge.

Edwards, R. G., Fishel, S. B., Cohen, J., Fehilly, C. B., Purdy, J. M., Slater, J. M., et al. (1984). Factors influencing the success of in vitro fertilization for alleviating human infertility. *Journal of in Vitro Fertilization and Embryo Transfer, 1*(1), 3.

Featherstone, M., & Hepworth, M. (1991). The mask of ageing and the postmodern life course. In M. Featherstone, M. Hepworth, & B. S. Turner (Eds.), *The body: Social process and cultural theory* (pp. 369–389). London: Sage.

Formanek, R. (1990). Continuity and change and "the change of life": Premodern views of the menopause. In R. Formanek (Ed.), *The meanings of menopause: Historical, medical and clinical perspectives* (pp. 3–41). Hillsdale, NJ: The Analytic Press.

Franklin, S. (1997). *Embodied progress: A cultural account of assisted conception.* London: Routledge.

Franklin, S., & Ragone, H. (1998). *Reproducing reproduction: Kinship, power, and technological innovation.* Philadelphia: University of Pennsylvania Press.

Greil, A. L. (1991). *Not yet pregnant: Infertile couples in contemporary America.* New Brunswick, NJ: Rutgers University Press.

Hepworth, M., & Featherstone, M. (1982). *Surviving middle age.* Oxford: Blackwell.

Inhorn, M. C. (1994). *Quest for conception. Gender, infertility, and Egyptian medical traditions.* Philadelphia: University of Pennsylvania Press.

Inhorn, M. C. (2003). *Local babies, global science: Gender, religion, and in vitro fertilization in Egypt.* New York: Routledge.

Inhorn, M. C., & Van Balen, F. (Eds.), (2003). *Infertility around the globe: New thinking on childlessness, gender, and reproductive technologies.* Berkeley, CA: University of California Press.

Kahn, S. M. (2000). *Reproducing Jews; A cultural account of assisted conception in Israel.* Durham, NC: Duke University Press.

Marsh, M., & Ronner, W. (1996). *The empty cradle: Infertility in America from colonial times to the present.* Baltimore, MD: The Johns Hopkins University Press.

Martin, E. (1987). *The woman in the body: A cultural analysis of reproduction.* Boston: Beacon Press.

Martin-Matthews, A., & Matthews, R. (2001). Living in time: Multiple timetables in couples' experiences of infertility and its treatment. In K. J. Daly (Ed.), *Minding the time in family experience: Emerging perspectives and issues* (pp. 111–134). Oxford, UK: Elsevier Science.

McKaughan, M. (1987). *The biological clock: Reconciling careers and motherhood in the 1980s.* New York: Doubleday.

McLean, A. (1990). Contradictions in the social production of clinical knowledge: The case of schizophrenia. *Social Science & Medicine, 9,* 969–985.

Nachtigall, R. D., Becker, G., Quiroga, S. S., & Tschann, J. M. (1998). The disclosure decision: Concerns and issues of parents of children conceived through donor insemination. *American Journal of Obstetrics and Gynecology, 178,* 1165–1170.

Nachtigall, R. D., Tschann, J. M., Quiroga, S. S., Pitcher, L., & Becker, G. (1997). Stigma, disclosure, and family functioning among parents of children conceived through donor insemination. *Fertility and Sterility, 68,* 83–89.

Ragone, H. (1994). *Surrogate motherhood: Conception in the heart.* Boulder, CO: Westview Press.

Sandelowski, M. (1993). *With child in mind: Studies of the personal encounter with infertility.* Philadelphia: University of Pennsylvania Press.

Sandelowski, M., Harris, B. G., & Holditch-Davis, D. (1990). Pregnant moments: The process of conception in infertile couples. *Research in Nursing and Health, 13*(5), 273–282.

Schwartz, P., & Mayaux, M. J. (1982). Female fecundity as a function of age. *New England Journal of Medicine, 306,* 404.

Scott, R. T., & Hofmann, G. E. (1995). Prognostic assessment of ovarian reserve. *Fertility & Sterility, 63,* 1–11.

Strathern, M. (1992). *After nature: English kinship in the late twentieth century.* Cambridge: Cambridge University Press.

Thompson, C. (2005). *Making parents: The ontological choreography of reproductive technologies.* Cambridge, MA: MIT Press.

Utian, W. H. (1990). The menopause perspective: From potions to patches. In M. Flint, F. Kronenberg, & W. Utian (Eds.), *Multidisciplinary perspectives on menopause* (pp. 1–7). New York: The New York Academy of Sciences.

Van Balen, F., & Inhorn, M. C. (2003). Interpreting infertility: A view from the social sciences. In M. C. Inhorn & F. van Balen (Eds.), *Infertility around the globe: New thinking on childlessness, gender, and reproductive technologies* (pp. 3–32). Berkeley, CA: University of California Press.

Whiteford, L. M. (1989). Commercial surrogacy: Social issues behind the controversy. In L. M. Whiteford & M. L. Poland (Eds.), *New approaches to human reproduction: Social and ethical dimensions* (pp. 145–169). Boulder, CO: Westview Press.

Zola, I. K. (1972). Medicine as an institution of social control. *The Sociological Review, 20*(4), 487–504.

 24

Inventing a New Death and Making It Believable

Margaret Lock

Medical anthropologists question some deeply entrenched cultural ideas of Western societies that are reflected in biomedicine. One of these central ideas is the philosopher René Descartes' notion, that humans are made up of separate and distinct entities of body and mind. This idea of dualism has often led biomedicine—particularly its North American version—to think of the body as a machine. Traditional surgery, for example, has primarily emphasized the removal of broken or diseased parts of the body. In order to effect a cure, surgical interventions depend upon the body's ability to heal itself after the diseased part is removed or repaired. In the past twenty years, remarkable advances in biomedical technology have contributed to the goal of replacing broken parts of the body-machine with the organs of brain-dead human donors.

The development of new biomedical technologies has pushed the frontiers of life—both in allowing the continued life of tiny premature infants (who would have died in the past) and in fending off death (with ventilators and feeding tubes) for an extremely long time. Biomedical technologies, in short, have come to require new definitions of death and life. Many medical anthropologists have contributed to discussions about the moral, cultural, and financial implications of these new technologies. The research on technologies of organ transplants has included a variety of topics including the lived experience of organ recipients, the relationship between donor families and recipients, and the illegal international trade in organs. In addition, there are important issues concerning how these technologies are interpreted and accepted in other cultures; that is the topic of selection 23 by Marcia Inhorn.

An important aspect of medical anthropology is to critically analyze the underlying beliefs and values that shape the culture of biomedicine and the practice of clinical care. The central idea of such analyses is the "cultural construction" of diverse realities. Creating new cultural realities about questions as basic as the definition of life, death, and what constitutes a person is a historical process. Cultures are always changing, sometimes slowly and sometimes quickly, through argumentative dialogues triggered by new discoveries or technologies.

This selection discusses the cultural construction of a new definition of death that was made necessary by new organ transplant technology. This new definition of brain death, in turn, made it possible for the organs of nonpersons to become a precious commodity. Organ transplantation is fraught with tensions that get to the heart of biomedicine and its new technologies.

As you read this selection, consider these questions:

- **What was the previous definition of death, and why did it become inadequate?**
- **How did the new definition of death get decided upon, and what were central arguments about it?**
- **What is the difference between whole-brain death and brain stem death?**
- **What does it mean that organs have become "commodified"?**
- **If healthy persons own their organs, is it their right to sell them?**
- **Why are there separate medical teams working with patients who are potential organ donors and with potential organ recipients?**

Context: Margaret Lock is an extremely influential medical anthropologist who taught, until recently, anthropology and social studies of medicine at McGill University. Her primary interest has been in anthropological analyses of the body in health and illness. Author or editor of seventeen books (many of which have won prestigious awards), her work has often utilized a cross-cultural comparison of culture and medicine in Japan and North America. Her 2002 book Twice Dead: Organ Transplants and the Reinvention of Death and her 1999 book Encounters with Aging: Mythologies of Menopause in Japan and North America are excellent examples of her insightful medical anthropological approach. Her most recent research has examined the emerging fields of genetics and epigenetics as they relate to nature–nurture debates and the cultural constructions of normal and abnormal; much of this work focuses on Alzheimer's disease and cognitive impairment.

Source: M. Lock (2002). "Inventing a New Death and Making It Believable." Anthropology and Medicine 9(2):97–115.

Did René Descartes simply make an error when he created the disembodied mind, as Antonio Damasio argues in his path-breaking book (1994)? Or did he construct a lie, or at least practice self-deception, in order that he might create a science of the body, one that troubled neither God nor the Church of the day because it did not impinge on their realms? We will never have a satisfactory answer, of course, but, error or lie, the effects of Descartes' thesis are still very much among us. It is not unreasonable to argue that, without the embedding of a disembodied mind in the discursive background of medical discourse that has a bearing on mind/body problems, the concept of brain-death may well never have been invented.

Until the 18th century recognition of death was a social convention. Whether the end point of life is recognized as putrefaction of the body—a body crawling with maggots—or the point at which a feather held in front of the nose stops fluttering, that condition must be agreed upon as equivalent to the moment of death. The transformation of the socially recognized process of dying into a declared moment of death demarcates the transition from life to death, with all that entails for the status of the involved individual. Once the management of death became, over 200 years ago, a medical rather than primarily a religious matter, efforts were made from the outset by the medical profession to measure and standardize death. The cessation of the heartbeat, determined with the assistance of the newly invented stethoscope, permitted doctors to declare death as the moment when the heart and lungs cease to function. But, from the outset, a deception was in effect built into the diagnosis, because the body continues to exhibit a great deal of biological activity after the heart stops beating. Once the technology of cardiopulmonary resuscitation became available the process of dying could be successfully reversed, exposing the deception, and demonstrating conclusively that selection of the moment of death along the continuum of dying entails a moral decision.

Declaration of cardiopulmonary death is the convention by which the death of most of us will be made social. What is informally recognized with the declaration of such a death is that, after efforts at resuscitation (if attempted) are discontinued, all concerned agree that an irreversible process of dying has set in about which nothing can be done. Today, however, for about 1% of all deaths in the so-called developed world, death is medically recognized as taking place in the first instance in the brain and not in the cardiorespiratory system.

A complex conjunction of technologies and events must intersect in the creation of such "living cadavers," as they were first named in the 1960s, and are now more familiarly known (but perhaps less accurately) as brain-dead bodies. First, an "accident" must take place—an automobile or plane crash; a drowning; a conflagration causing smoke inhalation; a major blow to the head; or a "cerebral accident" in which the brain suddenly floods with blood. These accidents frequently result, some of them inevitably so, in major trauma to the brain. Brain trauma is also caused by other accident-like events, among which gunshot wounds to the head or suicide attempts are the most common. More often than not victims of such severe trauma, because they can no longer breathe for themselves, cannot survive without the aid of a relatively simple piece of technology—the artificial ventilator.

Artificial ventilators or respirators—"breathing machines" as they were known in the first part of the 20th century, and then later as "iron lungs"—were developed on a large scale for the first time to combat the polio epidemics of the 1940s and 1950s. Over 400 different forms of positive pressure ventilators have been marketed in the ensuing years; these machines are part of the battery of indispensable technology without which intensive care units (ICUs) could not do their work. A ventilator, together with the responsible ICU staff, becomes, in effect, a simulacrum for much of the functioning of the lower brain-stem, and takes over the involuntary task of breathing for patients who are no longer able to cope independently. Certain of these individuals will make a partial or complete recovery, but the hearts of others will stop beating, or their blood pressure will drop irrevocably, and they will then die in spite of the ventilator. For a third class of patients, resuscitative measures are only a "partial success" (Ad Hoc Committee, 1968), so that with the assistance of the ventilator, the heart and lungs of such patients continue to function, but the brain is irreversibly damaged.

These brain-dead patients remain betwixt and between, both alive and dead; breathing with technological assistance but irreversibly unconscious. Without the artificial ventilator such entities could not exist, and even with technological management, their condition usually persists for only a few hours, days, or weeks, or very occasionally for months because, despite intensive care, the heart gives up, or the blood pressure cannot be sustained. Recently, however, with increased knowledge and experience, survival rates have lengthened (Shewmon, 1998; Shrader, 1986). One or two exceptional cases have been reported of over a year's duration (Shewmon, 1998), but there are no documented cases of anyone recovering from this state, *if* it has been correctly diagnosed. Most probably rather little attention would be paid to the condition of brain death, except for the fact that by far the majority of human organs used for transplantation are procured from brain-dead bodies. Living cadavers are, therefore, a scarce resource, valuable entities that are rigorously monitored and managed by the international medical community.

In order for organs to be procured from technologically-assisted brain-dead patients such individuals must be constituted among medical communities as no longer alive. This is the case today in North America, most European countries, and in many other parts of the world. However, in Japan, despite its sophistication and experience with biomedical technology, such patients count as not-yet-dead. Until 1997 when the law was modified in Japan it has not been possible to procure organs legally from the brain-dead, and even now it can only be done in highly restricted circumstances. In contrast to the situation in many other countries, the Japanese public, the legal profession, and even the majority of the medical profession in Japan, have not been convinced that a diagnosis of brain death, even though scientifically accurate, implies that brain-dead patients are dead (see Lock, 2002, for a full development of this argument).

LEGALIZING THE BRAIN-DEAD AS CORPSE-LIKE

After the first heart transplant was carried out in South Africa by Christiaan Barnard in late 1967, it was clear that the status of living cadavers urgently needed to be clarified, particularly so because more than one transplant surgeon was shortly thereafter charged with murder for removal of a beating heart from a patient. In one case, in Texas, a charge was dropped when it was decided by the medical examiner that the donor had been murdered by an assailant when his head was smashed in, and not several hours later by the transplant surgeon (*Newsweek*, 1967).

In the state of Virginia, in May 1972, four years after removal of Bruce Tucker's beating heart and its transplantation into a waiting patient, the involved surgeons, charged with wrongful death, learned that they were to be acquitted. The brother of the donor who had brought the case against the four doctors alleged that Bruce Tucker had not been dead at the time that his heart and kidneys were removed for transplantation, and that it was the removal of the organs that had caused his death. Tucker had been diagnosed as irreversibly unconscious, but as of 1968 no systematic criteria had been set out for confirming a diagnosis of brain death. In order to establish if Tucker could breathe independently, he had been removed from the ventilator for five minutes, and, once it was agreed that he was not breathing on his own, he was hastily reattached to the machine in order that oxygen would continue to circulate through his body and keep the organs in good condition for transplant.

It had been assumed prior to the hearing that the prosecution was likely to win the case due to some preliminary comments made by the judge, but apparently the judge's mind was swayed by the statements of expert witnesses. One physician insisted that the body exists only to support the brain and that "the brain is the individual" (Kennedy, 1973, p. 39). The donor's brother was particularly upset because the hospital had apparently made little effort to locate next of kin, and had treated Tucker's body as though it was unclaimed. After they were informed by the hospital administration and the police that next of kin could not be traced physicians had gone ahead with the procurement without permission and with no evidence that Tucker wished to be an organ donor. Tucker's brother gave evidence in court that he had telephoned the hospital three times, but he insisted that he had never been informed that his brother was to become an organ donor, and that he had eventually learnt of this event from the undertaker. This case, together with the one or two others like it in the United States, spurred the medical and legal establishment into creating standardized criteria to determine brain death. The Uniform Anatomical Gift Act was already in place as of 1968, designed to ensure non-commercial and voluntary donation of corpses and body parts for transplantation, but without efforts to standardize the determination of brain death, loopholes still remained. Across North America, the decision by the Virginia court permitted both transplant surgeons and intensivists working in ICUs who make brain death diagnoses to breathe easier.

In Japan, in 1969, a surgeon was also charged with murder, when he carried out the world's 30th heart transplant. The case was dropped without sentencing after two years, but it was clear that the doctor had lied at the hearing, and that the donor probably was able to breathe independently when his heart was removed. The recipient too, it was eventually decided, was not so ill that he needed a transplant. In Japan, over the years, numerous other charges have been laid against doctors who failed to obtain informed consent from relatives before procuring organs or who lied about the procedures they had carried out (Lock, 2002). These scandals contributed enormously to the fact that brain death was only legally recognized in Japan as the end of life in 1997. Aside from the first heart transplant of 1968 no other was carried out until 1999.

MAKING SUDDEN DEATH USEFUL

Standardized criteria for determining brain death were set in place in the United States in 1981, just before the Virginia court decision (President's Commission, 1981). Many other countries were enacting laws and guidelines about the same time, but the criteria vary in small but significant ways within some countries and from one country to another (Pallis, 1987). A battery of clinical tests (which also vary within and among countries, and are in any case not always consistently applied) are used to confirm the diagnosis. However, when making clinical decisions in connection with brain-dead patients, the diagnosis provides little information that will affect the therapeutic regime, for nothing can be done, given our current state of knowledge, to reverse the situation once the brainstem is extensively damaged.

When an elderly or a very sick person on a ventilator starts to show signs of irreversible brain damage, very often no special effort is made to diagnose brain death. There is no pressure to bring about a resolution to the situation. It is only for that relatively small number of patients who may become organ donors that a precision diagnosis is called for. Once it is confirmed that a donor has been located, then the assertive force of transplant technology comes into play, and attention is turned from the living cadaver to the condition of their organs (see also Hogle, 1995, 1999). Potential organ donors cannot breathe independently, but unlike most other patients on ventilators, they are neither elderly nor suffering from cancer or other invasive, degenerative, or infectious diseases. Almost all donors are basically healthy and very often they are young, although increasingly middle aged donors are made use of; almost without exception, donors have been victims of accidents or traumatic violence. The conjunction of certain forms of accidents and violence with ventilator use and also with transplant technology has produced an entity, the living cadaver, that prior to the 1950s did not exist, and since the 1970s has come to be thought of increasingly not only as dead but in short supply.

The proclaimed "shortage" of organs has been described as a public health crisis (Randall, 2000). People whose work is associated with transplant technology are told repeatedly how many thousands of patients die each year waiting for organs. In the United States, for example, roughly 30,000 potential recipients were awaiting transplants in 1993 and, as Arnold et al. note, "every day six of these patients die prior to receiving a heart or liver transplant." Those who need kidneys continue on dialysis (1995, p. 1). This shortage is exacerbated because we are better than we used to be at buckling up our seatbelts, and in any case over the past 10 years the number of automobile accidents has been cut in half. At the same time the "success rate" in obtaining agreement from patients and families to donate organs has remained unchanged (Caplan, 1988).

Under the circumstances, organ procurement agencies are particularly vigilant. Their employees give lectures and provide small incentives to medical personnel working in intensive care units. They also monitor how well ICUs succeed in procuring organs and, in the province of Québec, for example, send admonitory letters to units that do not provide the number of organs that could be expected to be procured, given how many victims of accidents are treated in the unit. Required request of all families of brain-dead patients is in place in many states in America. In some countries, including Spain, Belgium, France, Austria, Norway and Brazil, presumed consent is legalized, so that organs are automatically taken from potential donors unless they have opted out ahead of time or else family members speak up in a timely fashion and firmly stop the proceedings. In theory protests by family members do not have to be heeded, but in practice it appears that they are.

FROM SUSPENDED ANIMATION TO ORGAN TRANSPLANTS

The work of Alexis Carrel, the 1913 Nobel Prize winner in medicine, together with several other scientists, provided the necessary foundations so that transplant technology could mature over the course of this century. Carrel and his colleagues showed that not only could cells be kept in suspended animation, as was well known by the turn of the century, but that they could be made to function and reproduce independently of the human body (*McClure's*, 1913). Once this was demonstrated, it was then a short step to the experimental era of organ transplantation, although this technology was not destined to mature until the late 1970s, when powerful immuno-suppressants that function to reduce the rejection rate of transplanted organs came on the market.

It was evident as early as the 1950s that patient/ventilator entities were causing disquiet. For one thing, it was not clear what they should be called: "living cadavers," "ventilator brain," and "heart–lung preparations" were just a few of the terms bandied about. In a 1966 CIBA Foundation symposium, the focus of which was on organ transplants, certain impatience, characteristic of many professionals associated with the transplant world in connection with these new entities, was clear:

> [F]or how long should "life" be maintained in a person with irrevocable damage of the brain? . . . [W]hen does death occur in an unconscious patient dependent on artificial aids to circulation and respiration? [A]re there ever circumstances where death may be mercifully advanced? . . . [D]oes the law permit operations which "mutilate" the donor for the advantage of another person? (Wolstenholme & O'Conner, 1966, pp. vii–viii)

The thrust of questions such as the above becomes, in effect, a desire to know when individual patients whose organs have potential value for others can be counted as dead enough to be transformed into commodified objects. At what juncture can the "lie" of death slip by uncontested? Hybrid bodies of brain-dead patients—*faux vivants*—are produced and reproduced routinely today through discourse and practices at various sites including the media, state legislatures, politically driven commissions, professional literature, the laboratory, popular literature, and so on. But before this situation could be taken for granted a new death had to be invented.

INVENTING A NEW DEATH

The first attempt to define death based on the condition of the brain was made by French neurophysiologists, who coined the term *coma depassé* (irreversible coma) in 1959 to describe this condition (Jouvet, 1959; Mollaret & Goulon, 1959). With their usual aplomb, a group of Harvard doctors together with one lawyer, one theologian, and one historian when called together as a task force to examine ethical problems in connection with the "hopelessly unconscious patient" made no reference to the work of the French physicians. The chair of this 1968 Ad Hoc Committee was anesthesiologist Henry Beecher, well known for his concern of long standing about experimentation on human subjects. Together with his colleagues he "invented" the term "irreversible coma" which was used interchangeably with the concept of "brain death" for several years. The committee gave two reasons for redefining death: it stated that there were increased burdens on patients, families, and hospital resources caused by "improvements in resuscitative and support measures," and secondly, and more ominously, that "obsolete criteria for the definition of death can lead to controversy in obtaining organs for transplantation" (Ad Hoc Committee, 1968, p. 337). Over the years it has been repeated many times that the "real" reason for creating brain death was in order that organs could be procured legally.

With the publication of the Harvard Ad Hoc Committee report, two definitions of death became widely recognized, the "traditional" cardiopulmonary death, and brain death. Throughout the 1970s, articles appeared in medical journals in both North America and Europe arguing that the clinical tests used to diagnose brain death were reliable and replicable (Black, 1978; Grenvik et al., 1978; Mohanda & Chou, 1971). However, a 1978 two-part article in the *New England Journal of Medicine* pointed out that there was no official consensus in the United States about the best *criteria* for determining the diagnosis (in contrast to Argentina, Australia, Greece, and Finland, where consensus had been reached and relevant laws passed, and Canada, France, Great Britain, and Czechoslovakia, where criteria had been agreed upon and legal changes were, in most cases, pending). This same article cites 30 different sets of criteria laid out by various advisory groups to be used when making a diagnosis of brain death, including those outlined by the Harvard group, and by the Royal College of Physicians and Surgeons of the United Kingdom. The author, a neurologist, came to what appears to be a remarkable conclusion, namely, that "whole-brain damage from which survival has never been seen can be diagnosed by many different sets of criteria," and that the criteria chosen may depend ultimately on the methods considered most reliable (Black, 1978, p. 338).

By 1981, it was recognized in North America that consistent *public policy* with respect to redefining death was essential. In the United States, a Uniform Determination of Death Act was proposed, after extensive debate among the members of a special President's Commission, less than half of whom were physicians. This Act was immediately supported by the American Medical Association, and the American Bar Association, and subsequently adopted over the years by the majority of state legislatures. In the same year, the Law Reform Commission of Canada published a document entitled *Report on the Criteria for the Determination of Death,* which provided the basis for amendments to federal statutory law in connection with the recognition of death in Canada.

The President's Commission was mandated to "study and recommend ways in which the traditional legal standards can be updated in order to provide clear and principled guidance for determining whether such [brain-dead] bodies are alive or dead" (1981, p. 3). On the basis of this mandate, the Commission set out to write an unambiguous definition of death to be enshrined, for the first time ever, in law (Annas, 1988, p. 621). As part of this process, the Commission stated that it was necessary to rationalize and update what they characterized as "obsolete" diagnostic criteria present in the Harvard Ad Hoc Committee statement. The Commission worked against the position taken in writing by a good number of individual physicians, philosophers, and theologians, who argued that the law should not have the final word on death.

The Commission was explicit from the outset that their task of making a "determination of death" was quite separate from the matter of "allowing [someone] to die," although both arise from "common roots in society" (1981, p. 4). The report stressed that it was the death of a human being, "not the 'death' of cells tissues and organs," about which committee members were concerned. The Commission insisted that policy conclusions and the statute recommendation must "accurately reflect the social meaning of death and not constitute a mere legal fiction" (1981, p. 31). Although it was recognized that "functional cessation of vital bodily systems" can be used as standards to judge whether biological death has occurred, the importance of such findings, it was asserted, is for what they reveal about "the status of the human being," rather than about the various body systems.

Not surprisingly, it was recognized in the report that for the medical community, "a sound basis exists for declaring death even in the presence of mechanically assisted vital signs" (p. 31). But the Commission wished to know whether the scientific viewpoint was "consistent with the concepts of 'being dead' or 'death' as they are commonly understood in our society" (p. 31). The Commission concluded that:

> The living differ from the dead in many ways. The dead do not think, interact, autoregulate or maintain organic identity through time, for example. Not all the living can always do *all* of these activities, however; nor is there one single characteristic (e.g., breathing, yawning, etc.) the loss of which signifies death. Rather, what is missing in the dead is a cluster of attributes, all of which form part of an organism's responsiveness to its internal and external environment. . . . In setting forth the standards recommended in this Report, the Commission has used "whole brain" terms to clarify the understanding of death that enjoys near universal acceptance in our society. (President's Commission, 1981, p. 36)

The public was not polled or called in to give testimony before the Commission, and to this day we have no more than spotty anecdotal evidence on which to ground an assertion that brain death has "near universal acceptance" in the United States. However, given the confusion over the concept of brain death manifested by the media and the medical and legal professions in the years prior to the report of the Commission, it is highly unlikely that there could have been near universal acceptance of brain death among the public. In the early 1980s, very few people had much of an idea, aside from confusing images obtained from science fiction and movies such as *Coma,* as to what the term brain death signifies, a situation that no doubt persists to this day.

The Commission was at pains to establish a single set of standards which would be accepted throughout the United States. The difficulties of transporting bodies across state lines for the purposes of "treatment" (meaning, it seems, organ procurement) without clear public policy in place was raised as a major stumbling block. It was also emphasized that physicians must know as early as possible along the continuum of dying when a mechanically supported patient's brain ceases to function, in order that adequate care could be taken of organs designated for transplant.

As with the earlier Harvard Report, it is the interests of the organ transplant enterprise that determines the direction of these arguments. For example, it was explicitly stated that, even when the patient is on a respirator, internal organs undergo changes that make them less fit for transplant unless they are carefully perfused and certain medications are avoided. It is notable that these comments were made at exactly the time when powerful new immuno-suppressant drugs were becoming widely available, and the numbers of organ transplants carried out was rapidly on the increase throughout North America.

The Commission recommended that a concept of "whole-brain death," equated with an "irreversible loss of all brain function," be adopted. Determination of whole-brain death has been the standard diagnostic practice in the United States. This decision was made in part because members of the religious right who participated in the President's Commission argued forcibly that they could only support the equation of a brain-death diagnosis with death if it was the case that brain-dead individuals were without doubt no longer in any way alive. They argued for a black and white distinction between life and death and insisted that the whole brain must be recognized as dead. In fact, as the neurologists who participated in the commission well knew at the time, it is not possible to establish whole-brain death absolutely conclusively using any of the tests or procedures that are routinely carried out to determine this condition. In fact, it has been shown repeatedly that in many diagnosed cases of brain death some residual activity remains in the upper brain. This activity has no functional significance or prognostic value and will cease within days, but its existence means that in a strict sense of the term all activity of the brain has not entirely and absolutely ceased. The term whole-brain death is therefore misleading for those who insist that the point of death, when located in the brain, must be defined as absolutely no activity in the brain of any sort. The British did not fall into this epistemological conundrum because, as a result of a powerful case made by the neurologist Christopher Pallis, the concept of brain-stem death and not whole-brain death became recognized as the end of human life in that country. Pallis's argument was that, on the basis of neuro-anatomy, it is incontrovertible that if the brain-stem is irreversibly damaged and is no longer functioning then inevitably the upper brain must cease to function in due course—usually within hours or days. Whatever residual activity is left in the upper brain after irreversible damage to the brain-stem is of no consequence.

In the intervening years some countries have followed the United States and others, mostly in Europe, have followed the lead of the British. Yet others, like Canada, started out recognizing whole-brain death, but in recent years the professional society has put out guidelines in which brain-stem death is now the standard (*Canadian Journal of Neurological Sciences*, 1999).

CAPITALIZING ON AMBIGUITY

For the remainder of this paper I will focus on one particular site where brain-dead bodies exist in a space "entirely controlled by man and his technology" (Agamben, 1998, p, 164), and by means of which parts of their bodies can be put to utilitarian use. Observation of the management of the transition to a brain-dead body ready for commodification provides insight into ideas about what constitutes death, and how theories of person and identity are constructed and imbued with moral value. Death and dying can never be stripped of meaning and reduced to biology, and this is where ambiguity and, at times, deception creep into the proceedings.

The "worth" of brain-dead entities is constructed as part of the conceptual space (Bates, unpublished manuscript) in which standardized ICU practices, wherever their location, take place. Conceptual space is in part produced by medical knowledge and practices, which itself may be contested, but in addition this space is profoundly influenced by the discourse in connection with living cadavers emanating from other relevant sites; notably the media, the law, religious bodies, and popular culture are deeply implicated in the creation, management, and disposal of this ambiguous entity in the ICU. What is more, not everyone working in the ICU feels the same way about disposal of brain-dead bodies and their commodification so that organs can be procured. But once it is conventionally accepted that transplants making use of organs taken from brain-dead bodies is a worthwhile endeavor, then everyone in the ICU is complicit to some extent, and those who are uncomfortable about whether brain death "really" is death must reconcile their personal feelings with what is standardized practice.

WHEN BODIES OUTLIVE PERSONS

It is striking that despite legal recognition of whole-brain death and brain-stem death, respectively, and the publication of standardized guidelines for their determination by the various involved medical colleges and societies, these guidelines are rarely referred to in practice. The majority of the 32 intensivists and eight nurses in ICUs whom I interviewed in the latter part of the 1990s in Canada and the United States have never read these guidelines. Usually intensivists are simply taught what to do at the bedside without referral to written guidelines. However, today, in contrast to the 1970s, there is a high degree of (but not complete) standardization across hospitals with respect to clinical tests (although this is not the case with confirmatory tests such as the EEG).

Everyone agrees that the clinical examination for brain death is straightforward. The tests were described as "robust," "simple," and "solid" and, together with the apnea test (a requirement to see if the patient can breathe independently of the ventilator), they inform the physician about the condition of the lower brain—about the brain-stem. If there is no response to this battery of tests, then brain death can be provisionally diagnosed, because, as noted above, without brain-stem function the upper brain cannot survive. In practice, two specialists should make the diagnosis independently, and usually the tests are repeated after a suitable time interval (although this is not always the case today, even though guidelines inevitably recommend repeat tests). At this juncture, the death certificate is signed, and the ventilator is turned off unless the patient is to become an organ donor.

There is unanimous agreement among the intensivists interviewed that the clinical criteria for whole-brain death are infallible *if* the tests are performed correctly (even though whole-brain death cannot actually be diagnosed but must be inferred as having happened or else as imminent). There is also agreement that whole-brain death, properly diagnosed, is an irreversible state, from which no one in the experience of the informants has ever recovered, although five of those interviewed have been involved with cases where "errors" have occurred. However, although the physicians I talked to agree that a brain death diagnosis is robust, it does not follow that they believe that the patients are "dead" when sent for organ retrieval.

Among these intensivists, not one believes that a diagnosis of brain death signifies the end of biological life, despite the presence of irreversible damage and knowledge that this condition will lead, usually sooner rather than later, to complete biological death. As one intensivist put it, "It's not death, but it is an irreversible diagnosis, which I accept." There is implicit agreement that a diagnosis of whole-brain death indicates that, despite massive technological intervention, the brain has ceased to function as a site for the integration of biological activities in other parts of the body. At the same time a unanimous sentiment exists that the organs and cells of the body, including small portions of the brain, remain alive, thanks to the artificial brain-stem supplied by the ventilator and ICU staff. Indeed, if organs are to be transplanted, then they *must* be kept alive and functioning as close to "normal" as is possible; as Youngner et al. note, "maintaining organs for transplantation actually necessitates treating dead patients in many respects as if they were alive" (1985, p. 321).

Intensivists are aware that infants have been delivered from brain-dead bodies. It is not possible for them to disregard the fact that the brain-dead are warm and usually retain a good color, that digestion, metabolism, and excretion continues, and some know that the hair and nails continue to grow. Many also realize that some brain cells may still be firing and that endocrine and other types of physiological activity continue for some time. For the majority, although a brain-dead patient is not biologically dead, the diagnosis indicates that the patient has entered into a *second* irreversible state, in that the "person" and/or "spirit" is no longer present in the body. The patient has, therefore, assumed a hybrid status—that of a dead-person-in-a-living-body. However, rather than dwell on ambiguities or engage in extended discussion about conceptual ideas about death, most clinical practitioners are, not surprisingly, interested first and foremost in accuracy and certainty. In order to convey their certainty that an irreversible biological condition has set in, in addition to explaining about tests and examinations to families, they emphasize that the "person" is no longer present, even though the appearance of the entity lying in front of them usually does not give visual support to this argument.

Intensivists stated (Lock, 2002) that they say things such as the following to families at the bedside: "the things that make her her are not there any more," or "he's not going to recover. Death is inevitable." One doctor, who in common with many of his colleagues, chooses not to say simply that the patient is dead, because for him personally this is not the case, tells the family firmly that the patient is "*brain-dead*" but that there is "absolutely no doubt but that things will get worse." Another physician pointed out that it is difficult to assess what is best to say to the family, because in most cases one does not know if they have religious beliefs or not:

> I believe that a "humanistic" death happens at the same time as brain death. If I didn't believe this, then I couldn't take care of these patients and permit them to become organ donors. For me the child has gone to heaven or wherever, and I'm dealing with an organism, respectfully, of course, but that child's soul, or whatever you want to call it, is no longer there. I don't know, of course, whether the family believes in souls or not, although sometimes I can make a good guess. So I simply have to say that "Johnny" is no longer here.

One of the intensivists thinks of the brain-dead body as a vessel, and tells the family that what is left of their relative is only an empty container, because the "person has gone." For a doctor born in Latin America, the "essence" of the patient has gone, and this is what he tells the family. All the intensivists except one agreed that the absence of the person is evident *because* of an irreversible brain function, thus ensuring a permanent lack of consciousness, no awareness, and no sensation of pain. In other words, a sensate, suffering, individual has ceased to exist because their mind no longer functions, when discussing brain death. Families, she insisted, often find it difficult to accept that there is.

It is essential that the doctor takes control "a bit," argued one interviewee no chance of a reversal, and this is where the doctor cannot afford to appear diffident or equivocating. One doctor stated that "you can't go back to the family and say that their relative is brain-dead, you've *got* to say that they are dead—you could be arrested for messing up on this." He recalled that during his training he had described a patient as "basically dead" to his supervisor, who had responded abruptly by insisting: "He's dead. That's what you mean, basically." The task for intensivists then is to convince the family that, even though their relative appears to be sleeping, they are in fact no longer *essentially* alive; what remains is an organism or vessel that has suffered a mortal blow.

DOUBTS AMONG THE CERTAINTY

It is clear that these intensivists have few second thoughts about reversibility, but it is also evident that many of them nevertheless harbor some doubts about the condition of a recently declared brain-dead patient, and it is often those with the longest experience who exhibit the most misgivings. An intensivist with over 15 years of experience said that he often lies in bed at night after sending a brain-dead body for organ procurement and asks himself, "was that patient *really* dead? It is irreversible—I know that, and the clinical tests are infallible. My rational mind is sure, but some nagging, irrational doubt seeps in." This doctor together with the majority of other intensivists interviewed take some consolation from their belief that to remain in a severely vegetative state is much worse than to be dead. *If* a mistake is made, and a patient is diagnosed prematurely, or treated as though brain-dead when this is not indeed the case, then it is assumed that either they would have become brain-dead shortly thereafter, or permanent unconsciousness would have been their lot. But doubts continue to fester away at some people.

One intensivist, who came to North America from India as an immigrant when a child, stated that for him a brain-dead body is "an in-between thing. It's neither a cadaver, nor a person, but then again, there is still somebody's precious child in front of me. The child is legally brain-dead, has no awareness or connection with the world around him, but he's still a child, deserving of respect. I know the child is dead and feels no pain, is no longer suffering, that what's left is essentially a shell. I've done my tests, but there's still a child there." When asked by families, as he often is, if the patient has any consciousness, or feels pain, this intensivist has no difficulty in reassuring them that their child is dead, and is no longer suffering. He noted that it is especially hard for relatives when they take the hand of their child and sometimes the hand seems to respond and grasp back. This reflex response was noted by several of the intensivists and nurses as very disconcerting for families, especially when one is trying to convince them that the patient is no longer alive.

One doctor professed to a belief in a spirit or soul that takes leave of the body at death. For her, if brain damage is involved, this happens when the patient's brain is irreversibly damaged, at the moment of trauma or shortly thereafter. Another intensivist insisted at first, as did many of the individuals interviewed, that he had no difficulty with the idea of brain death: "it seems pretty straightforward to me. Do the tests, allow a certain amount of time; a flat EEG and you're dead." Then, 10 minutes later he said: "I guess I equate the death of a person with the death of the spirit because I don't really know about anything else, like a hereafter. I'm not sure anyway, if a hereafter makes a difference or not." When asked what he meant by the word "spirit," this intensivist replied: "I guess one would have to take it as meaning that part of a person which is different, sort of not in the physical realm. Outside the physical realm. It's not just the brain, or the mind, but something more than that. I don't really know. But anyway, a brain-dead patient, someone's loved one, won't ever be the person they used to know. Sure their nails can grow and their hair can grow, but that's not the essence."

A senior doctor, struggling to express his feelings, imbued the physical body with a will: "the body *wants* to die, you can sense that when it becomes difficult to keep the blood pressure stable and so on." This intensivist, although he accepts that brain death is the end of meaningful life, revealed considerable irresolution in going on to talk about the procurement of organs: "we don't want this patient to expire before we can harvest the organs, so it's important to keep them stable and alive, and that's why we keep up the same treatment after brain death." Yet another interviewee acknowledged that "real" death happens when the heart stops: "the patient dies two deaths."

For these physicians an organ donor is by definition biologically alive, or at least "partially" biologically alive, when sent to the operating room for organ retrieval, because there can be no argument about the liveliness of the principal body organs, aside from the brain. Perhaps most revealing of some confusion and occasional doubts in connection with the status of a brain-dead individual is that among the 32 doctors interviewed, only six had signed their donor cards or left other forms of advanced directives, and one other wasn't sure whether he had done so or not. When I pressed for reasons as to why people appeared hesitant, I was not given any very convincing reasons. Doctors said that their family would know what to do, or that they just didn't feel quite right about donation or, alternatively, that they supposed they should get it sorted out.

NURSING THE BRAIN-DEAD

Among the eight nurses I interviewed, all think of brain death as a reliable diagnosis, and they claim that they have no difficulties with it. When the first set of clinical tests indicate brain death, these nurses think of their patients as "pretty much dead," because none of them have ever witnessed a reversal of the diagnosis at the second set of tests. However, they do not change their care of or behavior towards brain-dead patients until after the second confirmation of brain death. If the patient is to become an organ donor then, even after brain death is confirmed, care of the living cadaver continues, but now it is in reality the organs that are being cared for.

While carrying out their work between the two sets of tests, all of the nurses continue to talk to their patients and, in addition to keeping their eyes on the monitors, pay their usual attention to the comfort and cleanliness of the body. Two nurses stated that they are acutely aware of the family at this time, and deliberately make their behavior around the patient as "normal" as possible, for their sakes. More often than not it is the nurse to whom the family has been putting their urgent questions, asking above all about the prognosis. In many cases nurses sense that a patient is brain-dead before the first set of tests are actually done, for they have been checking the pupils of the eyes regularly, looking for reflexes and noting when there is no longer any response to painful stimulation as when tubes are threaded into or taken out of the body.

After the second set of tests confirm whole-brain death the majority of the nurses now regard the patient in front of them as no longer fully human: "a brain-dead body can't give you anything back; there's only an envelope of a person left, the machine is doing all the work." When nurses continue to talk to brain-dead bodies and "care" for the organs, it is "out of habit," or "just in case a soul is still there," or "because the soul is probably still in the room" (see also Wolf, 1991; Youngner et al., 1985).

In common with the physicians, the majority of nurses believe that "it is what goes on in your head that makes you a person." One nurse insisted that the idea that nails grow after brain death does not make her at all uncomfortable. Confusion is apparent, as was the case among some physicians, in the way in which nurses talk at times about the brain-dead: "Once the patient has been declared brain-dead you still keep them on all of the monitors and the ventilator, for two reasons: first of all, the family wants to go in and see the patient *still alive,* and second, soon after, a few minutes after, we'll be asking them to consider organ donation" (emphasis added). One nurse insisted that brain death is not death, and that patients remain alive until the heart stops beating, which takes place in the operating room if organs are to be procured. Despite these ambiguities the ICU nurses with whom I talked are more conscientious than are the physicians about signing their donor cards—all but one senior nurse had done so.

One medical specialty, that of anesthesiologists who are also intensivists, sometimes find themselves in disturbing circumstances in connection with organ procurement. A woman who works in a children's hospital put it this way:

> Occasionally there is a patient who I've been looking after over the weekend in the ICU, working with closely, hoping that things will improve. The following week I will be having my turn on anesthesiology, and so I don't go to the ICU, and I look up and see them wheeling in the child so as we can procure organs from him. The child has taken a turn for the worse and become brain-dead in the day or so after I went off the ICU. For me, this is the most ghastly job that I have to do. (see also Youngner et al., 1985)

This same doctor added:

> Procurements are not a pretty sight. I always get the hell out of the operating room as soon as I possibly can. As soon as they've got the heart out. Everyone starts to scrabble at that point. It's ghastly, absolutely ghastly. I sort of have to sit down by the machines and just keep checking the dials every couple of minutes so as I don't have to watch what's going on. It's ghoulish, but you just have to try and focus on the fact that those organs are going to do some good. In a way I *have* to think of them still as a patient because they are under my care, and I guess the most important thing is that they are treated with respect, which isn't normally a problem at all. But with procurements, there's this conflict between the whole body and the organs. I can't really let myself think of it as a person any more. On the other hand, certainly if I've had contact with them before, and have been caring for them, then it's really hard for me to just accept that that process has ended. There really is a conflict. So I have to think of the body as a vessel, partly because I'm trying to protect myself. It's a really unpleasant emotion, especially because often there's no external trauma, so it's really hard to realize that this young person is dead.

In summary, none of these ICU specialists were opposed in principle to the idea of organ transplants, and all of them believe that it is appropriate for individuals to donate organs, with prior consent. They are more ambivalent than many of them care to admit, however, about the status of a living cadaver. While they agree that brain death is irreversible, they do not believe that brain-dead individuals are dead. Nevertheless, because they are convinced that no sentient being, no person, continues to exist once brain death is declared, they find themselves able to send brain-dead individuals off for organ procurement. Aside from a few qualms at times, persons are clearly located in brains, that is, in minds.

In addition to occasional doubts about the ontological status of brain-dead organ donors, the more mundane but terrifying anxieties created by the possibility of error always lurk in the shadows. All intensivists had heard about cases where errors have been made, and some have been directly involved with them. In hospitals where I have done research I am convinced that these ambivalences and anxieties are sufficient that, despite the pressures placed on ICUs by transplant personnel, caution is the overriding stance.

I make no claim that for these intensivists, being the direct heirs of Enlightenment philosophy, location of person in the brain is a "natural" move. For one thing a large number were schooled in quite different philosophic traditions before going into medical school. Without the weight of more than 30 years of systematization and routinization of brain death criteria, supplemented by positive recognition from the media and from professional, legal, and political quarters, few if any organs would be procured from brain-dead bodies, and few intensivists would be willing to participate in their procurement. This enormous apparatus permits intensivists, except when a few stubborn doubts surface, to convince themselves that individuals whose brains are irreversibly damaged and who will expire in short order when taken off the ventilator have the worth of corpses. Knowledge, particularly from the Christian tradition, buttressed by Enlightenment philosophy, although rarely referred to explicitly, contributes to widely-shared tacit knowledge making it appear rational to think of brain-dead bodies as objects that can be commodified. This same tacit knowledge has permitted a legitimizing discourse to gel at various key sites over the years.

In common with the public at large, intensivists participate in the rhetoric that meaning can be created for grieving relatives out of accidental, untimely deaths if organs can be procured and "live on" in other needy patients. In North American ICUs today one common story is that families recognize death too quickly and are prepared to move to the organ donation phase when considerable hope remains of patient recovery. Experienced ICU staff must then restrain both inexperienced colleagues and families. The metaphor of the gift of life is effective it seems in permitting people to restore a modicum of order to their lives after chance has played havoc and temporarily taken control. The rational mind does not account for the success of this rhetoric about saving the lives of strangers, or only partially so. For many involved families thoughts of transcendence are not far from the surface (Joralemon, 1995; Lock, 2002; Sharp, 1995). It seems that this rhetoric has successfully overcome any reservations grieving families who choose to donate organs may have about the status of their relative as living or dead.

CONCLUSIONS

The ambiguous status of the living cadaver makes it possible to arrive at more than one conclusion about its condition as alive or dead. In North America, a brain-dead body is clearly biologically alive in the minds of the majority of those who work closely with it, but it is no longer a person. On the basis of their well-founded trust in medical tests, intensivists permit themselves to persuade many relatives of brain-dead patients that this condition can safely be counted as death—a conclusion based on the condition of the brain. This is done in good faith because the patient is in a condition about which medicine can do nothing, one that will proceed inevitably to complete biological death. A brain-dead body, having no mind, takes on cadaver-like status, retains only the respect given to the dead, and can, therefore, be commodified. The stark reality of this transition is veiled by a rhetoric about the saving of the lives of desperate people—about the good that will come from organ donation.

The conceptual space in which ICU practitioners in North America work could not have come about without intervention by powerful mediators in the medical world. These medical experts in consort with representatives of the law, religious bodies, and judiciously selected philosophers ensured, on the basis of carefully structured debate that took place as part of the President's Commission, that brain death was legally recognized and that the Catholic Church was not unduly disturbed by this situation. Details about this debate have never been widely circulated among the public. When disputes arose at later dates they were quickly displaced by a judicious use of the powerful metaphor of the "gift of life" associated with the transplant world, and attention was directed by medicine and the media to the life-saving technology of organ transplants.

Even though procurement of organs from brain-dead bodies is today routine, complete consensus about the condition of brain death as the end of life has never been achieved, and the debate is currently opening up once again in part because, as a result of improved ICU technology, brain-dead patients can sometimes "live" for extended periods of time. Under these circumstances can this condition be counted as death? Or is this diagnosis of death perhaps better understood as a legalized fiction—a lie? And *does not* the technology simply prolong a state that could best be described as good-as-dead? Perhaps Descartes would have known how to deal with this intolerable ambiguity.

REFERENCES

Ad Hoc Committee of the Harvard Medical School to Examine the Definition of Death. 1968. A definition of irreversible coma. *Journal of the American Medical Association,* 205, 337–340.

Agamben, G. 1998. *Homo Sacer: Sovereign Power and Bare Life.* Stanford: Stanford University Press.

Annas, G. J. 1988. Brain death and organ donation: you can have one without the other. *Hastings Center Report,* 18, 28–30.

Arnold, R., Youngner, S., Shapiro, R. & Mason Spicer, C. 1995. Introduction: back to the future: obtaining organs from non-heart beating cadaver donors. In Arnold, R., Youngner, S., Shapiro, R. & Mason Spicer, C. eds. *Procuring Organs for Transplant: The Debate over Non-Heart-Beating Cadaver Donors.* Baltimore: Johns Hopkins University Press.

Bates, D. W. Y. William Harvey and the construction of coherence. Unpublished manuscript.

Black, P. 1978. Brain death. *New England Journal of Medicine,* 229, 338–344.

Canadian Journal of Neurological Science. 1999. Guidelines for the diagnosis of brain death. *Canadian, Journal of Neurological Science,* 26, 64–66.

Caplan, A. L. 1988. Professional arrogance and public misunderstanding. *Hastings Center Report,* 18, 34–37.

Damasio, A. R. 1994. *Descartes' Error; Emotion, Reason, and the Human Brain.* New York: Putnam.

Grenvick, A., Powner, D. J., Snyder, J. V., Jastremski, M. S., Babcock, R. A. & Loughhead, M. G. 1978. Cessation of therapy in terminal illness and brain death. *Critical Care Medicine,* 6, 284–291.

Hogle, L. 1995. Standardization across non-standard domains: the case of organ procurement. *Science, Technology & Human Values,* 20, 482–500.

Hogle, L. 1999. *Recovering the Nation's Body: Cultural Memory, Medicine and the Politics of Redemption.* New Brunswick, NJ: Rutgers University Press.

Joralemon, D. 1995. Organ wars: the battle for body parts. *Medical Anthropology Quarterly,* 9, 335–356.

Jouvet, M. 1959. Diagnostic électro-sous-corticographique de la mort du système Nerveux central au cours de certains comas. *Electroencephalography and Clinical Neurophysiology,* 11, 805.

Kennedy, I. 1973. The legal definition of death. *Medico-Legal Journal,* 41, 36–41.

Lock, M. 2002. *Twice Dead: Organ Transplants and the Reinvention of Death.* Berkeley: University of California Press.

McClure's Magazine. 1913. On the trail of immortality. *McClure's Magazine,* 40, 304–317.

Mohandas, A. & Chou, S. N. 1971. Brain death: a clinical and pathological study. *Journal of Neurosurgery,* 35, 211–218.

Mollaret, P. & Goulon, M. 1959. Coma depasse et necroses nerveuses contrales massives. *Revue Neurologique,* 101, 116–139.

Newsweek. 1967. When are you really dead? *Newsweek,* 18 December, 70, 87.

Pallis, C. 1987. Brain stem death—the evolution of a concept. *Medico Legal Journal,* 2, 84–104.

President's Commission for the Study of Ethical Problems in Medicine and Biomedical and Behavioral Research. 1981. *Defining Death: Medical, Legal and Ethical Issues in the Determination of Death.* Washington, DC: US Government Printing Office.

Randall, T. 2000. Too few human organs for transplantation, too many in need . . . and the gap widens. *Journal of the American Medical Association,* 265(13), 1223–1227.

Sharp, L. 1995. Organ transplantation as a transformative experience: anthropological insights into the restructuring of the self. *Medical Anthrolopology Quarterly,* 9, 357–389.

Shewmon, A. 1998. Chronic "brain death": meta-analysis and conceptual consequences. *Neurology,* 51, 1538–1545.

Shrader, D. 1986. On dying more than one death. *Hastings Center Report,* 16(1), 12–17.

Wolf, Z. R. 1991. Nurses' experiences giving post-mortem care to patients who have donated organs: a phenomenological study. *Scholarly Inquiry for Nursing Practice: An International Journal,* 5, 73–87.

Wolstenholme, G.E.W. & O'Conner, M. 1966. *Ethics in Medical Progress: With Special Reference to Transplantation.* Boston: Little, Brown.

Youngner, S. J. et al. 1985. Psychosocial and ethical implications of organ retrieval. *New England Journal of Medicine,* 313, 321–324.

Culture, Illness, and Mental Health

CONCEPTUAL TOOLS

■ ***Culture defines normality, and cultural rules determine who is crazy.*** How do you know if you're normal? How do you know if your emotional feelings are appropriate or if your thought processes are disturbed? These are difficult questions because we have to compare ourselves with others, and yet there are no cross-culturally universal standards for normal behavior or thinking. Historical and cultural contexts vary. Saintly behavior in one context may be considered deranged in another. Before the Civil War in the United States, there was a mental illness affecting African American slaves called drapetomania. The symptoms of this illness included repeated attempts to run away from the owner's plantation, and slaves with this "illness" had less value. In more recent history, homosexuality was officially diagnosed as a mental illness, and then, in a revision of the *Diagnostic and Statistical Manual* (*DSM*) of the American Psychiatric Association, it was decided that homosexuality was no longer an illness. The powerful novels of Aleksandr Solzhenitsyn, like *The Gulag Archipelago* (1973), show how psychiatry can become a powerful tool of social control by the state—when any political dissidence becomes de facto evidence of insanity. The problem of the definition of normality is exactly the same as the problem of cultural relativity: Although we need to be tolerant of a range of variation of the definitions of normal thought and behavior, absolute relativism, an "anything goes" approach—is not acceptable. Boundaries of health and illness are difficult to set. Recognition of this cultural relativity and the function of mental illness categories as agents of social control have played a role in labeling theory and the antipsychiatry movement (Szasz 1974).

■ ***Some mental conditions may be more pronounced or elaborated in particular cultural settings; these conditions have been labeled "culture-bound" or "culture-specific" syndromes*** (Simons and Hughes 1985). This concept in medical anthropology and cross-cultural psychiatry has caused significant debate. Culture-bound syndromes (CBSs) seem exotic and usually have vernacular ethnomedical labels depending on the locality where they were first described. For example, *latah* is an elaborated startle response that is founded in Malaysia (Simons 1985, 1996). People (usually older women) who have *latah* are often startled several times a day, because their response is so extreme and entertaining. Sometimes their attention can be captured and they mimic their tormentors; sometimes they say colorful obscenities. Another CBS is *koro,* an extreme anxiety reaction affecting males. A victim fears that his penis is shrinking up into his abdomen and that when it ascends all the way he will die. Epidemics of *koro* have been reported in China and Malaysia. Other CBSs include *pibloktoq* (arctic hysteria), *amok* (sudden mass assault), and the folk illness *susto* (soul loss or magical fright), which we will read about later (see selection 26). Some anthropologists have argued that the criteria for culture bound syndromes fit particular conditions in the United States, including premenstrual syndrome (PMS) (Johnson 1987) and obesity (Ritenbaugh 1978). Most medical anthropologists do not believe that mental disorders can actually be limited to a particular society with a particular culture; rather, society *constructs* illness labels, and social customs may function to put people at elevated risk for certain kinds of stressors that may result in mental illness (Hahn 1995).

■ ***Some cross-cultural psychiatrists believe that there are a very small number of universal mental illnesses, two of which correspond to biomedical labels of "schizophernia" and "depression."*** In contrast to labeling theorists who emphasize cultural relativity, some cross-cultural epidemiological studies of mental health have focused on commonalities of serious mental disorders. Schizophrenia-type illnesses—including cognitive impairment, auditory hallucinations, and inappropriate behaviors—appear to have some cross-cultural validity. There is also persuasive evidence that there is a genetic component to these illnesses. Depression-type illnesses are common throughout the world, although the local expression of the affective (emotional) disorder varies (Kleinman and Good 1985). Risk of depression-type illnesses also appears to have a genetic component. Evolutionary theorists have speculated as to why genes involved in the etiology of severe mental illnesses seem to persist in human populations (Allen and Sarich 1988). It is possible that mild expressions of these illnesses—for example, in creativity or social sensitivity—may be advantageous.

■ ***Different cultures have their own ethnopsychiatric systems for diagnosing and curing mental illness. All ethnopsychiatric systems are based on cultural assumptions and social role expectations.*** In ethnomedical studies, it is difficult to separate psychiatric practice from other kinds of medical interventions because other cultures may not rely on the same philosophical assumptions—for example, the separation of mind and body in Euro-American medicine. The cross-cultural study of ethnopsychiatric systems is very interesting (Gaines 1992), and more epidemiological studies of the effectiveness of traditional therapies is warranted. For example, H. Kristian Heggenhougen (1984) has shown the effectiveness of religious healers in treating heroin addiction in Southeast Asia. Medical anthropologists have also examined the cultural assumptions embedded in a psychiatric category system like the *DSM's* definitions of personality disorders. Charles Nuckolls has shown that U.S. pyschiatrists often arrive at diagnoses of personality disorders in the first few seconds of an interaction and that personality disorder categories hinge on definitions of appropriate gender attributes (Nuckolls 1996).

■ ***Social stress is a serious cause of illness.*** Generations of psychosomatic researchers have demonstrated that feelings of distress and hopelessness affect physical well-being. Although stress is difficult to define, its importance is obvious. Studies of stress show the interconnectedness of the physical, psychological, and social aspects of an individual. Recent studies by medical anthropologists have shown that the stresses of modernization and a growing discrepancy between rich and poor are serious world health problems (Des Jarlais, et al. 1995).

■ ***Mental health problems are not limited to the developed world.*** Problems such as unipolar depression are widespread throughout humanity, in rich and poor nations alike, and they result in a great deal of suffering and disability. In the field of global health, a new measure of the burden of disease focuses on disability-adjusted life years (DALYs) that are lost due to a specific health problem. On this measure, mental health problems rank very high. World mental health problems have been studied by some medical anthropologists (DesJarlais et al. 1995) and pose a major global challenge.

 25

Do Psychiatric Disorders Differ in Different Cultures?

Arthur Kleinman

This selection comes from a book, Rethinking Psychiatry *(Kleinman 1988), written for psychiatrists about cultural variation and mental health. The selection reviews a large and somewhat contradictory literature; as you will see when you critically review the literature, there is a lot that we do not know about the epidemiological distribution and symptomatological expression of mental illnesses across cultures.*

Here, Arthur Kleinman assumes that you understand what culture-bound syndromes are. The first part of the selection is about epidemiological studies of mental illness—the distribution across cultural groups and social categories—although it is difficult to evaluate this work because of the lack of international standardization of definitions. Despite these problems, it seems clear that rates of major mental illnesses vary from society to society. A famous study in this regard—Nancy Scheper-Hughes's Saints, Scholars and Schizophrenics *(1979)—demonstrates that traditional patterns of social organization and family interaction, in combination with worsening economic conditions, result in elevated rates of schizophrenia (and institutionalization) in Ireland.*

The second and third parts of the selection concern the symptomatology of mental illness and illness behavior *(how people react to their symptoms and seek help, or, in the case of depression, attempt suicide). This selection differs from many others in this book because it does not focus on a particular case; instead, it discusses a wide variety of cases. The answer to the question posed in the title is affirmative, but the ways in which psychiatric disorders vary remain complex.*

As you read this selection consider these questions:

- **If illnesses are socially constructed, how is it possible to compare mental illness rates and symptom complexes across cultures? How can one compare psychiatric diagnoses across cultures when standards of normal behavior differ from culture to culture? Is this a pointless endeavor?**
- **Although it is clear that family patterning or genetic predispositions are involved in schizophrenia and depression, the author says that the actual causes of these illnesses are not known. Why do you think this may be the case?**
- **What is *somatization* in the expression of psychological discomfort? Why might it be important for a healer to be aware of the process of somatization?**
- **Why is suicide considered an illness behavior in the context of depression? Why is the study of suicide interesting?**

Context: Arthur Kleinman is an eminent physician, medical anthropologist, and professor of psychiatry and anthropology at Harvard University. Focusing on the experience of illness in China, Taiwan, and the United States, he has written numerous books and articles on cross-cultural psychiatry, social stigma, disability, and chronic pain. By comparing and contrasting the human experience of mental illness in different cultures, this reading challenges us to consider the degree to which psychiatric (and medical) categories are really objective or universal. This reading, from a book for the lay-educated public, raises questions about how the ideas of culture should influence basic concepts in psychiatry.

Source: A. Kleinman (1988). "Do Psychiatric Disorders Differ in Different Cultures?" In *Rethinking Psychiatry: From Cultural Category to Personal Experience*, pp. 18–33. New York: Free Press.

EPIDEMIOLOGY

The prevalence data (total cases at a particular time) for schizophrenia—a serious mental disorder of unknown cause characterized by delusions, hallucinations, associations of unrelated ideas, social withdrawal, and lack of emotional responsiveness and motivation—indicate a band of prevalence rates ranging from roughly two to ten cases per thousand population across a range of populations (Sartorius and Jablensky 1976). Lower rates have been reported in less developed societies and the highest rates in North America and certain European societies (Fortes and Mayer 1969; Torrey 1980; Sikanerty and Eaton 1984). Although some incidence data (new cases in a defined period of time) are available for European societies, the data for non-Western societies are very limited and controversial. As we have seen in the World Health Organization studies, there is evidence for a wider range of incidence rates when the broader, heterogeneous sample of schizophrenic patients is used to calculate rates, and a narrower range when the more homogeneous sample is employed. Other studies report small-scale, preliterate societies with hardly any cases of schizophrenia and communities, often small, isolated Scandinavian ones,* with very high rates of schizophrenia (cf. Warner 1985 for the most comprehensive review).

It is hard to know what to make of these findings. They certainly represent a wider continuum than is suggested by the professional catechism that there is a relatively narrow band of prevalance of this psychiatric disorder cross-culturally. There are, furthermore, families that have much higher rates of this major mental illness than most others in the population. Twin studies, including those comparing twins of schizophrenic parents who are adopted out into nonschrzophrenic families, indicate that there is a significant genetic basis to this disorder.[1] But the genetic contribution is controversial; most models of the disorder invoke an interaction between social environment, genetic endowment, and neurobiological processes, making for a complex causal nexus. It is clearer to say in 1987 that the cause is unknown, as Carpenter, McGlashan, and Strauss (1977), leading psychiatric researchers who have devoted their careers to the study of schizophrenia, concluded a decade ago. Perhaps the chief epidemiological conclusion is simply the finding of patients with the core symptoms of schizophrenia in a very wide variety of societies. This mental illness is no myth.

* For example, Book et al. (1978) report a rate of 17 cases per 1000 for northern Sweden; and Torrey et al. (1984) report a rate of 12.6 per thousand for a high prevalence area in western Ireland.

Schizophrenia in developing societies is much more likely to present with an acute than an indolent onset; chronic mode of onset is more common in Western societies. DSM-III's diagnostic criteria strictly limit cases of schizophrenia to those that have had a course of at least six months. Acute onset cases that are of less than six months' duration are not diagnosed as schizophrenia by the standards of DSM-III. The WHO's ICD-9 does not have this requirement. Thus, different categories and different phenomena interact to create incommensurate findings. Acute onset psychosis of short duration is probably not the same disease as chronic onset long-duration psychosis (Stevens 1987). Whether acute onset and chronic onset psychoses of the same duration are indeed the same disorder is unclear. Schizophrenia is probably a group of syndromes. From the cross-cultural perspective, schizophrenia is organized as much by taxonomies as it is by disease processes.

Warner (1985) advances a substantial body of evidence to suggest that the occurrence and course of schizophrenia are strongly conditioned by the political economy. Unemployment and economic depression in the West and the development of capitalist modes of wage labor in non-Western societies appear to lead to greater numbers of individuals manifesting schizophrenia and fewer of them improving. . . . Warner also explains how analysts of the cross-cultural data base on the prevalence of schizophrenia could come to almost diametrically opposed views of the relative frequency of the disorder in non-Western and Western societies because of ideological commitments which lead psychiatrists to emphasize certain studies while discounting or even ignoring others.

The prevalence data for brief reactive psychosis—an acute psychosis closely associated with a serious stressful life event in a person without premorbid pathology and with recovery within days or weeks without any significant chronic symptoms or persistent disability—show that this disorder constitutes a much larger portion of acute psychoses in nonindustrialized, non-Western societies than in the industrialized West (Langness 1965; Manschreck 1978; Murphy 1982). Psychiatric researchers are concerned that such cases of brief reactive psychosis misdiagnosed as schizophrenia confound cross-cultural comparisons. But for the anthropologist, brief reactive psychoses are of particular interest because they are the one psychotic disorder that has enormously different prevalance rates cross-culturally. Moreover, they show great diversity in form—in an arc running from trance and possession states occurring outside culturally authorized settings to schizophreniform experiences—and such impressive cultural shaping that certain brief reactive psychoses are included in the culture-bound syndrome category. This group of psychiatric disorders is neither well-studied nor given a central place in psychiatry; yet for cultural analysis it is of very special significance. It is not surprising, then, that anthropological studies of individual brief reactive psychoses are more frequent than anthropological studies of schizophrenia. Studies disclose that of all forms of madness brief reactive psychoses bear the strongest causal relationship to immediate life event stressors, especially stressors that are of particular cultural salience, that they are the most culturally diverse of all psychoses, that they overlap with final common pathways of normal behavior (e.g., culturally approved trance states), and that they respond well to indigenous healing systems (Langness 1965; Kleinman 1980; Lewis 1971).

The epidemiology of nonpsychotic disorders around the globe is even more variable. Depression is the best case in point. The findings reveal a much greater range of variation than for schizophrenia. There simply are no studies in the non-Western world, however, comparable in rigor and standardization to the Epidemiological Catchment Area (ECA) studies sponsored by the NIMH in the United States. That set of studies, a particularly expensive undertaking involving investigators trained to use the same interview schedule (DIS), surveyed communities in five sites. Six-month prevalance rates (i.e., total number of cases detected in a period of six months) for affective disorders (chiefly depression) ranged from 4.6 to 6.5 percent. Lifetime prevalence rates (i.e., total number of individuals in the study population who experienced an episode of depressive disease sometime during their life) ranged from 6.1 to 9.5 percent. Major depression, as in earlier research, was found to be more common in women and in urban areas (Blazer et al. 1985; Myers et al. 1984; Robins et al. 1984).

Reviewing the English language literature for industrialized Western societies, Boyd and Weissman (1981) estimated the point prevalence (number of cases at a particular point in time) of clinical depression (not including manic-depressive disorder, a psychosis) in studies using newer, more reliable diagnostic techniques as 3.2 percent in males and 4.0 to 9.3 percent in females. The range of prevalence in reports from non-industrialized, non-Western societies is much greater.

Despite reports during the colonial period that depression was uncommon in India, Venkoba Rao (1984) states that recent studies indicate depression is a common disorder, though, because the variation of rates across different cultural areas in India is wide, he is uncertain just how common. Rao cites Indian rates of 1.5 to 32.9 per thousand in the general population. Among the highest rates currently reported are those for Africa: 14.3 percent for men and 22.6 percent for women in Uganda (Orley and Wing 1979). Ironically, an earlier generation of colonial psychiatrists, many of whom were paternalistic and racialist, claimed that depression was rare in Africa, India, and other non-Western culture areas owing to putative weaknesses in the cognitive and affective states of indigenous populations.[2]

Increased rates of depression in Africa and other non-Western cultures appear to be the result of the use of more culturally appropriate diagnostic criteria and standardized research methods in studies that sample the general population and therefore do not rely, as did an early generation of studies, on clinic-based figures that are biased by different patterns of help seeking. But Prince (1968) and H. B. M. Murphy (1982, p. 143) suggest, in addition to correction of methodological shortcomings, there has probably been a general increase in rates of depression in many non-Western societies due to the pressures and problems of modernization. Clearly, the findings of high rates of depression in Uganda must, at least in part, reflect the political chaos and murderous oppression that the members of that society have so tragically experienced.

Lin and Kleinman (1981) reviewed the epidemiological studies of mental illness in China since the early 1950s, which include some of the largest population surveys ever attempted, involving tens of thousands of respondents. They found that prior to 1981, with the exception of manic-depressive psychosis and involutional melancholia, a psychosis among the elderly, clinical depression was simply not reported. In the past few years the Chinese have begun to publish clinic-based studies that record higher rates of depression (an increase from 1 percent to 20 percent of outpatient samples), though rates still lower than in the West (see studies cited in Kleinman 1986). This increase is almost certainly the result of using newer Western-influenced diagnostic criteria and psychometric assessment tools. The WHO's comparative international study of *Depressive Disorders in Different Cultures* (Sartorius et al. 1983), a multicultural project involving centers in Japan, Iran, and other non-Western societies, does not cite prevalence rates among its findings. Tsung-yi Lin and his colleagues in Taiwan (1969) reported a great increase in the rates of neuroses including depression from the time of a first survey of three communities in the late 1940s to a second survey, conducted by the same research team with the same criteria and methods, 15 years later, during the period of Taiwan's rapid modernization. Clinicians in many non-Western societies have claimed similar increases, but pre -and postepidemiological surveys, like Lin's, are few in number. There is a strong possibility that, at least in some societies, the norms and idioms for expressing distress have changed so substantially that the expression, not necessarily the occurrence, of depression is more common. We do know, however, that the rates of depression and other neurotic conditions are elevated in refugee, immigrant, and migrant populations owing to uprooting, loss, and the serious stress of the acculturation process (Beiser 1985, Beiser and Fleming 1986). Selective uprooting of those most vulnerable to mental illness does not play a significant role in forced migrations of the most recent Southeast Asian and South American refugees in North America, so that the data on refugees probably are an accurate reflection of psychiatric casualties of uprooting and acculturation.[3] Furthermore, at least in North America, leading psychiatric epidemiologists claim to have incidence data that the rate of depression among young adults is on the rise (*Psychiatric News* 15 May, 1988).

Some advance has also been made in understanding risk factors for depression. In a classic study, Brown and Harris (1978) convincingly demonstrated that among working-class women in England, relative powerlessness, absence of affective support, and the social pressures of child rearing and no job outside the home significantly increased their vulnerability to serious life event stressors, like loss; those with marginal self-esteem were pushed over the edge into generalized hopelessness and clinical depression. Kleinman (1986) has found the same pattern of vulnerability and provoking agents among Chinese depressives, though the particular sources of their vulnerability differ. Good, Good and Moradi (1985) reported comparable findings among Iranian immigrants in the United States. Beiser (1987) has identified a mediating process in depressed and anxious Southeast Asian refugees to Canada: excessive nostalgia and preoccupation with self-perceptions of time past as ideally positive and future time as threatening and undesirable identify those at highest risk for developing distress at a later date. The causes of differential susceptibility remain a very important subject for cross-cultural comparisons.

For the other neurotic disorders, there is terribly little valid cross-cultural epidemiological data. In earlier epidemiological studies, either anxiety was mixed in with other neuroses or the criteria for distinguishing it from other disorders were not enumerated. In an earlier review of what cross-cultural literature does exist, my colleague Byron Good and I (1985) estimated that, with the exception of studies of Australian aborigines, anxiety disorders are diagnosed at a rate of 12 to 27 cases per thousand population. In the ECA studies, six-month prevalence rates of anxiety and somatoform (somatization disorder, hypochondriasis, psychogenic pain) disorders varied from 6.6 to 14.9 percent and lifetime rates from 10.4 to 25.1 percent (with differences largely due to different rates for phobias), making this combined category the commonest psychiatric condition in the United States. Iranian studies described prevalence rates of 27 and 8 per thousand in one project for anxiety disorders among villagers and city dwellers, respectively, and 48 and 38 per thousand for a mixed category of anxiety and somatoform disorders in another. Indian studies cite rates of 17.8, 20.5, and 12 per thousand population for the same category.

The studies of Australian aborigines are a marked contrast. Population surveys of 2,360 individuals turned up only one case of "overt anxiety" (Jones and Home 1973). The Cornell-Aro Mental Health Project in Nigeria conducted by the psychiatrist-anthropologist Alexander Leighton and his colleagues (1963b) reported high levels of anxiety symptoms (this study did not make disease designations) in village and town residents, 36 and 27 percent, and found high levels of respondents who were significantly impaired, 19 and 16 percent. By contrast, the Sterling County study in Nova Scotia by the same team of investigators (Leighton et al., 1963a) found far fewer anxiety symptoms (13 and 10 percent) but twice the rate of impairment (38 and 32 percent). As with their findings for depression, Orley and Wing's (1979) comparison of Ugandan village women and London women found higher rates of anxiety disorders in the former. (Given the high rates of infectious diseases, many undiagnosed, among rural dwellers in the non-Western world, it is extremely difficult to know what to make of attempts to diagnose their anxiety and somatoform disorders.) Many researchers of the common culture-bound syndromes—especially fright and soul loss disorders, neurasthenia, and *taijinkyofusho*, a Japanese phobic reaction associated with fear of others—hypothesize that these conditions may represent culturally authorized final common behavioral pathways for anxiety disorders (Carr and Vitaliano 1985; Simons and Hughes, eds., 1985). Consequently, the cross-cultural epidemiological literature on depression and anxiety disorders indicates that these are common around the globe, particularly in patients in general medical clinics, though precise determination of comparative rates is not feasible at present and reasons for the wider cross-cultural disparities are uncertain.

Studies also generally show that these disorders are found at higher rates among women (though several studies show the reverse) and members of lower socioeconomic classes in a number of societies. The most recent studies of depression and gender have supported Brown's model of the effect of powerlessness and low self-esteem on the etiology of depression in women (Finkler 1985; Kleinman 1986; Good and

Kleinman 1985; Lock 1986, 1987; Gaines and Farmer 1986). The definitive epidemiological data is not in, but women and certainly poor women appear to be at higher risk for mental illness in a number of societies.[4] For the major mental disorders, the social context . . . appears to be the chief source of cross-cultural diversity. But this is in part because genetic, temperament, and other biographical variables, which might explain why only some individuals exposed to the same pressures become ill, have not been systematically studied outside the Western world.

That research on American Indians and Hispanic Americans shows both very high and quite low rates in different studies warns us again of the importance of intracultural diversity. The association of depression with high rates of alcoholism in some (but not all) American Indian and Alaskan Native populations emphasizes as well the potentially important relationship between alcohol abuse and mental illness. . . . Alcoholism rates are rising in a number of areas around the world, though, as Heath (1986) sagely cautions, the evidence for a worldwide epidemic, which some mental health professionals claim is happening, is simply not there. Nonetheless, alcohol rates in East Asian societies (Japan, Hong Kong, Taiwan, even China), which were traditionally very low by Western standards, are now increasing, and this will complicate the cross-cultural epidemiology of mental disorders very considerably, because it will be necessary to determine if changes in rates of psychopathology are due to alcoholism (Lin and Lin 1984).

Our original question was, do psychiatric disorders differ cross culturally? The epidemiological rates indicate significant differences. This is even true without taking into account culture-bound syndromes and trance and possession psychoses which occur outside of culturally authorized ritual settings. Those disorders by definition are found only or principally in non-Western societies. The epidemiological data, however, do not sustain the radical cultural relativist argument that mental disorders are incomparable in greatly different societies. The chief mental disorders are diagnosable worldwide; research is quite clear on this point. Thus, we are once again left with evidence of both cross-cultural universals and particularities, cross-cultural support for the dialectical view that "life requires both the determination of the environment and the physical body" (Kitaro 1970, p. 100).

SYMPTOMATOLOGY

A salient international finding, often replicated as I have noted, is the marked predominance of somatic symptoms among depressed and anxious patients in non-Western societies, albeit these symptoms are also common in the West (Kleinman and Good, eds., 1985; Good and Kleinman 1985; Kirmayer 1984; H. B. M. Murphy 1982; Weiss and Kleinman in press).[5] Particular symptoms and symptom patterns differ across patients in different cultures. Because the literature relevant to symptomatology comes from studies of depression and anxiety disorders, I will focus principally on these conditions.

I have shown (1986) that headaches, dizziness, and lack of energy form a symptom cluster in ancient Chinese society and in contemporary Taiwan and China which is the core of neurasthenic illness behavior associated with mixed depressive and anxiety disorders. These symptoms have been culturally salient for centuries in Chinese society and still today carry considerable cultural meaning. Indeed, Chinese patients appear to selectively perceive, label, and communicate these symptoms out of the diffuse complaints of psychophysiological arousal and the multiform somatic effects of stress. The association of a culturally salient somatic language of complaints with depression and/or anxiety disorders has also been recorded for clinical samples in Saudi Arabia (Racy 1980), Iraq (Bazzoui 1970), Benin (Binitie 1975), Peru (Mezzich and Rabb 1980), India (Teja et al. 1971; Sethi et al. 1973), and Hong Kong (Cheung et al. 1981), and among depressed patients in many non-Western cultures (Marsella 1979).

Data from the WHO's cross-cultural study of depression in clinical research centers in Montreal, Teheran, Basel, Nagasaki, and Tokyo disclose both similarities and differences in symptomatology (Sartorius et al. 1983). Sadness, joylessness, anxiety, tension, lack of energy, decreased interest and concentration, and feelings of inadequacy and worthlessness were found in three-fourths to all of the depressed patients at each center. One-third had hypochondriacal ideas, and 40 percent had some somatic complaints, obsessions, and phobias. More personality disorders were detected in Western centers, where concepts of such disorders may fit the Western diagnostic categories better, than in non-Western ones. Psychomotor agitation was more frequent in Teheran and symptoms of self-reproach higher in Europe. Marsella et al. (1985) reflect on their participation in this project and conclude the WHO comparison was not organized to pick up more center-specific symptoms, and it didn't.

Field (1958), working among the Ashanti in West Africa, in local healing shrines, found that anxiety was commonly expressed as self-accusation or fears of witchcraft. Studies in Nigerian society report that generalized anxiety disorders among Yoruba are associated with three clusters of primary symptoms—worries, dreams of witchcraft, and bodily complaints (Collis 1966; Anumonge 1970; Jegede 1978). Each of these takes a form appropriate in Yoruba culture. Predominant worries expressed by patients were those associated with procreation and maintenance of a large family. Lambo (1962), himself a Yoruba psychiatrist, long ago noted the close correlation between "morbid fear of bewitchment" and "acute anxiety states in Africa."

The combination of universal and culture-specific symptoms of depressive and anxiety disorders had been reported for Iranians (Good et al. 1985), Chinese (Kleinman and Kleinman 1985), and American Indians (Manson et al. 1985). Research on American Indians has shown that certain signs that might be taken as evidence of severe depression in other groups are normative for members of this ethnic group, including "prolonged" mourning, "flat affect," auditory hallucinations of spirit beings, and visual hallucinations of the recently dead (O'Nell in press).

The research literature also points out that feelings of guilt are much less commonly associated with depression in the non-Western world than in the West. H. B. M. Murphy (1982) attributed guilt to the influence of the Judeo-Christian heritage, including its effects on Islam. Melancholia, the traditional term for depressive disorder in the West, acquired this moral meaning from *acedia*, a religious expression of depression (Jackson 1985). But the literature purporting to demonstrate low frequency and severity of guilt in the Third World is flawed by the absence of consistent definitions, operationalized criteria, and methods of assessment. This is because many writers *assume* that guilt is a sign of higher levels of personality functioning—stronger egos, more intense superego development, higher differentiation—on the basis of outmoded and unsubstantiated psychoanalytic and evolutionary schemes. Weiss and Kleinman (in press) note that in spite of substantial findings of guilt in India (Venkoba Rao 1973; Teja et al. 1971; Ansari 1969), discussions in the Indian literature minimize its significance or interpret it as milder or of a different kind. For example, Venkoba Rao (1973) distinguished karmic guilt (concerned with deeds in a previous life) from present guilt. He felt that karmic guilt might actually protect against the other type.

Sartorius et al. (1983) did not find major differences in guilt between depressive patients in the West and Japan. Escobar and his co-workers (1983), in keeping with H. B. M. Murphy's (1982) hypothesis, found Christian patients in Colombia to have the same degree of guilt in the course of depression as found in depressed patients in North America. I (1986) discerned less guilt among depressives in China than is reported from the West, and noted that low self-esteem was also less common. I reviewed the work of Cheung and her colleagues (1981) in Hong Kong suggesting no major difference in guilt there and in the West, and wondered if her subjects are Christians or otherwise acculturated to Western values in that highly Westernized community. Since there are few studies that systematically look for other idioms of expressing guilt in the non-Western world, the finding of low preoccupation with guilt could be an artifact of reporting and of the research methodology.

For example, Field (1958) noted that the expression of guilt among her Ashanti informants occurred only in an idiom of witchcraft. Levy (1973), studying Tahitians, demonstrated in a subtle ethnographic and psychological study that shame and guilt were not discrete feelings, but intermixed. Lutz (1985), Rosaldo (1980), and other psychological anthropologists have studied individuals in small-scale preliterate societies whose concepts of self and emotions are radically different than in the West. These anthropologists repeatedly show that different meanings of guilt, sadness, and other emotions significantly influence the experience of those emotions (Lutz and White 1986). Guilt understood and experienced as existential suffering, or as loss of face, or as self-accusation of witchcraft is not the same emotional phenomenon. Thus, anthropologists hold that simple dichotomies between high and low levels of guilt or its presence and absence in very different societies distort a much more complex picture cross-culturally.

Suicide has also been said to be less common among depressed patients in the Third World (Headley, ed., 1983); it probably is, with some notable exceptions like Japan, less common in non-Western societies generally (La Fontaine 1975). But since most cases in developing societies probably go unrecorded, and since there is great variation across rural/urban, time, and ethnic boundaries, the cross-cultural epidemiology of suicide is anything but clear. Indeed, the low prevalence of suicide has been explained as the result of the alleged low level of guilt—a decidedly weak foundation.

I (1982) found less suicide among Chinese depressives in Hunan, but explained this finding by suggesting that somatization protects against this and other negative sequelae of a more intrapsychic, existential experience of depression. This explanation needs to be weighed against a history of salience of suicide in Chinese culture (Hsieh and Spence 1982). Mezzich and Raab (1980) report lower tendency toward suicide among depressed Peruvians than among matched North American depressives. They attribute this difference to strong teaching by the Catholic Church against suicide. Venkoba Rao points out several cultural factors in India that may protect against suicide. These include the emphasis on family obligations over individual rights, the legitimation of suicide, at least historically, under ritual conditions (*sati*), and the concept of *karma* (which would lead individuals to avoid suicide lest they be reborn in a less desirable state).

Attempted suicide in a number of Asian and Middle Eastern societies, as in North America, is higher among women than among men. But, unlike North America, completed suicides also appear to me more common among women in these societies (Headley, ed., 1983). Reasons for suicide and means of carrying it out vary greatly, but there is significant evidence that relative powerlessness, absence of alternative means of communicating despair, traditional use of suicide as a sanctioned idiom of distress, and its place in cultural mythology make particular categories of women (generally the young but in certain cultures the elderly too) more likely, perhaps driven, to take this last alternative.

There is also evidence that social change contributes to fluctuating suicide rates. For example, suicide rates in various of the Pacific Island cultures are increasing rapidly as those societies experience the problems of modernization. Also a recent report from Sri Lanka reports that the suicide rate tripled between 1955 and 1974, when it was highest among the Tamil ethnic minority in the northeast (Kearney and Miller 1985). The authors explain the increase as the result of rapid population growth, increased competition for education and employment, and the breakdown of a stable society, placing great pressure especially on Tamils. It is unclear from their report whether these rates are associated with increased depression, or what has happened during the current era of civil war. Poverty, economic failure, and exam failure are other important social factors contributing to suicide around the globe. Much of the anthropological work on suicide has indicated that it may (and often does) occur in individuals without mental illness who are under great social pressure or for whom it is one of a very few culturally authorized expressions of severe distress (La Fontaine 1975).

The review of the findings of the WHO's cross-cultural comparison of schizophrenia, as noted earlier, also discloses important differences in the mode of onset and symptoms of schizophrenia. Barrett (in press), furthermore, offers evidence that the sense of a split or divided self that is so strongly associated with both professional and lay discourses on schizophrenia in the West may emerge as salient because of the Western conception of the person as a bounded individual self. Patients in the West report feeling a split in personality. This aspect of schizophrenia appears to be less central to the experience of the disorder in China and other non-Western societies. In those societies, the expression of a feeling of split personality is as uncommon as is the mythology of a self divided against itself.[6]

Thus, we can conclude that the symptomatology of mental disorders differs very substantially cross-culturally. For schizophrenia, major depressive disorder, and anxiety disorders there are also significant uniformities. If we lump together with these mental illnesses culture-bound disorders and trance-possession and other dissociative psychoses (occurring outside ritually prescribed settings), then the variation in the symptoms of mental illness is much greater. Thus, the research literature on symptomatology points to the same pattern of cross-cultural findings as do the other aspects of mental illness we have reviewed: there are certain significant similarities and many very significant differences.[7]

ILLNESS BEHAVIOR

Few researchers have actually compared the illness behavior—i.e., meaningful experience of symptoms and patterns of coping and help seeking—of appropriately matched samples of depressed or anxious patients in different societies. Research does disclose, however, greatly different patterns of help seeking for mental illness in different societies and ethnic groups (Lin et al. 1978; Lin, Kleinman and Lin 1982). These studies find, for example, that North American Indian, Asian, and Caucasian ethnic patients follow distinctive pathways to the mental health center, arrive there at very different points in the course of illness, and experience greatly divergent types of involvement of their family members. Response to psychiatric treatment also differs. Lin et al. (1986) review the literature demonstrating distinctive pharmacokinetic and pharmacodynamic responses to tricyclic antidepressants among East Asian and Caucasian groups, disclosing different physiological responses to treatment in these ethnic groups. That is to say, biology-culture interactions are important in treatment, and are probably also significant in perception of symptoms (cf. Hoosain 1986).

Perhaps the best way to get at cultural influences on illness perception and experience in mental illnesses like depressive and anxiety disorders is to analyze those culture-bound syndromes that bear a family resemblance to these disorders, because certain of these syndromes have been described in considerable detail. Manson et al. (1985) disclose that among Hopi one culture-specific syndrome overlaps extensively with depressive symptomatology, whereas several others that appear to overlap actually are distinctive. Johnson and Johnson (1965) discovered among the Dakota Sioux a syndrome called *towatl ye sni* (or "totally discouraged"). This syndrome cut across various Western categories of psychopathology, but struck the authors as especially close to depression. Yet the beliefs and behaviors labeled *towatl ye sni* were also strongly culturally shaped and included feelings of deprivation, the experience of one's thoughts traveling to the dwelling place of dead relatives, an orientation to the past as the best time, willing death to become nearer to the dead, and preoccupations with ghosts and spirits.

Prince and Tcheng-Laroche (1987) show that *taijinkyofusho* among Japanese can be glossed as a phobia of interpersonal relations but is different from DSM-III social phobia inasmuch as patients feel guilty about embarrassing others with their behavior (e.g., blushing, unpleasant body odor, stuttering) rather than fearful of others' criticisms. In *taijinkyofusho* the emphasis is on the fear of discomfiting others through their sense of shame, a fear thoroughly in concert with Japanese cultural sensibilities but quite foreign to North American fears. This experience suggests that psychiatric classifications of phobias are unsufficient as presently cast to model a major illness experience in Japanese society. While similarities have been found between agoraphobia and one type of neurasthenia in Japan, *shinkeishitsu* associated with obsessions and phobias, there are also divergences. Agoraphobia in North America is found predominantly in women, *shinkeishitsu* in men. Western sufferers are afraid of being alone in public; Japanese patients avoid contact with others (least with intimates or strangers, most with acquaintances). The illness behavior of the Japanese is best described as "anthropophobic."

Littlewood and Lipsedge (1987) argue that anorexia nervosa might be regarded as a culture-specific illness behavior in the West, at times associated with personality disorder, at other times part of a constellation of psychiatric depression with somatic delusions. These British psychiatrists point out anorexia nervosa is not highly prevalent outside the West, with the exception of the educated class of industrialized societies like Japan who have been strongly influenced by Western aesthetic standards which value extreme slimness and which view strict dieting as an emblem of moral discipline. The historian Caroline Walker Bynum (in press), who traces the lineaments of anorexia to various Christian saints, concludes:

> The cultures within which female non-eating occurs and achieves significance as a form of sanctity or empowerment are all cultures which, on the one hand, associate the female with body and sexuality and, on the other, expect females to suffer and to serve (especially to offer food to) others.

Anorectic women in medieval Italy and modern Portugal participate, she avers, not in behavior whose cause is physiological, but in cultures which share similar perceptions of women's roles and symbolism of being female. Historical analysis does not lend support, furthermore, to psychodynamic interpretations of the nature of mother–daughter conflict or patriarchal control as the basis for anorectic behavior. The "starving disease" epidemic of our time, she shows, is also more than the fight among a male-dominated culture and a resisting female subculture for control of the bodies of adolescent girls that feminist psychologists have made it out to be. The symbolic meaning in modern Portuguese peasant society and medieval Italy of noneating as purity through suffering that brings women, who are otherwise symbolically polluting, closer to God, Bynum regards as the most availing explanation for anorexia in those societies. The noneating living, like the consecrated incorrupt dead, "symbolize restraint or purity that harnesses and channels, but does not destroy, fertility" (see also Bell 1985; Pina-Cabral 1986). Brian Turner (1985, pp. 180–201), a sociologist who has canvassed the social historical significance of bodily practices in the West, links the cultural analysis of anorexia with the political and economic forces in contemporary capitalism's consumer society to show that this is a disorder whose sign—slimness—is promoted by food and drug and other industries for which this bodily product of hedonism and narcissism holds powerful commercial significance.

What can be generalized from these and many, many other accounts is that illness behavior is always strongly shaped by culture even when the associated disease processes can be diagnosed with an international nosology. Whatever the causes of anorexia, which are likely to be multiple and interactive, the experience of anorexia and other chronic disorders is inseparable from their cultural context.

COURSE AND OUTCOME

A final aspect of illness behavior, but one deserving special attention, is course and outcome of disorder. Here the literature is particularly murky. The example of better outcome for schizophrenia in less developed societies is a beam of clear light. One of the more interesting (and better-supported) hypotheses to explain this finding is Waxler's (1977) theory that where schizophrenia is popularly viewed as an acute problem and patients suffering from it are accordingly expected to recover just like those who suffer from other acute disorders, there the cultural message is reinforced by familial and community responses to the patient that encourage normalization and discourage acceptance of a disabled role. In this view, chronicity is in large measure the result of social messages and interpersonal reactions to the patient that impede the patient's sense of self-control and undermine his optimism and its psychophysiological effects. Other factors such as the economics of disability, the investment of certain mental health programs in maintaining patients in long-term patient roles, and the very high demands that industrialized societies make on former patients in the absence of effective supports have also been implicated as obstacles to better outcome from schizophrenia (Lin and Kleinman in press; Warner 1985; Estroff 1981; Waxier 1977). The medical profession may inadvertently abet these forces, since in North American and Western European society its members have been trained to treat schizophrenic patients with the expectation that there is little that can be done to help them recover from a disorder that until recently was regarded as progressively disabling. In fact, more recent long-term research shows that even in the West, the course of many schizophrenic patients is much more hopeful than the professional stereotype (see Bleuler 1978; Harding et al. 1987; Alanen et al. 1986).

If we take suicide as an outcome, then somatized illness experience in major depressive disorder in the Third World would have a better outcome than psychologized depression in the West, inasmuch as there is less suicide among the former group. But given what has already been said about the relationship of guilt and low self-esteem to depression, and taking into account the tendency toward lower suicide rates generally in much of the nonindustrialized world, it is difficult to be certain if somatization per se protects against suicide. However, because of the findings for schizophrenia in developing societies, it is important that research be undertaken to compare the course of depressive and anxiety disorders in Western and non-Western societies. A leading hypothesis should be that somatized depression may have an easier course and better outcome than psychologized depression, owing to less morbid preoccupation with, and negative expectation in, the personal experience of the illness.

Overall, then, chronicity and disability may be at least partially separable from physiological disease processes and their causes. Just as there is no one-to-one correlation of symptom to pathology, there are a variety of courses for the same disorder. The meanings of the illness experience and the social context of the sick person together with his biography also shape these outcomes (Osterweis et al., eds., 1987). It is unlikely that all or even most non-Western settings encourage processes of adaptation and rehabilitation, but clearly contemporary industrialized societies place certain categories of the sick under constraints that foster chronicity and disability. This is a topic that is likely to receive much greater attention in future cross-cultural research.

NOTES

1. The genetic theory of schizophrenia, which up until several years ago seemed well established, is now in considerable disarray. Inheritance has not been proved (see Barnes 1987a). There is evidence of abnormalities in dopamine receptors in key regions of the brain. The response of patients to antipsychotic drugs also points to dopamine neurotransmission as disordered. But other biological findings are controversial (e.g., alleged altered brain blood flow and larger ventricles). There is still, after more than 30 years of intensive biological investigation, no clear-cut understanding of the biology of schizophrenia (Haracz 1982; Lewontin, Kamin and Rose 1984; Barrett in press). This does not deter psychiatrists and those who write the advertisements for drug companies from asserting without any hesitation that schizophrenia is a biologically based disorder. This belief is a central tenet of professional orthodoxy.

   The most convincing research on the genetics of a mental illness comes from Egeland et al. (1987), who studied bipolar (manic-depressive) disorder, which has a 0.5 to 1 percent prevalence rate in the West, among Old Order Amish in the U.S. They established that a gene on chromosome 11 is associated with dominant inheritance. But there is only partial "penetration," meaning that environmental factors are still essential in the expression of the genetic vulnerability. Other research suggests different genetic factors in other populations in which bipolar disease has been studied.
2. The topic of colonial impediments to accurate psychiatric findings from India and Africa in the nineteenth and early twentieth centuries is reviewed in Weiss and Kleinman (in press).
3. The most recent Cuban migration to the U.S. did include patients with mental illness who were forced to depart for Florida. But this is not true of Vietnamese, Cambodian, Laotian, or South American refugee groups.
4. Showalter (1985) reviews evidence that the finding of greater rates of neurotic disorder among women seems to have been true as well of women in England during much of the nineteenth and twentieth centuries. Although her historical analysis indicates it affected women in all social classes, there is no epidemiological data to settle the issue.
5. This section of the chapter includes materials modified from a report of an NIHM contract for a Review of Cross-Cultural Studies of Depressive and Anxiety Disorders prepared by the author and his colleagues, Byron Good and Peter Guarnaccia, in May 1986.

6. One of the more impressive demonstrations of cultural differences in symptomatology of mental illness is the reports of Jilek-Aall et al. (1978) of the symptom patterns of Russian Doukhobor, Coast Salish Indian, and Mennonite patients, whom they treated in the Fraser Valley of British Columbia, Canada. These cross-cultural psychiatrists found "that while sexes could to some extent be differentiated on the basis of clinical symptoms, cultural factors came out as the more important differentiating criteria of symptom formation." For example, for the Doukhobor psychiatric patients, violent acts against property and relatively very paranoid delusions concerning legal authority and God or Devil were common. Prolonged mourning reactions, suicide attempts, identity confusion, marital maladjustment, and hallucinations of supernatural beings differentiated Canadian Indian patients from the other two ethnic groups; whereas gastrointestinal symptoms, hypochrondriasis, apathy, feelings of inadequacy and self-depreciation, guilt and fear of rejection or punishment by God, shame, sexual dysfunction, and general and phobic anxiety set Mennonite patients apart.
7. In a long-term study of manic-depressive disorder among Old Order Amish in Pennsylvania, Egeland (1986) describes how the biological bases of the disorder, group norms, and social conditions combine to form a pattern of expressing complaints that discloses just such uniformities and differences.

REFERENCES

Alanen, Y. O., et al. 1986. Toward Need-Specific Treatment of Schizophrenic Psychoses. New York: Springer Verlag.

Ansari, S. A. 1969. Symptomatology of Indian depressives. Transactions of the All India Institute of Mental Health 9:1–18.

Anumonge, A. 1979. Outpatient psychiatry in a Nigerian University general hospital. Social Psychiatry 5:96–99.

Barrett, R. in press. Schizophrenia and personhood. Medical Anthropology Quarterly.

Barzun, J. 1983. A Stroll with William James. Chicago: University of Chicago Press.

Bazzoui, W. 1970. Affective disorders in Iraq. British Journal of Psychiatry 117:195–203.

Beiser, M. 1958. A study of depression among traditional Africans, urban North Americans, and Southeast Asian Refugees. In Culture and Depression. A. Kleinman and B. Good, eds. Berkeley: University of California Press.

Beiser, M, and J. Fleming. 1986. Measuring psychiatric disorder among Southeast Asian refugees. Psychological Medicine 16:627–639.

Bell, R. 1985. Holy Anorexia. Chicago: University of Chicago Press.

Binitie, A. 1975. A factor-analytical study of depression across African and European cultures. British Journal of Psychiatry 127:559–563.

Blazer, D., et al. 1985. Psychiatric disorders: a rural/urban comparison. Archives of General Psychiatry 41:971–978.

Bleuler, M. 1978. The Schizophrenic Disorders: Long-Term Patient and Family Studies. New Haven, CT: Yale University Press.

Book, J. A., et al. 1978. Schizophrenia in a North Swedish geographical isolate 1900–1977. Clinical Genetics 14:373–394.

Boyd, J., and M. Weissman. 1981. Epidemiology of affective disorders. Archives of General Psychiatry 38:1039–1046.

Brown, G., and T. Harris. 1978. The Social Origins of Depression. New York: Free Press.

Bynum, C. W. in press. Holy anorexia in modern Portugal. Culture, Medicine, and Psychiatry.

Carpenter, W., T. McGlashen, and J. Strauss. 1977. The treatment of acute schizophrenia without drugs. American Journal of Psychiatry 134:14–20.

Carr, J., and P. Vitaliano. 1976. The Great Universe of Kota: Change and Mental Disorder in an Indian Village. Berkeley: University of California Press.

Cheung, F., et al. 1981. Somatization among Chinese depressives in general practices. International Journal of Psychiatry in Medicine 10:361–374.

Collis, R. J. M. 1966. Physical health and psychiatric disorders in Nigeria. Transactions of the American Philosophical Society New Series 56(4):1–45.

Escobar, J., et al. 1983. Depressive symptomatology in North and South American patients. American Journal of Psychiatry 140:47–51.

Estroff, S. 1981. Making It Crazy. Berkeley: University of California Press.

Field, M. D. 1958. Search for Security: An Ethno-Psychiatric Study in Rural Ghana. London: Faber & Faber.

Finkler, K. 1985. Symptomatic differences between the sexes in rural Mexico. Culture, Medicine, and Psychiatry 9:27–58.

Fortes, M., and D. Y. Mayer. 1969. Psychosis and social change among the Tallensi of Northern Ghana. In Psychiatry in a Changing Society. S. H. Foukes and G. S. Prince, eds. London: Tavistock.

Gaines, A., and P. Farmer. 1986. Visible saints: Social cynosures and dysphoria in the Mediterranean tradition. Culture, Medicine, and Psychiatry 10:295–330.

Good, B., et al. 1982. Toward a meaning-centered analysis of popular illness categories. In Cultural Conceptions of Mental Health and Therapy. A. Marsella and G. White, eds. Dordrecht, Holland: D. Reidel.

Good, B., and A. Kleinman. 1985. Culture and anxiety. In Anxiety and the Anxiety Disorders. J. P. Maser and A. H. Turns, eds. Hillsdale, NJ: Lawrence Erlbaum.

Good, M., J. D. Good, and R. Moradi. 1985. The interpretation of Iranian depressive illness. In Culture and Depression. B. Good and A. Kleinman, eds., Berkeley: University of California Press.

Gould, Stephen J. 1987. Animals and us. New York Review of Books 34(11):20–25.

Harding, C. M., et al. 1987. The Vermont longitudinal study of patients with severe mental illness. Parts 1 and 2. American Journal of Psychiatry 144:718–726, 727–735.

Headley, L. A., ed. 1983. Suicide in Asia and the Near East. Berkeley: University of California Press.

Heath, D. 1986. Drinking and drunkenness in transcultural perspective. Parts 1 and 2. Transcultural Psychiatry Research Review 23.

Hossain, R. 1986. Perception. In The Psychology of the Chinese People. M. Bond, ed. Hong Kong: Oxford University Press.

Hsieh, A., and J. Spence. 1982. Suicide and the family in premodern China. In Normal and Abnormal Behavior in Chinese Culture. T. Y. Lin and A. Kleinman, eds. Dordrecht, Holland: D. Reidel.

Jackson, S. 1985. Acedia: The sin and its relationship to sorrow and melancholia. In Culture and Depression. A. Kleinman and B. Good, eds. Berkeley: University of California Press.

Jegede, R. O. 1978. Outpatient psychiatry in an urban clinic in a developing country. Social Psychiatry 13:93–98.

Johnson, D., and C. Johnson. 1965. Totally discouraged: A depressive syndrome of the Dakota Sioux. Transcultural Psychiatry Research Review 2:141–143.

Jones, I., and D. Home. 1973. Diagnosis of psychiatric illness among tribal aborigines. Medical Journal of Australia 1:345–349.

Kearney, R., and B. Miller. 1985. The spiral of suicide and social change in Sri Lanka. Journal of Asian Studies 45:81–101.

Kirmayer, L. 1984. Culture, affect, and somatization. Parts 1 and 2. Transcultural Psychiatry Research Review 21(3):159–188, 237–262.

Kitaro, N. 1970. Fundamental Problems of Philosophy: The World of Action and the Dialictical World. D. A. Dilworth, trans. Tokyo: Sophia University.

Kleinman, A. 1980. Patients and Healers in the Context of Culture. Berkeley: University of California Press.

Kleinman, A. 1982. Neurasthenia and depression. Culture, Medicine, and Psychiatry 6(2):117–190.

Kleinman, A. 1986. Social Origins of Distress and Disease: Depression, Neurasthenia and Pain in Modern China. New Haven, CT: Yale University Press.

Kleinman, A., and J. Kleinman. 1985. Somatization. In Culture and Depression. B. Good and A. Kleinman, eds. Berkeley: University of California Press.

LaFontaine, J. 1975. Anthropology. In A Handbook for the Study of Suicide. S. Perlin, ed. New York: Oxford University Press.

Lambo, T. 1962. Malignant anxiety. Journal of Mental Science 108:256–264.

Langness, L. L. 1965. Hysterical psychosis in the New Guinea highlands: A Bena Bena example. Psychiatry 28:259–277.

Leighton, A., et al. 1963. The Character of Danger: Psychiatric Symptoms in Selected Communities, Vol. II. New York: Basic Books.

Leighton, A., et al. 1963. Psychiatric Disorder among the Yoruba. Ithaca, NY: Cornell University Press.

Levy, R. 1973. Tahitians: Mind and Experience in the Society Islands. Chicago: University of Chicago Press.

Lewis, I. S. 1971. Ecstatic Religion: An Anthropological Study of Spirit Possession and Shamanism. Harmoundsworth, England: Penguin.

Lin, K. M., and A. Kleinman. 1981. Recent development of psychiatric epidemiology in China. Culture, Medicine, and Psychiatry 5:135–143.

Lin, K. M., and A. Kleinman. in press. Psychopathology and clinical course of schizophrenia: A cross-cultural perspective. Schizophrenia Bulletin.

Lin, K. M., A. Kleinman, and T. Y. Lin. 1982. Overview of mental disorders in Chinese culture. In Normal and Abnormal Behavior in Chinese Culture. A. Kleinman and T. Y. Lin, eds. Dordrecht, Holland: D. Reidel.

Lin, N., et al. 1985. Modeling the effects of social support. In Social Support, Life Events and Depression. N. Lin et al. eds. New York: Academic Press.

Lin, T. Y. et al. 1969. Mental disorders in Taiwan 15 years later. In Mental Health in Asia and the Pacific. W. Caudell and T. Y. Lin, eds. Honolulu: East West Center Press.

Lin, T. Y., et al. 1978. Ethnicity and patterns of help-seeking. Culture, Medicine, and Psychiatry 2:3–14.

Lin, T. Y., and D. Lin. 1982. Alcoholism among the Chinese. Culture, Medicine and Psychiatry 6:109–116.

Littlewood, R., and M. Lipsedge. 1987. The butterfly and the serpent: Culture, psychopathology and biomedicine. Culture, Medicine, and Psychiatry 11:289–336.

Lock, M. 1986. Ambiguities of aging: Japanese experience and perception of menopause. Culture, Medicine, and Psychiatry 10:23–46.

Lock, M. 1987. Protests of a good wife and wise mother: Somatization and medicalization in modern Japan. In Health and Medical Care in Japan. M. Lock and E. Norbeck, eds. Honolulu: University of Hawaii Press.

Lutz, C. 1985. Depression and the translation of emotional worlds. In Culture and Depression. A. Kleinman and B. Good, eds. Berkeley: University of California Press.

Lutz, C., and G. White. 1986. The anthropology of emotions. Annual Review of Anthropology 15:405–436.

Manschreck, T. 1978. Towards an explanation of recent trends in suicide in Western Samoa. Man 22(2):305–330.

Manson, S., et al. 1985. The depressive experience in American Indian communities. In Culture and Depression. B. Good and A. Kleinman, eds. Berkeley: University of California Press.

Marsella, A. 1979. Depressive experience and disorder across cultures. In Handbook of Cross-Cultural Psychology Volume 6. H. Triandis and J. Draguns, eds. Boston: Allyn & Bacon.

Marsella, A., et al. 1985. Cross-cultural studies of depressive disorders. In Culture and Depression. A. Kleinman and B. Good, eds. Berkeley: University of California Press.

Mezzich, J., and E. Raab. 1980. Depressive symptomatology across the Americas. Archives of General Psychiatry 37:818–823.

Murphy, H. B. M. 1982. Comparative Psychiatry: The International and Intercultural Distribution of Mental Illness. New York: Springer-Verlag.

Murphy, J. 1982. Cultural shaping and mental disorders. In Deviance and Mental Illness. W. R. Gove, ed. Beverly Hills: Sage.

Myers, J. K., et al. 1984. Six-month prevalence of psychiatric disorders in three communities. Archives of General Psychiatry 41:959–967.

O'Nell, T. in press. Psychiatric investigations among American Indians and Alaska natives: a critical review. Culture, Medicine, and Psychiatry.

Orley, J., and J. Wing. 1979. Psychiatric disorders in two African villages. Archives of General Psychiatry 36: 513–520.

Osterweis, M., et al., eds. 1987. Pain and Disability. Washington, DC: National Academy Press.

Pina-Cabral, J. 1986. Sons of Adam, Daughters of Eve: The Peasant Worldview of the Alto Minho. London: Oxford University Press.

Prince, R. 1968. Changing picture of depressive syndromes in Africa. Canadian Journal of African Studies 1:177–192.

Prince, R., and F. Tcheng-Laroche. 1987. Culture-bound syndromes and international classifications of disease. Culture, Medicine, and Psychiatry 11(l):3–20.

Racy, J. 1980. Somatization in Saudi women. British Journal of Psychiatry 137:212–216.

Rao, A. V. 1973. Depressive illness and guilt in Indian culture. Indian Journal of Psychiatry 26:301–311.

Rosaldo, M. 1980. Knowledge and Passion: Ilongot Notions of Self and Social Life. London: Cambridge University Press.

Sartorius, N., and A. Jablensky. 1976. Transcultural studies of schizophrenia. WHO Chronicle 30:481–85.

Sartorius, N., et al. 1983. Depressive Disorders in Different Cultures. Geneva: WHO.

Sethi, B. B., et al. 1973. Depression in India, Journal of Social and Biological Structures 9(4):345–352.

Sikanerty R., and W. W. Eaton. 1984. Prevalence of schizophrenia in the Labali district of Ghana. Acta Psychiatrica Scandinavica 6:156–161.

Simons, R., and C. Hughes, eds. 1985. The Culture-Bound Syndromes. Dordrecht, Holland: D. Reidel.

Stevens, J. 1984. Brief psychosis: Do they contribute to the good prognosis and equal prevalence of schizophrenia in developing societies? British Journal of Psychiatry 151:393–396.

Teja, J. S., et al. 1971. Depression across cultures. British Journal of Psychiatry 119:253–260.

Torrey, E. F. 1980. Schizophrenia and Civilization. New York: Jason Aronson.

Torrey, E. F., et al. 1984. Endemic psychosis in western Ireland. American Journal of Psychiatry 141:966–969.

Turner, B. 1985. The Body and Society. Oxford: Basil Blackwell.

Warner, R. 1985. Recovery from Schizophrenia: Psychiatry and Social Economy. New York: Routledge and Kegan Paul.

Waxier, N. 1977. Is outcome for schizophrenia better in nonindustrialized societies. Journal of Nervous and Mental Disease 167:144–158.

Weiss, M., and A. Kleinman. in press. Depression in cross-cultural perspective. In Contributions of Cross-Cultural Psychology to International Mental Health. P. Dasein et al., eds. New York: Plenum.

26

The Epidemiology of a Folk Illness: Susto *in Hispanic America*

Arthur J. Rubel

This is a classic in the field of medical anthropology, and it represents the initial data collection of what became a larger and very significant study in the epidemiology of a folk illness called susto, *usually translated as "soul loss" or "magical fright." The important book from this study (the collaboration of a medical anthropologist, a psychological anthropologist, and a physician) is called Susto:* A Folk Illness *(Rubel, O'Neil, and Collado-Ardon 1984). This is a folk illness because it does not fit into the categorization system of biomedicine or psychiatry (the* DSM*). An epidemiological study of a folk illness involves the description of its distribution in regard to time, place, and person. Analysis of these data allows the researcher to make hypotheses about the causation of the illness. The symptom complex of susto reminds many students of "depression"—victims who have lost their souls feel tired and listless, have trouble sleeping, don't care about their appearance, have little appetite, and so forth. But the cultural meanings of* susto *are very different from what North Americans would call depression. The cultural interpretations of the cause of* susto, *in fact, differ for people of Indian descent and mainstream others of mixed descent (mestizos). You will notice that the Indian etiological theory is closely linked to the idea of* animism *(that all living things have souls). People get sick when their souls become separated from their bodies.*

In this selection, Arthur Rubel introduces us to the concept of stress, a concept that has much relevance to medical anthropology (Selye 1976). He also presents a fascinating model of the individual as a "linked open system" of physical, social, and psychological aspects that are clearly interconnected in the context of stress and support. The larger study is designed as a retrospective case-control study—a comparison of the life situations of people who have suffered from susto *and matched pairs who have not had the illness. Over the course of the longer study, it became possible to also do a prospective case-control study by following cases and controls over a ten-year period; one of the most surprising findings from this work was that people who had suffered from* susto *had a much greater likelihood of dying over this period. This selection considers the issue of the sick role and its associated claims for a "time out" from regular responsibilities in the context of difficult-to-meet social demands (this is something students may know from personal experience).*

As you read this selection, consider these questions:

- **What are the rights and responsibilities of the sick role? Why might this be a good thing? How might the sick role be abused, and what happens to a person who is suspected of not really being sick?**
- **Why are there ethnic differences in the etiological explanations of susto between Indians and non-Indians?**
- **How is the treatment of susto different, for example, from the treatment of depression in U.S. society? How do the two conditions differ with regard to the blaming-the-victim question?**
- **What is the role of the family in the cure? How might this fit with Lévi-Strauss's analysis (selection 15) of the role of belief in healing?**
- **What is epidemiological about this research?**

Context: Arthur Rubel was one of the founders of medical anthropology. Most of his career was spent at the University of California at Irvine (where he taught in the Department of Family Medicine), as well as Michigan State University. His research focused on the health of people living on both sides of the Mexican-U.S. border. He was particularly interested in the very important infectious disease of tuberculosis. This classic article on *susto*, or soul-loss illness, was remarkable in 1964 for two reasons. First, it was one of the first applications of the methods of epidemiology to the study of a folk illness; prior to this time, a folk illness had never been studied in such a systematic fashion. Second, it emphasized ethnic differences in beliefs about the etiology and curing of *susto*. This article describes the descriptive epidemiology of the illness—that is, its distribution in regard to time, place, and person. Rubel's early work has since prompted generations of medical anthropologists to study this interesting folk illness.

Source: A. J. Rubel (1964). "The Epidemiology of a Folk Illness: *Susto* in Hispanic America." *Ethology* 3(3):268-283.

This exploratory article seeks to assess the extent to which folk illness may be subjected to epidemiological studies, as are other illnesses. It is a working assumption of this paper that, in general, folk-illness phenomena are indeed amenable to such investigation if one is aware of special methodological problems which are concomitants of such research. A presentation of some of these general problems is followed by an examination of the Hispanic American folk illness which I refer to as *susto*.

METHODOLOGICAL PROBLEMS

A work which has as its announced goal the description, distribution, and etiology of folk illness faces a number of methodological problems. Not the least of these is an acceptable definition of folk illness. In these pages "illness" refers to syndromes from which members of a particular group claim to suffer and for which their culture provides an etiology, diagnosis, preventive measures, and regimens of healing. I apply the prefix "folk" to those illnesses of which orthodox Western medicine professes neither understanding nor competence—a definition which, although somewhat cumbersome, has the value of subsuming a number of seemingly bizarre syndromes which are reported in anthropological, medical, and psychiatric literature from many areas of the world.

Another problem of basic importance is that, when modern epidemiologists or research-oriented physicians engage in systematic research on folk health phenomena, they find it difficult to agree with the population that a health problem indeed exists; furthermore, they tend to disagree with their patients on even the most fundamental premises about health and illness. The two groups perceive the same condition from premises which are fundamentally divergent. The problem is compounded by the fact that the health professional must elicit medical history and descriptions of the discomfort from people who hold an opposing point of view.

In recent years anthropologists have elucidated the underlying logic whereby a number of folk peoples understand illness, diagnosis, and healing, e.g., the work of Frake (1961) among the Subanun, of Metzger and Williams (1963) on the Tzeltal, and of Rubel (1960) among Mexican-Americans. These are steps along the way, but such studies do not inform us which components of the population do in fact become ill, nor under what circumstances illness occurs, nor what courses the illness follows when it does manifest itself. Investigations of folk illness are presently at a stage where we can assert with some degree of confidence only that certain syndromes appear to be confined to particular cultural or linguistic groups, e.g., Algonkians, Eskimos, or Mexican-Americans, and do not appear among others. That is to say, if one may divide the study of folk illness into two complementary areas of achievement—illness as a culture complex and the epidemiology of folk illness—then I submit that the first of these represents our present state of knowledge.

Monographs, articles, and more casual reports on exotic cultures abound with allusions to certain seemingly bizarre notions about illness. Sometimes these descriptive writings discuss the folk concept in some detail, but more often they do not. Often such reports titillate the reader by providing a few clinical case histories which reflect cultural beliefs about health and illness, but only in rare instances is one provided detailed descriptions about an individual patient's medical history, his or her response to the onset of the folk illness, or close observations of the course which the illness follows. Even more rarely does the reader encounter an extensive corpus of cases assembled either from published sources or from field observations.

The large collections of library data on the basis of which Parker (1960) and Teicher (1960) discuss the folk illness known as *wiitigo* are extremely valuable. The scrupulous attention paid by these scholars to the intricacies of a folk illness points up some of the more pressing problems faced by researchers who utilize library resources to derive epidemiological inferences as to causality. For example, the case materials on the *wiitigo* illness are reported by such diverse observers as anthropologists, explorers, missionaries, trappers, and Indians. Moreover, in these as in other instances, the descriptive reports often span years or even centuries of time and define the population involved in only the grossest terms. In the absence of precise chronological, social, or cultural parameters it is hazardous to attempt to infer rates of prevalence or incidence of a folk illness, much less the relationships which obtain between these rates and such demographic variables as age, sex, or marital status. Yet it is precisely from such inferences and associations that we may hope to gain an understanding of the nature of folk illness.

The methodical field worker who seeks cases of folk illness within a precisely delimited locale and time span is confronted by the problem of defining beforehand what it is that he seeks. Oftentimes, though the symptoms of presumed patients remain constant from place to place, the labels by which a disability is identified vary considerably. For heuristic and practical purposes I suggest that, in the present state of the study of folk illness, when several symptoms regularly cohere in any specified population, and members of that population respond to such manifestations in similarly patterned ways, the cluster of symptoms be defined as a disease entity. For, as Leighton (1961:486) has commented, it will prove profitable to fasten our attention first on "the distribution of selected types of human patterns, and only later ask what the functional effect and consequences of these are. The determination of pathology is the last thing to be done rather than the first" (cf. also Blum 1962).

SUSTO IN HISPANIC AMERICA[1]

The general problems in the study of folk illness, to which we have alluded, apply equally to the investigation of a condition, here called *susto,* which is reported from many regions of the Spanish-speaking New World.[2] Though variously called *susto, pasmo, jani, espanto, pérdida de la sombra,* or other terms in different localities, the reference in this paper is always to a syndrome, rather than its variant labels, and for purposes of exposition this particular cluster of symptoms and its attendant beliefs and behaviors will be arbitrarily designated as *susto.*

Those who suffer from *susto* include Indian and non-Indian, male and female, rich and poor, rural dwellers and urbanites. In the United States it is endemic to the Spanish-speaking inhabitants of California, Colorado, New Mexico, and Texas (Clark 1959; Saunders 1954; Rubel 1960). In Hispanic America *susto* is often mentioned in the writings of anthropologists and others. In contrast to other well-known folk illnesses such as *wiitigo* and arctic hysteria, however, it is not confined uniquely either to the speakers of a single group of related languages or to the members of one sociocultural group. Peoples who speak unrelated aboriginal languages, e.g., Chinantec, Tzotzil, and Quechua, as well as Spanish-speaking non-Indians, appear to be equally susceptible to this syndrome.[3]

From the point of view of cultural analysis, the *susto* syndrome reflects the presence in Hispanic America of a trait complex which also occurs elsewhere in the world—a complex consisting of beliefs that an individual is composed of a corporeal being and one or more immaterial souls or spirits which may become detached from the body and wander freely. In Hispanic America, as elsewhere, these souls may leave the body during sleep, particularly when the individual is dreaming, but among peasant and urban groups they may also become detached as a consequence of an unsettling experience. The latter aspect of spirit separation from the corporeal being has attained such importance in Hispanic America as to justify being described as a cultural focus (Honigmann 1959: 128–129). I shall speak of it, together with its associated behavioral traits, as the *susto* focus. It is clearly distinct from the more widely diffused trait of soul separation. It is on the behavioral, rather than the cultural, nature of this focus that this paper concentrates.

Local embellishments on the basic cohering symptoms of *susto* make this entity appear far more inconstant than is really the case. When one concentrates on the constants which recur with great consistency among the various groups from which *susto* is reported, the basic syndrome appears as follows: (1) during sleep the patient evidences restlessness; (2) during waking hours patients are characterized by listlessness, loss of appetite, disinterest in dress and personal hygiene, loss of strength, depression, and introversion (Sal y Rosas 1958; Gillin 1945).[4]

A number of basic elements recur in the folk etiology of *susto.* Among Indians the soul is believed to be captured because the patient, wittingly or not, has disturbed the spirit guardians of the earth, rivers, ponds, forests, or animals, the soul being held captive until the affront has been expiated. By contrast, when a non-Indian is diagnosed as suffering from soul loss, the locale in which it occurred, e.g., a river or forest, is of no significance, nor are malevolent beings suspected.[5] In many though not all cases a fright occasioned by an unexpected accident or encounter is thought to have caused the illness.

The curing rites of the groups in which this syndrome manifests itself as a significant health phenomenon likewise share a number of basic features. There is an initial diagnostic session between healer and patient during which the cause of the particular episode is specified and agreed upon by the participants. The soul is then coaxed and entreated to rejoin the patient's body; in the case of Indians those spirits who hold the soul captive are begged and propitiated to release it, and in both Indian and non-Indian groups the officiant shows the soul the direction back to the host body. During healing rites a patient is massaged and often sweated, both apparently to relax him, and he is "swept" or rubbed with some object to remove the illness from his body. In the Peruvian highlands a guinea pig is utilized for the therapeutic rubbing, whereas some Guatemala Indians use hens' eggs, and in south Texas and parts of Mexico medicinal brushes are employed for the same purpose.

CASE HISTORIES

The fullest account of a case of *susto* (Gillin 1948) describes the condition of a Pokomam Indian woman from San Luis Jilotepecque in eastern Guatemala. The 63-year-old woman shared with neighbors a belief that her soul had been separated from the rest of her body and held captive by sentient beings. The capture of her soul was believed to have been precipitated when she discovered her husband philandering with a loose woman of the village. As a consequence of her discovery, the patient upbraided her husband, who retaliated by hitting his wife with a rock. When Gillin (1948: 348) encountered the woman,

> she was in a depressed state of mind, neglected her household duties and her pottery making, and reduced her contact with friends and relatives. Physical complaints included diarrhea, "pain in the stomach," loss of appetite, "pains in the back and legs," occasional fever. Verbalizations were wheedling and anxious; she alternated between moods of timorous anxiety and tension characterized by tremor of the hands and generally rapid and jerky movements, and moods of profound, though conscious, lethargy. Orientation was adequate for time and place and normal reflexes were present.

The next case (Rubel 1960) is from a small city in south Texas. The patient, Mrs. Benitez, was a non-Indian who had been born in Mexico but had resided in Texas for many years. She was in her middle thirties and was the mother of five children, all girls. Her husband had deserted his family more than five years before. During our acquaintance the patient was irregularly employed as an agricultural field laborer, but most of her family's income was in fact derived from welfare agencies. She was extraordinarily thin and wan and appeared much older than her years. She had had a long history of epileptoid attacks, involving the locking of her jaw and involuntary spasms of her legs, but she claimed not to be able to recall what had occurred during such seizures. She expressed a feeling of constant tiredness and of complete social isolation, and she maintained that she had suffered recurrently from soul loss.

Another case concerns a middle-aged man, a baker by profession and a non-Indian, from Mexiquito in southern Texas. One day, according to his sister, when the baker was following his usual custom of delivering breads and cakes to workers at a vegetable-packing warehouse during the noon lunch hour, he stepped into an open ice chute as he moved across a wooden platform. His leg bent under the weight of his falling body, his shoulders hit the flooring, and the breads and cakes scattered in all directions. Noting his ludicrous predicament, the onlooking laborers commenced to laugh; then, perceiving him to be in great pain, they rushed to his assistance. He was immediately taken home to his mother, who initiated a treatment for the loss of his soul which had presumably been occasioned by the accident. She also massaged the injured leg and requested a neighbor to collect the inner bark of a tree known as *huisatche chino,* which she prepared by boiling and administered to the victim for the next eight days. The laughter of the onlookers and the consequent mortification and helpless anger of the victim apparently seemed so important to the informant that she mentioned them three times during the course of her short tale.

Another case from Mexiquito in Texas involved a family whom I shall call the Montalvos. Mr. Montalvo is a Spanish-speaking, native-born American citizen who neither speaks English nor reads or writes in any language. Since he has been old enough to work he has been an agricultural field laborer, except for a brief period when he was employed by a small construction company. His wife, who is likewise able to converse only in Spanish, came from a hamlet in arid northeastern Mexico where she grew up poor, illiterate, and anxious. The pathos of her life is compounded by an ever-present fear that her illegal presence in this country may be discovered, resulting in her arrest and deportation. During the course of our acquaintance the family spent a large proportion of its meager income and a substantial amount of time in efforts to secure the Mexican documents required to establish her legal residence in this country. The Montalvos had a seven-year-old daughter, a five-year-old son, and an infant boy who died shortly after I made the family's acquaintance.

On a Sunday outing Ricardo, the older boy, suffered an attack of *susto.* The rest of the family romped in and about the water of a local pond, but Ricardo demurred. Despite coaxing and taunts, especially from his sister, Ricardo would have nothing to do with the water but climbed into the automobile and went to sleep. He slept throughout the afternoon and did not even awaken when he was taken home after dark and put to bed. That night he slept fitfully and several times talked aloud in his sleep. On the following morning the parents decided that Ricardo had suffered a *susto.* It was caused, they reasoned, not by fear of the water but by the family's insistence that he enter the pond—a demand to which he was unable to accede. They brought him to a local curer to have his soul coaxed back to his body and thus be healed of soul loss.

The next case involved Antonio, a young married man about 25 years of age, likewise a native-born American citizen who could neither read, write, nor communicate in English. He and his family before him were laborers employed in harvesting cotton and vegetables in south Texas and migrating every spring and summer to the north-central states for similar field labor. To all outward appearances Antonio seemed an outgoing fellow contented enough with his lot. He lived with his wife and children in a homemade shack with an earth-packed floor, walls of corrugated paper, and a roof of tin. There was, of course, no indoor plumbing, but Antonio and the owner of the lot on which his shack stood had fashioned a shower and water closet in an outhouse which both families used. Unlike her husband, Antonio's wife came from a hamlet in northeastern Mexico. She neither spoke nor understood English, but she was able to write Spanish by using self-taught block letters. Despite the family's impoverished condition she, too, seemed a cheerful and untroubled person.

On one occasion Antonio was sent to a hospital with a diagnosis of double pneumonia. His fever was successfully controlled, and he was placed in a ward for a recuperative period. One night he noticed a change in the condition of a wardmate, became alarmed, and tried to communicate his concern to the attendants, but for some reason he was unsuccessful. Some time later they discovered that the wardmate had died and removed the corpse from the room. Antonio was much upset by the incident. He became fitful, complained of restless nights, and exhibited little interest in his food or surroundings. Moreover, he found his body involuntarily "jumping" on the bed while he lay in a reclining position. After leaving the hospital he went home and asked that his mother, who lived in Mexico, be brought to his side. When she arrived she immediately began to coax his soul back to his body by means of a traditional cure (see below).

A woman from Laredo, Texas, suffered *susto* on at least two occasions, several years apart. Each instance occurred during the course of her family's seasonal migration for field labor in the north. Mr. Solis, the patient's husband, was a highly excitable and apparently alienated person who conceived of himself as earning a living "by the honest sweat of my brow" in face of the restricting regulations of the local and federal government and of the outright malice of his employers. His lack of other than agricultural skills and the absence of year-round employment in south Texas left the family no choice except migratory labor and precluded the children's regular attendance at school despite the family's strong motivation toward education and their manifest aspirations toward a better way of life. Mrs. Solis, though probably only in her middle forties, was constantly sickly, felt weak, and had no desire to eat anything, not even when she awoke in the morning. Moreover, she felt listless during the day and did not like to move about. She claimed she had suffered this condition for two years but had not brought it to a physician's attention.

The first episode *of susto* afflicted Mrs. Solis during her family's stay in an Indiana migrant labor camp. It occurred after she had unwillingly and helplessly witnessed an attack on a peaceable member of her husband's crew by drunken and bellicose members of another crew in which the victim was slashed in the abdominal region and removed to a hospital. Several years later, when she was pregnant, Mrs. Solis helplessly watched the family truck overturn, carrying with it the fruit of the crew's labor. As a consequence of this disturbing event she suffered a miscarriage and was again afflicted with *susto.*

In the seven cases of soul loss presented thus far—one from an Indian community in Guatemala and the remainder from non-Indian groups in south Texas—it has been possible to present relevant data on the patient's personality, on the family contexts, and on the causes presumed by the people involved to have precipitated the soul loss and illness. The following cases are less complete because all the relevant data are not available.

One case involved a young Chinantec Indian schoolboy from San Lucas Ojitlán in Oaxaca, Mexico. According to the boy's teacher, it was necessary one day to punish him for talking in class. The lad was instructed to stand by his desk with his hands outstretched and his palms up, and the teacher then slapped one upturned palm with a small wooden ruler. According to the instructor's account, the blows were not hard enough to have hurt the boy in a physical sense. Nevertheless, the illness which resulted from this chastisement was so serious as to keep the lad out of school for two weeks. During this period he was unable to eat and manifested considerable apathy. The child's mother recognized from these signs that her son's soul had left his body and had been captured by the spirit of the earth, and she took corrective steps which will be related later.

The following two cases are reported by Diaz de Solas (1957) from the Tzotzil-speaking Indians of San Bartolomé de Los Llanos in the Mexican state of Chiapas. In the first case an Indian mother seated her four-year-old son on a stone wall from which he could watch her while she gardened in the family corn field. After a while the child lost his balance and fell to the ground. Although he cried, he seemed to have been uninjured by the accident, nor was it thought that he had suffered *susto* as a result. The mother, however, lost her soul—a condition which the community considered to have been precipitated by her helplessness as she watched the child's fall.

The second case from San Bartolomé involved a man who suffered a *susto* as a result of an accident he was unable to prevent. This Indian was leading his heavily laden horse home from market, a trip which required the fording of a swiftly flowing stream. As they crossed the stream, the pack animal was swept downstream by the current. The owner saved himself, and was finally able to retrieve his horse, but the valuable load was lost. Subsequently the Indian sickened, and his condition was diagnosed as *susto;* his soul was presumed to have been taken captive by the spirit of the locale in which the accident occurred. In both the cases from San Bartolomé it was thought that the illness would continue until the annoyance suffered by the spirits, respectively of the earth and the river, had been expiated.

A very similar case occurred in another Tzotzil municipio, San Andrés Larrainzar, in the Chiapas highlands (cf. Guiteras-Holmes 1961: 269–275). An Indian was driving a horse laden with corn on a trip from one section (*paraje*) of San Andres to another, and in the course of his journey they were forced to cross the Rio Tiwó. The man drove his animal into the river whilst he himself crossed over a small bridge. The horse was carried away by the current until it finally came to rest against a fallen tree trunk. Although the owner was able to rescue his horse, his load was lost. He felt very sad about his loss, and then he suffered an *espanto* (note the sequence!). At the end of a month the patient felt sad and sick, and had no desire to eat anything; as a consequence of these symptoms a curer was called into the case.

Foster (1951:168–169) reports an incident in which a Popoluca Indian suffered the loss and capture of his soul. According to the patient's account,

> In August, 1939, I was in a boat near Cotzacoalcos [*sic*] which upset and threw me into the water. I struggled and tried to reach the shore, but couldn't make it. I was afraid of drowning. Finally I was rescued, but I became very ill. I couldn't eat; I couldn't even sit up. I was ill all through the fall and winter until March, getting worse and worse. I know what the matter was because I dreamed of Coatzacoalcos and knew my spirit was there.

The examples of *susto* reported in the preceding pages represent only a few of the references to the illness which were discovered in the literature. They have been selected for inclusion herein because they describe with some amplitude the circumstances surrounding the onset of a specific case of *susto* or because they provide some of the social or personality characteristics of the patients.

HEALING RITES

I now move to a discussion of the curing rites associated with the syndrome of *susto.* I shall first describe those utilized to heal some of the patients in the cases already presented and shall then refer to some generalized, but detailed, descriptions of healing procedures provided by the psychiatrist Sal y Rosas (1958) and the anthropologists Tschopik (1951), Weitlaner (1961), and Carrasco (1960).

In the case from San Luis Jilotepecque, Guatemala, described by Gillin (1948), the patient for whom the healing ceremonies were intended was the wife who had suffered from a philandering husband. The essentials of the treatment may be divided into several stages. During the first stage, that of diagnosis, the native curer pronounced to the patient a clear-cut and authoritative diagnosis of *espanto* or soul loss. Later the woman was required to consider and "confess" the actual events which had led up to the particular episode of soul loss (she had had a previous history of similar episodes). During the second stage, that of the actual healing rites, a group of persons who were socially significant to the patient was organized to attend a nocturnal ceremony. Some of them joined the patient and the healer in offering prayers to the Catholic saints of the village. Hens' eggs were then passed over the patient to absorb some of the illness. They were later deposited at the place where the soul loss had occurred, along with a collection of gifts to propitiate the spirits who held the patient's soul and who were now requested to release it. Following prayers and libations to the spirits, a procession was formed. It led from the place of the accident back to the woman's home, the healer making noises to indicate to the soul the appropriate direction. Finally, the patient was undressed, "shocked" by cold liquor sprayed from the mouth of the curer, then massaged, and finally "sweated" on a bed placed over a brazier filled with burning coals.

The essentials of the Pokomam ceremony, with the exception of certain details in the expiation rites, are found widely dispersed in Hispanic America among Indians and non-Indians alike. In the case involving the Chinantec schoolboy, for example, the healing rites were as follows.[6] The boy's mother proceeded to the schoolhouse, taking with her the shirt her son had worn on the day he had been punished. Inside the building she moved directly to the desk alongside of which her son had been chastised. She took his shirt, rolled it up, and proceeded to wipe the packed earth flooring, meanwhile murmuring:

> I come in the name of curer Garcia who at this time is unable to come. I come in order to reunite the spirit of my boy, José, who is sick. I come this time and this time only. It surely was not your intention to dispossess him of his spirit. Goodbye, I will return in four days to advise you as to his condition and to do whatever is necessary.

The mother then removed from her clothing a bottle of liquor mixed with the herb called *hoja de espanto* and sprayed some of this liquor from her mouth on the shirt, as well as on the earthen floor on which the desk rested, meanwhile crossing herself and making the sign of the cross over the wet shirt. She then picked up the shirt and excavated a little earth, which she carried home. Here her son donned his shirt, and the earth was placed in a receptacle containing liquor set beside the boy's cot. The mother next called on the services of a professional curer, who poured liquor from the receptacle into his own mouth and sprayed the patient on his face, chest, crown, and the back of his neck. The child was then placed on his cot, rolled in blankets, and a brazier of hot coals was placed under the cot to sweat him. Following the child's recovery, the curer went himself to the schoolhouse, where he offered thanks to the earth for releasing the child's soul and then ceremoniously bade it farewell.

Very similar ceremonies were employed to heal the Tzotzil Indian from San Andrés Larrainzar. In this instance a specialist was called into the case only after the illness had run its course unchecked for a month. His first act was to diagnose the entity as *susto* or soul loss. The healer then repaired to the ford where the mishap had occurred. Here he offered candles, incense, and a slaughtered cock to the local spirits. Returning to the home of his patient, he brought with him a quantity of water from the site where the incident had occurred; he required the patient to drink three glasses of this water and administered a small amount (mixed with salt) to the rescued horse. Following this he built a small altar in the patient's home on which incense and candles were offered.

In the non-Indian cases reported from Texas the cures, though similar in many respects, involved neither expiation nor propitiation. The major problem a Texas curer confronts is to induce the soul to return to the patient's body; it is not compounded by the conception of malevolent captors. In Antonio's case his mother placed him on the dirt floor of his shack, with his arms outstretched but his legs together so that he formed a human cross. She then dug a hole at the base of his feet, another above his head, and one at each of his extended hands, filling them with a liquid composed of water and medicinal herbs. Then she began to "sweep" the illness out of her son's body via the extremities, using a broom constructed of a desert bush with medicinal qualities. She and her son then prayed, entreating his lost and wandering soul to rejoin his body, after which she blew a spray of liquid from her mouth directly into her son's face, and Antonio sipped some of the medicinal liquid which his mother had scooped from the holes in the dirt floor.

Among the most meticulous descriptions of cures for *susto* are those provided by Sal y Rosas (1958: 177–184). In the main, his data pertain to the Quechua Indians of the Callejon de Huaylas region of Peru, but a number of his observations refer to other parts of that country as well. After diagnosis, according to Sal y Rosas, a patient reclines on a cot or on a blanket stretched on the floor, and alongside him is placed a mixture of various flower petals, leaves, and wheat or corn is placed beside him. The curer blesses the mixture and distributes it over the patient's body, commencing at his head and moving down to the legs and then the feet. Later the curer's helper carries the mixture, wrapped in the patient's clothing, to the locality where the illness was precipitated, scattering on his way a trail of petals, leaves, and flour to indicate to the soul the path by which it is to return to the body. He also leaves an offering of liquor, cigarettes, and coca leaves at the site as an inducement to the soul to return. He then holds up the patient's shirt and shakes it in the air to attract the soul's attention. Returning to the patient's house, the helper carefully follows the trail of petals, leaves, and flour and holds the shirt in plain sight so that the soul will encounter no trouble in finding its way. (In more serious cases of soul loss, the patient is rubbed with a live guinea pig, which is then taken and left as a gift to the spirits of the locality where the illness occurred, in exchange for the captive soul.)

Reports by Weitlaner (1961) and Carrasco (1960: 103–105, 110) of symptoms, etiology, and curing rites among Nahuatl-speaking and Chontal-speaking groups in western Mexico indicate that soul capture and its concomitant syndrome are remarkably similar to those reported among aboriginal groups with very different linguistic affiliations. Among these Chontal and Nahua groups the loss and capture of a soul is believed to be precipitated by a fall on a road or pathway, by slipping or falling near a body of water, or by a sudden encounter with animals, snakes, or even a corpse. Diagnosis and healing include the elicitation by a healer of the date, place, and other pertinent circumstances of the event the patient presumes to have brought on the illness. This is followed by expiation for the annoyance caused by the spirit guardians of the locale and by propitiation of these beings in exchange for the captive soul. The healer then attempts to coax and lead the absent soul back to its host body. Unlike other groups previously discussed, the Nahua and Chontal adorn their healing rites with elaborate symbolism in which ritual colors, numbers, and directions play important parts. Nevertheless, beneath these local embellishments, one quickly discerns the fundamentals of the widespread *susto* complex and the associated healing rites which these Indians share with the other groups mentioned.

SUMMARY OF DESCRIPTIVE DATA

One of the most noteworthy aspects of the *susto* phenomenon is the fact that a basic core of premises and assumptions—symptoms, etiology, and regimens of healing—recur with remarkable constancy among many Hispanic-American groups, Indian and non-Indian alike. In general, the following symptoms characterize victims of this illness: (1) while asleep a patient evidences restlessness, and (2) during waking hours he manifests listlessness, loss of appetite, disinterest in costume or personal hygiene, loss of strength and weight, depression, and introversion. In one unique instance, a Texas patient (Mrs. Benitez) subsumes under *susto* her epileptoid seizures in addition to the more usual loss of strength, depression, apathy, listlessness, and introversion. However, it should be noted that, when this victim of *susto* describes her own condition, she stresses the post-spasmodic depressive and introversive emotional states rather than the seizure itself.

Although Indian and non-Indian populations appear to be equally subject to *susto*, there are significant differences between them with respect to the nature of the causal agents. Unlike non-Indians, Indian groups conceive of the separation of the soul from the body as precipitated by an affront to the spirit guardians of a locality—guardians of the earth, water, or animals—although the offense is usually caused unwittingly by the victim. Intentional or not, however, the mischief must be expiated and the spirits of the site propitiated before they will release the captured soul.

There are also other features of the precipitating events which recur with remarkable constancy. Thus one salient feature of all the cases cited is role helplessness. Significantly, however, a victim's helplessness appears in association with only some kinds of problems in role behavior, but not with others. In none of the instances cited, for example, do we discover a victim helpless in the face of role conflicts or expectations which are products of his or her cultural marginality or social mobility.[7] In other words, *susto* appears to communicate an individuals inability to fulfill adequately the expectations of the society in which he has been socialized; it does not seem to mark those role conflicts and uncertainties Indians confront as they pass into Ladino society or the problems posed to upwardly mobile Mexican-Americans in the process of being assimilated into the Anglo-American society of Texas.

In cases of soul capture, a healing specialist visits the site at which the mishap occurred, where he propitiates the spirits and then coaxes the released soul back to the body of the victim along a path clearly indicated by the healer. Sickness which has "entered" the victim's body is removed either by sweeping it out by means of medicinal branches or by passing hens' eggs, a fowl, or a guinea pig across the body of the victim in such a manner as to absorb the illness, removing it from the victim. Inasmuch as non-Indian groups neither attribute soul loss to malevolent sentient beings nor consider the site at which a mishap occurred to be important, it follows that neither expiation nor propitiation occur in their healing rites. Finally, the rites of both groups share such other elements as medicinal "sweeping" to remove internalized illness, recollection and verbalization by the patient of the event precipitating the separation of his soul from the body, simulation of the "shock" which was the immediate cause of that separation, and entreaties directed to a soul to return to the victim. The constancy with which similar precipitating events, symptoms, and healing methods recur among a variety of groups in Hispanic America makes the syndrome amenable to systematic epidemiological investigation.

AN EPIDEMIOLOGICAL MODEL

Epidemiology has been described by Wade Hampton Frost as "something more than the total of its established facts. It includes their orderly arrangement into chains of inference which extend more or less beyond the bound of direct observation" (Maxcy 1941: 1). In what follows I shall attempt to order the descriptive data into such "chains of inference." Let me first make clear that it is not my intent to investigate the truth of informants' statements as to whether or not those who complain of illness associated with a presumed loss of soul are really ill. It has been my experience (one which I share with others who write of this phenomenon) that individuals who claim to suffer an *asustado* condition are characterized by, if nothing else, a distinctive absence of well-being—the minimal criterion for defining illness.

It is hoped that my conceptual model and the hypotheses it generates will result in a later test of those hypotheses and their verification, modification, or rejection as may be required. Underlying this model is an assumption which holds that the *susto* syndrome is a product of the interaction between three open systems, each linked with the others (Caudill 1958: 4–7). The three systems in question are (1) an individual's state of health, (2) his personality system, and (3) the social system of which he is a member. The interaction between these three linked open systems is portrayed in the following simple diagram (see Cassell et al. 1960).[8]

Finally, I proffer the following tentative hypotheses:

I. A *susto* syndrome will appear only in social situations which victims perceive as stressful. The syndrome is the vehicle by means of which people of Hispanic-American peasant and urban societies manifest their reactions to some forms of self-perceived stressful situations, but not others. People in these societies not only choose to assume the sick role but also elect the kinds of symptoms by which to make manifest to others an absence of well-being (cf. Parsons and Fox 1952; Weinstein 1962).

II. The social stresses which are reflected in the *susto* syndrome are intra-cultural and intra-societal in nature. Stresses occasioned by conflict between cultures or by an individual's cultural marginality or social mobility will be symbolized by symptoms of illness other than *susto.* In other words, the frustration or alienation which often result from efforts to identify with, and to be accepted by, members of a society or social stratum distinct from that into which one has been socialized will not be reflected by *susto.*

III. In Hispanic-American societies, the *susto* syndrome will appear as a consequence of an episode in which an individual is unable to meet the expectations of his own society for a social role in which he or she has been socialized.

Corollary 1: Because these societies differentially socialize males and females, and because society's expectations of male and female children differ from those held for mature men and women, it is expected that girls and women will be afflicted by *susto* and its concomitants as a consequence of experiences different from those which jeopardize the health of boys and men of the same society. For example, girls are socialized to be demure, dependent, and home-oriented, whereas boys are trained to show aggressiveness, independence, and orientations toward occupational and public responsibility roles. I should not expect many girls or women in these societies to manifest *susto* under circumstances where the society has no reason to expect a female to fulfill a responsibility successfully. Neither should one expect a young man to suffer ill effects from his inability to carry out successfully a task usually assigned to females. If, for example, a girl of the same age as the Mexican-American boy, Ricardo, refused to enter the water because of timidity, it is my belief that the soul-loss syndrome would not have appeared. The girl's timidity would have been a demonstration of appropriate female behavior, whereas Ricardo's behavior was a far cry from the expectations which Mexican-Americans hold for boys and men.

Corollary 2: Since Hispanic-American societies attach greater importance to the successful accomplishment of some tasks than of others, the more importance which socializers attach to a particular task, the greater the likelihood will be that *susto* will occur in association with failure to perform that task adequately. It follows that, although females and males both risk illness as a consequence of failure adequately to perform sex-specific and age-specific tasks, not all such tasks are equally risky.

IV. Although all persons in a society may believe in the concept of soul loss and its attendant illness, not all members of that society will actually fall victim

STATE OF HEALTH

1. Susceptibility to *susto* and other health conditions.
2. Relative severity and chronicity of illness.
3. Frequency of episodes.

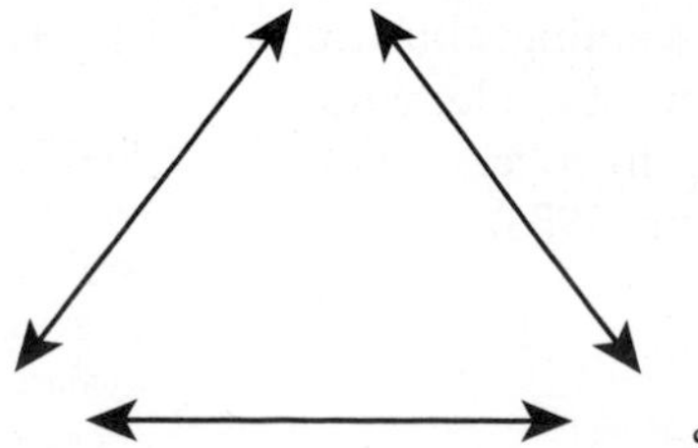

PERSONALITY SYSTEM

1. Self-perception of relative success or failure in fulfillment of social role expectations.
2. Individual's capacity to adapt to self-perceived inadequate role performances.

SOCIAL SYSTEM

1. Society's sex-specific and age-specific role expectations.

to this kind of illness. It is hypothesized that individual personalities act as contingency variables. That is, if two members of a society, matched for age and sex, fail to meet adequately the society's role expectations, one may respond to his self-perceived inadequacy by electing the sick role, i.e., *susto,* whereas the other may adapt in a different manner, e.g., by an expression of generalized anger or by displacement of hostility. Moreover, among those who do elect the *susto* syndrome, the severity, chronicity, and frequency of episodes will vary systematically with respect to personality and societal variables. The points which are of interest to us, of course, are (1) that some cultures provide *susto* as an adaptive mechanism to self-perceived social inadequacies, whereas others do not, and (2) that some but not all individuals with these cultural beliefs elect *susto* symptoms to indicate an absence of well-being.

Briefly, these hypotheses propose that *susto* illness in societies of Hispanic America may be understood as a product of a complex interaction between an individual's state of health and the role expectations which his society provides, mediated by aspects of that individual's personality.

SUMMARY

In this exploration of the health phenomenon which I call *susto,* I have sought to assess the extent to which this folk illness is amenable to epidemiological analysis. Despite localized embellishments on a general theme of soul-loss illness, there recurs in many societies a hard core of constant elements which lead one to conclude that this phenomenon is indeed subject to orderly description and analysis. Moreover, inferences of causality drawn from ethnographic data offer great potential for understanding the nature of folk illness and some facets of the relationships which obtain between health and social behavior. Finally, if one folk illness, *susto,* proves amenable to such investigation, other seemingly bizarre notions of illness demand the attention of epidemiologists and research physicians working in collaboration with anthropologists (see Fleck and lanni 1958).

NOTES

1. Field work was carried out among the Chinantec of San Lucas Ojitlan in 1950 and in the Tzotzil municipios of San Bartolomé de Los Llanos, San Andrés Larrainzar, and Santa Catarina Pantelhó in 1957 and 1961. Between 1957 and 1959 I engaged in a study of health and social life of Mexican-Americans in south Texas. Work among the Tzotzil was supported by the University of Chicago Man-In-Nature Project, in Mexiquito by the Hogg Foundation for Mental Health, and in Laredo by the Migrant Health Branch of the United States Public Health Service. To all these organizations I wish to acknowledge my gratitude. A preliminary version of this paper was presented at the annual meeting of the Society for Applied Anthropology in Pittsburgh, 1960, and a short version appeared in *Research Reviews* 8: 13–19 (Chapel Hill, 1961). I wish to express my gratitude to R. N. Adams, Harriet Kupferer, Duane Metzger, Ralph Patrick, and Richard Simpson for their considered criticisms. Remaining defects are solely the author's responsibility. Assistance in the preparation of this manuscript was provided by the Research Fund of the University of North Carolina at Greensboro, to which I am very grateful.
2. Foster (1953) remarks on the absence of this or a similar syndrome in either historic or contemporary Spanish life.
3. In some countries, according to Adams (1957), this syndrome has a "spotty" distribution from town to town, a discovery which affords an exciting opportunity to pursue controlled comparative studies of the functional relationship between *susto* and other aspects of social life.
4. It is noteworthy that among one of Peru's highland groups, the Aymara of Chuquito, a disease entity identified as *kat'a,* which Tschopik equates with *susto,* manifests itself in quite a different set of symptoms, although etiologically it is the equivalent of *susto* as described by Sal y Rosas, Gillin, and others (Tschopik 1951: 202, 211–212, 282–283). Furthermore, the Aymara rites for curing *kat'a* share all essential features with the Quechua rites described by Sal y Rosas (1958).
5. The importance of sentient beings in instances of Indian illness and their absence in cases of non-Indians are presumably a function of the utilization of sprites and other sentient beings in socialization procedures in Indian and non-Indian cultures. Fear of "bogy men" is, to be sure, used among both groups, but Indians to a far greater extent than Ladinos invoke the guardian spirits of woods, animals, caves, and streams (see Whiting and Child 1953).
6. For a curing rite remarkably similar in detail see Mak (1959:128–129).
7. A notable exception is found in the Cakchiquel town of Magdalena Milpas Altas, where *susto* is interpreted as associated with acculturation stresses (see Adams 1951: 26–27). Furthermore, in Magdalena, as in many other localities in Middle America, the kidnapper of Indian souls is depicted as a Ladino (Adams and Rubel 1964). This does not, however, require an assumption that Indian-Ladino relations are the context in which soul loss actually occurs, for available case histories lead us away from such an assumption.
8. This represents an adaptation of a model prepared by the Department of Epidemiology, School of Public Health, University of North Carolina, to the members of which I owe my training in epidemiology.

REFERENCES

Adams, R. N. 1952. An Analysis of Medical Beliefs and Practices in a Guatemalan Indian Town. Guatemala.

———. 1957. Cultural Surveys of Panama-Nicaragua-Guatemala-El Salvador Honduras. Washington.

Adams, R. N., and A. J. Rubel. Sickness and Social Relations. Handbook of Middle-American Indians (in press).

Blum, R. H. 1962. Case Identification in Psychiatric Epidemiology: Methods and Problems. Milbank Memorial Fund Quarterly 40: 253–289.

Carrasco, P. 1960. Pagan Rituals and Beliefs Among the Chontal Indians of Oaxaca. Anthropological Records 20: 87–117.

Cassel, J., R. Patrick, and D. Jenkins. 1960. Epidemiological Analysis of Health Implications of Culture Change: A Conceptual Model. Annals of the New York Academy of Sciences 84: 938–949.

Caudill, W. 1958. Effects of Social and Cultural Systems in Reactions to Stress. Memorandum to the Committee on Preventive Medicine and Social Science Research, Pamphlet, 14.

Clark, M. 1959. Health in the Mexican-American Culture. Berkeley.

Diaz de Solas, M. 1957. Personal Communication.

Fleck, A. C., and F. A. J. Ianni. 1958. Epidemiology and Anthropology: Some Suggested Affinities in Theory and Method. Human Organization 16: 38–41.

Foster, G. M. 1951. Some Wider Implications of Soul-Loss Illness Among the Sierra Pepoluca Homenaje a Don, Alfonso Caso, pp. 167–174.

———. 1953. Relationships Between Spanish and Spanish-American Folk Medicine. Journal of American Folklore 66: 201–247.

Frake, C. 1961. The Diagnosis of Disease Among the Subanun of Mindanao. American Anthropologist 63: 113–132.

Gillin, J. 1945. Moche: A Peruvian Coastal Community. Washington.

———. 1948. Magical Fright. Psychiatry 11: 387–400.

Guiteras-Holmes, C. 1961. Perils of the Soul. New York.

Honigmann, J. J. 1959. The World of Man. New York.

Leighton, A. 1961. Remarks. Milbank Memorial Fund Quarterly 39:486.

Mak, C. 1959. Mixtec Medical Beliefs and Practices. America Indigena 19: 125–151.

Maxcy, K. A., ed. 1941. Papers of Wade Hampton Frost, M.D. New York.

Metzger, D., and G. Williams. 1963. Tenejapa Medicine I: The Curer. Southwestern Journal of Anthropology 19: 216–234.

Parker, S. 1960. The Wiitiko Psychosis in the Context of Ojibwa Personality and Culture. American Anthropologist 62: 603–623.

Parsons, T., and R. Fox. 1952. Illness, Therapy, and the Modern Urban American Family. Journal of Social Issues 8: 31–44.

Rubel, A. J. 1960. Concepts of Disease in Mexican-American Culture. American Anthropologist 62: 795–815.

Sal y Rosas, F. 1958. El mito del Jani o Susto de la medicina indigena del Peru. Revista de la Sanidad de Policia 18: 167–210. Lima.

Saunders, L. 1954. Cultural Differences and Medical Care. New York.

Teicher, M. I. 1960. Windigo Psychosis. Seattle.

Tschopik, H. 1951. The Aymara of Chucuito, Peru: Magic. Anthropological Papers of the American Museum of Natural History 44: 133–308.

Weinstein, E. A. 1962. Cultural Aspects of Delusion. New York.

Weitlaner, R. J. 1961. La ceremonia Ilamada "Levantar la sombra." Typescript.

Whiting, J. W. M., and I. L. Child. 1953. Child Training and Personality. New Haven.

 27

Seeking to Escape the Suffering of Existence: Internet Suicide in Japan

Chikako Ozawa-de Silva

Many medical anthropologists focus their research on mental health and illness as seen from a cross-cultural perspective. Mental health is a very serious global health issue; mental illness—especially depression—causes much disability and suffering both in economically disadvantaged communities and in wealthy, technologically advanced societies. The influence of culture in the typology and experience of mental illness was explored in the selection by Arthur Kleinman (no. 25). The selection by Arthur Rubel (no. 26) illustrated cultural variations in the interpretation and treatment of affective disorders. In general, mental illnesses are divided into two types: psychotic ailments (like schizophrenia) and affective disorders, also known as mood disorders (like depression and anxiety). Suicide is most often understood as an extreme outcome of depression. Understanding suicide and life-threatening behaviors has been a concern of social scientists since the pioneering statistical work on this topic by Émile Durkheim in 1897.

This selection represents a different approach to understanding changing patterns of suicide in Japan. It is a humanistic approach that emphasizes cultural history, patterns of cultural change, and the lived experience of people contemplating suicide. As the author explains, Japanese culture has a particular history in relation to suicide. The recent increase in group suicide among young people in Japan—one of the wealthiest and healthiest societies in the world—is shocking. But increased wealth and technological sophistication do not necessarily bring more social integration. Emotional disorders like depression are both a cause and an effect of social isolation. In this case, individuals use the new Internet technology to find others with whom they can communicate about their experiences of loneliness and the "suffering of existence." One might think that increased social interaction through the Internet might be helpful or therapeutic, but in this case, it is not so.

As you read this selection, consider these questions:

- **Much of the "suffering of existence" described in this selection is experienced by teenagers and young adults. Is this part of the life cycle particularly stressful? Are these stresses to be found in all cultures?**
- **Does the Internet encourage social interaction or discourage it? What is the effect of the Internet on mental health?**
- **What do you think about using websites as an information source for research?**
- **Why is there the phenomenon of suicide pacts?**

Context: Chikako Ozawa-de Silva teaches medical anthropology and the anthropology of religion at Emory University. Her primary research focus has been the Japanese meditative-psychotherapeutic practice of Naikan. She received her PhD from Oxford University in 2001 and was a postdoctoral research fellow at Harvard's Department of Social Medicine and at the University of Chicago. Her work is informed by phenomenological approaches to issues of health and illness—approaches that have been major contributions of medical anthropological scholars at Harvard and Chicago. Ozawa-de Silva's work contributes to medical anthropology by bringing together Western and Asian (particularly Japanese and Tibetan) perspectives on the mind-body, religion, medicine, therapy, health, and illness.

Source: Original contribution based on "Too Lonely to Die Alone: Internet Suicide Pacts and Existential Suffering in Japan." *Culture, Medicine and Psychiatry*, December 2008.

INTRODUCTION

Japan is internationally known for the longevity of its citizens. Not only has it been credited with having the world's longest average lifespan, but Japan also has the most individuals over the age of 100: some 36,000 centegenarians, the vast majority of whom are women. At the same time, however, Japan also has the less favorable reputation of being a "suicide nation." This is partially due to highly ritualistic forms of suicide such as *hara-kiri* and the infamous *kamikaze* pilots. Moreover, in 1998 suicide rates shot up dramatically, and they have not returned to their previous levels since then. Many scholars and public officials have suggested a correlation between the higher rates of suicide and Japan's long-term economic recession. What is notable, however, is the increase of suicide among young Japanese, and the emergence of new forms of suicide, such as Internet suicide pacts.

Consider the following transcript, taken from the chat area of one of thousands of Japanese "suicide websites," that is, websites for people to discuss the issue of suicide:

> **Mina:** I decided to die today. I'm sorry I caused trouble.
> **NATO Dan:** Well, I won't stop you, as I don't think you are serious about it. If you do want to die, then please die quietly without causing trouble for other people. Jumping in front of a train is out of the question. I hear that a body that has died from freezing to death or from carbon monoxide still looks pretty. Well, I have to say that it's too late to regret it after you're dead. Good night. So, does my reaction satisfy you?
> **NATO Dan:** The way you are, you're going to be driven into a corner even in the afterlife, too.
> **Mina:** Mizuho-san, have you already died? Would you like to die together? After I've died, I am going to kill myself in the afterlife also.
> **Mina:** I will certainly not cause anyone any trouble. I ran away from home when I was at elementary school. I don't think there's anyone who remembers me. I'll hide in the woods and take poison, and die by falling into a hole made in the past.
> **Kantaro:** Wait, Mina. Don't die!
> [. . .]
> **Mika:** I really want to commit suicide. I really want to commit suicide because everybody bullies me and I don't want to go to school. God, I want to die. Aaah! I want to die!!!
> **Ruru:** It seems no one's around right now . . .
> **Ruru:** Mika-san, nice to meet you.
> **Ruru:** Mika-san, are you also bullied? GGGGGGGGGGGGGG.
> **Mika:** Would you like to go to Mt. Fuji's sea of trees? I was about to go. My regards. I am Mika. Let's be friends, shall we?
> **Ruru:** Me, too. I tried to kill myself many times and strangled my own neck. Recently my wrists . . . But I cannot die.
> **Mika:** When would you like to do it?
> **Ruru:** Personally, I prefer the winter break. The forest will be cold. If we wander around, I think we would die from hunger or the cold . . . Otherwise, shall we hang ourselves?
> **Mika:** Ruru-san, thank you! When shall we do it? I am always free! Please give me a call at home. (086) 922 4831. Other people, please don't give me nuisance calls! Ruru-san, only you can call me. Are we agreed?
> **Mika:** Ahhh . . .
> **Mika:** Death.
> **Ruru:** Got it. I will give you a call tonight. I have to go now as my class is about to end. I wonder when I can come again . . .
> **Marcy [Moderator]:** By any means, it's not that I want to prevent you from committing suicide. But I would want you two to understand the responsibility of posting these comments seriously, as it is disgusting. Mika asked for a suicide pal by posting her phone number. In general, such actions will give a sense of companionship and the courage to die to people who want to die, but who are half-heartedly suicidal, and who lack the courage to die by themselves. This is a state of mind arising out of a human "group mentality." Suicidal individuals tend to fall for such a technique, as they tend to have few friends. They can easily come to "depend" on "relationships of mutual trust." Ruru, please analyze your own head before calling. Mika, be aware that you might end up dragging along someone who might not commit suicide on her own. Anyway, I won't request that this correspondence be deleted, as these two seem to have already written down the contact information . . . Well, as it is your life, it is your freedom to put an end to it, but . . . please don't ask for company! (Za Keijiban 2003)

Only the contact information has been changed in these remarkable exchanges. Such suicide websites are part of a growing problem in Japan that has been classified as a new type of suicide, called Internet suicide pacts, where individuals, primarily young individuals, arrange to meet to commit group suicide. It is not known whether any of the individuals in the above dialogues ended up committing suicide, but Internet suicide pacts have led to serious concern about the presence of such Internet sites and questions about the nature of group suicides and suicide pacts in Japan.

Suicide has long been an important topic of study in various fields including anthropology. Its relevance for study is due not only to it being a locus for central issues such as the value of life, the meaning of death, suffering, and violence, but also because it is a topic that clearly reveals the necessity for explanatory models that mediate social and individual factors. One could broadly categorize the main approaches to suicide as falling into these two extremes: on the one hand, social, economic, and cultural analyses that emphasize social determinism, and on the other hand, analyses of individual factors such as psychology and psychopathology. Whereas discourse on suicide in the U.S. focuses predominantly on individual pathology and factors such as depression, discourse in Japan has focused on social pathology, economic factors, a "culture of suicide," and cultural aesthetics.

The recent rise of suicide in Japan, and of new forms of suicide, such as Internet suicide pacts, has revealed the inadequacy of either of these two approaches when taken independently. Durkheim, in his seminal work on suicide (1966), classified suicide into four different categories: (1) egoistic suicide, (2) altruistic suicide, (3) anomic suicide, and (4) fatalistic suicide, although he did not fully develop the concept of fatalistic suicide. Internet suicide pacts, as a form of group suicide, might on the surface appear to fall into his second category of suicide, altruistic suicide. However, altruistic suicide is characterized by an individual's self-sacrifice for a collective cause, as well as a sense of overintegration. The young Japanese who contemplate or engage in Internet suicide pacts seem to suffer from a lack of integration, however, yet they seek others to die with, and their deaths hardly appear to be a form of self-sacrifice for a larger cause. Internet suicide pacts, in particular, provide instances where the inseparability of agency and social forces becomes particularly evident. Given the statements of those who commit such suicides, such as "I am too lonely to die alone" and "It could have been anyone to die with," what is the meaning of an individual "choice" or "decision" to die, when this occurs in the context of an intersubjective decision by a group of strangers to die together, each of whom is too afraid or too lonely to die alone? In contrast to the popular Japanese discourse that suicide is one way that individuals can assert their autonomy in a collectivist Japanese society, suicide pacts seem to involve individuals giving up, or subordinating, their autonomy to a collective decision, a group choice.

DEATH IN A "SUICIDE NATION"

Japan has been known as a "suicide nation" (Takahashi 2001:26; Ueno 2005; Pinguet 1993:14) due to the various forms of suicide that have gained prominence in public attention, as well as the fact that suicide has been seen, in certain cases, as a moral action and as a last place to practice one's "free will" in a generally conformist society (Doi 2001). Until recently, suicide prevention was not a popularly acknowledged concept, but the recent sharp rise in suicide rates and new types of suicide, such as Internet suicide pacts, have attracted international attention and disturbed Japanese society to the extent that suicide prevention is now being taken more seriously. Until a decade ago, Japan's suicide rate stayed around 18 to 19 suicides per 100,000 people, roughly in the area of suicide rates for France and Germany (Takahashi 2001:25–26), but it surged suddenly in 1998 and has been elevated ever since. Since 1998, Japan has had the second-highest suicide rate among the G-8 nations (26.0 in 1998, 24.2 in 2005) after Russia (34.3 in 2004), significantly higher than France (17.8 in 2002), Germany (13.0 in 2004), Canada (11.6 in 2002), the U.S. (11.0 in 2002), Italy (7.1 in 2002), and the U.K. (6.9 in 2002) (Jisatsutaikougaiyou 2006:2).*

Suicide is also the leading cause of death in Japan among people under the age of 30. The year 2003 saw Japan's highest number of suicides historically, at 34,427, or 27 suicides per 100,000 members of the population, followed by 32,325 in 2004 (Keisatsu Chou 2004:4). These figures are all the more startling when one considers that there are 100 to 200 times as many unsuccessful suicide attempts as there are actual suicides (Takahashi 1999:24). When looking into suicide rates by gender, the suicide rate for men in 2005 was 36.1, compared with 12.9 for women, supporting a general tendency showing that men have higher suicide rates than women. The number of suicides among middle-aged men between 40 and 54 was five times higher than that among women in the same age category, a figure some have pointed at as evidence of the link between suicide and the recent economic recession and rise in unemployment (Desapriya and Iwase 2003:284). In the past, women's suicide rates were prominently high in the age group of women 80 and above, but since the sudden rise in suicide rates, the age curve, which used to increase steadily with age, has looked more even due to the rise of suicide among the youth and adults (such as age groups 15–19 and 40–44) and a decrease in the suicide rates of age groups 60 and above. Thus, for women, younger individuals are the main contributors to the rise of suicide. For men, the basic curve of suicide rates among different age groups before and after 1998 has not shown a significant change, although again, suicide rates among the elderly (75 and above) show a decrease in the last decade, despite a rise in overall suicides.

* The fact that the data from this report compare suicide statistics from different years is likely due to variances in the collection of suicide data in different countries, which means that the most recent official suicide rate for a given country may be a few years earlier or later than that for another country:

Most disturbing has been the rise of suicide rates among young Japanese. When comparing the sudden rise of suicides in 1998 against the previous year, women under the age of 19 show the most significant rise, with an almost 70% increase in suicides, followed by a 50% increase among men under 19 (Police Office Reports in Takahashi 2001:14). Both men and women between 20 and 29 show the next highest increases, and the third highest are those between 30 and 39. The age group of individuals over 80 years of age has not shown a significant increase in the number of suicides, and in some cases has gone down.

While Japanese cultural attitudes toward suicide in general have been tolerant, the public and mass media have not been inclined to view Internet suicide pacts in this way. Instead, they are seen as irresponsible, thoughtless acts, and those who engage in them are considered copy-cats or too weak-willed to die alone. It has also been said that such individuals are incapable of understanding life and its depth and weight, seeing it instead as something light and virtual, and therefore they view death in the same virtual way (Ohsawa 1996, 2005:102; Saito 2003; Usui 2002); computer games, television, films, and so on have been invoked and blamed for this (Machizawa 2003:113–114; Usui 2002). Thus, such individuals are merely irresponsible for choosing to die when they have no good reason to do so, and when they are not undergoing any serious kind of suffering. But how accurate and insightful is this popular view?

In the following sections I will examine the recent rise in suicide in Japan and the most common public explanations given for this, and then examine the specific case of Internet suicide pacts with a representative selection of ethnographic findings from my study of Japanese suicide-related websites. These findings suggest that, far from being conducted by individuals who are not undergoing any serious kind of suffering, Internet suicides are characterized by severe existential suffering, a loss of the "worth of living" *(ikigai)* or its absence in the case of many Japanese adolescents and young adults, and a profound loneliness and lack of connection with others.

SUICIDE OR SOCIAL MURDER? THE RHETORIC OF SUICIDE IN JAPAN

Although attempts have been made to understand suicide from sociocultural perspectives, suicide in the West has been predominantly understood through the lens of individual pathology, and many statistics indicate that more than 90% of individuals who attempt suicide suffer from psychiatric disorders such as depression or psychosis (Desjarlais 1995:74). In Japan, however, one of the dominant features in the rhetoric of suicide has been giving a positive cultural valence to certain forms of suicide (Pinguet 1993; Takahashi 1997, 1999, 2001; Traphagan 2004:319). In the cases of Mishima Yukio and Eto Jun, for example, two famous writers who took their own lives, the public reaction and mass media reports included praises of their heroism. Overall, Japanese cultural perceptions of suicide are more tolerant than those in the U.S., and in numerous cases suicides are viewed morally as a sign of maturity and responsibility.

When suicide in Japan is not aestheticized and is in fact seen as a pathology, it is typically as a "social pathology." Japan's economic downturn has been frequently cited as contributing to this social pathology, and to rising rates of depression and suicide. There has been a strong tendency in Japanese thought on suicide to blame society itself and to look outside the actual individuals involved for the cause of suicide (see, for example, Ueno 2005). However, while it is certainly necessary and helpful to broaden the view beyond the individual to include social, cultural, and economic dimensions, completely removing the individual can have negative repercussions if it overemphasizes social determining factors. Margaret Lock (1986), a medical anthropologist who works on Japan, has noted that socially oriented medical discourse in Japan can actually overdetermine the meaning of people's distress.

The Japanese government is highly aware of the recent steep rise in annual rates of suicide in Japan, but discussion around this issue has focused blame on the current social and particularly economic situation of Japan. The vast majority of news and journal articles discussing the issue attribute the rise in suicide to the economic recession, which they claim caused financial and psychological insecurity among middle-aged Japanese men in a society that had previously enjoyed extremely low levels of unemployment. However, suicide is the leading cause of death not among middle aged Japanese men, but among the youth. Nor does this majority view explain the suddenness of the rise in suicide rates over a very short period of time, or why this rise does not appear to correspond with any sudden change in Japan's economic situation. In 1998, the number of suicides suddenly shot up by 34.8% over the previous year. When looking just at adolescents, the increase was 53.5% over the previous year (from 469 deaths in 1997 to 720 deaths in 1998).

Thus, such an approach is insufficient, and it fails to take into account the more nuanced social dimensions of expectations, aspirations, and ideas about what Japanese call the "worth of living" *(ikigai),* that is, one's motivation in life. Although economic deprivation and poor physical conditions certainly contribute to mental distress, it is clear that material affluence, without attention to social relations, is no guarantee of mental well-being and happiness (Keyes 1998, 2002; Ryff et al. 2003). Moreover, as Kitanaka (2006) has shown, the rise of depression in Japan in the 1990s was not merely a result of economic hardship, but is connected to a complex range of factors including the campaigns of pharmaceutical companies and psychiatrists to make the concept of mild depression more widespread. The notion of mental illness had long been stigmatized in Japan (Ohnuki-Tierney 1984; Ozawa 1996; Ozawa-de Silva 2006, 2007; Roland 1988), and depression was not an exception. However, corresponding with the recent rise of depression has been the success of the pharmaceutical industry in publicizing depression as a *kokoro no kaze* (cold of the heart) (Schulz 2004; Kitanaka 2006:100), lessening the social stigma associated with depression and making it normal, something ordinary individuals could get, like a cold or the flu.

Another popular contention by scholars and the mass media in Japan has been that the growth of Internet access and use is partially to be blamed for the rise of suicide. Suicide Internet websites are one widely cited aspect of this. Although the exact relationship between the rise of the Internet and suicide remains unclear, Internet access does seem to have contributed to a rise in *hikikomori* (withdrawal syndrome), which refers to the more than one million Japanese who have stopped going to school or work for more than six months (but in many cases for several years, even over ten years), and who instead remain at home, never leaving their house, and sometimes never even leaving their own room (Borovoy 2006; Machizawa 2003:21; Saito 1998). There is a clear resemblance between *hikikoromi* and Internet suicide pacts, as their main communication tool is the Internet, and these individuals have reduced social interaction and social support. However, neither Internet suicide pacts nor *hikikomori* are easily explained by citing the economic recession as a primary reason.

Lastly, when it comes to adolescents, both the mass media and researchers have tended to attribute suicide to two main causes: *ijime* or "bullying" and the competitive school examination system called *jyuken jigoku* or "examination hell." They point out that many of the notes left by adolescent suicides say things like "I am a failure, because I did not make it into such-and-such university," or "I was afraid that I would fail the examination, and I lost hope in life," or "I have been bullied by such-and-such a person. They did this and that to me and therefore, I am going to die." These letters sometimes seem to indicate that the act of suicide itself is revenge against the bullies by listing the names of the students who bullied them. Interestingly, however, this aspect of suicide as revenge seems to be missing from most cases of Internet suicide pacts. It is clear therefore that one cannot simplify all cases of suicide into one or two reasons such as "examination hell" and "peer abuse," as important as these factors may be in many incidents of suicide. To attain a more nuanced understanding of this phenomenon, it is important to examine broader social and cultural factors that have been undergoing significant transformation in recent times in Japan.

SHINJYU AND INTERNET SUICIDE PACTS

Within the study of suicide, the term "suicide pact" is used to refer to an arrangement between two or more individuals to die together or at close to the same time. Unlike mass suicides, where a large group of people may choose to die together for religious, ideological, or military reasons, suicide pacts are typically made between individuals with a close personal relationship, such as close friends or lovers, and the reasons are diverse and usually highly personal in nature. The term in Japanese for these types of suicide pacts is *shinjyu,* for which there is no exact translation in English, and which has particular historical and cultural connotations.

It is difficult to say when Internet suicide pacts started taking place, as early cases were first treated as ordinary *shinjyu* (suicide pacts), before the category of Internet suicide pact was established *(Intānetto shūdan jisatsu,* literally "Internet group suicides"). However, Ueno (2005) notes that the first mention of Internet suicide pacts in *Asahi Shinbun,* a major Japanese newspaper, dates to October 2000, which noted at the time that there were 40,000 Japanese websites on suicide, 150 of which were devoted to "how to commit suicide." The first widely popularized case of an Internet suicide pact took place in February 2003, when a teenage girl found one man and two women dead in an apartment room, lying down side by side like the Japanese character for "river." There were numerous charcoal briquettes in a *shichirin* stove oven, and all the windows were sealed up with scotch tape. It later turned out that the man had set up his apartment to commit suicide, and had invited others to join him over the Internet; the two other women and the girl who later found them had agreed to do so.

Since this incident, a chain of suicide pacts have been recorded involving this method, which has become the most popular way of committing group suicide. In October 2004, seven young men and women were found dead in a car in the parking lot on a mountain in Saitama Prefecture. There were four *shichirin* in the car and all the windows had been sealed up with scotch tape. On the same day, another car was found nearby, parked outside a temple in Yokosuka, with the dead bodies of two women, aged 21 and 27, who had committed suicide by the same method of carbon monoxide poisoning, and who had possibly been connected with the other seven victims, making it a total of nine individuals who died due to an Internet suicide pact that day (*New York Times,* October 13, 2004). This was the largest number of individuals who had died through an Internet suicide pact until nine individuals died together in 2006 (Hi-ho Kai-in Support 2007).

At the end of 2006, entering the word "suicide" in the Japanese-language site of the popular search engine Google yielded 3,140,000 websites, and the phrase "suicide methods" *(jisatu no houhou)* returned 22,600 results. The suicide-related website Ghetto (http://www.cotodama.org/) reports having had 976,580 hits (visits to the site) since it was opened, and 821 hits in one day (as of December 18, 2006). Another website, *Jisatsu Saito Jisatsu Shigansha no Ikoi no ba,* which literally means "Suicide Site: A Relaxing Place for Suicidal People" (http://izayoi2.ddo jp/top/) reports having had over 3 million hits since it opened and as many as 1,121 hits on a single day as of December 18, 2006.

Since September 2003, I have been visiting over forty of these Japanese suicide websites in an attempt to understand better the nature of Internet suicides and the role these websites play in them. Although participant observation is a more standard model for ethnography in cultural anthropology, I found that closely monitoring the statements of numerous suicidal individuals on over forty Internet suicide sites provided a means for gaining insight into their suffering and their motivations for seeking out communication with others. Among the over 40,000 sites on suicide, I narrowed down the list of those to study by searching the Internet for phrases such as *jisatsu saito* (suicide sites), *shūdan jisatsu* (group suicide), or *jisatsu kurabu* (suicide club) in order to identify suicide websites that were organized and run by a regular moderator, with features such as a BBS and chat rooms. The regulation of suicide websites increased over the time I studied them; thus, by 2006 most suicide sites stated that any message containing information such as a telephone number, address, time/place to organize the suicide, and so on would be immediately deleted by the moderator. This was not the case in 2003.

Most suicide sites present themselves as functioning for the purpose of suicide prevention, that is, as spaces where suicidal individuals can openly share and discuss their troubles and suffering. The sites have many regular visitors, and they are often young (many identify as in their twenties or as junior and high school students, 14–18 years old). In some cases the moderator is completely invisible, but in others the moderator has a visible role and regularly responds to visitors' comments like a counselor.

A typical example is the suicide website called Ghetto, which is composed of two chat rooms (one open to all visitors and one restricted to members), several discussion forums with titles such as "Grassland for Suicidal Individuals," and a links section called "Suicide Station." The moderator states: "This site's main purpose is to discuss suicide and mental illness. We welcome those who may not particularly want to discuss only sensitive issues such as suicide, but who would like to be connected with others who may have similar problems. For those who are facing a serious situation but still want to live, we recommend that you call the national hotline *(inochi no denwa)*" (Ghetto 2006). The moderator further explains how certain activities are prohibited on the site, including "writing in private information such as addresses and telephone numbers," "spurring others on to actually commit suicide or other illegal acts," and "suicide announcements with precise information such as place, date and time" (Ghetto 2006).

During my study, I was struck by certain recurring themes, comments, and expressions. One of the most frequently expressed concerns on suicide sites is an absence of meaning. Some posts reflect a general existential concern, such as "Why was I born? Who am I anyway? Where am I going to go? I think there is no meaning to live as I do not even know that" (Ikizurasa kei no foramu, November 22, 2006). Others cite specific incidents that led to a sense of life having no meaning: "I turned 21 this year. There is something I have been thinking about for a long time. Why was I born in this world? When I was 10 years old, I was scolded badly by my parents. Since then I started thinking that there is no meaning for me to live and I've attempted suicide many times" (Ikizurasa kei no foramu, September 16, 2006). This comment hints at resentment, and hatred is indeed an emotion that surfaces in some of the posts in connection with an absence of meaning. One visitor wrote, "Why was I born? Why am I living? . . . I can hardly sleep nowadays as I hate everything" (Jisatsusha no Sougen, December 22, 2006). Several express that even though nothing is wrong with their life in terms of external conditions, such as family life, finance, and so on, they experience despair as a result of finding no meaning in life.

Conjoined with this absence of meaning is a sense of loneliness. Almost all the posts I came across on suicide websites made reference to how lonely the site visitors were. One individual wrote:

> My dependency got worse as I started to participate in chat rooms. I feel anxious when I am alone. I cannot leave the computer even for a second. I feel anxious that I am not needed by anyone. Just being told that I am necessary would be enough—I would have a peace of mind. I would do anything asked of me so as not to be disliked . . . I am lonely. I cannot live alone. I want to be strong . . . To be honest, I am becoming unsure of what I am living for . . . As I cannot believe in true love, I seek even just the words . . . I want to be loved and needed. (Nageki Keijiban, October 12, 2006)

Loneliness is often linked with an inability to interact socially. One comment notes, "I cannot stand loneliness! But I cannot trust people. I cannot trust anything except myself and my pet" (Nageki Keijiban, October 13, 2006). Loneliness is also experienced despite the physical presence of other people, as in the post of one student who wrote, "I am so lonely! Even at school, I am so lonely and I want to die" (Ikizurasa kei no foramu, December 13, 2006).

What is notable is how many of the posts do not give an explicit reason for this feeling of loneliness. The phrase *nanto naku,* meaning somehow or for some reason, occurs frequently, as in the following post: "For some reason, I am lonely . . . all alone . . . I wish I had not been born . . . Life is long . . . I will serve my life! Please come and fetch it [my life] if there is anyone who wants it" (Ikizurasa kei no foramu, November 1, 2006). Another wrote, "For some reason, I am living. For some reason, I want to die . . . but I am afraid of pain and I am also afraid of meeting Yama [the Lord of Death in Buddhism] in hell, and it does not matter much about living. I do not know what I want to do . . . I just want to die. I wonder why" (Jisatsusha no Sougen, December 24, 2006).

There are also comments in posts that explicitly call out for a change that will alleviate the loneliness being experienced, such as "I want to be alone, but I wish someone were there by me" (Ikizurasa kei no foramu, October 28, 2006), and "I do not want to be alone. Even though I am a failure, I still want someone to love me" (Kokoro no Hanazono, November 19, 2006). Some, however, express a loneliness that does not seem like it would be eliminated by merely meeting someone. One individual wrote simply, "I do not have any place" (Ikizurasa kei no foramu, December 21, 2006), and a schoolgirl commented, "I feel lonely whenever I am by myself . . . I feel like I would like to die, but then I am too afraid to commit suicide" (Kokoro no Hanazono, November 16, 2006).

Loneliness and an absence of meaning in life seem to be closely connected in the comments of these individuals, and both are given as reasons for suicide. There is often a sense of inner conflict: on the one hand, they experience intense loneliness when by themselves, but on the other hand, they feel mistrustful of others and do not like to be in social settings. In certain cases, these feelings seem to combine in the wish to die with others—in other words, to escape the pain of loneliness and absence of meaning in this life, but at the same time, to do so in connection with another person or persons, because to die alone would be too painful.

Thus, the following comments are common: "Are you suicidal and would you like to die with me? I don't have the guts to die alone. I'm asking for people who would like to die with me" (Omae ha mou shindeiru, December 24, 2005), and "Is there anyone who wants to die but who can't die alone? Please, let's die together" (Ikizurasa kei no foramu, November 7, 2006). The tone of suggestions to commit suicide together is often shockingly casual. One person wrote, in response to another post: "Sleeping pills won't kill you, as Kumagorou says. Is there anyone who would like to die using another method?" (Ikizurasa kei no foramu, November 6, 2006). Another wrote, "Would you die together? By the way, I live in Gunma prefecture" (Ikizurasa kei no foramu, November 4, 2006). Often, the tone is pleading or supplicatory: "I have been wanting to die and have been thinking about suicide methods. Please let me die with you" (Ikizurasa kei no foramu, Sepetember 15, 2006); "If it is all right with you, would you like to die with me?" (Ikizurasa kei no foramu, Sepetember 14, 2006); "I no longer wish to suffer. But I am too afraid to die alone. Is there anyone who wishes to die with me?" (Ikizurasa kei no foramu, August 14, 2006).

There are many posts that do not explicitly connect a wish to die with an absence of meaning. However, these posts do often express a certain uncertainty with regard to what to do in life, which seems to be a milder awareness of an absence of meaning. Such individuals seem to be on the borderline, as they do not wish to experience any pain that might be involved in dying, yet they also express the sentiment that neither living nor dying would make much difference to them. Committing suicide often has an active and intentional connotation, but these individuals express a great deal of passivity. They seek a painless death, and dying with others seems to be one way of eliminating some of the pain of death. One such individual wrote, "I'm so tired. What's the point of living any longer? But I don't want to die in pain. I want to vanish in a second" (Ikizurasa kei no foramu, October 15, 2006).

The last common theme that I found among the posts and discussions was a sense that one's social interactions were "fake," a sentiment connected with the idea of not being able to trust others. One person wrote, "Recently I'm not sure why I'm alive. I go to school, do some part-time job, and it's a nothing special, everyday life. But I can't make friends, perhaps because I don't trust people. I always suppress myself and show a fake self . . . The only thing I think about is life and death. I really wonder why I'm living" (Jisatsusha no Sougen, December 16, 2006). And another wrote, "I want to be normal. I'm pretending to be normal. If people find out that I'm not normal, then they will all leave me. I will then be all alone" (Kokoro no Hanazono, November 19, 2006). This sense of the pain of not being accepted for who one is comes through in statements made by those who have emerged from such a state as well, such as in this last comment: "By the way, my environment has changed and I am now surrounded by people who accept me so I stopped thinking about death at all. At one time I really wanted to die" (Ikizurasa kei no foramu, October 17, 2006).

BECOMING AN ADULT IN JAPAN AND THE "WORTH OF LIVING" *(IKIGAI)*

The rise of group suicide among strangers, exemplified by Internet suicide pacts, raises challenging questions about the nature and causes of suicide in Japan. In commenting on the death of the nine young Japanese in October 2004, who had arranged a group suicide over the Internet and died in their cars through carbon monoxide poisoning, caused by charcoal-burning stoves, one Japanese man wrote on a BBC News website:

> In 70s we were not rich but we had dreams. If we studied and worked hard, we could buy TV sets, cars and so on. We've never imagined that our companies go bankrupt or we get fired for a recession. We are pessimistic and vulnerable. Once we lost a life model, we have a difficulty finding new one [sic]. Now adults in Japan are struggling to find new dreams or purposes to live. We have to change or we can't show a brighter future where young people will want to live. (BBC News 2005)

Such comments point to both Japan's economic situation and the loss of a clear *ikigai* (literally "worth of living"), or reason to live, among both older and younger generations. As Traphagan notes, "For many Japanese, younger and older generations are perceived as having completely different core values, which leads to considerable stress between those generations" (Traphagan 2004:316,2003). In addition to these factors, one is naturally left to question the state of mind such individuals are in when contemplating and committing *shinjyu,* or suicide pacts, with relative strangers. One woman who died with a man she had just met over the Internet stated in her will: "It's sad to die alone. It could have been anyone" (Sasaki 2007).

While we commonly understand how social conditions can result in social suffering, anthropology has tended to focus on particular social conditions of deprivation, such as poverty, oppression, prejudice, and so on. This is not the case for the social suffering in Japan that we are investigating here. Although Japan did suffer from a long-term economic recession, the society has nevertheless succeeded in modernization and development in the post–World War II period, becoming a major capitalist power with tremendous success in terms of education, standard of living, and medical care. It is an affluent society in terms of material well-being, and it remains so despite the recent economic recession that has commonly been blamed for the recent rise in suicide rates and depression. Despite all this, the social and cultural environment that such individuals are born into is one within which they feel the absence of a clear *ikigai,* conjoined with a loss of traditional family values, changes in family structure, and a perceived failure to meet the aesthetic expectations of society. These and other complex factors seem to be resulting in a profound sense of loneliness and alienation.

A strong sense of isolation, loneliness, and alienation alone might not be so distinctive or unique, but the choice to die with others, especially strangers, is less usual. It is not hard to see such suicide pacts as a sad cry for individuals who are seeking reconciliation, connectedness, and unity with others and perhaps the world. In Japanese society, dying alone is stigmatized, and it is a cultural imperative for family members to be present when a person dies. Long writes, "The potential for loneliness of the dying seems to be a particular concern, expressed not only in words (for example, *kodoku na shi,* 'lonely death'), but also in the near obsession with *shini me ni au* (being there at the moment of death)" (2001:273). In most cases of individual suicide, one might not actively wish for others to die alongside oneself. In cases of group suicide, however, this wish to avoid a "lonely death" seems to obtain. Even the choice of the *shichirin* stove oven itself is significant, for it is a nostalgic symbol of comfort, togetherness, and communal action, like gathering around for a barbeque. This raises the question of whether modern Japanese are paying the price of pursuing "individualism" by a sense of loneliness and alienation. If suicide is not being used as a way to punish others, or make a dramatic statement, and if it is not arising as a form of sacrifice or corporate atonement, would it be possible to think that these suicides are something entirely different: an attempt to bring about healing from a state of existential loneliness?

The broader social and cultural situation in Japan has been affected by rapid structural and ideological changes following World War II, such as the decline of traditional extended family structures, changes in traditional values such as placing the family above the individual's needs, suspicion of the idea of religion, and changes in company structure such as the loss of lifelong job security. Many contemporary Japanese individuals are torn between adopting Western individualistic values and maintaining traditional values, as in the case of wondering whether they should put their own or others' happiness first. Traditionally *ikigai* would have been closely associated with social roles, such as one's job for men or caring for the family and one's in-laws for women. *Ikigai* has now become more of an open question for many Japanese, who must struggle to find a meaning for their existence without the traditional social roles to fall back upon.

Yamamoto-Mitani and Wallhagen's study among Japanese women caring for their elderly in-laws reveals a range of responses, from an acceptance of traditional social roles and finding one's *ikigai* in them ("Caregiving and ikigai, after all, for me, . . . they are inseparable") (2002:407), to a more ambivalent intermediate position ("I have to believe that taking care of Mother is my *ikigai.* I have to believe that, otherwise I feel empty") (2002:409), to a feeling that one's social role is a suppression of the self and should not be one's *ikigai* ("It is really sad if caregiving is my *ikigai*") (2002:407). They write that "[The] moral imperatives that underpin the lives of Japanese women are undergoing significant modification . . . The introduction of more Western institutions has also encouraged more individualistic views of self, family, and well-being" (2002:403).

Mathews notes how a strong sense of *ikigai* is linked with a feeling that one is needed, essential, not merely a nameless cog in the machine that could be replaced without anyone noticing; this accounts for why in his interviews "family as *ikigai* tended to breed less ambivalence than work" (1996:734). Yet the comments of suicidal individuals on websites seems to indicate that they are not integrated into any kind of framework—either work or family—that makes them feel essential and needed.

It therefore does not seem a coincidence that this lack of integration, feelings of worthlessness, a lack of *ikigai,* and loneliness are more prevalent among young persons than adults, who would already be integrated into larger networks that would create a sense of being needed and an *ikigai.* A younger person does not have a clearly defined role or position of responsibility within a family (as a caregiver and provider, for example, which a father or mother can be, either through company work or by taking care of the home) and has not yet assumed a position within a company or as a caregiver in his or her own family. Mathews (1996) has noted that for younger persons, *ikigai* comes not from the self's embeddedness in these networks, but from anticipation of future selves and, one would assume, future relational networks. It would seem therefore that the anticipation of *ikigai* serves as a kind of *ikigai* when a network of social embeddedness, obligation, and a feeling of being needed have not yet been established. In that case, what is missing in these young persons' lives is this sense of anticipation—that there is something in the future worth living for, and a clear set of paths to the future or scenarios that can be envisioned.

Further complicating this issue is the conflict of ideals Japanese youth face with regard to what it means to become an adult in Japan. While the influence of Western values is clearly visible in Japan, the model of adulthood presented through such values differs significantly from traditional Japanese notions, and when these models come into conflict, the difficulty of combining Western ideals into existing conceptions can result in tensions (Pike and Borovoy 2004). The liminal state between childhood and adulthood may be appealing to young Japanese because of the relative degree of freedom it affords. At the same time, however, the flip side of that freedom from entrapping social relations is a degree of uncertainty and isolation caused by the very same absence of those social relations. Remaining in such a state for a prolonged period of time, as happens with the many young Japanese who stay at home late into their twenties and thirties, could allow that uncertainty and disconnection to develop into anxiety; the prolongation of the period before transition into adulthood could make that transition all the more difficult and concerning. Thus it is not surprising that these themes—existential anxiety, loneliness, lack of satisfying social relations, and lack of a role or meaning for oneself—all appear regularly in the posts and conversations recorded on suicide websites.

LONELINESS AND EXISTENTIAL SUFFERING

There is no question that loneliness is a central factor in understanding the situation of suicidal individuals and those who participate in suicide Internet websites, and we have seen that comments on loneliness are very prevalent on such sites. Yet what role does loneliness play in understanding the phenomenon of Internet suicide? Work on loneliness in sociology, social psychology, and the health sciences has identified three essential characteristics of loneliness: that it involves perceived deficiencies in one's social world; that it is a subjective state experienced by the individual rather than an objective feature of the individual's social world; and that it is experienced as unpleasant and distressing (Kraus et al. 1993:37). As scholars have emphasized either the social factors involved in loneliness (social networks, number of friends, level of social interaction) or the individual factors (personality variables, cognitive bias), depending on their disciplinary approach (sociology favoring the former, psychology the latter), the proposed responses have likewise been for changes in the social situation or individual therapy (Carden 2006; Gardner 2005; Hawkley 2005; Kraus et al. 1993; Lopata 1969; Mahon 2006; Martina 2006; Renshaw and Brown 1993; Stack 1998; Tilburg 1991). Interestingly, this parallels our earlier discussion of the way suicide is viewed in Japan predominantly as a social ill or pathology, and in the West as an individual one, with corresponding theories for treatment and response.

Surveying the literature across a broad range of disciplines reveals the complexity of loneliness and the fact that it can refer paradoxically to both a dysfunction and cause of pain, which has been primarily the approach taken by the social and health sciences, and a beneficial quality that leads to deeper self-understanding, which is a quality more emphasized by philosophers (Nilsson 2006, Karnick 2005).* For example, Yalom notes three kinds of loneliness, of which, along with interpersonal and intrapersonal isolation, the third is existential isolation, a "'separation from the world,' where the person is confronted with an anxiety in the face of nothingness but also his own freedom. Loneliness is regarded as the deepest source of normal anxiety" (Nilsson 2006:95). Nilsson (2006) notes:

> Lindström and Lindhohm's study shows that loneliness is one category of existence. Furthermore, the same authors demonstrate the existential meaningfulness of loneliness and write: "It belongs to the mystery of love that one attempts to uphold another's loneliness and create a free space in which existential loneliness can be transformed into a mutually shared loneliness."

*Another dimension added by philosophical reflections on loneliness, such as those by Heidegger, Merleau-Ponty, Tillich, Buber, and others, is its ontological and existential nature.

Attention to the existential dimension of loneliness may help to explain how Internet suicide sites create a space of communication and acceptance where lonely and potentially suicidal individuals can enter in, express themselves, and feel accepted and understood by like-minded individuals who are also lonely, thereby transforming their individual loneliness into a shared loneliness, and their dysfunctional loneliness into a more beneficial form of loneliness, one less dominated by consuming mental pain and more conducive for introspection and growth. In a study examining the use of cell phone text messaging by Japanese schoolchildren, Ogata et al. (2006) showed that mobile phone use decreased feelings of loneliness and facilitated friendships and connectedness when used in an informed manner. It is worth noting that Internet suicide websites also contain forums for poetry; poetry as a literary form is solitary in terms of composition and typically understood in Japan as born from intense self-reflection and solitude, yet it is nevertheless a form of communication, and an intensely personal and meaningful one. Poetry is closely related to the idea of solitude and loneliness as positive forces for introspection, contemplation, and creativity.

Thus, it is important to distinguish between the negative dimension of loneliness, which we might call "afflictive loneliness"—borrowing from the Buddhist taxonomies of mental states, which note that certain mental states are afflictive when they disturb the peace of mind of the individual and are based in cognitive and affective distortions not in accord with reality and not conducive to happiness (Guenther and Kawamura 1975)—and nonafflictive loneliness, or solitude.

Furthermore, it is equally important to draw a distinction between existential suffering and clinical depression. Psychiatrists have noted that when people who are severely depressed are treated, it is often when they emerge from depression that they experience existential despair and can then become more prone to suicide than when they were actually depressed. This distinction has been employed by Havens and Ghaemi (2005:138) in their article suggesting the use of therapeutic alliance with patients with bipolar disorder who suffer from subsyndromal depression, often as a result of the medications prescribed to treat their bipolar disorder: "It is our view that many bipolar patients may not have clinical depression viewed as an endogenous disease entity, but rather they may be suffering from clinical *'despair,'* as defined by the existentialist philosophers Søren Kierkegaard (Kierkegaard 1989) and Karl Jaspers (Jaspers 1998). Patients may suffer, too, from a complete loss of hope for the future and a loss of any grounding in the world."

This is a point Arthur Kleinman has been making in his work on depression and neurasthenia in cross-cultural perspective (1986, 1988, 1991, 2006; Kleinman and Good 1985; Kleinman, Das, and Lock 1997).* His early work addresses the possible dangers inherent in the medicalization of human despair, and in his most recent work (2006:9, italics added) he explicitly states:

> Perhaps the most devastating example for human values is the process of medicalization through which ordinary unhappiness and normal bereavement have been transformed into clinical depression, existential angst turned into anxiety disorders, and the moral consequences of political violence recast as post-traumatic stress disorder. That is, *suffering is redefined as mental illness and treated by professional experts, typically with medication.*

Similarly, Victor Frankl (1992:125) writes:

> I would strictly deny that one's search for a meaning to his existence, or even his doubt of it, in every case is derived from, or results in, any disease. Existential frustration is in itself neither pathological nor pathogenic. A man's concern, even his despair over the worthwhileness of life is an *existential distress* but by no means a *mental disease.*

A clear recognition of this level of suffering would help in understanding the phenomenon of Internet suicide in Japan. The suffering caused by painful experiences, the loss of a loved one, or a change in one's circumstances is easier to understand, and suicides arising from these kinds of suffering evoke sympathy and understanding. A deeper understanding of pervasive, existential suffering, as evidenced by afflictive loneliness, would help reduce the tendency to see suicides that arise from this suffering as incomprehensible acts, or as merely the result of mental illness, as commonly understood. Social psychologists informed by an existentialist approach, for example, have noted that three things are correlated with reports of lower subjective well-being and suffering. These include (1) an inability to maintain a certain consistency of self-understanding across multiple social roles; (2) a sense of being therefore inauthentic or fake to one's true self; and (3) an inability to see actions of social duty as autonomous engagement (an ability that seems to increase with age and maturity) (Sheldon et al. 1997; Sheldon et al. 2005). This speaks to the comments made by visitors to Japanese suicide websites—comments on loneliness, feeling fake, being unable to relate to others—and supports the idea that this existential suffering is connected with a difficulty experienced in the process of entrance into adulthood and its concomitant establishment of a self-identity congruent with social relations and roles, that is, the reconciliation of individual autonomy with social relations and obligations that may be a prerequisite to a strong *ikigai.*

CONCLUSION

As noted, loneliness can be seen to involve two factors: the external environment and effect of social forces on the individual, and the attitude or perception of individuals themselves. A response to loneliness must therefore involve both these dimensions: on the one hand, changes to social structures that will reduce the social isolation of individuals, and on the other hand, methods for individuals to be able to change attitudes, perceptions and behaviors, and thereby to find increased social satisfaction from the situation they already find themselves in. A suitable response must acknowledge both the social factors involved in promoting loneliness and suffering, but also the individual cognitive biases, attitudes, and propensities of individuals that perpetuate them. This response would seek to effect social change, but also provide resources for individuals to change their own perceptions and modes of interaction. In such a way, individuals are not disempowered from being able to take positive action to change their own situation; yet by addressing social factors, it is not merely left up to individuals to fix their own problems—rather, a social network is created to support them in that process through education, opportunities for interaction, and so on. Both dimensions are necessary, because research has shown that loneliness depends both on the presence of social networks and on individuals' subjective evaluations of their social networks (Kraus et al 1993:38). My research on the Japanese therapeutic practice of Naikan has shown the powerful effect that a cognitive reevaluation of one's own situation—even, or especially, in the case of severe circumstances or trauma—can have on an individual's long-term affect, mental health, and well-being (Ozawa-de Silva 2006, 2007).

The case of Internet suicide pacts in Japan draws attention to the question of what kinds of choices are possible—what one is allowed to choose—within the

*Neurasthenia is a diagnostic category that was popularly used in the U.S. in the 19th century to refer to "both weakness of the nerves and nervous exhaustion" (Kleinman 1988:100). However, neurasthenia nowadays is often known as a Chinese version of major depression. In his work, Kleinman called attention to the fact that behind neurasthenia is the deep trauma of the Cultural Revolution in the People's Republic of China, which is a shared form of social suffering among those who experienced it.

contexts of one's culture. In Japan, suicide is culturally acceptable only in certain prescribed circumstances—when there is a clear reason for the person to commit suicide according to cultural norms. Outside of those circumstances, suicide is an individual act that causes trouble for others, for the collective, and is therefore socially proscribed. But if it is something that a group chooses, then the decision of the group becomes something that an individual can follow, is indeed obligated, according to cultural prescriptions, to follow; social obligation is thereby reconciled to individual choice. Such cultural considerations as these lead me to believe that if a solution to the problem of suicide in Japan is to be found, attention must be paid to the very traditions and structures that modern Japan has sought to cast off. This will happen not through a return to outmoded social relationships that are no longer possible or relevant, but through a deeper understanding of the values of interpersonal connections that were embodied in those roles and relationships and that now need to be cultivated again, albeit perhaps in different forms.

REFERENCES

BBC News. 2004. Have Your Say: Why Are Suicide Pacts on the Rise in Japan? Electronic document, http:/mews.bbc.co.uk/2/hi/talking_point/3737072.stm, accessed October 15.

Borovoy, Amy. 2006. *The Hidden: Sheltering and Rehabilitating the Emotionally Distressed in Japan.* San Jose, California. American Anthropology Association.

Brooke, James. 2004. "9 Die in Japan Suicides Tied to Web." Electronic document, *The New York Times,* October 13, 2004, http://www.nytimes.com/2004/10/13/international/asia/13japan.html?_r=1&oref=login.

Desjarlais, Robert, Leon Eisenberg, Byron Good, and Arthur Kleinman. 1995. *World Mental Health: Problems and Priorities in Low-Income Countries.* Oxford: Oxford University Press.

Doi, Takeo. 2001. *The Anatomy of Dependence.* Tokyo, New York, London: Kodansha International.

Durkheim, Émile. 1966. *Suicide: A Study in Sociology.* New York: The Free Press.

Frankl, Viktor. 1992. *Man's Search for Meaning.* Boston: Beacon Press.

Ghetto. 2006. Ghetto. Electronic document, http://www.cotodama.org, accessed December 18.

Havens, Leston L., and S. Nassir Ghaemi. 2005. Existential Despair and Bipolar Disorder: The Therapeutic Alliance as Mood Stabilizer. *American Journal of Psychotherapy* 59:2:137–147.

Hi-ho Kai-in Support. 2007. Hikite yaku ni hikizurarete shūdan jisatsu: Jisatsu saito no kyōfu (Lured into Group Suicide by Recruiters: The Danger of Suicide Websites). Electronic document, http://home.hi-ho.ne.jp/support/info/security/colum/column05.html, accessed March 10.

Ikizurasa kei no foramu. 2006. (The Forum about Difficulty in Living). Electronic document, http://8238.teacup.com/hampen/bbs, posted November 22, accessed December 1.

Jisatsusha no Sōgen. 2006. Jisatsusha no sōgen (The Field for Suiciders). Electronic document, http://www.cotodama.org/cgi-bin/ibbs/ibbs.cgi, posted December 22, accessed December 24.

Jisatsutaikougaiyou. 2006. Ikiyasui Shakai no Genjitsu wo Mezashite (Aiming for the Society for Comfortable Living). Electronic document, www8.cao.go.jp/jisatsutaisaku/sougou/taisaku/kaigi_2/data/sl.pdf, accessed March 16, 2008.

Keyes, Corey. 1998. Social Well-Being. *Social Psychology Quarterly* 61(2):121–140.

Kitanaka, Junko. 2006. Society in Distress: The Psychiatric Production of Depression in Contemporary Japan. Ph.D. dissertation, Department of Anthropology, McGill University.

Kleinman, Arthur. 1986. *Social Origins of Distress and Disease: Depression, Neurasthenia and Pain in Modern China.* New Haven, CT: Yale University Press.

———. 1988. *Illness Narratives: Suffering, Healing and the Human Condition.* New York: Basic Books.

———. 1991. *Rethinking Psychiatry: From Cultural Category to Personal Experience.* New York: The Free Press.

———. 2006. *What Really Matters: Living a Moral Life amidst Uncertainty and Danger.* Oxford and New York: Oxford University Press.

Kleinman, Arthur, and Byron Good. 1985. *Culture and Depression: Studies in the Anthropology and Cross-Cultural Psychiatry of Affect and Disorder.* Berkeley: University of California Press.

Kleinman, Arthur, Veena Das, and Margaret Lock. 1997. *Social Suffering.* Berkeley: University of California Press.

Kokoro no Hanazono. 2006. Kokoro no Hanazono (Flowerbed of the Heart). Electronic document, http://bbsl.nazca.co.jp/12/asiato01/, accessed December 22.

Kondo, Dorinne. 1990. *Crafting Selves.* Chicago: University of Chicago.

Lock, Margaret. 1986. Plea for Acceptance: School Refusal Syndrome in Japan. *Social Sciences and Medicine* 23(2):99–112.

Long, Susan. 2001. Negotiating the "Good Death": Japanese Ambivalence about New Ways to Die. *Ethnology* 40(4):271–289.

Machizawa, Shizuo. 2003. *Hikikomoru Wakamonotachi (Withdrawn Youths).* Tokyo: Daiwa Shobo.

Mathews, Gordon. 1996. The Stuff of Dreams, Fading: Ikigai and "The Japanese Self." *Ethos* 24(4):718–747.

Nageki Keijiban. 2006. Nageki Keijiban (Wailing BBS). Electronic document, http://wailing.org/freebsd/jisatu/index.html, posted October 12, accessed December 15.

Omae ha mou shindeiru. 2005. Omae ha mou shindeiru (You Are Already Dead). Electronic document, http://jamu.cc/2ch/test/read.cgi/xyz/. l, posted December 24.

Ohnuki-Tierney, Emiko. 1984. *Illness and Culture in Contemporary Japan.* Cambridge: Cambridge University Press.

Ohsawa, Masaki. 1996. *Kyoko no Jidai no Hate: AUM to Sekai Saishu Sensou (The End of the Era of Fiction).* Tokyo: Chikuma Shobo.

———. 2005. Fukanou sei no Jidai (The Era of Impossibility). *Sekai (The World)*, February issue.

Ozawa, Chikako. 1996. Japanese Indigenous Psychologies: Concepts of Mental Illness in Light of Different Cultural Epistemologies. *British Medical Anthropology Review* 3(2), Winter.

Ozawa-de Silva, Chikako. 2002. Beyond the Body/Mind? Japanese Contemporary Thinkers on Alternative Sociologies of the Body. *Body & Society* 8(2):21–38.

———. 2006. *Psychotherapy and Religion in Japan: The Japanese Introspection Practice of Naikan.* London: Routledge.

———. 2007. Demystifying Japanese Therapy: An Analysis of Naikan and the Ajase Complex through Buddhist Thought. *Ethos* 35(4):411–446.

Pinguet, Maurice. 1993. *Voluntary Death in Japan.* Cambridge: Polity Press.

Ryff, Carol D., Corey L. M. Keyes, and Diane L. Hughes. 2003. Status Inequalities, Perceived Discrimination and Eudaimonic Well-Being: Do the Challenges of Minority Life Hone Purpose and Growth? *Journal of Health and Social Behavior* 44(3):275–291.

Pike, Kathleen, and Amy Borovoy. 2004. The Rise of Eating Disorders in Japan: Issues of Culture and Limitations of the Model of "Westernization." *Culture, Medicine and Psychiatry* 28:493–531.

Roland, Alan. 1988. *In Search of Self in India and Japan.* Princeton, NJ: Princeton University Press.

Saito, Kan. 2003. Iki Kihaku sa, Kontei ni (On the Fundamental Thinness of Life). *Asahi Shinbun* (Asahi newspaper), May 2, morning edition.

Saito, Tamaki. 1998. *Shakai teki Hikiomori (Social Withdrawal).* Tokyo: PHP Shinsho.

Sasaki, Tishinao. 2007. Ōte masukomi intānetto shinjyū hōdō no otoshiana (The Catch of the Major Mass Media Reports on the Internet Suicide Pacts). Electronic document, http://homepage3.nifty.com/sasakitoshinao/pcexplorer_5.html, accessed January 3.

Schulz, Kathryn. 2004. Did Antidepressants Depress Japan? *New York Times,* August 22.

Sheldon, Kennon M. 2002. The Self-Concordance Model of Healthy Goal-Striving: When Personal Goals Correctly Represent the Person. In E. L. Deci and R. M. Ryan (Eds.), *Handbook of Self-Determination Research* (pp. 65–86). Rochester, NY: University of Rochester Press.

Sheldon, Kennon M., Richard M. Ryan, Laird J. Rawsthorne, and Barbara Ilardi. 1997. Trait Self and True Self: Cross-Role Variation in the Big-Five Personality Traits and Its Relations with Psychological Authenticity and Subjective Well-Being. *Journal of Personality and Social Psychology* 73(6):1380–1393.

Sheldon, Kennon M., Tim Kasser, Linda Houser-Marko, Taisha Jones, and Daniel Turban. 2004. Doing One's Duty: Chronological Age, Felt Autonomy, and Subjective Well-Being. *European Journal of Personality* 19:97–115.

Site Rank. 2005. Jisatsu Saito no Tōhyō Rankingu (Ranking of Suicide Sites). Electronic document, http://cat.jp.siterank.org/jp/cat/1100102562/, accessed January 15.

Takahashi, Yoshitomo. 1997. Culture and Suicide: From a Japanese Psychiatrist's Perspective. *Suicide and Life-Threatening Behavior* 27(1):137-145.

———. 2001. *Jisatsu no sain wo yomitoru (Reading a Signal of Suicide).* Tokyo: Kodansha.

Tillich, Paul. 1952. *The Courage to Be.* New Haven, CT: Yale University Press.

Traphagan, John. 2004. Interpretations of Elder Suicide, Stress, and Dependency among Rural Japanese. *Ethnology* 43(4):315–329.

Ueno, Kayoko. 2005. Suicide as Japan's Major Export: A Note on Japanese Suicide Culture. *Revista Espaco Academico* 44(January). Electronic document, http://www.espacoacademico.com.br/044/44eueno_ing.htm, accessed December 25, 2006.

Usui, Mafumi. 2002. Internet Shinrigaku (Internet Psychology), September 24. Electronic document, http://www.n-seiryo.ac.jp/~usui/net/, accessed February 17, 2007.

Yamamoto-Mitani, Noriko, and Margaret I. Wallhagen. 2002. Pursuit of Psychological Well-being *(Ikigai)* and the Evolution of Self-Understanding in the Context of Caregiving in Japan. *Culture, Medicine and Psychiatry* 26:399–417.

Za Keijiban. 2003. Jisatsu shitai hito ha oide yo bisshito shikate ageru kara (Come Here, Those of You Who Want to Commit Suicide, and I'll Give You a Stern Scolding!). Electronic document, http://psychology.dot.thebbs.jp/1050I36588.html, accessed September 26.

Part II

APPLYING MEDICAL ANTHROPOLOGY

The selections in the second part of this book show you how medical anthropology can be used to analyze and improve real human health problems. Most of these selections are case studies of medical anthropology in action. In reality, however, this division between understanding and applying medical anthropology is arbitrary; it is impossible to separate theory and practice in the social sciences, especially in the field of health and healing. We believe that *all* the different approaches described in the first part of the book have relevance to the analysis and solution of health problems. All the approaches are anthropological because they are based on fundamental concepts, such as culture, and basic methods, such as participant observation and cross-cultural comparison. All the approaches can contribute to our society's efforts to deal with health problems such as AIDS, malnutrition, and mental health. The underlying premise in the organization of this book is the dual goal of first understanding the diversity of theoretical perspectives in medical anthropology and then seeing how the discipline is applied to real human problems. Also, although it would have been easy to select all of the examples for this second part solely from the United States, because there is so much medical anthropological work done here, it is very important to have a range of ethnographic examples.

There *is* a field called applied anthropology, and some of the selections in this part of the book probably do not fit within a strict definition of that field. Applied anthropology often refers to research and analysis done by anthropologists on a specific problem and for a specific client. For example, a coalition of health care providers in an inner-city area may hire an anthropologist to help them understand why people with tuberculosis do not comply in taking the full course of their treatment medicine, or an international health organization aimed at improving children's nutrition in certain demonstration projects in Africa may hire an anthropologist to do background studies of traditional infant feeding practices. In both cases, the applied anthropologist is hired to do specific work and to deliver a specific product—usually a report. In these examples, the anthropologist would be asked for advice in improving the program; sometimes the anthropologist is regarded as a social and cultural troubleshooter, brought in to discover what went wrong. In a promising development, many of those in charge of health programs recognize the importance of social and cultural factors in the success of their projects, and therefore more applied medical anthropologists are now being asked to play a role in the design and management of those projects. Some anthropologists—such as those who work for the World Health Organization or the U.S. Centers for Disease Control and Prevention—claim that it is harder to design and implement successful health programs than to criticize such efforts from the sidelines. The greater recognition of applied medical anthropology is therefore a challenging opportunity for the field.

In applied medical anthropology, when a particular client defines a specific problem to be studied, it may seem to be an *atheoretical* enterprise—that is, simply a matter of applying the correct anthropological methods to the problem, like following a recipe in a cookbook. In reality, this is not the case because problems, theories, and methods are all linked. For example, there may be constraints on the medical anthropologist who is hired by a hospital. How critical can that person be and still keep the job? The client-employers want anthropologists to help them do their job better, so anthropologists may need to work within that system. In any case, there is not a single anthropological paradigm that can be applied to every problem. Research requires triangulation between a problem, an ethnographic context, and a theoretical orientation. For example, the problem might be the care of burn victims in a hospital setting, the setting might be the burn center itself and debridement (the removal of dead tissue), and the theoretical orientation might be the illness experience of patients, the psychology of pain, and the goals of the nursing staff. This example is from the work of a clinical anthropologist, Thomas Johnson, whose study of illness experience in a burn unit resulted in a small but significant change in debriding procedures (Johnson 1997). Patients said they could tolerate pain if they knew when it was going to end, but nurses doing the debridement had been working to get it done as quickly as possible. From listening to patients, the anthropologist realized that patients preferred to have predictable breaks during this painful process. By placing a large clock in the debridement room and agreeing upon a set schedule of debriding minutes followed by rest periods, the applied anthropologist was able to introduce an improvement for both patients and nurses. The problem, setting, and theory all worked together in focusing the research, implementation, and evaluation of a change. When looking at research proposals (or student's ideas for research papers), anthropologists look for the problem, the setting, and the theoretical orientation. Only after these three parameters are set can an appropriate methodology for research be selected.

The selections in Part II are divided into seven areas: case studies in explanatory models; working with the culture of biomedicine; ethnicity and health care; stigma and coping; gender and health; culture and nutrition; and global health issues and programs. Within each topic area, a wide variety of health problems are represented. But *how* are we to define health problems? Biomedicine defines health problems by categorizing human biological systems (neurology, orthopedics, internal medicine, ophthalmology, and so on) or points in the life cycle (pediatrics, obstetrics, geriatrics); it may also focus on specific diseases. Because anthropologists argue that health problems cannot be easily separated from aspects of sociopolitical organization, cultural beliefs, and ecology, it is impossible to define health problems as only *within* an individual human body. Clearly, this understanding of health problems requires a wider, socially oriented view, and medical anthropology offers a variety of angles (or lenses) for examining those problems. The same health issue—lower back pain, for example—might be seen through the lens of explanatory models if the goal is to improve the treatment or pain management of patients. On the other hand, this health issue might involve the political economy of health if the goal is to prevent back injuries that occur on the job. In fact, any single health problem may be explored from a diversity of medical anthropological perspectives; the "correct" perspective depends on what you want to know and what you want to do with that information. This diversity of perspectives is a strength of anthropology.

Students interested in further reading in applied anthropology may refer to the works listed in the references at the back of the book. There is also useful information on the Society for Applied Anthropology (SfAA) home page (http://www.sfaa.net) and the National Association of Practicing Anthropologists (NAPA) home page (http://www.practicinga-thropology.org). The film *Anthropologists at Work: Careers Making a Difference* (35 min,, VHS), distributed by the American Anthropological Association, is also a useful introduction.

Case Studies in Explanatory Models

CONCEPTUAL TOOLS

■ ***The study of explanatory models has many practical uses.*** Explanatory models (EMs) have been a major contribution of Arthur Kleinman and his colleagues, who introduced this concept to describe individuals' cognitive models of their own illnesses as these models relate to cultural issues in clinical settings. Kleinman has suggested that clinicians can elicit a patient's EM by asking questions like the following: What do you think caused your problem? Why do you think this illness happened at the particular time that it did? How bad do you think this illness is? What worries you most about this illness? What kind of treatment were you expecting to get? What are the most important results you expect to get from treatment? (see Brown, Gregg, and Ballard 1997; Kleinman 1988). These questions resemble those an anthropologist would ask to learn about a different ethnomedical system. In a clinical setting, asking these kinds of questions allows the health care provider to get the patient's cultural beliefs "out on the table" so that potential cultural problems might be avoided. If the patient thinks a condition is severe and will last a long time and the physician thinks the condition is mild and temporary, it is important to discuss this discrepancy in a way that does not condescend to the patient. Asking these questions also allows the health care provider to acknowledge legitimate differences in medical beliefs; it is a way to treat the patient with respect. In a public health or health education setting, eliciting EMs from community members (also called the folk model of illness) can help planners identify (or rule out) potential cultural conflicts. The case of *empacho* in selection 35 is an example of this. Ethnomedical beliefs about the etiology, diagnosis, and treatment of illnesses are important because when patients and healers rely on different ethnomedical systems there is increased risk of miscommunication. If people's behavior is logically linked to their modes of thinking, then it is essential to know what people think.

■ ***The fallacy of empty vessels is that people in other societies lack health knowledge.*** This idea is based on the important work of Steven Polgar, who developed this concept to describe cultural problems encountered in international health programs, but the idea is equally applicable in class-stratified, multicultural societies like the United States (Polgar 1962). The fallacy of empty vessels is that people in other societies (so-called target populations) do not have any health knowledge or beliefs. Rather, they are "empty vessels," waiting to be filled with the knowledge of scientific medicine developed in modern, rich countries. The fallacy implies that as soon as people are educated about new scientific knowledge for prevention and treatment, they will change their behaviors or accept the medical innovations. In reality, however, all peoples already have their own ethnomedical beliefs and practices, and these preexisting beliefs influence how new ideas are accepted. When one pours different liquid into already-filled vessels, a new mixture results, and when new biomedical ideas are introduced to people who already have an ethnomedical system, they are more likely to accept those ideas that fit with the preexisting system and reject those that do not. Such problems can be overcome, but only if one is aware of the fallacy of empty vessels. Understanding that people receive health messages within the context of their own beliefs is essential in order to achieve effective communication between physicians and patients, and health promoters and the public.

■ ***Questions of compliance or adherence are linked to issues of power.*** Anthropologists hold that, in general, people's behavior is understandable and logical within their own social and cultural context. The challenge, therefore, is to understand the "other's" point of view. The idea of eliciting EMs from patients, or of studying the folk models of illness in a population, is based on the belief that compliance (adherence) can be improved through better communication. One important factor left out of this equation, however, is that people's behavior is sometimes constrained by their particular conditions of social class. Another factor is that there are power differentials between the givers and receivers of health messages. Health care providers are in a more powerful position, and they may expect their suggestions to be followed simply because of these power differences. In this regard, health care providers may perceive patient noncompliance as a problem of disobedience, expecting the receivers of health messages to comply like obedient and powerless children. This attitude does not fit well with a model of partnership between patient and provider.

■ ***Medical pluralism exists in most social contexts.*** In general, simple one-to-one relationships between a single society and a single ethnomedical system do not exist. As biomedicine has dispersed in nearly all areas of the world, traditional medical systems continue to thrive. Medical pluralism means that multiple medical systems coexist in a single social context, and therefore people choose from a variety of medical-therapy options to deal with their complaints. The pattern of health-seeking between different modalities of health systems available is called the *hierarchy of resort* (Romanucci-Ross 1969).

 28

Ethnomedical Beliefs and Patient Adherence to a Treatment Regimen: A St. Lucian Example

William W. Dressler

This selection tests a relatively straightforward hypothesis: In the context of medical pluralism, are people who do not hold biomedical beliefs more or less likely to be noncompliant in taking medication for hypertension? In this research in St. Lucia, William Dressler uses the personalistic-naturalistic distinction in ethnomedical systems developed by George Foster (see selection 12). When a theoretical ideal typology is tested in a research setting, it often becomes evident that the original categorizations were less clear-cut than expected. Three belief systems (personalistic, naturalistic, and biomedical) coexist in St. Lucia. Dressler interviewed people diagnosed with hypertension in the biomedical clinic to see whether they took their prescribed hypertension medicine. Essential hypertension, or high blood pressure, is a particularly interesting phenomenon to examine because it is a symptomless disease. It is diagnosed from readings with a blood pressure cuff and a stethoscope; this raised pressure in the cardiovascular system is clearly linked to high risk for stroke and premature death. The disease can be controlled through medication, but that medicine often has to be taken for a lifetime. Because of this set of features, the problem of compliance in taking the prescription is particularly difficult.

In this example, Dressler is not looking specifically at explanatory models about a specific illness (as we will see in the next selection, also dealing with hypertension), but rather at people's overall ethnomedical cognitive models. Also notice how the anthropologist asks specific questions so that he may classify people by the quantitative analysis necessary to test the hypothesis. Although there is little mystery about the methodology of this research, it is not so obvious how to interpret the results.

As you read this selection, consider these questions:

- **What do you think are the advantages and disadvantages of doing anthropological research using the quantitative, hypothesis-testing approach described in this selection?**
- **How is it that a single society can have multiple and competing ethnomedical systems? Why don't some of these ethnomedical beliefs just die out?**
- **Is it possible for a symptomless disease to be an illness?**
- **How do you interpret the fact that language use becomes a powerful predictive marker of hypertension medication compliance?**
- **Are applied medical anthropologists correct in their assumption that human behavior is generally predictable and almost always changeable?**

Context: William Dressler is a medical anthropologist at the University of Alabama. His research interests include the biocultural relationships between racism and chronic disease in minority populations and the social construction of disease risk. He has conducted numerous field projects in Mexico, England, the Caribbean, and the United States. This selection presents a systematic study of the ways that different kinds of ethnomedical beliefs influence how people may or may not adhere to biomedical prescriptions. This is a very important consideration for health care providers and policy makers because people often do not follow the advice of their physicians. This kind of research can help improve communication and understanding between health care providers and their patients.

Source: W. A. Dressler (1980). "Ethnomedical Beliefs and Patient Adherence to a Treatment Regimen: A St. Lucian Example." *Human Organization* 39:88–91.

The study of "adherence to" or "compliance with" treatment regimens has become very important in recent years. These terms refer to the extent to which a patient persists in behaviors prescribed by a health professional (e.g., taking pills, changing diets), or restricts activities, such as smoking. These issues loom large in the treatment of chronic diseases such as high blood pressure (or essential hypertension). Hypertension is an asymptomatic disease which leads to heart disease, stroke, kidney disease and others if not treated, and treatment may last a lifetime. Yet an accepted estimate is that of all hypertensives, only one-fourth are under treatment, and only one-half of those adhere to their regimen (Kirscht and Rosenstock 1977).

This problem has stimulated the search for those factors, especially beliefs and attitudes, that are associated with adherence behavior (Blackwell 1973). These concerns converge with one of the more interesting theoretical issues in medical anthropology, namely, the relationship of ethnomedical beliefs to health-related behaviors.

A number of anthropologists have commented on the problem of adherence to treatment in relation to ethnomedical beliefs. Snow (1974) has reviewed much of the literature on folk medical beliefs among Black Americans, and she describes a wide range of beliefs dealing with both natural and supernatural causes and treatments of illness. She concludes that "the presence of an alternate medical system which at best is different from and at worst is in direct conflict with that of the health professional can only complicate matters. These beliefs . . . may greatly color the doctor/patient relationship and influence the decision to follow—or not—the doctor's orders" (1974:94). Similarly, Harwood (1971) and Logan (1973) have reviewed ethnomedical beliefs held by Hispanics in the New World. They have argued that an individual's commitment to (in the case of Hispanics) the humoral theory of medicine can seriously undermine the biomedical treatment of disease. Finally, Wiese (1976) suggests that food-related beliefs in Haiti might interfere with successful nutritional therapy.

Based on these studies, the hypothesis can be advanced that, within a mixed medical setting, the greater an individual's commitment to an ethnomedical belief system, the less likely it is that that individual will adhere to a treatment regimen prescribed within the Western medical setting.

I conducted research to evaluate this hypothesis in the West Indies, in a town in St. Lucia. The population of St. Lucia is predominantly Afro-American, and is descended from African slaves. Until recently, St. Lucia was a colonial dependency of Britain, although the original White settlers on the island were French. The French influence is most evident in language; virtually every St. Lucian speaks a French-English creole, locally termed Patois, as their first language (Lieberman and Dressler 1977).

The research reported here was conducted in a town of approximately five thousand inhabitants. The region is situated on the western coast of St. Lucia and is devoted to agriculture. The bulk of arable land is held by large estates planted in bananas, coconuts, citrus, and root crops. A large percentage of the population is employed as agricultural laborers. There is also a copra processing plant in the town, employing nearly three hundred persons. Other economic pursuits include fishing, small-scale retailing, and government service.

St. Lucia is especially appropriate for this study for two reasons. First, there is a very high prevalence of hypertension in St. Lucia. Despite the fact that hypertension is asymptomatic, the disease is of concern to the people of St. Lucia, and it occupies a prominent place in the ethnomedical belief system. Second, the medical system of St. Lucia is a mixed, traditional-Western system. Furthermore, the medical subsystems have coexisted for over a century, since the first Western-trained physicians visited St. Lucia in the 19th century.

THE MEDICAL SYSTEM

Foster (1976) has proposed two categories, the "naturalistic" and the "personalistic," to account for variation in ethnomedical belief systems. These categories will be used to describe the intracultural variation in ethnomedical beliefs in St. Lucia. There is, of course, a certain degree of overlap between these two categories. Nonetheless, they are useful in distinguishing two varieties of ethnomedical belief in St. Lucia, and they are emically valid. St. Lucians make a similar distinction themselves. Finally, the Western medical system is considered to be analytically and logically distinct.

The *personalistic system* refers to that subset of ethnomedical beliefs in which illness and other types of misfortune are explained by the active aggression of some agent which might be human, nonhuman, or supernatural (Foster 1976:775). In St. Lucia this set of beliefs is subsumed under the term *obeah*. Obeah is a West Indian form of sorcery. Obeah is not seen as a necessary or even sufficient cause of illness; however, these practices may be used to make any existing illness episode longer, more severe, and sometimes fatal. Persons who practice obeah are referred to as *jagajey* and obtain their power directly from Satan. There are a number of malevolent agents that can be used by a jagajey, and these agents can be dangerous in their own right.

If obeah is suspected in an illness, a *gade* will be consulted. A gade is an ethnomedical specialist who has the power and knowledge to counteract obeah. The gade gains knowledge through dreams and uses divination to diagnose. Other kinds of illnesses can be treated by a gade, but only the gade can fight obeah.

The *naturalistic system* refers to that subset of ethnomedical beliefs in which forces of nature—such as cold and dampness—are thought to be major causes of illness (ibid.). In St. Lucia these beliefs are subsumed under the term "bush medicine." The most important factors in the environment which cause illness are imbalances in hot and cold (referring to actual temperature) and dietary factors. There is a degree of etiologic specificity in these beliefs; particular kinds of factors are associated with specific illnesses. For example, hypertension (referred to simply as "the pressure") is believed to be caused by chemical fertilizers that were introduced during the expansion of the banana industry and are now used in the growing of staple crops.

When an illness is believed to have been caused by a natural force, the treatment will be in the form of a "bush tea" made from local plants. Many people seek the advice of a bush medicine specialist. These individuals are known by no special cover term; they are simply recognized as being particularly knowledgeable in the domain of bush medicine. These specialists typically do not charge for their services.

The *Western system* refers to the government health-care delivery system. The most important segment of that system is the health center. The island is divided into seven medical districts, each staffed by a District Medical Officer (DMO). The DMO is an M.D., usually a White expatriate, whose function is to treat patients attending general medical clinics throughout the district. The health center that was located in the research community was staffed by two registered nurses, several student nurses and aides and a dispenser, in addition to the DMO.

With respect to hypertension, the treatment practices were as follows: if a patient presented an elevated blood pressure reading and no other evidence of hypertension, a tranquilizer was given. If some other sign of hypertension was present, reserpine, an antihypertensive drug, was prescribed. Hypertensives were given 30-day prescriptions that could be refilled six times, at which time they returned to the DMO for evaluation of control. In the interim, their blood pressure was monitored by a nurse at two-week intervals. Those patients receiving tranquilizers were given a nonrefillable 30-day prescription.

METHODS

A sample of 40 hypertensives under treatment at the local health center was interviewed. This sample represents all those cases under treatment that could be contacted. The sample is thus not a probability sample, but neither is it merely accidental. The only systematic bias which might have occurred was an underrepresentation of males (as compared to a community-wide probability sample): there were 33 females and 7 males in the sample. Significance tests were used not for the purposes of generalizing to a universe, but to rule out the operation of random processes within the sample (Blalock 1972:239). Descriptive statistics for the sample are presented at the bottom of Table 1.

Adherence behavior was measured as a dichotomy on the basis of successful compliance with the medication regimen. During the course of an interview each respondent's most recent prescription for medication was examined. If the respondent had taken 70% or more of the tablets from the most recent prescription, and had properly refilled the prescription, then the respondent was considered to have successfully complied with the regimen. Using this criterion, 19, or 47.5%, of the respondents were compliant. This equals compliance rates found in most studies (Kirscht and Rosenstock 1977).

Ethnomedical beliefs were measured by presenting the respondents with statements and asking them first if they were aware of the statement, and second if they believed the statement to be true or false. The latter responses were used as evidence of commitment to beliefs. The following 16 items were used (the items were randomized on the interview schedule).

1. *Lespwi* are evil spirits who can hurt people.
2. *Bolom* are things that look like children but are really evil spirits.
3. *Lajablesse* are evil spirits who can hurt people.
4. A gade is a man who knows how to fight evil spirits and treat sicknesses.
5. If a person works obeah on you, it can make you sick or even kill you.
6. Jagajey are people who know how to work evil.
7. High blood pressure is caused by fertilizers (salt put on plants to make them grow).
8. *Gwenabafay, twatas,* or *citronel* can be used to make a bush tea for *empwida.*
9. A tea made with Indian cucumber is good for high blood pressure.
10. Empwida is caused by being hot and eating or drinking something cold.

TABLE I Descriptive Statistics and Correlation Matrix

	(1)	(2)	(3)	(4)	(5)	(6)	(7)	(8)	(9)
1. Language	—								
2. Travel	.533***	—							
3. Age	−.017	−.100	—						
4. Education	.731***	.406**	−.126	—					
5. Economic status	.060	276*	.026	.241	—				
6. Personalistic beliefs	.285*	.288*	−.012	.366*	−.059	—			
7. Naturalistic beliefs	.364**	.198	.063	.308*	.076	.519***	—		
8. Western beliefs	.344**	.172	.107	.239	.007	.168	.425**	—	
9. Adherence	−.040	−.156	−.208	.026	.174	−.319*	−.172	−.060	—
Mean	.60	.45	63.8	3.7	3.2	2.5	2.5	.48	
Standard Deviation	.49	.50	10.3	2.4	2.1	1.4	.78	.50	

[1] *p < .05
[2] **p < .01
[3] ***p < .001

11. Eating green paw-paw is good for high blood pressure.
12. A person will get high blood pressure if his blood is too rich.
13. If a person has high blood pressure, he should not put salt on his food.
14. If high blood pressure is not treated, it can cause a stroke.
15. A person who has high blood pressure must always take pills.
16. High blood pressure can never be cured.

Three subscales were formed for purposes of analysis. Scale reliability was assessed using the coefficient of internal consistency, "alpha" (Kerlinger 1973:451–52). The *personalistic scale* is made up of items 1–6 (alpha = .80). The *naturalistic scale* is made up of items 7–12 (alpha = .65). The *Western scale* is made up of items 13–16 (alpha = .65). Each scale shows an acceptable degree of reliability.

The following variables were included as potential predictors of adherence because they have been shown to affect health behavior in other contexts (Woods and Graves 1973). *Economic status* was measured as a four-item index of the acquisition of material culture (electricity, plumbing, toilet, concrete house; alpha = .84). *Education* is a seven-point scale of years of education completed. *Age* is the respondent's age in years. *Travel* was coded as a dichotomy, i.e., whether or not the respondent had ever traveled off the island. *Language* was coded as the language used during the interview (English = 1; Patois = 0).

A correlation matrix of all variables is presented in Table 1. The only variable significantly related to adherence to treatment is the personalistic belief scale; the higher an individual's acceptance of personalistic beliefs, the lower their compliance.

In order to control for the effects of the background variables, partial correlations were computed between the belief scales and adherence, controlling for economic status, education, age, travel, and language use. The partial correlation for adherence and personalistic beliefs was significant and negative (partial $r = -.29$, $p < .05$). The other partial correlations were not significant ($r = -.17$ for adherence and naturalistic beliefs; $r = -.06$ for adherence and Western beliefs).

DISCUSSION

It is of interest to examine the utility of Foster's (1976) scheme for classifying ethnomedical beliefs at the outset. There is, of course, a certain degree of ambiguity in applying the concepts of "personalistic" or "naturalistic." From one perspective, we could group these categories of belief under the rubric "ethnomedicine" and distinguish both from Western medicine. On the other hand, Western beliefs and bush medicine could be grouped as kinds of naturalistic beliefs and could be distinguished from personalistic beliefs. As it turns out, this seeming ambiguity reflects the empirical situation in St. Lucia accurately. When we examine the correlations among the three belief scales, personalistic and naturalistic beliefs are correlated, and naturalistic and Western beliefs are correlated, but personalistic and Western beliefs are uncorrelated. The personalistic and naturalistic systems share an emphasis on herbal and plant remedies, along with a lack of government recognition. The naturalistic and Western systems share an emphasis on natural forces or conditions as causes of disease. There is little or no similarity between personalistic and Western beliefs. Thus, this conceptual scheme proved useful in the analysis of the intracultural diversity of medical beliefs in St. Lucia.

Of additional interest are the patterns of relationships among the sociocultural variables and the three belief scales. In general, those individuals with greater English language facility, more exposure to the world through travel, and more education, tend to express more agreement with statements of medical beliefs of all kinds. These findings could be a methodological artifact. That is, individuals with greater English language facility and more education might answer more in the affirmative to please the investigator. It seems unlikely, however, that this would occur in the case of personalistic beliefs. On the other hand, it has been shown in a number of studies that "modernizing" individuals present more illness complaints. Perhaps modernizing individuals also express more concern with medical beliefs. Their concern with the cognitive domain of health might manifest itself both in more illness complaints *and* in an expression of more knowledge and affirmation of medical beliefs in an interview situation.

It is striking that these modernizing individuals express more agreement with statements of personalistic beliefs. These results run counter to the scholarly mainstream of research in modernization. The various conceptions of "modern" persons differ somewhat, but a recurring feature is that such persons believe in determinism and scientific knowledge and reject traditional beliefs.

These and other data clearly do not support this position. My findings corroborate those of Jahoda (1970), one of the few studies in this area. Jahoda examined the correlates of supernatural beliefs in a large sample of university students in Ghana. He found that "the modest trend was for subjects who had spent more years at the university and for those from a more literate home background to retain more supernatural beliefs" (ibid.: 126). If these results continue to be replicated in future research, the concept of "psychological modernization" will need revision. More research should be devoted to the modernization of traditional belief systems, the process that seems to be at work in St. Lucia, rather than the simple adoption of Western belief systems.

The only significant correlate of adherence to treatment for essential hypertension is the scale of personalistic beliefs. When sociocultural variables are controlled, the correlation is reduced somewhat, but the significant, inverse relationship remains.

It has been argued that the link between personalistic beliefs and adherence is motivational. It is hypothesized that those individuals believing in a personalistic system see themselves as under the control of external forces. Thus, there is little motivation for them to take their medication since control of their fate is out of their hands (Caplan et al. 1976:35). This hypothesis predicts that individuals should take *no* action to treat their illness. This is not consistent with the data in this study. Over half of the respondents (55%) report having used a bush tea for their high blood pressure, and this reported behavior is positively correlated with both personalistic beliefs ($r = .41, p < .01$) and naturalistic beliefs ($r = .36, p < .01$). Interestingly, the two behavioral responses (medication or bush tea) are independent of one another ($r = .05$, n.s.). Since these two behavioral responses are independent of one another, and related to personalistic beliefs in different directions, a motivational hypothesis fails to account for the observed correlations.

Some years ago, Buchler (1964) observed that people on Grand Caymans in the West Indies preferred to take medication in liquid form rather than as pills, which he related to their customary use of bush teas. Perhaps the same process is operating here. This would explain why individuals more committed to personalistic beliefs are more likely to use a bush tea, but less likely to take their pills as directed. This interpretation should be tested in future research.

In summary, partial support was found for the hypothesis I advanced. One dimension of ethnomedical beliefs does relate to adherence behavior, although the interpretation of that relationship is problematic. This is far from a definitive study. Rather, these data serve to illustrate some of the more general issues in the study of ethnomedical beliefs and health behavior.

REFERENCES

Blackwell, B. 1973. Patient Compliance. New England Journal of Medicine 289:249–52.

Blalock, H. M. 1972. Social Statistics. Second ed. New York: McGraw-Hill.

Buchler, I. R. 1964. Caymanian Folk Medicine: A Problem in Applied Anthropology. Human Organization 23:48–49.

Caplan, R. D., et al. 1976. Adhering to Medical Regimens. Ann Arbor: Institute for Social Research, The University of Michigan.

Foster, G. M. 1976. Disease Etiologies in Non-Western Medical Systems. American Anthropologist 78:773–82.

Harwood, A. 1971. The Hot-Cold Theory of Disease. Journal of the American Medical Association 216:1153–58.

Jahoda, G. 1970. Supernatural Beliefs and Changing Cognitive Structures among Ghanian University Students. Journal of Cross-Cultural Psychology 1:115–30.

Kerlinger, F. 1973. Foundations of Behavioral Research. Second ed. New York: Holt, Rinehart and Winston.

Kirscht, J. P., and I. M. Rosenstock. 1977. Patient Adherence to Antihypertensive Medical Regimens. Journal of Community Health 3:115–24.

Lieberman, D., and W. W. Dressler. 1977. Bilingualism and Cognition of St. Lucian Disease Terms. Medical Anthropology 1:81–110.

Logan, M. H. 1973. Humoral Medicine in Guatemala and Peasant Acceptance of Modern Medicine. Human Organization 32:385–96.

Snow, L. 1974. Folk Medical Beliefs and Their Implications for Care of Patients. Annals of Internal Medicine 81:82–96.

Wiese, H. J. C. 1976. Maternal Nutrition and Traditional Food Behavior in Haiti. Human Organization 35:193–200.

Woods, C. M., and T. D. Graves. 1973. The Process of Medical Change in a Highland Guatemala Town. Los Angeles: Latin American Center, UCLA.

 29

Health Beliefs and Compliance with Prescribed Medication for Hypertension among Black Women—New Orleans 1985–86

Centers for Disease Control and Prevention
Based on Work by Suzanne Heurtin-Roberts and Efrain Reisin

This brief selection is from the no-nonsense publication of the Centers for Disease Control and Prevention, the Morbidity and Mortality Weekly Report (MMWR). *The selection summarizes some important ethnographic research by Suzanne Heurtin-Roberts and Efrain Reisin on the relationship between ethnomedical beliefs (EM's) and compliance with taking prescribed antihypertension medicine. This research is important because it demonstrates that although there is variation in the African American community in regard to the belief in folk medical concepts, those who believe in the traditional ethnomedical categorizations are less likely to be compliant. The researchers also demonstrate that the medical staff at this inner-city hospital were generally unaware of the health beliefs of their patients, although medical anthropologists studying the ethnomedical beliefs within African American communities have known for a long time about the differences between "high blood" and "high pertension." These illness labels have been described in diverse regions of the United States: Washington State (Blumhagen 1980), western Michigan (Snow 1993), and eastern North Carolina (Mathews 1988).*

The folk model distinguishes between a chronic condition amenable to treatment and an episodic condition affected by emotional crises. "High blood" is considered to be a persistent condition of blood that is too thick, too rich, or too heavy. This blood is thought to rise up into the head and stay there, causing negative health consequences largely because the condition makes the heart work too hard. A variety of symptoms may indicate that "high blood" exists—red eyes, nosebleeds, headaches, tasting of blood—due to blood rising to the head. "High blood" is caused in part by individual predisposition and is exacerbated by a diet rich in red, heavy, and sweet foods (including pork and red wine). People with "high blood" generally have that condition for life, and they need to avoid certain foods to prevent dangerous episodes. "High blood" can be treated by drinking blood-thinning agents like epsom salts or pickle juice (Heurtin-Roberts and Reisin 1990). On the other hand, "high pertension," or tension, is an episodic, emotional condition in which the blood suddenly rises and then falls, making the victim more likely to "fall out" or faint. "High pertension" is largely a matter of an individual's predisposition, as well as the result of particular emotional contexts. It cannot be treated or cured; the best that can be done is to avoid emotional trauma.

The findings of this study show that women who recognized the ethnomedical categories were more likely to be noncompliant than were women who only recognized the biomedical category of hypertension. Of the women who believed in the folk medical categories, those who believed their condition was the untreatable "high pertension" were the least likely to be compliant in taking the necessary medicine. The fact that health care workers were unaware of these folk categories and did not attempt to elicit the EM's of their patients clearly adds to the problem of compliance.

As you read this selection, consider these questions:

- **What kind of confusion might arise if a health care provider does not know that her patient believes in "high pertension" instead of the biomedical category "hypertension"?**
- **Why would the MMWR consider this study important enough to publish it as timely medical news?**
- **What kind of education project seems to be suggested by this research? Do you think it would be best to focus on health care providers or patients?**
- **Why does it seem very logical that a person who believed that she had "high pertension" would not think that taking medication regularly would be an important thing to do?**
- **Why might a person who thinks she has "high blood" think that taking hypertension medication regularly is a reasonable thing to do?**

Context: Suzanne Heurtin-Roberts is a medical anthropologist and social worker who works for the federal government. She is the health disparities coordinator for the Behavioral Research Program of the National Cancer Institute at the National Institutes of Health. She is best known for her research on "high-pertension" among African Americans—the topic of this article. Her work for the NIH has had an impressive impact on health disparities research. For example, she helped push a $56-million research agenda on population health and health disparities. She was also responsible for organizing the "Guidelines for Qualitative Methods" for NIH proposals and reviewers, which has improved the quality of medical anthropological methods used in government-sponsored health research. Efrain Reisin is professor of medicine at the Louisiana State University Health Science Center, where he is the chief of nephrology and hypertension. At the time when this piece was published (1990), research into ethnic health disparities in the United States was just beginning. Moreover, most research on "compliance" did not recognize that there are logical reasons for health behaviors, including those that don't follow "doctor's orders." This article provided an important introduction to the medical anthropological view of this chronic disease problem.

Source: Centers for Disease Control (1990). "Topics in Minority Health: Health Beliefs and Compliance with Prescribed Medication for Hypertension among Black Women, 1985–86." *Morbidity and Mortality Weekly Report* 39(40):701–704.

In the United States, the prevalence of definite hypertension (i.e., having systolic blood pressure $\geqslant$ 160 mm Hg and/or diastolic blood pressure $\geqslant$ 95 mm Hg, and/or taking antihypertensive medication) is 1.5 times higher among blacks (25.7%) than among whites (16.8%).[1] Although hypertension-related mortality appears to be declining among blacks, this problem continues to be disproportionately higher among blacks than among whites, particularly in younger age groups.[2] Poor compliance with prescribed treatment is cited as the major reason for inadequate control of hypertension in blacks and whites.[3] Improved understanding of patients' beliefs about hypertension could aid the development of public health strategies to reduce or control the disease. This report summarizes a study of the relationship between beliefs about hypertension and compliance with antihypertensive treatment among black women who received health care at a public hospital clinic in New Orleans.

From May 1985 through July 1986, 54 (72%) of 75 black women aged 45–70 years receiving treatment for essential hypertension and possibly one other chronic disease unrelated to hypertension were included in the study. Each patient participated for 2 months. To elicit beliefs and attitudes about hypertension and general health, investigators interviewed each patient twice using a standardized questionnaire. Patients were visited in their homes at 2-week intervals to monitor blood pressure and compliance with prescribed medication. The 15 resident physicians who treated these patients at the clinic were interviewed about their awareness of patient health beliefs.

Based on medication diaries, field notes, and pill counts (at the initial visit and at 1 and 2 months after the initial visit), patient compliance was categorized as "poor" (pill use < 60%) or "good" (use > 80%). For women with pill use 60%–79% (n = 14) or for whom complete pill-use records were not available, diaries and field notes were used to determine whether compliance was "good" or "poor." The likelihood of poor compliance among women who professed folk beliefs was compared with the likelihood of poor compliance among women who believed in a biomedical model of hypertension.

The 54 patients conceptualized their disease as "pressure trouble" or simply "pressure." One group (n = 22) believed in the existence of the biomedical disease, hypertension; the other group (n = 32) believed instead in the existence of two diseases, "high blood" and "high-pertension," distinguished by folk etiology, symptomatology, and treatment.

Patients characterized "high blood" as a physical disease of the blood and heart in which the blood was too "hot," "rich," or "thick"; the level of the blood rose slowly in the body and remained high for extended periods. These participants considered "high blood" to be caused by heredity, poor diet, and "heat" (from either the body or the environment); to be predictable and controllable; and to be capable of resulting in illness or death. "High blood" was thought to be appropriately treated by dietary control (i.e., abstention from pork, hot or spicy foods, and "grease") and by various folk remedies such as ingestion of lemon juice, vinegar, or garlic water. Patients believed these treatments cooled and thinned the blood, causing its level in the body to drop.

Patients considered "high-pertension" to be a disease "of the nerves" caused by stress, worry, and an anxious personality. Unlike "high blood," "high-pertension" was believed to be volatile and episodic. These patients believed that at times of emotional excitement, the blood would "shoot up" rapidly toward the head, then "fall back" or "drop back" quickly. Rather than medication and dietary control, these patients considered the appropriate treatment for "high-pertension" to be mitigation of stress and emotional excitement through control of emotions and the social environment.

Of the 32 women who believed in either of the two folk illnesses, 20 (63%) complied poorly with antihypertensive treatment, compared with six (27%) of 22 who believed in biomedical hypertension (relative risk = 2.3; 95% confidence interval [CI] = 1.2–4.4). Differences in compliance were also related to self-diagnosis: women who believed they had "high-pertension" were 3.3 times as likely to comply poorly as women who believed they had biomedical hypertension (95% CI = 1.7–6.8). Those with "high blood" were 0.5 times as likely to be poor compliers (95% CI = 0.1–3.1). Patients who believed they had both folk illnesses were 2.4 times as likely to be poor compliers as those who believed they had biomedical hypertension (95% CI = 1.1–5.2).

The 15 resident physicians had limited knowledge of the existence among their patients of folk beliefs about hypertension. Only two physicians knew of their patients' beliefs about the role of blood and emotional states in hypertension. Although 12 of the 15 physicians were aware of folk terms for hypertension, eight believed such terms were simply folk expressions for the biomedical illness.

EDITORIAL NOTE

Compliance with drug therapy has been a major focus of research on the control of hypertension since 1979, when the Hypertension Detection and Follow-Up Program Cooperative Group[1] reported lower mortality in persons with moderate hypertension who received therapy. Although the benefits of drug therapy are well established, excess mortality associated with essential hypertension persists among black persons in the United States. The findings in this report suggest that physicians might decrease the excess mortality associated with hypertension through health education efforts and by taking into consideration their patients' beliefs.

This study (1) documented hypertension-related beliefs of a high-risk population under treatment, (2) demonstrated a measurable relationship between patients' perceptions of illness and compliance behavior, (3) determined that physicians treating these patients were unaware of their patients' perceptions of their illness, and (4) suggested the importance of training physicians to elicit patients' conceptions of the illness[4] before selecting a therapeutic regimen.

Limitations of the study sample are that it was small and facility-based and included only black women. Nonetheless, the findings about these patients' perceptions of hypertension are consistent with other studies that used larger, community-based samples of blacks[5, 6] and facility-based samples of whites.[7] These studies advocate educating physicians about the importance of patient beliefs about hypertension.

REFERENCES

1. Drizd T, Dannenberg AL, Engel A, NCHS. Blood pressure levels in persons 18–74 years of age in 1976–80, and trends in blood pressure from 1960 to 1980 in the United States. Hyattsville, Maryland: US Department of Health and Human Services, Public Health Service, CDC, 1986; DHHS publication no. (PHS)86-1684. (Vital and health statistics; series 11, no. 234).
2. National Heart, Lung, and Blood Institute. The 1988 report of the Joint National Committee on Detection, Evaluation, and Treatment of High Blood Pressure. Arch Intern Med 1988; 148:1023–38.
3. National Heart, Lung, and Blood Institute. The 1984 report of the Joint National Committee on Detection, Evaluation, and Treatment of High Blood Pressure. Arch Intern Med 1984; 144:1045–57.
4. Kleinman A. Patients and healers in the context of culture: an exploration of the borderland between anthropology, medicine, and psychiatry. Berkeley, California: University of California Press, 1980:105–6.
5. Snow L. Traditional health beliefs and practices among lower class black Americans. Western J Med 1983; 139: 820–8.
6. Wilson RP. An ethnomedical analysis of health beliefs about hypertension among low income black Americans [Dissertation]. Stanford, California: Stanford University, 1985.
7. Blumhagen D. The meaning of hypertension. In: Chrisman NJ, Maretzki TW, eds. Clinically applied anthropology. Boston: Reidel Publishing, 1982.

Working with the Culture of Biomedicine

CONCEPTUAL TOOLS

■ ***Biomedicine is an ethnomedicine of Western culture.*** In a cultural sense, a medical system is an organized set of ideas referring to a particular healing tradition (e.g., Chinese, Ayurvedic, homeopathic, or biomedical). Medical anthropologists use the term *biomedicine* to refer to the tradition of scientific, biologically oriented methods of diagnosis and cure. Biomedicine is a relatively recent tradition that is technologically sophisticated and often extremely successful in curing. Historically known as "allopathic medicine", biomedicine has grown extremely quickly in terms of knowledge and technology as have the prestige and professionalization of biomedical practitioners. The scientific medical system is international, cosmopolitan, dominant, and hegemonic. It is not, however, culture-free. The cultural and epistemological assumptions of biomedicine have been studied by medical anthropologists (Rhodes 1996), as have the significant and fascinating national and regional differences in the practice of biomedicine, especially between European countries and the United States (e.g., differences in the interpretation of schizophrenia or low blood pressure, or in rates and styles of surgery) (Payer 1988). When viewed as a cultural system, biomedicine becomes one ethnomedicine among many others. All ethnomedicines are rooted in cultural presuppositions and values, associated with rules of conduct, and embedded in a larger context (Hahn 1995). There is little doubt that *belief* in the healer and the power of the medicine by a patient and family plays a fundamental role in the process of healing. All medical systems manipulate symbols to invoke and enhance belief; in this regard, all medical systems involve symbolic healing processes (sometimes labeled a placebo effect).

■ ***An awareness of culture is important in biomedicine; however, it is not as simple as developing "cultural competence."*** Cultural competence is a movement in the training of contemporary health care professionals. It is aimed at making practitioners aware of and sensitive to the cultural beliefs and values of their patients. This is especially the case when patients are from immigrant groups or ethnic minorities. Despite widespread popularity, cultural competence remains a vaguely defined goal, with no explicit criteria established for its accomplishment or assessment; this may be due to the elusive nature of the central construct of culture. Medical anthropologists do not necessarily think that training in cultural competence is a bad thing. However, this training is often done in an overly simplistic way that can reinforce stereotypes. There is sometimes a kind of cookbook approach, one implying that all members of a certain ethnic group have exactly the same beliefs. On the contrary, anthropologists argue that culture is always changing, constructed, and contested—even if it tends to be conservative.

■ ***"Cultural humility" may be a useful alternative to "cultural competence."*** People working within the world of biomedicine often imagine that theirs is a culture-free realm dominated by science and rationality. This is far from the case, despite what these "natives" believe. The idea of cultural humility, first described in work by Melanie Tervalon and Jann Murray-Garcia (1998), emphasizes a process of cultural self-reflection and self-critique. In this approach, the largest barrier to culturally appropriate care is not the lack of knowledge about other health beliefs, but a failure of self-awareness necessary for a respectful attitude toward different points of view. In this sense, cultural competence is simply part of regular medical competence.

■ ***Illness behavior can be considered a "hierarchy of resort."*** When people perceive that they are ill, they act on this perception and seek medical care. Sociologists call these actions *illness behaviors*. The primary components of illness behavior include acceptance of the sick role and the seeking of therapeutic interventions. Studies of illness behavior center on patterns of seeking health care; these patterns are called a *hierarchy of resort*. In general, people's hierarchies of resort begin with seeking solutions at home, usually from a female figure called "Mom" (or a linguistic variation thereof—actually, "Mama" is very common in the languages of the world). If household remedies do not work, the patient and his or her family move up the hierarchy of resort to a health care specialist. Depending on the society, this second step may involve going to a biomedical doctor or to a folk healer. If the patient is not cured on this level, and financial resources permit, the patient will seek care from a different, often more specialized, medical practitioner. Ethnographic descriptions of medical decision making and therapy-seeking behaviors comprise important aspects of the anthropological description of medical systems.

30

Anthropology and the World of Physicians

Thomas Johnson

Anthropological analysis of biomedical concepts, beliefs, and practices is common in the field today. In working within the settings of biomedicine, applied medical anthropologists hope to contribute to the improvement of people's health and the quality of their health care. However, it is very difficult to change any health care setting, and anthropologists who study physicians have found that critical analyses of problems are not always appreciated by medical practitioners. Moreover, there is more than one way to try to make a difference—one can work outside the health care system or within the system. In the past, there have been some tensions between anthropologists working from these different perspectives.

For anthropologists working within biomedical settings, the attraction of working as a clinician may be strong because clinicians can have an immediate impact on patients' well-being. In this selection, Thomas Johnson describes his work in a hospital and offers insights about the culture of biomedicine that draw on his anthropological training. For instance, his observations about the meaning of time—for both patients and health care workers—clearly emphasize cultural constructions and differential experiences.

As you read this selection, consider these questions:

- **What are Thomas Johnson's goals in practicing his specialized form of applied medical anthropology?**
- **How does he gain acceptance into the world of clinicians?**
- **The method of "participant observation" is sometimes considered an oxymoron. How might that be the case here?**
- **Does a clinician trained in medical anthropology have an advantage in practicing his or her craft as a healer?**

Context*:* This autobiographical article was published in Anthropology Newsletter, the monthly publication of the American Anthropological Association, as part of a series called "Portrait of an Anthropologist." The purpose of the series was to illustrate the work of anthropologists working outside of academic settings (this includes approximately 50 percent of anthropology PhDs). This article was also written at a time when there were marked tensions between "critical medical anthropologists" and "clinically applied anthropologists." Johnson, who did his research in a hospital setting, originally gained additional clinical training as a psychologist to enhance his teaching of medical students and nurses. In the process, he found himself very attracted to performing clinical care. It is often difficult for individuals to do both things, and Johnson eventually became much more of a practitioner than a researcher. He works at the University of Alabama Medical Center, Huntsville.

Source: T. Johnson (1990). "Anthropology and the World of Physicians." *Anthropology Newsletter*, November-December.

Biomedicine has always fascinated me: the complex social organization of hospitals; the elaborate rituals and specialized language of practitioners; the poignancy of human emotions made exquisitely palpable in time of sickness; the powerful, even brutal molding of young people into physicians by the process of medical education. I have worked in medical settings for the past 25 years—from exploring every nook and cranny of a hospital as a maintenance worker/undergraduate sociology major, to discovering the existence of a specialty called medical anthropology that encouraged me to conduct ethnographic studies of hospital wards, indigent clinics and migrant farm worker health care as a graduate student. I learned about the power of medical education by immersing myself in the process—from cadaver dissection to bedside rounds—during dissertation research.

I concluded that the 1960s activist dreams I had about improving health care in this country could best be achieved by attempting to change the medical education process. Knowing that the most powerful professional socialization in medicine takes place in clinical settings rather than in the lecture hall, I became one of only a few nonphysician medical anthropologists whose primary teaching role has been in hospital wards and outpatient clinics. Ultimately, also I recognized that, for me at least, the immediacy of patient care was so rewarding that I completed another graduate degree in clinical psychology. With dual training and clinical credentials I consider almost everything I do—from leading a staff support group for nurses in a burn unit to being a psychotherapist—as a specialized type of applied medical anthropology.

With this background, I have spent most of the last fifteen years in clinical and teaching activities on the faculties of three medical schools and residency programs, although during that time I also taught for seven years in a graduate medical anthropology program. Currently, I am on the faculty of a family medicine residency program, in which I act as a consultant to residents and physician faculty in the care of their patients. I also give seminars and supervise residents in a required month-long clinical rotation in medical behavioral science.

Over the years, interacting with medical students and residents while interviewing a severely burned patient or a parent whose baby was stillborn an hour earlier not only has permitted me to influence medical practice, but has also allowed me to view with ever greater acuity the cultural contrasts between medicine and anthropology—differences in world views and epistemologies that must be understood to work successfully in medicine. My experiences suggest that any medical anthropologists desiring to work in biomedicine will have to struggle with these implicit, unspoken assumptions that characterize the culture of biomedicine. My purpose here is to present some of these distinctive features of biomedicine, particularly as they contrast with those of academic anthropology.

Most anthropologists recognize that culture can be defined in Kroeberian terms (as "acts, artifacts, beliefs, etc."), but it is also clear that culture is a phenomenon involving basic assumptions about the world. These assumptions, sometimes thought of as "core values," not only guide people in their activities, but also underlie group identity and serve boundary maintenance functions (defines who is "us" and who is "not us"). Because identity and boundary maintenance functions are a major feature of professionalization in complex cultures, many medical anthropologists may anticipate that being accepted by practitioners in a biomedical setting will be difficult. I have not experienced this to be true. In fact, I have found that physicians unconsciously divide the world moiety-like into two groups: practitioners and the public. Because *therapeutic activism* is a core value among practitioners, anyone willing to be even peripherally involved in the process of patient care will find acceptance. Anyone not involved in the therapeutic process is automatically relegated to the lay moiety.

Thus, although it is true that physicians may anticipate criticisms from a social scientist in their midst, once a medical anthropologist has demonstrated even a modicum of therapeutic activism, which initially involves passing what I call "ethnographic tests" (such as helping to remove an encrusted incisional drain without overt expressions of disgust or enduring caustic and insensitive remarks about patients without becoming defensive), ready acceptance will follow. Such inevitable ethnographic tests are not unlike those in traditional cross-cultural fieldwork settings where anthropologists are expected to accept offers of certain indigenous foods or to witness rituals like clitoridectomy or infanticide without overt judgmentalism. As in any cross-cultural setting, it is axiomatic that learning "medicalese"—both informally through informants and by taking a course in medical terminology—is essential for effective participation.

My participation in biomedical settings has led me to see inevitable epistemological differences between anthropology and biomedicine. For example, among my biomedical colleagues there is an unspoken assumption that medical science is rational and objective. This ethos of *positivism* provides for a sense of certainty and control in the face of sickness. The touch stone of this view is "hard data": an emphasis on quantification, which predisposes physicians to value phenomena that can be reduced to numerical equivalents, such as blood pressure, serum amylase levels, and the like, but to be much more uncomfortable with phenomena such as anxiety or depression (unless, of course, these can be "measured" using psychological testing).

Thus, the very modes of acquiring knowledge in medical anthropology and biomedicine stand in sharp contrast. In biomedicine, diagnosis based on the core value of *affective neutrality* is the *sine qua non* of inquiry. The term "diagnosis" literally means "to tell apart": not only to differentiate one disease from another, but also to separate those who are well or "in control" from those who are sick, which may effectively distance practitioners from patients. Of course, diagnosis is also a process that improves the confidence and reduces the anxiety of practitioners. Diagnosis emphasizes *explaining*, while knowledge acquisition in academic medical anthropology increasingly emphasizes *understanding*—bemoaning the decontextualization and disembodying of sickness and demanding that empathic attention be paid to the individual experiences and social contexts of people who are ill.

Whenever I am asked to render a diagnosis, I debate with myself to clarify if the process will permit me to better understand and help the patient, or if it will distance me because I am feeling uncomfortable.

In actual treatment activities, this key difference in the way physicians and medical anthropologists are predisposed to gather and value data creates an inevitable tension within me. Although the anthropological predilection to immerse oneself in the life-world of patients is compelling, unless one is actively involved in the therapeutic process it is difficult to appreciate how *too much* understanding actually can be paralyzing. When agonizing clinical decisions have to be made, I have experienced how too much empathy can lead to overwhelming feelings of vulnerability and uncertainty. Nonetheless, I see how dangerous it can be to objectify patients so that, in my own clinical work, I constantly challenge myself to walk a tightrope between explaining and understanding—between distancing and empathy—recognizing always the liabilities of each.

While treatment decisions ostensibly are attempts to "control" the diseases to be treated, I have noticed an unconscious tendency for physicians to want to control patients themselves (the term "patient management" is common in biomedicine, and betrays this posture—I insist on the term "disease management," but recognize that this still involves a cooperative effort between physician and patient). When hospitalized and seriously ill, illusions of control of patients and their diseases are easier; in primary care outpatient settings, however, patient behavior is frustratingly difficult to predict, making attention to the psychosocial dimensions of patient care—the grist for a medical anthropologist's mill—essential.

I have discovered that work in biomedicine demands constant attention to other unspoken assumptions about the world, such as the *concept of time*, which is viewed differently in medical and academic anthropology settings. In the latter, time is one's own, and scholarship that results from working in relative isolation is expected and valued. Time is something that one can "control," as when a long-distance runner consciously sets an individual pace. In biomedicine, time is both a scarce commodity and a compelling force, in relation to which practitioners see themselves as out of control. In clinical settings one responds almost exclusively to demands from others, there is never enough time to meet all the demands, and it is impossible to predict when demands will be made. Although it seems trivial on the surface, one of the most frustrating aspects of working as an anthropologist in the biomedical world is seldom being able to enjoy conversations over meals, which invariably are eaten hurriedly for fear that one's beeper will go off at any moment.

Availability is another important core value in biomedical culture. Carrying a beeper is a symbolic statement that one is "always available": this is a powerful anxiety-allaying mechanism, reassuring all that help is always close when the inevitable emergencies occur. Although there are seldom emergencies demanding my involvement, I have found it imperative (albeit sometimes annoying) to adopt the "beeper mentality" that exists in biomedicine. Interestingly, my academic anthropology colleagues regularly questioned the presence of my beeper with derogatory suggestions that I was "playing doctor." The importance of availability in clinical settings is also symbolized in daily ritual activities in clinical settings: "making rounds" on patients starting at 7:00 AM, being "on call" at night, or working on holidays become rites of intensification that solidify group identity. I have found that I must be available to participate in such activities, even at onerous times, to remain an effective part of the group.

In individual physicians, the behavioral and attitudinal manifestations of therapeutic activism, positivism, affective neutrality, time pressure and expectations of availability are often expressed and/or perceived by outsiders as arrogance. Successful medical anthropologists must not be put off by such a posture in physician colleagues, but recognize it as a psychological defense against the uncertainties that attend patient care—something I truly believe most of my academic colleagues have never experienced (here, I recognize my own apparent arrogance!).

In truth, unspoken assumptions within biomedicine can and sometimes do have negative effects on clinical reasoning and decision making. Unless physicians can step back and examine these assumptions within biomedicine, there is very real likelihood that medical practice will become a compulsion to change patients, rather than an opportunity to help them. There is a danger that these unconscious assumptions of biomedicine will be a source of clinical distortion. Thus, in every patient care consultation, my goal is to get medical students and residents to understand themselves, and not simply help them explain their patients' problems. My work is an attempt to help physicians become more genuine and flexible in their care of patients by better understanding the unconscious motivations and assumptions underlying their clinical activities.

31

A Teaching Framework for Cross-Cultural Health Care

Elois Ann Berlin
William C. Fowkes, Jr.

This selection concerning ethnicity and health care is essentially a lecture to clinicians and medical students about the fundamental characteristics of successful cross-cultural medical practice. The key is effective communication between patient and health care giver. Effective communication is a fundamental aspect of all human relationships, yet it is surprisingly difficult to achieve. In this selection, the authors use the acronym LEARN as a mnemonic device (Listen, Explain, Acknowledge, Recommend, Negotiate). It represents the key attributes of an effective cross-cultural communication process. The authors describe each stage in this communication process with a short case study from a multicultural hospital setting.

Language can be a barrier to effective communication because, in addition to different words and grammar, cultural beliefs and values underlie the communication process. Different cultural backgrounds, like different languages, represent communication obstacles that can be overcome. The challenge of communication and cooperation among people of different ethnic groups can be found in the LEARN acronym. Many times, health care providers fail to listen and to identify a patient's concerns. Often, people in power think of themselves as giving orders to subordinates, rather than teaching, explaining, and recommending. Along with this old-fashioned idea that the doctor's orders are the law to be obeyed, noncompliance is nothing more than disobedience. But this model no longer works. Today, a buzzword in clinical practice is the "therapeutic alliance" of physician and patient, meaning that healing requires a partnership based on mutual understanding, respect, and cooperation. Such a partnership is more difficult to achieve across the cultural divide of an ethnic boundary. The key to such a partnership is effective communication.

Other guides for cross-cultural clinical practice can be found in the collection Ethnicity and Health Care *(Harwood 1981), special issues of the* Western Journal of Medicine *(Barker and Clark 1992; Clark 1983), and chapters in behavioral science textbooks for medical students (Brown, Gregg, and Ballard 1997).*

As you read this selection, consider these questions:

- **Why is it important for doctors to know about cross-cultural medicine? After all, isn't medicine a universal science?**
- **Do you think that following the advice in the LEARN acronym would take more of a physician's time? Would it be worth the trouble?**
- **To what extent do social class differences and educational differences complicate effective communication between health care givers and patients?**
- **Do you think that medical school students would listen to this lecture? Could they learn from it?**

Context: Elois Ann Berlin is a medical anthropologist and professor emeritus in the Department of Anthropology at the University of Georgia. Her research is mainly biocultural and ethnobotanical, focusing on the adaptive use of food and medicines among the highland Maya of Chiapas, Mexico. William Fowkes is a physician and professor emeritus of medicine at Stanford University who specializes in family medicine and geriatrics. This selection was published at a time when biomedicine was beginning to make systematic attempts to improve cross-cultural understanding and communication in clinical settings, an effort that has since been termed "cultural competence." Yet while many cultural competency programs have been criticized for overgeneralizations regarding different social groups, this particular work is distinctive in that it focuses on the process of cultural understanding for health professionals in any setting, rather than the memorization of cultural particulars.

Source: E. A. Berlin and W. C. Fowkes (1983). "A Teaching Framework in Cross-Cultural Healthcare" *Western Journal of Medicine*, 139:130–134.

Health care providers are finding themselves dealing with increasingly diverse patient populations. Fueled by armed conflict, political unrest and economic instability, the influx of immigrants into the United States is prompting a structural shift in the demographic representation of minorities. The impact is especially acute in states like California, which are subject to secondary migration or relocation after preliminary resettlement. These migration patterns, in combination with reproductive patterns, set a trend that is predictive of what has been termed *minoritization.*

In addition to language and socioeconomic barriers recognized to stand between minority populations and the health care system,[1–3] there is an increasing awareness of the impact of diverse health and disease belief systems on the interaction of health care providers and patients of a different cultural heritage.[4–10]

Overcoming these obstacles is aided by the incorporation of new rolls for cross-cultural communication. At the Family Practice Residency at San Jose Health Center, we have begun to develop a set of guidelines for health care providers in a practice that serves a multicultural patient population. We have structured these guidelines around the following mnemonic:

Guidelines for Health Practitioners: LEARN

L *Listen* with sympathy and understanding to the patient's perception of the problem
E *Explain* your perceptions of the problem
A *Acknowledge* and discuss the differences and similarities
R *Recommend* treatment
N *Negotiate* agreement

It should be emphasized that the LEARN model is not intended to replace completely the normal structure of the medical interview. Rather, it is intended as a supplement to history taking. The difference in focus is between a patient's factual subjective report of onset and duration and characteristics of symptoms and a patient's theoretical explanation of the reasons for the problem.

DISCUSSION OF GUIDELINES

Listen

Interview techniques have been proposed that aid in elicitation of a patient's conception of the cause, process, duration and outcome of an illness as well as healing strategies and resources that the patient considers to be appropriate.[4, 6] Understanding a patient's conceptualizations and preferences constitutes the first step. Questions such as, What do you feel may be causing your problem? How do you feel the illness is affecting you? and What do you feel might be of benefit? are examples of the shift in focus.

Explain

Explanation or communication of a "Western medicine" model is the next step. This may be a biomedical model but often the provider is making an educated guess, for example, that a patient's diarrhea is indeed due to an intestinal virus as opposed to toxins from contaminated food or psychosocial stress. In the primary care setting, treatment is frequently initiated without a definite diagnosis or biomedical model. However, it is critical to the success of the interaction that the care-giver have a strategy and that the strategy be conveyed to the patient.

Acknowledge

Acknowledgment of a patient's explanatory model occurs next or is integrated into the previous explanatory step. Based on an understanding of the explanatory models of both patient and provider, areas of agreement can be pointed out and potential conceptual conflicts understood and resolved. Resolution may involve bridging the conceptual gap between disparate belief systems. In many instances there is no therapeutic dilemma involved and a patient's own model can be incorporated into the system of care. If the provider feels that a patient's explanatory model and its consequences may have possible deleterious effects, such as a toxic medicinal substance, then an attempt must be made to market a more appropriate model leading to the next step. An example of a counterproductive explanatory model and resultant intervention is the consumption of pickle brine for hypertension—called "high blood" by some southern blacks. "High blood" is characterized by too much blood and treated by avoiding rich foods and consuming pickle brine, an "astringent" substance. The high sodium content of pickle brine would likely be deleterious in the face of blood pressure elevation.[10]

Recommend

Within the constraints imposed by a patient's and provider's explanatory models, a treatment plan can be developed. Patient involvement in the treatment plan is important. This step constitutes an extension of such an effort to include cultural parameters when appropriate culturally relevant approaches can be incorporated into the recommendation to enhance the acceptability of the treatment plan.

Negotiate

Negotiation is perhaps the key concept of the proposed LEARN model. It is necessary to understand a patient's perceptions and to communicate the provider's perspective so that a treatment plan can be developed and negotiated. There may be a variety of options from the biomedical, psychosocial or cultural approaches that could be appropriately applied. The final treatment plan should be an amalgamation resulting from a unique partnership in decision making between provider and patient. A patient can truly be involved in the instrumentation of recovery if the therapeutic process fits within the cultural framework of healing and health.

APPLICATION OF GUIDELINES

To illustrate the application of the LEARN model, we have selected examples from the experiences of our staff and students. We have chosen a separate case to exemplify each concept of LEARN. Although all or most steps in the model are involved in every clinical encounter, the cases were chosen to best illustrate each concept specifically.

- Listen

A 28-year-old Vietnamese woman, a social work student, was first seen in the Family Practice Center in autumn of 1982 because of weight loss, mood swings, nervousness, sweaty palms and an increased number of bowel movements. She had lived in the United States for five years. Initially she volunteered that she had been extremely depressed ten years earlier and had once attempted suicide. She had an established diagnosis of retinitis pigmentosa and was legally blind. She was living with her mother and two siblings and was entering college to study social work. On initial examination there were findings consistent with retinitis pigmentosa. Lid lag was also noted. Initial laboratory studies elicited values consistent with mild hyperthyroidism and she was started on a regimen of propranolol hydrochloride taken orally.

She was seen regularly and had a constellation of symptoms including abdominal pain, mute attacks during which she could not open her mouth, twitching and palpitations. After taking propranolol she felt very fatigued and weak and had an episode of syncope after which she refused to take further medication. Additional symptoms developed including squeezing substernal chest pain. Repeat thyroid function testing was normal.

There was no apparent physical explanation for the symptoms and it was felt that she was suffering from anxiety and depression related to her disability and life stress. Supportive approaches were instituted with regular counseling visits. Relaxation training and a life journal were begun. The technique used for relaxation included both breathing exercises and visualization.

Shortly after these measures were instituted the patient presented in a very agitated state and said that the pleasant visual images she attempted to conjure turned "dark and scary." She also related that a childhood diary had been taken from her by one of her sisters and that the contents had been ridiculed. This made it very difficult for her to keep the recommended life journal. At this time, with encouragement, she related some very important events in her childhood. When she was 8 to 10 years of age her affliction was felt by her family to be due to her possession by an evil spirit, and a healer was summoned. The attempt at exorcism failed and this was interpreted as a sign that her illness was a form of punishment for her transgressions in a past life. She was virtually locked away in a back room for several years before the events that led to her immigration.

She stated she no longer held this set of beliefs, but she continued to worry about whether she was a good person. Her physician agreed with her rejection of the ideas held by her family and suggested that her studies in social work and her commitment to help people were indeed evidence of her goodness and worth.

She moved out of her home to campus housing and has improved somewhat. She continues to visit the Family Practice Center for supportive care.

Cultural Context

The medicoreligious beliefs of Vietnam derive from such a variety of sources that specification of exact religious context of the healing rituals of this patient's early life is difficult.

There have been historical interchanges of Ayurvedic medicine, with its roots in Galenic humoral pathology, influenced by Hinduism and Buddhism, especially in Southeast Asia.[11–16] Chinese medicine, which is more closely related to Confucian and Taoist religious philosophies, has made an additional contribution. More recent influences come from Catholicism and Western medicine. Local indigenous beliefs and practices also no doubt exert some influence.[17]

Attribution of illness to possession by spirits or demons is consistent with all of these religious traditions (including Catholicism, at least historically). Whichever temple and priest or shaman the patient's family applied to for help, her status as a victim of a malevolent source would have been validated by successful exorcism. This would have been confirmed by the return of her eyes to normal appearance. Failure of repeated exorcistic rites to alleviate the symptoms led to the conclusion that her deviant appearance was a mystical mark, a sign of evil committed in a former life. This conclusion transformed her from victim to perpetrator. In a family whose members include all of the living, dead and as yet unborn, the final diagnosis shamed the family in perpetuity. This was the justification for confining the child in the house and restricting her social interactions. The family was, literally, attempting to hide their shame. The psychologic burden that this explanation placed on the patient resulted in somatization of complaints. Mental illness, which bears strong negative sanctions for similar reasons, would have constituted yet another mark against the family.

The patient migrated with her family to the United States when she was an adolescent. The process of acculturation and an alternative biomedical diagnosis provided a context for a change of attitudes and perception of self-worth. Although several people whom the patient had consulted over time (social workers and health care providers) had felt that there was a troubling "cultural component" in her medical history, the patient had never been able to discuss it fully. Careful probing and an open, nonjudgmental attitude on the part of the resident physician allowed the patient to divulge the complete background information and to acknowledge the lingering self-doubt these experiences had produced. She was then able to initiate steps for improvement such as removing herself from the family context, which produced continuing stress and reinforced a negative self-image, and continuing her studies in a helping profession, which confirmed her goodness.

- Explain

A 21-month-old Mexican-American male infant with recurrent onset of fever, runny nose and noisy breathing was brought to the clinic by his mother. The mother noted that the child had been sleeping restlessly and making sighing noises while asleep.

On physical examination, he was found to have edematous mucous membranes and mucoid nasal discharge consistent with an upper respiratory tract infection (URI).

The mother stated that she was very concerned because two months earlier the child had had a major motor seizure that she associated with a high fever. She felt that the seizure had precipitated *susto* (fright disease), as evidenced by the sighing and restlessness during sleep, and wanted a regimen to control fever and prevent a worsening of the child's *susto*.

The resident physician discussed upper respiratory tract infections and their effects on breathing. He suggested a decongestant for relief of symptoms. He also confirmed the relationship of fever to seizures and advised continued use of antipyretics. He demonstrated the use of sponge baths to reduce fever and emphasized the importance of fever control in preventing seizures. In addition, he suggested that the mother consult a *curandera* (folk healer) concerning her questions about *susto*. The patient has subsequently been seen for routine visits and has had no further seizures or other significant problems.

Cultural Context

Susto is a Latin-American folk illness that is caused by fright.[18–22] The source or cause of fright might be anything from a simple startle response to an encounter with spirits. Children are particularly susceptible to *susto*. Symptoms vary widely, but the sighing and restlessness or poor sleep pattern exhibited by the patient are common manifestations. The mother's explanatory model for this case of *susto* was as follows:

> URI → fever → seizures → *susto* → sleep disturbance.

The provider was able to give a detailed biomedical explanation of that portion of the patient's explanatory model to which it was applicable and to recommend consultation with a folk specialist for that portion that lay outside the purview of modern medicine.

- Acknowledge

A 25-year-old Vietnamese woman was seen for a routine prenatal examination. As part of her evaluation she had blood drawn for laboratory testing. Within the next few days she returned with a variety of symptoms including weakness, fatigue and coryza. She attributed this to having blood removed, feeling that removal of blood weakens the system and causes illness.

Her provider, a Vietnamese physician, was aware of the belief and acknowledged it, but also explained how much blood volume she actually had and gave the example of persons donating blood, a much larger volume, without symptoms.

She was pleased with the explanation, seemed to feel less fearful and her symptoms abated.

Cultural Context

The probable influence of Chinese medicine or Ayurvedic medicine (or both) in Southeast Asia is seen in this patient's response to blood tests. Edwards[23] describes the following physiological process from Chinese medical theory: "The connection between food, [blood], sex and health is found in the transformational formula in which seven units of the precursor yields one unit of the subsequent product:

Food → blood → *jing* → *qi* → *shen*

Edwards defines the terms as follows: *jing* = "sexual fluid," which is a vital substance; *qi* = "breath" or "life energy" (also written *chi*); *shen* = "ethereal energy." A similar process has been described from Ayurvedic medical theory, which could be outlined as follows:

Food → chyle → blood → flesh → fat
bones → marrow → semen[24]

Because several physiological systems are involved in the production, transportation and storage process—that is, digestive, genitourinary, circulatory and respiratory—symptoms can be diffuse and varied. Since all descriptions indicate a geometric reduction between precursor and product, the consequences of interruption of the cycle would increase geometrically in seriousness at each earlier step in the process.

The patient's and the provider's explanatory models were similar in that they both believed blood loss to constitute a potential threat to health. Their explanations differed in the amount of blood that must be lost to pose a problem. By relating the amount of blood removed to the total blood volume and comparing this with the much larger quantities safely removed from blood donors, the physician was able to reassure the patient and to effect alleviation of symptoms.

- Recommend

A 38-year-old Mexican-American man was seen in the Family Practice Center for chronic genitourinary problems. He had experienced hematuria and right flank pain two years before. In addition there had been recurrent episodes over 18 years of right flank pain and dysuria, diagnosed as urinary tract infections. He did not use analgesics. Examination of the external genitalia and prostate was unremarkable. He had no abdominal or flank tenderness. Analysis of urine showed 50 to 100 leukocytes per high dry field. An intravenous pyelogram showed a localized hydronephrotic area in the upper pole of the right kidney.

He was seen by a urologist who carried out retrograde pyelograms. These showed a large calyceal diverticulum connected with the right collecting system, with hydronephrosis of the upper pole of the kidney.

Surgical treatment was recommended. The patient expressed considerable reluctance to have an operation. When questioned by his family physician he expressed concern that his "blood was low" and that he would have trouble going through an operation under the circumstances. His physician discussed the amount of blood that could be expected to be lost with a partial nephrectomy and also the total available blood supply in the body. He suggested that a surgical procedure be delayed for a period to allow the patient to "build up his blood" with appropriate medication. This was quite acceptable to the patient and the consultant urologist.

He subsequently underwent uneventful partial right nephrectomy.

Cultural Context

Blood is "hot" according to the hot-cold system of humoral pathology as practiced in Latin America. Blood is also associated with strength, both in the health and the sexual sense. Having a large supply of blood makes one strong and healthy, but is also associated with virility and hence with machismo. Menstrual blood, semen and sexual activity are very hot.[25] Men's blood is hotter than women's blood.

The patient felt a need to build up his blood supply in order to have reserve strength for an operation because he expected a significant amount of blood to be lost during it. He was willing to accept the recommendation that he take iron to help build blood. However, an equally acceptable way to build blood would have been to eat blood products such as fried blood or blood sausage. Organ meats are good for building up strength and blood supply. In the Mexican-American folk system, an abundant and varied diet builds physical reserves, including a healthy supply of blood.

By describing the surgical procedure, including control of bleeding, the resident physician was able to alleviate some of the patient's concerns about blood loss. The provider was then able to recommend a treatment plan acceptable to the patient by prescribing "blood building" medicines and by scheduling the operation following a delay of fixed duration that the patient concurred would be adequate to prepare himself.

• Negotiate

A 48-year-old black man was seen because of severe hypertension and congestive heart failure associated with far-advanced renal insufficiency. Initially he was managed conservatively. It became obvious, however, that he had reached a stage at which renal dialysis was his only hope for survival.

When he was approached about the possibility of hemodialysis he declined, stating that he was a devout Christian and felt that the Will of God was of prime importance and that he would wait for God's intervention rather than accept dialysis.

His physician acknowledged the importance of God's influence, but suggested that the opportunity for dialysis as a means to control his condition might be the way God had intended for him to survive. Indeed, there was nothing in the Bible that prohibited dialysis and God helps those who help themselves.

The following day the patient consented to hemodialysis and now has a functioning bovine shunt and is doing well.

Cultural Context

The socioreligious context of this patient's explanatory model was fundamentalist Protestantism. The direct intervention and control of health by God is supported in the Old Testament (Exodus 4:11): ". . . who maketh the dumb or deaf, or the seeing or the blind? Have not I the Lord?" The New Testament contains dozens of examples of the healing powers of Christ.[26] While one common alternative to treatment is faith healing,[27] this patient seemed to be relying on the Old Testament with healing based on direct intervention by God. He suggested that he felt that God did not intend him to die yet and would intervene on his behalf. The provider was able to call on other aspects of Christian beliefs such as "the Lord helps those who help themselves" and that God sometimes works through human agents: "For to one is given by the Spirit the word of wisdom; . . . to another the gift of healing by the same Spirit" (I Corinthians 12:8–9).

The implication was drawn that the physicians and dialysis might be the instruments through which God intended to intervene. Medical intervention was thus translated into a construct that did not violate the tenets of the patient's faith. By using beliefs from the patient's own religious background, the provider was able to negotiate acceptance of recommended biomedical treatment.

SUMMARY AND CONCLUSIONS

Given current demographic trends it is probably unrealistic to assume that health care providers can gain in-depth knowledge about the health-affecting beliefs and practices of every ethnic or cultural group they are likely to encounter in practice. The processes of acculturation, interethnic variation and social change also serve as confounding agents in predicting knowledge, behavior and attitudes. Social class differences, too, provide striking variability. We have, therefore, chosen a process-oriented model by which the cultural, social and personal information relevant to a given illness episode can be elicited, discussed and negotiated or incorporated.

However, it is common in our experience for patients of different beliefs to be reluctant to discuss this problem for fear of criticism or ridicule. It is certainly of value for providers who deal with culturally diverse patients to have some understanding of common basic conceptions of health, illness and anatomy held by these persons. Much work needs to be done in codifying these conceptions and making them available to professionals in medicine.

The foregoing examples serve to illustrate some of the means the members of a family practice residency program have used for enhancing communication and promoting the integration of patients' and providers' perceptions of needs and solutions into the therapeutic process.

REFERENCES

1. Bullough B, Bullough V: Poverty, Ethnic Identity and Health Care. New York: Appleton-Century-Crofts, 1972.
2. Quesada GM: Language and communication barriers for health delivery to a minority group. Soc Sci Med 1976 June; 10:323–327.
3. Language Access Task Force, Velez M (Chief Author): Health Care for Non-English Speaking Populations: Access and Quality. West Bay Health Systems Agency. San Francisco, Western Center for Health Planning, 1982.
4. Harwood A (Ed): Ethnicity and Medical Care. Cambridge, Mass, Harvard University Press, 1981.
5. Hill CE: A folk medical belief system in the American South: Some practical considerations. South Med 1976 Dec. pp 11–17.

6. Kleinman A, Eisenberg L, Good B: Culture, illness and care: Clinical lessons from anthropological and cross cultural research. Ann Intern Med 1978; 89:251-258
7. Martinez RA (Ed): Hispanic Culture and Health Care: Fact, Fiction and Folklore. St Louis, CV Mosby, 1978
8. Mason JC: Ethnicity and clinical care. Indiana Phys Assist Health Practitioner 1980 Nov; 30:30-39
9. Muecke MA: Caring for Southeast Asian refugee patients in the USA. Am J Public Health 1983; 73:431-438
10. Snow LF: Folk medical beliefs and their implications for care of patients: A review based, on studies among Black Americans. Ann Intern Med 1974; 81:82-96
11. Basham AL: The practice of medicine in ancient and medieval India. In Leslie C (Ed): Asian Medical Systems. Berkeley and Los Angeles, University of California Press, 1976, pp 18-43
12. Burgel JC: Secular and religious features of medieval Arabic medicine, In Leslie C (Ed): Asian Medical Systems, Berkeley and Los Angeles, University of California Press, 1976, pp 44–62
13. Gard RA: Buddhism. New York, George Braziller, 1962
14. Obeyesekere G: The impact of Ayurvedic ideas on the culture and the individual in Sri-Lanka. In Leslie C (Ed): Asian Medical Systems. Berkeley and Los Angeles, University of California Press, 1976, pp 201–226
15. Olness K: Indochinese refugees—Cultural aspects of working with Lao refugees. Minn Med 1979 Dec; 62: 871–874
16. Renou L: Hinduism. New York, George Braziller, 1961
17. Whitmore JK (Ed): An Introduction to Indochinese History, Culture, Language and Life—For Persons Involved with the Indochinese Refugee Education and Resettlement Project in the State of Michigan, Ann Arbor, Center for South and Southeast Asian Studies, University of Michigan, 1979
18. Klein J: *Susto*: The anthropological study of diseases of adaptation. Soc Sci Med 1978 Jan; 12:23–28
19. O'Nell CW, Selby HA: Sex differences in the incidence of susto in the Zapotec Pueblos: An analysis of the relationships between sex role expectations and a folk illness. Ethnology 1968; 7:95-105
20. O'Nell CW: An investigation of reported "fright" as a factor in the etiology of *susto*. "Magical Fright." Ethos 1975; 3:41-63
21. Rubel AJ: The epidemiology of folk illness: *Susto* in Hispanic America. Ethnology 1964; 3:268–283
22. Uzzell D: *Susto* revisited: Illness as a strategic role. Am Ethnol 1974; 1:369–378
23. Edwards JW: Semen anxiety in South Asian cultures: Cultural and transcultural significance. Med Anthropol, in press
24. Zimmer HR: Hindu Medicine. Baltimore, Johns Hopkins Press, 1948
25. Ingham JM: On Mexican folk medicine. Am Anthropol 1970; 72: 76–87
26. Henderson G, Primeaux M: Religious beliefs and healing. In Henderson G, Primeaux M (Eds): Transcultural Health Care. Menlo Park, Calif., Addison-Wesley, 1981, pp 185–195
27. Baer HA: Prophets and advisers in black spiritual churches: Therapy, palliative, or opiate? Cult Med Psychiatry 1981 Jun; 5:145–170

 32

Confronting "Culture" in Medicine's "Culture of No Culture"

Janelle S. Taylor

Anne Fadiman's The Spirit Catches You and You Fall Down: A Hmong Child, Her American Doctors, and the Collision of Two Cultures *(1997) is an influential book that many professors use in their medical anthropology courses. The story is written as a tragedy because the firmly held cultural beliefs of the little girl's Hmong parents clash with those of her physicians, and the outcome of the conflict seems both inevitable and tragic. The popularity of this book has come at a time of greater emphasis on "cultural competence" training for health care practitioners. Some policy makers believe that adding this education requirement will reduce racial and ethnic disparities in health measures.*

Historically, medical anthropologists have emphasized the importance of cultural knowledge and sensitivity in clinical treatment. They have argued that increased cultural understanding and improved cross-cultural communication will improve health care outcomes for minority groups. This idea is illustrated clearly with the LEARN model described by Berlin and Fowkes in selection 32; a significant goal in this approach is to improve so-called patient "compliance." Medical anthropologists whose work is aimed at improving health care—sometimes called clinical medical anthropologists—face a serious challenge, however, because cultural competence training often seems to tap an old-fashioned and static view of culture. There is an implicit understanding that culture belongs only to the "other" and that it is always an obstacle.

More recently, medical anthropologists have turned their research and analytical lens toward understanding the culture of biomedicine. This approach is not always appreciated by health care practitioners because it is seen to have little practical use in their daily work. But is this really the case?

In this selection, Janelle Taylor describes biomedicine as a culture that believes it has no culture. Yet health care practitioners and biomedical researchers are part of a larger society whose ideas, beliefs, and values are created by the dominant groups. Therefore, the physicians' knowledge is considered "real," while the patients' knowledge is considered "cultural." Moreover, the cultural and psychosocial dimensions of a patient's illness experience are frequently thought of as irrelevant—as "touchy-feely stuff" that needs to be ignored. Such beliefs are learned by medical students within the institutional culture of medical education. Nonetheless, in the contemporary world, every medical interaction has the potential to be a cross-cultural encounter. Given our increasingly diverse society, perhaps someday the consideration of culture might become simply part of competent medical care.

As you read this selection, consider these questions:

- **What does the author mean by this statement: "Physicians' medical knowledge is no less cultural for being real, just as patients' lived experiences and perspectives are no less real for being cultural"?**
- **How are medical students learning to think when they master the "narrative structure" required for successfully presenting a case during rounds?**
- **Why might people in power believe that only the "other" has culture?**
- **Might physicians' confidence in the truth of medical knowledge enhance their special power to alleviate suffering?**

Context: Janelle Taylor teaches medical anthropology at the University of Washington, where she also holds an appointment in women's studies and directs the critical medical humanities project. This selection was published in *Academic Medicine*, a journal that focuses on medical education, as part of a special series on the teaching of "cultural competence." The cultural competence movement has been met with ambivalence by many medical anthropologists, and Taylor's work cogently explains why this is the case. Much of her medical anthropological work on biomedical technologies has been informed by feminist theory. In 2004, she co-edited the book *Consuming Motherhood*; her most recent book is *The Public Life of the Fetal Sonogram: Technology, Consumption, and the Politics of Reproduction* (2008).

Source: J. Taylor (2003). "Confronting 'Culture' in Medicine's 'Culture of No Culture.'" Academic Medicine 78(6):555–559.

Efforts to promote cultural competence in medical education and practice that have blossomed over the past decade or so have thus far focused primarily on the task of providing cultural information about various specific immigrant communities. This focus has been fruitful, resulting in expanded and improved resources of many kinds—from courses to training seminars, translator services, highly informative Web sites,[1] and more—to assist practitioners caring for patient populations that have created (especially in those regions where successive waves of immigrants have congregated most densely) an enormously complex tapestry of linguistic, religious, and other kinds of diversity. In the wake of these accomplishments, cultural competence has earned a secure place among the formal educational goals of medical school curricula, and the moment may now be ripe to pause and consider future directions. With that in mind, in this article I present reflections from medical anthropology on the institutional culture of medical education, and suggest some reasons why achieving the broader goals of cultural competence curricula may require broader institutional changes.

As cultural competence programs have matured, a number of parties involved in promoting them have warned against a too-simple understanding of "culture."[2,3] One obvious concern is that materials intended to help foster awareness of and openness to difference may—depending upon how they are presented and how they are received—have the contrary effect of perpetuating more or less rigid stereotypes about what members of a particular "culture" believe, do, or want, and how they should be dealt with.[4–6] Some authors stress that a "culture" is not a static and timeless thing but is constantly changing as people make use of their cultural resources in creative and sometimes surprising ways.[7] Others emphasize that "culture" is multifaceted, encompassing linguistic, religious, educational, class, and many other dimensions of difference, which intersect in complex ways in the life experience and identity of any one individual.[2] It has been proposed that the term cultural "humility" ought to replace cultural "competence" as the goal of multicultural education in medicine.[4] It is also argued that "culture" must be situated in relation to "social" factors such as literacy or socioeconomic class standing.[8] The point has also been made repeatedly that not only patients and their communities have cultures, but that there is also a "culture" of medicine.[9,10]

It is tempting to remain at the level of theoretical discussions, and to imagine that what is needed are newer and better definitions for "culture." This temptation is perhaps especially strong for those of us who discuss cultural competence from the discipline of sociocultural anthropology, because we use the same key term, "culture," differently. Coming from anthropology, where "culture is now viewed by many to consist of sets of competing discourses and practices, within situations characterized by the unequal distribution of power"[11] (and where, it must be added, one enjoys the luxury of reflecting on culture at some distance from the urgencies of clinical care), the literature on cultural competence can give one the slightly spooky sensation of having encountered the Ghost of Anthropology Past.[12] Guarnaccia and Rodriguez note that

> in reviewing recent works on culturally-competent mental health, writers have often turned to earlier writings by anthropologists to present a definition of culture. In general, these definitions have reflected a static view of culture as the distinctive set of beliefs, values, morals, customs and institutions which people inherit . . . [whereas] more recent approaches to culture in anthropology provide a more dynamic perspective . . . viewing culture as a process in which views and practices are dynamically affected by social transformations, social conflicts, power relationships, and migrations.[2]

Merely to argue about how one ought to define "culture," however, is unlikely to be especially persuasive or helpful. The anthropologist, I am well aware, risks sounding a bit like Humpty Dumpty saying to Alice that "when *I* use a word, it means just what I choose it to mean, neither more nor less!" A more interesting and useful approach is to ask of cultural competence programs the same question that anthropologists ask of any sociocultural phenomenon that they wish to understand: How do systems of thought relate to what anthropologists sometimes call "systems of social action" (i.e., the observable patterns in the ways that people act and interact in society)? Specifically, in this case, how do particular ways of conceptualizing and talking about "culture" relate to the sociocultural organization of the institutions of medicine and medical education? To put it very bluntly, are there features of the culture of medicine that might tend to lead those who inhabit it to think of "culture" as a static set of ideas and beliefs that only other people possess?

MEDICINE AS A "CULTURE OF NO CULTURE"

In 1988 the sociocultural anthropologist Sharon Traweek published an innovative ethnographic study of an unusual type of human community: high-energy physicists working at the Stanford Linear Accelerator.[13]

As an ethnographer, Traweek sought to situate this community's systems of thought in relation to their systems of social action, contextualizing the science of high-energy physics in relation to the patterned ways that the community of physicists organized themselves socially. She was particularly interested in how this community reproduced itself—how it produced new generations of physicists who would assume their places in its social and professional hierarchies, while also assuming the community's values, assumptions, and goals as their own. She stated:

> I believe that to understand how scientific and technological knowledge is produced we must understand what is uncontested as well as what is contested, how the ground state is constructed as well as how the signals called data are produced. When I speak of the shared ground I do not mean some a priori norms or values but the daily production and reproduction of what is to be shared . . . the forces of stability, the varieties of tradition, in a community dedicated to innovation and discovery.[13]

What emerges from Traweek's study is a portrait of high-energy physics as "a culture of no culture"—that is, a community denfined by the shared cultural conviction that its shared convictions were *not* in the least cultural, but, rather, timeless truths.

Physicians obviously differ from physicists in many regards, not least in the fact that the central purpose they share with the medical community is not so much the production of new knowledge as it is the alleviation of human suffering caused by illness and injury. "Medical knowledge," furthermore, encompasses both formally codified knowledge and the quite different kinds of knowledge gained through clinical experience. In general terms, however, it is confidence in the *truth* of medical knowledge that underwrites physicians' special power to alleviate suffering. Medical knowledge is understood to be not merely "cultural" knowledge but *real* knowledge. In this perspective, it may be reasonable to describe medicine, no less than physics, as perceiving itself to be a "culture of no culture."

This presents obvious difficulties for the project of crafting cultural competence curricula that will go beyond focusing on "other" cultural groups, and attend to cultural dimensions of medicine itself. Lorna A. Rhodes notes that

> in both biomedical settings and the study of other kinds of medicine, it is hard to avoid the assumption that what needs to be explained are the "alternatives," the "other" perspectives, the "misunderstandings" or "misuses" of biomedicine rather than biomedicine itself.[14]

Or as Byron Good puts it, "Our convictions about the truth claims of medical science rest uneasily with . . . our desire to respect competing knowledge claims of members of other societies or status groups."[15]

One sees traces of this uneasiness in, for example, Anne Fadiman's book *The Spirit Catches You and You Fall Down: A Hmong Child, Her American Doctors, and the Collision of Two Cultures,* widely used as a text for teaching about issues of culture in medicine. Fadiman writes that

> for better or for worse, Western medicine *is* one-sided. Doctors endure medical school and residency in order to acquire knowledge that their patients do not have. Until the culture of medicine changes, it would be asking a lot of them to consider, much less adopt, the notion that . . . "our view of reality is only a view, not reality itself."[16]

Fadiman asserts that "medicine *is* one-sided" and that doctors have "knowledge that their patients do not have." At the same time, however, she leaves open the intriguing possibility that physicians *might* someday place their medical knowledge on an even footing with (culturally different) patients' knowledge, if and when "the culture of medicine changes." What would have to change? What is it about the culture of medicine that makes it appear, to its members, to be so devoid of culture?

To answer this question following Traweek's lead requires documenting the social processes by which "what is uncontested"—in this case, the conviction that medical knowledge is *real,* i.e., not "cultural"—is produced and reproduced, through the training of new generations.

Mary-Jo DelVecchio Good, writing of her ethnographic study of the training of Harvard University medical students, shows us, at least in part, how this takes place. To earn for themselves a place in the medical community, medical students must establish their competence. "Competence," with no modifier, means mastery of medical—i.e., *real*—knowledge. One of the key ways in which medical students establish their competence, according to Good, is by learning how to craft and perform what she calls "clinical narratives"—in other words, learning to transform what patients say into what physicians write on charts and say to each other. As Good's account shows, these narrative practices through which students demonstrate their "competence" leave precious little room for eliciting the kinds of information that might be necessary to establish "*cultural* competence." These narrative practices are, thus, part of what Frederic Hafferty[9] has referred to as medicine's "hidden curriculum":

Students were encouraged to learn new narrative forms, to create medically meaningful arguments and plots with therapeutic consequences for patients. In this process, they sharpened their biomedical "gaze" and developed their clinical reasoning. Throughout these exercises, the "psychosocial" aspects of most patients' illnesses, their social histories and emotional states, and their lives outside of the hospitals and clinics were largely irrelevant; these data from daily life were regarded as "inadmissible evidence" in the presentations made during everyday work rounds.[17]

In *The Spirit Catches You*, Fadiman quotes the physician Dan Murphy recounting his own experience of treating Lia Lee, the small sick child of Hmong immigrants who was at the center of the book's story, during one of her seizures. Murphy recalls agonizing over his inability to talk to Lia's parents, but at the same time describes precisely this experience of proving his competence by creating, under these circumstances, a "medically meaningful argument" and a "plot with therapeutic consequences":

> I thought it might be meningitis, so Lia had to have a spinal tap, and the parents were real resistant to that. I don't remember how I convinced them. I remember feeling very anxious because they had a real sick kid and I felt a big need to explain to these people, through their relative who was a not-very-good translator, what was going on, but I felt like I had no time, because we had to put an IV in her scalp with Valium to stop the seizures, but then Lia started seizing again and the IV went into the skin instead of the vein, and I had a hard time getting another one started. Later on, when I figured out what had happened, or not happened, on the earlier visits to the ER, I felt good. It's kind of a thrill to find something someone else has missed, especially when you're a resident and you are looking for excuses to make yourself feel smarter than the other physicians.[16]

His description makes all too clear how medical "competence" can be established and demonstrated by creating clinical narratives, even in the face of the bleakest inability to communicate across cultural difference.

Indeed, one might argue that establishing one's "competence" as a physician *requires* bracketing off questions of the patient's life experience. Byron Good, who carried out research jointly with DelVecchio Good among Harvard University medical students, quotes one student's explanation of what "presenting a case" to an attending physician involves:

> . . . basically what you're supposed to do is take a walking, talking, confusing, disorganized (as we all are) human being, with an array of symptoms that are experienced, not diagnosed, and take it all in, put it in the Cuisinart and puree it into this sort of form that everyone can quickly extrapolate from. They don't want to hear the story of the person. They want to hear the edited version. . . . You're not there to just talk with people and learn about their lives and nurture them. You're not there for that. You're a professional and you're trained in interpreting phenomenological descriptions of behavior into physiologic and pathophysiologic processes. So there's the sense of if you try to tell people really the story of someone, they'd be angry; they'd be annoyed at you because you're missing the point. That's indulgence, sort of.[15]

If, as Good and Good suggest, physicians-in-training establish their overall "competence" by learning to craft clinical narratives in a way that "justifies the systematic discounting of the patient's narrative,"[15] then what does "competence" mean when we attach to it the modifier "cultural"? However one defines "culture," does not attention to it demand, at the very least, taking an interest in what people think and say and what they have experienced—in short, "the story of the person"?

As long as these basic features of the "hidden curriculum" and institutional culture of medical education remain in place, no amount of fine-tuning the theoretical definitions that students are assigned to read on "touchy-feely Tuesdays" is likely to unsettle the tendency of medical education to produce and reproduce itself as a "culture of no culture."

RECONSTRUCTING "COMPETENCE": BEYOND "ADD CULTURE AND STIR"

Increased diversity among those who enter medical school, however, might go some distance toward unmasking the "culture" in this "culture of no culture."

Separate and self-contained though medical institutions in some respects are, they are also integrally a part of the broader sociocultural order in which they are embedded, and tend to reflect its patterns of thought and social action. These are less likely to appear necessary and natural, and thus more likely to become visible as "culture," to people who do not themselves emerge from its dominant segments. Guarnaccia and Rodriguez note that

> professional cultures are variants of the dominant culture focused on particular sectors of society and social problems. Thus, dominant cultural norms and values are built into the frameworks for the training of professionals, for assessment of clients, and for developing

> treatment approaches. For someone from a different culture to become a professional involves at least two processes of acculturation—one to the dominant culture and the other to that of the profession.[2]

This acculturation process can be stressful for professionals from minority cultural groups, who "frequently are in a conflicted position with multiple loyalties to clients and institutions."[2] Nor is the situation of such medical professionals, marked out within this "culture of no culture" as being individuals who have "culture," made any simpler when they are enlisted to serve as mediators, translators, or native informants.

The same dissonance that places such strain on medical professionals from minority groups can, however, also yield insights—which, if heeded, might perhaps help open paths toward change. Mary Canales and Barbara Bowers, writing of cultural competence within nursing, note that

> although the theoretical concepts of "cultural diversity" and "culturally competent care" have been supported and promoted by the largest professional nursing organizations, the practical application of these concepts has often created difficulties for nurse researchers, educators and clinicians. Historically, it has been nursing leaders and educators, operating from a predominantly White, dominant culture perspective, who have initiated and promoted the majority of the directives for professional nursing.[18]

The same certainly holds true for medicine as well. Canales and Bowers conducted in-depth interviews with Latina nurse educators as a way of exploring "cultural competence, particularly how to teach it, from the perspectives of nursing faculty who have often found themselves on the cultural margins within schools of nursing and society in general."[18]

What they found was that Latina participants were less concerned to present their students with information about specific cultural groups than to teach broader constructions of the Other and the phenomena of "Othering." Indeed, Canales and Bowers found that

> what was salient for these participants was the perception that competent care includes cultural competence. According to this theory of teaching practice, preparing students to become competent practitioners requires that students learn to care for those perceived as different from self; that they learn to care as connected members of a community and the larger society; and that students learn to care with a commitment towards changing existing social, health, and economic structures that are exclusionary.[18]

SUMMING UP

I have presented here some reflections from medical anthropology on the institutional culture of medicine and medical education. Medicine, I have argued, sees itself as a "culture of no culture," and its practitioners tend systematically to foster static and essentialist understandings of the "cultures" of patients. Even though requirements designed to address cultural competence are increasingly commonly incorporated into medical school curricula, medical students as a group may be forgiven for failing to take these very seriously as long as they perceive that they are quite distinct from the *real* "competence" that they need to acquire. To change this situation will require challenging the tendency to assume that "real" and "cultural" must be mutually exclusive terms. Physicians' medical knowledge is no less cultural for being real, just as patients' lived experiences and perspectives are no less real for being cultural. Whether this is a lesson that can effectively be conveyed within existing curricular frameworks remains an open question. Cultural competence curricula will, perhaps, achieve their greatest success if and when they put themselves out of business—if and when, that is, medical competence itself is transformed to such a degree that it is no longer possible to imagine it as *not* also being "cultural."

REFERENCES

1. Ethnomed: ethnic medicine from Harborview Medical Center. Department of Anthropology, University of Washington. (http://ethnomed.org/). Accessed 3/10/03.
2. Guamaccia PJ, Rodriguez O. Concepts of culture and their role in the development of culturally-competent mental health services. Hispanic J Behav Sci. 1996;18;419–43.
3. Sobo E, Seid M. Cultural issues in pediatric medicine: what kind of "competence" is needed? Paper presented at the annual meeting of the American Anthropological Association, New Orleans, LA, November 2002.
4. Tervalon M, Murray-Garcia J. Cultural humility versus cultural competence: a critical distinction in defining physician training outcomes in multicultural education. J Health Car Poor Underserved. 1998;9(2):117–25.
5. Turbes S, Krebs E, Axtell S. The hidden curriculum in multicultural medical education: the role of case examples. Acad Med. 2002;77:209–16.
6. Nuñez A. Transforming cultural competence into cross-cultural efficacy in women's health education. Acad Med. 2000;75:1071–80.

7. Santiago-Irizarry V. Culture as cure. Cultural Anthropology. 1996;11:3–24.
8. Green AR, Betancourt JR, Carrillo JE. Integrating social factors into cross-cultural medical education. Acad Med. 2002;77:193–7.
9. Hafferty FW, Franks R. Beyond curriculum reform: confronting medicine's hidden curriculum. Acad Med. 1998;73:403–7.
10. Costley A, Dasgupta S. The anatomy of intake rounds: examining the reproduction of biomedical culture in the training of pediatric residents. Paper presented at the annual meeting of the American Anthropological Association, New Orleans, LA November 2002.
11. Frank G. Venus on Wheels: Two Decades of Dialogue about Disability, Biography, and Being Female in America. Berkeley, CA: University of California Press, 1999.
12. Helmreich S. After culture: reflections on the apparition of anthropology in artificial life, a science of simulation. Cultural Anthropology. 2002;16;612–27.
13. Traweek S. Beamtimes and Lifetimes: The World of High Energy Physicists. Cambridge, MA: Harvard University Press, 1988.
14. Rhodes LA. Studying biomedicine as a cultural system. In: Johnson TM, Sargent CF (eds). Medical Anthropology: A Handbook of Theory and Method. New York: Greenwood Press, 1990.
15. Good B. Medicine, Rationality and Experience: An Anthropological Perspective. Cambridge, U.K.: Cambridge University Press, 1994.
16. Fadiman A. The Spirit Catches You and You Fall Down: A Hmong Child, Her American Doctors, and the Collision of Two Cultures. New York: Noonday, 1997.
17. Good MJD. American Medicine: The Quest for Competence. Berkeley, CA: University of California Press, 1995.
18. Canales MK, Bowers BJ. Expanding conceptualizations of culturally competent care. J Adv Nurs. 2001;36:102–11.
19. Taylor JS. The story catches you and you fall down: tragedy, ethnography, and "cultural competence." Medical Anthropology Quarterly. 2003;17:159–81.

 33

Anthropology in the Clinic: The Problem of Cultural Competency and How to Fix It

Arthur Kleinman
Peter Benson

In recent years, there has been a substantial effort made to teach "cultural competence" to health care providers. Some states have made cultural competence training a requirement for medical or nursing licenses. The purpose of these measures is to improve the quality of health care and patient satisfaction, avoid problems, and decrease health inequalities related to race and ethnicity. These are all admirable goals. However, there is little evidence that such training programs work. In 2003, the Institute of Medicine published an important report titled Unequal Treatment: Confronting Racial and Ethnic Disparities in Health Care. *This study demonstrated that there are indeed unconscious prejudices of health care providers when dealing with minorities or immigrant groups. The poor do not have access to the best medical care. Much of this is caused by inequities in the financing of health care and inequities in health insurance. There are some good reasons that minority groups distrust the health system. Problems in cross-cultural communication, which might be avoided with cultural competence training, were not a major contributor to health disparities.*

Cultural misunderstandings, like the ones described in Anne Fadiman's book The Spirit Catches You and You Fall Down *(1998), do occur. They cause serious difficulties for both practitioners and patients. Cross-cultural communication skills can be taught and developed, as we saw in the selection earlier in this section by Berlin and Fowkes on the LEARN model. An awareness of culture is important in biomedicine. However, it is not as simple as developing "cultural competence." The idea of cultural humility, first described in work by Melanie Tervalon and Jann Murray-Garcia (1998), emphasizes a process of cultural self-reflection and self-critique. In this approach, the largest barrier to culturally appropriate care is not the lack of knowledge about other health beliefs, but a failure of self-awareness necessary for a respectful attitude toward different points of view.*

As such, the idea of cultural competence is problematic for medical anthropology. It is based on simplistic notions of culture that can lead to unfortunate assumptions and stereotyping. It ignores the cultural beliefs and attitudes of health care providers. It fails to account for intracultural variations. Finally, it does not give providers an idea of what to do in the cross-cultural encounter—for example with the explanatory models approach. For most medical anthropologists, "cultural competence" should simply be part of regular medical competence.

As you read this selection, consider these questions:

- **Why is culture so difficult to define? Why do people working in the health care system tend to believe that they do not have culture? What does it mean to say that culture is not static?**
- **"Competence" implies that an individual has the knowledge and skills to do something. What is it that cultural competence courses are trying to teach?**
- **What do the authors mean by explanatory models? If a physician asked the "eight questions," how would you react?**
- **What is the new "cultural formulation," and how is it different from the explanatory model approach?**
- **How might perceptions of "what is at stake" influence a patient's ability to heal?**

Context*:* Arthur Kleinman is chair of the Department of Anthropology at Harvard University and professor of psychiatry and medical anthropology at Harvard Medical School, as well as author of dozens of books and hundreds of articles. Kleinman's writing on this topic was incorporated into the fourth edition of the *Diagnostic and Statistical Manual of Mental Disorders*. This article, written for a widely circulated Internet journal, was part of a series on social medicine. Kleinman's most recent book, *What Really Matters: Living a Moral Life amidst Uncertainty and Danger* (2007), is based on his career as a practicing psychiatrist. Peter Benson is an assistant professor of anthropology at Washington University. He has done fieldwork in Mexico on the political economics of globalized vegetable farming and in North Carolina on migrant labor and global tobacco companies.

Source: A. Kleinman and P. Benson (2006). "Anthropology in the Clinic: The Problem of Cultural Com-petency and How to Fix It." *PLoS Medicine* 3(10):e294.

Cultural competency has become a fashionable term for clinicians and researchers. Yet no one can define this term precisely enough to operationalize it in clinical training and best practices.

It is clear that culture does matter in the clinic. Cultural factors are crucial to diagnosis, treatment, and care. They shape health-related beliefs, behaviors, and values [1,2]. But the large claims about the value of cultural competence for the art of professional care-giving around the world are simply not supported by robust evaluation research showing that systematic attention to culture really improves clinical services. This lack of evidence is a failure of outcome research to take culture seriously enough to routinely assess the cost-effectiveness of culturally informed therapeutic practices, not a lack of effort to introduce culturally informed strategies into clinical settings [3].

PROBLEMS WITH THE IDEA OF CULTURAL COMPETENCY

One major problem with the idea of cultural competency is that it suggests culture can be reduced to a technical skill for which clinicians can be trained to develop expertise [4]. This problem stems from how culture is defined in medicine, which contrasts strikingly with its current use in anthropology—the field in which the concept of culture originated [5–9]. Culture is often made synonymous with ethnicity, nationality, and language. For example, patients of a certain ethnicity—such as, the "Mexican patient"—are assumed to have a core set of beliefs about illness owing to fixed ethnic traits. Cultural competency becomes a series of "do's and don'ts" that define how to treat a patient of a given ethnic background [10]. The idea of isolated societies with shared cultural meanings would be rejected by anthropologists, today, since it leads to dangerous stereotyping—such as, "Chinese believe this," "Japanese believe that," and so on—as if entire societies or ethnic groups could be described by these simple slogans [11–13].

BOX 1 CASE SCENARIO: CULTURAL ASSUMPTIONS MAY HINDER PRACTICAL UNDERSTANDING

A medical anthropologist is asked by a pediatrician in California to consult in the care of a Mexican man who is HIV positive. The man's wife had died of AIDS one year ago. He has a four-year-old son who is HIV positive, but he has not been bringing the child in regularly for care. The explanation given by the clinicians assumed that the problem turned on a radically different cultural understanding. What the anthropologist found, though, was to the contrary. This man had a near complete understanding of HIV/AIDS and its treatment—largely through the support of a local nonprofit organization aimed at supporting Mexican-American patients with HIV. However, he was a very-low-paid bus driver, often working late night shifts, and he had no time to take his son to the clinic to receive care for him as regularly as his doctors requested. His failure to attend was not because of cultural differences, but rather his practical, socioeconomic situation. Talking with him and taking into account his "local world" were more useful than positing radically different Mexican health beliefs.

Another problem is that cultural factors are not always central to a case, and might actually hinder a more practical understanding of an episode (see Box 1).

Historically in the health-care domain, culture referred almost solely to the domain of the patient and family. As seen in the case scenario in Box 1, we can also talk about the culture of the professional caregiver—including both the cultural background of the doctor, nurse, or social worker, and the culture of biomedicine itself—especially as it is expressed in institutions such as hospitals, clinics, and medical schools [14]. Indeed, the culture of biomedicine is now seen as key to the transmission of stigma, the incorporation and maintenance of racial bias in institutions, and the development of health disparities across minority groups [15–18].

CULTURE IS NOT STATIC

In anthropology today, culture is not seen as homogenous or static. Anthropologists emphasize that culture is not a single variable but rather comprises multiple variables, affecting all aspects of experience. Culture is inseparable from economic, political, religious, psychological, and biological conditions. Culture is a process through which ordinary activities and conditions take on an emotional tone and a moral meaning for participants.

Cultural processes include the embodiment of meaning in psychophysiological reactions [19], the development of interpersonal attachments [20], the serious performance of religious practices [21], common-sense interpretations [22], and the cultivation of collective and individual identity [23]. Cultural processes frequently differ within the same ethnic or social group because of differences in age cohort, gender, political association, class, religion, ethnicity, and even personality.

THE IMPORTANCE OF ETHNOGRAPHY

It is of course legitimate and highly desirable for clinicians to be sensitive to cultural difference, and to attempt to provide care that deals with cultural issues from an anthropological perspective. We believe that the optimal way to do this is to train clinicians in ethnography. "Ethnography" is the technical term used in anthropology for its core methodology. It refers to an anthropologist's description of what life is like in a "local world," a specific setting in a society—usually one different from that of the anthropologist's world. Traditionally, the ethnographer visits a foreign country, learns the language, and, systematically, describes social patterns in a particular village, neighborhood, or network [24]. What sets this apart from other methods of social research is the importance placed on understanding the native's point of view [25]. The ethnographer practices an intensive and imaginative empathy for the experience of the natives—appreciating and humanly engaging with their foreignness [26], and understanding their religion, moral values, and everyday practices [27,28].

Ethnography is different than cultural competency. It eschews the "trait list approach" that understands culture as a set of already-known factors, such as "Chinese eat pork, Jews don't." (Millions of Chinese are vegetarians or are Muslims who do not eat pork; some Jews, including the corresponding author of this paper, love pork.) Ethnography emphasizes engagement with others and with the practices that people undertake in their local worlds. It also emphasizes the ambivalence that many people feel as a result of being between worlds (for example, persons who identify as both African-American and Irish, Jewish and Christian, American and French) in a way that cultural competency does not. And ethnography eschews the technical mastery that the term "competency" suggests. Anthropologists and clinicians share a common belief—i.e., the primacy of experience [29–33]. The clinician, as an anthropologist of sorts, can empathize with the lived experience of the patient's illness, and try to understand the illness as the patient understands, feels, perceives, and responds to it.

THE EXPLANATORY MODELS APPROACH

One of us [AK] introduced the "explanatory models approach," which is widely used in American medical schools today, as an interview technique (described below) that tries to understand how the social world affects and is affected by illness. Despite its influence, we've often witnessed misadventure when clinicians and clinical students use explanatory models. They materialize the models as a kind of substance or measurement (like hemoglobin, blood pressure, or X rays), and use it to end a conversation rather than to start a conversation. The moment when the human experience of illness is recast into technical disease categories something crucial to the experience is lost because it was not validated as an appropriate clinical concern [34].

Rather, explanatory models ought to open clinicians to human communication and set their expert knowledge alongside (not over and above) the patient's own explanation and viewpoint. Using this approach, clinicians can perform a "mini-ethnography," organized into a series of six steps. This is a revision of the Cultural Formulation included in the fourth edition of the Diagnostic and Statistical Manual of Mental Disorders (DSM-IV) (see Appendix I in [35]) [36,37].

A REVISED CULTURAL FORMULATION

Step 1: Ethnic Identity The first step is to ask about ethnic identity and determine whether it matters for the patient—whether it is an important part of the patient's sense of self. As part of this inquiry, it is crucial to acknowledge and affirm a person's experience of ethnicity and illness. This is basic to any therapeutic interaction, and enables a respectful inquiry into the person's identity. The clinician can communicate a recognition that people live their ethnicity differently, that the experience of ethnicity is complicated but important, and that it bears significance in the health-care setting. Treating ethnicity as a matter of empirical evidence means that its salience depends on the situation. Ethnicity is not an abstract identity, as the DSM-IV cultural formulation implies, but a vital aspect of how life is lived. Its importance varies from case to case and depends on the person. It defines how people see themselves and their place within family, work, and social networks. Rather than assuming knowledge of the patient, which can lead to stereotyping, simply asking the patient about ethnicity and its salience is the best way to start.

Step 2: What Is at Stake? The second step is to evaluate what is at stake as patients and their loved ones face an episode of illness. This evaluation may include close relationships, material resources, religious commitments, and even life itself. The question, "What is at stake?" can be asked by clinicians; the responses to this question will vary within and between ethnic groups, and will shed light on the moral lives of patients and their families.

Step 3: The Illness Narrative Step 3 is to reconstruct the patient's "illness narrative" [38]. This involves a series of questions (about one's explanatory model) aimed at acquiring an understanding of the meaning of illness (Box 2).

The patient and family's explanatory models can then be used to open up a conversation on cultural meanings that may hold serious implications for care. In this conversation, the clinician should be open to cultural differences in local worlds, and the patient should recognize that doctors do not fit a certain stereotype any more than they themselves do.

BOX 2 THE EXPLANATORY MODELS APPROACH

- What do you call this problem?
- What do you believe is the cause of this problem?
- What course do you expect it to take? How serious is it?
- What do you think this problem does inside your body?
- How does it affect your body and your mind?
- What do you most fear about this condition?
- What do you most fear about the treatment?

(Source: Chapter 15 in [38])

Step 4: Psychosocial Stresses Step 4 is to consider the ongoing stresses and social supports that characterize people's lives. The clinician records the chief psychosocial problems associated with the illness and its treatment (such as family tensions, work problems, financial difficulties, and personal anxiety). For example, if the clinicians described in the case scenario in Box 1 had carried out step 4, they could have avoided the misunderstanding with their Mexican-American patient. The clinician can also list interventions to improve any of the patient's difficulties, such as professional therapy, self-treatment, family assistance, and alternative or complementary medicine.

Step 5: Influence of Culture on Clinical Relationships Step 5 is to examine culture in terms of its influence on clinical relationships. Clinicians are grounded in the world of the patient, in their own personal network, and in the professional world of biomedicine and institutions. One crucial tool in ethnography is the critical self-reflection that comes from the unsettling but enlightening experience of being between social worlds (for example, the world of the researcher/doctor and the world of the patient/participant of ethnographic research). So, too, it is important to train clinicians to unpack the formative effect that the culture of biomedicine and institutions has on the most routine clinical practices—including bias, inappropriate and excessive use of advanced technology interventions, and, of course, stereotyping. Teaching practitioners to consider the effects of the culture of biomedicine is contrary to the view of the expert as authority and to the media's view that technical expertise is always the best answer. The statement "First do no harm by stereotyping" should appear on the walls of all clinics that cater to immigrant, refugee, and ethnic-minority populations. And yet since culture does not only apply to these groups, it ought to appear on the walls of all clinics.

Step 6: The Problems of a Cultural Competency Approach Finally, step 6 is to take into account the question of efficacy—namely, "Does this intervention actually work in particular cases?" There are also potential side-effects. Every intervention has potential unwanted effects, and this is also true of a cultural-ist approach. Perhaps the most serious side-effect of cultural competency is that attention to cultural difference can be interpreted by patients and families as intrusive, and might even contribute to a sense of being singled out and stigmatized [3,11,12]. Another danger is that overemphasis on cultural difference can lead to the mistaken idea that if we can only identify the cultural root of the problem, it can be resolved. The situation is usually much more complicated. For example, in her influential book, *The Spirit Catches You and You Fall Down*, Ann Fadiman shows that while inattention to culturally important factors creates havoc in the care of a young Hmong patient with epilepsy, once the cultural issues are addressed, there is still no easy resolution [33]. Instead, a whole new series of questions is raised.

DETERMINING WHAT IS AT STAKE FOR THE PATIENT

The case history in Box 3 gives an example of how simply using culturally appropriate terms to explain people's life stories helps the health professionals to restore a "broken" relationship and allows treatment to continue. This case is not settled, nor is it an example of any kind of technical competency. But there are two illuminating aspects of this case. First, it is important that health-care providers do not stigmatize or stereotype patients. This is a case study of an individual. Not all Chinese people fit this life story, and many contemporary Chinese now accept the diagnosis of depression. Second, culture is not just what patients have; clinicians also participate in cultural worlds. A physicians too rigidly oriented around the classification system of biomedicine might find it unacceptable to use lay classifications for the treatment.

BOX 3 CASE SCENARIO: THE IMPORTANCE OF USING CULTURALLY APPROPRIATE TERMS TO EXPLAIN PEOPLE'S LIFE STORIES

Miss Lin is a 24-year-old exchange student from China in graduate school in the United States, Where she developed symptoms of palpitations, shortness of breath, dizziness, fatigue, and headaches. A thorough medical work-up leaves the symptoms unexplained. A psychiatric consultant diagnoses a mixed depressive-anxiety disorder. Miss Lin is placed on antidepressants and does cognitive-behavioral psychotherapy, with symptoms getting better over a six-week period; but they do not disappear completely.

Subsequently, the patient drops out of treatment and refuses further contact with the medical system. Anthropological consultation discovers that Miss Lin comes from a Chinese family in Beijing- one of her consins is hospitalized with chronic mental illness. So powerful is the stigma of that illness for this family that Miss Lin cannot conceive of the idea that she is suffering from a mental disorder, and refuses to deal with her American health-care providers because they use the terms "anxiety disorder" and "depressive disorder". In this instance, she herself points out that in China the term that is used is neurasthenia or a stress-related condition. On the anthropologist's urging, clinicians reconnect with Miss Lin under this label.

For the late French moral philosopher Emmanuel Levinas, in the face of a person's suffering, the first ethical task is acknowledgment [39]. Face-to-face moral issues precede and take precedence over epistemological and cultural ones [40]. There is something more basic and more crucial than cultural competency in understanding the life of the patients; what the patient, at a deep level, stands to again or lose. The explanatory models approach does not ask, for example, "What do Mexicans call this problem?" It asks, "What do you call this problem?" and thus a direct and immediate appeal is made to the patient as an individual, not as a representative of a group.

CONCLUSION

What clinicians want to understand through the mini-ethnography is what really matters—what is really at stake for patients, their families, and, at times, their communities, and also what is at stake for themselves. If we were to reduce the six steps of culturally informed care to one activity that even the busiest clinician should be able to find time to do, it would be to routinely ask patients (and where appropriate family members) what matters most to them in the experience of illness and treatment. The clinicians can then use that crucial information in thinking through treatment decisions and negotiating with patients.

This is much different than cultural competency. Finding out what matters most to another person is not a technical skill. It is an elective affinity to the patient. This orientation becomes part of the practitioner's sense of self, and interpersonal skills become an important part of the practitioner's clinical resources [41]. It is what Franz Kafka said "a born doctor" has: "a hunger for people" [42]. And its main thrust is to focus on the patient as an individual, not a stereotype; as a human being facing danger and uncertainty, not merely a case; as an opportunity for the doctor to engage in an essential moral task, not an issue in cost-accounting [43].

REFERENCES

1. Kleinman A (2004) Culture and depression. N Engl J Med 351:951–952.
2. Kleinman A (1981) Patients and healers in the context of culture: An exploration of the borderland between anthropology, medicine, and psychiatry. Berkeley (California): University of California Press. 427 p.
3. Kleinman A (2005) Culture and psychiatric diagnosis and treatment: What are the necessary therapeutic skills? Utrecht (Holland): Trimbos-Instituut. 25 p.
4. DelVecchio Good M (1995) American medicine: The quest for competence. Berkeley (California): University of California Press. 265 p.
5. Stocking GW Jr, editor (1996) *Volksgeist* as method and ethic: Essays on Boasian ethnography and the German anthropological tradition. Madison (Wisconsin): University of Wisconsin Press. 349 p.
6. Abu-Lughod L (1991) Writing against culture. In: Fox RG, editor. Recapturing anthropology: Working in the present. Santa Fe (New Mexico): School of American Research Press. pp. 137–162.
7. Clifford J, Marcus GE, editors (1986) Writing culture: The poetics and politics of ethnography: A School of American Research advanced seminar. Berkeley (California): University of California Press. 305 p.
8. Gupta A, Ferguson J, editors (1996) Culture, power, place: Explorations in critical anthropology. Durham (North Carolina): Duke University Press. 361 p.
9. Fischer MMJ (2003) Emergent forms of life and the anthropological voice. Durham (North Carolina): Duke University Press. 477 p.
10. Betancourt JR (2004) Cultural competence—Marginal or mainstream movement? N Eng J Med 351: 953–954.
11. Taylor J (2003) The story catches you and you fall down: Tragedy, ethnography, and "cultural competence." Med Anthropol Q 17:159–181.
12. Lee SA, Farrell M (2006) Is cultural competency a backdoor to racism? Anthropology News 47(3):9–10. Available: http://raceproject.aaanet.org/pdf/rethinking/lee_ferrell.pdf, Accessed 10 August 2006.
13. Green JW (2006) On cultural competence. Anthropology News 47(5): 3.
14. Taylor J (2003) Confronting "culture" in medicine's "culture of no culture." Acad Med 78:555–559.
15. Lee S, Lee M, Chin M, Kleinman A (2005) Experience of social stigma by people with schizophrenia in Hong Kong. Br J Psychiatry 186:153–157.
16. Keusch GT, Wilentz J, Kleinman A (2006) Stigma and global health: Developing a research agenda. Lancet 367:525–527.
17. Wailoo K (2001) Dying in the city of the blues: Sickle cell anemia and the politics of race and health. Chapel Hill (North Carolina): University of North Carolina Press. 352 p.
18. United States Department of Health and Human Services [HHS] (1999) Mental health: A report of the Surgeon General. Washington (D.C.): HHS. Available: http://www.mentalhealth.samhsa.gov/cmhs/surgeongeneral/surgeongeneralrpt.as. Accessed 10 August 2006.
19. Moerman DE (2002) Explanatory mechanisms for placebo effects: Cultural influences and the meaning response. In: Guess HA, Kleinman A. Kusek JW, Engel LW, editors. The science of the placebo: Toward an interdisciplinary research agenda. London: BMJ Books. pp. 77–107.
20. Goffman E (1959) The presentation of self in everyday life. New York: Anchor. 259 p.
21. Barth F (1987) Cosmologies in the making: A generative approach to cultural variation in Inner New Guinea. Cambridge: Cambridge University Press. 112 p.
22. Sahlins M (1978) Culture and practical reason. Chicago: University of Chicago Press. 259 p.
23. Holland D. Lachicotte W Jr, Skinner D, Cain C (1996) Identity and agency in cultural worlds. Cambridge: Harvard University Press. 368 p.
24. Kleinman A (1999) Moral experience and ethical reflection: Can medical anthropology reconcile them? Daedalus 128:69–99.
25. Geertz C (1983) Local knowledge. New York: Basic Books. 256 p.
26. Jackson M (1996) Things as they are. Bloomington (Indiana): University of Indiana Press. 288 p.
27. Geertz C (1972) The interpretation of cultures. New York: Basic Books. 480 p.
28. Marcus G, Fischer MMJ (1986) Anthropology as cultural critique. Chicago: University of Chicago Press. 228 p.
29. Slobodin R (1997) W. H. R. Rivers: Pioneer anthropologist, psychiatrist of the ghost road. Stroud (United Kingdom): Sutton. 299 p.
30. Barker P (1991) Regeneration. New York: Penguin. 256 p.
31. Sacks O (1996) An anthropologist on Mars. New York; Vintage. 352 p.
32. Konner M (1988) Becoming a doctor. New York: Penguin. 416 p.
33. Fadiman A (1998) The spirit catches you and you fall down. New York: Farrar, Straus and Giroux. 352 p.
34. Kleinman A, Benson P (2004) La vida moral de los que sufren de la enfermedad y el fracaso existencial de la medicina. Monograffas Humanitas 2:17–26.
35. [Anonymous] (1994) Diagnostic and statistical manual of mental disorders, 4th ed. Washington (D.C.): American Psychiatric Association. Available: http://www.psychiatryonline.com/resourceTOC.aspx?resourceID=l. Accessed 10 August 2006.
36. Novins DK, Bechtold DW, Sack WH, Thompson J, Carter DR, et al. (1997) The DSM-IV outline for cultural formulation: A critical demonstration with American

Indian children. J Am Acad Child Adolesc Psychiatry 36:1244–1251.

37. Mezzich JE, Kirmayer LJ, Kleinman A, Fabrega H Jr, Parron DL, et al. (1999) The place of culture in DSM-IV. J Nerv Ment Dis 187:457–464.
38. Kleinman A (1988) The illness narratives: Suffering, healing, and the human condition. New York: Basic Books. 304 p.
39. Levinas E (2000) Useless suffering. In: Smith MB, Harshav B, translators. Entre nous: Thinking-of-the-other. New York: Columbia University Press. pp. 91–101.
40. Levinas E (1998) Otherwise than being: Or beyond essence. Pittsburgh: Duquesne University Press. 205 p.
41. Goethe (1978) Elective affinities. New York: Penguin. 304 p.
42. Lensing LA (2003 February 28) Franz would be with us here. Times Literary Supplement. pp. 13–15.
43. Kleinman A (2006) What really matters: Living a moral life amidst uncertainty and danger. Oxford: Oxford University Press. 272 p.

Ethnicity and Health Care

CONCEPTUAL TOOLS

■ ***Race is not a useful biological category, but it is an important social category.*** Most people believe the word *race* is a scientific term with a specific biological meaning. This is not the case when it comes to humans. Human biologists, including biological anthropologists, do not have a clear idea of how to define a race or what the significance of that category is if they have defined it. It is not possible to define a race in terms of either physical appearance *(phenotype)* or genetic makeup *(genotype).* This is partially because there is no way to determine the number of characteristics used to define the categories; the more characteristics used, the more categories there are. Moreover, genetic traits are independently assorted at conception. And, after all, all humans are biologically unique on an individual level while at the same time all are members of the single species, *Homo sapiens.*

The term *race* is a historical artifact from an archaic biology. The idea that there are a few "races"—white, black, red, yellow—or their scientific-sounding equivalents—Caucasoid, Negroid, Mongoloid—simply doesn't make sense or serve a useful purpose in biological explanations (Goodman and Armelagos 1996). From an evolutionary perspective, it would make scientific sense to consider the concept of *populations* that might form breeding isolates, but for actual living humans, such breeding isolates do not seem to exist. On the other hand, race as a social category is of incredible importance because it has been used as a biological rationalization for patterns of exploitation (slavery) or socioeconomic injustice (racism). Race is a social construction that has real biological consequences—for example, higher disease rates and lower life expectancies for members of some minority groups.

■ ***The North American rule of racial hypodescent is one indication of the social construction of race.*** In the United States, a child who has one African American parent and one white parent is automatically socially classified as an African American. This does not make biological sense, because the child inherits one-half of her genes from each parent. This traditional social rule is called *racial hypodescent,* meaning that the offspring is put into the lower-ranking category. The same rule functions for children of mixed-caste marriages in India. There are historical reasons for racial hypodescent in the United States: Slave children became material property of the slave owner even if he was the biological father. Other social rules of racial classification operate in different societies, like Brazil, with their own economic histories (Harris 1980).

■ ***Ethnicity is a useful and important social construct.*** Often, when people in the United States use the term *race,* they are actually referring to social categories of identity and subcultural differences that should be called *ethnicity.* Ethnic categories are based on cultural distinctions of history, heredity, religion, language, and so forth. People identify with their own ethnic group, and they are identified by others as members of that group. At the same time, however, the boundaries between ethnic groups are permeable, bendable, and socially constructed, as shown in the important anthropological research of Fredrik Barth (1969). As is so evident in today's world, ethnic groups are often the focus of ethnocentrism, bigotry, and political violence.

■ ***Ethnicity interacts with social class.*** People may use the term *race* when they are actually referring to differences in social class, that is, differences in access to material resources like money, property, and education. People in the United States may think that they live in a classless society, largely because just about everybody thinks they are members of the struggling middle class. In actuality, the United States is a highly stratified society in terms of wealth, meaning that we have a much more significant problem of poverty than most other industrialized nations. Members of ethnic minorities are more likely to be poorer and less powerful. Racist beliefs on the part of the dominant white ethnic groups exacerbate the problems of socioeconomic inequity.

■ ***In a multicultural society, ethnocentrism is a constant problem.*** The degree to which people identify with their ethnic group depends on various factors, including the degree of hostility of the dominant group, the length of time since immigration, the agglomeration of minorities in ethnic enclaves, and so forth. When individuals begin to identify more with the dominant culture—often as a result of education and upward social mobility—they become *acculturated* (an old anthropological term meaning that they have lost their traditional culture). Although the United States retains the myth of the melting pot, we are not a culturally homogenized society.

Ethnocentrism, the tendency to judge others using your own cultural criteria, is characteristic of all the world's societies, but it is an everyday problem in a multicultural, multiethnic society. Ethnocentrism can only be overcome through tolerance and vigilance.

■ ***Knowledge about cultural variation in the folk models of illness is valuable and useful, but this is different from simple stereotyping.*** Individuals hold explanatory models of their illnesses; when people in a group share some characteristics of an explanatory model it is called a *folk model of illness.* But not every member of an ethnic group will have identical beliefs about health and illness (Harwood 1981). The health care provider must learn to elicit this information from patients and to be sensitive to the possibility that cultural factors may interfere with effective communication.

Medical anthropologists do not advocate an ethnic "cookbook" approach to medical care and public health. What *is* most important is that health providers understand the range of health beliefs in a population and that they treat the people who hold these beliefs with respect and not ethnocentric derision (Clark 1983).

 34

A Case of Lead Poisoning from Folk Remedies in Mexican American Communities

Robert T. Trotter II

It is important to realize that not all medical remedies are helpful or even harmless. This is the case for both biomedicine and folk medicine. Physician-caused illness, called iatrogenic *illness (Illich 1976), is a serious problem in the United States. Mistakes in hospital treatment—most often avoidable drug interactions—are a major cause of morbidity today. (The American Iatrogenic Association estimates that 80,000 deaths per year in the United States are in some way related to physician error.) Illnesses caused by folk medical treatments are less well documented, but they certainly exist. For example, Marcia Inhorn (1994) has shown how both biomedical and ethnomedical treatments of infertility may actually add to the problem of tubal-factor infertility.*

In general, medical anthropologists would expect that people would drop harmful treatments after they have had experience with them. But when the link between cause and effect is clouded—often because of a time delay in the effects—a faulty ethnomedical treatment might be continued. Also, because medical systems evolve, people often value novelty, and treatments are used (in both biomedicine and ethnomedicine) before they are completely tested.

This selection comes from a book of applied anthropology called Anthropological Praxis: Translating Knowledge into Action *(Wulff and Fiske 1987) that consists of first-person reports of how medical anthropologists' work made a difference in the world. To some students, the examples in* Anthropological Praxis *are self-congratulatory, but please do not let that stand in your way. This selection presents the case of a medical anthropologist who discovers a real public health threat in the course of a study and then takes action to remove that threat in his local area.*

The folk medical problem of empacho, *dealt with here, is something that we will encounter again in selection 48. Because this illness is not recognized by standard biomedicine, people turn to folk medicine for cures. The problem of lead-based treatment in Latino folk medicine has persisted and is reported in the epidemiological literature (Weller et al. 1992). If you live in a multicultural urban area, it is easy to find folk medicine pharmacies—New Age shops,* botanicas, *Chinese pharmacies, or homeopathic drug stores—and as a student of medical anthropology, you should see what is inside.*

As you read this selection, consider these questions:

- **What are greta and azarcon used for? Do the people buying these medicines know what they are made of? Do you know what your over-the-counter medicines are made of?**
- **How did Robert Trotter combine his interests in a research study and social action in this case?**
- **Why was there a need for a "communication bridge" in this case? Was the gap more than between the Hispanic community and the Anglo community?**
- **Are medical anthropologists being ethnocentric when they identify negative aspects of folk medical practices?**

Context: Robert T. Trotter is a regent's professor at the University of Northern Arizona. In his long career as an applied anthropologist, he has worked on diverse questions including HIV prevention and intervention, disabilities, addiction, ethnomedicine (curanderismo), migrant health in the United States, and corporations. In recent years, he has done research to improve the "plant culture" in a General Motors assembly plant. Author of six books, most of his work has focused on the southwestern United States. This selection was first published in a volume containing contributions from nominees for the Applied Anthropology "Praxis" Award. The essays in that volume used a common four-part applied anthropological format: (1) problem definition, (2) policy formation, (3) program implementation, and (4) evaluation. The problem in this case is clear, and it runs counter to the assumption that all ethnomedical treatments are benign.

Source: R. T. Trotter II (1987). "A Case of Lead Poisoning from Folk Remedies in Mexican American Communities." In *Anthropological Praxis,* Shirley Fiske and Robert Wulff (eds.). Boulder, CO: Westview Press.

PROBLEM AND CLIENT

Three sources of lead poisoning most commonly affect children in the United States: eating lead-based paint chips, living and playing near a smelter where even the dust has a high lead content, and eating off pottery with an improperly treated lead glaze. This [article] describes the discovery of a fourth source of lead poisoning, one resulting from folk medicine practices in Mexican American communities.

In summer 1981, a team of emergency room health professionals in Los Angeles discovered an unusual case of lead poisoning. They treated a child with classic symptoms of heavy metal poisoning. When they pumped the child's stomach, they found a bright orange powder. Laboratory analysis of the powder determined that it was lead tetroxide (PbO_4) with an elemental lead content of more than 90 percent. After being strenuously questioned, the child's mother admitted giving the child a powdered remedy called *azarcon*. She also said that the powder was used to treat a folk illness called *empacho*, which translates roughly as a combination of indigestion and constipation. Empacho is believed by people who treat it to be caused by a bolus of food sticking to the intestinal wall. Unfortunately, this case was not handled in a culturally sensitive way, and the child was not brought back for follow-up. However, a general public health alert was sent out (see MMWR 1981, 1982; Trotter et al 1984).

As a result of the public health alert, a second case of lead poisoning from azarcon was discovered in Greeley, Colorado, by a nurse from the Sunrise Health Center who was culturally sensitive to the parents' claim that the child was not eating paint (the most commonly suspected cause). Having read about the azarcon case in Los Angeles, the nurse asked the mother if she was treating the child for empacho, and, when she answered yes, asked if the mother was using azarcon as a remedy. Analysis of the powder that the mother was keeping with the family's medicines confirmed that it was lead tetroxide.

Until this time, the use of lead as a home remedy had been assumed to occur only in isolated cases, and no anthropological input had been sought. However, additional questioning by the Los Angeles County Health Department and by individuals at the Sunrise Community Health Center turned up apparent widespread knowledge of azarcon in both Mexican American communities. The U.S. Public Health Service decided at this point that an anthropologist's study of this potential problem would be useful.

About six months after the azarcon problem was discovered, I was called by a friend who worked in the Region VI office for the Public Health Service (PHS) in Dallas. He asked me if I had ever heard of a remedy called azarcon while I was doing my research on Mexican American folk medicine. I had not. He then told me about the cases found in Los Angeles and Greeley and asked me to look for azarcon in south Texas.

I searched all the herb shops in four towns, including the one in the market in Reynosa, Mexico, and talked with *curanderos* (folk healers) living on the U.S.-Mexican border. I did not find azarcon nor did I find anyone who knew what it was. I reported this fact to my friend, and we both were relieved that the problem seemed to be confined to the western United States. Not long after I received a packet of information from the Los Angeles County Health Department, which had conducted a small survey on azarcon. Among other findings they had discovered some alternate names for the preparation. I went back to the herb shops to look for azarcon under its alternate names because the common names of remedies often change drastically from region to region.

The most important alternate name turned out to be *greta*. When I asked for greta in Texas I was sold a heavy yellow powder that, when analyzed, was found to be lead oxide (PbO) with an elemental lead content of approximately 90 percent. The shop owners told me that greta was used to treat empacho. So we now had confirmation that two related lead-based remedies were being used to treat empacho in Mexican American communities. In fact, a wholesale distributor in Texas, which was also selling over 200 other remedies to retail outlets, was supplying greta to more than 120 herb shops (*yerberias*). This finding drastically shaped both the scope and the content of the health education project that we started soon after this discovery. Because of the geographical scope of the problem and the multiple compounds involved, in the end six interacting clients utilized applied anthropology services to deal with the threat of greta and azarcon.

My first client was the Region VI Office of PHS. As previously described, it sponsored my initial narrowly focused ethnographic study to find azarcon—before our knowledge of greta. The second client group that requested my help was the task force formed to create and implement a health education project directed at eliminating the use of azarcon in Mexican American communities in Colorado and California. The project was sponsored through a federally funded migrant and community health center, the Sunrise Health Center, but was funded by the foundation of a private corporation. Our objective was to develop culturally sensitive health awareness materials that would reduce the risk of people using azarcon without attacking or denigrating the folk medical system. We knew that attacks on folk beliefs would produce strong resistance to the whole campaign and make people ignore our message. I was asked to participate because of my research on Mexican American folk medicine, in the hopes that my ethnographic data could be used to help design a health awareness campaign that would encourage a switch to nonpoisonous remedies.

The technique behind this approach has been successfully used by all major advertising agencies for decades: It is relatively easy to get people to switch from one product to another when both products perform the same function. It is difficult or impossible to get people to stop using a product for which there is a felt need, regardless of the known potential for harm for that product, unless one provides an acceptable alternatative. Thus, it is easy to get a smoker to switch from Camel filters to Winstons but very hard to get that person to stop smoking altogether. So we decided that we would attempt to give people the alternative of switching from greta or azarcon to another remedy for empacho, such as *te de manzanilla* (chamomile), known to be harmless, rather than trying to get people to stop treating empacho altogether.

The discovery of greta use in Texas and Mexico produced a third client. The Food and Drug Administration (FDA) decided it needed basic ethnographic information on the use of greta. It wanted to know who used greta, what it was used for, how it was used, and where it could be purchased. Lead oxide is most commonly used as an industrial compound (as an adherent in marine paints) and as a color component in the paint used to make the "no passing" stripes on U.S. highways. It has never been considered either a food additive or a potential drug. Therefore, the FDA needed verifiable data that the compound was being used as a "drug." The FDA asked me to conduct a short, thorough ethnography in the herb shops where I had found the greta. This study included collecting samples and interviewing the owners (and a number of clients who wandered in to buy other remedies) about the ways that greta was used, what it was used to treat, how it was prepared, and the size of dose given for children and adults. These data allowed the FDA to determine that greta was a food additive and enabled it to exercise its authority to issue a Class I recall to ban the sale of these lead compounds as remedies. The information I gathered was important because herbal remedies do not normally fall under the jurisdiction of the FDA,[1] except in terms of the cleanliness requirements surrounding their packaging.

The discovery of greta in Texas caused the regional office of Health and Human Services (HHS) to request my assistance in creating and executing a survey along the U.S.-Mexican border to discover how much knowledge people had about greta and azarcon and how many people used them. HHS felt that the use might be much more extensive than was suggested by the relatively small number of poisonings discovered in clinics. The survey indicated that as many as 10 percent of the Mexican American households along the border had at one time used greta or azarcon. The survey also turned up several other potentially toxic compounds that included mercury and laundry bluing (Trotter 1985).

The fifth group to request data was the Hidalgo County Health Care Corporation, a local migrant clinic. It asked for a survey to determine the level of greta and azarcon use in the local population compared with their clinic population. The HHS regional survey had only sampled clinic populations. The Hidalgo County research project involved simultaneously sampling at the clinics and in the communities from which the clinic population is derived. Over a two-week period, a stratified random sample of informants at the clinic sites were given a questionnaire designed for the HHS regional survey. At the same time, a random stratified block cluster sample of households in the catchment communities were administered the same questionnaire. The results indicated that no significant difference existed between the two populations in terms of their knowledge about and use of greta and azarcon. The data showed trends that suggested that the clinic populations were more likely to treat folk illnesses than was the population at large.

My final client was the Migrant Health Service, a division of the PHS. The Migrant Health Service requested consultation on the necessity of a lead initiative for the entire United States, based on the results of the ethnographic and survey research conducted for other groups involved in the overall project. In the end, it was decided that a nationwide lead initiative was not necessary. Instead, the areas of high greta and azarcon use were targeted for a special initiative and received special notification of the problem.

PROCESS AND PLAYERS

The wide geographical distribution of greta and azarcon use, their employment as traditional remedies, and their inclusion in the treatment of a folk illness made this problem ideal for intervention by an anthropologist. Among other qualities, we tend to have a high ambiguity quotient: We tolerate poorly defined research objectives and virtually boundary-free problems that must be analyzed and solved simultaneously. The fact that the project rapidly developed a multiple-client base also made it very suitable for applied anthropology rather than for another social science. Anthropologists are often called upon to serve diverse, even conflicting, roles as culture brokers. Multiple clients are no different from multiple community interest groups. Serving as a go-between in one setting develops the skills for doing so in any other setting.

From this perspective, my participation was requested by various clients because medical anthropologists have become known for being comfortable and competent in dealing with the types of issues presented by the greta and azarcon problem (problems that do not fit existing, well-defined categories or public health procedures). I did not become involved through a disguised or accidental process; my expertise was specifically sought because of the clients' recognition that they wanted a particular set of skills. This was particularly clear for the group creating the health education program. It deliberately sought an anthropologist with current knowledge about the Mexican American folk medical system. I was chosen because several people in the group had either read articles I had written or had heard me speak publicly about folk medicine. Likewise the migrant health program of PHS wanted someone with the same knowledge base, and I had previously worked with several of the individuals there.

My role evolved into a combination of researcher, consultant, communication bridge, and developer of program elements. My goal was to help create a culturally sensitive and effective method for reducing the use of these two folk remedies without interfering with the overall use of folk medicine. Another of my critical roles was that of information broker between the various client groups, some of which had not previously been in communication. Some of these groups had severe organizational barriers to communication with one another. One such barrier was simply organizational distance; the Washington-based migrant health officials only dealt with the local programs within certain contexts, such as regional and national meetings, or when a problem occurred in the operation of a clinic. I provided a good temporary (higher intensity) communication bridge to facilitate the exchange of information for this project. In the same way, the PHS and FDA had little need for contact, except for the temporary mutual need to solve different aspects of the greta/azarcon problem. But each of these groups found it useful to have the information available to, or available from, the others.

My final role was that of a scholar to publish the results of the study. The group developing the health education project wanted my findings published in order to disseminate the information about greta and azarcon as widely as possible. The PHS wanted my results because it was finding it more and more difficult to put money into projects on the sole basis of an emotional appeal. The federal government (and increasing numbers of state and local governments) are reluctant to recognize "problems" that are not sufficiently documented and shown to be "real." One of the favored forms of documentation is publication in scientific journals. So following the normal process of publishing the results of an investigation allows an agency or organization to demonstrate a need for a specific program. The agency can support a request for a short-term (emergency) effort or can request a future increase in funds (or at least the maintenance of their prior funding levels). Scholarly documentation of problems and program effectiveness is particularly useful for programs that receive federal funds on an annual basis. When the preliminary results of my ethnographic research were published in *Medical Anthropology Quarterly* (Trotter et al. 1984), the officials in the migrant health program felt they could reasonably justify the expenditure of funds to deal with the part of the greta and azarcon problem that affected their clients.

Publication can provide other long-term benefits. Naming members of the nonscholar staff as co-authors of publications not only gives them appropriate recognition for their contributions but also can increase the opportunities for future funding. Sharing a publication and its visibility tends to be excellent public relations. Clients can use the prestige of being an author in the development of their own careers. This tends to improve the chances of the anthropologist securing additional consultant work from that source. It produces a win/win situation.

RESULTS AND EVALUATION

Because this project involved several clients, it also had multiple results and multiple levels of outcomes. The Sunrise clinic health education project resulted in considerable media exposure on the existence and dangers of greta and azarcon. This exposure included radio public service announcements broadcast on Spanish radio stations, a special television program aired in Los Angeles County, and an information packet sent to migrant clinics. These informational campaigns contained the suggestion that people switch to other remedies because greta and azarcon were hazardous.

The other major accomplishment of the Sunrise project was the production and distribution of a poster designed by Mexican American commercial design students at Pan American University. The students were provided an in-depth briefing on the problem and our investigations, then were turned loose to create a culturally appropriate poster. A small cash prize was given to the student with the best design. Twenty posters were completed and turned over to a group of Mexican American clients and staff at the clinic to judge for most effective design. The final poster, which combines the elements in two of the submissions, uses the culturally emotive symbol of La Meurte (a skeleton) to warn of the dangers of the use of greta and azarcon. The dominant impact of the poster is visual/emotional—to trigger the client into asking the clinic staff about greta and azarcon. The group felt that too many words would dilute the impact of the poster, so we did not attempt to incorporate the theme of product switch into the design. Posters with this design have been placed in over 5,000 clinics and other public access sites in each state with a concentration of Mexican Americans.[2]

The success of the overall campaign is demonstrated by the fact that some two years after the project was completed, interest had died down, and both greta and azarcon were hard to find in the United States. Another measure of the campaign's lasting success is illustrated by the doctor in El Paso who treated a child with classic lead poisoning symptoms. Not only did he recognize the probable cause of the symptoms (lead poisoning has such common symptoms that it is rarely suspected), he immediately asked the mother if the child was being treated with greta or azarcon. It turned out to be greta, and the child was immediately treated, with no serious long-term problems. The doctor was very happy that he had caught a problem that others might have missed, and we were pleased to discover that the project had at least a qualitative measure of success. Based on anecdotal information, the project appears to have had an important effect on public knowledge about these remedies and has reduced their use by some degree. However, no scientific effort was made to determine exactly how much change has occurred. Even with the increased information, these compounds will continue to be used regardless of the effectiveness of the campaign. Knowledge does not always drive behavior, as is evident in all the results of nonsmoking campaigns.

The work completed for the FDA was successful within the parameters set by the client. The data were sufficient to allow the agency to determine that the consumption of greta and azarcon fell within their jurisdiction, and it was able to successfully conduct a recall. Additionally, the data and the agency's recognition of its validity allow it to deal with future incidences of the sale of these two compounds as home remedies. This is a positive benefit because reuse of the compound is virtually assured by the fact that Mexico is the primary source of folk knowledge about the use of greta and azarcon and the source of the compounds themselves. Unfortunately, the public health sector in Mexico has not been able to devote many resources to this particular problem.

My work for the regional office of HHS resulted in data that allowed policy to be set and lead screening procedures to be amended at both national and regional levels to deal with this new source of lead poisoning. The basic policies dictated the creation of the new lead protocols. The agency pinpointed potential areas of high usage of the compounds and recommended cost-effective lead screening programs to be undertaken at selected sites. The screening is accomplished by drawing small samples of blood and testing it chemically for the effects or presence of lead. Because of the survey and accompanying ethnographic data the lead screening protocols for migrant and public health services were modified to include ethnomedical sources of poisoning, such as greta and azarcon. Clinics were alerted to this source, and a growing number of cases have subsequently been discovered that would have otherwise been overlooked.

The data provided to HHS also permitted cost avoidances. Just after the discovery of greta and azarcon there was a rush to do something, which included a preliminary decision to buy some very expensive equipment for a large number of clinics. However, the data allowed a more cost-effective decision to be made: to only do lead screening in those areas where there was a demonstrated risk. This approach avoided the purchase of equipment that would have been misused or not used at all because no funds were available to train clinic staffs to use these complex instruments after they were purchased.

The survey of greta and azarcon use (Trotter 1985) turned out to be an excellent educational and informational device. It was conducted at thirty migrant and public health clinics in Texas, New Mexico, and Arizona. As a result of the open-ended ethnographic structuring of the survey instrument, several other potentially toxic compounds, with regional but not universal usage, were also discovered. This finding alerted the local clinics both to the current use of home treatments of illnesses in their area and to some of the specific health education needs of their clients. In my opinion, the education benefits of conducting this type of survey have an untapped potential as an educational device for health care providers.

A project is only half successful, regardless of its results, if it does not produce additional opportunities for anthropologists to practice anthropology. These serendipitous results can be as simple as further work for the same client or as important as the development of new theories for the discipline. Yet rarely are these spin-offs mentioned or considered an important aspect of anthropological praxis. Even when a project has clear closure (rare for many of the types of applied problems tackled by anthropologists), the process of solving the problem should set up personal and professional relationships that carry beyond that temporary closure. Regardless of the products they produce, successful applied scientists are process oriented; they are constantly moving from one point on a continuum to the next.

The additional opportunities created by the greta and azarcon problem may have more long-lasting effects on the cross-cultural delivery of health care in the United States than the original projects had. The first spin-off was an invitation to participate in a program review for the Migrant Health Services division of PHS in Washington, D.C. The program review brought together a group of experts from around the United States to review, revise, and set new policies for the delivery of health care services in all migrant health clinics in the United States. The policies that were adopted are strongly cross cultural. They include the development of a Public Health Service Corps provider orientation package that specifically addresses cultural sensitivity, basic anthropological concepts of culture, and awareness of the qualitative aspects of migrant lifestyles, health beliefs, and medical needs. I am in the process of developing this package. Other policies and goals include statements on program coordination, continuity of care, information needs (e.g., research), and services. All have been shaped by the participation of anthropologists in the policy-making body.

Additionally, Indiana Health Centers, Inc., a private, nonprofit corporation that runs the migrant health clinics in Indiana, asked me to spend a week as a consultant for its program. The primary purpose of the consultation was to conduct public and clinic seminars on ethnomedicine and its importance to the delivery of health care to Mexican Americans. A latent purpose was to legitimize the use of culturally appropriate health services and to integrate them into the scientific medical system. One indication that the process worked is the clinic's decision to incorporate four of the most common Mexican American folk illnesses into their diagnostic system, which includes a computer coding and retrieval system. At the end of the year, the clinics will use these to set goals, determine funding and educational needs, and determine policy for the program, along with all other diagnostic data derived from their computer system.

To disperse the data as widely and rapidly as possible, four different articles on greta and azarcon were submitted to a variety of journals. Each article was targeted for a particular audience. The most important audiences were thought to be health professionals, medical anthropologists, public health personnel, and an international pharmacological audience. Each audience needed to know about the data and had an opportunity to help solve the problem of lead poisoning caused by folk remedies. However, this process of multiple submissions conflicts directly with the practice of avoiding prior publication.

The Hidalgo County Health Care Corporation was provided with reports showing that greta and azarcon use was comparable between their clinic and catchment populations. These data were also passed along to the regional and national offices of PHS. In this case the client used the data to create priorities for the next funding cycle. Each funding request requires goals and priorities, and better funding opportunities exist if the clinic demonstrates changing as well as expanding needs and services, especially in the area of patient education. The data allowed it to successfully compete for funding for its patient education goals by demonstrating a need for further health education on home remedies.

Perhaps the most important overall result of this project was the increased awareness of the utility of anthropology in solving culturally related health care problems in at least one segment of the medical care delivery system. For many years anthropologists have been saying that knowledge of folk medicine was important to the delivery of health care. But the only examples of how such knowledge was useful were couched in terms of "better rapport" with patients, "potentially reducing recidivism," or were tied to the "interface between culture and psychological processes." Patient rapport is an abominably low priority for practicing physicians and for most health clinics that are experiencing a patient overload. Likewise the cultural/psychological aspect has low prestige and is of interest to a small group of practitioners but not to the larger group dealing with physical medicine.

Now anthropologists are becoming visible to the greater part of medicine. Our discovery of the use of greta and azarcon and the subsequent discoveries that similar remedies are causing lead poisoning in Hmong, Saudi Arabian, and Chinese communities have finally demonstrated a clear link between anthropological research and the dominant biophysical side of modern medicine. Anthropological knowledge, research methods, and theoretical orientations are finally being used to solve epidemiological problems overlooked by the established disciplines. For some of our potential clients, this approach, for the first time, makes anthropology a potentially valuable source for consultation and for funding.

I was also invited by the Pennsylvania Department of Education, Migrant Education Division, to participate in its Project HAPPIER (Health Awareness

Patterns Preventing Illness and Encouraging Responsibility). Project HAPPIER, which has a national scope, is funded through discretionary (143c) funds from the Office of the Secretary of Education. The objective of the project was to provide a major health resource guide and the data necessary to target health education in migrant clinics and for migrant educators, nationwide. My initial role was to conduct an analysis of national migrant health education needs, including an eight-state survey of migrant health beliefs and health education needs, as seen from the perspective of the migrants themselves. Although the survey provided excellent information, several important cultural groups were not well represented. Therefore, the following year I helped conduct a separate needs assessment in Puerto Rico to gather data on one of the underrepresented groups. The goals of the surveys were to improve our knowledge about migrant health status in all three migrant streams and to provide information that would allow the states and Puerto Rico to offer migrant children sufficient health education to improve the health status of the current and the next migrant generation. The preliminary results of the study indicate that migrants both want and need health education. This finding points up the possibility of exploring a number of areas for research and program development (spin-offs from spin-offs).

Other opportunities that resulted from the original project included the more traditional requests for speaking engagements, lectures, and so on. These occasions afforded visibility that created new project opportunities and acted as a source of income. In most academic settings these activities also count toward merit and promotion points.

Although it is very important to direct one's best effort toward each project, I feel that the best applied anthropologists also follow what I call the "basic fission theory of anthropological praxis." Each project undertaken by an applied anthropologist should produce at least four others (up to the capacity, skill, and time commitment available to the individual anthropologist). One indicator of success in anthropological praxis is a continued demand for the services offered; it is easiest to generate this demand by current success. An anthropologist should look for spin-offs during a project, not just after it is completed.

THE ANTHROPOLOGICAL DIFFERENCE

I believe that the anthropological difference I added to the greta/azarcon project comes from the training that all anthropologists receive. It includes our strong focus on culture combined with our willingness to innovate, to look for explanations in areas that have been neglected by other investigators. The difference is not so much a part of anthropological theory and methods as it is a part of the personal orientation many of us have and that we try to pass along to others. For example, the health officials who originally investigated the case of lead poisoning in Greeley assumed that the little girl could only have contracted lead poisoning in the same way all other children get lead poisoning—from the environment.[3] In her case, the only accessible source of lead was a fence some 200 yards from her house. Although her parents insisted that she never played near that fence, they were ignored until the child had gone through chelation therapy and, in a follow-up screening, was determined to have re-elevated blood lead levels without access to the fence. Then the publicity on the California case caused a culturally sensitive worker (who had been exposed to transcultural nursing concepts) to ask about azarcon, and the case was solved.

Another anthropological contribution to this project was in the design and administration of the research requested by the clients. The methodological contributions an anthropologist can make to a project may be as important or even more important to the client than his or her contributions of theory. It is relatively easy to find someone who has a theoretical explanation for known behavior; it is also easy to find someone who can administer surveys. It is much harder to find someone who can combine ethnographic data collection and theory grounded in real behavior with survey methodology that can determine the scope of a behavior. These projects demanded both types of expertise. I had to discover both the basic patterns of and reasons for the continued use of home remedies in an urban-industrial society and a cultural context within which the educational and intervention process could take place. At the same time, I had the vitally important task of discovering how widespread the use of these remedies had become and if other hazardous remedies were being used to treat the same folk illness. A combination of ethnography and survey accomplished these goals.

The final area of anthropological contribution was in the design of the educational material and the programmatic responses to the problem of greta and azarcon. The major contribution there was to ensure that the materials used or developed were culturally appropriate rather than trying to force inappropriate change on people who would resent it, making the effort useless in the long run.

In some ways this cluster of projects indicates a potential new era for anthropology in health-related fields. In these instances the services of an anthropologist were deliberately sought because of the clients' sophisticated knowledge of the type of services they needed and the exact type of expertise they wanted. They needed descriptive ethnographic data to determine a method in which to produce a product switch from one remedy to other, nontoxic ones. In addition they needed a survey built on a solid ethnographic base that did not presume a closed field of knowledge about the subject. More and more of today's anthropologists are equally comfortable with quantitative and qualitative methods of data collection. This combination of research methods is actually stronger than either pure ethnography or pure statistical analysis, but it requires a much more methodologically sophisticated researcher. In some ways, the flexibility of approach—an eclectic orientation to methodology and analysis—has always marked the anthropological difference and may herald a subtle but real advantage not only for anthropological praxis but also for the future employment of anthropologists in many industries. If, as many claim, we are now in an information-driven age, anthropologists should have an advantage in the information service market, given the importance or centrality of communications research and information handling in the history of anthropology.

NOTES

1. Most of the people buying and selling greta and azarcon believe they are herbal compounds, probably because the overwhelming majority of Mexican American home remedies are botanicals.
2. Other Hispanic groups were not targeted for this campaign. A broad search among anthropologists working with other Hispanic populations in the United States indicated that the two compounds were not present in their ethnomedical pharmacopoeias.
3. Two traditional sources of lead poisoning are the consumption of lead paint chips, primarily by children living in dilapidated urban areas, and occupational exposure to high concentrations of lead by workers and children of workers in high lead use industries, such as battery manufacturing. The third source is environmental pollution. The most common victims of this type of poisoning are children whose normal hand-to-mouth activities give them an overdose of lead from playing on soil with a high lead content (such as that near heavily traveled roads or industries such as smelters that have high lead emission levels). Epidemiological investigations are conducted when a child or adult is detected as having high blood lead levels. These investigations invariably concentrate on discovering which of these sources caused the problem.

REFERENCES

Ackerman et al. 1982. Lead Poisoning from Lead Tetroxide Used as a Folk Remedy—Colorado. *MMWR* (Center for Disease Control, Morbidity and Mortality Weekly Report) 30(52):647–648.

Trotter, Robert T., II. 1985. Greta and Azarcon: A Survey of Episodic Lead Poisoning from a Folk Remedy. *Human Organization* 44(1):64–72.

Trotter, Robert T., II, Alan Ackerman, Dorothy Rodman, Abel Martinez, and Frank Sorvillo. 1984. Azarcon and Greta: Ethnomedical Solution to an Epidemiological Mystery. *Medical Anthropology Quarterly* 14(3):3,18.

Vashistha, et al. 1981. Use of Lead Tetroxide as a Folk Remedy for Gastrointestinal Illness. *MMWR* 30(43):546–547.

 35

Why Does Juan García Have a Drinking Problem? The Perspective of Critical Medical Anthropology

Merrill Singer
Freddie Valentin
Hans Baer
Zhongke Jia

Medical anthropological studies of health and ethnicity can be accomplished using a wide array of theoretical perspectives. This selection uses the political-economic perspective of critical medical anthropology (CMA) to examine the question of alcohol abuse in a Puerto Rican community in Hartford, Connecticut. The council's research and projects focus on ethnic communities that themselves reflect cultural variation (Cubans, Mexicans, Puerto Ricans, Dominicans, and so on). From the perspective of CMA, ethnicity is a variable that must be understood in the context of class stratification and international political-economic relations. To understand why a particular Puerto Rican man has a drinking problem, the authors argue, it is first necessary to recognize the wider, macro context.

The disease concept of alcoholism is discussed in the first part of this selection. This is a modern idea that medicalizes an individual's "out of control" behavior. As a disease, alcoholism does not provoke the same moral judgment as it did earlier in the twentieth century in the United States. Recently, alcoholism has been discussed using the model of an addiction to a toxic substance, again emphasizing the individual level. These medical models clearly have explanatory power, but the social epidemiological distribution of heavy drinking or problem drinking is not random. There are larger reasons—political, economic, historical, and social—why some people are more at risk for this problem. The CMA approach examines these other factors.

Notice that the research methodologies used by these CMA researchers are not very different from standard medical social science; in this example, the data set is based on interviews with a random sample of men from an ethnic enclave. But the interpretation *of the data emphasizes the macro factors.*

As you read this selection, consider these questions:

- **Given the political-economic argument the authors make, how can the variation in problem drinking rates between ethnic groups be explained?**
- **How did Juan García's life compare with the American dream? How do you think García would have explained his own drinking problem?**
- **How does this analysis show the relatedness of ethnicity and social class?**
- **Given the explanation of the health problem from the CMA perspective, what kinds of solutions are possible?**
- **Why does the Alcoholics Anonymous program work? Do you think it is cross-culturally valid?**

Context: Merrill Singer is a medical anthropologist at the Center for Health Intervention and Prevention and the Department of Anthropology at the University of Connecticut. He has written extensively about health disparities in minority populations, focusing on issues of substance abuse and HIV/AIDS. Hans Baer is a medical anthropologist at the University of Melbourne whose work has influenced scholarship in critical medical anthropology and political ecology, with studies in the United States, United Kingdom, Australia, and Germany. Freddie Valentin was a graduate student in social work and a research assistant at the Hispanic Health Council when this article was written. Zhongke Jia currently works in the Department of Public Health in Portland, Oregon. This group all worked as a research team at the Hispanic Health Council. This work is primary based on Singer's interviews with and participant observation among spiritualist healers; Juan Garcia is a fictional version of a key informant. This selection is a classic example of critical anthropology insofar as it challenges us to consider the larger historical and socioeconomic circumstances that influence how some groups are more susceptible to alcoholism than others.

Source: M. Singer, F. Valentin, H. Baer, and Z. Jia (1992). "Why Does Juan Garcia Have a Drinking Problem?" Medical Anthropology 14(1):77–108.

. . . anthropology, in spite of its limitations, may play a part in documenting what the West has done to other societies.

—Sidney Mintz (1989:794)

We will try to be objective but in no way will we be impartial.

—Manuel Maldonado-Denis (1980:26)

Critical medical anthropology as a named theoretical perspective is about a decade old (Baer and Singer 1982), although its main roots within the subdiscipline, as expressed in the work of researchers like Soheir Morsy, Alan Young, Anthony Thomas, and Ronald Frankenberg, are somewhat older. Because of its links to the social analysis of Marx and Engels, and because it began as a challenge to medical anthropology, critical medical anthropology has been a somewhat controversial approach. Those who do not embrace it have issued a number of potentially damaging critiques, including the argument that critical medical anthropology: (1) is not suited to the applied and practical agenda of medical anthropology; (2) does not foster scientific research; (3) tends to be concentrated on macro-level systems and hence overlooks the lived experience of illness sufferers; (4) does not effectively demonstrate the links between micro-processes and macro-forces; and (5) is a passing trend whose popularity rests primarily on anthropology's fickle tendency to follow fashion. . . .

. . . Consequently, this paper, which is concerned with articulating the perspective of critical medical anthropology: targets an applied issue; is based on empirical research; incorporates the individual level; is concerned with showing the direct casual links between on-the-ground sociocultural/behavioral patterns and the macro-level; and situates its approach within the broader perspective of the political economy of health, which is at least as old as anthropology itself.[1]

In this paper we examine the health issue of problem drinking among Puerto Rican men. Over the years, medical anthropologists have exhibited an enduring interest in substance use and abuse, although attention has been especially concentrated since the early 1970s (Agar 1973; Bennett 1988; Douglas 1987; Heath 1976, 1978, 1980, 1987a, 1987b; Partridge 1978), producing both the Alcohol and Drug Study Group of the Society for Medical Anthropology in 1979, and a rapid expansion of the anthropological substance literature in recent years. Anthropologists bring a range of perspectives to the study of drinking in particular, and they have made a number of significant contributions to this field. However, from the viewpoint of critical medical anthropology, we have argued that

> the anthropological examination of drinking has failed to systematically consider the world-transforming effects of a global market and the global labor processes associated with the evolution of the capitalist mode of production. Anthropological concentration on the intricacies of individual cases, while a necessary and useful method for appreciating the rich detail of cultural variation and insider understandings, has somewhat blinded researchers to the uniform processes underlying global social change, including changes in drinking patterns. While the literature notes some of the effects of incorporation into the capitalist world-system, rarely does it attempt to comprehend alcoholism in terms of the specific dynamics of this system. Rather, the central thrust has been to locate problem drinking within the context of normative drinking and normative drinking within the context of prevailing local cultural patterns. (Singer 1986a:115)

Although anthropological contribution to the U.S. Latino drinking literature has been somewhat limited, a number of studies are available (Ames and Mora 1988; Gordon 1978, 1981, 1985a; Gilbert 1985, 1987, 1988; Gilbert and Cervantes 1987; Page et al. 1985; Singer and Borrero 1984; Singer, Davison and Yalin 1987; Trotter 1982, 1985; Trotter and Chavira 1978). To date, most studies have been concerned with Mexican Americans. Drinking among Puerto Rican men has been a relatively neglected topic, although it has been suggested that this population is particularly at risk for alcohol-related problems (Abad and Suares 1974).

The goal of this paper is to deepen our understanding of problem drinking among Puerto Rican men by bringing to bear the perspective of critical medical anthropology. We begin with a review of the origin and perspective of critical medical anthropology after which we present the case of Juan García (pseudonym), a Puerto Rican man who in 1971 died with a bottle in his hand and booze in his belly. Following a location of this case in its historic[al] and political-economic contexts, we present findings from two community studies[2] of drinking behavior and drinking-related health and social consequences among Puerto Rican men and adolescents to demonstrate the representativeness of the case material. In this paper, it is argued that the holistic model of critical medical anthropology advances our understanding beyond narrow psychologistic or other approaches commonly employed in social scientific alcohol research. More broadly, we assert this perspective is useful in examining a wide range of topics of concern to the subdiscipline.

. . .

Specific concern within the political-economic perspective with issues of health—including, it bears noting, the special topic of problem drinking—can be traced on the one hand to Friedrich Engels' study of the working class of Manchester and on the other to Rudolf Virchow's examination of a typhus epidemic in East Prussia. Both of these seminal studies, which possibly constitute the earliest examples of medical anthropology field work, occurred in the 1840s. Each of these researchers undertook an intensive examination of local conditions, using ethnographic observation and informal interviewing, and attempted to describe and interpret research findings in light of broader political and economic forces. The current study, in fact, can be read as an extension and elaboration of the approach developed by Engels and Virchow in their respective work. Specifically, our analysis of problem drinking among Puerto Rican men, as well as studies of mood-altering substance use by other critical medical anthropologists (e.g., Stebbins 1987, 1990), is directly influenced by Engels' examination of drinking and opiate use in his Manchester study.

Beyond theory, critical medical anthropology is committed inherently to the development of appropriate practical expression. Indeed, the data for this essay were drawn from research that Singer and Valentín have conducted over the last seven years through the Hispanic Health Council, a community action agency dedicated to creating short- and long-term health improvements in the Latino community of Hartford, CT and beyond {e.g., Singer, Irazzary, and Schensul 1990; Singer et al. 1991). Critical medical anthropology rejects a simple dichotomy between "anthropology of medicine" and "anthropology in medicine" that separates theoretical from applied objectives. Rather, critical medical anthropologists seek to place their expertise at the disposal of labor unions, peace organizations, environmental groups, ethnic community agencies, women's health collectives, health consumer associations, self-help and self-care movements, alternative health efforts, national liberation struggles, and other bodies or initiatives that aim to liberate people from oppressive health and social conditions. In sum, through their theoretical and applied work, critical medical anthropologists strive to contribute to the larger effort to create a new health system that will "serve the people," including the area of alcoholism, which has proven to be an especially intractable problem under particular social conditions.[3] . . .

. . . The medicalization of problem drinking, however thoroughly institutionalized at this point, involved a process that began in 1785 with Benjamin Rush (Rush 1785/1943) but was only completed relatively recently. As the National Council on Alcoholism stated in an educational pamphlet a number of years ago: "The main task of those working to combat alcoholism . . . is to remove the stigma from this disease and make it as 'respectable' as other major diseases such as cancer and tuberculosis" (quoted in Davies 1979:449). A significant step in this process was a 1944 statement of the American Hospital Association proposing that "the primary attack on alcoholism should be through the general hospital" (quoted in Chafetz and Yoerg 1977:599). Four years later, the World Health Organization included alcoholism in its International Classification of Diseases. But it was not until 1956 that the American Medical Association declared alcoholism to be an officially recognized disease in U.S. biomedicine. Four years later, E. M. Jellinek published his seminal book, *The Disease Concept of Alcoholism*. Finally, in 1971 the National Institute on Alcohol Abuse and Alcoholism was established "premised on the belief that alcoholism is a disease and an important health problem" (Conrad and Schneider 1980:108).

Since then, the disease concept has become "everyone's official dogma, with medical organizations, alcoholics themselves, and well-meaning people speaking on their behalf urging governments and employers to accept and act on its implications" (Kendell 1979:367). And with notable success! As Schaefer (1982:302) points out, "Alcoholism is a growth industry. Empty hospital beds are turned into alcoholism 'slots'. The disease concept has become . . . integrated into the political and economic consciousness." While ambiguity remains about how much blame to lay at the feet of the drinker for causing his/her own problems, research indicates that the majority of people in the U.S. accept alcoholism as a bonafide if confusing disease (Mulford and Miller 1964; Chrisman 1985).

. . .

From the perspective of critical medical anthropology, the conventional disease model of alcoholism must be understood as an ideological construct comprehensible only in terms of the historic[al] and political-economic contexts of its origin (see Conrad and Schneider 1980; Mishler 1981). The disease concept achieved several things, including: (1) offering "a plausible solution to the apparent irrationality of . . . [problem drinking] behavior" (Conrad and Schneider 1980:87); (2) guaranteeing social status as well as a livelihood to a wide array of individuals, institutions, and organizations, within and outside of biomedicine (Trice and Roman 1972); and (3) limiting the growing burden on the criminal justice system produced by public drunkenness, the most common arrest made by police nationally (Park 1983). In the perspective of critical medical anthropology, however, it hinders *exploration of alternative, politically more challenging understandings of destructive drinking* (Singer 1986a). This point is argued below by presenting the case of Juan García in terms of contrasting conventional psychologistic and critical medical anthropological interpretations.

THE CASE OF JUAN GARCÍA

Juan was born in Puerto Rico in 1909. The offspring of an adulterous relationship, he deeply resented his father. At age eight, Juan's mother died and he went to live with an aunt, and later, after his father died, was raised by his father's wife. As expression of his undying hatred of his father, Juan took his mother's surname, García.

As a young man, he became romantically involved with a cousin named Zoraida, who had been deserted with a small daughter by her husband. They lived together for a number of years in a tiny wooden shack, eking out a meager living farming a small plot of land. Then one day, Zoraida's ex-husband came and took his daughter away. Because of his wealth and social standing, there was little Juan and Zoraida could do. In resigning themselves to the loss, they began a new family of their own.

Over the years, Zoraida bore 19 children with Juan, although most did not survive infancy. According to Juan's daughter, who was the source of our information about Juan:

> My mother went to a spiritual healer in Puerto Rico and they told her witchcraft had been done on her, and that all her children born in Puerto Rico would die; her children would only survive if she crossed water.

Given their intensely spiritual perspective, the couple decided to leave Puerto Rico and migrate "across water" to the US. It was to New York, to the burgeoning Puerto Rican community in Brooklyn, that Juan and Zoraida moved in 1946.

New to U.S. society and to urban life, Juan had great difficulty finding employment. Unskilled and uneducated, and monolingual in Spanish, he was only able to find manual labor at low wages. Eventually, he began working as a janitor in an appliance factory. Here, a fellow worker taught him to draft blueprints, enabling him to move up to the position of draftsman.

Juan's daughter remembers her parents as strict disciplinarians with a strong bent for privacy. Still, family life was stable and reasonably comfortable until Juan lost his job when the appliance factory where he worked moved out of state. At the time, he was in his mid-fifties and despite his efforts was never again able to locate steady employment. At first he received unemployment benefits, but when these ran out, the García family was forced to go on welfare. This greatly embarrassed Juan. Always a heavy drinker, he now began to drink and act abusively. According to his daughter:

> A big cloud came over us and everything kept getting worse and worse in the house. This was 1964, 1965, 1966. . . . The pressure would work on him and he used to drink and then beat my mother. But my mother wouldn't hit him back. . . . I went a year and a half without speaking to my father. He would say that I wasn't his daughter. We respected our father, but he lost our respect cause of the way he used to treat us. He would beat me and I would curse at him. . . . When my mother couldn't take the pressure any more, she would drink too. . . . My parents would get into fights and we had to get in between. Once they had a fight and my father moved out.

By the time Juan died of alcohol-related causes in 1971, he was a broken man, impoverished, friendless, and isolated from his family.

If we think of problem drinking as an individual problem, then it makes sense to say that Juan suffered from a behavioral disorder characterized by a preoccupation with alcohol to the detriment of physical and mental health, by a loss of control over drinking, and by a self-destructive attitude in dealing with personal relationships and life situations. Moreover, there is evidence that he was an insecure, emotionally immature individual who used alcohol as a crutch to support himself in the face of adversity. Finally, without probing too deeply, we even can find, in Juan's troubled relationship with his father, a basis in infantile experience for the development of these destructive patterns. In short, in professional alcohol treatment circles, among many recovered alcoholics, and in society generally, Juan could be diagnosed as having suffered from the disease of alcoholism.

In so labeling him, however, do we hide more than we reveal? By remaining at the level of the individual actor, that is, by locating Juan's problem *within* Juan, do we not pretend that the events of his life and the nature of his drinking make sense separate from their wider historic and political-economic contexts? As Wolf (1982) reminds us, approaches that disassemble interconnected social processes and fail to reassemble them falsify reality. Only by placing the subjects of our investigation "back into the field from which they were abstracted," he argues, "can we hope to avoid misleading inferences and increase our share of understanding" (Wolf 1982:3). To really make sense of Juan's drinking, to move beyond individualized and privatized formulationic, to avoid artificial and unsatisfying psychologistic labeling, the critical perspective moves to the wider field, to an historic[al] and political-economic appraisal of Puerto Ricans and alcohol.

HISTORIC AND POLITICAL ECONOMIC CONTEXT

When Columbus first set foot on Puerto Rico on November 19, 1493, he found a horticultural tribal society possessed of alcohol but devoid of alcoholism. While there is limited information on this period, based on the wider ethnographic record it is almost certain that the consumption of fermented beverages by the indigenous Taíno (Arawak) and Carib peoples of Puerto Rico was socially sanctioned and controlled, and produced little in the way of health or social problems. As Davila (1987:10) writes, the available literature suggests that "the Taíno made beer from a fermentable root crop called manioc, and . . . they might also have fermented some of the fruits they grew. However, the existing evidence suggests that alcohol was used more in a ritual context than in a social one." Heath notes that among many indigenous peoples of what was to become Latin America, periodic fiestas in which most of the adults drank until intoxicated was a common pattern. However, "both drinking and drunkenness were socially approved in the context of veneration of major deities, as an integral part of significant agricultural ceremonies, or in celebration of important events in the lives of local leaders" (Heath 1984:9). At times other than these special occasions, alcohol consumption was limited and nondisruptive, controlled by rather than a threat to the social group.

These and other features of Arawak life greatly impressed Columbus. He also was quick to notice the limited military capacity of the Indians, given their lack of metal weapons. Setting the tone for what was to follow, in one of his first log entries describing the Arawak, Columbus noted: "With fifty men we could subjugate them all and make them do whatever we want" (recorded in Zinn 1980:1). In effect, this was soon to happen, prompted by the discovery of gold on the Island. Under the Spanish *encomienda* system, ostensibly set up to "protect" the Indians and assimilate them to Spanish culture, indigenous men, women and children were forced to work long hours in Spanish mines. Within 100 years of the arrival of the Coloumbus, most of the indigenous people were gone, victims of the first phase of "primitive accumulation" by the emergent capitalist economy of Europe.

Once the gold mines were exhausted, the island of Puerto Rico, like its neighbors, became a center of sugar production for export to the European market (History Task Force 1979). Almost unknown in Europe before the thirteenth century, 300 years later sugar was a staple of the European diet. Along with its derivatives, molasses and rum, it became one of the substances Mintz (1971) has termed the "proletarian hunger-killers" during the take-off phase of the Industrial Revolution. In time, rum became an essential part of the diet for the rural laboring classes of Puerto Rico.

This process was facilitated by two factors. First, alcohol consumption among Spanish settlers was a normal part of everyday activity. Prior to colonial contact, in fact, the Spanish had little access to mood-altering substances other than alcohol. As Heath (1984:14) indicates, among the Spanish, alcoholic beverages were consumed "to relieve thirst, with meals, and as a regular refreshment, in all of the ways that coffee, tea, water, or soft drinks are now used. . . ." Alcohol "thus permeated every aspect of . . . life" among the settlers (Davila 1987:11). Second, there was a daily distribution of rum to day workers and slaves on the sugar plantations (Mintz 1971). Not until 1609 did King Felipe III of Spain forbid the use of alcohol as a medium for the payment of Indian laborers (Heath 1984). Rum distilleries, in fact, were one of the few industrial enterprises launched by the Spanish during their several hundred year reign in Puerto Rico. Commercial production was supplemented by a home brew called *ron cañita* (little cane rum) made with a locally crafted still called an *alambique* and widely consumed among poor and working people (Carrion 1983). . . .

The U.S. acquisition of Puerto Rico in 1898 as war booty from the Spanish-American War—an event marking the beginning of "a major political realignment of world capitalism" (Bonilla 1985:152)—ushered in a new phase in Puerto Rican history and Puerto Rican drinking. At the moment of the U.S. invasion of Puerto Rico, 91% of the land under cultivation was owned by its occupants and an equal percentage of the existing farms were possessed by locally resident farmers (Diffie and Diffie 1931). Intervention, as Mintz (1974) has shown, produced a radical increase in the concentration of agricultural lands, the extension of areas devoted to commercial cultivation for export, and the mechanization of agricultural production processes. Indeed, it was through gaining control over sugar and the related production "that the United States consolidated its economic hegemony over the Island" (History Task Force 1979:95). Shortly after assuming office, Guy V. Henry, the U.S. appointed Military Governor of Puerto Rico, issued three rulings that facilitated this process: a freeze on credit, a devaluation of the peso, and a fix on land prices. Devaluation and the credit freeze made it impossible for farmers to meet their business expenses. As a result, they were forced to sell their property to pay their debts and thousands of small proprietors went out of business. The fix on land prices ensured that farm lands would be available at artificially low prices for interested buyers. At the time, the principal buyers in the market were either North American corporations or Puerto Rican companies directly linked to U.S. commerce. As a result, within "the short span of four years, four North American corporations . . . dedicated to sugar production came to control directly [275,030 square meters] of agricultural land" (Herrero, Sánchez, and Gutierrez 1975:56). As contrasted with the rural situation prior to U.S. intervention, by 1926 four out of five Puerto Ricans were landless (Clark 1930). The inevitable sequel to the consolidation of coastal flat lands for sugar cane plantations was a large migration out of the mountains to the coast, and the formation of "a vast rural proletariat, whose existence was determined by seasonal employment" (Maldonado-Denis 1976:44).

In the newly expanded labor force of sugar cane workers, a group that formed a large percentage of the Puerto Rican population until well into the twentieth century, drinking was a regular social activity. Mintz, who spent several years studying this population, notes the importance of drinking in men's social interaction. During the harvest season, the day followed a regular cycle. Work began early, with the men getting to the fields at sunrise and working until three or four in the afternoon, while women stayed at home caring for children, cleaning, doing the laundry, and preparing the hot lunches they would bring to their husbands in the fields.

> It is in the late afternoon that the social life of the day begins. . . . After dinner the street becomes the setting for conversation and flirting. Loafing groups gather in front of the small stores or in the yards of older men, where they squat and gossip; marriageable boys and girls promenade along the highway. Small groups form and dissolve into the bars. The women remain home. . . . The bachelors stand at the bar drinking their rum neat—each drink downed in a swallow from a tiny paper cup. The more affluent buy half pints of rum . . . and finish them sitting at the tables. (Mintz 1960:16–17)

During this period, a deeply rooted belief, reflecting the alienated character of work under capitalism, began to be established. This is the culturally constituted idea that *alcohol is a man's reward for labor:* "I worked hard, so I deserve a drink" (Davila 1987:11). Gilbert (1985:265–266), who notes a similar belief based on her research among Mexican American men, describes the widespread practice of "respite drinking," "that is to say, drinking as a respite from labor or after a hard day's work." As Marx asserts, under capitalism

> labor is external to the worker, i.e., it does not belong to his essential being; . . . in his work, therefore, he does not affirm himself but denies himself. . . . The worker therefore only feels himself outside his work, and in his work feels outside himself. He is at home when he is not working, and when he is working he is not at home. His labor is not voluntary, but coerced; it is forced labor. It is therefore not satisfying a need; it is merely a means to satisfy needs external to it. Its alien character emerges clearly in the fact that as soon as no physical or other compulsion exists, labor is shunned like the plague. (Marx 1964:110–111)

Because labor for cane workers was not intrinsically rewarding, its performance required external motivation, a role which alcohol in part—probably because of its ability in many contexts to produce euphoria, reduce anxiety and tension, and enhance self-confidence, as well has having a low cost and ready availability—filled. Serving as a valued recompense for the difficult and self-mortifying work undertaken by men, alcohol consumption became culturally entrenched as an emotionally charged symbol of manhood itself. Vital to the power of this symbolism was the emergent reconceptualization of what it meant to be a man in terms of sole responsibility for the economic well-being of one's family. Although there existed a sexual division of labor prior to the U.S. domination of Puerto Rico, in rural agricultural life work was a domestic affair that required family interdependence and close proximity. Proletarianization produced a devaluation of female labor as homemaking, while relegating it to an unpaid status. Additionally, it "led to Puerto Rican masculinity being defined in terms of being paid laborers and *buenos proveedores* (good providers)" (De La Cancela 1988:42–43). In this context, drinking came to be seen as a privilege "earned by masculine self-sufficiency and assumption of the provider role" (Gilbert 1985:266; also see Rodriguez-Andrew et al. 1988). In the words of one of Gilbert's informants: " 'Yo soy el hombre de la casa, si quiero tomar, tomo cuando me de la gana' (I am the man of the house, and if I want to drink, I drink when I feel like it)."

The 1930s marked a significant turning point in the lives of the sugar cane workers as well as most other Puerto Ricans. Prior to the Depression, sugar cane provided one-sixth of Puerto Rico's total income, one-fourth of its jobs, and two-thirds of the dollars it earned from the export of goods. One out of every three factories on the Island was a sugar mill, a sugar refinery, a rum distillery, or molasses plant. The Depression nearly destroyed this economic base. Sugar prices fell drastically, while two hurricanes (1928 and 1932) all but demolished what remained of the damaged economy.

In response, control of Puerto Rico was transferred from the U.S. War Department to the Department of the Interior, and federal taxes on Puerto Rican rum sold in the U.S. were remitted to the Puerto Rican treasury, thus providing the island's Commonwealth government with $160 million in working capital. This money was used to build a number of government-owned manufacturing plants. However, concern in the U.S. Congress with "the crazy socialistic experiment going on down in Puerto Rico" (quoted in Wagenheim 1975:108) led to the sale of these factories to local capitalists. The Commonwealth government also launched Operation Bootstrap at this time "to promote industry, tourism and rum" (Wagenheim 1975:108). Operation Bootstrap was an ambitious initiative designed to reduce the high unemployment rate caused by the stagnation of a rural economy that had been heavily dependent on the production of a small number of cash crops for export. The program offered foreign investors, 90 percent of whom came from the United States, tax holidays of over ten years, the installation of infrastructural features such as plants, roads, running water and electricity, and most importantly, an abundant supply of cheap labor.

Significantly, however, as Maldonado-Denis (1980: 31–32) points out. "What is altered in the change from the sugar economy based on the plantation to the new industrialization is merely the form of dependency, not its substance." In line with the unplanned nature of capitalist economy—at the world level, displaced agricultural workers quickly came to be defined as both an undesired "surplus population" and a *cause* of Puerto Rico's economic underdevelopment. As Day (1967:441) indicates, in a capitalist economy "if there is some cost to maintain [a] . . . surplus, it is likely to be 'pushed out'." This is precisely what occurred. Between 1952 and 1971, the total number of agricultural workers in Puerto Rico declined from 120,000 to 75,000 (Dugal 1973). So extensive was the exodus from rural areas that it threatened "to convert many towns in the interior of the Island to ghost-towns" (Maldonado-Denis 1980:33). Male workers, in particular, were affected by industrialization, because over half of the new jobs created by Operation Bootstrap went to women (Safa 1986).

Although Juan and Zoraida understood their decision to leave Puerto Rico as part of an effort to protect their children from witchcraft, the folk healer's message and its interpretation by Juan and Zoraida must be located in this broader political-economic context. As Maldonado-Denis (1980:33) cogently observes, the "dislocation of Puerto Rican agriculture—and the ensuing uprooting of its rural population—is the result of profound changes in the structure of the Puerto Rican economy and not the result of mere individual decisions arrived at because of fortuitous events." However, "migrants do not usually see the larger structural forces that create [their] personal situation" and channel their personal decisions (Rodriguez 1989:13).

The first significant labor migration of Puerto Ricans to the U.S. began in the 1920s, with the biggest push coming after World War II. The focus for most migrants until the 1970s was New York City. As noted, it was to New York that Juan and Zoraida, along with 70,000 other Puerto Ricans, migrated in 1946. As many as 60% of these migrants came from the rural zones of the Island. They arrived during a post-war boom in the New York economy that created an urgent demand for new labor (Maldonado-Denis 1972). Employment was the primary motivation for migration and many found blue collar jobs, although often at wages lower than those of Euro-American and even African American workers performing similar toil (Maldonado 1976; Rodriguez 1980).

By the time of the post-war migrations, heavy alcohol consumption among men was woven deeply into the cultural fabric of Puerto Rico. However, as Coombs and Globetti (1986:77) conclude in their review of the literature on drinking in Latin America generally, "Until recently, most studies, conducted mainly in small communities or rural areas, found relatively few visible ill effects. Little guilt or moral significance was attached to alcohol use or even drunkenness." This description appears to hold true for Puerto Ricans as well. According to Marilyn Aguírre-Molina

> If we look at the Puerto Rican experience, we can clearly see how alcohol use and the alcohol industry are entrenched within the population . . . [D]istilled spirit is very available (at low cost), and part of the national pride for production of the world's finest rum. . . . Alcohol consumption has an important role in social settings—consumption is an integral part of many or most Hispanic functions. . . . At parties, or similar gatherings, a child observes that there's a great deal of tolerance for drinking, and it is encouraged by and for the men. A non-drinking male is considered anti-social. . . . Tolerance for drinking is further evidenced in the attitude that there is no disgrace or dishonor for a man to be drunk. . . . [I]t becomes evident that alcohol use is part of the socio-cultural system of the Hispanic, used within the contexts of recreation, hospitality [and] festivity. (Aguírre-Molina 1979:3–6)

Adds Davlia (1987:17), "In our culture, weakness in drinking ability is always humiliating to a man because a true man drinks frequently and in quantity. Therefore, for a Puerto Rican man not to maintain dignity when drinking would be an absolute proof of his weakness, as would be his refusal to accept a drink." Refusal to drink among Puerto Rican men, in fact, can be interpreted as an expression of homosexuality because drinking is defined as a diacritical male activity (Singer, Davison, and Yalin 1987). In Puerto Rico, these attitudes are supported by an extensive advertising effort by the rum industry, few restrictions on sales, ready availability of distilled spirits at food stores, and low cost for alcoholic beverages (Canino et al. 1987).

Most aspects of Puerto Rican life were transformed by the migration, drinking patterns included. According to Gordon

> Puerto Ricans have . . . adopted U.S. drinking customs and *added* them to their traditional drinking customs. . . . They follow the pattern of weekday drinking typical of the American workingman. . . . Weekday drinking among Puerto Ricans does not affect the importance of their traditional weekend fiesta drinking more commonly seen in a rural society (emphasis added). (Gordon 1985a:308)

. . .

While it is evident from Mintz's (1960) account of sugar cane workers that many Puerto Rican men had adopted working class drinking patterns even prior to migration, these behaviors were generalized and amplified following movement to the U.S. As a consequence of cultural pressure to maintain traditional drinking patterns as well as adopt U.S. working class norms, many Puerto Rican men have adopted a heavy drinking pattern. The development of this pattern was facilitated by the high density of businesses in poor, inner city neighborhoods that dispense alcohol, especially beer, for on- and off-premise consumption: multiple encouragements to drink in the media, including advertisements, films, and television programs (Maxwell and Jacobson 1989); and structural factors that have contributed first to a redefinition and ultimately to the marginalization of the Puerto Rican man. This last factor was especially important in transforming heavy drinking into problem drinking in this population.

As suggested above, the transition from yeoman farmer to rural proletariat began a process of reconceptualizing the meaning of masculinity among Puerto Ricans. This transition was completed with the migration. Work-related definitions of manliness and provider-based evaluations of self-worth became dominant. To be *un hombre hecho y derecho* (a complete man) now meant demonstrating an ability to be successful as an income earner in the public sphere. This is "the great American dream of dignity through upward mobility" analyzed so effectively by Sennett and Cobb (1973:169), a dream that threatens always to turn into a nightmare for the working man. And the name of this nightmare, as every worker knows so well, is unemployment. The fear of unemployment is not solely an economic worry, it is equally a dread of being blamed and of blaming oneself for inadequacy, for letting down one's family, for failing while others succeed. The "plea . . . to be relieved of having to prove oneself this way, to gain a hold instead on the innate meaningfulness of actions" is a central theme in the lives of working people (Sennett and Cobb 1973:246).

Juan's hard work, enabling his movement from janitor to draftsman, achieved without formal education or training, is the embodiment of the dream and the fear of the working man. During the period that Juan was successful at realizing the dream, his daughter remembers her family life as stable and happy. These golden years provided a stark contrast with what was to follow. Throughout this period Juan drank heavily, and yet he had no drinking problem. Alcohol was his culturally validated reward for living up to the stringent requirements of the male role in capitalist society. The swift turnaround in Juan's life following the loss of his job suggests that Puerto Rican male drinking problems should be considered in relationship to the problem of unemployment.

Several studies, in fact, indicate a direct association between unemployment and problem drinking. In his study of alcohol-related problems in Toronto, for example, Smart (1979) reports that 21% of unemployed respondents suffer from three or more alcohol-related problems compared to only 6% of employed workers. While an increase in consumption levels following unemployment has not been found in all studies of small groups of workers in particular settings (e.g., Iversen and Klausen 1986), a national study by McCornac and Filante (1984) of distilled spirit consumption and employment in the U.S. at the time of Juan's death supports this linkage. Their study concludes,

> The unemployment rate had a positive and significant impact on the consumption of distilled spirits in both the cross-sectional and pooled analyses. During a recessionary period, rising unemployment stimulates consumption while decreasing real per capita income decreases consumption. However, the two effects are not equal. From 1972–1973 to 1974–1975, the rate of unemployment rose by 37% . . . while real per capita income declined by less than 1%. Thus, the net effect of simultaneous changes in these two variables was

> to increase consumption by approximately 8%. The important implication of this finding is that the negative consequences of higher rates of unemployment can be extended to include the increased social and economic costs of an increase in the use of distilled spirits. (McCornac and Filante 1984:177–178)

Similarly, analysis of national data on long and short term trends in alcohol consumption and mortality by Brenner (1975) shows an increase in alcohol consumption and alcohol-related health and social problems during periods of economic recession and rising unemployment. His study, covering the years during Juan's period of heaviest drinking and subsequent death, finds that "National recessions in personal income and employment are consistently followed, within 2 to 3 years, by increases in cirrhosis mortality rates" (Brenner 1975:1282). Economic disruptions, he argues, create conditions of social stress, which in turn stimulate increased anxiety-avoidance drinking and consequent health problems. Research by Pearlin and Radabaugh (1976:661) indicates that anxiety is "especially likely to result in the use of alcohol as a tranquilizer if a sense of control is lacking and self-esteem is low." The key variable in this equation, as Seeman and Anderson (1983) stress, is powerlessness. Based on their study of drinking among men in Los Angeles, they argue, "The conclusion is inescapable that the sense of powerlessness is related to the experience of drinking problems quite apart from the sheer quantity of alcohol consumed" (Seeman and Anderson 1983:71). Increased alcohol consumption and alcohol-related problems and mortality have been found to be associated in several studies (Makela et al. 1981; Wilson 1984).

The major economic factor of concern here, of course, was the flight of the appliance factory where Juan was employed to a cheap labor market outside of the industrial Northeast. Juan was not alone in losing his job to the corporate transfer of production. About the same time, thousands of U.S. workers were being laid off by the "runaway shop"; 900,000 U.S. production jobs were lost, for example, between 1967 and 1971 alone (Barnet and Muller 1974). In New York City, during this period, 25% of the largest companies relocated, reflecting a shift away from a production-centered economy. This transition has intensified the problem of Puerto Rican unemployment (Maldonado-Denis 1980; Rodriguez 1980). Mills and his coworkers, in their study of Puerto Rican migrants in New York, found that lacking specialized job skills Puerto Rican workers are at the mercy of economic forces. During periods of economic upturn they are welcomed, but when the business cycle "is on the way down, or in the middle of one of its periodic breakdowns, there is a savage struggle for even the low wage jobs. . ." (Mills et al. 1967:82).

Consequently, at the time that Juan died in 1971, Puerto Ricans had one of the highest unemployment rates of all ethnic groups in the country. While 6% of all men in the U.S. were jobless, for Puerto Rican men the rate of unemployment was 8.8%. Significantly, the actual rate of unemployment for Puerto Rican men was even higher than these figures suggest because, as measured by the Department of Labor, the unemployment rate does not include numerous individuals who have given up on the possibility of ever locating employment. If discouraged workers were included, the "unemployment among Puerto Rican men would be more accurately depicted—not at the 'official' rate of 8.8 percent—but at the 'adjusted' (and more realistic) level of 18.7 percent" (Maldonado-Denis 1980:79–80).

For many older workers like Juan, whose age made them dispensable, and many younger Puerto Rican workers as well, whose ethnicity and lack of recognized skills made them equally discardable, the changing economic scene in New York meant permanent unemployment. Increased drinking and rising rates of problem drinking were products of the consequent sense of worthlessness and failure in men geared to defining masculinity in terms of being *un buen proveedor* (Canino and Canino 1980:537–538). As De La Cancela (1989:146) asserts, "living with limited options, uncertainty, and violence breeds fertile ground for ego exalting substance use among Latinos." Pappas identifies the general reasons in this ethnography of the effects of factory closing on rubber workers in Barberton, Ohio. Beyond a salary, a job provides workers with a feeling of purpose and means of participation in the surrounding social world. In addition to contributing to the experience of uselessness, loss of work fragments social networks and produces increased isolation, placing increased strain on domestic relations. Restriction of the quantity of outside social interaction "narrows the psychic space in which the unemployed maneuver" (Pappas 1989:86).

. . .

Within the context of Puerto Rican culture, these general processes take on a particular slant. Drinking among Latino males is commonly linked both in the alcohol literature and in popular thinking with the concept of *machismo,* or the notable Latino emphasis on appearing manly at all times, particularly in public. Some have gone so far as to lay blame for the high rates of drinking found among Latino males on *machismo.* It is certainly the case that drinking is culturally defined as a male thing to do, as a culturally approved means of expressing prowess as a male. But this does not lead directly to alcoholism. Rather, it is the combination of a cultural emphasis on drinking as proper, appropriate, and manly, with political and economic subordination in a system in which most alternative expressions of manliness are barred to Puerto Rican access that is of real significance (Singer 1987b). This interpretation underscores De La Cancela's (1986:292) argument that "just as capitalism obscures the necessity of institutionalized unemployment by defining the unemployed as somehow lacking in the required skills to succeed, *machismo* obscures the alienation effects of capitalism on individuals by embodying the alienation in male-female sex-role terms. . . ."

Unemployment blocked Juan, as it has so many other Puerto Rican men, from the major socially sanctioned route to success as a man. It did not, however, exterminate the ever present and powerful need to achieve the cultural values of *machismo* (mastery), *dignidad* (honor and dignity of the family), and *respecto* (respect of one's peers). In a sense, however counterproductive, drinking was all that was left for Juan that was manly in his understanding. Hard drinking replaced hard work, and alcohol, as a medium of cultural expression, was transformed from compensation for the sacrifices of achieving success into salve for the tortures of failure.

JUAN IS NOT ALONE

The "personal problems" of the unemployed workers of Barberton, like the problems experienced by Juan García, constitute part of the human fallout of so-called economic development. Although often portrayed as natural and inevitable, changes in the nature and location of production exact enormous human costs, costs that tend to be born disporportionately by the poor and working classes. The extent of the agony for Puerto Rican men is captured by Davila:

> I have a father who is an alcoholic and a brother who died of cirrhosis of the liver a year ago at the age of 42. I have a young son who is having alcohol problems of his own. I have cousins and uncles who have died of alcoholism. I have friends who likewise have died of alcoholism or are currently alcoholic. And I am a recovering alcoholic. . . . All the persons I have listed are Puerto Rican . . . they are all men. (Davila 1987:17–18)

A study comparing mortality differentials among various Latino subgroups residing in the U.S. during the years 1979–1981 found that the Puerto Rican population had a distinct pattern of mortality from chronic liver disease and cirrhosis. The age-adjusted death rate among Puerto Ricans from liver-related problems, which are common among heavy drinkers, is about twice that among Mexicans and almost three times the rate among Cubans. Further, the rate among Puerto Ricans is over two times the African American rate and triple the Euro-American rate (Rosenwaike 1987). In fact, New York Board of Health data for 1979–81 indicate that cirrhosis was the second leading cause of death among Island-born Puerto Ricans age 15–45 (cited in Gordon 1985b).

These data suggest that Juan's case, while having special features peculiar to his individual life course, is not, on the whole, unique. His life and his death, in fact, are emblematic of the broad experience of working class Puerto Rican men in the U.S., a conclusion supported by findings from our studies of drinking patterns and experiences among Puerto Rican men and adolescents in Hartford, CT. For both studies, the sampling frame consisted of all Puerto Rican households in high-density Puerto Rican neighborhoods as defined by census reports (25% Latino surnames). In the first of these studies, interviews were conducted with a randomly selected sample of Puerto Rican adolescents age 14–17 years. The sampling unit consisted of 210 adolescents (one adolescent subject per participating household), of which 88 were boys.

A series of national household surveys (Abelson and Atkinson 1975; Abelson and Fishburne 1976; Abelson et al. 1977) of drinking among adolescents indicates that over half of the adolescents in the U.S. report using alcohol during the past year, compared to 31% of the Puerto Rican adolescents in our sample. In the national samples, about one-third of participants report drinking within the month prior to the survey, compared to 14% in our sample. Similarly, Rachal et al. (1976), in a national sample of over 13,000 adolescents in grades 7–12, found that 55% reported usually drinking at least once a month, compared to 10% in our sample. Regarding the quantity of alcohol consumed per drinking episode, these researchers found that 55% of their sample reported more than one drink per drinking occasion, compared to only 19% in our sample. In short, as have other researchers (Welte and Barnes 1987), we found a lower drinking prevalence among Puerto Rican adolescents than tends to be found for the general U.S. adolescent population.

. . .

The existing literature suggests that *family controls* are a major factor limiting alcohol consumption among Latino youth to levels below those of their white counterparts. This was found to be a primary reason given for not drinking by the adolescents in our study. Based on his research among Mexican-Americans in Texas, Trotter (1985:286) states: "Unmarried children who smoke or drink in front of parents are often thought to be extremely disrespectful, and to shame their family." This explanation fits with the cultural understanding that drinking is an earned reward for assuming the responsibilities of employment and family support, roles not open to dependent children.

Our second study examined drinking patterns in 398 Puerto Rican men, 18–48 years of age, recruited to a research sample structured by type of residence (private home, rented apartment, housing project). These primary sampling units were chosen because of expected differences in socio-economic status and the sense from prior research that residents in rented apartments in low income neighborhoods often are under greater economic pressure than households in rent controlled housing projects or owners of private homes or condominiums. The housing project included in this study is located at some distance from the central city area and tends to be in better repair than other Hartford housing projects. Respondents living in targeted neighborhoods (selected because of census data indicating a high density Spanish surname population) were randomly recruited and interviewed in their place of residence.

Among the men in the sample, 84% were born in Puerto Rico and half had been living in the U.S. for under ten years. Most of the other men were born in the U.S., 37% in Hartford. Fifty-four percent were married or living with a partner, and 83% had a high school education or less. Data on these respondents indicate the economic difficulties faced by Puerto Rican men generally. Thirty-three percent reported that they were unemployed and looking for work and another 17% worked only part-time at the time of the interview. More than half of the men (55%) reported annual household incomes of under $8,000; 85% reported incomes under $15,000. Rates of unemployment for men across the three residential subgroups was as follows: private home: 3%; rented apartment: 44.3%; housing project: 68.5%. Additionally, rates of part-time employment across these three residence types were 12%, 19.8%, and 10.8%, respectively. These data are consistent with other research in Hartford indicating "that whites . . . on average have a higher socio-economic level than the Black and Hispanic samples, and *the Hispanic group is consistently ranked lowest* . . . in socio-economic indicators in Hartford" (AIDS Community Research Group 1988:9; emphasis in original).

About 80% of the men in our study reported that they have consumed alcohol. Of these, 31% indicated that they drink at least once a week. Regarding quantities normally consumed when drinking, we found that 53% of the drinkers reported having at least 3 drinks per drinking occasion. Ten percent indicated that they normally drink until "high" or drunk, although drinking for these effects was reported as a motivation for consumption by 41%. . . . Almost 20% of the men reported having eight drinks per drinking occasion at least 1–3 times per month during the last year. Another 7.5% reported this level of drinking 3–11 times during the last year. The majority of the men, however, reported lower levels of drinking.

. . . Approximately 10% of the men in the study reported they felt that their drinking was not completely under control during the last year. If a longer time period is included (since a man's first drink), approximately 20% reported having felt out of control.

Additionally, 34% of the men stated that drinking as a means of forgetting about problems was a very to somewhat important motivation for them to drink, while almost a quarter reported they drink because they have nothing else to do.

Data show that between 7–28% of the men reported at least one drinking-related problem. Notably, 28.4% of the men indicated that drinking has had a harmful effect on their home life or marriage.

Table I compares negative drinking consequences among Puerto Rican men (21 years-of-age and older) with findings among men from a national probability sample of the general population aged 21 or older (Cahalan 1982). The problem drinking scales displayed on this table were constructed by combining responses from several related questions following Cahalan (1982). In most cases, quite similar questions (pertinent to these scales) appear on both the national and Hartford instruments. Symptomatic drinking refers to signs of physical dependence and loss of control suggestive of Jellinek's gamma alcoholism (e.g., drinking to relieve a hangover, blackouts, having difficulty stopping drinking). Three variables used to construct this scale (tossing down drinks quickly, sneaking drinks, drinking before a party to ensure having enough alcohol) were not included in our survey, possibly resulting in a lower score for Puerto Rican men. Half of the variables used to construct an additional scale on psychological dependence for the national study were not included in our instrument and consequently this item is not included in the table.

In the national sample, 25% of the respondents were abstainers compared to 20% in our study. Additionally, it is evident from Table I that the prevalence of drinking-related problems is higher for the Hartford sample on most of the scales, supporting the epidemiological data suggesting higher problem drinking rates among Puerto Rican men. These differences are especially notable on the two scales (complaints about drinking by friends of spouses) that involve the impact of drinking on personal relationships. The final column on this

TABLE I Prevalence of Drinking-Related Problems among Men (21 years and older) over Last 12 Months

Drinking-Related Problems	Total National Probability Sample N = 751	Total Hartford Puerto Rican Sample N = 352*	Hartford Puerto Rican Drinkers N = 180*
Health problems associated with drinking	4.0	9.4	31.7
Acting belligerently under the influence	8.0	9.1	48.5
Friends complain about drinking	3.0	30.7	35.9
Symptomatic drinking	20.0	19.9	36.5
Job-related drinking problems	7.0	6.8	19.7
Problems with law, police, accidents	2.0	4.8	38.6
Engaging in binge drinking	1.0	4.5	50.0
Spouse complains about drinking	2.0	7.7	13.0

* Excludes participants under 21 years of age

table reports problem frequencies just for drinkers in the Hartford study (i.e., abstainers are not included). Positive responses on two of the scales, belligerence (getting into heated arguments while drinking) and binge drinking (being intoxicated for several days at a time), were reported by approximately half of the Puerto Rican drinkers.

Overall, we found high rates of heavy and problem drinking in our study of Puerto Rican men, with the heaviest and most problematic drinking occurring among men who lived in rented apartments in high density, low income, inner city neighborhoods. The correlation coefficients between employment and the problem drinking scales reported in Table I are displayed in Table II. As this table indicates, there is a negative correlation between being employed and all eight problem drinking scales. Unemployment, in sum, is a clear correlate of problem drinking in Puerto Rican men.

Our research suggests that the onset of drinking problems among Puerto Rican males is associated with a *post-adolescent transition* into the world of adult responsibilities and sociocultural expectations. Specifically, findings from our second study indicate this transition occurs in the mid-20s. After that point, rates of problem drinking continue to rise until Puerto Rican men are well into their forties (cf. Caetano 1983). Confronted repeatedly with setbacks in attaining regular and rewarding employment, and unable to support their families, many Puerto Rican men in Hartford drink to forget their problems and their boredom, while seeking through heavy and often problem drinking what they cannot achieve otherwise in society: respect, dignity, and validation of their masculine identity. While 38.5% of the men in our sample who reported two or more drinking-related health or social problems indicated that they drink to forget about their personal worries, the figure was 7.1% for problem-free drinkers. Similarly, 30.8% of problem drinkers reported drinking to release tension compared to 6.5% of problem-free drinkers. As our data show, not all Puerto Rican men become involved in problem drinking (or the use of other mind-altering drugs). Indeed, the majority do not. That so many do however reveals the folly of remaining at the micro-level in developing an explanation of this phenomenon.

TABLE II Zero-Order Correlation Coefficients between Employment and Drinking-Related Problems among Puerto Rican Men

Drinking-Related Problems	Correlation Coefficient (r)
Health problems associated with drinking	–.1805
Acting belligerently under the influence	–.0634
Friends complain about drinking	–.0069
Symptomatic drinking	–.1165
Job-related drinking problems	–.0573
Problems with law, police, accidents	–.2171
Engaging in binge drinking	–.3371
Spouse complains about drinking	–.1530

CONCLUSION

In this examination of the broader context of Juan's drinking, we see the intersection of biography and history, that critical link uniting "the innermost acts of the individual with the widest kinds of social-historical phenomena" (Gerth and Mills 1964:xvi). In reviewing the social environment of "Juan's disease," we have not, we believe, "depersonalize[d] the subject matter and the content of medical anthropology" (Scheper-Hughes and Lock 1986:137). The goal of critical medical anthropology is not to obliterate the individual nor the poignant and personal expressions produced by the loss and struggle to regain well-being. Nor does this perspective seek to eliminate psychology, culture, the environment, or biology from a holistic medical anthropology. Instead, by taking "cognizance of processes that transcend separable cases" (Wolf 1982:17), we attempt to unmask the ways in which suffering, as well as curing, illness behavior, provider–patient interactions, etc., have levels of meaning and cause beyond the narrow confines of immediate experience. As Mintz (1989:791) suggests, "When we can accurately specify the effects of policies readily imposed by external authority, the relationships between outside and inside, and between the living of life events and the weight of the world system, are clear." Situated in relationship to relevant history and political economy, Juan's drinking loses the bewildering quality commonly attached to destructive behavior. This is achieved by an exploration of the macro-micro nexus which includes and requires an examination of symbolic, environmental, and psychological factors, but does not reduce analysis to any of these factors.

. . .

As Juan's case reveals, however misdirected and self-destructive, problem drinking is a dramatic and nagging reminder that medical anthropology must be more than the study of health systems and political-economic structures, it must be sensitive also to the symbolically expressed experiential and meaning frames of struggling human beings reacting to and attempting to shape their world, although never "under circumstances chosen by themselves" (Marx 1963:15). In its disruptiveness, problem drinking, in any type of society or social system (Singer 1986a), brings to light the dynamic tensions between structure and agency, society and the individual, general processes and particular human responses. Addressing these issues is the special contribution of critical medical anthropology to the wider arena of the political economy of health.

Thus, we argue for the adoption of a broad theoretical framework designed to explore and explain macro-micro linkages and to channel praxis accordingly. The success of critical medical anthropology in providing such a framework will determine its utility and endurance.

NOTES

1 Other critiques of critical medical anthropology have been addressed in Singer, Baer, and Lazarus (1989) and Singer (1989c). A recent critique, noteworthy for its distortions of the perspective, was penned by McElroy (1990). She alleges that critical medical anthropology is antiscience because it does not take Western biological categories at face value, asserting instead that political-economic factors shape even scientific thinking. The failures of medical ecology notwithstanding (Singer 1989a; Baer 1990b; Trostle 1990), at issue is not the reality of biology or a questioning of biological factors in disease etiology. As a materialist approach, critical medical anthropology hardly rejects the natural science paradigm. Instead, we call for a better science of humanity, one that recognizes the social origins and functions of science. Moreover, as demonstrated by Scheder (1988), critical medical anthropology is as much concerned with the political economy of disease as it is with the political economy of illness, treatment or related domains. The point is that critical medical anthropology views disease as both naturally and socially produced, but views "nature" as both naturally and socially produced as well.

2 These studies were supported by National Institute on Alcohol Abuse and Alcoholism grants R23 AA06057 and R01 AA07161. Preparation of this paper was supported by the latter grant. Merrill Singer served as Principal Investigator for both grants, while Freddie Valentin was Project Director and Zhongke Jia was Data Manager on the second study.

3 Despite the focus of this paper, it should be emphasized that these conditions are not found only in capitalist society, nor are alcohol-related problems found exclusively in oppressed social classes and ethnic minority communities. These points are elaborated in Singer (1986a).

4 Most recently, a growing number of alcohol researchers have abandoned the notion of alcoholism in favor of alcohol dependency, because, it is believed, this labels a demonstrably organic condition. However, the barometers (e.g., DSM-III and ICD 10) used to measure this organic condition still include behavioral and experiential factors which anthropological researchers have long argued are open to sociocultural influence (e.g., "a narrowing of the personal repertoire of patterns of alcohol use," "a great deal of time spent drinking or recovering from the effects of drinking"). In this paper, we employ the term *problem drinking* to refer to drinking patterns associated with negative health and social consequences for the drinker and his social network.

REFERENCES

Abad, V., and J. Suares. 1974. Cross Cultural Aspects of Alcoholism among Puerto Ricans. Proceedings of the Fourth Annual Alcoholism Conference of the National Institute on Alcohol Abuse and Alcoholism. Washington, D.C.

Abelson, H., and R. Atkinson. 1975. Public Experience with Psychoactive Substances. Princeton, NJ: Response Analysis Corporation.

Abelson, H., and P. Fishburne. 1976. Nonmedical Use of Psychoactive Substances. Princeton, NJ: Response Analysis Corporation.

Abelson, H., et al. 1977. National Survey of Drug Abuse, 1977. Rockville, MD: NIAAA AIDS Community Research Group.

———. 1988. AIDS: Knowledge, Attitudes and Behavior in an Ethically Mixed Urban Neighborhood. Special Report to the Connecticut State Department of Health Services, Hartford, CT.

Agar, M. 1973. Ripping and Running. New York: Academy Press.

Aguirre-Molina, M. 1979. Alcohol and the Hispanic Woman. Paper presented at the Conference on Women in Crisis, New York, NY.

Ames, G., and J. Mora. 1988. Alcohol Problem Prevention in Mexican American Populations. In Alcohol Consumption among Mexicans and Mexican Americans. M. J. Gilbert, ed. Pp. 253–280. New York: Plenum.

Baer, H. 1989. The American Dominative Medical System as a Reflection of Social Relations in the Larger Society. Social Science and Medicine 28(ll):1103–1112.

———. 1990a. Kerr-McGee and the NRC. From Indian Country to Silkwood to Gore. Social Science and Medicine 30(2):237–248.

———. 1990b. Biocultural Approaches in Medical Anthropology: A Critical Medical Anthropology Commentary. Medical Anthropology Quarterly 4:344–348.

Baer, H., and M. Singer. 1982. Why Not Have a Critical Medical Anthropology? Paper presented at the Annual Meeting of the American Anthropological Association, Washington, DC.

Baer, H., M. Singer, and J. Johnsen. 1986. Introduction: Toward a Critical Medical Anthropology. Social Science and Medicine 23(2):95–98.

Barnet, R., and R. Muller. 1974. Global Reach. New York: Simon and Schuster.

Bennett, L. 1988. Alcohol in Context: Anthropological Perspective. Drugs and Society 2(3/4):89–131.

Bonilla, F. 1985. Ethnic Orbits: The Circulation of Capitals and Peoples. Contemporary Marxism 10:148–167.

Brenner, H. 1975, Trends in Alcohol Consumption and Associated Illnesses. American Journal of Public Health 65:1279–1292.

Brown, R. 1979. Rockefeller Medicine Men. Berkeley, CA: University of California Press.

Caetano, R. 1983. Drinking Patterns and Alcohol Problems among Hispanics in the U.S.: A Review. Drug and Alcohol Dependence 12:37–59.

Cahalan, D. 1982. Epidemiology: Alcohol Use in American Society. In Alcohol, Science and Society Revisited. E. Gomberg, H. White, and J. Carpenter, eds. Pp. 96–118. Ann Arbor, MI: University of Michigan Press.

Canino, G., et. al. 1987. The Prevalence of Alcohol Use and/or Dependence in Puerto Rico. In Health and Behavior: Research Agenda for Hispanics. The Research Monograph Series, vol. 1. M. Garria and M. Arana, eds. Pp. 127–144. Bloomington, IN: The University of Indiana Press.

Canino, I., and G. Canino. 1980. Impact of Stress on the Puerto Rican Family: Treatment Considerations. American Journal of Orthopsychiatry 50:535–541.

Carrión, A. 1983. Puerto Rico: A Political and Cultural History. Chicago, IL: Aldine.

Chafetz, M., and H. Demone. 1962. Alcoholism and Society. New York: Oxford University Press.

Chafetz, M., and R. Yoerg. 1977. Public Health Treatment Programs in Alcoholism. In Treatment and Rehabilitation of the Chronic Alcoholic. B. Kissin and H. Begleiter, eds. Pp. 593–614. New York: Plenum.

Chrisman, N. 1985. Alcoholism: Illness or Disease? In The American Experience with Alcohol. L. Bennett and G. Ames, eds. Pp. 7–22. New York: Plenum.

Clark, V. 1930. Puerto Rico and Its Problems. Washington, D.C: The Brookings Institution.

Coll y Toste, C. 1969. Historia de la esclavitud en Puerto Rico. San Juan, PR: Sociedad de Autores Puerutorriqueños.

Conrad, P., and J. Schneider. 1980. Deviance and Medicalization: From Badness to Sickness. St. Louis, MO: C. V. Mosby.

Coombs, D., and G. Globetti. 1986. Alcohol Use and Alcoholism in Latin America: Changing Patterns and Socio-cultural Explanations. The International Journal of the Addictions 21:59–81.

Davies, P. 1979. Motivation, Responsibility and Sickness in the Psychiatric Treatment of Alcoholism. British Journal of Psychiatry 134:449–458.

Davila, R. 1987. The History of Puerto Rican Drinking Patterns. In Alcohol Use and Abuse among Hispanic Adolescents. M. Singer, L. Davison, and F. Yalin, eds. Pp. 7–18. Hartford, CT: Hispanic Health Council.

Day, R. 1967. The Economics of Technological Change and the Demise of the Share Cropper. American Economic Review 47:427–449.

De La Cancela, V. 1986. A Critical Analysis of Puerto Rican Machismo: Implications for Clinical Practice. Psychotherapy 23(2):291–296.

———. 1988. Labor Pains: Puerto Rican Males in Transition. Centro Bulletin 2:41–55.

———. 1989. Minority AIDS Prevention: Moving beyond Cultural Perspectives toward Sociopolitical Empowerment. AIDS Education and Prevention 1:141–153.

De Ropp, R. 1976. Drugs and the Mind. New York: Delta.

Diffie, B., and J. Diffie. 1931. Puerto Rico: A Broken Pledge. New York: Vanguard Press.

Douglas, M., ed. 1987. Constructive Drinking: Perspectives on Drinking from Anthropology. New York: Cambridge University Press.

Dugal, V. 1973. Two Papers on the Economy of Puerto Rico. San German, Puerto Rico: The Caribbean Institute and Study Center for Latin America.

Elling, R. 1981. The Capitalist World-System and International Health. International Journal of Health Services 11:21–51.

Gerth, H., and C. W. Mills. 1964. Character and Social Structure. New York: Harbinger Books.

Gilbert, M. J. 1985. Mexican-Americans in California: Intraculrural Variation in Attitudes and Behavior Related to Alcohol. In The American Experience with Alcohol. L. Bennett and G. Ames, eds. Pp. 255–278. New York: Plenum.

———. 1987. Alcohol Consumption Patterns in Immigrant and Later Generation Mexican American Women. Hispanic Journal of the Behavioral Sciences 9:299–314.

———. 1988. Alcohol Consumption among Mexicans and Mexican Americans: A Binational Perspective, Spanish Speaking Mental Health Research Center. Los Angeles, CA: University of California.

Gilbert, M. J., and R. Cervantes. 1987. Mexican Americans and Alcohol. Monograph No. 11, Spanish Speaking Mental Health Research Center. Los Angeles, CA: University of California.

Gordon, A. 1978. Hispanic Drinking after Migration: The Case of Dominicans. Medical Anthropology 10:154–171.

———. 1981. The Cultural Context of Drinking and Indigenous Therapy for Alcohol Problems in Three Migrant Hispanic Cultures; An Ethnographic Report. In Cultural Factors in Alcohol Research and Treatment of Drinking Problems. Journal of Studies on Alcohol (Special Supplement No. 9). D. Health, J. Waddell, and J. Topper, eds. Pp. 217–240.

———. 1985a. Alcohol and Hispanics in the Northeast. In The American Experience with Alcohol. L. Bennett and G. Ames, eds. Pp. 297–314. New York: Plenum.

———. 1985b. State of the Art Review: Caribbean Hispanics and their Alcohol Use. Paper presented at the National Institute on Alcohol Abuse and Alcoholism Conference on the Epidemiology of Alcohol Use and Abuse Among U.S. Minorities, Bethesda, MD.

Heath, D. 1976. Anthropological Perspectives on Alcohol: An Historical Review. In Cross-cultural Approaches to the Study of Alcohol: An Interdisciplinary Perspective. M. Everett, J. Waddell, and D. Heath, eds. Pp. 42–101. The Hague: Mouton.

———. 1978. The Sociocultural Model of Alcohol Use: Problems and Prospects. Journal of Operational Psychiatry 9:56–66.

———. 1980. A Critical Review of the Sociocultural Model of Alcohol Use. In Normative Approaches to the Prevention of Alcohol Abuse and Alcoholism. T. Hartford, D. Parker and L. Light, eds. Pp. 1–18. NIAAA Research Monographs No. 3, DHEW Pub. No. ADM-79-847. Washington, D.C.: U.S. Government Printing Office.

———. 1984. Historical and Cultural Factors Affecting Alcohol Availability and Consumption in Latin America. Research Papers in Anthropology, No. 2, Department of Anthropology, Brown University, Providence, RI.

———. 1987a. A Decade of Development in the Anthropology Study of Alcohol Use: 1970–1989. In Constructive Drinking. M. Douglas, ed. Pp. 16–70. New York: Cambridge University Press.

———. 1987b. Anthropology and Alcohol Studies: Current Issues. Annual Review of Anthropology 16: 99–120.

Herrero, J., V. Sanchez Cardona, and E. Gutierrez. 1975. La Politicia monetaria del '98. El Nuevo Dia, 30 July 1975.

History Task Force. 1979. Labor Migration Under Capitalism: The Puerto Rican Experience. New York: Monthly Review Press.

Iversen, L., and H. Klausen. 1986. Alcohol Consumption among Laid-Off Workers before and after Closure of a Danish Ship-Yard: A 2-Year Follow-up Study. Social Science and Medicine 22:107–109.

Jessor, R. 1984. Adolescent Problem Drinking: Psychosocial Aspects and Developmental Outcomes. In Proceedings: NIAAA-WHO Collaborating Center Designation Meeting & Alcohol Research Seminar. Pp. 104–143. Rockville, MD: U.S. Department of Health and Human Services.

Keesing, R. 1987. Anthropology as Interpretive Quest. Current Anthropology 28:161–176.

Kendell, R. E. 1979. Alcoholism: A Medical or Political Problem? British Medical Journal 1:367–371.

Makela, K., et. al. 1981. Alcohol, Society and the State. Toronto: Addiction Research Foundation.

Maldonado-Denis, M. 1972. Puerto Rico: A Socio-Historic Interpretation. New York: Vintage Books.

———. 1980. The Emigration Dialectic: Puerto Rico and the USA. New York: International Publishers.

Maldonado, R. 1976. Why Puerto Ricans Migrated to the United States in 1947–73. Monthly Labor Review (September):7–18.

Marx, K. 1963. The 18th Brumaire of Louis Bonaparte. New York: International Publishers.

———. 1964. The Economic and Philosophic Manuscripts of 1844. New York: International Publishers.

Marx, K., and F. Engels. 1967. On Religion. New York: Schocken Books.

Maxwell, B., and Jacobson, M. 1989. Marketing Disease to Hispanics. Washington, DC: Center for Science in the Public Interest.

Mc ornac, D., and R. Filante. 1984. The Demand for Distilled Spirits: An Empirical Investigation. Journal of Studies on Alcohol 45:176–178.

McElroy, A. 1990. Bioculrural Models in Studies of Human Health and Adaptation. Medical Anthropology Quarterly 4:243–265.

McKinlay, J. 1986. A Case for Refocusing Upstream: The Political Economy of Illness. In The Sociology of Health and Illness: Critical Perspectives. P. Conrad and R. Kern, eds. Pp. 484–498. New York: St. Martin's Press.

Mills, C. W., et al. 1967. The Puerto Rican Journey. New York: Russell and Russell.

Mintz, S. 1960. Worker in the Cane. New Haven, CT: Yale University Press.

———. 1971. The Caribbean as a Socio-cultural Area. In Peoples and Cultures of the Caribbean. M. Horowitz, ed. Pp. 17–46. Garden City, NY: Natural History Press.

———. 1974. Caribbean Transformation. Chicago, IL: Aldine.

———. 1989. The Sensation of Moving. While Standing Still. American Ethnologist 169(4):786–796.

Mishler, E. 1981. The Social Construction of Illness. In Social Contexts of Health, Illness, and Patient Care. E. Mishler et al., eds. Pp. 141–168. Cambridge: Cambridge University Press.

Morgan, Lynn. 1987. Dependency Theory in the Political Economy of Health: An Anthropological Critique. Medical Anthropology Quarterly 1:131–154.

Morsy, S. 1990. Political Economy in Medical Anthropology. In Medical Anthropology: Contemporary Theory and Method. T. Johnson and C. Sargent, eds. Westport, CT: Praeger.

Mulford, H., and D. Miller. 1964. Measuring Public Acceptance of the Alcoholic as a Sick Person. Quarterly Journal of Studies on Alcohol 25:314–323.

Navarro, V. 1977. Social Security and Medicine in the U.S.S.R. Lexington, MA: Lexington Books.

Noble, D. 1979. America by Design: Science, Technology, and the Rise of Corporate Capitalism. New York: Alfred A. Knopf.

Osherson, S., and L. Amara Singham. 1981. The Machine Metaphor in Medicine. In Social Contexts of Health, Illness, and Patient Care. E. Mishler, et al., eds. Pp. 218–249. Cambridge: Cambridge University Press.

Page, B., L. Rio, J. Sweeney, and C. McKay. 1985. Alcohol and Adaptation to Exile in Miami's Cuban Population. In The American Experience with Alcohol. L. Bennett and G. Ames, eds. Pp. 315–332. New York: Plenum.

Pappas, G. 1989. The Magic City: Unemployment in a Working Class Community. Ithaca, NY: Cornell University Press.

Park, P. 1983. Social-Class Factors in Alcoholism. In The Pathogenesis of Alcoholism, vol 6, Psychosocial Factors. B. Kissin and H. Begleiter, eds. Pp. 365–104. New York: Plenum.

Partridge, W. 1978. Uses and Nonuses of Anthropological Data on Drug Abuse. In Applied Anthropology in America. E. Eddy and W. Partridge, eds. Pp. 350–372. New York: Columbia University Press.

Pearlin, L., and C. Radabaugh. 1976. Economic Strains and the Coping Functions of Alcohol. American Journal of Sociology 82:652–663.

———. 1982. Ethnic and Racial Variation in Alcohol Use and Abuse. In Special Populations Issues. Pp. 239–311. Washington, DC: U.S. Department of Health and Human Services.

Rachal, J., J. Williams, M. Brehm, B. Cavanaugh, R. Moore, and W. Eckerman. 1975. Final Report: A National Study of Adolescent Drinking Behavior, Attitudes, and Correlates. Research Triangle Park, NC: Research Triangle institute.

Rodriguez, C. 1980. Economic Survival in New York. In The Puerto Rican Struggle. C. Rodriguez, V. Sanchez Korrol, and J. Alers, eds. Pp. 31–46. Maplewood, NJ: Waterfront Press.

———. 1989. Puerto Ricans: Born in the U.S.A. Boston, MA: Unwin Hyman.

Rodriguez-Andrew, S., M. J. Gilbert, and R. Trotter. 1988. Mexican American Cultural Norms Related to Alcohol Use as Reflected in Drinking Settings and Language Use. In Alcohol Consumption among Mexicans and Mexican-Americans: A Binational Perspective. M. J. Gilbert, ed. Pp. 103–126. Los Angeles, CA: Spanish Speaking Mental Health Research Center, University of California.

Rosenwaike, I. 1987. Mortality Differentials among Persons Born in Cuba, Mexico, and Puerto Rico Residing in the United States, 1979–1981. American Journal of Public Health 77:603–606.

Rush, B. 1943. An Inquiry into the Effects of Ardent Spirits upon the Human Body and Mind. Quarterly Journal of Studies on Alcohol 4:321–341.

Safa, H. 1986. Female Employment in the Puerto Rican Working Class. In Women and Change in Latin America. J. Nash and H. Safa, eds. Pp. 84–105. South Hadley, MA: Bergin & Garvey.

Schaefer, J. M. 1982. Ethnic and Racial Variation in Alcohol Use and Abuse. In Special Population Issues. Pp. 239–311. Washington, D.C.: U.S. Department of Health and Human Services.

Scheder, J. 1988. A Sickly-Sweet Harvest: Farmworkers Diabetes and Social Equality. Medical Anthropology Quarterly 2:251–277.

Scheper-Hughes, N. 1990. Three Propositions for a Critically Applied Medical Anthropology. Social Science and Medicine 30(2):179–188.

Scheper-Hughes, N., and M. Lock. 1986. "Speaking Truth" to Illness: Metaphors, Reification, and a Pedagogy for Patients. Medical Anthropology Quarterly 17: 137–140.

Seeman, M., and C. Anderson. 1983. Alienation and Alcohol: The Role of Work, Mastery, and Community in Drinking Behavior. American Sociological Review 48:60–77.

Sennett, R., and J. Cobb. 1973. The Hidden Injuries of Class. New York: Vintage Books.

Singer, M. 1986a. Toward a Political-Economy of Alcoholism: The Missing Link in the Anthropology of Drinking. Social Science and Medicine 23:113–130.

———. 1986b. Developing a Critical Perspective in Medical Anthropology. Medical Anthropology Quarterly 17(5):128–129.

———. 1987a. Cure, Care and Control: An Ectopic Encounter with Biomedical Obstretics. In Encounters with Biomedicine: Case Studies in Medical Anthropology. H. Baer, ed. Pp. 249–265. New York: Gordon and Breach.

———. 1987b. Similarities and Differences in Alcohol Use and Abuse among Hispanic and Non-Hispanic Drinkers. In Alcohol Use and Abuse among Hispanic Adolescents. M. Singer, L. Davison, and F. Yalin, eds. Pp. 44–49. Hartford, CT: Hispanic Health Council.

———. 1989a. The Limitations of Medical Ecology: The Concept of Adaptation in the Context of Social Stratification and Social Transformation. Medical Anthropology 10(4):223–234.

———. 1989b. The Coming of Age of Critical Medical Anthropology. Social Science and Medicine 28(11):1193–1204.

———. 1989c. Keep the Label and the Perspective: A Response to "Emic" Critiques of Critical Medical Anthropology. Anthropology Newsletter 30(3):15,19.

———. 1990a. Postmodernism and Medical Anthropology: Words of Caution. Medical Anthropology 12:289–304.

———. 1990b. Reinventing Medical Anthropology: Toward a Critical Re-Alignment. Social Science and Medicine 30(2):179–188.

Singer, M., H. Baer, and E. Lazarus. 1989. Critical Medical Anthropology in Question. Social Science and Medicine 30(2):5–8.

Singer, M., and M. Borrero. 1984. Indigenous Treatment for Alcoholism: The Case of Puerto Rican Spiritualism. Medical Anthropology 8:246–273.

Singer, M., L. Davison, and F. Yalin, eds. 1987. Alcohol Use and Abuse among Hispanic Adolescents. Hartford, CT: Hispanic Health Council.

Singer, M., C. Flores, L. Davison, G. Burke, and Z. Castillo. 1991. Puerto Rican Community Mobilizing in Response to the AIDS Crisis. Human Organization 50(1):73–81.

Singer, M., R. Irizarry, and J. Schensul. 1990. Needle Access as an AIDS Prevention Strategy for IV Drug Users: A Research Perspective. Human Organization 50(2):142–153.

Smart, R. 1979. Drinking Problems among Employed, Unemployed and Shiftworkers. Journal of Occupational Medicine 21:731–735.

Stebbins, K. 1987. Tobacco or Health in the Third World? A Political-Economic Analysis with Special Reference to Mexico. International Journal of Health Services 17: 523–538.

———. 1990. Transnational Tobacco Companies and Health in Underdeveloped Countries: Recommendations for Avoiding a Smoking Epidemic. Social Science and Medicine 30(2):227–236.

Trice, H., and P. Roman. 1972. Spirits and Demons at Work: Alcohol and Other Drugs on the Job. Ithaca, NY: New York State School of Industrial and Labor Relations, Cornell University.

Trostle, J. 1990. Comments on Defining the Shape of Biocultural Studies. Medical Anthropology Quarterly 4:371–373.

Trotter, R. 1982. Ethnic and Sexual Patterns of Alcohol Use: Anglo and Mexican American College Students. Adolescence 17:305–325.

———. 1985. Mexican-American Experience with Alcohol: South Texas Examples. In The American Experience with Alcohol. L. Bennett and G. Ames, eds. Pp. 279–296. New York: Plenum.

Trotter, R., and J. Chavira. 1978. Discovering New Models for Alcohol Counseling in Minority Groups. In Modern Medicine and Medical Anthropology in the United States-Mexico Border Population. B. Velimirov, ed. Pp. 164–171. Washington, DC: Pan American Health Organization.

Wagenheim, K. 1973. The Puerto Ricans. New York: Anchor Books.

———. 1975. Puerto Rico: A Profile. New York: Praeger.

Wallerstein, E. 1979. The Capitalist World-Economy. Cambridge: Cambridge University Press.

Welte, J., and G. Barnes. 1987. Alcohol Use among Adolescent Minority Groups. Journal of Studies on Alcohol 48(4):329–346.

Wilson, R. 1984. Changing Validity of the Cirrhosis Mortalty–Alcoholic Beverage Sales Construct: U.S. Trends, 1970–1977. Journal of Studies on Alcohol 45:53–58.

Wolf, E. 1982. Europe and the People without History. Berkeley, CA: University of California Press.

Zinn, H. 1980. A People's History of the United States. New York: Harper & Row.

 36

Understanding "Masculinity" and the Challenges of Managing Type-2 Diabetes among African-American Men

Leandris Liburd
Apophia Namageyo-Funa
Leonard Jack

The historical legacy of slavery has had an enormous negative effect on the health of African Americans. Discrimination and racism still exist today, despite significant progress since the civil rights era. When leaders in the health field talk about health disparities, they are most often referring to the relatively poor health statistics of African Americans (Institute of Medicine 2003). Clearly these disparities are caused by social factors—economic deprivation and the experience of racism—rather than any biological differences (see Goodman in selection 5). African American men bear the largest share of these health inequalities; their lives are shortened primarily by cardiovascular and/or chronic diseases, and secondarily by higher rates of violence.

It is difficult for most white Americans to recognize the invisible privileges related to their skin color; in fact, it is difficult to imagine being a minority at all. Many of us run into the same limits when imagining the situation of the opposite gender. In much of medical anthropology, discussions of health and gender focus on women, and specifically on reproductive health. But males have gender, too. The cultural rules that shape the performance of "masculinity" often have negative health effects. Three factors seem particularly important: (1) males seek medical care less frequently and at a later point in the course of illness; (2) males generally pay less attention to their diet; and (3) males more often engage in risky behaviors including smoking, alcohol abuse, violence, and unsafe driving.

This selection describes a particular set of African American men who have been diagnosed with type-2 diabetes. Like all diabetics, they face the challenge of managing their disease through blood monitoring, diet, and insulin injections or pills. Diabetes is a major health problem in the United States and a growing problem in much of the world. This chronic disease is the leading source of amputations and blindness. All diabetics are fearful of these negative health outcomes, but African American men consistently fare worse in their management of the disease. This is not because of their ethnicity or their health beliefs; rather, it is a result of their poverty and relatively low levels of social support. This selection uses anthropologically based qualitative methods to describe the particular challenges older African American men face in dealing with diabetes.

As you read this selection, consider these questions:

- **What challenges do these diabetic men face? Are these problems related to their ethnicity, gender, or economic circumstances?**
- **Why is there a relationship between diabetes and depression?**
- **What do the authors mean by a difference between "black masculinity" and "hegemonic masculinity"?**
- **In your opinion, why are men in general, and African American men in particular, reluctant to go to the doctor?**

Context: Leandris Liburd is chief of the Division of Adult and Community Health and the Division of Diabetes Translation, in the National Center for Chronic Disease Prevention and Health Promotion at the Centers for Disease Control and Prevention (CDC). Apophia Namageyo-Funa works in the same division. Leonard Jack is an associate dean of Health Sciences at Jackson State University. During the 1990s, the CDC expanded its mission from a focus on infectious disease to one that includes chronic diseases and the prevention of all health problems. Approximately forty medical anthropologists work at the CDC. Liburd earned a PhD in anthropology from Emory University and an MPH from the University of Michigan. Her specialty is gender and African American health.

This research is related to a larger project for health promotion in minority communities called Racial and Ethnic Approaches to Community Health (REACH). The goal of that association is to benefit people of African descent through education, advocacy, and health policy in order to eliminate health disparities. This selection was originally published in the Journal of the National Medical Association.

Source: L. Leandris, A. Namageyo-Funa, and L. Jack (2007). "Understanding 'Masculinity' and the Challenges of Managing Type-2 Diabetes among African-American Men." *Journal of the National Medical Association* 99(5):550–558.

INTRODUCTION

From 1980–1998, the age-adjusted prevalence of diagnosed diabetes for men and women was similar.[1] However, in 1999, the prevalence for males began to increase faster than that for females. From 1980–2003, the age-adjusted prevalence of diagnosed diabetes increased 50% for men and 37% for women.[1] African-American men bear a greater burden of type-2 diabetes. In 2003, 7.0% of African-American men had diagnosed diabetes compared with 5.1% of white men, according to the Centers for Disease Control and Prevention (CDC):[2] Moreover, African-American men experience poorer levels of glycemic control and higher rates of diabetes-related complications, such as lower-extremity disease, visual impairment and end stage renal disease.[1, 3] The successful management of type-2 diabetes requires daily attention to a complex constellation of behaviors such as healthy eating, medication adherence, stress management, glucose monitoring and testing, management of hypoglycemia, physical activity and foot care.[4] Traditional diabetes self-management education appears to be effective in achieving the needed behavior changes in the short term but has not proved beneficial in sustaining these multiple and overlapping behaviors over time.[5]

While all people with type-2 diabetes are challenged by the long-term demands of managing their disease, little "male-centered" research has been done with men in general or African-American men in particular, i.e., we know little about the behavioral, psychosocial and cultural contexts in which men experience and manage type-2 diabetes. Such efforts could identify the unique social and cultural realities that either facilitate or impede men's ability to control type-2 diabetes.[6] We argue that a greater understanding of how "masculinity" mediates the illness experience of type-2 diabetes is an important area for inquiry if we are to improve health outcomes for African-American men. A large and growing body of literature is examining associations between masculine gender identity, male sex roles and health-related behaviors.[7–13] Such research has been conducted with men who have chronic diseases, such as prostate and testicular cancer, multiple sclerosis and coronary heart disease.[14,16] However, when research on masculinity and health is carried out with African-American men, the focus is more often HIV/AIDS, violence, homicide and substance abuse.[8,11]

A full examination of the broader sociocultural dimensions of disease management for people with diabetes is not feasible in the time frame typically allotted for patient encounters. Therefore, this research is important for physicians interested in not only providing the highest-quality clinical care but also understanding more holistically the toll that type-2 diabetes exacts on the minds, bodies and social relationships of their African-American male patients. In this paper, we examine the transcripts of in-depth interviews conducted with a small sample of African-American men with established type-2 diabetes for common threads associated with "masculinity" and posit how diabetes self-management is affected. We describe the sometimes paradoxical relationship between the requirements of diabetes self-management and the social and internalized expectations of black masculinity as revealed in the illness narratives of our study participants. According to Riessman,

> The illness narrative, a form of case study, emerged in response to biomedicine's focus on disease (not illness) and consequent neglect of patient experience. . . . [It] recognizes the importance of subjective reality in adaptation to chronic illness: how the disease is perceived, enacted and responded to by "self" and others. . . . [and] provides a way for sufferers to explain and contextualize their interrupted lives and changing relationships with the social worldly.[15]

We conclude with recommendations that encourage physicians to consider this knowledge in the care and counseling of their African-American male patients with type-2 diabetes and to connect these patients with community-based public health programs for ancillary behavioral interventions.

AFRICAN-AMERICAN MEN AND MASCULINITY

Gender identity is a key variable in decisions about health behaviors, including how to engage with the healthcare system. Competing ideologies and discourses of black masculinity defy the articulation of a monolithic masculine gender identity for African-American men. Indeed, there are complex theoretical debates within black masculinity studies, and a comprehensive review of these debates is beyond the scope of this paper. We also have no interest in perpetuating stereotypes of African-American men. However, in the interest of framing our thematic analyses and interpretations of the illness narratives, we synthesize some of the prevailing sociocultural perspectives of black masculinity.

"Masculinity" reflects a shared understanding of what it means to be a man: what one looks like, how one should behave and so forth.[18] The rules that guide gender behavior—and in this instance, masculinity—are culturally constructed and shift over time and place. Issues of class, age, ethnicity and sexual differentiation are also relevant in the construction of black masculinities.[19] "Black masculinity" and what some scholars describe as "hegemonic masculinity"[13] are mutually constituted. In other words, during specific historical periods, black and white men have valued similar ideologies about manhood, but institutionalized racism has kept many black men from achieving the same privileges and attributes of manhood as white men.[20] Economic, social and political independence, citizenship, honor, power and sexual prowess, for example, have all characterized manhood in the United States at different historical eras. Black men, however, have historically and to the present had to confront and overcome a legacy of lynching, disenfranchisement(s), segregation, economic alienation, and stereotypes of uncivilized and beastly sexuality in their quest for this manhood.[20] Unlike their white counterparts, African-American men have been denied the message from family, school and the larger society that "power and control are their birthright."[21] This is best evidenced by their economic marginality, high rates of incarceration, overrepresentation in hazardous occupations and prevalence of substance abused.[8,11,12] Over centuries of resistance to the denial of their manhood, black masculinity still emerges in diverse social constructions as equated with physical strength and endurance, pride and control.

A range of investigations of African-American manhood and masculinity have identified domains of manhood among African Americans to include self-determinism and accountability, family connectedness, pride, spirituality and humanism, and relationships with others.[22] In their qualitative examination of "manhood meaning" among a sample of 152 African-American men residing in five metropolitan areas in five states, Hammond and Mattis found 15 categories of meaning that coded manhood.[22] For example, almost 50% of the respondents indicated that manhood means being responsible and accountable for one's actions, thoughts and behaviors, and this responsibility-accountability extends beyond the self to include one's family and community. In addition, manhood was associated with being independent; self-governing; and able to manage one's life, including having the power and freedom to execute decisions. Being able to provide for oneself and family in ways that extend beyond economic provisions was also an important category of manhood. Lastly, of particular note, achieving personal growth and maturity across the life span was important in African-American manhood as well as having focus and stability across the multiple domains of one's life.[22]

According to Williams,

> Beliefs about masculinity and manhood that are deeply rooted in culture and supported by social institutions play a role in shaping the behavioral patterns of men in ways that have consequences for health. Men are socialized to project strength, individuality, autonomy, dominance, stoicism and physical aggression, and to avoid demonstrations of emotion or vulnerability that could be construed as weakness.[12]

In the healthcare arena, this can mean infrequent encounters with the healthcare system, delayed attention to symptoms, poor medication compliance and an unwillingness to talk openly about health concerns.[12] The masculine response has both positive and negative aspects that can be channeled to either support or undermine diabetes self-management. How is diabetes self-management negotiated within a framework of black masculinity? Additional research on the positive and negative masculine responses to the challenges of diabetes self-management among African-American men is desperately needed.

METHODS

The initial illness narratives study sought to explore cultural aspects of diabetes self-management among a small sample of African-American men living with type-2 diabetes.[23] This analysis is a thematic elaboration of data collected as part of the initial study. The questions asked in the initial study did not directly address masculinity and its relationship to diabetes self-management, but through the inductive process of ethnographic and

TABLE 1 Brief Profile of Participants

Simon Smith, 71, retired. Has had diabetes for 5 years. Pain associated with finger stick makes monitoring diabetes difficult.

Marcus Jones, 46, property manager. Has had diabetes for 25 years. Limited income affects his diabetes management.

Tom Hill, 55, single, owns a cleaning company. Has had diabetes for 2.5 years.

Randy Taylor, 53, religious leader, single, lives alone. Has had diabetes for 15–20 years and has complications.

William Brown, 57, unemployed, lives with wife. Has had diabetes for 20 years.

Michael West, 39, self-employed, married, cares for his son, does not have health insurance. Has had diabetes for 8 years.

John Ingram, 47, married, quality control check engineer. Has had diabetes for 2 years.

Jason Doe, 47, married, is a document specialist and reads about diabetes self-management. Has had diabetes for 8 years.

Lloyd Dixon, 43, is on disability. Has had diabetes 4–5 years and has not been managing his diabetes.

Percy Holmes, 45, caterer. Has had diabetes for 15–16 years and has heart disease. Is only recently attentive to his diabetes.

Vincent Washington, 52, is on disability. Has had diabetes for 15 years.

Allen Christian, 53, building inspector, lives with diabetic wife, is well read on diabetes and medications. Has had diabetes for 9 years.

Joe Williams, 67, married, construction worker. Has had diabetes for 12–15 years.

Donald Owens, 52, single. Has had diabetes for 2 years. Does not exercise because he does not want to lose weight.

Neil Gun, 70, retired, married. Has had diabetes for 4–5 years.

George Crowe, 69, retired, married and believes diabetes is an eating disorder. Has had diabetes for 12 years.

phenomenological research, themes associated with "masculinity" emerged.[24] Sixteen African-American men with established diabetes living in Raleigh, NC, participated in in-depth, semistructured interviews within an illness-narrative framework. The men were selected from the participant roster of Project DIRECT (Diabetes Intervention: Reaching and Educating Communities Together), a community diabetes demonstration project sponsored by CDC and previously described in this journal.[25-26] Additional details of the sampling and data collection methods and analysis are outlined elsewhere.[23] This article reports results on four questions from the interview guide[23] interpreted from the theoretical stance of masculinity: (1) What do you fear most about having diabetes? (2) In what ways have people treated you differently after learning you have diabetes? (3) In what ways has knowing that you have diabetes affected the way you see yourself? Finally, (4) What are some reactions when you tell people you have diabetes? Findings from this qualitative, ethnographic study cannot be generalized to the larger community of African-American men with type-2 diabetes because of the geographic location of the study, the sample size and the breadth of meanings associated with the lived experience of "black masculinity."

RESULTS

This analysis is an elaboration of the major theme of masculinity that emerged in the larger illness narratives study that is reported elsewhere.[23] A brief profile of the study participants is provided in Table 1. Topics and major themes that emerged from the four questions we identified from the in-depth interviews are outlined in Table 2. Consistent with usual procedures in reporting ethnographic research, we incorporated direct quotes from the transcribed interviews of respondents into the cultural analysis and interpretation of findings.[27] Actual names are replaced with pseudonyms.

What Do You Fear Most about Having Diabetes?

African-American men with diabetes living in southeast Raleigh have poorer glycemic control, more frequent complications, greater functional impairment and higher rates of complications than their white counterparts.[28] Braithwaite argues that "Men tend to be hesitant to acknowledge fear in any capacity."[11] The majority of men in this study, however, appeared very open in the interview about their fears related to complications of uncontrolled diabetes. Mr. Ingram, 47 years old and diagnosed with diabetes for two years, explains it this way:

> Black men have always had a problem in admitting things are not going right in their life. That's the way it was a long time ago, and that's going to be the way it's going to be in the near future until we start coming together as men [and] being able to confide in someone. It's hard to find someone to confide in because no sooner than we say keep it to yourself, we can't even get a block down the street before somebody's telling.

Among other men in the study, these fears were deeply embedded in their subconscious. For example,

TABLE 2 Topics and Major Themes across Groups

1. What do you fear most?
   - Loss of independence
   - Shortened life span
   - Compromised quality of life
2. In what ways have people in your life treated you differently after learning you have diabetes?
   - They have been accepting
   - They have provided social support
   - They have rejected me
3. In what ways has knowing that you have diabetes affected the way you see yourself?
   - Have recognized [new] physical limitation(s)
   - Am more anxious about [effects of] the disease
   - Haven't experienced any [negative] perceptions in self-image
   - Haven't experienced any limitations or changes in lifestyle
4. What are some reactions when you tell people that you have diabetes?
   - Empathy
   - Surprise
   - Curiosity

Mr. Washington shared, "Well, I keep dreaming I am going to lose some limbs." Only one respondent, Mr. Hill, said "I don't fear nothing. I worry more. If I have a worry, it's more about hypertension than diabetes."

The range of fears expressed by the men included: "death behind diabetes," "possibly losing a limb or eyesight," "taking the shots," "not being able to control my eating to the point where my sugar is just going sky high," and "what may be happening inside that I can't see." Taken together, their greatest fear was a loss of independence. Mr. Taylor described it this way:

> The greatest fear that I have is that I don't want to become an invalid. I don't want to have an amputation of my limbs and I don't want to get to the point that I can't take care of myself, and someone else will have to take care of me.

Mr. Ingram added to his response to this question that he did not have any fears about having diabetes "because if you fear, it tends to change the way you live and that fear tends to turn into stress, and the stress can actually become more problemsome than the disease itself."

In What Ways Have People in Your Life Treated You Differently After Learning You Have Diabetes?

Overwhelmingly, the men in this study have not been treated differently or ostracized by family members, friends or others in their social networks. They typically receive outpourings of social support, given the pervasiveness of diabetes in this African-American community. Mr. Jones, who has been diagnosed with diabetes for 25 years, remarked:

> Once they know [I have diabetes}, they're probably more helpful. They're supportive. They'll say, "I know it's 12:00 [noon]. Do you need to stop and get something to eat?" So, I'm thankful for that sort of stuff."

Within this supportive environment, however, the men still work to retain control over their bodies and diabetes self-management. When they feel that well-intended advice becomes badgering, they quickly remind people, "I know what I'm doing."

In describing how his relationships with his male friends have been affected by diabetes, Mr. Brown, who has had diabetes for 20 years, commented,

> So the people I hang out with seem straight [okay] with it [the diabetes]. But they're still bike riding and stuff and invite me to go . . . and they don't encourage me to drink no liquor or alcohol, so I get along with my friends really good.

Mr. Brown used to ride a motorcycle and consume alcohol with his friends. In the interest of his health, he declines to participate in these activities, but he is not made to feel "less of a man" in their eyes. Similarly, Mr. Brown added that his wife helps him with controlling the disease by "cooking according to my diabetes."

> She tries to help me on both diabetes and weight. She does the cooking and cooks right. Sometimes the food

> has no taste, and she stopped cooking the saucy stuff. But I don't always do my part like eating the right portion or eating late at night and then laying down on it, so I was gaining weight.

In one instance, however, a participant in the study shared that his short marriage ended in divorce after his wife learned of his erectile dysfunction. Even those men who were in stable and long-term intimate relationships expressed frustration and dismay over the negative impact diabetes had on their sexual functioning. For example, one participant commented:

> I'd like for sex to be like it was before I had it [diabetes]. We've been married for 39 years, and I had sugar mainly during that time. Now, when I attempt to have sex I don't get it right all the time. It's stressful to me sometimes, but my wife is understanding. I ain't going to say it's been a problem between us two, but it's been a problem to me.

For both of these men, the inability to adequately satisfy themselves and their partners sexually affected their comfort levels with this most intimate aspect of their relationships.

In What Ways Has Knowing That You Have Diabetes Affected the Way You See Yourself?

The way one sees oneself is a part of the personal and interpersonal significance of having diabetes. In other words, how the African-American man with type-2 diabetes perceives himself is mediated by how others see him. Mr. Smith, a 71-year-old diabetic man with advanced neuropathy in his right leg, commented that when people learn he has diabetes, "They are horrified! They think you're really sick." Yet, his response to our question was that having diabetes had not affected the way he sees himself. He was "just trying to figure out how best to handle it."

Mr. Holmes, diagnosed with diabetes for 15 years, replied that he sees himself "not really [in] any way—because I'd say nobody knows I've got major complications except myself, because I mean, the way I carry myself, people don't even know I have diabetes." It is important to Mr. Holmes to maintain his public appearance of strength, pride and mastery over his circumstances. The consequence of the primacy of his public persona is that he neglected to adhere to a treatment regimen to control his diabetes for 15 years. After suffering two heart attacks and neuropathy in one of his legs, he decided to "be a better manager" of his body.

Depression is a common problem among African-American men with type-2 diabetes.[31] Depression negatively affects diabetes self-management, glycemic control and quality of life.[32,33] Moreover, depression is too often underdiagnosed and undertreated in black men generally and black men with diabetes in particular.[31] Diabetes and depression are doubly alienating and threatening for black men. Mr. Owens acknowledged,

> Sometimes, knowing that I am diabetic and that I am limited, sometimes if I'm not careful, it can cause depression. It can cause a feeling that I'm different from everyone else, to the point that I can't do some of the normal things I used to; so at times it do create depression.

The men who expressed feelings of anxiety about having diabetes said they were depressed and worried because they could not see what was happening to their bodies. They felt a loss of control over what was happening to them. As one man noted, "I don't know. Sometimes if I'm not feeling well, I think, I don't know how much damage diabetes is doing to my heart and blood vessels that I can't see." In particular, the men felt that in living with diabetes they no longer have control over activities that require physical effort, which in turn leads them to view themselves in a negative light. Not all men felt that living with diabetes limited them physically, and some indicated that they were capable of carrying out their routine activities. Paradoxically, some of the men who stated there was no difference in their self-image admitted to having a physical limitation as a result of diabetes, yet they presented an upbeat attitude about it and did not look at the physical limitation as limiting what they were capable of achieving.

What Are Some Reactions When You Tell People You Have Diabetes?

In this study, it was clear that the men received some unexpected reactions. The way people react to the announcement of diabetes reveals whether or not diabetes is considered a culturally marked disorder in the community—specifically, how common or normative is diabetes in this community? This question also exposes the misinformation in local knowledge about diabetes onset, behavioral risk factors and disease management. Mr. Dixon stated, "I'm finding out now more and more and more people have it. And that I had nothing all these years to be ashamed [of]. A lot of people got diabetes." A majority of the responses were empathetic or surprised, and a few reflected curiosity about the disease and its clinical manifestation. The men who received empathetic reactions said the people they were telling had family members with the disease, and they understood what the men were going through. They offered encouragement by admonishing the men to take care of themselves and complimented them by saying the men "did not look sick." As Mr. Christian stated, "They be like, 'Oh man, really?' They say, 'But you don't look like it. You look different. Well are you taking care of yourself?'" The men who received surprised reactions said the people they were telling could not believe that a person who physically looked like themselves had diabetes. The men who received curious reactions said the people they were telling knew of someone with diabetes, and they wanted to obtain information that might help that friend better manage the disease. As one man stated, "They listen. People are now trying to become more educated about diabetes."

DISCUSSION

A diagnosis of diabetes can have a profound effect on a man's self-image. At the point of diagnosis, the patient is jarred by the awareness of having moved from a perceived physical state of "health" to one of "sickness." The expression of manhood as autonomy and nondependence is threatened by the potential loss of body parts, the ability to work and the ability to get around without assistance. The domino effect of these diabetes-related complications can result in the loss of considerable family freedom and flexibility. The entire family system is affected because sex roles shift; income is often reduced, living standards are subject to change; and specialized care for the diabetic man places added demands on the emotional, physical and financial resources of family members. If family resources are already stretched to the limit, a lower-extremity amputation, kidney dialysis or blindness can be devastating for the household. Manhood as "waymaking" for self and others is reconstructed in the face of diabetes-related complications. These concerns ground much of the fear associated with having type-2 diabetes.

Prevailing meanings of "masculinity" among African-American men can pose challenges to good diabetes management on several levels. For example, in wanting to maintain control over their own care to the extent possible, the men in this study set up boundaries around the social support they were willing to accept from their wives, family members and friends. Such coping skills where black men assert their agency to confront and manage the stresses associated with having type-2 diabetes were believed to position them for better health outcomes and quality of life. They were generally receptive to gestures that helped them control their diabetes, but they were opposed to being "policed" by even well-intentioned loved ones and friends. It seemed essential to them that they maintain at all times control over their bodies regardless of the clinical implications. Overall, the men in this community were not treated differently in any negative way because of diabetes, which is important to manhood as giving and receiving respect as well as being involved in one's community.[22]

According to Braithwaite,

> Men have traditionally been socialized that they should not cry, that they should be cavalier about certain things that affect them, that it is weak to show pain, and that it is cowardly to run from danger.[11]

We observed this in the men's responses to how diabetes has affected the way they see themselves. In this study, for example, the younger the men were at the time of diagnosis, the more dismissive they appeared in attending to the disease. These men continued to engage in behaviors that undermined good diabetes management even though they were putting their long-term wellness at stake—for example, drinking alcohol and eating foods they found pleasurable. If they were not feeling bad or hindered from accomplishing their daily obligations, the men continued to pursue their personal interests and desires, or as one man put it, "I went on with my life." Healthy eating, one of the cornerstones of good diabetes self-management, is particularly challenging for African-American men given that food, meal planning and preparation and other concerns of nurturance have traditionally rested in the purview of women. In addition, there are fewer options for healthy food choices for the men in this and other urban communities given the saturation of fast-food restaurants and convenience stores.

Erectile dysfunction among diabetic men is common and was an expressed concern of several men in this study as well.[29] Regardless of the causes of sexual dysfunction, the inability to achieve or maintain an erection sufficiently rigid for sexual intercourse, ejaculation or both can greatly affect not only male patients but also their partners, as was the case for several participants in this study. Sexual dysfunction is an organic sequela of diabetes that should be treated but is unfortunately underdiagnosed.[29] Underdiagnosis and undertreatment often occurs because either patients or healthcare providers find it difficult to talk about sexual health.[30]

Another example of tension among the performance of masculinity, how men see themselves and diabetes self-management among men in this study is in the area of physical activity. From childhood, they usually associated physical activity with participation in competitive team sports and male bonding. Learning to engage in physical activity for reasons other than the love of a game and the bragging rights for winning has been a challenge. Team sports can mean pounding, pushing and physical contact that is no longer appropriate for the man with type-2 diabetes. As the men aged and participated less in team sports, it became difficult for them to become interested in solitary and noncompetitive options such as walking. One of the men in the study also linked any type of "exercise" with weight loss, and he did not want to lose any weight. Therefore, he refused to participate in any type of physical activity. What are safe, accessible, team or group sport activities that would appeal to urban, working-class African-American men? This is an important question for physicians to investigate with their male patients who have type-2 diabetes.

Lastly, most of the men in this study were either unemployed, underemployed or on a fixed income. They did not always have the financial means to purchase medications and other diabetic supplies. Poorly tolerated side effects from certain prescription drugs were also common. In some instances, the men reported these concerns to their doctor, but more often than not, they "took matters into their own hands" and adjusted medication dosages or replaced prescription drugs with herbal medicines or other over-the-counter drugs. Physicians are encouraged to talk with their male patients about changes they may have made to the prescribed regimen, and to negotiate with them more appropriate or affordable drug regimens when possible. Clearly, an appropriate response will require optimal clinical care that recognizes the role of masculinity and how masculinity shapes male diabetes self-management behaviors and healthcare seeking behaviors. Public health programs are also needed to complement clinical care with community-based interventions that are designed to embrace cultural norms and support social norms that bond masculinity and health.

As for reactions from others when the people reveal they have diabetes, the disproportionate burden of diabetes experienced by the larger African-American community generally structures an environment of social support and empathy. A diagnosis of diabetes does not have to be "a death sentence," as one man commented. One can delay, and in many instances prevent, the development of diabetes-related complications and enjoy a full life. Men can take control of diabetes rather than diabetes taking control of them. If we continue to educate the community about the causes of diabetes and strategies for prevention, we can eliminate the misinformation and what one participant called "shame" associated in some circles with having this disease.

Fortunately, efforts to improve health among black men in the United States are emerging, such as the partnership between Morehouse School of Medicine and The 100 Black Men Inc. Together, these partners designed and implemented The 100 Black Men's Health Challenge, a healthy lifestyle program that seeks to promote the adoption of a personalized nutrition and physical activity plan and to encourage black men to establish and maintain a relationship with their primary care provider. Results from The 100 Black Men's Health Challenge will provide insight into how the leadership of national minority organizations can help institutionalize health-promoting social norms around diet, physical activity and healthcare-seeking behaviors.

Diabetes is an invisible but formidable foe. Men are rarely taught how to fight an enemy that they cannot see or touch, and thus must engage in a *performance* of masculinity that diabetes can erode. The participants in this study appeared at times to approach diabetes self-management like "shadow boxing"—jabbing and shuffling but never really knowing if they were defeating this opponent. Later, when they developed complications of uncontrolled diabetes, the outcome of a match that lasted for 15–20 years became clearer. In African-American communities where the prevalence of diabetes is high, many people come to believe that its negative outcomes—such as loss of limbs and independence, renal failure and blindness—are imminent and inevitable. The men in this study observed the devastation of diabetes in the lives of family members, friends and in their extended social networks, and feared like outcomes for themselves. Physicians can replace these fears with power by equipping men with the skills and knowledge needed to prevent these complications.

The study of gender can be considered the study of relationships—those between men and women, men and men, and women and women, and their relationships with the entire society. The formation of gender identities begins at birth and is learned through many channels, including families and social networks, community and government institutions, and the media, to name a few. Future efforts to prevent and control diabetes among African-American men will likely require the full participation of healthcare providers, medical institutions, national men's organizations, national diabetes organizations, diverse media and entertainment outlets, the African-American community and society at large. These combined commitments are necessary to nurture and reinforce a social context for manhood as health promoting particularly among African-American men with and at risk for type-2 diabetes.

REFERENCES

1. Centers for Disease Control and Prevention [CDC). National diabetes fact sheet: general information and national estimates on diabetes in the United States, 2005. Atlanta, GA: U.S. Dept. of Health and Human Services; 2005. www.cdc.gov/diabetes/pubs/factsheet05.htm.
2. Centers for Disease Control and Prevention. National diabetes fact sheet: general information and national estimates on diabetes in the United States, 2005. Atlanta, GA: U.S. Dept. of Health and Human Services; 2005. www.cdc.gov/diabetes/statistics/prev/national/tableraceethsex.htm.
3. Harris Ml, Eastman RC, Cowie CC, et al. Racial and ethnic differences in glycemic control of adults with type-2 diabetes. *Diabetes Care*. 1999; 22(3):403–408.
4. American Diabetes Association. Standards of medical care in diabetes. *Diabetes Care*. 2004;27(suppl 1):S15–S35.,
5. Jack Jr L. Diabetes self-management education research: An international review of intervention methods, theories, community partnership and outcomes. *Disease Management and Health Outcomes*. 2003; 11 (7):415–428.
6. Jack L. Diabetes and men's health issues. *Diabetes Spectrum*. 2004;17(4):206–208.
7. Sabo D, Gordon DF. Men's Health and Illness: Gender, Power, and the Body. Thousand Oaks, CA: Sage Publications; 1995.
8. Staples R. Health among Afro-American males. In: Sabo D and Gordon DF, Eds. Men's Health and Illness: Gender, Power, and the Body. Thousand Oaks, CA; Sage Publications; 1995:121–138.
9. Jack L. Toward men's health research agenda in health education: examining gender, sex roles, and health-seeking behaviors in context. *Am J Health Edu*. 2005; 36(5):309–312.
10. Forrester DA. Myths of masculinity: impact upon men's health. *Nurs Clin North Am*. 1936;21(l):15–23
11. Braithwaite RL. The health status of black men. In: Braithwaite RL Taylor SE, eds. Health Issues in the Black Community, 2nd ed. San Francisco, CA: Jossey-Bass Publishers; 2001:62–80.
12. Williams DR. The health of men; structured inequalities and opportunities. *Am J Public Health*. 2003;93(5):724–731.
13. Courtenay WH, Constructions of masculinity and their influence on men's well-being: a theory of gender and health. *Soc Sci Med*. 2000;50:1385–1401.
14. Gordon DF. Testicular cancer and masculinity. In Sabo D and Gordon DF, eds. Men's Health and Illness: Gender; Power, and the Body. Thousand Oaks, CA: Sage Publications; 1995:246–265.
15. Riessman CK. Performing identities in illness narrative: masculinity and multiple sclerosis. *Qualitative Res*. 2003; 3 (1):5–33.
16. Helgeson VS. The effects of masculinity and social support on recovery from myocardial infarction. *Psychosom Med*. 1991;53(6):621–633.
17. Summers MA. Manliness and Its Discontents: the Black Middle Class and the Transformation of Masculinity. 1900–1930. Chapel Hill, NC: University of North Carolina Press; 2004.
18. Edley N, Wetherell M. Masculinity, power and identity. In Mac an Ghaill M, ed. Understanding Masculinities. Buckingham: Open University Press; 1996:97–113.
19. Marriott D. Reading black masculinities in Mac an Ghaill M, ed. Under'standing Masculinities, Buckingham: Open University Press; 1996:185–201.
20. Estes S. I am a Man!: Race, manhood, and the civil rights movement. Chapel Hill, NC: The University of North Carolina Press; 2005.
21. Rybarczyk B. Diversity among American men: the impact of aging, ethnicity, and race. In: Kilmartin CT, ed. The Masculine Self. New York, NY: Macmillan Publishing; 1994:113–131.
22. Hammond WP, Mattis JS. Being a Man About It. Manhood Meaning Among African American Men. *Psychology of Men & Masculinity*. 2005:6(2):114–126.
23. Liburd LC, Namageyod-Funa A, Jack L, et al. Views from within and beyond. Illness narratives of African American men with type 2 diabetes. *Diabetes Spectrum* 2004;17[4]:219–224.
24. Morse JM, Field PA. Qualitative Research Methods for Health Professionals, 2nd ed. Thousand Oaks, CA. Sage Publications; 1995.
25. Herman WH, Thompson IJ, Visscher W, et al. Diabetes meliitus and its complications in an African-American community: Project DIRECT. *J Natl Med Assoc*. l998;90:147–156.
26. Engelgau MM, Narayan KM, Geiss LS, et al. A project to reduce the burden of diabetes in the African-American community: Project DIRECT. *J Natl Med Assoc*. 1998; 90(10); 605–6I3.
27. Hammersley M, Atkinson P. Ethnography: Principles in Practice, 2nd ed. London: Routledge: 1995.
28. Gregg EW, Geiss LS, Saaddine J, et al. Use of diabetes preventive care and complications risk in two African-American communities. *Am J Prey Med*. 2001;21[3]:197–202.
29. Penson DF, Wessells H. Erectile dysfunction in diabetic patients. *Diabetes Spectrum*. 2004;17(4):225–230.
30. Jack Jr L. A candid conversation about men, sexual health, and diabetes. *Diabetes Educ*. 2005; 3(6):810–817.
31. Fisher L, Laurencin G, Chesla CA, et al. Depressive affect among four ethnic groups of male patients with type 2 diabetes. *Diabetes Spectrum*. 2004;17(4):215–224.
32. Anderson RJ, Freedland KE, Clause RE, et al. The prevalence of comorbid depression in adults with diabetes. *Diabetes Care*. 2001;24(6):1069–1078.
33. Lustman PJ, Anderson RJ, Freedland KE, et al. Depression and poor glycemic control. *Diabetes Care*. 2000:23:934–942.

Stigma and Coping with Chronic Illness

CONCEPTUAL TOOLS

■ ***Stigma is the negative social attribution placed on people because of their disability or illness.*** Based on the famous work of Erving Goffman (1963), stigma is defined as a sociological phenomenon in which an individual is devalued and shunned because some illness or disability makes her or him different or "not normal." The stigmatized condition becomes the "master status" that overpowers all other social attributes. This is especially the case when a chronic condition is obvious and public. Stigma creates long-lasting suffering.

■ ***When stigmatized conditions are "invisible," they involve the dilemma of disclosure.*** Some illnesses, like genital herpes or deafness, as seen in the selections in this section, require a person with the affliction to decide when or if to disclose his or her status to another person. Disclosure risks not only social rejection for an individual but also the possibility that the negative information will become widely known.

■ ***Chronic illnesses have different and more complex social dimensions than acute illnesses.*** The rights and responsibilities of the "sick role" usually refer to time-limited illness experiences, when an individual is sick and then is cured. Chronic illnesses or disabilities do not follow the conventions of the sick role. Instead, chronic illnesses become part of people's core social identities. The illness experience is a continuing one, to which an individual must adjust. These adjustments can be difficult, especially because of sociocultural expectations about being "normal."

■ ***The anthropological study of aging has much in common with medical anthropology.*** Aging is a normal part of the human life cycle. In American society, however, the process of aging has been medicalized. A significant number of anthropological studies of communities of the elderly, including the particular contexts of nursing homes (Savishinsky 1991; Sokolovsky 1983), have shown how the lives of the elderly are shaped by their interactions with the medical system. In addition, the elderly often live in circumstances of age segregation, separated from their families, almost as if old age itself was a stigmatized condition.

■ ***Stigma is often the result of fear.*** Stigma is a type of xenophobia that possibly, in the historical past, functioned to encourage people to avoid contagion. Widespread fear in social groups, however, can result not simply in scapegoating and discrimination against individuals but also in violence and forced displacement of large groups of people. Social tensions between groups can lead to a lack of trust and cooperation in times of emergency. Fear of new diseases or fear of government entities can hamper the reporting of disease outbreaks. Combatting new emerging diseases, which can spread rapidly throughout the world because of airline travel, requires mutual trust and international cooperation.

 38

Coping with Stigma: Lifelong Adaptation of Deaf People

Gaylene Becker

Usually, when people think of an illness that carries stigma, they think of the classic case of leprosy, as we saw in selection 18. What comes to mind are images of dirty bandages, lost fingers or toes, open sores, or the social ostracism of being unclean. Stigma means that people fear the individual who is sick. The suffering from stigma can be worse than the physical pain. In fact, the irony that Hansen's disease (leprosy) is not very contagious must add to the suffering of stigma. Disfigurement from an illness—as in the case of neurofibromatosis, the condition of the so-called Elephant Man—is worse because people assume that the individual inside is also disfigured. Stigma is the grotesque side of the beauty myth (Wolf 1992).

Medical anthropologists have studied the illness experience of people with chronic health problems, including congenital conditions like the extremely short stature of little people or dwarfs (Ablon 1988). People with such conditions have to learn to adapt to their life situation physically, socially, and psychologically.

This selection concerns stigma and lifelong adaptations of deaf people, a group with no obvious physical disability. However, their disability affects their social interactions. In this selection, Gaylene Becker refers to deafness as an "invisible disability." Deaf people have to interact with the hearing world, but that interaction is sometimes difficult or emotionally painful. Often, hearing people condescend to deaf people, which is one theme of the award-winning film Children of a Lesser God. *Although deafness is not a disease, the deaf form a community with special needs. Several years ago, college students at Gallaudet University (a university for the deaf) engaged in a nationally recognized protest when a hearing president was appointed by the university's board of trustees. The Americans with Disabilities Act has guaranteed hearing-impaired people access to public facilities and events, but the issues of stigma still remain.*

As you read this selection, consider these questions:

- **Why might an "invisible disability" involve a different set of problems?**
- **Is the creation of social stigma simply part of human nature? Or does our culture define what is normal?**
- **To what extent does the term adapt used in this selection have the same meaning as the concept of adaptation used in the first part of this book?**
- **What are the advantages and disadvantages of hearing-impaired people attending separate schools or being mainstreamed? Is participation in a separate community a normal human need or an adaptation to ostracism?**

Context: Gaylene Becker (1943–2007) was a much-admired medical anthropologist at the University of California, San Francisco (UCSF), who brought a strong sense of social justice to her research. During her career, she explored issues ranging from infertility to aging, as well as the intersections between them (see selection 23). This selection represents her earlier investigations into the relationships between social stigma, chronic illness, and physical disabilities, under the guidance of George Foster and Joan Ablon at the UCSF–Berkeley joint medical anthropology program. Becker was one of the first people to receive a doctoral degree with a specific focus on medical anthropology. This classic article highlights some unique themes surrounding deafness: both the stigma of an invisible disability and the ways in which deaf people segregate themselves to avoid negative interactions with the hearing world.

Source: G. Becker (1981). "Coping with Deafness: Lifelong Adaptation of Deaf People." *Social Science & Medicine* 15:21–24.

INTRODUCTION

Mrs. Simpson[1] was sitting in her small, cluttered apartment in senior citizen housing, relating the story of her life. Suddenly, she became agitated, jumped up, and enacted a drama from her childhood.

> I was playing in the school yard with some other girls and a boy came along. He pointed at me. "Deafy," he screamed. "Deaf and dumb," and he threw something like acid in my face. It was a terrible day in my life. Why should he hate me just because I am deaf?

Stigma is a universal phenomenon. In every society certain conditions are stigmatized, whether they are based on physical "blemishes," or on behaviour that deviates from the norm.[2] Societies develop negative attitudes in response to the stigmatizing condition. Individuals with such a blemish or behaviour quickly become aware of the way others view them. The stigmatized individual must struggle with these negative attitudes and with the devalued status that accompanies them and develop strategies for handling the stigma. The individual who fails to do this cannot function adequately. In American society, failure to learn coping skills often results in institutionalization, or at best, existence on the fringes of society. When sufficient numbers of stigmatized people form a subsociety, they build coping strategies for dealing with stigma into their subculture.

This paper describes the ways in which older deaf people perceive and deal with stigma. The author studied 200 people in the San Francisco Bay Area who were born deaf or became deaf in the first few years of life. They were all over the age of 60 at the time of the study and communicated in American Sign Language. Fieldwork was conducted in sign language, utilizing traditional anthropological field techniques of participant observation and in-depth interviewing. The 200 people formed a natural group, and from this group 60 were selected for in-depth interviewing. Participant-observation activities took place wherever aged deaf people congregated—in senior citizen centers, at deaf clubs, at funerals, and in people's homes. The author did participant-observation almost daily during the one-year period of the research.

Deafness is called an invisible disability because it is only noticeable when a person attempts to communicate.[3] No visible indicators, such as the white cane of the blind person, give other people cues about what to expect in communication with a deaf person. Once the disability is known, the impact of it may be heightened.[4] Hearing people often "freeze" and withdraw from the situation or behave inappropriately. This type of behaviour is so common that Schlesinger and Meadow[5] have labeled it "shock withdrawal paralysis." Such a response to the deaf individual is in part due to the stigma attached to sign language, and is a continuous reminder to deaf people that they vary from the norm.

THE ROOTS OF STIGMA

The experience of stigma is inextricably intertwined with the condition of deafness for most deaf people and arises in the first few years of life. The great majority of aged deaf people had hearing parents with whom they were never able to satisfactorily communicate. These individuals did not begin to acquire language until they went to school at the age of five or six. The inability of parents to teach their children language and to socialize them created an emotional crisis that was exacerbated by the controversy over educational methods for deaf children. Parents faced a dilemma. They had to make a choice: whether to have their children learn the "oral" method that taught speech and lipreading, or whether to send children away to a school where they would learn sign language. One hearing parent said of this decision, "It was agonizing. My in-laws were against me. They said I just wanted to get rid of the deaf one—by sending him off to a state school. I decided it was in his best interest, but it wasn't easy to let him go."

American Sign Language was, and is, forbidden in oral schools, and its use brought punishment to the individual. In those state schools where it was used, the stigma surrounding it created a common bond among deaf children. In old age people still discuss their first awareness of being stigmatized. One woman said, "My father didn't want to send his child to an 'asylum'—it would bring shame on the family," while another respondent said, "My mother dragged me out of that school—she said it was not nice to sign."

In contrast, deaf individuals in the study group who had deaf parents did not experience these conflicts. Eight percent of the deaf population have deaf parents,[6] from whom they learn sign language and with whom they develop adequate communication. Meadow[7] found that such individuals have higher self-esteem than deaf people with hearing parents. Deaf people from deaf families see themselves as carrying on a cultural tradition to which little or no stigma is attached. Instead, they have a strong and positive identification that carries them through life.

American Sign Language, made up of signs, gestures, finger-spelling, facial expressions, and body language, is often embarrassing or frightening to the uninitiated. In any case, it is negatively perceived. It is distinct from English and follows different grammatical and syntactical construction.[8] Until the past few years, when sign language systems based on English were introduced, American Sign Language was the only system of manual signs in common use in the United States. Regardless of the type of education they received as children, in adulthood American Sign Language is the main means of communication for most deaf Americans.

The negative attitudes of hearing parents and the general public toward sign language creates conflict about the language for its users. One informant reported that whenever she started to leave the house to visit deaf friends, her mother said, "Oh, you're not going out with those deaf, are you?" (referring to her signing friends). The stigma attached to sign language further influenced deaf people's perspective of the world, so that they saw the world as being divided into two kinds of people: those who could hear and those who were deaf.

In adulthood deaf people demonstrate considerable ambivalence about their own language. Various informants talked to me about how sign language is "negative," making the sign with particular force. Many individuals talked about how they are "for" total communication, a recent innovative method in deaf education, because it combines sign language with speech and lipreading and is thus more acceptable. Most noticeable, however, is the way signs change in the privacy of the group. In groups of deaf people sign language becomes bigger and bolder than in public. Facial expression and body language take on new dimensions, and the richness of the language is exploited to its fullest.

IDENTITY

American Sign Language is a symbolic badge of identity in the deaf community. Identity provides the individual with a sense of self and enables him or her to relate that sense of self to the surrounding world. Clark and Kiefer[9] define identity as "that cognitive structure which gives a sense of coherence, continuity, and social relatedness to one's image of oneself." Deaf identity is crystalized early in life and is maintained throughout the life course. As individuals age, deafness defines their relationship to society.

Deaf-hearing interactions are characterized by ambiguity. Ambiguity regarding the degree of impairment in disability has the most negative impact on interpersonal relationships.[10] An informant commented, "People often talk to me and I can't answer. I shake my head and point to my ear. But they don't understand—they think I'm stuck up."

Regardless of the actual quantity of interaction with either hearing or deaf people, conflict is kept alive in the person's mind by the inconsistencies between self-perception with reference to the in-group and to the outside world. A deaf man said, "It's not very nice, but have you heard the expression, 'deafy'?" As the author nodded yes, he continued, "It's sad to say, but I know people I would have to call deafies. The major characteristic of the deafy is fear of association with hearing people."

The sign, deafy (the thumb is put against the ear and the fingers wave back and forth), is probably the most stigmatized expression in sign language. It symbolizes negative experience in deaf-hearing interaction, and stands for deaf and dumb, in the literal sense. In talking about oneself in front of hearing people, the expression is used in several ways: (1) by highly educated people as a form of irony or sarcasm, (2) by people with minimal English language skills who are forced to convey their lack of understanding of the situation to a hearing person, and (3) to express anger and frustration at the hearing world for its construed wrongs against the deaf. For example, in a bitter denouncement of the oral method, one informant finished up with "I didn't learn anything—that's why I'm a deafy."

Early fears about the hearing world have been maintained, characterized by the fear of being seen as a deafy by the hearing world. This often leads to negative predictions about the fate of any deaf-hearing interaction. For example, a number of deaf people predicted that a program that planned to integrate deaf and hearing aged would fail. In explanation, one informant said, "Deaf don't like to be around hearing." Another informant acknowledged this attitude, and said, "Some deaf people get mad dealing with hearing people, but my attitude is just to be calm—they (hearing people) will gradually get used to it (the deafness)."

Many deaf people indeed have feelings of inferiority which they express by the elaboration of signs that connote stupidity. Sign language has a large number of signs for inferior mental ability, e.g. stupid, ignorant, pea-brain, know-nothing, and dummy. One informant demonstrated how he felt about himself when he said to the researcher, "I'm dumb . . . You're hearing—smart," while another informant said of herself, "Me—no voice—dumb." This perception, which correlates hearing with intelligence and deafness with dumbness, was almost universal in individuals' comments and underlines the stigmatized way individuals see themselves.

THE INFLUENCE OF COPING MECHANISMS ON SELF-ESTEEM

Deaf identity is also shaped by social factors that engender a positive sense of self. The commonality of experiences, the frequent interaction with other deaf people, and successful communication about intimate aspects of everyday life help develop a sense of self-esteem that grows with time.[11]

In the process of personal development, deaf people have evolved a range of coping mechanisms to deal with stigma. The primary way they do this is a normalization process. The term "normalizing" has been used to describe the response of chronically ill and disabled people in different situations. In this context, normalizing refers to a strategy of social interaction. For example, Davis[12] uses the term to analyze the social behaviour of children with polio, while Strauss[13] discusses normalizing in terms of disease management. Normalizing is situational, and everyone experiences the need to normalize at one time or another. The concept covers a broad area of behavior. Normalization can occur within any group that is set apart by deviance or social marginality. Within the tightly knit reference group of elderly deaf that I studied the normalization process took place primarily within the group. The introduction of outsiders invites cognitive dissonance. During the initial field experience, people were reticent to talk to me. As a hearing person I was a threat to their feelings of normality. Outsiders serve as reminders (both in fact and fantasy) that the world is not necessarily the way it is perceived by the in-group. For this reason, the in-group seldom accepts outsiders who are not deaf. Even adult children of deaf parents who are native signers are on the margin of the group if they can hear.

In contrast, interaction within the in-group enhances feelings of normality, reinforces positive feelings about one's abilities and validates one's worth. An informant said, "At the suggestion of the minister, my parents finally sent me to the state school when I was 18 to learn sign language. I made a lot of friends there and it made me realize how lonely and friendless my childhood had been." He began to socialize with deaf people, going to the Deaf Club and to social events at the state school. After dating a number of deaf women, he met his wife-to-be. She had grown up in state schools and had an extensive network of friends from childhood. When they married, he was included in this social network and developed his own friendships within the group. As the years passed, he took on leadership responsibilities in the church and deaf social organizations in which he and his wife were members. His interactions with hearing people were gradually reduced and when he retired, his social life with hearing people ended.

This story records a typical reaction to the difficulties inherent in deaf-hearing relationships. Once the individual has begun to reconcile the dilemma of trying to function as a hearing person and to begin to accept his or her deafness as a reality of life, he or she can devote energy formerly used in frustrating interactions to develop more fully as a person and to establish meaningful relationships with peers.

Membership in a deaf community that integrates the use of sign language and shared experience fosters self-esteem. During the course of fieldwork with the aged deaf, a pattern in the interaction of deaf people could be observed to recur. When individuals were in a group of deaf people they were talkative, confident, outgoing, and relaxed. When they were interacting with people with normal hearing, whether alone or with only a few deaf people present, they became quiet and hesitant. Thus, their self-perceptions shaped two different kinds of behaviour, one convivial, sociable, and gregarious, the other wary, timorous, and withdrawn. This dichotomy in their behaviour reflects the ultimate ways in which they have adapted to their disability, and softened the effects of stigmatizing situations.

VALUES AND SOCIAL BEHAVIOR

Among the aged deaf I studied, being deaf is the single most important factor in their lives. One owes allegiance to deafness because of early communication problems where individuals could communicate only with peers. One must further the good of the community, putting it before oneself, if necessary. Conformity to a group norm serves important functions, especially for those who must continuously deal with their own nonconformity. Conformity decreases feelings of deviance and, at the same time, heightens feelings of belongingness, a process that occurs both consciously and unconsciously. This process is related to deviance disavowal. Davis[14] used this term in discussing the response of nonstigmatized individuals' behaviour toward the stigmatized. As part of the normalization process, however, the aged deaf dissociate themselves from others who suffer from a different social stigma: ethnic and racial minorities, the socially deviant, and those with other disabilities. For example, after stating that her hearing niece had been hospitalized in a mental institution, one woman added quickly, "But I never see her. I don't have anything to do with her."

In the process of normalization, symbols of stigma undergo a transformation in which the negative aspects of the symbol become a means of self-affirmation. One example is the single sign for "I love you." This has become a much-used symbol in the 1970's—in greeting one another, in speeches, on bumper stickers, and in graphics intended to educate the hearing world about deafness. The sign originated in the California School for the Deaf some 40 years ago when the school used the oral method and signing was prohibited. Students would arrange their fingers in the sign configuration and walk down the hall, dangling a hand casually at their side or holding it against their books.[15] Through this maneuver the students demonstrated deaf solidarity against a hearing world. The sign has thus undergone a profound transformation. The stigmatized origin of the sign has been forgotten, and it has become a powerful symbol of unity and affection that is now used by deaf people all over the United States.

CONCLUSION

In efforts to counteract what Goffman[16] refers to as spoiled identity, and to develop as individuals, aged deaf people have lived their lives on two levels: (1) the superficial interactions with hearing "strangers," and (2) the intimate interactions with deaf peers. As time passes, intimate interactions become increasingly important to the self-concept. The awkward, tension-laden interaction with strangers, although they are reminders of one's deafness, become easier to avoid as people age. By limiting the intensity and frequency of their contacts with the hearing world, elderly deaf people reduce the level of frustration with which they must live. The combination of deaf identity and a strong system of social support sustain elderly deaf people against isolation and loss of self-worth. Thus, they have created a climate that enables them to adapt to their disability.

REFERENCES

1. A pseudonym is used to protect confidentiality.
2. Goffman E. *Stigma Notes on the Management of Spoiled Identity.* Prentice-Hall, Englewood Cliffs, NJ, 1963.
3. Meadow K. P. Personal and social development of deaf persons. In *Psychology of Deafness for Rehabilitation Counselors* (Edited by Bolton B.). University Park Press, Baltimore, 1976.
4. Davis F. Deviance disavowal: the management of strained interaction by the visibly handicapped. *Soc. Probl.* 9, 120, 1961.
5. Schlesinger H. S. and Meadow K. P. *Sound and Sign,* Univ. of California Press, Berkeley, 1972.
6. Schein J. and Delk M. T. *The Deaf Population of the United States.* National Association of the Deaf, Silver Springs, MD, 1974.
7. Meadow K. P. Parental response to the medical ambiguities of deafness. *J. Hlth Soc. Behav.* 9, 299, 1968.
8. Stokoe W. C. Sign language structure: an outline of the visual communication systems of the American deaf. Occasional Papers No. 8, University of Buffalo, Buffalo, NY, 1960.
9. Clark M. M. and Kiefer C. Working paper on ethnic identity. Mimeo, Human Development Program, University of California, San Francisco, 1971.
10. Zahn M. A. Incapacity, impotence, and invisible impairments: their effects upon interpersonal relations. *J. Health and Hum. Behav.* 14, 115, 1973.
11. Mead G. H. *Mind, Self, and Society,* Univ. of Chicago Press, Chicago, 1934.
12. Davis F. *Passage through Crisis,* Bobbs Merrill, Indianapolis, 1963.
13. Strauss A. L. *Chronic Illness and the Quality of Life,* Mosby, St. Louis, MO, 1975.
14. Davis F. Deviance disavowal: the management of strained interaction by the visibly handicapped. *Soc. Prob.* 9, 120, 1961.
15. Goffman E. *Stigma: Notes on the Management of Spoiled Identity,* Prentice-Hall, Englewood Cliffs, NJ, 1963.

 38

Genital Herpes: An Ethnographic Inquiry into Being Discreditable in American Society

Marcia C. Inhorn

For many students, this selection will hit close to home. Sexually transmitted diseases (STDs) are a risk, a worry, and a problem to many sexually active college-age people. Some STDs are caused by viruses and cannot be cured with antibiotics, and there are now some antibiotic-resistant strains of bacterial STDs. The most famous STD today is HIV/AIDS, and it is causing massive mortality and untold suffering. On a global level, roughly one-half of the victims of HIV/AIDS are women—and most have "done" nothing more than have sex with their husbands. Nonetheless, they are often blamed for their condition (Farmer, Connor, and Simmons 1996).

Throughout the world, STDs are frequently stigmatized conditions that reflect on the morality of the patient (Gregg 1983). Often there is also a double standard in terms of stigma. In this selection, Marcia Inhorn analyzes the problem of information management—that is, the decision of whom to tell about one's condition. The problem of living with herpes is less a medical problem than a social and psychological one. The fact of having a secret, and the shame associated with having the truth come out, is part of the illness experience of people with genital herpes.

This selection may seem dated, in large part because the HIV/AIDS epidemic changed the situation enormously. At the time it was written, the emerging genital herpes epidemic seemed terrible and noteworthy. Many people had recognized that a marked increase in STD prevalence accompanied the sexual revolution of the late 1960s and 1970s (the era before AIDS). Some people did not consider these infections to be serious problems until the herpes epidemic and the emergence of other "new," untreatable, and potentially lethal STDs like AIDS. This attitude, however, ignored the fact that STDs, particularly in women, could result in long-term infertility. The big change in attitude came with AIDS; public health workers believe that the risk of AIDS has made the general population more careful about STDs.

This selection suggests that the media play an important role in the social construction of new epidemics—after all, new diseases are news. However, given the changing nature of epidemiological information and the suffering caused by stigma, the role of the media can be a two-edged sword. There is value in informing the public, but there is also the danger associated with irrational social reaction to epidemics.

As you read this selection, consider these questions:

- **Does the stigmatization of genital herpes mean that the normal rules of the sick role are not applicable?**
- **Why is information management a problem associated with this illness?**
- **What does the author mean by "discreditable"? Why would an infection make someone less creditable?**
- **What are the functions of self-help groups, like the voluntary association called HELP?**
- **Can the stigmatization of an illness change over time? Why?**

Context: Marcia Inhorn is professor of medical anthropology and international affairs at Yale University, where she is also chair of the Council on Middle East Studies. She is a past president of the Society for Medical Anthropology. She is an influential scholar, particularly in the area of gender, health, and new reproductive technologies. Inhorn has conducted multisited research on the social impact of infertility and reproductive technologies in Egypt, Lebanon, the United Arab Emirates, and Arab America; she is the author of three books on that subject and editor of six other volumes. This article was written and published while she was a graduate student at the University of California, Berkeley. It appeared in the *Medical Anthropology Newsletter*, a relatively informal publication that preceded the founding of the SMA's official journal, *Medical Anthropology Quarterly*. It was written at a time when there was a rapid increase in the incidence of genital herpes in the United States and before there were effective antivirals for its management.

Source: M. Inhorn (1986). "Genital Herpes: An Ethnographic Inquiry into Being Discreditable in American Society." *Medical Anthropology Newsletter* 17(3):59–63.

INTRODUCTION

In her widely acclaimed book *Illness as Metaphor,* Susan Sontag (1979) ruminates over Western society's use of illness as a symbol of corruption and decay and the subsequent social stigma attached to sufferers of those metaphorically manipulated afflictions. She states:

> Leprosy, in its heyday aroused a . . . disproportionate sense of horror. In the Middle Ages, the leper was a social text in which corruption was made visible; an exemplum, an emblem of decay. Nothing is more punitive than to give a disease a meaning—that meaning being invariably a moralistic one. Any important disease whose causality is murky, and for which treatment is ineffectual, tends to be awash in significance. (1979:57)

Writing in the late 1970s, she adds:

> In the last two centuries, the diseases most often used as metaphors for evil were syphilis, tuberculosis, and cancer—all diseases imagined to be, preeminently, the diseases of individuals. (1979:58)

Without question, if Sontag were to rewrite her thought provoking treatise for the 1980s, two "diseases of individuals" would have to be added to the list of metaphorical maledictions in the United States. The diseases, of course, are genital herpes and, most recently, acquired immunodeficiency syndrome (AIDS).

This paper will deal with only the first of these two recent additions—the condition that has been dubbed by the popular media as "the new scarlet letter." Genital herpes is a sexually transmitted disease (STD) that tends to affect otherwise healthy, predominantly Caucasian, educated, well-employed, middle- to upper-middle-class men and women and, in so doing, may exert upon these never-before-traumatized individuals a profound psychosocial impact out of proportion to the otherwise benign, non-life-threatening physical condition itself. The reason for the psychosocial ramifications, according to genital herpes patients,[1] is quite clear: namely, that the popular media have transformed genital herpes into a socially stigmatized condition of major proportions. This transformation, furthermore, has taken place only within the past five years, and its effects have diminished only slightly with the media's more current fascination over AIDS. Thus, to use Goffman's definition, the individual with genital herpes can now be seen as

> possessing an attribute that makes him different from others in the category of persons available for him to be, and of a less desirable kind—in the extreme, a person who is quite thoroughly bad, or dangerous, or weak. He is thus reduced in our minds from a whole and usual person to a tainted, discounted one. Such an attribute is a stigma, especially, when its discrediting effect is very extensive. (1963:3)

QUESTIONS AND METHODS

With this in mind, the question remains: What is it like to be an individual with genital herpes in the mid-1980s? This is the question to be addressed in this paper and is not unlike the one that other anthropologists, who have chosen to study so-called "marginal" members of their own societies, have asked in recent years.

This article represents the results of two months of field work among a group of American adults of heterogeneous backgrounds and origins who have been brought together because of their "marginalized" status as genital herpes patients. All of the individuals who participated in this study are members (or, in some cases, are temporarily attending meetings) of HELP, a nationwide, volunteer-run, self-help organization for individuals with genital herpes. Through observation of three meetings (two for both men and women and one for women only) of a large metropolitan chapter of HELP, many of the concerns of individuals with newly diagnosed or recurrent genital herpes were recorded, and volunteers were recruited for follow-up, confidential telephone interviews. Eight individuals (four men and four women), ranging in age from the mid-20s to late-30s, agreed to be interviewed, each interview lasting from one to two hours. In addition, three sexually active individuals (two women and one man) of the same age group who do not have genital herpes were interviewed to elicit representative attitudes toward this disease from the so-called "normal" sector of the sexually active heterosexual population.

These data were supplemented by a thorough search of the recent medical (including nursing) literature on genital herpes; the "popular" literature (including recent articles in the press); and six years' worth of *The Helper,* the quarterly publication for HELP members, published by the sponsoring American Social Health Association (ASHA) in Palo Alto, California (ASHA 1979–84).

This paper integrates information from these varied sources as the key issues in the life experiences of individuals with genital herpes are discussed. These issues fall into two broad categories: (1) clinical concerns, revolving primarily around prevention of recurrence or of transmission of the disease to sexual partners; and (2) problems of "information management," as first defined by Goffman (1963). This paper will address only the second category: issues of information disclosure—to lovers, friends, and family—and the importance of "disclosure selectivity" in the lives of individuals with genital herpes.[2] This will be followed by a discussion of the role of self-help groups in information management counseling, and, finally, of the role of the media in the recent stigmatization of this condition and the impact of this stigmatization on the lives of genital herpes patients.

TO TELL OR NOT TO TELL

For individuals with genital herpes, the greatest degree of discomfort often has very little to do with physical pain per se, but, rather, with the psychological suffering encumbered in the issue of "information management." In his now-classic book on stigma, Goffman (1963) explains the special problems of disclosure faced by those with a "discreditable" stigma, such as genital herpes. He states:

> when his differentness is not immediately apparent, and is not known beforehand (or at least known by him to be known to the others), when in fact his is a discreditable, not a discredited person, then the second main possibility in his life is to be found. The issue is not that of managing tension generated during social contacts, but rather that of managing information about his failing. To display or not to display; to tell or not to tell; to let on or not to let on; to lie or not to lie; and in each case, to whom, how, when, and where. (1963:42)

Indeed, Goffman's explication of the problems of the "discreditable" persona is quite germane to the discussion of genital herpes. Genital herpes is truly a discreditable condition—one that is essentially "invisible" (except, of course, when the individual is experiencing an outbreak and is having difficulty functioning), but, in certain instances, must be exposed with unpredictable outcomes to significant others. Indeed, this issue—more than anything else—seems to be *the* crucial variable in the lives of those with genital herpes; its importance cannot be underestimated.

Sexual Partners

Many individuals who volunteered information at HELP meetings, and other respondents, did not know precisely from whom or how they had contracted genital herpes. In most cases, however, this was not attributable to sheer number of sexual partners (i.e., so-called "promiscuity"), but, rather, to the insidious nature of the disease; namely, it may have appeared for the first time during periods of sexual inactivity or during periods of monogamy with a supposedly uninfected sexual partner.

For others, the disease was clearly contracted from a known sexual partner, who either did not tell of his or her problem or, in some cases, miscalculated the length of an outbreak and, hence, the period of contagion. For those who were "lied to" by their partners, a degree of anger or outright rage was felt by all.

Indeed, the issue of "honesty" was raised by all individuals interviewed and appears to be *the* major information management dilemma faced by genital herpes patients—or as Goffman would put it, "to tell or not to tell; to let on or not to let on; to lie or not to lie" (1963:42). Although the decision to disclose information about one's genital herpes is optional in most cases, it seems that, for most individuals, this matter of choice disappears—either morally or practically—when it comes to telling a potential sexual partner. Yet, the individual with genital herpes is caught in a "double bind" when it comes to forming intimate, "post-stigma" relationships, for, if this "failing" is revealed too soon, the other party may flee, while, if disclosed too late, guilt, accusations or dishonesty, and actual transmission of the stigmatized viral condition may ensue.

For example, one married man said he considers himself fortunate to be in a permanent relationship because of the disclosure implications faced by single men and women. He explained:

> If I weren't in a relationship, I know I'd have a lot more to deal with. Having to tell someone after two or three dates, "I have herpes. Will you go to bed with me?" is not a pleasant thought. I would say "No" myself if I didn't have it! So I see all these single people in the group [HELP] having to come up with little schemes to delay sex and build up other aspects of the relationship first.

Such "sex-delaying" schemes and ways to "break the news" are the topics of much conversation, both at the HELP meetings and in *The Helper*. At one meeting, the group leader suggested some "do's and don'ts" for telling a partner, including: (1) don't make it into a dramatic production; (2) don't use words like "incurable," "highly contagious," and "venereal"; (3) don't give more information than the person can handle (e.g., an hour on the statistics alone); (4) do present it in a matter-of-fact tone of voice; (5) do pick a quiet, relaxed moment to tell; (6) don't wait until you're in bed with your clothes off; and (7) don't wait until you've had sex with the person 16 times.[3] However, according to most informants, this suggested approach is easier said than done, and actual disclosure experiences ranged from "histrionics" on the part of several informants to avoidance of sexuality altogether in the case of others.

According to informants, the reason disclosure to intimates is so difficult is because of an overwhelming fear of rejection—a fear that appears to loom large in the minds of those with genital herpes. Several informants admitted that they now avoid, to a great degree, intimate relationships because of their fear of potential rejection. Others, primarily women, said that they had stayed in problematical relationships much longer than they would have had they not had genital herpes, because of their timidity in striking up new sexual partnerships. Virtually all informants stated that their sex lives had changed significantly as a result of genital herpes and that they were now much more circumspect about entering into new situations of intimacy.

Nevertheless, despite this overriding pessimism, actual experiences with new sexual partners suggest that the worst fears of rejection are rarely realized. Of the six individuals with genital herpes who had attempted to have post-herpes sexual relationships, only two could cite definite cases of rejection because of the disease; most informants had at least two, and often many more, instances of acceptance. Furthermore, of the three individuals interviewed who did not have genital herpes, two of them had already engaged in sexual relationships with partners whom they knew had herpes—and said that they would do it again if the situation ever arose. The third individual, furthermore, concurred that genital herpes would be a "superfluous" factor in deciding whether or not to have a relationship. All three individuals added, however, that their attitudes toward genital herpes had changed drastically—toward a more positive, enlightened view—over time.

Friends

Likewise, many of the individuals with genital herpes were extremely reluctant to tell their friends—or their "pre-stigma" acquaintances (Goffman 1963:35)—about their newly acquired problem. Although some individuals attending the HELP meetings said they had told most of their friends and acquaintances about their condition, two of those interviewed, both male, had not divulged this information to any pre-stigma acquaintances, and the other six said they had told only a few of their closest friends, most of whom had reacted supportively.

At least part of the reason why most individuals chose not to tell more than a few close friends was their paranoia over widespread exposure of their "failing" and a desire to uphold their pre-stigma reputation. This, in turn, was related to the aforementioned fear of rejection: of being made a pariah by one's larger circle of friends and acquaintances. This paranoia over exposure was understandable when one considers that most of the individuals attending the meetings—and certainly those interviewed—appeared to be bright, attractive, articulate, highly successful individuals, with positions of responsibility in the community. Widespread knowledge of the stigmatized condition would not only spoil the well-developed image, but might cast doubt on the so-called "moral character" of the individuals involved—especially considering the route of transmission of the disease. Thus, most of the individuals interviewed were extremely protective of their "secret," and the fear of exposure was a possibility that haunted many of their lives. As one woman stated:

> Some of my very closest friends don't even know. You have to *really* know who you trust, because if you tell one wrong person, and that person tells one person, then 101 people already know. If I have even a one-percent doubt in my mind, I don't tell.

Families

The fear of telling "Mom and Dad" was often even more pronounced in interviews with genital herpes patients. By telling parents or brothers and sisters about the condition, the genital herpes patient not only admits to his or her own sexuality, but that the sexual activity may have been of a questionable nature. Thus, unlike many other stigmatized conditions, in which family members are intimately involved in the individual's welfare (see, for example, Ablon 1984 or Ablon, Ames, and Cunningham 1984), genital herpes seems to be a condition with little involvement of the family group itself, since families, particularly parents, are rarely informed directly about their now "discreditable" member. Instead, informants, if they divulged this information at all, tended to choose only one member of the family, usually the "closest" sibling. In most cases, too, the disclosure was accompanied by promises of secrecy, especially regarding exposure to parents.

One informant, who told her brother about her condition, added:

> As for my parents, I *can't* tell them. The sad part is that if you had the flu or pneumonia, your family would stand by you. But you're a pariah if it's something like this.

Another informant, who also told a brother about herpes, explained:

> It's helped psychologically to have someone to talk to about it. Herpes is not one of your major two or three diseases, but it can get depressing. Most people are not in stable relationships when they get it, and they're lonely. Loneliness is the main aspect of the disease.

HELP: EDUCATIONAL AND SOCIAL FUNCTIONS

This last statement—that "loneliness is the main aspect of the disease"—explains why many individuals with genital herpes seek out HELP, if only temporarily. HELP, a program of the ASHA's Herpes Resource Center,[4] is the country's only self-help organization for individuals with genital herpes. Of the more than 80 local chapters nationwide, most are located in major metropolitan areas.

For many individuals, this volunteer-run, self-help organization is a source of clinical information,[5] but its major function is as a support system of "sympathetic others," who can serve as role models, confidantes, and advisors during both clinical and emotional crises. Many individuals use the group intensively during the primary stages of their illness and then later settle into less frequent attendance patterns or, in some cases, stop going. Others use the group less as a resource and more as a social club. As one informant stated: "The honest truth is that I go to HELP to meet a woman. Sometimes I just think it would be easier having a relationship with someone who already understands."

Meeting others with similar "moral careers" (Goffman 1963) for the purpose of trouble-free dating and sex may be a covert function of the group; in fact, several individuals at the meetings mentioned their desires to date someone who also had genital herpes, for this, they believed, would solve some of their anxieties over information disclosure and transmission. Herpes "dating services" were also discussed at meetings; however, several members shared their negative experiences with these services, which are expensive and seemingly ineffectual, according to informants.

However, when the issue of "endogamous" dating was raised at meetings, the group leader provided convincing clinical evidence to discourage this practice: namely, the possibility of contracting two different strains of herpes virus, thereby exacerbating the recurrence problem. As a result of these clinical discussions, most of the individuals interviewed said they preferred to have sexual relations with individuals who did not have genital herpes, despite the difficulties encumbered in having to divulge their "secret stigma."

THE MEDIA AND THE PROCESS OF STIGMATIZATION

Without question, if genital herpes were to be ranked today by degree of social stigma in the long list of STDs, it would take second place, with AIDs assuming the top position. If, however, one were to rank genital herpes by degree of social stigma in a list of STDs normally found among heterosexuals alone (thereby eliminating AIDS), it would surely attain top billing—outranking the now curable syphilis and gonorrhea. Indeed, if one were to rank genital herpes in terms of stigma among all the diseases known to American society, it would certainly fall among the top dozen diseases, and possibly even among the top four or five. The reason for this notoriety is believed to be due to the media—and a process of stigmatization that took place almost overnight. As one informant stated, "We are victims of the media."

According to everyone interviewed, including those without genital herpes, the media have caused most of the problems for individuals with genital herpes. Those who could remember—particularly those who had already contracted the disease by the end of the 1970s—say that the media seemed to pick up on genital herpes in the very early 1980s, with a strong emphasis on the "incurable," "recurrent" nature of the disease. This culminated in August 1982, when *Time* magazine printed a cover story in which genital herpes was called "the new scarlet letter" (Leo 1982). At HELP meetings and in interviews, several persons pointed directly to this article as the lynchpin in the subsequent "epidemic" of paranoia and fear of herpes in the United States.

Although the media's sensationalist enthusiasm for genital herpes diminished substantially with the onset of AIDS, resurgences of interest have continued to occur, as seen most recently in the "little Johnny Bigley" case, in which a three-year-old child, affected at birth by neonatal Herpes simplex Type 1, caused fearful parents to remove their children from his classroom, thereby creating nationwide panic. The fact that such a "herpes scare" could take place in 1985 indicates that fear of genital herpes is still very strong in the United States, that misinformation and misconceptions about the disease abound, and that a corrective educational effort by the media has yet to take place.

As a result, a great deal of anger is directed at the press; this was evident at HELP meetings, in interviews with informants, and even in *The Helper* publication, which had initially condoned the media's attention. One informant explained his frustration in this way: "Before the scarlet letter cover, you could screw around as much as you wanted—as long as you didn't have a conscience. But now, everything's changed." Or, as another informant concluded, "The best thing that ever happened to herpes was AIDS."

Even those individuals without genital herpes who were interviewed said they thought the media were responsible for the public's fear of the condition. One person noted that the media have done a further disservice ("adding insult to injury") by lumping herpes with AIDS in terms of health risk, even though they are "orders of magnitude different in their severity."

But how does this media-generated social stigma translate into everyday life for those with genital herpes? According to all informants, the innocent jokes and cruel remarks made about herpes hurt the most—turning otherwise average days into bad ones and even souring friendships. As one woman explained:

> It's still an "hysterical" issue for people—in both senses of the word. For instance, I'll be talking with a group of friends about our love lives, and someone will say, "Boy, you're lucky you didn't catch herpes from him!" Then everyone laughs. They would never in a million years imagine that I have it, and, if they knew, some of them probably wouldn't sit in the same room with me for fear of catching it. I never say anything, but I really think those kinds of remarks are insensitive. Nowadays, you never know who might have it—maybe even your best friend. So it's better to just keep your mouth shut.

Another said that herpes has become "funny" because (1) it is sexually transmitted, and (2) it is incurable. Underlying this humor, however, is a great deal of fear. He asserted:

> People always joke about that which they're most afraid of. There is a lot of ignorance out there, and where there's ignorance, there's fear, and where there's fear, there's humor. That's the syllogism.

Thus, although most informants could accept the jokes on an intellectual level, humor about herpes also presented something of a Catch 22; namely, most informants said their natural desire to lash out at these offensive remarks was curbed by their fear of exposure and subsequent rejection. Hence, most informants simply "kept their mouths shut" to prevent being "treated like a leper" in social settings. Indeed, the terms "leper" or "leprosy" were used at least once by five informants and by two of the individuals without herpes also interviewed. Although most informants said they did not regard themselves as "lepers," they acknowledged that the public may regard herpes as being like leprosy—contagious and to be avoided at all costs. This attitude, although understandable, is unfair considering the relatively benign nature of the disease, and has made living with herpes much more difficult, according to all those questioned.

CONCLUSION

The "invisible" nature of genital herpes is, in some senses, its most perplexing attribute—creating emotional, practical, and ethical dilemmas in the private, "discreditable" domain of information management (Goffman 1963). This article has attempted to explicate that domain, through an ethnographic inquiry into the lives of some marginalized members of our own society. Interviews with eight young adults, all affected by genital herpes, reveal how fear of disclosure—and subsequent rejection—plays a powerful role in the daily lives of these individuals. Deciding whether or not and how to tell friends, families, acquaintances, strangers, and worst of all, potential lovers about one's "secret stigma" proves to be a continuous conundrum for most. To tell or not to tell, to lie or not to lie, to let or not to let on—these are the questions that individuals with genital herpes must face with each relationship, new or old, and the answers are not easily forthcoming.

Most individuals opt to solve these problems in the following ways: (1) by dividing the world into two groups, a select group of trusted "insiders," and the "outsiders," who would be too distraught (e.g., parents), too rejecting, or too garrulous to be trusted with the secret; (2) by limiting sexual partners, so as to avoid transmission of the virus and, more important, to avoid the issue of disclosure to intimates; and (3) by joining HELP, a self-help group for genital herpes patients, which offers both emotional and clinical support.

These steps are necessary, informants insist, because of the recent stigmatization of the disease.

Namely, in the early 1980s, the media transformed genital herpes from an unknown, relatively benign, nonstigmatized condition into an "incurable, highly contagious, recurrent venereal disease, threatening the life, liberty, and happiness of every American who uses public toilets." This loathsome and leprous image, informants say, is entirely undeserved, for genital herpes is non-life-threatening, nonapparent, and easily preventable when proper precautions are taken. But because genial herpes has now been lumped with such stigmatized conditions as leprosy, AIDS, tuberculosis, and cancer, life has become difficult for those with the disease, who fear social outcasting, cruel humor, and other forms of outright stigmatization.

Whether genital herpes will continue to be stigmatized in American society remains to be seen. In all probability, the degree of stigma will diminish substantially if a vaccine to prevent transmission or, better yet, a true antiviral agent becomes available. But until that time, we, as medical anthropologists, have a rare opportunity to study the processes of stigmatization and marginalization at home. Once we understand how discreditable stigmas—the "new scarlet letters"—of our own complex society are created, maintained, and managed by individual members, we may be able to shed light on the phenomenon of acquired deviancy—on becoming society's discreditable members—the world over.

NOTES

1. I prefer to use the term "patient" rather than "victim" or "sufferer."
2. Information on clinical concerns of genital herpes patients may be obtained from the author.
3. Likewise, in an article on "Talking About Herpes" in *The Helper* (Summer 1984), some additional advice was preferred, including (1) don't tell a lie about herpes; (2) do assume that the person you are about to tell has little, if any, accurate information about herpes; (3) do be prepared to dispel fears and misconceptions; (4) don't worry in advance about telling (because it doesn't help); (5) don't feel as though you have to be a walking encyclopedia about every herpes-related nuance; (6) do use appropriate analogies wherever possible; (7) don't forget to emphasize how preventable herpes is; and (8) don't be surprised to learn that the person you are anxious to tell has wanted to tell you, too.
4. In 1982, the ASHA changed the name of its genital herpes self-help organization from Herpetics Engaged in Living Productively (HELP) to the Herpes Resource Center (HRC), because the term "herpetics" was viewed negatively by its membership. However, the acronym HELP is still used by the 80-odd local chapters, and the ASHA's publication is still called *The Helper*. Thus, the acronym HELP has been used throughout this paper to conform to current usage.
5. HELP also serves a number of other less widely discussed but important functions. These include (1) research fund drives; (2) lobbying; (3) provision of a telephone "hotline"; (4) symposia coordination; (5) epidemiological, demographic, and psychosocial surveys of the membership; (6) formulation of medical advisory boards; (7) public relations and media interviews, (8) legal advice; (9) announcements of clinical trials; (10) announcements of new clinics and chapters; and (11) review and evaluation of the medical and popular literature on genital herpes. To see how HELP compares with other national self-help organizations, refer to Borman et al. 1982; Borman and Lieberman 1976; Killilea 1976; and Silverman 1978.

REFERENCES

Ablon, J. 1984. Little People in America. New York: Praeger.

Ablon, J., G. Ames, and W. Cunningham. 1984. To All Appearances: The Ideal American Family. In Power to Change. E. Kauffman. ed. Pp. 199–235. New York: Gardner Press.

American Social Health Association. 1979–84. The Helper. J. A. Graves. ed. Palo Alto, CA: American Social Health Association.

Borman, L. D., L. E. Borck, R. Hess, and F. L. Pasquale. 1982. Helping People to Help Themselves: Self-Help and Prevention. In Prevention in Human Services. R. Hess. ed. Pp. 1–129. New York: The Haworth Press.

Borman, L. D., and M. A. Lieberman. 1976. Self-Help Groups. The Journal of Applied Behavioral Science (Special Issue) 12(3):261–463.

Goffman, E. 1963. Stigma: Notes on the Management of Spoiled Identity. Englewood Cliffs, NJ: Prentice-Hall.

Killilea, M. 1976. Mutual Help Organizations: Interpretations in the Literature. In Support Systems and Mutual Help. G. Caplan and M. Killilea. eds. Pp. 37–93. New York: Grune & Stratton.

Leo, J. 1982. The New Scarlet Letter. Time 120(5):62–66.

Silverman, P. R. 1978. Mutual Help Groups: A Guide for Mental Health Workers. Rockville, MD: National Institute of Mental Health.

Sontag, S. 1979. Illness as Metaphor. New York: Vintage Books.

39

Stigma in the Time of Influenza: Social and Institutional Responses to Pandemic Emergencies

Ron Barrett
Peter J. Brown

The ancient Greeks used the term stigma *to describe a permanent mark that branded someone as a criminal, traitor, or slave. In the 1960s, sociologists such as Erving Goffman and other anthropologists began using the term in a different way: Stigma described the social discredit that people experience for having certain physical or behavioral features, or belonging to certain groups. Prior to this, social scientists had mainly focused on why people deviate from social norms. After shifting their focus from deviance to social stigma, social scientists began asking why certain human features are stigmatized and not others. In the medical social sciences, researchers have been increasingly studying the impact of social stigma on human health and well-being. Infectious diseases provide important examples in this regard.*

Sometimes, the social stigma of an infectious disease is more contagious than the virus or bacteria itself. The stigma can also be more devastating than the disease, leading to social isolation, unemployment, loss of spouse and family, and psychological distress. Further, stigma can negatively impact the epidemiology and course of the diseases themselves, especially when they result in public panic, delayed treatment, noncooperation with surveillance efforts, or nonadherence to vaccination and other prevention and treatment programs. This article explores some of these issues and their impact on social responses to influenza pandemics and other major disease outbreaks.

This selection is an example of both critical and applied medical anthropologies. It is critical insofar as it challenges readers to think beyond simple biological models of parasite and host when looking at a particular disease outbreak. This article is very much focused on a broader sense of "environment" that includes social relationships between human beings, both historically and currently, and not just between humans and other animals or microbes. It is also an example of applied medical anthropology because it reaches out to health professionals and policy makers, and presents reasons for them to consider the impact of social stigma when attempting to manage pandemic emergencies.

As you read this selection, consider these questions:

- **In a practical sense, how do you go about reducing the fear and stigma associated with a particular infectious disease?**
- **Could one argue that a certain degree of social stigma be healthy because social isolation reduces the chances of further infection?**
- **To what extent might other forms of social discrimination, such as those against women, homosexuals, or ethnic minorities, impact people's attitudes toward certain diseases?**
- **What could happen when a society mainly focuses on certain kinds of diseases and not others?**
- **To what extent are people's anxieties about avian influenza (bird flu) linked to anxieties about other kinds of threats such as terrorism or economic collapse?**

Context: Peter Brown is a medical anthropologist in the Departments of Anthropology and Global Health at Emory University. His research interests include the political and ecological aspects of infectious diseases, obesity, and the provision of medical care in clinical settings. Ron Barrett is a medical anthropologist and registered nurse in the Departments of Family & Community Nursing and Anthropology at Emory. He has conducted research on religious healing and the stigma of leprosy in India, and end-of-life decision making in the United States. Brown and Barrett are editors of this book. This article has an applied aspect in that it attempts to shape health policy by educating other disciplines about the impact of social stigma in large-scale disease outbreaks and inspiring further research in this area. It was first presented at a multidisciplinary workshop at Harvard University on Asian flus and avian influenza at a time when there was a great deal of public interest in and fear about the possibility of a global pandemic of "bird flu."

Source: R. Barrett and P. Brown (2008). "Stigma in the Time of Influenza: Social Responses to Pandemic Emergencies." *Journal of Infectious Diseases* 137: S34–37.

The best models of influenza pandemics highlight the powerful influence of fear and stigma in the management of infectious disease emergencies. Analogous models based on recent epidemics of plague and severe acute respiratory syndrome illustrate the role of stigma in the delayed and disproportionate responses by affected populations and institutions. The historical model of the 1918 influenza pandemic presents similar themes across nations and localities. Although avian influenza has only recently attracted public and political attention, the recurring dynamics of fear and stigma have a very long history.

"Stigma" was originally a classical Greek term for a permanent mark that branded a person as a criminal, traitor, or slave. In recent decades, the word "stigma" has been used to describe the process of negative discrimination against people with certain physical, behavioral, or social attributes [1]. This concept of stigma as discrimination has been central to the medical social sciences, particularly in studies of disability, the social aspects of mental illness, race and gender disparities in health care, and the cultural constructions of biomedicine [2–4]. The social consequences of stigma can result in adverse health effects in general [5, 6], as well as in exacerbation of the effects of the epidemiology and pathology of certain diseases [7, 8]. It therefore can be argued that stigma is more than just a negative outcome of certain diseases; it is an illness in itself, comorbid with respect to its marked physical conditions.

The same argument can be made for the social stigma of infectious diseases. In many countries, the stigma of Hansen disease (HD), or leprosy, is far worse than the disease itself [9]. Although HD can be cured with antibiotics, the social mark of leprosy can last a lifetime. This stigma motivates widespread concealment, delaying early detection and treatment and furthering the spread of the infection [10]. Similar dynamics can be found for HIV infection and AIDS, a potentially stigmatized disease that some have described as the "new leprosy." As with HD, the stigma of AIDS can perpetuate the spread of HIV, especially when the costs of social exposure outweigh the benefits of early testing and treatment [10]. Farmer and Kleinman [11] explored these dynamics in the early years of the HIV/AIDS pandemic, tracing the ways in which the suffering of patients with AIDS and of their families is created by socioeconomic inequalities, compounded by the inappropriate use of resources, magnified by discrimination, augmented by fear, and amplified by the loss of social identity. Despite subsequent biomedical advancements, these observations are as true for the world today as they were 18 years ago [12].

By extension of these lessons to infectious diseases in general, stigma can be seen as a biosocial phenomenon with 4 essential elements. First, stigma can present major barriers against health care seeking, thereby reducing early detection and treatment and furthering the spread of disease. Second, social marginalization often can lead to poverty and neglect, thereby increasing the susceptibility of populations to the entry and amplification of infectious diseases. Third, potentially stigmatized populations may distrust health authorities and resist cooperation during a public health emergency. Finally, social stigma may distort public perceptions of risk, resulting in mass panic among citizens and the disproportionate allocation of health care resources by politicians and health professionals.

Issues of risk perception and resource allocation are particularly relevant to the prevention of avian influenza. Compared with many neglected health problems, the threats of avian influenza and bioterrorism currently receive a remarkable degree of attention and resources. They occupy a prominent position in many public health agendas, even if they exist only as worst-case simulations and nightmares in the public imagination [13]. In the same issue of *Science* that describes the public health risk from an outbreak of H5N1 influenza [14], an editorial entitled "Perceived Threats and Real Killers" argues that US health priorities have become overly focused on unknown risks from new diseases and the unknowable consequences of bioweapons at the expense of known threats such as influenza [15]. This argument does not question the value of disease surveillance and public health preparedness, and it does not exclude the possibility that biosecurity investments might be leveraged to improve the public health infrastructure and the surge capacity of primary health care facilities. Nevertheless, it is extremely difficult to predict an outbreak of virulent influenza or any other specific epidemics with any precision. We must look for common themes by relying on the history of previous epidemics and the social and epidemiological lessons that they provide.

FROM PLAGUE TO INFLUENZA IN WESTERN INDIA

Early in 2006, 3 separate outbreaks of avian influenza were detected in rural poultry farms in the western Indian states of Maharasthra and Gujarat [16]. The affected districts have strong trade and migration connections with the industrial city of Surat, one of the wealthiest and fastest-growing cities in India. These same connections played a major role in the Indian plague epidemic of 1994, when a small outbreak of bubonic plague in a nearby village quickly spread to Surat and developed into a larger epidemic of more-virulent pneumonic plague, with 197 confirmed cases and 54 related deaths in the city's underclass communities [17]. More than just an epidemic precedent, the plague in Surat provides important lessons with regard to the potential role of stigma in the social responses to future outbreaks.

Within a week after *Yersinia pestis* infection had been identified publicly, a half million people fled Surat, including 78% of the professional health care providers in the city's most affected areas [18]. Many of these émigrés were turned away from neighboring communities and cities. Trains passed through Surat without stopping, and ships refused cargo from the city. International flights to India were cancelled, outgoing passengers were quarantined (including Mother Teresa), and several Persian Gulf states banned Indian imports, resulting in billion-dollar losses and major declines in the Bombay Stock Exchange, including the SENSEX, a collection of stocks thought to represent the health of India's newly liberalized economy [19]. This "stigma epidemic" of 1994 spread much farther and faster than the pathogen itself, severely inhibiting disease containment and control efforts and creating additional social and health problems related to major economic losses.

Given the social reaction in 1994, there is cause for concern about a similar response in the event that avian influenza develops human-to-human transmissibility in this region. Yet the city of Surat also has made subsequent social reforms that may help to reduce public stigma and anxiety during such an emergency. There have been major improvements in sanitation and the provision of primary health care, resulting in improved public confidence in health authorities and their messages [20]. Moreover, in contrast to conditions in the surrounding state, relations have improved between the city's Hindu and Muslim communities, possibly reducing the risk of mutual accusation—including that of bioterrorism—that pervaded the previous epidemic [21]. Surat presents positive as well as negative lessons for social responses to infectious diseases.

IS INFLUENZA DIFFERENT?

Unlike the Indian plague epidemic of 1994, the 1918 influenza pandemic readily spread across many different demographic categories and populations around the world [22]. Thus, it is sometimes considered to have been more "democratic" than other infections, which suggests that social reactions to influenza may have been different from reactions to other, traditionally stigmatized diseases. Yet, in the United States, there were many local examples of public panic, discriminatory statutes, and avoidable mortality among systematically abandoned sick individuals [23]. At an international level, control of the 1918 influenza pandemic was impeded by wartime restrictions on the flow of information. The reason that the 1918 influenza pandemic became known as the "Spanish flu" was that Spain, a nonbelligerent nation in which the press was not subject to the same degree of censorship, was the first to announce the presence of the disease. Such labeling served to deflect blame from combatant countries such as the United States, where the first cases of influenza were detected.

Censorship converged with the rapid abatement of the disease to bury many historical details of the 1918 influenza pandemic. Yet, the fear of influenza remains a part of the historical memory of the pandemic, looming large in discussions of a possible avian influenza pandemic today. Such discussions often emphasize the enormously high mortality of the 1918 influenza pandemic without considering the distribution of that mortality. Colonial India experienced ~18 million deaths, possibly more than all other nations combined [24]. This was most likely due to malnutrition and the dense, unsanitary living conditions so often associated with poverty. Limited access to basic resources continues to be one of the best predictors of mortality during any disease outbreak, especially among the world's impoverished majority [25].

Fear of infection is exacerbated by projected scenarios of socioeconomic breakdown, chaos, food and fuel shortages, violence, and incivility. With this in mind, public health communications strive to motivate preparation rather than panic. Yet, public health officials face a no-win situation with respect to future disease threats: any level of concern may seem unduly alarmist if an epidemic does not occur, but no level of preparation will be considered sufficient if an epidemic does occur. When the swine influenza pandemic of 1976 never arrived, public health officials who urged mass vaccinations were later criticized for a very small percentage of adverse reactions to vaccination [26]. Such criticism dissuades public health officials from recommending aggressive primary prevention efforts.

Finally, the economic impact of stigma can impede early reporting by those who are at highest risk of infection during an influenza pandemic. The 6-point statement of principles developed during a 2006 conference on social justice and influenza in Bellagio, Italy, concerned problems of fear of discrimination, reprisal, and uncompensated loss of livelihood. The principles state that, because of vulnerability, "special efforts are needed to foster reporting by disadvantaged groups, as well as to protect them from negative impacts which could worsen their situation" [27]. This is especially relevant for poor agriculturalists in the poultry sector, such as those in Thailand, where significant delays in the reporting of avian influenza occurred [28]. Effective surveillance must account for the economic consequences of stigma.

CONCLUSION

The historical models discussed in this article illustrate the ways in which stigma and fear can severely impede efforts to manage the spread of an outbreak of virulent influenza. Yet, they also provide lessons for the mitigation or prevention of these social dynamics. Chief among these lessons is the importance of building a surge capacity for public trust. As with other surge capacities, this cannot happen without a preexisting public health infrastructure for all segments of the population, especially those who are the most susceptible. Community trust is strongly influenced by the degree to which officials and health care providers have addressed local health needs prior to epidemic emergencies. Only when these conditions are preestablished is it realistic to expect affected populations to cooperate with programs such as contact tracing and to distinguish isolation measures from the historical specter of quarantines. Hospitals and isolation centers should be seen as treatment zones to be sought rather than places of death to avoid.

In the earliest stages of an epidemic, care must be taken to support the social status of first-line health care providers and to ensure the safety of their immediate families. Otherwise, they may be forced to choose between the good of their families and the good of their larger society. At the same time, government transparency must be established from the very beginning. Official silence only reinforces misinformation and public mistrust. Without clear and reliable information, the unknown risks of infection can exacerbate stigmatization and create undue alarm [29].

Finally, it is important to note that transparency does not preclude optimism, even under the worst health conditions. In the last century, many nations experienced their largest declines in infectious disease–related mortality before the advent of antimicrobial drugs [30]. Even the 1918 influenza pandemic provides strong evidence that coordinated nonpharmacological interventions (NPIs) played a major role in reducing the incidence of cases and disease-related mortality in several major US cities [31]. In the event of a similar pandemic, it is imperative that such NPIs include the prevention and management of stigma.

REFERENCES

1. Goffman E. Stigma: notes on the management of spoiled identity. Englewood Cliffs, NJ: Prentice-Hall, 1963.
2. Murphy R. Physical disability and social liminality: a study in the rituals of adversity. Soc Sci Med 1988; 26:235–42.
3. Kleinman A. The illness narratives, suffering, healing, and the human condition. New York: Basic Books, 1988.
4. Wailoo K. Dying in the city of the blues: sickle cell anemia and the politics of race and health. Chapel Hill, NC: University of North Carolina Press, 2001.
5. Berkman LF, Syme SL. Social networks, host resistance, and mortality: a nine-year follow-up study of Alameda County residents. Am J Epidemiol 1979; 109:186–204.
6. Seeman TE, Knudsen L, Cohen R, Gurualnik J. Social network ties and mortality among the elderly in the Alameda County study. Am J Epidemiol 1987;126:714–23.
7. Barrett R. Self-mortification and the stigma of leprosy in northern India. Med Anthropol Q 2005; 19:216–30.
8. Dressler WW. Health in the African American community: accounting for health inequalities. Med Anthropol Q 1993; 7:325–45.
9. Waxler NE. Learning to be a leper: a case study in the social construction of illness. In: Mishler E, ed. Social contexts of health, illness and patient care. Cambridge: Cambridge University Press, 1992:169–92.
10. McGrath JW. The biological impact of social responses to the AIDS epidemic. Med Anthropol 1992; 15:63–79.
11. Farmer P, Kleinman A. AIDS as human suffering. Daedalus 1989; 118:135–62.
12. Nordström A. World AIDS Day [message]. New York: United Nations, 2006. Available at: http://www.un.org/events/aids/2006/whoadg.shtml. Accessed 10 January 2008.
13. Barrett R. Dark winter and the spring of 1972: deflecting the social lessons of smallpox. Med Anthropol 2006: 25:171–91.
14. Ferguson NM, Fraser C, Donelly CA, Ghani AC, Anderson RM. Public health risk from the H5N1 influenza epidemic. Science 2004; 304:968–9.
15. Glass RI. Perceived threats and real killers. Science 2004; 304:927.
16. US State Department, Embassy of the United States, New Delhi, India. Avian influenza update. Available at: http://newdelhi.usembassy.gov/acsinfluenza.html. Accessed 28 November 2006.

17. Barrett R. Human ecology and misattribution: the 1994 plague in western India. In: Clunan A, Lavoy P, eds. Terrorism, war, or disease? Unraveling the use of biological weapons. Stanford, CA: Stanford University Press (in press).
18. Shah G. Public health and urban development: the plague in Surat. Delhi: Sage Publications, 1997.
19. World Resources Institute. The Black Death revisited: India's 1994 plague epidemic. Washington, DC: World Resources Institute, 1996. Available at: http://archive.wri.org/item_detail.cfm?id=941§ion=pubs&page=pubs_content_text&z. Accessed 28 November 2006.
20. Swamy HMS, Vyas A, Narang S. Transformation of Surat: from plague to second cleanest city in India. Delhi: All India Institute of Local Self Government, 1999.
21. Shah M. The power of stigma: the plague in Surat, India [dissertation]. Stanford CA: Stanford University, Department of Anthropological Sciences, 2006.
22. Crosby AW. America's forgotten pandemic: the influenza of 1918. Cambridge: Cambridge University Press, 2003.
23. Barry JM. The Great Influenza: the epic story of the deadliest plague in history. New York: Viking Press, 2004.
24. Mills ID. The 1918–19 influenza pandemic: the Indian experience. Indian Econ Soc Hist Rev 1986; 23:1–40.
25. Kim JH, Millen JV, Irwin A, Gershman J. eds. Dying for growth: global inequality and health for the poor. Monroe, ME: Common Courage Press, 2003.
26. Neustadt RE, Fineberg HV. The epidemic that never was: policy making and the swine flu scare. New York: Vintage Books, 1983.
27. Bellagio Group. Bellagio Meeting on Social Justice and Influenza: statement of principles. Baltimore: Johns Hopkins Berman Institute of Bioethics, 2006. Available at: http://www.hopkinsmedicine.org/bioethics/bellagio/statement.html. Accessed 10 February 2007.
28. GRAIN. Fowl play: the poultry industry's central role in the bird flu crisis [briefing report]. Barcelona: GRAIN, 2006. Available at: http://www.grain.org/briefings/?id=194. Accessed 10 February 2007.
29. Gray GM, Ropeik DP. Dealing with the dangers of fear: the role of risk communication. Health Aff (Millwood) 2002; 21:106–16.
30. McKeown T. Determinants of health. Hum Nat 1978; 1:57–62.
31. Markel H, Navarro JA, Sloan A, Michelson JR, Stern AM, Cetron MS. Nonpharmaceutical interventions implemented by US cities during the 1918–1919 influenza pandemic. JAMA 2007; 298:644–54.

 40

AIDS as Human Suffering

Paul Farmer
Arthur Kleinman

This is a powerful selection. It compares the illness experience and deaths, of two people with AIDS. One is a gay man in a New York City hospital, and the other is a poor woman in rural Haiti. The selection's cross-cultural comparison emphasizes the social and cultural dimensions of AIDS and the fact that stigma and cultural values can greatly increase the human suffering from the disease.

The AIDS pandemic is a terrible thing. A pandemic *is a global epidemic; many people in the United States, who immediately think of homosexual men when one mentions AIDS, forget that the majority of people with AIDS are found in Third World countries. Many people in biomedicine think of AIDS as a disease and a scientific challenge but forget the human suffering of the illness experience.*

From the view of epidemiology, an epidemic *is a disease with greater-than-expected frequency (incidence). By definition, therefore, any newly discovered or identified disease is an epidemic. Epidemics are media events, in part because the discovery of a disease's biological cause makes for an exciting story. Throughout history, there has been a pattern of infectious diseases changing from epidemic to endemic (meaning the diseases are permanently transmitted within a population). In other words, new diseases in a population often begin with high mortality rates and then, through processes of mutual adaptation of host and pathogen over time, diseases may become both more common and less virulent. Whether AIDS will follow this pattern is a matter of conjecture. Recently, because of stunning advances in clinical treatments for people who are HIV positive, AIDS has become more like a long-term chronic disease. But this medical progress appears to be primarily among white males with medical insurance; there is less improvement among ethnic minorities. For people in Third World countries, where economic resources do not permit even HIV testing, the scientific breakthroughs in clinical treatment of AIDS seem unlikely in the foreseeable future.*

Medical anthropologists have contributed a great deal to the study of HIV transmission and prevention since the very beginning of the epidemic. The literature is large, and interested students might begin with an anthropology and AIDS bibliography (Bolton and Orozco 1994). The design of culturally appropriate prevention strategies has been another area of interest to many applied medical anthropologists.

Paul Farmer, one of the authors of this selection, has done anthropological fieldwork on the impact of the AIDS epidemic on a small Haitian community where, in one sense, AIDS was thought of as a disease that could be "sent" through sorcery (Farmer 1988). Toward the beginning of the AIDS epidemic, Haitians were singled out by the Centers for Disease Control as an ethnic "risk group" for the disease, and this erroneous epidemiological fact had some serious repercussions in terms of stigma and discrimination. Farmer is also a physician; he has worked in a rural health center in Haiti that has had marked success. The lessons learned from that project have been expanded to a nongovernmental agency called Partners in Health that has projects all over the world (Farmer, Connors, and Simmons 1996).

As you read this selection, consider these questions:

- **In what ways were Robert's and Anita's deaths different? How do those differences reflect cultural values? Which kind of death would you prefer?**
- **How is the stigma from HIV/AIDS different from something like a spinal-cord injury?**
- **Examine the nonmedical sources of human suffering caused by AIDS listed at the end of this selection. What kind of solutions would you suggest?**
- **How might culture be a factor in the distribution of disease? Could Robert or Anita have avoided their disease? How?**

Context: Both Paul Farmer and Arthur Kleinman teach at Harvard University and are very important figures in the field of medical anthropology. Both are physicians as well as anthropologists. Both are very famous, although Farmer is actually a former student of Kleinman. Kleinman has written 6 single-authored books, 24 edited books, and over 200 journal articles. Within medicine, Farmer's specialization is infectious disease, while Kleinman's is psychiatry. This article was written in 1989, which was toward the beginning of the HIV / AIDS epidemic in the United States. It is somewhat difficult for contemporary students to imagine the social context of this disease at that time. In the 1980s, AIDS was an untreatable and fatal medical mystery; people with the disease were highly stigmatized and discriminated against. The social epidemiology of AIDS at that time was sometimes referred to as the 4 Hs (homosexuals, hemophiliacs, heroin users, and Haitians). Paul Farmer, whose medical and anthropological work in Haiti is described in Tracy Kidder's book Mountains beyond Mountains, was already concerned with the health experiences of rural Haitians when the AIDS epidemic struck. Kleinman was interested in the social and cultural aspects of illnesses in general, and in this disease that caused immense social suffering in particular. During this period, there was a great deal of scientific activity searching for the cause and cure of AIDS—but at the same time, the human suffering of the people afflicted was being ignored. This article was published in the highly influential journal of the American Academy of Arts and Sciences.

Source: P. Farmer and A. Kleinman (1989). "AIDS as Human Suffering" *Daedalus*, special issue "Living with AIDS," 118(2):135–161.

That the dominant discourse on AIDS at the close of the twentieth century is in the rational-technical language of disease control was certainly to be expected and even necessary. We anticipate hearing a great deal about the molecular biology of the virus, the clinical epidemiology of the disease's course, and the pharmacological engineering of effective treatments. Other of contemporary society's key idioms for describing life's troubles also express our reaction to AIDS: the political-economic talk of public-policy experts, the social-welfare jargon of the politicians and bureaucrats, and the latest psychological terminology of mental-health professionals. Beneath the action-oriented verbs and reassuringly new nouns of these experts' distancing terminology, the more earthy, emotional rumblings of the frightened, the accusatory, the hate-filled, and the confused members of the public are reminders that our response to AIDS emerges from deep and dividing forces in our experience and our culture.

AIDS AND HUMAN MEANINGS

Listen to the words of persons with AIDS and others affected by our society's reaction to the new syndrome:

- "I'm 42 years old. I have AIDS. I have no job. I do get $300 a month from social security and the state. I will soon receive $64 a month in food stamps. I am severely depressed. I cannot live on $300 a month. After $120 a month for rent and $120 a month for therapy, I am left with $60 for food and vitamins and other doctors and maybe acupuncture treatments and my share of utilities and oil and wood for heat. I'm sure I've forgotten several expenses like a movie once in a while and a newspaper and a book."[1]
- "I don't know what my life expectancy is going to be, but I certainly know the quality has improved. I know that not accepting the shame or the guilt or the stigma that people would throw on me has certainly extended my life expectancy. I know that being very up-front with my friends, and my family and coworkers, reduced a tremendous amount of stress, and I would encourage people to be very open with friends, and if they can't handle it, then that's their problem and they're going to have to cope with it."
- "Here we are at an international AIDS conference. Yesterday a woman came up to me and said, 'May I have two minutes of your time?' She said, 'I'm asking doctors how they feel about treating AIDS patients.' And I said, 'Well, actually I'm not a doctor. I'm an AIDS patient, and as she was shaking hands, her hand whipped away, she took two steps backward, and the look of horror on her face was absolutely diabolical."
- "My wife and I have lived here [in the United States] for fifteen years, and we speak English well, and I do O.K. driving. But the hardest time I've had in all my life, harder than Haiti, was when people would refuse to get in my cab when they discovered I was from Haiti [and therefore in their minds, a potential carrier of HIV]. It got so we would pretend to be from somewhere else, which is the worst thing you can do, I think."

All illnesses are metaphors. They absorb and radiate the personalities and social conditions of those who experience symptoms and treatments. Only a few illnesses, however, carry such cultural salience that they become icons of the times. Like tuberculosis in *fin de siècle* Europe, like cancer in the first half of the American century, and like leprosy from Leviticus to the present, AIDS speaks of the menace and losses of the times. It marks the sick person, encasing the afflicted in an exoskeleton of peculiarly powerful meanings: the terror of a lingering and untimely death, the panic of contagion, the guilt of "self-earned" illness.

AIDS has offered a new idiom for old gripes. We have used it to blame others: gay men, drug addicts, inner-city ethnics, Haitians, Africans. And we in the United States have, in turn, been accused of spreading and even creating the virus that causes AIDS. The steady progression of persons with AIDS toward the grave, so often via the poor house, has assaulted the comforting idea that risk can be managed. The world turns out to be less controllable and more dangerous, life more fragile than our insurance and welfare models pretend. We have relegated the threat of having to endure irremediable pain and early death—indeed, the very image of suffering as the paramount reality of daily existence—to past periods in history and to other, poorer societies. Optimism has its place in the scale of American virtues; stoicism and resignation in the face of unremitting hardship—unnecessary character traits in a land of plenty—do not. Suffering had almost vanished from public and private images of our society.

Throughout history and across cultures, life-threatening disorders have provoked questions of control (What do we do?) and bafflement (Why me?). When bubonic plague depopulated fourteenth-century Europe by perhaps as many as half to three-fourths of the population, the black death was construed as a religious problem and a challenge to the moral authority as much or even more than as a public-health problem. In the late twentieth century, it is not surprising that great advances in scientific knowledge and technological intervention have created our chief responses to questions of control and bafflement. Yet bafflement is not driven away by the advance of scientific knowledge, for it points to another aspect of the experience of persons with AIDS that has not received the attention it warrants. It points to a concern that in other periods and in other cultures is at the very center of the societal reaction to dread disease, a concern that resonates with that which is most at stake in the human experience of AIDS even if it receives little attention in academic journals—namely, suffering.

A mortal disease forces questions of dread, of death, and of ultimate meaning to arise. Suffering is a culturally and personally distinctive form of affliction of the human spirit. If pain is distress of the body, suffering is distress of the person and of his or her family and friends. The affliction and death of persons with AIDS create master symbols of suffering; the ethical and emotional responses to AIDS are collective representations of how societies deal with suffering. The stories of sickness of people with AIDS are texts of suffering that we can scan for evidence of how cultures and communities and individuals elaborate the unique textures of personal experience out of the impersonal cellular invasion of viral RNA. Furthermore, these illness narratives point toward issues in the AIDS epidemic every bit as salient as control of the spread of infection and treatment of its biological effects.

Viewed from the perspective of suffering, AIDS must rank with smallpox, plague, and leprosy in its capacity to menace and hurt, to burden and spoil human experience, and to elicit questions about the nature of life and its significance. Suffering extends from those afflicted with AIDS to their families and intimates, to the practitioners and institutions who care for them, and to their neighborhoods and the rest of society, who feel threatened by perceived sources of the epidemic and who are thus affected profoundly yet differently by its consequences. If we minimize the significance of AIDS as human tragedy, we dehumanize people with AIDS as well as those engaged in the public-health and clinical response to the epidemic. Ultimately, we dehumanize us all.

ROBERT AND THE DIAGNOSTIC DILEMMA

It was in a large teaching hospital in Boston that we first met Robert, a forty-four-year-old man with AIDS.[2] Robert was not from Boston, but from Chicago, where he had already weathered several of the infections known to strike people with compromised immune function. His most recent battle had been with an organism similar to that which causes tuberculosis but is usually harmless to those with intact immune systems. The infection and the many drugs used to treat it had left him debilitated and depressed, and he had come east to visit his sister and regain his strength. On his way home, he was prevented from boarding his plane "for medical reasons." Beset with fever, cough, and severe shortness of breath, Robert went that night to the teaching hospital's emergency ward. Aware of his condition and its prognosis, Robert hoped that the staff there would help him to "get into shape" for the flight back to Chicago.

The physicians in the emergency ward saw their task as straightforward: to identify the cause of Robert's symptoms and, if possible, to treat it. In contemporary medical practice, identifying the cause of respiratory distress in a patient with AIDS entails following what is often called an algorithm. An algorithm, in the culture of biomedicine, is a series of sequential choices, often represented diagrammatically, which helps physicians to make diagnoses and select treatments. In Robert's case, step one, a chest X-ray, suggested the opportunistic lung parasite *Pneumocystis* as a cause for his respiratory distress; step two, examination of his sputum, confirmed it. He was then transferred to a ward in order to begin treatment of his lung infection. Robert was given the drug of choice, but did not improve. His fever, in fact, rose and he seemed more ill than ever.

After a few days of decline, Robert was found to have trismus: his jaw was locked shut. Because he had previously had oral candidiasis ("thrush"), his trismus and neck pain were thought to suggest the spread of the fungal infection back down the throat and pharynx and into the esophagus—a far more serious process than thrush, which is usually controlled by antifungal agents. Because Robert was unable to open his mouth, the algorithm for documenting esophagitis could not be followed. And so a "GI consult"—Robert has already had several—was called. It was hoped that the gastroenterologists, specialists at passing tubes into both ends of the gastrointestinal tract, would be better able to evaluate the nature of Robert's trismus. Robert had jumped ahead to the point in the algorithm that called for "invasive studies." The trouble is that on the night of his admission he had already declined a similar procedure.

Robert's jaw remained shut. Although he was already emaciated from two years of battle, he refused a feeding tube. Patient refusal is never part of an algorithm, and so the team turned to a new kind of logic: Is Robert mentally competent to make such a decision? Is he suffering from AIDS dementia? He was, in the words of one of those treating him, "not with the program." Another member of the team suggested that Robert had "reached the end of the algorithm" but the others disagreed. More diagnostic studies were suggested: in addition to esophagoscopy with biopsy and culture, a CT scan of the neck and head, repeated blood cultures, even a neurological consult. When these studies were mentioned to the patient, his silent stare seemed to fill with anger and despair. Doctors glanced uncomfortably at each other over their pale blue masks. Their suspicions were soon confirmed. In a shaky but decipherable hand, Robert wrote a note: "I just want to be kept clean."

Robert got a good deal more than he asked for, including the feeding tube, the endoscopy, and the CT scan of the neck. He died within hours of the last of these procedures. His physicians felt that they could not have withheld care without having some idea of what was going on.

In the discourse of contemporary biomedicine, Robert's doctors had been confronted with "a diagnostic dilemma." They had not cast the scenario described above as a moral dilemma but had discussed it in rounds as "a compliance problem." This way of talking about the case brings into relief a number of issues in the contemporary United States—not just in the culture of biomedicine but in the larger culture as well. In anthropology, one of the preferred means of examining culturally salient issues is through ethnology: in this case, we shall compare Robert's death in Boston to death from AIDS in a radically different place.

ANITA AND A DECENT DEATH

The setting is now a small Haitian village. Consisting of fewer than a thousand persons, Do Kay is composed substantially of peasant farmers who were displaced some thirty years ago by Haiti's largest dam. By all the standard measures, Kay is now very poor; its older inhabitants often blame their poverty on the massive buttress dam a few miles away and note bitterly that it has brought them neither electricity nor water.

When the first author of this paper began working in Kay, in May of 1983, the word *SIDA*, meaning AIDS, was just beginning to make its way into the rural Haitian lexicon. Interest in the illness was almost universal less than three years later. It was about then that Anita's intractable cough was attributed to tuberculosis.

Questions about her illness often evoked long responses. She resisted our attempts to focus discussions. "Let me tell you the story from the beginning," she once said; "otherwise you will understand nothing at all."

As a little girl, Anita recalls, she was frightened by the arguments her parents would have in the dry seasons. When her mother began coughing, the family sold their livestock in order to buy "a consultation" with a distinguished doctor in the capital. Tuberculosis, he told them, and the family felt there was little they could do other than take irregular trips to Port au-Prince and make equally irregular attempts to placate the gods who might protect the woman. Anita dropped out of school to help take care of her mother, who died shortly after the girl's thirteenth birthday.

It was very nearly the *coup de grâce* for her father, who became depressed and abusive. Anita, the oldest of five children, bore the brunt of his spleen. "One day, I'd just had it with his yelling. I took what money I could find, about $2, and left for the city. I didn't know where to go." Anita had the good fortune to find a family in need of a maid. The two women in the household had jobs in a U.S.-owned assembly plant; the husband of one ran a snack concession out of the house. Anita received a meal a day, a bit of dry floor to sleep on, and $10 per month for what sounded like incessant labor. She was not unhappy with the arrangement, which lasted until both women were fired for participating in "political meetings."

Anita wandered about for two days until she happened upon a kinswoman selling gum and candies near a downtown theater. She was, Anita related, "a sort of aunt." Anita could come and stay with her, the aunt said, as long as she could help pay the rent. And so Anita moved into Cite Simone, the sprawling slum on the northern fringes of the capital.

It was through the offices of her aunt that she met Vincent, one of the few men in the neighborhood with anything resembling a job: "He unloaded the whites' luggage at the airport." Vincent made a living from tourists' tips. In 1982, the year before Haiti became associated, in the North American press, with AIDS, the city of Port-au-Prince counted tourism as its chief industry. In the setting of an unemployment rate of greater than 60 percent, Vincent could command considerable respect. He turned his attention to Anita. "What could I do, really? He had a good job. My aunt thought I should go with him." Anita was not yet fifteen when she entered her first and only sexual union. Her lover set her up in a shack in the same neighborhood. Anita cooked and washed and waited for him.

When Vincent fell ill, Anita again became a nurse. It began insidiously, she recalls: night sweats, loss of appetite, swollen lymph nodes. Then came months of unpredictable and debilitating diarrhea. "We tried everything—doctors, charlatans, herbal remedies, injections, prayers." After a year of decline, she took Vincent to his hometown in the south of Haiti. There it was revealed that Vincent's illness was the result of malign magic: "It was one of the men at the airport who did this to him. The man wanted Vincent's job. He sent an AIDS death to him."

The voodoo priest who heard their story and deciphered the signs was straightforward. He told Anita and Vincent's family that the sick man's chances were slim, even with the appropriate interventions. There were, however, steps to be taken. He outlined them, and the family followed them, but still Vincent succumbed. "When he died, I felt spent. I couldn't get out of bed. I thought that his family would try to help me to get better, but they didn't. I knew I needed to go home."

She made it as far as Croix-des-Bouquets, a large market town at least two hours from Kay. There she collapsed, feverish and coughing, and was taken in by a woman who lived near the market. She stayed for a month, unable to walk, until her father came to take her back home. Five years had elapsed since she'd last seen him. Anita's father was by then a friendly but broken-down man with a leaking roof over his one-room, dirt-floor hut. It was no place for a sick woman, the villagers said, and Anita's godmother, honoring twenty-year-old vows, made room in her overcrowded but dry house.

Anita was diagnosed as having tuberculosis, and she responded to antituberculosis therapy. But six months after the initiation of treatment, she declined rapidly. Convinced that she was indeed taking her medications, we were concerned about AIDS, especially on hearing of the death of her lover. Anita's father was poised to sell his last bit of land in order to "buy more nourishing food for the child." It was imperative that the underlying cause of Anita's poor response to treatment be found. A laboratory test confirmed our suspicions.

Anita's father and godmother alone were apprised of the test results. When asked what she knew about AIDS, the godmother responded, "AIDS is an infectious disease that has no cure. You can get it from the blood of an infected person." For this reason, she said, she had nothing to fear in caring for Anita. Further, she was adamant that Anita not be told of her diagnosis—"That will only make her suffer more"—and skeptical about the value of the AIDS clinic in Port-au-Prince. "Why should we take her there?" asked Anita's godmother wearily. "She will not recover from this disease. She will have to endure the heat and humiliation of the clinic. She will not find a cool place to lie down. What she might find is a pill or an injection to make her feel more comfortable for a short time. I can do better than that."

And that is what Anita's godmother proceeded to do. She attempted to sit Anita up every day and encouraged her to drink a broth promised to "make her better." The godmother kept her as clean as possible, consecrating the family's two sheets to her goddaughter. She gave Anita her pillow and stuffed a sack with rags for herself. The only thing she requested from us at the clinic was "a beautiful soft wool blanket that will not irritate the child's skin."

In one of several thoughtful interviews accorded us, Anita's godmother insisted that "for some people, a decent death is as important as a decent life. . . . The child has had a hard life; her life has always been difficult. It's important that she be washed of bitterness and regret before she dies." Anita was herself very philosophic in her last months. She seemed to know of her diagnosis. Although she never mentioned the word *SIDA*, she did speak of the resignation appropriate to "diseases from which you cannot escape." She stated, too, that she was "dying from the sickness that took Vincent," although she denied that she had been the victim of witchcraft—"I simply caught it from him."

Anita did not ask to be taken to a hospital, nor did her slow decline occasion any request for further diagnostic tests. What she most wanted was a radio—"for the news and the music"—and a lambswool blanket. She especially enjoyed the opportunity to "recount my life," and we were able to listen to her narrative until hours before her death.

AIDS IN CULTURAL CONTEXT

The way in which a person, a family, or a community responds to AIDS may reveal a great deal about core cultural values. Robert's story underlines our reliance on technological answers to moral and medical questions. "Americans love machines more than life itself," asserts author Philip Slater in a compelling analysis of middle-class North American culture. "Any challenge to the technological-over-social priority threatens to expose the fact that Americans have lost their manhood and their capacity to control their environment."[3] One of the less noticed but perhaps one of the farthest-reaching consequences of the AIDS epidemic has been the weakening of North America's traditional confidence in the ability of its experts to solve every kind of problem. In the words of one person with the disorder, "The terror of AIDS lies in the collapse of our faith in technology."[4]

This core cultural value is nowhere more evident than in contemporary tertiary medicine, which remains the locus of care for the vast majority of AIDS patients. Despite the uniformity of treatment outcome, despite the lack of proven efficacy of many diagnostic and therapeutic procedures, despite their high costs, it has been difficult for practitioners to limit their recourse to these interventions. "When you're at Disney World," remarked one of Robert's physicians ironically, "you take all the rides."

Robert's illness raises issues that turn about questions of autonomy and accountability. The concept of autonomous individuals who are solely responsible for their fate, including their illness, is a powerful cultural premise in North American society. On the positive side, this concept supports concern for individual rights and respect for individual differences and achievement. A more ominous aspect of this core cultural orientation is that it often justifies blaming the victims. Illness is said to be the outcome of the free choice of high-risk behavior.

This has been especially true in the AIDS epidemic, which has reified an invidious distinction between "innocent victims"—infants and hemophiliacs—and, by implication, "the guilty"—persons with AIDS who are homosexuals or intravenous drug users. Robert's lonely and medicalized death is what so many North Americans fear: "He was terrified. He knew what AIDS meant. He knew what happens. Your friends desert you, your lover kicks you out into the street. You get fired, you get evicted from your apartment. You're a leper. You die alone."[5] The conflation of correlation and responsibility has the effect of making sufferers feel guilt and shame. The validity of their experience is contested. Suffering; once delegitimated, is complicated and even distorted; our response to the sufferer, blocked.

In contrast, in Haiti and in many African and Asian societies, where individual rights are often underemphasized and also frequently unprotected, and where the idea of personal accountability is less powerful than is the idea of the primacy of social relationships, blaming the victim is also a less frequent response to AIDS. Noticeably absent is the revulsion with which AIDS patients have been faced in the United States, in both clinical settings and in their communities. This striking difference cannot be ascribed to Haitian ignorance of modes of transmission. On the contrary, the Haitians we have interviewed have ideas of etiology and epidemiology that reflect the incursion of the "North American ideology" of AIDS—that the disease is caused by a virus and is somehow related to homosexuality and contaminated blood. These are subsumed, however, in properly Haitian beliefs about illness causation. Long before the advent of AIDS to Do Kay, we might have asked the following question: some fatal diseases are known to be caused by "microbes" but may also be "sent" by someone; is *SIDA* such a disease?

Differences in the responses of caregivers to Robert and Anita—such as whether to inform them of their diagnosis or undertake terminal care as a family or a community responsibility—also reflect the egocentered orientation in North American cities and the more sociocentric orientation in the Haitian village. An ironic twist is that it is in the impersonal therapeutic setting of North American health-care institutions that concern for the patient's personhood is articulated. It is, however, a cool bioethical attention to abstract individual rights rather than a validation of humane responses to concrete existential needs. Perhaps this cultural logic—of medicine as technology, of individual autonomy as the most inviolable of rights, and so of individuals as responsible for most of the ills that befall them—helps us to understand how Robert's lonely death, so rich in all the technology applied to his last hours, could be so poor in all those supportive human virtues that resonate from the poverty-stricken village where Anita died among friends.

A core clinical task would seem to be helping patients to die a decent death. For all the millions of words spilled on the denial of death in our society and the various psychotechniques advertised to aid us to overcome this societal silence, AIDS testifies vividly that our secular public culture is simply unable to come to terms with mortality.

A final question might be asked in examining the stories of Robert and Anita: just how representative are they of the millions already exposed to HIV? As a middle-class, white gay male, Robert is thought by many to be a "typical victim of AIDS." But he is becoming increasingly less typical in the United States, where the epidemic is claiming more and more blacks and Hispanics, and Robert would not be sociologically representative of the typical AIDS patient in much of the rest of the world. In many Third World settings, sex differences in the epidemiology of HIV infection are unremarkable: in Haiti, for example, there is almost parity between the sexes. Most importantly, most people with AIDS are not middle-class and insured. All this points to the fact that the virus that causes AIDS might exact its greatest toll in the Third World.

AIDS IN GLOBAL CONTEXT

Although the pandemic appears to be most serious in North America and Europe, per capita rates reveal that fully seventeen of the twenty countries most affected by AIDS are in Africa or the Caribbean. Further, although there is heartening evidence that the epidemic is being more effectively addressed in the North American gay community, there is no indication that the spread of HIV has been curbed in the communities in which women like Anita struggle. Although early reports of high HIV seroprevalence were clearly based on faulty research, even recent and revised estimates remain grim: "In urban areas in some sub-Saharan countries, up to 25% of young adults are *already* HIV carriers, with rates among those reporting to clinics for sexually transmitted diseases passing 30%, and among female prostitutes up to 90%."[6] In other words, the countries most affected are precisely those that can least afford it.

These figures also remind us that AIDS has felled many like Anita—the poor, women of color, victims of many sorts of oppression and misfortune. Although heterosexual contact seems to be the means of spreading in many instances, not all who contract the disease are "promiscuous," a label that has often offended people in Africa, Haiti, and elsewhere. *Promiscuous* fails utterly to capture the dilemmas of millions like Anita. In an essay entitled "The Myth of African Promiscuity," one Kenyan scholar refers to the "'new poor': the massive pool of young women living in the most deprived conditions in shanty towns and slums across Africa, who are available for the promise of a meal, new clothes, or a few pounds."[7]

Equally problematic, and of course related, is the term *prostitute*. It is often used indiscriminately to refer to a broad spectrum of sexual activity. In North America, the label has been misused in investigations of HIV seroprevalence: "the category *prostitute* is taken as an undifferentiated 'risk group' rather than as an occupational category whose members should, for epidemiological purposes, be divided into IV drug users and nonusers—with significantly different rates of HIV infection—as other groups are."[8] A more historical view reminds us that prostitutes have often been victims of scapegoating and that there has long been more energy for investigation of the alleged moral shortcomings of sex workers than for the economic underpinnings of their work.

The implications of this sort of comparative exercise, which remains a cornerstone of social anthropology, are manifold. The differences speak directly to those who would apply imported models of prevention to rural Haiti or Africa or any other Third World setting. A substantial public-health literature, reflecting the fundamentally interventionist perspective of that discipline, is inarguably necessary in the midst of an epidemic without cure or promising treatment. The same must be true for the burgeoning biomedical literature on AIDS. But with what consequences have these disciplines ignored the issue of AIDS as suffering? Whether reduced to parasite–host interactions or to questions of shifting incidence and prevalence among risk groups, AIDS has meant suffering on a large scale, and this suffering is not captured in these expert discourses on the epidemic.

The meaning of suffering in this context is distinctive not only on account of different beliefs about illness and treatment responses but because of the brute reality of grinding poverty, high child and maternal mortality, routinized demoralization and oppression, and suffering as a central part of existence. The response to AIDS in such settings must deal with this wider context of human misery and its social sources. Surely it is unethical—in the broadest sense, if not in the narrow technical biomedical limits to the term—for international health experts to turn their backs on the suffering of people with AIDS in the Third World and to concentrate solely on the prevention of new cases.

DEALING WITH AIDS AS SUFFERING

To what practical suggestions does a view of AIDS as human suffering lead?

Suffering Compounded by Inappropriate Use of Resources

The majority of all medical-care costs for AIDS patients is generated by acute inpatient care. In many ways, however, infection with HIV is more like a chronic disease. Based on cases of transfusion-associated HIV transmission in the United States, the mean time between exposure to the virus and the development of AIDS is over eight years. This period may well be lengthened by drugs already available. And as the medical profession becomes more skilled at managing the AIDS condition, the average time of survival of patients with the full-blown syndrome will also be extended. For many with AIDS, outpatient treatment will be both more cost-effective and more humane. For the terminally ill, home or hospice care may be preferred to acute-care settings, especially for people who "just want to be kept clean." Helping patients to die a decent death was once an accepted aspect of the work of health professionals. It must be recognized and appropriately supported as a core clinical task in the care of persons with AIDS.

Not a small component of humane care for people with AIDS is soliciting their stories of sickness, listening to their narratives of the illness, so as to help them give meaning to their suffering. Restoring this seemingly forgotten healing skill will require a transformation in the work and training of practitioners and a reorganization of time and objectives in health-care delivery systems.

The practitioner should initiate informed negotiation with alternative lay perspectives on care and provide what amounts to brief medical psychotherapy for the threats and losses that make chronic illness so difficult to bear. But such a transformation in the provision of care will require a significant shift in the allocation of resources, including a commitment to funding psychosocial services as well as appropriate providers—visiting nurses, home health aides, physical and occupational therapists, general practitioners, and other members of teams specializing in long-term, outpatient care.

Suffering Magnified by Discrimination

In a recent study of the U.S. response to AIDS, the spread of HIV was compared to that of polio, another virus that struck young people, triggered public panic, and received regular attention in the popular media. "Although these parallels are strong," notes the author, "one difference is crucial: there was little early sympathy for victims of AIDS because those initially at risk—homosexual men, Haitian immigrants, and drug addicts—were not in the mainstream of society. In contrast, sympathy for polio patients was extensive."[9] This lack of sympathy is part of a spectrum that extends to hostility and even violence, and that has led to discrimination in housing, employment, insurance, and the granting of visas.[10] The victims of such discrimination have been not only people with AIDS or other manifestations of HIV infection but those thought to be in "risk groups."

In some cases, these prejudices are only slightly muted in clinical settings. In our own experience in U.S. hospitals, there is markedly more sympathy for those referred to as "the innocent victims"—patients with transfusion-associated AIDS and HIV-infected babies. At other times, irrational infection-control precautions do little more than heighten patients' feelings of rejection. Blame and recrimination are reactions to the diseases in rural Haiti as well—but there the finger is not often pointed at those with the disease.

Although the President's Commission on AIDS called for major coordinated efforts to address discrimination, what has been done has been desultory, unsystematic, and limited in reach. While legislation is crucial, so too is the development of public-education programs that address discrimination and suffering.

Suffering Augmented by Fear

Underlying at least some of the discrimination, spite, and other inappropriate responses to AIDS is fear. We refer not to the behavior-modifying fear of "the worried well" but to the more visceral fear that has played so prominent a role in the epidemic. It is fear that prompts someone to refuse to get into a taxi driven by a Haitian man; it is fear that leads a reporter to wrench her hand from that of a person with AIDS; it is fear that underpins some calls for widespread HIV-antibody testing, and fear that has led some health professionals to react to patients in degrading fashion. The fact that so much of this fear is "irrational" has thus far had little bearing on its persistence.

Dissemination of even a few key facts—by people with AIDS, leaders of local communities, elected officials and other policy-makers, teachers, and health professionals—should help to assuage fear. HIV is transmitted through parenteral, mucous-membrane, or open-wound contact with contaminated blood or body fluids and not through casual contact. Although the risk of transmission of HIV to health-care professionals is not zero, it is extremely low, even after percutaneous exposure (studies show that, of more than 1,300 exposed health-care workers, only four seroconverted[11]).

Suffering Amplified by Social Death

In several memoirs published in North America, persons with AIDS have complained of the immediate social death their diagnosis has engendered. "For some of my friends and family, I was dead as soon as they heard I had AIDS," a community activist informed us. "That was over two years ago." Even asymptomatic but seropositive individuals, whose life expectancy is often better than that of persons with most cancers and many common cardiovascular disorders, have experienced this reaction. Many North Americans with AIDS have made it clear that they do not wish to be referred to as victims: "As a person with AIDS," writes Navarre, "I can attest to the sense of diminishment at seeing and hearing myself referred to as an AIDS victim, an AIDS sufferer, an AIDS case—as anything but what I am, a person with AIDS. I am a person with a condition. I am not that condition."[12]

It is nonetheless necessary to plan humane care for persons with a chronic and deadly disease—"without needlessly assaulting my denial," as a young man recently put it. The very notion of hospice care will need rethinking if its intended clients are a group of young and previously vigorous persons. Similarly, our cross-cultural research has shown us that preferred means of coping with a fatal disease are shaped by biography and culture. There are no set "stages" that someone with AIDS will go through, and there can be no standard professional response.

Suffering Generated by Inequities

AIDS is caused, we know, by a retrovirus. But we need not look to Haiti to see that inequities have sculpted the AIDS epidemic. The disease, it has been aptly noted, "moves along the fault lines of our society."[13] Of all infants born with AIDS in the United States, approximately 80 percent are black or Hispanic.[14] Most of these are the children of IV drug users, and attempts to stem the virus may force us to confront substance abuse in the context of our own society. For as Robert Gallo and Luc Montagnier assert, "efforts to control AIDS must be aimed in part at eradicating the conditions that give rise to drug addiction."[15]

There are inequities in the way we care for AIDS patients. In the hospital where Robert died, AZT—the sole agent with proven efficacy in treating HIV infection—is not on formulary. Patients needing the drug who are not in a research protocol have to send someone to the drugstore to buy it—if they happen to have the $10,000 per year AZT can cost or an insurance policy that covers these costs. Such factors may prove important in explaining the striking ethnic differences in average time of survival following diagnosis of AIDS. In one report it was noted that, "while the average lifespan of a white person after diagnosis is two years, the average minority person survives only 19 weeks."[16]

From rural Haiti, it is not the local disparities but rather the international inequities that are glaring. In poor countries, drugs like AZT are simply not available. As noted above, the AIDS pandemic is most severe in the countries that can least afford a disaster of these dimensions. A view of AIDS as human suffering forces us to lift our eyes from local settings to the true dimensions of this worldwide tragedy.

Compassionate involvement with persons who have AIDS may require listening carefully to their stories, whether narratives of suffering or simply attempts to recount their lives. Otherwise, as Anita pointed out, we may understand nothing at all.

NOTES

1. The first three of the four quotations cited here are the voices of persons with AIDS who attended the Third International Conference on AIDS, held in Washington, D.C. in June 1987. Their comments are published passim in 4 (1) (Winter/ Spring 1988) of *New England Journal of Public Policy*. All subsequent unreferenced quotations are from tape-recorded interviews accorded the first author.
2. All informants' names are pseudonyms, as are "Do Kay" and "Ba Kay." Other geographical designations are as cited.
3. Philip Slater, *The Pursuit of Loneliness: American Culture at the Breaking Point* (Boston: Beacon Press, 1970), 49, 51.
4. Emmanuel Dreuilhe, *Mortal Embrace: Living with AIDS* (New York: Hill and Wang, 1988), 20.
5. George Whitmore, *Someone Was Here: Profiles in the AIDS Epidemic* (New York: New American Library, 1988), 26.
6. Renée Sabatier, *Blaming Others: Prejudice, Race, and Worldwide AIDS* (Philadelphia: New Society Publishers, 1988), 15.
7. Professor Aina, ibid., 80.
8. Jan Zita Grover, "AIDS: Keywords," in *AIDS: Cultural Analysis/Cultural Activism* (Cambridge: MIT Press, 1988), 25–26.
9. Sandra Panem, *The AIDS Bureaucracy* (Cambridge: Harvard University Press, 1988), 15.
10. See Sabatier for an overview of AIDS-related discrimination. As regards Haiti and Haitians, see Paul Farmer, "AIDS and Accusation: Haiti, Haitians, and the Geography of Blame," in *Cultural Aspects of AIDS: Anthropology and the Global Pandemic* (New York: Praeger, in press). The degree of antipathy is suggested by a recent *New York Times*–CBS News poll of 1,606 persons: "Only 36 percent of those interviewed said they had a lot or some sympathy, 'for people who get AIDS from homosexual activity,' and 26 percent said they had a lot or some sympathy 'for people who get AIDS from sharing needles while using illegal drugs'" (*New York Times*, 14 October 1988, A12).
11. Infectious Diseases Society of America, 276.

12. Max Navarre, "Fighting the Victim Label," in *AIDS: Cultural Analysis/Cultural Activism* (Cambridge: MIT Press, 1988), 143.
13. Mary Catherine Bateson and Richard Goldsby, *Thinking AIDS: The Social Response to the Biological Threat* (Reading, Mass.: Addison-Wesley, 1988), 2.
14. Samuel Friedman, Jo Sotheran, Abu Abdul-Quadar, Beny Primm, Don Des Jarlais, Paula Kleinman, Conrad Mauge, Douglas Goldsmith, Wafaa El-Sadr, and Robert Maslansky, "The AIDS Epidemic among Blacks and Hispanics," *The Milbank Quarterly* 65, suppl. 2 (1987): 455–99.
15. Robert Gallo and Luc Montagnier, "AIDS in 1988," *Scientific American* 259 (4) (October 1988):48.
16. Sabatier, 19.

Gender and Health

CONCEPTUAL TOOLS

■ ***Gender and sex are different categories.*** In general, anthropologists use the term *sex* to refer to biologically based differences between men and women, and *gender* to refer to the more important and more pervasive social, cultural, economic, and political differences between men and women. Gender is a cultural construct, and cultural ideas about women's health and women's bodies differ from social group to social group and across historical periods. There are biomedical consequences to the cultural constructions of gender differences. Prevalence of disease is often different for women and men, not because of biology but because of differential access to resources or exposure to both social and epidemiological stressors. There are also problems of underreporting and underrecognition of some diseases, like heart disease, in women. Gender issues do not only pertain to women; male gender rules and expectations are also culturally constructed. This may be why men have lower life expectancies than women at every age and in every country reporting vital statistics to the World Health Organization (WHO). There is little doubt that gender roles affect health.

■ ***Women's reproductive health represents an important and widely studied area of medical anthropology.*** Historically, the study of women had been neglected in the field of anthropology, but this situation has changed in recent decades (Morgen 1989). Feminist perspectives (a type of critical theory) have made major contributions to our understanding of health and medical systems. Women's reproductive health issues include a wide variety of concerns, including obstetric practice in childbirth and the risk of maternal mortality; cultural beliefs about menstruation and health, diet, infertility, abortion, contraception, and menopause (Sargent and Brettell 1996). An important critique of the literature on women's health is that women have been "essentialized" as reproducers—their most essential characteristic has been their ability to reproduce. Consequently, women's health is equated with reproductive health, and other aspects of health are underemphasized.

■ ***There is little research on what women themselves deem to be their health concerns.*** There is little research based on what *women* have identified as their health problems. In general, the identification of women's health problems has not come from women themselves. We know even less about the health issues, concerns, and experiences of women who are not white and not middle class. There has been very little research examining the intersection of gender, race, class, age, sexual orientation, religion, and women's health. This absence of women's perspective is particulary ironic in that women are very often the "producers of health"—in other words, women are in charge of health issues on the household level.

■ ***New reproductive technologies, such as in vitro fertilization, represent interesting case studies of the process of medicalization.*** Medical anthropologists have documented enduring sexism in biomedicine, most often in the field of obstetrics (Hahn 1987). Historically, biomedicine has medicalized and often pathologized normal physiological processes, like pregnancy, childbirth, and breast-feeding. Normal stages in women's reproductive life cycle are turned into diseases. For example, "moodiness" around the time of the period becomes "PMS," which in turn becomes a psychiatric condition. Male medical authority has been allowed to define women's bodies and their health, and women's lives—especially their reproductive lives—have increasingly come under medical control.

■ ***The language of biomedicine and the speech of biomedical practitioners can demonstrate power relations.*** Medical anthropologists studying biomedicine are interested in issues of power relations, and power differentials are often involved in interactions between men and women. We can see this, for example, in the case of doctor–patient interactions in which male physicians may intimidate female patients in the course of giving instructions on health care. Medical arguments on women's health are often political or moral discussions (discourses) in the guise of health issues. For example, a recent study of beliefs about cervical cancer showed a marked difference between the Latina immigrants' beliefs and those of their physicians, who viewed cervical cancer as a consequence of immorality and "promiscuity" (Martinez, Chavez, and Hubbell 1997).

- ***Women's health is politicized.*** Women's health is often the site of political struggle. The most notable example, of course, is the continuing debate over abortion (Ginsburg 1989). Among the many other issues is the targeting of poor women in international birth control and population control efforts.

- ***Men have gender too, and this affects their health.*** Sometimes the word *gender* in medical anthropology has referred only to issues of women's health. In this regard, male gender and the health impacts of masculinity have not been studied thoroughly. Males die younger than women. Among other things, men have higher rates of alcohol abuse, suicide, road traffic fatalities, and death from violence.

 **41**

Medical Metaphors of Women's Bodies: Menstruation and Menopause

Emily Martin

This selection explores the cultural and historical underpinnings of medical knowledge about women's bodies and medical authority over women. Emily Martin's approach fits within epistemologically oriented critical medical anthropology (as in selection 21). Her approach critically examines the cultural assumptions as they developed and as they are used in a field of expertise—biomedicine. This type of analysis is more typical of the work by humanities scholars (more specifically, cultural studies) largely because it focuses on the underlying conditions of the discourse, *particularly the written communication of experts. This selection is part of Martin's book* The Woman in the Body: A Cultural Analysis of Reproduction *(1987). Because it is historical in its orientation, the primary sources of evidence in this analysis are texts (and textbooks) of medical knowledge.*

Feminist critiques like this one powerfully remind us of the processes through which objective facts are, in actuality, culturally constructed. Ethnographic studies of scientists in their laboratories and "doing science" have demonstrated that this production of knowledge is not value-neutral or culturally neutral; the studies of laboratory scientists (Latour 1986) are very much like the ethnographic studies of medical doctors working in clinics (Hahn and Gaines 1985) in that metaphors and stories are often used for communicating local cultural knowledge. The feminist analysis here demonstrates how the use of language and particular metaphors can influence how women are treated. Metaphors are shorthand for ways of thinking; they reflect implicit understandings among members of a social group. Metaphors, therefore, have real and practical implications for social relations, and these are important considering our previous readings on suffering and stigma.

Why are both menopause and menstruation considered pathological, or at least described with negative metaphors? Emily Martin traces these ideas to a more general medical metaphor of the body as a machine or a factory. The "product" of a female factory is a baby. As a factory, the body is organized with a centralized information system, and failure to follow the master plan must be seen as disorganization.

In a very readable book comparing medical beliefs in Germany, France, Britain, and the United States, Lynn Payer (1988) describes the U.S. ethnomedical system as being based on the metaphor of the body as a machine. It was for this reason, she argues, that U.S. biomedical researchers thought it feasible to build a mechanical heart, whereas European biomedical researchers saw this effort as folly. The idea is that the cultural metaphor of the machine with replaceable parts allowed and encouraged a type of habitual thinking. In the same way, gender-related metaphors in biomedical discourse encourage specific treatment of women.

As you read this selection, consider these questions:

- **In what types of metaphors are women "essentialized" as reproducers from the biomedical viewpoint?**
- **Is it possible for this type of analysis to fit with the evolutionary medical analyses introduced in the first part of this book?**
- **Is the use of negative metaphors in texts a male plot? Or do women themselves incorporate these cultural models in their discourse and thinking?**
- **How might this analysis fit with the creation of premenstrual syndrome as a pathology?**

Context: Emily Martin is a cultural and medical anthropologist who, for many years, has conducted ethnographic fieldwork on a variety of issues in China and Taiwan. Drawing on this breadth of experience, Martin has also become well known for her feminist analyses of biomedicine in which she exposes cultural biases in (supposedly objective) scientific texts about human reproduction and women's bodies. This article is a classic example of this latter work, drawing upon long-standing sociolinguistic theories about the ways that our use of language can shape human attitudes toward different kinds of people and their health states, ideas that began with the work of Benjamin Lee Whorf. Similar approaches can be found in Susan Sontag's *Illness as Metaphor* (1978) or George Lakoff and Mark Johnson's more general work on metaphors and human categories (1980).

Source: E. Martin (1988). "Medical Metaphors of Women's Bodies: Menstruation and Menopause." *International Journal of Health Services* 18(2):237–254.

It is difficult to see how our current scientific ideas are infused by cultural assumptions; it is easier to see how scientific ideas from the past, ideas that now seem wrong or too simple, might have been affected by cultural ideas of an earlier time. To lay the groundwork for a look at contemporary scientific views of menstruation and menopause, I begin with the past.

It was an accepted notion in medical literature from the ancient Greeks until the late 18th century that male and female bodies were structurally similar. As Nemesius, Bishop of Emesa, Syria, in the fourth century, put it, "women have the same genitals as men, except that theirs are inside the body and not outside it." Although increasingly detailed anatomical understanding (such as the discovery of the nature of the ovaries in the last half of the 17th century) changed the details, medical scholars from Galen in second-century Greece to Harvey in 17th-century Britain all assumed that women's internal organs were structurally analogous to men's external ones.[1]

Although the genders were structurally similar, they were not equal. For one thing, what could be seen of men's bodies was assumed as the pattern for what could not be seen of women's. For another, just as humans as a species possessed more "heat" than other animals and hence were considered more perfect, so men possessed more "heat" than women and hence were considered more perfect. The relative coolness of the female prevented her reproductive organs from extruding outside the body but, happily for the species, kept them inside where they provided a protected place for conception and gestation.[1, p. 10]

During the centuries when male and female bodies were seen as composed of analogous structures, a connected set of metaphors was used to convey how the parts of male and female bodies functioned. These metaphors were dominant in classical medicine and continued to operate through the 19th century:[2, p. 5]

> The body was seen, metaphorically, as a system of dynamic interactions with its environment. Health or disease resulted from a cumulative interaction between constitutional endowment and environmental circumstance. One could not well live without food and air and water; one had to live in a particular climate, subject one's body to a particular style of life and work. Each of these factors implied a necessary and continuing physiological adjustment. The body was always in a state of becoming—and thus always in jeopardy.

Two subsidiary assumptions governed this interaction: first, that "every part of the body was related inevitably and inextricably with every other," and second, that "the body was seen as a system of intake and outgo—a system which had, necessarily, to remain in balance if the individual were to remain healthy."[2, pp. 5–6]

Given these assumptions, changes in the relationship of body functions occurred constantly throughout life, though more acutely at some times than at others. In Edward Tilt's influential mid-19th century account, for example, after the menopause, blood that once flowed out of the body as menstruation was then turned into fat:[3, p. 54]

> Fat accumulates in women after the change of life, as it accumulates in animals from whom the ovaries have been removed. The withdrawal of the sexual stimulus from the ganglionic nervous system, enables it to turn into fat and self-aggrandisement that blood which might otherwise have perpetuated the race.

During the transition to menopause, or the "dodging time," the blood cannot be turned into fat, so it was either discharged as hemorrhage or through other compensating mechanisms, the most important of which was "the flush":[3, pp. 54, 57]

> As for thirty-two years it had been habitual for women to lose about 3 oz. of blood every month, so it would have been indeed singular, if there did not exist some well-continued compensating discharges acting as wastegates to protect the system, until health could be permanently re-established by striking new balances in the allotment of blood to the various parts. . . . The flushes determine the perspirations. Both evidence a strong effect of conservative power, and as they constitute the most important and habitual safety-valve of the system at the change of life, it is worth while studying them.

In this account, compensating mechanisms such as the "flush" are seen as having the positive function of keeping intake and outgo in balance.

These balancing acts had exact analogues in men. In Hippocrates' view of purification, one that was still current in the 17th century,[4, p. 50]

> women were of a colder and less active disposition than men, so that while men could sweat in order to remove the impurities from their blood, the colder dispositions of women did not allow them to be purified in that way. Females menstruated to rid their bodies of impurities.

Or in another view, expounded by Galen in the second century and still accepted in the 18th century, menstruation was the shedding of an excess of blood, a plethora:[4, p. 50] But what women did through menstruation men could do in other ways such as by having blood let.[5] In either view of the mechanism of menstruation process itself not only had analogues in men, it was seen as inherently health maintaining. Menstrual blood, to be sure, was often seen as foul and unclean[4, p. 50] but the process of excreting it was not intrinsically pathological. In fact, failure to excrete was taken as a sign of disease, and a great variety of remedies existed even into the 19th century specifically to reestablish menstrual flow if it stopped.[6]

By 1800, according to Laqueur's important recent study, this long-established tradition that saw male and female bodies as similar both in structure and in function began to come "under devastating attack. Writers of all sorts were determined to base what they insisted were fundamental differences between male and female sexuality and thus between man and woman, on discoverable biological distinctions."[1] Laqueur argues that this attempt to ground differences between the genders in biology grew out of the crumbling of old ideas about the existing order of politics and society as laid down by the order of nature. In the old ideas, men dominated the public world and the world of morality and order by virtue of their greater perfection, a result of their excess heat. Men and women were arranged in a hierarchy in which they differed by degree of heat. They were not different in kind.[1, p. 8]

The new liberal claims of Hobbes and Locke in the 17th century and the French revolution were factors that led to a loss of certainty that the social order could be grounded in the natural order. If the social order were merely convention, it could not provide a secure enough basis to hold women and men in their places. But after 1800 the social and biological sciences were brought to the rescue of male superiority. "Scientists in areas as diverse as zoology, embryology, physiology, heredity, anthropology, and psychology had little difficulty in proving that the pattern of male-female relations that characterized the English middle classes was natural, inevitable, progressive."[7, p. 180]

The assertion was that men's and women's social roles themselves were grounded in nature, by virtue of the dictates of their bodies. In the words of one 19th century theorist:[7, p. 190]

> the attempt to alter the present relations of the sexes is not a rebellion against some arbitrary law instituted by a despot or a majority—not an attempt to break the yoke of a mere convention; it is a struggle against Nature; a war undertaken to reverse the very conditions under which not man alone, but all mammalian species have reached their present development.

The doctrine of the two spheres—men as workers in the public, wage-earning sphere outside the home and women (except for the lower classes) as wives and mothers in the private, domestic sphere of kinship and morality inside the home—replaced the old hierarchy based on body heat.

During the latter part of the 19th century, new metaphors that posited fundamental differences between the sexes began to appear. One 19th century biologist, Patrick Geddes, perceived two opposite kinds of processes at the level of the cell "upbuilding, constructive, synthetic processes" summed up as anabolism, "disruptive, descending series of chemical changes" summed up as katabolism.[8] The relationship between the two terms was described in frankly economic terms:[8, p. 133]

> The processes of income and expenditure must balance, but only to the usual extent, that expenditure must not altogether outrun income, else the cell's capital of living matter will be lost—a fate which is often not successfully avoided. . . . Just as our expenditure and income should balance at the year's end, but may vastly outstrip each other at particular times, so it is with the cell of the body. Income too may continuously preponderate, and we increase in wealth, or similarly, in weight, or in anabolism. Conversely, expenditure may predominate, but business may be prosecuted at a loss; and similarly, we may live on for a while with loss of weight, or in katabolism. This losing game of life is what we call a katabolic habit.

Geddes saw these processes not only at the level of the cell, but also at the level of entire organisms. In the human species, as well as almost all higher animals, females were predominantly anabolic, males katabolic. Although in the terms of his saving–spending metaphor it is not at all clear whether katabolism would be an asset, when Geddes presents male-female differences, there is no doubt which he thought preferable:[8, pp. 270–271]

> It is generally true that the males are more active, energetic, eager, passionate, and variable; the females more passive, conservative, sluggish, and stable. . . . The more active males, with a consequently wider range of experience, may have bigger brains and more intelligence; but the females, especially as mothers, have indubitably a larger and more habitual share of the altruistic emotions. The males being usually stronger, have greater independence and courage; the females excel in constancy of affection and in sympathy.

In Geddes, the doctrine of separate spheres was laid on a foundation of separate and fundamentally different biology in men and women, at the level of the cell. One of the striking contradictions in his account is that he did not carry over the implications of his economic metaphors to his discussion of male-female differences. If he had, females might have come off as wisely conserving their energy and never spending beyond their means, males as in the "losing game of life," letting expenditures outrun income.

Geddes may have failed to draw the logical conclusions from his metaphor, but we have to acknowledge that metaphors were never meant to be logical. Other 19th century writers developed metaphors in exactly opposite directions: women spent and men saved. The Reverend John Todd saw women as voracious spenders in the marketplace, and so consumers of all that a man could earn. If unchecked, a woman would ruin a man, by her own extravagant spending, by her demands on him to spend, or in another realm, by her excessive demands on him for sex. Losing too much sperm meant losing that which sperm was believed to manufacture: a man's lifeblood.[9]

Todd and Geddes were not alone in the 19th century in using images of business loss and gain to describe physiological processes. Susan Sontag has suggested that 19th century fantasies about disease, especially tuberculosis, "echo the attitudes of early capitalist accumulation. One has a limited amount of energy, which must be properly spent. . . . Energy, like savings, can be depleted, can run out or be used up, through reckless expenditure. The body will start 'consuming' itself, the patient will 'waste away.'"[10, pp. 61–62]

Despite the variety of ways that spending–saving metaphors could be related to gender, the radical difference between these metaphors and the earlier intake–outgo metaphor is key. Whereas in the earlier model, male and female ways of secreting were not only analogous but desirable, now the way became open to denigrate, as Geddes overtly did, functions that for the first time were seen as uniquely female, without analogue in males. For our purposes, what happened to accounts of menstruation is most interesting: by the 19th century, the process itself is seen as soundly pathological. In Geddes' terms,[8, p. 244]

> it yet evidently lies on the borders of pathological change, as is evidenced not only by the pain which so frequently accompanies it, and the local and constitutional disorders which so frequently arise in this connection, but by the general systemic disturbance and local histological changes of which the discharge is merely the outward expression and result.

Whereas in earlier accounts the blood itself may have been considered impure, now the process itself is seen as a disorder.

Nineteenth century writers were extremely prone to stress the debilitating nature of menstruation and its adverse impact on the lives and activities of women.[11] Medical images of menstruation as pathological were remarkably vivid by the end of the century. For Walter Heape, the militant anti-suffragist and Cambridge zoologist, in menstruation the entire epithelium was torn away, "leaving behind a ragged wreck of tissue, torn glands, ruptured vessels, jagged edges of stroma, and masses of blood corpuscles, which it would seem hardly possible to heal satisfactorily without the aid of surgical treatment.[1, p. 32] A few years later, Havelock Ellis could see women as being "periodically wounded" in their most sensitive spot and "emphasize the fact that even in the healthiest woman, a worm however harmless and unperceived, gnaws periodically at the roots of life."[12, p. 284]

If menstruation was consistently seen as pathological, menopause, another function which by this time was regarded as without analogue in men, often was too: many 19th century medical accounts of menopause saw it as a crisis likely to bring on an increase of disease.[11, pp. 30–31] Sometimes the metaphor of the body as a small business that is either winning or losing was applied to menopause too. A late 19th century account specifically argued against Tilt's earlier adjustment model: "When the period of fruitfulness is ended the activity of the tissues has reached its culmination, the secreting power of the glandular organs begins to diminish, the epithelium becomes less sensitive and less susceptible to infectious influences, and atrophy and degeneration take the place of the active up-building processes."[13, pp. 25–26] But there were other sides to the picture. Most practitioners felt the "climacteric disease," a more general disease of old age, was far worse for men than for women. And some regarded the period after menopause far more positively than it is being seen medically in our century, as the "'Indian summer' of a woman's life—a period of increased vigor, optimism, and even of physical beauty."[11, p. 30]

Perhaps the 19th century's concern with conserving energy and limiting expenditure can help account for the seeming anomaly of at least some positive medical views of menopause and the climacteric. As an early 20th century popular health account put it:[14, p. 413]

> [Menopause] is merely a conservative process of nature to provide for a higher and more stable phase of existence, an economic lopping off of a function no longer needed, preparing the individual for different forms of activity, but is in no sense pathologic. It is not sexual or physical decrepitude, but belongs to the age of invigoration, marking the fullness of the bodily and mental powers.

Those few writers who saw menopause as an "economic" physiological function might have drawn very positive conclusions from Geddes' description of females as anabolic, stressing their "thriftiness" instead of their passivity, their "growing bank accounts" instead of their sluggishness.

If the shift from the body as an intake–outgo system to the body as a small business trying to spend, save, or balance its accounts is a radical one, with deep importance for medical models of female bodies, so too is another shift that began in the 20th century with the development of scientific medicine. One of the early 20th century engineers of our system of scientific medicine, Frederick T. Gates, who advised John D. Rockefeller on how to use his philanthropies to aid scientific medicine, developed a series of interrelated metaphors to explain the scientific view of how the body works:[15, pp. 170–171]

> It is interesting to note the striking comparisons between the human body and the safety and hygienic appliances of a great city. Just as in the streets of a great city we have "white angels" posted everywhere to gather up poisonous materials from the streets, so in the great streets and avenues of the body, namely the arteries and the blood vessels, there are brigades of corpuscles, white in color like the "white angels," whose function it is to gather up into sacks, formed by their own bodies, and disinfect or eliminate all poisonous substances found in the blood. The body has a network of insulated nerves, like telephone wires, which transmit instantaneous alarms at every point of danger. The body is furnished with the most elaborate police system, with hundreds of police stations to which the criminal elements are carried by the police and jailed. I refer to the great numbers of sanitary glands, skillfully placed at points where vicious germs find entrance, especially about the mouth and throat. The body has a most complete and elaborate sewer system. There are wonderful laboratories placed at convenient points for a subtle brewing of skillful medicines. . . . The fact is that the human body is made up of an infinite number of microscopic cells. Each one of these cells is a small chemical laboratory, into which its own appropriate raw material is constantly being introduced, the processes of chemical separation and combination are constantly taking place automatically, and its own appropriate finished product being necessary for the life and health of the body. Not only is this so, but the great organs of the body like the liver, stomach, pancreas, kidneys, gall bladder are great local manufacturing centers, formed of groups of cells in infinite numbers, manufacturing the same sorts of products, just as industries of the same kind are often grouped in specific districts.

Although such a full-blown description of the body as a model of an industrial society is not often found in contemporary accounts of physiology, elements of the images that occurred to Gates are commonplace. In recent years, the "imagery of the biochemistry of the cell [has] been that of the factory, where functions [are] specialized for the conversion of energy into particular products and which [has] its own part to play in the economy of the organism as a whole."[16, p. 58]

Still more recently, economic functions of greater complexity have been added: adenosine triphosphate (ATP) is seen as the body's "energy currency": "Produced in particular cellular regions, it [is] placed in an 'energy bank' in which it [is] maintained in two forms, those of 'current account' and 'deposit account.' Ultimately, the cell's and the body's energy books must balance by an appropriate mix of monetary and fiscal policies."[16, p. 59] Here we have not just the simpler 19th century saving and spending, but two distinct forms of money in the bank, presumably invested at different levels of profit.

Development of the new molecular biology brought additional metaphors based on information science, management and control. In this model, flow of information between deoxyribonucleic acid (DNA) and ribonucleic acid (RNA) leads to the production of protein. Molecular biologists conceive of the cell as "an assembly line factory in which the DNA blueprints are interpreted and raw materials fabricated to produce the protein end products in response to a series of regulated requirements."[16, p. 59] The cell is still seen as a factory, but, compared to Gates' description, there is enormous elaboration of the flow of information from one "department" of the body to another and exaggeration of the amount of control exerted by the center. For example, from a college physiology text:[17, pp. 7–8]

> All the systems of the body, if they are to function effectively, must be subjected to some form of control. . . . The precise control of body function is brought about by means of the operation of the nervous system and of the hormonal or endocrine system. . . . The most important thing to note about any control system is that before it can control anything it must be supplied with information. . . . Therefore the first essential in any control system is an adequate system of collecting information about the state of the body. . . . Once the CNS [central nervous system] knows what is happening, it must then have a means for rectifying the situation if something is going wrong. There are two available methods for doing this, by using nerve fibres and by using hormones. The motor nerve fibers . . . carry instructions from the CNS to the muscles and glands throughout the body. . . . As far as hormones are concerned the brain acts via the pituitary gland . . . the pituitary secretes a large number of hormones . . . the rate of secretion of each one of these is under the direct control of the brain.

Although there is increasing attention to describing physiological processes as positive and negative feedback loops, so that like a thermostat system, no single element has preeminent control over any other, most descriptions of specific processes give preeminent control to the brain, as we will see below.

In over-all descriptions of female reproduction, the dominant image is that of a signaling system. Lein, in a textbook designed for junior colleges, spells it out in detail,[18, p. 14]

> Hormones are chemical signals to which distant tissues or organs are able to respond. Whereas the nervous system has characteristics in common with a telephone network, the endocrine glands perform in a manner somewhat analogous to radio transmission. A radio transmitter may blanket an entire region with its signal, but a response occurs only if a radio receiver is turned on and tuned to the proper frequency . . . the radio receiver in biological systems is a tissue whose cells possess active receptor sites for a particular hormone or hormones.

The signal-response metaphor is found almost universally in current texts for premedical and medical students:[19, p. 885; 20, p. 129; 21, p. 115; emphasis added]

> The hypothalamus *receives signals* from almost all possible sources in the nervous system.
>
> The endometrium *responds directly* to stimulation or withdrawal of estrogen and progesterone. In turn, regulation of the secretion of these steroids involves a well-integrated, highly structured series of activities by the hypothalamus and the anterior lobe of the pituitary. Although the ovaries do not function autonomously, they *influence*, through *feedback* mechanisms, the level of performance *programmed* by the hypothalamic-pituitary axis.
>
> As a result of strong stimulation of FSH [follicle-stimulating hormone], a number of follicles *respond* with growth.

And the same idea is found, more obviously, in popular health books:[22, p. 6; 23, p. 6; emphasis added]

> Each month from menarch on, [the hypothalamus] acts as elegant interpreter of the body's rhythms, *transmitting messages* to the pituitary gland that set the menstrual cycle in motion.
>
> Each month, *in response to a message* from the pituitary gland, one of the unripe egg cells develops inside a tiny microscopic ring of cells, which gradually increases to form a little balloon or cyst called the Graafian follicle.

Although most accounts stress signals or stimuli traveling in a "loop" from hypothalamus to pituitary to ovary and back again, carrying positive or negative feedback, one element in the loop, the hypothalamus, part of the brain, is often seen as predominant. Just as in the general model of the central nervous system, the female brain-hormone ovary system is usually described not as a feedback loop like a thermostat system, but as a hierarchy, in which the "directions" or "orders" of one element dominate:[24, p. 1615: 19, p. 885; emphasis added]

> Both positive and negative feedback control must be invoked, together with *superimposition* of control by the CNS through neurotransmitters released into the hypophyseal portal circulation.
>
> Almost all secretion by the pituitary is *controlled* by either hormonal or nervous signals from the hypothalamus. . . . The hypothalamus is a collecting center for information concerned with the internal well-being of the body, and in turn much of this information is used *to control* secretions of the many globally important pituitary hormones.

As Lein puts it into ordinary language:[18, p. 84]

> The cerebrum, that part of the brain that provides awareness and mood, can play a significant role in the control of the menstrual cycle. As explained before, it seems evident that these higher regions of the brain exert their influence by modifying the actions of the hypothalamus. So even though the hypothalamus is a kind of master gland dominating the anterior pituitary, and through it the ovaries also, it does not act with complete independence or without influence from outside itself . . . there are also pathways of control from the higher centers of the brain.

So this is a communication system organized hierarchically, not a committee reaching decisions by mutual influence. The hierarchical nature of the organization is reflected in some popular literature meant to explain the nature of menstruation simply: "From first menstrual cycle to menopause, the hypothalamus acts as the conductor of a highly trained orchestra. Once its baton signals the downbeat to the pituitary, the hypothalamus-pituitary-ovarian axis is united in purpose and begins to play its symphonic message, preparing a woman's body for conception and childbearing."[22, p. 6] Carrying the metaphor further, the follicles vie with each other for the role of producing the egg like violinists trying for the position of concertmaster; a burst of estrogen is emitted from the follicle like a "clap of tympani."[21, p. 6]

The basic images chosen here—an information transmitting system with a hierarchical structure—have an obvious relation to the dominant form of organization in our society.[25] What I want to show is how this set of metaphors, once chosen as the basis for the description of physiological events, has profound implications for the way in which a change in the basic organization of the system will be perceived. In terms of female reproduction, this basic change is of course menopause. Many criticisms have been made of the medical propensity to see menopause as a pathological state.[26] I would like to suggest that the tenacity of this view comes not only from the negative stereotypes associated with aging women in our society, but as a logical outgrowth of seeing the body as a hierarchical information-processing system in the first place. (Another part of the reason menopause is seen so negatively is related to metaphors of production, which I discuss later.)

What is the language in which menopause is described? In menopause, according to a college text, the ovaries become "unresponsive" to stimulation from the gonadotropins, to which they used to respond. As a result the ovaries "regress." On the other end of the cycle, the hypothalamus has gotten estrogen "addiction" from all those years of menstruating. As a result of the "withdrawal" of estrogen at menopause, the hypothalamus begins to give "inappropriate orders."[18, pp. 79, 97] In a more popular account, "the pituitary gland during the change of life becomes disturbed when the ovaries fail to respond to its secretions, which tends to affect its control over other glands. This results in a temporary imbalance existing among all the endocrine glands of the body, which could very well lead to disturbances that may involve a person's nervous system."[27, p. 11]

In both medical texts and popular books, what is being described is the breakdown of a system of authority. The cause of ovarian "decline" is the "decreasing ability of the aging ovaries to respond to pituitary gonadotropins."[28] At every point in this system, functions "fail," and falter. Follicles "fail to muster the strength" to reach ovulation.[22, p. 18] As functions fail, so do the members of the system decline: "breasts and genital organs gradually atrophy,"[28 p. 598] "wither,"[22, p. 181] and become "senile."[21, p. 121] Diminished, atrophied relics of their former vigorous, functioning selves, the "senile ovaries" are an example of the vivid imagery brought to this process. A text whose detailed illustrations make it a primary resource for medical students despite its early date describes the ovaries this way:[21, p. 116]

> [T]he *senile ovary* is a shrunken and puckered organ, containing few if any follicles, and made up for the most part of old corpora albincantia and corpora atretica, the bleached and functionless remainders of corpora lutia and follicles embedded in a dense connective tissue stroma.

In more recent accounts, it is commonly said that ovaries cease to respond and fail to produce. Everywhere else there is regression, decline, atrophy, shrinkage, and disturbance.

The key to the problem connoted by these descriptions is functionlessness. Susan Sontag has written of our obsessive fear of cancer, a disease that we see as entailing a nightmare of excessive growth and rampant production. These images frighten us in part because in our stage of advanced capitalism, they are close to a reality we find difficult to see clearly: broken-down hierarchy and organization members who no longer play their designated parts represent nightmare images for us. One woman I talked to said her doctor gave her two choices for treatment of her menopause: she could take estrogen and get cancer or she could not take it and have her bones dissolve. Like this woman, our imagery of the body as a hierarchical organization gives us no good choice when the basis of the organization seems to us to have changed drastically. We are left with breakdown, decay, and atrophy. Bad as they are, these might be preferable to continued activity, which because it is not properly hierarchically controlled, leads to chaos, unmanaged growth, and disaster.

But let us return to the metaphor of the factory producing substances, which dominates the imagery used to describe cells. At the cellular level DNA communicates with RNA, all for the purpose of the cell's production of proteins. In a similar way, the system of communication involving female reproduction is thought to be geared toward production of various things: the ovaries produce estrogen, the pituitary produces follicle-stimulating hormone and luteinizing hormone, and so on. Follicles also produce eggs in a sense, although this is usually described as "maturing" them since the entire set of eggs a woman has for her lifetime is known to be present at birth. Beyond all this the system is seen as organized for a single preeminent purpose: "transport" of the egg along its journey from the ovary to the uterus[28, p. 580] and preparation of an appropriate place for the egg to grow if it is fertilized. In a chapter titled "Prepregnancy Reproductive Functions of the Female, and the Female Hormones," Guyton puts it all together: "Female reproductive functions can be divided into two major phases: first, preparation of the female body for conception and gestation, and second, the period of gestation itself."[19, p. 968] This view may seem commonsensical, and entirely justified by the evolutionary development of the species with its need for reproduction to ensure survival.

Yet I suggest that assuming this view of the purpose for the process slants description and understanding of the female cycle unnecessarily. Let us look at how medical textbooks describe menstruation. They see the action of progesterone and estrogen on the linking of the uterus as "ideally suited to provide a hospitable environment for implantation and survival of the embryo"[28, p. 576] or as intended to lead to "the monthly renewal of the tissue that will cradle [the ovum]"[18, p. 43] As Guyton summarizes, "The whole purpose of all these endometrial changes is to produce a highly secretory endometrium containing large amounts of stored nutrients that can provide appropriate conditions for implantation of a fertilized ovum during the latter half of the monthly cycle."[19, p. 976] Given this teleological interpretation of the purpose of the increased amount of endometrial tissue, it should be no surprise that when a fertilized egg does not implant, these texts describe the next event in very negative terms. The fall in blood progesterone and estrogen "deprives" the "highly developed endometrial lining of its hormonal support," "constriction" of blood vessels leads to a "diminished" supply of oxygen and nutrients, and finally "disintegration starts, the entire lining begins to slough, and the menstrual flow begins." Blood vessels in the endometrium "hemorrhage" and the menstrual flow "consists of this blood mixed with endometrial debris."[28, p. 577] The "loss" of hormonal stimulation causes "necrosis" (death of tissue).[19, p. 976]

The construction of these events in terms of a purpose that has failed is beautifully captured in a standard text for medical students (a text otherwise noteworthy for its extremely objective, factual descriptions) in which a discussion of the events covered in the last paragraph (sloughing, hemorrhaging) ends with the statement, "When fertilization fails to occur, the endometrium is shed, and a new cycle starts. This is why it used to be taught that 'menstruation is the uterus crying for lack of a baby.'"[29, p. 63]

I am arguing that just as seeing menopause as a kind of failure of the authority structure in the body contributes to our negative view of it, so does seeing menstruation as failed production contribute to our negative view of it. We have seen how Sontag describes our horror of production out of control. But another kind of horror for us is *lack* of production: the disused factory, the failed business, the idle machine. Winner terms the stopping and breakdown of technological systems in modern society "apraxia" and describes it as "the ultimate horror, a condition to be avoided at all costs."[30] This horror of idle workers or machines seems to have been present even at earlier stages of industrialization. A 19th century inventor, Thomas Ewbank, elaborated his view that the whole world "was designed for a Factory."[31] "It is only as a Factory, a *General Factory*, that the whole materials and influences of the earth are to be brought into play."[31, p. 23] In this great workshop, humans' role is to produce: "God employs no idlers—creates none."[31 p. 27] Ewbank continues:[31, p. 141]

> Like artificial motors, we are created for the work we can do—for the useful and productive ideas we can stamp upon matter. Engines running daily without doing any work resemble men who live without labor; both are spendthrifts dissipating means that would be productive if given to others.

Menstruation not only carries with it the connotation of a productive system that has failed to produce, it also carries the idea of production gone awry, making products of no use, not to specification, unsalable, wasted, scrap. However disgusting it may be, menstrual blood will come out. Production gone awry is also an image that fills us with dismay and horror. Amid the glorification of machinery common in the 19th century were also fears of what machines could do if they went out of control. Capturing this fear, one satirist wrote of a steam-operated shaving machine that "sliced the noses off too many customers."[32] This image is close to the one Melville created in *The Bell-Tower*, in which an inventor, who can be seen as an allegory of America, is killed by his mechanical slave,[32, p. 153] as well as to Mumford's[33] sorcerer's apprentice applied to modern machinery:[34, p. 180]

> Our civilization has cleverly found a magic formula for setting both industrial and academic brooms and pails of water to work by themselves, in ever-increasing quantities at an ever-increasing speed. But we have lost the Master Magician's spell for altering the tempo of this process, or halting it when it ceases to serve human functions and purposes.

Of course, how much one is gripped by the need to produce goods efficiently and properly depends on one's relationship to those goods. While packing pickles on an assembly line, I remember the foreman often holding up improperly packed bottles to show to us workers and trying to elicit shame at the bad job we were doing. But his job depended on efficient production, which meant many bottles filled right the first time. This factory did not yet have any effective method of quality control, and as soon as our supervisor was out of sight, our efforts went toward filling as few bottles as we could while still concealing who had filled which bottle. In other factories, workers seem to express a certain grim pleasure when they can register objections to company policy by enacting imagery of machinery out of control. Noble reports an incident in which workers resented a supervisor's order to "shut down their machines, pick up brooms, and get to work cleaning the area. But he forgot to tell them to stop. So, like the sorcerer's apprentice, diligently and obediently working to rule, they continued sweeping up all day long."[35, p. 312]

Perhaps one reason the negative image of failed production is attached to menstruation is precisely that women are in some sinister sense out of control when they menstruate. They are not reproducing, not continuing the species, not preparing to stay at home with the baby, not providing a safe, warm womb to nurture a man's sperm. I think it is plain that the negative power behind the image of failure to produce can be considerable when applied metaphorically to women's bodies. Vern Bullough comments optimistically that "no reputable scientist today would regard menstruation as pathological,"[36] but this paragraph from a recent college text belies his hope:[37, p. 525]

> If fertilization and pregnancy do not occur, the corpus luteum degenerates and the levels of estrogens and progesterone decline. As the levels of these hormones decrease and their stimulatory effects are withdrawn, blood vessels of the endometrium undergo prolonged spasms (contractions) that reduce the blood flow to the area of the endometrium supplied by the vessels. The resulting lack of blood causes the tissues of the affected region to degenerate. After some time, the vessels relax, which allows blood to flow through them again. However, capillaries in the area have become so weakened that blood leaks through them. This blood and the deteriorating endometrial tissue are discharged from the uterus as the menstrual flow. As a new ovarian cycle begins and the level of estrogens rises, the functional layer of the endometrium undergoes repair and once again begins to proliferate.

In rapid succession the reader is confronted with "degenerate," "decline," "withdrawn," "spasms," "lack," "degenerate," "weakened," "leak," "deteriorate," "discharge," and, after all that, "repair."

In another standard text, we read:[38, p. 624]

> The sudden lack of these two hormones [estrogen and progesterone] causes the blood vessels of the endometrium to become spastic so that blood flow to the surface layers of the endometrium almost ceases. As a result, much of the endometrial tissue dies and sloughs into the uterine cavity. Then, small amounts of blood ooze from the denuded endometrial wall, causing a blood loss of about 50 ml during the next few days. The sloughed endometrial tissue plus the blood and much serous exudate from the denuded uterine surface, all together called the *menstrum*, is gradually expelled by intermittent contractions of the uterine muscle for about 3 to 5 days. This process is called *menstruation*.

The illustration that accompanies this text captures very well the imagery of catastrophic disintegration: "ceasing," "dying," "losing," "denuding," and "expelling."

These are not neutral terms; rather, they convey failure and dissolution. Of course, not all texts contain such a plethora of negative terms in their descriptions of menstruation, but unacknowledged cultural attitudes can seep into scientific writing through evaluative words. Coming at this point from a slightly different angle, consider this extract from a text that describes male reproductive physiology, "The mechanisms which guide the *remarkable* cellular transformation from spermatid to mature sperm remain uncertain. . . . Perhaps the most *amazing* characteristic of spermatogenesis is its *sheer magnitude*: the normal human male may manufacture several hundred million sperm per day."[28, pp. 483–484; emphasis added] As we will see, this text has no parallel appreciation of the female processes such as menstruation or ovulation, and it is surely no accident that this "remarkable" process involves precisely what menstruation does not in the medical view: production of something deemed valuable. Although this text sees such massive sperm production as unabashedly positive, in fact, only about one out of every 100 billion sperm ever makes it to fertilize an egg: from the very same point of view that sees menstruation as a waste product, surely here is something really worth crying about!

When this text turns to female reproduction, it describes menstruation in the same terms of failed production we saw earlier:[28, p. 577 emphasis added]

> The fall in blood progesterone and estrogen, which results from *regression* of the corpus luteum, *deprives* the highly developed endometrial lining of its hormonal support; the immediate result is *profound constriction* of the uterine blood vessels due to production of vasoconstrictor prostaglandins, which leads to *diminished* supply of oxygen and nutrients. *Disintegration* starts, and the entire lining (except for a thin, deep layer which will regenerate the endometrium in the next cycle) begins to slough. . . . The endometrial arterioles dilate, resulting in *hemorrhage* through the weakened capillary walls; the menstrual flow consists of this blood mixed with endometrial debris. . . . The menstrual flow ceases as the endometrium *repairs* itself and then grows under the influence of rising blood estrogen concentration.

And ovulation fares no better. In fact part of the reason ovulation does not merit the enthusiasm that spermatogenesis does may be that all the ovarian follicles containing ova are already present at birth. Far from being *produced* as sperm is, they seem to merely sit on the shelf, as it were, slowly degenerating and aging like overstocked inventory:[28, pp. 567–568]

> At birth, normal human ovaries contain an estimated one million follicles, and no new ones appear after birth. Thus, in marked contrast to the male, the newborn female already has all the germ cells she will ever have. Only a few, perhaps 400, are destined to reach full maturity during her active productive life. All the others degenerate at some point in their development so that few, if any, remain by the time she reaches

> menopause at approximately 50 years of age. One result of this is that the ova which are released (ovulated) near menopause are 30 to 35 years older than those ovulated just after puberty; it has been suggested that certain congenital defects, much commoner among children of older women, are the result of aging changes in the ovum.

How different it would sound if texts like this one stressed the vast excess of follicles produced in a female fetus, compared to the number she will actually need. In addition, males are also born with a complement of germ cells (spermatogonia) that divide from time to time, and most of which will eventually differentiate into sperm. This text could easily discuss the fact that these male germ cells and their progeny are also subject to aging, much as female germ cells are. Although we would still be operating within the terms of the production metaphor, at least it would be applied in an evenhanded way to both males and females.

One response to my argument would be that menstruation just *is* in some objective sense a process of breakdown and deterioration. The particular words are chosen to describe it because they best fit the reality of what is happening. My counterargument is to look at other processes in the body, that are fundamentally analogous to menstruation in that they involve the shedding of a lining to see whether they also are described as breakdown and deterioration. The lining of the stomach, for example, is shed and replaced regularly, and seminal fluid picks up shedded cellular material as it goes through the various male ducts.

The lining of the stomach must protect itself against being digested by the hydrochloric acid produced in digestion. In the several texts quoted above, emphasis is on the *secretion* of mucus,[37, p. 419] the *barrier* that mucus cells present to stomach acid,[29, p. 776] and—in a phrase that gives the story away—the periodic *renewal* of the lining of the stomach.[37, p. 423] There is no reference to degenerating, weakening, deterioration, or repair, or even the more neutral shedding, sloughing, or replacement. As described in an introductory physiology text:[38, pp. 498–499]

> The primary function of the gastric secretions is to begin the digestion of proteins. Unfortunately, though, the wall of the stomach is itself constructed mainly of smooth muscle which itself is mainly protein. Therefore, the surface of the stomach must be exceptionally well protected at all times against its own digestion. This function is performed mainly by mucus that is secreted in great abundance in all parts of the stomach. The entire surface of the stomach is covered by a layer of very small *mucous cells*, which themselves are composed almost entirely of mucus; this mucus prevents gastric secretions from ever touching the deeper layers of the stomach wall.

The emphasis here is on production of mucus and protection of the stomach wall. It is not even mentioned, although it is analogous to menstruation, that the mucus cell layers must be continually sloughed off (and digested). Although all the general physiology texts I consulted describe menstruation as a process of disintegration needing repair, only specialized texts for medical students describe the stomach lining even in the more neutral terms of "sloughing" and "renewal."[39] One can choose to look at what happens to the lining of stomachs and uteruses negatively as breakdown and decay needing repair, or positively as continual production and replenishment. Of these two sides of the same coin, stomachs, which women *and* men have, fall on the positive side; uteruses, which only women have, fall on the negative.

One other analogous process is not handled negatively in the general physiology texts. Although it is well known to those researchers who work with male ejaculates that a very large proportion of the ejaculate is composed of shedded cellular material, the texts make no mention of a shedding process let alone processes of deterioration and repair in the male reproductive tract.[28, pp. 557–558]

What applies to menstruation once a month applies to menopause once in every lifetime. As we have seen, part of the current imagery attached to menopause is that of a breakdown of central control. Inextricably connected to this imagery is another aspect of the metaphor of failed production. Recall the metaphors of balanced intake and outgo that were applied to menopause up to the mid-19th century, later to be replaced by metaphors of degeneration. In the early 1960s, new research on the role of estrogens in heart disease led to arguments that failure of female reproductive organs to produce much estrogen after menopause was debilitating to health.

This change is marked unmistakably in the successive editions of a major gynecology text. In the 1940s and 1950s, menopause was described as usually not entailing "any very profound alteration in the woman's life current."[40] By the 1965 edition, dramatic changes had occurred: "In the past few years there has been a radical change in viewpoint and some would regard the menopause as a possible pathological state rather than a physiological one and discuss therapeutic prevention rather than the amelioration of symptoms."[41]

In many current accounts, menopause is described as a state in which ovaries fail to produce estrogen. The 1981 World Health Organization report defines menopause as an estrogen deficiency disease.[42] Failure to produce estrogen is the leitmotif of another current text:[19, p. 979]

> This period during which the cycles cease and the female sex hormones diminish rapidly to almost none at all is called the *menopause*. The cause of the menopause is the "burning out" of the ovaries. . . . Estrogens are produced in subcritical quantities for a short time after the menopause, but over a few years, as the final remaining primordial follicles become atretic, the production of estrogens by the ovaries falls almost to zero.

Loss of ability to produce estrogen is seen as central to a woman's life: "At the time of the menopause a woman must readjust her life from one that has been physiologically stimulated by estrogen and progesterone production to one devoid of those hormones."[19, p. 979]

Of course, I am not implying that the ovaries do not indeed produce much less estrogen than before. I am pointing to the choice of these textbook authors to emphasize above all else the negative aspects of ovaries failing to produce female hormones. By contrast, one current text shows us a positive view of the decline in estrogen production:[43, p. 799]

> It would seem that although menopausal women do have an estrogen milieu which is lower than necessary for *reproductive* function, it is not negligible or absent but is perhaps satisfactory for *maintenance* of *support tissues*. The menopause could then be regarded as a physiologic phenomenon which is protective in nature—protective from undesirable reproduction and the associated growth stimuli.

I have presented the underlying metaphors contained in medical descriptions of menopause and menstruation to show that these ways of describing events are but one way of fitting an interpretation to the facts. Yet seeing that female organs are imagined to function within a hierarchical order whose members signal each other to produce various substances, all for the purpose of transporting eggs to a place where they can be fertilized and then grown, may not provide us with enough of a jolt to begin to see the contingent nature of these descriptions. Even seeing that the metaphors we choose fit very well with traditional roles assigned to women may still not be enough to make us question whether there might be another way. Here I suggest some other ways that menstruation and menopause could be described.

First, consider the teleological nature of the system, its assumed goal of implanting a fertilized egg. What if a woman has done everything in her power to avoid having an egg implant in her uterus, such as birth control or abstinence from heterosexual sex? Is it still appropriate to speak of the single purpose of her menstrual cycle as dedicated to implantation? From the woman's vantage point, it might capture the sense of events better to say the purpose of the cycle is the production of menstrual flow. Think for a moment how that might change the description in medical texts: "A drop in the formerly high levels of progesterone and estrogen creates the perfect environment for reducing the excess layers of endometrial tissue. Constriction of capillary blood vessels causes a lower level of oxygen and nutrients and paves the way for a vigorous production of menstrual fluids. As a part of the renewal of the remaining endometrium, the capillaries begin to reopen, contributing some blood and serous fluid to the volume of endometrial material already beginning to flow." I can see no reason why the menstrual blood itself could not be seen as the desired "product" of the female cycle, except when the woman intends to become pregnant.

Would it be similarly possible to change the nature of the relationships assumed among the members of the organization—the hypothalamus, pituitary, ovaries, and so on? Why not, instead of an organization with a controller, a team playing a game? When a woman wants to get pregnant, it would be appropriate to describe her pituitary, ovaries, and so on as combining together, communicating with each other, to get the ball, so to speak, into the basket. The image of hierarchical control could give way to specialized function, the way a basketball team needs a center as well as a defense. When she did not want to become pregnant, the purpose of this activity could be considered the production of menstrual flow.

Eliminating the hierarchical organization and the idea of a single purpose to the menstrual cycle also greatly enlarges the ways we could think of menopause. A team which in its youth played vigorous soccer might, in advancing years, decide to enjoy a quieter "new game" where players still interact with each other in satisfying ways but where gentle interaction *itself* is the point of the game, not getting the ball into the basket or the flow into the vagina.

REFERENCES

1. Laqueur, T. Female orgasm, generation, and the politics of reproductive biology. *Representations* 14:1–82, 1986.
2. Rosenberg, C. E. The therapeutic revolution: Medicine, meaning, and social change in nineteenth-century America. In *The Therapeutic Revolution: Essays in the Social History of American Medicine*, edited by M. J. Vogel and C. E. Rosenberg, pp. 3–25. University of Pennsylvania Press, Philadelphia, 1979.
3. Tilt, E. J. *The Change of Life in Health and Disease*. John Churchill, London, 1857.

4. Crawford, P. Attitudes to menstruation in seventeenth-century England. *Past and Present* 91:47–73, 1981.
5. Rothstein, W. G. *American Physicians in the Nineteenth Century, from Sects to Science.* Johns Hopkins University Press, Baltimore, 1972.
6. Luker, K. *Abortion and the Politics of Motherhood.* University of California Press, Berkeley, 1984.
7. Fee, E. Science and the woman problem: Historical perspectives. In *Sex Difference: Social and Biological Perspectives*, edited by M. S. Teitelbaum, pp. 175–223. Doubleday, New York, 1976.
8. Geddes, P., and Thompson, J. A. *The Evolution of Sex.* Scribner and Welford, New York, 1890.
9. Barker-Benfield, G. J. *The Horrors of the Half-known Life: Male Attitudes Toward Women and Sexuality in Nineteenth-Century America.* Harper & Row, New York, 1976.
10. Sontag, S. *Illness as Metaphor.* Vintage, New York, 1979.
11. Smith-Rosenberg, C. Puberty to menopause: The cycle of femininity in nineteenth-century America. In *Clio's Consciousness Raised*, edited by M. Hartman and L. W. Banner, pp. 23–37. Harper, New York, 1974.
12. Ellis, H. *Man and Woman.* Walter Scott, London, 1904.
13. Currier, A. F. *The Menopause.* Appleton, New York, 1897.
14. Taylor, J. M. The conservation of energy in those of advancing years. *Popular Science Monthly* 64: 343–414, 541–549, 1904.
15. Berliner, H. Medical modes of production. In *The Problem of Medical Knowledge: Examining the Social Construction of Medicine*, edited by P. Wright and A. Treacher, pp. 162–217. Edinburgh University Press, Edinburgh, 1982.
16. Lewontin, R. C. et al. *Not in Our Genes. Biology, Ideology, and Human Nature.* Pantheon, New York, 1984.
17. Horrobin, D. F. *Introduction to Human Physiology.* F. A. Davis, Philadelphia, 1973.
18. Lein, A. *The Cycling Female: Her Menstrual Rhythm.* W. H. Freeman, San Francisco, 1979.
19. Guyton, A. C. *Textbook of Medical Physiology.* W. B. Saunders, Philadelphia, 1986.
20. Benson, R. C. *Current Obstetric and Gynecologic Diagnosis and Treatment.* Lange Medical Publishers, Los Altos, Cal., 1982.
21. Netter, F. H. *A Compilation of Paintings on the Normal and Pathological Anatomy of the Reproductive System.* The CIBA Collection of Medical Illustrations, Vol. 2. CIBA, Summit, NJ, 1965.
22. Norris, R. V. *PMS: Premenstrual Syndrome.* Berkeley Books, New York, 1984.
23. Dalton, K., and Greene, R. The premenstrual syndrome. *Br. Med. J.* May 1953, pp. 1016–1017.
24. Mountcastle, V. B. *Medical Physiology*, Ed. 14, Vol. II. C. V. Mosby, St. Louis, 1980.
25. Giddens, A. *The Class Structure of Advanced Societies.* Harper & Row, New York, 1973.
26. McCrea, F. B. The politics of menopause: The "discovery" of a deficiency disease. *Social Problems* 31(1): 111–123, 1983.
27. O'Neill, D. J. *Menopause and Its Effect on the Family.* University Press of America, Washington, D.C., 1982.
28. Vander, A. J. et al. *Human Physiology: The Mechanisms of Body Function*, Ed. 4. McGraw-Hill, New York, 1985.
29. Ganong, W. F. *Review of Medical Physiology*, Ed. 11. Lange Medical Publishers, Los Altos, Cal., 1983.
30. Winner, L. *Autonomous Technology: Technics-out-of-Control as a Theme in Political Thought.* The MIT Press, Cambridge, Mass., 1977.
31. Ewbank, T. *The World a Workshop: Or the Physical Relationship of Man to the Earth.* D. Appleton, New York, 1855.
32. Fisher, M. *Workshops in the Wilderness: The European Response to American Industrialization, 1830–1860.* Oxford University Press, New York, 1967.
33. Mumford, L. *The Myth of the Machine: Technics and Human Development*, Vol. 1. Harcourt, Brace and World, New York, 1967.
34. Mumford, L. *The Myth of the Machine: The Pentagon of Power*, Vol. 2. Harcourt, Brace and World, New York, 1970.
35. Noble, D. *The Forces of Production.* Knopf, New York, 1984.
36. Bullough, V. L. Sex and the medical model. *J. Sex Res.* 11(4): 291–303, 1975.
37. Mason, E. B. *Human Physiology.* Benjamin/Cummings Publishing Co., Menlo Park, Cal, 1983.
38. Guyton, A. C. *Physiology of the Human Body*, Ed. 6. Saunders College Publishing, Philadelphia, 1984.
39. Sernka, T., and Jacobson, E. *Gastrointestinal Physiology: The Essentials.* Williams & Wilkins, Baltimore, 1983.
40. Novak, E. *Textbook of Gynecology*, Ed. 2. Williams & Wilkins, Baltimore, 1944.
41. Novak, E., et al. *Novak's Textbook of Gynecology*, Ed. 7. Williams & Wilkins, Baltimore, 1965.
42. Kaufert, P. A., and Gilbert, P. Women, menopause, and medicalization. *Cult. Med. Psychiatry* 10(1): 7–21, 1986.
43. Jones, H. W., and, Jones, G. S. *Novak's Textbook of Gynecology*, Ed. 10. Williams & Wilkins, Baltimore, 1981.

 42

Turn-Taking in Doctor–Patient Dialogues

Candace West

This selection is an example of a sociolinguistic *analysis. The researcher examines speech events (things people actually say instead of a language's grammatical rules) in order to examine aspects of social reality. The speech events in this case are dialogues between patients and doctors. Among the topics sociolinguistics examines are pronunciation differences between social classes, dialect differences, and social context (Coulmas 1997). In this study, Candace West begins with the postulation that the social relationship between doctor and patient is asymmetrical. These social differences are apparent not only in patterns of speech but also in modes of dress—for example, the contrast between the doctor's white coat and the patient's open-backed examination gown. Social asymmetry is a key to the establishment of medical authority.*

One sociolinguistic variable is turn-taking, including interruptions and overlapping conversations. The social implications of two people talking at the same time vary in different cultural contexts. To a person from the northeastern United States, for example, overlapping conversations might be considered a sign of enthusiasm and friendliness; to someone from the southern United States, the same sociolinguistic behavior might be regarded as rude and obnoxious. Differences in speech patterns between men and women are the topic of a best-selling book by Deborah Tannen, You Just Don't Understand *(1990). Although people are often unaware of their speech behavior, this is at the root of many miscommunications.*

This study shows that doctors interrupt patients more often than vice versa, but it also suggests that male patients interrupt female doctors more often. The study raises issues of communication, authority, and trust in the healer (as discussed in selection 15), as well as the attributes of effective communication (the LEARN model discussed in selection 32).

As you read this selection, consider these questions:

- **What do dialogue interruptions signify in terms of either the patient or the doctor listening to the other?**
- **What does the author mean by "master-status"? How is this signified in the term lady doctor?**
- **Why do sociolinguists transcribe conversations with those diacritical marks and strange spellings? What information do these convey?**
- **From their own perspective, why do doctors interrupt patients?**

Context: Candace West is a linguist and professor of sociology at the University of California, Santa Cruz. Long before popular books such as *Men Are from Mars: Women Are from Venus*, West was studying gender differences in communication by closely analyzing conversations in particular cultural settings. By applying sociolinguistic methods to a clinical setting, this selection demonstrates the important role of professional relations in general, and gender relations in particular, in the communication of medical information between physicians and patients. In so doing, this kind of systematic study can help improve the practice of biomedicine.

Source: C. West (1984). "Turn-Taking in Doctor–Patient Dialogues." In C. West, *Routine Complications: Troubles with Talk between Doctors and Patients.* Bloomington: Indiana University Press.

Whatever else transpires in physicians' interactions with patients must somehow be reconciled with the organization of their turns at talk. To date, such activities as history taking, examination, diagnosis and treatment have not yet been consigned to computers. Hence, performance of these tasks relies largely on the face-to-face exchange of speech between doctors and their patients.

In everyday life, we appear to recognize the significance of orderly speech exchange for attainment of conversational goals. Getting across the content of a message often seems contingent on such matters as being able to get a word in edgewise, sustaining a train of thought without interruption, and receiving some indication that one's conversational partners are in fact listening.

But little attention has been paid to the implications of talk's turn-taking organization for participants in medical encounters. Part of the neglect may stem from an overemphasis on the importance of physicians' contributions to these exchanges. Physicians are, after all, the ones to perform examinations, issue diagnoses, and formulate "orders" for treatment. However, insofar as such tasks are dependent on patients' contributions to talk (e.g., expressing concerns, reporting symptoms, or indicating "where it hurts"), physicians' performance of their clinical work is ultimately contingent on the ordering of their talk with patients.

Elsewhere, the substance of spoken interaction is found to be a fundamental means of ordering social activities and organizing social relationships. For example, there is now an extensive body of research suggesting that males interrupt females far more often than the reverse, across a variety of situations (Argyle et al., 1968; Eakins and Eakins, 1976; McMillan et al., 1977; Natale et al., 1979; Octigan and Niederman, 1979; Willis and Williams, 1976). Findings of my own earlier work indicate that males' interruptions of females in cross-sex conversations constitute an exercise of power and control over their conversational partners (Zimmerman and West, 1975; West and Zimmerman, 1977; West, 1979; 1982; West and Zimmerman, 1983).

Of course, power is an important facet of many other social relationships, such as those between whites and Blacks, bosses and employees, and—of particular interest here—doctors and patients. Recall Parsons's perspective on the matter, summarized by Wolinsky (1980): "The practitioner must have control over the interaction with the patient, ensuring that the patient will comply with the prescribed regimen" (p. 163). Insofar as the physician–patient relationship is, as some have contended, *essentially* asymmetrical by our cultural standards, it is here that we would expect to find highlighted the dynamics of micropolitical exchange, through, among other things, a greater proportion of interruptions initiated by superordinate parties to talk:

> In front of, and defending the political-economic structure that determines our lives and defines the context of human relationships, there is the micropolitical structure that helps maintain it. This micropolitical structure is the substance of our everyday experience. The humiliation of being a subordinate is often felt most sharply and painfully when one is ignored or interrupted while speaking, towered over or forced to move by another's bodily presence, or cowed unknowingly into dropping the eyes, the head, the shoulders. (Henley, 1977:3)

. . . I report results of my analysis of the organization of turn-taking between patients and family physicians. My preliminary findings offer some empirical support for the archetypal relationship thought to exist between doctors and patients: Physicians interrupt patients far more often than the reverse, *except* when the doctor is a "lady." Then, I find that gender seems to have a greater impact than professional status where women physicians are concerned. Consideration of these results leads me to address such issues as the respective parts played by power, status, and gender in social interaction.

THE MODEL

Sacks et al. (1974) observe that speech exchange systems in general are arranged to ensure that (1) one party talks at a time and (2) speaker change recurs. These features are seen to normatively organize a variety of forms of talk, including casual conversation, formal debate, and high ceremony. Conversation is distinguished from other forms of exchange by its variable distributions of turn size, turn order and turn content. . . .

Within this framework, a turn at talk consists not merely of the temporal duration of an utterance but of the right and obligation to speak which is allocated to a particular speaker. Turns are built out of what Sacks et al. term "unit-types," consisting of possibly complete words, phrases, clauses or sentences, depending on their context. Further, unit-types are described as "projective" devices, in that they allow enough information prior to their completion to allow the hearer to anticipate an upcoming transition place. In other words, the end of a possibly complete unit-type is the proper place for transition to occur between speaker turns.

My prior research has led me to distinguish between two general categories of simultaneous speech *overlaps* (briefly, errors in transition timing) and *interruptions* (violations of speaker turns). Overlaps are defined as stretches of simultaneous speech initiated by a "next" speaker just as the current speaker arrives at a possible transition place (Zimmerman and West, 1975:113–115). Jefferson and Schegloff (1975) note that such instances of simultaneity are common where the current speaker stretches or drawls the final syllable of an utterance, or adds a tag-question to an otherwise complete statement:

(Dyad 19:305–307)

Patient: I live better and so I- they don't
bo:ther me too mu:ch,[y'know?]
Physician [O::kay.]

Here (as indicated by the brackets), the physician starts her "Okay" just at what would ordinarily be the proper completion point for the patient's utterance ("they don't bother me too much"). However, the patient's addition of a tag-question ("y'know?") results in their collision. I regard such an instance of simultaneous speech as a possible error in transition timing rather than as an indication that the physician is not listening. Indeed, one must listen very carefully in order to anticipate the upcoming completion of a current speaker's utterance and begin speaking precisely on cue, with no silence intervening between turns.

A related form of simultaneity "provoked" by careful listening is what Jefferson (1973) terms a "display of independent knowledge." For example, "saying the same thing at the same time" as someone else indicates not only that one is attending to them, but also that one is listening carefully enough to predict what they are going to say:

(Dyad 1:325–331)

Physician: An::d Ornade ha:s one called
isopropamide iodide, an:d it ha:s
uh, phenylpropanolamine an'::
Neosynephrine [Ye:ah it's a small amount- it's not that-]
Patient: [So it- a small amount's but not that-]=
Patient: = Right =
Physician: = It's six of one und half
a doz [en a the] other
Patient [Uh-huh]

In this excerpt, for example, just as the physician says "It's a small amount, it's not that" the patient independently produces the same thing—thus displaying her careful attention to both the form and content of the physician's emerging utterance.

In contrast, the fragment below illustrates an instance of interruption. An interruption is an initiation of simultaneous speech which intrudes deeply into the internal structure of a current speaker's utterance; operationally, it is found more than a syllable away from a possibly complete unit-type's boundaries (Zimmerman and West, 1975:113–115). Unlike overlaps or displays of independent knowledge, interruptions have no rationale for their occurrence in considerations of active listening (e.g., concerns for minimizing silence between speaker turns or displaying independent understanding). In fact, inasmuch as the rules for turn-taking assign the turnspace to the current speaker until a possible turn-transition point is reached (Sacks et al., 1974:706), an interrupting speaker is engaged in *violation of the current speaker's right* to be engaged in speaking. The following excerpt offers an illustration of the potential effects of such intrusion:

(Dyad 1:945–954)

((Here, the physician and patient have been discussing the effectiveness of sleeping pills when used over an extended time period. The physician argues that the patient will be better off doing without such medication; the patient argues that her anxieties over a forthcoming trip will interfere with her effectiveness on the job for which the trip is to be taken.))

Physician: . . . prob'ly settle dow:n gradjully, a
little bit, once yuh get used to it.
Patient: = The- press::[ure's gonna-]
Physician: [Well if it doe::sn',]
Physician: Seco<u>bar</u>:bital's not gonna help.
(.2)
Patient: We:ll,
(.2)
Physician: It's gonna make things worse.

The physician's intrusion ("Well if it doesn', Secobarbital's not gonna help") occurs where the patient is nowhere near completion of her utterance, and the patient drops out almost instantly, leaving her utterance hanging incomplete. As I note in the preface to this fragment, this physician and patient had been arguing about whether or not he ought to issue her a prescription for sleeping pills. One might imagine that his exasperation with the argument might have prompted him to cut off the patient's protests, especially since this patient was requesting refills for sixteen other medications (including Valium and Serax) prior to departing on her trip. However, the *method* used by the doctor to superimpose his opinion over that of the patient is interruption of her turn at talk, that is, violation of her speaking right. Later in this [article], I will focus on the content of such interruptions between speakers in the physician–patient exchanges in my collection.

INTERRUPTIONS IN MEDICAL DIALOGUES

Instances of simultaneous speech were first located in the 532 pages of transcribed exchanges. Using the criteria specified in the preceding discussion, I separated instances of interruption (i.e., deep intrusions into the internal structure of speakers' utterances) from other types of simultaneity. Then I compared the initiations of interruptions by physician and patient in each dyad in the collection.

Recall Parsons's suggestion that the physician–patient relationship is *essentially* an asymmetrical one. Distributions of physician-initiated and patient-initiated interruptions would lend support to such a claim.

Inspecting Table 1, we see that a total of 188 instances of interruption occurred. Of these, physicians initiated 67 percent (126) and patients initiated 33 percent (62). Thus, doctors interrupted patients far more often than vice versa. Interruptions display further patterned asymmetries according to patients' race and gender. For example, the ratios of physicians' interruptions to patients' interruptions are: 1.1 (or nearly equal) for white male patients; 1.8 for white female patients; 2.6 for Black male patients; and 4.4 for Black female patients. Moreover, in the two dyads characterized by more patient-initiated than physician-initiated interruption (those to which footnotes 1 and 2 are appended), the patient is hard of hearing on the one hand, and mentally retarded on the other.

TABLE 1 Interruptions in Encounters between Patients and Male Physicians

	Percentage of Physician Interruptions		*Percentage of Patient Interruptions*	
Black female patient, 16 years	91	(10)	9	(1)
Black female patient, 20 years	100	(1)	—	(0)
Black female patient, 31 years	77	(20)	23	(6)
White female patient, 17 years	100	(1)	—	(0)
White female patient, 32 years	67	(10)	33	(5)
White female patient, 36 years	69	(11)	31	(5)
White female patient, 53 years	73	(29)	27	(11)
White female patient, 58 years	80	(4)	20	(1)
White female patient, 82 years[1]	37	(7)	63	(12)
Black male patient, 17 years	56	(5)	44	(4)
Black male patient, 26 years	100	(7)	—	(0)
Black male patient, 36 years	67	(4)	33	(2)
White male patient, 16 years	100	(1)	—	(0)
White male patient, 16 years	67	(2)	33	(1)
White male patient, 31 years	60	(3)	40	(2)
White male patient, 36 years	58	(7)	42	(5)
White male patient, 56 years[2]	36	(4)	64	(7)
TOTAL	67	(126)	33	(62)

[1] This patient is hard of hearing.

[2] This patient is mentally retarded.

TABLE 2 Interruptions in Encounters between Patients and Female Physicians

	Percentage of Physician Interruptions		*Percentage of Patient Interruptions*	
Black female patient, 52 years	50	(7)	50	(7)
Black female patient, 67 years	40	(6)	60	(9)
Black male patient, 58 years	28	(5)	72	(13)
White male patient, 38 years	8	(1)	92	(11)
TOTAL	32	19)	68	(40)

With the exception of these exchanges, doctors interrupted patients more in every dialogue in this group. However, this group is comprised only of interchanges between patients and *male* physicians.

Table 2 presents the distribution of interruptions between patients and *female* physicians. And in this case we can see that the statistical asymmetries depicted in Table 1 are exactly reversed. Whereas male physicians (in the aggregate) contribute 67 percent of all interruptions relative to their patients' 33 percent, female physicians (in the aggregate) initiate only 32 percent of interruptions relative to their patients' 68 percent. Moreover, patients in exchanges with female physicians interrupt as much [as] or more than their physicians in each dyad in this collection.

Although the group of exchanges involving women doctors contains only four dyads, it is at least worth noting that the two interactions that approximate symmetrical relationships between the parties involved (the first two listed in Table 2) are same-sex exchanges between women doctors and women patients. These symmetries are more striking when one considers the differences in race and age between them (the patients in both dyads are Black and the physicians are white; the patients are both considerably older than their physicians). My earlier research on same-sex exchanges between white females conversing in public places also suggested that casual conversation between females tends to display symmetrical distributions of interruptions.

Obviously, the variety of race, age, and gender combinations in a sample of this size precludes extensive extrapolation regarding the composite effects of these factors. There is, for example, only one white male patient engaged in an exchange with a white female physician; similarly, there is only one sixty-seven-year-old patient involved in talk with a physician of half her years. Still, the consistency of patterns of physician and patient-initiated interruption displayed in Tables 1 and 2 offers some empirical evidence for the asymmetrical relationship posited between physicians and patients—*except* when the doctor is a "lady."

. . . Insofar as interruptions constitute violations of persons' rights to be engaged in speaking, there is ample evidence in the transcripts that patients' rights to speak are systematically and disproportionately violated by their male doctors. However, when physicians are women, the asymmetrical relationship between doctor and patient is exactly reversed: the posited asymmetry is stood on its head when women doctors are involved. In order to discuss the implications of these results, I move now to consider the relationship between asymmetrical patterns of interruption and interactional control.

Conversational Dominance

In previously comparing conversations between men and women and exchanges between parents and children, I suggested that males' use of interruptions might display dominance or control to females (and to any witnesses), just as parents' interruptions communicated aspects of parental control to children and to others present (West and Zimmerman, 1977:527). If patients can be likened to children (as claimed by Parsons and Fox, 1952), then we might regard the violations of their speaking rights by male physicians as displays of the physicians' interactional control. Parsons's contention was that patients' situational dependency on physicians, physicians' professional prestige, and their authority over patients all ensure physicians the necessary leverage for controlling interpersonal encounters. But, if physicians' control is to be exerted in actual dialogues with patients, one would expect some ready vehicle might be available in any medical exchange for demonstrating the physician's power.

While medical sociologists place heavy emphasis on social roles as determinants of behavior, the actual behaviors of persons in social roles remain to be enacted in everyday life. In short, such scripts as may exist for the physician–patient encounter must always be negotiated on the basis of situational exigencies. However, as Zimmerman notes:

> It would surely be odd if a society were designed so that its institutions were partly constructed of role-relationships, but lacked any systematic mechanism for articulating societal roles within the features of various interactional settings. . . . [And] stranger still if this articulation were itself not socially organized. Strangest of all would be a state of affairs in which the instantiation of a role in an actual situation had no bearing on the understanding of roles in general, or the sense of "objectivity" and transcendence of the role. (Zimmerman, 1978:12)

His observations invite us to look more closely at the ways in which the respective roles of patient and doctor might be played out in the organization of actual interactions between the two.

Hence, rather than regarding the physician's authority as superimposed onto encounters with patients in "well-rehearsed," script-like fashion (cf. Wilson, 1970), we must examine the dynamics of actual medical exchanges to see how power and control are constituted between participants in those exchanges. A telling example is offered by the fragment used earlier to demonstrate the potential effects of interruption itself. There, a disagreement between a (white male) physician and (white female) patient was ultimately resolved by the doctor's interruption of the patient's opinion (regarding sleeping pills) with his own contrary opinion ("They won't help"). In that excerpt we saw interruption used to advance the physician's (expert) perspective while simultaneously cutting off the patient's (lay) point of view.

Another example of the relationship between interruptions and interactional dominance was furnished by a friend—in this case, a male physician. Prior to writing up the results of this analysis, I discussed with him the tendency of male physicians to interrupt patients in these encounters. My friend did not find this trend a surprising one, and explained, "That's because so many patients are still answering your last question when you're trying to ask them the *next* one!" His "explanation" was of interest for two reasons. First, it fails as an explanation on the grounds that answers follow questions, not the other way around. Hence, a speaker interrupting an answer with a "next question" is disavowing the obligation to listen to the answer to a prior question. . . . But second, my doctor-friend's explanation was of empirical interest, since I had already begun to notice that a great many physician-initiated interruptions in these data were composed of doctors' questions to their patients.

Consider the following fragment, which shows the staccato pace at which physicians' "next" questions can follow their "last" ones:

(Dyad 20:053–074)

Patient: It us:ually be (1.0) ((she reaches down to touch her calf with her left hand)) i:n he:ah.
You: know, it jus' [be a li:l-
Physician: [Can y' pull up] yer cuff there for me? (.6) Duh yuh have the pain right no::w?
(.2)
Patient: Um-um. No, it [ha::ppens
Physician: [It's not happ'ning right now::?]

Patient: ss-°some- Only one: time when ah w [as heah.]
Physician: [Can y] uh take yer shoe: off for me please?
(.8)
((Patient removes her shoe))
Patient: [But I-]
Physician: [WHU:] :T'RE YUH DO::ING, when yuh <u>no:dice</u> the <u>pai:n</u>
(.4)
((Physician bends over to touch the muscles in the patient's legs))
Patient: We:ll, I thi:nk that- Well, <u>so:me</u>time I jus' be si:ttin' theah. (1.0) An' yih: know: ih ji:st- (1.2) ((she shrugs, holding up both palms)) Then I fee:l a liddul pai:n in theah. (.2) Yih know, ji:st- gra:dually (.4) It gradually c [ome o:n.]
Physician: [Take thi:s] shoe: off?

We can note here that each of the physician's intrusions into his (Black female) patient's turn at talk is patently reasonable and warranted by the external constraints of medical examination and treatment. To ask where a patient is feeling pain, how often, when, or under what conditions is all justified by, even required for, precise diagnosis of a problem (cf. Cicourel, 1975, 1978). However, when these inquiries cut off what the patient is in the process of saying, particularly when what she is saying is presumably the necessary response to a "prior" needed question, then the physician is not only violating the patient's rights to speak, but he is also systematically cutting off potentially valuable information *on which he must himself rely* to achieve a diagnosis (see also Frankel, 1984).

Just below, a similar pattern is evident:

(Dyad 2:085-099)

((Here, the doctor is inquiring about a recent injury to the patient's back caused by an auto accident.))
Patient: When I'm sitting <u>up</u>right. Y'know =
Physician: = More so than it was even before?
Patient: Yay::es =
Physician: = Swelling 'r anything like that thet chew've no:ticed?
(.)
Patient: Nuh:o, not the [t I've <u>nodi</u>-]
Physician: [TEN:::DER duh the tou] ch? press:ing any?
Patient: No::, jus'when it's- si::tting.
Physician: Okay: =
Patient: = Er lying on it.
Physician: Even ly:ing. Stan:ding up? walking aroun:d?
((singsong))
Patient: No: [jis-]
Physician: [Not] so mu:ch. Jis'- ly:ing on it. Si:tting on it. Jis' then.

In this excerpt, the longest pause to ensue between the Black female patient's response and the white male physician's next query is one tenth of one second (marked by the period in parentheses). And, on two occasions, the physician's "next" utterance cuts off the patient's completion of her answer to his "last" one. The staccato pacing and intrusions into the patient's turnspaces demonstrate that—in essence and in fact—a simple "yes" or "no" is all this doctor will listen to. Such practices also serve to demonstrate who is in control in this exchange.

In the case of both excerpts, it appears that the use of interruptions by male doctors is a *display* of dominance or control to the patient, just as males' and parents' interruptions (in my previous research) were employed to communicate control in cross-sex and parent–child exchanges. But also in these exchanges (as in the cross–sex and parent–child data), I find that the use of interruptions is *in fact* a control device, as the intrusions (especially when repeated) disorganize the local construction of conversational activities. Insofar as the over-arching conversational activity is, in the medical exchange, attending to the patient's health, we can only speculate on the potential benefits being lost when doctors interrupt their patients.

Although Parsons tends to equate physicians' interactional control over patients with the ability to treat them, I contend that this sort of control is more likely to hinder than to help physicians' efforts at healing. While it may be true, as he claimed, that patients consult physicians because they do not know what is wrong with them nor what to do about it (Parsons, 1951:439), it is equally true that physicians must listen to patients in order to know what brings them there for treatment. Thus, the doctor—as well as the patient—has much to lose when one or the other of them is unable to "get a word in edgewise."

The Case of Female Physicians

The above analysis notwithstanding, the fact remains that results for four of the 21 exchanges in this collection do not display the asymmetrical pattern implied by Parsons's description. Exchanges between two women doctors and two women patients evidence distributions of interruptions that approach symmetry. Moreover, exchanges between female physicians and male patients show the male patients (not the female physicians) interrupting most (92 percent of interruptions in one exchange and 72 percent in another). It must be noted that there are only two female physicians interacting with two male patients in the collection of materials I analyze. Thus, attention to these dyads approximates a variant of case study rather than a survey of such participants generally. However, since these proportions parallel—rather than contradict—the actual distributions of females and males in medicine (where women, notes Judith Lorber, are "invisible professionals and ubiquitous patients," 1975), they would seem to warrant at least preliminary consideration here.

Permit me a brief digression to recall a somewhat dated riddle concerning a father and son who go for a ride in the country in the father's new sports car. Speeding too quickly around a corner, the father loses control of the wheel, and the car crashes into an embankment. The father is killed instantly, but the son is rushed to the local emergency room, where he is met by the hospital staff on call for emergency treatment. A surgeon rushes over to the stretcher, pulls back the blanket, and exclaims: "My God! I can't operate—that's my son!" The punchline of the riddle is: How can this be? If the boy's father was killed in the accident, then who is the surgeon?

The answer to the riddle—more obvious now, perhaps, than when it first came into vogue—is that the surgeon is the boy's *mother.* The usefulness of the riddle, as a heuristic device, rests in its illumination of the sorts of auxiliary traits that have come to accompany the status of "surgeon" in our culture. As Everett Hughes observes:

> There tends to grow up about a status, in addition to its specifically determining traits [e.g., formal and technical competence], a complex of auxiliary characteristics which come to be expected of its incumbents. It seems entirely natural to Roman Catholics that all priests should be men, although piety seems more common among women. . . . Most doctors, engineers, lawyers, professors, managers, and supervisors in industrial plants are men, although no law requires that they be so. (1945:353–354)

In our society, notes Hughes, the auxiliary characteristics that have grown up around the status "physician" include "white," "Protestant," and "male." Therefore, when persons assume the powerful status of physician and are not possessed of whiteness, Protestantism, or maleness, there tends to be what Hughes terms a "status contradiction," or even a "status dilemma"—"for the individual concerned and for other people who have to deal with him" (1945:357).

The case of the "lady doctor" provides an illuminating example, the adjective "lady" (or "woman" or "female") only underscoring the presumed maleness of the status "physician." Hughes argues that particular statuses (e.g., "Black") serve as "master-status determining traits," that is, traits which tend to have more salience than any others with which they may be combined. Thus, for persons (e.g., women) whose master-status conflicts with other very powerful statuses (e.g., physician), there is likely to be a dilemma over whether they are to be treated as members of the social category "women" *or* as practitioners of the profession "physician." Most important, as noted above, dilemmas of status extend not only to the individuals possessed of conflicting status-determining characteristics, but to those who must "deal with" them as well.

In the context of this analysis, we are well-advised to remember Zimmerman's (1978) observation that the appropriate behaviors of persons occupying social roles remain to be acted out in everyday life. Hughes's (1945) description might lead us to an overly deterministic perspective that portrays "choices" between two conflicting status-determining characteristics (e.g., "woman" and "physician"), as if the resolution of status dilemmas were an individual matter. However, the issue is more complicated than can be described by the "choice" or "nonchoice" of individuals who are caught in status dilemmas, since they must interact with others in their social worlds. For example, the Black man who would "pass" as a white one must rely on others' willingness to read various physical characteristics and elements of demeanor as constitutive of his "whiteness." Similarly, the woman who would become a physician must rely on others' willingness to honor her displays of professionalism over those of her gender.

While the evidence is tentative, there is reason to believe that Hughes's (1945) and Zimmerman's (1978) analyses might be pertinent to findings here presented. Recall, for example, that the four female physicians included in these exchanges were among the first cohort of women ever to enter the residency program at the Center. Moreover, at the time they began their training, there was only one woman physician on the staff of the faculty at the Center. (At the time of this writing, there is still only one faculty member who might ease the special adjustments of this "new and peculiar" cohort, through what might be termed role modeling, mentoring, or special advising, Shapiro et al., 1978.) Even the faculty supervising residents displayed a heightened awareness of the "special" status of the first cohort of women. For example, those who assisted me in my data collection took great pains to include "our new women residents" in the final corpus of exchanges. Through such descriptions they helped make gender a salient characteristic for women residents (e.g., not once did I hear a doctor who was male described as a "man resident").

More pertinent still, for purposes of this data analysis, are the words of patients themselves. Consider the fragment below, excerpted from the final moments of one (white) female physician's first meeting with a new (Black female) patient:

(Dyad 11:740–747)

Physician: OKa:y!
(.6)
Patient: °O:kay.
(.6)
Physician: We:ll, I've enjo:yed mee:ting you! hh
(.2)
Patient: I ha:ve too::. Enjoy:ed meeting you:, cuz I've nev-.hh (.6) Nev:uh ha:d a fe:male docktuh befoah!-hunh-hungh-hungh-hungh!

"Enjoyable" or otherwise, meetings with female physicians are apparently rare in this patient's experience.

Another (Black male) patient, asked by his (white) female physician if he was having any problems passing urine, responded "You know, the *doctor* asked me that" (transcribing conventions simplified here). In this instance, it was difficult to tell who "the doctor" *was;* "the doctor" was *not,* evidently, the female physician who was treating him.

Finally, consider the excerpt below, in which a (white) female physician attempts to provide her professional opinion on a (Black male) patient's problem:

(Dyad 4:213–231)

((To this point, the patient has complained about his weight, and the doctor and patient have been discussing possible strategies for reducing. One suggestion offered by the physician was to slow down while eating; but the patient has *just countered* that suggestion with a complaint—he does not like cold food.))

Patient: . . . An' they take twe:nny 'r thirdy minutes
((five lines deleted))
Tuh eat.
Physician: Wull what chew [could DO:
Patient: [An' then by the] time they get through: their foo:d is col::d an' uh- 'ey li:kes it y'know
Physician: [engh-hengh-hengh-hengh-hengh] .hh
Patient: [An' th' they enjoy that] but I- I 'on't like cole foo:d.
(.2)
Physician: One thing yuh could d [o::
Patient: [Spesh'ly] food thet's not suhpoze: be col' =
Physician: = O: kay.h = is tuh ea:t, say, the meat firs'. Yuh know:, but if yuh have a sal:ad tuh eat, t'sa:ve that till after yuh eat the meat. (.) Cuz the sal:ad's suhpose tuh be co:ld.

Note that the physician's attempts to advance her solution are interrupted repeatedly by the patient's ongoing elaboration of his (already evident) problem.

In this same exchange, the patient earlier questioned his physician about a medication he is taking for high blood pressure. He said that he had heard a radio report indicating that this medicine "might" cause cancer. It was a controversial report since a great many people take that particular drug to help control their blood pressure elevations. The patient's concern is certainly one with which many of us can identify and it is especially poignant in these times (in which everything from saccharin to fluorescent lighting has been linked to some potentially serious health hazard). In the case of the patient's medication, the radio report was followed by a subsequent announcement advising people to continue taking their medicine since the research had confirmed no cause-and-effect relationship between the medication and cancer. The patient said that he never heard anything further (following the subsequent announcement).

Following this initial expression of concern, the doctor checked the patient's blood pressure and explained to him that she has looked into this problem. There is, she said, no alternative medication available, and there is, in her opinion, no better present alternative than to continue with his medication. At this juncture, the patient shifts to a slightly different complaint:

(Dyad 4:430–454)

Patient: . . . If there Wuz any way possible duh git me some diffrun type a pill thet li:ke yuh take twi:ce a da::y instead of three:, .hh an' have th' same effeck with this (allernate) 'n u:h wahdur pi:ll,
Physician: OhKa:y, that's egzackly what we: were try:ing tuh do:: .hh =
Patient: = Ah kno:w, but tho:se- I- (.) heard [what th'man sai:d.]
Physician: [We .ll.,]
(.)

Physician: Ay:::e- checked in:ta tha:t, oka::y?
an:::d (1.0) No:t No:t-extensively, I
didn' search all the lidda'chure =
Patient: = ((clears his throat))
(.4)
Physician: .h Bu::t uh:m (.6) ((sniff)) Ah feel
comf'trable us:in' thuh dru:::g?
An' would take it muhself::: °If I
needed tuh. ((Looking directly at the
patient))
(6.0)
Physician: So it ['s u:p- .hh It's u:p
tuh you::] :: =
Patient: [But if all they sa:y-
if there's any-] =Ah
know::w, it's u:h-uh
[bud it's u:h] Ah'm try:in'
Physician: [It's up tuh you:]
Patient: to: uh- .h ((clears throat)) i:s there:
any other ty::pe that chew could u:h
fi:gger . . .

To spare us, I have omitted the next several lines, in which the physician again asserts that there is nothing else the patient can take and in which the patient again asserts his desire to get around taking this medication. Below, however, is the resolution of their argument:

(Dyad 4:471–479)

Physician: If I brought cha some arduhcul(s)
saying thet this wuz Okay:::, would
juh bihlie:::ve me? .h
Patient: Ye:ah, su:re, defin [at'ly]
Physician: [Oka:y.]
(.)
Physician: O[Kay:,] o::kay=
Patient: [But u:h-] =((clears throat)) .h
Whether I would cha:nge to it'r no:t,
it would be a diff- y'know, a nuther
thi::ng,

The patient might "believe" this woman physician if she brought him some articles supporting her opinions, but whether or not he would follow her advice "would be a nuther thi::ng."

My concern here is not the possible carcinogenic effects of the drug (though important)—nor the alternatives to it. Rather, I am interested in the way in which this woman physician is "heard" by her (male) patient. . . . As noted earlier, Parsons claimed that the therapeutic practice of medicine is predicated on institutionalized asymmetry between physician and patient. In his view, physicians are in a position of situational authority vis-à-vis their patients, since only physicians are possessed of the technical qualifications (and institutional certification) to provide medical care.

Yet, in these excerpts we see that neither technical qualifications (conferred by the training and medical degree) nor personal assurances ("I would take this myself," "I checked into it") are sufficient for the woman physician to have her authority *(as a physician)* respected by the patient. Elsewhere, Hughes (1958) suggests that clients of professionals do not simply grant them authority and autonomy as faits accompli. Given a recent history of increasing challenges to medical authority in the United States (cf. Reeder, 1972), it is entirely possible that patients in general are taking increased initiative in their own health care and questioning physicians' opinions more frequently. But nowhere in these data did I find a patient who questioned the opinion of a male physician as forcefully or as repeatedly as the case noted here.

SUMMARY AND CONCLUSIONS

Employing the model of turn-taking in conversation of Sacks et al. (1974), I established a theoretical basis for distinguishing interruptions from other types of simultaneous speech events in an attempt to examine the empirical bases for such claims as Parsons's (1951, 1975) regarding the essential asymmetry of the physician-patient relationship.

Exchanges between patients and male physicians in this collection lend support to the asymmetrical archetype: Male doctors interrupt their patients far more often than the reverse, and they appear to use interruptions as devices for exercising control in their interactions with patients. However, there is no evidence to suggest that this pattern of physician-initiated interruption is conducive to patients' good health. If anything, it appears that this sort of control is likely to hinder physicians' efforts at healing. Moreover, where female physicians are involved the asymmetrical relationship is exactly reversed: Patients interrupt their female doctors as much or more in each exchange in this collection. Thus, my results for women physicians conflict with Parsons's description of the general pattern.

At present, any discussion of the implications of this gender-associated difference must be speculative. The corpus of materials does not constitute a random sample, and simple projections from these results to physicians and patients in general cannot be justified by the usual logic of statistical inference. But, in engaging in such discussion, I would hope to eliminate possible misinterpretations of its significance. I am not claiming that female physicians are "better listeners" than their male colleagues (although they may be). These analyses have focused on the distribution of interruptions *between* physicians and patients. Whereas female physicians in this collection were interrupted by patients far more often than vice versa, it makes as much sense to attribute this finding to their patients' gender-associated "disrespect" (particularly in light of Hughes's and Zimmerman's suggestions) as it does to attribute it to the physicians' own communication skills. Neither inference is entirely warranted at this point.

What *is* tenable, for the findings reported here, is the suggestion that gender may have primacy over professional status where women physicians are concerned, that gender may amount to a "master-status" (Hughes, 1945), even where other power relations are involved.

 43

Culture, Scarcity, and Maternal Thinking: Maternal Detachment and Infant Survival in a Brazilian Shantytown

Nancy Scheper-Hughes

This selection is an early report from the important and disturbing medical anthropological research by Nancy Scheper-Hughes, culminating in her book Death without Weeping *(1992). Based on research in an extremely poor shantytown neighborhood in northeastern Brazil where she had been a Peace Corps volunteer eighteen years earlier, this selection emphasizes questions drawn from medical anthropology, psychological anthropology, international health, and feminist studies. The research findings run counter to biosocial evolutionary analyses of the universality of "mother love." As such, they also challenge universal, biologically based gender roles, instead emphasizing the importance of culture and political-economic context in explaining human behavior. In many ways, the extreme poverty and hopelessness of the mothers of Alto do Cruzeiro are reminiscent of Colin Turnbull's dramatic, depressing ethnography of the Ik—a resettled African population whose circumstances resulted in loss of social cooperation and support and high death rates (Turnbull 1972). In this selection, Scheper-Hughes argues that high child mortality is the result of political economy, not medical technology. An important intervening variable appears to be maternal detachment from infants who are failing to thrive.*

From an ethnomedical perspective, the author discusses a folk category of doença de crianca *that is used by mothers to explain why certain children will not thrive and are destined for early death. There are other cultural attributes associated with these tragic circumstances: beliefs about sour or insufficient breast milk, sanctions against strong maternal sentiments toward children, and patterns of enculturation that routinize infant death.*

At the end of this ethnographic case study, Scheper-Hughes questions some generalized theories about motherhood and mother–infant relationships, including maternal bonding and maternal thinking. Mundane and avoidable circumstances of poverty—especially endemic hunger, lack of clean water, unsanitary conditions, inadequate housing, unemployment, and low wages—are often-repeated themes in medical anthropology. The human face of such situations—including physical and mental suffering—is illustrated more clearly by ethnographic accounts of scarcity and maternal behavior than by cold statistics.

As you read this selection, consider these questions:

- **What did the researcher gain by collecting reproductive histories of the women from Alto? Were you surprised by the statistics from that survey?**
- **Why don't women believe in the sufficiency of breast milk for infant feeding for the first six months (as recommended by the World Health Organization)?**
- **Why is infant mortality a women's health issue?**
- **Is there an advantage for mothers in limiting their attachment to infants? Or do you think that this is a question of cultural rules about the expression of feelings?**
- **Some people are offended by this selection. Why do you think that is the case?**
- **Is malnutrition a medical problem or a political problem?**

Context: Nancy Scheper-Hughes is a medical anthropologist at the University of California, Berkeley. She is well known for her contributions as a critical medical anthropologist working on issues of schizophrenia in Ireland, child survival in the developing nations, and the transnational trade in human organs. This selection is based upon a study of maternal attachment among women living in the favela slums of Brazil. The expanded analysis of this work was published in an award-winning book titled *Death without Weeping: The Violence of Everyday Life in Brazil.*

Source: N. Scheper-Hughes (1985). "Culture, Scarcity, and Maternal Thinking." *Ethos* 13(4):291–317.

Maternal practices begin in love, a love which for most mothers is as intense, confusing, ambivalent, poignantly sweet as any they will experience.

—Sara Ruddick (1980:344)

This paper is about culture, scarcity, and maternal thinking. It explores maternal beliefs, sentiments, and practices bearing on child treatment and child survival among women of Alto do Cruzeiro, a hillside shantytown of recent rural migrants. It is set in Northeast Brazil, a region dominated by the vestiges of a semifeudal plantation economy which, in its death throes, has spawned a new class: a rural proletariat of unattached and often desperate rural laborers living on the margins of the economy in shantytowns and invasion barrios grafted onto interior market towns. *O Nordeste* is a land of contrasts: cloying fields of sugar cane amidst hunger and disease; a land of authoritarian landlords and libertarian social bandits; of conservative Afro-Brazilian possession cults, and a radical, politicized Catholicism. In short, the Northeast is the heart of the Third World in Brazil—its mothers and babies heirs to the so-called Brazilian Economic Miracle, a policy of capital accumulation that has increased both the Gross National Product and the Gross National Indifference to a childhood mortality rate that has been steadily rising throughout the nation since the late 1960s.[1]

Approximately 1 million children under the age of 5 die each year in Brazil, largely the result of parasitic infections interacting with infectious disease and chronic undernutrition. Of these, few could be saved (for long) by the miracles of modern medicine. Infant and childhood mortality in the Third World is a problem of *political economy*, not of *medical technology*. Here, however, I will discuss another pair of childhood pathogens—maternal detachment and indifference toward infants and babies judged too weak or too vulnerable to survive the pernicious conditions of shantytown life. The following analysis of the reproductive histories of 72 women of Alto do Cruzeiro explores the links between *economic* and *maternal* deprivation, between material and emotional scarcity. It discusses the social and economic context that shapes the expression of maternal sentiments and the cultural meanings of mother love and child death, and determines the experiences of attachment, separation, and loss. It identifies a unifying metaphor of life as a *luta*, a struggle, between strong and weak, or between weak and weaker still, that is invoked by Alto women to explain the necessity of allowing some—especially their very sick—babies to die *"a mingua,"* that is, without attention, care, or protection. This same metaphor is prospected on to body imagery in mothers' perception of their bodies as "wasted" and their breasts as "sucked dry" by the mouths of their infants, producing the disquieting image of hungry women hungrily consumed by their own children.

Finally, it is argued that maternal thinking and practices are *socially produced* rather than determined by a psychobiological script of innate or universal emotions such as has been suggested in the biomedical literature on "maternal bonding" and, more recently, in the new feminist scholarship on maternal sentiments.

BACKGROUND/CASE STUDIES

Two events, occurring more or less simultaneously, first captured my attention and started me thinking about maternal behavior under particularly adverse conditions. One event was public and idiosyncratic, the other was private and altogether commonplace. One aroused community sentiments of anger and hostility; the other aroused no public sentiments at all. Both concerned the survival of children in similarly unfortunate circumstances.

Rosa

During a drought in the summer of 1967 while I was then a Peace Corps health and community development worker living in Alto do Cruzeiro in the interior market town of Ladeiras (a pseudonym), I was drawn one day by curiosity to the jail cell of a young woman from an outlying rural district who had just been apprehended for the murder of her infant son and 1-year-old daughter. The infant had been smothered, while the little girl had been hacked with a machete and dashed against a tree trunk. Rosa, the mother, became, for a brief period, a central attraction in Ladeiras as both rich and poor passed her barred window in order to rain down slurs on her head: "beast"; "disgraceful wretch"; "women without shame"; "unnatural creature." Face-to-face with the withdrawn and timid girl, I asked her the obvious, "Why did you do it?" And she replied, as she must have for the hundredth time: "to stop them from crying for milk." After a pause she added (perhaps to her own defense): *"bichinos não sente nada"*—little things have no feelings. Embarrassed, I withdrew quickly, and left the girl (for she was little more than that) alone to ponder her "crime."

Lourdes and Ze

I lived at that time on the *Alto*, not far from the makeshift lean-to of Lourdes, a young girl of 17, single and pregnant for the second time. Conditions on the Alto do Cruzeiro were then, as now, appalling: contaminated drinking water, food shortages, unchecked infectious disease, lack of sanitation, and crowded living conditions decimated especially the oldest and youngest residents of the hill. Lourdes's first born, Ze-Ze, was about a year old and severely marasmic (i.e., malnourished)—toothless, hairless, and unable even to sit up, he spent his days curled up in a hammock or lying on a piece of cardboard on the mud floor where he was harassed by stray dogs and goats. I became involved with Zezino after I was called on to help Lourdes with the birth of her second child, a son about whom a great fuss was made because he was both fair (*loiro*) and robust (*forte*). With Lourdes's limited energy and attention now given over to the newborn, Zezino's condition worsened and I decided to intervene. I carried him off to the cooperative day care nursery (*creche*) I had organized with the more activist women of the hill. My efforts to rescue Ze were laughed at by the other women, and Zezino himself resisted my efforts to save him with a perversity perhaps only equal to my own. He refused to eat and wailed pitifully whenever I approached him. The *creche* mothers advised me to leave Zezino alone. They said they had seen many babies like this one and that "if a baby *wants* to die, it *will* die" and that this one was completely *disanimado*, lifeless, without fight. It was wrong, they cautioned, to fight death. But this was a philosophy alien to me and I continued to do battle with the little boy until finally he succumbed: he ate, gained weight, his hair grew in, and his face filled out. Gradually, too, he developed a strong attachment to me. Long before he could walk he would spring to my back where he would wrap his spindly arms and legs around me. His anger at being loosed from that position could be formidable. He even learned to smile. But along with the other women of the *creche* I wondered whether Ze would ever be "right" again, whether he could develop normally after the traumas he had been through. Worse, there were the traumas yet to come since I had to return him to Lourdes in her miserable conditions. And what of Lourdes—was this fair to her? Lourdes did agree to take Zezino back and she seemed more interested in him now that he looked more human than monkey, while my own investment in the child began to wane. By this time I was well socialized into shantytown culture and I never again put so much effort where the odds were so poor.

I returned to the Alto in the summer of 1982, 18 years later. Among the women of the Alto who formed my research sample was Lourdes, still in desperate straits and still fighting to put together the semblance of a life for her five living children, the oldest of whom was Ze, now a young man of 20, and filling in as "head" of the household—a slight, quiet, reserved young man with a droll sense of humor. Much was made of the reunion between Zezino and me, and the story was told several times of how I had wisked Zezino off when he was all but given up for dead and had force fed him like a fiesta turkey. Ze laughed the hardest of all, his arm protectively around his mother's shoulders. When I asked Ze later in private the question I asked all my informants—Who has been your greatest friend and ally in life, the one person on whom you could always depend—he took a long drag on his cigarette and replied, "My mother, of course."

I introduce these vignettes as caveats to the following analysis. With respect to the first story, it was to point out that severe child battering leading to death is universally recognized as *criminally deviant* in *Nordestino* society and culture. It is, to this day, so rare as to be almost unthinkable, so abhorrent that the perpetrator is scarcely thought of as human. "Mother love" is a commonsense and richly elaborated motif in Brazilian culture, celebrated in literature, art, and verse, in public ceremonies, in music and folklore, and in the continuing folk Catholic devotion to the Virgin Mother. Nonetheless, selective neglect accompanied by maternal detachment is both widespread among the poorer populations of Ladeiras but "invisible"—generally unrecognized by those outside shantytown culture, even by professionals such as clinic doctors and teachers who come into frequent contact with severely neglected babies and young children. *Within* the shantytown, child death *a mingua* (accompanied by maternal indifference and neglect) is understood as an appropriate maternal response to a deficiency *in* the child. Part of learning how to mother on the Alto includes learning when to "let go."

I also want to point out, with reference to the second vignette, that although the data indicate that Alto mothers do sometimes withdraw care and affection from some of their babies, such behaviors do not invariably lead to death, nor are the distanced maternal emotions irreversible. One of the benefits of returning to the same community where I had previously worked was the chance to observe the positive outcomes of several memorable cases of selective neglect—children who, like Ze, survived and were later able to win their way inside the domestic circle of protective custody and love. It is also essential to note that selective neglect is not analogous to what we mean in the United States by "child abuse"; it is not motivated by anger, hate, or aggression toward the child. Such sentiments—part of the "classic" child abuse syndrome identified in the United States (Steele and Pollock 1968; Gill 1970; Bourne and Newberger 1979; Gelles 1973; Kempe and Heifer 1980)—appear altogether lacking among women of the Alto who are far more likely to express *pity for*, than anger against, a dependent child, who are disinclined to strike what is seen as an innocent and irrational creature, and who, to the best of my knowledge, never project images of evil or badness onto a small child.

THE SAMPLE: THE WOMEN OF O CRUZEIRO

My first sample of 72 Alto women was an opportunistic one, comprised of the first women to volunteer for the study following an open meeting I called at the *creche* and social center at the top of the hill. Many more women volunteered over the next several weeks than I could possibly have interviewed during the brief period of my stay (8 weeks). The only criterion for inclusion in the sample was that the woman had been pregnant at least once. All understood that I was studying reproduction and mothering within the context of women's lives on the Alto.

The interviews elicited demographic information, work history, patterns of migration, marital history. This was followed by a discussion of each pregnancy and its outcome. For each live birth the following information was recorded: location of, and assistance with, the delivery; mother's perceptions of the infant's weight, health status, temperament; infant feeding practices; history of early childhood illnesses, how treated, and outcomes, including mortality. Following the reproductive history I asked each mother a series of open-ended, provocative, and evaluative questions, including: Why do so many infants die here? What do infants need most in order to survive the first year of life? What could most improve the situation of mothers and infants here? Who has been your greatest source of comfort and support throughout your adult life? How many children are enough to raise? Do you prefer to raise sons or daughters and why?

As both psychological anthropologist and feminist I was concerned not only with raising questions about *behavior* and *practice* (i.e., *did* some of these women selectively neglect some of their infants and place them at risk) but also with questions of *meaning* and *motivation*, how and why they might do this. I wanted to know what infant death and loss meant to them, and how they explained and interpreted their actions as women and mothers. I wanted to know what were the effects of chronic scarcity and deprivation on women's abilities to nurture, to attend, indeed even to love. And, finally, I wanted to know what were the consequences of continual loss of infants and babies for the world views of Alto mothers, as, at a later stage, I hope to explore the consequences of selective neglect on the personalities, beliefs, and sentiments of those children—like Ze-Ze—who *do* survive in spite of their inauspicious and inhospitable early experiences. What follows here is a discussion of the initial findings from the first and exploratory stage of the research.

I was able to work efficiently during this initial period because I was both known and trusted on the Alto as the *Americana* who had once lived and worked with them. In fact, several of the older women and their adult daughters (now grandmothers and mothers) in my sample were the very same young mothers and toddlers with whom I had worked 20 years ago (1964–1966) in the construction and operation of a cooperative day care center for working mothers. My previous work and association with the midwives of the Alto and my attendance at numerous home births years ago now gave me access to the homes of young women who gave birth during the research period.

The women interviewed ranged in age from 17 to 71; the median age of 39 meant that most were still potentially fertile. A profile of the average woman in my sample could read as follows. She was born on an *engenho* (sugar plantation) where she grew up working "at the foot of the cane." She attended school briefly and while she can do sums with great facility, she cannot read. After marriage she moved several times always in search of better work conditions for her husband or a better life for the children, preferably a *vida na rua* (a life on urban streets) rather than in the *mata*, the rural backwaters. Her husband or present companion is a "good" man, but described as *meio-fraco*, weak-poor, unskilled, unemployed, or worse, sickly and dependent, or perhaps, a *cachazeiro*, a drunkard. They have been separated from time to time. She works at least part time in the marketplace, hiring herself out in the fields. The combined weekly household income in 1982, Cr$5000 ($25.00), put the family on the borders between *pobreza* and *pobretão*—poverty and absolute misery. The nuclear family is counted from above and below—including the little angels in heaven, and *os desgraçados*, the living but sinful children on earth.

REPRODUCTIVE HISTORIES

The 72 women reported a staggering *686* pregnancies and 251 childhood deaths (birth to 5 years). The average woman (speaking statistically) experienced 9.5 pregnancies, 1.4 miscarriages, abortions, or stillbirths, and 3.5 deaths of children. She has 4.5 living children. Many infants and toddlers were, however, reported by their mothers to be sick or frail at the time of the interview, and at least some of these could be anticipated to join the mortality statistics in the months and years ahead (see Table 1).

TABLE I Reproductive Histories Summary

Total pregnancies	686 (9.5/woman)
Total living children	329 (4.5/woman)
Miscarriages/abortions	85 } 101(1.4/woman)
Stillbirths	16
Childhood deaths (birth–5 yrs.)	251 (3.5/woman)
Childhood deaths (6–12 yrs)	5

N = 72 women; ages 19–71 median age 39.

TABLE 2 Sex and Age at Death (Birth–5 Years)

	Male	*Female*	*Total*		
Postpartum (1–14 days)	21	12	33	175 (70%)	205 (82%)
15 days–7 weeks	18	8	26		
2 mos.–6 mos.	57	59	116		
7 mos.–1 year	13	17	30		
13 mos.–2 years	12	15	27		
2½ yrs.–5 yrs.	8	11	19		
Totals:	129	122	251		

N = 251.

Alto babies are at greatest risk during the first year of life: 70% of the deaths had occurred between birth and 6 months, and 82% by the end of the first year. No doubt contributing to the high mortality in the first year is the erosion of breastfeeding which, the interviews with my older informants reveal, had begun on the plantation long before commercial powdered milk was available. All Alto infants are reared from birth on *mingaus* and *papas*, cereals of rice or manioc flour mixed with milk and sugar. The breast, when offered at all, is only a supplement to the staple baby food, *mingau*. Central to the precipitous decline in breastfeeding among Alto mothers[2] is not so much a positive valuation of commercial powdered milk as a pervasive devaluation of breastmilk related to women's often distorted perceptions of their bodies, and breasts in particular, to be discussed below.

Sex, Birth Order, and Temperament

I probed the circumstances surrounding each pregnancy, birth, and death, and I elicited infant care practices and mothers' theories of infant development and infant needs. In addition, I probed for patterns of preferential treatment or neglect, and I asked the women to share with me their thoughts and feelings about motherhood, family life, about joy and affliction, about loss and grief. Neither the reproductive histories nor the interviews revealed a strong sex or birth order bias.

The 72 mothers reported a total of 251 deaths of offspring from birth to 5 years; 129 males and 122 females (Table 2). Despite a fairly pervasive ideology of male dominance in Brazilian culture, the women of the Alto expressed no consistent pattern of sex preference, and virtually all agreed that a mother would want to have a balance between sons and daughters. Both sexes were valued in children, although for different reasons. Boys were said by mothers to be "easy" to care for and were independent from an early age. Sons could be sent out to "forage" in the market and were unashamed to beg or steal, if necessity came to that. Sons were also enjoyed for their skill in street games and sports, an important aspect of community life on the Alto. But daughters were highly valued as well: they were not only useful at home, but were a mother's lifelong friend and intimate. Alto mothers and daughters strive to stay in proximity to each other throughout the life cycle; distance, dissension, and alienation between mothers and daughters occurs, but is considered both tragic and deviant. "Obviously," Alto mothers would conclude, a woman would want to have at least one *casal* (a boy-girl pair) and preferably two pairs, spaced closely together.

With respect to birth order among the subset of completed families, the most "protected" cohorts were those children occupying a middle rank, neither among the first or last born. Although childhood deaths often occurred in runs, this usually reflected external life circumstances of the mother during that period of her reproductive career, and there were no strong correlations between birth order and survivability. However, the *casula*, the last born child to survive infancy, was particularly loved and indulged.

Far more significant with respect to maternal investment was the mother's perception of the baby's constitution and temperament—the infant's qualities of readiness for the uphill struggle that is life. The mothers readily expressed a preference for babies who evidenced early on the physical and psychological characteristics of "fighters" and "survivors." Active, quick, sharp, playful, and developmentally precocious babies were much preferred to quiet, docile, passive, inactive, or developmentally delayed babies. Mothers spoke fondly of those babies who were a little *brabo* (wild), who were *sabido* (wise before their years), and who were *jeitoso* (skillful with objects, words, tasks, people). One young mother explained:

> I prefer a more active baby, because when they are quick and lively they will never be at a loss in life. The worst temperament in a baby is one that is dull and *morto de espirito* [lifeless], a baby so calm it just sits there without any energy. When they grow up they're good for nothing.

The vividly expressed disaffection of Alto mothers for their quieter and slower babies was particularly unfortunate in an area where malnutrition, parasitic infections, and dehydrations artificially produce these symptoms in a great many babies. A particularly lethal form of negative feedback results when some Alto mothers reject and withdraw their affections from their passive and less demanding babies whose disvalued "character traits" are primarily the symptoms of chronic hunger. This pattern is revealed in the mother's explanations of their children's causes of death.

PERCEIVED CAUSES OF CHILDHOOD MORTALITY

Although uneducated and, for the most part, illiterate, the shantytown mothers interviewed were all too keenly aware that the primary cause of infant mortality was gastroenteric and other infectious diseases resulting from living in, as they so graphically phrased it, a *porcaria*, a pig sty. When asked why, *in general*, so many babies and young children of O Cruzeiro die, the women were quick to reply: "they die because we are poor, because we are hungry"; "they die because the water we drink is filthy with germs"; "they die because we can't keep them in shoes or away from this human garbage dump we live in"; "they die because we get worthless medical care: 'street medicine,' 'medicine on the run'"; "they die because we have no safe place to leave them when we go off to work."

When asked what it is that infants need most to survive the first year of life, the Alto mothers in my sample invariably answered "good food, proper nutrition, milk, vitamins." I soon became bored with its concreteness. The irony, however, was that not a single mother had stated either a lack of food or insufficient milk was a primary or even a contributing cause of death for any of her *own* children. Perhaps they must exercise this denial because the alternative—the recognition that a child is slowly starving to death—is too painful.

Table 3 offers a condensed rendering of these women's perceptions of the major pathogens affecting the lives of their children. Certainly naturalistic explanations predominated in which biomedical conceptions of contagion and infection blend with aspects of humoral pathology and belief in the etiological significance of teething. While a *vontage de Dens*, God's will, was understood as the ultimate cause of all human events (including the death of one's children), in very few instances did mothers attribute particular deaths to the immediate action or will of God or the saints. Human agency (although not necessarily guilt and responsibility) was imputed to the deaths of 101

TABLE 3 Causes of Infant/Childhood Deaths (Mothers' Explanations)

I.	*The Natural Realm* (locus of responsibility: natural pathogens)	
	A. Gastroenteric (various types of diarrhea)	71
	B. Other Infectious, Communicable Diseases	41
	C. Teething (*denticão*)	13
	D. Skin, Liver, Blood Diseases	13
	Total:	138
II.	*Supernatural Realm* (locus of responsibility: God, the saints)	
	A. *De Repente* (taken suddenly by God, saints)	9
	B. *Castigo* (punishment for sin of the parent)	3
	Total:	12
III.	*The Social Realm* (locus of responsibility: human agency is directly or indirectly implied)	
	A. Malignant Emotions (envy, shock, fear)	14
	B. *Resguardo Quebrado* (postpartum or illness precautions broken)	5
	C. *Mal Trato* (poor care, including poor medical care)	6
	D. *Doença de Crianca* ("ugly diseases" involving benign neglect)	39
	E *Fraqueza* (perceived constitutional weakness that involves maternal under-investment)	37
	Total:	101

of the children. This includes deaths attributed to poor care (*mal trato*), to uncontrolled pathogenic emotions (such as anger or envy resulting in evil eye, or fear resulting in the folk syndrome *susto* [magical fright]), and to breaking of customary precautions (*resguardas*) surrounding childbirth and the 40 days following, and attached to common childhood ailments. Finally, the interviews revealed a pattern of passive selective neglect expressed in the medium of folk diagnoses of *doença de crianca* (sickness of the child) and of *fraqueza* (weakness) implying in both cases a will toward death in the child.

Underlying and uniting these etiological notions is a world view in which all of life is conceptualized as *luta,* a power struggle between strong and weak. Death can be stronger than young life, and so mothers can speak of a baby whose drive toward life was not sufficiently strong or well developed, or who had an aversion (*disgosto*) to life. A pregnant woman who is "used up" (*acabado*) from too many previous pregnancies is said to transfer this weakness to the fetus who is then born frail and skinny, unfit for the *luta* ahead. Conversely, when a mother says that her infant suffered many crises during its first year but *vingou* (triumphed) in any case, she is giving proud testimony to the child's inner vitality, his or her will to live, to *lutar* (fight). If an infant succumbs to *denticão* (teething) it is understood that she died because the "force of the teeth" overwhelmed the delicate little system. The folk pediatric illness *gasto* is almost always fatal because the infant's alimentary canal is reduced to a sieve:

whatever goes into the mouth comes out directly in violent bouts of vomiting and bloody diarrhea. The baby becomes *gasto* (spent, wasted), his [her?] vital fluids and energy gone. Most disquieting, however, is the image mothers convey of those of their babies who were said to have died of thirst, their tongues blackened and hanging out of their mouths because their mothers were too weak, ruined, or diseased to breastfeed them. One young mother said:

> They are born already starving in the womb. They are born bruised and discolored, their tongues swollen in their mouths. If we were to nurse them constantly we would all die of tuberculosis. Weak people can't give much milk.

When I challenged a young and vigorous Alto woman about her inability to breastfeed, she responded angrily, pointing to her breast, "Look. They can suck and suck all they want, but all they will get from me is blood." Once again we have the metaphor of *a luta*—the struggle between weak and weaker over scarce resources. Another reason given by Alto mothers for their failure to breastfeed their babies for more than the first few weeks of life was that their infant had rejected the breast. And why not? For I was told repeatedly by mothers of newborns that their breastmilk was "foul" or "worthless" and for many different reasons. The milk was said to be either "salty" or "bitter" or "watery" or "sour" or "infected" or "dirty" or "diseased." In all, their own milk was rejected as unfit for infants and little more than a vehicle for contamination.

I do not know to what extent mothers' perceptions of breastmilk insufficiency is a function of their nutritional status or of their reliance on supplementary infant feedings of *mingau*, which surely interferes with the mother's own milk production. But I do know that once the breastmilk falters Alto mothers are quick to interpret this as a symptom of their own *fraqueza*, their physical and moral weakness. Similarly, when these young women refer to their breastmilk as scanty, curdled, bitter, or sour, they are also speaking metaphorically to the scarcity and bitterness of their lives as women of the Alto. What has been taken from these women is their faith in their ability to give. As the mothers stated earlier, "We have *nothing* to give our children" and "Weak people can't give much milk."

In all, the etiological system and body imagery can be understood as a projection, a microcosm of the hierarchical social order in which strength, force, and power win out. It is a response to, a defense against, and a reflection of the miserable conditions of Alto life. It is these survivor values and perceptions that make Alto mothers reluctant to care for those infants and babies seen as deficient in vital energy, in *animacão*. Multiple births fare poorly on the Alto: few twins and triplets survive infancy. An obstetrical nurse in Ladeiras reported that poor mothers will take the stronger of a set of twins and leave the smaller or frailer for the hospital staff to dispose of as they see fit. All the mothers agreed that it is best if the weak and disabled die as infants and that they die without a prolonged and wasted struggle. Celia, for example, could speak of her two infants having given her "no trouble" in dying. They just "rolled their eyes to the back of their heads and were still." It is the more gradual, protracted deaths—the deaths of *doença de crianca*—that Alto mothers particularly fear.

DOENÇA DE CRIANCA: ETHNOMEDICAL SELECTIVE NEGLECT

The Alto mothers spoke frequently and covertly of a cluster of childhood illnesses that are both greatly feared and from which they withdraw treatment and care. They used a euphemism, "sickness of the child," in order to avoid discussing the many anxiety-provoking symptoms and conditions subsumed under the term. The women volunteered that a child with a *doença de crianca* was best left to die a *mingua*, meaning a child allowed to slowly wither away without sufficient care, food, love, or attention. It meant, quite simply, a death by neglect. The women did not like talking about this subject, but neither did they deny or conceal their own behavior or their feelings.

Doença de crianca was used to refer to any serious childhood condition which, while not necessarily life-threatening, was believed likely to leave the mother with a permanently disabled, frail, or dependent child. Various paralyses, epilepsy, childhood autism, and developmental disabilities were discussed in this context. The symptoms that mothers particularly feared and which they were likely to label as symptoms of a "sickness of the child" included deliriums from high fevers, fit-like convulsions, extreme passivity and immobility, retarded verbal or motor skills, disinterest in food, play, social interaction, changes in skin color, loss of body liquids and body fat, sunken eyes. The etiology was multicausal; many things caused *doença de crianca* including frights (*pasmo*, *susto*), germs and other microbes, evil eye, and complications resulting from otherwise normal childhood illnesses. Measles, diarrhea, even a common cold could, without taking proper precautions, "turn into" (*virar*) a dreaded sickness of the child, thereby marking the child as beyond hope of a normal recovery.

The expansiveness and flexibility of the folk diagnosis allows Alto mothers a great deal of latitude in deciding which of their children are not favored for normal development and from which she may withdraw her attentions. The woman does not hold herself responsible for the death and nor is she blamed by the immediate female community (men seem to have little knowledge of the matter); the cause of death is a perceived deficiency in the child, not a deficiency in the mother. Thirty-nine babies were said to have died of a sickness of the child, but the same behaviors are implied in an additional 37 deaths attributed to *fraqueza* (innate weakness of the child). The following statements of mothers are indicative:

> There are various "qualities" of *doença de crianca*. Some die with rose colored marks all over their body; others die black colored. It's very ugly—with this disease it takes a very long time for them to die. It takes a lot out of the mother. It makes you sad. This sickness we don't treat. If you treat it the child will never be right. Some become crazy. Others are just weak and sickly their whole life.
>
> They die because they have to die. If they were meant to live, it would happen that way as well. I think that if they were always weak, they wouldn't be able to defend themselves in life. So, it is really better to let the weak ones die.
>
> There are two diseases we don't like to talk about because they are the ugliest things in the world. So we just say *doença de crianca* and leave it at that. One of these is what some people call *gotas de serena* [literally "evening mist"] which is a kind of madness, like rabies in a dog. The other is *pasmo,* a terrible paralysis that the child gets from a bad shock. His skin turns black and he just sits there still and dumb in the hammock, really lifeless. We are afraid of these sicknesses of the child. It is best to leave them die.
>
> (*Doença de crianca*) can come from many different things. It can come from a fright the child has, but also from dirty laundry, or from strong germs that enter through the fingernails. Look, we don't like talking about this. We don't mention its name. We are afraid of calling it up.

It became painfully apparent that Alto mothers were often describing the symptoms of severe malnutrition and gastroenteric illness further complicated by their own selective inattention. Untreated diarrheas and dehydration contributed to the baby's passivity, his or her disinterest in food, and developmental delays. High fevers often produced the fit-like convulsions that mothers feared as harbingers of permanent madness or epilepsy. Because these hungry and dehydraled babies are so passive and uncomplaining, their mothers can easily forget to attend to their needs, and can distance themselves emotionally from what comes to appear as an *unnatural* child, an angel of death that was never meant to live. Many such babies are left alone in their hammocks while their mothers are out working, and not even a sibling or a neighbor woman is within earshort when their feeble cries signal a final crisis, and so they die alone and unattended—*a mingua* as people say. A mother speaks of having "pity" for such a child, but her grief is as attenuated as her attachment to a baby who never demonstrated more than a fragile hold on life. The dead baby is washed and dressed in white satin and covered with sweet-smelling flowers. The coffin is simple: a cardboard or inexpensive wooden box decorated with a lining of purple tissue paper and a silver paper cross. Alto children form the funeral procession. In this way they are socialized to accept as natural and commonplace the burial of siblings and playmates; as later, perhaps they will have to bury their own children and grandchildren.

BONDING THEORY AND THE BIOLOGICAL BASIS OF MOTHER LOVE

In recent years there has been considerable interest in exploring the biological components of mother–infant attachment. The observations of species specific maternal behavior patterns such as nesting, grooming, and retrieving which have been studied in animal mothers immediately after birth led a number of ethnologists, human biologists, anthropologists, pediatricians, and developmental psychologists to posit the parallel existence of a sequence of largely *innate* behaviors in human mothers' responses to their newborn. Such maternal behaviors as smiling, gazing, cooing, nuzzling, sniffing, fondling, and enfolding the newborn immediately postpartum has been observed, recorded, and quantified in order to demonstrate the existence of a universal psychobiological script referred to as "mother–infant bonding" (Klaus and Kennell 1976).

Maternal bonding (or loving and attentive, if somewhat mindless, attachment to the newborn) is said to be "triggered" in mothers in response to instinctual infant behaviors, especially crying, sucking, clinging and smiling. The automatic "milk let-down" reflex in lactating mothers' responses to hungry infant cries is often cited as evidence of the unlearned and innate components of mothering. Klaus and Kennell and their associates have identified a "critical" or "sensitive" period for maternal bonding that is said to occur immediately postpartum:

> There is sensitive period in the first *minutes* and hours of life during which it is *necessary* that the mother and

> father have close contact with the neonate for later devlopment to be optimal. (Klaus and Kennell 1976:14)

If the mother and the infant are separated during this time (as is customary in hospital delivery), maternal bonding may be inhibited, suggest Klaus and Kennell, with consequences as serious as maternal indifference toward, or even rejection of, the infant when the two are reunited. Unlike other mammals, however, rarely are these consequences irreversible in *human* mothers:

> The process that takes place during the maternal sensitive period differs from imprinting in that there is not a point beyond which the formation of an attachment is precluded. This is the *optimal* but not the sole period for an attachment to develop. Although the process can occur at a later time, it will be more difficult and take longer to achieve. (Kennell, Trause, and Klaus 1975:88)

Support for the evolutionary genetic basis of human bonding has come from recent studies of hunter-gatherer populations. Research by Draper, Howell, and Konner (see Lee and DeVore 1976) indicates that the relationship between mother and infant in such small, mobile social groups is characterized by: a high degree of physical skin-on-skin contact (for over 70% of the day and night in the early months of life); continuous and prolonged nursing (up to 4 or 5 years); close, attentive, and seemingly "indulgent" maternal behavior. These behaviors "typical of most primate species living in large groups [and of most] hunter-gatherers known today . . . probably represent the usual social environment for development in our species going back millions of years" (SSRC Committee on Biosocial Science n.d.:2). Maternal bonding, therefore, is thought to be part of our evolutionary inheritance.

Alice Rossi suggests that while "biologically males have only one innate orientation, a sexual one that draws them to women, women have two such orientations, a sexual one toward men, and a reproductive one toward the young" (1977:5). Human mothering has a strong unlearned component, argues Rossi, because of the precarious timing of human birth. The extremely immature and dependent human neonate requires particularly close attention and care in order to assure its survival. Therefore, it was particularly advantageous for a "maternal instinct" to become genetically encoded in women's evolutionary psychology.

The by now extensive maternal-infant bonding literature[3] has had, among other effects, a profound influence upon changes in the obstetrical management of pregnancy, labor, and delivery in this country and elsewhere. Many hospitals now have "birthing rooms" and rooming-in wards in order to enhance early mother–infant interaction and maternal bonding. Unfortunately, however, some of the "disciples" of Klaus and Kennell enlarged the claims made for the significance of early bonding. This lead to the naïve belief among some health professionals that if early contact was *necessary* to ensure *optimal* parenting, perhaps this was *all* that was needed to ensure *competent* parenting. A number of hospital-based intervention programs, based on this shaky assumption, were launched in the 1970s when belief in the critical importance of early bonding was at its height (see Lamb 1982b). Some programs identified high-risk populations for "inadequate" parenting (usually this meant the poor, nonwhite teenage or single mothers, mothers of low birth-weight infants, previous child abusers) and manipulated the hospital environment in order to "promote" bonding in the high-risk mothers who were sometimes observed against a matched control group. Rarely was there any attention paid to providing a supportive environment for the mother and child once they left the hospital. Similarly, the child abuse literature is replete with references to abuse and neglect as the consequence of failures in early maternal bonding.[4]

Recently, the scientific basis of bonding theory has been called into question,[5] and several longitudinal studies have not supported claims for any *long-term* effects of early mother–infant interaction (Ali and Lowry 1981; Rutter 1972; Chess and Thomas 1982; Curry 1979; deChateau 1980; deChateau and Wiberg 1977). As the scientific status of maternal bonding has receded, however, a view of womanhood positing the powerful effects of reproduction and mothering on females has arisen among some feminists (Rosaldo and Lamphere 1974; Ortner 1974; Chodorow 1978; Marks and de Courtivron, eds. 1980; Ruddick 1980; Gilligan 1982; Greer 1984). Sara Ruddick, for example, in a widely cited article published in *Feminist Studies* (1980:346–347) posits certain

> features of the mothering experience which are *invariant* and nearly *unchangeable*, and others, which, though changeable, are nearly universal. It is therefore possible to identify interests that appear to govern maternal practice throughout the species.

These *interests* concern demands for the *preservation, growth,* and *acceptability* of offspring. Ruddick refers to women's experience of a "social-biological pride in the function of their reproductive processes" (1980:344) and of a "sense of well-being" when their children flourish. Although she acknowledges that some economic and social conditions, such as poverty and isolation "may make [maternal] love frantic" (p. 344), she nonetheless maintains that these "do not kill the love." And she adds, "For whatever reasons, mothers typically find it not only *natural* but compelling to protect and foster the growth of their children" (1980:344). In stating her strong case for a *generalized* mode of "maternal thinking" Ruddick does specify that her model is based on her "knowledge of the institutions of motherhood in middle-class, white, Protestant, capitalist, patriarchal America" (p. 347) and she does call upon others "to correct her interpretations and to translate across cultures."

This is precisely what I shall do for the remainder of this paper in response to both the "bonding" and the "maternal sentiments" literature.

CULTURE, SCARCITY, AND HUMAN NEEDS

I have seen death without weeping
The destiny of the Northeast is death
Cattle they kill
To the people they do something worse
—Traveling *repentista* singer, Brazil

Whenever we social and behavioral scientists involve ourselves in the study of women's lives—most especially thinking and behavior surrounding reproduction and maternity—we frequently come up against psychobiological theories of *human* nature that have been uncritically derived from assumptions and values implicit in the structure of the modern, Western, bourgeois family. Theories of innate maternal scripts such as "bonding," "maternal thinking," or "maternal instincts" are both culture and history bound, the reflection of a very specific and very recent reproductive strategy: to give birth to few babies and invest heavily in each one. This is a reproductive strategy that was a stranger to most of European history through the early modern period,[6] and it does not reflect the "maternal thinking" of a great many women living in the Third World today where an alternative strategy holds: to give birth to many children, invest selectively based on culturally derived favored characteristics, and hope that a few survive infancy and the early years of life. This reproductive strategy requires a very different conception of maternal thinking, and just as surely elicits different kinds of maternal attachments, feelings, and sentiments—such as, for example, those implicated in the selective neglect of "high risk" babies on the Alto do Cruzeiro. Since this reproductive strategy is characteristic of much of the world's poorer population today, it would seem that some revision of the maternal bonding/maternal thinking as a universal human script is in order.

As might be expected, women whose cumulative experiences lead them to resignation with respect to high fertility *and* to an expectation of frequent failure to rear healthy, living children will respond differently to their newborn than middle-class mothers with both greater control over their fertility *and* a high expectation for the health and viability of their children. Infant life *and* infant death carry different meanings, weight, and significance to Alto women than to the mothers generally studied in "bonding" research. Despite the fact that the birth and neonatal environment on Alto do Cruzeiro should be optimal for intense, early bonding to occur, mother–infant attachment is often muted and *protectively distanced*.

The traditional birth environment among Alto women is a home birth attended by a lay midwife and by several supportive female friends and relatives, especially the woman's mother. Virtually all the mothers in my sample over 40 gave birth at home with a traditional *parteira*; half the younger women still prefer home to hospital delivery, although "charity cases" are accepted in the maternity wing of the town hospital. Even those who do give birth in the town *maternidade* stay for less than 2 days and keep their newborns in a small crib next to the hospital bed.

Alto mothers and infants sleep together until the baby is considered old enough to sleep in its own small hammock or cot next to the mother's bed. Cosleeping lasts from 1 month to 6 months. Breastfeeding, although greatly attenuated, is the norm for the first few weeks (generally 1 month to 6 weeks in this sample). Although Alto infants are not tied to the mother's person in shawl or sling, the infant spends a good many hours of the day in the arms or, when slightly older, balancing on the hip of the mother or any one of a number of convenient mother surrogates: siblings of both sexes, neighbors, visiting anthropologists. There is a great deal of physical affection expressed toward infants who are frequently stroked, tickled, teased, sniffed (kissing is thought inappropriate), and babbled to by all in the household. In short, all the conditions conducive to "bonding," as described in the medical and psychological literature, can be said to obtain in O Cruzeiro.

Nonetheless, Alto mothers protect themselves from strong, emotional attachment to their infants through a form of nurturance that is, from the start, somewhat "impersonal," for lack of a better word. Many Alto babies remain not only unchristened but *unnamed* until they begin to walk or talk *or* until a medical crisis (and the possibility of death) prompts a hurried, emergency baptism. In such cases (and I have been present at several of these) the name given the child is incidental. In some cases I or another casual onlooker was asked to pick a name spontaneously. Often the infant simply inherits the name of the last infant to have died in the family. Unnamed babies are simply called *ne-ne* (baby) or given a Brazilian generic name, Ze (Joe) or Maria. Adult affection for the *ne-ne* is diffuse and not focused on any particular characteristics of the infant as a little persona.

The circulation of babies through informal adoption or abandonment is commonplace on the Alto. Mothers in dire straits will sometimes ask a current or former employer to take their baby as a foster child or even as a future household servant. Young and unmarried women will sometime leave a 5- or 6- month-old baby on the doorstep of an Alto woman known to be particularly tender-hearted. This happened to a dear friend and key informant during the summer of my stay in 1982, and brought back poignant memories to us both of the occasions during 1965–1966 when we had to cope with several babies abandoned at the cooperative day care center we had organized on the hill.

Given the extraordinary incidence of infant mortality on the Alto, child funerals are an almost daily occurrence and are dispatched with a quality of *la belle indifferance* that outsiders sometimes find quite shocking (see, for example, Scrimshaw 1978). The infant coffinmaker is a village level specialist found in every community of Northeastern Brazil. He sometimes works in the medium of cardboard, paper maché and scrap material. A brief wake is held in the home when an infant over 6 months dies. Household visitors are expected to admire the sweet angel, but not to grieve. Mothers are scolded by other women if they shed tears for an infant, and few do. There do exist cases of Alto women who refuse to forget the death of a particularly favored baby, but their emotions tend to be dismissed as inappropriate or even as symptomatic of a kind of insanity.

The mundaneness and the high expectancy of infant death is shared by physicians and politicians of the town. In pointing out to the mayor of Ladeiras the rather extraordinary rate of child mortality for the community he replied that he was aware of the problem and that he had, in fact, fulfilled a campaign promise in that regard: a free baby coffin to all registered voters according to their family's needs.

In all, what is constructed is an environment in which loss is anticipated and bets are hedged. "Mother love" with its attendant emotions of *holding, keeping*, and *preserving* is replaced by an estranged and guarded "watchful waiting." What makes this possible is a cultural conception of the child as human, but significantly less human than the grown child or adult. There is socialized in the Alto mother an emotion of estrangement toward the infant that is protective to her, but potentially lethal to the child. Maria Piers (1978:37) refers to this state of primitive unconnectedness as "basic strangeness":

> Basic strangeness precedes basic trust. It marks the beginning of life and its end. In the intervening years, however, many situations occur that drive us back partially or wholly into that state. Basic strangeness denotes the opposite of empathy. It is a state in which we "turn off" toward others and are unable to experience them as fellow human beings. Instead, we may value them as inanimate objects.

Piers suggests that the single most frequent cause of such total estrangement is "abject poverty" leading to physical weakness and hopelessness. In such a condition, "even one's own child may appear as a competitor" (1978:39). In human parenting nothing can be taken for granted, least of all that the parent would sacrifice her life and resources for her child. Human mothers who reach the limit of their endurance can and often do become both estranged from and indifferent toward their children. Certainly Piers's concept is worthy of further refinement and investigation.

However, I do not wish to suggest by the foregoing that Alto mothers never suffer the loss of their infants. Indeed, amidst the generally passive and emotionally flat narrations of their lives as women, workers, and mothers, the pain of a particularly unresolved or poignant loss would break through and shatter the equanimity and resignation that is the norm. There would be memories of *particular* babies in whom a mother's hopes for the future *had* been invested, and she would weep in the telling of *that* death of all the deaths and losses she had endured. In the presence of so "deviant" a response I would be at a loss for how to proceed, or indeed, whether to proceed at all. But invariably my Alto assistant, Irene, or another woman would come to the rescue. "No, Dona Maria," she would scold the grieving woman, "of course you will not go mad with grief. You *will* conform. You will go on. You have *your own life* ahead."

The reproductive and life histories of these shantytown women lead me to question the validity of such ill-defined terms as maternal bonding, attachment, maternal thinking, critical period, and separation anxiety that fill the literature on mother–infant interaction. The terms and concepts seem wholly inadequate to convey the experience of mothering under the less than optimum conditions that prevail throughout much of the world today. The classical maternal bonding model focuses altogether too much attention on too few critical variables and on too brief a period in the mother–child life cycle. The model grossly underestimates the power and significance of social and cultural factors that influence and shape maternal thinking over time: the cultural meanings of sexuality, fertility, death, and survival; mother's assessment of her economic, social support, and psychological resources; family size and composition; characteristics and evaluation of the infant—its strength, beauty, viability, temperament, and "winsomeness."

The bonding model has neither relevance to, nor resonance with, the experiences of the women of O Cruzeiro for whom the life history of attachments follows a torturous path marked by many interruptions, separations, rejections, and losses reflecting the precariousness of their own existence and survival. But it is also important to note that an early lack of attachment, an indifferent commitment, or even a hostile rejection of an infant does not preclude the possibility of an enfolding drama of mother–child attachments later on, as some of the memorable survivors of early and severe selective neglect, like Ze-Ze, would indicate. That there must be a biological basis to human emotions is not disputed. It is argued, however, that the nature of human love and attachments is a complex phenomenon, socially constructed and made meaningful through culture. A more contextualized model of maternal thinking and sentiments is needed.

Finally, in concluding this paper, I wish to make it abundantly clear that there are many conditions on the Alto do Cruzeiro that are hostile to child survival. Most serious are the ones I scarcely mentioned: contaminated water, unchecked infectious disease, food shortages, the absence of day care facilities, and grossly inadequate medical care. I have focused instead on maternal thinking and behaviors that may also contribute to childhood mortality in order to address the indignities and inhumanities forced on poor women who must make choices and decisions that no woman should have to make. In the final analysis, the selective neglect of children must be understood as a direct consequence of the "selective neglect" of their mothers who have been excluded from participating in what was once called the Economic Miracle of modern Brazil.

NOTES

1. See Paim, Netto-Dias, and De Araujo 1980. Also, see Wood 1977. A recent PAHO investigation of childhood mortality in a dozen urban and rural sites in eight Latin American countries found the city of Recife in Pernambuco, Northeast Brazil, to have the highest infant mortality of all urban centers sampled.
2. See Goldberg, Rodrigues, Thome, and Morris 1982; Grant 1983; Berquo, Cukier, and Spindel 1984. A recent UNICEF report noted that in Brazil the percentage of babies breastfed *for any length of time* has fallen from 96% in 1940 to under 40% in 1974. This same report cites another study which found that among a large sample of children of poor parents in the South of Brazil, bottle-fed babies were between three and four times more likely to be seriously malnourished than breastfed babies.
3. See, for example, Klaus and Kennell 1976, 1982; Kennel, Voos, and Klaus 1979; Klaus, Jerauld, and Kreger 1972; Lozoff, Brittenham, and Trause 1977.
4. See, for example, Hurd 1975 and Schwarzbeck 1977.
5. See, for example, Sveja, Campos, and Emede 1980; Lamb 1982a, 1982b, and 1982c; Korsch 1983.
6. Contemporary historians of European and American family life in the early modern period have described childrearing practices that were at best harshly pragmatic, and at worst sadistic and passively infanticidal. (See, for example, Aries 1962; de Mause 1974; Fox and Quitt 1980; Laslett 1965; Shorter 1975; Stone 1977.)

REFERENCES

Ali, Z., and M. Lowry. 1981. Early Maternal-Child Contact: Effect on Later Behavior. *Developmental Medicine and Child Neurology* 23:337–345.

Aries, Philipe. 1962. *Centuries of Childhood: A Social History of Family Life*. New York: Vantage.

Berquo, Elza, Rosa Cukier, and Cheywa Spindel. 1984. *Caracterizaçao e Determinantes Do Aleitamento Materno na Grande São Paulo e na Grande Recife*. CEBRAP—Centro Brasileiro de Analise e Planejamento, Nova Serie Numero 2.

Bourne, Richard, and Eli Newberger, eds. 1979. *Critical Perspectives on Child Abuse and Neglect*. Lexington, MA: Lexington Books.

Chess, Stella, and Alexander Thomas. 1982. Infant Bonding: Mystique and Reality. *American Journal of Orthopsychiatry* 52(2):213–222.

Chodorow, Nancy. 1978. *The Reproduction of Mothering: Psychoanalysis and the Sociology of Gender*. Berkeley: University of California Press.

Curry, M.A.H. 1979. Contact during the First Hour with the Wrapped or Naked Newborn: Effects of Maternal Attachment Behaviors at 36 Hours and Three Months. *Birth and Family Journal* 6:227–235.

DeChateau, P. 1980. *Parent–Neonate Interaction and Its Long-Term Effects: Early Experiences and Early Behavior* (E. G. Simmel, ed.). New York: Academic Press.

DeChateau, P., and B. Wiberg. 1977. Long-Term Effects on Mother–Infant Behavior of Extra Contact During the First Hour Post Partum. *Acta Paedietrica Scandinavica* 66: 145–151.

De Mause, Lloyd. 1974. *The History of Childhood*. New York: The Psychohistory Press.

Fox, Vivian, and Martin H. Quitt. 1980. *Loving, Parenting and Dying: The Family Cycle in England and America*. New York: The Psychohistory Press.

Gelles, Richard. 1973. Child Abuse as Psychopathology. *American Journal of Orthopsychiatry* 43(4):611–621.

Gilligan, Carol. 1982. *In a Different Voice: Psychological Theory and Women's Development*. Cambridge: Harvard University Press.

Gills, David. 1970. *Violence against Children*. Cambridge: Harvard University Press.

Goldberg, H., W. Rodrigues, M. Thome, and Morris. 1982. Infant Mortality and Breastfeeding in Northeastern Brazil. Paper presented at the Population Association of America Annual Meeting, San Diego, California.

Grant, J. 1983. The State of the World's Children, 1982–1983. UNICEF, Information Division, Geneva, Switzerland.

Greer, Germaine. 1984. *Sex and Destiny: Politics and Human Fertility*. New York: Harper & Row.

Hurd, J. L. M. 1975. Assessing Maternal Attachment: First Step toward the Prevention of Child Abuse. *Journal of Obstetric, Gynecologic and Neonatal Nursing* 4(4):25–30.

Kempe, H., and R. Helfer. 1980. *The Battered Child*. Chicago: University of Chicago Press.

Kennel, J. H., M. A. Trause, and M. H. Klaus. 1975. *Parent–Infant Interaction*. CIBA Foundation Symposium, No. 33. Amsterdam: Elsevier.

Kennel, J. H., V. K. Voos, and M. H. Klaus. 1979. Parent–Infant Bonding. *Handbook of Infant Development* (J. D. Osfsky, ed.). New York: Wiley.

Klaus, M. H. R. Jerauld, and N. C. Kreger. 1972. Maternal Attachment: Importance of the First Post-Partum Days. *New England Journal of Medicine* 286:460–463.

Klaus, M., and J. K. Kennell, eds. 1976. *Maternal-Infant Bonding*. St. Louis: C. V. Mosby (revised edition entitled *Parent–Infant Bonding*, 1982).

Korsch, Barbara. 1983. More on Parent–Infant Bonding. *Journal of Pediatrics* (February):249-250.

Lamb, Michael. 1982a. Maternal Attachment and Mother–Neonate Bonding: A Critical Review. *Advance in Developmental Psychology*. Vol. 2, pp. 1–39. Hillsdale, NJ: Lawrence Erlbaum Associates.

———. 1982b. Early Contacts and Maternal–Infant Bonding: One Decade Later. *Pediatrics* 70(5):763–768.

———. 1982c. The Bonding Phenomenon: Misinterpretations and Their Implications. *Journal of Pediatrics* 10(4): 555–557.

Laslett, Peter. 1965. *The World We Have Lost*. London: Methuen.

Lee, R. B., and I. De Vore. 1976. *Kalahari Hunter-Gatherers*. Cambridge: Harvard University Press.

Lozoff, B., G. M. Brittenham, and M. A. Trause. 1977. The Mother–Newborn Relationship: Limits of Adaptability. *Journal of Pediatrics* 91:1-12.

Marks, Elaine, and Isabelle De Courtivron, eds. 1980. *New French Feminisms*. New York: Schocken.

Ortner, Sherry. 1974. Is Female to Male as Nature Is to Culture? *Women, Culture, and Society* (M. Rosaldo and L, Lamphere, eds.), pp. 67–88. Stanford: Stanford University Press.

Paim, S., C. Netto-Dias, and J. DeAraujo. 1980. Influencia de Fatores Sociais e Ambientais na Mortalidade Infantil. *Boln. Of Sanit. Pan-Am* LXXXVIII:327–340.

Piers, Marta. *1978. Infanticide*. New York: W. W. Norton.

Rosaldo, Michelle, and Louise Lamphere. 1974. Introduction. *Women, Culture, and Society* (M. Rosaldo and L. Lamphere, eds.), pp. 1–16. Stanford: Stanford University Press.

Rossi, Alice. 1977. A Biosocial Perspective on Parenting. *Daedalus* 106(2):1–32.

Ruddick, Sara. 1980. Maternal Thinking. *Feminist Studies* 6:342–364.

Rutter, Michael. 1972. *Maternal Deprivation Reassessed*. New York: Penguin.

Schwarzbeck, C. 1977. Identification of Infants at Risk for Child Abuse: Observations and Inferences in the Examination of the Mother-Infant Dyad. *Child Abuse: Where Do We Go from Here?* Conference Proceedings, Feb. 18–20, 1977. Washington, D.C.: Children's Hospital National Medical Center, Child Protection Center, pp. 67–69.

Scrimshaw, Susan. 1978. Infant Mortality and Maternal Behavior in the Regulation of Family Size. *Population and Development Review 4:383–403.*

Shorter, Edward. 1975. *The Making of the Modern Family*. New York: Basic Books.

SSRC Committee on Biosocial Science, n. d. Biosocial Foundations of Parenting and Offspring Development. New York: SSRC, unpublished report.

Steele, Brandt, and Carl Pollock. 1968. A Psychiatric Study of Parents Who Abuse Their Children. *The Battered Child* (R. E. Heifer and C. H. Kempe, eds.), pp. 103–147. Chicago: University of Chicago Press.

Stone, Lawrence. 1977. *The Family, Sex, and Marriage in England, 1500–1800*. New York: Harper & Row.

Svejda, M. J., J. J. Campos, and R. N. Emede. 1980. Mother–Infant "Bonding": Failure to Generalize. *Child Development* 51:775–779.

Wood, Charles. 1977. Infant Mortality Trends and Capitalist Development in Brazil. *Latin American Perspectives* 4(4): 56–65.

Culture and Nutrition: Fat and Thin

■ ***Nutrition is a key aspect of health, and eating habits are largely shaped by culture and political economy.*** Nutritional anthropologists study how and what people in different cultures eat. This includes measures of actual food preparation and intake, as well as the symbolic meanings of food. Children's growth and development require the regular consumption of calories, protein, and essential micronutrients. Malnourished children are less able to survive inevitable bouts of infectious disease. There have always been food shortages, and still today many people of the world are malnourished. The social epidemiological distribution of malnutrition is never random.

■ ***Malnutrition can be in the form of protein-calorie malnutrition (PCM), micronutrient malnutrition, and overnutrition.*** Nutritional needs change over the life cycle, and lack of adequate food during gestation and childhood may have lifelong effects on physical and mental health. Food shortages have immediate impacts on children. PCM refers to overall nutritional intake and the bioavailability of energy from calories as well as protein; PCM may even be considered a biomedical label for hunger (Cassidy 1982). In some parts of the world, the traditional diet may be deficient in particular vitamins and minerals. Micronutrient malnutrition diseases include goiter and cretinism from iodine deficiency, night blindness from vitamin A deficiency, scurvy from vitamin C deficiency, and a host of others. In the developed world, overnutrition is a widespread and intractable problem.

■ ***Within the same household, everyone may not have the same access to food.*** Although children and pregnant women have the greatest nutritional needs, they do not always receive adequate or appropriate foods. The "breadwinner effect" is a common scenario in many cultures, in which people doing physical labor receive the largest portion of food. Sometimes a significant portion of the household budget may be used for nonnutritive consumables like cigarettes and alcohol. Within households, those most vulnerable are probably "weanlings"—toddlers who no longer get breast milk and who have to adapt to adult foods. Some nutritional interventions in Third World countries have emphasized the development of appropriate weaning foods (Dettwyler and Fishman 1992).

■ ***"Positive deviance" refers to exceptional cases that have good health outcomes.*** There is considerable variation among individuals within any society and culture. As medical anthropologists study how cultural patterns might play a role in causing health problems, they must also be on the lookout for individuals who have chosen different, successful strategies. Solutions to health problems may be found among such cultural innovators or "positive deviants." International health programs can develop and promote these local solutions.

■ ***Some nutritional problems require study on multiple levels of analysis.*** To understand nutritional problems, medical anthropologists often think it is useful to examine different levels—the individual, the household, the society, and the regional economy. For nutritional problems like anorexia nervosa, there are clearly several levels of interaction: individual beliefs, family dynamics, social pressures, cultural beliefs, and larger sociocultural contexts. Anthropologists study problems at all of these levels.

■ ***Obesity is a growing health problem in the United States and throughout the world.*** Overnutrition in calories, particularly fat, and declines in physical activity are the cause of this "epidemic." While there are both biological and cultural factors that predispose people to obesity, radical culture changes have created this serious problem.

 44

The Biocultural Approach in Nutritional Anthropology: Case Studies of Malnutrition in Mali

Katherine A. Dettwyler

Medical anthropological research dealing with nutritional issues is, almost by definition, biocultural in its approach. What foods people eat and how much they eat are determined not simply by hunger, a biological drive, but more importantly by political-ecological factors that determine the availability of food and cultural factors that shape the acceptability and preparation of food. Some scholars have questioned the "small but healthy" hypothesis, and nutritional anthropologists must be concerned about measures of childhood growth and development. Such measures reflect the biological consequences of nutritional intake. Researchers can assess the nutritional status of children by using standards, like the National Center for Health Statistics (NCHS) standards used in this selection.

Undernutrition takes two forms. First is overall protein and calorie deficit, as described here in case studies from the African country of Mali. Marasmus, a type of overall wasting, and kwashiorkor, an illness of protein deficiency often related to weaning, are particular types of malnutrition. In the poor countries of the world, there is a well-documented relation between undernutrition and infectious disease. Poorly nourished children have a harder time recovering from bouts of infectious disease, while at the same time illness episodes slow growth rates. This situation is often found in relation to inappropriate infant formula feeding wherein babies may be given an extremely diluted solution of "milk" made with water that is full of pathogens. The interaction of disease and malnutrition means that underweight children are more likely to die, as was sadly noted by the Brazilian shantytown mothers studied by Nancy Scheper-Hughes in selection 44.

Malnutrition can also be the result of the lack of a specific micronutrient such as iodine or vitamin A; a severe deficiency of iodine, for example, can result in goiter and mental retardation (Fernandez 1990; Greene 1977). Such consequences can be avoided by relatively simple programs of adding iodine to salt. Whether such well-aimed "magic bullets" will do much to solve problems of world hunger, however, is another question.

In this selection, Katherine Dettwyler provides individual case studies of child malnutrition in Mali. These are like the cases she describes in her book of anthropological fieldwork, Dancing Skeletons *(1994). Mali is one of the poorest countries of the world, and as a consequence, both child malnutrition and death rates are very high. This selection demonstrates that the relationship between socioeconomic status and malnutrition is not simple, for some of the cases here are the children of low-status mothers within a relatively prosperous extended family household. The vast majority of malnutrition in Third World countries does not have a single identifiable cause. Local agricultural production and the marketing of food are central factors, but issues regarding the status of women or cultural rules about child feeding also must be considered.*

As you read this selection, consider these questions:

- **What are the particular situations of these Malian mothers and children that result in child malnutrition and early death? In any one of these cases, how might these tragic outcomes have been avoided?**
- **Why is this study of malnutrition considered biocultural? Are there cultural factors that might not get included in regular nutrition surveys?**
- **What does the author mean when she says that in many instances children are severely malnourished because they "have fallen through the safety net of overlapping support systems that normally ensure a minimum level of nutrition and health for children in the community"? Why is she impressed that the traditional system is actually working?**
- **Do you think it is relevant that two of the case studies are of twins?**

Context: Katherine Dettwyler is author of the widely known book *Dancing Skeletons: Life and Death in West Africa*. In 1995, this book was awarded the Margaret Mead Award, for communication to the public, by the American Anthropological Association and the Society for Applied Anthropology. It is a very readable and personal account of field research on a medical anthropological topic in Mali, West Africa.

As a nutritional anthropologist, her primary interest is in breast-feeding; she is co-editor of *Breastfeeding: Biocultural Perspectives.* A proponent of an extended period of breast-feeding (up to four years) based on her biocultural and evolutionary approach in medical anthropology, Dettwyler speaks regularly to groups like the La Leche League. This article was written for a professional anthropological audience.

Source: K. Dettwyler, (1992). "The Biocultural Approach in Nutritional Anthropology: Case Studies of Malnutrition in Mali." *Medical Anthropology* 15(1):17–39.

Socioeconomic status is often cited as the most important factor influencing nutritional status in children, and, in general, national rates of malnutrition are negatively correlated with per capita income. As Pryer and Crook (1988:5) have stated, "Appalling environmental conditions and intense poverty are likely to be the two most important determinants of health and nutritional status of the slum and shanty town dwellers in many of the cities of the developing countries." Although not disputing this conclusion, a number of ethnographic studies have highlighted the role that cultural beliefs and practices regarding infant feeding and care also play in determining health and nutritional status in young children (Daniggelis 1987a, 1987b; Guldan 1988; Hull and Simpson 1985; Marshall 1985; Zeitlin and Guldan 1988).

The work of Zeitlin and her colleagues has focused on the role of psychosocial and behavioral aspects of child care and feeding in determining "positive deviance" in child health—those children who manage to thrive under conditions of environmental adversity (see Zeitlin, Ghassemi, and Mansour 1990 for a review of the literature on positive deviance). Others have focused on attributes of those children who fare particularly poorly under such conditions, including how they are perceived by their caretakers. For example, in a study of childhood deaths in northeastern Brazil, Scheper-Hughes found that mothers "gave up" on severely malnourished children and neglected them until they died (Scheper-Hughes 1987). Likewise, Mull and Mull report that among the Tarahumara of Mexico, children who are perceived as being "handicapped" may be allowed to starve to death, or are killed outright (Mull and Mull 1987). In Kenya, de Vries (1987) found that Masai infants who cry a lot are perceived as being fighters, with the personality and will necessary to survive the harsh conditions of life. These children are given more attention and nursed more often than quiet, placid babies. The quieter babies thus suffer and die more often from malnutrition.

The work of Bledsoe, Ewbank, and Isiugo-Abanihe (1988) and Bledsoe (1991) has focused on intrahousehold food distribution patterns and the effect of being a foster child on access to food and health care resources, growth, and health among the Mende of Sierra Leone. Bledsoe finds that, compared to "born" children of the household, young "fosters" have less access to food resources but are expected to perform more labor (Bledsoe 1991). Fosters also suffer more from malnutrition, but are taken to the hospital less often than "born" children (Bledsoe, Ewbank, and Isiugo-Abanihe 1988).

These examples could all be described as instances of "socio-cultural malnutrition," a term coined by Gokulanathan and Verghese to refer to growth failure in children that is "due to factors other than poverty and the lack of availability of food materials" (1969:118). Research in Mali (West Africa) suggests that sociocultural malnutrition contributes to the overall malnutrition picture. A number of studies in Mali have compared expenditures for food and dietary intakes of groups at different levels of socioeconomic status and from different parts of the country. All of these studies have concluded that relative income is not closely related to diet in Mali (Diakite 1968; Clairin et al. 1967; May 1968; Mondot-Bernard and Labonne 1982). Members of all social classes consume the same foods in the same quantities, and rising income is not correlated with an increase in quantity or an improvement in the nutritional quality of the diet.

In 1982 and 1983, and again in 1989, the author conducted research in a periurban community in Mali, focusing on the relationship between infant/child feeding beliefs and practices and the growth and development of children. The 1982–83 research was based on a mixed-longitudinal study of 136 children under four years of age. The 1989 research included a follow-up study of the children in the earlier sample. Previous publications based on this research have described the systems of beliefs concerning infant and child feeding practices (Dettwyler 1985, 1986), breast-feeding and weaning (Dettwyler 1985, 1987), the role of anorexia in malnutrition (Dettwyler 1989a), infant feeding styles (Dettwyler 1989b), and the relationship between relative poverty and nutritional status and growth in the entire sample (Dettwyler 1985, 1986).

Treating the growth data in cross section, average growth for all children in the 1982–83 sample during the first three years of life corresponds closely to the fifth percentile of NCHS standards (Hamill et al. 1979; . . .). A few children were growing at or above the NCHS fiftieth percentile, even though they came from relatively poor families (cf. "positive deviants," Zeitlin, Ghassemi, and Mansour 1990), while others were well below the fifth percentile, including some from relatively well-off families. The children in the latter group can be described as having fallen through the safety net of overlapping support systems that normally ensure a minimal level of nutrition and health for children in the community.

The data clearly indicate that relative poverty is not an accurate predictor of the observed variation in nutritional status and growth in this community, and that differences in maternal attitudes, experience, and other factors are responsible (Dettwyler 1986). In Mali, these factors include maternal age, marital problems, untreated illness, allocation of household resources, maternal attitudes, maternal competence and experience, support networks, and the position of the mother within the social structure of a polygynous, patrilineal society. In this paper, case studies of three families from the research community illustrate how sociocultural malnutrition in young children in Mali can be viewed as a consequence of the interactions among many factors. It is hoped that the case studies will demonstrate the value of a biocultural approach in which detailed ethnographic data, gathered in conjunction with traditional anthropometric measurements, can illuminate the intricate interactions between culture and biology.

DEMOGRAPHIC AND ETHNOGRAPHIC BACKGROUND OF THE SAMPLE

The study community of Farimabougou (a pseudonym) is one of approximately ten periurban communities located across the Niger River from the capital city of Bamako. During 1982 and 1983, a sample of 136 children were visited every four to eight weeks. The sample was constructed in a flexible, random manner, by walking the streets of the community, looking for families with young infants (not yet eating solid foods), explaining the project, and recruiting families willing to cooperate over an extended period of time. The study compounds were widely distributed and included all sectors of the community. A few infants, usually from neighboring compounds, were added to the study at the request of their mothers. Only three families dropped out of the study due to lack of interest. Several families were dropped because the index infant died during the measles epidemic that occurred during the initial month of the study. The final sample of 136 children came from 117 compounds and included 20 sibling pairs.

Growth data were collected at each visit, and multiple, semistructured interviews of mothers and other caretakers, as well as participant-observation of child feeding activities, were used to collect data on infant feeding beliefs and practices and infant health. Growth data included anthropometric measures of weight, and of arm, head, and chest circumference, as well as number of teeth erupted and general stage of motor and language development. Exact ages were determined from birth certificates, and the records of the local maternity clinic provided birth weights for some of the children.[1] All interviews were conducted by the author in Bambara, the native language of most of the informants, with the assistance of a Malian interpreter. A follow-up study of the same children was conducted in 1989. Approximately half of the children were relocated, measured again when possible, and their mothers interviewed again.

A brief description of the community will provide a wider context for the case studies that follow. Traditionally, the Malian economy has been based on subsistence agriculture. Bamako and Farimabougou, however, operate primarily on a cash economy. Most food is purchased in the daily market using cash obtained from the wage labor of fathers and, occasionally, mothers. Farimabougou is a poor community. In 1979, the World Bank defined the "urban poverty threshold" for Bamako as approximately $60.00 per month per household, and reported that the average income in Farimabougou is 40 percent lower than that of Bamako, with almost half of the households in Farimabougou below the urban poverty threshold (World Bank 1979).

In terms of ethnic identity, the parents of children in the study identify themselves primarily as Bambara or Mandinka (67%); the rest are divided among Fulani, Senoufo, Songhrai, Bobo, and Dogon. According to information provided by the Institut du Sahel (T. T. Kane, pers. comm. 1989), in 1989 Mali had a crude birth rate of 47/1,000 and a crude death rate of 20/1,000, resulting in a natural growth rate of 2.7 percent. The infant mortality rate was 130/1,000, and the juvenile mortality rate was 159/1,000. Life expectancy at birth was 47 years. The average number of births was 6.7 per woman. Data for these variables specific to Farimabougou do not exist.

During the 1982–83 study in Farimabougou, the average age for the introduction of solid foods was 7.9 months, with 14.4 months as the average age when children began eating the adult staples (millet and rice). The average age of weaning was 20.8 months, and women experienced an average duration of lactational amenorrhea of 10.1 months. The average pregnancy interval was 19.4 months, and the average interbirth interval was 26.5 months.

Two of the case studies reported here involved twins. According to local maternity clinic records, the rate of twinning in Farimabougou was 17.8/1,000 births in 1981 and 1982; this is almost identical to the rate reported by Imperato for the Bambara and Mandinka (17.9/1,000). According to Imperato:

> Twin births are extremely common among the Bambara and Malinke . . . Because twins are regarded among the Bambara and the Malinke as a blessing bestowed by the supreme being, their birth is received with great rejoicing. (Imperato 1977:119)

In terms of child care in general, and infant feeding practices in particular, twins are not treated differently from single births. Twins often start life smaller than singleton births, and must share one mother's milk. In two of the case studies below, being a twin undoubtedly adds yet another risk factor for malnutrition. At the same time, other sets of twins in the sample survived and flourished.

In 1982–83, the houses in Farimabougou were mostly of mud-brick construction with corrugated iron roofs and were located inside mud-walled compounds that were closely packed along narrow dirt streets. Compounds had neither running water nor electricity. Each compound had a pit latrine. Household garbage was thrown into a pit inside the compound, or out into the street.

The Malian diet is based on millet and rice, accompanied by various sauces. Animal protein in the diet comes from beef, mutton, or fish, which are often pounded before being added to the sauce. According to several food consumption surveys, with the exception of years of severe drought and of certain areas of far northern Mali, adult Malians have an adequate diet (Clarin et al. 1967; Diakite 1968; May 1968; Mondot-Bernard and Labonne 1982).

The traditional social organization of the Bambara consists of extended families living in large compounds, polygynous marriages, patrilineal descent, and patrilocal residence (N'Diaye 1970). This type of compound social organization is seldom realized in Farimabougou. Usually only one adult male from a rural family migrates to the city, and he usually has only one wife due to economic constraints. Thus, most of the children in the larger sample came from parents in monogamous marriages and lived in compounds containing only nuclear family members.

Except for a few Christian families, the people of Farimabougou are Moslem. For the most part, however, women do not strictly follow Muslim teachings. They are not secluded, they seldom go to the mosque or pray at home, they rarely fast during Ramadan, and they are not familiar with Koranic guidelines concerning infant feeding. Islamic beliefs coexist with traditional religious beliefs and practices. Sickness and death are usually attributed to Allah rather than to organic causes, witchcraft, or sorcery.

The majority of women who participated in the study were born in rural villages and had lived in the urban environment for less than 20 years at the time of the initial study. They have had little or no formal education, speak Bambara but not French, and can neither read nor write.

Health services for the residents of Farimabougou are provided primarily by traditional herbalists who sell leaves in the market, and by a government-run PMI (maternal/child health center) located approximately three kilometers away. Although the PMI visits are free, the numerous medicines that are usually prescribed are very expensive. Most children are born at the PMI, but mothers do not often take sick children to the PMI for treatment, preferring to try traditional cures first. The nearest hospital is located in downtown Bamako, at least 20 minutes away by public transportation. In 1982–83, few children had been vaccinated against any of the major childhood diseases, and oral rehydration solution as a treatment for diarrhea was virtually unknown. Measles, malaria, upper respiratory infections, and diarrhea were the major illnesses of young children. According to Imperato, who has written in detail about traditional Bambara beliefs concerning measles:

> Measles is the most important disease of childhood in Africa. It occurs throughout the continent, the incidence being highest in most areas every third year. Measles epidemics occur at the peak of the dry season in West Africa, from March through May, when stores of food and human nutritional levels are at their lowest . . . From 1958 through 1975, the annual number of measles cases reported in Mali has ranged from 10,000 to 40,000, with case mortalities of 15–20 percent. (Imperato 1977:138)

A serious outbreak of measles occurred during the initial study in May of 1982. There were only a few cases of measles in 1983.

Malaria affects children primarily during the rainy season (July–September). Only one child death was attributed to malaria during the initial study. Of the seven child deaths that occurred between the two studies, four were reported to be due to malaria, and three to measles.

In general, women welcome new pregnancies. Children are viewed as a source of wealth and prestige; the more children you have, the higher the family income will be, the more people there will be to support you when you are old, and the higher your status as a wife. Infertility is considered a tragedy. The Bambara believe that it is good luck to have a female child first, but both male and female children are valued. The growth data as well as interview data reveal no significant sex bias in terms of nutrition or health care. Thus, being a female is not a risk factor for malnutrition in this community. Although children are highly valued, there is little understanding of the importance of proper nutrition and health care during the first few years of life. Infant mortality rates are very high, and mothers seem resigned to the fact that many children die, even if you "search for medicine" for them. It is considered to be a much greater loss if an older child or an adult dies than if a young infant dies.

Compared to conditions in 1983, Farimabougou had changed little by 1989. Treated water was available from common stand-pipes located on the main roads, but most people continued to obtain water from the wells in their compounds. The community still lacked electricity, sewage treatment, and garbage disposal service. The major noticeable physical change was a building boom on the periphery of the community. Although construction of many houses has begun, few are completed. Block after block of half-finished cement houses, destined to be middle-class neighborhoods, surround the original mud-brick community.

In terms of health care, several changes were apparent. One is that many of the children under 3 years of age had been vaccinated against measles, tetanus, polio, and tuberculosis, primarily by a traveling van of health workers who visit the market periodically. Women said that measles no longer kills many children, and that only a few children in Farimabougou died of measles during the hot season of 1989. Women were still reluctant to take children to PMI for immunizations, however. The local PMI had acquired a bad reputation among mothers because of long waits and "rude treatment" by the health workers, and was used even less than it was in 1983. By 1989, many mothers had heard of oral rehydration solution, and approximately 10 percent reported that they use it for the treatment of diarrhea in young children. Other women still used traditional herbal cures for diarrhea or did not treat diarrhea at all.

The three case studies given here, involving seven children, represent children with some of the poorest growth in the sample. Their growth data are not as complete as those of some of the other children for several reasons. Often the children were too sick or miserable to measure, and one child died early in the study. However, their family situations, though unique in their specific combinations of factors, are not atypical. These case studies clearly illustrate that malnutrition is often the result of a complex set of factors acting in combination.

CASE STUDIES

Case Study 1: Children #5 and #6

Children #5 and #6 were fraternal twins, a boy named Al-Hassane and a girl named Assanatu (all the names have been changed). Birth records in the local PMI record their birth weights as 2.2 and 1.5 kilos, respectively; the records do not indicate if the twins were premature. Jeneba, the twins' mother, had been married before and given birth to four children. Two were still alive and lived with their father's brothers. The other two, a set of twin boys, had died at 6 months of age from diarrhea, according to Jeneba. After her first husband died in 1980, Jeneba remarried; she gave birth to Al-Hassane and Assanatu in 1981. Her second husband was a widower with teenaged children from his first marriage. He was employed at the national airport in a salaried position, but his wife did not know how much money he made.

Al-Hassane and Assanatu entered the study at the age of 8 months. . . . At 8 months of age, both children fell below the fifth percentile of NCHS standards for weight-for-age. The boy's weight, 6.3 kilos, falls in the "moderately malnourished" category according to the World Health Organization's system of classification by standard deviations below the median (between 2 and 3 SD below the median). The girl's weight, 5.0 kilos, places her in the "severely malnourished" category, more than three standard deviations below the median for her age. The children were receiving only breast milk at this time, although the girl sometimes ate a little millet porridge. The mother reported that because she had insufficient breast milk for twins, she had occasionally given them formula as a supplement when they were younger. However, their father had stopped providing money for this purpose.

At the next visit, when the children were 9 months of age, their mother was sick with malaria. The children were still nursing, and both had begun to eat solid food on a regular basis during the previous month. They had eaten no solid food for two days, however, because the mother was too ill to cook and had no one to help her. Pryer and Crook have noted that in urban regions of Third World Countries, "adults who are ill or malnourished are very likely to be unable to cope with the time-intensive demands of child care" (Pryer and Crook 1988). Jeneba's husband's older children, from his first marriage, were cooking for him and for themselves, but would not help their stepmother care for her children. At this visit, Al-Hassane's weight had dropped to 5.5 kilos, while Assanatu's had remained at 5.0 kilos. Both children now fell into the "severely malnourished" category.

At 10 months, the boy's weight had returned to 6.0 kilos, but the girl's remained at 5.0 kilos. A 24-hour dietary recall revealed that for breakfast they had eaten millet porridge flavored with sweetened condensed milk. For lunch, they had rice flavored with beef bouillon cubes; in the late afternoon, they had eaten some boiled sweet potatoes. According to their mother, they had not eaten any dinner the night before, because they were already asleep when the meal was served. She said that they were usually asleep when the evening meal was prepared.

At 11 months, Al-Hassane had regained his 8-month weight of 6.3 kilos, but Assanatu still had not gained any weight. At 12 months, the children were sick with fever and diarrhea, but both had gained a little weight since the previous month. At 15 months, Al-Hassane had lost 1.0 kilo of weight since the previous visit. His mother said he had been chronically ill with fever and diarrhea caused by teething and had refused to eat any food for the previous month. Assanatu had not been sick and had gained 0.5 kilo during the preceding three months. At this visit, the mother confided that she was thinking of leaving her husband because they were not getting along. She was especially upset over her stepchildren's refusal to accept her or her children as part of the family, and their refusal to help with the domestic labor.

The next month when I went to visit the compound, I was told that Jeneba had indeed taken the twins and left. After four months, I relocated them at her first husband's compound. At 19 months, Al-Hassane weighed 8.6 kilos (moderately malnourished), a gain of more than 3.0 kilos in four months. This weight gain represents marked catch-up growth in response to the changed environment, especially an improvement in diet; normal weight gain for males between 15 and 19 months is 0.80 kilos. Assanatu had gained 1.1 kilos in the same time period, which also represents some catch-up growth; normal weight gain for females is 0.75 kilos. However, at 7.1 kilos, she was still classified as "severely malnourished."

Jeneba said they had been completely healthy ever since she had moved. She now had access to money to provide them with proper food, as well as help with the domestic labor, and emotional support from her relatives. Her first husband's family was providing money for food and medical care. A 24-hour dietary recall at this time revealed that they had eaten rice porridge with sugar for breakfast. At the morning market, they had eaten meat brochettes (small pieces of beef cooked on a skewer). For lunch, they had rice with fish and onion sauce, with leftovers in the late afternoon. At night, they had eaten millet porridge.

. . .

Assanatu was always significantly smaller than her brother, especially for head circumference. Her weight gains and losses were never as dramatic as Al-Hassane's either. However, she was slightly advanced in motor development, suffered less from teething, and generally seemed more alert and happy. These differences may reflect the tendency of females to be less affected by stressful environmental conditions than males (Stini 1985; Stinson 1985). Assanatu seemed to respond by not growing in size, but continuing to advance developmentally. Al-Hassane was bigger, but developmentally delayed. Both children seemed to be treated the same by their mother, in terms of access to food and medical resources.

Follow-Up In 1989, contact was re-established with the family. According to Jeneba, Al-Hassane died at 3 years of age, when he had the measles. Assanatu had the measles at the same time, but recovered. Today, at almost 8 years of age, Assanatu's weight of 18.6 kilos is below the fifth percentile of NCHS standards. She would be considered "mildly malnourished" by the WHO classification. Her height, 121.0 centimeters, is just below the twenty-fifth percentile of NCHS standards, well within "normal" limits. The main legacy of her early childhood malnutrition is a small head circumference. Most brain growth occurs during the first 3 years of life, and inadequate nutrition during this time cannot be overcome by improved conditions in later childhood. Assanatu's head circumference, 47.3 centimeters, is the median for a child of only 18 months by NCHS standards, and falls well below those of the other girls her age in the follow-up study, whose head circumferences range from 49 to 53 centimeters. Her mother reports that she is "not very smart," and although she went to Koranic school for a while, she no longer attends "because she couldn't keep up." She also reports that Assanatu suffers often from malaria, and "doesn't like to eat very much." Jeneba never returned to her second husband, and he provides no support for Assanatu. They still live with her first husband's family, along with a man to whom Jeneba is not legally married. She has had one child with this man, and is now pregnant with her eighth child.

In this case, a variety of factors combined to provide a less than satisfactory environment for proper growth for the twins. In addition to beginning life with low birth weights and having to share their mother's breast milk, the twins did not receive supplementary solid foods on a regular basis until 9 months of age, by which time both were already severely malnourished. The late addition of solids to the diet is typical of this community. Although their father had a steady, salaried job, their mother had little direct access to this income; she was dependent on her husband's good will and could not always count on money for formula to supplement her breast milk. Marital discord led her to return to her first husband's family. Even though the twins belonged to a different patrilineage, her first husband's family welcomed them and provided help with child care, as well as financial and emotional support. The twins responded with substantial catch-up growth and improved health. Al-Hassane's poor nutritional status during the first 2 years of life undoubtedly played a role in his death from measles at the age of 3 years, and Assanatu's early deprivation has led apparently to some mild, but probably permanent, mental deficiencies.

It is interesting to speculate on the different paths taken by these two children. Assanatu seemed to conserve her resources through poorer physical growth. Did this allow her to survive by reserving scarce resources for fighting disease? Did Al-Hassane's strategy of spending resources on growth mean that there were insufficient resources for fighting disease? If so, how do we account for individual or population differences in resource allocation?

Assanatu's functional impairments affect her directly, but they also affect her family and the society at large. She will never be able to make as much of a contribution as she might have if she had been adequately nourished, and this observation holds for many children who survive severe cases of early childhood malnutrition.

Case Study II: Children #76 and #77

Children #76 and #77 were a set of identical twin girls, named Fatoumata and Oumou. They were their mother's first and second children. Their mother, Aminata, was approximately 16 years old, and unmarried. The twins' father, who had not been allowed to marry her, did not contribute anything to their support. Aminata lived in a large compound containing one elderly woman, this woman's four adult sons, and their wives and children. Aminata was the foster child of a wife of one of the adult men in the compound.

I first encountered the twins when they were 14 months of age. They were never officially part of the growth study, but lived in the compound next to a family that was, so I saw them on a regular basis. They were not included in the official growth study for several reasons. First, the original sample was constructed to maximize the spread of families throughout the town, and I tried not to include immediate neighbors. Second, the twins were often so sick and miserable that it seemed unkind to bother them by taking measurements. Third, and most important, I was conducting a naturalistic study of traditional Malian patterns of infant feeding and their effects on growth and development. In this case, I often gave Aminata advice, and occasionally money to buy fish, and for several months I brought her home-made formula (powdered milk, sugar, oil, water). In addition, when the twins had the measles, I bought the ingredients for oral rehydration solution and showed Aminata how to mix and administer it. Thus, the twins' growth after 14 months of age reflected in part my efforts on their behalf. Their growth data are included in the summary statistics for the sample reported elsewhere. Despite the paucity of growth data, and my interventions, their case is described here because it provides a particularly clear illustration of the constraints placed on women and their children by the social structure of a patrilineal society.

The twins were born at home, so birth weights are not available. I did not measure them when I first met them at 14 months of age. At 15 months of age, during the hot season, both twins caught the measles. Fatoumata had an especially serious case, probably because she was already more severely malnourished than her twin. For two weeks neither twin ate any solid food, and both became dehydrated. I provided oral rehydration solution and tried to convince their mother to take them to the hospital, but she refused. They eventually got better, though it took several months for them to recover fully and begin eating normally again. Following their bout with measles, at 19 months of age, Fatoumata weighed 4.2 kilos, which is more than five standard deviations below the median of the NCHS standards (anything more than 3 SD below the median is considered "severely malnourished"). Her sister Oumou weighed 5.9 kilos, which is between four and five standard deviations below the median. . . .

Although I did not measure their heights, photographs reveal that Fatoumata was already several centimeters shorter than her sister. My field notes from this visit describe them as follows: "reddish hair, no tissue in buttocks or thighs, sunken eyes, sunken fontanelles, sores on their faces, vacant stares, can barely crawl." At 19 months, they could not walk or talk. They were still nursing and eating only a little food, primarily rice or millet breakfast porridge.

Oumou began to walk when she was 24 months old, and Fatoumata at 26 months. At 26 months of age, after intermittent intervention by the author, Fatoumata weighed 7.2 kilos, and Oumou 7.8 kilos. Both of these weights fall between three and four SD below the median. The children were still nursing at this time, and were eating all the adult foods, including rice and millet with various sauces. The mother requested that I stop providing formula, because she "didn't have time to give it to them." At the time, I did not understand this statement, but as the study progressed, the truth of her assertion became apparent. The twins were weaned at 28 months of age, and their mother reported that they ate more food than before being weaned.

The twins were 3 years and 4 months old at the end of the study. They could walk, but not run, could say only the words for "mother" and "water," and spent their days standing listlessly in the doorway of their house. I never measured them again, but a photograph taken at the time, which includes my own daughter, Miranda, aged 3 years and 2 months, shows that they only reach the middle of Miranda's chest, and that Fatoumata, who had been more seriously ill with the measles, was even shorter than Oumou.

What factors contributed to malnutrition in this case? At first, I was inclined to attribute it to their mother's seemingly callous indifference to their welfare. On the scale of "maternal attitude" devised for the larger study (Dettwyler 1985, 1986), she epitomized the "below average" ranking.[2] She had asked me to stop bringing formula because it took too much time to give it to the children. In addition, she said that the children were a burden to her, that she had little chance of marrying with two small children, and that she would be in a better position for getting out of the compound if they died. As I probed into the motivations underlying these statements, the reality of her position in the family and the conditions of her life became clear.

As described earlier, Aminata lived in a compound based around four adult brothers and their elderly mother. When Aminata herself was 3 years old, she had been given to her father's sister as a foster child. A common practice throughout West Africa, child fostering involves sending young children to live with relatives for a variety of reasons (e.g., to provide labor for paternal relatives, to keep an elderly grandmother company in a rural village, or to help a female relative care for a newborn baby). Foster children often have low status in the household, and they may not be accorded the same access to scarce resources as the other children in the family (Bledsoe, Ewbank, and Isiugo-Abanihe 1988; Bledsoe 1991).

After several years, Aminata was passed on again as a foster child, from her aunt to this woman's daughter (her own cousin), who was a young adult at the time. This woman, in turn, had married into the family of four brothers, as the second wife of the third brother. In this strongly patrilineal, age-conscious society, a man's status in the family depends on his birth order, with the oldest surviving brother being the head of the family: Likewise, a woman's status depends both on the status of her husband and on her position as his first, second, third, or fourth wife. Generally speaking, first wives have higher status than later wives. This meant that Aminata was the foster child of the second wife of the third brother in a compound of four adult men. Thus, Aminata was the foster child of a woman who also had low status in the household.

In addition to her low structural position in a large, patrilineal family, Aminata was several years older than any of the children in the family. During 1982 and 1983, she was responsible for the vast majority of the heavy manual labor in the compound, including virtually all of the millet pounding, firewood chopping, water hauling, and clothes washing. She also did the majority of the cooking. Even though there were five other adult women in the household, Aminata was never allowed to rest. Partly to escape the drudgery of her existence, she used to "go out at night" with a group of boys and girls her own age.

When she was 15 years old, Aminata became pregnant by one of her "friends." The adult men of the compound did not approve of this man, and her life became even worse. The birth of twins, usually viewed as a blessing, was an excessive burden for an unmarried, adolescent girl. Her work load did not change while she was pregnant or after the twins were born, and she was routinely beaten by the women of the compound for her indiscretion in becoming pregnant before marriage. Although the twins' father wanted to marry Aminata, her foster fathers would not allow it.

On a relative scale of socioeconomic status, Aminata's compound would be considered "above average" for the community. It contained four adult male wage earners, all of whom were skilled laborers. The compound itself was large, with cement-block houses, and the other children of the family were only mildly malnourished, which is typical of children in the community. Therefore, money was available in the family; Aminata, however, had no access to it. If she needed money to take her children to the doctor or to buy the food I suggested, she had to ask her cousin, who in turn had to ask her husband. These requests were seldom granted. When she had to spend the day at the river washing clothes, she used to leave the children with a friend, because no one at her own compound would watch them for her.

She felt that there was little she could do to change her situation or to improve her children's health given her lack of resources. She really *didn't* have the time to give them formula or to administer oral rehydration solution every 15 minutes when they were dehydrated from measles or diarrhea. Pryer and Crook (1988:19) have noted, "especially during illness when appetite fails, small children need to be fed frequently during the day, which is very time consuming, and can be especially difficult for mothers from poor families who may have other domestic and economic responsibilities."

Follow-Up In 1989, I returned to Aminata's compound. She was no longer living there, but I was able to relocate her in a neighboring community. According to Aminata, the smaller of the twins, Fatoumata, died in 1984 of malaria. Shortly thereafter, Oumou was sent to live with Aminata's own parents (whom she had not seen in many years) in Mopti, a large port town on the Niger River northeast of Bamako. Once both the twins were "out of the way" (her phrase), Aminata's foster family arranged for her to be married to a man of their choosing.

Since her marriage in 1984, Aminata has had three more children, of whom two survive. The first child, a boy, is now 4 years old. The second, a girl, died in 1986 in Mopti while Aminata was visiting Oumou. According to Aminata, this child died from the measles. That was the last time Aminata saw Oumou, and she has no plans to visit her again. The third child, another boy, is now one year old. The two surviving children have weights and heights that place them in the "mildly malnourished" category.

Aminata reports that she is very happy in her marriage and content with her life. She married into a large extended family with many adult women to share the work. She is the first of two wives of one of the older brothers. The women take turns doing the domestic labor, and she only has to work two days each week. Looking back on her childhood and adolescence, she says that although she had to work very hard, she learned how to do everything well, so that now her life is comparatively easy. She says she tries not to think of Fatoumata and Oumou because it makes her sad. She feels no personal responsibility for Fatoumata's death, or for the death of her younger daughter. When I asked, "Do you think there is anything you could have done to prevent their deaths," she replied, "You can search for medicine, and give your children medicine, but if it is their time, Allah will take them no matter what you do." Aminata does not admit to any bad feelings toward her foster family, or blame them for contributing to Fatoumata's death or Oumou's separation from her.

Fatoumata and Oumou were two of the most severely malnourished children in the study. Their malnutrition, like that of Al-Hassane and Assanatu, had many contributing causes. If Aminata had not been a foster child, or if she had gotten pregnant by a man her foster fathers liked (so they could have been married), if she had had only one child instead of twins, or if the adult women of the compound had helped more with the household labor—if any one of a number of factors had been different, her children would have been healthier. The combination resulted in an impossible situation. As this case clearly illustrates, additional income for the family would not have resulted in any improvement in either her situation or the nutritional status of her children. Additional income and nutritional advice for Aminata, personally provided by the researcher, did not help either, as she had neither the time nor the energy to take care of her children.

Case Study III: Children #62, #62a, and #105

Child #105 was a boy named Umaru, and #62 and #62a were Umaru's nephews Mori and Bakari. Umaru is one of the success stories in Farimabougou, while Mori represents one of the more tragic failures. . . .

Umaru was his parents' fourteenth child, four of whom had died. Umaru contracted polio when he was about 10 months old, and had just recovered from the measles when he entered the study at 18 months of age. At that time, his weight of 8.3 kilos placed him in the "moderately malnourished" category (between 2 and 3 SD below the NCHS median for weight-for-age). His mother, Ma, reported that he had lost a lot of weight because of the measles. He was weaned at 24 months because his mother was pregnant again.

. . . Umaru gained weight fairly steadily over the course of the study, and his last weight of 11.3 kilos at 32 months, while still below the fifth percentile of NCHS standards, placed him in the "mildly malnourished" category typical of children in the community. In the original study, Ma was classified as "above average" in terms of maternal attitude. She was very devoted to her children. Because of his polio, she regularly took Umaru to the Chinese hospital at Kati, about 15 kilometers distant, for acupuncture treatments and physical therapy, and she spent many hours working with him at home to teach him to walk. She was very upset by the death of her first grandchild (#62, below), and distraught by the stillbirth of her own fifteenth child. This child, after 10 months of gestation, died during labor and had to be removed by Caesarian section. Her doctor warned her that she should not have any more children. Even though she had given birth to 15 children, and had 10 still surviving, she was sad that she would not be having more. While Ma was recuperating from surgery, her husband took over the cooking, clothes washing, and other domestic chores, actions that are highly atypical for Malian men. Umaru's father was devoted to his children and optimistic that Umaru would recover fully from the effects of polio.

Mori (#62) was his mother's first child. His mother, Sali, was Ma's oldest daughter, so Mori was Umaru's nephew. At birth, Mori weighed 3.9 kilos, which is above the ninetieth percentile of NCHS standards. Mori was weaned at 13 months of age, which is very early for this community, because his mother was pregnant again. When he entered the study at 15 months of age, his weight was 7.9 kilos, placing him in the "moderately malnourished" category. . . .

During the next month, Mori came down with the measles and spent 18 days in the hospital in Bamako, where he was fed through a subclavicular IV. At my next visit, when he was 16 months old, he had been home from the hospital for only a few days. His mother reported that, since coming home, he had "refused to eat" and would only drink a little water. During my visits, timed to coincide with meals, she made little effort to encourage him to eat or drink. She was not particularly interested in my suggestions for helping Mori eat, preferring to talk about her current pregnancy.

At 16 months, Mori's weight had dropped to 6.7 kilos. At 17 months, it had dropped again, to 6.4 kilos, which is more than four standard deviations below the median. When I came to remeasure him at 18 months, I was told that he had died several weeks before. During my last visit, after Mori's death, I witnessed a bitter exchange between Ma and Sali. Ma, Mori's grandmother, was sharply critical of her daughter, saying that she was not a good mother, did not care about her children, and was not willing to do what was necessary to keep them alive. Sali ignored her mother, replying that she (Sail) was young and did things the "modern" way. She blamed Mori's death on the measles and his own refusal to eat. She did not see any connection between the fact that Mori had been weaned early because of her subsequent pregnancy and his death from measles/malnutrition, and she felt no responsibility for his lack of food intake after his release from the hospital.

The fact that she had weaned Mori very early because of her subsequent pregnancy indicated that she and her husband were not observing the traditional postpartum sex taboo (until the baby is weaned, or at least until he can walk well). Her husband was a recent migrant from a rural village, and the only member of his family to migrate. When I first met them, the young couple was living with her parents, since the husband had no patrilineal relatives in the community. Shortly after Mori died, the couple moved out because of "arguments" between mother and daughter and moved in with friends of the father's who lived across town. The grandmother was not informed where they had moved, and they were lost to the study for more than a year.

According to Sali's father, his son-in-law was able to "get away" with not observing the traditional taboos, as well as with misguided allocation of scarce household resources, because he had no older agnates to put pressure on him. The fact that he was a recent migrant to the city, and the sole migrant from his family, suggests that he may have been overwhelmed by the opportunities of urban life and was not mature or responsible enough to forego personal pleasure for the health of his children. Certainly in a rural village, a young man of his age would not be in charge of his own compound and would not be allowed to make the kinds of choices he made. In addition, in a small rural village, the young couple would not have been able to simply pick up and move away, but would have had to stay under the supervision of elders with more experience. As Gokulanathan and Verghese note, "The gradual break-up of the extended family units under the influence of the wage economy and the movement of people produce changes in the family hierarchy. The authoritative person in the family may be a wage earning member, usually a younger person who may not be sufficiently informed about *either* the traditional ways *or* modern methods (Foster, 1962)" (Gokulanathan and Verghese 1969:123).

. . .

In the case of Umaru, we find very different circumstances from those of the other children described in these case studies. Umaru's mother was happily married, an experienced, older mother with 10 healthy surviving children. Her first eight children had been born in a rural village, and she was deeply suspicious of urban mores. Despite suffering from both polio and measles, Umaru has survived, even flourished. Although his family's income was only "average" for the community, and there were many other children to feed (Umaru had seven older siblings still at home), Umaru had exceptional parents. They were devoted to each other and to their children, and did not own any of the symbols of "modern" life such as a moped, a bicycle, or even a radio. If primary health care and health education in Mali had been better when Umaru was an infant, he probably would have been vaccinated against measles and polio.

By contrast, Sali's maternal attitude was defined as clearly "below average." She was inexperienced as a mother and rejected the traditional values epitomized by her parents. Her antagonism toward her mother, and the fact that her mother was recovering from a traumatic Caesarian still birth, made it unlikely that she would or could ask her mother for help or advice. Her focus was on her husband and on the acquisition of expensive symbols of modern, urban life, including a moped and multiple sets of fancy clothes. In Mori's malnutrition and subsequent death, many factors were at work. If even one had been different, he might have survived. As it was, the combination of inexperienced parents, early weaning, measles, traditional infant feeding practices, and poor maternal (and paternal) attitude were fatal.

CONCLUSIONS

Under certain circumstances, it may be possible to point to one factor as being primarily responsible for malnutrition in a community. Droughts, famines, warfare, and refugee camps garner worldwide attention and represent obvious single-cause reasons for widespread malnutrition in particular instances. For example, the relatively high rates of severe malnutrition in northern Mali following the drought of 1984–85 can be attributed to the failure of the rains and the subsequent devastation of animal herds on which the populations relied for subsistence.

Unfortunately for change agents and development agencies (and, of course, for the affected populations), the vast majority of malnutrition in Third World populations does not have one primary cause. Nor does it have a simple solution. If alleviating malnutrition were only a matter of increasing household income, providing nutrition education for all mothers, implementing family planning programs, or immunizing all children under five against the major childhood diseases, it would be difficult enough. But the widespread chronic mild and moderate malnutrition that affects Third World children under "normal" conditions is the result of an intricate web of interacting factors.

Without the constraint of poverty, Malian women such as Jeneba and Aminata would not have to stay in untenable household situations, and Sali and her husband would not have had to choose between gas for the moped and food for the children. Without the constraint of social institutions such as child fosterage, polygyny, patrilineality, and arranged marriages, girls would not find themselves in positions like Aminata's. Without traditional infant feeding practices such as weaning as soon as the mother gets pregnant again, and letting children themselves decide whether and how much they want to eat, children like Mori might not die. Without the stress of measles, compounded by the high temperatures of the hot season, or the stress of malaria during the rainy season, malnutrition by itself would not be so devastating. Without the constraint of inadequate primary health care, measles and malaria themselves would not be so serious a threat. Without the constraint of a contaminated environment due to the complete lack of sewage and garbage disposal, children would not get diarrhea so often. Without the constraints imposed by lack of running water and electricity, women would not have to spend hours every day hauling water, chopping firewood, and pounding millet, and would thus have more time and energy to devote to child care activities.

Given the conditions of life under which periurban Malian women raise children, it is surprising that the majority of children are *only* mildly malnourished. Like the cases described here, in many instances where children are severely malnourished it is because they have fallen through the safety net of overlapping support systems that normally ensure a minimal level of nutrition and health for children in the community. Rather than be chagrined when children fall through the cracks, one must be impressed with the number of children for whom the system works.

These three case studies are typical of the histories collected during the original 1982–83 study and the 1989 follow-up study. The details of each child's situation differed, but in every case of severe malnutrition, a variety of biological, social, and cultural factors contributed to the child's poor growth. Conversely, for those children who were growing much better than the average for this population, their household situations included few or none of the constraining factors faced by the women described above.

As the case studies presented here reveal, a truly integrated, biocultural approach in nutritional anthropology, including longitudinal case histories of individual children and of populations, is necessary if we are to understand all of the interactions between culture and biology that result in observed patterns of nutritional status, growth and development, morbidity, and mortality, and to use this understanding to design successful intervention programs to improve child health. It may not be possible, or necessary, to specify the exact contribution of each strand to the web, as they will be different for every child. It *is* possible to study and describe the web of causation, made up of many different factors that affect child growth and child health. To do so, however, requires that researchers begin from a biocultural perspective and have adequate training in both quantitative and qualitative research methodologies, training that enables them to see the faces behind the numbers.

Approaches such as "rapid ethnographic assessment" (Bentley, Pelto, and Straus 1988) can provide only a limited understanding of the causes of malnutrition in any particular community. Likewise, it is of little value to attempt to reduce the complex causes of malnutrition to one or two easily measurable factors, such as "socioeconomic status," "housing type," or "maternal educational level." In particular, researchers interested in alleviating childhood malnutrition must get beyond simplistic measures of socioeconomic status, and realize that all poor people are not the same—differences in individual and family circumstances have important effects on the health, nutritional status, and survival of children. Not all family members have equal access to the household's resources, nor do all parents put children's needs first. Finally, it is misleading, and ultimately futile, to think that malnutrition can be alleviated by any one "magic bullet" such as oral rehydration solution, Vitamin A enrichment, or breastfeeding promotion campaigns. To save a child from death by diarrhea today using oral rehydration solution, so that he can die tomorrow from malaria, is not a significant improvement. To increase family income, only to have that income spent on costly consumer goods or prestigious but nutritionally inferior "Western" foods, will not improve the nutritional status of children.

Policy planners must acknowledge that malnutrition has no easy solution. Programs to improve child health must address many, if not all, of the causes of malnutrition, including the difficult issues of the status of women in patrilineal societies and the disruptive forces of modernization. At the same time that multistranded programs to eliminate risk factors are implemented, other programs must be designed that strengthen the various strands of the safety net already operating in every community to ensure that more children survive and prosper.

NOTES

1. Birth certificates are filled out at the maternity clinic at the time of birth. If a child is not born at the clinic, he or she must be taken to the clinic within three days to register the birth. Therefore, the birth certificates are assumed to be accurate. Parents occasionally forge a birth certificate to enable a child to begin school before the official age of 8 years, but this practice did not affect the young children involved in this sample.
2. The "maternal attitude" scale divides mothers into three categories of "average," "above average," and "below average." A mother with an "above average" maternal attitude is one who always makes sure her child is awake and present at meals, fixes foods that the child especially likes, buys him extra food on a regular basis, takes him to the doctor when he is sick, and purchases the prescribed medications. A mother with a "below average" maternal attitude is one who lets her child sleep or play through meals, does not cater to his food preferences or buy him extra food, and is less likely to consult medical personnel when he is sick, spend money for prescribed medicines, or administer medications consistently.

REFERENCES

Bentley, M. E., G. H. Pelto, and W. L. Straus. 1988. Rapid Ethnographic Assessment: Applications in a Diarrhea Management Program. Soc. Sci. Med. 27(1):107–116.

Bledsoe, C. 1991. The Trickle-Down Model within Households: Foster Children and the Phenomenon of Scrounging. In The Health Transition: Methods and Measures. Health Transition Series No. 3. J. Cleland and A. G. Hill, eds. Pp. 115–131. Canberra: Australian National University Press.

Bledsoe, C. H., D. C. Ewbank, and U. C. Isiugo-Abanihe. 1988. The Effect of Child Fostering on Feeding Practices and Access to Health Services in Rural Sierra Leone. Soc. Sci. Med. 27(6):627–636.

Clairin, R., et al. 1967. L'Alimentation des Populations Rurales du Delta Vif du Niger et de l'Office du Niger. M.I.S.O.E.S. 1967 [cited in May 1968].

Daniggelis, E. 1987a. Infant Feeding Practices and Nutritional Status. Paper presented at the annual meeting of the American Anthropological Association, Chicago.

———. 1987b. Cash Fishing and Subsistence Plantations: The Impact of a Global-Economy on Samoan Children's Growth. M.A. thesis, Department of Anthropology, University of Hawaii.

Dettwyler, K. A. 1985. Breastfeeding, Weaning, and Other Infant Practices in Mali and Their Effects on Growth and Development. Ph.D. dissertation, Indiana University, Bloomington. Ann Arbor: University Microfilms.

———. 1986. Infant Feeding in Mali, West Africa: Variations in Belief and Practice. Soc. Sci. Med. 23(7):651–664.

———. 1987 Breastfeeding and Weaning in Mali: Cultural Context and Hard Data. Soc. Sci. Med. 24(8):633–644.

———. 1989a. The Interaction of Anorexia and Cultural Beliefs in Infant Malnutrition in Mali. American Journal of Human Biology l(6):683–695.

———. 1989b. Styles of Infant Feeding: Parental/Caretaker Control of Food Consumption in Young Children. American Anthropologist 91(3):696–703.

de Vries, M. W. 1987. Cry Babies, Culture, and Catastrophe: Infant Temperament Among the Masai. In Child Survival: Anthropological Perspectives on the Treatment and Maltreatment of Children. N. Scheper-Hughes, ed. Pp. 165–185. Boston: D. Reidel Publishing Company.

Diakite, S. 1968. Nutrition in Mali. In Proceedings of the West African Conference on Nutrition and Child Feeding. Pp. 87–97. Dakar, Senegal. Washington, DC: United States Department of Health, Education, and Welfare, Public Health Service.

Gokulanathan, K. S., and K. P. Verghese. 1969. Socio-Cultural Malnutrition (Growth Failure in Children Due to Socio-Cultural Factors). J. Trop. Pediatr. 15:118–124.

Guldan, G. S. 1988. Maternal Education and Child Caretaking Practices in Rural Bangladesh: Part 1, Child Feeding Practices: Part 2, Food and Personal Hygiene. Ph.D. dissertation, School of Nutrition, Tufts University.

Hamill, P. V. V., T. A. Drizd, C. L. Johnson, R. B. Reed, A. F. Roche, and W. M. Moore. 1979. Physical Growth: National Center for Health Statistics Percentiles. Am J. Clin. Nutr. 32:607–629.

Hull, V., and M. Simpson, eds. 1985. Breastfeeding, Child Health and Child Spacing: Cross-cultural Perspectives. London: Croom Helm.

Imperato, J. P. 1977. African Folk Medicine: Practices and Beliefs of the Bambara and Other Peoples. Baltimore: York Press, Inc.

Marshall, L. B., ed. 1985. Infant Care and Feeding in the South Pacific. New York: Gordon and Breach.

May, J. M. 1968. The Ecology of Malnutrition in the French Speaking Countries of West Africa and Madagascar. New York: Hafner.

Mondot-Bernard, J., and M. Labonne. 1982. Satisfaction of Food Requirements in Mali to 2000 A.D. Paris: Development Centre of the Organization for Economic Co-operation and Development.

Mull, D., and D. Mull. 1987. Infanticide among the Tarahumara of the Mexican Sierra Madre. In Child Survival: Anthropological Perspectives on the Treatment and Maltreatment of Children. N. Scheper-Hughes, ed. Pp. 113–132. Boston: D. Reidel Publishing Company.

N'Diaye, B. 1970. Groupes ethniques au Mali. Bamako: Edition Populaires.

Pryer, J., and N. Crook. 1988. Cities of Hunger: Urban Malnutrition in Developing Countries. Oxford: Oxfam.

Scheper-Hughes, N. 1987. Culture, Scarcity, and Maternal Thinking: Mother Love and Child Death in Northeast Brazil. In Child Survival: Anthropological Perspectives on the Treatment and Maltreatment of Children. N. Scheper-Hughes, ed. Pp. 187–208. Boston: D. Reidel Publishing Company.

Stini, W. A. 1985. Growth Rates and Sexual Dimorphism in Evolutionary Perspective. In The Analysis of Prehistoric Diets. R. I. Gilbert and J. H. Mielke, eds. Pp. 191–226. New York: Academic Press.

Stinson, S. 1985. Sex Differences in Environmental Sensitivity during Growth and Development. Yearbook of Physical Anthropology 28:123–147.

World Bank, Document of the. 1979. Report and Recommendations of the President of the International Development Association to the Executive Director on a Proposed Credit to the Republic of Mali for an Urban Development Project. June 12, 1979. Report WP-2595-MLI.

Zeitlin, M., and G. S. Guldan. 1988. Appendix IIC Bangladesh Infant Feeding Observations. In Maternal Education and Child Caretaking Practices in Rural Bangladesh: Part 1, Child Feeding Practices; Part 2, Food and Personal Hygiene, p. 106. Ph.D. dissertation, School of Nutrition, Tufts University.

Zeitlin, M., H. Ghassemi, and M. Monsour. 1990. Positive Deviance in Child Nutrition. Tokyo: United Nations University Press.

 45

An Anthropological Perspective on Obesity

Peter J. Brown
Melvin Konner

The subject of this selection is another kind of malnutrition in sharp contrast to the undernourished children in Mali in the previous selection. Obesity is a large problem in the developed world, especially in societies like the United States. Excess fat carries with it increased risk for cardiovascular disease, stroke, and certain kinds of cancer. As we saw in earlier selections about the diet of our prehistoric ancestors (see selections 2 and 7), most humans never lived with a predictable food surplus. Obesity was never a possibility for our ancestors, just as excessive fatness is not a worry for people currently living in the poorest segments of society.

In U.S. society, fat is a major concern for many people. Weight loss is a huge industry—and a profitable one, because studies show that most weight lost through dieting is eventually regained. Fear of fatness is an important factor in a simultaneous epidemic of anorexia nervosa and other eating disorders among young women generally from affluent families (Brumberg 1988). From a psychological standpoint, obesity and anorexia might be seen as flip sides of the same cultural coin. Overweight people face stigma and discrimination, whereas others are never satisfied with their weight and are literally dying to be thin. Obviously, questions of fat and thin are much more than purely biological and medical issues. In recent years there have been a number of excellent medical anthropological and feminist studies of the questions of eating disorders in contemporary America (Bordo 1993; Condit 1990).

This selection is an example of the biocultural approach to medical anthropology. It explores the interaction of genes and culture in an evolutionary context, and it argues that many human populations are predisposed to the problem of obesity. This is because humans evolved in environments that were prone to food shortages. In such contexts, individuals who are able to store energy reserves in the form of fat might be at a selective advantage. For many people throughout the world these food shortages still exist, as we saw in selection 45. The problem of hunger also continues to plague rich countries like the United States, but some people are hungry because they are dieting, and others are hungry because their food stamps have run out. The United States is a highly stratified society with huge differences in access to resources between rich and poor. In general, however, there is food in abundance so that it is easy for even the poor to become fat. As a consequence, because status markers must by definition be difficult to achieve, being thin ironically may become a symbolic marker of wealth. This selection explores the cultural meanings of the perfect body from a cross-cultural perspective. As is often the case, an anthropological perspective allows us to view a contemporary problem in a new way.

As you read this selection, consider these questions:

- **Why is central body fatness more of a risk for chronic disease than peripheral body fatness? What are the implications of this for gender differences in obesity?**
- **How might obesity be culturally constructed?**
- **Can you think of ways that the anthropological approach to obesity might yield practical suggestions to chronic disease prevention programs?**
- **What are some similarities and differences between this analysis and the Stone Agers in the fast-lane argument of selection 2?**
- **Why do you think plumpness is a marker of beauty for women in so many other cultures? What does this tell us about cross-cultural standards of beauty?**

Context: Peter Brown teaches medical anthropology at Emory University, and is co-editor of this book. He has an interest in cultural factors that help cause obesity, which is a precondition to an array of chronic diseases. Melvin Konner, a physician and anthropologist, also teaches at Emory University. Konner is author of eight books, including *The Tangled Wing: Biological Constraints on the Human Spirit* (2nd ed. 2002). His field of expertise is the interaction between biology and behavior, medicine and society, and nature and culture; he is a frequent public commentator on medical ethics, health care reform, child care, child welfare, and other policy questions. This article was presented to the New York Academy of Sciences before the "epidemic" of obesity became a widespread concern in the

United States The intended audience was primarily a medical one. Since that time, the incidence of obesity, and pediatric obesity in particular, has been rising precipitously not only in the United States, but throughout the world. Written by a cultural anthropologist and a biological anthropologist, the article attempts to place the human predisposition to fatness in a cross-cultural and evolutionary perspective.

Source: P. J. Brown and M. Konner. (1987)."An Anthropological Perspective on Obesity." *Annals of the New York Academy of Sciences* 499:29–46.

An anthropological approach to human obesity involves both an evolutionary and a cross-cultural dimension. That is, it attempts to understand how the human predisposition to obesity so evident in modern affluent societies may have been determined during our species' long evolutionary history as hunters and gatherers, as well as the variation in obesity prevalence in different societies, social classes, or ethnic groups.

The evolutionary success of *Homo sapiens* is best understood by reference to the operation of natural selection on our dual system of inheritance; that is, on genes and culture, but also, and perhaps especially, on their interaction. Human biology and culture are the product of adaptation to environmental constraints; traits that enhance an individual's ability to survive and reproduce should become common in human societies. In this view, the health and illness of a population can be conceived as measures of biocultural adaptation to a particular ecological setting. Changing patterns of morbidity and mortality, such as the epidemiological transition from infectious to chronic diseases, are the result of historical changes in lifestyle (i.e. culture) that affect health.

It is valuable to view obesity from this evolutionary perspective because of its great historical scope. The first appearance of the genus *Homo* occurred over two million years ago, and the first anatomically modern humans (*Homo sapiens sapiens*) became predominant about 40,000 years ago.[1] From either prehistoric point of departure, during most of human history, the exclusive cultural pattern was one of hunting and gathering. This original human lifestyle is rare, but a few such groups have been the subject of detailed anthropological study.[2]

Culture, in an anthropological sense, entails learned patterns of behavior and belief characteristic of a particular society. This second dimension of the anthropological perspective includes variables demonstrably related to the prevalence of obesity in a particular group—material aspects of lifestyle, like diet and productive economy—as well as more idealistic variables, the relationship of which to obesity is more speculative—such as aesthetic standards of ideal body type or the symbolic meaning of fatness.

Cross-cultural comparison thus serves two purposes, one relating to each of the two dimensions. First, technologically simple or primitive societies provide ethnographic analogies to amplify our understanding of prehistoric periods, or to test hypotheses about biocultural evolution. Such societies provide useful analogies to prehistoric societies, particularly in terms of economic production and diet. Second, cross-cultural comparison allows us to see our own society's health problems and cultural beliefs about health in a new way. In a heterogeneous society like the United States, where particular social groups have markedly high prevalences of obesity, attention to cultural variation in beliefs and behaviors has practical value for medicine. Going beyond the U.S. to the numerous cultural varieties in the anthropological record gives us a fascinating range of further variation for systematic analysis. Such analysis is likely to reveal relationships that may not appear in other approaches, and attention to this wider range of cultures becomes even more relevant as obesity becomes a factor in international health.

In this paper we argue that throughout most of human history, obesity was never a common health problem, nor was it a realistic possibility for most people. This was because, despite the qualitative adequacy of their diet, most primitive societies have been regularly subjected to food shortages. Scarcity has been a powerful agent of natural selection in human biocultural evolution. Both genes and cultural traits that may have been adaptive in the context of past food scarcities today play a role in the etiology of maladaptive adult obesity in affluent societies. Following this evolutionary argument about the origins of obesity, we turn our attention to the cross-cultural range of beliefs about ideal body characteristics and the social meanings of obesity. A prerequisite for both discussions is a review of some basic facts concerning the social epidemiology of obesity.

HUMAN OBESITY: THREE SOCIAL EPIDEMIOLOGICAL FACTS

Humans are among the fattest of all mammals,[3] the proportion of fat to total body mass ranges from approximately 10 percent in the very lean to over 35 percent in the obese.[4] In other mammals, the primary function of fat deposits is insulation from cold, but in humans, it is now widely accepted that much (but not all) fat serves as an energy reserve. The social distribution of adiposity within and between human populations is not random, and that distribution provides a key to understanding obesity. Three widely recognized social epidemiological facts about obesity are particularly salient for this discussion: (1) higher levels of fatness and risk of obesity in females represents a fundamental aspect of sexual dimorphism in *Homo sapiens;* (2) obesity is rare in unacculturated primitive populations, but the prevalence often increases rapidly during modernization; and (3) the prevalence of obesity is related to social class, usually positively; but among females in affluent societies, that relationship is inverted.

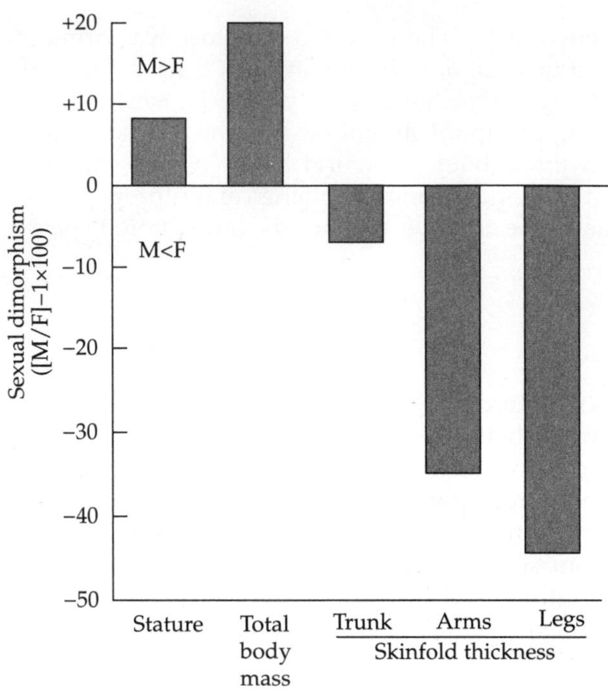

FIGURE 1 Sexual dimorphism in stature, body mass, and fat measures among white Americans aged 20 to 70 in Tecumseh, Michigan. Sexual dimorphism calculated by comparing male versus female means by ([M/F] -1×100); positive figures refer to greater male measures. Data are from Bailey.[4] Skinfold thicknesses are means of 4 sites (trunk) or 5 sites (arms and legs/thighs); the mean sexual dimorphism in all 17 fat measures is −19%.

Obesity and Gender

Differences in fat deposition are an important aspect of sexual dimorphism in *Homo sapiens*.[5] Sexual dimorphism is found in many primate species, and it is more pronounced in terrestrial, polygynous species. Humans are only mildly dimorphic in morphological variables like stature; a survey of human populations around the world reveals a range of dimorphism in stature from 4.7 to 9.0 percent.[6] The most significant aspects of sexual dimorphism reside predominantly in soft tissue. On average for young adults in an affluent society, adipose tissue constitutes approximately 15 percent of body weight in males and about 27 percent in females.[4]

Fatness, particularly peripheral or limb body fat, is the most dimorphic of the morphological variables, as shown in Figure 1. Adult men are larger than women in stature (+8%) and total body mass (+20%), whereas women have more subcutaneous fat as measured in skinfold thicknesses. Bailey's analysis of sex differences in body composition using data from white Americans in Tecumseh, Michigan, show, greater female skinfolds in 16 of 17 measurement sites (the exception is the suprailiac). In general, adult limb fatness was much more dimorphic than trunk fatness: trunk: –7.5% (mean of 5 measures); arms: –35.4% (mean of 4 measures); and legs/thighs: –46.7% (mean of 5 measures).[4]

It is noteworthy that peripheral body fat does not have the same close association with chronic diseases (i.e. Type II diabetes mellitus or hypertension) as centripetal or trunk fatness. Thus the sexual dimorphism in fat deposition may be unrelated to the dimension of obesity that most affects health. The developmental course of this dimorphism is also of interest. It is present in childhood, but increases markedly during adolescence, due to greatly increased divergence in the rate of fat gain.[7] Thus this divergence occurs at the time of reproductive maturation.

Although there is some population-specific variation in fat distribution, human sexual dimorphism in overall fat and peripheral fat appears to be universal. Although very small in stature and extremely lean by worldwide standards, the !Kung San, a hunting and gathering society of the Kalahari desert, show a similar pattern of sexual dimorphism, with a pronounced difference in measures of subcutaneous fat for women (see Figure 2). The sexual dimorphism of the !Kung San is about +6.7% for stature, +20% in weight, and –80% in midtriceps skinfolds.[8]

Sex differences are also seen in the prevalence of obesity. Despite methodological differences in the operational definition of obesity and in sampling frameworks, data from the 14 populations shown in

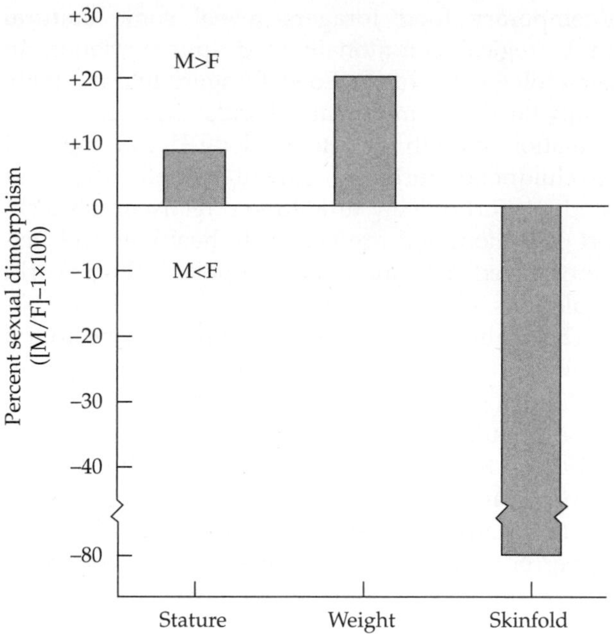

FIGURE 2 Sexual dimorphism in stature, weight, and midtriceps skinfolds among !Kung San hunter-gatherers of Botswana. Sample includes 527 men and women, aged 10–80, all living in a traditional lifestyle. Sexual dimorphism calculated by comparing male versus female means by ([M/F]−1 × 100); positive figures refer to greater male measures. Note the larger male/female difference in fat than among white Americans shown in Figure 1.

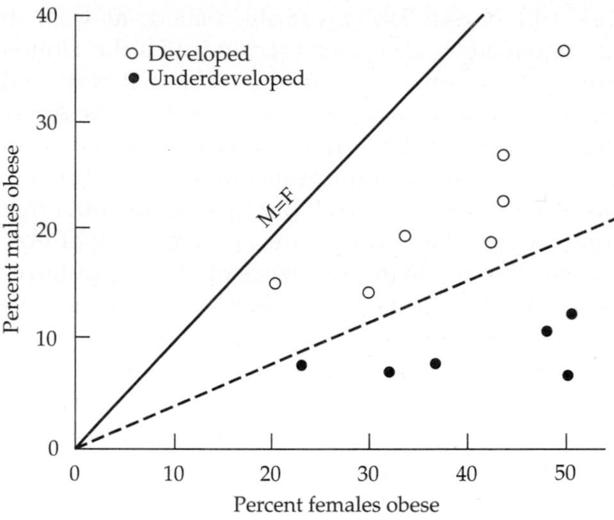

FIGURE 3 Gender differences in prevalence of obesity in 14 populations by general economic development. Only complete society prevalences were used, and underdeveloped populations were limited to groups with a significant degree of obesity. Operational definitions of obesity differ between studies. Populations include: Pukapuka, Rarotonga and New Zealand urban Maori,[13] Capetown Bantu, Guyana, Lagos (Nigeria), Puerto Rico, Germany, London,[12] U.S. Blacks, and U.S. Whites.[16] The unbroken line demarcates equal male/female obesity rates. The broken line indicates an apparent division between the proportion of gender difference in obesity between developed and underdeveloped countries.

Figure 3 show that in all of the surveys, females have a higher prevalence of obesity than males. Variations in the male/female ratio of proportions of obesity seen in this figure reveal a new regularity that remains to be explained—namely, that more affluent western populations have more equivalent male/female ratios of obesity prevalence than poor populations in the underdeveloped world.

Obesity and Modernization

The second social epidemiological fact regards culture change and the origins of obesity. It is significant that anthropometric studies of traditional hunting and gathering populations report no obesity. By contrast, numerous studies of traditional societies undergoing the process of modernization (or Westernization) report rapid increases in the prevalence of obesity.[9–12] A classic natural experiment study by Prior and colleagues compared the diet and health of Polynesian islanders at different stages of acculturation: the prevalence of obesity in the most traditional island (Pukapuka) was 15.4%; for a rapidly modernizing population (Rarotonga), it was 29.3%; and for urban Maoris it was 35.4 percent.[13] Trowell and Burkitt, whose recent volume contains 15 case studies of societies experiencing increased obesity and associated Western diseases during modernization, conclude that obesity is the first of these diseases of civilization to appear.[14]

Change in diet appears to be a primary cause for the link between modernization and obesity. More precisely, westernization of traditional diets involves decreased intake of fiber and increased intake of fats and sugar. The seeming inevitability of this change toward a less healthy diet is impressive but not well understood. We suspect that more is involved in this dietary change than the simple imitation of prestigious western foodways: the quick shift from primitive to high fat, high sugar diets with the advent of affluence may have evolutionary roots.

Obesity and Social Class

The third and possibly most important fact concerning the social epidemiology of obesity is its association with social class and ethnicity. Research primarily by Stunkard and colleagues have shown that social class and obesity are inversely related, at least in heterogeneous and affluent societies like the United States.[15,16] The inverse correlation of social class and obesity is very strong, particularly for females. A few studies, however, have found a weak association of class and obesity for groups including men, children, and certain ethnic groups.[17] But there is no doubt that social factors play a role in the epidemiology of obesity, and that the high prevalence of obesity for lower class women reflects that, "obesity may always be unhealthy, but it is not always abnormal."[15]

The association between socioeconomic class and obesity among adult women, therefore, merits special attention. This association is not constant through the life cycle. Garn and Clark describe a pattern of growth called "the socioeconomic reversal of fatness in females": in childhood, middle and upper class girls (and boys) are consistently fatter than poorer girls; at around the time of puberty, the relative level of fatness in the two groups switches; and in adulthood, lower class women are consistently fatter than middle and upper class women.[18]

In the traditional societies typically studied by anthropologists, the social epidemiology of adult obesity is not well documented. The data indirectly suggest, however, that the relationship of obesity and social class is often a positive one. Surveys from developing countries show a positive association between social class and obesity prevalence and, as expected, an inverse correlation between class and protein-calorie malnutrition.[19]

EVOLUTION AND OBESITY: DIET, FOOD SCARCITIES, AND ADAPTATION

Both genes and lifestyle are involved in the etiology of obesity, although the relative importance of either factor, and the ways in which they interact, are not thoroughly understood.[20] We suggest that both genetic and cultural predispositions to obesity may be products of the same evolutionary pressures, involving two related processes: first, traits that cause fatness were selected because they improved chances of survival in the face of food scarcities, particularly for pregnant and nursing women; second, fatness may have been directly selected because it is a cultural symbol of social prestige and an index of general health.

Cultural Evolution from Food Foraging to Food Production

For 95 to 99 percent of our history, humans lived exclusively as hunters and gatherers. Studies of contemporary food foragers reveal some cultural and biological commonalities despite variation in their ecological context. Food foragers live in small, socially flexible, seminomadic bands; experience slow population growth due to prolonged nursing and high childhood mortality; enjoy high quality diets and spend proportionately little time directly involved in food collection; and are generally healthier and better nourished than many contemporary third world populations relying on agriculture.

The reality of food foraging life is to be found somewhere between the Hobbesian "nasty, brutish, and short" and the "original affluent society," a phrase popularized by some anthropologists during the 1960s.[21] It is important to dispel romantic notions of food foragers, like the !Kung San of Botswana, as innocents leading a carefree existence; they suffer from a 50 percent child mortality rate, a low life expectancy at birth, and even a homicide rate that rivals that of many metropolitan areas. Yet, given the length of time that it has survived, food foraging must be considered a successful strategy of adaptation.

Approximately 12,000 years ago, some human groups shifted from a food foraging economy to one of food production. This shift required the domestication of plants and animals, an evolutionary process in which humans acted as agents of selection for domestic phenotypes. This economic transformation, known as the neolithic revolution, may be considered the most important event in human history because it allowed population growth and the evolution of complex societies and civilization. The current consensus among archeologists is that the new economy based on agriculture was something that people were effectively forced to adopt because of ecological pressures from population growth and food scarcities.[22] Nearly

TABLE 1 Late Paleolithic, Contemporary American, and Currently Recommended Dietary Composition[26]

	Late Paleolithic Diet	*Contemporary American Diet*	*Current Recommendations*
Total dietary energy (percent)			
Protein	34	12	12
Carbohydrate	45	46	58
Fat	21	42	30
P:S. ratio[a]	1.41	0.44	1.00
Cholesterol (mg)	591	600	300
Fiber (gm)	45.7	19.7	30–60
Sodium (mg)	690	2300–6900	1100–3300
Calcium (mg)	1580	740	800–1200
Ascorbic Acid (mg)	392.3	87.7	45

[a] Polyunsaturated: saturated fat ratio.

everywhere it has been studied, the switch from food foraging to agriculture is associated with osteological evidence of nutritional stress, poor health, and diminished stature.[23]

It is important to note that the beginning of agriculture is linked to the emergence of social stratification. Civilization was made possible by the political, economic, and military power of urban elites over agricultural surpluses collected in the form of tribute. For members of the ruling class, social stratification has numerous advantages, the most important of which is guaranteed access to food during periods of relative food scarcity. In state level societies, nutritional stress is never evenly distributed across the social spectrum. Functionally, the poor insulate the rich from the threat of starvation.

Obesity is thus not simply a disease of civilization. It is common only in certain kinds of civilized societies—ones with an absolute level of affluence so that even the poor have access to enough food to become obese. Trowell has suggested that obesity became common in Europe, first in elites and then the rest of society, only about 200 years ago.[24]

The Adequacy of Preindustrial Diets

The adequacy of the diet of food foragers, and by close analogy that of our prehistoric ancestors, has been the subject of considerable interest. New analytical techniques now being applied to skeletal populations by archeologists are expanding our knowledge of prehistoric diet.[25] A recent analysis of the nutritional components of the Paleolithic diet,[26] shown in Table 1, suggests that the diet of prehistoric food foragers was high in protein, fiber, and vegetable carbohydrates and low in sugar and saturated fats. There are striking similarities of this reconstructed stone age diet and the daily nutritional requirements recommended by the U.S. Senate Select Committee, in all areas except cholesterol intake. With this exception, the Paleolithic diet could be considered a model preventive diet, more stringent and thus probably more healthy even than the currently recommended one. But this fact reflects limitations in the availability and choice of foods rather than some primitive wisdom about a nutritionally optimal diet. Studies of culture change have repeatedly shown that when traditional populations with healthy diets have the opportunity, they readily switch to the less healthy (except in terms of abundance) Western diets.

Another method of estimation of the adequacy of the preindustrial diet is through cross-cultural comparison. Marjorie Whiting used ethnographic data from the Human Relations Area Files (HRAF) and nutritional studies to survey some major components of diet in a representative sample of 118 nonindustrial societies with economies based on food-foraging, pastoralism, simple horticulture, and agriculture.[27] (The HRAF is a compilation of ethnographic information on over 300 of the most thoroughly studied societies in the anthropological and historical record, cross-indexed for hundreds of variables. Subsamples of societies are chosen for representativeness of world areas and economic types.) In general, the quality of nonindustrial diets is high, the mean percent of calories derived from fat and carbohydrates falling within the recommended U.S. standards, and the percentage of protein nearly twice the recommended amount.[26] For the 84% of societies where food supply is adequate or plentiful, therefore, the diet seems superior to that of the United States. The major inadequacy of preindustrial diets and productive economics, however, is their susceptibility to food shortages.

The Ubiquity of Food Shortages

Food shortages have been so common in human prehistory and history that they could be considered a virtually inevitable fact of life in the past. Whiting's cross-cultural survey found some form of food shortages for all of the societies in the sample. . . . In 28.7 percent of the societies, food shortages are rare, occurring every 10 to 15 years, whereas in 24.3 percent they happen every 2 to 3 years. Shortages occur annually or even more frequently in 47 percent of the societies. Half of these are annual shortfalls, which Whiting described as happening "a few weeks preceding harvest, anticipated and expected, recognized as temporary," and in the other 23.5 percent of the societies, shortages are more frequent than once a year. This distribution has great evolutionary significance.

. . . For the 113 societies with adequate data, 29.3 percent had severe shortages that were characterized by the exhaustion of emergency foods, many people desperate for food, and starvation deaths—in short, a famine. Moderate shortages, in which food stores were used up, where emergency foods were used, and where people lost considerable weight, were found in 34.4 percent of the societies. Finally, 36.3 percent had mild food shortages, with fewer meals than usual, some weight loss, but no great hardships.[27] Two examples, one archeological and one ethnographic, will serve to illustrate these patterns and their relationship to the relative reliance on food foraging or food production.

The southwestern United States, where we today find Native American groups like the Pima, with endemic obesity and a high prevalence of type II diabetes,[28] was in the prehistoric past the frequent site of food shortages. Tree-ring analysis has been used to calculate the frequency of ecological stresses and resulting food shortages affecting these people, the builders of the impressive kivas and cliff dwellings. The data from southern New Mexico suggest that, between 600 and 1249 A.D., every other year had inadequate rainfall for dry farming, and that there was severe stress (more than two successive years of total crop failures) at least once every 25 years.[29] The complex agricultural societies of the prehistoric southwest expanded quickly during a period of uncharacteristically good weather. Despite a variety of social adaptations to food shortages, when lower rainfall pattern resumed, the complex chiefdomships could not be maintained: the population declined, and the culture devolved back to food foraging.

Medical studies of the !Kung San hunter-gatherers have found that adults were in generally good health, but exhibited periodic mild caloric undernutrition.[30] Seasonal variation in the availability of food resulted in an annual cycle of weight loss and weight gain in both food-foraging and food-producing societies. Agriculturalists, however, experience greater seasonal swings of weight loss and gain. Seasonal weight loss among the !Kung, although it varied by ecological region and year, averaged between 1 and 2 percent of adult body weight.[8, 31] Seasonal weight losses among African agriculturalists are more severe, averaging 4 to 6.5 percent of total body weight in typical years.[32]

Biological and Cultural Adaptations to Scarcity

Food shortages suggest a hypothesis of the evolution of obesity. Because shortages were ubiquitous for humans under natural conditions, selection favored individuals who could effectively store calories in times of surplus. For three-fourths of the societies, such stores would be depleted, or at least called on, every two to three years, and sometimes more frequently.

Medical data on famine victims show that, in addition to outright starvation, malnutrition from food shortages has a synergistic effect on infectious disease mortality, as well as decreasing birth weights and rates of child growth.[33] Females with greater energy reserves in fat have a selective advantage over their lean counterparts in withstanding the stress of food shortage, not only for themselves, but for their fetuses or nursing children. Humans have evolved to "save up" food energy for the inevitability of food shortages through the synthesis and storage of fat. Moreover, females, whose reproductive fitness depends upon their ability to withstand the nutritional demands of pregnancy and lactation, appear to have been selected for more slow-releasing peripheral body fat than males.

In this evolutionary context the usual range of human metabolic variation must have produced many individuals with a predisposition to become obese; yet they would, in all likelihood, never have the opportunity to do so. Furthermore, in this context there could be little or no natural selection against such a tendency. Selection could not provide for the eventuality of continuous surplus because it had simply never existed.

There is little evidence that obesity, at least moderate obesity, reduces Darwinian reproductive fitness. A follow-up study of participants to the Third Harvard Growth Study found a positive correlation between fatness and fertility when holding both social class and ethnicity constant.[34] The influence of social class is important and complex: in developed countries, fatness, lower social class, and fertility are all positively associated, whereas in underdeveloped countries, fatness and fertility are associated only in upper socioeconomic classes.[35] A minimal level of female fatness may increase lifetime reproductive success because of its association with regular cycling as well as earlier menarche. In preindustrial societies, social status is related, both symbolically and statistically, to fertility and fatness.

It is likely that under some conditions fatness is an adaptation to successful completion of pregnancy. Recommended weight gain during pregnancy is between 20 and 30 pounds, and failure to gain weight (which may be caused by inadequate caloric intake) is considered a clinically ominous sign.[36, 37] Especially for women with lower gains and lower pregravid weight, weight gain is positively correlated with birth weight and negatively correlated with perinatal mortality. The energy cost of pregnancy is estimated to be 80,000 kcal (300 kcal/d), assuming no change in energy output[38]—a reasonable assumption for nonindustrial societies. Intrauterine growth retardation associated with working during pregnancy is greatest against the background of low pregravid weight and low pregnancy weight gain.[39] Failure to supplement usual intake adequately will result in a depletion of pregravid tissue reserves.

The ongoing energy cost of lactation, if milk is the sole primary infant food, is higher than that of pregnancy, and lactation in traditional societies may last up to four years and be superimposed on early pregnancy. Estimated needed supplements, converted to energy in milk with high efficiency (around 90%), range from 500 kcal/d in the early postpartum period to 1000 kcal/d by the end of the first year.[36,40] Well-fed women with high pregnancy weight gains can supplement less and safely attain a deliberately negative energy balance during lactation by drawing on prepartum fatty tissue reserves.[41] At the other extreme, experimental interventions in Gambia[42] and Guatemala[43] provided caloric supplementation to pregnant and lactating women. In the Gambian case, women readily took supplements larger than the above-mentioned estimates, and supplemented women who completed pregnancy in the lean season experienced a six-fold reduction of the proportion of low-birth-weight infants, ending up with an incidence typical of developed countries (4.7%). In both populations, supplements during lactation also increased the duration of postpartum infertility.

Using the figure 80,000 kcal for pregnancy, and a conversion rate of 9.1 kcal/g, pregnancy with no supplementation could be maintained by pregravid tissue reserves amounting to 8.8 kg of fat. Viewed from the perspective of the costs of shortage rather than the costs of pregnancy per se, an annual or less frequent shortage of the length and type experienced by the Gambian women, whether occurring during pregnancy or lactation, would be cushioned against by excess fat amounting to 15 to 20% of body weight. In as much as women in traditional societies spend the great majority of their reproductive lives either pregnant or nursing, an ideal of plumpness would be adaptive throughout that period. A custom such as the fattening hut for brides-to-be (see below) might provide a critical head-start on this lifelong reproductive energy drain.

Humans have also evolved other cultural mechanisms to minimize the effects of food shortages, including economic diversification, storage of foods, knowledge of possible famine foods, conversion of surplus food into durable valuables to be exchanged for food in emergencies, and cultivation of strong social relations with individuals in other regions.[44] These mechanisms act as buffers between environmental fluctuation and biological adaptation.

THE SOCIAL MEANING OF OBESITY: CROSS-CULTURAL COMPARISONS

Fatness is symbolically linked to psychological dimensions such as self-worth and sexuality in many societies of the world, including our own, but the nature of that symbolic association is not constant. In mainstream U.S. culture, obesity is socially stigmatized[45] even to the point of abhorrence. Weight loss is a major industry in the U.S., with annual expenditures of over five billion dollars. Most cultures of the world, by contrast, view fatness as a welcome sign of health and prosperity.

In an obesity-prevention campaign in a Zulu community outside of Durban,[46] one of the health education posters depicted an obese woman and an overloaded truck with a flat tire, with a caption "Both carry too much weight." Another poster showed a slender woman easily sweeping under a table next to an obese woman who is using the table for support; it has the caption "Who do you prefer to look like?" The intended message of these posters was misinterpreted by the community because of a cultural connection between obesity and social status. The woman in the first poster was perceived to be rich and happy, since she was not only fat, but had a truck overflowing with her possessions. The second poster was perceived as a scene of an affluent mistress directing her underfed servant.

Given the rarity of obesity in unacculturated pre-industrial societies, it is not surprising that many groups have no ethnomedical definition of or concern with obesity. Given the frequency of food shortages, it is equally predictable that thinness, rather than fatness, will be deemed a serious medical symptom. The Tupinamba of Brazil have no descriptive term for fat people, but are reported to fear the symptom of thinness (*angaiuare*).[47] In the preindustrial context, thin people are to be pitied; this is the case for food foragers like the !Kung San, where culturally defined thinness (*zham*) is viewed as a symptom of starvation.

It may be large body size rather than obesity per se that in agricultural societies becomes an admired symbol of health, prestige, prosperity, or maternity. The agricultural Tiv of Nigeria, for example, distinguish between a very positive category, too big (*kehe*), and an unpleasant condition, to grow fat (*ahon*).[48] The first is a compliment—sign of prosperity that also refers to the seasonal weight gain of the early dry season when food is plentiful. The second term refers to a rare and undesirable condition.

Even in the industrialized U.S., there is ethnic variation in definitions of obesity. Some Mexican-Americans have coined a new term, *gordura mala* (bad fatness), because the original term *gordura* continues to have positive cultural connotations.[49] There has also been historical variation in clinical standardized definitions of obesity in American medicine. Between 1943 and 1980, definitions of ideal weights declined for women but not for men; more recently, upward revision of those standards has been proposed, due to an apparent disjunction in some data sets between cosmetically ideal weights and the weights at which mortality is minimized. This, however, remains controversial.[50,51] In any case, the definition of obesity is ultimately linked to cultural conceptions of normality, beauty, and health.

Cross-Cultural Variation in Ideal Body Type

In addition to the basic association between plumpness and health, culturally defined standards of beauty may have been a factor in the sexual selection for phenotypes predisposed to obesity. In a classic example, Malcom described the custom of fattening huts for the seclusion of elite Efik pubescent girls in traditional Nigeria.[52] A girl spent up to two years in seclusion before marriage, and at the end of this rite of passage she possessed symbols of womanhood and marriageability: a three-tiered hairstyle, clitoridectomy, and fatness. This fatness was a primary criterion of beauty as it was defined by the elites, who had the economic resources to participate in this custom. Similar fattening huts were found in other parts of West Africa.

Among the Havasupai of the American Southwest, if a girl at puberty is thin, a fat woman stands (places her foot) on the girl's back so that she will become attractively plump. In this society, fat legs, and to a lesser extent arms, are considered essential to beauty.[53] The Tarahumara of Northern Mexico, whose men are famous as long-distance runners, reportedly consider large, fat thighs as the first requisite of beauty; a good-looking woman is called a "beautiful thigh."[54] Among the Amhara of the Horn of Africa, thin hips are called "dog hips" in a typical insult.[55] A South African Bemba courting song has the following verse: "Hullo Mama, the beautiful one, let us go to town/You will be very fat, you girl, if you stay with me."[56]

But how common is such a cultural connection between beauty and fat? There has been no systematic cross-cultural survey of definitions of feminine beauty or ideal body type among the societies of the world. The lack of a survey reflects, in part, the failure of ethnographers and historians to report adequately on this cultural element. Of the 325 cultures coded by the Human Relation Area Files, only 58 have adequate data to estimate some characteristic of ideal female body type.

TABLE 2 Cross-Cultural Standards of Female Beauty

	Number of Societies	*Percent of Category*
Overall Body		
Extreme obesity	0	0
Plumpness/moderate fat	31	81
Thin/abhorence of fat	7	19
Breasts		
Large or long	9	50
Small/abhorence of large	9	50
Hips and Legs		
Large or Fat	9	90
Slender	1	10
Stature		
Tall	3	30
Moderate	6	60
Small	1	10

The data summarized in Table 2 must be considered cautiously for a number of reasons: Because of the paucity of ethnographic data, a representative sample is impossible. Although limited to sources rated good or better, there is potential ethnographer bias toward the exotic. Observations cover a wide historical time span, often characterized by substantial cultural changes. There is the problem of relative standards; given the endemic obesity in modern society, what we consider normal may be fat to members of a society where obesity is uncommon. There is no consideration of intracultural diversity. Because the unit of analysis is a culture, the HRAF data base is skewed toward demographically small and technologically simple societies; the HRAF data base does not include the U.S. or modern European societies.

Granting the weaknesses of the data base, some guarded generalizations still seem possible. Cultural standards of beauty seem to be based on the normal characteristics of the dominant group of a society; they do not refer to physical extremes. No society on record has an ideal of extreme obesity. On the other hand, the desirability of plumpness or being filled out is found in 81 percent of societies for which there is data. This standard, which probably includes the clinical categories of overweight and mild obesity, apparently refers to the desirability of subcutaneous fat deposits. For societies where data on ideal standards on hips and legs is available, it appears that plumpness in peripheral body fat is commonly preferred. Societies that favor plumpness as a standard of beauty are found in all of the major world culture areas, with the exception of Asia. There appears to be no trend in preference for breast-size or stature. Ethnographic discussion of beauty in other societies often emphasizes cultural enhancements to the body, such as scarification, clothes, body paint, jewelry, and other adornments, rather than attributes of the body itself.[57] Standards of sexual beauty are based upon images of nubile, postpubertal, young-adult years in virtually all societies.

Fatness may also be a symbol of maternity and nurturance. In traditional societies where a woman attains her proper status only through motherhood, this symbolic association increases the cultural acceptability of obesity. A fat woman, symbolically, is well taken care of, and she in turn takes good care of her children. Fellahin Arabs in Egypt describe the proper woman as an "envelope for conception," and therefore a fat woman is a desirable ideal because she has more room to bear the child, lactate abundantly, and give warmth to her children.[58]

Although there is cross-cultural variation in standards of beauty, this variation falls within a certain range. American ideals of thinness occur in a setting where it is easy to become fat, and preference for plumpness occurs in settings where it is easy to remain lean. In context, both standards require the investment of individual effort and economic resources; furthermore, each in its context involves a display of wealth. In poor societies the rich impress the poor by becoming fat, which the poor cannot do. In rich societies even the poor can become fat, and avidly do; therefore, the rich must impress by staying thin, as if to say, "We have so little doubt about where our next meal is coming from, that we don't need a single gram of fat store." Cultural relativism in feminine beauty standards, therefore, may be limited by evolutionarily determined human universals on the one hand and by lawful cross-cultural variation on the other.

The ethnographic record concerning body preferences in males is very weak. The HRAF data base includes only 12 societies with adequate information to gauge ideal male body type. In all of these societies, the expressed preference was for a muscular physique and for tall or moderately tall stature. Other characteristics mentioned include broad shoulders and being well filled out. One extreme in this admiration of large body size would be Japanese Sumo wrestlers whose program to build large bodies is really purposeful obesity; similar patterns of fattening young male wrestlers is found in Polynesia.[59] With few exceptions (e.g. the !Kung San)[8] human societies admire large body size, but not necessarily fatness, as an attribute of attractiveness in men. All of these physical characteristics can be considered as indicators of general health and nutritional status. Large body size and even obesity, however, are desirable because they symbolize economic success, political power, and social status in some societies.

Big Men, political leaders in tribal New Guinea, are described by their constituents in terms of their size and physical well-being (as well as other attributes). A Big Man may be described as a tall forest beech tree or as a man "whose skin swells with 'grease' [or fat] underneath."[60] Large body size may, in fact, be an index of differential access to food resources. This is seen in chiefdomships, as in ancient Polynesia, where hereditary political leaders sit at the hub of a redistribution system in which chiefly families are assured a portion of each family's harvest. The spiritual power (*mana*) and noble breeding of a Polynesian chief is expected to be seen in his physical appearance. One ethnographer in Polynesia was asked, "Can't you see he is a chief? See how big he is?"[61] The Bemba of South Africa believe that fatness in a man demonstrates not only his economic success but also his spiritual power in fending off the sorcery attacks.[62] A similar symbolic association can be assigned to deities. The corpulence of the seated Buddha, for example, symbolizes his divinity and otherworldliness.

Cultural variation in the meaning of fatness is also found among ethnic groups in the United States. Massara's ethnographic study of the cultural meanings of weight in a Puerto Rican community in Philadelphia[63] documents the positive associations and lack of social stigma of obesity. In addition, quantitative evidence[64] suggests that there are significant differences in ideal body preferences between this ethnic community and mainstream American culture. Positive evaluations of fatness may also occur in lower class Black Americans[65] and Mexican Americans.[17] There is also heterogeneity within these ethnic groups; upwardly mobile ethnics more closely resemble mainstream American culture in attitudes about obesity and ideal body shape.

In contrast to these ethnic minorities, and most of the cultures of the world, the ideal of female body shape in dominant middle/upper class America is thin. Studies suggest that females hold this cultural value more strongly than males,[66] who tend to be more satisfied with their own current body shape. Over the past three decades cosmetic ideals of female body shape have gotten thinner,[67] even thinner than medical ideals. Cultural beliefs about attractive body shape, therefore, place pressure on females to lose weight, and appear to be involved in the etiology of anorexia and bulimia. Neither the socioeconomic reversal of fatness in females nor the social history of symbolism of thinness has been adequately examined. Thinness, like tanning, is a contemporary symbol of economic status and leisure time for women. Both may be unhealthy, and both represent reversals of previous ideals.

Finally, although we have focused on the role of food shortages in human history, they are unfortunately not limited to the past. The drought and famine in the Horn of Africa and the Sahel have justifiably received world attention. Even in the United States, arguably the richest nation in human history, an estimated 20 million people are hungry.[68] This continuing worldwide epidemic of hunger presents a powerful and tragic counterbalance to our contemplation of the new epidemic of obesity and a reminder of the sometimes harsh realities of our history.

SUMMARY

An anthropological perspective on obesity considers both its evolutionary background and cross-cultural variation. It must explain three basic facts about obesity: gender dimorphism (women > men), an increase with modernization, and a positive association with socioeconomic status. Preindustrial diets varied in quality but shared a tendency to periodic shortages. Such shortages, particularly disadvantageous to women in their reproductive years, favored individuals who for biological and cultural reasons, stored fat. Not surprisingly, the majority of the world's cultures had or have ideals of feminine beauty that include plumpness. This is consistent with the hypothesis that fat stores functioned as a cushion against food shortages during pregnancy and lactation. As obesity has increased, the traditional gap between males and females in its prevalence has narrowed. Under Western conditions of abundance, our biological tendency to regulate body weight at levels above our ideal cannot be easily controlled even with a complete reversal of the widespread cultural ideal of plumpness.

REFERENCES

1. Pilbeam, D. 1984. The descent of hominoids and hominids. Sci. Am. 250: 84–96.
2. Lee, R. B. & I. DeVore, Eds. 1968. Man the Hunter. Aldine. Chicago, IL.
3. Pitts, G. C. & T. R. Bullard. 1968. Some interspecific aspects of body composition in mammals. In Body Composition in Animals and Man. National Academy of Science, Washington, D.C. Pub. No. 1598:45–70.
4. Bailey, S. M. 1982. Absolute and relative sex differences in body composition. In Sexual dimorphism in Homo sapiens. R. L. Hall, Ed. Praeger Scientific. New York.
5. Pond, C. M. 1978. Morphological aspects and the ecological and mechanical consequences of fat deposition in wild vertebrates. Ann. Rev. Ecol. Syste. 9: 519–570.
6. Stini, W. A. 1978. Malnutrition, body size and proportion. Ecol. Food Nutr. 1:125–132.
7. Tanner, J. M. 1962. Growth at Adolescence. Blackwell Scientific. Oxford.
8. Lee, R. B. 1979. The !Kung San: Men, Women, and Work in a Foraging Society. Harvard University Press. Cambridge, MA.
9. Page, L. B., A. Damon & R. C. Moellering. 1974. Antecedents of cardiovascular disease in six Solomon Islands societies. Circulation 49: 1132–1146.
10. Zimmet, P. 1979. Epidemiology of diabetes and its macrovascular manifestations in Pacific populations: the medical effects of social progress. Diabetes Care 2: 144–153.
11. West, K. 1978. Diabetes in American Indians. In Advances in metabolic disorders. Academic Press. New York.
12. Christakis, G. 1973. The prevalence of adult obesity. In Obesity in Perspective. G. Bray, Ed. 2: 209–213. Fogarty International Center Series on Preventive Medicine.
13. Prior, I. A. 1971. The price of civilization. Nutr. Today 6(4): 2–11.
14. Trowell, H. C. & D. P. Burkitt. 1981. Western Diseases: Their Emergence and Prevention. Harvard University Press. Cambridge, MA.
15. Goldblatt, P. B., M. E. Moore & A. J. Stunkard. 1965. Social factors in obesity. J. Am. Med. Assoc. 192: 1039–1044.
16. Burnight, R. G. & P. G. Marden. 1967. Social correlates of weight in an aging population. Milbank Mem. Fund. 45: 75–92.
17. Ross, C. E. & J. Mirowsky. 1983. Social epidemiology of overweight: a substantive and methodological investigation. J. Health Soc. Behav. 24: 288–298.
18. Garn, S. M. & D. C. Clark. 1976. Trends in fatness and the origins of obesity. Pediatrics 57: 443–456.
19. Arteaga, P. J. E. Dos Santos & J. E. Dutra De Oliveira. 1982. Obesity among school-children of different socioeconomic levels in a developing country. Int. J. Obesity 6: 291–297.
20. Stunkard, A. J., T. I. A. Sorenson, C. Hanis, T. W. Teasdale, R. Chakaborty, W. J. Schull & F. Schulsinger. 1986. An adoption study of obesity. N. Engl. J. Med. 314: 193–198.
21. Sahlins, M. 1972. Stone Age Economics. Aldine. Chicago, IL.
22. Wenke, R. J. 1980. Patterns in Prehistory. Oxford. New York.
23. Cohen, M. N. & G. J. Armelagos, Eds. 1984. Paleopathology at the Origins of Agriculture. Academic Press. New York.
24. Trowell, H. 1975. Obesity in the western world. Plant Foods for Man 1:157–165.
25. Gilbert, R. I. & J H. Mielke, Eds. 1985. The Analysis of Prehistoric Diets. Academic Press. New York.
26. Eaton, S. B. & M. Konner. 1985. Paleolithic nutrition: a consideration of its nature and current implications. N. Eng. J. Med. 312: 283–289.
27. Whiting, M. G. 1958. A cross-cultural nutrition survey. Doctoral Thesis. Harvard School of Public Health. Cambridge, MA.
28. Knowler, W. C., D. J. Pettitt, P. J. Savage & P. H. Bennett. 1981. Diabetes incidence in Pima Indians: contribution of obesity and parental diabetes. Am. J. Epidemiol 113: 144–156.
29. Minnis, P. E. 1985. Social Adaptation to Food Stress: A Prehistoric Southwestern Example. University of Chicago Press. Chicago, IL.
30. Truswell, A. S. & J. D. L. Hansen. 1977. Diet and nutrition of hunter-gatherers. In Health and Disease in Tribal Societies. Ciba Foundation, Eds. 213–226. Elsevier. Amsterdam.
31. Wilmsen, E. 1978. Seasonal effects of dietary intake in the Kalahari San. Fed. Proc. Fed. Am. Soc. Exp. Bio. 37: 65–71.
32. Hunter, J. M. 1967. Seasonal hunger in a part of the west African savanna: a survey of body weights in Nangodi, north-east Ghana. Trans. Inst. Br. Geog. 41: 167–185.

33. Stein, Z. & M. Susser. 1975. The Dutch famine, 1944–1945, and the reproductive process. Pediatr. Res. 9: 70–76.
34. Scott, E. C. & C. J. Bajema. 1982. Height, weight and fertility among participants of the third Harvard growth study. Hum. Biol. 54: 501–516.
35. Garn, S. M., S. M. Bailey & I. T. T. Higgens, 1980. Effects of socioeconomic status, family life, and living together on fatness and obesity. In Childhood Prevention of Atherosclerosis and Hypertension. R. Lauer & R. Skekelle, Eds. Raven Press. New York.
36. Eastman, N. J. & E. Jackson. 1968. Weight relationships in pregnancy. Obstet. Gynecol. Surv. 23: 1003–1025.
37. Naeye, R. L. 1979. Weight gain and outcome of pregnancy. Am. J. Obstet. Gynecol. 135:3–9.
38. Blackburn, M. W. & D. H. Calloway. 1976. Energy expenditure and consumption of mature, pregnant and lactating women. J. Am. Diet. Assoc. 69: 29–37.
39. Naeye, R. L. & E. C. Peters. 1982. Working during pregnancy: effects on the fetus. Pediatrics 69: 725–727.
40. Thomson, A. M., F. E. Hytten & W. Z. Billewicz. 1970. The energy cost of human lactation. Br. J. Nutr. 24: 565–572.
41. Butte, N. F., C. Garza, J. E. Stuff, E. O. Smith & B. L. Nichols. 1984. Effect of maternal diet and body composition on lactational performance. Am. J. Clin. Nutr. 39: 296–306.
42. Prentice, A. M., R. G. Whitehead, M. Watkinson, W. H. Lamb & T. J. Cole. 1983. Prenatal dietary supplementation of African women and birth-weight. Lancet 1: 489–492.
43. Delgado, H., A. Lechug, C. Yarbrough, R. Martorell, R. E. Klein & M. Irwin. 1977. Maternal nutrition—its effect on infant growth and development and birth spacing. In Nutritional Impacts on Women. K. S. Moghissi & T. N. Evans, Eds. Harper & Row. Hagerstown, MD.
44. Colson, E. 1979. In good years and bad: food strategies of self-reliant societies. J. Anthropol. Res. 35: 18–29.
45. Cahnman, W. J. 1968. The stigma of obesity. Sociol Q. 9: 294–297.
46. Gampel, B. 1962. The "Hilltops" community. In Practice of Social Medicine. S. L. Kark & G. E. Steuart, Eds. E. & S. Livingstone. London.
47. Evreux, Y. 1864. Voyage dans le Nord du Bresil Fait durant les Annees 1613 et 1614. F. Denis, Ed. A. Franch. Paris and Leipzig.
48. Bohannan, P. & L. Bohannan. 1969. A source notebook on Tiv religion (5 vol.). Human Relations Area Files. New Haven, CT.
49. Ritenbaugh, C. 1982. Obesity as a culture-bound syndrome. Cult. Med. Psychiatry 6: 347–361.
50. Metropolitan Life Foundation. 1983. Height and Weight Tables. Metropolitan Life Insurance Company.
51. Burton, B. T., W. R. Foster, J. Hirsch & T. B. Van Itallie. 1985. Health implications of obesity: an NIH consensus development conference. Intl. J. Obesity 9: 155–169.
52. Malcom, L. W. G. 1925. Note on the seclusion of girls among the Efik at Old Calabar. Man 25: 113–114.
53. Smithson, C. L. 1959. The Havasupai Woman. U. Utah Press. Salt Lake City, UT.
54. Bennett, W. C. & R. M. Zingg. 1935. The Tarahumara: an Indian Tribe of Northern Mexico. U. Chicago Press. Chicago, IL.
55. Messing, S. D. 1957. The Highland Plateau Amhara of Ethiopia. Doctoral dissertation (Anthropology). U. Pennsylvania. Philadelphia, PA.
56. Powdermaker, H. 1960. An anthropological approach to the problem of obesity. Bull. N.Y. Acad. Sci. 36: 286–295.
57. Brain, R. 1979. The Decorated Body. Harper & Row. New York.
58. Amnar, H. 1954. Growing Up in an Egyptian Village. Routledge & Kegan Paul. London.
59. Beaglehole, E. & P. Beaglehole, 1938. Ethnology of Pukapuka. Bernice P. Bishop Museum. Honolulu, HI.
60. Strahern, A. 1971. The Rope of Moka. Cambridge University Press. New York.
61. Gifford, E. W. 1929. Tongan Society. Bernice P. Bishop Mus. Bull. 61. Honolulu, HI.
62. Richards, A. I.1939. Land, Labour and Diet in Northern Rhodesia: an Economic Study of the Bemba Tribe. Oxford University Press. London.
63. Massara, E. B. 1979. Que gordita! a study of weight among women in a Puerto Rican community. Ph.D. dissertation. Bryn Mawr College. Philadelphia, PA.
64. Massara, E. B. 1980. Obesity and cultural weight evaluations. Appetite 1: 291–298.
65. Styles, M. H. 1980. Soul, black women and food. In A Woman's Conflict: The Special Relationship between Women and Food. J. R. Kaplan, Ed. Prentice-Hall. Englewood Cliffs, N.J.
66. Garner, D. M., P. E. Garfinkel, D. Schwartz & M. Thompson. 1980. Cultural expectations of thinness in women. Psychol. Rep. 47: 483–491.
67. Fallon, A. E. & P. Rozin. 1985. Sex differences in perceptions of desirable body shape. J. Abnorm. Psychol. 94: 102–105.
68. Physician Task Force on Hunger in America. 1985. Hunger in America: the Growing Epidemic. Harvard University School of Public Health. Boston, MA.

Global Health Issues and Programs

■ ***Many medical anthropologists work in the field of global health, most often as consultants to specific programs.*** Since the World Health Organization's 1978 proclamation for primary health care (PHC), there have been efforts to institute basic health services and prevention programs on a worldwide basis. PHC represented a change from previous international health programs aimed at single disease eradication. The idea of PHC was to bring health *to the people,* to empower communities through health initiatives, and to decrease mortality through "horizontal" efforts—as opposed to fighting disease through "vertical" programs. PHC work requires sensitivity to local cultural beliefs and values, as well as cooperation with and empowerment of local people. Medical anthropology has made significant contributions to this field (Lane and Rubinstein 1996).

■ ***Primary health care programs often center on mother and infant health.*** The child survival initiatives have used relatively simple technologies—oral rehydration therapy (ORT), childhood immunizations, promotion of breast-feeding, and the use of growth charts to identify malnourished children for supplementary feeding. These programs clearly work in lowering infant and child mortality (Basch 1990; Coreil and Mull 1990).

■ ***Medical anthropologists study the culture and organization of global health programs themselves.*** There is a culture to global health programs and policies, just like there is a culture to clinical biomedicine. Health policies develop out of political processes, and local sociocultural contexts shape the implementation of programs. Medical anthropologists have shown that cultural factors *within the health program* are sometimes important obstacles to the success of a project (Foster 1987). An excellent example of an ethnography of a health policy and its implementation is Judith Justice's *Policies, Plans, and People* (1986).

■ ***Some medical anthropologists strive to promote cooperation of traditional ethnomedical practitioners within international health programs.*** Traditional healers and lay midwives are health workers who often cooperate with biomedical practitioners. For example, Edward Green (1985) has helped organize and train local traditional healers in Swaziland to use oral rehydration therapy. Another area of substantial work is the supplementary training of traditional birth attendants (TBAs) in efforts to reduce maternal mortality (Cosminsky 1986).

■ ***Anthropologists working with global health issues and programs must look beyond cultural differences that may influence the acceptance of health-innovations and analyze the political–economic circumstances that create health problems.*** Sometimes medical anthropologists working in global health projects are expected to be the experts in "culture" and to work toward the cultural acceptability of an innovation. Although this is important work, it is also important to explain the bigger picture. Political and economic constraints, a history of colonial exploitation, or unjust local governments can play significant causal roles in perpetuating health problems in the developing world. This is what Paul Farmer calls "structural violence." The hallmark of anthropology is a holistic approach to understanding human societies and their problems—especially their health problems.

 46

Saving the Children for the Tobacco Industry

Mark Nichter
Elizabeth Cartwright

Incorporating ethnographic studies into international health programs has required some modification of traditional anthropological methods to make fieldwork briefer and more focused. These new methodologies include protocols called focused ethnographic studies (FESs) (Bentley, Pelto, and Pelto 1990; Gove and Pelto 1993). Medical anthropologists have planned a significant role for PHC including programs aimed at oral rehydration therapy, as we will see in selection 47; safe motherhood initiatives; interventions against acute respiratory infections (ARIs) (Nichter 1993); and introduction of appropriate weanling foods (Dettwyler and Fishman 1992). As this selection explains, nearly all of these international health efforts have been aimed at infectious diseases in children. Two lessons are apparent when reviewing this intensive PHC work: First, cultural factors must be considered in designing successful community-based programs; second, the underlying political and economic processes that result in the disastrous health conditions of the Third World are seldom addressed by international health projects.

This selection examines a different international health problem—the proliferation of tobacco use in the poor countries of the world. As cigarette smoking has decreased in the United States, there has been an extended effort to expand the market in developing countries. Cigarette companies have long been a powerful political force in the United States; tobacco growers were given federal subsidies, and the companies were able to promote an addictive and lethal product to the American public with impunity. Only recently have these companies told the complete truth about their product. Critics of cigarette marketing in the Third World argue that this is tantamount to exporting chronic disease and death. The marketing strategies of multinational tobacco companies to expand international sales include saturation campaigns with persuasive ads wherein cigarettes are depicted as consumables of modern, wealthy, and sophisticated people.

There are ironic contradictions between U.S. trade policy and "agricultural" development on the one hand and health policies on the other hand. This selection is a good example of a political-economic analysis applied to an international health problem. The emphasis is on the interrelation of macroeconomic factors (tobacco company profits), health consequences (the coming Third World epidemics of lung cancer and chronic diseases), household economic costs (money to purchase cigarettes), and American ideological models of free choice and individual responsibility. Part of the mission of medical anthropology is to remind people of the bigger picture of health problems; this selection does just that.

As you read this selection, consider these questions:

- **Why do tobacco companies need to recruit new smokers in the Third World? Does the early death of smokers hurt their business?**
- **What does it mean to say that children are innocent and therefore more in need of international health interventions?**
- **Is this selection cynical? What steps of action and intervention does it suggest? What are some obstacles that you might anticipate?**
- **Why might people in Third World countries be attracted to U.S. products like baby formula and cigarettes?**
- **Why are local governments not inclined to regulate cigarette smoking for their own populations?**

Context: Mark Nichter is a medical anthropologist and Regents Professor of Anthropology, Public Health, and Family medicine at the University of Arizona. He has conducted ethnographic research throughout South and Southeast Asia—including India, Sri Lanka, and the Philippines—and has received both the Margaret Mead and the Rudolph Virchow awards for his extensive contributions to medical anthropology. Elizabeth Cartwright is a medical anthropologist who has focused on chronic disease among Mexican migrants, in addition to authoring several visual anthropology projects. This article is an excellent example of how critical medical anthropology can reveal the large-scale political and economic forces affecting individual health behavior, especially in the context of international development.

Source: M. Nichter and E. Cartwright (1991). "Saving the Children for the Tobacco Industry." *Medical Anthropology Quarterly* 5(3):236–256.

Over the last 15 years, the United States has played a significant role in fostering child survival and safe motherhood programs on a global scale. Under these programs massive immunization and oral rehydration efforts have been initiated and have achieved impressive adoption rates in many Third World settings. At the recent World Summit on Children researchers estimated that immunization programs have saved the lives of nearly two million children and oral rehydration has saved another one million (Potts 1990; United Nations International Children's Emergency Fund [UNICEF] 1990). We juxtapose this image of success with the sobering realization that chronic ill health related to tobacco consumption is dramatically increasing among adults in Third World countries. This escalating health problem affects not only the present but future generations in both direct and indirect ways.

We argue that "primary health care" and "child survival" need to be considered within a context of pathogenic trends in life-style which accompany "defective modernization" (Simonelli 1987). In addition, we question the focus of these international programs on children, often to the neglect of households, which are, after all, the units of health production (Berman, Kendall, and Bhattacharyya 1991).[1]

We maintain that the effects of tobacco consumption need to be viewed not just in relation to the health of smokers but also to the health and welfare of all household members. In this article, therefore, we examine how tobacco consumption negatively influences household health in three ways. First, smoking leads to and exacerbates chronic illness, which in turn reduces adults' ability to provide for their children. Smoking also daily diverts scarce household resources which might be used more productively. And third, children living with smokers are exposed to smoke inhalation and have more respiratory diseases. In short, we adopt an expanded concept of child survival that is both household-centered and diachronic. Unless such a perspective is adopted, the success in child survival that may be realized by immunizing children and keeping them rehydrated will be vitiated by a second child survival crisis arising from the chronic ill health or the death of their parents.

We maintain that the disease focus of child survival programs, like the individual responsibility focus of antismoking campaigns, diverts attention away from the political and economic dimensions of ill health.[2] Saving the children, the symbols of innocence, puts the United States in a favorable light in a turbulent world and competitive international marketplace, but it also deflects attention from other issues. One such issue is that families with young children represent a huge potential market for American products, such as tobacco, which undermine household health. While U.S. support of child survival programs received significant positive press coverage, tobacco more quietly became the eighth largest source of export revenue for the United States in 1985–86 (Wharton Econometrics 1987). Fostering tobacco consumption in the Third World may be healthy for the U.S. trade balance but not for those populations whose health is endangered by increased tobacco accessibility and advertising.

In this article we shall document the environmental and human impact of a cash crop so appealing as an immediate source of tax revenue and profit for First and Third World governments that policy makers surreptitiously support the tobacco industry even while speaking publicly in favor of antismoking initiatives.

TOBACCO PRODUCTION, THE ECOSYSTEM, AND ENVIRONMENTAL HEALTH

Recently, Maurice King (1990) has argued that primary health care policy must be contextualized in relation to the sustainability of the environment. King largely focuses his attention on population growth and the resource capacity of local ecosystems in the context of a rapidly deteriorating environment. Sustainability must, however, be viewed even more broadly. It needs to be viewed in relation to the carrying capacity of adults and how this is impacted by a mix of life-style and environmental factors that contribute to chronic ill health and incapacitating disease.

In this light it has been estimated that throughout the globe more than 100 million people, including workers and their dependents, rely for their livelihood on tobacco-based agriculture, manufacturing, and commerce (Tobacco Journal International 1988). Economically, tobacco has become a very attractive crop in many developing countries for the taxes and export earnings it generates. For example, 47% of Malaysia's taxes (Fischer 1987:20) and 55% of Malawi's export earnings (Madeley 1983:124) derive from tobacco sales. The Brazilian government receives $100 million per month from this source (Mufson 1985).

The Third World presently accounts for 75% of the total tobacco acreage under production (Stanley 1989), with most plots averaging less than one hectare in size (Muller 1983:1304). To help small farmers participate in tobacco production, international tobacco companies, the World Bank, and the Food and Agricultural Organization (FAO) have made available loans, extension advice, seed, and pesticides to farmers (Motley 1987; Muller 1983:1304). Since 1980, the World Bank has loaned more than $1 billion (U.S.) for agricultural projects supporting tobacco production (Stanley 1989:12).

In most cases this assistance has rendered tobacco more profitable than competing food crops. Additionally, the heavy consumption of cigarettes worldwide makes the demand for tobacco, as well as its price, more consistent than many other primary products (Muller 1983). Increasing rates of tobacco consumption in developing countries further adds to the marketability of this crop.

However, there are many long-term environmental and health costs associated with tobacco cultivation. An enormous amount of firewood is necessary to cure tobacco leaves, for example. Given an average of 2–3 hectares of forest needed to flue-cure one ton of tobacco, Madeley (1983:1310) has estimated that 2.5 million hectares of trees are cut worldwide each year for tobacco curing. This is approximately one out of every eight trees harvested on an annual basis. The absence of adequate wood for the curing process has become a major constraint on tobacco production in Southern Brazil, Pakistan, Kenya, and Nigeria (Muller 1983:1305).

In areas vulnerable to erosion, tree-felling reduces the productivity of soil needed for growing food crops. It may also increase the time and energy necessary for gathering firewood for household use. In addition, farmers and field hands may be exposed to hazardous levels of pesticides in countries where there are fewer health regulations for farmworkers pertaining to protective clothing and length of exposure (Madeley 1983:1310). Existing regulations are often also difficult to enforce, though the pesticides are usually highly toxic varieties that are banned in the United States. Since tobacco requires 8 to 16 times the number of applications of pesticides as food crops, the health risks from its cultivation both through direct exposure and contamination of drinking water are considerably greater (Madeley 1983:1310).

PREVALENCE OF TOBACCO USE

Worldwide, one billion smokers consume 5 trillion cigarettes per year or 14 cigarettes per day per smoker (Chandler 1986:39). On an international scale, it is estimated that about 50% of adult males and 10% of adult females are smokers (Stanley 1989:5). In developed countries, however, these proportions are 51% and 21% (Stanley 1989), with notable differences among national groups. For example, in Japan and the USSR rates of smoking among males are 66% and 65% respectively, while among females the rates are 14% and 11%. In the United States, on the other hand, the rates for males are considerably lower but are more nearly equal for the two sexes (32% and 27% for males and females respectively). The U.S. rates are closer to Latin American figures which, however, show almost consistently higher rates for males and lower rates for females than the U.S. rate. . . . In [some] Asian countries . . . , percentages of male smokers are 50% to 100% higher than in the United States, while percentages of women smokers are much lower.

Specific data for smoking prevalence do not exist for much of the Third World. [Data] are incomplete in that they do not differentiate type of smoker by amount of tobacco consumed, smoker's age, or duration of habit. These various lacunae make cross-national comparisons difficult.[3] For example, while rates of smoking appear particularly high among both urban and rural areas in the Pacific, the quantity of tobacco consumed may be much less than in Asia or Africa.

Regional patterns of tobacco consumption exist and are manifested in distinct public/private, gender, and age cohort smoking behavior. In China, for example, smoking prevalence among males increases sharply between the age of 20 and 24, while among females it increases after age 45.[4] . . . While urban smoking rates globally are generally higher than rural rates, this is not always the case. Higher rates of smoking have been reported among Chinese peasants than among urban dwellers. In one survey 81% of male peasants were found to smoke (Tomson and Coulter 1987) as compared to a countrywide average of 61%.

Trends in Tobacco Use

In the United States, smoking prevalence has been declining steadily since 1974 at an annual rate of approximately 2% (cf. Cohen 1981). Between 1974 and 1985, 1.3 million people per year quit smoking. The number of ex-smokers has been offset, however, by the addition of approximately one million new young American smokers a year (Pierce, Fiore, and Novotny 1989). Notably, teenage girls are the chief segment of the North American population who are increasing their consumption of tobacco (Greaves and Buist 1986:8). In 1987, U.S. consumers smoked 1.5% less than in 1986 and 10% less than in 1981.

The American tobacco industry, however, has been little affected by the decline in domestic tobacco consumption. Over this time period, U.S. cigarette exports have increased 56%, and production has increased 5% (Grise 1988). In developing countries, 54% of adult males and 8% of adult females are presently believed to smoke (Stanley 1989). This calculation includes both traditional forms of smoking and the rapidly increasing use of manufactured cigarettes.[5] Tobacco consumption worldwide is estimated to have increased by 73% over the last 20 years, particularly in the Third World. This increase represents not simply *more* people becoming smokers, but a larger *percentage* of the world's population acquiring tobacco habits. Between 1970 and 1985 increases in cigarette consumption exceeded population growth by significant amounts in Africa, Asia, and South America. . . .

Traditional uses of tobacco tend to predispose men more than women to adopt highly refined packaged cigarettes. In much of Africa, Asia, the Pacific, and Latin America, women generally start smoking later than men (Waldron et al. 1988). Social sanctions commonly prohibit young women from smoking commercial cigarettes but are often less restrictive about the consumption of locally grown tobacco products. Sanctions may reflect women's lack of access to Western goods and do not result in a sex difference in overall tobacco consumption (Waldron et al. 1988). Access to goods like tobacco is associated with women's work opportunities and their acquisition of disposable income. Cigarette companies are presently attempting to capitalize on women's enhanced income worldwide by selling cigarettes as a marker of status change (Gupta and Ball 1990).

MARKETING OF CIGARETTES

On a worldwide scale, the tobacco industry spends approximately $12.5 billion annually on advertising. Not surprisingly, cigarettes rank among the top three most advertised products in the world (Jacobson 1983). In 1988 the U.S. tobacco industry spent $2.5 billion for advertising and promotion, or about $6.5 million a day. In contrast, the U.S. Office of Smoking and Health has a total annual budget of $3.8 million (Cohen 1981). This discrepancy between expenditures for tobacco promotion versus expenditures for health through smoking cessation is not limited to the United States. In 1983, $10,000 (U.S.) was spent by the Argentinean government on antitobacco campaigns, while tobacco companies reportedly spent $40 million (U.S.) on marketing and publicity (Baragiola 1986).

Cigarette smoking is escalating rapidly among adolescents in several developed countries (Mintz 1987). It has been well documented in the West that 90% of persons who smoke cigarettes have begun by the age of 19 (Kandel and Logan 1984). This trend reflects a greater availability of cigarettes to teens, and it is associated with an increased number of misconceptions regarding the risk of addiction and individual vulnerability to smoking-related diseases (Leventhal, Glynn, and Fleming 1987:3376). Within the context of the family, researchers have found that adolescents whose parents and older siblings smoke are more likely to become smokers themselves (Chassin et al. 1984:239).

Over three-quarters of the world's young people aged 15–24 live in Third World countries. This population constitutes an immense marketing opportunity, as well as an extremely vulnerable audience for advertising campaigns. Cigarette advertising in developing countries has been largely directed toward men, but women and adolescents are being increasingly targeted as well (Taha and Ball 1985). Even when not specifically targeted, adolescents interpret cigarette advertisements in ways very similar to adults (Aitken, Leathar, and O'Hagan 1985:785). Research suggests, for example, that adolescents find it difficult to comprehend the long-term risks of smoking (Aitken et al. 1987; Amos, Hillhouse, and Robertson 1989; Charlton 1990; Roberts 1987; Stebbins 1987). Teens are also more susceptible to the images of romance, success, sophistication, popularity, and adventure which advertising suggests they could achieve through the consumption of cigarettes (McCarthy and Gritz 1987; Yankelovich et al. 1977). As two critics of this form of advertising in Kenya observe, however:

> The cruel irony is that the majority of Kenyans (like many of the target groups for Western advertisements) will never have the successful careers, the high consumption life styles or the sense of satisfaction depicted in the advertisements. Yet when they buy the attractively packaged cigarettes they are buying part of the myth. Along with their deadly products, the tobacco industry pedals the myth of the Western ideal of development. (Currie and Ray 1984:1137; see also Stebbins 1987:529)

Rather than being regarded simply as objects to consume, cigarettes become indices of social membership for adolescents who are searching for their identities or who wish to escape the immediate reality into which they have been born (Baudrillard 1981). The growing number of adolescent smokers at home and abroad suggests that the impact of these forms of tobacco promotion may be formidable.

HOUSEHOLD EXPENDITURES ON TOBACCO

How much of a drain on household income is tobacco consumption among those living at the margin? Little household-based data exist on expenditure for tobacco in relation to household income. One study in São Paolo, Brazil, found that expenditure for cigarettes in a low-income population ranged from 3.1 to 14.6% ($\bar{x}$ = 9.8%) of family income (Silveira et al. 1982). This was higher than expenditures for either transportation (5.8%) or milk (8.3%) among the same families. Brazil is the fifth largest cigarette market in the world, and cigarettes are the most heavily advertised product. Over 40% of Brazil's 120 million people are under the age of 15, 70% of its people live in urban areas, and television reaches three-quarters of all households. Sixty percent of males and 26% of females in urban areas of Brazil smoked in 1978 (Jacobson 1983:37).

A 1979 study by Nichter (1991) in South India among subsistence level agricultural households of the Shudra and Harijan castes found that tobacco was consumed in one form or another (smoking, snuff, in conjunction with betel nut) in virtually every household. Sixty-five percent of a sample of males over age 25 (*N* = 100) were smokers of "beedies" or cigarettes. Respondents smoked for relaxation, as a means of social exchange, to reduce hunger, control toothache, enhance digestion, and assist with routine defecation.

Among two convenience samples of households (*N* = 50) of male smokers (where female tobacco consumption habits were assumed to vary randomly), weekly modal expenditure on all forms of tobacco was 5 rupees (median expenditure = Rs. 4.5). In 1979, the daily wage for agricultural labor was Rs. 5–6 (U.S. $.63–.75) in this region. Among a sample of smokers (*N* = 25) having a mean estimated yearly household income of Rs. 2500 (U.S. $312), tobacco purchases were estimated to account for 10% of total household income. Among a second sample (*N* = 25) having a mean estimated annual household income of Rs. 3,600 (U.S. $450), tobacco accounted for 7% of annual income. These annual tobacco expenditures equaled annual household health care expenses in both samples (Nichter 1991).

In a study conducted in 1988–89 in Alexandria, Egypt, Marcia Inhorn (personal communication) found that 151 of 190 (79%) lower-class male heads of household had smoked cigarettes. Of the 145 regular cigarette smokers, 102 (70%) smoked between one and three packs per day at a daily cost of £1–3 (U.S. $.40–1.20) for the lowest priced, Egyptian-manufactured brand. Cigarette expenditures for most men were between £30–90 per month. Although monthly combined household incomes ranged from £40–400 per month, the majority (65%) ranged from £50–200. On a regular basis, expenditures for cigarettes thus accounted for between one-third and one-half of all disposable income in the majority of households. In nuclear family households supported by a cigarette-smoking husband, the husband's need for "pocket money" to buy cigarettes was often regarded by wives as the major reason for their inability to provide proper nourishment for their children. Although a small number of husbands had intentionally "weaned" themselves from cigarettes to less expensive water-pipe tobacco, the majority of Egyptian men in this study were addicted to cigarettes, having begun smoking in most cases during their late adolescent years.

MORBIDITY/MORTALITY

In 1989 the World Health Organization estimated that 2.5 million people die each year of tobacco-related deaths, approximately one death every 13 seconds (Ile and Kroll 1990). One-and-a-half to two million of these deaths occurred in developed countries, with the United States accounting for approximately 400,000 deaths per year (Peto 1990).[6] The two biggest tobacco producers outside the United States, China and India, also have high tobacco-induced mortality rates which are predicted to rise even higher. Peto has estimated that fewer than 100,000 Chinese people now die of tobacco-related diseases a year, but by the year 2025 two million Chinese (mostly male) will die a year. In India as in China, some 60–80% of adult males smoke. Gupta (1989) has conservatively estimated that in this decade 630,000 to one million adults will die per year from tobacco induced diseases.

Beyond the fatalities, the estimated lost productivity associated with chronic diseases related to smoking is staggering. The Office of Technology Assessment of the U.S. Congress has calculated that in 1985 the direct costs of treating smoking-related diseases in the United States was $22 billion. The indirect costs from lost income because of illness and premature deaths attributable to tobacco was $43 billion (Stanley 1989:27). These figures are rough estimates of the price one country is paying for tobacco use. It is impossible to calculate comparable costs among impoverished populations in developing countries.

Overshadowing these figures on fatalities and lost productivity among tobacco users are considerations of "significant others" indirectly affected by the inability of an adult to support them, for those directly affected by tobacco-related ill health are often responsible for the economic well-being of children, pregnant or lactating mothers, and older relatives. Expensive treatment regimens and disabilities resulting in lost wages can severely deplete family resources.

Fatal and disabling diseases either induced or exacerbated by tobacco that have been reported in the medical literature include: lung cancer, chronic obstructive lung disease, heart disease, myocardial infarctions, peripheral vascular disease, and hypertension. These diseases develop in a manner which is dose-dependent and increases with time of exposure (Peto 1986)—i.e., the earlier a person starts smoking and the higher the tar content of the tobacco smoked, the greater the risk of developing pathological problems (Tominaga 1986:131).

Manufactured cigarettes bearing international brand names which are sold in the Third World often have much higher tar and nicotine levels than those sold in the West. . . . The median tar level in the United States is 20 mg/cigarette, while in Indonesia it is 36 mg/cigarette (Stanley 1989:4). The use of filter-tips in Western countries has become increasingly popular, as have low-tar cigarettes. Cigarettes produced in the Third World, however, are often unfiltered, as are traditional tobacco products such as beedies. Yach (1986:286) notes a disturbing trend in which people from the lowest social classes in both Nigeria and South Africa smoke cigarettes with the highest tar and nicotine contents. Access to "safer" cigarettes varies between richer and poorer nations, as well as between social classes within individual countries.

Because there is a 20–25 year time lag before health problems related to smoking manifest themselves, current disease rates reflect the consequences of habits acquired decades ago. The Council on Scientific Affairs of the American Medical Association cites increased usage of cigarettes as the major contributing cause of increasing rates of lung cancer in the Third World (Council on Scientific Affairs 1990:3318). Further epidemiological profiles of Third World adults are sure to reflect changing trends in both active and passive smoking. An increasing number of children smoke and/or are exposed to adults who smoke (Nath 1986:33). It is estimated that approximately 200 million children now under 20 years of age will die from tobacco use (Peto and Lopez 1990:1).

Passive smoke inhalation constitutes a significant health risk by increasing susceptibility to acute respiratory tract infections. Acute lower respiratory tract infections are the second major cause of death among children in the Third World, accounting for some three to four million infant and child deaths per year, or approximately one-third of the total global infant child mortality (Berman and McIntosh 1985; Gadomski 1990; World Health Organization 1988). The cumulative incidence of acute respiratory tract infections increases significantly with the presence of a smoker in the household (Chen et al. 1988).[7] This holds true for children of parents who do and do not have histories of asthma or wheezing. . . .

In sum, smoking directly affects the health of children either when they themselves smoke or when they are the passive recipients of their parents' smoke. Indirectly, their health is also affected by the health of their caretakers: with increased absenteeism, decreased productivity, and more money spent on illness treatments, families with members who have tobacco-related illnesses are likely to have fewer resources to spend on nutritious food and health care.

UNITED STATES POLICY AND COMPLICITY

This year the first author interviewed a U.S. marketing executive in East Africa who said,

> It is our moral duty to help educate those in the Third World and to help Third World nations become self-sufficient so they can stand on their own two feet and be full partners in international trade. Literacy is good for business and good for democracy. There are some who say that taking advantage of an illiterate population through image advertising is immoral. They may have a point. The innocence of an illiterate population is easily exploited. When that population can read, however, it's a question of free choice. Once literate, you have to respect a man's choice. They are on their own.

Notwithstanding antismoking legislation at home, the U.S. government has exerted its influence in developing the world tobacco market in several ways. In the 20 years following World War II, one billion dollars in Food for Peace (PL480) funds were spent supplying Third World countries with tobacco as a means of reducing the U.S. surplus and creating a market for cigarettes in the Third World (Motley 1987; Stebbins 1988; Taylor 1984). As Stebbins notes,

> Despite its name, the Food for Peace program's main function was not to combat hunger and malnutrition, but to develop new markets for American agricultural products, to dispose of surplus commodities and to further U.S. foreign policy. (1988:9)

More recently, U.S. trade policy has protected the American tobacco industry. Countries such as Japan, South Korea, and Thailand (to name but the most recent examples) have been pressured to open their doors to American cigarette sales and advertising or suffer trade sanctions (American Public Health Association 1988; Connolly 1988a, 1988b; Connolly and Walker 1987; U.S. Department of Agriculture 1988). When South Korea resisted American tobacco industry advertising, it was met with a retaliatory list of possible trade sanctions which would go into effect should restrictions continue (John 1988:28). Section 301 of the revised 1974 United States Trade

Act protects American export industry from "discriminatory" trade restrictions, including foreign monopolies in tobacco sales, importations, and advertising. As Schmeisser has noted, the tobacco industry has used the 1974 Trade Act to enlist the services of the executive branch of the U.S. government to "arm twist offending foreign powers into a more magnanimous trade posture" (Schmeisser 1988:18). The Food and Agricultural Organization (FAO) and the World Bank have meanwhile promoted tobacco production through multimillion dollar loans to several Third World countries, including India and Pakistan.

U.S. foreign policy on health matters is inconsistent. Small children are worth saving, apparently because they are innocent, while their older brothers and sisters and their parents are fair game for the tobacco industry. The marketing executive quoted above introduced a curious variation on the theme of innocence by equating it with illiteracy. While it may be immoral to influence those unable to read through advertising, literacy renders people responsible for their actions as free agents. This argument fosters victim-blaming: the poor of the Third World who "choose" to smoke processed cigarettes, often to affiliate with a highly advertised fantasy good life (commodity fetishism), are, by this reasoning, held accountable for their own poor judgment (or Western taste?).

Several health activists interviewed by the first author in India and the Philippines expressed the opinion that antismoking campaigns need to play a greater role in primary health care programs. Immunization emerged as a metaphor which was extended to antismoking campaigns. Children need to be immunized against the false consciousness of cigarette image advertisements, just as they need to be immunized against polio and measles.[8] Emotional appeals targeted at parents who smoke were also suggested as a means of making them more aware that they were risking their ability to care for their children.

While these tactics merit consideration, polluted environments, poor occupational health conditions, and other more immediate health risks serve to minimize the impact of such messages.[9] "Immunization" programs, in the form of antismoking messages, may also divert attention from issues essential to successful antismoking programs. A national policy which fosters the accessibility of cigarettes may be masked by token policy gestures such as legislation that bans cigarette advertisements on the radio while allowing billboard advertisements in bus terminals. Such actions give the appearance of an antismoking position which is in fact not sustained for reasons related to profit and tax revenues.

Incorporating smoking education within existing primary health care programs is insufficient (Milio 1985:610). What is needed is to reduce public access to cigarettes. Such a program, however, requires political will of a different order from what is necessary to mount a mass media antismoking campaign (Stebbins 1990:233). The political will must be strong enough to withstand significant losses from tax revenues and survive a public outcry if tobacco taxes are raised.

SUMMARY AND CONCLUSIONS: LESSONS FOR INTERNATIONAL HEALTH AND MEDICAL ANTHROPOLOGY

The foregoing data suggest that it will be difficult for the many Third World countries that derive substantial revenue from internal cigarette sales (external sales are another matter) to escape the paradoxes contained in the following scenario.

1. At a time when incomes are falling in much of the Third World, increased funds are needed to maintain social welfare programs and child survival efforts.[10]

2. Significant tax revenue is generated by cigarette taxation in an environment in which tobacco consumption is increasing. (For example, 12% of Brazil's revenue comes from tobacco sales, "enough to pay all expenses for medical care in the country including drugs and hospitalization, or 40% of all social benefits of the country" [Lokshin and Barros 1983:1314].)

3. Existing consumer demand increases as a result of advertising. Advertising targets new markets and populations who are not already brand loyal. Young people and women increasingly are the targets of carefully planned campaigns.

4. The age of initiation into smoking decreases, particularly in urban areas. A younger age of initiation translates into a younger age when the negative health effects of smoking are realized. These effects are increasingly apparent in the 35–45 age range.

5. A significant number of adults are affected by chronic disease during the time when their carrying capacity for the young and the old (especially women) is high. This begins to have a noticeable impact on the household production of health.

6. Short-term assets from cigarette tax revenues are offset by the costs of long-term health care and loss of productivity. However, politicians, whose tenures in office are relatively short, look to tobacco as an immediate source of revenues which enable them to finance

programs of high visibility in order to marshal public support. Child survival programs provide highly visible proof of government action which is also internationally applauded.

7. Faced with massive chronic health problems linked to smoking, in the context of poor environmental and occupational health conditions, child survival programs and adult health care programs will compete for very limited funds.

...

A greater awareness of U.S. complicity in propagating tobacco consumption in the Third World and the toll it is likely to take challenges our national values, our national stake in appearing to be morally right and committed to the development of "health for all." Research revealing the tobacco industry's role in the household production of ill health shifts attention from our collective public efforts to "save the children" to our support of cigarette sales in Third World countries as a means of establishing a more equitable balance of trade. Such research recontextualizes the problem as one involving serious ethical questions concerning free trade and market justice.

The concept of "market justice" ultimately lays responsibility for poor health in the hands of the consumer/citizen in the name of free trade as a democratic principle tied to individual rights. Factors that predispose and condition humans to engage in "voluntary behavior" associated with health risk need to be examined critically. So does a behavioral model of public health rooted in the "market justice/individual responsibility" paradigm of health education (McLeroy, Gottlieb, and Burdine 1987). Several questions need to be raised. Do people freely choose their own risks in an environment saturated by market images (Foege 1990)? How has a desire to engage in risky behavior been fostered? Have particular segments of a population been targeted for promotion of products associated with risky behavior? Who profits from the promotion of risk-taking behavior? To what extent have people become immune to antismoking messages? What images have been employed to reduce the impact of health education messages?

Beauchamp (1976, 1985), among others (e.g., Neubauer and Pratt 1981), has argued for the formulation of a new critical paradigm of public health that is sensitive to the production and representation of so-called voluntary risks. This paradigm challenges attempts to limit public attention to the behavior of the smoker or drinker (Beauchamp 1976:12). Central to this emergent paradigm is the critical examination of "market justice" as a means of opening dialogue about a counter ethic. Since a major American tobacco company is presently affiliating itself with the Bill of Rights in its latest marketing campaign, research exposing the household and environmental costs of a "free" international tobacco trade are timely.[11]

The case of tobacco illustrates why medical anthropologists interested in public health need to pay as much attention to the social relations of consumption and the semiotics of consumables as they do to modes of production and world systems penetration of local markets.[12] Each contributes in profound and multiple ways to international health. International health must be situated within what Baudrillard (1981:200) has termed our true environment, "the universe of communication" as well as within the market, its economic equivalent. Within this environment the illusion of freedom is fostered through objects of immediate gratification, such as cigarettes, alcohol (Singer 1986), and sugar (Mintz 1985), which establish group membership, affiliate one with the "good life," take the edge off frustrated aspirations, blur the contradictions of everyday life, and make the intolerable tolerable for the moment. At issue is the hidden cost in human suffering and ecological destruction paid for expressions of personal freedom shaped by market interest. Taking stock of this issue constitutes an agenda for international health as important as vaccine development. Pathogens come in all shapes and sizes.

NOTES

1. While progress in international health has unquestionably been made when measured in terms of reduction in mortality among infants and young children, international progress may be criticized for approaching health problems among the poor with acute-care strategies, while in actuality these problems more closely resemble chronic illnesses (Chen 1986).
2. Social scientists (Crawford 1979; Neubauer and Pratt 1981; Winkler 1987), as well as people in public health (Allegrante and Green 1981; Bush 1986; Godin and Shephard 1984), have identified the attention to the physical body as a means of diverting attention from the body politic. It has been suggested, for example, that such a tactic underlies support for the fitness movement in the United States, where responsibility for ill health is placed upon the individual rather than on those complicit in manipulating national tastes for fast driving, irresponsible sex, drinking, smoking, etc., through the media. Individuals are also held responsible for their own health in situations where illnesses result from environmental pollution and hazardous working conditions (Alexander 1988).
3. Also missing are data on the meaning of smoking in different cultures. Prevalence data must be viewed critically and in relation to the meaning of tobacco consumption and exchange (Black 1984; Marshall 1981).

4. Other countries have similar age-related tobacco consumption trends as China. For example, in the Philippines 30% of the population are smokers. Eighty percent of Philippine smokers are males aged 26–35 who consume at least half a pack a day. The majority of these smokers come from the lower socioeconomic classes (Aung-Thwin 1987).
5. The *Multinational Monitor* (Motley 1987) has published a much larger table of "smokers worldwide," summarizing data available from the World Health Organization and numerous other sources. In most cases, figures cited exceed those noted from Stanley (1989). The validity of these figures varies depending on the survey methods employed and the sample size. The figures are meant to provide some estimate of smoking prevalence.
6. In contrast to these statistics, the U.S. tobacco industry proclaimed in 1980 that "many eminent scientists hold the view that no case against smoking has been proved" (Ashton and Stepney 1983).
7. Chapman et al. (1990) argue that the risks associated with passive smoking particularly threaten the cigarette industry, because passive smoking shifts attention from the arena of individual and personal freedom to social responsibility and larger units of analysis.
8. An immunization model has been applied in U.S. smoking prevention programs. See, for example, Evans, Rozelle, and Maxwell (1981); Hurd et al. (1980); McAlister, Perry, and Maccoby (1979); and Perry, Maccoby, and McAlister (1980); as well as Duryea, Ransom, and English (1990) for a critical commentary.
9. While significant, tobacco is far from being the only factor increasing respiratory diseases. Breathing the air in Mexico City is equivalent to smoking two packs of cigarettes every day (Wayburn 1991). Poorly regulated occupational settings, as well as the larger polluted living environment, have been clearly implicated in contributing to the increased prevalence of various cancers and pulmonary disorders. Antismoking campaigns need to be situated within this wider context to weigh all causative factors appropriately. It would be a shame to see tobacco habits scapegoated at the expense of ignoring such issues as improper disposal and regulation of industrially produced toxins. On the use of smoking as a "whipping boy," see Alexander (1988), Brown et al. (1990), and Sterling (1978).
10. At a time when increases in foreign aid for child survival are unlikely and the average incomes of many Third World nations throughout much of Africa and Latin America are reported as falling 10 to 25 percent (Chernomas 1990), governments are being encouraged to explore new means of community financing (Bossert 1990; Chen 1986).
11. Those engaged in developing a critical public health paradigm may gain much from anthropological studies looking beyond the physical body to the social body, body politic, and consumer body (O'Neill 1985; Scheper-Hughes and Lock 1987). King (1990) draws attention to the deep conviction within Western civilization that we are able to control the natural world, thus enabling all communities to develop indefinitely. This notion of progress defines modernist thinking and has been critiqued by Bateson in his discussion of *creatura* (1972) and by Toulman (1982) in his definition of a new cosmology that draws upon ecological wisdom.
12. Of course it may be argued that the mode of consumption is simply a mode of production of self-identity.

REFERENCES

Aitken, P. P., D. S. Leathar, and F. J. O'Hagan. 1985. Children's Perception of Advertisements for Cigarettes. Social Science and Medicine 21(7):785–797.

Aitken, P. P., et al. 1987. Children's Awareness of Cigarette Advertisements and Brand Imagery. British Journal of Addiction 82:615–622.

Alexander, J. 1988. Ideological Construction of Risk: An Analysis of Corporate Health Promotion Programs in the 1980s. Social Science and Medicine 26(5): 559–567.

Allegrante, J., and L. Green. 1981. When Health Policy "Becomes Victim Blaming." New England Journal of Medicine 305:1528–1529.

American Public Health Association. 1988. Limiting the Exploration of Tobacco Products. American Journal of Public Health 78(2):195–196.

Amos, A., A. Hillhouse, and G. Robertson. 1989. Tobacco Advertising and Children—The Impact of the Voluntary Agreement. Health Education Research 4:51–57.

Ashton, H., and R. Stepney. 1983. Smoking: Psychology and Pharmacology. Cambridge, England: Cambridge University Press.

Aung-Thwin, M. 1987. Insecurity Hindering Philippine Tobacco Industry. Tobacco Journal International 6:399–400.

Baragiola, A. M. 1986. Tabaquismo: Aspectos sanitorias, educativos y sociales. Revista Argentina de Analysis, Modificación y Terapía del Compartamiento 2(4):49–54.

Barthes, Roland. 1973. Mythologies. London: Paladin Press.

Bateson, Gregory. 1972. Steps to an Ecology of Mind. New York: Ballantine Books.

Baudrillard, Jean. 1981. For a Critique of the Political Economy of the Sign. St. Louis, MO: Telos Press.

Beauchamp, Dan E. 1976. Public Health as Social Justice. Inquiry 18(1):3–14.

———. 1985. Community: The Neglected Tradition of Public Health. Hastings Center Report, December:28–36.

Becker, Marshall. 1986. The Tyranny of Health Promotion. Public Health Reviews 14:15–25.

Berman, Peter, Carl Kendall, and Karabi Bhattacharyya. 1991. The Household Production of Health: Putting the People at the Center of Health Improvement. Social Science and Medicine. (In press.)

Berman, S., and K. McIntosh. 1985. Acute Respiratory Infections. Reviews of Infectious Diseases 7(5):29–46.

Black, P. 1984. The Anthropology of Tobacco Use: Tobain Data and Theoretical Issues. Journal of Anthropological Research 40(4): 475–503.

Bossert, T. 1990. Can They Get Along without Us? Sustainability of Donor Supported Health Projects in Central America and Africa. Social Science and Medicine 39(9): 1015–1023.

Brown, L. R., et al. 1990. State of the World, 1990: Worldwatch Institute Report on Progress toward a Sustainable Society. New York: W. W. Norton.

Bush, Roger. 1986. Health Promotion—An Ethical Perspective. The Western Journal of Medicine 144(l):102–103.

Chandler, William. 1986. Banishing Tobacco. Worldwatch Paper 68. Washington, DC: Worldwatch Institute.

Chapman, Simon, et. al. 1990. Why the Tobacco Industry Fears the Passive Smoking Issue. International Journal of Health Sciences 20(3):417–427.

Charlton, A. 1990. Children's Advertisement Awareness Related to Their Views on Smoking. Health Education Journal 45:75–78.

Chassin, Laurie, et. al. 1984. Predicting the Onset of Cigarette Smoking in Adolescents: A Longitudinal Study. Journal of Applied Social Psychology 14(3):224–243.

Chen, Lincoln. 1986. Primary Health Care in Developing Countries: Overcoming Operational, Technical and Social Barriers. Lancet 2(2):1260–1265.

Chen, Y., et. al. 1988. Chang-Ning Epidemiological Study of Children's Health: Passive Smoking and Children's Respiratory Diseases. International Journal of Epidemiology 17(2):348–355.

Chernomas, Robert. 1990. The Debt Depression of the Less Developed World and Public Health. International Journal of Health Services 20(4):537–543.

Cohen, Nicholas. 1981. Smoking, Health and Survival: Prospects in Bangladesh. Lancet 1(2):1090–1093.

Connolly, Gregory. 1988a. The American Liberation of the Japanese Cigarette Market. World Smoking and Health 13:20–25.

———. 1988b. Tobacco and United States Trade Sanctions. In Smoking and Health 1987: Proceedings of the 6th World Conference on Smoking and Health. M. Aoki, S. Hisomichi, and S. Tominaga, eds. Pp. 351–354. New York: Elsevier Science.

Connolly, Gregory, and Bailus Walker, Jr. 1987. Restrictions on Importation of Tobacco by Japan, Taiwan and South Korea. New England Journal of Medicine 316(22):1416–1417.

Council on Scientific Affairs. 1990. The Worldwide Smoking Epidemic. Journal of the American Medical Association 263(24):3312–3318.

Crawford, Robert. 1979. Individual Responsibility and Health Politics in the 1970's. In Health Care in America. S. Reverby and G. Rosner, eds. Pp. 249–268. Philadelphia: Temple University Press.

Currie, Kate, and Larry Ray. 1984. Going Up in Smoke: The Case of British American Tobacco in Kenya. Social Science and Medicine 19(11):1131–1139.

Duryea, E. J., M. V. Ransom, and G. English. 1990. Psychological Immunization: Theory, Research, and Current Health Behavior Applications. Health Education Quarterly 17(2):169–178.

Evans, R. I., R. M. Rozelle, and S. Maxwell. 1981. Social Modeling Films to Deter Smoking in Adolescents: Results of a Three-year Field Investigation. Journal of Applied Psychology 66:399–414.

Fischer, P. M. 1987. Tobacco in the Third World. Journal of the Islamic Medical Association 19:19–21.

Foege, William H. 1990. The Growing Brown Plague. Journal of the American Medical Association 264(12):1580.

Gadomiski, Anne, ed. 1990. ALRI and Child Survival in Developing Countries. Workshop Report. Baltimore, MD: Johns Hopkins Institute for International Programs.

Gallup Organization, Inc. 1988. The Incidence of Smoking in Central and Latin America. Conducted for the American Cancer Society. Princeton, NJ: Gallup Organization.

Godin, Gaston, and Roy Shephard. 1984. Physical Fitness—Individual or Societal Responsibility? Canadian Journal of Public Health 95:200–202.

Greaves, L., and M. Buist. 1986. The Tobacco Industry Weeding Women Out. Broadside 7(7):3–4.

Grise, U. N. 1988. Tobacco Situation and Outlook Optimistic for Next Several Years. Tobacco International 190(6):7–8.

Gupta, Prakash. 1989. An Assessment of Excess Mortality Caused by Tobacco Usage in India. In Tobacco and Health: The Indian Scene. L. D. Sanghvi and P. Notari, eds. Pp. 57–62. UICC Workshop. Bombay, India: Tata Memorial Centre.

Gupta, Prakash, and Keith Ball. 1990. India: Tobacco Tragedy. Lancet 334:594–595.

Hurd, P. D., et al. 1980. Prevention of Cigarette Smoking in Seventh Grade Students. Journal of Behavioral Medicine 3:15–28.

Ile, Michael L., and Laura A. Kroll. 1990. Tobacco Advertising and the First Amendment. Journal of the American Medical Association 264(12):1593–1594.

Jacobson, Bobbie. 1983. Smoking and Health: A New Generation of Campaigners. British Medical Journal 287:483–484.

John, G. A. 1988. Section 301 Charges by CEA and the Korean Monopoly Response. Tobacco International 190:6, 28.

Kandel, D. B., and J. A. Logan. 1984. Patterns of Drug Use from Adolescence to Young Adulthood: Periods of Risk for Initiation, Continued Use and Discontinuation. American Journal of Public Health 74:660–666.

King, Maurice. 1990. Health Is a Sustainable State. Lancet 336:664–667.

Leeder, S. R., et al. 1976. Influence of Personal and Family Factors on Ventilatory Function of Children. British Journal of Preventive Social Medicine 30:219–224.

Leventhal, Howard, Kathleen Glynn, and Raymond Fleming. 1987. Is the Smoking Decision an "Informed Choice"?: Effect of Smoking Risk Factors on Smoking Beliefs. Journal of the American Medical Association 257(24):3373–3376.

Lokshin, Fernando, and Fernando Barros. 1983. Smoking or Health: The Brazilian Option. New York State Journal of Medicine 83(13):1314–1316.

Madeley, John. 1983. The Environmental Impact of Tobacco Production in Developing Countries. New York State Journal of Medicine 83(13):1310–1311.

Marshall, Mack. 1981. Tobacco Use and Abuse in Micronesia: A Preliminary Discussion. Journal of Studies on Alcohol 49:885–893.

McAlister, A., C. Perry, and N. Maccoby. 1979. Adolescent Smoking: Onset and Prevention. Pediatrics 63:659–662.

McCarthy, W. J., and E. R. Gritz. 1987. Madison Avenue as the Pied Piper: Cigarette Advertising and Teenage Smoking. Paper presented at the annual meeting of the American Psychological Association, New York City, August 13.

McLeroy, K. R., N. Gottlieb, and J. Burdine. 1987. The Business of Health Promotion: Ethical Issues and Professional Responsibilities. Health Education Quarterly 14(1):91–109.

Milio, Nancy. 1985. Health Policy and the Emerging Tobacco Reality. Social Science and Medicine 21(6):603–614.

Mintz, Morton. 1987. The Smoke Screen: Tobacco and the Press, an Unhealthy Alliance. Multinational Monitor 8(7,8):15–17.

Mintz, Sidney. 1985. Sweetness and Power: The Place of Sugar in Modern History. New York: Penguin.

Mosley, William Henry. 1984. Child Survival: Research and Policy. Population and Development Review 10:3–23.

Motley, Susan. 1987. Burning the South: U.S. Tobacco Companies in the Third World. Multinational Monitor, July/August, 8(7/8):7–10.

Mulfson, S. 1985. Cigarette Companies Develop Third World as a Growth Market. Wall Street Journal. 5 July:A1, A16.

Muller, Mike. 1983. Preventing Tomorrow's Epidemic. The Control of Smoking and Tobacco Production in Developing Countries. New York State Journal of Medicine 83(13):1304–1309.

Nath, Uma Ram. 1986. Smoking: Third World Alert. Oxford: Oxford University Press.

Neubauer, Dean, and Richard Pratt. 1981. The Second Public Health Revolution: A Critical Appraisal. Journal of Health Politics, Policy and Law 6(2):205–228.

Nichter, Mark. 1991. Anthropology's Contribution to Health Service Research in the Third World. (Unpublished manuscript in the files of the first author.)

O'Neill, John. 1985. Five Bodies. The Human Shape of Modern Society. Ithaca, NY: Cornell University Press.

Peach, H. 1986. Smoking and Respiratory Disease Excluding Lung Cancer. In Tobacco: A Major International Health Hazard. D. G. Zaridze and R. Peto, eds. Pp. 61–72. Lyon, France: International Agency for Research on Cancer.

Perry, C., N. Maccoby, and A. McAlister. 1980. Adolescent Smoking Prevention: A Third Year Follow-up. World Smoking and Health 1:40–45.

Peto, Richard. 1986. Influence of Dose and Duration of Smoking on Lung Cancer Rates. In Tobacco: A Major International Health Hazard. D. G. Zaridze and R. Peto, eds. Pp. 23–33. Lyon, France: International Agency for Research on Cancer.

———. 1990. Future Worldwide Health Effects of Current Smoking Patterns. Paper presented at WHO Workshop, Perth, Australia, April 3.

Peto, Richard, and A. D. Lopez. 1990. Proceedings. Seventh World Conference on Tobacco and Health. Perth, Australia, April 3.

Pierce, J. P., M. C. Fiore, and T. E. Novotny. 1989. Trends in Cigarette Smoking in the United States. Projections to the Year 2000. Journal of the American Medical Association 261(l):61–65.

Potts, Malcolm. 1990. Mere Survival or a World Worth Living In? The Lancet 36:866–868.

Rothwell, K., and R. Maseroni. 1988. Tendancies et effets du tabagisme dans le monde. World Health Statistics Quarterly 41:228–241.

Roberts, J. L. 1987. The Name of the Game—Selling Cigarettes on BBC TV. London: Health Education Authority.

Scheper-Hughes, Nancy, and Margaret Lock. 1987. The Mindful Body: A Prolegomenon to Future Work in Medical Anthropology. Medical Anthropology Quarterly (n.s.) 1:6 41.

Schmeisser, Peter. 1988. Pushing Cigarettes Overseas. New York Times Magazine July 10:16–22, 62.

Silveira, Lima, et. al. 1982. Implicaçcoés Medicas e Socioeconômicas do Tabagismo em Familias de Baixa Renda em Sao Paulo. Jornal Pediatrico (Rio) 52:325–328.

Simonelli, Jeanne. 1987. Defective Modernization and Health in Mexico. Social Science and Medicine 24(1):23–36.

Singer, Merrill. 1986. Toward a Political-Economy of Alcoholism: The Missing Link in the Anthropology of Drinking. Social Science and Medicine 23(2):113–130.

Stanley, Kenneth. 1989. Control of Tobacco Production and Use. (Unpublished manuscript in the files of the authors.)

Stebbins, Kenyon R. 1987. Tobacco or Health in the Third World: A Political Economy Perspective with Emphasis on Mexico. International Journal of Health Services 17(3):521–536.

———. 1988. Tobacco, Politics, Economics and Health: Implications for Third World Populations. Paper presented at the annual meeting of the American Anthropological Association, Phoenix.

———. 1990. Transnational Tobacco Companies and Health in Underdeveloped Countries: Recommendations for Avoiding an Epidemic. Social Science and Medicine 30(2):227–235.

Sterling, Theodore. 1978. Does Smoking Kill Workers or Working Kill Smokers, or the Mutual Relationship between Smoking, Occupation and Respiratory Disease. International Journal of Health Services 8(3):437–452.

Taha, Ahmed, and Keith Ball. 1985. Tobacco and the Third World: The Growing Threat. East African Medical Journal 62:735–741.

Taylor, Peter. 1984. The Smoke Ring: Tobacco, Money and Multinational Polities. New York: Pantheon Books.

Tobacco Journal International. 1988. Counting the Multitudes of the World's Tobacco People. Tobacco Journal International 3:166, 170.

Tominaga, S. 1986. Spread of Smoking to the Developing Countries. In Tobacco: A Major International Health Hazard. D. G. Zaridze and R. Peto, eds. Pp. 125–133. Lyon, France: International Agency for Research on Cancer.

Tomson, D., and A. Coulter. 1987. The Bamboo Smoke Screen: Tobacco Smoking in China. Health Promotion 2(2):93–108.

Toulman, Steven. 1982. The Return to Cosmology. Berkeley: University of California Press.

Tuomkilehto, Jaakko, et. al. 1986. Smoking Rates in Pacific Islands. Bulletin of the World Health Organization 64(3):447–456.

United Nations International Children's Emergency Fund (UNICEF). 1990. The State of the World's Children. New Delhi: UNICEF.

United States Department of Agriculture. 1988. World Tobacco Situation. Foreign Agricultural Service Report. FT 8–88.

Waldron, Ingrid, et al. 1988. Gender Differences in Tobacco Use in Asian, African and Latin American Societies. Social Science and Medicine 27:1269–1275.

Wayburn, E. 1991. Human Health and Environmental Health. Western Journal of Medicine 154:341–343.

Wharton Econometrics. 1987. The Importance of Tobacco to the United States Foreign Trade. Washington, DC: United States Department of Health and Human Services.

Winkler, Daniel. 1987. WHO Should be Blamed for Being Sick? Health Education Quarterly 14(1):11–25.

World Health Organization. 1988. Can Community Health Workers Deal with Pneumonia? World Health Forum 9:221–224.

Yach, Derek. 1986. The Impact of Smoking in Developing Countries with Special Reference to Africa. International Journal of Health Services 16(2):279–292.

Yankelovich, S., et al. 1977. A Study of Cigarette Smoking among Teenage Girls and Young Women: Summary of the Findings. Washington, DC: U.S. Government Printing Office.

Yu, Jing Jie, et al. 1990. A Comparison of Smoking Patterns in the People's Republic of China with the United States: An Impending Health Catastrophe in the Middle Kingdom. Journal of the American Medical Association 264(12):1575–1579.

47

Ethnomedicine and Oral Rehydration Therapy: A Case Study of Ethnomedical Investigation and Program Planning

Carl Kendall
Dennis Foote
Reynaldo Martorell

As we have seen, the interest of medical anthropologists in the ethnomedical systems of other societies can have practical value. This selection demonstrates that preexisting ethnomedical beliefs make a difference in regard to the acceptance of a health promotion message. It is an example of the fallacy of empty vessels that may plague international health programs. In the case study presented here, the health planners did not take into account the fact that the Hondurans might have their own folk models for the causes of diarrhea that could hamper the acceptability of oral rehydration therapy. This case study is particularly interesting not only because of the role of traditional ethnomedical beliefs but also because of the effect of the anthropologists' study on the health program.

Dehydration due to diarrhea has been a major cause of childhood mortality in the developing world. On a worldwide scale, millions of dehydration deaths can be prevented if children are kept properly hydrated during diarrhea episodes with a mixture of water, salt, sugar, and other minerals; this is called oral rehydration therapy (ORT).

This intervention does not cure the diarrhea and it has no effect on the sources of infection, but there is no doubt that it is a simple, appropriate technology that can save many lives. When babies are sick with diarrhea, they often have little appetite (and ORT doesn't taste very good), so applying ORT requires work and patience by the mother.

In this case, the local ethnomedical system includes four causes of diarrhea. The researcher discovered that the public health messages about ORT were widely known in the village, but the treatment was not always used. One of the causes of the diarrhea, empacho, *was thought to be significantly different from the other causes, and it therefore required a different remedy. We have already read about treatments for* empacho *in the case of dangerous folk medical treatments in Texas (selection 34). Because it is believed that there is a clogging or obstruction of the digestive tract, a traditional treatment for* empacho *is a purgative. This treatment is dangerous for a child sick with diarrhea because it exacerbates the problem of dehydration. In both the Texas example and the Honduras example described here, a sizable percentage of children with diarrhea were not being treated with ORT and were, in fact, being put at greater risk.*

The anthropologists discovered this problem and reported it to their international health program. What should be done with this cultural information? In this case, there was a confrontation between the biomedical culture and the local ethnomedical system. This case study raises issues of cross-cultural communication, which we explored with regard to clinical medicine (see selection 32). It may be that the LEARN model of cross-cultural medicine (Listen, Explain, Acknowledge differences, Recommend, and Negotiate) is also applicable to international health programs.

As you read this selection, consider these questions:

- **Why did the ORT program planners include a component of ethnomedical research in their overall scheme? Why was the ethnomedical advice ignored by the central program staff?**
- **What makes empacho so different from other causes of diarrhea? Why does the purgative therapy make sense from this ethnomedical viewpoint?**
- **Did the anthropologists suggest that to circumvent the problem of empacho the ORT program actually lie to the local people? Is this ethical?**
- **How might the LEARN model (see selection 32) have been applied in this case?**

Context: This article was written during a period when there was much research on oral rehydration therapy (ORT) as a strategy for preventing child death from diarrhea dehydration. This simple technology of home-based primary health care has saved millions of lives. Despite this effectiveness, ORT is still not accepted for the treatment of some cases of diarrhea in the developing world. This classic article illustrates how local health beliefs can influence health decision making, of both the parents of sick children and decision makers in the Ministry of Health. Carl Kendall is a well-known medical anthropologist who has worked on a wide variety of health problems in the developing world, particularly Latin America. He is a professor of global and community health, and director of the Center for Health Equity, at the Tulane University School of Public Health and Tropical Medicine. Dennis Foote works for the Academy for Educational Development, a large NGO in the international health and development field; he is currently vice president and senior technology advisor of the Global Learning Group. Reynaldo Martorell is chair and a distinguished professor of global health and nutrition in the Hubert Department of Global Health, Rollins School of Public Health, Emory University. A biological anthropologist by training, Martorell is a world expert on child health and nutrition.

Source: C. Kendall, D. Foote, and R. Martorell (1984). "Ethnomedicine and Oral Rehydration Therapy." *Social Science and Medicine* 19:253–260.

INTRODUCTION

The World Health Organization (WHO) has designated diarrheal disease control a primary objective.[1] A component of this control program is the promotion of home-based oral rehydration therapy (ORT). Oral rehydration therapy has been shown, both in clinical trials and in the field to be a safe and effective therapy for dehydration. WHO promotes a dry sealed packet containing 3.5 g sodium chloride, 2.5 g potassium chloride, 2.5 g sodium bicarbonate and 20 g glucose that is added to one liter of clean water in the home. Reaching millions of rural households with this simple solution will tax existing health delivery systems, and WHO has called for operational or applied research to improve delivery of these services.

WHO and other agencies supporting oral rehydration activities acknowledge that ORT programs and promotional campaigns must be appropriate to the social and cultural context of the program.[2] Anthropologists have been encouraged to participate, and bring to the problem skills and research tools appropriate for both operational research and larger questions involved in the extension of coverage of ORT. Among these tools are ethnomedical models, such as Kleinman's explanatory models.[3] Ethnomedical models have been used principally to explain outcomes, particularly program failure.[4] Although they are often mentioned as useful for planning and for operational research, the lack of case-histories in the literature suggests their relative neglect in practice. This paper presents a case study of ethnomedicine and program planning, including a subsequent evaluation of a program that incorporates an ethnomedical perspective to promote acceptance and use of home-based ORT. Points are illustrated with current results from the Mass Media and Health Practices Evaluation, a longitudinal study of 750 families in 20 sites in Honduras, conducted concurrently with the ethnographic investigation. The paper concludes with a discussion of the need for and difficulties in the application of ethnomedical perspectives in investigation and early program planning.

THE PROGRAM

PROCOMSI (Proyecto de Comunicacion Masiva Aplicada a la Salud Infantil or Mass Communication Project Applied to Infant Health) is a health promotion project administered jointly by the Academy for Educational Development and the Division of Education of the Honduras Ministry of Health. Primary emphasis is placed on home-based ORT. The program promotes WHO authorized packets of ORS called, in Honduras, Litrosol. A number of preventive behaviors, including exclusive breast-feeding of young infants, are encouraged as well. The project has been active in Honduras for three years.

The project consists of an integrated program of radio, print materials and health worker training to teach or reinforce changes in a variety of practices and beliefs surrounding infant diarrhea. The method for using these media, with proper testing and program modification procedures, was institutionalized by the country's Ministry of Health for broader use in health education efforts.

The methods are innovative in several respects:

heavy use of research for planning;

intensive use of pretesting and formative evaluation in message and project design;

use of an integrated campaign format through multiple channels;

and concentration on a very focused set of objectives.

...

The study involves a sample of 750–800 families distributed over 20 communities. Each family is visited monthly over a period of two years by a field worker who asks survey questions, makes observations and/or measures the children. Initial findings point to high levels of exposure to campaign components, learning new information and trying the advocated behaviors. The results are being intensively evaluated by the Institute for Communication Research, Stanford University. The data on which this paper is based are drawn from that evaluation. The project has used a behavior-oriented and context appropriate promotional strategy to inform a predominantly rural population of approximately 350,000 people about the preparation and use of ORT. Radio, print materials and face-to-face instruction were the principal tools of the campaign.

THE RESEARCH

The paper reports results from several research activities associated with ORT production and evaluation in Honduras. First, in a single community, interviews were conducted on beliefs and practices related to diarrhea. Next, a pre-intervention survey was conducted in this community. During the spring of 1980 the research site was visited repeatedly. Interviews were conducted with four key informants and Ministry of Health staff. In June 1980, all households in the community were administered an interview schedule to collect baseline data on household size and composition, maternal histories, morbidity, mortality, hygiene and sanitation and other measures. Two years later, the community was restudied to measure morbidity, program campaign recall, and recognition and use of ORT. These studies served as the basis for the design of the Mass Media and Health Practices (MMHP) Evaluation discussed above. In addition, the Academy for Education Development (AED), the implementors of the project, conducted a developmental investigation, prior to program development. This investigation focused on diarrheal disease treatment, literacy, radio listening habits and household characteristics.

THE SITE OF THE EVALUATION'S ETHNOMEDICAL RESEARCH

Los Dolores (a pseudonym), the site of research, consists of five linked hamlets scattered in mountainous terrain at altitudes of 1000 and 1600 m. Wet and dry seasons are sharply demarcated. Rainfall is commonly 1000 mm per year and during winter (*invierno*) which extends from May to October, streams are high. By contrast during the dry summer (*verano*) low stream flow is only 1–2 liters/second/km.[5] A peak of diarrhea incidence is reached during the month of June, just after the start of the rainy season.

The soils support extensive stands of needleleaf and broadleaf evergreens and deciduous shrubs, as well as some deciduous broadleaf vegetation. The valley floors are most heavily farmed, but because of population pressures on these lands, some villagers must often farm plots with slopes in excess of 45 degrees. All household heads in Los Dolores possess lands, although the plots are quite small (<5 *manzanas*). Rural countrypeople grow corn, sorghum, beans, potatoes and some rice; sugar cane is grown for cash but none of the farms of Los Dolores could be considered commercial-scale.

Los Dolores is culturally representative of the 20 sites chosen for the evaluation, which share Ladino culture.

THE SOCIAL CONTEXT AND THE SITES OF THE MMHP EVALUATION

Evaluation sites are found, as in Los Dolores, in Honduras' Health Region I. In Central America, the local political-administrative unit is the *municipio* or municipality containing a headquarters (*cabecera*) and a number of villages (*aldeas*) and hamlets (*caserios*). The *municipios* in the evaluation sample are Sabanagrande, Yuscaran and Danli. The ethnographic evaluation site is an *aldea* in Yuscaran. Although the three municipios are ecologically distinctive, the conditions of rural life are remarkably similar.

A typical rural community is a locale with a number of town centers connected by paths. These centers are clusters of houses often no more than 50 m apart. Many of these adjacent households are connected by ties of kinship. The houses are predominantly adobe, one-story high, with tile roofs. Often they are only a single room with a cooking area attached to an exterior wall. Most floors are of dirt. The houses contain two or three beds for the seven inhabitants. The plot surrounding the house is divided into areas for play and reception of guests, areas for the drying of grains, and areas for micturation, defecation and disposal of garbage.

All *aldeas* are linked to their *cabeceras* by roads, although six of the sites included in the study become inaccessible during the rainy season. Irregular bus service is found in most of the *aldeas* of Sabanagrande and many in Danli, but not in Yuscaran. All *aldeas* have primary schools for grades 1 to 6, and all *cabeceras* have secondary schools.

Only three *aldeas* have completed piped-water systems, although others much like Los Dolores have partially completed networks. None of the *aldeas* have a.c. electric power networks, although some rural inhabitants use automobile batteries to power televisions, and an occasional household near a power line will receive electricity. Latrine programs were begun in 1980 in almost all *aldeas*. No *aldeas* have completed the program and most latrines are little used.

The 5345 people enumerated in the initial baseline sample are overwhelmingly young. 4.2% of the total population was less than a year old at the time of the census, 24.8% less than 5 years of age, and 58% less than 12 years of age. Little difference is found between sites.

Rural Honduran households are predominantly organized into conjugal family households. The 747 households included in a census had a mean household size of 7.16 members. Households in Los Dolores, composed mostly of the conjugal pair and offspring, have a mean size of 5.83 (SD 3.29).

Most household heads in the evaluation sample are small landowners producing subsistence crops of corn and beans. Although self reports of land ownership are notoriously unreliable, of the 521 households for which both ownership and area data are available, 85% of the sample own their own land (although few have full legal title). Ownership of land is skewed, with 5.4% of households owning 53.9% of the land. . . .

COSMOPOLITAN MEDICAL SERVICES

The physician or nurse nearest Los Dolores is located in the Ministry of Health facility in the county seat, 1½ hours' walk away. A Ministry of Health center there is staffed by a graduate medical student completing his or her year of obligatory rural social service, and two auxiliary nurses. Although there are no pharmacies, several stores in town stock medicines which are prescribed, often, by shopkeepers and clerks. Local, part-time curers also serve as heath care providers, prescribing and injecting medicines. The countrypeople (*campesinos*) of Los Dolores occasionally use the hospital facilities available in Tegucigalpa, the nation's capital, 1½ hours by bus from the county seat, when one is available. The Ministry has two local unpaid representatives in Los Dolores, a recently appointed *guardian* (village health worker) who works with the auxiliary nurses, and a *representante* who works with the health promoter in sanitation projects. Neither of these individuals, a recently married couple in their twenties, are local healers.

LOCAL MEDICAL SERVICES

There are no *injectadores* (persons who dispense medication by injection) or *purteras* (traditional or trained midwife) in Los Dolores. Several women will assist family and friends in childbirth, but refuse the vocation of midwife. Nearby communities provide these healers, however. Several men and women are *sobadores* or masseurs. A *sobador* massages the body and prescribes medicines for a number of diseases. These include *empacho,* to be described below, and *fluxion,* a flux or chill that is felt to enter the body. A large number of herbal remedies are known to older men and women. Younger householders claim not to know these remedies and appear to prefer commercially packaged medicines.

FOLK MEDICAL ATTRIBUTIONS OF CAUSE

A key goal in the promotion of ORT was to express program messages in a rural vocabulary using lay understanding of diarrhea. Both the initial evaluation and the developmental investigation demonstrated the importance for treatment decisions of folk medical attribution of disease causality. The results of these investigations have been reported elsewhere,[6] but for purposes of the paper, a brief summary is provided.

Interviews with key informants concerning diarrheal etiology and treatment revealed a number of folk illnesses associated with diarrheal symptoms believed to be causes of diarrhea.[7] These are:

1. *empacho*
2. *ojo* (evil eye)
3. *caida de mollera* (fallen fontanelles)
4. *lombrices* (worms).

Episodes of diarrhea are believed to be caused by these folk illnesses when the diarrhea is especially severe and when the episode is refractive. As has been pointed out elsewhere,[8] folk diagnosis is often a pragmatic activity involving trial and error appraisal of a medicine's efficacy. These folk illnesses are the attributions of last resort. Since the effect of ORT on morbidity is small, but its impact on mortality high, these complicated diarrheas, which are diagnosed pragmatically in episodes of long duration, are important for reaching those cases of diarrhea that are likely to be fatal.

Empacho is a painful condition of the gut characterized by explosive evacuations and flatulence. Locally it is differentiated by cause; for it is believed that it can be brought on by eating the wrong kinds of food (foods that are heavy (*pesado*) or a combination of foods that are improperly balanced along the hot-cold spectrum); eating at improper times or missing a meal or eating foods that are incompletely cooked or raw. *Empacho* also produces a special skin quality that is used as a diagnostic indicator. A masseur or masseuse (*sabador* or *sabadora*) treats *empacho* by massaging the body and administering a purgative. Purgatives are considered to be any substance (most frequently oils, sometimes "salts," but also absorbents) that promotes evacuation. This evacuation serves to clean (*limpiar*) the gut of its improperly digested contents which are considered dirty (*sucio*).

Rural countrypeople are aware of the potent effect of purgatives and prescribe milder purgatives to children; nevertheless, the use of purgatives may contribute to the high mortality attributed to diarrhea which accounts for 24% of all reported infant and child deaths in Honduras.[9]

Evil eye, the result of malicious, penetrant visual rays, produces fever. A diagnostic sign is a lack of symmetry in the eyes. Local informants make a sharp distinction between *mal de ojo*, a condition of red, sore eyes and *ojo* or sometimes *mal de ojo*, produced by penetrant rays. Treatment for the latter involves bundling, as for any fever, and spraying the skin with a number of liquids. Purgatives are not used since etiology does not involve contamination of the gut.

Fallen fontanelles are believed to be caused by improper maternal handling of an infant. According to local ethnoanatomy, the infant's palate is incompletely developed. Thus the tissue underlying the fontanelles can fall. Treatment is specific to the ethnoanatomical effect, involving pushing up on the roof of the mouth and tapping on the heels of the inverted child and/or sucking on the fontanelles.

Worms are considered a normal symbiote of the gut, but when mistreated, leave their "sack" and wander through the body causing illness. If left untreated by a purgative the worms could cause a fatal illness—worm fever (*fiebre de lombrices*). Most episodes of worm-caused diarrhea are felt to be benign, however, and are not treated by the administration of medicines. If the diarrhea continues too long, however, treatment is sought. This treatment often involves the administration of mild local purgatives. Worms, as a normal symbiote, are not the same category of calamity as the other folk illnesses mentioned above. Worm fever, on the other hand, is treated much like *empacho*, discussed below.

FOLK MEDICAL TREATMENT DECISIONS

The original study could uncover no resistance to the incorporation of ORT to cases of diarrhea attributed to *ojo* or *caidu*. However, cases of *empacho* are generally thought to require the administration of a purgative, and it was felt that parents would resist the use of ORT for the treatment of this disease, and continue to use folk remedies. Since it was felt that *empacho* would have to be addressed by the program, a convenience sample of ten mothers in Los Dolores were asked if they knew about a range of illnesses, including *empacho*. These illnesses include those attributed as primary causes of mortality in Honduras by the Ministry of Heath, and an additional group of folk illnesses. Respondents were asked if they had heard of the disease, and if it was curable. All responded "yes" to both questions. They were then read a list of healers and asked "Can healer *X* cure disease *Y*"?. . .

Almost uniformly, respondents believed that although cosmopolitan medical staff could cure diarrhea and dysentery, they would be unsuccessful in treating either *empacho* or *ojo*. Since the source of ORT would be the Ministry of Health (and a fictitious physician, "Dr. Salustiano," a major campaign figure), the staff felt that program messages were unlikely to be successful in convincing rural parents to treat episodes of diarrhea attributed to *empacho* with ORT.

No mothers interviewed in 1980 knew about dehydration. Those who recognized the word thought it was a synonym for malnutrition (*desnutrición*), this followed from the use of pre-mixed oral and intravenous solutions called *suero* that mothers were familiar with. These expensive solutions, literally translated into English as whey or serum are prescribed during *empacho*, since the gut is thought to need rest.

NON-USE OF ETHNOMEDICAL RESULTS IN PLANNING

A natural outcome of these findings could have been the promotion of ORT as a purgative, or at least as a specific treatment for *empacho*. A medical consultant to the implementation project, Dr. M. M. Levine, was among the first to suggest such a strategy. Two factors, however, militated against the promotion of ORT as a purgative or as a cure for *empacho*.

The first was the expressed resistance on the part of Ministry staff physicians to both the illness label "*empacho*" and the use of "purgative" in PROCOMSI activities. *Empacho* was not considered a disease entity and physicians did not want the program to appear to support purgative use.

The second difficulty was that the implementors' survey research activities did not often encounter *empacho* attributed as a cause of diarrhea. When questioned "what causes diarrhea?" respondents would most often reply dirty water or worms. The reasons for these attributions will be discussed later. Because of these difficulties, a resistant Ministry and inadequate survey research justification, the implementors ignored *empacho* as an impediment to ORT use. ORT was promoted then, not as a purgative but as salts that were good for diarrhea and avoided dehydration, the latter a concept unknown to rural countrypeople and laboriously taught in the campaign, which began in March 1981.

THE TWO-YEAR IMPACT SURVEY

In May of 1980 and again 2 years later (June 1982) all households were censused and standardized interviews were conducted in all households containing children under 5 years of age in Los Dolores. The 2–year impact survey measured:

1. Diarrhea morbidity and treatment, including use of ORT (2 weeks/month and 6 month recall of episodes, with "diarrhea" defined by the mother);
2. Breastfeeding and nutrition (breastfeeding and weaning practices, list of foods consumed) for children less than 3 years of age;
3. Household demographic changes, including mortality; and
4. PROCOMSI campaign exposure, recall and recognition.

. . .

RESULTS

Morbidity

The morbidity survey was conducted in June 1982. For the two week period prior to the visit to each household with a child under five, mothers reported 12 episodes of diarrhea. There 12 episodes totaled 70 days of diarrhea with a mean duration of 5.8 days (SD 2.48). No child was reported as having had more than one episode, and specific incidence of diarrhea in children less than 60 months of age for a 2 week period between 1 and 22 June was 375/1000. During the entire month (18 May–22 June) a total of 17 episodes were reported in 17 of 32 children, for a total of 122 days of diarrhea (mean duration 6.58 days, SD 3.5) for a 1 month incidence of 531/1000 in children less than 60 months of age. . . . Clearly diarrhea is a salient problem. Information was collected for episodes (three in total) that occurred as long as 6 months prior to the intervention. There are grounds for suspecting that memory effects were responsible for the low number of cases reported, although diarrhea is highly seasonal. There are no grounds for suspecting that the three cases reported between 1 and 6 months prior to the survey were in any way especially salient cases.

The evaluation has currently analyzed diarrheal morbidity for two data sweeps, the first in June and July of 1981 during the rainy season, and the second in March of 1982, during the dry season. 36% of the children were reported to have had diarrhea in the previous two weeks of the rainy season of 1981 while 21.5% were said to have been sick during the dry season of 1982.

. . .

Combining information on diarrhea from all appropriate questions, we have estimated that *at least* 56.0% of children in wave 1 and 45.0% in wave 2 were ill with diarrhea in the previous 6 months. We emphasize the words "at least" because of the effects of memory loss. Clearly, diarrheal diseases are a major public health problem in Honduras as they are in these other areas. . . .

The MMHP evaluation data and the data collected in Los Dolores are comparable. There were 18 children less than 3 years of age in 17 out of 44 households in Los Dolores. Of these 18 children, 7 had completed breastfeeding at the time of the survey. Mean duration of breastfeeding was 16.85 months (SD 6.2 months). Only one mother reported never breastfeeding, and only one of the mothers reported breastfeeding for less than two months. Other mothers were still breastfeeding children at 27 and even 34 months. . . . Thirteen of the 18 children less than 3 years of age were reported to have had an episode of diarrhea in the previous month, but only 3 of the 7 children still breastfeeding had reported episodes.

Although the numbers are too small to be significant and are confounded by age, diet and behavioral differences, some impact of breastfeeding on diarrheal incidence may be reflected in these data. All mothers suspended powdered or cow's milk, as well as meat, eggs and many other foods during episodes of diarrhea. Breastfeeding mothers, however, continued breastfeeding during episodes.

CAMPAIGN EXPOSURE, RECALL AND RECOGNITION, JUNE 1982

. . . All families claimed awareness of the ORT packet and its use; all could name it. All families claimed to have heard about it both through radio and by word of mouth. No mothers, except mothers in those households with posters, reported the posters as a source of information about the program. Although no mother knew the word dehydration or about ORT packets before program implementation, 12 of the 24 mothers correctly defined dehydration as the loss or absence of fluids in the body. Three of the 24 mothers could correctly recall the five components stressed in the mixing messages (mix with 1 liter of water, use all of one packet, give whole liter in 1 day, shake the bottle, throw left-over away after 1 day). Fourteen other families missed only a single component: the amount of fluid to give a child per day (1 liter). It appears that the promotion campaign has been successfully conducted in Los Dolores.

A survey of mothers in the MMHP evaluation sample, conducted in April 1982 demonstrates similarly high figures for the sample. 85.3% of families reported owning a radio; 77.5% of the total sample had a working radio. Coverage of the population, expressed as the percentage of all mothers remembering hearing at least one spot on the previous day, is 38.9%. The percentage of listeners who report having heard a spot between 6 a.m. and 9 p.m. by hour varies between 60.5 and 78.9%.

46.6% of the sample reported having seen a PROCOMSI health poster and could describe it, much higher than the percentage for Los Dolores. 92.5% of the total MMHP sample could identify "Litrosol" in April 1982. For preparation of ORS, 94.2% of the sample who had used Litrosol reported mixing it with one liter of water. 95.7% reported using all of one packet. 59.7% reported giving the whole liter in 1 day. 83.5% reported agitating the bottle to mix the solution. 32.6% reported throwing away the solution after 1 day.

USE

Of the 20 cases of diarrhea reported in the previous 2 weeks, 11 used ORT. Use does not imply that each and every case followed PROCOMSI's therapeutic regimen. For the most part, mothers gave less ORT than the prescribed liter per day. Nine cases did not use ORT. Eight of these diarrheal episodes were attributed to *empacho*.

Initial findings of the survey demonstrate that for March 1982 during the dry season 26.1% (55/211) of diarrheal episodes that occurred during the last 2 weeks were treated with ORT. The percentage of cases varied from *municipio* to *municipio*. . . .

This variation may have been due to the availability of Litrosol. The figures are not directly comparable with Los Dolores because of seasonal differences and the ethnographer's presence. Approximately 40% of these diarrheal episodes were treated with purgatives. Unfortunately, attributions of cause by treatment are not yet available from the evaluation.

DISCUSSION

The program appears to have been successful in providing knowledge about ORT, and in achieving its use in the home. On the other hand, over a 6-month period, 9 out of 20 diarrheal episodes in children were not treated with ORT. Although there are grounds for suspecting the quality of recall of the three episodes that were reported to have occurred prior to 1 month, only one of the episodes reported did not use Litrosol, and this was the only non-*empacho* episode in which Litrosol was not used. With this one exception, the diarrheas which were not treated with ORT were attributed to *empacho*. The initial findings from ethnographic investigation early in the program were confirmed: those episodes of diarrhea attributed to this folk illness are treated with purgatives, and not with ORT.

Two reasons were given earlier to explain why a promotional strategy for ORT appropriate to this folk illness was not approved: (1) the rejection by the Honduran cosmopolitan medical community of the public discussion of *empacho* and the promotion of ORT as a purgative in a Ministry of Health program; and (2) the relatively few mothers who reported *empacho* as a cause of diarrhea.

As reported earlier, lay treatment does not proceed directly from recognition of symptoms to diagnosis. In fact, diagnosis is negotiated among family and health specialists during the course of the illness and its treatment. *Empacho* is rarely diagnosed early in an episode and when diagnosed is considered a serious and potentially fatal illness. In addition, *empacho* is characterized by other symptoms as well as diarrhea, such as abdominal pain. These "primary" symptoms are perhaps more salient than diarrhea as evidence of *empacho*. These are among the reasons that frequency of the *empacho* response to survey items could have been low. These results blunted the urgency of both evaluators' and implementors' attempts to promote a cure for *empacho* in the program. In fact, the term "*empacho*" which can be considered a symptom or an illness, overlaps incompletely with the disease category "diarrhea." Some biomedical researchers believe that *empacho* may be characterized by an etiology different from that of most diarrheas; one suspicion is a rotaviral agent, and another food allergies or other disorders of digestion.

A detailed discussion of the first reason for rejection of a strategy for *empacho* is beyond the scope of this paper. However, it involves issues raised, for example, in Hahn and Kleinman about the truth status of ethnomedical events.[10] In contrast to biomedicine, ethnomedicine appears to offer results of dubious reliability and little precision.

In this case, however, program planners might have been willing to accept the findings of PROCOMSI's initial developmental investigation. Why did these findings not corroborate the importance of *empacho* in treatment decisions about diarrheal disease? The answer to this question, briefly put, is that the validity of findings from "what if" survey formats can be greatly challenged. Especially when laboratory findings cannot be used to corroborate assessments, only an intensive case-by-case review can control for issues of validity of disease categories and criteria for attribution.

Whatever the final results of the microbiological and metabolic investigations currently being planned for *empacho,* the findings that were significant for program planning and for interpretation of results were collected using research techniques appropriate to a subject area broadly defined here as "ethnomedicine." However, this example reinforces the results of many other ethnographic studies conducted in conjunction with social change programs; that is, that such findings are usually not accorded independent status for purposes of planning. It is hoped that the successful ethnomedical investigation in the PROCOMSI project will not only advance diarrheal disease control and health education efforts, but will also promote ethnomedical investigation, as an independent and appropriate operational research tool.

REFERENCES

1. World Health Organization. Scientific Working Group Reports 1978–1980. Programme for Control of Diarrhoeal Diseases. Unpublished reports. World Health Organization, Geneva. The WHO diarrhoeal diseases control programme. *Wkly Epid.* Rec. 54 No. 16,121–123, 1979. World Health Organization. *Progamme for control of Diarrhoeal Diseases—Training Modules,* 1980.
2. See Ref. 1, for example, WHO environmental health and diarrhoeal disease prevention. Report of a Scientific Working Group, Diarrhoeal Diseases Control Programme, Document No. R-680, p. 15 and United States Agency for International Development. *Health Sector I, Honduras.* Project Paper, Project No. 522–0153.
3. Kleinman A. International health care planning from an ethnomedical perspective: critique and recommendations for change. *Med. Anthrop.* 2, 71–94. Kleinman A. *Patients and Healers in the Context of Culture.* University of California Press, Los Angeles, 1980.
4. cf. Wellin E. Directed culture change and health programs in Latin America. *Millbank Meml Fund Q.* 44, 111–128.
5. Agency for International Development Resources Inventory Center. *National Inventory of Physical Resources, Central American and Panama: Honduras.* AID/RIC GIPR No. 5, 1966.
6. Kendall C, Foote D. and Martorell R. Anthropology, communications, and health: the mass media and health practices program in Honduras. *Hum. Org.* 42, 353–360; . . .
7. A number of environmental causes are also felt to produce diarrhea, as well as a number of other conditions, states and agents, such as *lombrices.* These are described in Ref. 6. They are not discussed further in this article.
8. Young J. *Medical Choice in a Mexican Village.* Rutgers University Press, New Brunswick, 1981; and Kleinman A. *op. cit.* Ref 3.
9. Direccion General de Estadistica y Censos. *Anuario Estadistico, 1978.* Tegucigalpa, Ministerior de Economia, 1980.
10. Hahn R. A. and Kleinman A. Belief in pathogen, belief as medicine; "voodoo death" and the "placebo phenomenon." *Med. Anthrop Q.* 4, No. 4, 3ff., 1983.

48

New Challenges to the AIDS Prevention Paradigm

Edward C. Green

HIV/AIDS is probably the greatest global health challenge faced by humanity at the beginning of the twenty-first century. For most people in North America, however, HIV/AIDS is now completely off the radar screen. It is thought to be an epidemic of the recent historical past. Although it caused much suffering (as described in the selection by Farmer and Kleinman), we tend not to think about it because it now primarily affects poor people living in Africa and Asia. Before 2003, when anti-retroviral (ARV) drug cocktails became available at a reduced price in the developing world, infection with HIV/AIDS was a death sentence. ARVs have changed that, and in the best-case scenario, HIV/AIDS might be considered a manageable chronic disease, albeit one that requires a good deal of medical attention. In the past, the only strategies that public health practitioners had were prevention campaigns. These efforts primarily emphasized the use of condoms and involved the distribution of condoms. Unfortunately, such campaigns were not successful. But even in the era of ARVs, the importance of AIDS prevention remains paramount.

Medical anthropologists have been actively involved in AIDS prevention since the beginning of the pandemic. In most of the world, HIV is transmitted through heterosexual intercourse, and women often have higher rates of the disease than do men. Many infected women did nothing riskier than have sex with their husbands. In many cultural contexts, it can be very difficult (even dangerous) for women to ask their husbands to use a condom. Similarly, in contexts characterized by poverty, women have few opportunities to earn money, and this is one reason "transactional" sex occurs. One Haitian woman once told anthropologist Paul Farmer that if we want to stop the spread of AIDS, then we should give women jobs. Anthropologists have played an important role in getting public health practitioners to revise their simplistic ideas of "prostitution."

In the history of AIDS prevention, Uganda has been a special and positive case. With impressive political support, there was a home-grown social movement to acknowledge and destigmatize the virus and decrease its spread. This was accomplished, in large measure, through behavior change aimed at discouraging "concurrent" sexual partners. This selection describes this behavioral change from an anthropological point of view. It also suggests that this model may be applicable in other societies. In today's world, HIV/AIDS is clearly associated with poverty, but anthropologists believe that cultures are always changing and that people's behavior can change to improve their health.

As you read this selection, consider these questions:

- **What is the difference between "risk reduction" and "risk avoidance" strategies in relation to sexually transmitted diseases like HIV?**
- **How is the behavioral change approach different than a medical approach? Which approach needs the contributions of social scientists?**
- **Why might the ABC plan proposed by the author be attractive to people from the West with a conservative orientation?**
- **How might Uganda's approach be described as culturally appropriate?**

Context: Edward Green is an applied medical anthropologist and a senior research scientist at the Harvard School of Public Health and Center for Population and Development Studies. He is also the director of the AIDS Prevention Research Project at Harvard. He is author of five books and editor of one, and has written over 250 peer-reviewed journal articles, book chapters, conference papers, and commissioned technical reports. His books include *Rethinking AIDS Prevention: Learning from Successes in Developing Countries (2003)* and *Indigenous Theories of Contagious Disease (1999)*. Green has worked in a large number of developing countries affected by the HIV/AIDS pandemic on projects funded by the U.S. Agency for International Development. Much of his work has involved integrating indigenous and "modern" health care systems by encouraging traditional healers to work together with biomedical public health practitioners. Green has advocated the ABC approach—that is, "Abstain, Be Faithful, or use Condoms," which was based on the Uganda experience. This approach found much political resonance in the United States, but it also received a good deal of criticism. This selection, written for a newsletter read by anthropologists, encourages the rethinking of AIDS prevention.

Source: E. Green (2003). "New Challenges to the AIDS Prevention Paradigm." *Anthropology News*, September, pp. 5–6.

Evidence is mounting that the global model of HIV/AIDS prevention, designed by Western experts, has been largely ineffective in Africa. The model is based on risk-reduction or "remedies" interventions (condoms, treating sexually transmissible infections with drugs), rather than on risk avoidance (mutual monogamy, abstinence or delay of age of first sex). This dichotomy is imperfect because reduction in number of sexual partners would have to be classified as risk reduction, not avoidance. The remedies-based global model does not promote partner reduction, nor even address multi-partner sex.

John Richens proposed the term primary behavior change (PBC) to denote fundamental changes in sexual behavior, including partner reduction, that do not rely on devices or drugs. He, I and a very few others have suggested treating AIDS as a behavioral issue that calls for behavioral solutions, although not to the exclusion of risk reduction remedies. The dominant paradigm model treats AIDS as a medical problem requiring medical solutions. PBC deals with the problem itself, getting at what is needed for primary prevention, while the medical model deals with symptoms.

RISK REDUCTION MODEL

The dominant prevention paradigm was developed for high-risk groups in US cities like San Francisco. Part of the risk reduction model was to not address sexual behavior. It was argued that this would amount to making value judgments, which is unscientific and would only drive away those who needed to be reached. AIDS experts settled for risk or harm reduction approaches, which assume that behavior is difficult or impossible to change; therefore efforts ought to be made to mitigate the consequences of risky behavior. Thus condoms and clean needles (if legal) were provided to reduce risk of sexually transmitted and blood-to-blood HIV infection respectively. There was and is no discouragement of any form of sexual behavior, or injecting drug use. AIDS experts applauded themselves for their open-mindedness and realism.

This approach might have been suitable for San Francisco or Bangkok. But when exported to Africa and other parts of the world, and despite claims to the contrary, there was little attempt to adapt the model to other cultural settings or epidemic patterns. In the US, Europe and most of Asia, HIV infections are concentrated in a few fairly well-defined high risk groups. In (sub-Saharan) Africa, most infections are found in the general population. Actually, many are opposed to this distinction, arguing, "Let's not single out particular risk groups. That will stigmatize them—blame the victims—and make the general public feel that they are not at risk. So our message should be, 'We are *all* at risk of AIDS'" This has a nice, egalitarian ring; we are all in this thing together. Nevertheless, differences in epidemiological patterns and cultural settings are real, calling for—among other things—different approaches to prevention.

AIDS PREVENTION IN AFRICA

How has the Western risk reduction model fared in Africa? Most efforts have focused on condoms. There is no evidence to date that mass promotion of condoms has paid off in decline of HIV infection rates at the population level. The UNAIDS multi-center study, published in a special edition of *AIDS* in 2001, found that condom user levels made no significant difference in determining HIV prevalence levels. And a 2003 UNAIDS review of condom effectiveness, by Hearst and Chen, concludes, "There are no definite examples yet of generalized epidemics that have been turned back by prevention programs based primarily on condom promotion."

Some argue that not enough condoms are being used in Africa to have made a difference yet, that condoms would have an impact if only we exported them in the billions instead of the mere tens of millions. Maybe, but what we do know from recent UNAID data is that, after 15+ years of intense condom social marketing in Africa, the result today is an average of only 4.6 condoms available (not necessarily used) per male per year in Africa. That figure was actually a bit higher in the mid-1990s; it has declined somewhat even since then in spite of the explosion of AIDS in southern Africa. The problem seems to be low demand.

UGANDA'S APPROACH

In addition to condoms, the other relatively expensive AIDS prevention programs currently funded by major donors are mass treatment of STIs, voluntary counseling and testing and prevention of mother-to-child transmission through Nevirapine. Like condom marketing, remedies rather than behavior change. These programs, along with condom social marketing, had not yet started in Uganda when infection rates began to decline in the late 1980s. Yet Uganda has experienced the greatest decline of HIV infection of any country. Its home-grown prevention program was based largely on behavioral change. Reacting to Western advice, President Museveni said in 1990, "Just as we were offered the 'magic bullet' in the early 1940s, we are now being offered the condom for 'safe sex.' We are being told that only a thin piece of rubber stands between us and the death of our continent. I feel that condoms have a role to play as a means of protection, especially in couples who are HIV-positive, but they cannot become the main means of stemming the tide of AIDS."

Uganda's largely home-grown approach to AIDS led to a delayed age of first sex, less casual sex, and relatively high condom user rates among the few who still engage in casual sex. Uganda also pioneered approaches in reducing stigma, bringing discussion of sexual behavior out into the open, involving HIV-infected people in public education, persuading individuals and couples to be tested and counseled, and improving the status of women. The genius of Uganda's ABC program (Abstain, Be faithful, or use Condoms) is that it focuses on what *individuals themselves* can do to change (or maintain) behavior, and thereby avoid or reduce risk of infection. But it also tackled the difficult social and institutional problems that only committed governments can impact in the near- to intermediate-term. These programs were led by the government (especially the Ministry of Health) but also involved many NGOs and community-based local organizations.

PROVIDING MORE OPTIONS

It has been difficult for Western donor agencies and consulting firms involved in AIDS prevention to accept evidence that suggests what they have been doing may not have been very effective in Africa; meanwhile something they have not supported has worked better. Some have dismissed the ABC approach as simplistic or narrow. Yet the ABC approach adds primary behavior change (the A and B of ABC) to existing programs that, for the most part, do not go beyond "C," beyond condom (and drug) remedies. Adding primary behavior change provides people with more behavioral options for preventing HIV infection than are currently available, and these are sustainable options that do not depend on relatively high-cost Western imports.

References

Note: These are references to the Conceptual Tools, part introductions, and article introductions only.

TO THE INSTRUCTOR

Anderson, Robert. 1996. *Magic, Science and Health: The Aims and Achievements of Medical Anthropology.* Fort Worth, TX: Harcourt Brace.

Foster, George, and Barbara Anderson. 1978. *Medical Anthropology.* New York; Wiley.

Hahn, Robert A. 1995. Sickness and Healing: An Anthropological Perspective. New Haven, CT: Yale University Press.

Helman, Cecil, G. 1994. *Culture, Health and Illness.* Oxford: Butterworth Heinemann.

Janzen, John M. 2002. *The Social Fabric of Health: An Introduction to Medical Anthropology.* Boston: McGraw-Hill.

Landy, David, ed. 1977. *Culture, Disease, and Healing: Studies in Medical Anthropology.* New York: Macmillan.

Logan, Michael, and Edward E. Hunt, eds. 1978. *Health and the Human Condition.* North Scituate, MA: Duxbury.

McElroy, Ann, and Patrcia K. Townsend. 1996. *Medical Anthropology in Ecological Perspective.* Boulder, CO: Westview Press.

Sargent, Carolyn F., and Thomas M. Johnson, eds. 1996. *Medical Anthropology: Contemporary Theory and Method.* Westport, CT: Praeger.

Singer, Merrill and Hans Baer. 2007. *Introducing Medical Anthropology: A Discipline in Action.* Lanham, MD: Altamira Press.

Todd, Harry F., Jr., and Julio L. Ruffini, eds. 1979. *Teaching Medical Anthropology.* Vol. 1. Washington, DC: Society for Medical Anthropology.

Wiley, Andrea S., and John S. Allen. 2009. *Medical Anthropology: A Biocultural Approach.* New York: Oxford University Press.

Winkelman, Michael. 2008. *Culture and Health: Applying Medical Anthropology.* San Francisco: Jossey-Bass.

TO THE STUDENT

Anderson, Robert. 1996. *Magic, Science and Health: The Aims and Achievements of Medical Anthropology.* Fort Worth, TX: Harcourt Brace.

McElroy, Ann, and Patricia K. Townsend. 1996. *Medical Anthropology in Ecological Perspective.* Boulder, CO: Westview Press.

Podolefsky, Aaron, and Peter J. Brown, eds. 1997. *Applying Anthropology: An Introductory Reader.* Mountain View, CA: Mayfield.

Sargent, Carolyn F., and Thomas M. Johnson, eds. 1996. *Medical Anthropology: Contemporary Theory and Method.* Westport, CT: Praeger.

PART I. UNDERSTANDING MEDICAL ANTHROPOLOGY: BIOSOCIAL AND CULTURAL APPROACHES

Brown, Peter J., Marcia Inhorn, and Daniel Smith. 1996. *Disease, Ecology, and Human Behavior. In Medical Anthropology: Contemporary Theory and Method,* edited by Carolyn Sargent and Thomas Johnson, pp. 183–219. Westport, CT: Praeger.

Diamond, Jared. 1987. "The Worst Mistake in Human History." *Discover*, May: 64–66.

Goodman, Alan, and Thomas Leatherman, eds. In press. *Building a New Biocultural Synthesis: Political-Economic Perspectives on Human Biology.* Ann Arbor: University of Michigan Press.

Hahn, Robert A. 1995. *Sickness and Healing: An Anthropological Perspective.* New Haven, CT: Yale University Press.

Harrison, G. A., et al. 1988. *Human Biology: An Introduction to Human Evolution, Variation, Growth, and Adaptability.* Oxford: Oxford University Press.

Johnston, Francis E., and Setha Low. 1984. "Biomedical Anthropology: An Emerging Synthesis in Anthropology." *Yearbook of Physical Anthropolagy 27*: 215–227.

Jurmain, Robert, Harry Nelson, and William Turnbaugh. 1984. *Understanding Physical Anthropology and Archaeology.* St. Paul, MN: West.

Kendall, Carl. 1990. "Public Health and the Domestic Domain: Lessons from Anthropological Research on Diarrheal Diseases." In *Anthropology and Primary Health Care,* edited by Denis Mull and Jeannine Coreils, pp. 173–195. Boulder, CO: Westview Press.

Lee, Richard. 1992. "Art, Science, or Politics: The Crisis in Hunter-Gatherer Studies." *American Anthropologist 94*: 31–54.

McElroy, Ann, and Patricia K. Townsend. 1996. *Medical Anthropology in Ecological Perspective.* Boulder, CO: Westview Press.

McKeown, Thomas. 1979. *The Role of Medicine: Dream, Mirage, or Nemesis.* Princeton, NJ: Princeton University Press.

McNeill, William H. 1976. *Plagues and Peoples.* New York: Doubleday.

Moore, Lorna, et al. 1980. *The Biocultural Basis of Health: Expanding Views of Medical Anthropology.* St. Louis, MO: Mosby.

Payer, Lynn. 1988. *Medicine and Culture.* New York: Penguin.

Singer, Merrill. 1997. "Farewell to Adaptationism: Unnatural Selection and the Politics of Biology." *Medical Anthropology Quarterly 10*: 496–515.

Turshen, Meredith. 1984. *The Political Ecology of Disease in Tanzania.* New Brunswick, NJ: Rutgers University Press.

Ware, Norma. 1992. "Suffering and the Social Construction of Illness: the Delegitimation of Illness Experience in Chronic Fatigue Syndrome." *Medical Anthropology Quarterly* 6: 347–361.

Weller, Susan, and A. K. Romney. 1988. *Systematic Data Collection*. Newbury Park, CA: Sage.

Wiley, Andrea. 1992. "Adaptation and the Biocultural Paradigm in Medical Anthropology: A Critical Review." *Medical Anthropology Quarterly* 6: 216–236.

Young, James. 1981. *Medical Choice in a Mexican Village*. New Brunswick, NJ: Rutgers University Press.

EVOLUTION, HEALTH, AND MEDICINE

Armelagos, George. 1997. "Disease, Darwin, and the Third Epidemiological Transition." *Journal of Human Evolution* 5: 212–220.

Eaton, S. Boyd, Marjorie Shostak, and Melvin Konner. 1988. *The Paleolithic Prescription: A Program of Diet and Exercise and a Design for Living*. New York: Harper & Row.

Ewald, Paul. 1994. *Evolution of Infectious Disease*. Oxford: Oxford University Press.

Johnson, Allen, and Timothy Earle. 1987. *The Evolution of Human Societies: From Foraging Group to Agrarian State*. Palo Alto, CA: Stanford University Press.

Konner, Melvin. 2003. *The Tangled Wing: Biological Constraints on the Human Spirit*. New York: Holt Paperbacks.

Nesse, Randolph, and George C. Williams. 1994. *Why We Get Sick: The New Science of Darwinian Medicine*. New York: Random House.

Nesse, Randolph, and George C. Williams. 1991. "The Dawn of Darwinian Medicine. " *The Quarterly Review of Biology* 66: 1–22.

Shostak, Marjorie. 2000. *Nisa: The Life and Words of a !Kung Woman*. Cambridge, MA: Harvard University Press.

Solway, J. S., and R. B. Lee. 1990. "Foragers, Genuine or Spurious? Situating the Kalahari San in History." *Current Anthropology* 31: 109–146.

Whitaker, Elizabeth D. 1996. "Ancient Bodies, Modern Customs, and Our Health." In *Applying Anthropology*, edited by A. Podolefsy and P. J. Brown, pp. 36–45. Mountain View, CA: Mayfield.

HUMAN BIOLOGICAL VARIATION

Armelagos, George. 1997. "Disease, Darwin, and the Third Epidemiological Transition." *Journal of Human*. Evolution 5: 212–220.

Boas, Franz. 1940. *Race, Language, Culture*. New York: Macmillan.

Bogin, Barry. 2001. *The Growth of Humanity*. New York: Wiley-Liss.

Frisancho, A. Roberto. 1993. *Human Adaptation and Accommodation*. Ann Arbor: University of Michigan Press.

Goodman, Alan H., Deborah Heath, and M. Susan Lindee. 2003. *Genetic Nature/Culture: Anthropology and Science beyond the Two-culture Divide*. Berkeley: University of California Press.

Goodman, Alan, and Thomas Leland Leatherman. 1998. *Building a New Biocultural Synthesis: Political-Economic Perspectives on Human Biology*. Ann Arbor: University of Michigan Press.

Lasker, Gabriel. 1969. "Human Biological Adaptability." *Science 14*: 1480–1486.

BIOARCHAEOLOGY AND THE HISTORY OF HEALTH

Armelagos, George, and John R. Dewey. 1970. "Evolutionary Responses to Human Infectious Diseases." *BioScience* 157: 638–644.

Caldwell, John. 1982. *Theory of Fertility Decline*. San Francisco: Academic Press.

Cohen, Mark N. 1989. *Health and the Rise of Civilization*. New Haven, CT: Yale University Press.

Cohen, Mark N., and George J. Armelagos, eds. 1984. *Paleopathology at the Origins of Agriculture*. New Haven, CT: Yale University Press.

Kunitz, Stephen. 1983. *Disease Change and the Role of Medicine: The Navajo Experience*. Berkeley: University of California Press.

Kunitz, Stephen J. 1994. *Disease and Social Diversity: The European Impact on the Health of Non-Europeans*. New York: Oxford University Press.

McKeown, Thomas. 1979. *The Role of Medicine: Dream, Mirage, or Nemesis?* Princeton, NJ: Princeton University Press.

McNeill, William H. 1976. *Plagues and Peoples*. Garden City, NY: Doubleday.

CULTURAL AND POLITICAL ECOLOGIES OF DISEASE

Alland, Alexander. 1970. *Adaptation in Cultural Evolution*. New York: Columbia University Press.

Baer, Hans. 1996. "Toward a Political Economy of Health in Medical Anthropology. " *Medical Anthropology Quarterly* 10: 451–454.

Bourgois, Philippe. 2003. *In Search of Respect: Selling Crack in El Barrio*. Cambridge: Cambridge University Press.

Brown, Peter J. 1986. "Socioeconomic and Demographic Effects of Malaria Eradication: A Comparison of Sri Lanka and Sardinia." *Social Science and Medicine* 22(8): 847–861.

Brown, Peter J. 1997. "Culture and the Global Resurgence of Malaria." In *The Anthropology of Infectious Disease: International Health Perspectives*, edited by Marcia Inhorn and Peter Brown, pp. 119–141. Newark, NJ: Gordon & Breach.

Burnet, M., and D. O. White. 1978. *The Natural History of Infectious Disease*. Cambridge: Cambridge University Press.

Durham, William H. 1991. *Coevolution: Genes, Mind, and Culture*. Palo Alto: Stanford University Press.

Edgerton, Robert. 1992. *Sick Societies: The Myth of Primitive Harmony*. New York: Free Press.

Farmer, Paul. 1993. *AIDS and Accusation: Haiti and the Geography of Blame*. Berkeley: University of California Press.

Kidder, Tracy. 2003. *Mountains beyond Mountains*. New York: Random House.

McKeown, Thomas. 1988. *The Origins of Human Disease*. New York: Blackwell.

Moran, Emilio F., ed. 1990. *The Ecosystem Approach in Anthropology: From Concept to Practice.* Ann Arbor: University of Michigan Press.

Oaks, Stanley C., et al., eds. 1991. *Malaria: Obstacles and Opportunities.* Washington, DC: National Academy Press.

Ormerod, W. E. 1976. "Ecological Effects of Control of Sterk African Trypanosomiasis." *Science 191*: 815–821.

Sterk, Claire E. 1999. *Fast Lives: Women Who Use Crack Cocaine.* Philadelphia: Temple University Press.

Trostle, J., and J. Sommerfeld. 1996. "Epidemiology and Medical Anthropology." *Annual Review of Anthropology 25*: 253–274.

Wiley, Andrea. 1992. "Adaptation and the Biocultural Paradigm in Medical Anthropology: A Critical Review." *Medical Anthropology Quarterly* 6: 216–236.

ETHNOMEDICINE AND HEALERS

Csordas, Thomas, and Arthur Kleinman. 1996. "The Therapeutic Process." In *Medical Anthropology: Contemporary Theory and Method,* edited by Carolyn F. Sargent and Thomas F. Johnson, pp. 3–20. Westport, CT: Praeger.

Dow, James. 1986. "Universal Aspects of Symbolic Healing: A Theoretical Synthesis." *American Anthropologist 88*: 56–69.

Eisenberg, Leon. 1977. "Disease and Illness: Distinctions Between Professional and Popular Ideas of Sickness." *Culture, Medicine and Psychiatry 1*: 9–23.

Hahn, Robert A. 1995. *Sickness and Healing: An Anthropological Perspective.* New Haven, CT: Yale University Press.

Hahn, Robert A., and Arthur Kleinman. 1983. "Belief as Pathogen, Belief as Medicine." *Medical Anthropology Quarterly* 14(4): 3, 16–19.

Kleinman, Arthur. 1980. *Patients and Healers in the Context of Culture.* Berkeley: University of California Press.

Moerman, Daniel E. 1991. "Physiology and Symbols: The Anthropological Implications of the Placebo Effect." In *The Anthropology of Medicine: From Culture to Method,* edited by L. Romanucci-Ross, D. E. Moerman, and L. R. Tancredi, pp. 129–146. Westport, CT: Bergin & Garvey.

Payer, Lynn. 1988. *Medicine and Culture.* New York: Penguin.

Payer, Lynn. 1994. *The Disease Mongers.* New York: Wiley.

Rhodes, Lorna Amarasingham. 1996. "Studying Biome0dicine as a Cultural System." *In Medical Anthropology: Contemporary Theory and Method,* edited by Carolyn Sargent and Thomas Johnson. Westport, CT: Praeger.

BELIEF AND HEALING

Berger, Peter L., and Thomas Luckmann. 1967. *The Social Construction of Reality: A Treatise in the Sociology of Knowledge.* Garden City, NY: Anchor.

Janzen, John. 1978. *The Quest for Therapy: Medical Pluralism in Lower Zaire.* Berkeley: University of California Press.

McCord, Colin, and Harold Freeman. 1990. "Excess Mortality in Harlem." *New England Journal of Medicine* 322: 173–177.

Moerman, Daniel E. 1998. *Native American Ethnobotany.* Portland, OR: Timber Press.

Sontag, Susan. 1978. *Illness as Metaphor.* New York: Farrar, Straus & Giroux.

THE MEANING AND EXPERIENCE OF ILLNESS

Casteneda, Carlos. 1973. *The Teachings of Don Juan.* New York: Simon & Schuster.

Chagnon, Napoleon. 1968. *Yanomamo: The Fierce People.* New York: Holt, Rinehart & Winston.

DesJarlais, Robert. 1992. *Body and Emotion: The Aesthetics of Illness and Healing in the Nepal Himalayas.* Philadelphia: University of Pennsylvania Press.

Desowitz, Robert S. 1987. *The Thorn in the Starfish: How the Human Immune System Works.* New York: Norton.

Hahn, Robert A., and Atwood D. Gaines, eds. 1985. *Physicians of Western Medicine: Anthropological Approaches to Theory and Practice.* Dordrecht: D. Reidel.

Harner, Michael. 1968. "The Sound of Rushing Water." *Natural History*, June/July.

Harner, Michael. 1990. *The Way of the Shaman.* San Francisco: Harper & Row.

Jones, David E. 1972. *Sanapia: A Comanche Medicine Woman.* New York: Holt, Rinehart & Winston.

Katz, Pearl. 1990. "Ritual in the Operating Room." In *American Culture: Essays on the Familiar and Unfamiliar,* edited by L. Ploicov, pp. 279–294. Pittsburgh: University of Pennsylvania Press.

Katz, Richard. 1982. *Boiling Energy.* Cambridge, MA: Harvard University Press.

Konner, Melvin. 1982. *The Tangled Wing: Biological Constraints on the Human Spirit.* New York: Holt, Rinehart & Winston.

Konner, Melvin. 1987. *Becoming a Doctor: A Journey of Initiation in Medical School.* New York: Penguin.

Laderman, Carol, and Marina Roseman, eds. 1996. *The Performance of Healing.* New York: Routledge.

Murphy, Robert, and Yolanda Murphy. 1985. *Women of the Forest.* New York: Columbia University Press.

Shostak, Marjorie. 1981. *Nisa: The. Life and Words of a !Kung Woman.* London: Allen Lane, Penguin Books Ltd.

Tylor, Edward B. 1889. *Primitive Culture: Researches in the Development of Mythology, Philosophy, Religion, Language, Art, and Custom.* New York: Holt.

BIOMEDICINE, TECHNOLOGY, AND THE BODY

Hahn, Robert A. 1995. *Sickness and Healing.* New Haven, CT: Yale University Press.

Inhorn, Marcia. 2003. *Local Babies, Global Science: Gender, Religion and in Vitro Fertilization in Egypt.* New York: Routledge.

Inhorn, Marcia. 1996. *Infertility and Patriarchy: The Cultural Politics of Gender and Family Life in Egypt.* Philadelphia: University of Pennsylvania Press.

Inhorn, Marcia. 1994. *Quest for Conception: Gender, Infertility, and Egyptian Medical Traditions.* Philadelphia: University of Pennsylvania Press.

Lock, Margaret. 1994. *Encounters with Aging: Mythologies of Menopause in Japan and North America.* Berkeley: University of California Press.

Lock, Margaret. 2001. *Twice Dead: Organ Transplants and the Reinvention of Death.* Berkeley: University of California Press.

Rapp, Ryana. 2000. *Testing Women. Testing the Fetus: The Social Impact of Amniocentesis in America.* New York: Routledge.

CULTURE AND MENTAL HEALTH

Allen, J. S., and Sarich, V. M. 1988. "Schizophrenia in an Evolutionary Perspective." *Perspective in Biology and Medicine 32*: 132–153.

DesJarlais, Robert, Arthur Kleinman, et al., eds. 1995. *World Mental Health: Problems, Priorities and Responses in Low-Income Countries.* New York: Oxford University Press.

Gaines, Atwood. 1992. *Ethnopsychiatry: The Cultural Construction of Professional and Folk Psychiatries.* Albany: State University of New York Press.

Hahn, Robert A. 1995. *Sickness and Healing: An Anthropological Perspective.* New Haven, CT: Yale University Press.

Heggenhougen, H. Kristian. 1984. "Traditional Medicine and the Treatment of Drug Addicts: Three Examples from Southeast Asia." *Medical Anthropology Quarterly l6*(os) (1): 3–7.

Johnson, Thomas. 1987. "Premenstrual Syndrome as a Culture-Specific Disorder." *Culture, Medicine and Psychiatry 11*: 337–356.

Kleinman, Arthur, 1988. *Rethinking Psychiatry.* New York: Free Press.

Kleinman, Arthur and Byron Good, eds. 1985. *Culture and Depression: Studies in the Anthropology and Cross-Cultural Psychiatry of Affect and Disorder.* Berkeley: University of California Press.

Nuckolls, Charles. 1996. *The Cultural Dialectics of Knowledge and Desire.* Madison: University of Wisconsin Press.

Ritenbaugh, Cheryl. 1978. "Obesity as a Culture Bound Syndrome." *Culture, Medicine and Psychiatry 6*: 347–361.

Rubel, Arthur J., Carl W. O'Nell, and Rolando Collado-Ardon. 1984. *Susto: A Folk Illness.* Berkeley: University of California Press.

Scheper-Hughes, Nancy. 1979. *Saints, Scholars and Schizophrenics: Mental Illness in Rural Ireland.* Berkeley: University of California Press.

Selye, Hans. 1976. *Stress in Health and Disease.* Boston: Butterworths.

Simons, Ronald. 1985. "Latah." In *The Culture-Bound Syndromes*, edited by Ronald C. Simons and Charles C. Hughes. Dordrecht and Boston: D. Reidel.

Simons, Ronald. 1996. *BOO: Culture, Experience, and the Startle Reflex.* New York: Oxford University Press.

Simons, Ronald C., and Charles C. Hughes, eds. 1985. *The Culture-Bound Syndrome.* Dordrecht and Boston: D. Reidel.

Solzhenitsyn, Aleksandr. 1973. *The Gulag Archipelago, 1918–1956.* New York: Harper & Row.

Szasz, Thomas. 1974. *The Myth of Mental Illness: Foundations of a Theory of Personal Conduct.* New York: Harper & Row.

PART II. APPLYING MEDICAL ANTHROPOLOGY

Chambers, Erve. 1985. *Applied Anthropology: A Practical Guide.* Englewood Cliffs, NJ: Prentice-Hall.

Eddy, Elizabeth M., and William L. Partridge, eds. 1987. *Applied Anthropology in America.* New York: Columbia University Press.

Johnson, Thomas M. 1997. "Anthropology and the World of Physicians." In *Applying Cultural Anthropology*, edited by Peter J. Brown and Aaron Podolefsky, pp. 271–274. Mountain View, CA: Mayfield.

van Willigen, John. 1993. *Applied Anthropology: An Introduction.* Westport, CT: Bergin & Garvey.

van Willigen, John, Barbara Rylko-Bauer, and Ann McElroy, eds. 1989. *Making Our Research Useful: Case Studies in the Utilization of Anthropological Knowledge.* Boulder, CO: Westview Press.

Wulff, Robert M., and Shirley J. Fiske, eds. 1987. *Anthropological Praxis: Translating Knowledge into Action.* Boulder, CO: Westview Press.

CASE STUDIES IN EXPLANATORY MODELS

Blumhagen, Dan. 1980. "Hypertension: A Folk Illness with a Medical Name." *Culture, Medicine and Psychiatry 4*: 197–227.

Brown, Peter J., Jessica Gregg, and Bruce Ballard. 1997. "Culture, Ethnicity, and the Practice of Medicine." In *Human Behavior for Medical Students*, edited by Alan Stoudemire. New York: Lippincott.

Foster, George M. 1994, *Hippocrates' Latin American Legacy: Humoral Medicine in the New World.* Langhorne, PA: Gordon & Breach.

Harwood, Alan. 1977. *Rx-Spiritist as Needed: A Study of a Puerto Rican Community Mental Health Resource.* New York: Wiley.

Harwood, Alan. 1988. *Rx: Spiritist As Needed: A Study of a Puerto Rican Community Mental Health Resource.* Ithaca, NY: Cornell University Press.

Harwood, Alan. 1981. *Ethnicity and Medical Care.* Cambridge, MA: Harvard University Press.

Heurtin-Roberts, Suzanne, and Efrain Reisin. 1990. "Folk Models of Hypertension among Black Women: Problems in Illness Management." In *Anthropology and Primary Health Care*, edited by J. Coreil and J. D. Mull. Boulder, CO: Westview Press.

Kleinman, Arthur. 1988. *Rethinking Psychiatry.* New York: Free Press.

Konner, Melvin. 1993. *Medicine at the Crossroads: The Crisis in Health Care.* New York: Pantheon.

Leslie, Charles M. 1972. "The Professionalization of Ayurvedic and Unani Medicine." In *Medical Men and Their Work: A Sociological Reader*, edited by E. Freidson and E. J. Lorber, pp. 39–54. Chicago: Aldine.

Leslie, Charles M. 1976. *Asian Medical Systems: A Comparative Study.* Berkeley: University of California Press.

Logan, Michael H. 1977. "Anthropological Research on the Hot-Cold Theory of Disease: Some Methodological Suggestions." *Medical Anthropology 1*: 87–108.

Mathews, Holly F. 1988. "Sweet Blood Can Give You Sugar: Black American Folk Beliefs about Diabetes." *City Medicine* 2: 12–16.

Polgar, Stephen. 1962. "Health and Human Behavior: Areas of Interest Common to the Social and Medical Sciences." *Current Anthropology 3*: 159–205.

Romanucci-Ross, Lola. 1969. "The Hierarchy of Resort in Curative Practices: The Admiralty Islands." *Journal of Health and Social Behavior 10*: 201–209.

Snow, Loudell F. 1993, *Walkin' over Medicine.* Boulder, CO: Westview Press.

Sontag, Susan. 1978. *Illness as Metaphor.* New York: Farrar, Straus & Giroux.

Sontag, Susan. 1990. *Illness as Metaphor and AIDS and Its Metaphors.* New York: Doubleday.

WORKING WITH THE CULTURE OF BIOMEDICINE

Committee on Understanding and Eliminating Racial and Ethnic Disparities in Health Care. 2004. *Unequal Treatment: Confronting Racial and Ethnic Disparities in Health Care.* Washington, DC: National Academies Press.

Fadiman, Anne. 1998. *The Spirit Catches You and You Fall Down.* New York: Farrar, Straus & Giroux.

Hahn, Robert. 1995. *Sickness and Healing.* New Haven, CT: Yale University Press.

Kleinman, Arthur. 2007. *What Really Matters; Living a Moral Life amidst Uncertainty and Danger.* Oxford: Oxford University Press.

Payer, Lynn. 1988. *Medicine and Culture.* New York: Henry Holt.

Rhodes, Lorna A. 1991. *Emptying Beds: The Work of an Emergency Room Psychiatric Unit.* Berkeley: University of California Press.

Taylor, Janelle S. 2004. *Consuming Motherhood.* New Brunswick, NJ: Rutgers University Press.

Taylor, Janelle S. 2008. *The Public Life of the Fetal Sonogram: Technology, Consumption, and the Politics of Reproduction.* New Brunswick, NJ: Rutgers University Press.

Tervalon, Melanie, and Jann Murray-Garcia. 1998. "Cultural Humility Versus Cultural Competence: A Critical Distinction in Defining Physician Training Outcomes in Multicultural Education." *Journal of Health Care for the Poor and Underserved* 9(2): 117–225.

ETHNICITY AND HEALTH CARE

Barker, Judith, and Margaret Clark, eds. 1992. "Cross-Cultural Medicine: A Decade Later." *Western Journal of Medicine* 157: 247–374.

Barth, Fredrik, ed. 1969. *Ethnic Groups and Boundaries. The Social Organization of Culture Difference.* London: Allen & Unwin.

Brown, Peter J., Jessica Gregg, and Bruce Ballard. 1997. "Culture, Ethnicity, and the Practice of Medicine." In *Human Behavior for Medical Students,* edited by Alan Stoudemire. New York: Lippincott.

Clark, Margaret, ed. 1983, "Cross-Cultural Medicine." *Western Journal of Medicine* 139: 805–932.

Committee on Understanding and Eliminating Racial and Ethnic Disparities in Health Care. 2004. *Unequal Treatment: Confronting Racial and Ethnic Disparities in Health Care.* Washington, DC: National Academies Press.

DelVecchio Good, Mary-Jo, Paul Brodin, Byron Good, and Arthur Kleinman, eds. 1992. *Pain as Human Experience: An Anthropological Perspective.* Berkeley: University of California Press.

Goodman, Alan, and George Armelagos. 1996. "The Resurrection of Race: The Concept of Race in Physical Anthropology in the 1990s." In *Race and Other Misadventures,* edited by L. R. L. Reynolds. Dix Hills, NY: General Hall.

Harris, Marvin. 1980. *Patterns of Race, in the Americas.* Westport, CT: Greenwood.

Harwood, Alan, ed. 1981. *Ethnicity and Medical Care.* Cambridge, MA: Harvard University Press.

Illich, Ivan. 1976. *Medical Nemesis: The Expropriation of Health.* New York: Pantheon Books.

Inhorn, Marcia. 1994. *Quest for Conception: Gender, Infertility, and Egyptian Medical Traditions.* Philadelphia: University of Pennsylvania Press.

Weller, Susan C., Lee M. Pachter, Robert Trotter, and Roberta Baer. 1992. "Empacho in Four Latino Groups: A Study in Intra- and Inter-Cultural Variation in Beliefs." *Medical Anthropology 15*: 109–136.

Wright, Lawrence. 1994. "One Drop of Blood." *The New Yorker 70*: 46–55.

Wulff, Robert M., and Shirley J. Fiske, eds. 1987. *Anthropological Praxis: Translating Knowledge into Action.* Boulder, CO: Westview Press.

Zborowski, Mark. 1952. "Cultural Components in Response to Pain." *Journal of Social Issues 8*: 16–30.

Zborowski, Mark. 1969. *People in Pain.* San Francisco: Jossey-Bass.

STIGMA AND COPING

Ablon, Joan. 1988. *Living with Difference: Families with Dwarf Children.* New York: Praeger.

Bolton, R., and G. Orozco. 1994. *The AIDS Bibliography: Studies in Anthropology and Related Fields.* Arlington, VA: American Anthropological Association.

Eisenberg, David, et al. 1993. "Unconventional Medicine in the United States." *New England Journal of Medicine 328*: 246–252.

Farmer, Paul. 1988. AIDS *and Accusation: Haiti and the Geography of Blame.* Berkeley: University of California Press.

Farmer, Paul, Margaret Connors, and Janie Simmons. 1996. *Women, Poverty and AIDS: Sex, Drugs and Structural Violence.* Monroe, ME: Common Courage Press.

Goffman, Erving. 1963. *Stigma: Notes on the Management of Spoiled Identity.* Englewood Cliffs, NJ: Prentice-Hall.

Gray, John. 1993. *Men Are from Mars, Women Are from Venus. A Practical Guide for Improving Communication and Getting What You Want in Your Relationships.* New York: HarperCollins.

Gregg, Charles T. 1983. *A Virus of Love and Other Tales of Medical Detection.* Albuquerque: University of New Mexico Press.

Hahn, Robert A. 1995. *Sickness and Healing: An Anthropological Perspective.* New Haven, CT: Yale University Press.

Kidder, Tracy. 2003. *Mountains beyond Mountains.* New York: Random House.

Kleinman, Arthur. 1988. *The Illness Narratives: Suffering, Healing and the Human Condition.* New York: Basic Books.

Murphy, Robert F. 1987. *The Body Silent.* New York: Holt.

Murphy, Robert F., and Buell Quain. 1955. *The Trumaí Indians of Central Brazil.* Locust Vally, NY: J. J. Augustin.

Murphy, Yolanda, and Robert Murphy. 1985. *Women of the Forest.* New York: Columbia University Press.

Price, Reynolds. 1994. *A Whole New Life.* New York: Atheneum.

Savishinsky, Joel S. 1991. *The Ends of Time: Life and Work in a Nursing Home.* Westport, CT: Bergin & Garvey.

Sokolovsky, Jay, ed. 1983, *Growing Old in Different Societies: Cross-cultural Perspectives.* Belmont, CA: Wadsworth.

Wolf, Naomi. 1992. *The Beauty Myth: How Images of Beauty Are Used against Women.* New York. Anchor Books.

GENDER AND HEALTH

Coulmas, Florian, ed. 1997. *The Handbook of Sociolinguistics.* Oxford: Blackwell.

Ginsburg, Faye D. 1989. *Contested Lives: The Abortion Debate in an American Community.* Berkeley: University of California Press.

Hahn, Robert A., ed. 1987. "Obstetrics in the United States: Woman, Physician, and Society." *Medical Anthropology. Quarterly 1*: 227–320.

Hahn, Robert A., and Atwood D. Gaines, eds. 1985. *Physicians of Western Medicine: Anthropological Approaches to Theory and Practice.* Dordrecht: D. Reidel.

Lakoff, George, and Mark Johnson. 1980. *Metaphors We Live By.* Chicago: University of Chicago.

Latour, Bruno. 1986. *Laboratory Life: The Construction of Scientific Facts.* Princeton, NJ: Princeton University Press.

Martin, Emily. 1987. *The Woman in the Body: A Cultural Analysis of Reproduction.* New York: Beacon.

Martinez, Rebecca, Leo Chavez, and Alan Hubbell. 1997. "Purity and Passion: Risk and Morality in Latina Immigrants' and Physcans' Beliefs about Cervical Cancer." *Medical Anthropology 17*: 337–362.

Miller, Barbara D. 1987. "Female Infanticide and Child Neglect in Rural North India." In *Child Survival: Anthropological Perspectives on the Treatment and Maltreatment of Children,* edited by Nancy Scheper-Hughes, pp. 95–112. Dordrecht: D. Reidel.

Morgen, Sandra, ed. 1989. *Gender and Anthropology: Critical Reviews for Research and Teaching.* Washington, DC: American Anthropological Association.

Payer, Lynn. 1988. *Medicine and Culture.* New York: Penguin.

Sargent, Carolyn F., and Caroline B. Brettell, eds. 1996. *Gender and Health.* Upper Saddle River, NJ: Prentice-Hall.

Scheper-Hughes, Nancy. 1992. *Death without Weeping: The Violence of Everyday Life in Brazil.* Berkeley: University of California Press.

Sontag, Susan. 1978. *Illness and Its Metaphor.* New York: Farrar, Straus & Giroux.

Tannen, Deborah. 1990. *You Just Don't Understand: Women and Men in Conversation.* New York: Morrow.

Turnbull, Colin M. 1972. *The Mountain People.* New York: Simon & Schuster.

CULTURE AND NUTRITION: FAT AND THIN

Bordo, Susan. 1993. *Unbearable Weight: Feminism, Western Culture, and the Body.* Berkeley: University of California Press.

Brumberg, Joan Jacobs. 1988. *Fasting Girls: The Emergence of Anorexia Nervosa as a Modern Disease.* Cambridge. MA: Harvard University Press.

Cassidy, Claire. 1982. "Protein-Energy Malnutrition as a Culture-Bound Syndrome." *Culture, Medicine, and Psychiatry 6*: 325–345.

Condit, Vicki Bentley. 1990. "Anorexia Nervosa: Levels of Causation." *Human Nature 1*: 391–413.

Dettwlyer, Katherine, and Patricia Stuart-Macadam, eds. 1995. *Breastfeeding: Biocultural Perspectives.* Piscataway, NJ: Aldine Transaction.

Dettwyler, Katherine A. 1994. *Dancing Skeletons: Life and Death in West Africa.* Prospect Heights, IL: Waveland.

Dettwyler, Katherine, and Claudia Fishman. 1992. "Infant Feeding Practices and Growth." *Annual Review of Anthropology 21*: 171–204.

Fernandez, Renate L. 1990. *A Simple Matter of Salt: An Ethnography of Nutritional Deficiency in Spain.* Berkeley: University of California Press.

Greene, Lawrence S., ed. 1977. *Malnutrition, Behavior, and Social Organization.* New York: Academic Press.

Konner, Melvin. 2003. *The Tangled Wing: Biological Constraints on the Human Spirit.* New York. Holt Paperbacks.

GLOBAL HEALTH ISSUES AND PROGRAMS

Basch, Paul F. 1990. *Textbook of International Health.* New York: Oxford University Press.

Bentley, Margaret, Perti Pelto, and Gretel Pelto. 1990. "Applied Anthropological Research Methods: Diarrhea Studies as an Example." In *Anthropology and Primary Health Care,* edited by J. Coreil and J. D. Mull. Boulder, Co: Westview Press.

Coreil, Jeannine, and J. Denis Mull, eds. 1990. *Anthropology and Primary Health Care.* Boulder, CO: Westview Press.

Cosminsky, Sheila. 1986. "Traditional Birth Practices and Pregnancy Avoidance in the Americas." In *The Potential of the Traditional Birth Attendant,* edited by A. Mangay-Maglacas and J. Simons. WHO Offset Publication No. 95. Geneva: World Health Organization.

Dettwyler, Katherine, and Claudia Fishman. 1992. "Infant Feeding Practices and Growth." *Annual Review of Anthropology 21*: 171–204.

Foster, George. 1987. "Bureaucratic Aspects of International Health Agencies." *Social Science and Medicine 25*: 1039–1048.

Gove, Sandy, and Gretel H. Pelto. 1993. "Focused Ethnographic Studies in the WHO Programme for the Control of Acute Respiratory Infections." *Medical Anthropology 15*: 409–424.

Green, Edward C. 2003. *Rethinking AIDS Prevention: Learning from Successes in Developing Countries.* Westport, CT: Praeger.

Green, Edward C. 1999. *Indigenous Theories of Contagious Disease.* London: AltaMira Press.

Green, Edward C. 1985. "Traditional Healers, Mothers and Childhood Diarrheal Disease in Swaziland: The Interface of Anthropology and Health Education." *Social Science and Medicine* 20(3): 277–285.

Justice, Judith. 1986. *Policies, Plans, and People: Foreign Aid and Health Development.* Berkeley: University of California Press.

Lane, Sandra D., and Robert A. Rubinstein. 1996. "International Health: Problems and Programs in International Health." In *Medical Anthropology: Contemporary Theory and Method,* edited by Carolyn Sargent and Thomas Johnson, Westport, CT: Praeger.

McCord, Colin, and Harold Freeman. 1990. "Excess Mortality in Harlem." *New England Journal of Medicine 322*: 173–177.

Nichter, Mark. 1993. "Introduction: Anthropological Studies of Acute Respiratory Infection." *Medical Anthropology 15*: 319–334.

Credits

S Boyd Eaton, Marjorie Shostak, and Melvin Konner, "Stone Agers in the Fast Lane: Chronic Degenerative Diseases in Evolutionary Perspective," American Journal of Medicine, April 1988, 84, pp. 739-749. Used by permission.

R. Nesse, "How is Darwinian Medicine Useful?" Western Journal of Medicine, 2001, 174, pp. 358-360. Used by permission of the author.

Barry Bogin, "The Tall and Short of It," Discover Magazine, February 1998. Used by permission of Barry Bogin.

Alan Goodman, "Why Genes Don't Count (for Racial Differences in Health)," American Journal of Public Health, 2000, 90 (11), pp. 1699-1702. Used by permission.

Nina Jablonski and George Chaplin, "Skin Deep," Scientific American, Oct 2002, vol 287 (4), pp. 74-81. Used by permission of Scientific American.

George J. Armelagos, "Health and Disease in Prehistoric Populations in Transition," Diseases in Populations in Transition, Alan C. Swedlund, ed. Copyright © 1990. Reproduced with permission of Greenwood Publishing Group, Inc., Westport, CT.

Thomas McKeown, "Determinants of Health," Human Nature Magazine, April 1978.

Peter J. Brown, "Cultural Adaptations to Endemic Malaria in Sardinia," Medical Anthropology 5:3, 1981. Reprinted with permission of Gordon and Breach Publishers.

Farmer P. Social Inequalities and Emerging Infectious Diseases. Emerg Infect Dis [serial on the Internet]. 1996 October-December. Available from http://www.cdc.gov/ncidod/eid/vol2no4/farmer.htm.

Merrill Singer, "Why Is It Easier to Get Drugs than Drug Treatment in the US?" Unhealthy Health Policy: A Critical Anthropological Examination, Altamira Press, pp. 287-302. Used by permission of Rowman & Littlefield Publishing Group.

Reproduced by permission of the American Anthropological Association from American Anthropologist volume 78(4), pp. 773-782. 1976. Not for sale or further reproduction.

Claude Levi-Strauss, "The Sorcerer and His Magic," Les Temps Modernes, No. 41 (1949) pp. 3-24.

Daniel Moerman, Meaning, Medicine and the "Placebo Effect", Cambridge University Press, 2002. Reprinted with permission of Cambridge University Press.

Robert A. Hahn, "The Nocebo Phenomenon: Concept, Evidence, and Implications for Public Health," Preventive Medicine, Vol.26, No.5, (September 1997), pp.607-611. Used by permission.

Nancy E. Waxler, "Learning To Be A Leper: A Case Study in the Social Construction of Illness," Social Contexts of Health, Illness and Patient Care, Elliot Mishler, editor, pp. 169-194. Reprinted with the permission of Cambridge University Press.

L Hunt, "Strategic Suffering: Illness Narratives as Social Empowerment Among Mexican Cancer Patients," Narrative and the Cultural Construction of Illness and Healing, C Mattingly and C. Garro, eds., University of California Press, 2000, pp. 88-107. Used by permission of University of California Press.

Melvin Konner, "Transcendental Medication," The Sciences, May/June 1985. Used with the permission of the New York Academy of Sciences, 7 World Trade Center, 250 Greenwich Street, 40th Floor, New York, NY 10007, www.nyas.org

DW Blumhagen, "The Doctor's White Coat: The Image of the Physician in Modern America," Annals of Internal Medicine, vol 91:111-116, 1979. Used by permission.

M. Inhorn, "Religion and Reproductive Technologies," Anthropology News, Feb 2005, pp. 17-18. Reproduced by permission of the American Anthropological Association from American News Volume 46(2), 2005. Not for sale or further reproduction.

Arthur Kleinman, "Do Psychiatric Disorders Differ in Different Cultures?", Rethinking Psychiatry: From Cultural Category to Personal Experiences, chap 3, pp. 34-52. Reprinted with the permission of The Free Press, a Division of Simon & Schuster, Inc., from RETHINKING PSYCHIATRY: From Cultural Category to Personal Experience by ArthurKleinman. Copyright © 1988 by The Free Press. All rights reserved.

Arthur J. Rubel, "The Epidemology of a Folk Illness: Susto in Hispanic America," Ethnology 3(3):268-83. Used by permission.

C. Friese, G. Becker, RD Nachtigall, "Rethinking the Biological Clock: Eleventh-Hour Moms, Miracle Moms, and Meaning of Age-Related Infertility," Social Science and Medicine, 63(6): 1550-1560. Used by permission.

William W. Dressler, "Ethnomedical Beliefs and Patient Adherence to a Treatment Regimen: A St. Lucian Example," Human Organization, vol 39, pp. 88-91. Reproduced by permission of the Society for Applied Anthropology from William W. Dressler, "Ethnomedical Beliefs and Patient Adherence to a Treatment Regimen: A St. Lucian Example," Human Organization, vol 39, pp. 88-91.

M. Lock, "Inventing a New Death and Making it Believable," Anthropology and Medicine, 9 (2): 97-115. Used by permission.

Robert T. Trotter II, "A Case of Lead Poisoning from Folk Remedies in Mexican American Communities," Anthropological Praxis: Translating Knowledge into Action, Robert M. Wulff, Editor. From ANTHROPOLOGICAL PRAXIS by ROBERT WULFF. Reprinted by permission of WESTVIEW PRESS, a member of Perseus Books Group.

Thomas Johnson, "Anthropology and the World of Physician," Anthropology Newsletter, Nov/Dec.

Linda Hunt, "Beyond Cultural Competence," The Park Ridge Center Bulletin for Health, Faith and Ethics, Dec 2001, Vol 4. Used by permission of the author.

Merrill Singer, Freddie Valentin, Hans Baer, and Zhongke Jin, "Why Does Juan Garcia Have a Drinking Problem? The Perspective of Critical Medical Anthropology," Medical Anthropology, 14:1, pp. 77-108. Used by permission.

Elois Ann Berlin and William C. Fowkes, Jr. "A Teaching Framework for Cross-Cultural Health Care," Western Journal of Medicine, 139:130-134. Used by permission of Dr. Elois Ann Berlin.

Gaylene Becker, "Coping with Stigma: Lifelong Adaptation of Deaf People," Social Science and Medicine, Vol 15, 1981, pp. 21-24. Used by permission.

Janelle Taylor, "Confronting 'Culture' in Medicines of 'Culture of No Culture'," Academic Medicine, 78(6): 555-559. Used by permission.

Leandris Liburd, et al, "Understanding 'Masculinity' and the Challenges of Managing Type-2 Diabetes Among African-American Men," Journal of the National Medical Association, 99(5):550-558. Used by permission.

Reproduced by permission of the American Anthropological Association from Medical Anthropology Quarterly Volume 17(3), pp. 59-63, 1986. Not for sale or further reproduction.

Robert F. Murphy, "The Damaged Self," The Body Silent, pp. 85-111.

Paul Farmer and Arthur Kleinman, "AIDS as Humman Suffering," Daedalus, 118:2 (Spring, 1989), pp. 135-162. © 1989 by the American Academy of Arts and Sciences. Used by permission.

Arthur M. Kleinman, Barry R. Bloom, Anthony Saich, Katherine A. Mason, and Felicity Aulino. (2008) Introduction: Avian and Pandemic Influenza: A Biosocial Approach. The Journal of Infectious Diseases 197:s1, S1-S3. Used by permission.

Emily Martin, "Medical Metaphors of Women's Bodies: Menstruation and Menopause," International Journal of Health Services, Vol. 18 (2), pp. 237-254. Used by permission of Baywood Publishing Company, Inc.

Candace West, "Turn-Taking in Doctor-Patient Dialogues," Routine Complications: Troubles with Talk between Doctors and Patients. Reprinted with permission of Indiana University Press.

Rayna Rapp, "Accounting for Amniocentesis," Knowledge Power and Practice: The Anthropology of Medicine and Everyday Life, Shirley Lindenbaum and Margaret Lock, editors, pp. 56-78. Used by permission of University of California Press.

Nancy Scheper-Hughes, "Culture, Scarcity, and Meternal Thinking: Maternal Detachment and Infant Survival in a Brazilian Shantytown, Ethos 13:4, Winter 1985. Reproduced by permission of the American Anthropological Association from Ethos Volume 13(4), pp. 291-317, 1985. Not for sale or further reproduction.

Katherine A. Dettwyler, "The Biocultural Approach in Nutritional Anthrology: Case Studies of Malnutrition in Mali," Medical Anthropology, 15:1, pp. 17-39.

Peter J. Brown and Melvin Konner, "An Anthropological Perspective on Obesity," Annals of the NY Academy of Sciences, 1987.

Carl Kendall, Dennis Foote, and Reynaldo Martorell, "Ethnomedicine and Oral Rehydration Therapy: A Case Study of Ethnomedical Investigation and Program Planning," Social Science and Medicine, Vol. 19, pp. 253-260. Used by permission.

Mark Nichter and Elizabeth Cartwright, "Saving the Children for the Tobacco Industry," Medical Anthropology Quarterly, 5:3, Sept 1991.

Reproduced by permission of the American Anthropological Association from Medical Anthropology Quarterly Volume 5(3), pp. 236-256, 1991. Not for sale or further reproduction.

E. Green, "New Challenges to the AIDS Prevention Paradigm," Anthropology News, Sept 2003, pp. 5-6. Reproduced by permission of the American Anthropological Association from Anthropology News Volume 44(6), pp. 5-6, 2003. Not for sale or further reproduction.

Index